Yearbook of International Humanitarian Law

Yearbook of International Humanitarian Law

H. Fischer
General Editor

Avril McDonald
Managing Editor

Volume 4
2001

T·M·C·Asser Press

Published by T.M.C.Asser press,
P.O. Box 16163, 2500 BD The Hague, The Netherlands
www.asserpress.nl

T.M.C.Asser press English language books are distributed exclusively by:

Cambridge University Press, The Edinburgh Building, Shaftesbury Road,
Cambridge CB2 2RU, UK,
or
for customers in the USA, Canada and Mexico:
Cambridge University Press, 40 West 20th Street, New York, NY 10011-4211, USA

www.cambridge.org

Cover photograph: Kabul, Cemetery
Courtesy of ICRC/Franco Pagetti

ISBN 90-6704-169-6
ISSN 1389-1359

T.M.C. Asser Instituut – Institute for Private and Public International Law, International Commercial Arbitration and European Law
Institute Address: R.J. Schimmelpennincklaan 20-22, The Hague, The Netherlands; Mailing Address: P.O. Box 30461, 2500 GL The Hague, The Netherlands; Tel.: (31-70)3420300; Fax: (31-70)3420359; Internet: www.asser.nl.
Over thirty years, the T.M.C. Asser Institute has developed into a leading scientific research institute in the field of international law. It covers private international law, public international law, including international humanitarian law, the law of the European Union, the law of international commercial arbitration and increasingly, also, international economic law and the law of international commerce.
Conducting scientific research, either fundamental or applied, in the aforementioned domains, is the main activity of the Institute. In addition, the Institute organizes congresses and postgraduate courses, undertakes contract-research and operates its own publishing house.
Because of its inter-university background, the Institute often cooperates with Dutch law faculties as well as with various national and foreign institutions. The Institute organizes *Asser College Europe*, a project in cooperation with East and Central European countries whereby research and educational projects are organized and implemented.

CORRESPONDENTS

The Yearbook of International Humanitarian Law *extends its sincere thanks and appreciation to its correspondents, without whose assistance the compilation of this volume would not have been possible:*

AFRICA
Dr Jose Doria, *Angola*
Mr Adel Maged, *Egypt*
Dr Kinthure Kindiki, *Kenya*
Professor Khadija Elmadmad, *Morocco*
Mr Abdul Tejan-Cole, *Sierra Leone*
Dr Phenyo Rakate, *South Africa*
Dr Khoti Kamanga, *Tanzania*

ASIA-PACIFIC
Professor Tim McCormack, *Australia*
Mr David Boyle, *Cambodia*
Professor Yong Zhang, *P.R. China*
Mr Fadillah Agus, *Indonesia*
Ms Suzannah Linton, *Indonesia*
Professor Hideyuki Kasutani, *Japan*
Professor Seigo Iwamoto, *Japan*
Dr Surya P. Subedi, *Nepal*
Ms Treasa Dunworth, *New Zealand*

EUROPE
Dr Thomas Desch, *Austria*
Mr Peter Kustor, *Austria*
Mr Oleg Starovoitov, *Belarus*
Professor Eric David, *Belgium*
Professor Ivo Josipović, *Croatia*
Professor Maja Seršić, *Croatia*
Mr Jan Hladik, *Czech Republic/Slovakia*
Mr Peter Otken, *Denmark*
Mr Tanel Kerikmäe, *Estonia*
Mr Andres Parmas, *Estonia*
Professor Miodrag Starčević, *Federal Republic of Yugoslavia*
Professor Lauri Hannikainen, *Finland*
Professor Paul Tavernier, *France*
Mr Sascha Rolf Lüder, *Germany*
Mr Gregor Schotten, *Germany*
Dr Maria Gavouneli, *Greece*
Dr Péter Kovács, *Hungary*
Professor Colm Campbell, *Ireland*
Mr Ray Murphy, *Ireland*
Dr Valentina della Fina, *Italy*
Dr Rosa Dinuzzi, *Italy*
Professor Sergio Marchisio, *Italy*
Dr Fabio Raspadori, *Italy*
Dr Guilliano Salberini, *Italy*
Gredimanos Mesonis, *Lithuania*
Rytis Satkausas, *Lithuania*
Professor Nico Keijzer, *the Netherlands*
Ms Elies van Sliedregt, *the Netherlands*
Professor Igor Blishchenko, *Russian Federation*
Professor Antoni Pigrau I Solé, *Spain*
Mr A.P.V. Rogers, *United Kingdom*

MIDDLE EAST
Mr Mehrdad Molaei, *Iran*
Professor Djamchid Momtaz, *Iran*
Dr Mustafa Mari, *Occupied Palestinian Territories*

NORTH AMERICA
Professor René Provost, *Canada*
Mr Joseph Rikhof, *Canada*
Professor William A. Schabas, *Canada*
Mr Burrus M. Carnahan, *USA*
Commander Ronald Neubauer, *USA*

CENTRAL AND SOUTH AMERICA
Professor José Alejandro Consigli, *Argentina*
Mr Gabriel Valladares, *Argentina*
Professor Carlos Dettleff Beros, *Chile*
Professor Hernan Salinas Burgos, *Chile*
Professor Rafael A. Prieto Sanjuan, *Colombia*
Ms Fatima Andrada, *Paraguay*
Professor Alfonso Velázquez, *Paraguay*

CORRESPONDENTS-AT-LARGE
Mr Michael Cottier
Mr Jann Kleffner
Ms Suzannah Linton
Ms Avril McDonald
Mr Mutoy Mubiala

TABLE OF CONTENTS

CORRESPONDENT'S REPORTS

DOCUMENTATION

ABBREVIATIONS

ABl	Amtsblatt
AC	Appeal Cases
ACTR	Australian Capital Territory Reports
AD	Annual Digest of Public International Law Cases
Adelaide LR	Adelaide Law Review
ADF	Australian Defence Force
AFDI	Annuaire français de droit international
Afr. JI & CL	African Journal of International & Comparative Law
Air Force LR	Air Force Law Review
AJIL	American Journal of International Law
Albany LR	Albany Law Review
All ER	All England Law Reports
ALR	Australian Law Reports
Amer. Univ. JIL & Pol.	American University Journal of International Law and Policy
Amer. Univ. ILJ	American University International Law Journal
Amer. Univ. LR	American University Law Review
AP	Additional Protocol
AP	Associated Press
APL(s)	Anti-personnel landmine(s)
ARABSAT	Arab Satellite Communications Organization
Arizona JI &CL	Arizona Journal of International and Comparative Law
ASEAN	Association of South East Asian Nations
ATCA	Alien Tort Claims Act (USA)
Australian YIL	Australian Yearbook of International Law
Austrian JPIL	Austrian Journal for Public International Law
Austrian Rev. Int. & Eur. L	Austrian Revue of International and European Law
AVM	Anti-vehicle landmine
Berkeley JIL	Berkeley Journal of International Law
B.O.	Boletín Oficial de la República Argentina
BGBl	Bundesgesetzblatt (Austria)
Boston Univ. ILJ	Boston University International Law Journal
Boston College Int. & Comp. LR	Boston College International and Comparative Law Review
BTF	Balkans Task Force
BYIL	British Yearbook of International Law
Calif. Western ILJ	California Western International Law Journal
Can. JL & Jur.	Canadian Journal of Law and Jurisprudence
Canadian YIL	Canadian Yearbook of International Law
Case Western Reserve JIL	Case Western Reserve Journal of International Law
CCW	Convention on certain Conventional Weapons
CD	Conference on Disarmament
CENTCOM	Central Command
CHR	(United Nations) Centre for Human Rights
CIA	Central Intelligence Agency
CICR	Comité International de la Croix Rouge
CID	Criminal Investigation Division
CIS	Commonwealth of Independent States
CIVPOL	Civilian Police

CLA	Chief Legal Advisor
CLJ	Criminal Law Journal
CLR	Commonwealth Law Reports
CMAC	Court Martial Appeal Court
Cmnd.	Command Paper
Colorado JI Environ. L & Pol.	Colorado Journal of International Environmental Law and Policy
Colum. HRLR	Columbia Human Rights Law Review
Columbia JTL	Columbia Journal of Transnational Law
Cornell ILJ	Cornell International Law Journal
Cr. App. R	Criminal Appeals Reports
CRC	Convention on the Rights of the Child
Criminal LF	Criminal Law Forum
Criminal LR	Criminal Law Review
CSP	Conference of States Parties
CTBT	Comprehensive Test Ban Treaty
CTS	Commonwealth Treaty Series
CWC	Chemical Weapons Convention
Dalhousie LJ	Dalhousie Law Journal
Denver JIL & Pol.	Denver Journal of International Law and Policy
DLR	Dominian Law Reports
DMU	Detainee Management Unit
DoD	Department of Defense (USA)
Duke JCIL	Duke Journal of Compartive and International Law
ECCAS	Economic Community of Central African States
ECHR Rep.	European Convention on Human Rights Reports
ECHR	European Convention on Human Rights
ECOMOG	ECOWAS Monitoring Group
ECOSOC	UN Economic and Social Council
ECOWAS	Economic Community of West African States
EHRR	European Human Rights Reports
Emory ILR	Emory International Law Review
EJIL	European Journal of International Law
ERW	Explosive Remnants of War
EU	European Union
Eur. Ct. HR	European Court of Human Rights
Eur. Comm. HR	European Commission of Human Rights
Eur. J. Crime, Crim. L & Crim. Jus	European Journal of Crime, Criminal Law and Criminal Justice
Ex D	Exchequer Digest
F	Federal
F Supp.	Federal Supplement
FCJ	Federal Court of Justice (Canada)
FCR	Federal Court Reports
FDC	Force Detention Centre
FDTL	East Timorese Defence Force
Fed. Rep.	Federal Reporter
Fordham ILJ	Fordham International Law Journal
FRETILIN	Frente Revolucionaria Timor Lest Independence
FRY	Federal Republic of Yugoslavia
GA Res.	(United Nations) General Assembly Resolutions
GA	(United Nations) General Assembly

GAOR	(United Nations) General Assembly Official Records
GC	Geneva Conventions
Georgetown Int. Environ. LR	Georgetown International Environmental Law Review
GrCC	Greek Criminal Code
GU	Gazzetta Ufficiale (Italian Official Gazette)
GYIL	German Yearbook of International Law
Hague YIL	Hague Yearbook of International Law
HCJ	High Court of Justice
HRLJ	Human Rights Law Journal
HRQ	Human Rights Quarterly
I/A Court HR	Inter-American Court of Human Rights
I/A Comm. HR	Inter-American Commission of Human Rights
ICA	International Council on Archives
ICBL	International Campaign to Ban Landmines
ICBS	International Committee of the Blue Shield
ICC	International Criminal Court
ICCPR	International Covenant on Civil and Political Rights
ICCROM	International Centre for the Study of the Preservation and Restoration of Cultural Property
ICJ	International Court of Justice
ICJ Rep.	International Court of Justice Reports
ICL Yearbook	Yearbook of the International Law Commission
ICLQ	International and Comparative Law Quarterly
ICOM	International Council of Museums
ICOMOS	International Council on Monuments and Sites
ICRC	International Committee of the Red Cross
ICTR	International Criminal Tribunal for Rwanda
ICTY	International Criminal Tribunal for the Former Yugoslavia
IFLA	International Federation of Library Association and Institutions
IFOR	Implementation Force
IHL	International Humanitarian Law
IJ Est. & Coastal L	International Journal of Estuarine and Coastal Law
ILC Yearbook	Yearbook of the International Law Commission
ILM	International Legal Materials
ILR	International Law Reports
ILSA JI & CL	ILSA Journal of International and Comparative Law
IMT	International Military Tribunal (in Nuremberg)
IMTFE	International Military Tribunal for the Far East (in Tokyo)
Indian JIL	Indian Journal of International Law
INTELSAT	International Telecommunications Satellite Organization
Int. LF	International Law Forum
INTERFET	International Force in East Timor
IRA	Irish Republican Army
IRRC	International Review of the Red Cross
ISAF	International Security Assistance Force
Israel LR	Israel Law Review
Israel YB	Israel Yearbook
Israel YB HR	Israel Yearbook on Human Rights
J Armed Conflict L	Journal of Armed Conflict Law
JIL & Prac.	Journal International Law and Practice
JPI	Judicial Police Inspectors

KFOR	Kosovo Force
LAS	League of Arab States
Leiden JIL	Leiden Journal of International Law
LNTS	League of Nations Treaty Series
LOAC	Law of Armed Conflicts
Loy. LA Il & CLJ	Loyola Los Angeles International and Comparative Law Journal
Loyola I & CLJ	Loyola International and Comparative Law Journal
LQR	Law Quarterly Review
Maryland JIL & T	Maryland Journal of International Law and Trade
MCC	Military Criminal Code
Melbourne JIL	Melbourne Journal of International Law
Melbourne Univ. LR	Melbourne University Law Review
Mich. JIL	Michigan Journal of International Law
Mich. LR	Michigan Law Review
Mil. LR	Military Law Review
MLR	Modern Law Review
MNF	Multinational Force
Monash LR	Monash Law Review
Moscow JIL	Moscow Journal of International Law
MPYBUNL	Max Planck Yearbook of United Nations Law
MPYIL	Max Planck Yearbook of International Law
NATO	North Atlantic Treaty Organisation
NCOs	Non-Commissioned Officers
NGO	Non-Governmental Organisation
NILR	Netherlands International Law Review
NLR	Naval Law Review
Nordic JIL	Nordic Journal of International Law
Notre Dame JL	Notre Dame Journal of Law
NPC	New Penal Code
NQHR	Netherlands Quarterly of Human Rights
NY Univ. JIL & Pol.	New York University Journal of International Law and Politics
NYIL	Netherlands Yearbook of International Law
NZLR	New Zealand Law Review
ÖAD	Österreichische Außenpolitische Dokumentation
OAS	Organization of American States
OECS	Organization of Eastern Caribbean States
OIOS	(UN) Office of Internal Oversight Services
ONU	Organisation Nations Unies
ONUC	United Nations Force in the Congo
OPCW	Organisation for the Prohibition of Chemical Weapons
OSA	Operational Support Arrangement
OTP	Office of the Prosecutor (of the ICTR and/or ICTY)
PD	Probate Division, English Law Reports
PKF	Peace Keeping Force
PMG	Peace Monitoring Group
POW	Prisoner of War
Proc. ASIL	Proceedings of the American Society of International Law

QB	Queen's Bench
RBDI	Revue Belge de droit international
RDI	Rivista di diritto internazionale
RDPC	Revue de droit pénal et de criminologie
Receuil des Cours	Collected Courses of the Hague Academy of International Law
RGDIP	Revue générale de droit international public
RIAA	Reports of International Arbitral Awards
RICR	Revue International de la Croix Rouge
RQDI	Revue Québécoise de Droit International
RSC	Rules of the Supreme Court
RSCDPC	Revue de science criminelle et de droit pénal comparé
SADC	South African Development Community
SASC	South African Security Council
SC	(United Nations) Security Council
SC Res.	Security Council Resolution
SCOR	Security Council Official Records
SCR	Supreme Court Reports
SCU	Serious Crimes Unit
SFOR	Stabilization Force
SFRY	Socialist Federal Republic of Yugoslavia
SG	(United Nations) Secretary-General
SIPRI	Stockholm International Peace Research Institute
SOFA	Status of Force Agreement
Stanford JIL	Stanford Journal of International Law
SZIER/RSDIE	Schweizerische Zeitschrift für internationales und europäisches Recht / Revue Suisse de droit international et de droit européen
Texas ILJ	Texas International Law Journal
Texas LR	Texas Law Review
TIAS	
Tilburg For. LR	Tilburg Foreign Law Review
TLPS	Timorese Police Force
Transn. L & Contemp. Probs.	Transnational Law and Contemporary Problems
TRC Report	(South African) Truth and Reconciliation Commission Report
UNAMET	United Nations Mission in East Timor
UNAMIR	United Nations Assistance Mission for Rwanda
UNCHR	United Nations Commission on Human Rights
UNCHS	United Nations Centre for Human Settlements
UNCIVPOL	United Nations Civilian Police
UNCTAD	United Nations Conference on Trade and Development
UN Doc.	United Nations Documents Series
UNDP	United Nations Development Program
UNEF	United Nations Emergency Force (in the Sinai)
UNEP	United Nations Environmental Programme
UNESCO	United Nations Educational, Scientific and Cultural Organisation
UNFICYP	United Nations Force in Cyprus
UN GAOR	United Nations General Assembly Official Records
UNGCI	United Nations Guards Contingent in Iraq
UNHCR	United Nations High Commission for Refugees

UNHFOR	United Nations Human Rights Field Office in Rwanda
UNICEF	United Nations (International) Children=s (Emergency) Fund
UNIDIR	United Nations Institute for Disarmament Research
UNIFIL	United Nations Interim Force in Lebanon
UNIIMOG	United Nations Iran/Iraq Military Observer Group
UNIKOM	United Nations Iraq/Kuwait Observer Mission
UNITAF	United Nations Unified Task Force
UNITAF	United Nations Task Force (in Somalia)
UNOMSIL	United Nations Observer Mission in Sierra Leone
UNOSOM	United Nations Operation in Somalia
UNPF	United Nations Peacekeeping Force
UNPROFOR	United Nations Protection Force (in Bosnia and Herzegovina)
UNSC	United Nations Security Council
UNTAC	United Nations Transitional Authority in Cambodia
UNTAET	United Nations Transitional Authority in East Timor
UNTS	United Nations Treaty Series
UNWCC	United Nations War Crimes Commission
USDOD	United States Department of Defence
Vanderbilt JTL	Vanderbilt Journal of Transnational Law
Virginia JIL	Virgina Journal of International Law
Virginia LR	Virginia Law Review
WCR	War Crimes Reports
WHO	World Health Organisation
Whittier LR	Whittier Law Review
WLR	Weekly Law Reports
Yale LJ	Yale Law Journal
Yale JIL	Yale Journal of International Law
Yb Eur. Conv. HR	Yearbok of the European Convention of Human Rights
Yb ILC	Yearbook of the International Law Commission
YIHL	Yearbook of International Humanitarian Law
Yug. Rev. IL	Yugoslav Review of International Law
ZaöRV	Zeitschrift für ausländisches öffentliches Recht und Völkerrecht
ZöR	Zeitschrift für öffentliches Recht (Austrian Journal of Public and International Law)

ARTICLES

TRANSITIONAL JUSTICE IN AFGHANISTAN: CONFRONTING VIOLATIONS OF INTERNATIONAL HUMANITARIAN AND HUMAN RIGHTS LAW[1]

Peter G. Danchin[2]

1. INTRODUCTION

After more than two decades of war and foreign interventions, including the recent US-led military campaign following the 11 September 2001 terrorist attacks, Afghanistan has now entered a period of transition and rebuilding. It joins a host of other countries – from South Africa to Sierra Leone to East Timor – seeking to move from a repressive and violent past to a future based on democracy, the rule of law and respect for fundamental human rights and international humanitarian law. Afghanistan presents one of the most confronting case studies of 'transitional justice', what Teitel has described as the issue of how societies deal with their 'evil pasts'.[3]

In the case of war-torn Afghanistan, the challenge is overwhelming. A recent report on human rights and reconstruction in the country describes the situation as follows:

> 'For the past 23 years, foreign interventions have fueled a series of brutal wars that entrenched the power of unaccountable warlords, divided the country along ethnic lines, and destroyed its already-limited infrastructure and economic base. During this period the people of Afghanistan experienced widespread violations of all their fundamental human rights, ranging from political killings to systematic impoverishment ... Throughout the world, the reconstruction of Afghanistan is seen as a litmus test for whether the universal values of human rights and development will help define the parameters of global security, or whether the narrow military interests of powerful states will predominate. At stake is not only the ability of the Afghans to enjoy their fundamental rights, but the very legitimacy of the United Nations as the unbiased

---

2. B.A., LL.B. (Hons) (Melb.), Ll.M. (Columbia), J.S.D. Candidate (Columbia). Lecturer in International Affairs and Director, Human Rights Program, School of International and Public Affairs, Columbia University. I wish to thank Peter Bouckaert, Lorna Davidson, Dennis Dijkzeul, Horst Fischer, Avril McDonald and Gino Scarselli for their comments and suggestions on earlier drafts of this article.

3. R. Teitel, *Transitional Justice* (New York, Oxford University Press 2000) p. 3.

Yearbook of International Humanitarian Law
Volume 4 – 2001 – pp. 3-51

guardian of international law and guarantor of peace and security for all peoples of the world.'[4]

This article considers the question of how to confront the long history of systematic and widespread violations of international humanitarian and human rights law perpetrated by previous Afghan regimes, warring factions, terrorist groups and other relevant actors (including foreign military personnel). Two general arguments are advanced. First, the scale and scope of atrocities in Afghanistan, combined with the current unstable political and fragmented social environment make the pursuit of both accountability and justice on the one hand and truth and reconciliation on the other extremely problematic, at least at this early stage in the country's transition. Second, the actions of the US, both inside Afghanistan as part of its military campaign against the Taliban and Al Qaeda and in other parts of the world as part of its ongoing war against terrorism, are serving to undermine long-established principles of international humanitarian and human rights law, and threaten to impede the transition to peace, security and the rule of law in Afghanistan.

Perceiving new threats and modes of armed conflict, the US has failed to comply with even those international obligations to which it has expressly consented. This has served to further expose a long-standing exceptionalist stance towards international law, which has troubling implications not only for the coherence and progressive development of the humanitarian and human rights treaty regimes but also for future efforts to end impunity and bring to justice those suspected of committing atrocities.[5]

The inquiry proceeds in three stages. Part Two provides a brief historical background to the last two decades of armed conflict in Afghanistan and sets the post-September 11 political and military situation in the context of applicable norms of international law. Part Three then addresses the application of international humanitarian and human rights law to the various armed conflicts (both international and internal) that have occurred in Afghanistan. In relation to the role of the US, the combatant-civilian distinction which is so central to humanitarian law and the categorization and treatment of detainees under both humanitarian and human rights law is examined. Finally, Part Four assesses the normative and institutional choices faced by Afghanistan as it begins to navigate the divide between seeking justice for past abuses on the one hand and dealing with the political realities and entrenched power relations on the other.

---

4. Center for Economic and Social Rights, *Human Rights and Reconstruction in Afghanistan* (May 2002) ('CESR Report') pp. 1-2.

5. Koh attributes these developments to the larger phenomenon of a post-World War II legal system placed under increasing stress by the end of the 'post-Cold War era' on September 11. He has suggested that traditional legal dichotomies between 'war and peace, public and private, domestic and international, and civil and criminal' have become 'muddied' and that we are witnessing a 'transition from global optimism [the period from 1989 to 2001] to pessimism [the post-September 11 period]' and that this transition may be seen in three areas of the law: the use of force, the rise of the global justice system, and the relationship between civil liberties and national security. H. Koh, 'The Law Under Stress After September 11', *Yale L Rep.* (2002) pp. 12 at 13-14.

2. HISTORICAL BACKGROUND

Afghanistan has a long history of dynastic rule and coexistence of various religious and ethnic minorities.[6] In 1747, after Ahmad Shah Abdali was chosen as king by a Loya Jirga, he unified Afghanistan under the Durrani Pashtun dynasty, which ruled unbroken until the coup against Zahir Shah in 1973. The history of foreign interventions in Afghanistan began as early as the 1840s due to the country's geographic location at the frontiers of the British and Russian empires in Asia. Throughout much of the nineteenth century, Britain and Russia competed to utilize Afghanistan's geopolitical importance as a buffer against the other's expansion. Britain invaded Afghanistan twice between 1840 and 1878, until finally establishing the Durand Line in 1893, which sought to divide Afghans along tribal lines and to secure the frontier areas between Afghanistan and the Indian subcontinent.[7]

In 1880 the 'Iron Amir', Amir Abdul Rahman, became king of Afghanistan with British consent and was the first Afghan leader to seek to centralize and strengthen the state. It was not until after the third Anglo-Afghan war in 1919, however, that Afghanistan finally gained its independence from Britain and its first constitution. King Amanullah Khan initiated a broad-ranging program of Western-style domestic reforms and modernization which met with clerical opposition. This led to a rebellion in 1928 which saw the king exiled in 1929 and the rise to power of the short-lived and ruinous reign of the Saqaoists. It took a number of years for King Nadir Shah, who defeated the Saqaoists, to restore order and to regenerate the country's trade, infrastructure and education sectors. Then, in 1933, the last of the Durrani kings, Zahir Shah, ascended to the throne and ruled Afghanistan without any major changes until the mid-1950s.

After the Second World War, British influence in the region waned and Afghanistan under Prime Minister Sardar Muhammad Daud Khan (Zahir Shah's cousin and brother-in-law) turned to the Soviet Union for military and economic aid. Between 1953 and 1963, Daud Khan embarked on a policy of development, reform and modernization which produced some positive results (especially for Soviet financiers) but overall did not achieve much for the general population. After Daud was removed from power by Zahir Shah, the next decade, from 1963 to 1973, saw four prime ministers come and go, each with similar economic development plans and each one similarly ineffective. Then, in 1973, Muhammad Daud Khan overthrew King Zahir Shah[8] with the assistance of the pro-Soviet communist parties proclaiming Afghanistan a republic and himself both president and prime minister.

---

6. Various religions such as Zoroastrianism, Graeco-Buddism and Islam have existed in Afghanistan under successive ruling dynasties, including the Ghaznavid, Ghorid, Lodhi, Safavid and Moghul empires. Today, the country has a population of approximately 27 million people comprised of a number of ethnic groups: Pashtun (38%), Tajik (25%), Hazara (19%), minor ethnic groups (Aimaks, Turkmen, Baloch and others) (12%), and Uzbek (6%).

7. The Durand Line, established by Britain in 1893, was an artificial colonial division between present day Pakistan and Afghanistan that still divides the ethnic Pashtun tribes.

8. Zahir Shah was exiled to Rome, where he remained until the events of 11 September 2001.

After his return to power, Daud sought to marginalize the Parchamis, whom he suspected of being under Soviet influence, and looked instead to the West for economic assistance. By 1977, Daud had removed most People's Democratic Party of Afghanistan (PDPA) members from power and introduced a new constitution that banned the PDPA altogether. This prompted the two factions of the PDPA to seek more urgently to overcome their internal divisions. On 19 April 1978, 15,000 protesters took to the streets of Kabul in support of the PDPA, prompting the arrest and imprisonment a week later of the parties' leaders. The next day, the military staged a coup that removed Daud from power (killing him and his family in the presidential palace) and installed Nur Mohammad Taraki, the leader of the Khalq faction of the PDPA, as president of Afghanistan. Taraki immediately faced disagreements between and struggles for supremacy within each of the two PDPA factions and turned to the Soviet Union in an attempt to solidify his hold on power.[9] The Taraki government then initiated a program of radical land reform that resulted in mass repression in the countryside and the arrest and summary execution of many thousands of Afghans.[10] The attempt to reform rural society through terror provoked armed uprisings throughout Afghanistan and the start of guerrilla warfare.

2.1 Afghanistan's civil war (1979-2001)

This rapidly deteriorating situation in the late 1970s led to what is regarded as the first phase in Afghanistan's 23-year period of war – the Saur revolution and subsequent Soviet occupation. The power struggle between Taraki and his erstwhile disciple, Hafizullah Amin, was finally resolved in September 1979 when Amin prevailed and ordered Taraki's assassination. Amin immediately requested Soviet troops to protect Kabul so that he could redeploy the Afghan army to fight the Mujahidin (or 'jihad fighters'), who were by then intensifying their armed resistance. Fearing instability on its southern border and keen to establish firmer control in Afghanistan, on 24 December 1979, the USSR airlifted thousands of troops into Kabul, assassinated Amin and installed the Parcham leader Babrak Karmal as president.

The Soviet occupation had the effect of inflaming the nationalist and Islamic sentiments of the population and led to popular uprisings and war throughout Afghanistan. The Soviet troops and Karmal government sought to crush the uprisings with mass arrests, torture, and extra-judicial killings of dissidents, and with aerial bombardments and executions in the countryside.[11]

---

9. In December 1978, Afghanistan signed a Treaty of Friendship, Good Neighborliness, and Cooperation with the USSR that obliged the Soviets to provide military aid if requested by Afghanistan.

10. See Human Rights Watch, *Backgrounder on Afghanistan: History of the War* (2002) p. 1.

11. This ensured the collapse of the Afghan economy by turning more than a third of the population into refugees (five million out of a total population of 16 million), forcing the abandonment of more than half of the country's farming villages due to the aerial bombardment, and leaving only 20 to 25 percent of arable land being cultivated: see ESCR Report, *supra* n. 4, p. 59.

It is estimated that over one million Afghans died during this period, mostly in aerial bombardments, while the Mujahidin based in Pakistan and Iran continued their armed resistance. Recognizing the conflict between the Mujahidin and Soviet forces as a Cold War battleground implicating important energy resources in the Persian Gulf, the US and Saudi Arabia initiated covert operations in Afghanistan, providing massive military and financial support to the resistance. Throughout the 1980s, the US provided between $2-3 billion in weapons and supplies through the CIA and Pakistan's Inter-Service Intelligence Agency (ISI) as part of the largest US covert action program since the end of the Second World War. By 1987, the US was providing more than 65,000 tons of arms *per annum* to the Mujahidin, and in particular to the faction of Gulbuddin Hekmatyar. The CIA and the Pentagon worked with the ISI to forge unity among various Afghan and religious groups in Pakistan and to create a network of *deeni madrasas* (religious schools) in Pakistan and bases in Afghanistan to train the Mujahidin.[12]

In 1988, UN-mediated negotiations to end the war finally culminated in the Geneva Accords under which the Soviet Union agreed to remove all troops by February 1989. While still providing substantial financial assistance, the Soviets left behind a proxy communist government headed by Dr Najibullah, Karmal's former deputy, who managed to cling to power until early-1992. During this period and without *bona fide* commitments from either Afghanistan's neighbors or the international community, the UN attempted in vain to implement a transitional process acceptable to all the parties. The various Mujahidin factions, however, refused to negotiate with the government and continued their armed struggle. Following the Soviet withdrawal from Afghanistan, the US and its allies effectively abandoned any efforts to establish a peace process although some effort was made to support the continuing UN relief and humanitarian assistance operations. Afghanistan was thus left to its own resources to deal with the legacies of a huge flow of armaments, a burgeoning drug trade, a destroyed infrastructure and an impoverished population.

In early-1992, phase two of Afghanistan's 23-year civil war began when the forces of Ahmed Shah Massoud (a Tajik leader), General Abdul Rashid Dostum (head of a powerful Uzbek militia formerly allied with Najibullah), and the Hazara faction Hizb-i Wahdat formed a coalition called the Northern Alliance. Following a mutiny on 15 April non-Pashtun militia forces formerly allied to the government took control of Kabul airport and prevented President Najibullah from leaving Afghanistan. Massoud entered Kabul and installed a coalition government. The new government, however, excluded the Hizb-i Islami led by Gulbuddin Hekmatyar, who rejected the arrangement and launched massive and indiscrimi-

---

12. During this period, militant religio-political groups and *madrasas* proliferated in Pakistan. Today there are 58 registered religious political parties and 24 armed religious militias in the country. See S. Shafqat, 'From Official Islam to Islamism: The Rise of Dawat-ul-Irshad and Lashkar-e-Taiba', in C. Jaffrelot, *Pakistan: Nationalism without a Nation?* (New Delhi, Manohar/London, Zed Books 2002) pp. 131 at 133-134.

nate rocket attacks on Kabul that continued intermittently until February 1995.[13] In June 1992, Burhanuddin Rabbani (the Tajik leader of Jamiat-i Islami or 'Society of Islam') became president of the Islamic State of Afghanistan. Fighting continued, however, between the Hazara faction of Hizb-i Wahdat and Abd al-Rabb al-Rasul Sayyaf's Ittihad-i Islami, with many civilians being abducted and killed. In January 1994, Hekmatyar joined forces with General Abdul Rashid Dostum and successfully ousted Rabbani and his Defence Minister Massoud, thus initiating a full-scale civil war in Kabul which, by 1995, had reduced a third of the city to rubble.[14]

It was in the context of this chaos and lawlessness created by warring Mujahidin factions that the Taliban first emerged and the third phase of Afghanistan's civil war began. The Taliban (meaning 'students') were former Mujahidin and *madrasa* students who coalesced around Mullah Mohammad Omar, a former *mujahid* from Kandahar province. The group also included commanders in other Pashtun parties and former Khalqi PDPA members. The Taliban were disillusioned with the results of their victory over the communists and sought to restore stability to Afghanistan by enforcing a strict form of Islamic law (they adhered to an extreme form of Sunni Islam closely related to Saudi Wahhabism) and attacking local warlords who had carved up the country among the various factions. Also trained by Pakistan's ISI in *madrasa* and training camps, the Taliban demonstrated disciplined military prowess and defeated various Mujahidin factions, driving Massoud from Kabul to the north and securing control of 27 out of 30 provinces. Under Massoud's leadership, the Northern Alliance continued to fight the Taliban from the north, and received arms and financial assistance from Iran, Russia and India allowing them to control about five to ten percent of the country.

In 1997, the Taliban renamed the country the Islamic Emirate of Afghanistan and vigorously enforced their interpretation of Islamic law.[15] Between 1997 and 1998, the Taliban sought to gain more control in northern Afghanistan where Dostum still held large areas of land in and around Mazar-i Sharif in an alliance with Hizb-i Wahdat (which had a stronghold in the large Hazara population). After one of Dostum's deputies, General Abdul Malik Pahlawan ('Malik'), struck a deal with the Taliban, they were able to enter Mazar-i Sharif, prompting Pakistan, Saudi Arabia and the United Arab Emirates to recognize the Taliban as the official government of Afghanistan.[16] But the alliance with Malik proved to be short-lived,

---

13. The framework for an Afghan interim government forged by Pakastani-based Mujahidin in the Peshawar Agreement of 24 April 1992 collapsed only months after its implementation.

14. Human Rights Watch report, *supra* n. 10, p. 3.

15. Mullah Omar assumed the title *amir-ul momineen* (commander of the faithful). In order to enforce Islamic law, the Taliban created the Ministry of Promotion of Virtue and Prevention of Vice which was responsible for enforcing all decrees regarding moral behavior. This included comprehensive policies that were especially repressive towards women (prohibiting work outside the home in areas other than health care, virtually eliminating education for women and girls and requiring a draconian dress code) but also rigidly restricted the freedom of men in many areas of personal and social life.

16. Despite the fact that the Taliban had control of over 80 percent of the country, it failed to achieve international recognition as the legitimate government of Afghanistan. The UN continued to regard Rabbani's government as the *de jure* government of Afghanistan in exile (the 'Islamic State of

and when the Taliban sought to disarm local Hazaras, thousands of Taliban soldiers were taken prisoner and summarily executed Malik and Hizb-i Wahdat. In August 1998, however, the Taliban at last captured Mazar-i Sharif, massacring at least 2,000 people in the process, mainly Hazara civilians. Thus, during this period, the country was divided along ethnic lines, with the Taliban controlling the capital Kabul and over two-thirds of the country (including the predominantly ethnic Pashtun areas in southern Afghanistan) while opposing factions, under the banner of the Northern Alliance (or 'United Front for the Salvation of Afghanistan', as they later renamed themselves) had their strongholds in the ethnically diverse north.

As discussed in the next two sections, the conflict between the Taliban and the Northern Alliance resulted in serious violations of international humanitarian and human rights law on both sides, including indiscriminate aerial bombardment and shelling, summary executions and the widespread use of antipersonnel mines. Taliban offensives included scorched earth tactics in the Shomali plains north of Kabul, summary executions of prisoners in the north-central province of Samangan, and forced relocation and conscription. At the same time, the Northern Alliance carried out summary executions, burnt houses and looted in areas under its control, the principal targets being ethnic Pashtuns and others suspected of supporting the Taliban.

By 2001, Afghanistan was a country crippled not only by incessant civil war but also by the effects of a severe three year drought that resulted in the failure of crops and the death of most of its livestock. Life expectancy at birth was approximately 46 years old, and the overall literacy rate of people above the age of 15 was 31 percent, making it amongst the lowest in the world. During 23 years of civil war, the country lost a third of its population (over 1.5 million people are estimated to have died as a direct result of armed conflict) while another five million fled as refugees to Iran and Pakistan. A large part of the remaining population was left internally displaced.

2.2 Al Qaeda and the 'war against terrorism' (2001-2003)

In addition to the incessant meddling of neighboring countries,[17] the war in Afghanistan had a further unique and ultimately disastrous dimension that soon led

---

Afghanistan'), a position later confirmed in the Bonn Agreement of 5 December 2001. See *infra* n. 34 and accompanying text. The response of the Organization of the Islamic Conference was to leave the Afghan seat vacant until such time as the question of legitimacy could be resolved through negotiations among the warring factions.

17. Although there have been numerous agreements by Afghanistan's neighbors and other states involved in the conflict to end arms supplies as part of a larger peace process, none of these agreements has included enforcement mechanisms. On 21 July 1999, at a meeting in Tashkent of the Group of Six-plus-Two, comprising the countries bordering Afghanistan plus the US and Russia, the delegates signed an agreement, subsequently known as the Tashkent Declaration, in which they agreed 'not to provide military support to any Afghan party and to prevent the use of our territories for such purposes'.

to its fourth phase. The Saudi multi-millionaire Osama bin Laden, who had left Afghanistan in 1990, returned in 1996. He lived first under the protection of the Jalalabad *shura* (tribal council) until the Taliban took control of Jalalabad and Kabul in 1997. He then moved to Kandahar where he developed a close relationship with the Taliban leader Mullah Muhammad Omar. During this period, bin Laden continued to develop an international network of Islamic fighters from various countries (known as 'Al Qaeda') dedicated to carrying out acts of violence against embassies, military targets and civilians linked to the US. His fighters also fought alongside Taliban troops during their ongoing struggle with the Northern Alliance forces.

In August 1998, the US launched 79 cruise missiles against bin Laden's training camps near the Pakistan border and at a pharmaceutical plant in Sudan's capital Khartoum which US officials linked to bin Laden's operations. The strikes followed the bombings of the US embassies in Nairobi and Dar es-Salaam which killed more than 200 people, including 12 Americans, and an earlier truck bombing in 1996 that killed 19 members of the US military services and wounded nearly 400 others in an apartment building being used as military barracks in Saudi Arabia. On 15 October 1999, the UN Security Council imposed sanctions on the Taliban in order to pressure them to turn over bin Laden, banning Taliban-controlled aircraft from takeoff and landing and freezing the Taliban's assets abroad.[18] On 12 October 2000, a US warship, the *USS Cole*, was bombed while refueling in the Yemeni port of Aden by two suicide bombers in a fiberglass skiff loaded with explosives, killing 17 American sailors. In the wake of several arrests by Yemeni authorities, the Yemeni Prime Minister said that preliminary evidence suggested bin Laden's involvement, although no more conclusive evidence has subsequently come to light.

The Taliban's continuing failure to hand over bin Laden led to an expansion by the Security Council on 19 December 2000 of the sanctions regime, including an arms embargo on the Taliban, a ban on travel outside Afghanistan by Taliban officials of deputy ministerial rank and the closing of Taliban offices abroad.[19] On 9 September 2001, Massoud was assassinated when suicide bombers disguised as journalists detonated a hidden device in a video camera.[20] Then, dramatically, on 11 September 2001, international terrorists, including members of the organization Al Qaeda, carried out attacks on the Pentagon in Washington DC and on the World Trade Center in New York City killing over 3,000 people. The terrorists hijacked four civilian aircraft and flew them into these targets (with one aircraft crashing in Pennsylvania), killing all passengers on board and causing mass deaths and injuries to civilians and massive destruction of property. The next day, the Security

---

18. SC Res. 1267 (1999).

19. SC Res. 1333 (2000).

20. United Front leaders have claimed that the assassins were linked to Osama bin Laden, and many observers believe that the assassination was designed to deprive the United Front of its most effective leader in the aftermath of the events of September 11: see Human Rights Watch report, *supra* n. 10, p. 5.

Council adopted a resolution unequivocally condemning the attacks, declaring them to be a 'threat to international peace and security' and recognizing the 'inherent right of individual or collective self defense in accordance with the Charter'.[21]

On 28 September, the Security Council, acting under Chapter VII of the Charter, unanimously adopted a resolution directed towards combating terrorists and all states which support, harbor, provide safe haven to, finance, supply weapons to, help recruit or aid terrorists, and requiring all member states to cooperate in a wide range of areas – from suppressing and financing of terrorism to providing early warning, cooperating in criminal investigations, and exchanging information on possible terrorist acts.[22] The resolution also provided for the establishment of a new 'terrorism committee' of the Security Council, consisting of all members of the Council, to which all member states were required to report within 90 days on the steps they had taken to implement the resolution. Thus, Resolution 1373 quickly established a new comprehensive legal framework – backed by Chapter VII enforcement power – for states to address the threat of international terrorism through mutual cooperation and coordination of their criminal justice systems.

A week later on 7 October, the US Ambassador to the UN, John Negroponte, delivered a letter to the President of the Security Council stating that the US, together with other states, had 'initiated actions in the exercise of its inherent right of individual and collective self-defense' against Al Qaeda terrorist training camps and military installations of the Taliban regime in Afghanistan on the basis of 'clear and compelling information' that Al Qaeda, supported by the Taliban regime in Afghanistan, had a 'central role in the attacks'.[23] The letter further stated that while still at the early stages, the US 'may find that our self-defense requires further actions with respect to other organizations and other States'. Thus was born the 'Bush doctrine' – the asserted right to use military force in 'self defense' against any state which aids, harbors or supports international terrorists or terrorist organizations.[24] As of 7 October 2001 (and likely earlier), a US-led coalition of armed forces commenced 'self defense' operations in Afghanistan in order to destroy the Al Qaeda terrorist organization and to remove the Taliban regime from power.

The military tactics employed by the US and its allies (the 'international coalition') were to use overwhelming air power in conjunction with covert operations in cooperation with Northern Alliance forces. The international coalition rearmed anti-Taliban forces, provided them with tactical support through US special forces

21. SC Res. 1368 (2001).

22. SC Res. 1373 (2001).

23. Letter from the Permanent Representative of the US to the President of the UN Security Council (S/2001/946).

24. For discussion on self-defense and state responsibility for terrorist acts, see *infra* n. 58 and accompanying text

liaisons on the ground, and gave aerial bombing support.[25] The result was that Afghan anti-Taliban forces conducted most of the ground offensives and subsequently took military control of the areas they captured. This in turn meant that ethnically-based factions and individual warlords, once more, gained a stranglehold on power in provincial areas in the absence of an expanded international security force beyond Kabul.[26] As Ahmed Rashid has observed:

> 'In the 1980s, Washington backed anti-Soviet Afghan militias which in victory produced the factionalism that brought the Taliban to power. Now, the same forces, which with US backing ousted the Taliban, are threatening to return the country to warlordism all over again ... Warlords whose armies acted as proxy US ground forces in the Taliban campaign are now refusing to disarm or accept the writ of the country's fledgling interim government.'[27]

The international coalition's military campaign against the Taliban and Al Qaeda is now largely completed, although US and allied special operations forces continue to search for Al Qaeda forces in various parts of the country. Due to the secrecy of the Pentagon and general lack of access to conflict areas, accurate and independently verifiable details of the effects of the war remain unavailable. Despite the ability of the US to target its weaponry with precision accuracy, however, estimates by some observers of Afghan civilian casualties due to coalition bombing and special operations have ranged from 3,000 to 3,500.[28] In

---

25. See S.B. Glasser, 'U.S. Backing Helps Warlords Solidify Power', *Washington Post* (18 February 2002); Human Rights Watch, 'Dangerous Dealings: Changes to U.S. Military Assistance After September 11', Vol. 14(1)(G) (February 2002) at pp. 6-8.

26. See Human Rights Watch Briefing Paper, 'Afghanistan: Return of the Warlords', June 2002 (noting the reemergence of figures associated with the Taliban as well as the extremist Islamist movement led by the former Afghan Prime Minister Gulbuddin Hekmatyar in several southern provinces).

27. A. Rushid, 'Fledgling Afghan Government Faces Scourge of Warlordism – Local Leaders Who Ousted Taliban With Aid of U.S. Are Restoring Old Fiefs', *Wall Street Journal* (16 January 2002).

28. Most casualties are believed to have resulted from 'collateral damage' due to the US bombing of heavily populated metropolitan areas where military installations and other strategic targets were also located. In isolated cases, it appears that bombs were dropped on hospitals, schools, mosques and groups of fleeing refugees: see e.g., M.W. Herold, *A Dossier on Civilian Victims of United States' Aerial Bombing of Afghanistan: A Comprehensive Accounting* (2002) available online at www.cursor.org/stories/civilian_deaths.htm (suggesting that the US targeted civilian infrastructure, including the Kajaki dam and other power stations, radio stations, the Kabul telephone exchange, the Al Jazeera Kabul office, trucks and buses containing refugees, and numerous civilian trucks carrying fuel and oil). There have also been reports of US strikes on a Red Cross warehouse in Kabul (which was allegedly used by the Taliban for supplies) and a Red Crescent clinic in Kandahar on 31 October 2001 killing 15-25 civilians. Note, however, that there is disagreement over the numbers of civilian casualties and that the figures suggested by Herold have been challenged as being excessive: see J. Muravchik, 'Racking Up Afghan Casualties', *Wall Street Journal Europe* (21 August 2002) at A8 (arguing that the figure of over 3,500 civilian casualties is unsubstantiated).

addition, the US has employed its full arsenal of weapons, including JDAM-type bombs, cluster bombs and devastating sub-atomic 'daisy cutter' bombs.[29]

As discussed further below, both civilian casualties and the use of certain types of weapons raise the question of potential violations of international humanitarian law. But perhaps the most volatile political dimension of the most recent phase of the armed conflict in Afghanistan has centered on the issue of the legal status and treatment of detainees. Since the commencement of US military operations on 7 October 2001, thousands of individuals have been detained by anti-Taliban Afghan forces and by the US armed forces. These include both Taliban and 'foreign' Al Qaeda fighters from over two-dozen countries. In addition to Afghan nationals, many Pakistani nationals are reportedly among the detainees, as well as smaller numbers of Saudis, Yemenis and others from Arab States, Uzbeks, Chechens from Russia, Chinese, Europeans, and others.[30] The US military has been screening and interrogating detainees in Afghan custody in order to identify persons it wishes to prosecute or detain or who may have useful intelligence information (primarily in relation to the whereabouts of Taliban or Al Qaeda leaders, or knowledge about the inner workings of the Al Qaeda terrorist network). The US has taken custody of several hundred detainees held by Afghan forces, and has transferred them to its own detention facilities: a US military detention facility located outside Kandahar and detention facilities in offshore Navy ships, such as the *USS Peleliu*. In addition, US military forces have also directly taken custody of persons while carrying out military operations inside Afghanistan. In January 2002, the US began transferring these persons from the detention facilities in the immediate theater of conflict to a more permanent detention facility at the US military base in Guantánamo Bay, Cuba. According to the Department of Defense, as of 28 January 2002, 482 prisoners were being held by US forces in Afghanistan and at Guantánamo Bay, about one fifth of whom were Saudi nationals.

2.3 Post-war transition and rebuilding: the Bonn Agreement

As the full effects of the US-led military campaign became apparent in late-2001, the UN began to make arrangements for Afghanistan's political transition and rebuilding.[31] The UN has in fact long been engaged in the country, both in trying to

---

29. Weapons employed by the Air Force have included medium-sized Tomahawk and cruise missiles; fuel air bombs; B-52 carpet bombs; BLU-82 sub-atomic bombs (known as 'daisy cutters' which destroy everything in a 600 yard radius); 1,000 and 2,000 pound JDAM (Joint Direct Attack Munition) bombs; and Aerojet/Honeywell CBU-87 cluster bombs. As of 30 November 2001, it is estimated that US bombers had dropped approximately 600 cluster bombs in Afghanistan. Assuming a failure rate of 12 percent, this suggests that there are currently about 14,500 unexploded bomblets in the Afghan countryside and villages adding to the existing proliferation of landmines: see M. Steen, 'US Cluster Bombs Add to Afghan Landmine Tragedy', Reuters News Service (5 December 2001).

30. See Human Rights Watch, Backgrounder, *Afghanistan: Return of Foreign Fighters and Torture Concerns* (December 2001).

31. See Security Council Meeting 4414, SC/7210, 13 November 2001 (Secretary General's Special Representative, Lakhdhar Brahimi, outlining plans for political transition in Afghanistan and stressing the need for a 'home-grown solution that was aided by the international community' in order

end the inter-Afghan fighting that followed the Soviet withdrawal in 1989, and in delivering humanitarian assistance to large numbers of people both in Afghanistan and in refugee camps in neighboring countries.[32] Recognizing that Afghanistan presented a radically different situation compared with recent international peace-building operations in Kosovo and East Timor, the UN opted for a model closer to its earlier assistance missions that provided development support to post-conflict societies.[33] On 5 December 2001, the UN brokered talks in Bonn, Germany, which culminated in an agreement for Afghanistan's future political framework, which was fully endorsed by the Security Council the following day.[34] The Secretary General, Kofi Annan, stated that the Bonn Agreement represents a 'historic opportunity for the people of Afghanistan to emerge from a cycle of conflict and devastating poverty into a future in which there can be reconstruction and peaceful development'.[35]

The Bonn Agreement provided for a transfer of power from Burhanuddin Rabbani (whom the UN still recognized as the leader of the *de jure* government of Afghanistan in exile) to an Interim Authority that was to be established on 22 December 2001.[36] Six months after the establishment of the Interim Authority, an

---

to create a 'stable, representative and accountable government with both internal and external legitimacy').

32. The UN Special Mission to Afghanistan (UNSMA) operated for many years on a relatively minor budget. In 1997, for example, UNSMA received $3.1 million for its peacemaking operations and 30-person staff in Kabul and Islamabad: see Press Release, UN General Assembly, Fifth Committee, GA/AB/3130, 16 December 1996. Following the negotiation of the Bonn Agreement, on 28 March 2002, the Security Council endorsed the establishment, for an initial period of 12 months, of a UN Assistance Mission in Afghanistan (UNAMA) in order to integrate all existing UN elements into a single mission: see Report of the UN Secretary General, *The situation in Afghanistan and its implications for international peace and security*, A/56/875-S/2002/278 (18 March 2002) at Ch. VI, para. 94 et seq.

33. Thus, whereas sustained grassroots peace-building, peacekeeping and institutional construction have been pursued in other conflicts prior to establishing self-governing institutions, in Afghanistan the strategy was to assemble a broadly-based administration as quickly as possible in order to establish security and a partnership with the international community (which would assume a supportive role): see J. Dobbins, the US Special Envoy for Afghanistan, Remarks at a US Institute of Peace conference titled 'Afghanistan: Prospects for Peace and Reconstruction' (15 January 2002). As has been pointed out, however, this strategy creates a 'divide between formal authority and practical influence, increasing the risk that the political consensus established in the Bonn Agreement and recently reaffirmed at the Loya Jirga Kabul will spin out of control': S. Chesterman, 'Afghanistan: The Hard Part for the UN Starts Now', *International Herald Tribune* (5 July 2002) (arguing that the success of the UN mission in Afghanistan requires the Bonn Agreement to be seen not as a final status agreement but as a framework for further negotiations and for the UN to be able to exert significant political influence over that process).

34. Agreement on provisional arrangements in Afghanistan pending the re-establishment of permanent government institutions, S/2001/1154, 5 December 2001 (the 'Bonn Agreement'), endorsed by SC Res. 1383 (2001), 6 December 2001.

35. Report of the Secretary General, *supra* n. 32, para. 7.

36. Art. I, sec. 2 of the Bonn Agreement provides that the Interim Authority is to consist of an Interim Administration presided over by a Chairman, a Special Independent Commission for the Convening of the Emergency Loya Jirga, and a Supreme Court of Afghanistan, as well as any other courts established by the Interim Administration. The Interim Authority is the sole repository of

Emergency Loya Jirga was required to decide on a Transitional Authority. This should be a 'broad-based transitional administration' mandated to govern Afghanistan until such time as a 'fully representative government can be elected through free and fair elections', which must be held no later than two years after the convening of the Emergency Loya Jirga.[37] The Bonn Agreement also required a Constitutional Loya Jirga to be convened within 18 months of the establishment of the Transitional Authority in order to adopt a new constitution for Afghanistan.[38]

The Interim Authority chosen at Bonn in December 2001 was headed by Hamid Karzai, a Pashtun tribal leader, who was also later elected by the Emergency Loya Jirga held in June 2002 as President of the Transitional Authority. The overall composition of both the Interim and Transitional Authorities, however, was heavily influenced by the renewed military and political power of Afghanistan's warlords.[39] The three main ethnically-based armed militias in northern Afghanistan managed to secure representation in the Interim Administration. The Panjshiri Tajik leadership of Jamiat, the dominant element within the United Front (formerly, the Northern Alliance), which assisted the US-led coalition in the ousting of the Taliban, secured the three most critical departments in the Interim Administration – defense, interior and foreign affairs.[40] Hizb-i Wahdat received control of the planning department whose head, Haji Mohammad Mohaqiq, was

---

Afghan sovereignty, represents Afghanistan in its external relations, and occupies Afghanistan's seat at the UN, its specialized agencies and other international bodies: Art. I, sec. 3.

37. Art. I, sec. 4 of the Bonn Agreement.

38. This requires the Transitional Authority to establish a Constitutional Commission with the assistance of the UN: Art. I, sec. 6. Until a new Constitution is adopted, the Constitution of 1964 and existing laws and regulations constitute the applicable legal framework in the country (with some exceptions relating to the Bonn Agreement itself, international legal obligations to which Afghanistan is a party, and several provisions in the 1964 Constitution relating to the monarchy and executive and legislative bodies).

39. Four main groups signed the Bonn Agreement: the Northern Alliance, the Pakistan-based Peshawar Front, the Iran-backed Cyprus Group, and the Rome Process representing former King Zahir Shah. The 30-member cabinet of the Interim Administration included 11 Pashtuns, eight Tajiks, five from the Shi'a Hazara population, three Uzbeks, with the rest drawn from other minorities. Despite efforts to the contrary by the Special Independent Commission for the Convening of the Emergency Loya Jirga and the UN, warlords such as General Abdul Rashid Dostum and Commander Atta Mohammed selected themselves to the Loya Jirga, while in the west of the country, Ismail Khan reportedly manipulated the selection process: see Human Rights Watch briefing paper, *supra* n. 26 at p. 11.

40. Mohammad Qasim Fahim, the commander-in-chief of the Northern Alliance's Jamiat forces, became the Defense Minister in the Interim Administration; Yunus Qanooni, who led the Northern Alliance delegation, became the Interior Minister; and Abdullah Abdullah, who retained his position as foreign secretary, became the Foreign Affairs Minister. General Abdul Rashid Dostum, the military governor of Herat and commander of Junbish, initially denounced the Bonn Agreement but was ultimately assigned the post of deputy defense minister. Similarly, Ismail Khan, an ally of Jamiat leader Burhannudin Rabbani, pledged to recognize the Interim Administration while proclaiming autonomy for five western provinces: see P. Baker, 'Afghan Factions Criticize Accord: Some Leaders Vow to Boycott Regime', *Washington Post* (7 December 2001) cited in Human Rights Watch, *Paying for the Taliban's Crimes: Abuses Against Ethnic Pashtuns in Northern Afghanistan*, Vol. 14(2)(C) (April 2002) at p. 7.

also designated one of the five deputy chairmen of the Interim Cabinet.[41]

The Bonn Agreement requires the Interim Administration to establish with UN assistance an independent Human Rights Commission and a Judicial Commission, which together will have the task of ensuring that international humanitarian and human rights law and standards are implemented in the particular social, political and cultural context of Afghanistan.[42] Importantly from a transitional justice perspective, the Bonn Agreement makes two further stipulations: first, that the Interim Authority and the Emergency Loya Jirga act in accordance with 'basic principles and provisions contained in international instruments on human rights and international humanitarian law to which Afghanistan is a party';[43] and second, that the UN shall have the 'right to investigate human rights violations and, where necessary, recommend corrective action'.[44]

On 9 March 2002, a national workshop on human rights was convened in Kabul by the then-UN High Commissioner for Human Rights, Mary Robinson, with participants representing a wide spectrum of Afghan society and numerous human rights NGOs and institutions. The workshop produced four working groups which should proceed to formulate proposals for the establishment of the independent Human Rights Commission; the development of a national programme of human rights education; approaches to human rights monitoring; investigation and remedial action; and the advancement of the rights of women. Achieving accountability for humanitarian and human rights law violations and establishing transitional justice mechanisms more broadly – including proposals for the establishment of a Truth Commission to uncover the atrocities committed over two decades of war – will involve components of these proposals. At the same time, the Security Council has sought to link development aid to improved human rights performance,[45] and it is clear that the $4.5 billion reconstruction process will be a test

---

41. The cabinet of the subsequent Transitional Administration named by President Karzai in late-June 2002 differed only slightly from that of the Interim Administration.

42. Art. II, sec. 2 stipulates that a Judicial Commission will be established to 'rebuild the domestic justice system in accordance with Islamic principles, international standards, the rule of law and Afghan legal traditions'. Art. III, sec. C, para. 6 stipulates that a Human Rights Commission will be established with its responsibilities to include 'human rights monitoring, investigation of violations of human rights, and development of domestic human rights institutions'.

43. Bonn Agreement, Art. V, sec. 2. The Interim Authority is also required to 'respect international law' (Art. V, sec. 3) and to 'ensure the participation of women as well as the equitable representation of all ethnic and religious communities in the Interim Administration and Emergency Loya Jirga' (Art. V, sec. 4).

44. The UN is also responsible for the 'development and implementation of a programme of human rights education to promote respect for and understanding of human rights': Annex II – Role of the United Nations During the Interim Period, sec. 6. The advancement of the rights and participation of women and the integration of a gender perspective will be a primary focus for these institutions. In this regard, the Office of the High Commissioner for Human Rights has seconded a human rights adviser to the Office of the Special Representative in Kabul to provide advice in the initial stages of developing a human rights programme. In addition, the work of the Special Rapporteur of the Commission on Human Rights, Kamal Hossain, remains integral to this process: see Report of the Secretary General, *supra* n. 32, para. 43.

45. SC Res. 1401 of 28 March 2002.

case for a rights-based development approach that prioritizes basic needs, guarantees local participation, addresses the root causes of poverty, and establishes effective procedures for accountability and remedies for victims.

Outside Kabul, the overall human rights situation in Afghanistan remains precarious. There have been reports of civilian massacres involving reprisal killings and summary executions and the taking and retaking of areas by warring factions. Gross violations of the human rights of women and girls are continuing in many areas, including rape and other forms of sexual violence, abductions and kidnappings, as well as forced marriages and trafficking. The existence of millions of Afghan refugees and internally displaced persons is also creating great insecurity and instability in the country. Pending the creation of a national army, the unwillingness of the US and UK to expand the International Security Assistance Force (ISAF) beyond Kabul to other major cities and surrounding areas has allowed these violations to continue largely unchecked.[46]

Each of these factors has been recognized by the General Assembly[47] and the UN Commission on Human Rights,[48] both of which have called upon all Afghan parties to adhere strictly to their obligations under human rights instruments and international humanitarian law. The Secretary-General has further urged the Security Council to 'support the wish of the Afghan people for the expansion of the [ISAF]' so as to minimize the 'likelihood of large-scale hostilities erupting again between existing armed factions'.[49] A recent independent mission to Afghanistan

---

46. Under the Bonn Agreement, it was agreed that 'responsibility for providing stability and law and order throughout the country resides with the Afghans themselves'. Given that it would take some time to reconstitute Afghanistan's security and armed forces, however, a request was made to the Security Council to consider authorizing the early deployment of a UN-mandated force to 'assist in the maintenance of security for Kabul and its surrounding areas' and which could, 'as appropriate, be progressively expanded to other urban centers and other areas': Annex I – International Security Force, sec. 3. On 20 December 2001, the Security Council, acting under Chapter VII of the UN Charter, authorized an International Security Assistance Force (ISAF) for a period of six months to assist the Interim Authority maintain security in 'Kabul and its surrounding areas'. Despite repeated requests by both the Afghan administration and the Secretary-General, the Security Council has refused to expand the mandate of the ISAF to areas outside of Kabul and its immediately surrounding areas. See Report of the Secretary-General, *supra* n. 32, paras. 58-59 (noting that while the ISAF remains limited to Kabul, the main threats to the Interim Administration emanate from the provinces).

47. *Question of human rights in Afghanistan*, A/Res/56/176, 7 February 2002 (calling upon all Afghan parties, *inter alia*, to 'facilitate the provision of efficient and effective remedies to the victims of grave violations and abuses of human rights and of international humanitarian law and to bring the perpetrators to justice in accordance with international standards' and to 'treat all suspects and convicted or detained persons in accordance with relevant international law').

48. *The situation of human rights in Afghanistan*, Comm. HR Res. 2002/19, E/CN.4/2002/L.31, 22 April 2002 (calling upon the Interim Authority, its successors and all Afghan groups, in application of the Bonn Agreement, to 'adhere strictly to their obligations under human rights instruments and international humanitarian law, *inter alia*, in relation to the treatment of prisoners' and strongly condemning the 'past violations and abuses of human rights and international humanitarian law in Afghanistan by the Taliban and others', including torture, the use of child soldiers, civilian massacres and summary executions, the killing of foreign correspondents, Iranian diplomats and UN personnel, and the gross violations of the human rights of women and girls).

49. A/56/875-S/2002/278 at pp. 9, 21.

has warned that 'without an international force to maintain peace, disarm warlords, oversee the transition to a more representative government and establish mechanisms for human rights accountability, Afghanistan is likely to slide into renewed war once the world's attention shifts to the next global crisis'.[50] Thus, until the overall human security situation in the country is adequately addressed, the broad scope of activities of UNAMA – political, human rights and rule of law, gender, relief, recovery and reconstruction – will remain at risk of unraveling.

3. VIOLATIONS OF INTERNATIONAL HUMANITARIAN AND HUMAN RIGHTS LAW

3.1 Some preliminary questions

Before one can address the controversial question of modes of accountability for individual violations of international humanitarian and human rights law, it is first necessary to discuss three prior and interrelated issues: first, who are the potential perpetrators and actors; second, what is the scope of application of the relevant conventional and customary norms of international law; and third, what is the nature of the armed conflict (or multiple armed conflicts) that has existed at different periods over the last 23 years in Afghanistan, and how does this relate to the two prior issues?

In relation to the first issue, the analysis is divided into four parts in accordance with the different types of potential perpetrators: (a) Mujahidin and other warring Afghan factions, including Taliban forces; (b) forces of the Soviet Union and neighbouring states; (c) members of Al Qaeda and other international terrorist networks; and (d) US-led military forces involved in the post-September 11 armed conflict in Afghanistan.

In relation to the second issue, Afghanistan is a party to the four Geneva Conventions of 1949 (although not the two Additional Protocols of 1977), and to most of the human rights conventions.[51] Thus, almost the full scope of international humanitarian and human rights law is potentially applicable to abuses committed during periods of both armed conflict and peacetime in Afghanistan over the last two decades.

In relation to the third issue, some preliminary comments are necessary. For some years, both scholars and practitioners have been observing the gradual convergence of international human rights and humanitarian law.[52] Indeed, today

---

50. CESR Report, *supra* n. 4, at p. 2.

51. Afghanistan is a party to the Convention on the Prevention and Punishment of the Crime of Genocide; International Covenant on Civil and Political Rights; International Covenant on Economic, Social and Cultural Rights, the Convention against Torture and Other Cruel, Inhuman or Degrading Treatment or Punishment; and the Convention on the Rights of the Child. Afghanistan has signed but not ratified the Convention on the Elimination of All Forms of Discrimination Against Women.

52. See e.g., T. Meron, 'The Humanization of International Humanitarian Law', 94 *AJIL* (2000) p. 239.

we no longer refer to the 'laws of war' but rather to 'international humanitarian law', reflecting the influence of the human rights movement and principles of humanity. In many respects, the older body of the law of armed conflict, which derives historically from medieval notions of chivalry and reciprocity guaranteeing 'fair play' and minimizing unnecessary suffering in times of armed conflict, is being 'humanized' to accord with a more modern conception of individual human dignity that is thought to prevail in all circumstances.

This can be seen in a number of areas. As compared with the Lieber Code and early Hague law, the guarantees against torture, arbitrary arrest and detention, discrimination, and of due process in the 1949 Geneva Conventions and 1977 Additional Protocols reflect the unmistakable influence of the Universal Declaration of Human Rights; the domain of legitimate reprisals (collective responsibility of the many for violations by a few) has diminished and been influenced by the emphasis in human rights law on individual responsibility; violations of humanitarian law are increasingly subject to prosecution in third states under the principle of universal jurisdiction; the classic distinctions in thresholds of applicability between 'international' and 'non-international' armed conflicts has begun to break down with increasing calls for the formulation of fundamental standards of humanity that protect an 'irreducible core of non-derogable norms';[53] and we have seen the emergence of the notion of 'crimes against humanity' with no *a priori* nexus to armed conflict.

While these convergences are welcome developments, it is important to realize that significant differences between human rights and humanitarian law remain. Humanitarian law regulates aspects of a struggle for life and death between contestants who operate on the basis of formal equality; it allows the killing of 'combatants' and, in some circumstances, it may tolerate the killing and wounding of civilians as 'lawful collateral damage, where the military necessity is sufficiently great; it permits deprivation of personal freedom without conviction in a court of law; it allows an occupying power to resort to internment and limits the appeal rights of detained persons; and it permits far-reaching limitations on freedoms of expression and assembly'. Thus, while humanitarian law attempts to impose constraints on the savagery of war, especially regarding unnecessary suffering of civilians and inhumane methods and means of warfare, it nevertheless permits violations of some fundamental human rights. It is of importance, therefore – as will be seen in the case of Afghanistan – to determine whether the threshold requirements of either an international or internal armed conflict have been met or whether states remain bound by the full array of international obligations that exist under human rights law and other regimes providing for the protection of the rights of the individual.

---

53. See e.g., T. Meron and A. Rosas, 'A Declaration of Minimum Humanitarian Standards', *AJIL* (1991) p. 375; A. Eide, A. Rosas and T. Meron, 'Combating Lawlessness in Gray Zone Conflicts through Minimum Humanitarian Standards', 89 *AJIL* (1995) p. 215; D. Petrasek, 'Moving Forward on the Development of Minimum Humanitarian Standards', 92 *AJIL* (1998) p. 557. See also Minimum Humanitarian Standards: Analytical Report of the Secretary-General Submitted pursuant to Commission on Human Rights resolution 1197/21, UN Doc. E/CN.4/1998/87 (1998).

Once an international armed conflict may be said to exist, the killing of any person meeting the definition of a 'combatant' is permissible and the rights of civilians and detainees are governed primarily by the Geneva Conventions. While human rights law continues to apply in such situations and fill any 'gaps' in the humanitarian law regime, it may be limited or derogated from by states, leaving only a small 'core' of human rights norms applicable.[54] Where there is a conflict between the two legal regimes, the law of armed conflict – as the *lex specialis* – will prevail.[55] In the case of Afghanistan, the issue of thresholds of applicability is complex for two reasons. First, as we have seen, the cycle of war in Afghanistan has moved through at least four phases since the Saur revolution and Soviet occupation in 1979, with certain periods of hostilities having a more international, and others a more internal, character. Even during periods of largely internal armed conflict, Russia, the US, and neighboring states have been deeply involved in providing military and financial assistance to the warring Afghan factions. Thus, as in the case of the fighting in the former Yugoslavia after 1991, which was held to have mixed internal and international aspects,[56] difficult determinations need to be made regarding the consecutive phases of the Afghan wars in order to determine which rules apply to different perpetrators at different times. That said, the characterization of the different phases of conflict in Afghanistan – at least in relation to the most serious abuses of humanitarian law – is arguably less critical now in the wake of the progressive jurisprudence of the International Criminal Tribunal for the Former Yugoslavia (ICTY), which has expanded the crimes for which individuals may incur individual responsibility under international law, whether committed in international or internal conflicts.[57]

Second, the unprecedented nature of the events of September 11 and the consequent initiation by a US-led coalition of states of a global and ongoing 'war on terrorism' has further complicated the question of thresholds of applicability. In order to justify its 7 October 2001 military offensive in Afghanistan, the US attributed the legal responsibility for the September 11 attacks by Al Qaeda – an international terrorist organization – to the Taliban regime, and thus to the state of Afghanistan itself.[58] At the same time, the US advanced the so-called 'Bush doctrine', suggesting that its self-defense may require further actions with respect

---

54. See *Advisory Opinion, Legality of the Threat or Use of Nuclear Weapons, ICJ Reps.* (1996) p. 226, para. 25.

55. Meron, *supra* n. 52, pp. 266-273.

56. See Decision on the Interlocutory Appeal on Jurisdiction, *Prosecutor* v. *Duško Tadić*, 35 *ILM* (1996) p. 32, para. 77; *Prosecutor* v. *Tadić*, Opinion and Judgment, case IT-94-1-T (7 May 1997), 36 *ILM* (1997) p. 908.

57. Ibid.

58. Under international law the question of state responsibility for terrorist acts is unsettled. See L. Henkin, *International Law: Politics and Values* (Dordrecht, Martinus Nijhoff Publishers 1995) p. 125; I. Brownlie, *International Law and the Use of Force by States* (Oxford, Clarendon Press 1981) p. 370. However, the question of the extent of control required by the Taliban over Al Qaeda's terrorist operations appears to have been settled by SC Res. 1368 (2001): a state which aids, harbours or supports terrorists who carry out armed attacks against another state will be held responsible under international law and may be subject to a use of force in self-defense.

to other organizations and other states which aid, harbor or support international terrorists or terrorist organizations. This notion has prompted one scholar to suggest that following the initiation of US military strikes in Afghanistan on October 7 (and arguably even before that date), there was not one but two armed conflicts in existence: one between the US and Afghanistan (and hence the Taliban), and another – not limited to Afghanistan – between the US and Al Qaeda.[59] If this argument is accepted, it has significant implications not only for the stability of the inter-state system but also for the protection of individual human rights.[60] The better view is that the long-running internal armed conflict in Afghanistan between the Taliban and Northern Alliance became 'internationalized' on 7 October by the initiation of US military strikes and thus the rules of humanitarian law that regulate international armed conflicts became applicable at that point.[61]

3.2 Mujahidin and warring Afghan factions

Since the 20 April 1978 coup that removed Muhammad Daud Khan from power and the consequent Soviet occupation, Afghanistan has been a country ravaged by the brutality of war. Apart from abuses by Soviet forces (which are discussed in the

59. G. Aldrich, 'The Taliban, al Qaeda, and the Determination of Illegal Combatants', Presentation made at the Conference on the 'Twenty Fifth Anniversary of the Additional Protocols to the Geneva Conventions', The Hague, 7 June 2002. Reprinted in 4 *Humanitäres Völkerrecht* (2002) p. 202.

60. The main consequence would be that any member of Al Qaeda in any state or territory would be a 'combatant' (or, in the US view, an 'unlawful combatant') under international humanitarian law and hence a legitimate target for US military action. If accepted, such a position would represent a radical change to both humanitarian and general international law regarding the use of force.

61. There is some uncertainty regarding the exact point at which an international armed conflict commenced. Some commentators have argued that the August 1998 bombing by Al Qaeda of the US embassies in Nairobi and Dar-es-Salaam constitutes the relevant date or, failing that, the September 11 terrorist attacks themselves. See, for example, J. Paust, 'Responding Lawfully to International Terrorism: The Use of Force Abroad', 8 *Whittier LR* (1986) p. 711 These arguments assume, however, that an international armed conflict may arise between a state and a non-state international terrorist organization not linked to any particular state or territory. The better view is that the US military offensive of 7 October marked the point at which an international armed conflict began, at least as between the US and Afghanistan, and hence constituted the point at which international humanitarian law became applicable. A further complication is the question whether an 'armed attack' under Art. 51 of the UN Charter may be equated with the concept of an 'international armed conflict' for the purposes of humanitarian law (i.e., whether once a state has been subject to an armed attack – albeit by a non-state actor – the threshold for the application of the rules of humanitarian law that regulate international armed conflicts is thereby crossed). It is clear that the Security Council, NATO and the community of nations have accepted that while the US was attacked by a non-state terrorist organization, it was nevertheless subject to an 'armed attack' for the purposes of Art. 51, thus justifying the use of force in self defense. This issue affects the characterization under humanitarian law of the September 11 terrorist acts themselves (which cannot constitute war crimes unless there was an international armed conflict in existence when they were committed). Such acts may still, however, constitute crimes against humanity, violations of treaties governing matters such as hijacking, aircraft safety, terrorism etc., or simply crimes under domestic law: see *infra* n. 93 and accompanying text. See also T. Franck, 'Terrorism and the Right of Self-Defence', 95 *AJIL* (2001) p. 839 (arguing that self-defense is not limited to armed attacks by states, nations or belligerents);

next section), gross humanitarian and human rights violations have been committed over the last two decades by Afghan government troops, members of the different *mujahidin* factions and by the militias of any local military leader able to establish control over a pocket of territory. As territory has changed hands during different periods, entire local populations have been targeted for reprisals and collective punishment, including deliberate and arbitrary killings and torture.

One of the earliest reports on the unfolding human rights catastrophe in Afghanistan was written by Helsinki Watch in 1984. Covering the first phase of armed conflict in Afghanistan from the time of the Soviet invasion and occupation in 1979, the report documented mass destruction in the countryside (including the killing of farmers, destruction of food supplies, livestock and agricultural infrastructure); crimes against the rural population (including indiscriminate bombing); reprisal killings and massacres; summary executions and random killings; the widespread use of anti-personnel mines; and arbitrary arrest, forced conscription and widespread use of torture.[62] At the same time, fundamental civil liberties and independent institutions were brutally repressed in the cities.[63] Given that the armed conflict may be characterized as international during this period, the vast majority of these practices by Soviet and Afghan forces constitute violations of both international humanitarian law and the non-derogable rights protected by human rights law.[64]

After the Soviet withdrawal in 1989, the war in Afghanistan has generally been regarded as an internal armed conflict for the purposes of international humanitarian law and thus subject to common Article 3 of the four Geneva Conventions and Additional Protocol II (to the extent that it is customary law). During the period between 1989 and the rise of the Taliban around 1995, intense fighting between warring Afghan factions continued to result in gross and widespread violations of humanitarian and human rights law. These abuses were characterized by acts of torture, ill-treatment and extrajudicial executions of prisoners on the basis of political affiliation or ethnic origin and death sentences imposed by special courts

---

62. Helsinki Watch, *'Tears, Blood and Cries': Human Rights in Afghanistan Since the Invasion 1979-1984*, December 1984.

63. See A. Hyman, *Afghanistan under Soviet Domination, 1964-1981* (New York, St Martin's Press 1982) p. 81.

64. Indiscriminate bombing not directed at a specific military objective violates AP I, Art. 51(4); reprisals against villages and villagers violates AP I, Arts. 51(6) and 52(1); summary executions violate ICCPR, Arts. 6 and 7 and AP I, Art. 51(2); placing mines in inhabited areas or in homes violates AP I, Arts. 51(4b), (5b), 35(2); burning bodies of the slain and mining corpses with grenades violates AP I, Art. 34(1); destruction of agriculture violates AP I, Art. 54 (starvation of civilians as a method of warfare); stealing the property of civilians violates Geneva IV, Art. 33; attacks on and desecration of mosques violates AP I, Art. 52(3); suppression of freedoms of speech, press, political activity, association, assembly and movement; torture; detention in inhumane conditions; trial without due process all violate fundamental rights protected under the ICCPR (some of which may be derogated from in a time of public emergency threatening the life of the nation). See Helsinki Watch report, *supra* n. 62, pp. 167-170.

without the benefit of a fair trial.[65] There were also accounts of thousands of unarmed civilian women killed by unexpected and deliberate artillery attacks on their homes, as well as rapes, beatings and massacres by armed groups.[66] These practices violate common Article 3 and the customary laws of war applicable in non-international armed conflicts.

During the third phase of civil war between 1995 and 2001, most of the serious violations of humanitarian law (including, in some instances, atrocities rising to the level of crimes against humanity) resulted from the ongoing conflict between Taliban and Northern Alliance forces to the north of Kabul. Both the Taliban and the Northern Alliance resorted to indiscriminate aerial bombardment and shelling, summary executions and the widespread use of anti-personnel mines. Between 1991 and 2001, Taliban offensives were characterized by scorched-earth tactics in the Shomali plains north of Kabul, summary executions of prisoners in the north-central province of Samangan, and forced relocation and conscription. Northern Alliance forces between 1996 and 1998 sent volleys of rockets into crowded areas of Kabul, and there were also reports of summary executions, burning of houses and looting, mainly of ethnic Pashtuns and others suspected of supporting the Taliban. The atrocities and reprisals discussed previously which were committed by both sides in Mazar-i Sharif between 1997 and 1998 are representative of the impunity and war crimes committed during this phase of the conflict.[67] The two groups of victims most directly affected by the ongoing conflict were the Hazaras – a Shia Muslim ethnic group targeted by the Taliban as a form of collective punishment for suspected collaboration with the Northern Alliance[68] – and women generally.[69]

Following the collapse of the Taliban regime in November 2001 during the fourth phase of armed conflict in Afghanistan, further serious violations of humanitarian and human rights law by Afghan forces occurred. The UN and other agencies have reported the killings of hundreds of Taliban prisoners who were sealed in truck containers, suffocated and later buried in mass graves near Dasht-e Leili while being transferred by Northern Alliance forces to the Sheberghan prison near Mazar-i-Sharif.[70] At the same time, in the security vacuum created by the

---

65. See Amnesty International, *Afghanistan: Reports of torture, ill-treatment and extrajudicial executions of prisoners 1992* (noting violations of the ICCPR and the Torture Convention).

66. See Amnesty International, *Women in Afghanistan: A Human Rights Catastrophe*, May 1995. See also the Human Rights Watch report, *The Forgotten War: Human Rights Abuses and Violations of the Laws of War Since the Soviet Withdrawal* (1991).

67. See *supra* n. 15 and accompanying text.

68. See Human Rights Watch, *Afghanistan: Massacres of Hazaras in Afghanistan*, Vol. 13(1), 19 February 2001. See also Report of the situation of human rights in Afghanistan submitted by Mr Kamal Hossain, Special Rapporteur, in accordance with HR Commission resolution 2000/18, E/CN.4/2001/43, 9 March 2001, at paras. 40-4.

69. See Human Rights Watch, *Humanity Denied: Systematic Denial of Women's Rights in Afghanistan*, Vol. 13(5), October 2001.

70. See P. Constable, 'Afghans Condemn Killings of Taliban – Investigation into Deaths is Uncertain', *Washington Post* (22 August 2002) at p. A10 (noting that while the Afghan government has condemned the killings it has not carried out any investigations); B. Dehghanpisheh, J. Barry and

ISAF being restricted to Kabul, ethnic Pashtuns throughout northern Afghanistan have been targeted for reprisals for their association with the Taliban and have faced widespread abuses, including killings, sexual violence, beatings, extorsion and looting. The three main ethnically-based parties and their militias in northern Afghanistan that formerly comprised the Northern Alliance (and which are now well-represented in the transitional government[71]) have been implicated in these violations – the mainly ethnic Uzbek Junbish-i Milly-yi Islami of General Abdul Rashid Dostum, the mainly ethnic Tajik Jamiat-e Islami led in Mazar-i Sharif by Ustad Atta Mohammad, and the ethnic Hazara Hizb-i Wahdat led in the north by Haji Mohammad Mohaqiq, as well as non-aligned armed Uzbeks, Tajiks, and Hazaras seeking to capitalize on the vulnerability of disarmed Pashtun communities.[72] Due to the fact that after October 7 the conflict in Afghanistan once again became 'internationalized', the rules of humanitarian law applicable to international armed conflicts apply in full to the conduct of these hostilities and there can be little doubt that these abuses constitute grave breaches of the Geneva Conventions and of customary humanitarian law.

As the situation currently stands, there are violators of international humanitarian and human rights law on all sides and in relation to all phases of the armed conflict. Some of these perpetrators are in the custody of the new Afghan authorities, others are in the custody of the US-led military coalition both inside and outside Afghanistan, while still others are either in control of provincial areas[73] or in positions of power In the new Afghan Transitional Government itself. Those in the first category comprise mainly Taliban commanders who are alleged to have committed war crimes and the most serious human rights abuses. They are being detained by former Northern Alliance officials who have returned to power and who, as in the case of General Abdul Rashid Dostum, are themselves implicated in gross violations of humanitarian and human rights law, and by the United States.

R. Gutman, 'The Death Convoy of Afghanistan', *Newsweek* (26 August 2002) (noting that General Abdul Rashid Dostum was in charge of the militia forces accused of committing the abuses and continues to run the region in the north of the country near Mazar-e Sharif, making any government investigation of the deaths unlikely); 'Dead on Arrival – A War Crime in Afghanistan', *The Economist* (22 August 2002) at p. 34 (noting mounting pressure on 'local and international authorities to uncover the truth', including whether US forces in the area at the time had knowledge of the use of containers to transport detainees).

71. See *supra* n. 40 and accompanying text.

72. See Human Rights Watch, *supra* n. 40 (noting that in other parts of the north, commanders affiliated with the three major parties have established *de facto* authority over large areas, marking the return to a virtual monopoly of power by individual warlords).

73. Note, for example, the recent standoff between the Afghan Transitional Authority and Padsha Khan Zadran, a warlord in control of significant areas in southeast Afghanistan who rejects the leadership of Hamid Karzai and is seeking a formal position in the central government. Following the Bonn process, Zadran was appointed as the governor of Paktika province but another local warlord blocked him from taking office in Gardez. In April 2002, Zadran carried out a revenge rocket attack on Gardez, killing 36 people, including numerous civilians. In a direct affront to Karzai, Zadran now claims effective control of three southeastern provinces which the Transitional Authority has assigned to other regional leaders. See I. Fisher, 'Warlord Pushes for Control of a Corner of Afghanistan: Karzai Warns Armed Response is Possible', *New York Times* (6 August 2002) at p. A8.

3.3 Soviet and neighboring forces pre-September 11

In addition to the question of individual accountability for abuses by warring Afghan forces, account must also be taken of the role played by neighboring and other states in fueling Afghanistan's civil war. As discussed above, Afghanistan became the paradigmatic site for Cold War geopolitical struggle sponsored by various outside parties – Russia, Pakistan, Iran and other neighboring countries,[74] with the US and India influencing the conduct of the war in other ways. This aspect of the conflict raises difficult questions of state responsibility, violations of specific international conventions and, in some cases, individual accountability for serious violations of humanitarian and human rights law.

The most blatant violations relate to the period of Soviet occupation between 1979 and 1988. During this time, at least four types of violations may be identified: first, indiscriminate bombing of civilian areas by the Soviet air force, causing mass destruction to the countryside and thousands of civilian casualties; second, massacres of civilians by specialized commando units in areas where resistance forces were operating, including the widespread use of torture, rape and arbitrary detention; third, the widespread use of anti-personnel mines camouflaged as everyday objects; and fourth, the forcible transfer of Afghan children to the Soviet Union for up to ten years of education.[75]

These abuses constitute grave breaches of the Geneva Conventions (which apply in full given that this was an international armed conflict) and of non-derogable human rights. In both instances, Russia is required under international law to hold individual perpetrators accountable.[76] The indiscriminate use of landmines also violates conventional and customary humanitarian law rules prohibiting the use of weapons which 'employ a method or means of combat which cannot be directed at a specific military objective'.[77]

---

74. See Human Rights Watch, *Crisis of Impunity: The Role of Pakistan, Russia, and Iran in Fueling the Civil War*, Vol. 13(3), July 2001.

75. See Helsinki Watch, *supra* n. 62.

76. The Geneva Conventions and AP I oblige the contracting parties to make grave breaches of the protective provisions liable to punishment and to take all suitable measures to ensure compliance with the Conventions: Geneva I, Arts. 49, 50; Geneva II, Arts. 50, 51; Geneva III, Arts. 129, 130; Geneva IV, Arts. 146, 147; AP I, Art. 85. Under Art. 2 of the ICCPR, states are required to 'respect and ensure' the rights recognized in the Covenant. Furthermore, any acts amounting to genocide or crimes against humanity (widespread or systematic attacks directed against a civilian population whether during peace or wartime) – either of which may be applicable in the case of Soviet atrocities in Afghanistan – are subject to individual responsibility under international law.

77. During the Soviet occupation, thousands of 'butterfly mines', known as PFM-1s, were randomly disseminated by helicopter over large areas of Afghanistan. In general, mines placed without customary precautions and which are unrecorded, unmarked, or are not designated to destroy themselves within a reasonable time may be 'blind weapons' in relation to time and are thus prohibited. Contact mines may also violate prohibitions on the use of weapons 'the primary purpose of which is to spread terror among the civilian population': AP I, Art. 51(2). The main source of international law governing the use of landmines is the 1981 Protocol on Prohibitions or Restrictions on the Use of Mines, Booby Traps and Other Devices (Protocol II), annexed to the 1981 Convention on Prohibition or Restrictions on the Use of Certain Conventional Weapons Which May Be Deemed to Be Exces-

As regards the issue of outside support and provision of military and financial assistance to the warring Afghan factions by several states, two legal issues arise. First, do these states bear any responsibility under international law for their actions in directly and indirectly sustaining and manipulating the ongoing conflict;[78] and second, was the level of foreign interference such that during the third phase of the Afghan war the armed conflict between the Taliban and Northern Alliance is better characterized as international rather than internal?

From 1994 on, the Taliban were strongly supported by Pakistan which sought to secure valuable trade routes to Central Asia. In September 1995, the Taliban took control of Herat with substantial assistance provided by Pakistan. During the ongoing civil conflict in 2000 and 2001 between the Taliban and the Northern Alliance, Pakistan assisted the Taliban forces by facilitating the recruitment of fighters, offering military training, planning and directing pivotal military operations, and allowing arms for the Taliban to transit its territory. In late-2000, Pakistani aircraft assisted with troop rotations for Taliban forces during combat operations. Saudi Arabia and the United Arab Emirates also provided financial support to the Taliban. The Northern Alliance, on the other hand, obtained their arms primarily from Iran and Russia, with Tajikistan providing the necessary transit territory. Iran provided rockets, ammunition and mines and also military training to Northern Alliance forces. The Russian Federation enabled the transportation of Iranian aid, while providing direct assistance itself, including crucial support services and helicopters.[79] At different periods prior to the fourth phase of the conflict, the US and Saudi Arabia similarly provided direct financial and covert military assistance to mujahidin and Taliban forces. The Northern Alliance also received substantial military assistance dating back to the Soviet occupation in 1979, mainly from Iran (including large shipments of weapons, aerial resupply between 1996 and 1998 and military training for anti-Taliban forces in northern Afghanistan).[80] At the same time, Russia and several of the Central Asian States of

---

sively Injurious and to Have Indiscriminate Effects: Final Act, app. C, opened for signature 10 April 1981, UN Doc. A/CONF.95/15 (1980) ('Land Mines Protocol') which gives effect to several principles of customary law relating to the protection of the civilian population.

78. See Draft Articles on Responsibility of States for internationally wrongful acts, adopted by the ILC at its fifty-third session (November 2001), Art. 2 ('Draft Articles on State Responsibility'). On the issue of state responsibility for the conduct of armed forces, see F. Kalshoven, 'State Responsibility for Warlike Acts of the Armed Forces: From Article 3 of the Hague Convention IV of 1907 to Article 91 of Additional Protocol I of 1977 and Beyond', 40 *ICLQ* (1991) pp. 827, 853-858 (noting that in the *Nicaragua* case the ICJ recognized the possibility in principle for a state to become directly responsible for conduct of a foreign armed force that cannot, under the terms of Art. 43 of Protocol I, be regarded as part of its armed forces).

79. Although there have been numerous agreements by Afghanistan's neighbors and other states involved in the conflict to end arms supplies as part of a larger peace process, none of these agreements has included enforcement mechanisms. On 21 July 1999, at a meeting in Tashkent of the Group of Six-plus-Two, comprising the countries bordering Afghanistan plus the US and Russia, the delegates signed an agreement, subsequently known as the Tashkent Declaration, in which they agreed 'not to provide military support to any Afghan party and to prevent the use of our territories for such purposes'.

80. Human Rights Watch, *supra* n. 74, pp. 35-40.

the former Soviet Union have, to varying degrees, aided the Northern Alliance.[81] As is now well-known, after 7 October 2001, the US and its coalition partners switched allegiances and provided massive financial and military assistance to the Northern Alliance as its proxy force on the ground to oust the Taliban regime and the Al Qaeda terrorist network as part of its war against terrorism.[82]

Any conduct of either the Taliban or Northern Alliance forces in breach of an international obligation will be considered an act attributable to an outside state if those forces are in fact 'acting on the instructions of, or under the direction or control of, that State in carrying out the conduct'.[83] This raises something of a paradox for the US which, following the September 11 terrorist attacks, sought to attribute the unlawful acts of Al Qaeda to the Taliban regime on the basis of an apparently broader test of attribution than that established in the *Nicaragua* and *Tadić* cases. On the basis of that test – or even on the basis of the stricter 'effective' or 'overall' control tests laid out in *Nicaragua* and *Tadić* respectively[84] – violations of humanitarian and human rights law committed by Taliban and Northern Alliance forces may be attributable, in different ways and to varying degrees, to Russia, the US, Pakistan, Saudi Arabia and several of the other neighboring states if the requisite degree of control can be established. In addition, certain instances of direct military assistance provided to rebel Afghan groups could amount to an illegal use of force in breach of Article 2(4) of the UN Charter.[85] If such attribution can be established, the responsible state is under an obligation to make full reparation for the injury caused by the internationally wrongful act.[86]

Finally, the interference of outside states also relates to the second issue of characterization of the third phase of the Afghan conflict. As argued by Meron in

81. Ibid., pp. 40-49 (noting the direct role of Russia in arranging for the transportation of Iranian aid and providing assistance to Massoud and other anti-Taliban leaders, and the indirect support provided by Tajikistan, Uzbekistan, Turkmenistan and Kyrgyzstan in allowing cargo to transit through, and military bases and training camps to operate in, their territories)

82. Apart from questions of attribution and state responsibility, these actions also raise potential violations of the United States' 'Leahy Law'. Section 563 of the Foreign Operations Appropriations Act for Fiscal Year 2001 prohibits the provision of funds under the Act to 'any unit of the security forces of a foreign country if the Secretary of State has credible evidence that such unit has committed gross violations of human rights, unless the Secretary determines that ... the government of such country is taking effective measures to bring the responsible members of the security forces unit to justice': P.L. 104-208. Given the long history of abuses by Northern Alliances forces, US military assistance post-7 October 2001 appears to be in direct violation of this law.

83. Draft Articles on Responsibility of States for internationally wrongful acts, adopted by the ILC at its fifty-third session (November 2001), Art. 8 (Conduct directed or controlled by a state) ('Draft Articles on State Responsibility'). On the issue of state responsibility for the conduct of armed forces, see F. Kalshoven, 'State Responsibility for Warlike Acts of the Armed Foreces: From Article 3 of the Hague Convention IV of 1907 to Article 91 of Additional Protocol I of 1977 and Beyond', 40 *ICLQ* (1991) pp. 827, 853-858 (noting that in the *Nicaragua* case the ICJ recognized the possibility in principle for a state to become directly responsible for conduct of a foreign armed force that cannot, under the terms of Art. 43 of Protocol I, be regarded as part of its armed forces).

84. *Tadić* Appeals Decision, *supra* n. 56, paras. 137-138.

85. Such military assistance may also have violated the Tashkent agreement. See *supra* n. 17.

86. Draft Articles on State Responsibility, *supra* n. 83, Art. 31 (injury' includes any damage, whether material or moral, caused by the internationally wrongful act of a state).

rejecting the approach of the ICTY in the *Tadić* case, the question of attribution under the law of state responsibility is a related, but ultimately different, question to that of characterizing the nature of an armed conflict under international humanitarian law.[87] At the same time, it has been accepted that a conflict may have a mix of international and internal dimensions such that the rules of humanitarian law may apply in different ways as between the different parties to the conflict. For present purposes it is sufficient to note that the degree and scope of outside involvement in the Afghan civil war during the 1990s was such that certain aspects of an otherwise internal conflict may have become internationalized.[88] As in the *Tadić* case, this will affect the application of the rules of humanitarian law in any future trials for war crimes committed during this period.

3.4 Al Qaeda and foreign 'terrorists'

In addition to the individual responsibility of Afghan fighters and outside military forces under international law, it is necessary to consider the role played by members of Al Qaeda and other foreign 'terrorist' fighters operating within Afghanistan. As discussed in the next section, the legal status of international terrorists under humanitarian law has become a matter of considerable controversy following the September 11 attacks on New York and Washington, DC. While it is unclear exactly how many Al Qaeda and non-Afghan fighters have been captured in the course of US-led operations in Afghanistan, it is known that thousands of such individuals have been detained by anti-Taliban Afghan forces and US armed forces both in Afghanistan and in Guantánamo Bay, Cuba. Thus, the question of individual responsibility under international (and domestic) law for terrorist and related acts will be a central issue in any future criminal trials whether in Afghanistan, the US or before an international tribunal. For reasons discussed more fully below, however, while these issues raise complex questions of international law, there is only a remote prospect in reality of trials of such persons before an international tribunal. More likely is trial before a US military tribunal or domestic court, but even here the US to date has shown little willingness to conduct trials of alleged terrorists or persons suspected of violating humanitarian law.

Despite assertions by the Bush administration to the contrary, international terrorism and terrorism in war are not new phenomena and were clearly contemplated during the drafting of the Geneva Conventions and Additional Protocols.[89] During times of peace, acts of terrorism are prohibited both under numerous offence-specific international conventions and by the internal legislation of all states and are thus subject to prosecution and punishment under national criminal law. During times of armed conflict, the legal determination of terrorist acts depends on two criteria: first, the status of the person committing the violence

87. See *supra* n. 56 and accompanying text.

88. See H.-P. Gasser, 'Internationalized Non-International Armed Conflicts: Case Studies of Afghanistan, Kampuchea, and Lebanon', 33 *Amer. Univ. LR* (1983) p. 149.

89. See J.J. Paust, 'Terrorism and the International Law of War', 64 *Mich. LR* (1974) p. 1.

and second, the rules of humanitarian law governing the protection of specific categories of persons and the methods and means of warfare. In relation to the first criterion, only members of the armed forces of a party to an armed conflict have a right to participate directly in hostilities. If other persons resort to violence, they breach the law and their actions may constitute acts of terrorism. In relation to the second criterion, even members of the armed forces legitimately entitled to use violence may themselves become terrorists if they violate the rules of humanitarian law.[90] Article 51(2) of Additional Protocol I, under which acts or threats of violence 'the primary purpose of which is to spread terror among the civilian population' are prohibited, confirms that terrorism is not an authorized method of warfare. Terrorist attacks against civilians causing death or serious injury are grave breaches under Article 85 of Protocol I and are thus regarded as war crimes.[91]

Applying these principles to the various terrorist acts of Al Qaeda during the period following Osama bin Laden's return to Afghanistan in 1996, the position under international law is as follows. Regardless of the status of Al Qaeda or foreign fighters as either lawful or unlawful combatants in the context of the ongoing Afghan armed conflict, the deliberate targeting of civilians in Afghanistan is a war crime giving rise to individual responsibility and subject to prosecution under international law.[92] The legal position in relation to Al Qaeda's terrorist attacks on targets in Africa, Yemen and the US on or prior to September 11 2001 is complicated by the grey area that exists between war and peace in the context of international terrorism. Assuming these acts to have been committed during times of peace, they would constitute crimes under the various offence-specific international conventions discussed previously and would also be liable to prosecution under domestic criminal law.[93] Some commentators have suggested that the September 11 attacks themselves constitute crimes against humanity under customary law (which does not require a nexus to a state of armed conflict and which makes such crimes subject to universal jurisdiction).[94]

---

90. See H-P. Gasser, 'Prohibition of terrorist acts in international humanitarian law', *IRRC* No. 253 (1986) pp. 200 at 202-205 and the same writer in this volume at p. 329.

91. In relation to non-international armed conflicts, common Art. 3 makes clear that terrorist acts of any kind against persons not taking part in the hostilities are absolutely prohibited. In identical terms to Art. 51(2) of AP I regarding international armed conflicts, Art. 13 of AP II stipulates that acts or threats of violence 'the primary purpose of which is to spread terror among the civilian population' are prohibited.

92. The more difficult question is whether a member of Al Qaeda fighting alongside the Taliban who takes up arms against opposing forces (whether of the Northern Alliance forces or US forces) is thereby committing a crime. This will depend on whether the Al Qaeda member is a 'combatant' for the purposes of international humanitarian law: see *infra* n. 107 and accompanying text.

93. Jurisdictional questions would arise in relation to whether the state on whose territory the crime was committed or the state of nationality of either the perpetrator or the victims were parties to the relevant treaty. In relation to US domestic law, acts of terrorism may be prosecuted under the US Antiterrorist Act of 1990, 18 U.S.C. §2331 (2000).

94. Given the high degree of orchestration and planning behind the September 11 attack on the World Trade Center (the Pentagon being a military rather than civilian target), a case can be made that the 'systematic' requirement of crimes against humanity is satisfied: see D.A. Mundis, 'The Use of

Whether the attacks constitute war crimes remains a matter of divided opinion.[95]

3.5 US military actions post-September 11

In considering how to confront violations of humanitarian and human rights law in the transition now occurring in Afghanistan, it is finally necessary to consider the role played by the US in the context of the post-September 11 war on terrorism. This role has been problematic for at least three reasons. First, in determining the status of persons captured on the battlefield and subsequently detained in Afghanistan and in Cuba, the US has adopted an evasive – perhaps even *mala fides* – approach towards the basic protections of international humanitarian law. On 13 November 2001, the US President issued a Military Order entitled the 'Detention, Treatment, and Trial of Certain Non-Citizens in the War Against Terrorism'.[96] Section 2 of the Order provides for the trial in military commissions of any non-US citizen whom the President determines is or was a member of Al Qaeda or has engaged in, aided or abetted, or conspired to commit acts of international terrorism that have damaged or threaten to damage US citizens, national security, foreign policy, or the economy; any individual who has knowingly harbored any such persons; or where 'it is in the interest of the United States that such individual be subject to this order'. The unprecedented scope of the Order permits detention of persons of different nationalities with varying degrees of involvement in the fighting in Afghanistan, association with Al Qaeda or the Taliban, and connection to the events of September 11 or future acts of international terrorism.

3.5.1 *Status of detainees under international humanitarian law*

Immediately following the release of the Order, a number of concerned states and human rights NGOs questioned whether the determination by the US of the status of detainees being held at Guantánamo Bay and other military locations complied with the requirements of international humanitarian law. As already discussed, both the US and Afghanistan are parties to the four Geneva Conventions, which together provide a comprehensive legal framework for determining the status and ensuring the protection of captured combatants and civilians during situations of armed conflict.[97] Under Geneva III and IV, different regimes of protection apply

---

Military Commissions to Prosecute Individuals Accused of Terrorist Acts', 96 *AJIL* (2002) pp. 320, 327.

95. As discussed, *supra* n. 61, the uncertainty relates to the fact that the September 11 attacks were carried out by a non-state terrorist organization. The Bush administration has stated that the scale of the attack 'created a state of armed conflict': see November 13 Military Order, *infra* n. 96, sec. 1(a) (although the Order does not specify exactly with whom).

96. 66 *Fed. Reg.* 57,833 (16 November 2001).

97. While the two Additional Protocols of 1977 contain further extensive provisions on these issues, neither Protocol has been ratified by the US or Afghanistan. Several of these provisions, however, are regarded as being representative of customary international humanitarian law: see T. Meron, *Human Rights and Humanitarian Norms as Customary Law* (Oxford, Oxford University Press

depending on the status of persons not, or no longer, taking an active part in hostilities. An individual may either be a 'prisoner of war' under Geneva III (Treatment of Prisoners in War)[98] or a 'protected person' under Article 4 of Geneva IV (Protection of Civilian Persons in Time of War).[99] According to the authoritative Commentary to the Geneva Conventions of the International Committee of the Red Cross, *all* detainees must fall within the protections of one of these two conventions: 'There is no intermediate status; nobody in enemy hands can fall outside the law.'[100] In the event of 'any doubt' as to whether an individual is entitled to POW status, that person must be treated as a POW 'until such time as their status has been determined by a competent tribunal'.[101]

On 7 February 2002, the Bush Administration issued a statement indicating that the US would (after some initial uncertainty) apply the Geneva Conventions to those persons detained on the battlefield in Afghanistan.[102] In applying the Conventions, however, the US determined that Taliban detainees were not entitled to POW status as, in its view, they did not meet the requirements of Article 4 of Geneva III. Although comprising the armed forces of the government in effective control of Afghanistan, they were said not to wear uniforms sufficiently to distinguish themselves from the civilian population and not to conduct their operations in accordance with the laws and customs of war. In relation to Al Qaeda detainees, the US claimed that, as members of a non-state international terrorist organization, these individuals fell outside of the Geneva law altogether. They were akin to saboteurs or spies, which operate within the territory of an adversary out of uniform and without openly carrying arms. In both cases the detainees were said to be 'unlawful' or 'non-privileged' combatants, a term which does not appear in the Geneva Conventions but which derives from the World War II-era decision of the US Supreme Court *Ex Parte Quirin*.[103] Despite their suggested status as unlawful combatants, the US indicated that it would for the most part treat Taliban and Al Qaeda detainees 'in a manner that is reasonably consistent with the Geneva

---

1991); G. Aldrich, 'Prospects for United States Ratification of Additional Protocol I to the 1949 Geneva Conventions', 85 *AJIL* (1991) pp. 1 at 19 (arguing that much of Protocol I is 'clearly a codification of customary law').

98. Geneva III, Art. 4A sets out the requirements for POW status.

99. Paust has noted that during an armed conflict 'all persons who are not prisoners of war, including so-called unprivileged or unlawful combatants who may or may not have prisoner of war status, have at least various non-derogable rights to due process under the Geneva Civilian Convention and Geneva Protocol I'. See J.J. Paust, 'Antiterrorism Military Commissions: Courting Illegality', 23 *Mich. JIL* (2001) pp. 1 at 7, n. 15.

100. Commentary, J. Pictet, ed., *IV Geneva Convention Relative to the Protection of Civilian Persons in Time of War* (Geneva, International Committee of the Red Cross 1958) p. 51.

101. Geneva III, Art. 5.

102. *Status of Detainees at Guantanamo*, Fact Sheet, White House, Washington DC, 7 February 2002.

103. 317 US 1, 32 (1942) (eight German saboteurs captured on US territory were denied POW status and tried before a special military commission).

Conventions, to the extent they are appropriate' and that they would receive 'humane treatment'.[104]

The blanket denial of POW status to the Guantánamo detainees constitutes an unprecedented interpretation of humanitarian law which deviates both from prior US practice and general state practice under the Geneva Conventions. For present purposes, it is unnecessary to join the debate on competing constructions of Article 4 of Geneva III.[105] It is sufficient to observe that, regardless of the correct interpretation, an Article 5 tribunal must be established to resolve the legal status of each detainee.[106] Such tribunals were convened by the US in the Vietnam and Gulf Wars in cases where doubt existed as to whether captured enemy personnel warranted

---

104. DoD News Briefing – Secretary Rumsfeld and Gen. Myers11 January 2002, 2:10 pm (Pentagon), DoD News Briefing – ASD PA Clarke 14 January 2002 – 12:30 pm. Reproduced in this volume at pp. 657-658.

105. Most legal scholars agree that the Taliban should be accorded POW status under Geneva III. See 'Agora: Military Commissions', 96 *AJIL* (2002) pp. 320 et seq; Paust, *supra* n. 99. The status of members of Al Qaeda under humanitarian law, however, is more controversial. Following the authoritative ICRC commentaries, Al Qaeda members should be accorded the status of 'protected persons' under Geneva IV who may be prosecuted in the same manner as all other civilians who are prohibited from taking a direct part in hostilities. Alternatively, they may in some cases have attained the status of POWs in accordance with Geneva III, Art. 4A(2); AP I, Art. 44; and relevant customary norms. The US Department of the Army Field Manual further confirms this position stating that if a 'person is determined by a competent tribunal, acting in conformity with Art. 5 [Geneva III] not to fall within any of the categories listed in Article 4 [Geneva III], he is not entitled to be treated as a prisoner of war. He is, however, a 'protected person' within the meaning of Article 4 [Geneva IV]' (citations omitted): U.S. Department of the Army, Field Manual 27-10, The Law of Land Warfare, 15 July 1976, § 73. There is, however, at least one difficulty with this position. Geneva IV, Art. 70 provides that protected persons shall not be 'arrested, prosecuted or convicted by the Occupying Power for acts committed or for opinions expressed before the occupation ... with the exception of breaches of the laws and customs of war'. If Al Qaeda members were accorded the status of protected persons, the US would thus be prohibited from prosecuting them for terrorist acts such as those committed on September 11, 2001. Presumably, however, they could be prosecuted for war crimes committed in Afghanistan prior to 7 October 2001. Clearly, Art. 70 is in need of revision if the rules of humanitarian law are to remain relevant in the wake of September 11.

106. On 25 February 2002, a petition was lodged with the Inter-American Commission on Human Rights, of which the US is a member, seeking certain provisional measures in relation to the Guantánamo detainees. See Detainees in Guantánamo Bay, Request by the Center for Constitutional Rights, the Human Rights Clinic at Columbia Law School and the Center for Justice and International Law for Precautionary Measures Under Article 25 of the Commission's Regulations, 25 February 2002. On 13 March, the Commission upheld the petition and ruled that the US must immediately convene a 'competent tribunal' as required by Art. 5 of Geneva III to resolve the legal status of each of the detainees. The US has challenged the Commission's ruling, arguing that it has already conducted multi-agency, case-by-case screening procedures on the battlefield in Afghanistan which render an Art. 5 tribunal unnecessary. See Response of the United States to Request for Precautionary Measures – Detainees in Guantánamo Bay, Cuba, 12 April 2002. It is questionable, however, whether these screening procedures comply even with the US Army's internal code of conduct. The relevant provisions in the US Army Field Manual – which stand as the US interpretation of its obligations under international humanitarian law – require a 'competent tribunal' to comprise a board of 'not less than three officers' in determining whether a person claiming treatment as a POW, and who has committed a 'belligerent act or has engaged in hostile activities in aid of the armed forces', is entitled to that status. See FM, ibid., Ch. 3, Sec II, Art. 71, 'Interim Protection'.

POW status.[107] In several instances, detainees were found to be civilians who had taken no part in the hostilities and were transferred to refugee camps. Only a competent tribunal is able to properly assess the differing circumstances and degrees of involvement of individuals detained on the battlefield in the Taliban and Al Qaeda ranks. Whatever determinations of status are made, the US assertion of blanket 'unlawful combatant' status creates a dangerous and vague grey area between combatant and civilian status that not only violates the object and purpose of the Geneva Conventions but leaves the Guantánamo detainees without any defined legal rights protecting their fundamental human dignity under international law.

3.5.2 *Rights and future trials of detainees under international humanitarian law*

The second problematic feature of US military actions post-September 11 has centered on the volatile issue of whether the ongoing detention and proposed future trials of detainees in military commissions accord with the rights of prisoners under humanitarian law and the rights of all persons under international human rights law.[108] In establishing its own mechanisms to determine the rights of prisoners and to prosecute individuals for crimes under international law, the US has undermined well-defined international standards and has adopted a generally unilateralist

107. AP I, Art. 44 indicates that humanitarian law is progressively developing in such a way that criteria such as the uniform requirement are subordinate to the issue of whether individuals are members of a party to the armed conflict. Art. 44 deals mainly with combatants using methods of guerrilla warfare and ensures that once captured such persons are given 'protections equivalent in all respects to those accorded to prisoners of war' under Geneva III: see AP I, Art. 44(4). During the Vietnam war, the US granted captured Viet Cong fighters POW status despite their lack of uniform or identifying insignia. The curious logic of the current US position means that even soldiers of the Northern Alliance – who operated as proxy forces for the US in the fourth phase of the armed conflict in Afghanistan and who similarly fail to meet the uniform criteria -may be regarded as 'unlawful combatants'. If accepted, this position would have far-reaching and illogical consequences in any future war crimes trials in Afghanistan. As 'unlawful combatants', Northern Alliance soldiers could be prosecuted along with Taliban and Al Qaeda members as common criminals in accordance with AP I, Art. 45 for merely taking part in the hostilities both against each other and against the US and other international military forces ('lawful combatants'). Even if this were the case, however, such persons must at a minimum be treated in accordance with the fundamental guarantees of AP I, Art. 75 (provided that Geneva IV, to the extent that it is applicable, does not grant more favorable treatment). See D. Fleck, ed., *The Handbook of Humanitarian Law in Armed Conflicts* (Oxford, Oxford University Press 1995) p. 68.

108. Several cases are currently before the US courts seeking to challenge the indefinite detention of individuals captured on the battlefield in Afghanistan and subsequently transferred to the US military base in Guantánamo Bay, Cuba: see e.g., *Coalition of Clergy* v. *Bush*, case No. 02-570, 21 February 2002 (petition for *habeas corpus* rejected in federal court in California); *Fawzi Khalid Abdullah Fahad Al Odah* v. *US*, case No. 02-828, July 2002 (federal action brought by 11 Kuwaiti nationals and their family members alleging that their arbitrary detention on Guantánamo Bay violates customary international law and constitutional due process standards); *Shafiq Rasul* v. *Bush*, case No. 02-299, July 2002 (*habeas corpus* proceeding brought in the District of Columbia on behalf of Guantánamo Bay detainees).

position towards the norms and mechanisms of international justice. Both of these factors bear on questions of transitional justice in Afghanistan, where the rights of prisoners and the conduct of any future criminal trials (whether domestic or international or a combination of the two) will be influenced normatively and procedurally by the US approach

Photographs revealing the detainees kneeling, shackled, wearing blacked-out goggles and ear mufflers has raised questions about possible violations of 'humane treatment'[109] and the 1984 Torture Convention. In relation to future trials before military commissions, President Bush's November 13 Military Order has come under withering attack both within and outside of the US. Section 4 of the order requires the Secretary of Defense to formulate rules for the conduct of 'full and fair trials' subject to a few minimum requirements. The Order, however, provides for no right of judicial appeal or other independent review mechanism; sentencing (including imposition of the death penalty), not on the basis of unanimity but rather a two-thirds majority of commission members present; a standard of proof to be decided by the Secretary of Defense; no express presumption of innocence; the possibility of secret proceedings and hearsay evidence; no requirement that a defendant be given adequate time to prepare a reasonable defense; no explicit disclosure obligations on the prosecution, including of the nature of the charges filed against him or her; and no explicit right for defendants to select their own attorney. Furthermore, the proposed military commissions will lack any independence from the executive branch. The President has accorded to himself, or the Secretary of Defense, the power to determine who will be tried, to appoint the members of the commission, to select the panel that will review convictions and sentences, and to make the final decision in any case. The US State Department has repeatedly criticized states such as Burma, China, Russia, Sudan, Turkey, Egypt, Nigeria and Malaysia for the use of military tribunals to try civilians. Indeed, the State Department's annual Country Reports on Human Rights Practices monitor and evaluate other states in relation to the extent to which they guarantee the right to a 'fair public trial', which is defined to include many of the due process rights omitted by the November 13 Military Order.

The Order violates many of the protections contained in Articles 82 to 108 of Geneva III which apply to the detention and trial of POWs. These provisions require *inter alia* that POWs be tried by the same courts and according to the same procedure, be sentenced to the same penalties for the same acts, and have the same right of appeal as members of the armed forces of the Detaining Power. This requires the US to provide POWs the same rights accorded to its own forces under the Uniform Code of Military Justice. Article 105 further provides for the rights of defense, including the right to counsel of the accused's choice; the right to confer privately with counsel; the right to call witnesses; and the right to an interpreter. 'Protected persons', on the other hand, are entitled to the protection of Articles 71 to 76 of Geneva IV. This includes the right to a regular trial; the right to counsel of

109. Geneva III, Art. 25.

the accused's choice, who must be allowed to visit freely and be provided with the necessary facilities for preparing the defense; the right to call witnesses; the right to an interpreter; the right of appeal 'provided for by the laws applied by the court'; the right to be visited by the delegates of the Protecting Power (a neutral state appointed to monitor compliance with the Geneva Conventions); and the right to be detained and serve sentences in the occupied territory.

Any person who does not benefit from greater protection under these provisions is entitled to the protection of Article 75 of Additional Protocol I (at least to the extent that it is customary law in relation to the US and Afghanistan). Article 75(4) requires that proceedings be conducted before an 'impartial and regularly constituted court respecting the generally recognized principles of regular judicial procedure'. Those principles are deemed to include a range of procedural rights, such as the provision of 'all necessary rights and means of defense'; the right to be presumed innocent; freedom from compelled self-incrimination; and the right to be advised of remedies. Article 75(4) also prohibits *ex post facto* application of criminal law and requires respect for the principle of *non bis in idem*.[110]

A number of these violations were remedied on 21 March 2002 when the Secretary of Defense issued rules and regulations under section 6 of the Military Order.[111] The rules provide for the appointment of military defense lawyers with the possibility of hiring civilian lawyers of the defendant's own choosing (although at his or her own expense); the proof of guilt beyond a reasonable doubt; the right to call witnesses; and the presumption of innocence. A limited right of appeal is also now provided to a three member Review Panel comprising of military officers appointed by the Secretary of Defense (but which may also include civilians temporarily commissioned as military officers by the President). While these rules bring the proposed commissions more closely in line with the relevant provisions of Geneva III, several deficiencies remain. Any evidence which has 'probative value to a reasonable person' is admissible as are secret evidence and anonymous witnesses. Thus, while under the Uniform Code of Military Justice courts martial follow strict rules of evidence, in the military commissions hearsay evidence will be admissible. This is not a violation of international humanitarian law *per se* (the Geneva Conventions do not prohibit hearsay evidence) but it does provide a lesser evidential standard than under US military law. The right to appeal to a three member Review Panel does not accord with

---

110. Note also that Geneva IV, Art. 146, mirrored in all four Conventions, requires that any person prosecuted for violations of the Geneva Conventions, irrespective of their status under humanitarian law, must be provided with 'safeguards of proper trial and defense, which shall not be less favorable than' those provided for in Arts. 105 and following of Geneva III. These include the same rights of defense and appeal as those accorded to POWs. If a POW or protected person is willfully deprived of these rights of a fair and regular trial, the persons responsible for such a failure will themselves have committed a grave breach of the Geneva Conventions. See Geneva III, Art. 130; Geneva IV, Art. 147.

111. US Department of Defence, Military Commissions Order No. 1, Procedures for Trials by Military Commissions of Certain Non-United States Citizens in the War Against Terrorism, 21 March 2002.

Article 106 of Geneva III, which guarantees that POWs be accorded the same appeal rights as US soldiers (who have the right of appeal to the civilian courts after they exhaust their remedies within the military justice system). This has particular relevance to the imposition of the death penalty. Finally, the independence and impartiality of the proposed commissions remains in doubt. It is the President or the Secretary of Defense who ultimately decides who is to be tried, appoints the members of the commissions, selects the panels that will review convictions and sentences, and makes final decisions in individual cases. Given the broad scope of persons subject to the President's Order, the ambiguity surrounding which offences may be tried before the commissions and the prospect of indefinite detention (even following acquittal before a military commission), it is clear that the proposed military commissions do not accord with either the spirit or the letter of international humanitarian law.

Apart from its obligations under humanitarian law, the US is also bound by norms of conventional and customary human rights law. In 1992, the US ratified the International Covenant on Civil and Political Rights (ICCPR), which requires State Parties to respect and ensure to 'all individuals within its territory and subject to its jurisdiction' the rights recognized in the Covenant.[112] The ICCPR applies at all times – in times of war and peace – although states may derogate from certain provisions in a time of 'public emergency which threatens the life of the nation', but only to the extent 'strictly required by the exigencies of the situation'. Any state wishing to avail itself of this right of derogation must immediately inform the UN Secretary-General.[113]

On 14 September 2001, the President proclaimed a national emergency,[114] but the US has not officially sought to exercise its right of derogation under Article 4 of the Covenant. Accordingly, human rights scholars and NGOs have argued that the President's November 13 Military Order providing for the detention of certain individuals and the establishment of military commissions is in violation of various provisions of the ICCPR. The vague scope of section 2, which seeks to

112. ICCPR, Art. 2. For a discussion of the obligations imposed on States Parties by Art. 2 of the Covenant, see O. Schachter, 'The Obligation to Implement the Covenant in Domestic Law' in L. Henkin, ed., *The International Bill of Rights: The Covenant on Civil and Political Rights* (New York, Columbia University Press 1981) pp. 311-331. One question that has arisen is whether the obligations of the US under the Covenant extend to its activities in Guantánamo Bay at all, i.e., whether the holding of 'battlefield detainees' at the military base in Cuba may be considered as being 'within [US] territory and subject to its jurisdiction'. See e.g., T. Buergenthal, 'To Respect and Ensure: State Obligations and Permissible Derogations' in ibid., at pp. 72, 73-75 (arguing that the phrase 'within its territory and subject to its jurisdiction' in Art. 2(1) of the Covenant should be read as a disjunctive conjunction and that a State Party that 'denies to an individual subject to its jurisdiction the rights guaranteed in the Covenant violates its obligations even if the individual is not within its territory at the time the violation is committed)'. See also *Cyprus* v. *Turkey,* 18 *YB Eur. Conv. HR* (1975) p. 83 (Commission holding that States Parties to the European Convention on Human Rights are 'bound to secure the said rights and freedoms to all persons under their actual authority and responsibility, whether that authority is exercised within their own territory or abroad)'.

113. ICCPR, Art. 4.

114. Proclamation 7463, Declaration of National Emergency by Reason of Certain Terrorist Attacks.

define a broad class of persons who may be subject to detention for involvement in acts of 'international terrorism', arguably violates the right to security and liberty of the person and the prohibition on arbitrary arrest and detention.[115] The denial of minimum due process rights to the Guantánamo detainees, including the right of *habeas corpus*, the right to challenge the lawfulness of their detention in a civilian court and the entitlement to trial within a reasonable time, also arguably violate the ICCPR.[116] Finally, the failure to specify those criminal acts encompassed by the term 'international terrorism' may place the US in violation of the Covenant's non-derogable prohibition on the imposition of 'ex-post facto laws'.[117] This issue may become especially relevant if it is sought to convict individuals for international crimes solely on the basis of membership in a terrorist organization such as Al Qaeda without proof of any direct involvement in specific acts.

Further questions have been raised regarding the fairness of future trials conducted by military commissions, especially given the likelihood of imposition of the death penalty. The ICCPR requires a 'fair and public hearing by a competent, independent and impartial tribunal established by law'. This includes the presumption of innocence, the right to be informed of charges, the right to adequate time for the preparation of a defense, the right to legal assistance of one's own choosing, and the right to examine witnesses. Whether the commissions, which remain wholly subject to the discretion of the executive, will satisfy these standards remains the subject of controversy.[118] The Covenant also guarantees that anyone

---

115. ICCPR, Art. 9(1).

116. Art. 9(3)-(4). While Art. 9 may be subject to lawful derogation, the US has not sought to derogate and these obligations must therefore be held to be in full force and effect. Furthermore, the Human Rights Committee has stated that even in times of national emergency, the right to *habeas corpus* and judicial review of detention cannot be suspended: see General Comment No. 29, States of Emergency (Art. 4), 31 August 2001. Under the US Constitution, *habeas corpus* may only be suspended in the case of 'rebellion' or 'invasion', and only then by Congress (although this appears only to apply to persons held on US territory). In *Rasul* and *Odah* (see *supra* n. 108) it was held that in relation to petitions for writs of *habeas corpus* on behalf of aliens detained by the US at Guantánamo Bay, the Supreme Court's ruling in *Johnson* v. *Eisentrager*, 399 U.S. 763 (1950) was controlling and barred the Court's consideration of the merits of these two cases. *Johnson* v. *Eisentrager* involved a petition for writs of *habeas corpus* filed by 21 German nationals captured in China for engaging in espionage against the US following the surrender of Germany, but before the surrender of Japan, at the end of World War II. A US military commission sitting in China convicted the prisoners for violations of the laws of war and repatriated them to a US prison in Germany. Justice Robert Jackson, in an opinion for a divided Supreme Court, held that no court was able to extend the writ of *habeas corpus* to aliens held outside the sovereign territory of the US (at p. 778). The position was different in relation to 'citizens' (both in US territory and abroad) and 'friendly aliens' lawfully present or seeking residence within US territorial jurisdiction. But both enemy and friendly aliens captured incident to war have no right to *habeas corpus* (at p. 776). This decision leaves at least two areas of uncertainty: first, in relation to 'enemy combatants' who may be US citizens held outside of US territory, and second, in relation to enemy combatants who are aliens but who are present in US territory. In *Rasul* and *Odah*, the Court held that Guantánamo Bay was not within the sovereign territory of the US simply because it exercises 'jurisdiction and control over that facility' (at p. 28).

117. Art. 15.

118. See A. Neier, 'The Military Tribunals on Trial', *New York Review of Books* (11 February 2002) at p. 13. See also 'Agora: Military Commissions', 96 *AJIL* (2002) p. 83.

convicted of a crime shall have the right to judical review of his or her conviction and sentence 'by a higher tribunal according to law'. Whether the military review board established by the rules issued by the Secretary of Defense satisfies this obligation is similarly an open question. Given that Geneva III guarantees final appeals to the civilian courts for POWs interred by the US, it would be incongruous for the ICCPR – which applies to States Parties at all times, not just during war – to establish a lower standard.

What is clear is that the holding of prisoners in Cuba rather than on US soil is an attempt to ensure that no individual (or interested state) is able to seek or obtain a legal remedy in a judicial forum. US domestic courts petitioned on *habeas corpus* grounds by the parents of several Guantánamo detainees have held that they have no jurisdiction in relation to Guantánamo Bay.[119] The US has not acceded to the Optional Protocol to the ICCPR and it is therefore not possible for any detainee to initiate an individual communication to the UN Human Rights Committee; nor has it recognized the competence of the Committee to receive and consider communications from other States Parties alleging violations of the Covenant.[120] The US has also withdrawn its acceptance of the jurisdiction of the International Court of Justice following the 1986 *Nicaragua* case and it is therefore impossible for any state to bring an action for alleged violations of the ICCPR in the World Court (although an action under the Vienna Convention on Consular Relations may be brought under the specific jurisdiction clause in Article 1 of the Convention's Optional Protocol).

In conclusion, the November 13 Military Order sets a dangerous precedent by the world's reigning superpower. It sets a differential standard of justice for citizens and non-citizens, it seeks to derogate from both constitutional and international standards of due process and, by situating detention facilities outside of the US, it seeks to deny the availability of any judicial *fora* able to provide effective remedies. This sends a strong message to an increasing number of states, such as China, Burma, Colombia, Egypt, Kyrgyzstan, Malaysia, Nigeria, Peru, Russia, Sudan and Turkey as they wage their own 'wars on terrorism', and reverses the consistent and long-standing opposition of the US to the use of military tribunals in other countries in the name of states of emergency and national security.[121] It also ignores the availability of other domestic and international alternatives. Various commentators following the events of September 11 have suggested other prefer-

119. When, on 5 April 2002, it was discovered that a prisoner being held at Guantánamo Bay, Yasser Esam Hamdi, was an American citizen, he was immediately transferred to a military jail in Norfolk, Virginia. As a US citizen and alleged 'enemy combatant', it was unclear whether Hamdi retained his right to lodge a petition of *habeas corpus* in federal court demanding that the government either charge him with a crime or set him free. As this raised the opportunity for challenge to the detention and status of all prisoners being held at Guantánamo – and thus the suspension of *habeas corpus* in relation to 'enemy alien belligerents' in general – Hamdi was immediately removed: see K. Seelye, 'U.S. Moves Taliban Prisoner Born in America to Virginia', *New York Times* (5 April 2002).

120. Art. 41.

121. Human Rights Watch, *Past U.S. Criticism of Military Tribunals*, Washington, 28 November 2001.

able *fora* to prosecute and try international terrorists. Anne-Marie Slaughter has suggested that 'Al Qaeda should be tried before the world' and has advocated the establishment of an international tribunal to try accused terrorists.[122] Conversely, Harold Koh has said that 'we have the right courts for Bin Laden' and has argued that the US should try suspected international terrorists in its own federal courts as it has done on numerous prior occasions (including in relation to the 1993 bombing of the World Trade Center and the August 1998 bombings of the US embassies in Tanzania and Kenya).[123] The confusion of the war and justice paradigms in combating international terrorism, as represented by the move to establish military tribunals, has potentially far-reaching and devastating effects for the international human rights movement which, over the last half century, has sought to create a culture of rights and respect for human dignity in all parts of the world.

3.5.3 *US violations of international humanitarian law*

Third and finally, in its conduct of the war against the Taliban and Al Qaeda in Afghanistan, the US may itself have committed serious violations of humanitarian law regarding civilian casualties and the use of certain types of weapons. Thus, a further volatile and sensitive issue to be taken into account in considering transitional justice in Afghanistan is the question of future trials or investigations regarding war crimes committed by US forces. In the area of civilian casualties, the guiding principle of humanitarian law is that civilians may not be the direct object of attack, and that civilian status is lost only where individuals take an active part in hostilities (rather than merely on the basis of support or affiliation). The critical presumption is that if there is any doubt regarding whether someone is a combatant or a civilian, he or she must be presumed to be a civilian.[124] The principle of proportionality is also critical here, especially in relation to the volatile issue of 'collateral damage'. Attacks are prohibited if they cause incidental loss of civilian life, injury to civilians, or damage to civilian objects that is excessive in relation to the anticipated concrete and direct military advantage of the attack.[125]

Given the well-known complexities in this area of the law, for present purposes it is sufficient to note that several US military actions conducted in Afghanistan

---

122. A.-M. Slaughter, 'Terrorism and Justice: An international tribunal comprising US and Islamic judiciary should be set up to try terrorists', *Financial Times* (11 October 2001).

123. H. Koh, 'We Have the Right Courts for Bin Laden', *New York Times* (23 November 2001).

124. See Fleck, op. cit. n. 107, at pp. 211 et seq. ('neither the civilian population as such, nor individual civilians, shall be attacked, killed, wounded or taken prisoner without sufficient reason': AP I, Art. 51(2); AP II, Art. 13).

125. See H. Fischer, 'The Principle of Proportionality', available at www.crimesofwar.org. A closely related issue is the targeting of objects. Under AP I, Art. 52, military objectives are limited to those objects which by their nature, location, purpose or use make an effective contribution to military action and whose total or partial destruction offers a definite military advantage. This raises difficult questions in relation to objects with dual military and civilian uses such as bridges, roads, power installations and communications networks. Such questions are sure to arise in the context of the US-led strikes in Afghanistan (for example, in relation to the bombing of Red Cross and other food storage facilities in Kabul and the targeting of the civilian infrastructure noted above: see *supra* n. 28).

have raised questions regarding conformity with these norms of humanitarian law. While many deaths were likely the result of lawful collateral damage, several incidents have sparked controversy. In particular, on 1 July 2002, a team of American military experts was sent to the province of Uruzgan in central Afghanistan to investigate the circumstances under which US aircraft bombed an Afghan wedding celebration, killing an estimated 48 civilians and wounding 117.[126] In late-November 2001, questions were also raised by Amnesty International and other NGOs regarding the uprising and killings that occurred in the Qalai Janghi fort outside Mazar-i Sharif.[127] These and related incidents have led Afghan leaders to voice serious concerns about US military tactics in their ongoing war on terrorism.[128]

The second area of concern is the use of certain types of weapons. As noted above, the US has employed its full arsenal of conventional weapons in Afghanistan.[129] In January 2002, after coalition forces provided the UN Mine Action Programme (MAPA) with a list of 103 sites where cluster bombs were used, the UN began clearing an estimated 25,000 unexploded cluster bomblet units (CBU) dropped in Afghanistan by US warplanes.[130] This raises questions under conventional and customary humanitarian law, which prohibit the waging of war in a manner that causes unnecessary suffering, especially in relation to weapons that are either cruel or excessive in the nature and degree of suffering they cause or are incapable of distinguishing combatants from civilians.

While the use of cluster bombs and similar weapons remains unsettled under international law, these are questions that should be – but for the reasons discussed

126. See *Pentagon Team to Examine Bomb Error*, BBC News, 8 July 2002 (noting that the US had acknowledged that there were civilian deaths when an AC-130 attack helicopter raided villages 250 miles south-west of Kabul). See also D. Usborne, 'UN keeps damning report on Afghan massacre secret', *The Independent*, 31 July 2002 (noting in relation to the 1 July wedding party incident that the UN no longer intended to release a report written by a UN fact-finding team that included allegations that the US had under-reported civilian casualties and removed evidence from the site suggesting a 'cover-up').

127. J. Huggler, 'How our Afghan allies applied the Geneva Convention: Prisoners massacred, the dead plundered for boots, guns and even gold teeth', *The Independent* (29 November 2001). General Abdul Rashid Dostum, currently the Transitional Afghan deputy Defence Minister, was in command of the Northern Alliance forces during this incident.

128. UN Integrated Regional Information Network. Mounting Concern over Civilian Casualties', UN Integrated Regional Information Network, 7 January 2002 (noting concerns by both Hamid Karzai and Lakhdar Brahimi following reports that 52 civilians in the eastern province of Paktia were killed in a coalition strike).

129. See *supra* n. 29 and accompanying text.

130. From a total of 103 sub-munition strikes, 78 were struck by a total of 1,210 CBUs equaling a total of 244,420 sub-munitions. See 'UN to Clear Coalition Cluster Bombs', UN Integrated Regional Information Network, 2 January 2002. See also Human Rights Watch Report, 'Fatally Flawed: Cluster Bombs and Their Use by the United States in Afghanistan', 18 December 2002 (arguing that the US did not take all feasible precautions to avoid civilian casualties as required by international humanitarian law when it used cluster bombs in or near populated areas; problems included lack of accuracy in targeting during attacks, large numbers of explosive duds remaining after attacks resulting in the deaths of many civilians, and difficulties in clearance).

in Part 4 below are most unlikely to be – investigated and confronted in any future comprehensive process of transitional justice in Afghanistan.

4. TRANSITIONAL JUSTICE IN POST-WAR AFGHANISTAN

The discussion in Part 3 set out the full scale and scope of violations of humanitarian and human rights law in Afghanistan over the last two decades. As the Transitional Authority now begins the task of rebuilding Afghanistan's legislative, judicial and administrative institutions, how does it prioritize critical competing needs, and what does international law require in relation to holding individual perpetrators of atrocities accountable and in dealing with victims of the crimes? In trying to reconcile justice for past abuses and dealing with political realities and entrenched power relations, what are the factors that should be taken into account in designing an effective transitional justice policy for Afghanistan?

The unique nature of the Afghan transition raises a host of questions which challenge existing models of transitional justice employed so enthusiastically elsewhere. In a state ravaged by decades of internal and international armed conflict, should more pressing societal needs, such as establishing military and civil security, instituting humanitarian programs to deal with massive human insecurity, and rebuilding essential systems of governance, take priority over justice and reconciliation processes? From whose perspective should the desirability of establishing domestic or international courts or a Truth and Reconciliation Commission (TRC), or determining the priority of competing normative regimes be judged, the Afghan people themselves or the international community? If a TRC process is to be established, for example, how will the divisions between Afghanistan's various religious and ethnic groups – between Pashtuns, Tajiks, Hazaras, Uzbeks, and other minor ethnic groups – impact on this process? To what extent will a domestic or international court or a TRC be able to deal with the long history of outside involvement by surrounding states and terrorist groups in fomenting armed conflict and human rights atrocities in Afghanistan?

There is at least a degree of consensus between the new Afghan administration and the UN – at the level of principle if not on the details of implementation – that genuine accountability for humanitarian law and human rights abuses, tied to some process of truth telling and reconciliation, are structural requirements for future stability in the country. It is equally clear, however, that the inherent tensions between these objectives – between different transitional justice mechanisms and between norms based on human rights standards, Afghan cultural traditions and Islam – have yet to be comprehensively explored and resolved.

4.1 Rebuilding the legal system

In facing these challenges, the new government has had to confront two main clusters of problems: first, the question of how to achieve far greater cooperation and coordination to strengthen the peacekeeping-development nexus; and second, how to undertake post-conflict judicial and legal reconstruction alongside continuing military operations.

4.1.1 *Aid and reconstruction*

Chronic lack of resources hamper all transitional administrations. This is exacerbated by the fact that donor countries rarely provide sufficient resources in a timely fashion and have an even worse record in following through on pledges. Recent aid and reconstruction efforts in the former Yugoslavia and East Timor have revealed two general priorities: first, they must target local actors and capacity within an overall nation-building framework; and second, they must be provided in a timely fashion so that a black market economy cannot predominate.[131] In this respect, the Afghan transition represents a certain degree of progress and innovation. In order to address the problem of multiple actors engaging in redundant and competitive development work, the Karzai government has created the Afghan Assistance Coordination Authority (AACA), headed by the senior World Bank official, Ashraf Ghani. This Authority has developed a National Development Framework (NDF) that establishes a 'road map for recovery' and forces the donor community to coordinate among themselves while taking the priorities of the local government into account. This is intended to diminish the notoriously supply- rather than demand-driven, effects of development aid and to foster 'local ownership'.[132] Even so, of the international aid dispersed so far in Afghanistan, only approximately ten percent has been allocated to the Afghan government, the rest going to UNAMA. Furthermore, some of the largest donors have refused to pool their funds into a trust fund for the whole of Afghanistan.

4.1.2 *Rule of law and judicial reconstruction*

The Herculean task of seeking to establish the rule of law and legal institutions under international administration has become a fast-emerging area of study and policy innovation in recent years. The main challenge has been how to resolve the inherent tension between building capacity for sustainable local institutions while at the same time maintaining respect for international standards of justice. The more complex the political and security environment, the more acute the tension and the more resources that are needed. Thus, in situations of great human insecurity and scarce resources, improvisation and pragmatism are likely to trump principle at the level of practice. Given the level of devastation of both infrastruc-

---

131. See B. Rubin, 'Afghanistan and Threats to Human Security', International Symposium on Human Security, *Human Security and Terrorism - Diversifying Threats under Globalization - from Afghanistan to the Future of the World*, Tokyo, 15 December 2001.

132. S. Chesterman, *Tiptoeing Through Afghanistan: The Future of UN State-Building*, International Peace Academy, Transitional Administrations Project, September 2002.

ture and institutions in Afghanistan, the Transitional Authority has decided that, in accordance with the express terms of the Bonn Agreement, its first priorities in the area of legal reform and rebuilding are to establish independent Judicial and Human Rights Commissions.[133]

In assessing the UN experiments in judicial reconstruction in Bosnia, Kosovo, East Timor and Afghanistan over the last few years, the New York-based International Peace Academy has drawn three broad 'lessons learned'. First, the administration of justice should be amongst the top priorities of a post-conflict peace operation. Despite the fact, for example, that Bosnia has received more per capita international aid than Europe under the Marshall Plan, it remains in a legal and political quagmire. The main reason for this has been a failure to prioritize the promotion of the rule of law.[134] Similarly, the rule of law and the administration of justice have not been amongst the top priorities in Afghanistan, with the result that the peace achieved in Bonn remains dangerously fragile and provides a weak foundation for any subsequent reconciliation processes.

Second, in a post-conflict environment which lacks functioning law enforcement and judicial systems, rule of law functions may need to be temporarily transferred to the military. A key issue in all transitions is the role of the military in ensuring security, and it is increasingly being argued that this should include assuming policing functions to protect certain individuals and groups, to secure mass graves for exhumations, and to arrest war crimes suspects. This raises issues regarding the power of arrest and seizure of documentation which may contain information for future prosecutions.[135]

---

133. These priorities accord closely with the three prerequisites to long-term security in Afghanistan suggested recently by a coalition of human rights and development NGOs, the Consortium for Response to the Afghanistan Transition (CRAFT): (1) *rule of law* (determining, publishing and distributing applicable law; establishing the Judicial Commission mandated under the Bonn Agreement as soon as possible; providing governmental salary support; building institutional capacity by training ministry staff, judges, bar members and legal educators; providing basic equipment and law texts); (2) *human rights* (establishing an effective and independent Human Rights Commission; building the capacity of Afghan civil society to promote and protect human rights; providing human rights education; addressing women's rights; and establishing structures to monitor human rights); and (3) *governance* (building local institutions and the Bonn commissions): see Report of the Consortium for Response to the Afghanistan Transition, *Filling the Vacuum: Prerequisites to Security in Afghanistan*, March 2002, pp. 5-7.

134. International Peace Academy Conference Report, *You, the People: Transitional Administration, State-Building and the United Nations*, 18-19 October 2002, at Part V (arguing that the Bosnian governments failed to involve local communities and independent professionals in reconstruction planning and implementation, thus impeding the development of legal and judicial institutions and infrastructure).

135. See International Peace Academy, *Managing Security Challenges in Post-Conflict Peacebuilding*, IPA Workshop Report, 22-23 June 2001, at p. 7 (discussing the feasibility of creating an international arresting team separate from the military peacekeeping presence). In East Timor, INTERFET troops were authorized to detain persons suspected of committing serious offences under international law and were required to deliver them to the Force Detention Centre in Dili. See further I. Martin, 'Justice and Reconciliation: Responsibilities and Dilemmas of Peace-makers and Peace-builders,' in A.H. Henkin, ed., *The Legacy of Abuse: Confronting the Past, Facing the Future* (The Aspen Institute and New York University School of Law 2002) at p. 84.

Third, once the security environment stabilizes and the process of civil reconstruction commences, sustainability should take precedence over temporary standards in the administration of basic law and order.

In Afghanistan, the immense difficulty of undertaking post-conflict reconstruction alongside continuing military operations has become starkly apparent. The ISAF has been restricted to Kabul and its immediate environs while US Special Forces in the countryside have focused their operations entirely on the 'war against terrorism' (as opposed to also protecting civilians from violent reprisals or securing war criminals and evidence for future trials).[136] The prioritization of military over political strategies has undermined both the Transitional Authority in Kabul and re-entrenched the warlords in the provinces. The need to quickly develop a civil service and national police force and for military forces to assume temporary policing functions has not occurred on anything like the scale required. Until these problems are adequately addressed, there are no means by which to reduce the grip of rearmed warlords and for demilitarization to begin. As stated recently by UN Special Rapporteur Kamal Hossain, resources are urgently needed to recruit and develop a national police force and this is 'universally recognized by all sections of the Afghan people to be the number one priority'.[137]

To date, the state of development of the justice sector has been disappointing.[138] Given the experiences in Kosovo and East Timor, it is clear that failure to engage immediately with rule of law questions can result in a missed opportunity for the maximum impact of international engagement. A document from the Office of the SRSG in Afghanistan in May 2002 stated that a 'strategic, comprehensive, Afghan led, integrated program of justice sector reform can only begin with a comprehensive sectoral review and assessment of domestic needs, priorities, initiatives and capacities for reconstruction and development of this crucial sector'.[139] These assumptions are debatable if they require delays until the security environment allows for a thorough review. Rather it appears as though the rule of law and transitional justice have not been priorities for UNAMA (even taking into account its assistance rather than leadership role), the Transitional administration or the donor

136. See Human Rights Watch, 'All Our Hopes Are Crushed: Violence and Repression in Western Afghanistan', Vol. 14, No. 7, November 2002 (arguing that the UN approach of a 'light footprint' has proven ineffective to protect human rights and that American military forces have maintained relationships with local warlords that have undercut efforts by US diplomats and aid agencies to strengthen central authority and the rule of law).

137. Statement by Dr Kamal Hossain, Special Rapporteur on the Situation of Human Rights in Afghanistan, 58th Session of the Commission on Human Rights, 26 March 2002, at para. 10.

138. See e.g., International Crisis Group, *Afghanistan: Judicial Reform and Transitional Justice,* 28 January 2003 (observing that the judicial and human rights commissions have, to date, achieved little and that the Chief Justice of the Supreme Court, Fazl Hadi Shinwari, has rapidly placed political allies in key positions and advocated the return of a strict form of sharia law in Afghanistan).

139. Office of the SRSG for Afghanistan (UNAMA) (UNAMA-OSRSG, Kabul, May 2002), cited in Simon Chesterman, Justice Under International Administration: Kosovo, East Timor and Afghanistan, International Peace Academy, Transitional Administration Project, September 2002, at p. 11.

community. Indeed, in the AACA's National Development Framework, the justice system is barely mentioned.

4.2 International obligations and mechanisms for accountability

International human rights law has traditionally provided states with a wide discretion in implementing international obligations to respect and ensure rights.[140] At the same time, international criminal law has focused principally on the power rather than the duty of states to punish violations committed outside their territorial jurisdiction.[141] In more recent times, however, international law has required states to punish certain human rights crimes – such as genocide and torture – committed in their territorial jurisdiction, to investigate violations and to punish the perpetrators.[142] It is also well established that individual violations of international humanitarian law entail criminal sanctions.[143] Thus, it is clear that modern international criminal law (which encompasses specific violations of both humanitarian and human rights law) imposes obligations directly on individuals, making them liable to punishment, and imposes duties on states with respect to matters usually left to their discretion. The significance of these developments is that an amnesty law or an exercise of prosecutorial discretion that is valid under domestic law may nevertheless breach a state's international obligations.

In applying these principles to the last two decades of abuses in Afghanistan, it is clear that under international law the transitional government is under a duty to investigate allegations of war crimes, crimes against humanity, torture, extra-legal executions, disappearances and other serious violations of humanitarian and human rights law and to hold individual wrongdoers responsible. In certain

---

140. Human rights treaties such as the ICCPR emphasize 'obligations of result' leaving the determination of means of protecting rights to states: see Schachter, *supra* n. 112, p. 311. Increasingly, however, human rights treaties specify 'obligations of means' as well as result: see D. Orentlicher, 'Setting Accounts: The Duty to Prosecute Human Rights Violationa of a Prior Regime', 100 *Yale LJ* (1991) pp. 2537.

141. When international criminal law has required states to punish offences committed in their territory, the duty has traditionally applied to crimes committed against foreign nationals: see Orentlicher, *supra* n. 140, pp. 2551-2555, nn. 63-65.

142. While the ICCPR does not specify a duty to punish violations of rights, it is well accepted that a state State Party fails in its duty to ensure those rights protecting physical integrity if it does not investigate violations and seek to punish those who are responsible. See e.g., Report of the Human Rights Committee, 37 UN GAOR Supp. (No. 40) Annex V, general comment 7(16), para. 1, UN Doc. E/CN.4/Sub.2/Add.1/963 (1982) (complaints about ill-treatment under Art. 7 of the Covenant must be investigated effectively by competent authorities and those found guilty must be held responsible). In addition, a state's failure to punish repeated or notorious violations breaches the customary obligation to respect fundamental human rights: ibid., p. 2552.

143. Arts. 49, 50, 129, and 146 of Geneva I, II, III, and IV respectively enjoin the High Contracting Parties to enact legislation providing 'penal sanctions' for grave breaches of the Conventions. Further, common penal provisions of the Conventions confer universal jurisdiction over grave breaches of any Convention making the perpetrators *hostes humani generis*. The duty to punish or surrender those who have committed grave breaches is not conditioned in any way that suggests any restrictions on jurisdiction. See M. Bothe, ed., *National Implementation of International Humanitarian Law* (Dordrecht, Martinus Nijhoff Publishers 1990) pp. 73-78.

instances, the government may also be required to ensure that individuals whose rights have been violated have an effective remedy before a competent body and that they receive adequate compensation.[144]

The fact that discharging these various obligations in the volatile and fragile situation of post-conflict Afghanistan will prove extremely hazardous does not relieve the state of its duties as a matter of international law. A state cannot evade its duty to punish atrocious crimes merely to appease disaffected military forces, newly returned warlords or to promote national reconciliation.[145]

4.2.1 *International versus domestic justice*

The question of individual criminal accountability for past abuses was not addressed in direct terms during the Bonn process. Given the number and diversity of potential defendants, any prosecutorial strategy will need to have strictly defined limits and objectives. This raises the prospect of selective prosecutions, a practice which does not *per se* violate international law, provided that appropriate criteria are employed for selecting defendants.[146] In this respect, any future domestic or international prosecutions are likely to face at least three major dilemmas. The first concerns the relevant time period during which past abuses may be investigated and prosecuted. If it extends all the way back to the first phase of Afghanistan's 23-year old civil war, this will create an enormous group of potential defendants. The second is whether prosecutions will be brought only against Afghan perpetrators or whether attempts will be made to extradite and prosecute foreign perpetrators who may have committed war crimes and serious human rights violations.[147] The third dilemma is whether prosecutions will be brought only against members of the Taliban or also against those members of the Northern Alliance and other armed groups suspected of committing war crimes and serious human rights abuses. In the current political configuration, it seems inconceivable that prosecutions will be brought against those warlords and military commanders who now enjoy renewed positions of power either in the central Transitional Authority or in the provincial capitals.

The desperate economic and humanitarian plight of the country, in conjunction with the complexity of both the political landscape and scope of violations,

---

144. See ICCPR, Art. 2(3). See also *Velasquez Rodriguez* case, Inter-Am. Ct. H.R. (Ser. C) No. 4, para. 174 (1998) (judgment). As it is difficult to envisage either the warlords or surrounding states assuming responsibility for violations of international law and providing reparations to victims, presumably, the new, fiscally-limited Afghan government will need to assume this responsibility.

145. Note that the Restatement (Third) of the Foreign Relations Law of the United States takes the position that a complete failure to punish repeated or notorious violations of rights protected by customary law generates state responsibility for a breach of the law: § 702 and Comment *b*.

146. Most domestic penal systems reflect a priority on prosecuting persons responsible for the most serious offences. Any prosecutorial strategy should not, however, be arbitrarily directed towards any particular group of scapegoats in a system of past atrocities: see K. Davis, *Discretionary Justice: a preliminary inquiry* (Baton Rouge LA, Louisiana State University Press 1969).

147. In relation to Afghan perpetrators currently in custody, see *supra* n. 70.

suggests that Afghanistan is unlikely to prove the exception to the rule. Apart from those individuals in detention and facing trials in US military commissions or domestic courts, this raises the very real likelihood of impunity for the perpetrators of the worst abuses.

The question then arises whether international criminal justice institutions and forms of accountability have any role to play in the Afghan transition, especially given the likely obstacles facing domestic prosecutions. While several commentators have suggested the creation of international justice mechanisms in the wake of 11 September, this has been largely in the context of combating international terrorism. There has been no indication that the Security Council intends to establish an *ad hoc* Tribunal for Afghanistan,[148] and the ICC will have no jurisdiction over any crimes within its mandate committed in Afghanistan prior to July 2002. Furthermore, given the strongly unilateralist stance of the Bush administration towards the ICC and international justice more generally, any proposals for an *ad hoc* Tribunal to prosecute war crimes and other atrocities committed during the Afghan wars would almost certainly be vetoed (especially if such a tribunal were to have jurisdiction over individual violations of humanitarian law alleged to have been committed by US and allied forces).

In any event, both the scale of the atrocities and the number of victims is overwhelming and certainly far too great, even in an ideal world, to carry out international criminal prosecutions of all those individuals who have committed atrocities and serious violations of international humanitarian and human rights law. Any enmity existing between different ethnic and religious groups for past violations is arguably best dealt with by local processes and the imposition of domestic penalties rather than by an international criminal tribunal.

Thus, the only remaining realistic possibility may be the creation, with international assistance, of a special court – perhaps linked to a complementary truth commission – along similar lines to the Special Court and Truth and Reconciliation Commission currently being established in Sierra Leone.

Whatever approach is adopted, the lessons learned to date in applying international justice norms and mechanisms to states in transition suggest that a fully integrated approach is required that pays close attention to the realities and history of the relevant conflict and the need at the local level to reestablish the rule of law and to achieve effective legal and institutional reform.

Lustration and other political mechanisms by which to gradually diminish the official power of the warlords and other individuals implicated in abuses is another means of dealing with violators. In relation to the rebuilding of the Afghan national

148. As noted by Brown, while the creation of *ad hoc* tribunals has advanced the cause of international justice, it has also raised questions of fairness and political privilege. Why, for example, were such tribunals created for the Former Yugoslavia and Rwanda but not for Chechnya, Somalia, Cambodia, or the Persian Gulf War? The answer lies in the source of their creation – the Security Council – and hence the full range of political and strategic factors that influence that body (including the veto of the permanent five members). See B. Brown, 'Primacy or Complementarity: Reconciling the Jurisdiction of National Courts and International Criminal Tribunals', 23 *Yale JIL* (1998) pp. 383 at 386.

army and police force, for example, the UN Special Rapporteur on Human Rights, Asma Jahangir, has strongly urged the Karzai administration to establish stringent screening procedures to ensure that individuals suspected of committing atrocities be excluded.[149]

4.3 A truth commission for Afghanistan?

Given the extraordinary degree of political, social and economic instability and the devastated condition of Afghan judicial and other governmental institutions (which, as discussed, make prosecutions in the immediate term impossible), the question of whether to establish a TRC in post-war Afghanistan has now inevitably arisen.

Hamid Karzai's conception of justice for the Afghan people appears to rest on a combination of truth, reconciliation and presumably reparations for victims.[150] However, official investigations of past abuses leading to some form of societal closure and consensus regarding a troubled history, and acknowledgment of victims by an official institution, appear to be utopian objectives, at least for the immediate future, given the pressing security and humanitarian challenges facing the country.

The findings of early NGO consultations with the Afghan people themselves bear this out and suggest that reconciliation and forgiveness on the one hand and justice and reparations on the other rank well behind the desire for stability, security, protection of basic human rights, education and adequate health and humanitarian services.[151] Further, the traditional scenario justifying truth commissions of former evil oppressors and their innocent victims does not apply so neatly in the Afghan context. Truth commissions were established in Latin America because disappearances, torture and other gross violations of human rights were committed in secret. In countries such as Argentina, El Salvador and Chile, authoritarian regimes created state systems designed specifically to conceal the facts and carry out covert acts of terror. Truth commissions were therefore needed to expose the violations, their invisible victims, and the systems that made them possible. In Afghanistan, by contrast, the nature and extent of atrocities committed by each of the different groups of actors are well known.

Similarly, the reasons (although not of course the question of attribution of responsibility) for those atrocities appear to be relatively uncontroversial among Afghans. For these and related reasons, a convincing case for a TRC in Afghanistan must rest not only on the usual truth and reconciliation grounds but less obviously on specific grounds of seeking to link these objectives to further-reaching questions of security (especially lustration processes and subsequent

149. Afghannews.net, 'UN urges Afghanistan to screen police, army recruits', 6 February 2003. Available at www.afghannews.net/news.

150. See UN Press Release, Human Rights Committee, Seventy-fourth session, 18 March 2002.

151. See CESR Report, *supra* n. 4; United States Institute of Peace, *Rebuilding Afghanistan: A Framework for Establishing Security and the Rule of Law*, 11 December 2001.

internationally-assisted prosecutions of key individuals implicated in human rights abuses) and rebuilding the country's legal – especially constitutional and judicial – systems and institutions. In this respect, an Afghan TRC could constitute the first step in the critical process of building a 'culture of rights' in Afghanistan. Early attempts to implement the guiding principles of both the Bonn Agreement and the National Workshop on Human Rights – that is, to establish a transitional justice policy based on 'international human rights standards, Afghan cultural traditions and Islam' – are falling victim to the low priority accorded to rebuilding the justice system on Afghanistan's political agenda.

These difficult problems could be mitigated to some extent by a well-designed TRC fully integrated with the ongoing work of the Judicial and Human Rights Commissions in drafting a new Afghan constitution and undertaking various human rights-related activities. An Afghan TRC, for example, could meticulously document the many abuses of the past, provide a forum for thousands of victims to tell their stories and claim reparations, and seek to entrench in the hearts and minds of all Afghans a forward-looking human rights culture built on the rule of law, democracy and constitutionalism. Such a non-legal victim-oriented institution could also provide a unique forum (apart from the Loya Jirga) for substantive and wide-ranging discussions on how best to reconcile Afghanistan's national laws and practices with its international human rights treaty obligations. In the complex and contentious areas of women's rights and the relationship between religion and human rights, these discussions and deliberations with thousands of Afghans could gradually seek to illustrate the importance of human rights to the future of the country and begin to forge the consensus needed for a broadly-accepted Afghan constitution.[152] Without the involvement of the people themselves in both confronting the repression and abuses of the past and building a normative framework for the future, Afghanistan's constitutional and legal institutions will remain dangerously fragile and irrelevant. In this respect, a broadly conceived Afghan TRC may be a necessary, albeit, insufficient, precondition to both later prosecutions (whether domestic or international) and the ongoing work of drafting a new constitution and rebuilding the legal system.

5. CONCLUSION

A little over a decade ago, Louis Henkin suggested that ours was the 'age of rights', and that human rights was the 'idea of our time'.[153] If this had indeed been an article of faith amongst the community of nations, on 11 September 2001, the Age of

152. The ICG has similarly argued that '[a]s Afghanistan seeks a balance between secular and religious law, modernity and tradition, it is essential that women are fully represented in the process at all levels. Therefore, they must be involved in all efforts at consultation and the drafting of laws, the commissions, the teaching of law and the rebuilding of the courts.' ICG Report, International Crisis Group, *Afghanistan: Judicial Reform and Transitional Justice*, 28 January 2003, p. 21.

153. L. Henkin, *The Age of Rights* (New York, Columbia University Press 1990) p. xvii.

Rights was dramatically and tragically confronted with what some now see as the emergence of the Age of Terrorism. While acknowledging, for example, that since the end of the Cold War, human rights had become the 'dominant moral vocabulary in foreign affairs', Michael Ignatieff questioned whether after 11 September 'the era of human rights has come and gone'. He noted that 'Rome has been attacked, and Rome is fighting to re-establish its security and hegemony', and that, accordingly, the international human rights movement will have to engage soon in 'the battle of ideas: it has to challenge directly the claim that national security trumps human rights'.[154] That battle of ideas has now begun in earnest and is today being waged in a number of different *fora* and in relation to a number of issues, each raising its own problems and implications for the future promotion and protection of human rights and humanitarian law.[155]

Ignatieff has argued that America's 'capacity to shape outcomes in Afghanistan, still less to create a state, is constrained by the way it won the war against the Taliban'.[156]

More than any others, two factors – the effects of US imperialism and overriding security concerns – threaten to undermine attempts to establish transitional justice mechanisms and institutions in the fraught political and economic conditions of post-Taliban Afghanistan. The lessons of other transitional societies suggest that addressing individual criminal responsibility for serious violations of international humanitarian and human rights law is pivotal to the creation of a stable, accountable government subject to the rule of law. Without appropriate judicial mechanisms for both past and ongoing atrocities in Afghanistan and the exclusion of war criminals from participation in the transitional government or its new armed forces and police, these objectives will remain elusive.

This article has sought to show how overriding security concerns in the conduct of the US-led 'war on terrorism' are leading to the systematic undermining of long-established principles and protections of international law. This approach to combating international terrorism and 'terrorist states' has troubling implications for future transitional justice policies and institutions in Afghanistan for at least three reasons. First, it will affect the way in which the Afghan authorities interpret and apply the relevant protections and obligations under the Geneva Conventions and human rights treaties. The US category of 'unlawful combatants', for example,

---

154. M. Ignatieff, 'Is the Human Rights Era Ending?', *New York Times* (5 February 2002).

155. For present purposes it is sufficient to observe that the new US military and political strategy of 'preventive war' and 'anticipatory self defense' has profound implications for the traditional international rules of *jus ad bellum* which, in turn, will affect the future evolution of *jus in bello*. See further P. Danchin, 'Human Rights,' in *A Global Agenda: Issues Before the 56th General Assembly of the United Nations* (US/UNA, Rowman & Littlefield Publishers 2002) pp. 1-33 (discussing the new paradigm of terrorism and human rights in a post-September 11 world).

156. M. Ignatieff, 'Nation-Building Lite', *New York Times Magazine* (28 July 2002) at pp. 26, 28-29. Ignatieff further suggests (at p. 29) that the 'winning strategy paired Special Forces teams and air power with local commanders and their militias. When victory came, America thought it had won the war, but the warlords in the Northern Alliance thought they had. Now they dominate the Kabul government and insist that they, rather than the Americans, should shape the peace.'

affects the rights and duties of not only members of the Taliban and Al Qaeda forces but also those of the Northern Alliance and other armed groups. Second, the blanket denial of POW status and the refusal to convene an Article 5 tribunal in cases of doubt affects the status and rights of persons currently being detained by the Afghan authorities. Third, the willingness of the US to derogate from international standards regarding the rights of prisoners offers an unfortunate precedent. Accordingly, the incentives for the Transitional Authority (which has even greater and more pressing security concerns than the US) to comply with international humanitarian and human rights law in designing a transitional justice policy and rebuilding the legal system have been gravely damaged by the post-September 11 actions of the US government. It is difficult to envisage the US playing a positive leadership role in the creation of an enduring and effective post-Taliban system of justice while at the same time maintaining on the one hand its exceptionalist stance towards the international rule of law, human rights and the ongoing struggle for universal justice and on the other its aggressive, imperial security policy regarding the use of force.

While it may well be true that an overly hurried and optimistic transition towards democratization and criminal accountability for warlords could lead to increased ethnic conflict and destabilizing violence,[157] the far greater danger for Afghanistan is that impunity for past abuses will ensure not only future violations but also the continued rule of the gun over the rule of law. Whatever institutional responses are adopted – whether domestic courts, an international *ad hoc* tribunal, a mixed international-national tribunal or a truth commission linked to justice mechanisms – the primary objectives should be the creation of a genuine and popularly supported constitutionalist culture of human rights, the rebuilding of Afghanistan's legal system and the establishment of effective monitoring and accountability mechanisms to deter future abuses. Nation-building and reconstruction in Afghanistan face overwhelming challenges – the legacy of 23 years of brutal war, desperate poverty and a destroyed infrastructure and economic base. The extent to which these processes are likely to result in a durable peace, however, will depend in no small part on the extent to which, in accordance with the terms of the Bonn Agreement, the new Afghan government complies with its obligations under international humanitarian and human rights law.

---

157. See e.g., J. Snyder, *From Voting to Violence: Democratization and Nationalist Conflict* (New York, W.W. Norton 2002) (arguing that because ethnic conflict is most likely to break the early stages of democratic transitions, outside forces should hold back from promoting democracy and favor instead the 'gradual development of the rule of law, an impartial bureaucracy, civil rights, and a professional media, followed by the holding of free elections').

COMPUTER NETWORK ATTACK: THE NORMATIVE SOFTWARE[1]

Michael N. Schmitt[2]

1. INTRODUCTION

As the United States, assisted by a number of its allies, continues to mount asymmetrical attacks against terrorists and their supporters, the centrality of technology to 'future war' is becoming increasingly apparent. In a matter of months, US Forces successfully routed, with almost no hostile fire casualties, a battle-hardened and ruthless adversary in a combat environment that frustrated the potent Soviet army for a decade. Operation ENDURING FREEDOM follows close on the heels of Operation ALLIED FORCE, the 1999 NATO campaign that defeated, without friendly casualties, the Yugoslav military. In that conflict, as in the most recent one, exploitation of technological wherewithal proved a decisive factor in determining the victor.

This article surveys the international law governing one new facet of military technology, computer network attack, of an ancient form of conflict, information operations (IO). Information operations are 'actions taken to affect adversary information and information systems while defending one's own information and information systems',[3] whether during peacetime, crises, or 'war', and at the strategic, operational or tactical levels of armed conflict.[4] IO

2. Michael N. Schmitt, Professor of International Law and Director, Executive Program in International and Security Affairs, George C. Marshall European Center for Security Studies, Garmisch-Partenkirchen, Germany. The views expressed herein are those of the author in his personal capacity and do not necessarily represent those of any US or German government agency.

3. Joint Chiefs of Staff, Department of Defense Dictionary of Military and Associated Terms, Joint Publication 1-02, 12 April 2001 at p. 203. For US forces, Information Operation policy is set forth in, *inter alia,* Information Operations, Department of Defense Directive (DODD) S-3600.1, 9 December 1996; Joint Chiefs of Staff, Joint Doctrine for Information Operations, Joint Publication 3-13, 9 October 1998; Joint Chiefs of Staff, Joint Doctrine for Command and Control Warfare, Joint Publication 3-13.1, 7 February 1996; Implementing Instruction for Information Warfare/Command and Control, Chief of Naval Operations Instruction 3430.26, 18 January 1995; Information Operations, Air Force Doctrine Document 2-5, 5 August 5 1998. Many US military publications are available on-line through the Joint Electronic Library at http://www.dtic.mil/doctrine/jel/.

4. At the strategic level, information operations can be employed to 'achieve national objectives by influencing or affecting all elements (political, military, economic, or informational) of an adversary's or potential adversary's national power while protecting similar friendly elements'. At the oper-

Yearbook of International Humanitarian Law
Volume 4 – 2001 – pp. 53-85

can include such diverse activities as operations security, psychological operations, military deception, electronic warfare, physical attack, and computer network attack.[5] Its defining characteristic is that it is intended either to deny information to another or, alternatively, to leverage information to one's own advantage.

A key subcategory of information operations is information warfare (IW), i.e., 'information operations conducted during time of crisis or conflict to achieve or promote specific objectives over a specific adversary or adversaries'.[6] The defining aspect of IW is not what is affected (as a subset of IO, by definition the objective is affecting information, or the use thereof), but rather the circumstance in which it occurs – crisis or conflict. Espionage is the best example available to differentiate the two labels. Peacetime espionage is clearly an information operation. However, it does not constitute information warfare unless performed during a crisis or armed conflict.

Despite the current preoccupation with IO and IW, strategies and tactics to exploit information while deceiving or blinding an opponent are as ancient as warfare itself. Alcibiades used information warfare to convince the Chians to revolt against Athens in the 20th year of the Peloponnesian Wars;[7] the Mongols exploited superior information networks to compensate for numerically inferior forces in their battles across the face of Eastern Europe during the Thirteenth Century; and the use of balloons as observation platforms during the American Civil War represented archetypal information warfare. Undeniably, getting inside an opponent's OODA (observe, orient, decide, act) loop[8] has been a – perhaps *the* – key objective for combat commanders since the tribes of Israel stood before the walls of Jericho.

What is new is computer network attack (CNA). CNA can constitute IW or simply amount to IO. Defined as operations intended to 'disrupt, deny, degrade, or destroy information resident in computers and computer networks, or the computers and networks themselves',[9] the *means* used to mount the attack – a data

---

ational level, the focus of information operations is 'on affecting adversary lines of communication (LOCs), logistics, command and control (C2), and related capabilities and activities while protecting similar friendly capabilities and activities'. Finally, at the tactical level the objective is to affect adversary 'information and information systems relating to C2, intelligence, and other information-based processes directly relating to the conduct of military operations….'Joint Publication 3-13, ibid. at I-2 – I-3.

5. Idem at I-9. Or an operation may represent a combination. See e.g., A. Lungu, *War.Com:* 'The Internet and Psychological Operations', No. 28 *Joint Force Quarterly* (Spring/Summer 2001) at p. 13.

6. Joint Publication 1-02, *supra* n. 3, at p. 203.

7. Thucydides, *The Peloponnesian War*, book 8, para. 8.8.

8. OODA: Observe, orient, decide, act. 'Getting inside an opponent's OODA loop', i.e., being able to asses the situation and act thereon more quickly than an opponent (and then do the same for the new situation that has been created), is the purpose of information warfare.

9. Joint Publication 1-02, *supra* n. 3, at p. 88. The USAF Intelligence Targeting Guide, AF Pamphlet 14-210, 1 February 1998, para. 11.4.3, sets out seven employment concepts:
Corruption – The alteration of information content; the manipulation of data to make it either nonsen-

stream – set CNA apart from other forms of IO.[10] Examples include gaining external control of a computer system, spreading computer 'viruses' that destroy or alter data, using 'logic bombs' that activate in a system upon a pre-defined occurrence or at a set time, transmitting 'worms' that multiply in a computer network to overload it, and monitoring and/or seizing data with 'sniffers'. Whether conducted during peacetime or armed conflict, the objectives of such operations vary widely. The goal may simply be data collection or observation. Or the intention may be to reroute or block fund transfers. Media broadcasts can be jammed or altered and booby trapped computer chips can be imbedded in weapons systems or dual use assets. Of course, any military operation in which computers play a part could be disrupted with properly targeted CNA.[11]

Computer network attack is new wine in old bottles for a number of reasons. To begin with, it 'weaponizes' previously benign objects – computers systems. Although integral to warfare for a number of decades, only recently have they become capable of directly harming an adversary. Consider attacks on electrical grids, such as those that, somewhat controversially, occurred during Operations

---

sical or inaccurate. Destroying existing knowledge.

Deception – A specific type of corruption; the alteration of, or adding to, information to portray a situation different from reality. Creating false knowledge to include masquerading.

Delay – The reversible slowing of the flow of information through the system, and the slowing of the acquisition and dissemination of new knowledge.

Denial – The reversible stopping of the flow of information for a period of time; although the information may be transmitted and used within friendly territory, the adversary is denied access to it. The prevention of the acquisition and dissemination of new knowledge.

Disruption – The reduction of the capacity to provide and /or process information (reversible). This is a combination of delay and corruption. The delay of the acquisition and dissemination of new knowledge and the destruction of existing knowledge.

Degradation – The permanent reduction in the capacity to provide and/or process information.

Destruction – The destruction of information before it can be transmitted; the permanent elimination of the capacity to provide and/or process information.

10. Thus, e.g., electronic attack (EA) would not fall within this category. For instance, using an electromagnetic pulse to destroy a computer's electronics would be EA, whereas transmitting a code or instruction to a system's central processing unit to cause the power supply to short out would be CNA.

11. As an illustration of possible targets, consider a proposed 'Top 10' list of information warfare targets in the United States, all of which are targetable via CNA:

1. Culpeper, Viginia, electronic switch which handles all federal funds and transactions;
2. Alaska pipeline which currently carries ten percent of all US domestic oil;
3. Electronic switching system which manages all telephones;
4. Internet;
5. Time distribution system;
6. Panama Canal;
7. Worldwide Military Command and Control System (WMCSS);
8. Air Force satellite control network;
9. Strait of Malacca, the major maritime link between Europe-Arabian peninsula and the Western Pacific and East Asia; and
10. National Photographic Interpretation Center (Washington).

A.T. Gumahad, 'The Profession of Arms in the Information Age', No. 15 *Joint Force Quarterly* (Spring 1997) at pp. 14, 18.

DESERT STORM and ALLIED FORCE.[12] Using computers, a technologically adept attacker could obtain similar (perhaps improved) effects, with both *de minimus* risk to its own forces and greater ability to limit collateral damage to civilian objects and incidental injury to civilians. With the advent of CNA, today the computer is no less a weapon system than an F-16 armed with precision weapons.

CNA also dramatically decreases the time required to create tactical, operational, or even strategic effects in a conflict. Launch-to-impact lag can be less than seconds, an extraordinary advantage for a force attempting to get inside an opponent's OODA loop. Despite this attractive feature, time compression of such magnitude renders fail-safe mechanisms impractical for those launching an attack, while often denying the attacker's foe the opportunity to fully assess the nature and source of the attack before having to respond. Further complicating matters is the fact that, although capabilities to do so are improving, it remains difficult to know the identity of an attacker who is determined to either mask it or, more ominously, feign a different one. Or the attack may have been mounted through 'neutral' states; indeed the attacker, because of automatic routing mechanisms, may not be able to control, or even accurately predict, the cyber pathway to the target. Each of these factors heightens the risk of unintended consequences in an attack, or the response thereto, and hinders de-escalation in the face of an accidental attack (or one causing unintended and unforeseeable consequences).

Beyond the temporal factor, CNA dramatically expands the possible scope of an attack. The interconnectedness of today's cyber-world makes possible striking 'targets' numbering in the millions. Entire states could be affected, for instance, by destroying data in a government pension, airline reservation or tax ministry computer systems. Air traffic control nets can be attacked, as can water treatment facilities, factories, educational institutions, oil distribution pipelines and electrical grids. More 'modestly', CNA might be used to impact a state's military. Consider the devastating warfighting consequences of destroying or altering data resident in systems used for recalling reserve forces, controlling logistics or monitoring enemy order of battle. Indeed, during Operation DESERT STORM, US forces transmitted 100,000 electronic messages and made 700,000 phone calls daily.[13] A decade later, reliance on such CNA-vulnerable systems has increased dramatically.

Note the extent to which CNA presents new target sets and new ways to attack traditional targets, thereby opening up both insidious and beneficial prospects. Attacking many potential target sets was heretofore impractical. For instance,

---

12. On electrical grid attacks, see J.W. Crawford, 'The Law of Noncombatant Immunity and the Targeting of National Electrical Power Systems', 21 *Fletcher Forum of World Affairs* (Summer/Fall 1997) at p. 101. Legal issues regarding the two campaigns are discussed in US Department of Defense, Conduct of the Persian Gulf War: Final Report to Congress, app. O (1992), and Independent International Commission on Kosovo, Kosovo Report, ch. 6 (2000).

13. Testimony of Director of Central Intelligence George J. Tenet before the Senate Committee on Government Affairs, June 24, 1998, available online at http://www.cia.gov/cia/public_affairs/speeches/archives/1998/dci_testimony_062498.html.

comprehensively targeting financial, media, or communications sectors in a developed country is extremely complicated for even the most advanced militaries. However, each sector is extremely vulnerable to computer network attack. So too are the medical, educational, and other key segments of societal infrastructure that are, by humanitarian law, immune from attack.

The urge to exploit attacks on these newly targetable targets will inevitably rise as the capability to conduct them increases. Computer network attack also gives rise to new methods of attacking traditional targets, in great part due to the surgical precision resident in much CNA technology. As an example, rather than destroying the dual-use electrical generation assets on which air defence or command and control nets often depend, it may be possible to simply turn them off during an attack, thereby minimizing the risk of incidental injury and or collateral damage (as well as the international condemnation that such injury and damage may result in).

Finally, CNA offers 'war on the cheap'. For little more than the price of a computer, Internet access and a talented hacker, a state can field at least a rudimentary capability. This reality makes CNA particularly attractive to those who face dramatically superior forces, either because those forces may be vulnerable to computer network attack themselves (consider the dependence of NATO forces on computers) or because CNA permits an attacker to asymmetrically target centers of gravity other than military forces, especially civilian populations.[14] It should come as little surprise, therefore, that many countries are developing information warfare competencies.[15]

2. THE NORMATIVE CONTEXT

The absence of CNA specific law means that prescriptive norms designed for kinetic uses of force must be applied to such operations. However, the unique features of computer network attack render traditional applications of the *jus ad bellum* (the international law governing *when* a state may resort to the use of force) and *jus in bello* (the international law governing *how* force may be applied in armed conflict) somewhat lacking. The problem is less one of *lacunae* than it is interpreting the existing law in a manner that suits evolving concepts and conduct of warfare, maintains fidelity to the spirit underlying the international law

14. CIA Director Tenet made just this point when testifying before the Senate. 'Many of the countries whose information warfare efforts we follow realize that in a conventional military confrontation against the US, they cannot prevail. These countries recognize that cyber attacks – possibly launched from outside the US – against civilian computer systems in the US – represent the kind of asymmetric option they will need to 'level the playing field' during an armed crisis against the United States'. Idem.

15. Statement of Jack L. Brock, Director, Defense Information and Financial Management Systems Accounting and Information, General Accounting Office, Testimony Before the Permanent Subcommittee on Investigations, Committee on Governmental Affairs, US Senate, Information Security: Computer Attacks at Department of Defense Pose Increasing Risks, 22 May 1996 (GAO/T-AIMD-96-92), attached report, pp. 1-11.

governing uses of force, and fairly reflects the normative expectations of a global community which must apply, and is subject to, that body of law. Three queries lie at the heart of the matter: 1) When is initiating a computer network attack against a target state unlawful under the *jus ad bellum* if an armed conflict is not yet already underway? 2) When is use of computer network attack permissible in self-defence and when may armed force be used in self-defence against a computer network attack? and 3) Once in an international armed conflict, what are the *jus in bello* limits on computer network attack?[16]

Before addressing these questions, it is essential to recognize that the normative context of information operations generally, and computer network attack specifically, is far from limited to the *jus ad bellum* and *in bello*. Information operations, whether during peace or war, are subject to an array of legal regimes. Arms control agreements often prohibit, expressly or implicitly, Parties from interfering with 'national technical means of verification' of compliance therewith,[17] whereas the 1961 Convention on Diplomatic Relations provides for the inviolability of diplomatic communications.[18] Interference with navigational assets that endanger the safety of civil aircraft and maritime vessels would be unlawful in most circumstances.[19] International communications law imposes other limits on IO, again principally during peacetime.[20] The International Telecommunications Convention, for instance, provides that 'Members reserve the right to stop the transmission of any private telegram [or other private telecommunication] which may appear dangerous to the security of the State or contrary to its laws, to public order or to decency, provided that they immediately notify the office of origin ... except when such notification may appear dangerous to the security of the State.'[21] States may also be Party to bilateral communications agreements that limit their IO options. Finally, numerous agreements exist that are designed to preclude the chance of the inadvertent outbreak of hostilities. Perhaps the best example is the 1988

16. For useful surveys of the subject, see M.N. Schmitt and B.T. O'Donnell, eds., *Computer Network Attack and International Law,* (Newport RI, Naval War College International Law Studies 2002); T.C. Wingfield, *The Law of Information Conflict: national security law in cyberspace* (Falls Church VA, Aegis Corp. 2000) pp. 124-125; Ch. Joyner and C. Lotrionte, 'Information Warfare as International Coercion: Elements of a Legal Framework', 12 *EJIL* (2001) p. 825.

17. The Start II treaty, for example, explicitly relies on national technical means of verification to verify the nature of heavy bombers. See various provisions in Treaty on Further Reduction and Limitation of Strategic Offensive Arms, 3 January 1993, US-USSR, Senate Treaty Document No. 1, 103d Cong. (1993) available online at http://www.ceip.org/programs/npp/start2text.htm. The agreement was ratified by the US Senate in 1996 and the Russian Duma in 2000.

18. Vienna Convention on Diplomatic Relations, Art. 27, 18 April 1961, 23 *UST* 3227, 500 *UNTS* 95.

19. See e.g., Convention on International Civil Aviation, 7 December 1944, 61 Stat. 1180, *TIAS* 1591, 15 *UNTS* 295, esp. annex 10.

20. State practice suggests that telecommunications treaties are generally deemed suspended during armed conflict. See Department of Defense, Office of General Counsel, *An Assessment of International Legal Issues in Information Operations*, section V, 2nd edn. (1999) reprinted in Schmitt, op. cit. n. 16, at appendix.

21. Constitution and Convention of the International Telecommunication Union, 22 December 1992, Art. 34, Senate Treaty Document No. 104-134 (1996).

Agreement on the Prevention of Dangerous Military Activities between the United States and the Soviet Union, which prohibits interference with command and control networks in a manner which could cause harm to personnel or damage to equipment of the Armed Forces of the other Party', when those forces are operating in close proximity.[22]

The *situs* of an operation is particularly relevant. The law of the sea requires 'innocent passage' when the vessel of one state transits the territorial waters of another.[23] Information operations directed against a coastal state would certainly not be innocent. Information operations could be mounted from space, pass through it, or target space-based assets.[24] Yet, certain space law principles bound space operations. Consider that of non-interference with satellites except in self-defence or when authorized by the Security Council pursuant to Chapter VII of the United Nations Charter.[25] As to land-based operations, the activities of military forces stationed abroad are usually governed by status of forces and stationing agreements with the 'receiving state'. The United States, for example, is Party to over 100 such agreements. These instruments typically mandate that the receiving state be notified of military activities conducted from its soil, often require respect for host nation law, may specifically forbid any interference with the receiving state's communications, and establish jurisdictional competence in the event host nation laws are violated.[26] Of particular concern with regard to host nation law is espionage. Although espionage is not prohibited in international law, espionage against the host state would certainly violate its laws, thereby, in certain circumstances, subjecting participants to prosecution.[27]

---

22. Agreement on Prevention of Dangerous Military Activities, Art. II, 12 June 1989, USSR-US, 28 *ILM* (1989) p. 879. The United States treats the Russian Federation as the successor to the rights and duties found in the agreement.

23. Innocent passage is continuous and expeditious travel through another state's territorial sea. It may be exercised in the absence of consent by the coastal state regardless of the type of vessel, its cargo, or how it is propelled. Of course, activities consented to by the coastal state, such as military exercises, are always permissible. United Nations Convention on the Law of the Sea, Arts. 17-18, 10 December 1982, UN Doc. A/CONF.62/122), 21 *ILM* (1983) p. 1261 (entered into force on 16 November 1994)

24. On the military uses of space, see B. Cheng, 'Properly Speaking, Only Celestial Bodies Have Been Reserved for Use Exclusively for Peaceful (Non-Military) Purposes, but not Outer Void Space', in M.N. Schmitt, ed, *International Law Across the Spectrum of Conflict* (Newport RI, Naval War College 2001) p. 81. See also, D.S. Anderson and C.R. Dooley, 'Information Operations in the Space Law Arena: Science Fiction Becomes Reality', in Schmitt, op. cit. n. 16, pp. 265-310.

25. Regarding the exceptions, note that Art. 41 of Chapter VII of the United Nations Charter explicitly mentions 'complete or partial interruption of ... means of communications' as enforcement mechanisms available to the Security Council.

26. The model Status of Forces Agreement is that for NATO. Agreement between the Parties to the North Atlantic Treaty regarding the Status of Their Forces, 19 June 1951, 4 *UST* 1792, 199 *UNTS* 67. On the topic generally, see D. Fleck, ed., *The Handbook of the Law of Visiting Forces* (Oxford, Oxford University Press 2001).

27. On espionage, see D.M. Crane, *Fourth Dimensional Intelligence: Thoughts on Espionage, Law, and Cyberspace*, in Schmitt, op. cit. n. 16, pp. 311-321.

During periods of armed conflict, the law of neutrality would restrict belligerent activities that might affect or involve a non-participant.[28] For instance, the principle of neutrality precludes neutrals from allowing their facilities or assets to be used by one party to the conflict to the detriment of the other. In the context of information warfare, satellite imaging perhaps best illustrates this principle. An imaged belligerent would appear to have the right to interfere with imaging in the event a neutral conducting it refused to stop providing its opponent data. In fact, the US Department of Defense has opined that 'if a belligerent nation demanded that the US government deny GPS navigation services to its enemy, and if the US were unable or unwilling to comply, the belligerent may have a right to take necessary and proportional acts in self-defense ...'[29] The sole exception to the general prohibition on usage of neutral assets is relaying communications, which is permitted, so long as the service is provided impartially, by the 1907 Hague Convention Respecting the Rights and Duties of Neutral Powers and Persons in Case of War on Land.[30] Complicating the neutrality issue is the fact that the exorbitant costs have led to the creation of international consortia – such as INTELSAT, INMARSAT (now privatised), ARABSAT and EUTELSAT – which cooperate to launch satellites that typically provide information of both civilian and military utility. A situation might arise during an armed conflict in which a satellite system is jointly operated by both belligerents and neutrals, thereby raising thorny problems of whether the data may be either used by the belligerent partner or provided to a non-partner belligerent. Moreover, consortia agreements sometimes provide that the systems are to be used for 'peaceful' purposes, although the precise scope of these restrictions is often contested.[31]

The point of the preceding discussion, which was not an exhaustive analysis, is to illustrate that a great deal of international and domestic law would limit, or alternatively enable, the conduct of information operations. Moreover, the issue of whether conventional law survives the outbreak of hostilities and, if so, as between which Parties, is extraordinarily complex. Obfuscating analysis is the fact that the existing legal regimes were not established with computer network attack in mind. Whether they apply to CNA at all, and, if so, to what extent, is far from settled. Given this jurisprudential morass, legal review by experts must be an integral part of virtually every decision to mount an information operation, especially when a component of that operation involves computer network attack. With this caveat at hand, attention now turns to the core issues of the *jus ad bellum* and *jus in bello*.

28. See G.K. Walker, 'Information Warfare and Neutrality', 33 *Vanderbilt J Transnational L* (2000) p. 1079 for a discussion of neutrality.

29. *Assessment, supra* n. 20.

30. Hague Convention (V) Respecting the Rights and Duties of Neutral Powers and Persons in Case of War on Land, Arts. 8 and 9, 18 October 1907, 36 Stat. 2310, TS No. 540, available online at the ICRC treaty site, http://www.icrc.org/ihl.

31. See e.g., Agreement Relating to the International Telecommunications Satellite Organization, 20 August 1971, 23 *UST* 3813, *TIAS* No. 7532 (1973). Art. III (d), (e) prohibit the use of certain 'specialized telecommunications services' for military purposes.

2.1 When is initiating a computer network attack against a target state unlawful under the *jus ad bellum* if an armed conflict is not yet already underway?

The core prohibition on the use of force in the *jus ad bellum* is Article 2(4) of the United Nations Charter. It provides that 'all Members shall refrain in their international relations from the threat or use of force against the territorial integrity or political independence of any state, or in any other manner inconsistent with the Purposes of the United Nations'. The final prohibitory clause is the key to the article, for it captures those uses of force that do not immediately affect either territorial integrity or political independence but that threaten the core Purpose set forth in Article 1, the maintenance of international peace and security.[32] Further, the prohibition extends to mere *threats* to use force. Therefore, threatening any use of computer network attack that would violate Article 2(4) if the threat were carried out would be wrongful in and of itself.

There have been periodic suggestions that the scope of the prohibition is limited to uses bearing on territorial integrity and political independence.[33] However, this proposition is inconsistent with the *travaux préparatoire*, which demonstrate that the references to territory and independence were actually amendments to a draft (the Dumbarton Oaks Proposals) that read, 'All members of the Organization shall refrain in their international relations from the threat or use of force in any manner inconsistent with the purposes of the Organization.' Subsequent inclusion of the additional verbiage was simply meant to reassure smaller states that both cited categories were among the uses of force captured by the article.[34] The weight of scholarly opinion supports this broad interpretation of Article 2(4).[35] By it, *any*

---

32. UN Charter, Art. 1(1). Similar prohibitions are found elsewhere. For instance, the General Assembly, in its resolution regarding the Declaration on Principles of International Law Concerning Friendly Relations and Cooperation Among States in Accordance with the Charter of the United Nations, has provided that 'Every State has a duty to refrain in its international relations from the threat or use of force against the territorial integrity or political independence of any State, or in any other manner inconsistent with the purposes of the United Nations. Such a threat or use of force constitutes a violation of international law and the Charter of the United Nations and shall never be employed as a means of settling international issues.' *GA Res.* 2625 (XXV), *UN GAOR* , 25th Sess., annex, art. 1, *UN Doc.* A/Res/2625 (1970), reprinted in 65 *AJIL* (1971) p. 243 and in D. Rauschning, K. Wiesbrock and M. Lailach, eds., *Key Resolutions of the United Nations General Assembly, 1946-1997* (Cambridge, Cambridge University Press 1997) at p. 3.

33. This was the British position in the *Corfu Channel* case before the International Court of Justice. See discussion in I. Brownlie, *International Law and the Use of Force by States* (Oxford, Clarendon Press 1963) pp. 265-266. For an interesting analysis of the issue, see A. D'Amato, *International Law: Process and Prospect* (Irvington NY, Transnational Publishers 1995) pp. 57-73.

34. See Doc. 1123, I/8, 6 UNCIO Docs. 68 (1945); Doc. 784, I/1/27, 6 UNCIO Docs. 335 (1945); and Doc. 885, I/1/34, 6 UNCIO. Docs. 400 (1945). See also Brownlie, ibid, at pp. 265-269.

35. See e.g., Y. Dinstein, *War, Aggression and Self-Defense*, 3rd edn. (Cambridge, Cambridge University Press 2001) pp. 81-83; J. Mrazek, 'Prohibition of the Use and Threat of Force: Self-Defense and Self-Help in International Law', 27 *Canadian YIL* (1989) at pp. 81, 90; A. Randelzhofer, 'Article 2(4)', in B. Simma, ed., *The Charter of the United Nations A Commentary* (Oxford, Oxford University Press 1995) pp. 106, 117-118.

instance of computer network attack that amounts to a transnational use of force is prohibited, except those for which exceptions exist in the Charter.

Application of the prohibition to computer network attack thus centres on the meaning of 'force'.[36] The principle that treaty text should be interpreted 'in accordance with the ordinary meaning to be given to the terms of the treaty in their context and in light of its object and scope'[37] might suggest that the term is to be understood kinetically, i.e., as classic physical armed force. Were this so, computer network attack, standing alone, would not be violative of Article 2(4) because data transmission, disruption, or destruction are not forceful actions. They might violate other legal regimes, but not that governing that governing the use of force.

This overly narrow interpretation ignores the object and scope of the Charter. In fact, the absence of the qualifier 'armed' is meaningful. In the 1986 *Nicaragua* case, for instance, the International Court of Justice held that the arming and training of guerrilla forces (but not funding them) is a use of force by the state providing the arms and training.[38] For the Court, the meaning of 'force' reaches beyond the narrow confines of launching a physical, kinetic attack.

Yet, it is also the case that 'force' cannot be so expansively understood that it incorporates, for example, economic or political coercion. At the San Francisco Conference, a Brazilian proposal to extend the scope of the article to economic coercion was voted down.[39] Other international agreements setting forth the prohibition on the use of force, such as the Inter-American Treaty of Reciprocal Assistance and the Pact of the League of the Arab States, are consistent with the approach taken by the Charter drafters.[40] Moreover, later proposals to extend the prohibition to economic or political coercion met with little success. For instance, when the subject arose during deliberations in the General Assembly over the

36. On the applicability of Art. 2(4), see D. Silver, 'Computer Network Attack as a Use of Force under Article 2(4) of the United Nations Charter', in Schmitt, op. cit. n. 16, pp. 73-97.

37. Vienna Convention on the Law of Treaties, 23 May 1969, Art. 31(1), 1155 *UNTS* 331, 8 *ILM* (1969) p. 679. This point was reiterated by the International Court of Justice in *Competence of the General Assembly for the Admission of a State to the United Nations* case. There, the Court noted 'the first duty of a tribunal which is called upon to interpret and apply the provisions of a treaty is to endeavour to give effect to them in their natural and ordinary meaning in the context in which they occur'. *ICJ Rep.* (1950) pp. 4, 8.

38. *Military and Paramilitary Activities* (*Nicaragua* v. *US*), *ICJ Rep.* (1986) pp. 4, 119, para 228 [hereinafter Nicaragua]. It must be noted that for jurisdictional reasons the Court was not actually applying Art. 2(4) *qua* 2(4), but instead the customary international law prohibition on the resort to force.

39. 6 UNCIO Docs. 334, 609 (1945); Doc. 2, 617 (e)(4), 3 UNCIO Docs. 251, 253-54 (1945).

40. Inter-American Treaty of Reciprocal Assistance, Art. 1, 7 September 1947 *TIAS* 1838, 21 *UNTS* 77: '… undertake in their international relations not to resort to the threat or the use of force in any manner inconsistent with the provisions of the Charter of the United Nations or of this Treaty'. See also Pact of the League of Arab States, Art. 5, 22 March 1945, 70 *UNTS* 238, which only speaks of force: 'Any resort to force in order to resolve disputes arising between two or more member States of the League is prohibited.'

Declaration on Friendly Relations, consensus proved impossible to achieve.[41] Ultimately, the formal explanation of the Declaration's Principle prohibiting the use of *force*, which has text identical to that of Article 2(4),[42] was framed in terms bearing on the use of armed force, without mentioning either economic or political coercion.[43] By contrast, it is probative that the corollary explanation of the Principle on *non-intervention* did include economic and political interference within its scope.[44]

This brief survey suggests that whereas mere economic and political coercion will not suffice to contravene Article 2(4), acts that do need not necessarily include physical or kinetic force. Of course, the resulting gap between the defined points on the coercive continuum begs the question of how to assess the legality of information operations, information warfare, and computer network attack against the Article 2(4) standard.

A useful approach is to dispense with instrument-based criteria in lieu of consequence-based standards. Charter interpretation is typically instrument-based in the sense that prohibitions tend to be expressed in terms of the instrument employed to effect coercion on the target state – economic mechanisms, political pressure and physical force (either directly or through an agent). Paradoxically, however, economic or political coercion may be more disruptive to community values, such as political and human security, than limited instances of the use of armed force. Consider the suffering generated by UN's economic sanctions on Iraq over the past decade. Indeed, some have argued that the sanctions are more disruptive of Charter ends than the localized and restricted episodes of armed conflict that have periodically occurred.[45] Yet the use of military force falls within Article 2(4)'s purview (with substantial disagreement over compliance with the prescription), whereas sanctions (aside from the issue of their imposition pursuant to Chapter VII) do not.

This seeming dissonance between ultimate Charter goals and the prescriptive norms designed to achieve them is the product of a very rational cost-benefit analysis. Although the international community is in fact concerned with conse-

---

41. UN Doc. A/AC.125/SR.114 (1970). See also Special Committee on Friendly Relations, Report, 24 UN GAOR Supp. No. 19, UN Doc. A/7619, at 12 (1969); D.W. Bowett, 'Economic Coercion and Reprisals by States', 13 *Virginia JIL* (1972) p. 1.

42. Declaration on Friendly Relations, *supra* n. 32, annex: 'States shall refrain in their international relations from the threat or use of force against the territorial integrity or political independence of any State, or in any other manner inconsistent with the purposes of the United Nations. Such a threat or use of force constitutes a violation of international law and the Charter of the United Nations and shall never be employed as a means of settling international issues.' The resolution was adopted by acclamation.

43. Rather, the explanation contains references to 'war of aggression', 'violate existing international boundaries', 'organizing ... irregular forces or armed bands ... for incursion', etc. Idem.

44. 'No State may use or encourage the use of economic, political or any other type of measures to coerce another State in order to obtain from it the subordination of the exercise of its sovereign rights and to secure from it advantages of any kind.' Idem.

45. The situation led the UN to set up the 'Oil for Food Programme', under the UN's Office of the Iraq Programme. Details on the programme, as well as all relevant UN Secretary General reports on the situation, are available online at http://www.un.org/Depts/oip/.

quences of an action, fashioning an easily applied consequence-based standard would have been difficult. As a result, a form of prescriptive shorthand has been employed in the Charter. Uses of kinetic force are more likely to threaten common community values and more likely to spiral out of control, than economic or political coercion; hence, the greater opprobrium associated with the former. After all, it is far easier to ask the simple question of whether force has been used than it is to identify and appraise the consequences of a particular action. Some highly deleterious consequences may slip through the prescriptive crack, but ease of application, and the greater overall preservation of community values that results, justifies the loss.

2.1.1 *Evaluating CNA as a violation of Article 2(4)*

Computer network attack and other forms of information operations challenge the prevailing paradigm. A classic use of force generally causes, or is intended to cause, physical damage or human injury; economic and political coercion *generally* do not. However, the consequences of CNA range freely between minor inconvenience and irritation to death and monumental physical destruction. To simply exclude application of Article 2(4) to a 'means of warfare' which can generate unthinkable consequences would be to sacrifice substance on the altar of form. Thus, a technique for reasonably interpreting Article 2(4) in the light of changed circumstances (emergence of IO), while maintaining fidelity to its underlying *raison d'être*, is crucial.

First, it is fair to interpret any use of computer network attack (or other form of IO) that causes physical damage to property or injury to human beings as a prohibited use of *armed* force. Even in the prevailing conflict paradigm, numerous means of warfare are available that can produce damage or injury without releasing kinetic force – biological, chemical, neutron weaponry, and certain non-lethals such as acoustic devices. No one would suggest these are not weapons or that their employment would not be a use of force in the Article 2(4) context. There is no reason to exclude IO from a like understanding.

From an analytical point of view, what is particularly telling as one searches for a way to characterize other uses of information operations is that in the cases just cited a consequence-based approach is actually being utilized. These and similar examples demonstrate the viability of such an approach in determining whether actions, like the arming and training of guerrilla forces in the *Nicaragua* case, breach the Article 2(4) standard despite the absence of physical force.

Perhaps the most fruitful tactic for shaping use of force criteria is to ask how the consequences of economic or political coercion, which does not violate the standard, differ from armed force, which does. In other words, to what extent does an information attack create consequences that are more or less like those of our two known data points, economic/political and physical coercion? Although it is always dangerous to generalize, seven criteria are particularly distinctive when comparing the two coercive genre [and understanding why one is encompassed in Article 2(4), while the other is not].

1) *Severity*: Although economic or political sanctions can potentially cause great human suffering, armed attack is more likely to result in human injury or physical damage. Since human well-being is the foremost shared community value, there is a greater community incentive to definitively prohibit the latter.
2) *Immediacy*: The results of an armed attack are usually immediate, while the consequences of economic and political activities may not be apparent for some time. Immediacy is a greater community threat because it affords less opportunity for peaceful resolution.
3) *Directness*: The cause-effect relationship tends to be closer in an armed attack, with consequences less dependent on external factors. Therefore, proscribing armed attack is more likely to effectively avoid the threatened consequence than prohibiting economic or political coercion.
4) *Invasiveness*: Whereas acts of economic and political coercion tend to occur outside a state, albeit with effects within it, the use of armed force usually involves crossing into the target state. This represents a greater violation of the international law principle of territorial inviolability.
5) *Measureability*: It is typically difficult to measure the consequences of economic or political coercion, as they tend to be diffuse and intangible. In contrast, and despite the reality of reverberating effects, the consequences of an armed attack are often tragically apparent. This has the benefit of helping to ensure that community reaction thereto is less speculative than that, which would ensure *vis-à-vis* economic or political coercion.
6) *Presumptive Legitimacy*: Certain acts are presumptively illegitimate under both domestic and international legal regimes. Foremost among these is the exercise of violence. Alternatively, community expectations regarding other categories of acts, such as economic competition, tend to be permissive.
7) *Responsibility*: Whereas states still tend to enjoy a relative monopoly on armed force, those entities capable of applying economic or political coercion range from multinational corporations to non-governmental organizations. Thus, acts involving armed force, are likelier to be assessed as state acts than those based on economic or political coercion. Although this criterion really poses issues of state responsibility rather than the lawfulness of the act in question, since Article 2(4) limits state actions, it remains relevant to this inquiry.

Using this approach, analysis of a particular information operation would be both quantitative and qualitative; it requires an assessment of the degree (quantitative analysis) to which the various criteria (qualitative analysis) are or are not implicated. The technique has the benefit of trying to approximate the appraisal the international community is likely to make of a particular action's lawfulness. In the absence of a bright line test, it is this reaction, based on the normative expectations of the community, which matters.

It is useful to illustrate how the approach would play out in practice. Thomas Wingfield has very usefully set out examples of the types of queries that the various criteria would suggest.[46]

Severity

How many people were killed?

How large an area was attacked? (scope)

How much damage was done within this area? (intensity)

Immediacy

Over how long a period did the action take place? (duration)

How soon were its effects felt?

How soon until its effects abated?

Directness?

Was the action distinctly identifiable from parallel or competing actions?

Was the action the proximate cause of the effects?

Invasiveness

Did the action involve physically crossing the target country's borders?

Was the locus of the action within the target country?

Measureability

How can the effects of the action be quantified?

Are the effects of the action distinct from the results of parallel or competing actions?

What is the level of certainty?

Presumptive Legitimacy

Has this type of action achieved a customary acceptance within the international community?

Is the means qualitatively similar to others presumed legitimate under international law?

Responsibility

Is the action directly or indirectly attributable to the acting state?

But for the acting state's sake, would the action have occurred?

Overall Analysis

Have enough of the qualities of a use of force been identified to characterize the information operation as a use of force?

Reduced to basics, with this technique the reasonably foreseeable consequences of an information operation are evaluated holistically in terms of the aforementioned criteria to estimate where along the coercive continuum the operation in question should be placed. The closer the net analysis lies to kinetic use of force point, the greater the likelihood of the act being deemed a use of force in violation of Article 2(4).

---

46. Wingfield, op. cit. n. 16, at pp. 124-125, commenting on the criteria as explicated in M.N. Schmitt, 'Computer Network Attack and the Use of Force in International Law: Thoughts on a Normative Framework', 37 *Columbia JTL* (1999) p. 885.

Consider two illustrative examples. In the first, an unknown entity launches a computer network attack against a government security studies centre that educates senior officials from Europe and Eurasia. As a result of the attack, the distance learning programs are disrupted; faculty research is destroyed; e-files of required readings are deleted; both alumni data and the files necessary to in-process the next class are rendered inaccessible; and program participants begin receiving e-mails on their student computers threatening them for participating in the centre's activities.

In the second example, a state intelligence service launches a computer attack against an East European capital's electrical grid during a bitter winter freezing spell. Although redundant systems continue to provide some essential services, the disabling of many heating systems threatens the lives of the elderly and ill. Additionally, interference with the communications net impedes the ability to contact emergency service agencies and slows their response. Many stores must close temporarily, forcing the government to turn to relief agencies for food, medicine, and other essentials. Roadways are gridlocked because the systems that control traffic flow are affected and the commuter transport net is running at greatly decreased capacity. Sewage treatment plants lose capacity and the city's primary water treatment plant must tenuously rely on emergency generators, thereby raising concerns about the possibility of disease spreading. One hospital is open only for emergency treatment after several of its emergency generators fail.

The first case is clearly not a use of force. Although there is substantial disruption of an educational institution, there are no injuries or property damage (severity), the impact will occur over time (immediacy), the attack was purely cyber in nature and merely affected data (presumptive legitimacy under international law), the border was only crossed electronically (invasiveness), and it is unclear whether a state is involved or not (responsibility). While the operation's consequences are relatively direct and measurable, a comprehensive analysis would argue against characterization as a use of force.

By contrast, the second example approximates a use of force even though no kinetic forces were launched and no injuries or physical damage directly and immediately resulted from the attack. A foreseeable consequence is substantial injury or even death, and the extent of property damage will grow as the interference continues (severity). Such outcomes will in great part be ascertainable (measurability) and will begin to appear soon after the attack (immediacy). Although many of the effects will not be direct since the immediate target was the electrical grid, not activities dependent on it, the causal connection is clear and uninterrupted (directness). Finally, the attack is traceable to a state (responsibility), and activities that interfere with essential human services are presumptively illegitimate (legitimacy).

2.1.2 *CNA as a threat to the peace, breach of the peace or act of aggression*

There are two Charter-based exceptions to the Article 2(4) prohibition on the use of force. The first is action authorized by the Security Council under Chapter VII. Pursuant to Article 39, the Security Council is competent to 'determine the existence of any threat to the peace, breach of the peace, or act of aggression and … decide what measures shall be taken in accordance with Articles 41 and 42 [discussed *infra*], to maintain or restore international peace and security'. Step one in a Chapter VII analysis, therefore, is determining whether an act is a 'threat to the peace, breach of the peace, or act of aggression'. Could an information operation rise to this level? Without delving deeply into interpretation of the terms, the answer is undoubtedly yes.

In the 1974 Definition of Aggression Resolution, the General Assembly depicted aggression as ranging from 'the use of armed force by a state against the sovereignty, territorial integrity or political independence of another state, or in any manner inconsistent with the Charter of the United Nations' or allowing territory to be used by another state to commit an act of aggression to sending armed bands against another state.[47] Although General Assembly resolutions are not binding, the resolution's adoption by acclamation suggests that it is a widely accepted understanding of the term. Thus, any computer network attack falling within its ambit would justify a Chapter VII response.

Unfortunately, since the Definition of Aggression Resolution's listing is non-exhaustive, it will be difficult to determine whether many acts of computer network attack comprise aggression or not. However, CNA need not rise to the level of aggression for the Security Council to authorize Chapter VII action. Rather, by the terms of Article 39, all that is necessary is a finding that an act constitutes either a breach of the peace or a threat thereof. For the purposes of analysis, it is the breach of peace standard that is most relevant, for even if a computer network attack does not represent a breach, the Security Council could find that it risked provoking an 'unpeaceful' response [best interpreted as a use of force as that term is used in Article 2(4)]. It is important to note that the legality of the possible response to the threat to the peace is not relevant to a determination of whether a threat has occurred.[48] Thus, computer network attacks that do not even constitute a wrongful use of force under Article 2(4), but threaten to provoke an unjustified armed response, could be characterized as a threat to the peace, thereby providing a basis for imposition of Chapter VII measures.

And what is the standard by which the Security Council should judge actions as threats or not? In the *Tadić* case, the International Criminal Tribunal for the Former Yugoslavia (ICTY) held that any such finding must occur in the context of the 'Purposes and Principles of the Charter'.[49] In light of the scope of the Purposes articulated in Article 1 and the Principles set forth in Article 2, and in the absence of an effective mechanism to appeal its determinations, a fair reading of Article 39 is that a threat to the peace is whatever the Security Council says it is. Practice has demonstrated that the Council has enormous discretion in finding a threat to the

---

47. Definition of Aggression, Art. 1, GA Res. 3314 (XXIX); UN GAOR, 29th Sess., Supp. No. 31, at 142; UN Doc. A/9631 (1975), 13 *ILM* (1974) p. 710.

48. On this point, see J. Frowein, 'Chapter VII', in Simma, op. cit. n. 35, at pp. 605, 612.

49. *Prosecutor* v. *Tadić,* ICTY Case No. IT-94-1-AR72, Decision on the Defence Motion for Interlocutory Appeal on Jurisdiction, Appeals Chamber, 35 *ILM* (1995) p. 43 (1996).

peace. For instance, in 1991 the Council found the fighting between Yugoslavian forces and those of secessionist Croatia and Slovenia, essentially an internal matter, to be a threat to international peace.[50] Similarly, in 1993-1994 the Council determined that the internal situation in Haiti threatened international peace and security and authorized the use of force (the situation was ultimately resolved peacefully) to restore the government that had been overthrown by a military coup.[51] But the Council has gone further. For instance, in 1992 it found that the Libyan government's refusals to turn over suspects in the bombing of Pan Am Flight 103 (the Lockerbie bombing) 'constitute a threat to international peace and security'.[52] In 1993 it set up the ICTY after deciding that violations of international humanitarian law in the area threatened international peace and security;[53] and in 1994, after making a like determination, the Council established a similar tribunal to address the genocide and other international humanitarian law violations in Rwanda.[54] More recently, and even before the events of 11 September 2001, the Security Council repeatedly labelled the Taleban's acquiescence in allowing Afghan territory to be used as a base for terrorist camps and training, its refusal to cooperate with law enforcement, and its failure to turn over Usama bin Laden, to be such a threat.[55] The point of these examples is to illustrate the broad discretion enjoyed by the Council in finding a threat to the peace; it would enjoy equal discretion in finding, or not finding, that particular instances of computer network attack constitute a threat.

2.1.3 *The use of CNA to enforce Security Council Resolutions*

Should it determine there to be a threat to the peace, breach of the peace, or act of aggression, under Article 41, the Security Council may then authorize measures in response thereto *not* involving the use of armed force. Specifically cited as non-exhaustive, non-forceful options are 'complete or partial interruption of economic relations and of rail, sea, air, postal, telegraphic, radio, and other means of communication ...' Information operations could easily play a part in any such measures and, so long as they did not amount to 'armed force' (see discussion *infra*), would be perfectly legitimate. They may even offer attractive methods for enforcing Article 39 actions. Recall that the use of naval forces to enforce an Article 41 embargo during the Gulf War engendered controversy because the implied authorization of the use of force seemed to exceed the scope of the article's limitation to non-forceful steps – hence, coinage of the term 'Article 41 ½' measure.[56] Computer network attack could escape the dilemma of imposing sanctions without

50. SC Res. 713 (1991).
51. SC Res. 841 (1993); SC Res. 940 (1994).
52. SC Res. 748 (1992).
53. SC Res. 827 (1993).
54. SC Res. 955 (1994).
55. See e.g., SC Res. 1267(1999), SC Res. 1333 (2000), and SC Res. 1363 (2001).
56. Ph. Weckel, 'Le Chapitre VII de la Charte et son Application par le Conseil de Sécurité', 37 *Annuaire Français de Droit International* (1991) pp. 165, 202.

effective means of enforcement. For instance, it could be used to track financial transactions with a country, disrupt transportation into and out of the target state and interfere with communications.

In the event the Article 41 measures prove inadequate or the Security Council decides that attempting to resolve the situation non-forcefully would be fruitless, under Article 42 it may take whatever forceful actions it deems necessary to 'maintain or restore international peace and security'. Obviously, if an Article 42 authorization justifies the use of armed force, it would justify any information operation intended to accomplish the same objective. The sole limitation would be that the operation would have to comply with international humanitarian law.[57]

The legitimacy of using computer network attack to enforce a Security Council mandate would be patent regardless of to whom the mandate was issued. When the mandate is simply an invitation to member states to act, as was the case with Security Council Resolution 678, which authorized the expulsion of the Iraqis from Kuwait in 1990-1, states complying therewith tend to have wide authority to select the means they will employ to do so. Computer network attack is certainly one such potential arrow in their quiver. The same is true when the Security Council 'out-sources' to a regional organization, as is the case with SFOR and KFOR. Because the Council has authorized 'all necessary measures' to accomplish the mandate, the sole issue is whether a proposed information operation is rationally related to accomplishing the mandated objectives (and not otherwise illegal under international law, e.g., a human rights violation). That an enforcement operation is being mounted by an UN force, as with UNTAET in East Timor, does not alter the analysis.

In so far as computer network attack opens up new possibilities for 'striking' targets, as well as new targets, its availability may well facilitate the goal of maintaining collective security through minimal force. Many circumstances offer the possibility of CNA serving as an 'intermediate step' between Article 41 non-forceful measures and the outright use of force under Article 42; the more numerous the options open to the international community in applying sanctions, the easier it becomes to surgically craft effective enforcement mechanisms. For instance, if broadcasting facilities are being used to incite genocide, a computer network attack on them would be more congruent with the community norm of minimizing violence than would a conventional operation. Similarly, computer network attack may permit very discrete interference with the financial assets of a target state's leadership as a means of pressuring it to comply with international norms, without causing its citizenry the suffering often associated with embargoes.

---

57. On this topic, see J. Bialke, 'United Nations Peace Operations: Applicable Norms and the Application of the Law of Armed Conflict', 50 *Air Force Law Review* (2001) p. 1; Ch. Greenwood, 'International Humanitarian Law and United Nations Military Operations', 1 *YIHL* (1998) p. 3. In 1999 the UN Secretary-General issued a bulletin entitled *'Observance by United Nations Forces of International Humanitarian Law'*, ST/SGB/1999/13 (1999), reprinted in A. Roberts and R. Guelff, *Documents on the Laws of War*, 3rd edn. (Oxford, Oxford University Press 2000) p. 721, and *available at* http://www.un.org/peace/st_sgb_1999_13.pdf. In it, the Secretary-General sets forth those IHL standards applicable to UN operations.

Finally, it has become questionable whether Article 2(4) effectively captures the full extent of the prohibition on the use of force. In particular, are there other exceptions to the prohibition on the use of force that fall beyond the four corners of the Charter? For nearly half a century, the prevailing view has been that Article 2(4) and customary law on the use of force (which crystallized following the Second World War) were coterminous. This was the position taken by the International Law Commission when in 1966 it announced, 'the great majority of international lawyers today hold that Article 2, paragraph 4, together with the other provisions of the Charter authoritatively declares the modern customary law regarding the threat or use of force'.[58] Although the International Court of Justice has rejected an assertion that customary and Charter law on the use of force were identical (made by the United States in the *Nicaragua* case), it ultimately found no marked divergence of customary law from the Charter principle.[59]

That said, recent state practice, particularly the NATO air campaign against the Federal Republic of Yugoslavia in 1999, suggests at least the possibility of an emergent customary law norm permitting humanitarian intervention. Absent Security Council authorization under Chapter VII, such operations would seemingly violate Article 2(4). However, some suggest that humanitarian intervention may be legitimate in the absence of Council authorization in certain limited circumstances. This is possible because customary law emerges and/or evolves over time. Even if Article 2(4) and customary law were relatively indistinguishable in decades past, the evolutionary nature of the latter opens the possibility of gradual divergence. While this is not the forum to resolve the extent of any such departure, it should be noted that information operations could certainly play a role in humanitarian interventions, perhaps even in a stand-alone fashion. For instance, computer network attack could be targeted against rail networks being used to forcibly displace a civilian population. It could also be used to counter hate propaganda or disrupt paramilitary communications. Assuming, solely for the sake of analysis, that a non-Chapter VII humanitarian intervention is lawful, computer network attacks mounted as a component thereof would be equally legitimate. And, since a humanitarian intervention is an exception to the general prohibition on the use of force, it would not be necessary to analyse information operations in the fashion described above. If the CNA were not a use of force, it would not be prohibited (by this corpus of law); if it were, then it would fall within the exception. Of course, as with any other force employed to intervene, the CNA would, viewed in the context of the overall operation, have to comply with such requirements as necessity (no reasonable alternative to the use of force exists) and proportionality (only that amount of force necessary to achieve the legitimate objectives may be employed).

---

58. II *International Law Commission Yearbook* (1996) p. 247, cited with approval by the International Court of Justice in *Nicaragua, supra* n. 38 at p. 99.

59. *Nicaragua, supra* n. 38, at pp. 96-97.

2.2 When is use of computer network attack permissible in self-defence and when may armed force be used in self-defence against a computer network attack?

The second exception to the general prohibition on the use of force is found in Article 51 of the UN Charter: 'Nothing in the present Charter shall impair the inherent right of individual or collective self-defence if an armed attack occurs against a member of the United Nations until the Security Council has taken measures necessary to maintain international peace and security.' The article represents an acknowledgment of the reality that the Security Council may not always act, or act quickly enough, in the face of an attack on a state.

Until 11 September 2001, it was not altogether clear whether Article 51 encompassed armed attacks by non-state actors. However, the prevailing view of states today appears to be that so long as it is an 'armed attack' that has been mounted, the article applies regardless of the character of the attacker. For instance, the Security Council specifically cited self-defence in its resolutions concerning the 9/11 attacks.[60] Moreover, NATO's invocation of Article V of the North Atlantic Treaty, since that article is premised on Article 51 of the UN Charter, is apt evidence of at least the 19 NATO Member States' stance.[61] Recall that both the resolutions and the invocation occurred at a time when the links between al-Qaeda, the Taleban *de facto* Afghan government and the terrorist attacks was not altogether clear. By this approach, computer network attack mounted by a terrorist organization would activate the victim's Article 51 right to self-defence.

In a related matter, there is the issue of whether there are differences, a half-century after promulgation of the Charter, between the customary international law right of self-defence and Article 51. In 1986, the International Court of Justice acknowledged the existence of a customary international law right;[62] therefore, to the extent a state is a non-Party, it enjoys the right to self-defence as a matter of customary international law. Of course, this is a relatively unimportant departure given the inclusivity of UN membership. The applicability of Article 51 to attacks by non-state actors might have been another point of departure, with self-defence against them relying on customary international law. However, as just noted, that point of view appears to be out of vogue. Thus, to the extent that a state is justified in acting in self-defence, either against computer network attack or by employing computer network attack as a means of defence, it is irrelevant whether the attacker is a state or not or whether the victim is a Party to the Charter.

60. See e.g., SC Res. 1368 (12 September 2001), which recognized 'the inherent right of self-defence in accordance with the Charter'. See also SC Res. 1373 (28 September 2001).

61. Following a briefing by the US to the North Atlantic Council on 2 October 2001, NATO Secretary-General Lord Robertson stated that 'individuals who carried out these attacks were part of the world-wide terrorist network of Al-Qaeda ... [and that] ... the attack ... was directed from abroad and shall therefore be regarded as an action covered by Article V'. NATO Update, 3 October 2001, available online at http://www.nato.int/docu/update/2001/1001/e1002a.htm.

62. *Nicaragua*, *supra* n. 38, at pp. 102-104.

It is equally uncomplicated to dispense with the first question posed at the onset of this section: When may computer network attack be used in self-defence? The answer is always, so long as the operation meets the traditional criteria for acts in self-defence – proportionality, necessity, and immediacy – and is consistent in its execution with international humanitarian law.[63] If an 'armed attack' justifies the use of physical force in response, it would be ludicrous for it not to also justify computer network attack. On the contrary, since CNA may offer a less violent option for self-defence than traditional armed force, to hold otherwise would run contrary to the Charter's underlying purpose of minimizing conflict.

The harder question is what constitutes 'armed attack' as that term of art is used in Article 51, for its scope will determine when a state may respond forcefully in self-defence against computer network attacks.[64] To begin with, the idioms 'use of force' and 'armed attack' are not coincident. As noted by the International Court of Justice (ICJ) in *Nicaragua*, acts that are 'uses of force' may not be 'armed attacks'.[65] This is a sensible interpretation in light of the Charter's general tenor. If a principal aspiration of the Charter is to minimize conflict, then it is logical to set a low threshold for violation of the prohibition on the use of force and a high threshold for allowing a state to act forcibly in self-defence. The gap is safeguarded by the great discretion enjoyed by the Security Council in authorizing enforcement measures if a use of force not amounting to an armed attack threatens international peace and security.

How then to define 'armed attack?' Given the existence of a high threshold designed to limit recourse to self-defence to those cases truly requiring it, the sensible approach is to apply the standard set forth *supra* in the context of 'armed force'. An 'armed attack' occurs through the application of 'armed force', which is force that directly causes physical damage to property or injury to human beings. This narrow definition does not deny any remedy to victims of less severe forms of CNA. On the contrary, if the attack amounts to a 'use of force' in violation of Article 2(4), the attacker risks condemnation for violating a *jus cogens* norm, a serious charge indeed. That states do not relish being labelled law-breakers was well-illustrated by the United State's withdrawal from compulsory jurisdiction under the optional clause of the ICJ Statute in the wake of the Court's 1986 finding that it had illegally used force against Nicaragua. Moreover, victim states are entitled to seek Security Council assistance *à la* Chapter VII to virtually any computer network attack, even those not qualifying as a use of force.

The question then becomes *when* is an act of self-defence appropriate against a computer network attack. It arises in two contexts. First, when may a state defend itself against a future computer network attack that meets the requirements of

63. See Dinstein, op. cit. n. 35, at pp. 207-213 for a discussion of these requirements.

64. On CNA and self-defence, see Y. Dinstein, 'Computer Network Attacks and Self-Defense', in Schmitt, op. cit. n. 16.

65. *Nicaragua*, *supra* n. 38 at p. 102. The Court noted that the provision of weapons or logistical or other support is not an 'armed attack', but might constitute a use of force. The distinction makes sense in the context of the Charter's general disapproval of the resort to violence.

'armed attack'? Second, and more problematic, when may a state defend itself against CNA that does not meet those requirements, but that is being used to 'prepare the battlefield' for a follow-on armed attack, either cyber or kinetic in nature? Consider, for instance, attacks to disrupt an early-warning system, reserve call-up database or supply distribution system.

Although the Charter seems to suggest that an armed attack must occur before the right to self-defence arises, any such interpretation would be absurd in an era when a single attack can be catastrophic. It is now widely accepted that some defensive action prior to an armed attack, generally labelled 'anticipatory self-defence', can be justified. The most cited standard is that articulated by US Secretary of State Daniel Webster.[66] For Webster, the requisite precondition, known as the *Caroline* standard, is 'a necessity of self-defence, instant, overwhelming, leaving no choice of means, and no moment for deliberation'.[67]

More recently, Yoram Dinstein rejected the terminology 'anticipatory' in favour of 'interceptive' on the basis that the former term suggests that preventive actions in the face of a 'foreseeable' armed attack are legitimate. For Dinstein, the question is whether or not the 'other side has committed itself to an armed attack in an ostensibly irrevocable way'.[68] As he explains:

> 'The crucial question is who embarks upon an irreversible course of action, thereby crossing the Rubicon. This, rather than the actual opening of fire, is what casts the die and forms what may be categorized as an incipient armed attack. It would be absurd to require that the defending State should sustain and absorb a devastating (perhaps a fatal) blow, only to prove an immaculate conception of self-defence.'[69]

This is a particularly useful articulation in the context of computer network attack. As to the first scenario, CNA as an armed attack, the linchpin is whether the operation has begun, rather than whether the electrons have been launched. Thus, an order to an information operations unit to commence an armed attack via CNA might be sufficient to justify an interceptive response. As to the second scenario, CNA as a prelude to an armed attack, the dispositive issue is whether the attack is part of the operational flow or instead a discrete, isolatable act.

In the application of this approach, it is imperative to bear the criteria for self-defence – necessity, proportionality and immediacy – in mind. The extent of defensive options available to the victim of an impending armed attack will often determine the appropriateness of any interceptive measures. For instance, a technologically advanced state may be able use cyber-defences instead of traditional armed force against preparatory CNA, whereas a technologically backward one

66. For instance, the standard was cited with approval by the Nuremberg Tribunal. International Military Tribunal (Nuremberg), Judgement and Sentences, 41 *AJIL* (1947) pp. 172, 205.

67. Letter from Daniel Webster to Lord Ashburton (6 Augustus 1842), 29 *British and Foreign State Papers* (1840-1) pp. 1129, 1138.

68. Dinstein, op. cit. n. 35, at p. 172.

69. Ibid.

may have to resort to armed force immediately. Or the initial computer network attack may be part of an overall operation, but is so preparatory that it can hardly be deemed an element of the core armed attack. Early efforts to gather intelligence in order to conduct deliberate campaign planning might well fall into this category. Of course, if the CNA is an early phase of an operation, the proportionality of the response will be measured with respect to the overall attack and defensive actions may be directed against any (legitimate) target that will effectively counter the attack, not just the facilities from which the computer network attack was dispatched.

Restated, it is permissible to respond with armed force against a computer network attack that has been or is about to be launched, either as an armed attack in and of itself or as a preparatory step in a follow-on armed attack, when: 1) the CNA is an armed attack because it can cause physical damage or human injury *or* is part of a larger operation that constitutes an armed attack; 2) the CNA is an irrevocable step in an imminent (near-term) and probably unavoidable attack; and 3) the defender is reacting in advance of the attack itself during the last possible window of opportunity available to effectively counter the armed attack.

2.3 Once in an international armed conflict, what are the *jus in bello* limits on computer network attack?

Computer network attack presents novel challenges and opportunities for international humanitarian law (IHL). First, it employs a new weapon system – a computer and code – the capabilities of which are only now starting to become apparent. Second, because CNA does not necessarily result in the release of kinetic energy, its use often offers a low-collateral damage and incidental injury alternative to conventional attacks. In the same vein, it can be extraordinarily precise. Third, the interconnectedness of military and civilian systems poses the risk of unintended second, third and fourth tier effects (also know as reverberating effects) on civilians and civilian objects from an attack on a legitimate military objective. Finally, the increasingly wired nature of the civilian sector renders it an attractive target for computer network attack by those prepared to ignore the humanitarian law limits.

Despite the fact that computer network operations are a rapidly evolving aspect of modern warfare, IHL remains silent on their use. Indeed, the humanitarian law relevant to CNA was scripted decades before the advent of the technology that makes it possible. That said, any suggestion of the inapplicability of IHL to CNA because the latter post-dates the former is baseless. In *Legality of the Threat of Nuclear Weapons*, the ICJ explicitly rejected an analogous argument offered in the context of nuclear weapons.[70] Further, international humanitarian law requires Parties to review new 'weapons, means or methods' of warfare to assess whether

70. Legality of the Threat *or Use of Nuclear Weapons* (Advisory Opinion), *ICJ Rep.* (1996) p. 226, 35 *ILM* (1999) p. 809, para. 85.

their employment can comply with the strictures of IHL, a requirement echoed in many domestic regulations.[71]

There are essentially two questions with respect to conducting computer network attacks during international armed conflict: What can be attacked and how can the attacks be conducted. In order to address them, reference shall be made to the 1977 Additional Protocol I to the Geneva Conventions. Although numerous states, including NATO members the United States and Turkey, are not Parties to the Protocol, the provisions cited herein are generally understood to reflect customary international law and, thus, bind non-Parties.[72]

The core provision on legitimate targets is Article 48:

> 'In order to ensure respect for and protection of the civilian population and civilian objects, the Parties to the conflict shall at all times distinguish between the civilian population and combatants and between civilian objects and military objectives and accordingly shall direct their operations only against military objectives.'

At first glance, this would seem to prohibit any operation against anything other than a military objective, which is defined in Article 52.2 as 'those objects which by their nature, location, purpose or use make an effective contribution to military action and whose total or partial destruction, capture or neutralization, in the circumstances ruling at the time, offers a definite military advantage'. By this interpretation, any computer network attack directed against a civilian or civilian object would be prohibited. However, such an analysis would be overly restrictive. Indeed, state practice demonstrates that some types of operations that target civilians, most notably psychological operations, are considered legitimate.[73]

Instead, the Article prohibits 'attacks', a Protocol term of art. Article 48 merely states the general prohibition; specific prohibitions follow and clarify what is intended. Thus, Article 51(2) provides that 'the civilian population as such, as well as individual civilians, shall not be the object of *attack*'; 52(1) states that 'civilian

---

71. Protocol Additional (I) to the Geneva Convention of 12 August 1949, and Relating to the Protection of Victims of International Armed Conflicts, Art. 36, 12 December 1977, 1125 *UNTS* 3, 16 *ILM* (1977) p. 1391, reprinted in Roberts and Guelff, op. cit. n. 57, at p. 419. For the United States, the weapon review is required by Department of Defense Instruction 5000.2, Operation of the Defense Acquisition System, 23 October 2000, para. 4.7.3.1.4.

72. For example, although not a Party to Protocol I, the United States considers many of its provisions to be declaratory of customary international law. For a non-official, but generally considered authoritative, delineation of those viewed as declaratory, see M.J. Matheson, 'Session One: The United States Position on the Relation of Customary International Law to the 1977 Protocols Additional to the 1949 Geneva Conventions', 2 *Amer. Univ. JIL & Pol.* (1987) p. 419. See also International & Operational Law Division, Office of the Judge Advocate General, Department of the Air Force, Operations Law Deployment Deskbook, tab 12, no date, and comments by the then-State Department Legal Advisor Abraham D. Sofaer in 'Agora: The US Decision Not to Ratify Protocol I to the Geneva Conventions on the Protection of War Victims', 82 *AJIL* (1988) p. 784.

73. United States doctrine for the conduct of psychological operations is set forth in Joint Chiefs of Staff, Joint Doctrine for Psychological Operations, Joint Pub 3-53, 10 July 1996.

objects shall not be the object of *attack*'; 51(4) proscribes 'indiscriminate *attacks*'; and 52(2) requires that '*attacks* ... be limited to strictly military objects'.

But what, then, are 'attacks'? Fortunately, Protocol I defines the term in Article 49: '"Attacks" means acts of violence against the adversary, whether in offence or defence.' That the term 'operations' in Article 48 should be understood in the sense of their nature (i.e., as attacks), rather than strictly their targets (i.e., military objectives or not), is further reinforced by the *Commentary* to the Protocol, which states that the word 'should be understood in the context of the *whole* of the Section; it refers to military operations during which *violence* is used'.[74] If that is so, are computer network attacks acts of violence?

Violence is usually considered in the context of the application of physical force.[75] By this perspective, computer network attacks would be allowed against any target, military or not, because they involve no physical force. Any such assertion would be flawed in much the same way that taking a similar approach to the concept of 'armed force' and 'armed attack' was unsound in the *ad bellum* framework. Although physical force has typified methods and means of warfare throughout history, and is accordingly reflected in the style of the *lex scripta*, no one would deny IHL's applicability to, for instance, non-physical means such as chemical or biological weapons. Thus, the proper understanding of violence is causation of injury (or significant suffering) to persons or damage to property (including damage to intangible assets with tangible meaning, such as money or stock); the quintessence of targeting restrictions is consequence, not means or method. The various provisions that articulate their proscriptions in terms of consequences, without referring to their causal mechanism, further illustrate the Protocol's consequence-based nature. Consider the prohibition on creating 'widespread, long-term, and severe damage' to the environment[76] or that which disallows attacks on dams, dykes, or nuclear electrical generation stations that might result in 'severe losses among the civilian population'.[77] Indeed, the core IHL principle of proportionality involves a consequence-based balancing test.[78]

This analysis leads to the conclusion that targeting civilians or civilian objects with CNA in a manner that could foreseeable cause either injury or damage is prohibited; however, CNA targeting of military objectives is not, nor is targeting civilians or civilian objects if neither injury nor damage results.[79] IHL does not forbid irritating or inconveniencing the civilian population.

---

74. Commentary on the Additional Protocols of 8 June 1977 to the Geneva Conventions of 12 August 1949, para. 1875, Y. Sandoz, Ch. Swinarski and B. Zimmerman, eds. (1987).

75. E.g., the term is defined in the *Merriam-Webster's Collegiate Dictionary*, 10th edn., as 'exertion of physical force so as to injure or abuse'. F. Mish, ed. (Springfield MA, Merriam-Webster Inc. 1998).

76. Protocol I, *supra* n. 71, Arts. 35.3 and 55.1.

77. Ibid., Art. 56.1.

78. Protocol I, *supra* n. 71, Arts. 51.5(b) and 57.2(a)(iii).

79. But see E. Haslam, 'Information Warfare: Technological Changes and International Law', 5 *Journal of Conflict and Security Law* (2000) p. 173.

It remains to define 'military objective'. The Protocol's *Commentary* provides further clarification to the definition in Article 52(2) cited above.[80] Objectives which make an effective contribution include objects 'directly used' by the military, such as military equipment, locations 'of special importance for military operations in view of [their] location', and otherwise civilian objects that are being used by the military, such as a hotel now serving to house troops. Attacks that yield a definite military advantage are those where the military advantage gained by the operation is more than 'potential or indeterminate'.[81]

These are fairly restrictive standards. Taken together they suggest that an attack must have a direct effect on military operations. However, the United States has adopted a much broader interpretation than that contained in the Protocol or its *Commentary*. The seminal *Commander's Handbook on the Law of Naval Warfare*, for example, cites economic targets that 'indirectly but effectively support and sustain the enemy's war-fighting capability' as military objectives.[82] This divergence has enormous implications for computer network attack operations because the vast majority of potential economic targets that indirectly but effectively support and sustain a war effort depend to some degree on computer systems and networks. Quite simply, the interdependency that characterizes modern societies means they are packed with potential targets that contribute to war's economic base. The lack of symmetry in the two approaches is tangible, particularly in coalition operations. No one would argue, for example, that a factory producing armaments is immune from computer network attack but what about factories that produce non-military items for export? Would they be targetable by the US standard because export earnings contribute to a state's ability to arm its forces? What about the communications net on which commerce relies? Or systems storing data for financial institutions? Or inland waterways used for the transport of goods?

Lest the dilemma be exaggerated, it deserves reiterating that the interpretive divergence is only relevant to the extent injury (or significant suffering) or property damage (or a constructive equivalent thereof in the case of intangible property) occurs. This reality may prove useful in remedying grey area cases. For instance, consider the April 1999 bombing of the Radio Televivizije Srbije (Radio-Television Serbia) headquarters during Operation Allied Force, the attack that formed the basis for the *Bankovic* litigation before the European Court of Human

---

80. Protocol I, *supra* n. 71, Art. 52.2. On military objectives, see H. Robertson, 'The Principle of Military Objective in the Law of Armed Conflict', in *The Law of Military Operations*, Michael Schmitt, ed. (Newport RI, Naval War College Press 1998) p. 197.

81. Commentary, *supra* n. 74, paras. 2020-2024.

82. US Navy/Marine Corps/Coast Guard, *The Commander's Handbook on the Law of Naval Operations* (NWP 1-14M, MCWP 5-2.1, COMDTPUB P5800.7), para. 8.1.1 (1995) reprinted in its annotated version as Vol. 73 of the US Naval War College's International Law Studies series. This assertion is labelled a 'statement of customary international law'. The Handbook cites General Counsel, Department of Defense, Letter of 22 September 1972, reprinted in 67 *AJIL* (1973) p. 123, as the basis for this characterization.

Rights.[83] The affair focused great attention on the question of whether media facilities are valid targets; the case's dismissal on jurisdictional grounds in December 2001 has only served to continue the debate. Through computer network attack, the controversy surrounding attacks against broadcasting facilities need not even surface. Without causing injury or damage, CNA can simply shut off offending broadcasts, thereby rendering the present 'dispute' moot.

In addition to the 'military objective' issue, the protection of 'civilians' poses a number of quandaries.[84] Most notable is the matter of illegal combatants, one currently capturing international attention in the context of terrorists. Article 51(3) of Protocol I provides that civilians are not to be attacked 'unless and for such time as they take a direct part in hostilities'. A 'direct part' is described in the *Commentary* as engaging in 'acts of war which by their nature or purpose are likely to cause actual harm to the personnel or equipment of the enemy forces'.[85] By this standard, computer network attack directed against civilians engaged in combat would be acceptable even if the CNA resulted in injury or death. Thus, for example, the al-Qaeda organization can clearly be targeted with computer network attack without having to delve into whether or not it, or any of its subordinate units, merits combatant status. There are prisoner of war status issues to resolve to be sure, but the fact that the organization can be attacked based on its participation in the conflict is unassailable.

More problematic is the status of those who conduct computer network attacks. To the extent that the CNA either amounts to an 'attack' or constitutes an essential facet of ongoing military operations (even though not in and of itself qualifying as an attack), the operators are valid targets, either through kinetic or cyber means. If not members of the armed forces, such individuals would qualify as illegal combatants. States should bear this in mind as they develop CNA capabilities and staff organizations tasked to conduct the operations. Electing to contract out computer network attack functions or directly employing civilians to conduct attacks may well expose those involved to physical risk and subject them to charges of illegally participating in the conflict.

In addition to the general prohibition on attacking civilians and civilian objects, there are a number of specific restrictions that apply to CNA operations. For

---

83. *Bankovic & Others* v. *Belgium, the Czech Republic, Denmark, France, Germany, Greece, Hungary, Iceland, Italy, Luxembourg, the Netherlands, Norway, Poland, Portugal, Spain, Turkey and the United Kingdom*, European Court of Human Rights Application No. 52207/99.

84. Protection of civilians and civilian objects is provided for in Protocol I, Arts. 51.2 and 52. The Statute of the International Criminal Court also prohibits the direct targeting of civilians or civilian objects. Rome Statute of the International Criminal Court, Art. 8.2(b)(i) & (ii), UN Doc. A/Conf. 183/9, 17 July 1998, at Annex II, reprinted in 37 *ILM* (1998) p. 999, and M.C. Bassiouni, *The Statute of the International Criminal Court: A Documentary History* (Ardsley NY, Transnational Publishers 1998) p. 39 and available online at www.un.org/law/icc/texts/romefra.htm.

85. Commentary, op. cit. n. 74, para. 1944. It has even been asserted that mission-essential civilians working at a base during hostilities, though not engaged directly in acts of war, are legitimate targets. Letter from DAJA-IA to Counselor for Defense Research and Engineering (Economics), Embassy of the Federal Republic of Germany (22 January 1988), cited in W.H. Parks, 'Air War and the Law of War', 32 *Air Force LR* (1992) pp. 1, 34.

instance, Parties to Protocol I are prohibited from attacking dams, dykes, and nuclear electrical generating stations if the attack might trigger the release of 'dangerous forces' that can cause 'severe losses among the civilian population'.[86] Interestingly, computer network attack revives the possibility of attacking such facilities because they are vulnerable to cyber-neutralization (e.g., blocking their transmission of electricity) without risking the type of damage that might result in a release of their dangerous forces (water or radiation).

Along the same lines, Parties to Protocol I are forbidden to conduct attacks likely to cause widespread, long-term and severe damage to the environment.[87] Again, CNA offers interesting prospects for targeting facilities that might pose such a risk if attacked with conventional weaponry. For instance, rather than attacking POL storage facilities and hazarding massive release of their contents, POL distribution systems can be shut down by denial of power. The same approach could be taken, for example, with facilities containing toxic chemicals; simply shut them down, perhaps with tactics as simple as denying them electricity.

Although additional targeting restrictions exist in both conventional and customary IHL, this is not the place to exhaustively catalogue them. Rather, the point is that while CNA must comply with both, at the same time it may offer new opportunities for conducting military operations within the bounds of the law.

2.3.1 *Limits on the use of CNA*

Beyond the broad question of what computer network attack may be targeted against, it is necessary to explore limits on how CNA may be conducted. A major limitation is that prohibiting the use of indiscriminate weapons. Indiscriminate weapons are those that cannot be directed at a specific military objective or otherwise comply with the requirements of IHL.[88] Basically, a weapon is indiscriminate when its effects are not controllable.

A computer is, of course, not inherently indiscriminate; on the contrary, properly used it can mount an exceptionally surgical attack. Yet it is only part of a weapon system in which the code that is transmitted comprises the actual 'destructive force'. To the extent this code is designed to spread randomly, as many viruses and worms are, the weapon system as a whole is indiscriminate. Moreover, even if the code were not specifically intended to travel arbitrarily, use of code that cannot be controlled would also run counter to the prohibition. For instance, launching a

86. Art. 56. The United States opposes this provision and believes it does not reflect customary international law.

87. Protocol I, *supra* n. 71, Arts. 35.3 and 55. See also ICC Statute, *supra* n. 84, Art. 8.2(b)(iv). The US opposes this provision. On the issue of environmental damage during armed conflict, see J.E. Austin and C.E Bruch, eds., *The Environmental Consequences of War: Legal, Economic, and Scientific Perspectives* (Cambridge, Cambridge University Press 2000); M.N. Schmitt, 'Green War: An Assessment of the Environmental Law of International Armed Conflict', 22 *Yale JIL* (1997) pp. 1-109; R.J. Grunawalt, J.E. King and R.S. McClain, eds., 'Protection of the Environment During Armed Conflict and Other Military Operations', 69 *US Naval War College International Law Studies* (1996).

88. Protocol I, *supra* n. 71, Art. 51.4 (b) and (c).

virus against a military network tied into civilian systems without being able to preclude its transmittal into and through the latter would amount to use of an indiscriminate weapon.

One essential caveat is in order. The prohibition on the use of indiscriminate weapons occurs in the context of barring indiscriminate attacks; indeed, in Protocol I the restriction is found in Article 51(4), the paragraph on indiscriminate attacks. Thus, for the prohibition to apply, the indiscriminate weapon must be capable of an 'attack', i.e., capable of causing human injury or property damage. CNA with indiscriminate code that does not produce these consequences would not violate the prohibition; most of the viruses launched through the Internet to date would fall into this category.

In addition to the prohibition on indiscriminate weapons, it is forbidden to use discriminate weapons indiscriminately. Specifically, indiscriminate use is the launching of an attack that is 'not directed at a specific military objective'.[89] The distinction is subtle. Indiscriminate weapons cannot be aimed sufficiently; indiscriminate use involves not aiming with sufficient care; and aiming at civilians or civilian objects directly is an attack against protected persons or objects. Thus, with reference to computer network attack, a particular virus or worm might be capable of being directed against specific military objectives, but if it is simply launched haphazardly into the cyber world, the attack is indiscriminate. Essentially, culpable disregard of the consequences makes an attack indiscriminate. Recall, though, that there must be an 'attack' as that term is used in IHL.

Even if a computer network attack is directed against a military objective it must still comply with the principle of proportionality. Proportionality is a recognition that military operations often have unintended, albeit foreseeable, effects on the civilian population and civilian objects. By this principle, articulated in Articles 51 and 57 of Protocol I, an attack is prohibited if it 'may be expected to cause incidental loss of civilian life, injury to civilians, damage to civilian objects, or a combination thereof, which would be excessive in relation to the concrete and direct military advantage anticipated'.[90] The Protocol's *Commentary* describes a concrete and direct advantage as one that is 'substantial and relatively close[;] ... advantages which are hardly perceptible and those which would only appear in the long term should be disregarded'.[91] Most commentators agree that the advantage evaluated against the incidental injuries and collateral damage is that resulting from the overall operation, not the individual attack itself.[92] Reduced to basics, proportionality calculations are balancing tests. Unintended incidental injury to civilians and collateral damage to civilian objects is weighed against the overall

89. Ibid., Art. 51.4(a).

90. Protocol I, *supra* n. 71, Arts. 51.5(a) and 57.2(a)(iii) and (b). On proportionality, see W.J. Fenrick, 'The Rule of Proportionality and Protocol Additional I in Conventional Warfare', 98 *Military LR* (1982) p. 91; J.G. Gardam, 'Proportionality and Force in International Law', 87 *AJIL* (1993) p. 391.

91. Commentary, *supra* n. 74, para. 2209.

92. This position has been formally adopted by a number of states upon becoming Party to the Protocol, through the mechanism of understandings/declarations/reservations. All are available on the ICRC's IHL site at www.icrc.org/ihl.

military advantage that the attacker gains from the operation.

Proportionality calculations for computer network attacks are performed in the same fashion as those accomplished in advance of a kinetic attack. Consider a computer network attack against an airfield jointly used by civilian and military aircraft. The attack involves the generation of false approach data for air traffic controllers during periods of poor visibility. As a result of the attack, a number of aircraft, both civilian and military, will almost certainly crash on landing; mid-air collisions are also highly likely. Although the impact on civil aviation is unintentional, it is almost certainly inevitable given the dual-use nature of the facility. Proportionality would be calculated no differently in this scenario than in one involving a conventional strike against the airfield – estimate collateral damage and incidental injury and determine whether or not the military advantage of disrupting military operations at the field, given the circumstances of the conflict, justify them. Of course, the test is easier to describe than perform, for it requires comparing two completely different values against each other. How many civilian lives is disruption of the airfield for an hour worth? For a day? For the duration of the conflict? Despite the extraordinary difficulty of making such assessments, there is little difference between performing them for cyber and kinetic attacks.

In the context of proportionality, the practical, rather than juridical, aspects of computer network attack are of particular importance. Most noteworthy is the issue of reverberating effects. Reverberating effects, as noted *supra*, are the second, third, fourth (and so on) tier-effects that result from an attack on a legitimate target. They are not directly and immediately caused by the attack but lie in the attack's chain of causation; in tort terms, they would not have occurred 'but for' the attack. Often cited examples include the impact of air strikes against the electrical grids serving Baghdad and Belgrade during Operations DESERT STORM and ALLIED FORCE respectively. Claims of reverberating effects ranged from loss of heating and refrigeration to interference with the medical equipment functioning and shutting down drinking water pumping stations.[93]

CNA represents a double-edged sword with regard to reverberating effects. On the positive side, in some circumstances the precision capabilities of computer network attack enable operations that can achieve an objective without generating reverberating effects. For instance, an alternative to striking an electrical grid in order to disable command and control might be to target the C2 system nodes directly through computer attack. On the other hand, and somewhat ominously, the increasingly interconnected nature of modern societies amplifies computer network attack's risk of complex reverberating effects. Exacerbating the problem is the fact that the complicated relationships within and between networks render an accurate estimate of likely reverberating effects highly elusive. This reality does not relieve the attacker of the duty of including them in the proportionality calculation. As computer network attack matures as a method of warfare, cyber targeteers, operators and commanders will need to have ready access to experts capable of

93. 'NATO Denies Targeting Water Supplies', BBC World Online Network, 24 May 1999, http://news.bbc.co.uk/hi/english/world/europe/newsid_351000/351780.stm.

making such estimates.[94] In the United States, for example, the Joint Warfare Analysis Center currently is already modelling foreign infrastructures and contingent outcomes.

This latter point bears on duty of care requirements. Article 57 of Protocol I sets forth the requisite precautions in attack. Specifically, those who plan or decide on an attack must do everything feasible to verify that the targets are valid military objectives; take all feasible precautions to minimize collateral damage and incidental injury; and not conduct disproportionate attacks. Additionally, if there is a choice of targets for obtaining a like military advantage, the one selected should generally be that causing the least collateral damage and incidental injury. Should it become apparent during an attack that the target is not a military objective or that attacking it will generate disproportionate civilian consequences, the attack must be aborted. Finally, when an attack will affect the civilian population, the attacker must warn the civilian population, if doing so is reasonable in the circumstances.

The opportunities CNA presents for minimizing collateral damage and incidental injury through precision and non-kinetic effect have been discussed, as has the possibility that computer network attacks may offer the option of striking alternative targets to achieve similar results. These are positive factors in complying with the duty of care. In contrast, the near instantaneous launch-to-impact nature of most CNA means that effectively there will seldom be the chance to cancel an attack once launched. An exception might be a logic bomb that sits idle in a targeted system until activated by a particular condition (e.g., a particular date or predetermined instrumentation reading). In such cases, if the attacker still had access to the system in which it resides, it may be possible to recall or deactivate the bomb.

Verifying the nature of computer attack targets is facilitated by the fact that they can be 'interrogated' using advanced network mapping and sensor technologies. However, over-reliance on the technology is risky because a technologically adept opponent may effectively create ruses as to the nature of a potential target or its relationship to other systems.[95] For instance, CNA makes it possible to alter data in an enemy's intelligence systems regarding order of battle and force disposition or even to create false data intended to mislead the enemy. While ruses are legal under IHL, they would certainly complicate an opponent's ability to verify target status; in the event the ruse became known to the opponent, it would diminish confidence in target intelligence generally, a negative prospect with respect to encouraging precautions in attack.

---

94. A typical Information Operations Cell is illustrated in JP 3-13, *supra* n. 3, at figure IV-4 and accompanying text. It includes an IO officer from J-3; representatives from J-2, 4, 5, 6, 7, supporting combatant commands, and service and functional components; a judge advocate; and public affairs, counterintelligence, civil affairs, targeting, special operations, special technical operations, electronic warfare, psychological operations, military deception, and operations security experts.

95. 'Ruses of war' are not prohibited. Such ruses are acts which are intended to mislead an adversary or to induce him to act recklessly but which infringe no rule of international law applicable in armed conflict and which are not perfidious because they do not invite the confidence of an adversary with respect to protection under that law.' Protocol I, *supra* n. 71, Art. 37.2

More treacherously, an opponent might perfidiously create the impression that a civilian entity is a military objective (a violation of IHL in itself) in order to lure its opponent into attacking it.[96] For example, one could create the cyber-feedback that a neutral diplomatic facility was a military headquarters, thereby enticing an opponent to attack its systems. Alternatively, an opponent could perfidiously (i.e., unlawfully) create the cyber-impression that an actual military objective enjoys protected status under IHL. It would be possible, for example, to cause an enemy's systems to appear to be receiving the codes and signals established by the International Telecommunications Union, International Civil Aviation Organization and International Maritime Consultative Organization to distinguish medical units and transports when the objects involved were in fact military in nature.[97] Finally, it would be equally perfidious to route a computer network attack through a civilian system, or otherwise feign civilian origin, to make it appear harmless.[98]

3. CONCLUSION

As should be apparent, computer network attack presents international law with significant challenges. In the *jus ad bellum* realm, it forces paradigmatic shifts in the way such established concepts as 'use of force', 'armed force' and 'armed attack' are considered. In particular, it inevitably leads to consequence-based analysis. Interestingly, the use of computer network attack may actually foster community ends, especially as a tool available for use in Chapter VII operations.

On the other hand, when considered in the *jus in bello* context, it seems clear that, albeit a new form of warfare, the existing normative architecture is generally adequate *vis-à-vis* computer network attack. In fact, in some cases, CNA operations achieve the ends of international humanitarian law better than more traditional ones. As might be expected with any new method and means, some interpretive play is necessary; consequence-based interpretation of the term 'attack' is an apt example of this need.

Despite the general sufficiency of IHL as applied to computer network attack, one potentially dangerous lacuna is the apparent permissibility of targeting civilians and civilian objects with computer operations that do not amount to an 'attack'. This can have a dramatic impact on the well-being of the civilian population. Unfortunately, the compliance strategies likely to characterize much of Twenty-first Century warfare gives an incentive to such operations; after all, to the extent one is trying to compel an opponent to do or not to do something rather than defeat him, operations that motivate the population to pressure its leadership into compliance are appealing.

---

96. 'Acts inviting the confidence of an adversary to lead him to believe that he is entitled to, or is obliged to accord, protection under the rules of international law applicable in armed conflict, with intent to betray that confidence' are perfidy. Ibid., Art. 37.1.

97. Protocol I, *supra* n. 71, annex, Art. 11.

98. Ibid., Art. 37.1(c).

The development of computer network attack tactics and capabilities has outpaced comprehensive reflection on the appropriate architecture to govern it. Fortunately, the gap is beginning to narrow. Indeed, there is a lively informal debate underway over whether a permissive (facilitating use) or restrictive (protecting vulnerabilities) regime is preferable in responding to the issues raised in this article. To date, the jury remains hung.[99] Whether international law will ultimately adapt itself to computer network attack in a fashion consistent with core community values has yet to be seen.

99. See Report of the Secretary-General on Developments in the Field of Information and Telecommunications in the Context of International Security, UN Doc. A/54/213 (1999). Russia has repeatedly called for a multilateral treaty to limit 'information weapons'. For a discussion of a possible treaty, see P. Johnson, 'Is it Time for a Treaty on Information Warfare?', in Schmitt, op. cit. n. 16, at pp. 439-455. See for a discussion of CNA in the context of both law and ethics that concludes that a new convention is required, W.J. Bayles, 'The Ethics of Computer Network Attack', 31 *Parameters: Journal of the US Army War College* (Spring 2001) No. 1, at p. 44.

THE LAW OF SENTENCING IN INTERNATIONAL CRIMINAL LAW: THE PURPOSES OF SENTENCING AND THE APPLICABLE METHOD FOR THE DETERMINATION OF THE SENTENCE[1]

Jan Christoph Nemitz[2]

1. INTRODUCTION

'Sentencing is an art and not a science'. This statement of Lord Lane[3] expresses, with all due respect, what sentencing should not be. Although it cannot be denied that the process of determining a sentence is far from being a mathematical exercise, the result of which can be verified or falsified by reference to some unquestionable law of nature, both the legislator and the judiciary must strive for the development of a law of sentencing which is based on a comprehensive set of statutory provisions. The very term '*law* of sentencing' indicates that the meting out of a sentence is more than the exercise of a skill that only judges are vested with. The use of the term 'art', conversely, to describe sentencing gives the impression that the act of sentencing is beyond objective understanding and control. When we speak of art, we acknowledge that while views on the outcome can be manifold, objective criteria for a 'correct' assessment are few: there's no accounting for taste. This is unacceptable when looking at the significance of the law of sentencing for the pursuit of various sentencing purposes. To base the determination of the sentence on legal grounds enhances the review possibilities with regard to sentencing judgments. This contributes to an even sentencing practice, which in turn leads to just and comprehensible sentencing judgments. Such a practice is necessary in order to achieve public acceptance of the criminal justice system in general and of sentencing verdicts in particular. Such acceptance is imperative for the achievement of several sentencing purposes, especially that of affirmative (or positive) general prevention.

The process of sentencing plays an important role in the administration of criminal justice in every penal system. This is true in the realm of national criminal law, and it is, if possible, even more important in the international criminal law arena, where criminal tribunals are often criticised for being politically influenced

---

2. Dr. jur. (Freiburg i. Br.), Ass. jur. (Konstanz), jur. Mag. (Stockholm); Research Assistant at the Max Planck Institute for Foreign and International Criminal Law, Freiburg im Breisgau, Germany.

3. Quoted in A. Ashworth, *Sentencing and Criminal Justice*, 3rd edn. (London, Butterworths 2000) p. 34.

Yearbook of International Humanitarian Law
Volume 4 – 2001 – pp. 87-127

and biased. It is therefore indispensable for the success of those tribunals that their sentences are widely perceived as the outcome of an impartial and fair trial, reflecting the conception of justice of as many people worldwide as possible.

How can the 'success' of a tribunal be assessed? This question is closely related to the question of which purposes of punishment should be pursued by a tribunal's sentencing procedure: if the success of a tribunal depends on whether or not a perpetrator is punished, the tribunal's sentences pursue repressive aims of sentencing like retribution or just deserts. If success is seen rather in the preventive effect a tribunal might have in the fight against recidivism and criminality as such, preventive purposes of sentencing such as deterrence or rehabilitation will dominate the sentencing process.

This Article discusses which sentencing purposes should be pursued in international criminal law (2). It examines the jurisprudence of post-World War II tribunals (2.1) and the jurisprudence of the ICTR and the ICTY (the *ad hoc* Tribunals) (2.2). After a general discussion of several sentencing purposes (2.3), the concept of affirmative general prevention is explored in more detail (2.4). The differences that might arise out of disparities in the sentencing procedures on the international and national levels are dealt with in the following chapter (3), before some issues relating to the determination of the applicable law of sentencing are addressed (4). After a general introduction to the method of sentencing in international criminal law (5), the process of determining a sentence is discussed, with a special focus on the concept of the gravity of the crime (6). The issue of multiple convictions which are based on the same conduct (7), and the relationship between single and multiple sentences, are examined at the end of this study (8).

2. THE PURPOSES OF PUNISHMENT IN INTERNATIONAL CRIMINAL LAW

It has been shown that the sentencing process is strongly influenced by the underlying purposes of sentencing. To determine which of these purposes should be pursued is of more than merely theoretical interest since they provide the framework within which each individual sentence is meted out. Thus, a system prioritising the concept of rehabilitation will generally lead to sentences which do not necessarily correspond to the seriousness of the crime: if there is no need to resocialise the accused, the sentence may be disproportionally low; if resocialisation of the accused is unlikely, the sentence runs the risk of being disproportionally harsh. On the other hand, if retribution is seen as the primary sentencing purpose, this deed-oriented approach could also lead to unwelcome sentences if, for instance, the personality of the accused demands some mitigation. Therefore, every criminal justice system, international and national, has to determine which sentencing purposes it wants to pursue and which goals it wants to achieve.

The different concepts of sentencing purposes have been discussed in national criminal justice systems for centuries, and national legislation – together with jurisprudence and scholarly works – has generally rather detailed views on the various purposes to which sentencing is directed. In the realm of international criminal law, however, the question of which sentencing purposes should be pursued and – possibly even more important – which sentencing purpose should dominate if two or more of them collide (*antinomy*) has not yet been extensively discussed.[4] Furthermore, the question whether the nature of international crimes and of the international justice system require an emphasis on other aims of punishment than in national systems has scarcely been examined. Even the jurisprudence of the *ad hoc* Tribunals in The Hague and Arusha – the most comprehensive source on this issue – is not consistent in this respect: while some sentencing judgments have hardly addressed this issue, others have discussed it in detail.

2.1 The purposes of punishment pursued by post-World War II Tribunals

Retributive purposes of sentencing were emphasised in the Statutes of both the International Military Tribunal in Nürnberg (IMT)[5] and the International Military Tribunal for the Far East (IMTFE) in Tokyo[6]. Article 1 of the IMT Statute provides that a tribunal shall be established 'for the just and prompt trial and punishment of the major war criminals of the European Axis'.[7] Similarly, Article 1 of the IMTFE Statute reads that a tribunal was 'established for the just and prompt punishment of the major war criminals' in the Far East.[8] Apart from this wording, nothing else can be found in the Statutes on other sentencing purposes justifying and guiding the Tribunals' sentencing processes. Likewise, their judgments did not expressly mention any specific aim of punishment. The judges did not discuss the possible deterrent effect the judgments might have or their significance for the prevention of these crimes. Instead, the implicit purpose of the sentencing judgments was a repressive one: the major war criminals of the Axis Powers committed heinous crimes, therefore they would be punished and would get what they deserved.

An explanation for the lack of a deeper discussion of other sentencing purposes may be found in the fact that these Tribunals almost exclusively dealt with the highest-ranking defendants. It would have been rather odd to reason that an accused like Hermann Göring was entitled to some mitigation because of his promising resocialisation prospects. It is also clear that these judgments were intended to convey the strong message that even in times of war and dictatorship there are norms so fundamental that they have to be followed by everybody, in all circumstances.

---

4. Cf., however, K. Ambos and C. Steiner, 'Vom Sinn des Strafens auf innerstaatlicher und supranationaler Ebene', *Juristische Schulung* (2001) pp. 9 et seq. (with further references).

5. Established by the London Agreement of 8 August 1945.

6. Established by an order of the Supreme Commander of the Allied Powers, General Douglas McArthur, on 19 January 1946.

7. It is interesting to note that the wording of Art. 1 of the London Agreement read: '[...] for the trial of war criminals [...]', meaning that there was no statutory restriction to criminals of the Axis Powers.

8. Referring to Japanese war criminals, the Potsdam Declaration of 2 August 1945 stated that 'stern justice shall be meted out to all war criminals'.

In contrast to the final judgments of the IMT and the IMTFE against the major war criminals, some of the prosecutors before the IMT and some judges in subsequent trials explicitly addressed the issue of preventive sentencing purposes. The British Prosecutor Sir Hartley Shawcross dismissed the idea of summarily executing the offenders without a further trial by claiming that in doing so, 'the Rule of Law [could not] be raised and strengthened on the international as well as upon the municipal plane', and he added that 'future generations [would not] realise that right is not always on the side of the big battalions'.[9] Similarly, the French Prosecutor François de Menthon stated that 'our decision must be inscribed as a decisive act in the history of International Law in order to prepare the establishment of a true international society excluding recourse to war and enlisting force permanently in the service of the justice of nations; it will be one of the foundations of this peaceful order to which nations aspire on the morrow of this frightful torment'.[10]

Additionally, in one of the trials conducted under Control Council Law No. 10, Judge Powers held that one 'should reflect on the fact that if these trials have a reason for existence, it is to encourage respect for the rules applicable to warfare'.[11] Some other judges made similar statements – although not in the Majority Judgement – in which they highlighted the importance of the trials and the judgments for both the rule of law in general and for the comparatively 'young' body of international criminal law in particular.[12] In doing so, the concept of affirmative general prevention as a purpose of sentencing entered the arena of international criminal jurisprudence. According to this aim of sentencing, the infliction of punishment is justified by arguing that the public has to be reassured that the law is applied and enforced; only if this goal is achieved, will the public both accept and respect the law. In the long run, this understanding will contribute to the prevention of human rights violations.

However, such explicit statements in favour of affirmative general prevention remained the exception to the rule. It is therefore not surprising that a Trial Chamber of the ICTY interpreted the number of death penalties rendered by the IMT as evidence for the assumption that this sentencing practice 'would indicate

---

9. Quoted from *The Trial of German Major War Criminals*, Part 2 (London, His Majesty's Stationery Office 1946) p. 45.

10. Ibid., Part 4, p. 377.

11. Judge Powers, Dissenting Opinion in the *Wilhelmstraßen* case, quoted from XIV *Trials of War Criminals before the Nuernberg Military Tribunals under Control Council Law No. 10* (Washington DC, Government Printing Office 1952) p. 876.

12. Judge Jaranilla of the IMTFE regarded some of the penalties imposed by the Tribunal as being too lenient, fearing that this 'action may be construed as weakness and failure'. Quoted in B.V.A. Röling and C.F. Rüter, eds., *The Tokyo Judgment*, Vol. I (Amsterdam, University Press Amsterdam 1977) p. 514. This statement seems to express a concern for the acceptance of international criminal law by the public. Judge Pal, in his Dissenting Opinion, emphasised that the prosecution and punishment of war criminals is 'a weapon with which to enforce respect for the tenets of international law with its underlying principles of international justice'. Ibid., Vol. II, p. 575.

an inclination towards general deterrence and retribution'.[13] One can even go a step further, stating that of these two sentencing aims, retribution was the main one: the wording of the Statutes, the sentences handed down, and the absence of any references to other sentencing purposes in the judgments of the IMT and the IMTFE demonstrate that the judges followed the approach outlined by the US Chief Prosecutor Jackson in his opening address: '[...] it [is] hard to distinguish between the demand for a just and measured retribution, and the unthinking cry for vengeance which arises from the anguish of war'.[14]

In the decades following the post-World War II trials, international criminal law did not attract much attention in international legal research let alone in international legal practice. This changed profoundly in the early-1990s with the advent of the *ad hoc* Tribunals for the former Yugoslavia and Rwanda. It soon became apparent that the sentencing decisions rendered by these Tribunals devoted much more consideration and diligence to the discussion of sentencing purposes than those of the IMT and the IMTFE. Similarly, the Security Council resolutions establishing the Tribunals provide some guidance in this respect. In doing so, they seem to give repressive purposes priority over preventive ones: both resolutions state that the Tribunals shall 'bring to justice the persons who are responsible' for the crimes under the Statutes.[15] Additionally, according to both resolutions, the *ad hoc* Tribunals were 'established for *the sole purpose* of prosecuting persons' (emphasis added) who are criminally responsible for jurisdictional crimes.[16] This wording is similar to that of the Statutes of the IMT and the IMTFE. Furthermore, both resolutions state that the serious violations of humanitarian law should be 'effectively redressed'; this, again, indicates a rather repressive approach to sentencing.[17]

On the other hand, both resolutions also refer to deterrence as a purpose of punishment. They express the Security Council's determination to establish the Tribunals in order to 'put an end to such crimes' and to ensure 'that such violations are halted'.[18] The pursuit of this sentencing purpose corresponds to the fact that the *ad hoc* Tribunals were established under Chapter VII as a means to maintain or to restore international peace and security: future war criminals should be deterred by the prospect of being sentenced in The Hague or Arusha. However, the heinous crimes committed in and around Srebreniċa two years after the establishment of the ICTY and one year after the establishment of the ICTR demonstrate at least the empirical shortcomings when trying to measure the deterrent effect that the Tribunals have had: while it is easy to show the failure of deterrence, it is very

13. *The Prosecutor* v. *Dražen Erdemović*, Case No. IT-96-22-T, Sentencing Judgement, 29 November 1996, para. 62.

14. Quoted in *The Trial of German Major War Criminals*, Part 1 (London, His Majesty's Stationery Office 1946) p. 51.

15. SC Res. 827 (1993); SC Res. 955 (1994).

16. Ibid.

17. For a discussion of the difference between the concepts of 'redress' and 'retribution', see W.A. Schabas, 'Sentencing by International Tribunals: A Human Rights Approach', 7 *Duke JCIL* (1997) p. 498 at p. 502.

18. SC Res. 827 (1993); SC Res. 955 (1994).

difficult to prove its success. What can be said is that deterrence as a sentencing aim plays a more prominent role in the instruments establishing the *ad hoc* Tribunals than in those that established the IMT and the IMTFE some 50 years before.

Next to retribution and deterrence, the tribunals of The Hague and Arusha pursue yet another preventive aim of punishment: affirmative general prevention. Although this concept is not explicitly mentioned in either the relevant Security Council Resolutions or the Statutes, reference to this purpose of punishment can be found in the Tribunals' endeavour to 'contribute to the process of national reconciliation'.[19] The Rwandese government stressed the importance of this concept when it stated that those 'who were taught that it was acceptable to kill as long as the victim was from a different ethnic group or from an opposition party, cannot arrive at national reconciliation unless they learn new values'.[20] An important part of this educational process can be fulfilled by the fair conduct of criminal trials and the imposition of sentences that are proportionate to the crime. Thus, the legal conscience of the public and the people's trust in the law have to be either developed or reinforced. Both a trial and a conviction can contribute to this process by conveying the unambiguous message that an act was wrong – i.e., criminal – since the value which was harmed or destroyed was protected by international law. If the public accepts that violations of human rights must not be answered by similar violations – because these human rights are inviolable and absolute – the process of reconciliation will be facilitated. If, however, breaches of those values remain unpunished, respect for international criminal law and the values protected therein will be severely damaged.

2.2 Sentencing purposes in the jurisprudence of the *ad hoc* Tribunals

2.2.1 *Retribution and deterrence*

The early jurisprudence of the *ad hoc* Tribunals seems to indicate that retribution and deterrence are the main purposes of punishment.[21]

In the first sentencing judgment of the ICTY, Trial Chamber I stressed the importance of retribution in the sense of the just deserts concept 'as legitimate grounds for pronouncing a sentence for crimes against humanity, the punishment having to be proportionate to the gravity of the crime and the moral guilt of the accused'.[22] This wording makes it clear that retribution must not be understood in

19. Ibid.

20. UN Doc. S/PV.3453 at p. 14; quoted in P. Akhavan, 'The International Criminal Tribunal for Rwanda: The Politics and Pragmatics of Punishment', 90 *AJIL* (1996) p. 504 et seq.

21. *The Prosecutor* v. *George Rutaganda*, Case No. ICTR-96-3, Judgement, 6 December 1999, para. 456; *The Prosecutor* v. *Omar Serushago*, Case No. ICTR-98-39-S, Sentence, 5 February 1999, para. 20; *The Prosecutor* v. *Žejnil Delalić et al.*, Case No. IT-96-21, Judgement, 16 November 1998, para. 1234; *The Prosecutor* v. *Jean Kambanda*, Case No. ICTR-97-23-S, Judgement and Sentence, 4 September 1998, para. 28.

22. *Supra* n. 13, para. 65.

the sense of giving in to a desire for revenge but rather as being the purpose of a sentence which is both justified and restricted by the guilt of the accused.[23]

Similarly, the importance of deterrence has been pointed out in another sentencing judgment, with a special emphasis on the 'deterrence of high level officials, both military and civilian'.[24] However, in contrast to this and the other above-mentioned judgments in which deterrence was cited as one of the main purposes of sentencing, the Appeals Chamber showed a more reluctant attitude when ruling on the importance of this concept, contradicting the Trial Chamber's argument that deterrence is the most important sentencing purpose.[25] Instead, it only mentioned its 'general importance' and stated that no 'undue weight' should be given to deterrence as a sentencing factor.[26] However, the Appeals Chamber did not clarify in which situations the weight attributed to deterrence has to be considered as being 'undue', and did not support its argument that undue weight should not be given to this sentencing aim. As to the latter, one can think of two possibilities. Firstly, the Chamber could have been of the opinion that in a situation in which there is a conflict between deterrence and another sentencing purpose, e.g., just deserts, the latter should prevail. Secondly, the judges might have been of the opinion that the defendant should not be abused as a mere means to achieve criminal/political goals; it is indeed difficult to justify why a perpetrator should receive a more serious sentence just because the offence for which he is convicted was on the increase.[27]

What can be inferred from the decision of the Appeals Chamber is that the imposition of exemplary sanctions is not permitted in the jurisprudence of the *ad hoc* Tribunals: respect for the proportionality principle and the prohibition of according undue prominence to deterrence show that the approach of imposing a disproportionally severe sentence on the defendant in order to deter others has no basis in the Tribunals' sentencing decisions. Thus, the sentencing judgment in *Jelisić*, in which Trial Chamber I of the ICTY held that it 'must pronounce an

---

23. Cf., *The Prosecutor* v. *Zlatko Aleksovski*, Case No. IT-95-14/1-A, Judgement, Appeals Chamber, 24 March 2000, para. 185; see also loc. cit. n. 17, at p. 502; for a critical view on the pursuit of repressive sentencing purposes by the *ad hoc* Tribunals, see K. Ambos and S. Wirth, in A. Klip and G. Sluiter, eds., *Annotated Leading Cases of International Criminal Tribunals. The International Criminal Tribunal for Rwanda 1994-1999* (Antwerp, Intersentia 2001) p. 708. It can be argued, however, that the consistent practice of the *ad hoc* Tribunals to pursue, among others, repressive goals of sentencing has already become a rule of international customary law.

24. *The Prosecutor* v. *Žejnil Delalić et al.*, *supra* n. 21, para. 1234. It is not clear from the wording of the judgment whether or not the Chamber was of the opinion that deterrence should play a more significant role in cases against high-ranking perpetrators than in trials against low-ranking defendants.

25. *The Prosecutor* v. *Žejnil Delalić et al.*, Case No. IT-96-21-A, Judgement, Appeals Chamber, 20 February 2001, para. 803. The Appeals Chamber's reasoning has to be interpreted as an *obiter dictum*, because the ruling on the issue in question was not based on this statement. Nevertheless, it is an authoritative interpretation that can be taken into consideration in future judgments.

26. Ibid., paras. 801-803; *The Prosecutor* v. *Duško Tadić*, Case No. IT-94-1-A*bis*, Judgement in Sentencing Appeals, Appeals Chamber, 26 January 2000, para. 48.

27. For an example in English national law cf., *R.* v. *Le and Stark* (1998), *Criminal LR* (1999) p. 96.

exemplary sentence both from the viewpoint of punishment and deterrence'[28] must be interpreted in light of the Appeals Chamber's ruling.

2.2.2 *Rehabilitation of the offender*

With regard to the importance of the rehabilitation of the offender, the jurisprudence of the Tribunals does not display a uniform approach. In *Erdemović*, Trial Chamber I of the ICTY held that the nature of the jurisdictional crimes 'rule out consideration of the rehabilitative function of punishment'. However, the Chamber went on to say that it did not want to deny 'any rehabilitative and amendatory function to the punishment' with regard to the age of the defendant, his health, and his role in the criminal plan. Immediately thereafter, the Chamber stated that rehabilitation 'must be subordinate to [...] an attempt to stigmatise the most serious violations of international humanitarian law and [...] to preclude their reoccurrence'.[29] The sentence which the Chamber imposed, however, seems to contradict this argumentation: taking into consideration personal circumstances of the accused, such as his age, his family status, 'the lack of danger he presents', his corrigible personality, his desire to surrender, his showing of remorse, his timely guilty plea and his overall cooperation with the ICTY, the Judges sentenced him to ten years imprisonment.[30] After the ensuing judgment of the Appeals Chamber, the case was remitted to another Trial Chamber which reduced the sentence to five years.[31]

The sentencing purpose of rehabilitation has also been given considerable weight in two other sentencing judgments of the ICTR. In *Musema*, the judges held that 'there is cause to believe that the accused has undergone a profound change and that there are good reasons to expect his re-integration into society'.[32] Similarly, in *Serushago*, Trial Chamber I stated that the age of the accused, his cooperation with the Prosecutor and his public expression of remorse 'would suggest possible rehabilitation'.[33]

---

28. *The Prosecutor* v. *Goran Jelisić*, Case No. IT-95-10-T, Judgement, 14 December 1999, para. 116.

29. *Supra* n. 13, para. 66.

30. Ibid., para. 111.

31. *The Prosecutor* v. *Dražen Erdemović*, Case No. IT-96-22-T*bis*, Sentencing Judgement, 5 March 1998, paras. 16 et seq. Although in this judgment the issue of duress might have had a significant impact on the reduced length of the sentence, Trial Chamber II*ter* accorded considerable weight to post-crime circumstances, such as the defendant's cooperation with the authorities and his confession: this demonstrates the pursuit of rehabilitative aims of punishment.

32. *The Prosecutor* v. *Georges Ruggiu*, Case No. ICTR-97-32-I, Judgement and Sentence, 1 June 2000, para. 68. The defendant was sentenced to two sentences of 12 years imprisonment (to be served concurrently) for direct and public incitement to commit genocide and persecution as a crime against humanity.

33. *Supra* n. 21, para. 39. For a critical appraisal of this sentence cf., K. Ambos and J.C. Nemitz, in Klip and Sluiter, eds., loc. cit. n. 23, at pp. 838-840.

In other sentencing judgments, the purpose of rehabilitation was mentioned, but it was not accorded much importance.[34] The most suitable approach towards the consideration of this aim of punishment in international criminal law was adopted in *Blaškić*. In its Judgement, Trial Chamber I held that 'in a case as serious as this [...] the Trial Chamber must find that their [i.e., the personal circumstances that might be considered in a rehabilitative sense] weight is limited or even non-existent when determining the sentence'.[35] This ruling corresponds with the established practice of both the Appeals Chamber and the various Trial Chambers to consider the gravity of the offence as the most important factor in determining the sentence; to give rehabilitative considerations undue prominence in the sentencing process would violate the proportionality principle and obstruct the pursuit of other sentencing purposes.

Another argument which can be made in this respect is the fact that the Security Council's resolutions establishing the *ad hoc* Tribunals do not mention rehabilitation as an aim of punishment. Thus, without denying that rehabilitative considerations might be weighed in the sentencing process, their impact on the length of the sentence should be limited, unless the disregard for the rehabilitation of the offender is unjustified to a degree that might endanger the pursuit of another sentencing purpose, e.g., affirmative general prevention.

2.2.3 *Affirmative general prevention*

According to this theory, the purpose of a sentence is to influence the legal consciousness of the accused, the victim, the witness and the general public in order to reassure them that the legal system is implemented and enforced. Additionally, the process of sentencing aims at conveying the message that certain rules have to be obeyed, and it supports the internalisation of these rules and moral attitudes in the minds of the public.[36]

This educational function of sentencing has been repeatedly mentioned in the jurisprudence of the Tribunals. In the first sentencing judgment in *Erdemović*, Trial Chamber I held that 'reprobation (or stigmatisation) is one of the appropriate purposes of punishment'.[37] Furthermore, the need to contribute to national recon-

---

34. Cf., *The Prosecutor* v. *Clément Kayishema and Obed Ruzindana*, Case No. ICTR-95-1-T, Sentence, 21 May 1999, para. 2 (with further references); *The Prosecutor* v. *Žejnil Delalić et al., supra* n. 21, para. 1233.

35. *The Prosecutor* v. *Tihomir Blaškić*, Case No. IT-95-14, Judgement, 3 March 2000, para. 782 (referring to the Judgement in *Furundžija*, in which the judges ruled that 'this may be said of many accused and cannot be given any significant weight in a case of this gravity'. *The Prosecutor* v. *Anto Furundžija*, Case No. IT-95-17/1-T10, Judgement, 10 December 1998, para. 284).

36. 'Public reprobation and imposition of punishment is, according to this theory, a useful and necessary means to demonstrate the continued validity of the norm and to prevent imitation of the offender's conduct by others'. T. Weigend, 'Sentencing and Punishment in Germany', in M. Tonry and R.S. Frase, eds., *Sentencing and Sanctions in Western Countries* (Oxford, Oxford University Press 2001) p. 209 (with further references).

37. *Supra* n. 13, paras. 64-65; cf., also *The Prosecutor* v. *Tihomir Blaškić, supra* n. 35, para. 763 (referring to *Erdemović*).

ciliation has been given as justification for the imposition of a sentence.[38] In countries like Rwanda and Guatemala, where the murderers and the relatives of the victims have to live next to each other, the reconciliatory function of a punishment is of vital importance for the maintenance of peace.[39]

The stigmatisation of the offender's behaviour is also important to demonstrate public reprobation. Here, again, punishment is used as a means to enable the public to distinguish right from wrong. In some judgments, ending impunity has been mentioned as a sentencing purpose. In *Kupreškić*, the Trial Chamber held that 'another relevant sentencing purpose is to show the people of not only the former Yugoslavia, but of the world in general, that there is no impunity for these types of crimes. This should be done in order to *strengthen the resolve of all involved not to allow crimes against international humanitarian law* to be committed as well as *to create trust in and respect for the developing system of international justice*' (emphasis added).[40] This shows that ending impunity is pursued in order to achieve the same goal which is pursued by the concept of affirmative general prevention: to reassure the public that the legal system has been upheld and to influence the people not to violate this system.In a similar vein, Trial Chamber II*quater* ruled in *Delalić et al.*, that 'punishment of high-ranking political officials and military officers will demonstrate that such officers cannot flout the designs and injunctions of the international community with impunity'. The judges went on to state that the imposed sentences of imprisonment are 'a useful means to return the area to peace'.[41] This ruling demonstrates that the Chamber, by adjudicating on high-ranking offenders, wanted to create or reaffirm the general public's trust in the not so well-known body of international criminal law, thus contributing to international and national peace and reconciliation.

Likewise, Trial Chamber I of the ICTR explicitly referred to the similarities of the concepts of national reconciliation and restoration of peace. In doing so, the Chamber had recourse to the wording of the Rwandan Organic Law No. 8/96,[42] according to which the culture of impunity has to be eradicated in order to achieve reconciliation within the country.[43]

---

38. Cf., *The Prosecutor* v. *George Rutaganda*, Case No. ICTR-96-3-T, Judgement and Sentence, 6 December 1999, para. 455; *The Prosecutor* v. *Clément Kayishema and Obed Ruzindana*, *supra* n. 34, para. 1.

39. For a critical view on the ability of the punitive criminal justice model to contribute to the process of national reconciliation by punishing a limited number of perpetrators cf., M. A. Drumbl, 'Sclerosis. Retributive Justice and the Rwandan Genocide', 2 *Punishment and Society* (2000) pp. 292 et seq.

40. *The Prosecutor* v. *Zoran Kupreškić et al.*, Case No. IT-95-16, Judgement, 14 January 2000, para. 848.

41. *Supra* n. 21, para. 1234.

42. Rwandan Organic Law on the Organisation of Prosecutions for Offences constituting the Crime of Genocide or Crimes against Humanity, committed since 1 October 1990, adopted on 30 August 1996, published in the Gazette of the Republic of Rwanda, 35th year, No. 17, 1 September 1996.

43. *The Prosecutor* v. *Jean Kambanda*, *supra* n. 21, para. 27; the Chamber went on to state that the sentences have to be directed at retribution 'and over and above that [...] at deterrence'. Ibid., para. 28.

These examples from the jurisprudence of the Tribunals show that the concept of affirmative general prevention has been accorded increased significance since the trials of Nuremberg and Tokyo, both as an aim and as a justification of punishment. Additionally, the preamble of the ICC Statute indicates that the sentencing rationales of this Court will be more than retribution and deterrence: Paragraph 11 explicitly mentions the resolve of the States Parties 'to guarantee lasting respect for and the enforcement of international justice'. For the first time in the short history of international criminal tribunals, the sentencing purpose of affirmative general prevention has been written into the statute of such a court, and it is submitted that this purpose should be the most important one in the sentencing process of the ICC.[44] This is so partly because of the shortcomings of the other sentencing purposes and partly because of the 'advantages' of this aim of punishment.

2.3 The shortcomings of the concepts of just deserts, deterrence and resocialisation

The concept of retribution, even in the 'modern' sense of just deserts rather than revenge, is not suitable to be the prevailing aim of punishment in international criminal law. Although it is difficult to deny that every imposition of a sentence entails a retributive element in the sense that a negative action – the commission of the crime – is countered by an action that is perceived as negative by the accused – fine, imprisonment, this reasoning should not play the dominant role in the international criminal justice system. Firstly, utilitarian theories based on the concept of crime prevention have gained importance in the last decades; secondly, the heinous nature of the international crimes falling under the jurisdiction of the *ad hoc* Tribunals and the ICC makes it impossible to state that the perpetrator of various crimes against humanity deserves a sentence of so and so many years imprisonment.[45] On the other hand, one has to acknowledge that the sentencing purpose of just deserts plays a significant role in the domestic penal systems of many states, and this must also be taken into consideration in international criminal law.

The sentencing purpose of deterrence also has some shortcomings. One of these is the fact that sentences cannot have a deterrent effect unless the offender makes a rational decision before committing the crime. In armed conflicts, however, many perpetrators act in the heat of a combat situation. Others make a rational decision to commit a crime because they think they are on the right side and justified, if not obliged, to do so. If one reads the statements of members of Serbian paramilitary forces who have committed crimes against Kosovar Albanian civilians but who

---

44. Cf., also Ambos and Steiner, loc. cit. n. 4, p. 13 (with further references in fn. 66); the importance of this sentencing purpose in international criminal law is also highlighted in R. Lahti, 'Towards a Rational and Humane Criminal Policy – Trends in Scandinavian Penal Thinking', 1 *Journal of Scandinavian Studies in Criminology and Crime Prevention* (2000) p. 150.

45. Cf., H. Arendt, quoted in M. J. Osiel, 'Why prosecute? Critics of Punishment for Mass Atrocity', 22 *Human Rights Quaterly* (2000) pp. 128 et seq.

consider themselves to be innocent, since they 'only did what they had to do',[46] the concept of deterrence as a sentencing purpose seems doubtful. Another problematic aspect of the deterrence theory is the fact that this purpose can only be achieved if there is a significant chance of the perpetrator being apprehended. To date, such a tight system of international criminal prosecution does not exist. Therefore, deterrence should not play a significant role in the sentencing process until the risk of being prosecuted for international crimes is considerably higher than it is today. However, one exception has to be made. If the current development continues, it can be argued that the risk of being prosecuted is greater for high-level perpetrators than for those lower down the hierarchy.[47] Therefore, the imposition of a sentence against the former perpetrators might have a stronger deterrent effect on those in similarly high positions – who may wish to enjoy medical treatment in Switzerland one day instead of concluding their lives in a prison cell abroad – than on ordinary soldiers.

The concept of reconciliation also has shortcomings. Although there might be situations where there is a need to resocialise the offender, provided that he has a 'corrigible personality',[48] most of the perpetrators who have already appeared before the *ad hoc* Tribunals and who will appear before the ICC will not require resocialisation programmes. In general, international criminal courts have to limit themselves to the prosecution of more or less top level politicians and military commanders. These people are usually socialised in a sense that they could go on living in their community once the situation in which the crimes were committed has been brought to an end. To grant these defendants the benefit of their social background would be inappropriate considering the gravity of the crimes. If these defendants cooperate with the prosecutor, enter a guilty plea or publicly express remorse, this should, as a general rule, be considered in mitigation of the punishment. In these cases, the reason for mitigation is not the fact that such behaviour displays a corrigible personality; instead, the mitigating effect is justified by the fact that the public's trust in the legal system could be damaged if those circumstances would not have any impact on the length of the sentence. Thus, it is the sentencing purpose of affirmative general prevention that is pursued when granting mitigation in the above-mentioned circumstances.

Having examined the shortcomings of the sentencing purposes of just deserts, deterrence and resocialisation, more can be said about why the concept of affirmative positive prevention should play the dominant role among the different sentencing purposes underlying the sentencing process in international criminal law.

---

46. Cf., B. Schirra, 'Die Gräuel der Frenkie Boys', *Die Zeit* (49/1999).

47. The fate of Mr Pinochet and Mr Milošević, to name only two, illustrates this development (for a critical appraisal of the Pinochet case, see S. Wirth, 'Staatenimmunität für internationale Verbrechen – das zweite *Pinochet*-Urteil des *House of Lords*', 22 *Juristische Ausbildung* (2000) pp. 70 et seq.).

48. *Supra* n. 13, para. 111.

2.4 Advantages of the concept of affirmative general prevention

The jurisdictional crimes of the *ad hoc* Tribunals and the ICC differ to a large extent from the common crimes that national courts are primarily concerned with. In most cases, states or similar organisations will have enabled, facilitated or tolerated the commission of crimes, thus making previously deviant behaviour accepted by at least part of the public. Additionally, even in recent times, many people tend to believe that in situations of public turmoil or armed conflict, ordinarily criminal acts are permitted, if not necessary.[49] Together with educational programmes and political efforts, it is the task of a sentencing process to reinforce that there are human rights that no one can dispose of, even in times of war. The public must see that international crimes are punished in order to internalise the sanctity of these rights and values. It is therefore submitted that affirmative general prevention should be the most important aim of punishment in international criminal law.

Criminal justice systems the world over, through their constitutional, criminal, and criminal procedural laws, try to ensure that the sentences they render are perceived by the public as being necessary and just. Thus, they wish to convey the message that there are binding rules the violation of which will cause serious consequences for the perpetrator. In the long run, this will lead to an internalisation of values by the public, who learns to differentiate between 'right or wrong'.

At the national level, this process of internalisation has been largely achieved. At the international level, however, the situation is different.[50] Although the concept of international humanitarian law has been known at the latest since the First Geneva Convention of 1864 and the Hague Convention respecting the Laws and Customs of War on Land of 1907, little has been done since those days to establish and promote respect for and adherence to this area of law. National or international prosecutions of massive human rights violations are still the exception that proves the rule. However, to have a law without applying it is worse

---

49. In an interview with *Le Monde*, the French General Marcel Bigeard stated that the torture inflicted by French troops on Algerians during the Algerian war was 'a necessary evil'. Quoted in J. Hénard, 'Erinnerung ohne Reue', *Die Zeit* (50/2000) p. 21. Similarly, Robert Elliott, a judge of the civil district court of Columbus, Ohio, who, in the late stages, was involved in the trial against Lt. William Calley, held: 'Keep in mind that war is war and it is not at all unusual for innocent civilians to be numbered among its victims [...] It was so when Joshua took Jericho in ancient Biblical times [...] Now Joshua did not have charges brought against him for the slaughter of the civilian population of Jericho. But then "the Lord was with Joshua" we are told'. Quoted in M. Bilton and K. Sim, *Four Hours in My Lai* (New York, Penguin Group 1992) p. 356. Telford Taylor highlighted this problem by saying: 'The trouble is no one sees the Vietnamese as people. They're not people. Therefore it doesn't matter what you do to them'. Quoted in G.D. Solis, *Son Thang. An American War Crime* (New York, Bantam Books 1997) p. 115.

50. 'Wer im Kriege erlebt hat, mit welcher Leichtfertigkeit sich auf beiden Seiten hohe Kommandobehörden über das Völkerrecht hinwegsetzten, weil sie es für eine Angelegenheit von untergeordneter Bedeutung hielten, wird zugeben müssen, daß der erzieherischen Wirkung der Strafe im Kriegsvölkerrecht ebenso große, wenn nicht noch größere Bedeutung zukommt als im staatlichen Strafrecht', H.-H. Jescheck, *Die Verantwortlichkeit der Staatsorgane nach Völkerstrafrecht* (Bonn, Röhrscheid Verlag 1952) p. 196.

than not having a law at all: if the authorities turn a blind eye to violations, ordinary soldiers and their commanders will not feel obliged to respect what are perceived as merely paper rules. As Bilton and Sim put it with regard to the rules of engagement given to every US soldier in Vietnam: 'There was nothing wrong with these regulations; [...] they simply never became part of the soldiers' reality because they were never seriously enforced, and without emphatic enforcement they corresponded as much to the world of the "common grunt" as road maps of Mars.'[51]

Therefore, the developing system of international criminal justice in general, and every sentencing process in particular, have to spread the idea that violations of fundamental human rights are always prohibited, no matter how 'just' the cause may be for which these crimes were committed. Thus, those who already behave according to the law will be encouraged to defend the legal order because they see this order being enforced. Those who have not yet internalised these rules will, hopefully, change their attitude when learning of the trial procedure and the sentence.[52]

It could be argued, however, that the concept of affirmative general prevention does not provide clear guidance when determining a sentence: it is rather difficult to determine what length of sentence will reassure the public that justice has been done. But this apparent shortcoming reveals yet another advantage of this sentencing purpose. As with the concept of just deserts, the purpose of affirmative general prevention cannot be separated from the proportionality principle. It is fair to assume that the punishment which is proportionate to the crime – i.e., reflecting the harm caused by the offence(s) and the culpability of the offender –is most suitable to convince the perpetrator, the victim and the general public that the criminal justice system has been upheld and enforced in a just way. Additionally, it is fair to say that the goal of affirmative general prevention can only be achieved if a punishment has been imposed on the perpetrator, i.e., if moral blame has been expressed in the sentence. Thus, the pursuit of affirmative general prevention can be combined with the notion of just deserts providing for the possibility to pursue both repressive and preventive goals of sentencing.[53]

The prominent role of the theory of affirmative general prevention also illustrates the punitive approach's need to deal with the phenomenon of *Makrokriminalität*.[54] In this context, it is primarily the prosecution of high-ranking perpetrators that is important to achieve an educational effect. In this respect, a Trial Chamber of the ICTY held that 'one of the missions of the International

51. Bilton and Sim, op. cit. n. 49, at p. 376.

52. Expectations in this context, however, should not be unduly optimistic. According to a general public survey (GPS) conducted in England and Wales in October 2000, 60 percent of those polled thought that sentencing has little impact on crime levels and only 31 percent thought that it has quite a lot or a great deal of impact; cf., 'The Halliday Report (Making Punishments Work: Review of the Sentencing Framework for England and Wales)', July 2001, p. 109.

53. Similarly A.M. Danner, 'Constructing a Hierarchy of Crimes in International Criminal Law Sentencing', 87 *Virginia LR* (2001) p. 489.

54. For an analysis of this concept see H. Jäger, *Makrokriminalität. Studien zur Kriminologie kollektiver Gewalt* (Frankfurt a.M., Suhrkamp 1989).

Criminal Tribunal is to contribute to the restoration of peace in the former Yugoslavia. To do so, it has to identify, prosecute and punish *the principal political and military officials* responsible for the atrocities committed since 1991 in the territories concerned' (emphasis added).[55] This does not mean that international criminal tribunals should not prosecute offenders of lower ranks if they can be apprehended: it might even be a prosecutorial strategy to start with the ordinary private in order to later hold the highers-up accountable for these crimes; however, in situations like the one in Rwanda, with about 125,000 people imprisoned and awaiting trial, the punitive approach faces severe practical difficulties that might favour a more restorative model with regard to low-ranking perpetrators.[56]

Finally, the effectiveness of affirmative general prevention as a sentencing purpose demands that international criminal courts must be perceived as being independent, impartial, neutral, unbiased and non-political. Otherwise, their rulings and sentences will not be accepted as being just by the defendant, the victims, the witnesses and the general public.

3. SENTENCING AT THE INTERNATIONAL LEVEL VS. SENTENCING AT THE NATIONAL LEVEL

When discussing various sentencing purposes in international criminal law, one has to take into consideration that the way in which the various aims of punishment are pursued in national criminal jurisdictions might differ. Therefore, the relationship between the sentencing procedures at the international and national levels deserves some attention.

Contrary to many national systems, the statutes of the existing international criminal courts do not allow the imposition of the death penalty; on the other hand, they provide for a term of life imprisonment which does not exist in the penal systems of a number of states.[57] A further, and perhaps more important, distinction is that the international community, starting with the International Military Tribunals and continuing with the *ad hoc* Tribunals, the ICC and the newly constituted 'special' *sui generis* courts established to prosecute international crimes in Sierra Leone and East Timor, has taken a punitive approach to addressing *Makrokriminalität*. National legal systems, however, have responded in differing ways to this type of criminality, e.g., with amnesties, truth commissions and restorative justice initiatives like the *gacaca* courts in Rwanda.[58] These different ways in responding to mass delinquency not only can lead to disparities in the sentencing process of the various international courts but also to disparities in the jurispru-

55. *Supra* n. 28, para. 133.
56. Cf., Drumbl, op. cit. n. 39, at pp. 300 et seq.
57. E.g., Colombia, El Salvador, Nicaragua, Norway and Venezuela.
58. However, *Gacaca* trials will not deal with the masterminds of the Rwandan genocide but only with offenders from the other three categories of guilt established by the government in the Rwandan Organic Law, *supra* n. 42.

dence at the international and national levels.

With regard to the often immense number of perpetrators of international crimes, a more or less clear distinction between the international and the national plane has to be accepted, and the principle of complementarity in the ICC Statute is a result of this thinking. The Statute's references to national laws of sentencing are few but important: according to Article 80 of the ICC Statute, the States Parties are free to apply the penalties prescribed in their own national laws. This means, *inter alia*, that domestic courts are not bound by the Statute to impose sentences of life imprisonment and they are free to sentence a defendant to death.[59] This compromise formula was necessary in order to achieve consensus during the negotiations in Rome, and it was accepted at the expense of a more coherent sentencing practice. Thus, the unfortunate example of Rwanda, where high-ranking perpetrators receive custodial sentences from the ICTR while low-ranking offenders can be sentenced to death before national courts, might be repeated in the relationship between the ICC and the domestic courts of states applying capital punishment.

To some degree, this situation is unsatisfactory because it runs the risk of creating double standards in sentencing. Bearing in mind that international courts and their decisions have to be accepted by the global public in order to be able to achieve the sentencing purpose of affirmative general prevention, different sentencing standards might hamper the pursuit of this aim: in states with very poor prison conditions, international criminal courts can lose support when people learn that the detainees have a TV set in their cells and their own toilet. The ICC and all the other international criminal courts, however, have the opportunity to 'lead by example'. Therefore, the courts must devote much diligence to their sentencing judgments in order to convince the persons directly concerned and the general public that just decisions have been made and that just punishments have been imposed. In doing so, they have the chance to provide guidance that might be followed by national jurisdictions.

It is, however, important that the different international criminal courts do not differ in substance on issues of sentencing. Although the principle of *stare decisis* is not applicable in the jurisprudence of these courts, and although there is no legal obligation to have recourse to each others' decisions, international criminal courts should strive for a consistent approach to sentencing in order to contribute to a coherent law of sentencing. Significant disparities in the sentencing tariffs of these courts could undermine their acceptance by the public, thus sending contradictory signals to national jurisdictions, which will surely look to the international jurisprudence for guidance in their domestic trials.

---

59. For an extensive survey of the difficult negotiation process that ultimately led to the wording of this article, cf., W.A. Schabas, 'Life, Death and the Crime of Crimes', 2 *Punishment and Society* (2000) pp. 263 et seq.

4. THE DETERMINATION OF THE APPLICABLE LAW OF SENTENCING

Before discussing the sentencing method applicable in international criminal law, it is necessary to first examine the legal grounds upon which this sentencing law is based.

Confronted with a similar question in *Erdemović*, the Appeals Chamber had to determine whether or not a rule exists under international law with regard to duress as a defence to the killing of civilians. Since the Statute did not explicitly mention this issue, the Judges were obliged to explore whether a rule of international customary law or a general principle of law would apply. Following this approach, they acknowledged the traditional sources of international law as embodied in Article 38 of the ICJ Statute.[60] This means, that their Statutes are always the starting point for the determination of the applicable law of the *ad hoc* Tribunals, followed by international treaty law. With respect to a number of sentencing questions, however, the Statutes do not provide any guidance. Thus, one could argue that the drafters of the Statutes deliberately wanted to leave *lacunae* which should be filled by judicial interpretations of the Statutes, having recourse to the principles of interpretation as embedded in Article 31(1) of the 1969 Vienna Convention of the Law of Treaties.[61] With regard to sentencing purposes, however, an interpretation of the statutory provisions and rules is not enough in order to find out whether or not a primary rationale of sentencing exists in international criminal law. Therefore, it is far from clear that the drafters of these provisions wanted the judges to answer every sentencing issue by having recourse to the Statutes and the Rules. Instead, the judges, the defence counsels and the prosecutors should base their findings on the other sources of international law if the statutory provisions and their interpretation are not sufficient.[62]

---

60. Cf., *The Prosecutor* v. *Dražen Erdemović*, Case No. IT-96-22-A, Joint Separate Opinion of Judge McDonald and Judge Vohrah, 7 October 1997, para. 40; Separate and Dissenting Opinion of Judge Li paras. 2 et seq.; Separate and Dissenting Opinion of Judge Cassese, para. 11; Separate and Dissenting Opinion of Judge Stephen, paras. 24 et seq.; Art. 21 of the ICC Statute adopts a similar approach.

61. Although the 1969 Vienna Convention of the Law of Treaties is not directly applicable for an interpretation of the Statutes, which are annexes to Security Council Resolutions 827 and 955, the principles of interpretation embedded in these provisions reflect general principles of legal interpretation.

62. The Appeals Chamber has taken a somewhat different approach in *Aleksovski*: after an examination of the applicability of the *stare decisis* principle in some national legislation, the Chamber held: 'References to the law and practice in various countries and in international institutions are not necessarily determinative of the question as to the applicable law in this matter. Ultimately, that question must be answered by an examination of the Tribunal's Statute and Rules, and a construction of them which gives due weight to the principles of interpretation (good faith, textuality, contextuality, and teleology) set out in the 1969 Vienna Convention on the Law of Treaties', *The Prosecutor* v. *Zlatko Aleksovski*, *supra* n. 23, para. 98. The approach taken by Judges Cassese and Stephen in *Erdemović*, *supra* n. 60, however, contradicts this ruling. Since the question of duress as a defence to murder was not addressed in the Statute, the judges searched for and found an answer to this question in international customary law (Separate and Dissenting Opinion of Judge Cassese, para. 44) or in the general principles of law (Separate and Dissenting Opinion of Judge Stephen, para. 66). Judges McDonald and

Similarly, so far a rule of international customary law has not been established with regard to various other sentencing issues. In order to determine whether or not such a customary rule has evolved, one has to have recourse to the practice of states and intergovernmental organisations[63] and ask whether this practice was adopted because the actors were of the opinion that they were following the applicable law.[64]

The role of international criminal tribunals in the law-making process is of special importance in this context. The question is whether the decisions of these tribunals can contribute to the development of customary international law or whether they can only be referred to as 'subsidiary means for the determination of rules of law'.[65] To make a distinction between these two categories is a difficult task,[66] which becomes even more complicated by additionally taking into consideration the general principles of law recognised by legal systems of the world.[67] Where to draw the line? Do, for example, the decisions of the military tribunals in Nürnberg and Tokyo and of the other post-World War II courts constitute customary international law, general principles of law, or are they merely subsidiary agencies? And what about the jurisprudence of the ICTY and the ICTR? What role do they play in the development of international law?

As to the former, the role of the IMT and the IMTFE shall not be discussed in this context since the contribution of their judgments to the exploration of sentencing issues is rather limited.

With regard to the *ad hoc* Tribunals, however, the situation is different: their sentencing decisions have already ruled on important issues; thus, it is necessary to find out whether these decisions contribute to the body of international customary law or whether they can only be referred to as subsidiary means for the determination of rules of law according to Article 38(1)(d) of the ICJ Statute. Three possible answers can be offered: firstly, one can argue that the ICTR and the ICTY, established under Chapter VII of the UN Charter as subsidiary organs of the Security Council,[68] are accorded – at least partial – international legal personality. This is

Vohrah adopted the same approach but ultimately relied on an interpretation of the goals and aims of the Tribunal, thus leaning more towards the ruling in *Aleksovski* (Joint Separate Opinion of Judge McDonald and Judge Vohrah, para. 75).

63. Cf., B. Simma, 'Das Völkergewohnheitsrecht', in H.P. Neuhold, W. Hummer and Chr. Schreuer, eds., *Österreichisches Handbuch des Völkerrechts*, Vol. 1, 3rd edn. (Vienna, Manz 1997) p. 197.

64. V.D. Degan, *Sources of International Law* (The Hague, Nijhoff Publishers 1997) pp. 142 et seq.; M. Virally, 'The Sources of International Law', in M. Sørensen, ed., *Manual of Public International Law* (London, Macmillan 1968) p. 139.

65. Art. 38(1)(d) ICJ Statute.

66. As Sir Lauterpacht stated, 'the distinction between the evidence and the source of many a rule of law is more speculative and less rigid than is commonly supposed. [...] The imperceptible process in which the judicial decision ceases to be an application of existing law and becomes a source of law for the future is almost a religious mystery into which it is unseemly to pry'. Sir H. Lauterpacht, *The Development of International Law by the International Court* (London, Stevens 1958) p. 21.

67. Cf., Art. 38(1)(c) ICJ Statute; Art. 21(1)(c) ICC Statute.

68. Cf., Arts. 7(2), 29 UN Charter.

reflected in the fact that they can conclude international agreements in certain areas of law.[69] Therefore, it is submitted that their decisions can contribute to the development of international customary law.[70] The same reasoning can be applied to the decisions of the ICC once it has commenced its work. According to Article 1 of the ICC Statute, the Court will be a permanent institution; it will conclude a relationship agreement with the United Nations,[71] and there will be several organs:[72] in sum, the ICC will fulfill the necessary requirements of an international organisation. Thus, its decisions will be important sources for the development of international customary law.

Secondly, the decisions of the *ad hoc* Tribunals could be seen as law-determining agencies according to Article 38(1)(d) of the ICJ Statute. This would lead to a somewhat unwanted result: while the judgments of *national* courts undoubtedly contribute to the customary law-making process,[73] the decisions of *international* courts would be seen as being of lesser importance. Therefore, a third view is gaining support. It posits that the decisions of international courts have an impact which goes beyond what is stated in Article 38(1)(d) of the ICJ Statute, and their jurisprudence carries more weight than the jurisprudence of national courts.[74] This assumption is mainly based on rulings of these very same international courts, a fact which only at first sight weakens the reasoning. In his Separate and Dissenting Opinion in *Erdemović*, Judge Cassese held that decisions issued by those post-World War II tribunals which had been established under Control Council Law No. 10 carry more legal authority than decisions of courts established under and applying national law.[75] In a similar vein, Judges McDonald and Vohrah stressed the difference between international and national criminal courts, implicitly agreeing with the Prosecution's view that the jurisprudence of the former 'must be given considerably more weight than any national decision' in the process of

69. Cf., the Agreement on Security and Order which was concluded on 14 July 1994 between the ICTY and the Ministry of Justice of the Netherlands, printed in *Basic Documents* of the ICTY, 1998. In the words of Jaenicke: 'The legal capacity of subsidiary organs with external or operational functions to act on the international or national plane follows from their status as organs of the UN [and] the internationally recognized legal personality of the UN [...]'; G. Jaenicke, in B. Simma, ed., *The Charter of the United Nations* (Oxford University Press 1995) Art. 7 mn 26; see also with respect to international courts in general R. Bernhardt, 'Customary International Law', in R. Bernhardt, ed., *Encyclopedia of Public International Law*, Vol. 1 (Amsterdam, Elsevier 1992) p. 900.

70. Cf., generally D.P. O'Connell, *International Law*, Vol. 1, 2nd. edn. (London, Stevens 1970) p. 32; Bernhardt, ibid.; J.-G. Castel, *International Law chiefly as interpreted and applied in Canada* (Toronto, University of Toronto Press 1965) p. 16; W. Wengler, *Völkerrecht*, Vol. 1 (Berlin, Springer 1964) p. 175; for a critical view cf., K. Doehring, *Völkerrecht* (Heidelberg, C.F. Müller 1999) pp. 131 et seq.

71. Cf., Art. 2 of the ICC Statute.

72. Cf., Art. 34 of the ICC Statute.

73. Cf., A. Verdross and B. Simma, *Universelles Völkerrecht: Theorie und Praxis* (Berlin, Duncker & Humblot 1984) 3rd edn., para. 555 (referring to the ICJ's *Lotus* case).

74. Cf., C. Kreß, 'Zur Methode der Rechtsfindung im Allgemeinen Teil des Völkerstrafrechts', 111 *Zeitschrift für die gesamte Strafrechtswissenschaft* (1999) p. 603 (with further references).

75. *The Prosecutor* v. *Dražen Erdemović*, *supra* n. 60, Separate and Dissenting Opinion of Judge Cassese, paras. 21, 26, 28.

developing international customary law as long as they were established under and applied international law.[76] Additionally, in *Krstić*, Trial Chamber I of the ICTY stated that it 'considered the international case-law on the crime of genocide, in particular, that developed by the ICTR' when interpreting Article 4 of the ICTY Statute; it is only at the end of the paragraph, after having referred to the work of international committees and the relevant discussions of the process establishing the ICC, that the 'Trial Chamber also looked for guidance in the legislation and practice of States, especially their judicial interpretations and decisions'.[77] Thus, this ruling also seems to indicate that the judges gave more authority to decisions of international tribunals than to those of national courts.[78] It can be expected that the higher authority of international courts' decisions will become increasingly evident with the establishment of the ICC: while Article 21 of the ICC Statute does not explicitly mention the term international customary law, it is likely that the chambers will prioritise the jurisprudence of international criminal tribunals when determining 'the principles and rules of international law'.

The growing significance of the jurisprudence of international criminal courts can also be exemplified by reference to Section 10 of UNTAET Regulation No. 2000/15.[79] This section encompasses the law on sentencing applicable for the panels of judges within the District Court of Dili which has been established in East Timor by the Transitional Administration in order to prosecute serious criminal offences, including genocide, crimes against humanity and war crimes. According to Section 10, 'the panel shall have recourse to the general practice regarding prison sentences in the courts of East Timor *and under international tribunals*' (emphasis added).

The enhanced importance of the jurisprudence of international criminal courts can be justified by their status, by their expertise and by their independence: the *ad hoc* Tribunals have been established on the basis of the UN Charter. This means that the legitimacy of the Tribunals is founded in the assent of the vast majority of the world's states that have granted the Security Council the necessary powers to restore and maintain international peace and security. As to expertise, the Tribunals are today the only institutions that are exclusively preoccupied with adjudication in matters of international criminal law. This specialisation and the fact that the international judges represent different criminal justice systems contribute to the legal significance of their judgments and confer a greater authority on them than on judgments rendered by national courts. Furthermore, the fact that, as in the case of the *ad hoc* Tribunals, none of the judges come from countries that were directly

---

76. Ibid., Joint Separate Opinion of Judges McDonald and JudgeVohrah, paras. 53 et seq. Additionally, the judges referred to a national case that was 'quashed by the superior court in the French zone for contravening Control Council Law No. 10 *and thus is of doubtful authority*' (emphasis added), ibid., para. 48.

77. *The Prosecutor* v. *Radislav Krstić*, Case No. IT-98-33-T, Judgement, 2 August 2001, para. 541.

78. Cf., Kreß, loc. cit. n. 74, p. 603.

79. United Nations Transitional Administration in East Timor Regulation No. 2000/15 on the Establishment of Panels with Exclusive Jurisdiction over Serious Criminal Offences, 6 June 2000.

involved in the respective armed conflicts increases the authority of their jurisprudence.[80] The same will apply, *mutatis mutantibus*, to the jurisprudence of the ICC.

For these reasons, it is submitted that the judgments of the Tribunals and the ICC should have a greater impact on the development of international customary law than decisions of national courts.

5. THE METHOD OF SENTENCING

The Statutes of the *ad hoc* Tribunals offer little guidance regarding how the pursuit of the various aims of punishment identified can be transformed into specific sentencing tariffs. The Trial Chambers are obliged to take into account such factors as the gravity of the offence and the individual circumstances of the convicted person.[81] Rule 101 of the Rules of Procedure and Evidence of the ICTY and the ICTR offers some more assistance, stating that the chambers should take into account any aggravating and mitigating circumstances – including substantial cooperation with the Prosecutor by the convicted person – as well as the general practice regarding prison sentences in the courts of the former Yugoslavia and Rwanda, respectively.[82] This general practice provision is also included in the Statutes of both Tribunals[83] but it has no significant impact on their sentencing process. It has been stated in various judgments that this provision does not bind a Trial Chamber to follow the general practice of the courts of the former Yugoslavia, as 'it only obliges the Trial Chambers to take account of that practice'.[84]

Rule 145 of the ICC's Rules of Procedure and Evidence is more comprehensive in this respect. For the first time in the comparatively short history of international criminal instruments, the principle of culpability is explicitly mentioned in this Rule. Additionally, the Rule's wording provides a 'mixed' approach to the issue of mitigating and aggravating circumstances. Whereas Paragraph 1(c) mentions a number of 'neutral' circumstances that can be used both in favour and to the detriment of the accused, e.g., the degree of participation of the convicted person in the crime or his education, Paragraph 2 lists two specific mitigating and five aggravating circumstances.[85]

80. The post-World War I trials in Germany, with their unduly lenient verdicts, demonstrated the risk that is attached to national trials in the perpetrators' own state.

81. Art. 24(2) ICTY Statute; Art. 23(2) ICTR Statute.

82. The Appeals Chamber has already ruled that this provision does not comprise the general practice regarding prison sentences of the courts in the different *entities* that emerged from the dissolution of the former Yugoslavia, because these courts are not '"courts of the former Yugoslavia" within the meaning of Article 24 (1) of the Statute'; *The Prosecutor* v. *Goran Jelisić*, Case No. IT-95-10-A, Judgement, 5 July 2001, paras. 114 et seq.

83. Art. 24(1) ICTY Statute; Art. 2 (1) ICTY Statute.

84. *Supra* n. 25, para. 813 (with further references) However, if this general practice diverges from the sentencing practice of an *ad hoc* Tribunal, the practice of the Tribunals should be thoroughly explained (for the ICTY: *The Prosecutor* v. *Dragoljub Kunarać, Radomir Kovać and Zoran Vuković*, Case No. IT-96-23-T & IT-96-23/1-T, Judgement, 22 February 2001, para. 829).

85. Other aggravating circumstances than the ones mentioned in para. 2(b) may also be taken into consideration, cf., para. 2(b)(vi).

However, like the Statutes and Rules of the Tribunals, the provisions of the ICC are rather silent on the issue of how to actually mete out the sentence. In what way do the various circumstances have to be weighed against each other? What is the relationship between circumstances directly influencing the commission of the criminal act and those circumstances that occurred before or after the act? Is it, for instance, possible to accord a guilty plea the same mitigating significance as the diminished mental capacity of the accused during the commission of the crime? Is it possible to consider an aggravating circumstance to the detriment of the accused if this circumstance is a necessary statutory prerequisite of the crime?[86] What impact do sentencing purposes have on the determination of the sentence? Is it possible to consider the absence of a mitigating circumstance in aggravation of the sentence?

6. METING OUT THE SENTENCE: THE IMPORTANCE OF THE GRAVITY OF THE OFFENCE

Whereas the jurisprudence of the post-World War II tribunals did not provide much guidance for the process of meting out sentences in international criminal law, the chambers of the *ad hoc* Tribunals have already decided on a number of important sentencing issues. In doing so, the judges have tried – but not yet entirely succeeded (cf., 6.1.2 and 6.2.2.) – to establish a consistent sentencing practice, thus contributing to an international sentencing law which will certainly be further developed by the ICC.

One of the most important issues the chambers had – and still have – to deal with is the concept of the gravity of the offence. Thus, the determination of the content of this concept deserves a closer look.

As argued in Part 1 of this Article, the notions of just deserts and affirmative general prevention are among the most important sentencing purposes in international criminal law. Both require a sentencing process which is based on the principle of proportionality, i.e., the sentence must be – as much as possible – proportionate to the gravity of the crimes in order to avoid 'excessive disparities in sentences imposed for the same type of conduct'.[87] Thus, the determination of the seriousness of the offence committed by the perpetrator is one of the crucial tasks of an international judge. In the words of the Appeals Chamber, it is

86. This problem could arise if a superior is accused of intentionally launching an attack in the knowledge that such attack will cause incidental loss of life or injury to civilians or damage to civilian objects or widespread, long-term and severe damage to the natural environment which would be clearly excessive in relation to the concrete and direct overall military advantage anticipated (Art. 8(2)[b][iv] ICC Statute). The question is whether the fact that the accused was acting in the capacity of a superior can be considered as an aggravating circumstance in the sentencing process, although such an order can only be issued by a superior, in other words: would it be inappropriate to consider the same circumstance twice?

87. *Supra* n. 77, para. 698 (with reference to *supra* n. 25, paras. 756-758).

'by far the most important consideration, which may be regarded as the litmus test for the appropriate sentence'.[88]

The Statutes of the *ad hoc* Tribunals and the Rules of Procedure and Evidence do not elaborate on how the gravity of the offence shall be determined, nor do they say which aggravating or mitigating circumstances impact on offence seriousness and which do not. The answer to this question is not only of dogmatic interest: chambers of both Tribunals have already decided that 'the application of mitigating circumstances must not in any way diminish the gravity of the offence'.[89] Since the gravity of the offence is the most important factor when determining the sentence, it is important to clarify whether or not, for example, the guilty plea of the accused can be considered within the offence seriousness or not.[90]

As the Tribunals have not yet exhaustingly ruled on the content of the notion of the gravity of the crime, it is submitted that this question should be answered by referring to national jurisdictions in order to discover whether or not a general principle of law exists. This means that several jurisdictions representing major legal systems of the world should be examined, a task that cannot be comprehensively undertaken here. Instead, some references shall be made to English, Swedish and German law, as national criminal jurisdictions with a common law legacy and those stemming from the civil law tradition apply a similar interpretation of the concept of the gravity of the crime.

According to English law, the gravity of an offence consists of the harmfulness of the conduct or the danger arising out of the conduct and the culpability of the offender; whereas, for example, a large number of victims falls under the harmfulness category, the premeditated commission of a crime affects the culpability of the perpetrator. Factors like a guilty plea or cooperation with the prosecutor, however, can only be admitted outside the seriousness of the offence.[91]

The Swedish criminal law takes a similar approach, although under a different label. Instead of the gravity of the offence (or offence seriousness), Chapter 29 § 1(1) of the Swedish Criminal Code (*brottsbalken*, BrB) speaks of the penal value of the crime (or crimes) according to which the punishment should be meted out: this penal value mainly depends on the degree of harmfulness (or risk of

---

88. *The Prosecutor* v. *Žejnil Delalić et al.*, *supra* n. 21, para. 1225; this ruling has been endorsed by *The Prosecutor* v. *Žejnil Delalić et al.*, *supra* n. 25, para. 731 ('the gravity of the offence is the primary consideration in imposing sentence').

89. *The Prosecutor* v. *Stevan Todorović*, Case No. IT-95-9/1-S, Sentencing Judgement, 31 July 2001, para. 114; *The Prosecutor* v. *Georges Ruggiu*, *supra* n. 32, para. 80; *The Prosecutor* v. *Jean Kambanda*, *supra* n. 21, para. 37.

90. According to the German *Bundesgerichtshof* (BGH), circumstances posterior to the commission of the crimes can influence the guilt of the perpetrator as expressed in the gravity of the crime, provided that the circumstance admits of the conclusion that the perpetrator's guilt at the time of the commission of the crimes was higher or lower (so called *doppelspurige Indizkonstruktion*); cf., H.-J. Bruns, *Strafzumessungsrecht. Gesamtdarstellung* (Köln, Carl Heymanns Verlag 1974) 2nd edn., pp. 592 et seq.; BGH *Monatsschrift des Deutschen Rechts* 1954, p. 693.

91. A. Ashworth, *Sentencing & Criminal Justice*, 3nd edn. (London, Butterworths 2000) pp. 139 et seq.

harm) of the crime and the culpability of the offender when committing the crime.[92] Aggravating and mitigating circumstances, such as the organised commission of the criminal act or the provocation by the victim, heighten or reduce the harmfulness or the culpability, whereas the voluntary surrender of the offender or his bad health can only be considered outside the penal value.[93]

The central concept in the German law of sentencing is the guilt principle, on the basis of which the sentence shall be meted out (para. 46 (1) of the German Criminal Code [*Strafgesetzbuch*, StGB]).[94] The guilt of the offender is determined by the harmfulness of the offender's conduct and his blameworthiness. All circumstances concomitant with the commission of the crime, or allowing for the conclusion that the offender's culpability during the commission of the crime was heightened or reduced, affect his guilt. According to the Federal Court of Appeals (*Bundesgerichtshof*, BGH), all these circumstances provide for 'a margin [*Spielraum*] that is limited at the bottom by the penalty already proportionate to guilt and at the top by the penalty still proportionate to guilt'.[95] Within this margin, the judge has to determine the final sentence, taking into consideration general and/or special deterrence.

The approach of these jurisdictions is mirrored in some of the *ad hoc* Tribunals' decisions. Whereas many judgments do not clearly distinguish between factors relevant for an assessment of the gravity of the offence and (other) aggravating or mitigating circumstances,[96] some of the chambers have applied a more differentiated approach.

In *Blaškić*, Trial Chamber I distinguished between specific *material* circumstances directly affecting the gravity of the crime and specific *personal* circumstances of the offender which are relevant for the individualisation of the sentence.[97] Whereas the former comprises factors such as the number of victims or the superior position of the offender, the latter refers to circumstances posterior to the commission of the crimes, such as cooperation with the prosecutor, voluntary

---

92. A. von Hirsch and N. Jareborg, 'Sweden's Sentencing Statute Enacted', *Criminal LR* (1989) pp. 275, 277. This article includes English translations of the most important sentencing provisions of the Swedish Criminal Code. A bilingual German translation of the Swedish Criminal Code and an introduction into Swedish Criminal Law can be found in K. Cornils and N. Jareborg, *Das schwedische Kriminalgesetzbuch – Brottsbalken* (Freiburg i.Br., Edition Iuscrim 2000).

93. Cf., Chapter 29 paras. 2, 3 and 5 of the Swedish Criminal Code.

94. 'Guilt' in the sense of this provision is a broader term than the notion of guilt as one of the prerequisites for criminal responsibility.

95. 7 BGHSt 28, at 32; quoted in Weigend, loc. cit. n. 36, p. 204.

96. Cf., *The Prosecutor* v. *Dario Kordić and Mario Čerkez*, Case No. IT-95-14/2, Judgement, 26 February 2001, paras. 846 et seq.; *supra* n. 32, paras. 46 et seq.; *The Prosecutor* v. *Alfred Musema*, Case No. ICTR-96-13-T, Judgement and Sentence, 27 January 2000, paras. 1001 et seq.; *The Prosecutor* v. *Goran Jelisić supra* n. 28, paras. 121-134; *The Prosecutor* v. *Georges Rutaganda*, *supra* n. 21, paras. 466-473; *The Prosecutor* v. *Zlatko Aleksovski*, Case No. IT-95-14/1-T, Judgement, 25 June 1999, paras. 235-243; *The Prosecutor* v. *Omar Serushago*, *supra* n. 21, paras. 27-42; *The Prosecutor* v. *Anto Furundžija*, *supra* n. 35, paras. 281-284; *The Prosecutor* v. *Jean Paul Akayesu*, Case No. ICTR-96-4-T, Sentence, 2 October 1998, paras. 24-32.

97. *The Prosecutor* v. *Tihomir Blaškić*, *supra* n. 35, para. 765.

surrender and the character of the defendant.[98] Thus, the judgment admits of the conclusion that mitigating circumstances directly referring to the offence and the culpability of the defendant affect the gravity of the crime, whereas circumstances posterior to the commission of the crime can only be assessed outside offence seriousness. This ruling is supported by the decision of Trial Chamber II*quater* of the ICTY in *Delalić et al.* The judges held, that 'the most relevant factors are those central to the circumstances of the crime for which the accused has been found guilty. [...] the question of sentence must depend on the particular circumstances of the crime itself and the role of the accused therein'.[99]

This ruling corresponds with the law in the national jurisdictions mentioned above, and it is submitted that it should also be followed in the jurisprudence of the ICC. Thus, the gravity of the offence is determined by the harmfulness of the crime and the culpability of the offender as expressed in the commission of the criminal act. These two elements are affected by those aggravating and mitigating circumstances concomitant with and directly influencing the commission of the crime.[100] According to the principle of proportionality between offence seriousness and punishment, these factors should be most important when it comes to the determination of the sentence, providing for a margin within which every sentence is guilt proportionate. As a second step, those mitigating circumstances posterior to the commission of the crime should be assessed in order to determine the individual sentence within the margin determined by the gravity of the crime. Only in very exceptional cases should these mitigating circumstances reduce the sentence under the lowest point of this margin.[101] This sentencing approach can contribute to a coherent and foreseeable sentencing practice, and it serves the pursuit of the primary sentencing purposes of international criminal tribunals, namely affirmative general prevention and just deserts.

6.1 The inherent gravity of the offence

The first element to be considered when determining the seriousness of the crime is the inherent, or jurisdictional, gravity of the offence. Every crime mentioned in an

---

98. The Chamber made clear that the character was not so much considered in order to examine the defendant's reasons for the crime – in that case, the character could be relevant for the gravity of the crime, but rather in order to give a prediction about his rehabilitation prospects, ibid., para. 780.

99. *The Prosecutor* v. *Žejnil Delalić et al.*, *supra* n. 21, para. 1218; similarly, in *Erdemović*, Trial Chamber I distinguished between those mitigating circumstances contemporaneous with the commission of the crimes and those following the carrying out of the crimes; the Chamber did not, however, elaborate on the issue whether the former circumstances were more important than the latter; cf., *supra* n. 13, paras. 86 et seq.

100. The individual circumstances of the convicted person, e.g., his age, social background or health condition, are generally part of the mitigating and aggravating circumstances; although they are explicitly mentioned in Art. 24 (2) of the ICTY Statute and Art. 23(2) of the ICTR Statute, their significance in the sentencing process can only be derived from their status as either aggravating or mitigating factors. Individual circumstances of a neutral character, e.g., an average age of the offender, do not have an impact on the sentencing decision.

101. Increasing the sentence beyond the margin would violate the guilt principle.

international criminal tribunal's statute has certain legal characteristics that determine its seriousness *per se*.[102] As Trial Chamber I held in *Todorović*, 'the crime of persecution, a crime against humanity, [...] is inherently very serious. This crime, like other crimes against humanity, requires that the acts of the accused be related to a widespread and systematic attack on a civilian population of which the accused has knowledge'.[103]

To determine – if only theoretically – the inherent gravity of every jurisdictional crime is important mainly for three reasons: it prevents substantive disparities in sentencing, it contributes to the establishment of a ranking of crimes, and it facilitates the application of the principle that circumstances constituting an element of a crime should not be considered a second time as an aggravating factor.

6.1.1 *The inherent gravity of the offence and disparities in sentencing*

The jurisdictional crimes of the statutes of the *ad hoc* Tribunals and the ICC represent 'the most serious crimes of concern to the international community as a whole'.[104] This is mirrored in the fact that the widespread and flagrant commission of these crimes both in the former Yugoslavia and in Rwanda constituted a threat to international peace and security triggering Security Council action under Chapter VII of the UN Charter. With regard to genocide, the inherent gravity of this crime lies in the offender's special intent to destroy, in whole or in part, a national, ethnic, racial or religious group; it is for this subjective element of the offence that Trial Chamber I of the ICTR named it 'the crime of crimes'.[105] As to crimes against humanity, it is the statutory requirement that the crime has to be committed as part of a widespread or systematic attack against civilians that makes them particularly harmful. Additionally, persecution as a crime against humanity has to be committed with the intent to target the victim because of his or her race or political or religious beliefs.[106] Finally, grave breaches of the Geneva Conventions and violations of the laws and customs of war constitute crimes committed in armed conflicts. This jurisdictional 'war nexus' contributes to the inherent gravity of the offence, since victims are particularly vulnerable in situations of an armed conflict.

What all these crimes have in common is that they are generally committed with the toleration or even active participation of a state or a comparable organisation. On the one hand, this fact increases the risk of becoming a victim of what is labelled *Makrokriminalität*,[107] and on the other hand it reduces the risk of the offenders being held criminally responsible after the situation has returned to normal. Therefore, the statutory crimes mentioned in the *ad hoc* Tribunals'

102. *Supra* n. 35, paras. 803 et seq.
103. *Supra* n. 89, para. 32. Similarly, *The Prosecutor* v. *Jean Kambanda*, *supra* n. 21, para. 43.
104. Para. 4 of the Preamble and Art. 5(1) of the ICC Statute.
105. *The Prosecutor* v. *Jean Kambanda*, *supra* n. 21, para. 16.
106. Art. 5(h) ICTY Statute; cf., also *The Prosecutor* v. *Tihomir Blaškić*, *supra* n. 35, para. 244. Contrary to the Statutes of the ICTY and the ICC, Article 3 of the ICTR Statute requires a discriminatory intent for every sub-characterisation of a crime against humanity.
107. Cf., Jäger, op. cit. n. 54.

Statutes and those in the ICC Statute have an inherent gravity different to that of 'ordinary' crimes. This factor has to be considered by international judges when meting out the appropriate sentences. Otherwise, disparity in sentencing would run the risk of violating the principle of proportionality and endanger the achievement of the various goals of punishment.

6.1.2 *The inherent gravity of the offence and the establishment of a ranking of crimes*

The comparability of the various violations of international humanitarian law has already been extensively discussed in ICTY jurisprudence. In *Todorović*, the Defence claimed that the case was comparable to that of *Erdemović*, arguing that the punishment for her client should be similar to that of the latter.[108] A similar argument was put forward by the Defence in *Jelisić*.[109] The Trial Chambers and the Appeals Chamber have been rather reluctant to develop a ranking of the jurisdictional crimes, or a tariff of sentences arising from this ranking, although Trial Chamber I stated in *Aleksovski*, that 'it is crucial to establish a gradation of sentences'[110] a ruling supported in the Judgment of the Appeals Chamber in the same case.[111] Such a ranking of crimes and sentences has not yet been established. Accordingly, the Appeals Chamber held in *Furundžija*, 'that, at this stage, it is not possible to identify an established *penal regime*. [...] It is thus premature to speak of an emerging *penal regime*, and the coherence in sentencing practice that this denotes'.[112]

Nevertheless, it should be one of the goals of international criminal jurisprudence to develop a coherent sentencing pattern, as this would make sentencing practice more foreseeable, transparent and reliable. This is all the more important as neither the Statutes of the Tribunals nor the ICC provide for statutory sentencing margins specifically designed for each offence.

The sentencing method outlined above will further these goals. Sentencing circumstances not directly related to the commission of the crime, e.g., a guilty plea, should only play a minor role compared to the inherent gravity of the offences and the sentencing factors concomitant with the commission of these offences.

The most disputed issue so far with respect to a ranking of crimes concerns whether or not a crime against humanity, all else being equal, is a more severe offence than a war crime. This question has been answered in the affirmative by four out of five judges of the Appeals Chamber in *Erdemović*,[113] whereas the

108. *Supra* n. 89, para. 109.

109. *The Prosecutor* v. *Goran Jelisić*, *supra* n. 82, para. 97.

110. *The Prosecutor* v. *Zlatko Aleksovski*, *supra* n. 96, para. 243.

111. *The Prosecutor* v. *Zlatko Aleksovski*, *supra* n. 23, para. 184.

112. *The Prosecutor* v. *Anto Furundžija*, Appeals Chamber, 21 July 2000, para. 237. In *Jelisić*, however, the Appeals Chamber seemed to indicate that this perception might change, cf., *The Prosecutor* v. *Goran Jelisić*, *supra* n. 82, para. 96.

113. *Supra* n. 61, Joint Separate Opinion of Judge McDonald and Judge Vohrah, paras. 20 et seq.; Separate and Dissenting Opinion of Judge Stephen, para. 5 Judge Cassese joined the majority in this

majority of the judges in *Tadić* rejected this view.[114] At the moment, it seems that the latter view prevails. In *Furundžija*, the Appeals Chamber relied on the majority's view in *Tadić*, stating that 'there is in law no distinction between the seriousness of a crime against humanity and that of a war crime'.[115] Similarly, Trial Chamber II of the ICTY held in *Kunarać, Kovać and Vuković*, that it is 'wrong to resort to some abstract comparison of *per se* gravity of the crimes',[116] and Trial Chamber I seemed to support this opinion in *Krstić*.[117]

It is submitted, however, that this view fails to attribute appropriate weight to the different statutory elements of a crime against humanity and a war crime.[118] A murder as a crime against humanity is inherently more serious than a murder as a war crime, because the former was committed as part of a widespread or systematic attack against civilians and with knowledge of this attack. The contextual element of a widespread or systematic attack implies a higher risk for potential victims, because every crime against humanity contributes to a large-scale commission of similar crimes. Thus, the objective gravity of the crime is greater than a comparable war crime. Similarly, the fact that the offender must have acted with knowledge of such an attack aggravates his intent, as he knows that his criminal behaviour contributes to the attack and to a higher risk for potential victims. While these circumstances can also apply to a war crime, they are not statutory elements of a war crime.[119] Therefore, the inherent, i.e., the statutory, gravity of a crime against humanity is greater than that of a war crime, and this should be taken into consideration in the process of determining the sentence.

---

issue, Judgement, Disposition; Judge Li dissented, Separate and Dissenting Opinion of Judge Li, paras. 20 et seq.

114. *The Prosecutor* v. *Duško Tadić, supra* n. 26, para. 69; Judge Cassese dissented, ibid., Separate Opinion of Judge Cassese, para. 1.

115. *The Prosecutor* v. *Anto Furundžija, supra* n. 112, para. 242.

116. *Supra* n. 84, para. 851.

117. *Supra* n. 77, para. 700.

118. For a thorough discussion of this issue cf., A.M. Danner, 'Constructing a Hierarchy of Crimes in International Criminal Law Sentencing', 87 *Virginia LR* (2001) pp. 453 et seq.; M. Frulli, 'Are Crimes Against Humanity More Serious Than War Crimes?', 12 *EJIL* (2001), pp. 329 et seq.; J.C. Nemitz, 'Sentencing in the Jurisprudence of the International Criminal Tribunals for the Former Yugoslavia and Rwanda', in H. Fischer, C. Kreß and S.R. Lüder, eds., *International and National Prosecution of Crimes under International Law. Current Developments* (Berlin, Verlag Arno Spitz 2001) pp. 615-620; M. Bohlander, 'Prosecutor v. Duško Tadić: Waiting to Exhale', 11 *Criminal LF* (2000) pp. 234-248.

119. Cf., Arts. 2, 3 ICTY Statute and 4 ICTR Statute. The wording of Art. 8(1) of the ICC Statute ('The Court shall have jurisdiction in respect of war crimes in particular when committed as part of a plan or policy or as part of a large-scale commission of such crimes') does not differ in substance from these provisions: a plan, a policy or a large-scale commission are not elements of a war crime, but rather guiding circumstances for the Prosecutor's decision to commence an investigation, cf., W.F. Fenrick, in O. Triffterer, ed., *Commentary on the Rome Statute of the International Criminal Court. Observers' Notes, Article by Article* (Baden-Baden, Nomos 1999) Art. 8, mn 4.

6.1.3 *The inherent gravity of the offence and the prohibition against considering an element of the offence as an aggravating circumstance in sentencing ('Doppelverwertungsverbot')*

The development of a ranking of crimes demonstrates the importance of the principle to not consider a circumstance to the detriment of the convicted person in the sentencing phase if this circumstance has already been considered as an element of the offence. This principle is of special importance in jurisdictions where fixed sentencing margins are attached to each offence. Here, the aggravating factor constituting an element of the offence leads to an increased sentencing margin within which the final sentence is meted out. To review the same circumstance in aggravation within the increased sentencing margin would violate the principle that the offender shall only be punished once for his criminal behaviour.

If, however, no specific sentencing margins are provided for each offence, it is less clear why this principle should apply. One of the reasons is the inherent gravity of the offence. In *Blaškić*, Trial Chamber I held that persecution as a crime against humanity is a crime 'which, *in itself*, justifies a more severe penalty' (emphasis added). This ruling was based on a discriminatory intent being a statutory element of persecution,[120] whereas other crimes against humanity do not require discriminatory intent.[121] Therefore, the judges would not have been allowed to consider as an aggravating factor that the crime was committed on a discriminatory basis. This principle has been upheld in *Todorović*, where the Prosecutor had submitted 'that the discriminatory nature of Stevan Todorović's crime' and 'the fact that many of Stevan Todorović's victims were civilians, including women and children, should also be considered' as an aggravating circumstance.[122] The Chamber, however, disagreed with this contention, stating that these factors had already been 'encompassed in a consideration of the offence'.[123] This ruling shows that the jurisprudence of the *ad hoc* Tribunals is filling in the gaps in the international law of sentencing, thus contributing to a coherent and more dogmatic body of law.

Although we have seen that the inherent gravity of an offence is for several reasons important in the sentencing process, it must be noted that it can only provide a rather vague sentencing tariff; other circumstances must be reviewed, including those influencing offence seriousness and those posterior to the commission of the crime.

120. *Supra* n. 35, para. 785.

121. Art. 5 ICTY Statute; cf., also Art. 7 ICC Statute. Art. 3 ICTR Statute, however, requires a discriminatory intent for each crime against humanity.

122. *Supra* n. 89, paras. 52, 53.

123. Ibid., para. 57; similarly, but less clear: *The Prosecutor* v. *Dragoljub Kunarać, Radomir Kovać and Zoran Vuković*, *supra* n. 84, paras. 852, 867 874 and 879.

6.2 The gravity of the offence and individual, aggravating and mitigating circumstances

6.2.1 *The gravity of the offence and the individual circumstances of the convicted person*

The Statutes of the *ad hoc* Tribunals provide that the judges have to consider the individual circumstances of the convicted person together with the gravity of the offence.[124] The aim of these provisions is to individualise the sentence, i.e., to make it fit the perpetrator. Additionally, Rule 101(B) of the Rules of Procedure and Evidence states that, *inter alia*, any aggravating circumstances should be considered together with any mitigating circumstances, including the substantial cooperation of the convicted person with the Prosecutor before or after conviction. Yet, the relationship between these categories of sentencing circumstances is not very clear. Individual circumstances can be relevant for the determination of the gravity of the crime, e.g., the age of the perpetrator,[125] or they can be part of the behaviour of the offender after his commission of the crime, e.g., his family situation and social background.[126] Furthermore, they can constitute aggravating circumstances, e.g., the demonstration of lack of respect for the judicial proceedings, or mitigating circumstances, e.g., the assistance given to victims. Therefore, it is not possible to strictly differentiate between the factors constituting the gravity of the crime, the individual circumstances of the offender, and any aggravating and mitigating circumstances. This raises the question of which sentencing factors should be considered under the heading of the individual circumstances of the convicted person. The answer is found by having recourse to the role the individual circumstances play in the sentencing process. This role is twofold: first, a reference to the offender's personal circumstances at the beginning of the sentencing decision serves as a presentation of the convicted person to the reader and to the judges of the Appeals Chamber.[127] Their principle significance for the sentencing process, however, lies in their impact on the punishment.[128] This means that they are either considered as aggravating or as mitigating circumstances. Therefore, it is appropriate to review all individual circumstances constituting aggravating or mitigating circumstances within these two categories. However, as long as they provide a comprehensive impression of the defendant's personality, they should also be mentioned at the beginning of the sentencing judgment.

---

124. Art. 23(2) ICTR Statute and Art. 24(2) ICTY Statute.

125. Cf., *The Prosecutor* v. *Žejnil Delalić et al., supra* n. 21, para. 1284 (Landžo).

126. Cf., *The Prosecutor v. Dražen Erdemović, supra* n. 31, para. 16.

127. Cf., for the German law M. Schmehl and W. Vollmer, *Die Assessorklausur im Strafprozeß*, 3rd edn., (München, C.H. Beck 1994) p. 142.

128. Cf., for the German law G. Pfeiffer, *StPO. Strafprozeßordnung. Gerichtsverfassungsgesetz*, 3rd edn., (München, C.H. Beck 2001), § 267 mn 2, 5.

6.2.2 *The gravity of the offence and aggravating circumstances*

As stated, the Statutes of the *ad hoc* Tribunals do not provide for a method according to which the gravity of the offence and aggravating circumstances have to be considered in the sentencing process. In some judgments, the gravity of the offence was discussed as part of the aggravating circumstances,[129] while in others, it remained unclear according to which construct the gravity of the offences and the aggravating circumstances were considered.[130] The *Akayesu* decision did not even mention the factors upon which the defendant's life sentence was based.[131] This incoherence in sentencing reduces the transparency of sentencing decisions, thus making it more difficult for both the Defence and the Prosecutor to examine possible grounds for appeal. Therefore, the Chambers should first consider the *inherent* gravity of the offence before determining the gravity of the offence with the help of the applicable aggravating and mitigating circumstances.

In spite of these differences in structure, the aggravating circumstances that have been taken into consideration are very similar. With regard to the objective element of harm, several Trial Chambers have reviewed, *inter alia*, the way in which the crimes were committed,[132] the number of victims and their particular vulnerability,[133] and the superior authority position of the defendant.[134] The culpability of the offender was considered in aggravation when the crime was committed with premeditation.[135]

All these circumstances have in common that they are concomitant with the commission of the crime, which means that they increase the seriousness of the offence. However, the question remains as to whether circumstances posterior to the commission of the crimes, e.g., the defendant's disrespectful courtroom behaviour, can aggravate the sentence. This question was answered in the affirmative in *Delalić et al.*, where Trial Chamber II*quater* took into consideration Mr Mucić's 'lack of respect for the judicial process' and his and Mr. Delalić's conspiracy 'about the fabrication of evidence to be given at trial'; additionally, the

129. *The Prosecutor* v. *Georges Ruggiu*, *supra* n. 32, paras. 47 et seq.; *The Prosecutor* v. *Alfred Musema*, *supra* n. 96, paras. 1001 et seq.; *The Prosecutor* v. *Georges Rutaganda*, *supra* n. 21, paras. 468 et seq.; *The Prosecutor* v. *Omar Serushago*, *supra* n. 21, para. 27; *The Prosecutor* v. *Anto Furundžija*, *supra* n. 35, paras. 281 et seq.

130. *The Prosecutor* v. *Dario Kordić and Mario Čerkez*, *supra* n. 96, paras. 846 et seq.; *The Prosecutor* v. *Zlatko Aleksovski*, *supra* n. 96, paras. 235 et seq.

131. *The Prosecutor* v. *Jean Paul Akayesu*, *supra* n. 96, paras. 24 et seq.

132. *The Prosecutor* v. *Dragoljub Kunarać, Radomir Kovać and Zoran Vuković*, *supra* n. 84, para. 867; *The Prosecutor* v. *Goran Jelisić*, *supra* n. 28, para. 130; *The Prosecutor* v. *Clément Kayishema and Obed Ruzindana*, *supra* n. 34, para. 18; *The Prosecutor* v. *Žejnil Delalić et al.*, *supra* n. 21, paras. 1275, 1277.

133. *The Prosecutor* v. *Dragoljub Kunarać, Radomir Kovać and Zoran Vuković*, *supra* n. 84, para. 858; *The Prosecutor* v. *Tihomir Blaškić*, *supra* n. 35, para. 784.

134. Cf., *The Prosecutor* v. *Zoran Kupreškić et al.*, *supra* n. 40, para. 852; *The Prosecutor* v. *Georges Rutaganda*, *supra* n. 21, paras. 469, 470.

135. *The Prosecutor v. Tihomir Blaškić*, *supra* n. 35, para. 793 (with further references).

Chamber stated that the 'allegations[136] that Mr. Mucić participated in the threatening of a witness in the courtroom [were] particularly relevant aggravating conduct, which the Trial Chamber is entitled to take into account in the determination of the appropriate sentence'.[137]

The review of such post-offence conduct is complex. As a general rule, the defendant can only be sentenced for the criminal behaviour for which he has been indicted and convicted.[138] He must not be sentenced for conduct which is not related to this offence.[139] The Federal Court of Appeals in Germany (*Bundesgerichtshof*) and many German scholars are trying to bypass this obstacle by using disrespectful courtroom behaviour as circumstantial evidence: if post-offence conduct admits of the conclusion that the offender's culpability at the time of the commission of the crime was increased, the courts may consider it in aggravation. In this sense, post-offence conduct is used as circumstantial evidence for an aggravated gravity of the offence.[140] On the other hand, such conduct can be considered when deciding upon the rehabilitative prospects of the defendant. In this case, the conduct would not affect the gravity of the offence, but it would nevertheless qualify as 'any relevant information that may assist the Trial Chamber in determining an appropriate sentence'.[141]

The Appeals Chamber seems to have adopted the second approach when it stated that such 'behaviour is relevant to a Trial Chamber's determination of, for example, remorse for the acts committed or, on the contrary, total lack of compassion'.[142] However, the decision does not explicitly state whether or not the relevant post-offence conduct constituted a separate aggravating circumstance or was used in order to negate the existence of a mitigating circumstance (like remorse). This question has been answered in the latter sense by Trial Chamber II of the ICTY. It stated in *Kunarać, Vuković and Kovać* that the lack of remorse shown by the defendant was 'treated as negating remorse as a possible mitigating circumstance *rather than as an aggravating factor*' (emphasis added).[143] It is submitted that this approach should be followed by the other chambers as it respects the principle that the defendant can only be punished for behaviour that is directly related to the offence. Thus, aggravating post-offence conduct may only be considered in

---

136. In this context, the use of the term 'allegations' is at least misleading: as the Appeals Chamber has ruled in *Delalić et al.*, 'only those matters which are proved beyond reasonable doubt against an accused may be the subject of an accused's sentence or taken into account in aggravation of that sentence', *supra* n. 25, para. 763. The use of the term 'allegations', however, gives the impression that this circumstance was not proved beyond reasonable ground.

137. *The Prosecutor* v. *Žejnil Delalić et al.*, *supra* n. 21, paras. 1244, 1251.

138. *The Prosecutor* v. *Dragoljub Kunarać, Radomir Kovać and Zoran Vuković*, *supra* n. 84, para. 850.

139. Ibid.

140. Cf., Bruns, op. cit. n. 90, p. 566.

141. Cf., Rule 85(A)(vi) of the *ad hoc* Tribunals' Rules of Procedure and Evidence.

142. *The Prosecutor* v. *Žejnil Delalić et al.*, *supra* n. 25, para. 788.

143. *The Prosecutor* v. *Dragoljub Kunarać, Radomir Kovać and Zoran Vuković*, *supra* n. 84, para. 854.

assessing the rehabilitative potential of the defendant and in negating any mitigating circumstances.

6.2.3 *The gravity of the offence and mitigating circumstances*

An enormous number of mitigating factors has been considered in the judgments of the *ad hoc* Tribunals and it serves no purpose to enumerate them here.

One of them, however, is of particular importance, thus justifying a closer look: the guilty plea of the offender.

On the one hand, the guilty plea is a mitigating circumstance posterior to the commission of the crime and it should therefore – as a general rule – be accorded less weight than a mitigating circumstance concomitant with the commission of the crime. On the other hand, however, the special significance of an accused's guilty plea is indicated by the fact that a number of judgments have already demonstrated that it has been attributed substantial weight in the sentencing process.[144]

In order to determine what impact this circumstance should have, one has to look at the justifications for granting or negating mitigation of punishment. In *Erdemović*, Judge Cassese justified the reduction of punishment by referring to the particular difficulties the Prosecutor of an international criminal tribunal faces when conducting an investigation: in these cases, the collection of evidence is generally more difficult than in national investigations and the trials are also more expensive.[145] In the second Sentencing Judgement in the same trial, Trial Chamber II*ter* stated that the granting of mitigation in exchange for a guilty plea could contribute to national reconciliation, 'for it is the truth that cleanses the ethnic and religious hatreds and begins the healing process'.[146] The Chamber further held that the guilty plea must be given appropriate weight, as this 'is important for encouraging other suspects or unknown perpetrators to come forward'.[147] This argumentation has also been adopted by Trial Chamber I of the ICTR. In *Kambanda*, the judges stated that the guilty plea of the accused 'is likely to encourage other individuals to recognise their responsibilities during the tragic events which occurred in Rwanda in 1994'.[148] Furthermore, a guilty plea was considered as a mitigating circumstance when the judges were convinced that it displayed a showing of remorse: in *Ruggiu*, Trial Chamber I held that 'the

144. Cf., *The Prosecutor* v. *Stevan Todorović*, *supra* n. 89, paras. 75-88, 114; *The Prosecutor* v. *Georges Ruggiu*, *supra* n. 32, paras. 53-55; *The Prosecutor* v. *Goran Jelisić*, *supra* n. 28, para. 127; *The Prosecutor* v. *Omar Serushago*, *supra* n. 21, paras. 31-33, 35, 41; *The Prosecutor* v. *Jean Kambanda*, *supra* n. 21, paras. 52-61; *The Prosecutor* v. *Dražen Erdemović*, *supra* n. 31, 5 March 1998, para. 16 (ii); *The Prosecutor* v. *Dražen Erdemović*, *supra* n. 13, paras. 97, 111.

145. Cf., *The Prosecutor* v. *Dražen Erdemović*, *supra* n. 60, Separate and Dissenting Opinion of Judge Cassese, para. 8. This reasoning corresponds with the argumentation in English law, for example, cf., *R.* v. *Fearon* (1995), *Criminal LR* (1996) p. 213 ('The law required sentencing judges to give a discount for guilty pleas however strong the case might be'); *R. v. Buffrey* (1993), *Criminal LR* (1993) p. 320.

146. *The Prosecutor v. Dražen Erdemović*, *supra* n. 31, para. 21.

147. Ibid.

148. *The Prosecutor* v. *Jean Kambanda*, *supra* n. 21, para. 61.

accused's acknowledgement of his mistakes [sic] and crimes is a healthy application of reason and sentiment, which illustrates the beginning of repentance'.[149]

However, bearing in mind the importance of the concept of the gravity of the crime for the determination of the sentence, the question remains whether or not these reasons really justify a significant mitigating effect of a guilty plea. To start with, the assumption that a lenient sentence for Dražen Erdemović would motivate other perpetrators to come forward was far too optimistic; the low probability of being apprehended by national authorities or international troops seems to outweigh the wish to voluntarily surrender to The Hague or Arusha. However, the question should not be whether or not a guilty plea generally justifies a mitigation of punishment at all. It is rather the extent of mitigation that should be discussed.

The jurisprudence of the *ad hoc* Tribunals varies in this respect. In *Jelisić* and *Kambanda*, the offenders' guilty pleas did not lead to any reduction of the sentence for one or more of the following three reasons: firstly, the guilty plea did not demonstrate sincere remorse;[150] secondly, the accused was confronted with overwhelming evidence;[151] thirdly, in the case of *Kambanda*, the enormous gravity of the crimes to which the accused pleaded guilty and his position as Prime Minister of Rwanda;[152] In *Erdemović* and *Serushago*, however, the impact of the guilty pleas was substantial. In the latter case, the Chamber held 'that exceptional circumstances in mitigation surrounding the crimes committed [...] may afford [the offender] some clemency'.[153] It is submitted, however, that the *ad hoc* Tribunals and the ICC should not give much weight to guilty pleas.

The starting point for every consideration of a mitigating factor has to be the following question: does the granting of mitigation for certain conduct of the accused serve the sentencing purposes of the court? As stated above, it is submitted that the pursuit of just deserts, encompassing the repressive goal of retribution, and the notion of affirmative general prevention are the most important sentencing purposes in international criminal law. The former, however, does not justify a reduction of the punishment for a guilty plea: as the guilty plea is a factor posterior to the commission of the crime, it cannot affect its gravity. Since the aim of the just deserts principle is to sentence the offender for what he has done, the punishment has to be proportionate to the crime, not to the offender's conduct before or after it.

The sentencing purpose of affirmative general prevention is better suited to justify the mitigating effect of a guilty plea. Although in general also dependant on the proportionality principle, it can be argued that public opinion expects a more lenient sentence to be imposed on an accused who pleads guilty. This assumption

149. *Supra* n. 32, para. 55.

150. *Supra* n. 28, para. 127. Similarly, German jurisprudence requires a showing of remorse in order to consider the guilty plea in mitigation, cf., German Federal Court of Appeals (BGH) *Strafverteidiger* 1991, pp. 106, 108; cf., for the English law *R.* v. *Sharkey and Daniels* (1994), 16 *Criminal Appeal Reports (Sentencing)* 1995, p. 260.

151. The accused knew that photographs were produced at trial in which he could be seen committing crimes, cf., *The Prosecutor* v. *Goran Jelisić*, *supra* n. 28, para. 127.

152. *The Prosecutor* v. *Jean Kambanda*, *supra* n. 21, para. 62.

153. *The Prosecutor* v. *Omar Serushago*, *supra* n. 21, para. 42.

corresponds to the above-mentioned ruling in *Erdemović*, according to which the acknowledgement of personal guilt can contribute to the process of national reconciliation, thus fulfilling a goal of affirmative general prevention.

Mitigation of punishment for a guilty plea can also be granted for rehabilitative purposes, provided that two conditions are met. Firstly, the guilty plea must demonstrate a sincere expression of remorse: if the plea was made for purely tactical reasons, it should not be considered in mitigation. Secondly, the reduction of the punishment must not go below what is needed in order to pursue the goal of affirmative general prevention. This follows from the assumption that in international criminal law the latter sentencing purpose shall outweigh the pursuit of rehabilitative goals.

The argument that international trials are very arduous and expensive and that a guilty plea justifies a lesser punishment, because it saves the international tribunal a lot of money, is also only applicable if the two restrictions mentioned above are met. Otherwise, it would lead to the inappropriate result that the higher the position of the accused, the higher the discount granted for his guilty plea should be: as a general rule, the trial against an ordinary soldier is less time-consuming than proceedings against high-level politicians and high-ranking people from the military. On the other hand, the crimes of these latter offenders are generally more serious than those committed by ordinary soldiers.[154] However, as a mitigating circumstance posterior to the commission of the crime, a guilty plea cannot reduce the seriousness of an offence. Therefore, a guilty plea should not be given much weight when determining the sentence in such cases.

Another reason against any substantial reduction of punishment based on a guilty plea in international criminal proceedings is the fact that this might contribute to an increasing practice of plea bargaining. The case of *Todorović* is an illustrative example in this respect. In an agreement between the Defence and the Prosecution, the former withdrew his motion in which the accused challenged the legality of his arrest in the Federal Republic of Yugoslavia, while the latter withdrew counts 2 to 27 of the Second Amended Indictment; as a result, the accused pleaded guilty to count 1 of this Indictment (persecution).[155] Thus, although the Prosecution and the Defence agreed on those facts which constituted the underlying offences for the other counts as being true, the accused was only sentenced for the persecution count. Considering the gravity of these criminal acts, such a plea bargain agreement can hamper the pursuit of the sentencing purposes of affirmative general prevention and just deserts.

---

154. 'There is no doubt that abuse of positions of authority or trust will be regarded as aggravating', *The Prosecutor* v. *Žejnil Delalić et al.*, *supra* n. 21, para. 1220; this reasoning was upheld by the Appeals Chamber, *supra* n. 25, para. 736.

155. *The Prosecutor* v. *Stevan Todorović*, *supra* n. 89, paras. 2-17.

7. MULTIPLE CONVICTIONS BASED ON THE SAME CONDUCT

Due to the fact that different offences under the Statutes of the *ad hoc* Tribunals penalise the same criminal conduct – for example, 'wilful killing' as a grave breach of the 1949 Geneva Conventions and 'murder' as a violation of the laws or customs of war[156] – the convicted person is often *charged* with different crimes based on the same criminal conduct. While such practice has been acknowledged in the jurisprudence of both Tribunals,[157] the question whether multiple *convictions* for the same conduct of the convicted person are justified has given rise to some controversy in the jurisprudence of the Tribunals. Closely related to this issue is the question as to whether multiple *sentences* can be imposed for different crimes based on the same conduct: the imposition of multiple convictions can be important for the sentencing process, since the number of convictions may influence the severity of the sentence. Furthermore, conviction for a crime aggravates the social stigmatisation of the convicted person and it may diminish the prospects of an early release under the laws of the state of enforcement.[158]

The Trial Chambers addressed the problems arising out of multiple convictions in different ways. While some Chambers did not discuss them at all and briefly referred to the possibility of imposing multiple or single *sentences*,[159] the judgments of *Kayishema and Ruzindana* and *Akayesu* examined the possibility of multiple convictions based on the same facts in more detail, although this issue was discussed under the heading of 'cumulative charges'.[160]

In the former judgment, Trial Chamber II of the ICTR mentioned two situations in which multiple convictions based on the same facts were appropriate: '(1) where offences have differing elements, or (2) where the laws in question protect differing societal interests'.[161] In *Akayesu*, Trial Chamber I added a third situation:

---

156. 'The content of the offence of murder under Article 3 is the same as for wilful killing under Article 2'. *The Prosecutor* v. *Žejnil Delalić et al., supra* n. 21, para. 422. This ruling was upheld in *The Prosecutor* v. *Tihomir Blaškić, supra* n. 35, para. 181.

157. In *Delalić et al.*, the Appeals Chamber stated 'that, prior to the presentation of all of the evidence, it is not possible to determine to a certainty which of the charges brought against an accused will be proven'; *The Prosecutor* v. *Žejnil Delalić et al., supra* n. 25, para. 400. Therefore, the Prosecution must have the right to present cumulative charges and the Trial Chamber may subsequently determine which of these charges will be proved; cf., also *The Prosecutor* v. *Dragoljub Kunarać, Radomir Kovać and Zoran Vuković, supra* n. 84, para. 548; *The Prosecutor* v. *Zoran Kupreškić et al., supra* n. 40, paras. 720 et seq.

158. *Supra* n. 25, Separate and Dissenting Opinion of Judge David Hunt and Judge Mohamed Bennouna, para. 23.

159. E.g., *The Prosecutor* v. *Tihomir Blaškić, supra* n. 35, paras. 805 et seq.; *supra* n. 28, paras. 136-140.

160. *The Prosecutor* v. *Clément Kayishema and Obed Ruzindana, supra* n. 34, paras. 625-650; *The Prosecutor* v. *Jean-Paul Akayesu*, Case No. ICTR-96-4-T, Judgement, 2 September 1998, paras. 461-470.

161. *The Prosecutor* v. *Clément Kayishema and Obed Ruzindana, supra* n. 34, para. 627.

'where it is necessary to record a conviction for both offences in order fully to describe what the accused did'.[162]

It was in *Kupreškić et al.*, however, that the issue of multiple convictions – and of multiple offences in general – was discussed at length for the first time. In this case, Trial Chamber II referred to a number of national jurisdictions and judgments of international tribunals in order to deduce general principles applicable in international criminal law.[163] As a result, the Chamber followed the approach of the US Supreme Court as expressed in the *Blockburger* test:

> 'The applicable rule is that where the same act or transaction constitutes a violation of two distinct statutory provisions, the test to be applied to determine whether there are two offences or only one, is whether each provision requires proof of an additional fact which the other one does not.'[164]

This ruling was upheld by the Appeals Chamber in *Delalić et al.*, stating 'that multiple criminal convictions entered under different statutory provisions but based on the same conduct are permissible only if each statutory provision involved has a materially distinct element not contained in the other. An element is materially different from another if it requires proof of a fact not required by the other'.[165]

The reasoning behind this 'materially distinct element' test is to prevent the perpetrator from being convicted twice for the same criminal act. This prohibition can be derived from the guilt principle and the *ne bis in idem* principle. Therefore, the perpetrator can only be convicted for multiple offences if his conduct violated different statutory provisions containing different levels of offence seriousness, i.e., none of these offences can be a lesser included crime. On the other hand, it also means that the perpetrator *must* be convicted for multiple offences based on the same conduct if these offences express a *different gravity of the crime*. According to the guilt principle and the principle of proportionality, a sentence must correspond to the guilt of the perpetrator, i.e., it must mirror the gravity of the totality of the crimes he has committed. This argument also corresponds to the pursuit of the sentencing purposes of just deserts and affirmative general prevention. In other

162. *The Prosecutor* v. *Jean-Paul Akayesu*, *supra* n. 160, para. 468. Additionally, the Chamber held that multiple convictions for the same facts are not allowed if '(a) one offence is a lesser included offence of the other [...], or (b) where one offence charges accomplice liability and the other offence charges liability as a principal'; ibid.

163. *The Prosecutor* v. *Zoran Kupreškić et al.*, *supra* n. 40, paras. 637-719. For an illustrative and thorough discussion of this ruling and the general issue of multiple offences in the jurisprudence of the *ad hoc* Tribunals, see C.-F. Stuckenberg, 'Multiplicity of Offences: Concursus Delictorum', in Fischer, Kreß, Lüder, eds., op. cit. n. 118, pp. 573 et seq.; cf., also S. Walther, 'Cumulation of Offences', in A. Cassese, P. Gaeta and J. R. W. D. Jones, eds., *The Rome Statute of the International Criminal Court – A Commentary* (Oxford, Oxford University Press 2002).

164. *Blockburger* v. *US* (1932), 284 U.S. 299, 304, 52 S. Ct. 180.

165. *Supra* n. 25, para. 412; in the same sense *The Prosecutor* v. *Dragoljub Kunarać, Radomir Kovać and Zoran Vuković*, *supra* n. 84, paras. 549-557; *The Prosecutor* v. *Dario Kordić and Mario Čerkez*, *supra* n. 96, paras. 811-826.

words, a perpetrator should only be convicted for multiple offences based on the same conduct if each of these offences encompasses one or more statutory elements which contain a different gravity of the crime.

It follows that one of the most important questions in this respect refers to the definition of a 'materially distinct element' of each statutory provision. The majority of the Appeals Chamber held in *Delalić et al.*, that every element of a statutory crime qualifies for this test, i.e., both those exclusively referring to the underlying offence, like murder, wilful killing or rape, and those mentioned in the *chapeaux* of the statutory provisions, like the requirement of a widespread or systematic commission of crimes against humanity or the existence of an international or national armed conflict.[166] This ruling, however, was criticised by Judges *Hunt* and *Bennouna* for being 'highly artificial'. In their view, only elements relating to the offender's conduct and mental state as expressed in the underlying offence should be taken into consideration when applying the 'materially distinct element' test. Accordingly, the judges held that a rape under Article 2 or under Article 3 has no element which a rape under Article 5 does not have.[167]

It is submitted, however, that this approach does not correspond to the above-mentioned reasoning behind the 'materially distinct element' test. As we have seen, multiple convictions for the same acts are justified if each offence includes one or more elements which make them differ in their respective offence seriousness. The seriousness of a statutory provision, however, is often not only expressed in the definition of the underlying offence – like murder or rape – but also in elements of the provision's *chapeau*. This can be exemplified by a comparison of the definitions of rape as a war crime and rape as a crime against humanity.

In these cases, the contextual requirement of an international or internal armed conflict in the case of rape as a war crime,[168] or a widespread or systematic attack on the civilian population – in the case of rape as a crime against humanity, relate to the seriousness of the respective offence. Both elements express different levels of offence seriousness: the inherent gravity of a rape as a crime against humanity is materially different – and it may be added, more serious[169] – than that of a rape as a war crime, as the former is part of a widespread or systematic attack on civilians and the latter is not. With respect to the requirement of an armed conflict, however, it is necessary to distinguish between the different international statutes: the requirement that rape as a war crime has a nexus to an armed conflict of either national or international character is only present in Article 5 of the ICTY Statute. Article 3 of the ICTR Statute and Article 7 of the ICC Statute do not require a link to an armed conflict. It follows that there are no reciprocal unique elements in the case of a rape as a war crime and a rape as a crime against humanity under Article 5

166. *Supra* n. 25, para. 412; ibid., Separate and Dissenting Opinion of Judges Hunt and Bennouna, para. 25.

167. Ibid., para. 33.

168. *The Prosecutor* v. *Dragoljub Kunarać, Radomir Kovać and Zoran Vuković, supra* n. 84, paras. 400-402.

169. Cf., *The Prosecutor v. Duško Tadić, supra* n. 26, Separate Opinion of Judge Cassese.

of the ICTY Statute.[170] Thus, under the ICTY Statute, a multiple conviction based on the same conduct could not be imposed for rape as a war crime and rape as a crime against humanity; [171] under the ICTR and the ICC Statutes, however, this would be possible.

Therefore, to compare only the underlying offences in order to determine whether or not the relevant statutory provisions contain materially distinct elements would not sufficiently take into consideration that the elements of the *chapeaux* can also express the different gravity of the crimes for which the offender is convicted. These elements also fulfil the 'materially distinct elements' test mentioned above. Since the accused has to be convicted of the totality of his criminal conduct, it follows from the guilt principle and the principle of proportionality that multiple convictions based on the same criminal acts have to be imposed in these cases.

8. SINGLE SENTENCE OR MULTIPLE SENTENCES?

While some chambers of the *ad hoc* Tribunals have imposed multiple sentences on each count and held that these sentences had to be served concurrently,[172] a single sentence has been rendered in a large number of cases.[173] To date, however, no chamber has ruled that multiple sentences have to be to be served consecutively.

It is not possible to determine whether these two approaches have led to a substantial difference in the length of the sentences. In cases where multiple sentences have been imposed, they have to be served concurrently, which means that only the highest sentence has to be served. In cases in which a single sentence has been imposed, the chambers have not elaborated on the way in which the sentence was apportioned. It is possible that at least in some of these judgments the highest single sentence was aggravated by the other crimes for which the offender was convicted (*Asperationsprinzip*). Thus, the imposition of a single sentence may have led to a harsher sentence than the imposition of multiple sentences which had to be served concurrently. The former approach was adopted in Article 48 of the Criminal Code of the Socialist Federal Republic of Yugoslavia, according to which the court had to assess the sentence for each of the criminal acts for which the accused had been convicted before determining the composite sentence.

170. In a similar vein, the requirement of the victim being a 'protected person' (grave breach; war crime) or a 'civilian' (crime against humanity), and the requirement of the existence of an 'international or internal armed conflict' (grave breach; war crime) or an 'armed conflict' (crime against humanity under the ICTY Statute) are not reciprocal elements which denote different levels of offence seriousness.

171. The jurisprudence of the ICTY, however, would accept a multiple conviction in this case, cf., *The Prosecutor* v. *Miroslav Kvocka et al.*, Case No. IT-98-30/1-T, Judgement, 2 November 2001, para. 219; *The Prosecutor* v. *Goran Jelisić*, *supra* n. 82, para. 82 (with further references).

172. *The Prosecutor* v. *Zoran Kupreškić et al.*, *supra* n. 40, para. 866 (with further references).

173. E.g., *The Prosecutor* v. *Radislav Krstić*, *supra* n. 77, para. 727; *The Prosecutor* v. *Dragoljub Kunarać, Radomir Kovać and Zoran Vuković*, *supra* n. 84, paras. 883-890; *The Prosecutor* v. *Dario Kordić and Mario Čerkez*, *supra* n. 96, Disposition.

Article 78(3) of the ICC Statute contains a similar provision. In the case of multiple convictions, 'the Court shall pronounce a sentence for each crime and a joint sentence specifying the total period of imprisonment. This period shall be no less than the highest individual sentence pronounced and shall not exceed 30 years imprisonment or a sentence of life imprisonment in conformity with article 77, paragraph 1 (b)'. It is submitted that this practice should also be followed by the other international criminal tribunals. A sentence which has been meted out following this approach is best suited to guarantee that the length of the sentence reflects the totality of the perpetrator's criminal conduct, because every conviction is part of – and adds to – the final sentence. On the contrary, in the case of multiple convictions leading to multiple sentences to be served concurrently, the highest single sentence alone does not mirror the totality of the perpetrator's criminal conduct, provided that one accepts that the plurality of crimes adds to the totality of the criminal conduct.

Furthermore, the procedural rights of the parties are strengthened if a single sentence is pronounced for each crime (and a joint sentence for the total period of imprisonment), as both the Prosecutor and the Defence can claim a violation of the proportionality principle with respect to each single sentence. Additionally, the fact that the judges have to give reasons for the length of imprisonment for each conviction is likely to enhance the transparency of the sentencing process.

If one of the single sentences is quashed, it lies within the discretionary powers of the judges to decide whether or not the final sentence has to be altered. Thus, the quashing of a single sentence *may* affect the final sentence, whereas the quashing of one of multiple sentences *cannot* have an effect on the final sentence provided that the other sentences are to be served concurrently and the highest single sentence is upheld.

Finally, it is submitted that the judges, when pronouncing the final sentence, shall not take into consideration those circumstances that were already referred to when meting out the various single sentences. Otherwise, the perpetrator might be punished twice for the same conduct and the sentence imposed might not correspond to the totality of his criminal behaviour.

9. CONCLUDING REMARKS

Compared to domestic criminal justice systems, the international law of sentencing is still in an embryonic state. However, it is fair to expect that this situation will soon improve. Already today, the jurisprudence of the *ad hoc* Tribunals shows that their chambers devote much more diligence to sentencing issues than the international post-World War II tribunals. At the same time, scholars from all over the world contribute to an ongoing exploration of this legal field. With the establishment of the International Criminal Court and other international criminal tribunals, the number of sentencing judgments will steadily grow, and important issues like a ranking of crimes and symmetrical sentencing tariffs will be increasingly investigated.

It has been submitted herein that the judgments of the *ad hoc* Tribunals established by the UN Security Council should play a more important role in the development of the international customary law of sentencing than the judgments of national courts. The same should be true of the judgments of the ICC. This approach is based on the international status of these tribunals, their particular expertise and the fact that they can be perceived as being truly independent as they are not 'victors' courts.

Aside from this issue, this study has primarily focused on the sentencing purposes that should be pursued in international criminal law and the sentencing method applicable in the jurisprudence of international criminal tribunals. It has been shown that these two issues are closely intertwined and that they depend on each other. With regard to sentencing purposes, it is submitted that the concepts of affirmative general prevention and just deserts should be the most important aims of punishment to be pursued by international criminal courts. As to the former, the educational task of punishment is especially important in international criminal law, considering that this area of law is rather new and that it needs to be 'implanted' in the minds of the public all over the world. As to the latter, one has to acknowledge the human desire to see that the perpetrator gets what he 'deserves' and that his guilt is settled by a proportionate punishment.

At the time of writing these lines, the world remained in a state of shock following the monstrous terrorist attacks on the World Trade Center and the Pentagon. If those responsible for these attacks are punished by a court of law, few people will think that they should be sentenced for purely preventive reasons. Many will think that the offenders also deserve to be punished for what they did, and the jurisprudence of international criminal tribunals should take this attitude into consideration as they also deal with crimes of enormous gravity.

When examining the method of meting out a sentence according to international criminal law, this paper primarily focused on the notion of the gravity of the crime, which is the central element of sentencing in both international and national law. Since the pursuit of the sentencing purposes of affirmative general prevention and just deserts requires a sentence that is proportionate to the gravity of the crime, the determination of the content of this concept is a central issue in the law of sentencing. In this context, it is submitted that mitigating circumstances posterior to the commission of the crime should not lead to a substantial reduction of the punishment. This is particularly important with regard to the guilty plea of the offender: although the *ad hoc* Tribunals, for a variety of reasons, have a strong interest in reducing the length of their trials, this endeavour must not lead to sentences which do not mirror the seriousness of the totality of the offences committed. Otherwise, public acceptance of the sentencing judgments, and of the Tribunals' work in general, will be jeopardised and the pursuit of affirmative general prevention of international crime will be impeded.

TWENTY-FIVE YEARS AFTER THE ADOPTION OF ADDITIONAL PROTOCOL II: BREAKTHROUGH OR FAILURE OF HUMANITARIAN LEGAL PROTECTION?[1]

Heike Spieker[2]

1. INTRODUCTION

On 12 December 2002, the international community celebrated the twenty-fifth anniversary of the opening for signature of 1977 Protocol II Additional to the Geneva Conventions of 12 August 1949, and Relating to the Protection of Victims of Non-International Armed Conflicts. In view of today's armed hostilities around the globe, this anniversary raises the questions whether international humanitarian law provides substantive regulation protecting civilians in non-international armed conflicts; whether such legal protection is effectively countering the sufferings of the civilian population and what are now the main challenges for the international community *vis-à-vis* internal armed conflicts.

In 2001, 24 major armed conflicts were reported, 22 of a non-international character and 11 of eight or more years duration.[3] Eleven out of 20 humanitarian emergencies were counted in non-international conflicts.[4] Between 1990 and 2001, 57 different major armed conflicts in 45 different locations were counted, all but three of them[5] – apart from armed conflicts in the context of military operations in the framework of Chapter VII of the UN Charter – being non-international.[6] The

---

2. Heike Spieker is Head of the International Relations and International Law Division at the German Red Cross Headquarters, Berlin, Germany.

3. *SIPRI Yearbook* (Stockholm, Stockholm International Peace Research Institute 2002). For 1998, the SIPRI counted 27 major armed conflicts, with only two being international (*SIPRI Yearbook* 1999). In at least six of these conflicts, the intensity of the fighting had increased to a higher level than in the previous year, and 13 of the major armed conflicts incurred at least 1,000 deaths during the year. For the year 2000, the number of 25 non-international armed conflicts had gone down to 23 of 25 (*SIPRI Yearbook* 2001). Although these figures seem to indicate a declining trend, it seems that this does not constitute a sustainable development.

4. Government of the United States of America, Global Humanitarian Emergencies: Trends and Projections, 2001-2002, from: http://www.reliefweb. The remaining nine humanitarian emergencies were mostly due to natural disasters.

5. The three international armed conflicts being the conflicts between Iraq and Kuwait, India and Pakistan and Eritrea and Ethiopia: *SIPRI Yearbook* (2002) p. 6.

6. *SIPRI Yearbook* (2002) p. 6.

Yearbook of International Humanitarian Law
Volume 4 – 2001 – pp. 129-166

suffering of civilians in armed conflicts has been widely reported.[7] The proportion of war victims who are civilians among casualties of armed hostilities has leaped to a minimum of an estimated 75 percent.[8] Armed hostilities, the majority of which were internal, have claimed more than five million lives since the 1990s.[9]

Prior to Additional Protocol II of 1977, common Article 3 of the 1949 Geneva Conventions[10] was the only humanitarian law treaty regulation on the protection of the civilian population in non-international armed conflicts. Additional Protocol II has been simultaneously both enthusiastically praised for its progressive and more detailed regulation by humanitarian law of non-international armed conflicts and harshly criticised for its shortcomings, deficiencies and non-regulation compared to Protocol I and given the practical needs.[11] Compared to the content and comprehensiveness of Additional Protocol I, Protocol II appears as a 'torso', with a comparatively poor status of protection granted. Today, Additional Protocol II has 153 States Parties,[12] compared to 190 for the four Geneva Conventions.[13]

Asking whether the Protocol II 'torso' has made any difference to the fate of the civilian population as such and to individual civilians in non-international armed conflicts already seems to imply a negative answer – taking only the conduct of hostilities in Liberia, Sierra Leone, Colombia, East Timor and the former Yugoslavia as examples. Non-international armed conflicts since the last decade of the Twentieth Century have been characterised by a diverse set of antagonistic groups, variously driven by political ambitions and economic motives, with ethnicity or religious beliefs being widely used as a tool to define and motivate certain groups. Conflict resolution has been hampered by the fact that today's non-governmental parties to a conflict often tend to break apart into factions. All sides have access to

7. See for example, S/RES/1265 (1999), preamble, para. 4, where the UN Security Council expressed its grave concern about the fact that civilians account for the vast majority of casualties in armed conflicts and are increasingly targeted by combatants and armed elements, and recognised the resultant impact this will have on durable peace, reconciliation and development. See also a detailed ICRC survey in its 1999 'People on War' Report: http://www.icrc.org/eng/onwar.

8. See Report of the Secretary-General to the Security Council on the Protection of Civilians in Armed Conflict, S/2001/331, para. 3; other sources speak of nine out of every ten war casualties being civilians, R.A. Dallaire, 'The Changing Role of UN Peacekeeping Forces: The Relationship between UN Peacekeepers and NGOs in Rwanda', in J. Whitman and D. Pocock, eds., *After Rwanda, The Coordination of United Nations Humanitarian Assistance* (Basingstoke, Macmillan/New York, St. Martin's Press 1996) at p. 205.

9. UN Secretary-General, Millennium Report of the Secretary-General: 'We, the peoples: the role of the United Nations in the 21st century' [A/54/2000], http://www.un.org./millennium/sg/report/ch3.htm at para. 193.

10. 1949 Geneva Convention I for the Amelioration of the Condition of the Wounded and Sick in Armed Forces; Geneva Convention II for the Amelioration of the Condition of the Wounded, Sick and Shipwrecked Members of Armed Forces at Sea; Geneva Convention III Relative to the Treatment of Prisoners of War; Geneva Convention IV Relative to the Protection of Civilian Persons in Time of War.

11. On this issue, see for example, H. S. Levie, ed., *The Law of Non-International Armed Conflict* (Dordrecht, Martinus Nijhoff Publishers 1987).

12. Additional Protocol I has 160 States Parties; ICRC, http://www.icrc.org/eng/party_gc.

13. Out of 191 members of the United Nations, from http://www.un.org/Overview/unmember.html.

weapons and financial resources; the fighting often takes place in remote locations and all perceive their vital interests to be at stake.[14] Very often, these same vital interests with regard to the possession and control of economic goods are those needed for the functioning of modern industrial societies.[15] The consequences of such non-international armed conflicts have been the flow of refugees and internally displaced people, cross-border movement of armed personnel as well as the undermining of economic and political structures in neighbouring states through illicit trade in natural resources and arms. [16]

In 1999, the Secretary-General of the United Nations emphasised that the protection of the civilian population is one of the UN's priorities. He recommended a 'clear course of action for the Security Council to compel parties to a conflict to better protect civilian populations and to respect the rights guaranteed to civilians by international law'.[17] Member States of the United Nations pledged in the Millennium Declaration to expand and strengthen the protection of civilians in complex emergencies, in conformity with international humanitarian law.[18] In his second report in 2001, the UN Secretary-General stated that 'the realities of distressed populations have not changed'.[19] Although the recent 2002 report was able to state 'new contexts' provided for the protection of civilians in armed conflicts given the fact that 'since the previous report, some of the world's most protracted and violent conflicts are reaching resolution or coming to an end', the cases of Angola, Sierra Leone and Afghanistan 'confirmed the critical nature of the protection of civilian populations, including their right to humanitarian access, even in conflicts approaching resolution and through the transitional phase when peace is consolidated'.[20] The Secretary-General identified three global issues that will seriously challenge the capacity of Member States to protect civilians, in

---

14. *SIPRI Yearbook* 2001, under Part I.1.

15. M. T. Klare speaks of 'resource wars', such resources being in particular gold, diamonds, valuable minerals and old-growth timber. As in Angola and Sierra Leone, ethnic, political, and regional antagonisms are very often interwoven with the use of armed hostilities over economic resources, in *Resource Wars, The New Landscape of Global Conflict* (New York, Henry Holt 2001) pp. 109 et seq. He sees such 'resource wars' as part of an interconnected geopolitical system, 'a global landscape in which competition over vital resources is becoming the governing principle behind the disposition and use of military power' which will become 'the mostdistinctive feature of the global security environment' in the future, pp. 213 et seq.

16. *SIPRI Yearbook* (2002) p. 6 and government of the United States of America, Global Humanitarian Emergencies: Trends and Projections, 2001-2002, US Department of State, 11 January 2002, under 'Summary', from: http://www.cia.gov/nic/pubs/other_products/global_humanitarian_pub.htm.

17. Report on the Protection of Civilians in Armed Conflict, S/1999/957 of 8 September 1999, para. 68.

18. A/RES/55/2 of 13 September 2000, para. 26.

19. Report of the UN Secretary-General to the Security Council on the Protection of Civilians in Armed Conflict. *Supra* n. 8, para. 2.

20. Report of the UN Secretary-General to the Security Council on the Protection of Civilians in Armed Conflict, S/2002/1300, of 26 November 2002, para. 11. The Report takes it as a 'now well known fact that civilians, rather than combatants, are the main casualties of conflicts today, with women and children constituting an unprecedented number of the victims' (para. 12).

particular in non-international armed conflicts: first, the increased focus on gender-based violence in humanitarian crisis and conflict situations;[21] second, the commercial exploitation of conflict;[22] and, third, the rise of terrorism and the involvement of terrorist organisations in armed conflicts.[23]

Often remarked upon and analysed as having changed is the nature of armed conflicts in general[24] and of non-international armed conflicts in particular.[25] Yet assertions of that kind are extremely difficult to evaluate.[26] To some extent they depend particularly on information available on such conflicts and on their impact on the affected population, on the awareness of the international community of non-international armed conflicts and their consequences and on the political will to attach international concern to the problem. Nevertheless, it may be maintained that the number, shape, conduct of hostilities, participants, and victims of armed conflicts have changed since the adoption of common Article 3 of the Geneva Conventions of 1949 and Additional Protocol II of 1977. In particular, the global changes after the end of the Cold War exposed enormous national, religious, anthropological and ethnical incompatibilities and gave rise to a great number of respectively motivated clashes. The lack of 'good governance' in many states on all continents is an additional factor nourishing armed hostilities. Today, non-international armed conflicts are more numerous and more brutal and entail more bloodshed than international armed conflicts; the conduct of hostilities in Liberia, Southern Sudan, East Timor and Colombia as well as the former Yugoslavia and the Great Lakes region, are only some recent examples. Civilian casualties are caused by governmental and non-governmental parties to armed conflicts alike.[27] The extent of civilians becoming the principal victims of armed hostilities has reached new dimensions.

---

21. '(...), a grave and continuing problem that has been heightened by reports of sexual exploitation and abuse and trafficking of women and girls perpetrated by humanitarian workers and peacekeepers'. *Supra* n. 20, para. 54.

22. 'The illicit and illegal exploitation of natural resources is a growing problem that serves to fuel conflict and increasingly involves and harms the security of the civilian population.' *Supra* n. 20, para. 58.

23. 'The responses of States to acts of terrorism must remain cognizant of the need to protect civilian life and property and be undertaken with full respect to international humanitarian and human rights law. Every effort to strengthen the international protection of civilians in armed conflict is a victory against terrorism which, by its very nature, seeks to undermine civilian status and weaken the legal and institutional frameworks through which civilian men, women and children are shielded from the violence of war.' *Supra* n. 20, para. 61.

24. R.A. Dallaire, 'The Changing Role of UN Peacekeeping Forces: The Relationship between UN Peacekeepers and NGOs in Rwanda', in Whitman and Pocock, op. cit. n. 8, at p. 205.

25. For a comprehensive overview of recent discussions see P.F. Rogers, *Politics in the next 50 years*, University of Bradford, Department of Peace Studies, Peace Studies Papers, Fourth Series, Working Paper No. 1, http://www.brad.ac.uk/acad/peace/pubs/psp1.pdf 2000) pp. 1-40 and M. Kaldor, *New & Old Wars, Organised Violence in a Global Era* (Cambridge, Polity Press 1999).

26. *Supra* n. 19, para. 3.

27. See further L. Zegveld, *Accountability of Armed Opposition Groups in International Law* (Cambridge, Cambridge University Press 2002) p. 2.

The question whether or not Additional Protocol II has had a positive impact on the situation of civilians in non-international armed conflicts and entails progress in humanitarian legal protection is a question of the adequacy of the existing legal framework for protecting the civilian population in non-international armed conflicts. The present contribution will not attempt to provide a comprehensive overview of the existing law on the protection of the civilian population in non-international armed conflicts. It will neither describe the corpus of relevant treaty law[28] nor provide a commentary on the issue.[29] Moreover, it will not develop a comprehensive analysis of existing customary law[30] on the protection of the civilian population in non-international armed conflicts.[31] The specific protection

---

28. Mention should only be made of the fact that common Article 3 GC constitutes the 'minimum standard' of international humanitarian law being applicable in all armed conflicts. *Case Concerning Military and Paramilitary Activities In and Against Nicaragua of 27 June 1986, ICJ Rep.* (1986) para. 218. Under Additional Protocol II, the core protection of the civilian population is regulated by Arts. 13 to 18 in particular, setting out many of the provisions of common Article 3 GC in more detail and extending the protection afforded to civilians, detainees and medical personnel. These provisions grant protection to civilians and specific civilian objects as well as regulate the forced movement of civilians and humanitarian assistance operations. G.H. Aldrich compares the development of international humanitarian law for non-international armed conflicts to a cosmological ''big bang' that gives birth to a new universe. While the law applicable to non-international armed conflicts may still be seen as no more than a baby universe, the development is so new and unexpected that any predictions about further enlargement in the early part of the next century are bound to be very uncertain,' 'The Hague Peace Conferences: The laws of war on land', in 94 *AJIL* (2000) pp. 42-63 at p. 61.

29. For a concise summary see Zegveld, op. cit. n. 27, at pp. 76-93.

30. Any attempt would be condemned to inadequacy in comparison with the Study on Customary International Humanitarian Law in preparation by the International Committee of the Red Cross. The Study will supposedly prove that many rules are applicable to both international and non-international conflicts. T. Meron, 'The humanization of humanitarian law', 94 *AJIL* (2000) pp. 239 et seq., at p. 261; see also T. Meron, 'The continuing role of custom in the formation of international humanitarian law', 90 *AJIL* (1996) pp. 238 et seq., at p. 245 et seq.

31. It has been and still is extensively discussed whether common Art. 3 GC and Additional Protocol II respectively, *in toto* codify or have crystallised as customary law. See Constitutional Court of Colombia, Ruling No. C-574/92, Section V, B2c, 28 October 1992, and Ruling No. C-225/95, Section VD, 18 May 1995, in M. Sassòli and A. Bouvier, *How Does Law Protect in War* (Geneva, ICRC 1999) pp. 1357-1370, or T. Meron, *Human Rights and Humanitarian Norms as Customary Law* (Oxford, Oxford University Press 1989) pp. 73 et seq. and G.H. Aldrich, 'The Hague Peace Conferences: The Laws of War on Land', 94 *AJIL* (2000) pp. 42-63. See also in particular the International Court of Justice in the *case Concerning Military and Paramilitary Activities In and Against Nicaragua of 27 June 1986, ICJ Rep.* (1986) para. 218, and *Report of the UN Secretary General on Aspects of Establishing an International Tribunal for the Prosecution of Persons Responsible for Serious Violations of International Humanitarian Law Committed in the Territory of the Former Yugoslavia of 3 May 1993*, UN Doc. S/25704. The ICTY Appeals Chamber held that many of the Provisions of Additional Protocol II can now be regarded as declaratory of existing rules or as having crystallised into emerging rules of customary law, or as having been instrumental in their evolution as general principles: *The Prosecutor* v. *Duško Tadić*, case No. IT-94-1-A, Appeals Chamber, Decision on the Defence Motion for Interlocutory Appeal on Jurisdiction, 2 October 1995, para. 117. Art. 4 of the ICTR Statute of qualifies those provisions of Additional Protocol II being prone to 'serious violations' as constituting customary law. In particular Art. 4 AP II on fundamental guarantees is widely accepted as customary law: *Prosecutor* v. *Jean-Paul Akayesu*, case No. ICTR-96-4-T, Trial Chamber, Judgement of 2 September 1998, para. 616, and L. Moir, *The Law of Internal Armed Conflict* (Cambridge, Cambridge University Press 2002) pp. 133-192. The assumption of codification of customary law has

granted by international human rights law and its limitations[32] will not be elaborated.[33] An answer to the question of the adequacy of the existing legal framework will be approached by analysing the problems of applicability of international humanitarian law in non-international armed conflicts, recent practice of armed hostilities in such conflicts and implementation and enforcement of the law.

2. PROBLEMS OF APPLICABILITY OF HUMANITARIAN LAW IN NON-INTERNATIONAL ARMED CONFLICTS

An examination of the problems of applicability of humanitarian law norms in non-international armed conflicts is the initial, but crucial, step in any observation on the question of adequacy.

2.1 Problems in defining situations of 'non-international armed conflict'

Modern international humanitarian[34] law does not legally define the situation of armed conflict.[35] However, the jurisprudence of the ICTY has explicitly elaborated

---

recently been questioned by A. Rubin, 'Review Article. The Independent International Commission on Kosovo', 6 *Journal of Conflict and Security Law* (2001) pp. 147 et seq., at p. 148. In the *Kordić* Decision on the Defense Motion, the ICTY extended the list of customary law provisions with Art. 13(2) AP II, concerning unlawful attacks on civilians: *Prosecutor* v. *Dario Kordić* and *Mario Cerkez*, case No. IT-95-14/2-PT, Decision of 2 March 1999, para. 31.

32. Limitations on the protection granted by human rights law constitute in particular the derogation clauses and the fact that human rights law in general is not legally binding on non-governmental actors, i.e., in the case of non-international armed conflicts, on non-governmental parties of the conflict.

33. Cf., especially R. Provost, *International Human Rights and Humanitarian Law* (Cambridge, Cambridge University Press 2002).

34. On the development of the concept of armed conflict and its relationship to the notion of 'war', see K.J. Partsch, 'Armed Conflict', in R. Bernhardt, ed., *Encyclopedia of Public International Law*, Vol. I (Amsterdam, North-Holland 1992) pp. 249-252.

35. The Geneva Conventions refer to such a definition insofar as they clarify that the Conventions shall apply to all cases of declared war or of any other armed conflict which may arise between two or more of the High Contracting Parties' (common Art. 2(1) GC). This determination of the field of application is reiterated by Art. 1(3) AP I and indirectly repeated in Art. 1(1) AP II, while Additional Protocol II explicitly exempts internal disturbances and tensions from the notion of 'armed conflict'. The rather widely accepted definition as applied in continued jurisprudence by the ICTY states that 'an armed conflict exists whenever there is a resort to armed force between States or protracted armed violence between governmental authorities and organized armed groups or between such groups within a State': *The Prosecutor* v. *Duško Tadić*, Decision on Jurisdiction, *supra* n. 31, para. 70. This definition is repeated and elaborated in *The Prosecutor* v. *Duško Tadić*, Trial Chamber, Opinion and Judgement, of 7 May 1997, para. 561; *Prosecutor* v. *Žejnil Delalić, Zdravko Mucić, Hazim Delić* and *Esad Landžo*, case No. IT-96-21-T, Trial Chamber, Opinion and Judgement of 16 November 1998, paras. 182 f., and *Prosecutor* v. *Anto Furundžija*, case No. IT-95-17/1-T, Trial Chamber, Judgement of 10 December 1998, para. 59. In a less detailed manner, the ICTR Trial Chamber stated in the *Akayesu* case that the term 'armed conflict' in itself suggests the existence of open hostilities between armed

on the questions of temporal[36] and geographical[37] scope of the armed conflict as well as a 'sufficient connection' between the armed conflict and potential infringements of the law.[38]

According to the traditional concept of international humanitarian law, and notwithstanding various semantic differences,[39] there exists a classical distinction with regard to its applicability, i.e., the distinction between international armed conflict, non-international armed conflict and merely internal or domestic situations of tensions or disturbances.[40] An international armed conflict is the traditional and 'normal'[41] situation in which the provisions of international humanitarian law are applicable.[42] It is still a fact that in non-international armed conflicts a more limited range of humanitarian law provisions is applicable compared to the much more numerous and elaborate rules for international armed conflicts.[43] Both

---

forces which are organized to a greater or lesser degree: *Prosecutor* v. *Jean-Paul Akayesu*, *supra* n. 31, para. 620.

36. The ICTY Chamber in the *Čelebići* case base its findings on 'continuing armed violence at least from (...) 6 March 1992 until (...) November 1995', ibid., para. 185; the Trial Chamber in the *Furundžija* case found an armed conflict during the general time-frame of the acts of the accused in Bosnia-Herzegovina, ibid., para. 59; the ICTR Trial Chamber in the *Akayesu* case in a similar manner generally observed that 'there existed at the time of the events alleged in the Indictment an armed conflict not of an international character'. *Supra* n. 31, para. 621.

37. In the *Čelebići* case, the ICTY Trial Chamber referred to the applicability of rules of international humanitarian law. With regard to the geographical factor, the Chamber stated that 'for the norms of international humanitarian law to be applicable', 'there does not have to be actual combat activities in a particular location'. *Supra* n. 36, para. 185. In the specific case, the Chamber found it was not necessary that there was an armed conflict 'in the Konjic municipality itself'. It held that 'combat activities' in 'the larger territory of which it [i.e., Konjic municipality] forms part' were sufficient for the determination of an armed conflict. The ICTR Trial Chamber stated in *Akayesu* that 'the mere fact that Rwanda was engaged in an armed conflict meeting the threshold requirements of Common Article 3 and Additional Protocol II means that these instruments would apply over the whole territory hence encompassing massacres which occurred away from the 'war front'. *Supra* n. 35, para. 636.

38. Cf., *Čelebići*, *supra* n. 36, paras. 193-197. In the *Furundžija* case, the Trial Chamber relied on the accused being an 'active combatant' participating in a practice at least endorsed by a party to the conflict, *supra* n. 35 para. 65; Trial Chamber, *Le Procureur* v. *Zlatko Aleksovski*, case No. IT-95-14/1-T, Judgment 25 June 1999, para. 45.

39. Concerning the different uses of the expression 'armed conflict' and of its qualifications, cf., Partsch, loc. cit. n. 34, pp. 250-252.

40. J. Pictet, *Commentary on the IV Geneva Convention Relative to the Protection of Civilian Persons in Time of War* (Geneva, ICRC 1958) pp. 35 et seq.

41. Including the specific case of armed conflicts in which peoples are fighting against racist regimes in the exercise of their right of self-determination, Art. 1(4) AP I, which is sometimes clarified as a distinct type of non-international armed conflicts: M. Bothe, K.J. Partsch and W.A. Solf, eds., *New Rules For Victims of Armed Conflicts* (The Hague, Martinus Nijhoff 1982); Art. 1 AP II, 2.2.; Moir, op. cit. n. 31, at p. 101.

42. Cf., with further references Y. Sandoz, Chr. Swinarski and B. Zimmermann, eds., *Commentary on the Additional Protocols of 8 June 1977 to the Geneva Conventions of 12 August 1949* (Geneva, ICRC 1987) para. 4458.

43. The development of humanitarian rules for non-international armed conflicts in international treaties and custom is described for example by Sassòli and Bouvier, op. cit. n. 31, at pp. 68-70 and 88-90; C. Greenwood, 'Scope of Application of Humanitarian Law', in D. Fleck, ed., *Handbook of Humanitarian Law in Armed Conflicts* (Oxford, Oxford University Press 1995) pp. 39-49; and T. Meron, 'Is International Law Moving towards Criminalization?', 9 *EJIL* (1998) pp. 18-31 at 25, and in

common Article 3 GC and Additional Protocol II set out the prerequisite of a non-international armed conflict. It follows from the wording of common Article 3 GC that a non-international conflict constitutes an armed conflict without the involvement of at least two classical subjects of international law, that is, states, generally[44] referred to as a 'non-international armed conflict'. The contrast to international armed conflicts is provided by Article 1(1) AP II which defines non-international armed conflicts as 'all armed conflicts which are not covered by Article 1 [of AP I]', while Article 1(3) and (4) AP I determine the applicability of Additional Protocol I in situations of international armed conflict. Thus, non-international armed conflicts are defined by reference and in opposition to armed conflicts.

Finally, the traditional concept of international humanitarian law pays tribute to the principle of the sovereignty of states,[45] based on the fact that in situations qualifying as mere internal or domestic armed conflicts states do not apply humanitarian law rules at all and exclusively rely on instruments of domestic public and criminal law. Additional Protocol II (Article 1(2)) and the ICC Statute (Article 8(2)(d) and (f))[46] refer to such internal situations as 'situations of internal disturbances and tensions, such as riots, isolated and sporadic acts of violence and other acts of a similar nature'. In other words, despite different categorisations and sub-categorisations on the basis of various criteria and for differing purposes, states have made it clear that they distinguish – in general and in all lack of clarity – between situations where international law in general and international humanitarian law in particular is applicable on the one hand and situations on the other hand where the applicability of international humanitarian law is denied.

2.1.1 *Modern trends in international humanitarian law*

Notwithstanding the distinction between types of armed conflict regulated by humanitarian law, the increased impact and awareness of non-international armed conflicts is not least mirrored in the recent legal regulation of such conflicts, as well as in state practice and doctrine.[47]

The scope of the 1980 Certain Conventional Weapons Convention has been broadened[48] to apply to international armed conflicts and, in addition, to apply to 'situations referred to in Article 3 common to the Geneva Conventions of 12

Prosecutor v. *Tadić*, Appeals Chamber, Decision on the Defence Motion for Interlocutory Appeal on Jurisdiction, *supra* n. 31, paras. 100-127.

44. Cf., for example, Sandoz et al., op. cit. n. 42, para. 4458.

45. J. Pictet, op. cit. n. 40, at pp. 35 et seq.

46. The ICC Statute is explicitly based on this traditional concept in that Art. 8 on the definition of war crimes distinguishes between international and non-international armed conflicts and exempts 'internal situations' from this definition.

47. Cf., for example, Zegveld, op. cit. n. 27, at pp. 33-38.

48. Amendment of 21 December 2001: http://www.icrc.org/ihl.nsf; the Protocol on Prohibitions or Restrictions on the Use of Mines, Booby-Traps and Other Devices had already been amended in 1966.

August 1949',[49] as well as international armed conflicts, while at the same time excluding 'situations of internal disturbances and tensions (...) as not being armed conflicts'. The 1997 Anti-Personnel Landmines Convention[50] reemphasises the aspect of application in non-international conflicts by obliging States Parties 'never under any circumstances' to undertake to use such mines (Art. 1). The 1999 Second Protocol on the Protection of Cultural Property[51] excludes application in 'situations of internal disturbances and tensions', but does apply 'in the event of an armed conflict not of an international character'.[52] The 2000 Optional Protocol to the Convention on the Rights of the Child on Involvement of Children in Armed Conflict prohibits directly involving persons younger than 18 years in hostilities or their forced recruitment into the armed forces in both international and non-international armed conflicts.[53] There is an absolute prohibition on the recruiting or using in hostilities of persons younger than 18 by armed groups.[54] Although lacking legally binding force, the 1990 Turku Declaration of Minimum Humanitarian Standards[55] had earlier stated that such standards are applicable 'in all situations, including internal violence, disturbances, tensions, and public emergency, and which cannot be derogated from under any circumstances'.[56]

The effort to assimilate the legal regulation of non-international conflicts to the regime of international conflicts is also increasingly apparent in international criminal law. The ICTY and ICTR have jurisdiction over crimes committed in major armed hostilities between governmental armed forces and non-governmental armed groups and such groups among themselves. Decisions and judgements of the ICTY and ICTR are exclusively based on their Statutes and are legally binding in specific trials alone. Yet, their jurisprudence[57] has encouraged a certain conformity of international criminal law in international and in non-international armed conflicts. This has influenced the jurisdiction of the International Criminal Court and the offences incorporated in its Statute. While Article 8 on war crimes retains the distinction between international and non-international armed conflict,[58] and excludes application to 'situations of internal disturbances and

---

50. Amendment Art. 1(2).

51. Convention on the Prohibition of the Use, Stockpiling, Production and Transfer of Anti-Personnel Mines and on their Destruction of 18 September 1997.

52. Second Protocol to the Hague Convention of 1954 for the Protection of Cultural Property in the Event of Armed Conflict of 26 March 1999.

53. Art. 22(1) and 2.

54. Arts. 1 and 2, respectively.

55. Art. 4 of the Optional Protocol provides: 'Armed groups that are distinct from the armed forces of a State should not, under any circumstances, recruit or use in hostilities persons under the age of 18 years.'

56. Declaration of 2 December 1990. Revised 1996. Published by the Institute for Human Rights, Åbo Akademi University, Turku/Åbo 1996.

56. Art. 1.

57. In particular, the jurisprudence of the ICTY; cf., Decision on the Defence Motion for Interlocutory Appeal on Jurisdiction, *supra* n. 31, paras. 71 et seq. and paras. 86-93; for an inclusion in Art. 2 of the ICTY Statute cf. the Trial Chamber of the ICTY in the *Čelebići* case, 16 November 1998, *supra* n. 36, para. 317.

58. Art. 8(2)(c) and (e) ICC Statute.

tensions',[59] it assimilates offences in international and in non-international armed conflicts to a certain extent.

Several military manuals[60] provide for the application of humanitarian law rules in international as well as non-international conflicts, and the German military manual extends such application to the whole body of humanitarian law.[61] However, concluding mention should be made of the fact that neither States- nor non-States Parties to a conflict[62] make extensive use of the possibility provided by common Article 3(2) sentence 3 GC to make special agreements with the aim of widening the scope of applicable provisions and in particular of rendering rules for international conflicts applicable in non-international ones.[63]

These developments evidence an increasing general tendency to overcome traditional differences in the legal covering of international and non-international armed conflicts in certain aspects. At the same time they reveal an interesting double dichotomy: whereas in 1977 the attempt to reach an identical protection of the civilian population in international and non-international armed conflicts failed, some parts of international humanitarian law in the meantime have incorporated concrete steps to give preference to the protection granted by international humanitarian law against the preservation of national sovereignty in non-international armed conflict. However, notwithstanding the trend to merge international humanitarian law applicable in both international and non-international armed conflicts, state practice generally still retains a clear distinction between international and non-international armed conflicts and internal disturbances and tensions.

2.1.2 *Distinction between non-international armed conflict and internal disturbances and tensions*

While one might doubt whether the traditional paradigm of international humanitarian law to distinguish between three different types of armed hostilities remains helpful or relevant today,[64] it remains the basis for the existing humanitarian law regime. The problem arising out of this paradigm is one of legal definition. To define a non-international armed conflict as a conflict which neither constitutes an

---

59. Art. 8(2)(d) and (f) ICC Statute.

60. L.C. Green, *The Contemporary Law of Armed Conflict* (Manchester, Manchester University Press 1993 and 2000) pp. 59 et seq.; Meron, loc. cit. n. 30, at p. 261; A. Cassese, *International Law* (Oxford, Oxford University Press 2001) pp. 66-69.

61. Greenwood, loc. cit. n. 43, at p. 41.

62. Zegveld, op. cit. n. 27, p. 148.

63. M.S. Elewa, 'Genocide at the Safe Area of Srebrenica: A Search For a New Strategy For Protecting Civilians in Contemporary Armed Conflict', 10 *Michigan State Univ.-DCL JIL* (2001) pp. 429 et seq., at p. 436. Selected examples are referred to by Moir, op. cit. n. 31, pp. 67-88, 119-132 and 141.

64. See for instance Moir, ibid., p. 51: 'If this trend continues [i.e., that the distinction between internal and international armed conflict is becoming less important], then there may shortly be a body of international humanitarian law which applies to all armed conflicts.' For the debate on this issue refer to fn. 93 et seq., on p. 51.

international one nor internal disturbances and tensions is legally correct and incontestable. It is the actual application of these formally rigid definitions and distinctions in today's highly complex conflict situations that constitutes the problem. As demonstrated particularly by the various conflicts and sub-conflicts on the territory of the former Yugoslavia, the actual qualification of a conflict as international,[65] non- international or merely internal is not an issue of merely academic interest and jurisprudential practice, but concerns the application of international humanitarian law and the regulation of conflicts in practice.

2.1.2.1 Intensity of the conflict and organisation of the parties to the conflict

In order to distinguish non-international armed conflicts and internal disturbances and tensions, the jurisprudence of the ICTR is of particular relevance. The ICTR Trial Chamber in the *Akayesu* case had recourse to the criteria of the intensity of the conflict and a sufficient organisation of the conflict parties in qualifying the armed conflict in Rwanda.[66]

Concerning the criterion of the intensity of the conflict, the Tribunal first clarified that ascertaining the intensity of a non-international conflict does not depend on the subjective judgement of the parties to the conflict.[67] The Tribunal then referred to the qualification of the Rwandan conflict as 'a war, an internal [i.e., non-international] armed conflict' by 'all observers to the events, including UNAMIR and UN Special rapporteurs'[68]

With regard to the criterion of organisation of the parties to the conflict, the Chamber first distinguished 'mere acts of banditry or unorganized and short-lived insurrections' from 'genuine armed conflicts' and excluded the former from the scope of common Article 3 GC.[69] It then simply stated that the Rwandan governmental forces on the one hand and the RPF on the other hand were 'well-organized and considered to be armies in their own right'.[70] The Tribunal thus considered such acts of banditry and unorganised and short-lived insurrections as types of internal disturbances and tensions not qualifying as non-international armed conflicts.

65. On the distinction between international and non-international armed conflicts, including the problem of coincidence of both types, cf. in particular Judgement of the Appeals Chamber, *Prosecutor* v. *Duško Tadić*, case No. IT-94-1-A, of 15 July 1999, paras. 84-137. With regard to 'the conflicts in the former Yugoslavia', the Appeals Chamber referred to the involvement of the Armed Forces of Croatia in Bosnia- Herzegovina and of the Yugoslav National Army (JNA) in Croatia as three distinct subjects of international law, thus rendering the armed conflict an international one (para. 72). At the same time, the Chamber identified the use of armed violence between Bosnian Government forces and Bosnian Serb rebel forces in Bosnia-Herzegovina (as well as Croatian Government and Croatian Serb rebel forces in Croatia). From this finding, it drew the conclusion that these conflicts were to be qualified as non-international ones (para. 72). See also Trial Chamber, Opinion and Judgement, *Prosecutor* v. *Dusko Tadić*, of 7 May 1997, paras. 566-595.

66. *Akayesu*, 2 September 1998, *supra* n. 31, para. 620.

67. Ibid., para. 603.

68. Ibid., paras. 620-621.

69. Ibid., para. 620.

70. Ibid., para. 621.

In the *Rutaganda* case,[71] the ICTR trial chamber was satisfied that 'there existed an internal [i.e., non-international] armed conflict' on the basis of these criteria and the criteria of Article 1(1) AP II. Additionally, it relied on the fact that the RPF had stated to the International Committee of the Red Cross that it considered itself bound by the rules of international humanitarian law.[72] A very similar approach was taken in the *Ruzindana* case.[73]

In sum, substantial indications with regard to when an armed conflict is deemed to be sufficiently intense to qualify as a non-international armed conflict in the sense of common Article 3 GC and Article 1(1) AP II have not been provided by the jurisprudence. Sub-criteria as to when an organisation of the non-state actors in particular meets the threshold of sufficiency are also not provided by recent jurisprudence or by legal writing.

2.1.2.2 Aim and objective of the parties to the conflict

The criterion of aim and objective being pursued by the parties to the conflict might be another distinctive element distinguishing non-international armed conflicts and internal disturbances and tensions. However, although the ICTY made use of this criterion,[74] it did not elaborate on its substance. Relevant jurisprudence is scarce and substantive criteria are little. The ICTY Trial Chamber introduced the criteria of the 'aim and objective' which is pursued by the parties to the conflict. It did so with regard to the question if a former international armed conflict was continued after a certain date or 'alter[ed] fundamentally in its nature'.[75] Nor did it examine the conditions under which the aim and objective of an armed conflict may characterise the conflict as either international or non-international. The Trial Chamber indirectly had recourse to this criterion in the *Kunarac* judgement, attributing the criterion of 'pursu[ing] military goals and the objective of territorial gain' to armed conflicts in relation to situations below this threshold.[76] In sum, the definition of a non-international armed conflict is still 'termed in the abstract', and whether or not a situation can be described as an 'armed conflict', meeting the criteria of Common Article 3, is to be decided upon on a case-by-case basis'.[77]

---

71. *Prosecutor* v. *Rutaganda*, case No. ICTR-96-3, Judgement of the ICTR, 6 December 1999.

72. Ibid., para. 436.

73. 'It has been established, beyond a reasonable doubt, that there was an armed conflict, not of an international character, in Rwanda. This armed conflict took place between the governmental armed forces, the FAR, and the dissident armed forces, the RPF, in the time of the events alleged in the Indictment, that is from April to July 1994. It has also been shown, beyond a reasonable doubt, that Rwanda was bound by Common Article 3 and Protocol II, which were applicable to 'the situation in Rwanda in 1994'. The Parties in this non-international conflict confirmed their readiness to comply with the rules of these international humanitarian instruments.' *Prosecutor* v. *Clément Kayishema and Obed Ruzindana*, Judgement, case No. ICTR-95-1-T, 21 May 1999, para. 597.

74. *Čelebići,* 16 November 1998, *supra* n. 36, para. 224.

75. Ibid., para. 234.

76. *Prosecutor* v. *Dragoljub Kunarac, Radomir Kovac and Zoran Vuković*, case No. IT-96-23-T and IT-96-23/1-T, 22 February 2001, para. 579.

77. *Rutaganda*, 6 December 1999, *supra* n. 71, para. 91.

A further problem is that it is not clear which are the competent organs to make the determination whether a particular situation constitutes a non-international armed conflict or an internal disturbance or tensions, i.e., not only the criteria to be applied in making the determination as to the character of a situation but also the 'identity, jurisdiction and authority of the characterising agent'[78] applying the criteria is open to interpretation and partial discretion.[79]

The lack of accepted criteria to distinguish domestic situations from non-international armed conflicts prevents humanitarian law from being applied and prevents the civilian population affected by armed hostilities from enjoying the protection granted by humanitarian law. To achieve acceptance that at least a minimum standard – as embodied in common Article 3 GC and, possibly, Additional Protocol II – is applicable would secure and enhance the protection of the civilian population in non-international armed conflicts. Yet, any discretion of states to accept the application of common Article 3 GC and/or Additional Protocol II is limited when courts or tribunals and international institutions in general are competent to interpret and apply the law,[80] a framework which admittedly still constitutes the exception rather than the rule.

On the other hand, the positive effect of a lack of agreed distinctive criteria is the flexibility provided by such lacuna.[81] Doors might be opened to apply international humanitarian law in situations which traditionally would not necessarily qualify as non-international armed conflicts. In theory, weaknesses in protecting the civilian population and discretion in qualifying armed hostilities are balanced by an increased flexibility in applying international protective standards; in practice, the benefits of such increased flexibility and an enhancement of the protection of the civilian population in non-international armed conflicts generally remain dependant on the decisions of individual governments.

2.2 Scope of application of common Article 3 and Additional Protocol II

Common Article 3 GC does not distinguish between armed conflicts not of an international character and situations below this threshold, i.e., between the application of international humanitarian law and domestic criminal law. At the same time, both common Article 3 GC and Article 1 AP II refer to non-international armed conflicts of a certain specificity. This raises the question whether both common Article 3 GC and Article 1 AP II address in principle the same situation with a different threshold of applicability or whether both provisions cover

---

78. Provost, op. cit. n. 33, at pp. 243, 280 et seq.

79. Cf., the overview of actual conflicts that have having been evaluated by states as being regulated or not regulated by common Article 3 GC in Provost, ibid., at p. 268.

80. Zegveld, op. cit. n. 27, at pp. 12-14.

81. This factor is underestimated by Provost, op. cit. n. 33, at p. 290: 'A crucial problem common to both humanitarian law and human rights with respect to applicability of their norms is that so much turns on self-characterisation. More often than not, the state will simply disregard all relevant legal criteria and rely on strictly political considerations to officially label a situation as an armed conflict or a state of emergency.'

substantially different conflict situations.[82] Whereas common Article 3 GC addresses an 'armed conflict not of an international character occurring in the territory of one of the High Contracting Parties', Article 1(1) AP II refers to 'non-international armed conflicts' 'which take place in the territory of a High Contracting Party between its armed forces and dissident armed forces or other organised armed groups which, under responsible command, exercise such control over a part of its territory as to enable them to carry out sustained and concerted military operations and to implement this Protocol'. Thus Article 1(1) AP II adds five criteria[83] which have to be fulfilled in addition to the situation of a non-international armed conflict in order to entail its applicability.[84] While common Article 3 GC is applicable in any non-international armed conflict, provided that the hostilities amount to a non-international armed conflict and are not mere internal disturbances or tensions,[85] the threshold of application of Article 1 AP II is considerably higher[86] and its scope narrower[87] and more restrictive than that of common Article

---

82. Moir, op. cit. n. 31, at pp. 101 et seq., and Provost, op. cit. n. 33, at p. 248, distinguish between four different types of armed violence, differentiating between situations covered by common Art. 3 GC and those regulated under Additional Protocol II. Cf., also Bothe et al., eds., op. cit. n. 41. Art. 1 AP II, 2.2., distinguish between four categories of 'non-interstate conflicts': '(a) internal disturbances and tensions to which international human rights instruments are applicable; (b) non-interstate armed conflicts defined in common Art. 3 of the Conventions; (c) non-interstate armed conflicts defined in Art. 1 of Protocol II; (d) non-interstate armed conflicts falling under the definition of Art. 1 of Protocol I (wars of national liberation)'.

83. Additional Protocol II 'develops and supplements' the underlying principles of common Art. 3 GC. S.-St. Junod, 'General introduction to Protocol II', in Sandoz et al., eds., op. cit. n. 42.

84. For example, the ICTR qualified the conflict having taken place in Rwanda in 1994 as 'an internal [i.e., non-international] armed conflict within the meaning of Additional Protocol II' because the 'material conditions' of Additional Protocol II had been fulfilled, *Akayesu*, 2 September 1998, *supra* n. 31, para. 627.

85. Zegveld, op. cit. n. 27, at pp. 135-140, points to the fact that that the ICTY and ICTR as well as the Inter-American Commission on Human Rights have set down minimum conditions, while the UN SC and the UN Commission on Human Rights have applied common Art. 3 GC to various groups lacking any real effectiveness.

86. Green points to the fact that no group which has been recognised as a national liberation movement so far has had such control of any part of the national territory as would entail the applicability of Additional Protocol II in the strict sense (1993 and 2000), op. cit. n. 60, at pp. 66: 'The definition of a non-international armed conflict in Protocol II has a threshold that is so high in fact that it would exclude most revolutions and rebellions, and would probably not operate in a civil war until the rebels were well-established and had set up some form of *de facto* government (...).' Furthermore, Guatemala is an example where non-governmental conflict parties used guerrilla warfare tactics and did not necessarily seek territorial control, so that certain applicability criteria of Art. 1(1) AP II have to run vain due to the very nature of the actual tactics. See also A.G. Peterson, 'Order Out of Chaos: Domestic Enforcement of the Law of Internal Armed Conflict', in 171 *Mil. LR* (2002) pp. 1 et seq., at p. 21. Provost, op. cit. n. 33, at p. 264, considers AP II to be a 'regression, given that it requires basically the same conditions as did recognition of belligerence, but without triggering the full application of all humanitarian rules for international armed conflicts.' The high threshold for applicability of Additional Protocol II has prevented the ICTY Prosecutor from invoking the Protocol in the context of the conflict in former Yugoslavia: Zegveld, op. cit. n. 27, at p. 144 and fn. 30.

87. Zegveld, ibid., at p. 84: 'The protection provided by the Protocols sweeps more widely (i.e., covers the whole civilian population), but it is not absolute. The protection provided by Common Article 3 is absolute, but its sweep is narrower (i.e., it is confined to protecting persons in detention).'

3 GC, thus rendering Additional Protocol II applicable in more specified[88] situations.

Yet, the general and underlying type of conflict which both provisions address is the very same, only the quality of hostilities and the threshold of applicability differ considerably. All non-international armed conflicts without exception are regulated by common Article 3 GC. Once the higher threshold of Additional Protocol II is met, common Article 3 GC remains applicable and the situation is governed by both common Article 3 GC and Additional Protocol II. To understand non-international armed conflicts according to Additional Protocol II to be of a different type than those in the sense of common Article 3 GC[89] would prevent the application of common Article 3 in situations where a conflict governed by Additional Protocol II loses one or more of the specific criteria. Such an interpretation would not only be artificial but would essentially weaken and undermine the protection of the civilian population.

2.3 Binding force for non-governmental parties to the conflict

As treaty law provisions, both common Article 3 GC and Additional Protocol II are binding on their States Parties, thus at first sight excluding non-state actors to a non-international armed conflict. However, the wording of common Article 3 GC indicates the obligation for non-governmental parties: 'each Party to the conflict shall be bound'. It is in this wording that the International Court of Justice found common Article 3 GC to have developed into customary law.[90] The ICTY and ICTR confirmed the article as customary and applied it as entailing the international criminal responsibility of non-governmental individuals who have been involved in the commission of serious violations of international humanitarian law during a non-international armed conflict.[91] The nature of the binding force[92] of both common Article 3 and AP II on non-States actors to a non-international armed conflict remains debatable, however, because the legal personality of non-state entities under international law is still problematic. Although the subject is controversial, it is widely accepted that specific non-state entities, such as recognised insurgents, national liberation movements, international governmental organisa-

---

88. According to Aldrich, the applicability of Additional Protocol II is 'perversely (...) far too narrow. (...). This scope of application is reminiscent of the standard in customary law for the recognition of belligerency and the consequent application of all the customary laws of war'. 'The Hague Peace Conferences: The Law of War on Land', loc. cit. n. 28, at p. 60. Moir takes a more pragmatic approach: 'The conditions contained in Article 1 of the [Additional] Protocol [II] mean that it applies only to the most intense and large-scale conflicts.' Op. cit. n. 31, at p. 101.

89. Moir, ibid., at pp. 101 et seq.

90. International Court of Justice, *Military and Paramilitary Activities in and Against Nicaragua (Nicaragua v. United States of America), ICJ Rep.* (1986) para. 218.

91. *Prosecutor* v. *Blaškić*, case No. IT-95-14-T, Trial Chamber, Judgement of 3 March 2000, paras. 164-167, and *Akayesu*, 2 September 1998, *supra* n. 31, para. 608. Cf., also on this the comprehensive study by Provost, op. cit. n. 33, at pp. 94-102.

92. Zegveld, op. cit. n. 27, at p. 5, prefers the term 'accountability', covering both the substantive obligations of the relevant actors and their responsibility for breaches of these violations.

tions and individuals are generally endowed with some of the rights and duties of international legal subjects.[93] But, it is highly debated whether and to what extent non-governmental actors that are parties to a non-international armed conflict but which are not recognised as 'belligerent insurgents' constitute subjects under international law.

The UN Security Council commonly urges 'all parties to a conflict to comply with humanitarian law'.[94] The same entreaty is to be found, for example, in the 2001 Amendment to the 1980 UN Weapons Convention.[95] The Amendment simultaneously emphasises that 'each party to the conflict' shall be bound to apply the prohibitions and restrictions of the Convention and Protocols[96] and explicitly clarifies that such application to a party to the conflict which is not a High Contracting Party, but has accepted[97] the Convention or Protocols, 'shall not change their legal status'.[98]

In conclusion, and although the matter remains open,[99] it is today generally accepted that both common Article 3 GC and respective customary law is binding on both governmental and non-governmental parties to a conflict.[100] Regarding

---

93. Cassese, op. cit. n. 60, at p. 66.

94. See in particular S/RES/1265 (1999), paras. 4 and 9. Cf., also the Inter-American Commission on Human Rights, 'Third Report on the Situation of Human Rights in Colombia', OAS Doc. OEA/Ser.L/V/II, doc. 102 (1999), chapter IV, paras. 13 and 85 as well as Report No. 55/97 on Argentina, case No. 11.137, para. 174: 'Common Article 3's mandatory provisions expressly bind and apply equally to both parties to internal conflicts, i.e., government and dissident forces. Further references of the practice of the UN Security Council and the UN Commission on Human Rights are in Zegveld, op. cit. n. 27, at p. 11 fn. 5.

95. Convention on Prohibitions or Restrictions on the Use of Certain Conventional Weapons Which May be Deemed to be Excessively Injurious or to Have Indiscriminate Effects of 10 October 1980, Amendment Art. 1, of 21 December 2001.

96. Para. 3.

97. I.e., acceptance either explicitly by declaration or implicitly by application of the Convention or Protocols.

98. Para. 6.

99. For a comprehensive overview, see Sandoz et al., eds., op. cit. n. 42, Protocol II, Part I; Provost, op. cit. n. 33, at pp. 76 et seq.; Moir, op. cit. n. 31, at pp. 52-58. Cf., also Report of the Secretary-General to the Security Council on the Protection of Civilians in Armed Conflict, *supra* n. 8, para. 7; and Zegveld, op. cit. n. 27, at pp. 9 et seq., with references in fn. 1, pp. 14-26.

100. J. Pictet, *Commentary I on the Geneva ConventionCommentaries on the Geneva Conventions of 12 August 1949*, Vol. I, Geneva Convention for the Amelioration of the Condition of the Wounded and Sick in Armed Forces in the Field (, Geneva, ICRC 1952), Art. 3(1)(B), pp. 51-52: 'Each of the parties will thus be required to apply Art. 3 by the mere fact of that Party's existence and of the existence of an armed conflict between it and the other party. The obligation is absolute for each of the parties. (...) On the other hand, what justification is there for the obligation on the adverse party in revolt against the established authority? (...) But if the responsible authority at their head exercises effective sovereignty, it is bound by the very fact that it claims to represent the country, or part of the country. (...) If it does not apply it [Art. 3], it will prove that those who regard its actions as mere acts of anarchy or brigandage are right.' See also Green, op. cit. n. 60, at pp. 60 and 187: 'The intent of the Conventions is that Article 3 should apply to both sides equally, regardless of whether the revolutionary authorities have made any declaration of intent to comply.' *Prosecutor* v. *Zoran Kupreskić, Mirjan Kupreskić, Vlatko Kupreskić, Drago Josipović, Dragan Papić and Vladimir Santić*, case No. IT-95-16-T, Judgement of the ICTY Trial Chamber of 14 January 2000, paras. 551 et seq.

Protocol I, a textual assumption of applicability is more difficult to uphold.[101] Various arguments[102] focus particularly on the principle of legislative jurisdiction,[103] the interpretation of treaty law and common sense supporting the binding force of Additional Protocol II provisions for non-governmental parties to a conflict. It is now widely accepted that its provisions and, as far as they are constitute customary law, the respective customary law do obligate all parties to a conflict alike.[104]

Notwithstanding this general conclusion, it should be remembered that the question of the binding force of common Article 3 GC and Additional Protocol II on non-governmental parties to a non-international armed conflict is one of the most difficult methodological problems of international humanitarian law. Modern humanitarian law sometimes shows a tendency to over-emphasise the individual nature of obligations in this area of law.[105] Such an approach does not sufficiently take into account the traditional basis and scope of humanitarian law. To understand the members of non-state actors to a non-international armed conflict as a group of individuals who would individually be bound[106] to humanitarian law is an adequate justification for the application of norms of international criminal law, but does not justify the binding force of humanitarian law as such on non-state actors. Considerations of reciprocity[107] are convincing either as to aspects of concrete bilateral relations or to general philosophical reflections, but limited to these.

The question has to be answered by analogy to the issue of the binding force of norms of customary law on new states. Not only seceding and dismembering but also newly emerging states in general are expected by the international community to accept existing norms of customary law which have developed prior to their

---

101. Any mention of 'the Parties to the conflict' was removed from the text of Additional Protocol II in the fourth session of the Diplomatic Conference in 1977.

102. See Moir, op. cit. n. 31, pp. 97 et seq.

103. 'The answer is provided in most national legislations; by the fact of ratification, an international Convention becomes part of law and is therefore binding upon all the individuals of that country.' Pictet, op. cit. n. 40, Art. 3(1)(B), p. 34.

104. Sandoz et al., eds., op. cit. n. 42, Protocol II, Part I, para. 4444: 'The question is often raised how the insurgent party can be bound by a treaty to which it is not a High Contracting Party. [...] the commitment made by a state not only applies to the government but also to any established authorities and private individuals within the national territory of that State and certain obligations are therefore imposed upon them. The extent of rights and duties of private individuals is therefore the same as that of the rights and duties of the State. Although this argument has occasionally been questioned in legal literature, the validity of the obligation imposed upon insurgents has never been contested.' With the same conclusion, see for example, Cassese, op. cit. n. 60, at p. 69. Provost, op. cit. n. 33, at p. 89 states: 'The ICTR and ICTY offer no justification for restricting the application of humanitarian law to the state, and indeed there seems to be no policy or legal reason to do so, quite the contrary.'

105. Provost, op. cit. n. 33, at pp. 90, 94 et seq. and pp. 96-102.

106. On the question of the international legal personality of private individuals, see, for example, the brief summary of Cassese, op. cit. n. 60, at pp. 69 et seq.

107. Cf., Green, op. cit. n. 60, at p. 57; Provost, op. cit. n. 33, at pp. 156-161 denies the principle of reciprocity as a basis for the binding force of common Art. 3 GC and Additional Protocol II for non-state actors.

coming into being, although, in a strict sense, they have not participated in either state practice or *opinio iuris* for their development. These norms have been developed by other states, i.e., those existing prior to the emergence of the new states in question. The effect of the binding force of common Article 3 GC and Additional Protocol II on non-state parties to non-international armed conflicts is similar to this rule of international law. Customary humanitarian law for non-international armed conflicts, as far as it is embodied in common Article 3 GC and Additional Protocol II, is binding on non-state actors involved in such conflicts although they have not participated in its development in the strict sense. Non-state conflict entities acquire partial subjectivity under international law, insofar as they are bound by humanitarian law. The international community expects these actors to be and to feel bound by these norms because a non-binding force of customary humanitarian rules for non-state entities in non-international armed conflicts would be practically unworkable and therefore not feasible.

3. RECENT PRACTICE OF ARMED HOSTILITIES IN NON-INTERNATIONAL ARMED CONFLICTS

The conduct of hostilities in recent non-international armed conflicts caused extraordinary suffering of the civilian population. It is impossible to analyse all non-international armed conflicts since 1977 in a comprehensive manner in the present framework or even to examine those which received the most international attention. However, recent non-international armed conflicts reveal several distinctive features. These features will be examined with a view to answering the question whether and to what extent conduct of hostilities in non-international armed conflicts is covered by existing humanitarian law.

3.1 Directly targeting the civilian population

Directly targeting the civilian population, that is, making the civilian population as such, groups of civilians or individual civilians the direct object of attack, has become a rather common feature of military conduct in non-international armed conflicts and often even a characteristic feature of hostilities. For example, all parties to the conflict in southern Sudan have resorted to this method of warfare, while the targeting of the civilian population in the form of the practice of so-called 'ethnic cleansing' in Bosnia-Herzegovina[108] and in Kosovo is well known.[109] Such direct attacks on the civilian population are often conducted with the aim of eliminating or at least expelling a specific group among the civilian population from a

108. See Srebrenica Report of the Secretary-General pursuant to General Assembly resolution 53/35 'The fall of Srebrenica', A/54/549, 15 November 1999, http://www.un.org/peace/srebrenica.pdf.

109. The Kosovo Report, Independent International Commission on Kosovo,at p. 25: http://www.reliefweb.int./library/documents, p. 25.

specific territory or with terrorising the civilian population to put pressure on the government.

Attacks on the civilian population, be it the population as such or as individual civilians, are prohibited by Article 13(2) AP II, as are acts or threats of violence the primary purpose of which is to spread terror among the civilian population. It is assumed that the customary law study conducted by the International Committee of the Red Cross will find the same prohibition to constitute customary law. A strong indication is the fact that the UN Security Council has 'strongly condemn[ed] (...) the deliberate targeting of civilians in armed conflicts'.[110] Currently lacking is any regulation on the proportionality of losses among the civilian population which are not the result of direct targeting, but which are caused incidentally or collaterally.

The elimination or expulsion of specific parts of the civilian population seems to be widely motivated by psycho-sociological and/or religious factors. In this context, the sometimes extensive use of psychological methods of warfare or 'propaganda' and the use of the media is remarkable. The effect of such practices is specifically crucial with respect to practices of genocide and 'ethnic cleansing'.[111]

While neither common Article 3 GC nor Additional Protocol II provide for any prohibition of psychological methods and means of warfare, nor is there any such prohibition under existing customary law, the exertion of psychological influence or the use of 'propaganda' is almost inherent in any conduct of hostilities, be it in the context of an international or non-international armed conflict.[112] In this respect, it might even be counterproductive to consider legal coverage of this phenomenon. In that context, the Secretary-General of the United Nations acknowledged that 'combating hostile propaganda (...) may require a more immediate and intense effort by the international community, (...)'[113] – and probably such effort would have to be undertaken outside the area and outside the set of tools of international humanitarian law. Although it is theoretically not impossible to regulate psychological warfare, the implementation of any such provision would most probably be rather difficult. To draw the line between 'legal' and 'illegal' expressions of opinions poses already problems in the relation between states in terms of the *domaine réservé*; it is even more difficult in the context of non-international conflicts where the freedom of expression is protected as a customary human right.

In the framework of international criminal law, prohibition as a war crime of the

110. S/RES/1265 (1999), para. 2.

111. Report of the Secretary-General to the Security Council on the Protection of Civilians in Armed Conflict, *supra* n. 8, para. 39: 'If the first casualty of war is the truth, the next victims are those who are unable to draw attention to their need for protection.'

112. The genocide in Rwanda, for instance, was extensively abetted by the use of broadcasts and newspaper articles: Ubutabera, Independent Journal Providing Information on the International Criminal Tribunal for Rwanda, Arusha, No. 13, July 1997, in Sassòli and Bouvier, op. cit. n. 31, pp. 1280 et seq.

113. Report of the Secretary-General to the Security Council on the Protection of Civilians in Armed Conflict, *supra* n. 8, para. 41.

intentional directing of attacks against civilian objects exists only in relation to international armed conflict (Art. 8(2)(b)(ii) ICC Statute),[114] and similarly with the offences of attacking undefended civilian towns, villages, dwellings or buildings (Art. 8(2)(b)(v)) and intentionally launching an attack and thereby causing incidental loss of life or injury to civilians or damage to civilian objects or widespread, long-term and severe damage to the natural environment (Art. 8(2)(b)(iv)).

Neither common Article 3 GC nor Additional Protocol II provide for precautionary measures to be taken for the protection of the civilian population, either directly or indirectly through the obligation to ensure respect for protective rules as contained in common Article 1 GC and Article 1(1) AP I[115] for international conflicts. Indeed, the exact meaning and concrete consequences for States Parties to the Geneva Conventions and Additional Protocol I is far from clear and is the subject of intense interpretation and discussion.[116] Whether customary law is able to fill this lacuna; whether the obligation of governments to protect civilians under their jurisdiction from the negative effects of non-international armed conflicts may be derived from humanitarian law; and whether states even have a duty to prevent and repress acts committed by non-governmental parties to such conflict[117] remains doubtful.

3.2 Denial of access to vulnerable populations

The problem of access to vulnerable populations is intrinsic in almost every[118] armed conflict and non-international armed conflict in particular. Armed hostilities, such as those in Liberia, Sudan, Sierra Leone, the DRC, Afghanistan, Chechnya and Colombia, imply situations of deliberate denial of access to a suffering civilian population, paralleled by variously motivated interests of the international humanitarian community to provide humanitarian assistance and more accidental hindrances of access to the victims. Very often, such situations coincide with practices of starvation of the civilian population employed as a method of warfare in non-international conflicts.

The UN Secretary-General in his recent report on the protection of the civilian population reaffirmed the crucial importance of access to victims,[119] stating that to 'secure humanitarian access' is one of three key areas for practical actions setting the stage for an effective transition to peace and remaining essential throughout the process. Notwithstanding the importance of a clear separation of civilians and combatants and the swift re-establishment of the rule of law, justice and reconcilia-

114. In contrast to the list of war crimes of in international conflicts, Art. 8(2)(a) ICC Statute.

115. 'The High Contracting Parties undertake to respect and to ensure respect for the present Convention/for this Protocol in all circumstances.'

116. The problem will be one of the centre issues to be discussed in the framework of the 28th InternationalConference of the Red Cross and the Red Crescent in 2003.

117. Zegveld, op. cit. n. 27, pp. 92 et seq., at 173-177.

118. S/RES/1265 (1999), paras. 7 and 9.

119. Report of the Secretary-General on the Protection of Civilians in Armed Conflicts, *supra* n. 20, para.11.

tion during transition,[120] access to vulnerable populations remains difficult. In most conflict situations, humanitarian assistance continues to be manipulated, delayed and even denied, while a lack of safety and security of humanitarian personnel, the deliberate or *de facto* denial of access to populations – in particular through directly targeting the civilian population and relief personnel[121] – and a lack of structural engagement with non-state parties[122] to a conflict are the major obstacles to effective and efficient access.

Access to a suffering civilian population is a prerequisite for any protection, whether such protection be provided by means of relief or effective legal protection. Article 18(2) AP II provides that relief actions shall be undertaken, provided certain preconditions are met: Firstly, the civilian population has to suffer undue hardship due to a lack of the supplies essential for its survival (such as foodstuffs and medical supplies). Secondly, the High Contracting Party has to give its consent to the provision of relief. Thirdly, it must be ensured that relief actions are of an exclusively humanitarian and impartial nature and are conducted without any adverse distinction.

According to common Article 3(2) GC, an impartial humanitarian body, such as the International Committee of the Red Cross, may offer its services to the Parties to the conflict. Such offer therefore may not be considered as an interference in the domestic affairs of a state on whose territory a non-international armed conflict is taking place. Article 18 AP II provides the only other detailed treaty provision regulating the delivery of humanitarian assistance and access to victims in non-international armed conflicts. The wording of paragraph 2 is in several respects rather problematic, for example, regarding the difficulties of defining what hardship is 'undue' within the meaning of Article 18(2).[123] In addition, relief organisations, both governmental organisations, and more important in this context, non-governmental and particularly Red Cross/Red Crescent components, are often and widely blamed for operating partially and on the basis of unjustifiable distinctions.

Yet, maybe the most crucial criterion is the precondition of consent of the High Contracting Party. From the legal point of view, it is accepted that where the civilian population does suffer undue hardship owing to a lack of supplies, the High Contracting Party is legally obliged to give its consent, without any discretion. The problem remains of ascertaining when the threshold of undue hardship is reached. In cases where such consent is deliberately and arbitrarily denied or withdrawn by any government, this government is inflicting[124] starvation of civilians as a method of combat and also breaching the protection of objects indispensable to the survival of the civilian population incorporated in Article 14 AP II.

---

120. Ibid., para. 15.

121. Ibid.; the other two key areas are a clear separation of civilians and combatants and the swift re-establishment of the rule of law, justice and reconciliation during transition.

122. Ibid., paras. 19 and 25-29.

123. See Sandoz et al., eds., op. cit. n. 42, para. 4881 et seq., and Bothe et al., eds., op. cit. n. 41, Art. 18, 2.4.1.

124. See Sandoz et al., ibid., para. 4885.

From a practical viewpoint, the application of Article 18(2) is rendered considerably problematic in situations where efficient governmental structures are missing or where access to the victims is hindered by non-governmental parties to the conflict exercising effective control. Although the scope of Article 18(2) addresses only state actors, it is especially the prohibition of starvation according to treaty and customary law which is binding on all parties to the conflict and which, at least partly,[125] reconciles the deficiencies of the regulation on relief operations. Yet, replacement of the criterion of consent by criteria focusing on the perceived needs of the civilian population and the extent of the humanitarian emergency would be both unrealistic at present and not necessarily helpful in terms of the discretion in applying such criteria. 'Consent' of the parties will not become obsolete before clearer preconditions for governmental and non-governmental deliverance of humanitarian assistance have been developed.

With respect to the questions of the right of victims to receive humanitarian assistance, the right of the international community – comprising states and non-governmental organisations – to grant and offer humanitarian assistance and the legal details and consequences of these rights in non-international armed conflicts, treaty law is silent and we must rely exclusively on customary law.[126] The same is true for any regulation of the involvement of relief personnel and their protection in an environment of non-international armed conflict. Neither privileges or immunities nor duties of relief personnel in non-international conflicts, nor, in particular, the safety and security and respective protection of the personnel are regulated under treaty law.[127] However, this regime is supplemented by the sanctioning mechanism of Article 8(2)(e) ICC Statue on other serious violations of the laws and customs applicable in non-international armed conflicts, which embodies a further development of the law. Subparagraph (e) prohibits 'intentionally directing attacks against personnel, installations, material, units or vehicles involved in a humanitarian assistance or peacekeeping mission in accordance with the Charter of the United Nations, as long as they are entitled to the protection given to civilians or civilian objects under the international law of armed conflict' ((e)(iii)).[128]

Admittedly, development of the law in recent years indicates that the international community intends to apply the provisions of Additional Protocol I on relief

125. Zegveld, op. cit. n. 27, pp. 86-89.

126. H. Fischer, ed., *International law in humanitarian assistance, Network on Humanitarian Assistance*, 2nd edn. (Luxembourg, European Communities 1998) p. 54.

127. The UN General Assembly in this sense expressed its concern for the 'continuous erosion (...) of respect for the [- general -] principles and rules of international humanitarian law' (preambular para. 7) and urged 'all other parties involved in armed conflicts (...) to ensure the security and protection of all humanitarian personnel and United Nations and associated personnel' with only a general reference to 'international humanitarian law, in particular their [i.e., all other parties involved in armed conflicts] obligations under the Geneva Conventions of 12 August 1949 and the obligations applicable to them under the Additional Protocols thereto' (preambular para. 14); A/RES/56/217 of 19 February 2002.

128. War crimes against personnel involved in humanitarian assistance and peacekeeping missions and their respective installations and material are criminalised in Art. 8(2)(e)(iii) ICC Statute.

operations and personnel to non-international armed conflicts.[129] Such customary basis for the regulation of humanitarian assistance in non-international conflicts entails all the advantages[130] that customary provisions have in comparison to treaty law. But not least the experiences in Liberia, Sudan, the Democratic Republic of Congo, Afghanistan and Chechnya render the disadvantages and weaknesses quite evident, especially for the sake of clarity and facilitating negotiations. The value of the forthcoming ICRC study on customary humanitarian law will be tremendous, but for negotiation purposes written rules are always more unambiguous and more convincing than equally legally binding but 'virtual' norms. Treaty provisions are not but often seem to be more obligatory than customary rules. The fact that humanitarian treaty law is silent on a substantial regulation of delivering humanitarian assistance in non-international armed conflict constitutes a definite gap and a clear deficiency of the existing protection of the civilian population in non-international armed conflicts.

3.3 Displacement of the civilian population

The conflicts in Angola, Burundi, the DRC, Colombia and Indonesia and the former Yugoslavia,[131] for example, were widely characterised by substantive displacement of the civilian population, resulting either in refugees or internally displaced persons. The relevant treaty provision is Article 17 AP II, which does not prohibit displacement absolutely. It only prohibits the ordering of displacement for reasons related to the conflict in principle, while explicitly allowing it for the sake of the security of the civilian population involved or imperative military reasons. In that case, all possible measures shall be taken so that the civilian population may receive, under satisfactory conditions, shelter, hygiene, health, safety and nutrition in case of such displacement.

Displacement of the civilian population is another issue where existing law[132] is insufficient. Article 17 AP II has proven inadequate for those situations where displacement is not the effect of military planning but either effected upon decisions of governmental or non-governmental individuals or by the actual circumstances. The conduct of hostilities may either directly or indirectly – i.e., in particular when the economic situation in a conflict area is worsened as result of

---

129. Fischer, loc. cit. n. 126, at p. 51.

130. Such advantages are especially the fact that the development of customary norms is not dependent on the ratification by Governments and that under certain circumstances the development of customary law might be much quicker than negotiation, ratification and entering into force of international treaties.

131. C.M. Carey, 'International Displacement: Is Prevention Through Accountability Possible? A Kosovo Case Study', 49 *Amer. Univ. LR* (1999) pp. 243 et seq.

132. See also UN Secretary-General, http://www.un.org./millennium/sg/report/ch3.htm at para. 210. The recent report of the UN SG takes account of the fact that 'since the previous report [2001], an increasing number of States, United Nations organizations and regional and non-governmental organizations are making use of the Guiding Principles on Internal Displacement (E/CN.4/1998/53/Add.2, annex) to strengthen legal frameworks on the protection of internally displaced persons.' *Supra* n. 20, para. 13.

the hostilities – lead to population movements, caused by any party to the conflict. In addition, the caveat of 'imperative military reasons' gives discretion to any party to the conflict and the criteria of 'satisfactory conditions' must be perceived as making a mockery of the overwhelming majority of civilians who are exposed to forced displacement.

In contrast to the regime for international conflicts in the ICC Statute (cf., Art. 8(2)(a)(vii)), Article 8 of the Statute does not contain any provision on unlawful deportation or transfer or unlawful confinement; such violations of common Article 3 GC are not implied.[133] A general clause which might fill this lacuna is also missing in Article 8(2)(c). This is all the more surprising as the fundamental guarantee of the prohibition of acts of terrorism and the spreading of terror according to Article 4(2)(d) and Article 13(2) AP II are not qualified as sufficiently serious as to be sanctioned by a provision on the criminal responsibility for (serious) violations.

3.4 Separation of civilians and fighters

A distinctive feature of both common Article 3 and Additional Protocol II is the lack of a definition and regulation of 'combatants'.[134] Although the reason for this approach is clear, it might under certain circumstances be useful to rethink the renunciation to non-state fighters of such status in non-international armed conflicts.[135] As a result of armed hostilities, the intermingling of refugees, internally displaced persons and other civilians and armed fighters, both inside the territory of the hostilities and in neighbouring states, is a common feature of non-international armed conflicts in particular. A second phenomenon is the movement of combatants into camps and settlements of refugees and internally displaced persons.

The civilian population is thus threatened from the violence of armed fighters and from the reaction of governments to such situations. An additional factor is that there are several examples where governmental countermeasures have endangered the civilian population by their punitive effects and thereby added to the civilian suffering.[136] The result is that the civilian population suffers directly and indirectly from the negative effects of its lack of separation from armed fighters. A prerequisite to any separation is the distinction between fighters and civilians. Such distinction is presently only indirectly and implicitly provided by existing international humanitarian law applicable in non-international conflicts. Article 13(3) AP II

133. If such acts are indeed less serious as violation of common Art. 3 GC than the list contained in Art. 8(2)(c) remains questionable.

134. On the problem of defining the notions of 'civilian' and 'civilian population' in the context of common Article 3 GC and Additional Protocol II, see Zegveld, op. cit. n. 27, at pp. 75 et seq.

135. See also Moir, op. cit. n. 31, at pp. 91-96 and 274.

136. *Supra* n. 20, para. 34: 'Examples of such responses, which have themselves resulted in further threats to civilian security and rights to protection, include regroupment camps, forced relocation, protected villages and, in the Middle East, punitive measures directed at civilians. Such actions violate international humanitarian and human rights law and should be condemned.'

refers only indirectly to such distinction insofar as it distinguishes between civilians and those taking 'a direct part in hostilities'.[137]

In light of this implicit distinction between civilians being protected by the regulation on the protection of the civilian population contained in Articles 13-18 AP II and those being deprived of such protection, it might be worth considering a specific legal status for 'combatants' in non-international armed conflicts. Such status would have to be distinguished from any form of 'recognition of belligerency'.[138] It is not necessarily excluded that a recognised status on the basis of clear criteria and prerequisites might clarify and enhance the binding nature of humanitarian norms on non-governmental conflict parties in non-international armed conflicts and thereby improve the protection of the civilian population. Yet, any such recognised legal status could only contribute to facilitating a separation between civilians and armed fighters; actual separation would not be achieved nor would governments be impeded from disproportionate action against suspected fighters.[139]

3.5 Shortcomings of existing legal coverage

Humanitarian law currently applicable in non-international armed conflicts is characterised by considerable shortcomings in several respects. Examples are the issues of target selection, proportionality and precautionary measures, where treaty provisions are at best rudimentary,[140] and customary rules, which remain at least vague or questionable.

In other cases, the problem is less the insufficiency of the existing law but more the fact that certain problems and effects by their very nature cannot satisfactorily be regulated by legal provisions. This holds true, for example, for displacement of the civilian population which is not ordered or forced as such but which is simply caused by refugees or internally displaced persons having to leave because of intolerable living conditions.

---

137. 'Civilians shall enjoy the protection afforded by this Part, unless and for such time as they take a direct part in hostilities.' Art. 13(3) AP II.

138. Cf., Aldrich, loc. cit. n. 31, at pp. 42-63, and Moir, op. cit. n. 31, at pp. 4-20.

139. The UN Secretary-General focuses therefore on the following practical actions and requirements: '(a) commitment by Governments to remove refugee camps and internally displaced person settlements from border areas and to the separation and internment of combatants; (b) rapid deployment of United Nations multidisciplinary assessment teams to assist and support the separation of combatants and civilians; (c) provision of support to States hosting refugees in order to strengthen the capacity of law enforcement authorities through an appropriate security package, notably to strengthen police units in refugee situations; (d) promotion of the use of the aide-mèmoire and the Agenda for Protection by Governments in situations where combatants and civilians are intermingled, as a means of ensuring that their responses to perceived security threats meet international legal standards'. *Supra* n. 20, para. 40.

140. J.-M. Henckaerts, 'The Study on Customary Rules of International Humanitarian Law', in M. Hector and M. Jellema, eds., *Protecting Civilians in 21st Century Warfare* (The Hague, The Netherlands Red Cross 2001) p. 23.

A third shortcoming of existing legal regulation is its inability to deal with the characteristic of current non-international armed conflicts that atrocities are committed by governmental and non-governmental armed forces alike.[141] The 'classical' constellation of non-international armed conflicts, where insurgents fight against the governmental forces, has become much less typical than preceding the adoption of Additional Protocol II, and in particular much less characteristic of contemporary non-international armed conflicts. These are in themselves principally heterogeneous, varying within opposite extremes in terms of numbers of non-governmental actors, control over territory and population, and lines of organisation and military hierarchy.[142] Nowadays, non-international armed conflicts very often do not match the traditional phenomena, constellations and structures – constellations and structures which underlie the concept of both common Article 3 GC and Additional Protocol II.

It is therefore much more important to prove that any legal regulation of the conduct of non-international armed conflicts, be it by treaty or customary law, is not only binding upon governmental but also upon non-governmental parties to the conflict. As much as newly developed states have to accept the set of pre-existing norms of customary international law, each individual non-governmental party to a non-international armed conflict is new to the circle of traditional addressees of humanitarian rules, i.e., states having developed rules of international humanitarian law, and has to accept the legally binding force of common Article 3 GC and Additional Protocol II.

Yet, such legal obligation of non-governmental armed forces may only be efficient where the obligation is known to an individual fighter and is perceived and accepted by him as legally binding. The obligation to grant access to a suffering civilian population in the Democratic Republic of the Congo, for instance, has only a chance of being implemented and 350,000 resulting deaths[143] prevented when all members of all parties to the conflict have a perception of such – legal – obligation. In addition, even given such perception, both observance of the existing law and its preventive effectiveness are only feasible where non-state actors in a non-international armed conflict may profit from any utility and advantage through either the observance of rules and/or the avoidance of negative consequences from sanctions of violations. Such presumption entails questions of code of conduct, military hierarchy and discipline within non-governmental armed forces in particular. These questions are probably among the most eminent aspects of 'inadequacy' of existing legal coverage of non-international armed conflicts.

---

141. Cf., for example, UN Secretary-General, http://www.un.org./millennium/sg/report/ch3.htm at para. 210.

142. See also Zegveld, op. cit. n. 27, at p. 1.

143. *Supra* n. 20, para. 20.

4. IMPLEMENTATION AND ENFORCEMENT OF THE LAW

4.1 Implementation

Implementation of humanitarian norms is of crucial importance for the effectiveness and efficiency of international humanitarian law.[144] Generally, implementation measures consist of those introducing humanitarian law norms into a national or international legal system in order to make such norms part of this system and render them practically applicable.[145] In not only transforming provisions from one area of law into another but also transcribing abstract norms into concrete rules regulating conduct in a specific situation, implementation is the prerequisite for any application of international humanitarian law or its observance in a specific armed conflict.

Implementation of norms for international as well as for non-international armed conflicts typically has first of all to be effected in times of peace. This constitutes a difficulty in itself since implementation of humanitarian law is very often not a priority of governments. Implement of norms applicable in non-international armed conflicts is even more difficult and in practice hardly ever effected efficiently because such implementation measures have not only to address the conduct of governmental but also of non-governmental armed forces. On the one hand, such implementation presupposes a government's readiness to accept the potential possibility of being engaged in a non-international armed conflict – a situation that seems hardly conceivable for many governments. On the other hand, the law has to actually regulate the conduct of members of non-governmental armed forces – in their capacity as nationals of the state. Generally, humanitarian law is implemented into the domestic public and criminal law of a state, i.e., two areas of law which have to prove their effectiveness and efficiency under the circumstances of a non-international armed conflict. By its very nature, such implementation is built on very weak ground.

---

144. For a comprehensive introduction see Sassòli et al., op. cit. n. 31, at pp. 219-261.

145. Art. 80 AP I uses the term 'execution' of the Geneva Conventions and Additional Protocol I. 'The concept of execution in this article should be understood at two different levels. The first level covers measures introducing all or the relevant parts of the treaty into the legal order of each Contracting Party in accordance with the rules of its constitution (...). (...) In addition, the application of some provisions requires preparatory steps such as the designation or establishment of organizations and the introduction of procedures. Finally, some treaty provisions require development or clarification to be fully and uniformly effective. These various measures may be taken either at a legislative level or by the executive in its widest sense. The second meaning of 'execution', which is also contained in this article, is that of its actual application. Some measures must be taken continuously, for example, dissemination; others are only conceivable in situations falling within the material scope of application of the Protocol, (...).' Zimmermann, in Sandoz et al., eds., op. cit. n. 42, Art. 80, paras. 3288-3290.

4.2 Enforcement mechanisms

Classical mechanisms for the enforcement of international humanitarian law include the principle of reciprocity,[146] public opinion,[147] the institution of the protecting power,[148] the International Fact-Finding Commission established pursuant to Article 90 AP I,[149] sanctions, state responsibility and individual criminal responsibility. In the context of the present observations, the areas of international criminal responsibility and coercive military measures merit greater attention.

4.2.1 *International criminal law*

With the emerging partial legal subjectivity of individuals in international – humanitarian – law, the concept of individual criminal responsibility deriving directly from international law in addition to the concept of state responsibility has achieved a rather comprehensive acceptance. Since the legal personality of non-governmental parties to a conflict as such[150] is still widely discussed, the international criminal responsibility of their individual members is of crucial importance.

Although prosecution of violations of humanitarian law is not a new concept, the widely pursued objective not to let perpetrators of serious violations of humanitarian law go unpunished and to challenge the 'culture of impunity'[151] reached a new dimension with the establishment of the two *ad hoc* International Criminal Tribunals for the Former Yugoslavia[152] and for Rwanda[153] and with the entering

---

146. For recent observations on the impact of reciprocity considerations on international humanitarian law and human rights law see Provost, op. cit. n. 33, pp. 121-181.

147. A positive impact of international public opinion in the context of non-international armed conflicts presupposes a minimum of public presence of the non-governmental conflict parties in the international public and a certain advantage from the observance of humanitarian law for the non-state actors.

148. The concept of protecting powers is presently of no practical relevance in recent (non-international) armed conflicts. More recent initiatives to revitalise the concept have not been practically successful; cf., results of the workshop organised by the Swiss Federal Department of Foreign Affairs and the German Red Cross on the topic 'Ensuring Respect for International Humanitarian Law – Towards Appropriate Mechanisms', held during the 27th International Conference of the Red Cross and Red Crescent, Geneva, 31 October-6 November 1999, published in M. Bothe, ed., *Towards a Better Implementation of International Humanitarian Law,* 43 Bochumer Schriften zur Friedenssicherung und zum Humanitären Völkerrecht (Berlin, Arno Spitz 2001) pp. 139-141.

149. On the mandate of the Commission in the non-international armed conflict in Colombia see F. Kalshoven, 'Protocol II, The CDDH and Colombia', in K. Wellens, ed., *International Law: Theory and Practice* (The Hague, Martinus Nijhoff 1998) pp. 597-622.

150. Zegveld, op. cit. n. 27, pp. 133-163.

151. *Supra* n. 119, para. 46. On the criminalisation of acts committed in non-international armed conflicts see T. Meron, 'International Criminalization of Internal Atrocities', 89 *AJIL* (1995) pp. 554 et seq.

152. Report of the UN Secretary-General Pursuant to Paragraph 2 of Security Council Resolution 808 (1993) of 3 May 1993, S/25704, Introduction, paras. 4-11.

153. S/RES/955 (1994), preamble, paras. 6-8.

into force of the Statute of the International Criminal Court (ICC).[154] The Secretary-General of the United Nations and the Government of Sierra Leone concluded an agreement on the establishment of a Special Court for Sierra Leone in January 2002.[155] Extraordinary 'internationalised' Chambers are contemplated for Cambodia, while Special Panels for Serious Crimes, composed of both national and international judges, are operating in East Timor.[156]

The International Criminal Tribunals for the Former Yugoslavia and Rwanda and the International Criminal Court can exercise jurisdiction over war crimes, crimes against humanity and genocide in non-international armed conflicts. Despite challenges on this point,[157] it is confirmed jurisprudence of the ICTY that violations of common Article 3 GC are comprised in the list of offences described in Article 3 ICTY Statute.[158] Article 4 ICTR Statute explicitly refers to violations of common Article 3 and of Additional Protocol II. The sanctioning mechanism of the ICC Statute covers serious violations under the notion of war crimes in Article 8, i.e., 'serious violations of article 3 common to the Geneva Conventions' are listed in Article 8(2)(c) and 'other serious violations of the laws and customs [of war]' in subparagraph (e) in situations of 'armed conflict not of an international character'.[159] Yet, the enumeration of serious violations of common Article 3 GC given in the ICC Statute is less comprehensive compared to the list of grave breaches (Art. 8(a)).[160] It does not cover all provisions of Additional Protocol II ensuring humane treatment in general. Moreover, a general clause entailing individual criminal responsibility of inhuman treatment of persons not taking part in hostilities (Art. 4(1) AP II and common Art. 3) is not implied.

In the jurisprudence of the ICTY, Article 5 ICTY Statute on crimes against humanity allows for its application both in international and in non-international

---

154. Entry into force on 1 July 2002. On the recent progress in the area of international criminal law cf., H.-P. Kaul, 'The Continuing Struggle on the Jurisdiction of the International Criminal Court', in H. Fischer, C. Kreß and S.R. Lüder, eds., *International and National Prosecution of Crimes under International Law*, 44 Bochumer Schriften zur Friedenssicherung und zum Humanitären Völkerrecht (Berlin, Arno Spitz 2001) pp. 123-125.

155. Agreement for and Statute of the Special Court for Sierra Leone of 16 January 2002, http://www.icrc.org/ihl.nsf.

156. A. McDonald, 'The Year in Review', 3 *YIHL* (2000) p. 170.

157. *Prosecutor* v. *Dragoljub Kunarac, Radomir Kovac and Zoran Vuković*, Judgement of the ICTY Appeals Chamber of 12 June 2002, paras. 51 and 54.

158. Recently confirmed by the ICTY in ibid., para. 68, and *Prosecutor* v. *Dario Kordić* and Mario Cerkez, 26 February 2001, *supra* n. 31, paras. 162 et seq.

159. Whereas Art. 2 ICTY Statute covers only international armed conflicts, Art. 3 ICTY Statute confers jurisdiction over any serious violation of international humanitarian law not covered by Arts. 2, 4 or 5. Despite several contests, it is confirmed jurisprudence of the ICTY that violations of common Art. 3 GC are comprised in this clause and in the list of offences according to Article 3 ICTY Statute; recently confirmed by the ICTY in: *Prosecutor* v. *Dragoljub Kunarac, Radomir Kovac and Zoran Vuković*, 12 June 2002, *supra* n. 81, para. 68, and *Prosecutor* v. *Dario Kordić and Mario Cerkez*, 26 February 2001, *supra* n. 31, paras. 162 et seq.

160. A comprehensive analysis is provided by A. Zimmermann in O. Triffterer, ed., *Commentary on the Rome Statute of the International Criminal Court*, (Baden Baden, Nomos 1999) Art. 8, para. 2.

armed conflicts.[161] In contrast to the Statute of the ICTY, Article 7 ICC Statute, as well as Article 3 ICTR Statute, do not refer to the criterion of any armed conflict. Within their scope of application, crimes against humanity may be committed either in international or in non-international armed conflicts or even in internal disturbances and tensions. The prohibition of genocide as incorporated in Article 4 ICTY Statute (Art. 2 ICTR Statute) and Article 6 ICC Statute applies irrespective of any armed conflict, by implication thus applying also in internal as well as international armed conflicts. However, the requirement of there being a targeted group is extremely distinct and the necessary intent is highly specialised.[162] Only where these criteria are met may these provisions exert their protective effects with regard to the protection of the civilian population in non-international armed conflicts.

Without detracting from the progress that has been made in international criminal and humanitarian law through the enhancement of international prosecution of violations and through the demand for justice and accountability, it cannot be overlooked that prosecution and punishment of perpetrators is far from being the perfect remedy[163] and ideal reaction to violations. International prosecution is only possible where the international community is willing to implement and support it: the decision whether or not to establish tribunals or special courts too often appears to be rather arbitrary, and support is widely discretionary. Domestic prosecution relies on states' ability and willingness to prosecute violations of humanitarian law, including to implement and exercise the principle of universal jurisdiction, to cooperate in particular in terms of evidence and extradition and to adapt national legislation to standards of international humanitarian and criminal law.[164] Further, although amnesties[165] may have counterproductive effects, as Sierra Leone may illustrate,[166] in specific situations they may be more helpful to secure peace and reconciliation than criminal prosecutions. Thirdly, where they are not a substitute for but complement judicial prosecutions, truth and reconciliation mechanisms may be a helpful instrument to overcome a violent past.[167] Following

161. *Prosecutor* v. *Dragoljub Kunarac, Radomir Kovac and Zoran Vuković*, 22 February 2001, *supra* n. 81, para. 411.

162. *Prosecutor* v. *Radislav Krstić*, ibid., para. 481.

163. See also McDonald, loc. cit. n. 156, at p. 171.

164. Report of the Secretary-General to the Security Council on the Protection of Civilians in Armed Conflict, *supra* n. 8, para. 12.

165. On amnesties, see Sassòli et al., op. cit. n. 31, at pp. 209 and 250 as well as cases Nos. 129, South Africa, *AZAPO* v. *The President of the Republic of South Africa*, pp. 970 et seq. at 971 and 976, Colombia, *Constitutional Conformity of Protocol II*, pp. 1357 et seq. at 1369. Cf., further M.P. Scharf, 'Swapping Amnesty for Peace: was there a duty to prosecute international crimes in Haiti?', 31 *Texas ILJ* (1996) pp. 1 et seq.; and T. McCormack, 'Selective Reaction to Atrocity: War Crimes and the Development of International Criminal Law', 60 *Albany LR* (1997) pp. 681 et seq.

166. Report of the Secretary-General to the Security Council on the Protection of Civilians in Armed Conflict, *supra* n. 8, para. 10; C. Schocken, 'The Special Court for Sierra Leone: Overview and Recommendations', 20 *Berkeley JIL* (2002) pp. 436 et seq.; B. Akinrinade, 'International Humanitarian Law and the Conflict in Sierra Leone', 15 *Notre Dame JL* (2001) pp. 391 et seq.

167. C. Stahn, 'Accommodating Individual Criminal Responsibility and National Reconciliation: The UN Truth Commission for East Timor', 95 *AJIL* (2001) pp. 952 et seq.; S. Braun, 'Forgiveness, South Africa's Truth Commission, and Military Trials: America's Options in Dealing with Crimes

the institution of the truth commission in South Africa, several commissions have recently been established, including in Nigeria, Panama, Sierra Leone and East Timor.[168] The UN Secretary-General clearly reaffirmed the need 'to draw a distinction between punitive and restorative justice'[169] and emphasised that 'the demand for justice and accountability must be balanced with the political pressures to move forward'.[170]

4.2.2 *Coercive military measures*

Experience from the last decade in particular has shown that the international community has made increased use of coercive military measures to enforce international humanitarian law in non-international armed conflicts.

4.2.2.1 The trigger mechanism of Chapter VII of the UN Charter

Non-international armed conflicts can have a profound effect on international peace and security. On the basis of the qualification of a situation as an act of aggression or a threat to or breach of international peace and security in accordance with Article 39 UN Charter, the UN Security Council may determine, *inter alia*, military sanctions according to Article 42.[171] While specific agreements according to Article 43, providing the Security Council with armed forces under its own command, are still pending,[172] it is generally accepted[173] that Article 42 also provides the legal basis for Security Council authorisation of the use of force by Member States of the United Nations in order to restore or maintain international peace and security. It has been discussed whether situations of non-international armed conflicts may qualify as threats to or even breaches of international peace and security and, if so, whether the situation as such may be the basis for enacting the mechanism of Chapter VII UN Charter or whether 'internationalising

---

Against Humanity in Light of the Terrorist Attacks on September 11, 2001', 12 *Hamline Journal of Public Law & Policy* (2002) pp. 493 et seq.; M. Kamali, 'Accountability for Human Rights Violations: A Comparison of Transitional Justice in East Germany and South Africa', 40 *Columbia JTL* (2001) pp. 89 et seq.

168. Report of the Secretary-General to the Security Council on the Protection of Civilians in Armed Conflict, *supra* n. 8, para. 13.

169. Report of the UN Secretary-General to the Security Council on the Protection of Civilians in Armed Conflict, *supra* n. 20, para. 49.

170. Ibid., para. 50.

171. Notwithstanding the possibility of non-military sanctioning measures according to Art. 41 UN Charter and competences of the UN General Assembly in the area of peace and security. The General Assembly, for example in the cases of Myanmar, El Salvador and Sudan, has characterised as non-international armed conflicts internal hostilities which the state did not consider to be more than internal disturbances and strives; see Provost, op. cit. n. 33, at p. 299.

172. See the recent initiative of the UN SG to conclude Stand-by Agreements between the United Nations and Member States with regard to peacekeeping missions; www./un.org/depts/dpko/rapid/sba.html.

173. Cf., J.A. Frowein, 'Commentary to Article 39 UN Charter, paras. 16-23', in B. Simma, ed., *The Charter of the United Nations* (Oxford, Oxford University Press 1994).

elements', such as cross-border influx of refugees or transborder military activities, have to be ascertained.[174]

Regarding the situation of the Kurdish civilian population in northern Iraq in 1991, the UN Security Council maintained that the consequences of the 'repression of the Iraqi civilian population (...) threaten[ed] international peace and security in the region'.[175] However, it did so on the basis of having stated that this repression had 'led to a massive flow of refugees towards and across international frontiers and to cross-border incursions which threaten international peace and security in the region'.[176] Seized with the situation in Haiti in 1993, the Security Council focused on 'mass displacements of population, becoming or aggravating threats to international peace and security' and an increase in 'the number of Haitians seeking refuge in neighbouring Member States'.[177] When the Council qualified the situation in Rwanda to be a threat to international[178] peace and security, it referred to the death of 'many thousands of innocent civilians (...), the internal displacement of a significant percentage of the Rwandan population, and the massive exodus of refugees to neighbouring countries'.[179] Affirming that the situation in Kosovo in 1998 amounted to a threat to international[180] peace and security, the Security Council based its decision, *inter alia*, on the 'flow of refugees into northern Albania, Bosnia and Herzegovina and other European countries as a result of the use of force in Kosovo'.[181] When the Council renewed this determination after the Kosovo conflict in 1999, it referred to the rights of refugees[182] and 'the other States of the region' (para. 10).[183]

Without referring to such cross-border influences of violent internal situations, the Security Council determined the situation in Somalia to constitute a threat to international peace and security. The Council based its decision solely on 'the heavy loss of human life and widespread material damage resulting from the conflict in the country' and on its 'consequences on stability and peace in the region'.[184] Similarly, within the framework of the UNPROFOR[185] mandate, the

---

174. Ibid.; P. Malanczuk, *Akehurst's Modern Introduction to International Law*, 7th edn., (London, Routledge 1997) p. 426. A connected question is whether there are any limits on the Security Council's discretion to assess what constitutes a threat to international peace and security.

175. S/RES/688 (1991), para. 1.

176. S/RES/688 (1991), preamble, para. 3.

177. S/RES/841 (1993), preamble, paras. 9 and 11.

178. Although the Security Council literally referred to a 'threat to peace and security in the region', the subsequent statement to act 'under Chapter VII of the Charter of the United Nations' clarifies the context of Article 39 UN Charter; S/RES/918 (1994), under B.

179. S/RES/918 (1994), preamble, para. 8.

180. Although the Security Council literally referred to a 'threat to peace and security in the region', the subsequent statement to act 'under Chapter VII of the Charter of the United Nations' clarifies the context of Article 39 UN Charter; S/RES/1199 (1998), preamble, para. 14.

181. S/RES/1199 (1998), preamble, para. 7.

182. S/RES/1244 (1999), preamble, paras. 4 and 7.

183. S/RES/1244 (1999), preamble, para. 10.

184. S/RES/733 (1992), preamble, para. 3.

185. UNPROFOR was deployed in a situation which in any case had both qualities of international and non-international armed conflict.

Security Council qualified the situation in Bosnia-Herzegovina as a threat to international peace and security,[186] based on a continuing violation of the Sarajevo Airport Agreement of 5 June 1992 and the importance of delivering humanitarian assistance[187] as well as on abuses committed against the civilian population, particularly on ethnic grounds.[188] On the basis of these qualifications, it authorised the mission to use military armed force.[189]

In conclusion, situations of non-international armed conflicts have been qualified as threats to international peace and security in the framework of Chapter VII UN Charter, and the Security Council has enacted Article 42 UN Charter and authorised Member States to use military armed force to intervene in such conflicts. With the exception of Somalia, qualifications and authorisations have been based on certain cross-border effects of international situations.

4.2.2.2 The discretion under chapter VII UN Charter

With a view to the question of protection of the civilian population in non-international armed conflicts, one may state that the use of Chapter VII UN Charter as an instrument to put an end to non-international armed conflicts and to restore international peace and security is at least intended[190] as an additional means of enhanced protection of the civilian population. The UN Security Council stated that 'the deliberate targeting of civilian populations (...) and the committing of systematic, flagrant and widespread violations of international humanitarian law and human rights law (...) in situations of armed conflict may constitute a threat to international peace and security'.[191] The Council expressed not only its determination to ensure peacekeeping mandates in order to effectively protect civilians,[192] but further reaffirmed its readiness to consider such situations and, where necessary, to adopt appropriate steps.

This action taken by the UN Security Council reveals two problems. Firstly, such imposition of military sanctions in a non-international armed conflict entails increased risks for the civilian population because of the potential danger of intensifying the fighting and aggravating the violence. Secondly, on the basis of the existing legal structure and framework of the United Nations, Security Council decisions are up to a certain extent discretionary and even arbitrary[193] and in this

186. S/RES/770 (1992), preamble, para. 5.

187. S/RES/764 (1992), preamble, paras. 3 and 10.

188. S/RES/769 (1992), para. 4.

189. S/RES/836 (1993), para. 9.

190. For example, the UN Secretary-General: '(...) real dilemma (...). The fact that we cannot protect people everywhere is no reason for doing nothing when we can. Armed intervention must always remain the option of last resort, but in the face of mass murder it is an option that cannot be relinquished.' http://www.un.org./millennium/sg/report/ch3.htm, para. 218.

191. S/RES/1314 (2000), para. 9, S/RES/1265 (1999), para. 10.

192. S/RES/1265 (1999), para. 11.

193. N. Mandela, address delivered at the Independent International Commission on Kosovo's final seminar on 25 August 2000, in Independent International Commission on Kosovo: *The Kosovo Report*, p. 5; http://www.reliefweb.int./library/documents.

respect unpredictable. Council decisions and often especially the lack of decisions are to a considerable extent perceived to be unjust and are in that respect counter-productive to the protection of the civilian population. Military sanctions according to Chapter VII UN Charter are presently used as counter-measures against infringements of the protection of the civilian population in non-international armed conflicts. But in order to achieve more effectiveness, the international community needs to develop a more stringent and cohesive concept of security, thus enhancing predictability and acceptance of this mechanism.

4.2.3 *'Humanitarian intervention'*

In the context of the protection of the civilian population by third states,[194] the problem of the so-called 'humanitarian intervention' has at least to be mentioned. Definitions of the term 'humanitarian intervention' are as manifold as efforts to justify certain actions in international relations within the system of the non-use of force of the Charter of the United Nations.[195]

In its classical sense, 'humanitarian intervention' may be defined as a coercive action by one or more states involving the use of armed force in another state without the consent of its authorities, and with the purpose of preventing wide-spread suffering or death among the inhabitants.[196] To a great extent, the discussion has centred around the problem of authorisation.[197] Debate and practice since 1990 have focused on the problem whether the Security Council of the United Nations and/or regional bodies and/or individual states and groups of states can legitimately authorise such intervention. Much of the debate has concentrated on the

---

194. A. Roberts: '(...) the debate on the subject has been spurred by the strong sense that there were crises (...) in which the international community should have intervened promptly but failed to do so.' 'The So-Called 'Right' of Humanitarian Intervention', 3 *YIHL* (2000) p. 3.

195. See Green, 1993 and 2000, op. cit. n. 60, p. 192; Roberts, ibid., pp. 3 at 5 et seq.; R. Wedgwood, 'NATO's Kosovo Intervention: NATO's Campaign in Yugoslavia', 93 *AJIL* (1999) pp. 828 et seq.; J.I. Charney, 'NATO's Kosovo Intervention: Anticipatory Humanitarian Intervention in Kosovo', 93 *AJIL* (1999) pp. 834 et seq.; R.A. Falk, 'NATO's Kosovo Intervention: Kosovo, World Order, and the Future of International Law', 93 *AJIL* (1999) pp. 847 et seq.; J. Lobel and M. Ratner, 'Bypassing the Security Council: Ambiguous Authorisations to Use Force, Cease-Fires and the Iraqi Inspection Regime', 93 *AJIL* (1999) pp. 124 et seq.; and L. Henkin, 'NATO's Kosovo Intervention: Kosovo and the Law of 'Humanitarian Intervention'', 93 *AJIL* (1999) pp. 824 et seq. One of the more recent examples for such an effort is the judgement of the Independent International Commission on Kosovo's judgement on the lawfulness of the NATO involvement in Kosovo: '(... the NATO military intervention was illegal but legitimate. (...) the intervention was justified (...) because the intervention had the effect of liberating the majority population of Kosovo from a long period of oppression under Serbian rule'; Independent International Commission on Kosovo: *The Kosovo Report*, Executive Summary, p. 2; http://www.reliefweb.int./library/documents.

196. U. Beyerlin, 'Humanitarian Intervention', R. Bernhardt, ed., *Encyclopedia of Public International Law*, Vol. II (Amsterdam, Elsevier 1995) pp. 926-933.

197. For example, the UN Secretary-General held that UN authorised intervention maybe necessary, in http://www.un.org./millennium/sg/report/ch3.htm, paras. 217 et seq. The Independent International Commission on Kosovo in its report suggested 'to close the gap between legality and legitimacy' and proposed a 'principled framework' for humanitarian intervention, *Supra* n. 109, pp. 1 and 85; http://www.reliefweb.int./library/documents.

question whether there is a right of humanitarian intervention in those cases in which the UN Security Council, even though it may have formally recognised the gravity and urgency of a threat to international peace and security, is unable to reach agreement on specific military action.

The present contribution will not analyse this problem.[198] In the framework of the protection of the civilian population, it coincides in many respects with the problem of access to vulnerable populations in general and the criterion of consent of the party to the conflict concerned to the delivery of humanitarian assistance. To a considerable extent, any 'right to – humanitarian – intervention' encounters parallel difficulties and doubts, particularly with regard to the 'soft' application of 'hard law' criteria for any such intervention. As debates in the UN General Assembly in 1999 and 2000 on the military operation in Kosovo have shown, up to now the international community has not reached a satisfactory agreement on the existence of a 'right to humanitarian intervention' beyond the UN Charter – a fact which is not necessarily obstructing the protection of the civilian population in non-international armed conflicts.[199]

5. CONCLUDING REMARKS

Despite possibly 'changing trends'[200] in today's most protracted and violent non-international armed conflicts due to the fact that the conflicts in Angola, Sierra Leone and Afghanistan appear to have ended, the question still has to be answered whether Additional Protocol II is effectively counteracting the suffering of the civilian population and constitutes a failure or entails progress in humanitarian legal protection.

The above overview of the distinctive features of recent non-international armed conflicts and the suffering inflicted on the civilian population has revealed several shortcomings and lacunae, in particular with respect to proportionality; detailed criteria and conditions for the granting of access to a suffering civilian population; prohibition of forced displacement; and granting distinction and separation between civilians and combatants. Enforcement mechanisms with regard to the protection of the civilian population in non-international conflicts are generally rather weak, in particular coercive military measures, which lack a concise and coherent approach. Moreover, the catalogue of offences under the ICC Statute is partially deficient. Yet, it is clear that the cause of frustration and even despair is

---

198. For comprehensive studies cf. for example, Roberts, loc. cit. n. 194, at pp. 3 et seq., and R.B. Lillich, 'Humanitarian Intervention Through the United Nations: Towards the Development of Criteria', 53 *ZaöRV* (1993) pp. 557 et seq.

199. As the Independent International Commission on Kosovo states in its Kosovo Report: 'NATO air campaign did not provoke the attacks on the civilian Kosovar population but the bombing reacted an environment that made such an operation feasible.' *Supra* n. 109, at p. 26; http://www.reliefweb.int./library/documents.

200. *Supra* n. 20, para. 11.

the fact that norms are being violated at all: it is the fact of commission of violations and it is the scope of such infringements.

The yardstick for the efficiency of rules for the protection of the civilian population in non-international armed conflicts as contained in Additional Protocol II and common Article 3 is the degree to which their existence is able to contribute to the prevention of violations of these norms. And it is clear that Additional Protocol II and common Article 3 GC, be it on a treaty law or on a customary law basis, are not sufficiently adhered to in practice. Most of the disappointment and often helplessness among governments and writers stems from the fact that law in general and humanitarian law in particular neither prevents the commission of breaches of the law[201] nor seems to limit the extent of such infringements.

One could imagine a regulation of non-international conflicts equivalent to the regime of international ones or with even higher standards.[202] But that would not help very much as long as there are no better chances for a better observance of the already rudimentary rules.[203] However, such divergence entails the problem of existing regulation on the one hand and questions with regard to possibly most effective and efficient implementation and enforcement on the other hand.

Generally, the mere existence of a legal norm might prevent the actual infringement of the law whenever and wherever decisions are being taken on a most abstract level and in an environment where lawful behaviour constitutes a value and/or where it may provide an advantage of any kind. From a psycho-sociological point of view, the crucial element is the actor in armed hostilities – in inter-state relations as well as in intra-state relations. Even in international relations between governments, on the international level, this is far from being realised, self-understood – and functioning. In the typical constellations of non-international armed conflict, the actors may not only be manifold but also characterised by completely unstructured, conflicting and contradictory backgrounds, interests and motivations. In contrast to international armed conflicts, the different legal relationships, considerations and reasoning are much less abstract and much more personal.[204]

It is worth considering whether, and eventually the extent to which, effective and efficient implementation and enforcement of the law can contribute to the prevention of infringements. In the context of non-international armed conflicts,

---

201. On the – insoluble – problem of the relevance of law, legal institutions and legal instruments. see J.G. Merrills, *International Dispute Settlement* (Cambridge, Cambridge University Press 1991 and 1998): 'To some, the answer to all the world's problems is to be found in legal codes and international tribunals. To others, observing the disregard for legality which is a feature of most international crises, law at best has a marginal role in world affairs, and at worst is a pious illusion.' p. 292.

202. Some authors even already observe a rather comprehensive legal coverage of non-international armed conflicts; cf., for example, Moir, op. cit. n. 31, p. 275: '(...) constitutes a fairly extensive corpus of law, undoubtedly capable of offering civilians adequate protection were it to be applied.'

203. This would only be wrong if rules would not be observed just because of the fact that they are rudimentary – which is definitely not the case.

204. Admittedly also within states and governments arguments are being built and decisions being taken by individuals for more or less personal motivations; but in situations of non-international armed conflict the impact is much more direct and unfiltered and much less tempered by external or at least sociological factors.

such implementation and enforcement has to be effected on a personal basis, i.e., directed at the individual and not at abstract entities.[205] Individual criminal responsibility is one aspect of such an approach. However, it is not the only one and maybe not even the best one. Prosecution and punishment of those who violate the law cannot be a substitute for preventing violations.[206] Attention needs to shift from repression of those who violate the law to the area of prevention. Yet, the crucial question is how to achieve such idealistic objectives.

What is needed is both an international as well as a domestic environment where the acquisition of certain principles and patterns of behaviour – even in non-international hostilities – constitutes a value and provides an advantage. Apart from sociological considerations and approaches, such acquisition has to be enacted by states – who are the 'natural' actors in international law. Traditional approaches to implementing and enforcing international humanitarian law, which more or less follow the lines of international conflicts, did fail to a considerable and well-known degree. Maybe these approaches were bound to fail because they did not sufficiently address and affect the crucial actors in non-international armed conflicts: i.e., very often individuals and only rather by chance organised groups of individuals.

The importance of reaching the relevant actors cannot be overestimated. However, the crucial question remains how to reach individuals and groups of individuals and how to persuade them to bring their individual behaviour in line with international principles and norms in situations where the domestic authorities are not able or not willing to enforce such observance. This challenge is not a specific one for the area of international humanitarian law in non-international armed conflict but is inherent in any area of law with a repressive character. Any attempt to approach the challenge will imply elements of legislative implementation, dissemination, 'preventive dissemination' to potentially crucial target groups and training. Yet, of key importance is to create a general climate in the international community wherein observance of humanitarian norms for the protection of the civilian population is expected from everybody – even from non-state actors in non-international armed conflicts, from groups and from individuals.

Such expectation itself may only be effective where non-governmental conflict parties benefit from the observance of the law. Efforts of the international community have to focus on the creation of incentives for such benefit. Possible incentives might include an international general awareness/sphere for non-

---

205. Merrills answers the question whether there is any value in legal rules without procedures for adjudication in the positive: 'First, because in practice where legal rules exist they are normally followed, and secondly because although international disputes are generally resolved without adjudication, law will frequently play a significant part in defining the points in issue, and providing a framework for negotiation, conciliation or the presentation of a state's case in a political forum', op. cit. n. 201, at p. 293.

206. Fenrick states: 'The success or failure of international humanitarian law must be measured in terms of lives saved and injuries not suffered. It is not measured by the number of prosecutions of the number of convictions.' 'The Law Applicable to Targeting and Proportionality After Operation Allied Force: A View from the Outside', 3 *YIHL* (2000) pp. 53 at 79 et seq.

governmental conflict parties, exemption from criminal prosecution for those having participated in the hostilities, as well as an increase in pressure on governments and non-state actors; pressure by military means being the last resort. In principle, the international community has to take note of the fact that non-state actors in today's non-international armed conflicts play the crucial role in the application and observance of humanitarian law. Recognition of their partial subjectivity under humanitarian law combined with an increased international concern for non-international hostilities and an increased international involvement in such situations, not necessarily by military means, might give the protection of the civilian population in non-international armed conflicts a chance. It is this context that globalisation might play the crucial role: the attempt to create awareness in populations, societies, communities and individuals that the observance of international humanitarian law is expected – even in situations of non-international conflict.

Such globalisation necessarily and essentially has to be accompanied by a further development of humanitarian law for the protection of the civilian population in non-international armed conflicts. If there is one lesson from the history and sociology of law, then it is that renouncing legal norms – their existence, their further development, their implementation and their enforcement – has never brought any progress nor any improved protection for anybody.

THE EVOLVING JURISPRUDENCE AND PRACTICE OF EAST TIMOR'S SPECIAL PANELS FOR SERIOUS CRIMES ON ADMISSIONS OF GUILT, DURESS AND SUPERIOR ORDERS[1]

Suzannah Linton and Caitlin Reiger[2]

1. INTRODUCTION

After 24 years of occupation by Indonesia and nearly 500 years of Portuguese colonisation, East Timor gained its independence on 20 May 2002 when the United Nations formally handed over the reins of power to a popularly elected President. Justice for the immense suffering of the people of East Timor while under Indonesian rule is a major issue for the local and international communities. Of particular importance is the question of individual criminal responsibility for atrocities committed during the last year of the occupation, when the weeks following the referendum on independence held on 30 August 1999 saw unparalleled devastation wreaked upon the civilian population and infrastructure.

On 6 June 2000, the United Nations Transitional Administration in East Timor (UNTAET)[3] passed Regulation 2000/15 establishing Special Panels within the District Court of Dili, each to be composed of two international judges and one East Timorese, with jurisdiction to hear cases of Serious Crimes (Regulation 2000/15').[4] These are defined as genocide, war crimes, crimes against humanity, torture, and also sexual offences and murder under the Indonesian Penal Code if committed between 1 January 1999 and 25 October 1999.[5] The international crimes are

2. Suzannah Linton is Visiting Fellow, Center for Civil and Human Rights at the Law School, University of Notre Dame. She has worked on accountability for gross violations of human rights in many countries, including East Timor, where she served with the United Nations Transitional Administration. Caitlin Reiger is the co-founder and Senior Legal Advisor of the Judicial System Monitoring Programme in Dili, East Timor. Comments and opinions expressed are strictly personal to the authors. This article reflects legal developments up to 31 May 2002 and includes first-hand observations of the trial process before the Special Panels for Serious Crimes. Judgments examined in this article are on file with the authors, alternatively viewable at http://www.jsmp.minihub.org.

3. UNTAET was established by the Security Council under Chapter VII of the UN Charter, UN Doc. S/Res/1272 (1999). For the purposes of this article, references to UNTAET shall include the East Timor Transitional Administration.

4. UNTAET Regulation 2000/15 on the Establishment of Panels with Exclusive Jurisdiction over Serious Criminal Offences, UNTAET/REG/2000/15, 6 June 2000 ('Regulation 2000/15').

5. Kitab Undang-Undang Hukum Pidana (KUHP, or Indonesian Penal Code), available in Bahasa Indonesia at http://www.asiamaya.com.

defined in detail, following almost verbatim the subject matter jurisdiction of the Rome Statute of the International Criminal Court (ICC Statute).[6] Thus, the East Timor experiment is in some ways a trial run of many of the substantive legal provisions that will be applied at the ICC. Other substantive legal provisions, such as most of the defences and the procedure for a guilty plea, also replicate the ICC Statute.[7]

The Special Panels apply the laws applicable in East Timor, that is, those of Indonesia as amended or replaced by UNTAET and, where appropriate, applicable treaties and recognised principles and norms of international law, including the established principles of the law of armed conflict.[8] These are supplemented by a uniform code of criminal procedure, the Transitional Rules of Criminal Procedure, which regulates the conduct of all criminal proceedings.[9]

Trials in relation to atrocities committed during 1999 have been held before the Special Panels for Serious Crimes at the District Court of Dili since early 2001.[10] One of the most interesting and unique features of these cases is the fact that almost every accused person admits to being involved in some aspect of the crime with which he is charged, for example, that he killed.[11] But they usually claim that they did so because they were 'ordered' to or because they were forcibly coerced by someone perceived to have influence, be it a village leader, militia leader or Indonesian military official. The frequency of these claims indicates a pattern of coercive behaviour by pro-Jakarta forces, the low rank of the militia members who have been tried to date, as well the desire of many of them to acknowledge their involvement in crimes and be reconciled with their communities.

This paper examines how the issues of the guilty plea, superior orders and duress have been handled by the Special Panels, and explores whether their practice and jurisprudence in these respects are consistent with international standards of due process and fair trial, and the practice and jurisprudence of the *ad hoc* International

6. Rome Statute of the International Criminal Court, opened for signature 17 July 1998, UN Doc. A/CONF.183/9 (entered into force 1 July 2002), adopted by the United Nations Diplomatic Conference of Plenipotentiaries on the Establishment of an International Criminal Court on 17 July 1998.

7. A notable exception is superior orders, where UNTAET's drafters chose to revert to the positions adopted by the *ad hoc* Tribunals for Yugoslavia and Rwanda; see discussion at section 5.1 *infra*. The procedure for a guilty plea is contained in Regulation 2000/30 on Transitional Rules of Criminal Procedure, 25 September 2000, UNTAET/REG/2000/30 ('Transitional Rules of Criminal Procedure').

8. S. 3, UNTAET Regulation 1999/1 on the Authority of the Transitional Administration in East Timor, UNTAET/REG1999/1, 27 October 1999.

9. Transitional Rules of Criminal Procedure, *supra* n. 7

10. Regulation 2000/15 envisaged several panels operating simultaneously. However, for virtually the entire period covered by this study, there has been just one panel of judges, although its composition has varied in part. We use the singular in relation to specific cases and the plural when referring to the general practice.

11. There are no indications that the confessions arise from improper conduct of the investigative authorities and this has never been an issue in Serious Crimes cases thus far. However, the lack of legal representation for suspects during police questioning has been an ongoing problem, due to the few defence counsel available.

Criminal Tribunals for the former Yugoslavia (ICTY) and Rwanda (ICTR), as well as earlier case-law from the post-World War II prosecutions.

The study opens with a brief examination of international law and jurisprudence on admissions of guilt and allegations of coercion, whether in the form of superior orders or duress. As the relevant historical and legal developments in East Timor have been extensively covered elsewhere,[12] including in the Correspondents' Reports sections of the 2000 and 2001 volumes of the *Yearbook of International Humanitarian Law*,[13] they will not be examined here. The practice of the Special Panels concerning admissions of guilt, duress and superior orders will be examined in Parts 2, 3 and 4, respectively. Finally, some conclusions are offered.

2. ADMISSIONS OF GUILT, DURESS AND SUPERIOR ORDERS IN INTERNATIONAL LAW

2.1 **International law and admissions of guilt**

The guilty plea procedure *per se* derives from common law practice, which places a particular importance on the entering of a plea to the charge, enabling the accused to plead innocent or guilty at the start of the proceedings. Civil law jurisdictions, on the other hand, treat an admission of guilt as part of the evidence to be considered and evaluated in the course of a trial. The advantages of the guilty plea procedure are considered to include minimising costs, the saving of court time and avoiding the inconvenience and trauma of a trial, particularly to victims and witnesses.

An admission of guilt is a matter of procedural law that can involve issues of substance, for example, when an equivocal plea (a guilty plea that is accompanied or qualified by words describing facts which may negate criminal responsibility) is made. A court faced with a plea in such circumstances will need to distinguish two separate issues: (1) what it is that the accused is seeking to achieve with his statement – to be excused from responsibility or to have his punishment reduced; and (2) whether the applicable law accepts the situation raised by the accused as a

12. See generally J. Dunn, *Timor: A People Betrayed* (Brisbane, Jacaranda Wiley 1983); C. Budiardjo and Liem Soei Liong, *The War Against East Timor* (London, Zed Books Ltd. 1984); J. Taylor, *Indonesia's Forgotten War: The Hidden History of East Timor* (London, Zed Books Ltd. 1991); Catholic Institute for International Relations and the International Platform of Jurists for East Timor, *International Law and the Question of East Timor* (London and Leiden, CIIR and IPJET 1995); J. Taylor, *East Timor: The Price of Freedom* (London, Zed Books Ltd. 1999); S. Linton, 'Rising From The Ashes: The Creation Of A Viable Criminal Justice System In East Timor', 25 *Melbourne Univ. LR* (2001) p. 122; S. Linton, 'Prosecuting Atrocities At The District Court Of Dili', 2 *Melbourne JIL* (2001) p. 414; S. Linton, 'Cambodia, East Timor and Sierra Leone: Experiments in International Justice', 12 *Criminal LF* (2001) p. 185; S. Linton, 'New Approaches to International Justice in Cambodia and East Timor', *IRRC* No. 845 (2002) p. 93; M. Ruffert, 'The Administration Of Kosovo and East Timor by the International Community', 50 *ICLQ* (2001) p. 613; H. Strohmeyer, 'Collapse and Reconstruction of a Judicial System: The United Nations Missions in Kosovo and East Timor', 95 *AJIL* (2001) p. 46.

13. See 3 *YIHL* (2000) pp. 471-482 and in this volume at pp. 492-497.

complete defence or simply a mitigating factor. If the answer is one that requires evidence to be brought to prove the assertion, the case may be better dealt with by way of a full trial.

This common law institution has found its place in international criminal fora, which deal with cases that are by their nature complex and necessarily involve lengthy hearings. Article 20(3) of the ICTY's (Art. 19(3) ICTR's) Statute provides that

> 'the Trial Chamber shall read the indictment, satisfy itself that the rights of the accused are respected, confirm that the accused understands the indictment, and instruct the accused to enter a plea. The Trial Chamber shall then set the date for trial.'

The jurisprudence of the *ad hoc* International Criminal Tribunals indicates that, if accepted, a guilty plea should in principle give rise to a reduction in the sentence,[14] but this depends on the circumstances of the case.[15]

At the ICTY, the admission of guilt provision was first tested in the *Erdemović* case. Rule 62 of the then-applicable Rules of Procedure and Evidence provided, *inter alia*, that upon transfer to the Tribunal, the accused was to be brought before the court as soon as possible and permitted to enter a plea; if the plea was guilty, the Chamber was to instruct the Registrar to set a date for the pre-sentencing hearing.

Neither Rule 62 nor Article 20(3) gave the judges of the ICTY adequate guidance on how to deal with a guilty plea, and the Trial Chamber's acceptance of the guilty plea made by *Erdemović* on 31 May 1996 was eventually overturned by a majority of the Appeals Chamber for being flawed.[16] Guidance on how to deal with a guilty plea came in the form of a test identified by Judges McDonald and Vohrah:

(a) The guilty plea must be voluntary. It must be made by an accused who is mentally fit to understand the consequences of pleading guilty and who is not affected by any threats, inducements or promises.

(b) The guilty plea must be informed, that is, the accused must understand the nature of the charges against him and the consequences of pleading guilty to them. The accused must know what he is pleading guilty to;

---

14. *Prosecutor* v. *Stevan Todorović*, case No. IT-95-9/1-S, Sentencing Judgement, 31 July 2001.

15. *Prosecutor* v. *Jean Kambanda*, case No. ICTR 97-23-A, Judgement, 19 October 2000, where despite the former Prime Minister's guilty plea, a Trial Chamber of the ICTR imposed the maximum penalty, a life sentence. This was upheld on appeal.

16. *Prosecutor* v. *Drazen Erdemović*, case No. IT-96-22-T, Trial Chamber II, Judgement, 29 November 1996; *Prosecutor* v. *Drazen Erdemović*, case No. IT-96-22-A, Appeals Chamber, Judgement, 7 October 1997, with Joint Separate Opinion of Judge McDonald and Judge Vohrah ('Joint and Separate Opinion of Judges McDonald and Vohrah'), and Separate Opinions from Judges Cassese, Stephen and Li ('Separate Opinion of Judge Cassese', 'Separate Opinion of Judge Stephen', 'Separate Opinion of Judge Li'). By four votes (Judges Cassese, McDonald, Stephen and Vohrah) to one (Judge Li), the Appeals Chamber found that the guilty plea was not informed; By four votes (Judges Cassese, McDonald, Stephen and Vohrah) to one (Judge Li), the Appeals Chamber held that the case must be remitted to a Trial Chamber, other than the one which sentenced the Appellant, so that the Appellant could enter a fresh plea in full knowledge of the nature of the charges and the consequences of his plea.

(c) The guilty plea must not be equivocal. It must not be accompanied by words amounting to a defence contradicting an admission of criminal responsibility.[17]

The judges recognised that an accused who pleads guilty waives certain crucial fair trial rights. This waiver may therefore only be admitted under very stringent conditions and it is the duty of the Trial Court to ensure that an accused understands and readily accepts the consequences. For example, by pleading guilty, the accused waives the presumption of innocence, the right to a full trial and to test the prosecution case through the cross-examination of witnesses and calling evidence in his defence. A court faced with a guilty plea is therefore required to be particularly vigilant. This test was eventually adopted with amendment in both the ICTY and ICTR Rules of Procedure and Evidence.[18] It has since been successfully applied by ICTY Trial Chambers in the cases of *Jelisić*[19] and *Todorović*,[20] and *Plasvić*,[21] without being appealed to the Appeals Chamber. At the ICTR, former Prime Minister *Jean Kambanda* pleaded guilty to the charges against him and was sentenced to life imprisonment. His appeal, challenging, *inter alia*, the Trial Chamber's acceptance of his guilty plea and sentence, was rejected by the Appeals Chamber.[22] The current procedure for the handling of an admission of guilt therefore appears to provide satisfactory guidance to the judges of the ICTY and ICTR.

Drawing on this, Article 64(8)(a) of the ICC Statute provides that '[t]he Trial Chamber shall satisfy itself that the accused understands the nature of the charges. It shall afford him or her the opportunity to make an admission of guilt in accordance with Article 65 or to plead not guilty'. Article 65 sets out in detail the procedure for proceedings on an admission of guilt. These provisions have been adopted in East Timor and will be examined later.

---

17. *Erdemović* Appeal Decision, Joint and Separate Opinion of Judges McDonald and Vohrah, ibid., para. 8.

18. Rules of Procedure and Evidence of the International Criminal Tribunal for the Former Yugoslavia (adopted 11 February 1994 and subsequently amended), Doc. IT/32/Rev.20 ('ICTY Rules of Procedure and Evidence') ('ICTY Rules of Procedure and Evidence') and Rules of Procedure and Evidence of the International Criminal Tribunal for the Former Yugoslavia (adopted 29 June 1995 and subsequently amended), ('ICTR Rules of Procedure and Evidence').

19. Prosecutor v. *Goran Jelisić*, case No. IT-95-10-T, Judgement, 14 December 1999.

20. *Prosecutor* v. *Stevan Todorović*, *supra* n. 14.

21. On 2 October 2002, Biljana Plavsić, former Bosnian Serb President, pleaded guilty to persecution on political, racial and religious grounds as a crime against humanity. At her first appearance before the tribunal, she had entered a not-guilty plea. The Prosecution dropped all other charges in its Amended Consolidated Indictment of 7 March 2002. The parties filed a plea agreement that set out in detail what it was that Ms Plavsić agreed to. She agreed to the legal elements of the crime of persecution based on political, racial and religious grounds which the Prosecution was required to prove beyond reasonable doubt, and the specific rights that she was waiving by pleading guilty. It also emphasized that she had taken full legal advice and entered into the agreement voluntarily and without undue influence; her legal advisors also entered the agreement.

22. *Prosecutor* v. *Jean Kambanda*, *supra* n. 15.

2.2 International law and duress

Duress, namely acting under a threat from a third person of severe and irreparable harm to life or limb, entails that no criminal responsibility is incurred by the person acting under that threat.[23] To qualify as duress, this physical threat must be 'imminent, real, and inevitable'.[24] Duress is often termed 'necessity', but necessity is in fact a broader heading than duress, encompassing threats to life and limb generally and not only when they emanate from another person.[25] International law on the issue of duress resulting in the taking of human life reflects the fundamental division between common and civil law jurisdictions. In civil law countries, duress in such situations affords a complete defence; in common law countries it does not.

Neither the Charter of the International Military Tribunal at Nuremburg (IMT)[26] nor Control Council Law No. 10[27] addressed the issue of duress as a defence, leaving it up to the respective judges to decide what international law actually provided. The general position in relation to duress adopted in the post-World War II cases was set out in *Einsatzgruppen*:

> 'Let it be said at once that there is no law which requires that an innocent man must forfeit his life or suffer serious harm in order to avoid committing a crime which he condemns. The threat, however, must be imminent, real, and inevitable. No court will punish a man who, with a loaded pistol at his head, is compelled to pull a lethal lever. Nor need the peril be that imminent in order to escape punishment.'[28]

In adopting the ICTY and ICTR Statutes, the Security Council left open the question whether duress is available in international law as a defence. It fell to the judges to make this determination.

The opportunity arose in 1997 in *Erdemović*. There, a majority of the Appeals Chamber found that duress does not afford a complete defence to a soldier charged with a crime against humanity or a war crime involving the killing of innocent human beings.[29] However, each of the judges expressed different views in separate or dissenting opinions. Judge Cassese was adamant that the only logical conclusion in the absence of a specific international rule was that the general rule that duress

---

23. *Erdemović* Appeal Decision, Separate Opinion of Judge Cassese, *supra* n. 16, para. 14.

24. *Trial of Otto Ohlendorf et al., ('Einsatzgruppen'),* Trials of War Criminals Before the Nuremburg Military Tribunals under Control Council Law No. 10, (US Govt. Printing Office, Washington DC 1950) Vol. IV, p. 480.

25. *Erdemović* Appeal Decision, Separate Opinion of Judge Cassese, *supra* n. 16, para. 14.

26. Charter of the International Military Tribunal (IMT), in Agreement for the Prosecution and Punishment of the Major War Criminals of the European Axis (London Agreement), 8 August 1945, 82 *UNTS* p. 280 ('IMT Charter').

27. Control Council Law No. 10, Punishment of Persons Guilty of War Crimes, Crimes Against Peace and Against Humanity, 20 December 1945, 3 *Official Gazette Control Council for Germany 50-55* (1946) ('Control Council Law No.10').

28. *Einsatzgruppen, supra* n. 24, p. 480.

29. *Erdemović* Appeal Decision, *supra* n. 16, para. 19.

could amount to a defence in certain limited situations must prevail.[30] Judge Stephen concluded that 'despite the exception which the common law makes to the availability of duress in cases of murder where the choice is truly between one life or another, the defence of duress can be adopted into international law as deriving from a general principle of law recognized by the world's major legal systems, at least where that exception does not apply'.[31] In contrast, Judges McDonald and Vohrah embarked upon a detailed investigation of 'practical policy considerations' of national jurisdictions in relation to pleas of duress, and concluded that 'duress cannot afford a complete defence to a soldier charged with crimes against humanity or war crimes in international law involving the taking of innocent lives'.[32] Judge Li rejected duress as a complete defence to the massacre of innocent persons but accepted that it could constitute a mitigating circumstance.[33]

The majority's choice of the term 'soldier' may suggest that this ruling is limited to members of the regular armed forces, and does not apply to irregular combatants such as militias or paramilitaries. Also notable is the use of the term 'innocent life', which could be interpreted to suggest that a value judgement may be made by the soldier as to whether a victim is innocent or not.

In contrast, the ICC Statute recognises duress as a full defence. Article 31(1)(d) provides that a person shall not be criminally responsible if:

> 'the conduct which is alleged to constitute a crime within the jurisdiction of the panel has been caused by duress resulting from a threat of imminent death or of continuing or imminent serious bodily harm against that person or another person, and the person acts necessarily and reasonably to avoid this threat, provided that the person does not intend to cause a greater harm than the one sought to be avoided. Such a threat may be: made by other persons; or constituted by other circumstances beyond that person's control.'

This provision has been adopted in East Timor.

2.3 International law and obedience to superior orders

International law is unsettled on the consequences of international crimes committed pursuant to superior orders.[34] There are two divergent legal positions:(1) that obedience to superior orders is not a defence and may only lead to a mitigated sentence (conviction); and (2) that obedience to superior orders provides a complete defence to charges if proved (acquittal).

---

30. *Erdemović* Appeal Decision, ibid., Separate Opinion of Judge Cassese, paras. 41and 49.

31. *Erdemović* Appeal Decision, ibid., Separate Opinion of Judge Stephen, para. 64.

32. *Erdemović* Appeal Decision, ibid., Joint and Separate Opinion of Judges McDonald and Vohrah, paras. 77 and 88.

33. *Erdemović* Appeal Decision, ibid., Separate Opinion of Judge Li, para. 5.

34. For a concise identification of the main issues, see A. Eser, 'Defences in War Crimes Trials', in Y. Dinstein and M. Tabory, eds., *War Crimes in International Law* (Dordrecht, Martinus Nijhoff 1996) pp. 251-173.

2.3.1 *Superior orders as a mitigating factor*

Article 8 of the Charter of the IMT prohibited the use of superior orders as a defence but permitted its application as a mitigating factor.[35] The Tribunal's judgement found

> 'that a soldier was ordered to kill or torture in violation of the international law of war has never been recognised as a defence to such acts of brutality, though as the Charter here provides, the order may be urged in mitigation of the punishment'.[36]

The IMT judgement also introduced the concept of moral choice – whether the subordinate faced a situation where there was no moral choice, that is, where he did not have freedom to choose between actions that were right and wrong without suffering serious harm.[37]

Superior orders requires the existence of an order given by someone with the competence to issue orders to the recipient, who in turn must be legally bound to obey the order. As the earlier cited IMT judgement made clear, if the order is manifestly unlawful there is no duty to obey. The Statutes of the ICTY and ICTR have adopted the IMT's absolutist position of principle and deny recourse to superior orders as a defence. However, the Secretary-General's Report on the ICTY Statute stresses, the court may 'consider the factor of superior orders in connection with other defences such as coercion or lack of moral choice'.[38] Although the ICTY/ICTR position has drawn criticism for failing to take into account the more nuanced approach adopted by the post-World War II war crimes tribunals, literature and manuals of military law, which indicated that superior orders could in certain limited situations amount to a defence,[39] it is this concept of superior orders as a mitigating factor that is applied in East Timor.

2.3.2 *Superior orders as a complete defence, but in limited circumstances*

The alternative legal position is that obedience to superior orders is or should be a defence because it is a key element of the hierarchical nature of the military command structure which relies on the maintenance of discipline within it, and

---

35. IMT Charter, *supra* n. 26, Art. 8: 'The fact that the Defendant acted pursuant to orders of his government or of a superior shall not free him from responsibility, but may be considered in mitigation of punishment, if the Tribunal determines that Justice so desires.'

36. Trials of the German Major War Criminals, Proceedings of the International Military Tribunal, Sitting at Nuremberg, Germany 1947 (London, H.M. Stationery Office 1950) Vol. 22, p. 447 ('IMT Judgement').

37. Ibid. 'The true test, which is found in varying degrees in the criminal law of most nations, is not the existence of the order, but whether moral choice was in fact possible.'

38. Report of the Secretary-General, UN Doc. S/25704, para. 57.

39. T. Meron, *War Crimes Law Comes of Age* (Oxford, Oxford University Press 1999) p. 224. Also generally on the development of the law since 1945, see Y. Dinstein, *The Defence of Obedience to Superior Orders in International Law* (Leiden, Sijthoff 1965); L.C. Green, *Superior Orders in National and International Law* (Leiden, Sijthoff 1976).

also because commanding officers are made responsible for the acts of subordinates by way of the doctrine of command responsibility. Policy reasons aside, its proponents claim that, despite the sanctified position of the IMT Charter in international law, the law in fact applied then was a recent change and State practice and *opinio juris* have now moved away from the IMT rule towards the earlier position – some of the post-World War II jurisprudence is certainly accommodating of superior orders as more than a mere mitigating factor.[40] For example, in the *Hostages* case, the tribunal found that if the illegality of the order was not known to the subordinate, and he could not reasonably have been expected to know of its illegality, no wrongful intent necessary to the commission of a crime exists and the subordinate will be excused.[41]In the 1950s, the influential US Army Field Manual reverted to the pre-1944 position that recognised superior orders as a defence in limited situations.[42] The International Law Commission too gradually moved away from the absolutist position of total denial towards one recognising that it may be available in limited circumstances.[43]

In 1998, the drafters of the ICC Statute opted for a limited recognition of a superior orders defence. Article 33 stresses the basic principle that orders from a superior are not a defence. It then sets out a stringent test for determining what international law recognises as 'superior orders' and permits this to be raised as a defence where: (a) The person was under a legal obligation to obey the orders of the Government or the superior in question; (b) The person did not know that the order was unlawful; and (c) The order was not manifestly unlawful. Under paragraph 2, an order to commit genocide and crimes against humanity (but not war crimes), is manifestly unlawful. A superior order to commit such offences would thus not be accepted as a defence.

This test has the effect of distinguishing between superior orders and 'orders'. For the former, custom requires that there must be an order, either oral or written, addressing the accused or a group to which the addressee belongs, requiring certain actions or omissions leading to the commission of an international crime.[44] Furthermore, there has to be a superior-subordinate relationship, although not

40. Meron, op. cit. n. 39, at p. 101, see also L.C. Green, 'Superior Orders and the Reasonable Man', in *Essays on the Modern Law of War*, 2nd edn. (Ardsley, Transnational Publishers Inc. 1999) pp. 245-282.

41. *US* v. *Wilhelm List et al*, (Hostages), Trials of War Criminals before the Nuremberg Military Tribunals under Control Council Law No. 10 (US Govt. Printing Office, Washington DC 1950) Vol. XI, p. 1236.

42. See para. 509(a) of US Army Field Manual 27-10 (1956): The fact that the law of war has been violated pursuant to an order of a superior authority, whether military or civil, does not deprive the act in question of its character as a war crime, not does it constitute a defense in the trial of an accused individual, *unless he did not know and could not reasonably have been expected to know that the act ordered was unlawful.* (emphasis added).

43. See for example, Report of the International Law Commission on the work of its Thirty-Ninth Session, 4 May -17 July 1987 (1987), 2 *YILC*, Part, 1 and 7, and commentary on superior orders at UN doc. A/42/10 (1987) p. 9.

44. O. Trifterer, ed., *Commentary on the Rome Statute of the International Criminal Court, Observer's Notes, Article by Article* (Baden-Baden, Nomos, 1999) p. 582.

necessarily a military one, with the person giving the order having the right to demand obedience by the subordinate.

Under customary law, an accused who willingly joins a criminal enterprise cannot then raise the issue of superior orders.[45] *Einsatzgruppen*[46] and *Milch*[47] confirmed that voluntary membership in a criminal or illegal enterprise prohibits the availability of duress as a defence. This established a line of jurisprudence that duress or necessity cannot excuse from criminal responsibility the person who freely and knowingly chose to become a member of a unit, organisation or group institutionally intent upon actions contrary to international humanitarian law.[48] Moreover, superior orders cannot mitigate if the accused was prepared to carry out the unlawful act anyway.[49]

The moral choice test continues to apply in custom: the accused must have not have had freedom to choose between actions that were right and wrong.[50] Article 33 of the ICC Statute is felt by some to reflect the changes in customary international law and to have incorporated an understanding of some of the realities of combat situations and the demands of military discipline.[51] Its detractors claim that it overturns the cherished Nuremberg position and flies in the face of customary international law in permitting superior orders as a defence.[52]

2.4 Distinguishing duress from superior orders

Superior orders and duress are often confused because of their common element of coercion and the mistaken belief that soldiers are obliged to obey all orders of their superiors. Duress can arise as a result of an extreme degree of pressure from anyone whilst superior orders only arise from someone with whom one has a superior-subordinate relationship which legally obliges the recipient to obey the order.

Particular difficulty has arisen where there are threats going beyond the inherent coercion in a relationship of unequal power. The question is whether such extra coercion by a superior could amount to duress and thus possibly a defence. The

45. In illustrating how to use the superior orders doctrine, the tribunal in *Einsatzgruppen* raised an example of a sailor who voluntarily joins a pirate ship. He 'must not be heard to answer that he was ignorant of the probability he would be called upon to help in the robbing and sinking of other vessels. He who willingly joins an illegal enterprise is charged with the natural development of that unlawful undertaking. What SS man could say that he was unaware of the attitude of Hitler toward Jewry?', *Einsatzgruppen, supra* n. 24, p. 92.

46. Idem., p. 91.

47. Trial of Erhard Milch, Trials of War Criminals before the Nuremberg Military Tribunals under Control Council Law No. 10 (US Govt. Printing Office, Washington DC 1950) Vol. III, p. 964.

48. *Erdemović* Appeal Decision, *supra* n. 16, Separate Opinion of Judge Cassese, para. 17.

49. *Erdemović* First Trial Chamber Judgment, *supra* n. 16, para. 53.

50. The question of the moral choice was considered by the trial chamber and the five appellate judges as key in the *Erdemović* case, *supra* n. 16.

51. C. Garraway, 'Superior Orders and the International Criminal Court: Justice delivered or justice denied?', 81 *IRRC* (1999) No. 836, pp. 785-794.

52. P. Gaeta, 'The Defence of Superior Orders: The Statute of the International Criminal Court versus Customary International Law', 10 *EJIL* (1999) pp. 172 et seq.

Erdemović case illustrates the difficulties that courts face with coercive situations involving orders, and the need for the two legal concepts of superior orders and duress to be clearly distinguished. The first Trial Chamber stressed the now well-established position that the overriding duty of a soldier faced with a manifestly unlawful order is to disobey; this duty only recedes in the face of the most extreme duress.[53] It also found that while a complete defence based on moral duress and/or a state of necessity stemming from superior orders is not absolutely excluded, its conditions of application are particularly strict.[54] More precisely, it said that these must be sought not only in the existence of a superior order – which must first be proven – but also and especially in the circumstances characterising how the order was given and how it was received.[55] The Chamber felt that this called for a case-by-case approach which assesses the objective and subjective elements characterising duress or the state of necessity and examination of whether the accused in his situation did not have a duty to disobey, and whether he had the moral choice to do so or try to do so.[56]

This seemed to merge the concepts of duress and superior orders. On the Appeals Chamber, Judges Cassese, McDonald and Vohrah were clear about the need to separate the two. Judges McDonald and Vohrah rejected the submission that when duress is accompanied by a superior order that is a reason against allowing duress as a defence because obedience to superior orders *per se* had been specifically rejected as a defence in the Statute.[57] The judges were clear that obedience to superior orders is merely a factual circumstance to be considered when determining whether the defence of duress is made out on the merits; the fact that the Appellant obeyed an order of a superior does not go to the preceding legal question of whether duress may ever be pleaded as a defence.[58] They rejected the possibility of a hybrid defence of the sort suggested by the Trial Chamber, stressing that the two were distinct and duress could occur without superior orders.[59] Judge Cassese stressed that there is no necessary connection between the two and that superior orders may be issued without being accompanied by any threats to life or limb.[60] He raised the situation of a subordinate faced with an order from his superior. Ordinarily, he would be obliged to obey. But if the order is manifestly illegal under international law, the subordinate is under a duty to refuse to obey it. If, following such a refusal, the order is reiterated under a threat to life or limb, then the defence of duress may be raised. Superior orders would become legally irrelevant although it would come into play again as a mitigating factor if the duress is rejected. Equally, duress may be raised entirely independently of superior orders,

53. *Erdemović* Trial Chamber Judgment, *supra* n. 16, para. 18.
54. Ibid., para. 19.
55. *Idem.*
56. *Idem.*
57. *Erdemović* Appeal Decision, Joint Separate Opinion Judges McDonald and Vohrah, *supra* n. 16, para. 36.
58. *Idem.*
59. Ibid., para. 35.
60. Ibid., Separate Opinion of Judge Cassese, para. 15.

for example, where the threat issues from a person of the same or lower rank. Judge Cassese concluded that where duress is raised in conjunction with manifestly unlawful superior orders, the accused may only have a defence if he first refused to obey the unlawful order and then only carried it out after a threat to life or limb.[61]

3. ADMISSIONS OF GUILT BEFORE EAST TIMOR'S SPECIAL PANELS

3.1 The law of East Timor

Section 29A of the Transitional Rules of Criminal Procedure is taken directly from Article 65 of the ICC Statute and provides that an accused may make an admission of guilt either before or during trial.[62] In deciding whether such a plea is valid and can be accepted by the court, the Special Panel must determine that the following criteria are satisfied:

(a) The accused understands the nature and consequences of the admission of guilt;
(b) The admission is voluntarily made by the accused after sufficient consultation with defence counsel; and
(c) The admission of guilt is supported by the facts of the case that are alleged in the indictment and admitted by the accused; any materials presented by the prosecutor which support the indictment and which the accused accepts; and any other evidence, such as the testimony of witnesses, presented by the prosecutor or the accused.

If the Special Panel accepts the guilty plea and convicts the accused, it can proceed directly to conviction and sentencing.[63] If, on the other hand, the Special Panel is not satisfied that the criteria have been established, or if it decides that the interests of justice so require, 'it shall consider the admission of guilt as not having been made' and proceed to trial in the ordinary way.[64]

3.2 Issues arising from admissions of guilt made to the Special Panels

3.2.1 *Introduction*

In 2001, the first year of operation, the Special Panels took a cautious approach and accepted an admission of guilt only once, in the very first case.[65] The cases where

61. *Idem.*
62. Transitional Rules of Criminal Procedure, *supra* n. 7, s. 29A.
63. Ibid., s. 29A.2.
64. Ibid., s.29A.3 and s.29A.4.
65. *General Prosecutor* v. *Joao Fernandes*, Judgement of 25 January 2001, Special Panel for Serious Crimes, case No. 001/00.C.G.2000 (English) ('Joao Fernandes Trial Judgement').

the admissions were rejected involved partial admissions, confessions that did not entirely match the allegations of the Prosecutor, or allegations that someone 'forced' or 'ordered' the accused to commit the crime.[66] Up to May 2002, the panels had accepted another two such admissions, possibly marking the start of a more flexible approach.[67] Interestingly, faced with guilty pleas by the lead defendant at the commencement of the trial in a multiple-accused, multiple-incident crimes against humanity case, the panel only made its decision to accept that plea after concluding the trial and assessing evidence and the submissions of the parties.[68]

3.2.2 *Admissions accompanied by allegations of coercion*

Confronted with claims of coercion that seem to crisscross from duress to superior orders in almost every case, the Special Panels are rarely able to decide at the plea stage whether the allegations are of duress or superior orders. Rather than make a wrong decision, they have preferred to err on the side of caution and refused to accept the admission as a guilty plea and proceeded to determine the matter by way of a full trial. This is consistent with the guidance given by Judge Stephen in the *Erdemović* Appeals Chamber judgment. He noted that the Trial Chamber had rejected the plea of duress because of a lack of supporting evidence and proceeded to the sentencing stage.[69] He cautioned that at the plea stage, a Trial Chamber should not place the onus of proof upon an accused.[70] If the claim by the accused alerts the court to circumstances that may in the course of a trial form a sufficient basis for a defence of duress, the Trial Chamber should enter a plea of not guilty and set a date for trial. At the plea stage, matters of proof or evidence do not and cannot arise; the absence of evidence of duress is not a ground for rejecting the plea of duress and regarding the guilty plea as unambiguous.[71]

The case of *Joao Fernandes*, in which an admission was accepted by a Special Panel as a guilty plea, illustrates the confusion caused by admissions accompanied by allegations of coercion in Serious Crimes cases.[72] The first to come before the Special Panel, it is also the only case in which there has been a detailed consideration of the Section 29A procedure. Fernandes was charged with murder in violation of Article 340 of the Indonesian Penal Code for the killing of a village chief, Domingos Goncalves Perreira, during a massacre at the police station in

---

66. This occurred in cases such as *Julio Fernandes*, *Yoseph Leki*, *Manuel Lete Bere*, *Jose Valente*, *Agustinho da Costa*, *Gaspar Leite* and *Lospalos*, all of which are discussed at later stages of this paper.

67. *Public Prosecutor* v. *Marcurious de Deus*, case No. 13/2001, Decision, 18 April 2002, and *Public Prosecutor* v. *Augusto dos Santos*, case No. 6/2001, Decision, 15 May 2002.

68. *Public Prosecutor* v. *Joni Marques & Ors*, case No. 9/2000 ('*Lospalos* Case'), Decision, 11 December 2001.

69. *Erdemović* Appeal Decision, Separate Opinion of Judge Stephen, *supra* n. 16, para. 22.

70. Ibid., para. 22.

71. Ibid., para. 18.

72. *Erdemović* Appeal Decision, ibid., *Joao Fernandes* Trial Judgement, *supra* n. 65.

Maliana on 8 September 1999.[73] Like the original ICTY Trial Chamber in *Erdemović*, the Special Panel judges (Italian, Burundian and East Timorese) were faced in their first case with an admission of guilt. Fernandes admitted to killing Perreira but said that he did so on the orders of the Indonesian Army and the local militia leader. From the judgment, it is clear that the Special Panel had no doubt that he was making an admission of guilt; that what he was saying was that he committed the crime because he was ordered to do so. To the panel this was not about a defence but about mitigation. It therefore accepted that the guilty plea satisfied Section 29A and on 25 January 2001 sentenced him to 12 years imprisonment.[74]

On appeal, Fernandes both challenged his sentence and complained that the Special Panel had failed to consider the fact that he was forced to kill on the basis of superior orders as duress. In its decision of 29 June 2001, the Court of Appeal unanimously rejected the appeal as groundless.[75] There was little to discuss on the duress-superior orders issue as Regulation 2000/15 clearly provides that superior orders are not a defence, and if accepted by the court, may only serve to mitigate sentence. Duress on the other hand, if proven, is a complete defence. The Special Panel was found to have correctly regarded what the accused told them as an admission of guilt; the allegation that he was ordered to commit the crime amounted simply to a call for mitigation of sentence.

The fact that the case was appealed indicates several possibilities. The 12-year sentence could have prompted the defence to attempt to use the appeal as a chance to obtain trial *de novo* and a lighter sentence or acquittal. Also, in the course of proceedings, it seemed as if defence counsel were confused about the distinction between superior orders and duress, a distinction clearly set out in UNTAET Regulation 2000/15.[76] It is also possible that there was a genuine and serious misunderstanding between the Bench and the accused about what he was saying as a result of inadequate translations.[77] That the accused was himself confused cannot be discounted because virtually every Serious Crimes accused (and sometimes counsel too) seems to believe that (1) every instruction is a superior order and must

73. Penal Code of Indonesia, *supra* n. 5, Art. 340: '[t]he person who with deliberate intent and with premeditation takes the life of another person, shall, being guilty of murder, be punished by capital punishment, life imprisonment or a maximum imprisonment of twenty years'.

74. *Joao Fernandes* Trial Judgement, *supra* n. 65, para. 6.

75. *Joao Fernandes* v. *Prosecutor General*, Criminal Appeal No. 2 of 2001 (29 June 2001), 'Ruling of the Court of Appeal of East Timor'. The decision of the majority is hereafter referred to as '*Joao Fernandes Appeal – Majority Decision*' and the Separate Opinion of Judge Frederick Egonda-Ntende is referred to as '*Joao Fernandes Appeal – Judge Egonda-Ntende Separate Opinion*'.

76. JSMP trial observation notes, on file with Caitlin Reiger.

77. The languages used in the courts of East Timor are Tetum, Bahasa Indonesia, English and Portuguese as the official languages; other East Timorese languages are also used. The inability of the administrators of the courts to provide adequate translation has been the focus of concern for the detrimental impact on due process and fair trial: see Judicial System Monitoring Programme, *Justice in Practice: Human Rights in Court Administration*, Thematic Report No. 1, November 2001.

be obeyed; (2) whenever there is a superior order, there is duress; (3) duress and superior orders negate any criminal responsibility.[78]

One of the crucial issues that was not addressed by the Court of Appeal majority was how the Special Panel could have been so certain about what Joao Fernandes was trying to tell them when it did not investigate whether: (1) he and his counsel knew the difference between duress and superior orders; (2) he and his counsel knew the difference between a defence and a mitigating factor under the new law of East Timor or the consequences of pleading to one or the other; and (3) what was actually being sought with the claim of duress in the form of orders was not a lighter sentence but an acquittal. The quality of questions put by the Special Panel to the accused was raised in the Separate Opinion of Judge Egonda-Ntende, discussed in the following section.

In the two 2002 cases in which the Special Panel accepted guilty pleas, the accused also claimed that they were acting under orders, raising the possibility of an equivocal plea. However, both *Marcurious de Deus*[79] and *Augusto dos Santos*[80] made clear in their respective statements to the court that they were not forced to commit the crimes charged. Although the Special Panels did not question either of the men about their understanding of the different implications of this distinction, the judges did take care to confirm that the accused had discussed their admissions with defence counsel. In its judgment in the *dos Santos* case, the Special Panel noted that, as part of his admission of guilt, the accused stated that he was scared and followed the orders of his superior, the local militia commander Horacio de Araujo.[81] The Court also accepted that the accused 'lived in a very coercive environment' that put many young men under pressure 'to join criminal activities', yet it still held that the plea was unequivocal.[82]

3.2.3 *The duty of the court to accept only informed admissions of guilt*

A diligent court cannot just accept the word of an accused person at face value.[83] This is the guidance given by Judge Egonda-Ntende in *Joao Fernandes*, the sole voice on the Appeal Chamber who spoke out against the Special Panel's procedural handling of the guilty plea. The official record of the trial indicated to him that the Presiding Judge of the Special Panel had not taken sufficient care to ensure

78. In several cases, defence counsel have argued that the existence of superior orders proves that the accused could not have had the requisite intent. In *Jose Valente*, an international public defender claimed that the attempted plea of guilty could in fact only be a plea to manslaughter and not murder, with which the accused was charged. *The Public Prosecutor* v. *Jose Valente*, case No. 3/2001, Decision, 19 June 2001. In the *Lospalos* case, one of the defence counsel, in closing submissions, claimed that her client could not be found guilty as he had been ordered to participate in the crimes charged. *Supra* n. 68.

79. Supra n. 67.

80. Supra n. 67

81. Ibid, at para. 60(c).

82. Ibid., at para. 60(d).

83. *Joao Fernandes* Appeal, Judge Egonda-Ntende Separate Opinion, p. 30, *supra* n. 75.

that the accused genuinely understood the consequences of agreeing with the charges.[84] Fernandes was an illiterate farmer and the Presiding Judge had simply reiterated the words of Section 29A.1 to him. As there was nothing in his answers to indicate a problem, the court accepted the admission as a guilty plea meeting the requirements of Section 29. However, Judge Egonda-Ntende found that the judge had not ascertained if Fernandes had actually understood what he was saying and that by pleading guilty he was giving up rights such as the presumption of innocence, the right to a trial and the right to challenge witnesses. This is reminiscent of criticism by Judges McDonald and Vohrah of the ICTY Appeals Chamber of the first *Erdemović* Trial Chamber's handling of his guilty plea.

A trial court is expected to take great care to ensure the fairness of the proceedings, and to be particularly diligent when the accused are uneducated or otherwise labouring under disadvantages that put them in a weaker position than their accusers. In the *Fernandes* case, it seemed to Judge Egonda-Ntende that reasonable enquiries had not been made of the accused. The case had come to the Court of Appeal on a point that suggested lack of understanding and/or miscommunication between the accused and the Special Panel on whether he was making an admission of fact with duress being raised as a defence or an admission of guilt with superior orders being raised as a mitigating factor. Judge Egonda-Ntende read Section 29A.1 to mean that it is not enough for a court merely to repeat the words of a statute without complying with the intent of those provisions and that proactive questioning was needed to fulfil the duty.[85] He found that what was required was a set of questions that could elicit responses from the accused to show whether he understood the nature and consequences of an admission of guilt.

Judge Egonda-Ntende's imposition of a strict duty is consistent with the jurisprudence of the ICTR/ICTY Appeals Chamber, in particular the guidelines agreed to by the majority in *Erdemović*, and the overriding concern to ensure that proceedings are fair.[86] When rejecting the appeal of *Jean Kambanda*, the ICTR Appeals Chamber stressed that '[t]he duty of a Trial Chamber to inform an accused person of the possible sentence is not to be mechanically discharged. The proceedings have to be read as a whole, inclusive of the submissions of the parties'.[87] An unresolved issue is whether a trial court is required to explain in detail the elements of the crimes with which the accused is charged, and each and every consequence of

---

84. Ibid., pp. 28-31. There is often confusion about the official record. Clarification by simply examining the transcripts offers no remedy, for there continues to be no transcription facilities in the courts of East Timor. The official record is compiled by a rapporteur judge who makes notes on a laptop computer, relying on multiple levels of translation that are often of poor quality and sometimes third-hand. In his Separate Opinion, Judge Egonda-Ntende raised the problem of the inconsistent reporting contained in the court record and the judgments of the Special Panel. Similarly, whilst they do not seek rectification by way of corrigenda, both prosecution and defence privately complain that the judgments of the Special Panel contain many factual inaccuracies and mistakes.

85. *Joao Fernandes* Appeal, Judge Egonda-Ntende Separate Opinion, p. 31, *supra* n. 75.

86. *Erdemović* Appeal Decision *supra* n. 16: Joint Separate Opinion, para. 7; Separate Opinion of Judge Cassese, para. 10.

87. *Jean Kambanda* v. *The Prosecutor*, *supra* n. 15, para. 76.

making a guilty plea, or whether the trial court's obligations are satisfied if it simply makes reasonable enquiries or provides a basic explanation. This was raised by Judge Shahabuddeen, a member of the Trial Chamber to which the *Erdemović* case was remitted. He observed that both the Statute of the ICTY[88] and the Appeals Chamber left the Trial Chamber discretion as to the way that it complies with its obligations. He did not feel that a detailed parsing of the elements of the crime was required but, like Judge Egonda-Ntende of the East Timor Court of Appeal, stressed that the court has to make sufficient enquiries to ensure that the accused understands the charge. He suggested that an explanation of the elements of the charge, or of relevant elements, should only be necessary where something in the status or condition of the accused (such as his being legally unrepresented), or something in what he says when making his plea or some critically important element or other special reason alerts the trial judge to a need to give such an explanation in order to ensure that the accused understands what he is pleading to.[89]

In the *Leite* case, the Special Panel discovered the importance of adequate questioning just in time. At the preliminary hearing, the accused, an East Timorese former member of the Indonesian Army (TNI) in Aileu district, admitted that he fatally shot the victim who was hiding in bushes, and pleaded guilty to the charge of murder. The court initially accepted the plea. During further questioning at the next hearing, as part of the application of the Section 29A procedure, the accused elaborated that while he had been ordered to shoot anything that moved, he first thought he had shot only an animal in the bushes. As the presence of the requisite element of deliberate intent to commit murder was thrown into doubt, the court abandoned the procedure and the matter proceeded to trial.[90]

3.2.4 *Evidence and admissions of guilt*

In East Timor and at the ICC, an admission of guilt must be supported by the facts of the case as alleged in the indictment and admitted by the accused; any materials presented by the prosecutor which support the indictment and which the accused accepts; and any other evidence, such as the testimony of witnesses, presented by the prosecutor or the accused. East Timor's Transitional Rules of Procedure provide that the court may accept all evidence that is 'relevant and has probative value with respect to issues of dispute'.[91] In the *Joao Fernandes* case, the official record indicated to Judge Egonda-Ntende of the Appeals Chamber that the Special Panel had not distinguished between those documentary materials simply presented to it and those actually admitted as evidence, as well as between witness

---

88. Statute of the International Tribunal of the Former Yugoslavia, SC Res. 827, 48 UN SCOR (3217th mtg) (1993), 32 *ILM* p. 1203.

89. *Prosecutor* v. *Erdemović*, case No. IT-96-22-T*bis*, Sentencing Judgment, 5 March 1998; Separate Opinion of Judge Shahabuddeen, p. 3.

90. *The Public Prosecutor* v. *Gaspar Leite aka Gaspar Leki*, case No. 5/2001. On 14 September 2002, Leite was acquitted of murder but convicted of criminal negligence causing death under section 339 of the Indonesian Penal Code and sentenced to 11 months imprisonment.

91. Transitional Rules of Criminal Procedure, *supra* n. 7, s. 34.1.

statements and oral testimony.[92] Judge Egonda-Ntende's second objection to the Special Panel's acceptance of Fernandes' plea was that it was not supported by the facts. Judge Egonda-Ntende was concerned that the Special Panel failed to evaluate the material before it and to establish if in fact it was fully agreed to by the parties. There was nothing in the official record detailing the nature of the evidence against Joao Fernandes nor at what point the evidence was admitted on the record of trial:

> 'On the record of the trial court, all we have is the Presiding Judge asking, "Do you agree with the evidence and witness statements presented by the Public Prosecutor?" The record must particularise the evidence and the witness statements that are being referred to, and it is preferable that the defendant signifies his acceptance in respect of each item of evidence, or material, after its purport has been made clear to him.'[93]

In other words, an assortment of materials was simply handed over and accepted as evidence, with no effort to distinguish which of the materials or evidence were submitted in support of the indictment, and what was accepted by the accused as the factual basis underlying his plea. Judge Egonda-Ntende therefore found that these materials had been erroneously entered into the official record as evidence pursuant to Sections 33-37 of the Transitional Rules of Criminal Procedure, and that the conviction based on such materials was void.

By way of comparison, Rule 62*bis* of the ICTY's Rules of Procedure and Evidence requires that there must be a sufficient factual basis for the crime and the accused's participation in it. That can be proved either on the basis of independent indicia or on the lack of any material disagreement between the parties about the facts of the case. In *Jelisic*, the Trial Chamber confirmed that a guilty plea alone does not provide a sufficient basis for conviction of an accused for 'it is still necessary for the judges to find something in the elements of the case upon which to base their conviction both in law and in fact that the accused is indeed guilty of the crime'.[94] In this particular case, and others such as *Todorović*[95] and *Kambanda,*[96] the parties expressly agreed on the facts and the crimes alleged but the Trial Chambers still applied conventional standards for admissibility and evaluation.

Thus, agreement between the parties on the facts does not absolve the Trial Chamber of its duty to assess the admissibility of evidence and evaluate its relevance and probative value. The practice of the Special Panels does not demonstrate a clear understanding of this, although the situation appears to have improved since *Fernandes*. In *dos Santos*, the defence counsel agreed that the content of two witness statements submitted by the prosecutor supported the

---

92. *Joao Fernandes* Appeal, Judge Egonda-Ntende Separate Opinion, p. 33, *supra* n. 75.
93. Ibid., p. 32-33.
94. *Prosecutor* v. *Goran Jelisić*, *supra* n. 19 para. 25.
95. Supra n. 20.
96. Supra n. 15.

admission made by the accused.[97] However, in the court's decision and during the discussions in court, there is no other explanation of what these statements contained. Similarly, in *de Deus*, the defence counsel did not dispute the prosecutor's submission that the admission was supported by the material before the court, but the judgment does not detail what the evidence relied upon contained, merely listing the names of four witnesses who gave statements, and the numerical references of some additional documents on the court file.[98]

A diligent trial court should satisfy itself that there is consistency between the indictment, the statement(s) of the accused and independent evidence that is tendered in support. Seen together, all of this should establish a sufficient factual basis for the crime and the accused's involvement that convinces the court of guilt beyond reasonable doubt. Only this would warrant accepting the plea and entering a conviction. Commentary on the ICC Statute's Article 65(1), which is applied in East Timor, notes that the trial court hearing the guilty plea has in effect to embark on a 'trial factual basis procedure' and ensure that sufficient facts are shown to warrant a conviction if the defendant was to stand trial.[99] This would mean that, at the guilty plea stage, the evidence must convince the court of the accused's guilt beyond reasonable doubt.[100]

3.2.5 *Perceptions of impartiality and what happens when an admission is not accepted as a guilty plea*

Following the procedure for the ICC, the Transitional Rules of Criminal Procedure provide for trial on the merits following rejection of an attempted admission of guilt pursuant to the test of Section 29A1. A finding of not guilty is entered by the court. The procedure for trial, set out in Section 30, does not preclude the case being tried on its merits by the same panel that rejects the guilty plea; the wording used is 'it shall order that the trial be continued under the ordinary trial procedures provided in this Regulation'.[101] Deliberately omitted from this provision were the last nine words of Article 65(4)(b) of the ICC Statute: '... and may remit the case to another Trial Chamber'.

This has been interpreted to mean that the same panel that heard the submissions and evidence relating to the guilty plea may be the same one that tries the accused. The challenging realities of work in East Timor have sometimes meant that issues such as perceptions of impartiality and objectivity have been overlooked. Perhaps the drafters of the law had some foresight about the problems that would come to plague the Serious Crimes enterprise in East Timor, including the difficulty of

97. *The Public Prosecutor* v. *Augusto dos Santos*, *supra* n. 67, para. 51. Counsel told the court that part of the accused's motivation to plead guilty was to spare those witnesses from the need to testify.

98. *The Public Prosecutor* v. *Marcurious Jose de Deus*, *supra* n. 67, at p. 9 and notes taken during the hearing on 2 April 2002, on file with Caitlin Reiger.

99. Trifterer, op. cit. n. 44, at p. 829.

100. Contrast this with Judge Stephen, *Prosecutor* v. *Erdemović*, *supra* n. 16.

101. Transitional Rules of Criminal Procedure, *supra* n. 10, s 29A.3.

finding judges to fill the Special Panels. For most of the time since the creation of the Special Panels, there has only been one Special Panel.[102] Thus, even if there had been a desire to have a different panel for the trial, there was no alternative but to conduct the trial before the same judges. If a guilty plea is rejected for failing the test of Section 29(A)1, the pretence of holding a 'normal trial' based on a plea of not guilty requires that the earlier admissions cannot be used against the accused during the ensuing trial. This is because the court is to treat the admission as if it was never made: it is null and void, and no adverse implications to the accused can be drawn from it.[103] It would thus be preferable if a completely new Trial Chamber were to hear the matter, for the risk of bias is undoubtedly greater when a case goes to the same panel that heard and rejected the guilty plea. Fair trial standards require that the panel must be impartial, which is a difficult task when one has heard an accused say that he committed the crime with which he is charged.

Subsequent reliance at trial on statements made before the Special Panel during an unsuccessful attempt to plead guilty has regularly occurred in Serious Crimes cases, for example in *da Costa* and *Tavares*.[104] In the former case, one of the judges had been replaced between the preliminary hearing and the trial; in the latter, the panel was entirely the same. The issue of use of material concerning the rejected guilty plea has not been litigated, and the judgments do not address the matter at all, suggesting that it is not considered an issue.

Such materials were also used in the judgement of the panel in *Valente*,[105] but the circumstances indicate that this was not improper. The same Special Panel that rejected the purported confession tried the accused and eventually convicted him. In the course of the trial, the accused made no oral statement but his defence counsel submitted a written list of factual admissions and also quoted from the defendant's admissions at the preliminary hearing. In its written decision, the Special Panel relied extensively on the defendant's earlier statement to the court as part of the evidence that supported its conclusion.[106]

The rules are aimed at protecting accused persons, and there is no doubt that renewed admissions of guilt will be detrimental to an accused, as he himself erodes the presumption of innocence. Yet, it would be unduly restrictive to read them as preventing an accused from voluntarily reiterating his statements or reusing evidence submitted from the earlier proceeding, provided that the decision is an informed one, preferably made with the advice of defence counsel. Regardless of whether or not the panel is the same one that heard the plea, the general prohibition against using materials from the earlier proceeding should not prevent submissions

---

102. See Justice in Practice: Human Rights in Court Administration, Judicial System Monitoring Programme, Thematic Report No 1, November 2001, Dili, ('Justice in Practice: Human Rights in Court Administration') p. 14.

103. Trifterer, op. cit. n. 44, at p. 830.

104. *Public Prosecutor* v. *Agustinho da Costa*, case No. 07/2000, Judgment, 11 October 2001; *Public Prosecutor* v. *Augusto Asameta Tavares*, case No. 2/2001, Decision, 28 October 2001.

105. *The Public Prosecutor* v. *Jose Valente*, *supra* n. 78.

106. Ibid. For example, at page 5 the panel stated that 'The statements of the Defendant must be considered with the facts and with the statements of the witnesses before the court.'

and evidence by an accused in the course of trial from being treated as 'fresh' submissions. Thus, if as in *Valente*, the accused acting through his defence counsel wishes to resubmit evidence or pleadings in the course of the new proceedings, that would seem to be consistent with his fundamental right to conduct his defence in the way that he sees fit. It would then be perfectly in order for the trial court to rely on such material in reaching its decision, as was done in *Valente*.

3.3 Assessing the handling of the guilty plea by the Special Panel

The cogent opinion of Judge Frederick Egonda-Ntende of the Court of Appeal in *Joao Fernandes* clearly points to significant weakness in the Special Panel's practice on admissions of guilt. Responsibility for the lack of infrastructural support, for example, transcribing facilities and adequate multilingual translation, rests with the administrators of the judicial system, initially UNTAET's Department of Justice, which became part of the East Timor Transitional Administration in the year before full independence. Some of the problems in East Timor may also be due to the fact that none of the judges of the Special Panels have expertise in or experience of working in the field of international criminal law, and as international observers have pointed out, they have not been provided with training or adequate resources in order to develop their capacity in this area.[107] These deficiencies may also explain the unsatisfactory way that duress and superior orders have been handled, as will be seen in the following sections.

The problems may also be read as indicating that the ICC's provision on admissions of guilt does not provide judges of internationalised domestic tribunals with adequate guidance, and needs to be supplemented if its procedural streamlining purpose is to be achieved. It may well be that international judges of the ICC would not need to be given detailed rules on how to conduct such hearings, but East Timor's Special Panels have clearly had difficulty in grasping the rationale behind certain legal norms, for example, the reasoning behind rules that require investigations to be made of an accused to ascertain that a guilty plea meets the standards set down in law. It would seem that such courts would benefit from clear legislative guidance to ensure that standards of evidence and burdens of proof do not fall by the wayside simply because there is a guilty plea. Even if there is a guilty plea, the court needs to ensure that accused can only be convicted if the evidence of that guilt is convincing in accordance with the basic criminal standard, whether it is to satisfy the 'intimate conviction' in civil law or beyond reasonable doubt in common law.

A key element missing in all Special Panel and most related Court of Appeal decisions to date has been analysis and reliance on international standards. Given that under the basic law of East Timor (Regulation 1999/1, the very first law adopted by UNTAET) all laws and decisions must be consistent with the key

---

107. See *Justice in Practice: Human Rights in Court Administration*, pp. 10-12, *supra* n. 77. See also *East Timor: Justice past, present and future,* Amnesty International, AI Index ASA 57/001/2001, 27/7/01.

human rights treaties (ICCPR, ICESCR, etc), it is surprising that decisions in these United Nations' courts are rarely made with reference to those international norms or international jurisprudence. It is perhaps excusable that this does not occur in the many Serious Crimes cases which are processed as domestic crimes under the Indonesian Penal Code, but even in the single crimes against humanity case to be heard at the time of writing (*Lospalos*), the submissions of the parties on international criminal law were simply reprinted in the judgement without any analysis or application by the Special Panel. And, as the foregoing examination reveals, many of the problems of the Special Panel's handling of the *Fernandes* case are similar to those that arose in *Erdemović*, yet no lessons appear to have been learnt from the latter case.

Although in a minority, the standards of due diligence demanded by Judge Egonda-Ntende of a court faced with a guilty plea are in line with international practice and should be utilised in order to improve the quality of justice in East Timor. In the particular context of the East Timorese cases, it is suggested that where (1) the accused is uneducated or illiterate, or suffering from any kind of intellectual or mental disadvantage; (2) defence counsel appear not to understand the issues (as occurred in *Erdemović* and certain Serious Crimes cases[108]); and (3) the accused raises coercion in the form of both superior orders and duress, this should alert the panel to the necessity of giving an explanation in order to ensure that the accused understands what he is pleading to. If any doubts remain, or if it is clear that a possible defence is at issue, the panel must proceed to a full trial. As discussed in section 3.2.2 above, the recent cases of *de Deus* and *dos Santos* indicate some improvement in the quality of the more recent practice, although this seems largely due to the Special Panel's reliance on the presence of international defence counsel as a safeguard. The post-*Fernandes* practice suggests that that the Special Panels now shy away from taking decisions at the pre-trial stage and prefer to proceed to trial whenever the issue of coercion is raised. It could be that Judge Egonda-Ntende's criticisms in that case have caused a crisis of confidence in the panel when faced with allegations of coercion at the plea stage. Yet, every accused who has gone to trial following a rejected admission of guilt has in fact been convicted, suggesting that the approach of the Special Panels is in fact over-cautious and that the duress-superior orders confusion could perhaps be sorted out at the plea stage by improving the quality of questioning of the accused. A panel could follow the guidance of Judge Egonda-Ntende and international jurisprudence such as *Erdemović, Jelisić* and *Kambanda* and explain the provisions of Regulation 2000/15 on duress and superior orders to an accused (and to counsel if need be) and then carefully question the accused to establish exactly what it is that he is saying. This would save the time, expense and trauma of going to trial, matters which are not lightly to be dismissed in East Timor.

---

108. For example, in the *Soares* case, defence counsel argued that superior orders were a defence. *Public Prosecutor* v. *Carlos Soares*, *supra* n. 67.

4. DURESS

4.1 The law of duress in East Timor

Under the Indonesian law applicable at the time of commission of the offences falling within the jurisdiction of the Special Panels, duress was not expressly recognised as a defence although *force majeure* (undefined) was.[109] Section 19(d) of UNTAET Regulation No. 2000/15, following Article 31(1)(d) of the ICC Statute, permits duress as a defence in certain circumstances. There must have been:

1. a threat of imminent death or of continuing or imminent serious bodily harm;
2. the accused must have acted necessarily and reasonably to avoid the threat; and
3. the accused must not have intended to cause a greater harm than the one sought to be avoided.

4.2 Issues arising from the use of the ICC Statute's provision on duress in East Timor

4.2.1 *How is the test of duress being applied?*

The test formulated at Rome is being strictly applied in East Timor. Duress is correctly being treated by the Special Panels as an extreme situation. No one has been acquitted on the grounds of duress, possibly because of the striking fact that corroborating evidence of duress has never been submitted by defence counsel. The general practice can be illustrated through the following cases.

In *Julio Fernandes*,[110] the accused, a member of the resistance forces (FALINTIL) was charged with murder in violation of Article 340 of the Indonesian Penal Code. He admitted to killing a captured militiaman but claimed that he had been forced to do so by an angry crowd: an equivocal plea. The Special Panel declined to accept this as a guilty plea under Section 29A1 of the Transitional Rules of Procedure and referred the case for trial. During the trial, Fernandes claimed he had stabbed his victim twice during a tense situation with an hysterical crowd shouting, 'kill him, kill him'. The extremity of the situation was confirmed by prosecution witnesses who had been present. According to defence counsel, (1) the victim would probably have been killed anyway; (2) there was duress resulting from the threat of imminent death coming from the crowd; and (3) the victim had already been seriously maltreated and there was no evidence that the wounds inflicted by Julio Fernandes caused his death.

On 27 February 2001, Fernandes was convicted and sentenced to seven years imprisonment for deliberate and premeditated murder.[111] The Special Panel found

---

109. Art. 48, Indonesian Penal Code, *supra* n. 5.

110. *Prosecutor* v. *Julio Fernandes*, case No. 2/2000, Trial Decision, 1 March 2002, p. 11.

111. Ibid. The East Timorese judge dissented, finding the accused guilty of unpremeditated murder only.

that Fernandes had approached the victim, questioned him and, having listened to his answers, decided to kill him and only then stabbed him twice: 'It was not an instinctive reaction to a very peculiar situation, but a decision reached by reasoning.'[112] In rejecting the allegation of duress, the Special Panel found that the crowd was not threatening Fernandes, but calling on him, as a representative of the FALINTIL, to punish the captured militiaman in an 'official way'. It rejected the allegation that the crowd would have threatened his life had he refused to kill him in light of the fact that another person had refused to kill him and had walked away unscathed.[113] The argument that the victim would have died anyway (the 'wasted sacrifice', an issue discussed at length by the Appeals Chamber judges in *Erdemović)*, was not considered at all. This rejection of duress was later confirmed on appeal.[114]

In *Bere*,[115] the accused argued coercion, interchangeably claiming superior orders and duress. He was charged with murder in violation of Article 340 of the Indonesian Penal Code for the killing of Joao Goncalves on an undetermined day at the end of September 1999. Bere was by his own admission a member of the Daderus Merah Putih milita and he admitted stabbing the victim with a sword, but claimed to have been acting under pressure and following an order. At the preliminary hearing, his guilty plea was rejected and the case proceeded to trial.

Bere gave a number of contradictory statements about the circumstances that led to the killing. It seems that he, his old friend Raimundo Bere Mau and two others (who both testified in court) were part of a group that drove from West Timor to East Timor that night, having been told to do so by TNI (Indonesian army) members. He said he went along because he was afraid of the TNI. The accused was contradictory about the purpose of the trip, interchangeably claiming both that the mission was tasked with collecting the body of Joao Goncalves and disposing of his body in East Timor and killing him and disposing of the body in East Timor. Bere spoke repeatedly of 'orders' and duress, for example:

> 'I was invited to pick up a dead body and bring it to East Timor, but it was still alive and therefore I was ordered to kill. I had big argument with Raimundo. If I'd refused he would have shot me.'[116]

---

112. Ibid., at p. 8.

113. It should be noted that on appeal, Judge Egonda-Ntende noted that the Special Panel had made findings that were not based on the evidence before them, in particular that there was no evidence that this other person had been asked to kill the victim, and that other person had in fact stated that the shouts of the crowd were not directed at him. *Julio Fernandes* v. *Prosecutor General,* Criminal Appeal No. 7 of 2001, Ruling of the Court of Appeal, 29 June 2001, with Separate Opinion of Judge Frederick Egonda-Ntende, Nos. 13 and 14.

114. See the discussion at para. 20 of the Separate Opinion of Judge Egonda-Ntende, ibid. The majority ultimately found that the question of duress was not fundamental to the basis of the appeal: para. 12 of majority decision.

115. *The Prosecutor* v. *Manuel Goncalves Leto Bere*, alias Manuel Leto Bere, case No. 10/2000, Decision, 15 May 2001.

116. Note that during the trials interpreters regularly translate the Bahasa Indonesia word 'jemput' as 'invite', which in English creates the impression that the accused had a choice. This is not

There were numerous other inconsistencies in the accused's testimony, such as whether the victim was alive or dead when they reached him and put him in the vehicle. The two witnesses who were present did not hear any argument between Raimundo and the accused, and also stated categorically that when they got to the victim he was still alive. He was even able to walk and sit in the car despite having been seriously wounded.

The Special Panel rejected the allegation of duress due to the conflicting statements and the lack of any corroborating evidence. It was also persuaded that the accused would hardly fear his long-time friends (the two TNI officers Raimundo and Rui), with whom he had worked together on many occasions. The Special Panel did not consider if, in principle, Bere, as a member of the Daderus Merah Putih militia, was eligible to claim duress. It did, however, find that he had killed under superior orders, warranting mitigation of sentence. He was sentenced to 14 years.

In the *Lospalos* crimes against humanity case, none of the claims of duress brought by the multiple accused were accepted. One of the accused, Manuel da Costa, had claimed that another accused, Joni Marques, had threatened him and forced him to participate in the ambush and murder of a group of clergy. The panel was not satisfied that da Costa acted under duress when he joined the operation to kill the clergy and actually took part in the killings:

> 'It is unreasonable that Manuel da Costa, a militiaman who had joined the group more than ten years earlier and holding a high position, did not know the purpose and could feel threatened that he was going to be killed by one of his colleagues. The alleged duress is based on a hypothetical threat to have his legs crushed or even to be killed, but no one in the group had been killed for refusing to follow an order from the commander until that time. Manuel alleges having joined Team Alfa because he was threatened and tortured. As already decided by the Panel in the case of *The Prosecutor v. Josef Leki*, the alleged duress has to be current; not the alleged duress to join a group. There is a difference between being forced to join a group and to be engaged in a particular operation of a group. The words of Manuel to Joni Marques at the time when the grenade was thrown into the water sound like a comment only about the accomplishment of the operation, rather than a refusal to obey an order from Joni Marques ('Why throw the grenade if they are all dead?').'[117]

4.2.2 *Voluntary participation in a criminal undertaking*

In *Erdemović*, Judge Cassese found that the first thing that must be done is to determine whether the situation leading to duress was voluntarily brought about by the accused.[118] In particular, the trial court is first required to examine whether the group of which the accused was a member and with whom he had voluntarily

---

necessarily so, for in Bahasa Indonesia, 'jemput' can include picking someone up or fetching a person and the expectation is that the person is compliant.

117. *Lospalos* Decision, *supra* n. 68, paras. 935-936.

118. *Erdemović* Appeal Decision, Separate Opinion of Judge Cassese, *supra* n. 16, para. 50.

enlisted was purposefully intent upon actions contrary to international humanitarian law and the appellant either knew or should have known of this when he joined it, or, if he only later became aware of it, that he then failed to leave the group or otherwise disengage himself from such actions. If the answer is in the affirmative, he cannot plead duress. Equally, he could not raise this defence if he in any other way voluntarily placed himself in a situation which he knew would entail the unlawful execution of civilians.

In only one East Timorese case, that of *Yoseph Leki*, has it been found that there was a threat of imminent death or bodily injury to the appellant. Yet duress was denied to the accused because the panel felt he had voluntarily associated with the criminal activities of the group. The practice of the Special Panels is to reject claims of duress on the basis that there were other choices available to the accused and that he deliberately chose the criminal option. This is particularly clear in the situations where accused persons claim that they were forced to join militias. In these cases, there is surprisingly little informed assessment of the feasibility of those options to someone in the accused's position.

During the trial of *Jose Valente*, the defence submitted that the accused had no choice but to cooperate with the local militia as his parents were members of the armed resistance, FALINTIL.[119] The accused testified that he had been detained and tortured by the Indonesian special forces, KOPASSUS. He was only released after agreeing to obtain information on FALINTIL, and was forced to join the militia in the mid-1980s. Valente told the court that 'those who controlled us forced us'. The panel found that there was no evidence of duress, perhaps because the defence case consisted only of the accused's evidence. Unanswered are the questions of whether, such evidence being present, the subjective circumstances outlined by Valente could convince a court that he joined the militias under duress, and whether that duress could have continued for a considerable period of time, even amounting to years.

There are many reliable reports about the criminality of the East Timorese militia groups, including those of the International Commission of Inquiry, the Special Rapporteurs and Indonesia's KPP-HAM.[120] But in no case has a Special Panel entered into any substantive analysis of the militias by way of evidence submitted in the course of proceedings or summoned *proprio motu* by the court. The sorts of questions that one would expect the Special Panel to have asked by now include the following: What was the relationship between the militias and the Indonesian authorities? Were they legal or illegal organisations? How were they

119. *Public Prosecutor* v. *Jose Valente*, *supra* n. 78.

120. Report on the Investigation of Human Rights Violations in East Timor (2000), KPP-HAM (Investigation Commission of the Indonesian Commission on Human Rights), ('KPP-HAM Report') para. 51; Report of the International Commission of Inquiry on East Timor to the Secretary-General, UN Doc A/54/726, S/2000/59 (2000) ('Report of the International Commission of Inquiry'); Report of the Joint Mission to East Timor by the Special Rapporteur of the Commission for Human Rights on Extrajudicial, summary or arbitrary executions, the Special Rapporteur on torture, and the Special Rapporteur on Violence Against Women, UN Doc. A/54/660, 10 December 1999 ('Report of the Special Rapporteurs').

funded, equipped and trained? Who did they take their orders from? How were they structured? Were they controlled centrally? What was the purpose of the militias – were their activities directed at achieving a lawful or illegal purpose? Was the commission of serious offences, whether or not international crimes, a routine part of their activities? Was their sole or dominant intent and purpose that of violently and brutally bringing about a certain course of events? Did they achieve those means through criminal methods?

Without having asked such questions, the Special Panels have proceeded on the basis that the militias were a criminal organisation pursuing criminal activities. In light of this, one is led to suspect that the judges draw on personal opinions and extraneous sources. This sort of practice led to the situation in *Leki*, where the Special Panel made findings of fact about Indonesia's role in the East Timor carnage without any evidence being submitted by the parties, without the issues being litigated, by relying on a test of 'what even the humblest and most candid man in the world can assess' and by drawing on extraneous sources of information.[121] Another contributing factor may be the already mentioned poor quality of translation in the Serious Crimes cases.[122] Although less than half of the accused who have come before the Special Panels to date have explicitly stated (in English translation) that they were forced or threatened into joining the militias, the rest refer (in English translation) to 'being selected' or 'invited' to join local militias. While this is often considered by the court to be voluntary participation, this is not always an accurate conclusion. An 'invitation' to join the militia from an armed and feared militia leader who controls the area where the invitee and his family live is not likely leave him with a choice. One of the ten accused in the *Lospalos* case, Gilberto Fernandes, testified to having been employed as a cook at the KOPASSUS (Special Forces) base.[123] He said that one of the officers noticed he had a 'good attitude' and from then on he was considered part of the militia. During questioning, he denied 'joining' the militia, inferring that he was essentially 'appointed' and that this was not his choice.

In the circumstances of East Timor, it is dangerous to assume that because a person was a militiaman he was voluntarily associated with it and willingly went along with criminal activities. In June 1999, Amnesty International reported that:

> 'There are many credible reports of people being coerced into joining militia groups. Recruitment operations have targeted whole villages. In one case, 12 people in Atara village in Ermera District were killed on 16 May 1999, apparently because the village had refused to join the militia group Tim Pancasila. A number of other people described to Amnesty International how they had been threatened, beaten or detained because they had refused to join militia groups.'[124]

121. Case No. 5/2000, *The Prosecutor* v. *Yoseph Leki*, Judgement, 11 June 2001, p. 7.

122. *Supra* n. 77.

123. KOPASSUS are the special forces of the Indonesian Army. They are believed to have established, trained, equipped and directed the militias.

124. Amnesty International, East Timor: Seize the Moment, AI Index: 21/49/99, 21 June 1999.

The frequency of accused raising this issue in Serious Crimes cases suggests that there was indeed massive forced recruitment of civilians into the militias in East Timor, that is, involuntary participation.

The Special Panels have taken a rigid position.[125] This is illustrated by the case of *Yoseph Leki*, who was found to have voluntarily joined the Laksaur militia. He said that he could not flee the village for the hills as he had several young children and elderly relations, and did not consider fleeing with his family to the site of a notorious church massacre as a viable option. By way of comparison, child soldiers forcibly recruited into the armed forces cannot be said to have voluntarily exposed themselves to the danger. Certainly the age of the person will have a role but that in itself requires a subjective look at the facts of the case, rather than a blanket ruling to the effect that those who did not have the courage to stand up to the militias and flee to the hills did in fact exercise a decision to 'be with the guns',[126] to use the words of the Special Panel, and therefore cannot have recourse to the defence of duress.

The exact circumstances of how Leki joined the militia (two notorious Laksaur leaders, Olivio Moruk and Igidio Manek, were allegedly involved) were not examined in detail by the panel and the coercion at that particular point was not explored. Yet, the Special Panel refused to accept that he had no choice. It argued that while no one was expected to be a hero, others had been able to refuse to join the militia and had fled rather than resort to criminal activity. It may well be that the court simply did not believe him, for it found inconsistencies in Leki's testimony about his exact role leading up to 25 September 1999 and that he had carried arms since he joined the militia in June 1999 and was present with arms during the 25 September 1999 attack.

Having rejected the argument that Leki was forced to join the militia, the Special Panel then found he had been coerced into killing the victim. Prosecution witnesses (there were no defence witnesses) corroborated his claim that on 26 September 1999, he killed Paulino Cardoso under duress. One witness confirmed that Norberto Ximenes 'jumped and aimed his rifle at Yoseph Leki and said, 'Shoot him or I'll shoot you'. Another eyewitness told the Special Panel that Norberto had shot the victim, who was still alive, and then 'faced Leki ... Joseph [sic] Leki was the last to arrive. Then Norberto pointed the gun to Joseph [sic] Leki and spoke to him: 'If you don't shoot, I will kill you'.[127]

The Special Panel acknowledged that this amounted to duress, but denied the defence to Leki, holding that duress is not an available defence to a perpetrator who deliberately joined the common purpose of the group with knowledge of the intention to commit the crime.[128] The Special Panel found that Leki had the option,

---

125. In Mateus Tilman, the court held that he could have left the militia at any time during the months preceding the events charged, despite his claims that he had been forced to join. *The Prosecutor* v. *Mateus Tilman*, case No. 8/2000, Judgement, 14 June 2001. Also, in *Jose Valente*, the court held that he did not have to go with the militia group when they attacked independence supporters. *Supra* n. 78. Other examples include *Agustino da Costa, supra* n. 104, and *Augusto Asameta Tavares, supra* n. 104.

126. *Prosecutor* v. *Yoseph Leki, supra* n. 21, p. 8.

127. Ibid., p. 7.

128. Ibid., p. 9.

up to the very last moment when the duress occurred, to avoid the situation by simply refusing to contribute to the attacks. There is no record that the Special Panel asked the fundamental question of why Norberto had to point a gun at Leki to make him kill the victim. If Leki really was 'with the guns', as claimed by the Special Panel, why did this person have to coerce him? Did he in fact refuse to kill, which would have been consistent with his claim that he was not a willing member of the group? If he had been voluntarily involved, as claimed by the panel, could Leki not have changed his mind about his involvement in criminal activity? Criminal law in most countries recognises that a person may escape liability if he is able to withdraw effectively from the criminal venture, but active and meaningful steps are needed for this. For example, an erstwhile accomplice may withdraw from the enterprise by trying to prevent the commission of the offence by the perpetrator, by informing the police. Something obviously transpired between Norberto and Leki which led Norberto to point his gun at Leki, but the Special Panel failed to address this crucial issue. It is also pertinent to recall the example given by Judge Cassese in the *Erdemović* case.[129] He suggested that a subordinate faced with a manifestly unlawful order is under a duty to refuse to obey the order but if his refusal is met with a reiterated order to perform the task under a threat to life or limb, then the defence of duress may be raised. Yet the Special Panel's judgment in *Leki* does not tell us who Norberto was and whether he had any authority to give orders to the accused and whether those orders had to be obeyed. Perhaps the most troubling aspect of the *Leki* decision is the fact that it has been regularly cited as the leading authority on duress in subsequent cases before the Special Panels, including the *Los Palos* case.

4.3 Assessing the handling of duress by the Special Panels

Issues of proof are obviously crucial and yet posterity must record the extraordinary fact that in no Serious Crimes case so far has any witness (apart from the accused) been called by the defence, even in cases where the accused has not made a confession.[130] The lack of appreciation of the actual demands of fair trial and due process norms extends to the court's application of the Transitional Rules of

---

129. Separate Opinion of Judge Cassese, *supra* n. 16, para.15.

130. This issue is clearly linked to the considerable resource disparity between the small East Timorese public defenders' office and the larger, internationally-run Serious Crimes prosecution and investigation unit. Necessary facilities such as transport to remote districts, telephones and money for witness expenses have not been made available to the public defenders. Surprisingly, this has not concerned the Special Panel, which has never in the course of proceedings inquired about the conditions under which the defence operate and whether there is a level playing field enabling them to develop their case on the same terms as the prosecution, let alone taking steps to assist in the creation of suitable conditions for the exercise of the right of defence. It is also suggested that in the particular circumstances of East Timor, where poorly trained local defence counsel have struggled to defend their clients with minimal resources, the interests of justice would require the Special Panel to ensure that at all stages of the proceedings the defence is being given equal opportunity to find evidence and develop its case as that enjoyed by the Prosecution. See Judicial System Monitoring Programme, *The Prosecutor* v. *Joni Marques and 9 others* (The *Lospalos* case), A JSMP Trial Report, February 2002, p. 23.

Criminal Procedure. In the *Leki* case, the Special Panel effectively blocked the appearance of four defence witnesses in a case where the defence was of duress. At the end of the preliminary hearing, defence counsel advised the court that he was trying to contact witnesses in West Timor. However, the Court did not consider this to be a formal application to present evidence and the case was listed for trial. Then, at the commencement of the trial, the defence counsel presented a list of four witnesses who were prepared to testify in favour of the accused. However, the Special Panel dismissed this application to present evidence on the basis that it was 'ill-timed', as Section 29 of the Transitional Rules of Criminal Procedure requires that such matters are resolved at the preliminary hearing, when the court shall determine what evidence the defence intends to present to the court, as well as granting additional time to present additional evidence. The Transitional Rules of Criminal Procedure also state that during the trial the court has the power to call any additional witnesses it wishes to hear after the parties have completed their submissions. Thus, legally, the panel could have called those four witnesses.[131] East Timor's transitional legal system is a hybrid one, based on the Indonesian-Dutch civil law model as amended by UNTAET. This envisages a pro-active judiciary that seeks to establish the truth rather than arbitrate an adversarial process between prosecution and defence. Given this, the passivity of the Special Panel in 'getting to the bottom of things' is surprising.

A disturbing feature that arises from this study is that the Special Panels seem to have divided the East Timorese into two groups: 'good' people who fled to the hills and 'bad' people who chose to stay in their villages. The latter are regarded as not being worthy of the defence of duress, without serious consideration of the choices that individuals had to make and their subjective circumstances in an extreme situation. There is surprisingly little effort to establish what an accused means when he claims to have been forced to commit a crime, or the circumstances in which the accused say they joined the militia and whether it can be said to have been under duress or not. One rare incidence of judicial activity on this front occurred in the *Leki* case, when the sole East Timorese judge began vigorously pursuing a line of questioning to the accused about the links between the militia and the TNI, only to be stopped by the presiding judge (Burundian). No reason was publicly given for the halting of that questioning.

For the Special Panels to do justice in Serious Crimes cases, they must base their decisions upon a thorough examination of the realities of East Timor. That would mean assessing issues such as the power structures, the players and the political dynamics that operated in East Timor and eventually led to the violence of September 1999. The situation in East Timor during 1999 cannot be meaningfully divorced from the history of the Indonesian occupation since 1975, which was characterised by widespread violence, terror, intimidation and regular harassment by the Indonesian armed forces, particularly of those identified as having family members working with the resistance movement or who were suspected of such

131. Section 33.2, Transitional Rules of Criminal Procedure, *supra* n. 7.

involvement themselves. Such people were often specifically targeted to prove their allegiance through involvement in, for example, militia activity. Many East Timorese have reported the complexity of public versus private allegiances throughout the 24 year occupation, such as working with the Indonesians to deflect attention from their clandestine resistance activities or to take the pressure off their families, who in turn may have been targeted. This raises questions of the linkage between repression in a time of occupation and coercion. The pragmatic and shifting choices that people made to avoid suspicion and to keep out of trouble are not only complex but extremely difficult to assess for the purpose of legal categorisation.

During 1999, the pattern of capture, abduction, torture, murder and forced recruitment into militias intensified with the emergence of the second option given to the people of East Timor: independence should they reject autonomy within Indonesia.[132] This context was described by one of the East Timorese public defenders during the closing submissions of the *Lospalos* trial. She outlined the nature of the environment that the accused, Hilario da Silva, faced *vis-à-vis* powerful militia figures and the TNI in his village. The militia had been given the authority by the Indonesian military to terrorise the ordinary population and was protected by them. The reality was that ordinary people had no choice; to stay alive, one did as one was told. In response to the suggestion that the accused could have reported threats to the police, counsel stated that:

> 'The people who should have received such reports were not just involved but were main actors! ... At that time Team Alfa was very very powerful. They can kill anybody, they can do anything and commit any crime. They manipulated and used ordinary people and intimidated them to follow the wish of the Indonesian armed forces ... Ordinary people were scared and did such things.'[133]

The Special Panel rejected the argument on the basis that there was no evidence that da Silva had been forced to participate but only ordered to do so. Here too, as in all other Serious Crimes cases, the Special Panel did not investigate if the defence was being provided with the means to find evidence of what was being alleged.

Duress to join a group engaged in criminal activities and duress to commit a crime when part of that group each requires its own evidence. The two may in certain situations be linked and the Special Panels need to be more flexible and carry out a balanced assessment that examines both issues thoroughly. There certainly does come a point where a judicial assessment has to be made about whether the extent of a person's involvement with the militias has become more about voluntary participation rather than participation under duress. This is not a call for the Special Panels to excuse anyone who raises the cry of duress because

---

132. See KPP-Ham Report, para. 124, *supra* n. 120. Also, see Amnesty International, Paramilitary attacks jeopardise East Timor's future, ASA 21/026/1999 of 16 April 1999; Amnesty International, East Timor: Seize the Moment, AI, *supra* n. 124.

133. Independent Observer notes, on file with Caitlin Reiger.

they were forced to join the militias, but for a more diligent assessment of the realities of the environment at the time or times of the alleged duress.

5. SUPERIOR ORDERS

5.1 The law in East Timor

Under Section 21 of Regulation 2000/15, the fact that someone accused of Serious Crimes acted pursuant to an order of a Government or a superior shall not relieve him of criminal responsibility, but may be considered in mitigation of punishment if the panel determines that justice so requires.[134] Here the drafters chose to reject the ICC Statute's provisions and revert to the IMT/ICTY/ICTR position. By doing so, they placed upon the Special Panels an obligation to examine customary international law to determine the content of the law on superior orders, in particular, the test for identifying superior orders described earlier.

Section 21 introduced a new concept to East Timor, replacing Article 51 of the Indonesian Penal Code, which recognised superior orders as a defence in certain circumstances.[135] Article 51 provides that:

(1) Not punishable shall be the person who commits an act for the execution of an official order issued by the competent authority.

(2) An official order issued incompetently shall not exempt the punishment unless it was considered in good faith by the subordinate to be issued competently and its execution lied [sic] within the limit of his subordination.

It should be noted that Article 51 can be raised by accused on trial at Indonesia's Ad Hoc Court for Human Rights, which is currently processing cases arising from the East Timor violence, and in East Timor itself for cases pursued as 'Ordinary Crimes'. This may explain why so many East Timorese accused and their defence counsel seem to be confused about superior orders and duress under Regulation 2000/15, and continue to believe that because an act was committed pursuant to someone's order, the perpetrator is neither morally nor criminally responsible for his actions.

5.2 Retroactivity and the removal of a legitimate defence

The fundamental principle of *nullum crimen nulla poena sine lege* requires that no one be tried or punished for acts that were not criminal at the time they were

134. Regulation 2000/15, *supra* n. 4, s. 21.

135. *Supra* n. 5. Indonesian law is derived from Dutch law and Art. 51 is not unusual. For example, it is similar to Arts. 122-124 of the 1994 French Penal Code, which provides that: '[1] A person is not criminally responsible if that person performs an act prescribed or authorised by legislative or regulatory powers. [2] A person is not criminally responsible if that person performs an act ordered by a legitimate authority, except if that act is manifestly unlawful.'

committed.[136] Given that superior orders were a defence at the time that the offences were committed and continue to be applicable in Ordinary Crimes cases in East Timor, there appears to be a legality problem with Section 21's prohibition of its use as a defence by Serious Crimes accused. This is a very important issue for the majority of East Timor's Serious Crimes defendants who have been tried to date, charged with violating the Indonesian Penal Code and not with international crimes.

Retroactive laws were also a problem with the post-World War II German and Japanese cases. The controversy over the legality of the subject matter jurisdiction of the IMTs is well recorded.[137] Less attention has been focused on the legality aspect of the doctrine of obedience to superior orders. This provided a defence under domestic law in Germany and Japan at the time the crimes were committed. The courts have tended to avoid the issue of legality by relying on the rationale that whatever local laws said, soldiers are not automatons and are only bound to obey lawful and are obliged to disobey manifestly unlawful orders[138] or 'the rule that superior orders is not a defence to a criminal act is a rule of fundamental criminal justice that has been adopted by civilized nations extensively'.[139]

As the *Dover Castle* case before the Leipzig court revealed, German military doctrine was that the subordinate was bound to obey the orders of his superiors, but when that order involved a criminal act, it was the superior alone who was responsible unless the subordinate was found to have been an accomplice.[140] German National Socialist law embraced the concept of the *Führerprinzip*, under which the leader's orders were to be obeyed, and it was the leader who would be responsible for the consequences of that order. Until 1944, Allied military codes, such as that of the United States and the United Kingdom, reflected the classic position as stated in Oppenheim's International Law, which recognised a limited defence of superior orders.[141] The position was revised during the Second World War to the effect that 'members of the armed forces are bound to obey lawful orders only and that they cannot therefore escape liability if, in obedience to a command, they commit acts

136. See Universal Declaration of Human Rights, Art. 11(2); International Covenant on Civil and Political Rights, Art. 15.

137. From the start, defence counsel strenuously objected to prosecutions not specifically criminalized by international treaties or custom, let alone domestic law, but on the basis of a law passed after the acts had been committed.

138. *Einsatzgruppen, supra* n. 24, p. 472.

139. In *Re List and others (Hostages Trial)*, United States Military Tribunal at Nuremburg, Feb. 19 1949, War Crimes Reports, 8, (1949) reported in *Annual Digest and Reports of Public International Law Cases, 1948*, ed. H. Lauterpacht, p. 34.

140. *Dover Castle*, 16 *AJIL* (1922) p. 704. According to L.C. Green, under section 47(2) of the German Military Penal Code 1882, while the subordinate was bound to obey the orders of his superior, he would be punished as an accomplice to a criminal act if he knew that the order concerned an act criminal by either civil or military law and this was still German law at the end of the Second World War. 'Superior Orders and the Reasonable Man', in Green, op. cit. n. 40, at p. 260.

141. See *U.S. Dep't of the Army Rules of Land Warfare*, at 347 (Field Manual 27-10). Oppenheim's *International Law*, Vol. 2 (1906) took the position that members of the armed forces who commit violations ordered by their commander the member cannot be punished, for the commander is the one responsible: see Green, op. cit. n. 40, at p. 262.

which both violate unchallenged rules of warfare and outrage the general sentiment of humanity'.[142] The United States' Field Manual was amended shortly after to the effect that all those who violate the accepted laws and customs of war may be punished, and that superior orders 'may be taken into consideration in determining culpability, either by way of defence, or in mitigation of punishment'.[143]

As noted, the two international military tribunals excluded superior orders as a defence. The Nuremburg Tribunal avoided the problem of the *ex post facto* removal of the defence that had applied in Germany by stressing that a soldier 'was ordered to kill or torture in violation of the international law of war has never been recognised as a defence to such acts of brutality, though as the Charter here provides, the order may be urged in mitigation of the punishment'.[144] The tribunal in *Einsatzgruppen* specifically attacked the myth of absolute obedience to superior orders in German law by way of reference to the accused Seibert's testimony which indicated he saw that he had choice in the matter of obeying superior orders and in its examination of German precedent on the superior orders doctrine'.[145]

In the *Masuda* (Jaluit Atoll) case, defence counsel pointed out that the then-applicable Japanese law required complete obedience and that it was impossible to apply 'the liberal and individualistic ideas which rule usual societies unmodified to this totalistic and absolutistic military society'.[146] The court rejected this, focusing on manifest unlawfulness and convicted the accused. It found that:

> 'an order illegal in itself and not justified by the rules and useages of war, or in its substance clearly illegal so that a man of ordinary sense and understanding would know as soon as he heard the order read or given that it was illegal, will afford no protection for a homicide, provided the act with which he may be charged has all the ingredients in which may be necessary to constitute the same crime in law.'[147]

Bassiouni has raised the issue of legality in relation to new laws in former Soviet bloc nations that do not recognise the legal effects of superior orders or by declaring laws permitting superior orders as a defence to be null and void.[148] He cites the case of two East German border guards, who carried out 'shoot to kill' orders on the basis of then-applicable laws, and were convicted of manslaughter with the defence of superior orders being denied.[149] Clearly such orders would be manifestly unlawful. Yet Bassiouni argues that for such accused persons, the removal of the superior orders defence 'would not work as a way of policy preven-

---

142. Lauterpacht's amendments to the 1940 and 1944 editions of International Law, cited in Green, op. cit. n. 40, at p. 263.

143. *Supra* n. 141, Field Manual 27-10. Also see British Manual Amendment 34, April 1944.

144. IMT Judgment, *supra* n. 36, pp. 235-236.

145. *Einsatzgruppen, supra* n. 24, p. 472, 473, also p. 483-488.

146. The Trial of Admiral Masuda, cited in Green, op. cit. n. 40, at p. 265.

147. Ibid.

148. M.C. Bassiouni, *Crimes Against Humanity in International Law*, 2nd revised edn. (The Hague, Kluwer Law International 1999) p. 483.

149. Ibid.

tion but as retributive vengeance against those who may not have been in a position to exercise a moral choice'.[150]

The principle of legality enshrined in Article 15 of the ICCPR addresses itself to new laws that turn previously lawful actions into criminal actions, permitting a person to be prosecuted and punished. A defence provides an excuse, a justification to criminal actions. If a defence is accepted, the accused is acquitted and incurs no moral or legal guilt. This does not mean that no crime was committed; what it does mean is that the accused was not proven to be guilty of the charges against him and the presumption of innocence remains intact. If obedience to superior orders as a defence mean that a person's actions that are otherwise criminal acts become lawful, would retroactively removing the defence not violate the principle of retroactivity? This proposition finds support in the writings of Bassiouni, who argues that this would clearly be a violation of the principle of legality for it removes the legal basis for the legitimacy of the order that was followed.[151] Finally, the prohibition on retroactive criminal law bars the imposition of a heavier penalty than was prescribed by law at the time of the offence. In East Timor, when obedience to superior orders is raised by an accused under Section 21 of Regulation 2000/15, this will invariably be accompanied by an admission of particular conduct. If a conviction is entered, any sentence that is not mitigated to zero will be heavier than what existed at the time of the offence. Thus, one could argue that section 21 is null and void and its use in Serious Crimes cases is a grave violation of a fundamental principle of justice.

No Special Panel has considered this issue, although in the recent case of *de Oliveira* it was found that Regulation 2000/15 violates the prohibition against retroactive criminal laws insofar as it seeks to regulate the offences of murder and rape under the Indonesian Penal Code.[152] The case required examination of the broad definition of individual criminal responsibility contained in Regulation 15/2000, as the court found that the accused, a member of the Mahidi militia, was not the main perpetrator in the killing of Fernando Gomes.[153] Gomes' house had been set alight while he and his family were still inside by a group of militia that included the accused. When Gomes ran out of the house, he was shot by another militia member. The accused was found to have been the one who had first summoned Gomes out of the house. Although de Oliveira had been charged with murder under Article 340 of the Indonesian Penal Code, the Special Panel convicted him of the lesser offence of being an accomplice to murder.[154] The court

150. Ibid.

151. Ibid.

152. *Public Prosecutor* v. *Anigio De Oliveira*, case No. 7/2001, Decision, 27 March 2002 (currently only available in Portuguese).

153. S 14.3 of Regulation 2000/15 is taken from the ICC Statute and sets out a broad range of bases for individual criminal responsibility; these include committing, ordering, aiding, abetting, otherwise assisting with the crime, or in any other way contributing to the commission of a crime by a group. The prosecutor had charged de Oliveira with several of these modes of responsibility for the murder. *Supra* n. 4.

154. Art. 56, Indonesian Penal Code, *supra* n. 5.

did not address the impact of its finding of illegality in relation to the grounds for excluding such criminal responsibility set out in Regulation 2000/15, but it would seem to follow from the court's reasoning that the removal of a defence could possibly be found to be illegal at international law if the matter is litigated

5.3 Superior orders in Serious Crimes cases

As of 31 May 2002, all but three accused claimed to have been acting under orders as a means of justifying or explaining their conduct.[155] Of the 18 defendants who claimed to be acting under orders from either militia leaders or the Indonesian armed forces, the Special Panels accepted it as a mitigating factor for sentencing purposes in 15 cases. In virtually all of these cases, the accused also claimed some duress, generally described as the fear of being killed if the orders were not obeyed. These claims have been rejected and, as of 31 May 2002 there were no acquittals on the grounds of duress or otherwise.

Given the Special Panel's receptivity to superior orders as a mitigating factor, it seems that all accused are now raising it as a matter of strategy. However, it is not clear how much it weighs in mitigation. In this context, it should be recalled that the law does not require that the court must mitigate sentence, merely that the court may mitigate punishment in those circumstances where it is in the interests of justice.[156]

What is the test used by the Special Panels for determining the existence of superior orders? The Special Panels have been deciding the existence of superior orders on an ad-hoc, case-by-case basis without applying any discernable test or standard, whether that enshrined in Article 33 of the ICC Statute or otherwise.

Several cases usefully illustrate the practice of the Special Panels. *Agustinho da Costa* was a member of Team Pancasila militia and was charged with the murder of an UNAMET staff member.[157] The accused claimed to have done everything pursuant to orders of the TNI commander (*babinsa*) in his village.[158] According to the accused, the *babinsa* had been present at all of the militia activities to 'assist' and command them, although he did not directly participate. Da Costa claimed that he was ordered to join the militia four months before the incident. At the preliminary hearing, he stated that he was not guilty because everything he did was in

155. The only cases where superior orders have not been claimed are *Public Prosecutor* v. *Mateus Tilman* (case No. 8/2000); the lead defendant in the *Lospalos* case, Joni Marques; and *Public Prosecutor* v. *Carlos Soares Carmona* (case No. 3/2000), which is the only case not to directly involve politically-related violence but instead involved the murder of a person accused of witchcraft.

156. S. 21, Regulation 2000/15, *supra* n. 4.

157. *Prosecutor* v. *Agustinho da Costa*, *supra* n. 104.

158. *Babinsa* is an abbreviation of Bintara Pembina Desa, which is the title of a non-commissioned officer of a 'trainer' rank at the village level. The role of the *babinsa*s in the TNI structure is discussed by Dr Peter Bartu in 'The militia, the military, and the people of Bobonaro District' in D. Kingsbury, ed., *Guns and Ballot Boxes: East Timor's Vote for Independence* (Melbourne, Monash Asia Institute 2000) pp. 81, 83. It is possible that 'Paul', as a *babinsa*, was also a militia leader, but no clear evidence was ever led on this point.

obedience to the orders of his commander, failing which he believed he would have been killed. He told the court that he had acted under compulsion:

> 'I was forced, I was following an order. If I did not obey the order, I would be killed. They told me that I would be in trouble. I felt afraid. ...It was not on my own decision, my own initiative, my own will.'[159]

The Special Panel rejected the guilty plea for being ambiguous, and in its judgement found that as the accused stayed in his village rather than flee, as did so many others, he must have supported the militia and its criminal activities and thus could not claim duress. The panel convicted him to 15 years; the sentence was mitigated by the existence of superior orders. Without applying any identifiable test or standard, the Special Panel found that 'the defendant was ordered to look for and kill pro-independence and FALINTIL supporters' and that he 'carried out an order of Paul Babinsa [sic]'.[160] Yet, the only evidence of superior orders that emerged from this trial came from the accused. The panel accepted the existence of superior orders without establishing whether the accused was under a legal obligation to obey the *babinsa*, by investigating the relationship between the TNI and militias in the village, and more particularly the role of the *babinsa*, including whether the latter had the legal competence to give orders and whether his orders had to be obeyed by the accused. In reaching the conclusion that there was a superior order, the judgment did not consider if an order to kill the UNAMET worker – who was in fact subjected to a particularly gruesome death, involving being hacked and the chopping off of his hands and tongue – would have been manifestly unlawful and recognised as such by the accused. Likewise, the duty of the accused to disobey such an order, even if formally valid, received no consideration. Finally, da Costa was found to have been voluntarily part of a criminal enterprise and denied duress as a defence, yet this did not prevent the panel from accepting the claim of superior orders.

The case of *Prosecutor* v. *Manuel Lete Bere*[161] is also revealing. Its facts have already been examined.[162] Relevant here is the allegation by the Daderus Merah Putih militiaman that he stabbed the victim with a sword both under duress and following an order. Bere told the court he had been ordered to kill the victim and feared that his friend Raimundo would have shot him if he refused.

Whilst it rejected this as a duress situation, the Special Panel found that the accused had killed under the orders of Manuel Lopez, a local commander of the TNI. Again, there was no application of a discernable test or standard for establishing the finding of superior orders. There was no examination of the power

159. *Prosecutor* v. *Agustinho da Costa*, *supra* n. 104.

160. The second *Erdemovic* Trial Chamber also accepted there had been superior orders and coercion on the basis of the accused's word alone, but this was not during trial but in the course of a guilty plea. *Prosecutor* v. *Drazen Erdemovic*, Sentencing Judgment, *supra* n. 89.

161. The Prosecutor v. *Manuel Goncalves Leto Bere alias Manuel Leto Bere*, *supra* n. 115.

162. *Supra*, p. 192.

structures and the legal relationships between the players in this incident, in particular whether Bere was legally obliged to obey the order, that order being given by someone with legal competence to give such an order. The illegality of the order was not considered. Furthermore, the only evidence about the role of Manuel Lopez in the incident was the testimony of a witness Y., present during the incident, who said 'the order to kill the victim came from Manuel Lopez, the Daderus Merah Putih leader'. As noted, the accused had in fact claimed that a certain Raimundo forced him to commit the crime and he is not recorded as having said anything to suggest that the killing itself was done under specific orders from Manuel Lopez. Thus, the very existence of the order accepted by the Special Panel as a superior order is itself dubious.

In the *Lospalos* crimes against humanity case, superior orders were considered in much the same way. Although in closing submissions both the prosecutor and one of the defence counsel referred to international jurisprudence, the court entered into no substantive examination of the law whatsoever. The submissions were simply reproduced in the judgement. The only mention of superior orders in the court's findings is at the end in the discussion of the sentencing for each accused, where the court simply made findings of fact that several of the accused were acting under superior orders. On the issue of the militias, all that the Special Panel did was to confirm general findings made by other bodies, such as the International Commission of Inquiry, and take note of oral evidence by certain accused about the linkage. If a standard is discernable, it is that every order was treated as a superior order. Joni Marques, the lead defendant and one of the key figures in Team Alfa, was the only one of the ten accused who did not claim he was ordered to commit the crimes. Each of the others claimed that they were forced by Joni Marques to participate in the crimes charged. All except one, Manuel da Costa, were found to have been ordered by Joni Marques, and this was considered in mitigation of their sentences. There was no examination of whether Team Alfa was a legitimate institution and whether Joni Marques could lawfully issue orders to subordinates, who were *then* legally obliged to obey. These subordinates, like Joni Marques himself, were convicted of crimes against humanity, and customary international law is clear that orders to commit crimes against humanity are manifestly unlawful.

Manuel da Costa was himself a platoon commander of Team Alfa and the Special Panel found that he joined the operation to kill a group of clergy at the request and not the order of Joni Marques.[163] The issue of who was the more senior militia member with legal capacity to give orders, if at all, was not considered. This issue of rank was, however, given some consideration in the case of *Francisco dos Santos Laku*.[164] Laku was not a militia member but was an East Timorese member of the TNI, of the rank of sergeant, charged with murder for handing over a pro-independence supporter to militia members, who subsequently killed the man. Although he asserted that he was only following the orders of a Sergeant Alo, the

163. See *supra* n. 116 for discussion on the translation of the Bahasa Indonesia word 'jemput' as 'invite' when it does not necessarily mean the person had a choice.

164. *Prosecutor* v. *Francisco dos Santos Laku*, case No. 8/2001, Judgment 25 July 2001.

court held that these could not be viewed as superior orders since they were both of the same rank. Nevertheless, in sentencing Laku to eight years' imprisonment for the murder, the panel stated that it accepted that the accused was acting under the orders of the Indonesian government and that this had been taken into account as a mitigating factor.

5.3.1 *Can militia legitimately raise the issue of superior orders?*

As noted above, the nature and role of the militias has yet to be analysed in any of the proceedings of the Special Panels. This is partly a reflection of the fact that in only one case so far has the prosecution called a witness to provide detailed and specific evidence about the militias.[165] Had they seen fit to understand the phenomenon of the East Timorese militias in a meaningful way and thus really 'get to the bottom' of what happened and why it happened, the Special Panels could easily have exercised the option of summoning expert witnesses. They have never done so.

Unravelling the relationship between the militias is crucial as this impacts upon many legal issues, including whether they were part of the state apparatus and thus had legal authority to issue orders and demand compliance. The linkage to the state is important for determining whether they could commit war crimes (they would have to be sufficiently linked to Indonesia to do so) and whether criminal acts by them would trigger Indonesia's international obligations. Particularly relevant is the question of whether the militias were, as is almost universally alleged, a criminal organisation involved in criminal activities.

International experts agree that the East Timorese militias were extra-legal paramilitary organisations closely linked to the Indonesian regime, whose objectives and working methods were criminal.[166] The Serious Crimes cases have involved a variety of persons with different degrees of involvement with the militias – core militia members, those who got involved on a casual basis and those who say they were 'forced' to join the militias – even if all of them are 'small fish'. Can all or any of these categories benefit from a claim of superior orders? To what extent is a court of law able to look at the subjective circumstances of why the accused was associated with the militias? Unfortunately, the questions are not being asked and the prosecution, even the defence, proceed on the basis that the militias were obviously a criminal organisation and there is no need for litigation with evidence presented to a court of law. Thus, the Special Panels conclude that the militias were a criminal organisation *per se* and even make findings about how they acted under the direction and control of the Indonesian security forces.

---

165. In a recent trial, *Public Prosecutor* v. *Lino de Carvalho* (case No. 9/2001), the Public Prosecutor did call a police investigator to testify about the militia structures and links with the TNI. At the time of writing, this trial was not yet concluded.

166. See D. Kingsbury, 'The TNI and the Militias' and P. Bartu, 'The Militia, the military and the People of Bobonaro District', both inDamien Kingsbury, ed., *Guns and Ballot Boxes: East Timor's Vote for Independence* (Clayton, Monash Asia Institute 2000). See also the reports listed in n. 120.

Various reports of experts, including the UN Special Rapporteurs, the Indonesian KPP-HAM and others, have described the close links between the militias and the Indonesian armed forces, particularly the Special Forces KOPASSUS.[167] The UN Special Rapporteurs, for example, stated that although most of the atrocities during 1999 were committed by the militias, they had 'little doubt as to the direct and indirect involvement of TNI and police in supporting, planning, assisting and organising the pro-integration militia groups', particularly 'to convey strategic and tactical plans for acts of violence against supporters of independence'.[168] Testimony of militiamen before the Special Panels reveals that the militias often shared barracks with the military and received training and arms from them as well as engaging in joint operations and patrols. Furthermore, there is extensive material suggesting that the militias were used as a front for the Indonesia military to commit atrocities directly, such as participating in militia activities while dressed as militia.[169] Many have observed that the widespread and systematic destruction of September 1999, notably the forced evacuation of the population to West Timor, destruction of property and violence against the person, could not have been achieved with such success in so short a time without extensive support and assistance from institutions of state.[170]

There is then the contradictory practice whereby those who are considered to have voluntarily joined the militias are unable to claim a defence by way of duress, yet those same persons are able to benefit from mitigation by way of superior orders. Superior orders is a doctrine that builds on legitimate power structures such as within the armed forces of a state; it would be unacceptable for someone from the Mafia to be permitted to claim he was following superior orders and thus benefit from mitigation or even be excused of liability in countries which accept this as a defence. In East Timor, the issue is whether the Special Panels are correct to mitigate the sentences of convicted militia members because they claim that they committed crimes as a result of superior orders. UNTAET Regulation 2000/15 does not have a provision along the lines of Articles 9 and 10 of the IMT Charter, which enabled that tribunal to declare organisations such as the SS (*Schutzstaffel*) criminal, thus opening up the possibility of prosecutions for membership of a criminal organisation and involvement in its criminal activities following an earlier judicial determination of the nature of the group. It is unfortunate that Section 21 of Regulation 2000/15 has no statutory filter that would exclude subordination within a criminal organisation. However, such filters are

---

167. See Report of the Special Rapporteurs, *supra* n. 120, para. 59-61; see also Chapter II, KPP-Ham Report, *supra* n. 120; Report of the International Commission of Inquiry, *supra* n. 120, paras. 135-141.

168. Report of the Special Rapporteurs, ibid.

169. See Chapter II, KPP-HAM Report, *supra* n. 120; J. Dunn, 'Crimes Against Humanity in East Timor, January to October 1999: Their Nature and Causes', in *Masters of Terror: Indonesia's Military and Violence in East Timor in 1999*, Canberra Papers on Strategy and Defence No. 145 (Canberra, Strategic and Defence Studies Centre, ANU 2002) pp. 60-74.

170. Report of the International Commission of Inquiry, *supra* n. 120, paras. 136-142; Conclusions, KPP-HAM Report, *supra* n. 120.

part of the test in customary international law, which denies recourse to duress and superior order for such persons. As noted, the Special Panels do not seek guidance in the rules of customary international law and there is now a practice whereby the logic of the finding of voluntary participation in a criminal enterprise is not followed through.

5.3.2 *The question of manifest unlawfulness*

The doctrine of obedience to superior orders requires that a distinction is made between manifestly unlawful and plain unlawful orders. A manifestly unlawful order cannot lead to mitigation of sentence by way of superior orders; whether an unlawful order may do so falls within the inherent discretion of the court as to the mitigation it is prepared to concede. An order to kill unarmed civilians sheltering in a church would surely be unlawful, even for the many uneducated East Timorese farmers and fishermen who, for different reasons, committed Serious Crimes as or alongside militias and appear before the Special Panel as accused. But would such persons have had the capacity to distinguish between unlawful and manifestly unlawful orders? Could they fairly be expected to distinguish between those East Timorese who actively supported independence but did so peacefully, those who simply voted against autonomy and those who resisted the Indonesians by armed force, and know that just one of these could be a legitimate target of attack in an armed conflict? Could such people really be expected to know that the IMT at Nuremburg found that individuals have international duties which transcend the national obligations of obedience imposed by the individual state?

The answer would certainly depend on the circumstances and subjective facts; for example, seasoned militia members such as Joni Marques and Manuel da Costa in *Lospalos* told the Special Panel that they had received training from the Indonesian armed forces and should not be able to raise such an argument. Professional soldiers can be reasonably assumed to have received training on how to conduct themselves, dictated by both their specific rules of engagement as well as international humanitarian law. This concurs with judicial practice in military cases such as *Calley*, which also asserted a common sense standard for the average man.[171] The ordinary low-ranking militia member would not have access to training of the kind that Marques and da Costa received, which even included international training with foreign soldiers. They would not have had knowledge of international humanitarian law, nor have been subjected to the 'discipline' of the regular TNI soldiers. Certainly, they would have known that to kill a group of nuns and priests who had been distributing food to refugees would be criminal. Even manifestly unlawful. But, did the lower ranking members of Team Alfa know that they did not have to obey manifestly unlawful orders? Did they genuinely believe that they were obliged to follow all orders they received, regardless of how horrific? Should it make a difference to a court of law? Fairness suggests that questions should at

171. *United States* v. *Calley*, 48 CMR 19 (CMA 1973).

least be asked, but the Special Panel has not made the necessary enquiries.

In the case of *Joao Fernandes*, the majority of the Court of Appeal examined Article 51 of the Indonesian Penal Code, which provides for superior orders as a defence and found that:

> 'this demands, for the exclusion of the penal responsibility, that the agent that had acted by executing an official order given by the competent authority – which wasn't the appellant's case, seeing that neither the militia chief Natalino Monteiro nor the Maliana POLRES commander nor the Indonesian armed forces (TNI) had legal competence to order the killing of people, nor the appellant had a legal obligation to execute that order'.[172]

This touches on the doctrine of manifestly unlawful orders – from this it is clear that the two appellate judges viewed an order to kill as manifestly unlawful in itself, regardless of whether the giver of the order had the legal competence to issue any such orders. In the particular circumstances of the case, where the killing allegedly ordered was of civilians sheltering in the police station, such an order was manifestly unlawful, even for the low-ranking accused. He was obliged to disobey the order, but chose to obey and took part in the operation. Yet, despite the unlawfulness of the order, the logical connection was not made that Fernandes could not therefore claim the benefit of mitigation by way of superior orders under Regulation 2000/15.

5.4 Conclusions on superior orders before the Special Panels

This foregoing study clearly reveals substantial weaknesses with the treatment of superior orders in East Timor. Section 21 of Regulation 2000/15 may itself be null and void because it denies Serious Crimes accused the right to raise superior orders as a defence, as was permitted under the then-applicable law and which continues to be allowed to accused in Ordinary Crimes cases and those on trial in Indonesia. Virtually every person convicted of Serious Crimes and serving sentence has been detrimentally affected by this provision. As for the Special Panels, the practice and jurisprudence on superior orders reveal that every order is being accepted as a superior order without testing against the standards set by customary international law.[173] Many of the decisions reached are inconsistent with international practice, for example, permitting those who act on the basis of a manifestly unlawful order to claim mitigation by way of superior orders.

---

172. *Joao Fernandes* Appeal – Majority Decision, *supra* n. 75, p. 8.

173. Contrast the practice of the Special Panels with the IMT, which held that 'Superior orders ... cannot be considered in mitigation where crimes as shocking and extensive have been committed consciously, ruthlessly and without military excuse or justification.' Judgment of the International Military Tribunal for the Trial of the German Major War Criminals, Nuremberg, 30th September and 1st October, 1946. London: HMSO, Cmd. 6964, Reprinted 1966, pp. 90-92. See also *Einsatzgruppen*, *supra* n. 24, p. 480, where it was held that to plead superior orders, 'one must show an excusable ignorance of their illegality'.

Given the frequency with which such claims are accepted, superior orders have become a 'consolation prize' for those whose claims of duress have been rejected. Compassion towards low-ranking persons is not unusual: one need only look at the five year sentence ultimately meted out to Drazen Erdemović at the ICTY for his role in the slaughter at Srebrenica. Yet the practice of the Special Panels is not consistent, and the consequences of a finding that a person participated voluntarily in a criminal enterprise are not followed through to deny recourse to both duress and superior orders. Moral judgements are in fact being made about people without closely examining the subjective circumstances that led to their association with the militias.

In order that the doctrine of superior orders is justly implemented in a society such as East Timor's, it would seem essential to consider local concepts of power and authority. Traditional East Timorese society was a structured one, with hereditary villager elders (*liurai* and *dato*) commanding deep respect and loyalty from a predominantly rural community. In occupied East Timor, and elsewhere across Suharto's Indonesia, the cultural norms of the dominant Javanese islanders were introduced. The hereditary leaders were replaced with hand-picked *kepala desa* [village leaders] who were civil servants. Javanese culture emphasises a focus on avoiding conflict, extreme respect for hierarchy and authority, as well as a specific concept of centralised power in the figure of authority.[174] The cultural imperative was that people in higher positions must be respected and never contradicted through the voicing of an alternative viewpoint.[175] This meant that one had to follow the instructions of a person in a higher position; legal obligation either from the capacity of the person to give orders, or the obligation to obey, was simply not a consideration. In such an environment, the majority of those being tried by the Special Panels (being low-ranking, non-hardcore militia members whose association may not have been voluntary), would have felt obliged by the applicable social norms to obey *kepala desa, babinsa* and others in authority positions, such as Indonesian soldiers and policemen, probably also the militia members, who had open and blatant support from those in power. Further incentive to obey such persons came from the fact that such authority was backed up by the brute force of an occupying power. This discussion is linked to the issue of what a reasonable man in East Timor may consider to be manifestly unlawful.[176] While we do not suggest the

174. F. Magnis-Suseno, 'Langsir Keprabon: New Order leadership, Javanese culture, and the prospects for democracy in Indonesia', in G. Forrester, ed., *Post Suharto Indonesia: Renewal or Chaos?* (Singapore, Institute of Southeast Asian Studies 1999) p. 218.

175. Ibid., at p. 219: 'In the Javanese conception, behaving in a respectful and rukun [avoidance of open conflict] way will in the end always pay dividends since the community will live in harmony and be free from disturbances, and individuals are protected and provided for by their community and their leaders.'

176. L.C. Green suggests that 'the standard of measurement cannot be universal, but must depend on whether the accused is a civilian or a serviceman and whether the offence is of a kind that can be considered as being civil in character though committed by a soldier. If the act is essentially military in character and has been committed in war conditions, then the palpability must be looked at from the point of view of the reasonable soldier ...', Green, op. cit. n. 40, at p. 281.

introduction of cultural relativity, we do suggest that the reality of everyday life in such societies is a relevant factor particularly when considering the actions of civilians. It is unfortunate that the Special Panels have not demonstrated sensitivity towards this, given that the mixed panel mechanism itself was designed to meet local needs.

Despite the overarching need to search for the truth and make decisions that are informed, findings have been based on extraneous sources of information, as occurred in *Leki*. The responsibilities of the court as fact-finder have also been evaded by the practice of simply incorporating the reports of others, as in *Lospalos* ,and as Judge Egonda-Ntende noted in *Joao Fernandes*, lax evidentiary standards. Given that superior orders presume legitimate power structures, the Special Panel's generosity in the area of superior orders creates a series of parallel implications that the militias were legitimate organisations with an official hierarchy, permitting its leaders the legal competence to give orders to subordinates who were in turn obliged to obey them. We do however recognise, that such assessments must be tempered with the reality that the Special Panels have adopted an ad hoc approach that does not rely on recognised tests of international or other law.

6. CONCLUDING REMARKS

This study of admissions of guilt, duress and superior orders before the Special Panels reveals disturbing practices. The problems that were observed and examined all impact upon the ability of the Serious Crimes process to meet international standards.

The world's first internationalised domestic tribunal is providing an abundance of lessons for future experiments in international criminal justice. Even if an impressive rate of concluding trials in the face of tremendous obstacles has been achieved, the truth is that the overwhelming majority of these cases have been of ordinary murder and not the more demanding international crimes.[177] This paper has revealed that the quality of the process and the decisions themselves leave much to be desired. The wealth of international jurisprudence going back to Nuremburg is being ignored, and lessons that have been learnt in other institutions, such as in the course of the *Erdemović* litigation at the ICTY, have not been taken on board. Despite the huge influence of the ICC Statute, the Serious Crimes project operates as though it was disconnected from the norms and demands of customary international law. Some may argue that this is because the provisions taken from the ICC Statute are complete in themselves and there is no need to look beyond the laws passed by UNTAET in East Timor. Whether cases are processed as domestic

---

177. At 31 May 2002, the Special Panels had concluded 15 trials against a total of 24 individual accused, all of whom have been convicted and sentenced. Of these cases, only the *Lospalos* case involved charges of crimes against humanity. Six of the ten accused in that case were acquitted of some charges but convicted on others. A further 12 cases involving crimes against humanity were due to be heard by the Special Panels but had not yet been completed at the time of writing.

crimes under the Indonesian Penal Code or as international crimes, the issues that arise from admissions of guilt, duress and superior orders are not easy. Yet, the issues examined herein reveal that fundamental and unnecessary mistakes are being made, and that some of those failings arise from a reluctance to examine and apply substantive and procedural international law in order to reach decisions of an international standard. Some of the problems identified have included findings of facts being made in the absence of evidence on issues not litigated by the parties, inconsistencies, blanket rulings that prevent a case-by-case assessment, ad hoc approaches and effective discrimination against entire groups of people. It seems that few of the transitional justice benefits claimed for accountability mechanisms (such as the creation of an accurate and detailed historical record that casts light on the roots and chronology of mass violence, the provision of a meaningful platform for victims, acknowledgment of their suffering and contribution towards social repair and reconciliation) have been delivered by the Serious Crimes project. Whether this is because of the unrealistic expectations of the judicial mechanism per se or flaws in the East Timor process must be the subject of further, more detailed study.

There are many reasons why the road to justice in East Timor has been so rocky, and any attempt to understand them must begin with an appreciation that for the process to have come so far is in itself a remarkable achievement. When UNTAET took over the administration of the half-island, it really was faced with a catastrophic situation, with no courts, no judges, no prosecutors, no police force, no prisons; and that was just the criminal justice system. It is no exaggeration to say that the entire system had to be built from scratch, and UNTAET faced major challenges in finding personnel who were up to that job. To a certain extent, mistakes must be seen in the context of an evolving judicial system, but 'teething problems' are clearly not an excuse for much of what we have observed in the handling of Serious Crimes cases. The role of the Court of Appeal is therefore crucial for providing recourse to appeal for accused persons, and guidance for the Special Chambers. Extraordinarily, the Court of Appeal has been allowed to lie dormant since the departure of Judge Egonda-Ntende in November 2001, thus depriving Serious Crimes accused of the fundamental right to appeal convictions since then. The weakness and malfunctioning of the infant criminal justice system has been and remains the subject of concern for many observers and the UN itself. The former Special Representative of the Secretary-General and Transitional Administrator for East Timor, Sergio Vieira de Mello, has conceded that 'the justice system is still in a nascent state and needs continued close attention', adding that 'the lack of resources, including interpreters and court staff, has led to delayed hearings and unduly prolonged detention of suspects'.[178] The Serious Crimes project, even if it is dominated by international employees of the United Nations, has to be seen as a part of that weak structure and the ongoing challenges of creating a democratic

178. Sergio Vieira de Mello, Statement on the occasion of the Security Council Open Debate on the situation in East Timor, New York (30 January 2002). See also Report of the Secretary-General on the Transitional Administration in East Timor, 17 April 2002, UN Doc. S/2002/432 at pp. 17-18.

nation founded solidly on justice, rule of law and respect for human rights.

For all its blemishes, the Serious Crimes project offers the closest that the East Timorese have ever had to justice for crimes committed against them in the course of their struggle for freedom. It appears increasingly likely that the Serious Crimes project will be terminated by the end of 2003, and best efforts will have barely scratched the surface. At the time of writing, a draft law on amnesties and pardons introduced by President Xanana Gusmao remains pending before East Timor's Parliament. The draft law seeks to amnesty a broad range of criminal activity, including some actions that qualify as Serious Crimes. Proceedings before Indonesia's Ad Hoc Court for Human Rights in East Timor, the preferred option of the UN Secretary-General and the international community, are surpassing all expectations of a show trial.[179] Rather than bringing those accountable for atrocities to justice and uncovering the truth of what happened in East Timor, it seems to be used as a vehicle to whitewash the role of Indonesia in the carnage. Justice in the form of an *ad hoc* International Criminal Tribunal for East Timor, the preferred option of the International Commission of Inquiry, the UN Special Rapporteurs, Nobel Peace Prize winner Bishop Carlos Belo, many NGOs and countless ordinary East Timorese, seems in the post-September 11 and Bali Bomb world to be a lost cause.

Thus, the hopes for some sort of equilibrium will increasingly focus on East Timor's Commission for Reception, Truth and Reconciliation.[180] The Commission's mandate is threefold: to establish an accurate record of what happened in East Timor by examining the pattern and scope of human rights violations in the context of the country's unhappy history since 1974; to establish a Community Reconciliation Process to facilitate the return and reintegration of those who have committed less serious crimes by use of traditional justice mechanisms which are ultimately approved by a court of law; and to make recommendations to the government. The Community Reconciliation Process is designed to complement the investigation and prosecution of Serious Crimes, in that the General Prosecutor approves the cases which are dealt with through this mechanism, and amnesties may not be given for offences that amount to Serious Crimes. Given the limitations of the justice system, it appears increasingly likely that the commission will have to take on an even greater responsibility for uncovering and recording the history of human rights violations in East Timor than originally planned.

179. See International Crisis Group, Indonesia: The Implications of the Timor Trials, 8 May 2002; Human Rights Watch, Justice Denied for East Timor: Indonesia's Sham Prosecutions, the Need to Strengthen the Trial Process in East Timor, and the Imperative of UN Action, 20 December 2002.

180. The Commission was established by UNTAET Regulation 2001/10 of 13/7/01, UNTAET/REG/2001/10. For an examination of the work of the commission, see C. Stahn, 'Accommodating Individual Criminal Responsibility and National Reconciliation: The UN Truth Commission for East Timor', 95 *AJIL* (2001) p. 952.

TRANSITIONAL JUSTICE IN PEACE OPERATIONS: SHAPING THE TWILIGHT ZONE IN SOMALIA AND EAST TIMOR[1]

Michael Kelly[2]

1. INTRODUCTION

Much has been written about transitional justice in the circumstances of organised states progressing towards democracy.[3] Another category of transitional justice demanding equal study and resolution has, however, emerged. That is the interim administration of justice in the vacuum of the disrupted state following traumatic internal conflict, usually involving war crimes and crimes against humanity. Two things are characteristic of this circumstance: first, the requirement for a deployed international military force to do 'something' about fundamental law and order while waiting for the civil administrative 'cavalry' to arrive; second, the fact that a civil administrative element will eventually have to take over from the military and will also be required to do 'something' about the immediate law and order problem but in a manner that leads into the long term reconstruction and 'end state' process. In the future, this environment may also include the operation of the International Criminal Court (ICC), where many issues of jurisdiction, investigation, prosecution and the impact on long term rehabilitation will need to be managed.

Two examples of the worst case 'justice vacuum' scenarios faced by the international community have been Somalia and East Timor. This paper will look at general principles that have emerged from these case studies, concentrating on the issue of the interim administration of justice by military forces deployed on peace operations. In both cases, there was in place a coalition force facing an immediate problem of restoring order, which was followed on by a UN force and administration that faced the challenge of leading the transition from interim arrangements to a self-sustaining indigenous apparatus.

2. Michael Kelly is Director of the Australian Defence Force Military Law Centre and Deputy Director of the Asia Pacific Centre for Military Law. He served with the Australian Defence Force in Somalia in 1993 and in East Timor in 2001-2002 and on secondment with the International Committee of the Red Cross in Bosnia and Croatia in 1996.

3. M.E. Fischer, ed., *Establishing Democracies* (Boulder CO, Westview Press 1996); R.G. Teitel, *Transitional Justice* (New York NY, Oxford University Press 2000); A.J. McAdams, ed., *Transitional Justice and the Rule of Law in New Democracies* (Notre Dame ID, University of Notre Dame Press 1997); and N.J. Kritz, ed., *Transitional Justice: How Emerging Democracies Reckon with Former Regimes*, Vols. I-III (Washington DC, United States Institute of Peace Press 1995) are a sample.

Yearbook of International Humanitarian Law
Volume 4 – 2001 – pp. 213-251

In looking at these two examples of complex emergency, this paper will focus on the approach taken by Australian forces to the interim justice issue. The reason for this focus on the Australian perspective is due to the unique solutions Australian forces have applied to the interim administration of justice and the fact that these solutions have been relatively successful. A comparison of the two cases is instructive in assessing whether there are general principles that can be applied across cultural and circumstantial contexts. They also serve to illustrate particular elements that can complicate the problem such as where there is a continuing high level security threat or where there is no remaining local expertise to draw on.

In the case of Somalia, the Australian contingent occupied an area closely aligned with the Bay Province, whose capital was Baidoa. This contingent was subordinate to the UNITAF HQ in Mogadishu, and UNOSOM II briefly, and while able to exercise great discretion in its Area of Operations was not in a position to dictate overall policy approaches to the issue. In East Timor, however, the Australian approach became critical as Australia was in the policy setting position.

2. THE CASE OF SOMALIA

2.1 Restoring and maintaining order

2.1.1 *The legal foundations and the reluctance to act*

Operations in Somalia and East Timor were to unfold in similar phases with some similarities but very different results. In Somalia, a UN-mandated coalition force led by the United States, known as UNITAF (Unified Task Force), deployed in December 1992 in response to a massive humanitarian crisis resulting from a number of years of civil war.[4] Somalia had effectively ceased to exist as a state, having no functioning government, administration or infrastructure. Under Security Council Resolution (UNSCR) 794,[5] UNITAF was to use all necessary measures to secure the environment for humanitarian relief. UNITAF handed off to a UN 'Blue Helmet' force known as UNOSOM II in May 1993. This had a mandate under UNSCR 814[6] to engage in pro-active nation building with a distinct focus on law and order.

It quickly became apparent to UNITAF that the area presenting difficulty for the force would be the handling of detainees and regulating relations with the community in maintaining order and providing security for relief operations. The UNITAF Commander was given a framework of rules of engagement which addressed this issue in broad terms. From this he was to produce policy guidance

4. For a good summary of the background and lead up to the intervention, see J.L. Hirsch and R.B. Oakley, *Somalia and Operation Restore Hope: Reflections on Peacemaking and Peacekeeping* (Washington, United States Institute of Peace Press 1995).

5. SC Res 794, 47 UN SCOR (3101st mtg), UN Doc. S/RES/794 (1992).

6. SC Res 814, 48 UN SCOR (3188th mtg), UN Doc. S/RES/814 (1993).

and procedures. The rules of engagement specified that 'detention of civilians was authorised'. This was permitted where persons were interfering with the accomplishment of the mission or where persons otherwise used or threatened deadly force against UNITAF members, relief material, distribution sites or convoys. Persons who committed criminal acts in areas under the control of UNITAF members could also be detained. Persons detained were to be handed over to the US Military Police. This was qualified in the case of the Australian contingent, as a matter of national policy, by restricting detention to serious crimes such as rape and murder or crimes against the person. These qualifications were later adopted by HQ UNITAF. Most property related crimes were excluded, except theft of relief material. Neither UNSCR 794 nor the Rules of Engagement indicated what was to be the overall legal framework for this action or for relations with the community in general, given that there was no government to negotiate with and hence no Status of Forces Agreement or Memorandum of Understanding.

Subject to this broad authority, the UNITAF Commander was then obliged to produce clearer guidelines and procedures. The detainee handling regime that was put in place by HQ UNITAF was tailored to the circumstances. It was determined that the standard of the facilities must be of at least the minimum required for Prisoners of War for the temporary holding of no more than 48 hours.[7] The standards were based on accepted principles of international law and, in particular, those specified in the Fourth Geneva Convention. The process for handling detainees eventually crystallised as follows: a) detainee held for no more than 48 hours in the contingent locality; b) basic evidence to establish *prima facie* case obtained; c) detainee backloaded to UNITAF detention facility at Mogadishu University for no more than 72 hours; d) 'probable cause' report prepared by legal officer; e) report submitted to UNITAF Staff Judge Advocate (SJA); f) SJA reports to UNITAF Commander as to whether probable cause made out; and g) if probable cause made out detainee moved to Mogadishu central prison to await trial.[8]

For the Australian contingent, this system no longer applied once a justice administration was reestablished in Baidoa, but it worked well as a streamlined means of processing detainees with appropriate legal checks built in. Within the policy would be seen a number of contra-indications to the official US position that the laws of occupation did not apply to the UNITAF mission. In the second policy guideline issued 24 December 1992, it was stated that:

> 'The *obligation* of CTF (Combined Task Force) personnel to *protect the population* and detain civilians varies with the location of the incident ... Civilian detainees are categorised as either criminal or hostile in nature.
>
> For *areas under military control ..., a commander* shall *protect the population not only*

7. UNITAF, Staff Judge Advocate After Action Report (SJA AAR) p. 16, TAB E (1) & (2).
8. Memorandum to All Subordinate Unified Task Force Commanders, 'Detainee Policy', Lieutenant General Johnston, 9 February 1993.

from attack by military units, but also from crimes, riots, and other forms of civil disobedience.'[9] (emphasis added)

This was further evidenced in the US Army Military Police Special Operating Procedure for Operation Restore Hope, which outlined the authority for detention and procedures to be followed. Under the paragraph headed 'Authority to Detain' the guidance stated:

> 'Detainment of local nationals is authorised and directed once it is determined by competent authority to be necessary for imperative reasons of security to the US Armed Forces in the *occupied territory*.'[10] (emphasis added)

This document outlined the treatment of detainees and in effect constituted a summary of the provisions of the Fourth Convention regarding internment and detention.

The major flaw, however, was that no system was put in place for dealing with detainees against whom 'probable cause' was made out and who were taken to the Mogadishu Prison. Prior to deployment, the SJA had raised this issue with the UNITAF command, stating, 'there may be a requirement for a system of tribunals that operate in the absence of a host nation government. There may be a need to establish some kind of civil code and promulgate it in the native language.'[11] Neither of these points were addressed in the event. At one point, plans had been made by the US Judge Advocates for the convening of 'Article Five' Military Tribunals with the material and guidelines being sent from the US Third Army SJA at Fort McPherson Georgia to HQ UNITAF.[12] The purpose of these tribunals is merely to determine the status of a person as to whether he is entitled to be designated as a Prisoner of War with the consequent treatment and privileges attaching to that status. It was originally intended that such tribunals would be able to deal with detainees who had threatened the security of the force or the relief effort and

---

9. Signal from Commander Joint Task Force (CJTF) Somalia, 'Commander's Policy Guidance, Civilian Detainees, Vehicle accidents, Medical Care and Reporting Requirements', 24 December 1992. Other specifications included, 'Civilians shall be detained only in exceptional circumstances ... Exceptional circumstances should include the detention of civilians:
(1) who are suspected of crimes of a serious nature (i.e., willful killing, torture or inhumane treatment, rape, willfully causing suffering or serious injury to body or health, etc.) that the failure to detain would be an embarrassment to the US, or
(2) whose release immediately following a hostile encounter would likely endanger CTF forces or persons under the protection of CTF forces.
Civilians will not be detained solely for interrogation purposes. However, civilians who have been detained under exceptional circumstances may be interrogated provided the atmosphere remains entirely voluntary.'

10. United States Army, 720th Military Police Battalion, Joint Task Force Somalia, APO AE 09896-0631, Special Operating Procedure, 'Detainee Confinement Facility, Operation Restore Hope', Lieutenant Colonel A.J. Stamilio.

11. UNITAF, SJA AAR, TAB A (1).

12. Facsimile transmission, US Third Army SJA to Major Coulter dated 6 December 1992. Art. 5 refers to Art. 5 of the Geneva Convention Relative to the Treatment of Prisoners of War of 12 August 1949.

possibly against the faction leaders and their forces who were hostile to UNITAF.[13] It was determined that the Article Five tribunal format would not be appropriate and would be too cumbersome in the circumstances of Operation Restore Hope for simple criminal offenders, or even to determine the status of those attacking UNITAF forces.[14]

Following serious accusations against the faction leader Omar Jess and his subsequent apprehension[15] by UNITAF, there was some speculation that a 'war crimes' tribunal would be convened to deal with him. This was based in particular on evidence that his forces had been responsible for the massacre of a large number of civilians just prior to UNITAF deploying into the Kismayo area. However, a political decision was made not to proceed against Jess and he was released.[16] It was also determined that no tribunals would be convened to deal with the local community due specifically to uncertainty over the legal basis for the exercise of such jurisdiction resulting from the reluctance to acknowledge the application of the laws of occupation.[17]

2.1.2 *Attempts to stimulate a local solution*

The desire not to have to deal with offenders was perfectly understandable. The alternative, however, was to throw the problem over to UNOSOM II which proved never to be in a position, either in terms of having a legal plan or capability, to do anything about the detainees. By not having a plan, UNITAF was in breach of all acceptable human rights standards.[18] It was an aspect of the operation that none of the contingents had given any thought to or made any preparation for. The other alternative was to re-establish some form of local justice administration which would have satisfied all obligations and avoided any burden on the force. Initially there were some attempts at reconstituting an indigenous law enforcement regime

13. Interview with Colonel F.M. Lorenz (USMC), former UNITAF SJA, Townsville 27 June 1994.

14. UNITAF, SJA AAR, p. 43.

15. Memorandum for the Record, 'Kismayo Incident', Lieutenant Colonel F.R. Moulin Deputy SJA HQ UNITAF, 26 December 1992, UNITAF, SJA AAR, TAB Q (2). J. Perley, 'Somali Clan Killed Dozens of Rivals, US Officials Say', *New York Times* (29 December 1992) p. 1. Memorandum for the Record, from Task Force Kismayo Surgeon Major T.P. Pfanner, 'Observations at gravesite Near Kismayo Airport' (3 January 1993) UNITAF, SJA AAR, TAB Q (2). 'Given the similar times of death of the bodies and their conditions, it would seem logical to conclude that this scene represents a site of mass murder and probable torture. The involved persons appeared to be prominent members of their society or at least affluent by local standards. I personally observed at least 14 bodies and suspect many more are present to include possibly mass graves.'

16. Briefing by HQ UNITAF Judge Advocates attended by author on 8 February 1993.

17. UNITAF, SJA AAR, p. 44. F.M. Lorenz (UNITAF SJA), 'Confronting Thievery in Somalia: The Use of Non-Lethal Force During Operation Restore Hope', paper dated 13 April 1993, pp. 6, 9.

18. That is the requirement to follow detention with a fair trial as specifically required by Art. 71 of the Fourth Convention. See also Arts. 9-11 of the UDHR and Art. 9 of the ICCPR. Even if the extent of the plan was to work vigorously towards enabling the local justice system to try offenders, this would have satisfied the requirements of Art. 71, which states that offenders be brought to trial as rapidly *as possible*.

based on the desire to relieve the patrolling and security burden on the force.[19] The US was under domestic legal constraint in this respect as its Foreign Assistance Act (FAA) prohibits the training, advice or financial support of foreign police, prisons or other law enforcement agencies, (except in Central America and the Caribbean).[20] Ironically, had the application of the laws of occupation been acknowledged, this could have been used to distinguish the situation from the coverage of the FAA.[21] It would also have been possible to seek an exemption for the circumstances that applied in Somalia but Lieutenant General Johnston, CENTCOM, the Joint Chiefs of Staff (JCS) and Washington were all against involvement on the basis that it represented more 'mission creep'. This attitude changed as the realisation dawned of the importance of putting effort into such an initiative.[22] The expedient adopted to allow some limited involvement and to partially circumvent the restrictions of the FAA was to term this group the Auxiliary Security Force (ASF).[23] It was hoped by UNITAF that UNOSOM would fill the remaining holes by providing most of the logistic support with help from donor countries specifically volunteering for this task.

A Police Committee was constituted in Mogadishu but it became plagued by factional differences. The mistake made was that political representatives were allowed on the Committee rather than confining membership to former senior police commanders and administrators.[24] There were three key deficiencies in relation to the ASF. First was the factional problem in Mogadishu; second, the ASF was unarmed and had no chance of reestablishing order in the armed camp that was Somalia without the force itself being armed, while at the same time, a disarmament campaign was ongoing. Finally, even if the ASF did apprehend someone there was still no judiciary to hand a suspect over to. Overcrowded prisons would simply become more overcrowded and the violations of human rights standards only exacerbated. Even the Police Committee had pressed for a judiciary to be reconstituted side by side with the efforts to get the ASF going as, 'without a judicial system, the police could not be effective'.[25]

The next step was therefore to attempt to get a judiciary functioning. Moves began in an unplanned way from two separate sources. The UNITAF SJA Colonel F.M. Lorenz had been contacted by some former judicial officers from southern

---

19. Hirsch and Oakley, op. cit. n. 4, at p. 88.

20. UNITAF, SJA AAR, TAB S (1).

21. Even had the domestic legal restriction not been a factor, there was no real enthusiasm in the senior levels of command for getting involved with the local police beyond getting something on the streets of Mogadishu to control the crowds so that UNITAF troops did not have to. Anything else was considered 'beyond the mission'. Interview with Colonel Lorenz, *supra* n. 13.

22. Hirsch and Oakley, op. cit. n. 4, at pp. 87-89.

23. UNITAF, SJA AAR, p. 46. Also personal observations of author in dealings with LTCOL Spataro.

24. Interview with Brigadier Ahmed Jama, Washington, 3 January 1995. Brig. Jama was approached to join the committee but declined due to the policy of allowing non-police officials on the committee, which he claimed politicised it.

25. Memorandum from Provost Marshal to UNITAF J-3, 'Auxiliary Security Force', 27 January 1993.

Mogadishu who had a plan to reconstitute a judiciary. At the same time the US Liaison Office (USLO) representative, Mr Phillip Ives, had been in contact with some former jurists in northern Mogadishu. As a result of this contact, a meeting between the two groups and all former Somali jurists who could attend was arranged for 3 March 1993 at UNOSOM Headquarters. The meeting was well attended and produced some concrete results. It was decided that a steering committee would be formed to work on the creation of a broad-based Law Association to take justice reconstruction issues further but also to examine aspects of constitutional reform and the shape of the new Somalia. The general consensus was that the basis of the justice administration should be the 1962 Somali Penal Code and further meetings were agreed upon.[26]

Difficulties were soon to emerge, however. The Political Committee in Mogadishu, made up of the warlords, was highly suspicious and did not wish to encourage such uncontrolled interest groups developing, particularly if they cut across clan and factional certitudes. Their suspicions may have been well founded as the jurists asked to be permitted to send representatives to the Addis Ababa peace conference. They felt they were better qualified to discuss the future shape of Somalia than 'the thugs who will run the meeting', as one of them stated.[27] While there was some support for reestablishing the police force, there was never any substantive commitment to assisting a judiciary to compliment it on the part of UNITAF or the UN in these crucial early days.[28] The Steering Committee languished due to this lack of support and the hostility of the warlords.

2.1.3 *The dividend of inaction*

This failure also had serious consequences for the morale of the troops and their relationship with the community.[29] Because there was no system of justice or framework for dealing with offenders against the security and property of the force, they found themselves in an invidious position. On the one hand, it was highly corrosive of morale for the troops to apprehend bandits responsible for mass

---

26. Report by J. Hirsch of USLO to US State Department, 'Somali Jurists Meet at UNOSOM', 3 March 1993. F.M. Lorenz, 'Will the Rule of Law Replace the Law of the Gun?' 48 *Washington State Bar News* (1994) p. 19. Also personal observations of the author, who was in attendance at the 3 March meeting and the meetings with the southern Mogadishu jurists.

27. Interview with Dr Abdullahi Ossable Barre, former judge of the Supreme Court of Somalia, 3 March 1993, UNOSOM Headquarters Mogadishu.

28. Once again, this was considered 'beyond the mission'. The initiatives in this direction came from proactive individuals, such as Phillip Ives and Colonel Lorenz. There was no official encouragement of their efforts but only 'mild scepticism'. It was questioned as an unnecessary involvement. Because of this attitude, as Colonel Lorenz states, 'Other than meeting and talking these things through I guess we really did not provide any substantial support ... we didn't do a lot.' Interview with Colonel Lorenz, op. cit. n. 13.

29. Most troops deployed with a sense of mission and goodwill but soon became disillusioned with the inactive operation in those places where local commanders did not engage in civic action, succumbing to the laager mentality. M.J. Mazarr, 'The Military Dilemmas of Humanitarian Intervention', 24 *Security Dialogue* (1993) pp. 157-158.

murder and robbery and be forced to let them go or hand them over to village elders who had no power to do anything with the more serious bandits. There was no means of bringing even Somalis who killed members of the force to trial. On the other hand, the troops lost face with the community and the bandits when this was realised. Often troops in Mogadishu would be derisively stoned and sniped at with rifle fire as they drove by. Grenades were sometimes thrown at vehicles, such as in the case of five Belgian troops injured this way in Kismayo.[30] There was nothing that could be done with intruders into the encampments but hand them over to the elders or let them go.[31] Even in Mogadishu the central prison proved to be unreliable, with key bandits being able to secure release. As a result, the prison was abandoned in favour of the temporary detention facility at the Mogadishu University compound. In effect, given the limited scope of the UNITAF detention facility, long term detentions effectively ceased.[32] In this environment of frustration and tension, some troops determined that their only option was to administer rough justice themselves or snapped under the strain and used inappropriate lethal force in cases of simple theft.[33]

The most notorious incident occurred in Belet Weyn where a Somali who was caught within the perimeter of the Canadian contingent was tortured and beaten to death.[34] This was only the most severe of what was not an uncommon practice of administering some form of physical punishment to those caught stealing or breaching perimeters as a means of discouraging further attempts and seeing some 'justice' done. It was incumbent on those who put the troops in such a position to provide a proper framework for handling criminal activity. Not only was the failure to establish a proper law enforcement regime a breach of the obligations of laws of occupation but it also seriously threatened the morale, safety and standards of the troops.

The US command adopted a restrictive view of the mission which predisposed them to oppose the application of the laws of occupation. The US advisers were apprehensive as to the potential obligations which the law might impose.[35] In

30. Briefing HQ Australian Forces Somalia, 6 February 1993.

31. Lorenz, op. cit. n. 17, at pp. 7-8.

32. Ibid., at p. 5.

33. Ibid., at p. 4. See also M. Martins, 'Rules of Engagement for Land Forces: A Matter of Training, Not Lawyering', 143 *Military LR* (1994) at p. 130.

34. P. Cheney, 'Canada... Canada', *The Sunday Star* (Toronto, 10 July 1994) Section F. Report of the Board of Inquiry: Canadian Airborne Regiment Battle Group, Phase I, Volumes XI and XII, National Defence Headquarters, 31 August 1993. Commission of Inquiry into the Deployment of Canadian Forces to Somalia, 1997.

35. 'Although we would not seek to enter as an occupying force, recent experience in Iraq demonstrates that if we establish control over an area with no government infrastructure, we may be held to occupation force standards. Under international law, an occupying force is responsible for the public welfare, to include safety, sanitation and a whole host of other requirements. We have to make every effort to limit our responsibility in these areas, to ensure that we act within our capabilities, and be certain that the primary mission is still accomplished.' Memorandum from UNITAF SJA to Commanding General, 'JTF Legal Issues and Legal Office Staffing', 1 December 1992, UNITAF, SJA AAR, TAB A (1). Interview with Colonel Lorenz, *supra* n. 13. This modified initial US legal opinions as indicated by a document dealing with 'Special Command Responsibilities and Obligations Concerning the Somali Population.' Dated 18 December 1992 and faxed to Australia

particular, they were concerned that occupation of a part of Somalia meant accepting obligations for all of the country under the law and that the law would require them to remain in Somalia until order was restored.[36]

---

for the guidance of the Australian contingent on 21 December 1992. This was an annex to a general guidance and directive document to be provided to commanders at relevant levels in UNITAF. It stated that the operation would:

'... impose special responsibilities on commanders concerning legal actions and *legal responsibilities* toward the Somali population in areas under the commander's control. Commanders should ensure their level of legal and civil affairs staffing is sufficient in light of these special and unique considerations.

2. Command Responsibilities:

A. *Safety and Security of the local population*. In the area under his control, a commander must protect the population not only from attack by military units, but also from crimes, riots, and other forms of civil disobedience. To this end, commanders will:

(1) Demand and enforce such obedience as may be necessary for the security of his forces and the maintenance of law and order.

(2) Where necessary, establish rules of law necessary to fulfil this obligation.

(3) Detain those accused of criminal acts or other violations of public safety and security.

(a) Such detention shall include reasonable due process for the detainee under the circumstances.

(b) Persons so detained will not be detained or incarcerated together with persons entitled to Prisoner of War (POW) status.

(c) The period of detention will continue until the accused person, along with available evidence of his crime, can be turned over to authorities of a follow-on peacekeeping organization or a properly constituted local government.

B. *Hygiene and Public Health.* To the fullest extent possible, the commander has the duty of ensuring and maintaining, with the cooperation of international, national, and local authorities, medical services and public health and hygiene in the area under his control.

(a) In particular, commanders must apply those prophylactic and preventative measures necessary to combat the spread of contagious diseases and epidemics among those refugee populations that can be expected to gather in secure areas.

(b) The absence or ineffectiveness of international, national, or local medical or health organisations does not relieve the commander of this responsibility.

C. *Food and Medical Supplies.* It is the specific purpose of (the Operation) to provide and allow the passage of food, medical supplies, and other necessities of life to the Somali population. In those areas under the commander's control, it is his responsibility to ensure that required goods are in fact provided to the fullest extent of his ability. Ideally, this function will be fulfilled in cooperation with International Relief Organizations, but failures on the part of those organizations do not relieve the commander of this responsibility.'

Clearly later policy deliberations resulted in the dramatic scaling back of this directive, although no official modification was passed on to the contingent commanders. This document was in effect an acknowledgment of the applicability of the laws of occupation as 'legal responsibilities'.

36. The deployment of UNITAF into the southern areas of Somalia only was a point of some controversy. The mandate in UNSCR 794 clearly authorised the intervening force to deploy and exert authority throughout Somalia. The worst affected famine areas and fighting were occurring in the south, however, which is where the relief agencies were experiencing the most difficulty. As the mission was, in the eyes of the US Administration and in terms of the specific UNITAF mandate, about enabling the relief agencies to do their job, this limited deployment would be justified by that criteria. As noted, UNSCR 794 did refer to much broader issues such as the restoration of 'peace, stability and law and order with a view to facilitating the process of a political settlement under the auspices of the United Nations, aimed at national reconciliation in Somalia', as well as the prevention of breaches of international humanitarian law. These objectives would certainly have been facilitated by a nationwide deployment by UNITAF, it being infinitely more capable of doing so than UNOSOM II ever was. See United Nations Department of Public Information Reference Paper, *The United Nations and the Situation in Somalia* (April 1995) pp. 7-9. J.R. Bolton, 'Wrong Turn in Somalia', 73 *Foreign Affairs* (January/February 1994) pp. 59-61.

Had a different approach been adopted during the UNITAF phase to play a more constructive role in Somalia, it is asserted that much could have been achieved and confusion in critical areas avoided. With the correct approach to the crisis and armed with the provisions of the law of occupation, issues of disarmament; relief and reconstruction management; the maintenance of order; police and judiciary revival; the exercise of necessary functions of the sovereign; the facilitating of political participation; and marginalisation of the warlords could all have been addressed with a much greater probability of success. This would have circumvented the delicate political issue debated at various stages as to whether Somalia should become a 'Trusteeship' as a means of providing the framework for more interventionary reconstruction. To gauge the merits of an alternative approach to the overall UNITAF policy, the Australian experience will now be examined.

2.2 The Australian force in Somalia

The legal assessment made by the Australian contingent was that the presence of UNITAF forces in southern Somalia was governed by the laws of occupation. An examination of the mission and the provisions of these laws revealed that they could, in effect, serve an extremely useful purpose and provide the force with the guidelines it needed in the approach to be taken to securing the environment. At the same time they could assist in achieving longer term reconstruction objectives. Although the laws of occupation require that the force attempt to restore and maintain public order, the Battalion commander regarded this as both implicit in the mission and desirable in any event.[37]

The most important factor in arriving at this assessment was that there was no government in Somalia. The force deployed under a Security Council mandate but it had not been 'invited' into the country or deployed pursuant to a treaty or agreement with the 'host' state.[38] Both UNITAF as a whole and the individual national contingents had occupied a clearly distinguishable area and discrete areas of responsibility. In the case of the Australian Battalion Group, the Humanitarian Relief Sector (HRS) boundaries were clearly defined by HQ UNITAF, as noted above, relating roughly to the old provincial boundaries. Within this assigned territory and the UNITAF Area of Operations as a whole, there was no question that there was any other force able or prepared to challenge the authority of UNITAF or to exert authority themselves, even in the absence of UNITAF. The

---

37. Conference between LtCol Hurley and author, Battalion Headquarters Baidoa, 13 February 1993. He was later to say:
'A facet of command relationship that I had never experienced before existed in the personal authority given to the HRS commander. In the absence of any form of civil government at any level and the failure of the UN to provide resident local UN political officers, HRS commanders became military governors.' D.J. Hurley, 'Operation Solace', *Australian Defence Force Journal* (January/February 1994) No. 104, p. 31.

38. These points are relevant to assessing what if any aspects of the law of occupation applied to the deployment. The principal issue in this respect is whether the deployment is with or without the consent of the sovereign.

force was capable of exercising control and in fact staked out clear areas of authority that are traditionally exercised by the sovereign. It appears that this could readily be described as the partial occupation of the territory of one High Contracting Party by another[39] within the meaning of Article 2 of the Fourth Geneva Convention. There was no widespread disorder or rebellion that cast any doubt over Australian or UNITAF control or authority, an authority that was accepted by the vast majority of inhabitants of the occupied area. In fact, through their elders and by their clearly demonstrated reaction to the force, the people of the Bay region not only welcomed the intervention but repeatedly petitioned the Australian contingent and UNOSOM to have the troops remain.[40]

2.2.1 *The Auxiliary Security Force (ASF)*

From the beginning, the re-establishment of a police force in the area was a high priority of the Australians and detailed intentions in this respect were communicated to HQ UNITAF on 8 February 1993.[41] Working towards this objective was implied in the mission to establish a secure environment for humanitarian relief operations and was part of efforts to meet the Hague Regulations obligation to restore law and order. Apart from previous service in the police force, the criteria for selecting the ASF were based on: no past commission of crimes against the Somali people; no physical handicaps; and having served at least two years in the police force before the outbreak of the civil war. Prior to raising the force, a meeting was held with the community leaders on 18 February 1993 to advise them of the plan and elicit their support and input. The position of the commander of the ASF was obviously crucial and a person was nominated by the Australian Battalion Commander, LtCol Hurley who proved acceptable to all parties.[42] The ASF commenced operation in Baidoa on 15 February 1993 with an initial force of 20 personnel.[43] Eventually, 260 ASF were recruited and distributed throughout the Bay region.[44] Initially, the ASF was remunerated on a food for work basis with the assistance of the World Food Program (WFP) and the ICRC.[45] Later, they were paid intermittently in Somali shillings by UNOSOM. Copies of the old police regu-

---

39. Somalia had ratified the Conventions in 1969. All contingents of UNITAF were from states which had ratified the Fourth Geneva Convention.

40. The Somali Democratic Movement (SDM) representatives and the elders of the Bay Region presented a petition to Admiral Howe when the SRSG visited Baidoa on 11 April 1993, requesting that the Australians be retained in the area beyond the scheduled departure date of 20 May 1993. (Observations of the author at the conference held in Baidoa courthouse with Admiral Howe and the Bay leadership on 11 April 1993.)

41. Maj. R.H. Stanhope, Minute to LtCol. J.M. Smith, Army Force (ARFOR) SJA, 8 February 1993. (In possession of author.)

42. 1st Battalion RAR Group Post Operation Report (1 RAR POR), 31 May 1993, Enclosure 4, p. 6.

43. Maj. R.H. Stanhope (OC CMOT), Minute to ARFOR SJA, 8 February 1993.

44. Capt. S. Bagnall, Australian Liaison Officer, Minute to Provost Marshall's Office, 16 April 1993.

45. P. Vercammen, *Auxiliary Security Force in Baidoa.* Report to UNOSOM, 10 April 1993.

lations and police handbooks were obtained and distributed as it had been a long time since the police had worked or trained and they were in need of refreshing.[46]

2.2.2 *Police cells and prisons*

The Australian contingent was also responsible for the supervision of the police cells and prisons. This was a humanitarian responsibility which rested with the force but was in effect shared with the ICRC. The ICRC provided food for the prisoners and also for the ASF and prison guards in a food for work arrangement, while the contingent refurbished the cells and prison to bring them up to an acceptable humanitarian level. The contingent also had a responsibility to monitor the treatment of prisoners and the security of the prison.

The prison itself was solidly built but not many of the cells were in a condition to be used so that initially there were a number of inmates per cell. Although this was better than the circumstances of many of their compatriots on the outside, who were living in stick or plastic shelters, it was still a cause of concern. Overcrowding would clearly become a major problem without some form of judiciary and trial process to deal with these persons. Early in the deployment, no resources were being provided by UNOSOM to assist in this rebuilding program so the Australian contingent applied what resources were available and commenced work without waiting. The engineers deployed all over the Baidoa HRS, restoring prisons, police cells and courts.

2.2.3 *The judiciary*

The next key aspect of the reconstruction process involved the judiciary. This posed unique problems, however: who had survived from the judiciary; who could be trusted; who had the appropriate qualifications; would they be prepared to sit in judgement on key bandit and warlord figures; how would they be received by a community which had become used to anarchy? The reliability of the judges and their qualifications was an important point, as in the later years of the Barre regime judges had been appointed who had no legal training but who were persons upon whom Barre could rely. The fact that someone had been a judge was therefore insufficient by itself for them to be accepted for service by the force.

The Australian contingent's legal officer had been working with the Americans on this issue and attended meetings held by the Staff Judge Advocate Colonel Lorenz at HQ UNITAF with the group of jurists from south Mogadishu. The key figure in that group was a Dr Abdullahi Ossable Barre, a former professor at the University of Mogadishu and Judge of the Supreme Court. He was very familiar with the judiciary personnel of Somalia. At one meeting with Dr Ossable and former Ministry of Justice official Mr Dali Warsame Mohamed on 22 February 1993, a list was obtained of former court workers and judges from the Bay region

46. These materials were supplied by the UNITAF Provost Marshall, LtCol. Spataro, in English. Also included were extracts of the Criminal Procedure Code.

down to the administrative assistants with details of specific appointments and structures. Dr Ossable was able to advise which of these people were still alive. This list was sent down to the CMOT in Baidoa, who proceeded to track the individuals down.

Following the meeting at HQ UNOSOM between the northern and southern Mogadishu Somali jurists on 3 March 1993, an eight-person Technical Committee was formed to determine the process of reestablishing a court hierarchy. Elected to a key position on this committee was Dr Ossable. At the meeting, Dr Ossable had maintained that the laws created by the Barre regime should be considered a nullity and that the courts could proceed on the basis of the old criminal code as it had existed in the period of democracy prior to Barre. This position was supported by attendees at the meeting and the Steering Committee.[47] These were significant developments but, inexplicably, UNOSOM declined to have a representative at the meeting, was very reluctant to allow the use of UNOSOM HQ for the meeting, and did not encourage or participate in the process subsequently. Nor was there a representative present from the UNITAF contingents other than the HQ UNITAF SJA office and the Australian legal officer.

Taking advantage of the situation created by the meeting, the Australians met with Dr Ossable and other members of the Steering Committee. From this meeting, agreement was obtained that Dr Ossable and another former judge from Mogadishu, Mr Mohamed Mohamed Isgow, would travel down to Baidoa as representatives of the Steering Committee to meet with the surviving judges that had been located. The meeting took place on 6 March 1993 and included the Australian Commanding Officer, the Officer Commanding the CMOT, the legal officer and the UNOSOM political representative at the political representative's residence in Baidoa. At this meeting it was determined: (a) who was to be nominated to positions in the various courts; and (b) that the old Somali penal code, as it existed in 1962, would be applied, without the political crimes created by the Barre regime.

It was not problematic to disregard the political crimes created by the Barre regime as these had been imposed via separate legislation, special courts and security police distinct from the civil police and courts.[48] Barre's introduction of these laws was considered by the surviving Somali legal authorities represented by the Steering Committee to be unconstitutional in any event, and the agreement with the reconstituted judiciary to ignore them was based on that presumption which they themselves had highlighted.[49] These authorities asserted that the Barre laws could not be considered as part of the local law which either Somalis or the interventionary force were obliged to respect. As a result of the meeting, the courts were delineated in terms of personnel and structure for the Bay region based on the

47. Observations of the author, who attended the meeting, later confirmed by Dr Ossable and Mr Mohamed Mohamed Isgow of the committee at a meeting in Baidoa on 6 March 1993.

48. M. Ganzglass, 'Evaluation of the Judicial, Legal, and Penal Systems of Somalia', Report to the Special Representative of the UN Secretary-General (SRSG) UNOSOM II, 22 April 1993, pp. 4-5, 35.

49. Discussions between author and Baidoa judiciary as well as Dr Ossable and other members of the Mogadishu Steering Committee.

pre-civil war model. This structure was as follows: Maxamada Degmada – District Courts for each of the main towns; Maxamada Gobolka – Regional Court located in Baidoa for the Bay region; and Maxamada Rafkaanka – Court of Appeal located in Baidoa for the Bay region.

Jurisdiction between the District Courts and Regional Court was distinguished by the seriousness of the crime, in that District Courts could only hear matters which carried a maximum sentence of under three years in prison. Five District courts were to be established initially in the major towns of Dinsoor, Qansaxdhere, Berdaale, Buurhakaba and Baidoa. As there was no Somali Supreme Court functioning, and there was no likelihood of it being re-established in the near future, it was agreed between the Steering Committee and the local judges, with the contingent's concurrence, that the regional curial system would have to be autonomous for the interim and that the Regional Court of Appeal would be the final appeal court for the Bay region until further notice. The next step was to get the courts working as soon as possible. A building was therefore identified at the police compound which could be refurbished for use as a court. Co-location at the police compound had the added attraction of easing the burden on the contingent's assets in terms of providing security.[50] In the interim, some tents were set up at the back of the police compound for the judges to commence working from.[51] While ideally such facilities ought to be separated to preserve the image of impartiality, the security situation did not permit this, and moreover the old court buildings were too badly damaged to be used.

For most of the deployment, an infantry section was based at the police station to man an observation post and to provide security. With this umbrella, the courts commenced work within a few days of the meeting, despite early teething problems. The engineers refurbished the court building utilising their own materials and materials that were obtained through UNOSOM from Kenya. By the time the contingent departed, the Court House was fully functional. By the end of the Australian deployment, the judiciary was functioning well and was independent of the contingent or UNOSOM. The courts were not only able to deal with criminal matters but also family and civil disputes and continued to do so after the forces left.[52]

2.2.4 *Criminal Investigation Division (CID)*

In the later stages of the deployment, further enhancement of the police effectiveness occurred with the establishment of the CID. The ordinary police or ASF were

---

50. In the longer term it was envisaged that the courts would be able to move away from the police compound to emphasise the concept of separation between the police and judiciary. This had, in fact, been the case prior to the civil war.

51. The first case was heard on 19 March 1993 and dealt with a car thief who was given five years imprisonment. (Field notes by author.)

52. P. Vercammen, Report to UNOSOM, 24 March 1993. Personal observations of author and discussions with local Somalis while based at Police Compound. Interview with Superintendent Bill Kirk, Canberra, 15 August 1995.

not trained for or capable of careful investigations of major crimes or gathering reliable criminal intelligence. There had been a CID prior to the civil war which was assigned this role. There was, however, a reluctance to approve the reestablishment of the CID within the Police Committee in Mogadishu. It will be recalled that this committee was constituted from political nominations by the warlords of the two main armed factions in Mogadishu and only some former Somali police officials.[53] The hostility of the Committee appeared to be based on a jealousy of the progress of Baidoa and the hostility of the Mogadishu factions to the Rahanweyn. The Committee asserted that they did not want Baidoa to get too far ahead of the country in that no other area had managed to establish a CID unit. Given the uncertain future of the Mogadishu-based Police Committee and its questionable legitimacy, it was determined that this opposition should be ignored and the force pressed ahead with its plans.

The re-establishment of the CID was to some extent incidental. Former CID personnel had been encountered in the course of conducting investigations into key bandits in the area. As the investigations proceeded, these people were asked to render assistance, and in this way their loyalty and effectiveness could be evaluated. As confidence in them grew, they were requested to seek out additional reliable and capable CID survivors who were also tested and carefully observed in the same process. From an initial group of five, a formal sub-unit of the police was eventually created of 20 hand-picked personnel.

The CID were provided with initial direction from, and assigned specific investigations by, the Australians in the areas and matters with which the force was primarily concerned. They were tasked, in the first instance, with investigating major crimes, such as murder, rape and organised crime; corruption monitoring; and monitoring major crime figures held in the cells and prison to ensure they were securely held and that their cases were ready for trial. They were then tasked to support the prosecutor in the actual conduct of trials, in marshalling witnesses and safeguarding evidence. Finally they were to provide security-related information to UNITAF.

2.2.5 *Prosecutions*

As mentioned earlier in discussing the re-establishment of the judiciary, one of the key elements in the negotiations was the acceptance that the system would continue to operate on the basis of the 1962 Somali Penal Code. Somali criminal law was based on the Italian penal code of 1931 known as the 'Rocco Code' after Professor Arturo Rocco, who chaired the Italian commission which drafted it. The Somali version also included some elements of Islamic law and Somali custom. The Somali Criminal Procedure Code of 1963 was based upon an amalgamation of the pre-independence Italian Criminal Procedure Code of 1935, the British

53. M. Ganzglass, 'The Restoration of the Somali Justice System', in W. Clarke and J. Herbst, eds., *Learning From Somalia: The Lessons of Armed Humanitarian Intervention* (Boulder CO, Westview Press 1997) pp. 24-25.

Criminal Procedure Ordinance of 1956, and the Indian Evidence Act of 1872, which in turn is derived mostly from British criminal procedure. This reflected the amalgamation of the British and Italian colonial territories. The civil laws were based on Egyptian civil law.

It had been a priority of the Battalion to identify major bandit elements and war criminals within Baidoa and to try to eliminate them from the local scene by either having them dealt with in Mogadishu or processed through the local courts once these were firmly reestablished. In the course of justifying the detention of certain individuals, investigations were necessary to support accusations and enable the detainees to go to trial. The most significant initial detention that was made was of the bandit Hussein Barre Warsame, whom the Australian CI team had identified as having been responsible for serious crimes against international humanitarian law during the civil war and who remained a significant intimidating factor in Baidoa.

In the course of the Warsame investigation, given the time limitations, it was determined to proceed with charges based on 30 murders which had been committed personally by Warsame. Other evidence concerning Warsame's crimes indicated the terrible nature and extent of the threat he represented for the community.[54] Warsame was the chief weapon in the regime of intimidation and terror established by the overall warlord of the area, Hassan Gutaale Abdul (Gutaale).

Warsame was arrested on 13 March 1993. Just as the investigation was concluded, however, it was found that Warsame had escaped custody. It became apparent that Gutaale had travelled to Mogadishu and was able to obtain Warsame's release by means of a loyal Aideed judge, who certified on 20 March 1993 that there was no evidence against Warsame, that he was in poor health and

54. Two men were walking towards Warsame's house … Warsame called out to the two people to stop walking past his house and that they were to change over to the other side of the street. The two people said to Ganey (Warsame's nickname), 'This is our country and we are Baidoa citizens, and you come from far away. How can you order us?' After they said this, Ganey said, 'I chased Siad Barre's soldiers away and I can do what I want.' They said to him, 'We don't obey your orders,' and they refused to cross over to the other side of the street. Ganey then stood up where he was and raised the AK 47 rifle up and shot the two men dead. He shot his rifle at the men until he ran out of bullets. He then removed that magazine and replaced it with another.
Some days later, about the same time, I was walking home from the ICRC warehouse, when I had to pass by Warsame's place. I used to go past his place every day. I saw an old man who was carrying one bag of rice and two tins of oil … Warsame was sitting down and he called out to the man with the articles to stop and put his load on the ground. He pointed his rifle at the man. The man put the articles on the ground and Warsame sent one little boy out to pick up the load. The man would not let the little boy take the rice. Warsame then told the little boy to get out of the way. Warsame then stood up and fired his rifle into the man. He fired at his head and then lowered the shots down the man's body. The man fell over dead and Warsame walked over to the man's body and helped the little boy pick up the articles and take them back to his house. I felt terrible to see the mess that the body was in. There was blood everywhere. I left the area straight away.' Extracts from a statement by Mohamed Osman Ahmed, 22 March 1993. These single incidents illustrate the wealth of evidence of random killing that characterised the manner in which the regime of terror was maintained in the Bay region. Evidence also showed that this formed part of a deliberate pattern of attritional extermination through single and mass killings and starvation, which opened up opportunities to resettle SLA clan members in the area.

was entitled to temporary freedom. Warsame's release shattered confidence in the efficacy of the Mogadishu system, and the responsible judge was arrested by UNITAF and held at the UNITAF detention facility. Subsequently, an inquiry was conducted by the Somali Steering Committee. After receiving a response from the Australian contingent, the inquiry accepted that procedural irregularities had occurred and orders were made for the re-arrest of Warsame.[55] However, Warsame had disappeared into his clan area in Mogadishu and was not seen again. From that point on, UNITAF would no longer entrust important detainees to the Mogadishu prison, while the Australian force came to rely solely on the locally reconstructed cells and prisons in Baidoa.[56]

There were a number of positive results from the investigation conducted into Warsame's crimes. The first of these is that the exact extent and nature of the organised banditry network in Baidoa came to light.[57] The other positive factor from the investigations was that Warsame was no longer able to operate in Baidoa and had to remain in hiding in Mogadishu. The material that had been gathered during the course of the investigation was deposited with the Baidoa Chief Prosecutor, so that if Warsame were arrested, prosecution could commence immediately with probative evidence and identified witnesses.

With the revelation of the extent to which people in Baidoa and the Bay area had been dispossessed of their property, including homes and farmland, it was determined that one method of undermining the bandit organisation would be to encourage the dispossessed to commence reclamation action before the reestablished courts, based in many cases on original title deeds still held by them. The dispossessed responded to this encouragement with the first case commencing on 8 April 1993 and soon the courts were making orders for the return of property. The Battalion was prepared to and did provide security backup to enforce these orders where necessary. Combined with the prosecution action, this strategy resulted in the Bay area ceasing to be a source of funds for Aideed and wealth for his local bandit agents, and thereby reducing criminal activity to unremarkable levels.

2.2.5.1 The Gutaale trial

It had also become clear that something had to be done about the key figure in the bandit empire, Gutaale. It was Gutaale that had run the extortion operation of relief flights at the airfield. He had been responsible for the large scale attacks and

55. Report by Steering Committee, 1 April 1993.

56. With the exception of the Gutaale case, as described at section 2.2.5.1 *infra*.

57. An example of the method of property acquisition is provided by an extract from the statement of Ali Tabut Mohamed, 25 March 1993:

'In early April 1992 I was in the Pharmacy when a man I know as Ganey ... came into the shop. He got two persons to tie me up and beat me with a stick. They broke my right small finger and they also broke one of my toes on my left foot. They then took me to the Police Station in central Baidoa when I was again beaten ... There Ganey told me not to ever go back to the Pharmacy as he would shoot me. He took my lock to the door and replaced it with one of his own ... About ten days later I noticed that the Pharmacy was now a Tea Shop and the Tea Shop was run by Ganey's wife.'

looting raids on NGO compounds in which so many had died. It was Gutaale who directed the takeover of property and land and resettlement of Duduble clan elements in the area as the gradual Rahanweyn extermination progressed, bearing all the hall marks of genocide which he was instrumental in promoting.[58] Gutaale took his orders from one of Aideed's trusted subordinates, Colonel Arabee, who paid occasional visits to Baidoa from Mogadishu. Achieving Gutaale's removal could serve a number of purposes. First and foremost, the force considered it was obligated to do something about the evidence of Gutaale's activities. This obligation, it was assessed, stemmed from the Fourth Geneva Convention and Hague Regulations. In addition, it was believed that an obligation may have stemmed from Article 146 of the Fourth Geneva Convention to seek out and prosecute those guilty of committing grave breaches as detailed in Article 147 of the Convention. The assessment was made that common Article 3 to the Geneva Conventions of 1949 applied to the widespread internal conflict in Somalia, and that the crimes alleged of Gutaale amounted to serious breaches in violating the provisions of Article 3.[59] The issue would then have been whether common Article 3 offences constitute grave breaches, in relation to which the view was not certain. Regardless of the answer to that question, it was firmly believed that international jurisdiction pertained to breaches of common Article 3 and crimes against humanity generally.[60] Given the evidence suggesting genocidal activities by Gutaale and his

---

58. The evidence uncovered in the investigations and supported by the observations of the NGOs satisfied the test outlined in Art. 2 of the Convention on the Prevention and Punishment of the Crime of Genocide.

Apart from the killings, Gutaale attempted to use starvation as his key weapon, by raiding NGO warehouses, attacking convoys and a host of other tactics designed to prevent food reaching the Rahanweyn. He also pursued the Marehan/Barre/Morgan method of targeting women and children to choke off the next generation. Certainly a *prima facie* case against Gutaale existed. Given the extent of the deaths (40 percent of the population, including 70 percent of the children) his efforts to deny food, progressively slaughter the survivors, and to colonise the area with his own ethnic group, it could be inferred he intended to destroy the Rahanweyn. In any event the evidence indicated that he directed and participated in the destruction of a large 'part' of the Rahanweyn in the region. In terms of legal responsibility under the Genocide Convention it should be noted that Art. 4 states:

'Persons committing genocide or any of the other acts enumerated in Article 3 shall be punished, whether they are constitutionally responsible rulers, public officials or private individuals.'

59. The SLA, as part of Aideed's SNA forces, were part of the civil war being waged against Ali Mahdi and various other factions. It was, without question, party to the armed conflict which was continuing at the time of the offences. See J.S. Pictet, ed., *The Geneva Conventions of 12 August 1949: Commentary: IV Geneva Convention Relative to the Protection of Civilian Persons in Time of War* (Geneva, ICRC 1958) p. 36. Additional Protocol II did not apply as Somalia had not become a party to the Protocols.

60. See the recent jurisprudence from the International Criminal Tribunal for the Former Yugoslavia (ICTY) emerging from the *Tadić* cases, *Prosecutor* v. *Duško Tadić A/K/A 'Dule'* (Decision on the Defence Motion on Jurisdiction), 10 August 1995, especially paras. 65-74 in reference to common Art. 3 and paras. 75-83 on crimes against humanity. See also International Court of Justice in the *Nicaragua* case (Military and Paramilitary Activities (*Nicaragua* v. *US*)) *ICJ Rep.* (1986) p. 4 (Merits Judgment of 27 June 1986) relating to the customary law status of common Art. 3.

militia, it was felt that the force could also have been open to claims that it bore prevention and punishment obligations under the Genocide Convention.[61]

An implied obligation to facilitate law enforcement action against Gutaale arose from the mandate given the force in UNSCR 794, in that he had been a major threat to the relief effort. It will also be recalled that the Resolution warned that those guilty of violations of international humanitarian law would be held individually responsible, therefore implying a mandate to take action to give effect to this warning. This became a specific obligation with the introduction of UNSCR 814. As indicated above, with the Australian force committed to become part of UNOSOM, the objectives set out in that Resolution applied to the contingent. The Resolution noted:

> ... with deep regret and concern at the continuing reports of widespread violations of international humanitarian law and the general absence of the rule of law in Somalia... Convinced that the restoration of law and order throughout Somalia would contribute to humanitarian relief operations, reconciliation and political settlement, as well as to the rehabilitation of Somalia's political institutions and economy.

and therefore tasked UNOSOM:

> To assist in the re-establishment of Somali police, as appropriate at the local, regional or national level, to assist in the restoration and maintenance of peace, stability and law and order, *including in the investigation and facilitating the prosecution of serious violations of international humanitarian law.*

The legal position then, with respect to mandate and obligations, seemed clear. On the one hand, action could be taken against those posing a serious threat to law and order under law of occupation provisions and the Security Council Resolutions. On the other hand action was authorised in relation to those crimes which violated international humanitarian law. Gutaale's crimes may have fitted both categories as it could be argued that they had taken place in the context of a Geneva Convention common Article 3 conflict and also appeared to be part of a genocidal campaign against the Rahanweyn.

If a trial could be successfully mounted, it could provide the vehicle for enabling the courts and investigation system to deal with serious crimes and major figures while at the same time promoting the courts in the eyes of the community. It was strongly felt that if Gutaale was removed from the scene, it might hasten the downfall of the bandit organisation and reverse the colonisation of the area by his clan. A warning could also be transmitted to all the warlords of Somalia regarding their accountability.

---

61. Convention on the Prevention and Punishment of the Crime of Genocide, 9 December 1948, 78 *UNTS* 1948 p. 277. Art. 1 of the Genocide Convention states:
'The Contracting Parties confirm that genocide, whether committed in time of peace or in time of war, is a crime under international law which they undertake to prevent and to punish.' See also P. Hakewill, 'Murderous Complacency', *The Australian* (6 April 1995) p. 15.

It was therefore decided that Gutaale should be targeted for investigation to determine if it would be possible to put him on trial in the limited time remaining to the contingent in Baidoa. Gutaale was arrested on 29 March 1993 and he was then processed back to the UNITAF detention facility.

It was determined from the evidence gathered that two major incidents would form the basis of the prosecution. The first concerned the massacre of 15 bush people in Baidoa at around 0700 hours on 20 August 1992, by use of a Fiat APC driven by Gutaale with which he intentionally ran over a group of displaced persons in the centre of the town. Of the 15 dead, eight were women and seven children. The incident occurred in front of a large number of townsfolk who recalled in graphic detail the result.[62] The second incident involved an attack led by Gutaale on the Red Cross compound on or about 5 August 1992, in which 16 Somali Red Cross workers were killed. Altogether therefore, charges were framed involving 31 counts of murder with additional counts of robbery.

The trial commenced on 24 April before the Maxamada Gobolka (Regional Court) sitting in Baidoa. Eleven eye witnesses gave testimony as to Gutaale's involvement in the murders and identified him in court. After an initial trial and appeal, the sentence of death was imposed on Gutaale. It was determined that no extenuating circumstances had been made out under Article 39 of the penal code but that aggravating circumstances did exist, as indicated under Article 40 of the Somali penal code, and so there were no grounds upon which to mitigate the sentence.[63] The President of the Court of Appeal, in exercising his final review function, raised no objection to the conduct of the proceedings, which he had monitored closely, and rejected the final plea for pardon or commutation.

Regarding the legitimacy of the tribunals, the Somali argument that they preserved a continuing validity pre-dating the civil war, there having been no intervening act of a sovereign government to affect their operation, was concurred with by the Australians.[64] It was felt that they also derived authority

---

62. 'The APC drove down the market street very fast. People had to get out of its way or it would have run them over. The APC went past me, it then turned around up the street further and came back down the street at high speed. The APC then ran straight at a large group of people standing at the side of the road. I had to jump out of the way as I would have been run over. I looked and saw the APC run over a lot of people. They were bush people from the refugee camps. The APC then stopped a short distance away and then reversed back over all the people it had run over. There were dead people everywhere.
The APC then drove forward again and roared off up the road. The people on the APC were all laughing at this. I went over to help the people who had been run over. No one on the ground lived, they all died. I along with a lot of the commercial people (shop keepers), helped pick up the dead people. Altogether there were seven children killed and eight women. The bodies were all crushed, some had their heads run over, there was blood everywhere. We loaded all the dead people onto two trucks that came from the Red Cross.' Extract from the statement by Hassan Isaak Ali of 5 April 1993. All the witnesses were able to identify the driver as Gutaale.

63. Under Arts. 228-229 of the Somali Criminal Procedure Code, the higher courts have discretion to raise or lower sentences in cases taken on appeal. A. Wekerele, *Somalia: A Country Law Study* (Washington DC, Library of Congress 1990) p. 11.

64. Affirmed in discussions with representatives of the Baidoa Judiciary and the Mogadishu Steering Committee on 6 March 1993 in Baidoa.

from the contingent's sanction, in accordance with the obligations and rights delineated by the laws of occupation relating to the restoration and maintenance of order and the Security Council Resolutions. The trials were assessed by the contingent as having been conducted in accordance with the standards prescribed by the laws of occupation. The execution was then duly carried out by the ASF, in accordance with the specifications of Article 94 of the Code, by firing squad in the regional prison.[65] There was no intervention in the death sentence as it was felt it could not be asserted that the punishment was clearly disproportionate to the crime, within the terms of Article 67 of the Fourth Geneva Convention. It was also felt that the sentence adhered to other general principles of sentencing such as communal defence, given the fact that Gutaale would almost certainly have been freed from the regional prison by his force at some stage and resumed his activities with the added threat of revenge attacks. It was also considered to be consistent with the Security Council mandates to facilitate prosecutions and secure the environment for humanitarian relief, given that Gutaale had been a major threat in this respect. In accordance with the UN's Economic and Social Council (ECOSOC) rules on the death penalty, the execution was carried out with the minimum possible suffering.[66] All aspects of this process had been discussed in consultation

---

65. Art. 94 *Punishment of Death*:
'The punishment of death shall be carried out by shooting inside a penitentiary, or any other place prescribed by the Minister of Grace and Justice.' M.R. Ganzglass, *The Penal Code of the Somali Democratic Republic* (New Brunswick NJ, Rutgers University Press 1971) p. 112.

66. *Safeguards Guaranteeing Protection of the Rights of Those Facing the Death Penalty*, Economic and Social Council Resolution 1984/50, adopted 25 May 1984.
'In countries which have not abolished the death penalty, capital punishment may be imposed only for the most serious crimes, intentionally committed with lethal or extremely grave consequences.
Capital punishment may be imposed only for a crime for which the death penalty is prescribed by law at the time of its commission.
Persons below 18 years of age, pregnant women, new mothers or persons who have become insane shall not be sentenced to death.
Capital punishment may be imposed only when guilt is determined by clear and convincing evidence leaving no room for an alternative explanation of the facts.
Capital punishment may be carried out only after a final judgement rendered by a competent court allowing all possible safeguards to the defendant, including adequate legal assistance.
Anyone sentenced to death shall have the right of appeal to a court of higher jurisdiction.
Anyone sentenced to death shall have the right to seek pardon or commutation of sentence.
Capital punishment shall not be carried out pending any appeal, recourse procedure or proceeding relating to pardon or commutation of the sentence.
Where capital punishment occurs, it shall be carried out so as to inflict the minimum possible suffering.'
These rules have no binding force, particularly if it is accepted in the case of Somalia that the laws of occupation applied. It was nevertheless felt that their spirit should be observed as closely as possible. While there is no definition of 'minimum possible suffering' accompanying the rules, Gutaale's death was instantaneous, as confirmed by medical examination, and was certainly not accompanied by any mistreatment or prolongation. Given that there was no further possibility for appeal the ECOSOC rule could not be complied with in this respect, although the President of the Court of Appeal filled the role of final reviewer and dealt with petitions for pardon and commutation. As far as the laws of occupation were concerned, the Australians also felt that Arts. 68, 70 and 75 of the Fourth Geneva Convention,

with the UNITAF SJA, UNOSOM officials and an expert on Somali criminal law.

2.2.5.2 The consequences of the trial and the strategy

The effects of the trial were immediate and dramatic. Gutaale's clan, which were of the Duduble from Mogadishu, began to leave Baidoa immediately. His force also disintegrated and fled the next day. Confidence within the community began to rise visibly and within days gold could be seen on sale in the markets again. It was clear that the removal of this single individual was a major factor in re-establishing a satisfactory level of law and order within the Bay region. In addition, during the course of the investigations, other action was being taken against key figures in the bandit chain of command, so that by the conclusion of Gutaale's trial, of the top six, all were either in prison awaiting trial (three), had fled to Mogadishu (two), or, in Gutaale's case, dead.

The trial had been monitored closely by UNITAF and UNOSOM and the results were officially approved and received with much approbation.[67] As a consequence, requests were then received from Admiral Howe, the UN Secretary General's Special Representative in Somalia, for Australian assistance in facilitating the prosecution of other notable bandits, particularly in the Kismayo area.[68] This was not possible, in view of other important force administration tasks still to be performed in the short time remaining before re-deployment of the contingent back to Australia. A plan was provided by the Australians, however, for an investigation and justice reconstruction advisory team. This team could have provided a capability for intervention at key points of weakness in the reconstruction process and assisted in the resolution of significant and serious crimes, particularly those involving major international humanitarian/human rights law violators and criminals who constituted a threat to reconstruction and the security of UNOSOM.[69]

The Australians became involved in consultations concerning a plan for the reconstruction of the justice administration within Somalia. The overall concept that was developed was to build regional arrangements based on the Baidoa model.[70] UNOSOM would provide the central administration and responsibility

---

which would have been pertinent to the matter were the trial conducted by the Contingent, had been complied with.

67. 'Because UN officials and the Somalis seeking peace are so eager for the system to work, the outcome of the Gutalli [sic] case was hailed as a triumph of justice', C. Wilke, 'Law and Order Somali Style – Ravaged by War and Famine, Somalia Strives to turn Chaos into Civilization by Re-establishing the Rule of Law', *Boston Globe Sunday Magazine* (27 June 1993). J. Schofield, 'Australians Help Convict Somali Bandit of Murder', *The Age* (4 May 1993) p. 11.

68. Memorandum, SRSG Admiral Howe to LTG Bir UNOSOM Forces Commander, 7 May 1993.

69. Minute to HQ UNOSOM, from HQ AFS, 18 May 1993.

70. M. Ganzglass, 'Evaluation of the Judicial, Legal and Penal Systems of Somalia: Report to the Special representative of the UN Secretary General UNOSOM II, 22 April 1993', pp. 18-21, 28, 31, 33, 37. Mr Ganzglass and Ms Wright travelled throughout Somalia, making a full evaluation of the justice

for the national operation, including in the breakaway northern Somaliland. The plan that was produced specified the appointment of 152 administrative personnel operating on a budget of US$ 41m.[71] At a meeting on 16 May 1993 at HQ UNOSOM, the SRSG presented the plan to then-Under-Secretary General for Peace Keeping, Kofi Annan.[72] Unfortunately, the later deterioration of the situation in Mogadishu and an initial lack of support at UN HQ in New York prevented the full and timely implementation of this plan.

Notwithstanding that the justice reconstruction plan was never effectively put into full operation, some steps were taken to build on the Australian experience and efforts. A Police Training Academy was established in Baidoa to capitalise on the ASF and CID progress there. After the departure of UNOSOM, the Baidoa and Bay region continued to progress well, with outside help supplied by the European Community and the Life and Peace Institute among others, up to September 1995.[73] The governing council of the Bay Region continued to function, with key issues such as ways of funding the police and judiciary salaries being dealt with.[74] There was no evidence of any attempts to subvert the legal regime re-established by the contingent.[75] This came to an end on 16 September 1995 when Aideed, with 600 men and 30 'technicals', sallied out from Mogadishu and overran Baidoa and other areas in the Bay and adjacent regions.[76]

---

situation. Mr Ganzglass was later to sum up his impressions of Baidoa as follows:
'I visited Baidoa as a State Department consultant in UNOSOM's effort to rebuild the Somali police and judiciary and am familiar with the Australian efforts ... With the consent of local leaders they rebuilt the courts and police stations, and established a rule of law. One judge I met, who remembered me as his teacher in a course on the Somali penal code, was now teaching police the rudiments of the penal code. When the Australians left in May 1993, the entire Bay Region was peaceful ... In all the zones controlled by the Marines and the US army, there were no organised programs to work with local councils and rebuild courts and police stations or to train and equip the police. The US regarded such efforts as 'mission creep'. The Australians regarded it as essential to their mission to restore security to the area ... Haiti today is a good example of what we should have done in Somalia – recruit and train a police force and restore the judicial system. The pity is that the successful Australian effort was not implemented throughout the operational area and expanded to the north and northeast.' 8 *World View* (Spring 1995) p. 3.

71. A. Wright (Police, Judicial & Prison Policy Advisor to SRSG), 'Task Force on Police, Judicial and Prison Issues', Memorandum detailing strategy, 20 April 1993. Also Budgetary Details document provided to author.

72. Meeting held at HQ UNOSOM, 16 May 1993.

73. Discussions between the author and immigrant and refugee Somalis in Washington D.C. in January 1995, whose family members in Somalia had advised them of their moves.

74. Telephone report received from Mr Alexandros Yannis of the European Community (Somalia Operations) Nairobi HQ, 7 September 1995.

75. ABC journalist Mr James Schofield, letter to Maj. M.J. Kelly, dated 9 June 1995. Discussions with Somalis from Baidoa attending the UN Plainsboro Lessons Learned Conference on Somalia, 13-15 September 1995. See also details of general situation laid out in the comprehensive Life and Peace Report *Local Administrative Structures in Somalia: A Case Study of the Bay Region*, of June 1995.

76. Reuters reports of 17 and 19 September 1995. See also ongoing and archived reports of the situation in Baidoa and Somalia in general maintained by Mr Michael Marin on the 'Nomad Net' World Wide Web site.

2.3 Conclusion

This examination of the Australian contingent's experience in Somalia has shown that the approach that this contingent took to the public security function was based on the assessment that the laws of occupation applied *de jure* to their circumstances. From this body of laws were drawn guidelines, standards and many answers to the difficult issues that emerge from the public security problems in an armed intervention into a collapsed state. These issues included detention action; due process as a consequence of detention; applicable criminal laws and procedures; the relationship with the civil community; the handling of major violators of international humanitarian law and criminals posing a threat to the delivery of humanitarian relief; and the reconstruction of the local justice administration. Many questions are posed by this approach, including, was the assessment that the laws of occupation applied correct; if so, how would they apply in the context of a coalition operation; how far do the rights of the occupying power extend; what is the exact nature and scope of the obligations of the occupying power; and to what extent can an occupying power intervene in the measures taken by a local community in its approach to justice in the context of a collapsed state.

3. EAST TIMOR

3.1 Introduction

Between 20 September 1999 and 21 February 2000, a multinational force under unified command, with Australia as the lead nation, deployed to East Timor under the authority of the United Nations Security Council.[77] The deployment of the multinational force, known as the International Force for East Timor (INTERFET), was prompted by an humanitarian crisis in East Timor resulting from a collapse of law and order. INTERFET was replaced on 23 February 2000 with a peacekeeping force under UN command, which formed part of the UN Transitional Authority in East Timor (UNTAET).

Numerous actors had a role in creating the framework for the operation, including, the *de facto* 'host nation' Indonesia, the former colonial power Portugal, the United Nations itself, Australia as lead nation and all those nations actually or potentially contributing to the multinational force. It is noteworthy that there was no regional alliance equivalent to NATO to provide cohesion amongst troop contributing nations. Consequently, *ad hoc* arrangements regarding command and control and other key issues were required. The overarching operational framework for the deployment was under determination at a time when the situation on the ground was both in crisis and constantly changing.

---

77. UN Security Council Resolution 1264, UN Doc. S/RES/1264 (15 September 1999).

3.2 The context for INTERFET's deployment

3.2.1 *Pre-ballot*

The island of Timor, of which East Timor forms a part, has a history dominated by colonial occupation. The Portuguese first colonized it in 1520. Thereafter, the Spanish, Dutch and the British subjected it to successive colonization attempts. However, treaties in 1860 and 1893 affirmed Portuguese sovereignty over East Timor.

Japanese troops occupied Timor during the Second World War, but after the cessation of hostilities East Timor reverted to Portuguese possession. However, in 1975 Portugal flagged its intention to withdraw from East Timor. Subsequent internal and external negotiations concerning the future of East Timor accompanied a decline into civil war, with two main groups emerging. One group, *Uniao Democratica Tomorense*, favored some form of continued association with Portugal, whereas *Frente Revolucionaria Timor Lest Independence* (FRETILIN) supported complete independence. On 28 November 1975, FRETILIN issued a unilateral declaration of independence proclaiming the establishment of the Democratic Republic of East Timor. Other political groups in East Timor then issued a joint declaration of independence from Portugal in favour of integration with neighboring Indonesia (which had sovereignty over West Timor following independence from the Netherlands).

On 7 December 1975, Indonesia invaded East Timor and seized control of the region by force. On 17 July 1976, Indonesia annexed East Timor, proclaiming it to be its 27th province. The purported annexation of East Timor was never recognized by the United Nations but was recognized by Australia in 1979.[78]

The Indonesian military presence in East Timor met with violent opposition by FRETILIN, which conducted a campaign of insurgency. The intensity of the violence varied, but included saturation bombing by Indonesian forces and the constant ambushing of Indonesian ground forces by FRETILIN fighters. A ceasefire was attempted in 1983 but was short-lived. Indonesian military action was accompanied by attempts to integrate East Timor into Indonesia, through actions such as the forced movement of the local civilian population and the resettlement of Indonesian farmers in East Timor. *Bahasa* Indonesian was imposed as the official language in schools and the education process included a focus on the Indonesian State ideology of *Pancasila*.

---

78. See 8 *Australian YIL* (1978-1980) pp. 281-282 for extracts of speeches by the Australian Foreign Minister on Australia's *de jure* recognition of Indonesia's incorporation of East Timor. The recent public release of Australian government documents in relation to the Indonesian invasion and subsequent purported annexation of East Timor reveal more details of the government's thinking on the question of the extension of recognition to Indonesia's incorporation of East Timor. See 'Recognition by Australia of Indonesian Incorporation of East Timor – Submission to the Foreign Minister' in Department of Foreign Affairs and Trade, *Australia and the Indonesian Incorporation of Portuguese Timor 1974-1976: Documents on Australian Foreign Policy* (2000) pp. 839-840.

Although figures are uncertain, it is estimated that tens of thousands have died in conflict in East Timor since 1975, with several hundred 'disappearances'. Allegations of human rights abuses against Indonesian authorities declined after 1989, as the Indonesian authorities implemented a policy of 'opening up' East Timor to outside scrutiny. However, on 12 November 1991, at the Santa Cruz Cemetery in Dili, a significant event occurred. A parliamentary delegation from Portugal had been scheduled to arrive in East Timor on 4 November 1991. Pro-independence demonstrations had reportedly been planned. On 28 October 1991, two pro-independence activists who, with others, had been hiding in a church in Dili, were shot and killed. The Portuguese delegation's visit was postponed and a memorial mass and march to Santa Cruz cemetery were organized for one of the deceased activists. The security forces opened fire on the crowd. According to official figures, ten protesters were killed but other reports estimate the number of fatalities at about 100.

Following international condemnation, the Indonesian government established a seven-person commission of inquiry. It found that up to 50 people may have been killed and that security forces had used excessive force in responding to civil unrest. Criminal charges were subsequently brought against protesters and army and police personnel involved. Human rights groups criticized the trials of protesters for not conforming to international standards or with Indonesia's own Code of Criminal Procedure. Protesters received prison sentences of between nine years and life whereas security personnel received sentences from eight to 18 months.

In early-1999, the then-Indonesian President B.J. Habibie surprisingly announced a dramatic change in Indonesia's policy regarding East Timor. A major element of that policy was a popular consultation through referendum to be held in East Timor on the issue of integration with Indonesia. Three agreements were entered into on 5 May 1999 variously between Indonesia, Portugal and the United Nations, providing a framework for the resolution of East Timor's future status. That framework envisaged the People's Assembly implementing the results of the popular consultation in October 1999.

The UN established the United Nations Mission in East Timor (UNAMET) to organize and conduct the popular consultation in order to ascertain whether the people of East Timor accepted or rejected a constitutional framework proposed by Indonesia.[79] This framework provided for special autonomy for East Timor within the unitary Republic of Indonesia. President Habibe stated that the Indonesian government accepted that a vote against the proposal would be the equivalent of a vote for independence for East Timor. The ballot was originally scheduled for 8 August 1999[80] but eventually took place on 30 August 1999.

---

79. UN Security Council Resolution 1246, UN Doc. S/RES/1246 (15 June 1999).
80. Ibid.

3.2.2 *Post-ballot*

On 4 September 1999, the UN announced the results of the ballot, namely, a 78.5 percent vote against unity with Indonesia – effectively a 78.5 percent vote for independence. President Habibie announced that he accepted the ballot's outcome and directed Indonesian security forces to maintain order in East Timor. However, within hours of the announcement of the ballot results, pro-integration militias went on a rampage in Dili and other towns in East Timor.

On 6 September 1999, Australia began evacuating its nationals in East Timor with up to 150,000 civilians already being displaced by the violence. On 7 September 1999, Indonesia imposed martial law in East Timor. From 8 to 12 September, a UN Security Council mission traveled to Jakarta and Dili. On 10 September, the UN began evacuating all but essential staff from East Timor. Australia announced that it was canceling joint military exercises with Indonesia and that its general defence ties with Indonesia were under review.[81]

The Security Council mission reported that the violence in East Timor after the ballot could not have occurred without the involvement of large elements of the Indonesian military and police, concluding that the Indonesian authorities were either unwilling or unable to provide an environment for the peaceful implementation of the 5 May agreements. The mission also concluded that this situation had not altered with the imposition of martial law.[82] On 12 September 1999, the Indonesian government agreed to accept the assistance of the international community to restore peace and security in East Timor and to implement the result of the popular consultation. Thereafter, the Security Council adopted resolution 1264 on 15 September 1999 and, *inter alia*:

> *Determining* that the present situation in East Timor constitutes a threat to international peace and security; and
> *Acting* under Chapter VII of the Charter of the United Nations;
> *Authorizes* the establishment of a multinational force under a unified command structure … with the following tasks: to restore peace and security in East Timor; to protect and support UNAMET in carrying out its tasks; and, within force capabilities, to facilitate humanitarian assistance operations; and
> *Authorizes* the States participating in the multinational force to take all necessary measures to fulfil this mandate.[83]

The multinational force began its deployment to East Timor on 20 September 1999. By that stage, the East Timorese infrastructure had been badly damaged. In Dili, few buildings were undamaged. The towns of Ainaro and Cassa had been completely destroyed, and an estimated 70 percent of Atsabe, Gleno, Lospalus,

81. *The Weekend Australian* (11-12 September 1999) p. 2.

82. Report of the UN Secretary General on the Situation in East Timor, UN Doc. S/1999/1024 (4 October 1999).

83. UN Doc. S/RES/1264 (15 September 1999).

Maliana, Manatuto and Oecus had been either burnt down or leveled. Extensive damage was also reported in Suai and Liquica. About 20 percent of Vineque had been destroyed, but Bacau was relatively undamaged. The judicial and detention systems were not operating and no commercial activity was being conducted. There was no effective administration, as administrative officials apparently left the territory after the announcement of the ballot results.

By the time of the deployment of the multinational force, the Indonesian armed forces still had significant numbers of personnel in East Timor, particularly in Dili. A contingent of Indonesian police remained in Dili with a substantial security detachment providing support. After consultations in New York and Dili, the Indonesian armed forces undertook to cooperate with the multinational force in the implementation of Resolution 1264, through a Joint Consultative Security Group established in Dili, with UNAMET participation.[84] On 24 September 1999, Indonesia lifted martial law and rapidly withdrew from the territory.

On 26 October 1999, the United Nations Transitional Authority (UNTAET) was established pursuant to Security Council Resolution 1272.[85] INTERFET formally transferred its responsibilities provided by UNSCR 1264 to UNTAET on 23 February 2000. UNTAET was given authority to 'exercise all legislative and executive authority including the administration of justice'.

3.3 The INTERFET deployment[86]

3.3.1 *The international force*

INTERFET was established under unified command rather than UN command. Major General Peter Cosgrove, at the time the Commander of the Australian Defence Force's (ADF) Deployable Joint Force Headquarters (DJFHQ), based in Brisbane, was designated Commander INTERFET (COMINTERFET). Headquarters INTERFET was formed by the DJFHQ, with supplementary support from other contributing states. Although the figures varied throughout the INTERFET deployment, 22 contributing nations were represented in INTERFET with a total force strength of approximately 12,600. Australia provided the largest contingent of 5,521 ADF personnel.[87]

---

84. Report of the UN Secretary General on the Situation in East Timor, UN Doc. S/1999/1024 (4 October 1999).

85. UN Security Council Resolution 1272, UN Doc. S/RES/1272 (24 October 1999).

86. Unless otherwise indicated, Colonel Mark Kelly, the inaugural Chief of Staff HQ INTERFET, provided the information contained in this section in a presentation to the ADF's Operations Law Course, RAAF Base Williamtown, 11 May 2000.

87. The Australian contribution was: HQ INTERFET (including a command support unit); a brigade headquarters; three infantry battalions; an engineer regiment; two artillery batteries (employed in security and civil affairs duties); a construction squadron; a brigade administrative support battalion; an aviation reconnaissance squadron; an aviation regiment; a field hospital; a force support battalion; a RAAF expeditionary combat support squadron; a RAAF airfield defence squadron; a RAN frigate; two landing craft heavy; and a clearance diving team. In addition, RAN sea lift and support units and RAAF

3.3.2 *Application of international law to the operation*

The complex nature of the international legal framework for the INTERFET deployment has already been noted. Issues which impacted on the framework included: the sovereign rights, if any, of Indonesia over East Timor and the recognition, if any, by members of the INTERFET coalition of those rights; the residual rights, if any, of Portugal as the former colonial power; the effect of the *de facto* control of East Timor by Indonesia as recognized by the 5 May 1999 agreements between Indonesia, Portugal and the UN; the effect of the unilateral act of Indonesia's People's Consultative Assembly on 20 October 1999 to withdraw Indonesian claims of sovereignty over East Timor; and the effect of UN Security Council Resolutions 1264 and 1272.

The controversial status of Indonesia's authority in East Timor itself contributed to the complexity of the multinational deployment and distinguished it from peace operations such as that which commenced in Kosovo in mid-1999.[88] Neither the UN nor most of the states contributing troops to the INTERFET coalition had recognized Indonesian sovereignty over East Timor following the Indonesian invasion in 1975 and purported annexation on 17 July 1976.[89] In fact, in a series of resolutions following the 1975 Indonesian invasion and subsequent purported annexation of East Timor, the UN Security Council and General Assembly rejected Indonesian claims of sovereignty over the territory.[90] For the UN and these states, the status of East Timor at the time of the INTERFET deployment was that of a UN-designated non-self governing territory.[91] The notable exception to this view was that of the coalition's lead nation, Australia.

Notwithstanding the UN's position regarding sovereignty, its acceptance of the reality of Indonesian control over East Timor was reflected in various framework documents, such as the 5 May 1999 agreements between Indonesia, Portugal and the UN and UN Security Council Resolution 1264 (1999) establishing INTERFET. Thus, although operative paragraph 3 of Resolution 1264 authorized 'the States participating in the multinational force to take all necessary measures' to fulfill its mandate, other provisions envisaged a continuing, although temporary, role for Indonesia in East Timor. Paragraph 5, for example, underlined the government of Indonesia's 'continuing responsibility under the Agreements of 5 May 1999 ... to

---

airlift capabilities supported the force. Source: Briefing paper provided by Strategic Command Division, HQ ADF.

88. United Security Council Resolution 1244 (1999) establishing KFOR and authorizing its deployment into Kosovo expressly recognized the sovereignty of the Federal Republic of Yugoslavia over Kosovo.

89. See the series of UN resolutions regarding Indonesian sovereignty referred to above.

90. See for example, General Assembly Resolutions 3485 of 12 December 1975, 31/53 of 1 December 1976, 32/34 of 28 November 1982 and Security Council Resolutions 384 (1975) and 389 (1976) of 22 April 1976.

91. This was, for example, the NZ view as reported in the written comments of LtCol. L.P. Maybee, Command Legal Officer, HQ Land Command, NZDF, presented to the ADF 'INTERFET Lessons Learnt Conference', Australian Defence Force Academy, Canberra, 17 March 2000.

maintain peace and security in the interim phase between the conclusion of the popular consultation and the start of the implementation of its result'.

Differing views on the status of Indonesia's claims to East Timor had an effect on key issues, such as the drafting of the framework documents[92] for the deployment and the determination of the law applicable in East Timor after the multinational force was deployed.[93]

Consistent with ADF policy, the principles[94] of the LOAC were applied, where relevant, by way of guidelines.[95] The same approach was taken with respect to international human rights law. The *rationale* behind the ADF approach has consistently been that the key international humanitarian and human rights law instruments usually reflect best practice, and, compliance with them, where relevant, is the appropriate expectation for force standards. Maintenance of the legitimacy of a peace operation is considered a key to mission success.

The ADF has adopted a similar approach to the law of military occupation in its deployment on peace operations. The Australian position is that a UN mandated force can be in at least *de facto* occupation of the area of operations. The INTERFET deployment drew extensively upon the law of occupation for the establishment of an interim justice system. While it is the ADF view that the law of occupation does not require an armed conflict for it to apply *de jure*,[96] INTERFET forces were not occupying East Timor because Indonesia consented to the deployment. Here, the law of military occupation provided a framework of guiding principles.

---

92. Australia, as lead nation, negotiated a diplomatic agreement (covering matters often contained in Status of Forces Agreements) with Indonesia on behalf of all participating nations.

93. In Kosovo, the applicable law was clearly that of the Federal Republic of Yugoslavia but for East Timor there were arguments about whether Indonesian law or Portuguese law was the most appropriate legal regime.

94. The NZ position was different in relation to the application of LOAC. The NZ position was that not only the principles but the rules of LOAC applied to the deployment on the basis that the UN Secretary General's Bulletin of 12 August 1999 states that the principles and rules apply to enforcement actions or peacekeeping operations. The ADF position, by contrast, is that the Secretary General's Bulletin did not apply the principles and rules of LOAC to INTERFET as the Bulletin only applies to UN commanded forces or to peace enforcement or peace keeping operations where UN forces are a party to a conflict. The NZDF position was contained in the written submission of LtCol. Maybee, ibid., to the INTERFET Lessons Learnt Conference.

95. Comments of LtCol. Kelly, Directorate of International and Operations Law, Defence Legal Office, INTERFET Lessons Learnt Conference, transcript p. 134.

96. It will be recalled that the Australian contingent strongly advocated the application of the law of military occupation of the multinational force in Somalia. See also M.J. Kelly, *Peace Operations: Tackling the Military, Legal and Policy Challenges* (Canberra, Australian Government Publishing Service 1997). As we have seen, that law was in fact applied by the ADF in Somalia to good effect. This interpretation of the law has subsequently been asserted by Australia at the Meeting of Experts on the Fourth Geneva Convention of 1949 in Geneva, October 1998. Guidelines on the application of this approach have also been promulgated as Defence Legal Office policy.

3.3.3 *The legal framework for the operation*

3.3.3.1 Establishing the framework

As the lead nation for INTERFET, Australian authorities, in particular, the Department of Defence,[97] the Attorney-General's Department and the Department of Foreign Affairs and Trade (DFAT) assumed responsibility for the conception, drafting and negotiation of the framework documents. That responsibility normally falls to the UN Legal Adviser whenever an operation is UN commanded and controlled. These framework documents supplemented those created externally, such as the relevant Security Council Resolutions and the agreements of 5 May 1999.

The following framework documents were adopted:

—Exchange of Diplomatic Notes Constituting an Arrangement Between the Government of Australia and the Government of the Republic of Indonesia Concerning the Status of the Multinational Force in East Timor – which came into effect on 24 September 1999 and was known as the Status of Forces Arrangement (SOFA);

—Exchange of Diplomatic Notes Constituting an Arrangement Between the Government of Australia and UNTAET – which applied to the activities of the multinational force operating under a unified command structure in East Timor (INTERFET) from 26 October 1999;

—Agreement on Participation in INTERFET.

Difficulties experienced in reaching agreement with Indonesian authorities for certain technical issues has prompted the suggestion that, in future operations, rather than seek formal agreement by a process of negotiation, the mechanism of a unilateral declaration be employed in appropriate circumstances. The consent of the other party would thereafter be assumed if that party did not object. That is, after declaring the Australian position and intended course of action, operations would be conducted accordingly.[98] It is suggested that relevant circumstances for the use of this mechanism would be the strength of the UN mandate underpinning the operation.

---

97. Within the Department of Defence, primary responsibility for all aspects of this documentation development process was vested in the Directorate of Agreements within the Defence Legal Office in Canberra.

98. Ibid., Comments Cmdr. Letts, Naval Command, transcript p. 98.

3.3.3.2 Investigating alleged crimes against humanity[99]

A key reason for the Security Council's authorisation of the deployment of INTERFET was its deep concern over 'the continuing violence against and large-scale displacement, and relocation, of East Timorese civilians'.[100] However, no international tribunal has yet been established to try individuals alleged to have perpetrated atrocities in East Timor and the UN, at least for the initial period of the INTERFET deployment, had only limited investigative resources[101] available to conduct investigations of possible crimes against humanity.

The main challenge for INTERFET in relation to crimes against humanity, or indeed other serious violations of local criminal law, was the type and extent of INTERFET's involvement. Ultimately, that involvement was restricted to the conduct of limited investigations and attempts to preserve some crime scenes. A note on Guidance for the Multinational Peacekeeping Force in East Timor on the Preservation of Evidence provided by the Office of the High Commissioner for Human Rights was applied by INTERFET forces. The limited INTERFET involvement was driven in large part by a lack of available personnel resources – availability both in terms of numbers of military police and of personnel with relevant expertise (including, for example, forensic skills and crime investigation training). An additional reason for the limited INTERFET involvement related to perceptions that other agencies had a higher primary responsibility and possessed greater relevant expertise – particularly organisations such as the Office of the UN High Commissioner for Human Rights.

It is clear from the East Timor experience that some investigative role into alleged perpetration of international crimes will virtually always be required in future peace operations. Furthermore, this investigative role will most likely be required from the very commencement of the deployment.[102] External pressure for the peace force to be involved more extensively in such investigations than was the case for INTERFET will probably be applied from a variety of sources.[103] In future operations, particularly if other, more appropriate, agencies cannot deploy in sufficient time and the political will is present, an intervening military force may need to consider developing a more extensive crimes against humanity/war crimes

99. The expression 'crime against humanity' rather than 'war crimes' has been preferred to avoid the controversies of whether or not the acts in question in East Timor occurred in the context of an armed conflict. A 'crime against humanity' means certain acts, including murder, rape, deportation or forcible transfer, committed as part of a widespread or systematic attack directed against civilian population. For the most comprehensive treaty definition of the crime, see Art. 7 of the Rome Statute of the International Criminal Court – accessible at www.un.org/icc/part2.

100. Preamble to UN Security Council Resolution 1264 (1999).

101. At the time of INTERFET's arrival in East Timor, CIVPOL had only two members on the ground (Maj. Freeman Legal Officer, INTERFET Combined Legal Office, INTERFET Lessons Learnt Conference, transcript p. 118).

102. Here it is noted that the ADF did not deploy a trained investigator until after seven days after INTERFET troops deployed to East Timor. Comments of Maj. Freeman, ibid.

103. AD HQ fielded offers from civilian organisations during the INTERFET operation, *inter alia*, to provide civilian forensic teams to be attached to INTERFET.

investigative capability. Any such capability could include a mortuary, a forensic laboratory, forensic specialists, Military Police investigators, trauma counselors, translators and organic logistic support.[104]

3.3.3.3 The management of detainees

Within hours of deploying to East Timor, INTERFET troops found it necessary to detain a number of East Timorese.[105] To ensure that detainees received their basic legal rights, the Commander of INTERFET (COMINTERFET) directed that detainees were to be conveyed to the Force Detention Centre (FDC) as soon as practically possible, preferably within 24 hours but no later than 36 hours after being apprehended. Within 72 hours of a detainee's arrival at the FDC, the Senior Legal Advisor at the INTERFET Combined Legal Office was to review the detainee's case and, where appropriate, make arrangements for the transfer of the detainee to the appropriate Indonesian authorities. The SOFA with Indonesia provided, *inter alia*, that INTERFET could, in furtherance of its mandate, detain a person who was committing or had attempted to commit offences in relation to persons or property. Furthermore, the SOFA required detainees to be handed over to the appropriate authorities for the purpose of dealing with the alleged offender. However, handing detainees over to Indonesian civilian police proved unsatisfactory because of the collapse of the civil administration (including the judiciary and court system) in East Timor.[106] The detainees were simply released by Indonesian police soon after the transfer of custody.

With the collapse of the Indonesian judicial and detention systems, INTERFET faced the challenge of balancing the rights of detainees to natural justice and due process against the need to maintain detention. On 21 October 1999, INTERFET addressed this balance through the establishment of the Detention Management Unit (DMU) as an interim judicial system pending the reestablishment of a civil judiciary. Once again, the Australians relied on the Fourth Geneva Convention and the law of occupation as the guide for establishing the DMU regime.[107]

---

104. This structure was suggested in a written submission by Maj. O'Kane, SO2 Legal, HQ WESTFOR, in a written submission to the INTERFET Lessons Learnt Conference.

105. For example, it was reported on 22 September 1999, that INTERFET had 'arrested eight East Timorese – including members of the militia – for carrying weapons in the capital Dili', M. Blenkin and J. Martinkus, 'Militia Disarmed: Peacekeepers Arrest Eight', *The Daily Telegraph*, 1st edn. (22 September 1999) p. 3.

106. On 4 October 1999, the Secretary-General reported: 'The Indonesian police ... appear to have withdrawn from the territory [East Timor]. In Dili, there is a token presence of 12 persons, comprising of senior officers, investigators and basic administrative staff ... The Indonesian police have confirmed that the judicial and detention systems are not operating. With regard to detainees, the multinational force has established basic, short-term legal and practical provisions for preventive detention, in consultation with UNAMET and the International Committee of the Red Cross (ICRC). UN Doc. S/1999/1024 (4 October 1999), para. 13.

107. For a full account of the establishment of the DMU and its process, see B. Oswald, 'The INTERFET Detainee Management Unit in East Timor', 3 *YIHL* (2000) p. 347.

3.4 UNTAET and the Peacekeeping Force (PKF)

Following on from INTERFET, the issue of the transition to the United Nations Transitional Administration in East Timor (UNTAET) and the role the PKF would play in maintaining civil order arose. The issue for UNTAET once again became the establishment of a legal framework for the interim administration of justice that would be supportable and ensure the legitimacy of the mission in the perception of the international community and local population. UNTAET sought to establish an independent state and was therefore presented with the issue of transition to a new state polity and succession.[108] UNTAET involved the total assumption of sovereign functions by a UN administration, pending a lengthy process to create an indigenous, legitimised polity. It also had to contend with an almost total absence of local administrative capability. This process involved establishing local administrative capabilities at the same time as actually administering; registering an electorate and political parties/candidates; conducting an election; creating a constitutional assembly which drafted a constitution and then became the national Legislative Assembly; conducting a presidential election, and transferring to independence on 20 May 2002.[109] Given the scope of the task, to date the mission has proven to have been very successful, with the main area of difficulty being the administration of justice.

The UNTAET mission involved the careful balancing of many sensitivities and challenges, which increased as the operation matured and progress was made. The most pressing initial issue was reconciling the conflicted elements of East Timor, and dealing with the security threat emanating from both the West Timor based militia and the domestic law and order situation. Also to prove problematic was interpreting the UNTAET mandate and the responsibilities of the UNTAET elements in relation to it. This included balancing the roles and interests of the UNTAET civil administration, UN agencies, the Peacekeeping Force; the international Civilian Police (CIVPOL); the Human Rights Office; UNHCR; the UNTAET Justice Department, including the Office of the General Prosecutor and its Serious Crimes Investigation Unit; the emerging East Timorese Police Service; and the emerging East Timorese Defence Force. Critical to establishing the conditions under which UNTAET could terminate the mission were the construction of a sound relationship with the Indonesian government, the West Timorese-based TNI and their Commander in Denpasar, MajGen. Da Costa, and encouraging, assuaging and engaging the East Timorese political actors. Finally it was vital to engage concurrently in managing popular expectations and ameliorating their

108. The UNTAET administration was a fully responsible UN 'government' providing all the organs of administration and staffing them with predominantly expatriate personnel. This was established under Security Council Resolutions 1272 (1999) of 25 October 1999 and 1338 (2001) of 31 January 2001 and through the promulgation of UNTAET Regulation No. 1999/1 of 27 November 1999. A later regulation (No. 2001/28 of 19 September 2001) established the Council of Ministers of the Transitional Government in East Timor.

109. See UNSG Reports to UNSC S/2000/53 of 26 January 2000, S/2000/738 of 26 July 2000, S/2001/42 of 16 January 2001, S/2001/436 of 2 May 2001, S/2001/983 of 18 October 2001.

conditions. The challenge was to do all of this in the context of a devastated environment.

As was to be expected all of this was subject to budgetary constraints and funds would never be adequate to tackle all he challenges effectively. At the same time much effort had to go into ensuring that the East Timorese would have a viable and sustainable future with the withdrawal of the 'artificial' UN public sector and its dependent economy.

It is interesting to note the provisions under UNTAET Regulation No. 1999/1 of 27 November 1999 concerning the applicable law in East Timor.[110] Through these provisions, the UNTAET administration drew on the existing body of Indonesian law. Indonesian criminal law is based on its Dutch colonial predecessor, which shared the Napoleonic heritage of the Portuguese Criminal Code. Notwithstanding the fact that only Australia had formally recognized Indonesian sovereignty over East Timor, after 25 years of Indonesian rule, it was logical that the Indonesian Code be relied upon given the local familiarity with it and the excising of some of the political laws which had been utilised for repression. This was supplemented by a Regulation on Transitional Rules of Criminal Procedure to ensure fairness in accordance with fundamental international human rights standards.[111] UNTAET was provided with the ability to promulgate laws and the SRSG/Transitional Administrator was empowered to issue Directives.[112]

One problem which emerged was the attitude to the Regulations exhibited by the SRSG. This was illustrated in the deployment of the East Timorese Defence Force (FDTL) in the period leading up to the elections on 30 August 2001. Under

---

110. These state:
'3.1 Until replaced by UNTAET regulations or subsequent legislation of democratically established institutions of East Timor, the laws applied in East Timor prior to 25 October 1999 shall apply in East Timor insofar as they do not conflict with the standards referred to in section 2, the fulfillment of the mandate given to UNTAET under United Nations Security Council resolution 1272 (1999), or the present or any other regulation and directive issued by the Transitional Administrator.
3.2 Without prejudice to the review of other legislation, the following laws, which do not comply with the standards referred to in section 2 and 3 of the present regulation, as well as any subsequent amendments to these laws and their administrative regulations, shall no longer be applied in East Timor: Law on Anti-Subversion; Law on Social Organizations; Law on National Security; Law on National Protection and Defence; Law on Mobilization and Demobilization; Law on Defence and Security.
3.3 Capital punishment is abolished.'
See UNSG Reports to UNSC S/2000/53 of 26 January 2000; S/2000/738 of 26 July 2000; S/2001/42 of 16 January 2001; S/2001/436 of 2 May 2001; and S/2001/983 of 18 October 2001.

111. UNTAET/REG/2000/30 of 25 September 2000.

112. Section 4 Regulations issued by UNTAET:
'In the performance of the duties entrusted to the transitional administration under United Nations Security Council resolution 1272 (1999), the Transitional Administrator will, as necessary, issue legislative acts in the form of regulations. Such regulations will remain in force until repealed by the Transitional Administrator or superseded by such rules as are issued upon the transfer of UNTAET's administrative and public service functions to the democratic institutions of East Timor, as provided for in United Nations Security Council resolution 1272 (1999).'
Section 6 Directives:
'6.1 The Transitional Administrator shall have the power to issue administrative directives in relation to the implementation of regulations promulgated.'

UNTAET/REG/2001/1 of 31 January 2001, as amended by UNTAET/REG/2001/9 of 29 June 2001, the FDTL was prohibited from being mobilized or utilized in matters linked to internal public order, police issues or social conflicts. The SRSG determined that he wanted over 200 FDTL personnel deployed to assist with security for the election and to boost their profile and the confidence of the people. This was strenuously objected to by the PKF as it violated the Regulations, sent the wrong message to the FDTL and the people about their role, could not be logistically sustained and would interrupt the FDTL training. In the end, a different approach was taken, employing 66 personnel on civil assistance tasks, which did not violate the Regulations and achieved the intention of the SRSG. This points, however, to the need for personnel in such key positions to understand the critical concepts upon which such missions must be founded in terms of promotion of the rule of law.

UNTAET was built upon a broad Security Council Resolution mandate fleshed out by UNTAET Regulations based on the authority of that mandate. It was administered through a combination of function based and remedial departments which attempted to transition to indigenous staff and developing institutions through employment policy and consultative mechanisms. This approach was reasonably adequate from the perspective of establishing the perception of legitimacy for UNTAET although one significant weakness was the administration of justice.[113] The approach taken by the UN in East Timor while viable still remains very much an *ad hoc* solution and suffers from the usual problems of delay in marshalling the human and financial resources, although aspects of this are often a matter of international willpower. It also results in significantly variable aspects of quality and approach, which ideally ought to be neutralised through a professional cadre under an organised response mechanism. There certainly is a growing number of personnel with experience in performing these functions, but it has to be said that in the UNTAET experience the energy of a few compensated for the inactivity, apathy or incompetence of many. Nowhere was the issue of the variable quality of personnel more damaging than in the justice administration and CIVPOL area, which was subject to internal personnel turmoil, allegations of political interference and incompetence.

For the PKF, the UNTAET experience involved a difficult balancing act between the security function of defeating and deterring the known militia threat emanating from across the Tactical Coordination Line (TCL) in West Timor and supporting internal security. This meant establishing modes of operating and procedural arrangements with key stakeholders such as CIVPOL, UNHCR and the Serious Crimes Unit (SCU). There came a stage, dating roughly from July 2001, when the nature of returnees from West Timor changed from straightforward refugees to former functionaries, TNI, POLRI and militia members of the Indonesian regime and their families. A difficult balance had to be struck between the rights of refugees/returnees under the Refugee Convention and the Statute of the

---

113. See the Amnesty International Report on this subject (East Timor, Justice Past, Present and Future, AI Index: ASA 57/001/2001 of July 2001). While this report contains many justified criticisms the enormity of the task and the lack of human and financial resources must also be taken into account.

UNHCR[114] and the potential threat posed by these persons both in terms of their need to face justice, the activities they may have become involved in upon return and the reaction of the communities they were returning to in East Timor.

There were particular concerns for the PKF as tension emerged relating to the need to interview returnees for intelligence-gathering purposes. This was not helped by a certain level of mutual suspicion stemming from the different military and NGO/Agency 'sub-cultures' on the part of both UNHCR and PKF personnel, and by actions by some PKF elements that could be perceived as insensitive to prioritising human rights standards as the militia threat diminished and the environment began to normalise.[115] There were also some failures by PKF to facilitate technical requirements in the processing of detainees through to CIVPOL.[116] These matters were resolved through patient negotiation of guidelines and standards and the breaking down of the 'sub-cultural' suspicions. This was formalised in a number of Appendices to Annex L of the PKF Operational Order (OPORD) 8 which covered step by step procedures for returnee processing, interview guidelines, reconciliation meetings, 'go and see' visits and family meetings.[117] These guidelines also involved some compromise to prosecution objectives by the SCU, as the arrangements for reconciliation meetings meant that suspects would not be arrested at the meetings in order to facilitate the larger objective of encouraging large-scale returns and therefore resort to normal process when full return occurred. Compromise on the part of UNHCR occurred in terms of ensuring that no SCU suspects would be part of 'go and see' visits, and the acceptance that many returnees would lose their protected status as SCU suspects. UNHCR also undertook to assist low-level information gathering by PKF during the processing of returnees. In this context, the PKF developed operational coordination with the SCU involving the opening of field offices by the SCU and the dovetailing of intelligence operations and databases. The opening of the SCU field offices enhanced cooperation with the PKF at the tactical level, improved SCU effectiveness in the

114. Convention relating to the Status of Refugees of 28 July 1951 (entered into force on 22 April 1954), Article I of the Protocol relating to the Status of Refugees of 31 January 1967. Statute of UNHCR annexed to General Assembly Resolution 428 (V) of 14 December 1950.

115. These incidents were relatively minor matters involving the access to and questions asked of returnees by PKF intelligence personnel and in one case the temporary detention and questioning of a significant ex militia figure by the PKF in a way that cut across UNHCR objectives. (These matters were observed by and involved the author in his official capacity as Chief Legal Adviser (CLA) to the PKF Force Commander in East Timor from 24 July 2001 to 31 January 2002).

116. There were a number of technical requirements in the processing of detainees which included the time frames for charging and bringing before an investigating judge. There were times when the PKF was not expeditious in handing over detainees to CIVPOL to allow them sufficient time to deal with process requirements or when detainees were held longer than the period allowed to the PKF. (Observations and dealings of the author as CLA).

117. UNTAET PKF Operations Order, 08-0,1 File Number: 3313-1, 8 December 2001, Annex L Appendices 1-6. 'Go and See' visits were arrangements made by UNHCR with refugees to assist in the defeat of misinformation campaigns in West Timor about the state of affairs in East Timor and to reassure them about the local acceptance of their return. They would then be transported back to West Timor. The hope was that participants would influence or lead their families and refugee communities to return. These visits might involve figures who were of a security concern or interest.

gathering of evidence, and reinforced local confidence in the justice process and security environment.[118]

The PKF also executed an Operational Support Arrangement (OSA)[119] with CIVPOL in order to bring some rigor to the provision of support to what were essentially normal policing activities, such as cordon and search operations. PKF support was provided to these missions because the capabilities of CIVPOL and the emerging East Timorese Police Force (TLPS) were still inadequate. The main emphasis of the OSA was to ensure that there was a framework for using the PKF in this role that equated with proper standards relating to the role of a military force in a democracy with proper civil oversight and the priority of authority spelled out. This had the added significance of promoting these values within East Timor with an eye to how the FDTL would relate to the civil political regime as it emerged.

Tensions between CIVPOL and the PKF surfaced from time to time, due to the difficult working environment in which the security mandate of the PKF and the role of CIVPOL had a degree of overlap. These tensions were exacerbated by the lack of capability of CIVPOL.[120]

The efforts of the second DSRSG, Mr Dennis McNamara, to remedy many of the UNTAET justice administration deficiencies demonstrates that one determined and insightful individual in a key position can achieve a great deal, even with limited resources. It must be stressed, however, that the criticisms of UNTAET are those of detail in a broadly successful mission.[121]

3.5 Conclusion

The INTERFET/UNTAET missions in East Timor posed an array of challenges across all aspects of the operations – particularly in the legal field. The challenges faced by INTERFET/UNTAET reflected many of the common experiences and issues that have recurred in the course of recent complex peace operations. From the perspective of the promotion of the rule of law and defining the international humanitarian and human rights legal norms that should apply in such situations, the operation was a successful evolution in the approach that has been adopted by Australia since the deployment to Somalia described above. It is not suggested here

118. Observations of the author. The author was involved in the arrangements described as well as the execution of the guidelines with UNHCR.

119. Operational Support Arrangement between the UNTAET Civil Police Commissioner and the PKF Commander executed on 22 March 2002. Drafted by the author and the legal adviser to the CIVPOL Commissioner, Mr Wayne Hayde.

120. This lack of capability arose from insufficient numbers, resources and variable level of training and standards in the various CIVPOL contingents.

121. These are observations by the author. This period covered the constitutional assembly elections and formation of the assembly; the drafting of the constitution; the conclusion of key agreements with Indonesia; the Presidential election; the return and reintegration of the militia families and members; the establishment of the Truth and Reconciliation Commission; the conclusion of guidelines on the processing of returnees; the conduct of reconciliation meetings; cooperation between CIVPOL and PKF; the management of the operational deployment of the East Timorese Defence Force; and the establishment of the indigenous government.

that the operations ran perfectly or that they represent models for doctrinaire replication. However, the Australian approach to the issue of the interim administration of justice confirmed the existence of some fundamental general principles and issues that must be planned for and considered before any future military deployment into complex emergency situations.

In Somalia a reluctance to be proactive on this issue was the cancer at the heart of the mission that eventually killed it. While there is always a reluctance in the military to avoid 'mission creep' Somalia demonstrated that there are key points of intervention that it is in the interests of the military to address to facilitate an earlier withdrawal. It took much subsequent soul searching and added experiences to confirm the need to tackle rule of law matters right from the commencement of an operation. One of the key problems in Somalia was not only the lack of capability but the lack of legal analysis and preparation to enable remedial action to occur and to sustain the perception of legitimacy. UNTAET showed the benefit of this lesson but also highlighted that faith in the rule of law must be painstakingly built with the disrupted community and this will depend not only on the sense of security generated by the mission but by the behaviour of the security elements of the mission and the manner of maintaining order. UNTAET also illustrated the need to take positive action to avoid a dependence on the military for law and order support which will retard the development of indigenous law and order. It is essential that the military not be used to mask or delay the effort that should exerted on the standing up of the local capability.

One thing is certain, any deployment into the collapsed state environment will involve the military in a situation of the interim administration of justice to some degree and this must always be prepared and planned for. This includes everything from the legal framework to the logistics of looking after detainees. The UNTAET experience also confirms the need identified in Somalia and in subsequent operations for the international community to concentrate on developing an ability to deploy a capable police response and for the peacekeeping forces to be adequately trained in basic human rights principles and non-lethal force techniques. The peacekeeping forces also need to be adequately equipped and structured for their inevitable role in the interim administration of justice and the transition to civil authority. The Brahimi Report on Peace Operations has posed many suggestions which go directly to the heart of the international response to the interim administration of justice and the professionalisation issue.[122] If implemented effectively, or at least if the issues raised are adequately addressed, an operation will be more likely to succeed and in a way that leads to continuing viability with less need for international oversight or intervention. The rule of law is a key element to creating the 'virtuous circle' of mutually supporting factors rather than the 'viscous circle' that often begins with the insecurity and corruption generated by an inadequate or dysfunctional administration of justice.

---

122. *Report of the Panel on United Nations Peace Operations*, L. Brahimi, Chairman, of 21 August 2000, A/55/305-S2000/809 (available at http://www.un.org/peace/reports/peace_operations/) See in particular paras. 39-47, 76-83, 86-91, 118-125 and 219-225.

CURRENT DEVELOPMENTS

THE YEAR IN REVIEW[1]

Avril McDonald[2]

---

2. Dr Avril McDonald is Head of the Section of International Humanitarian Law and International Criminal Law at the TMC Asser Institute for International Law, The Hague and Managing Editor of the *Yearbook of International Humanitarian Law*.

1. INTRODUCTION

The defining moments of 2001, the terrorist attacks of September 11 against the United States of America, marked a turning point in international law and relations. By their scale and audaciousness, overnight they helped to propel the issue of international terrorism to the top of the international security agenda and particularly that of the USA, with consequences for many branches of international law, including the *jus ad bellum*, the *jus in bello*, international law relating to terrorism, international human rights law and international criminal law, that were just beginning to be felt as the year closed.

The September 11 attacks were immediately characterised by the United States as an act of war, an armed attack on such a scale as to constitute an armed conflict.[3] Its immediate response was to declare a so-called 'Global War on Terrorism'. Avowedly acting in self-defense, on 7 October the US launched armed attacks against Afghanistan, not because Afghanistan was considered to be legally responsible for the September 11 attacks but for harbouring and refusing to surrender members of Al Qaeda, including its leader, Osama Bin Laden, and refusing to dismantle terrorist training camps. Although the main target of the attacks was Al Qaeda, the armed conflict that ensued was an international armed conflict between the US and its allies and the state of Afghanistan, notwithstanding that the US never recognised the Taleban as the government of Afghanistan.

Outside Afghanistan, the 'war against terrorism' was fought on many fronts, and mainly in ways that did not involve the use of armed force. But it became increasingly clear that in fighting international terrorism, there would be a blurring of the clear distinctions between various branches of international law. In particular, counter-terrorism was assimilated with armed conflict. The apparent perception of some states that international terrorism, and particularly the possibility of the use of weapons of mass destruction by terrorists, is their number one security problem encouraged an increasingly militaristic approach to dealing with the phenomenon of terrorism. Some states and international organisations appropriated the language of warfare to describe the actions of terrorists, such as the attacks of September 11, even though, legally these were not acts of aggression or war crimes, at least as we have generally understood these concepts, but violations of international terrorism conventions and possibly crimes against humanity.

Some states applied the laws governing the conduct of hostilities to terrorists outside situations of armed conflict, or at least were operating in a legally very grey area, outside human rights law, outside normal criminal law enforcement. An example was given when, on 3 November 2001, an unmanned American Predator

3. Addressing Congress on 20 September 2001, President Bush said: 'On September 11th, enemies of freedom committed an act of war against our country.' Address Before a Joint Session of the Congress on the United States Response to the Terrorist Attacks of September 11, 37 Weekly Comp. Pres. Doc. 1347, 1347 (20 September 2001). Section 1 of the US Military Order of November 13, 2001, establishing military commissions to try persons detained on the battlefield in Afghanistan as well as elsewhere, stated that the attacks by Al Qaeda and other international terrorists are on 'a scale that has created a state of armed conflict that requires the use of United States Armed Forces'.

drone operating out of a US base in Djibouti fired a Hellfire missile at an automobile in Yemen which was believed to be carrying an Al Qaeda leader named Qaed Salim Sinan al-Harethi. Al-Harethi and five other passengers were killed.[4]

At the same time, the US government's initial treatment of persons captured on the battlefield of Afghanistan and refusal to grant them POW status suggested that Geneva law was not being applied where it was actually applicable.[5]

The growing disenchantment of the USA under the Bush administration with multilateralism was apparent throughout 2001, as the US set itself up in opposition to a number of international initiatives aimed at strengthening international law, in particular in the realm of arms control.

2. CONFLICTS, ARMED FORCES AND COMBATANTS

2.1 Types of conflicts

Almost all of the major armed conflicts in 2001 were intrastate. According to the SIPRI Yearbook, referring to internal armed conflicts: 'The central point of contention in all of the conflicts was control over either government or territory. However, the diversity of state and non-state actors reveals multiple and overlapping objectives related to political power, economic gain and ideological belief.'[6] Despite being non-international in character, SIPRI reported that '[a]ll of them were directly influenced by external actors.' Moreover, many of them spilled over the borders of the state, posing a threat to neighbouring states and provoking regional insecurity.

2.2 Types of actors

2.2.1 *Mercenaries*

Some progress on the subject of mercenaries was achieved during the year. The most significant development was the entry into force on 20 October 2001 of the International Convention against the Recruitment, Use, Financing and Training of Mercenaries, 30 days after the deposit of the 22nd instrument of ratification.[7] But

---

4. See S.M. Hersh, 'Manhunt: The Bush administration's new strategy in the war against terrorism', *The New Yorker*, 23 and 30 December 2002.

5. For a discussion of some of the legal issues raised by the Al Qaeda attacks and the resultant war on terror, see A. McDonald, 'Terrorism, Counter-Terrorism and the Jus in Bello', in M.N. Schmitt and G.L. Beruto, eds., *Terrorism and International Law: Challenges and Responses* (San Remo, International Institute of Humanitarian Law 2003) pp. 57 et seq.

6. SIPRI Yearbook 2002: Armaments, Disarmament and International Security (Oxford, Oxford University Press 2002) Chapter 1.

7. The first 22 States Parties to the Convention were Azerbaijan, Barbados, Belarus, Cameroon, Croatia, Cyprus, Georgia, Italy, Libya, Maldives, Mauritania, Qatar, Saudi Arabia, Senegal, Seychelles, Suriname, Togo, Turkmenistan, Ukraine, Uruguay and Uzbekistan. Nine other states had

the subject of mercenarism and the problems it gives rise to were also addressed by almost all of the sub-organs of the UN organisation. Work on the subject in the various fora identified several common themes, in particular, the rise of new types of mercenarism and its link with other forms of serious international criminality; the impact of mercenarism on respect for international law; the need for compliance with existing international law; and the need for the adoption of new law at the international, regional and national levels.

On 11 January 2001, the Special Rapporteur to the UN Economic and Social Council, Mr Enrique Bernales Ballesteros, issued his Report on the question of the use of mercenaries as a means of violating human rights and impeding the exercise of the right of peoples to self-determination.[8] The Report found that mercenaries are involved in almost every armed conflict, and although mercenaries are still engaged in traditional activities,[9] there is also a need breed of mercenaries, who are engaged in activities outside situations of armed conflict, and connected with terrorism, organised crime, illegal exploitation of natural resources, trafficking in weapons, *inter alia*.[10]

The Special Rapporteur stated: 'Such persons are terrorists because of the nature of the criminal act carried out, but mercenaries by virtue of their function.'[11] Many of these persons are motivated not by ideological reasons but by financial reward.[12] Mr Ballesteros observed that since 'they do not exactly match the definition given in article 47 of Protocol Additional I, the definition itself should be re-examined. The point being made by the Special Rapporteur's office is that they are indeed mercenaries and that customary legal definitions suffer from shortcomings and limitations and fail to cover situations and activities which are of a mercenary nature.'[13] The Special Rapporteur noted that the private security and military assistance companies that recruit many mercenaries are also becoming increasingly internationalised.[14] 'The Special Rapporteur referred to 'the failure of international law to predict the new operational modalities for mercenary activities', and advised that 'greater rigour and precision must be achieved in concepts and definitions, avoiding generalizations and ensuring clear legal regulations; private

---

signed the Convention, but had not yet ratified it: Angola, Congo, DR Congo, Germany, Morocco, Nigeria, Poland, Romania, Yugoslavia and Costa Rica.

8. E/CN.4/2001/19, 11 January 2001, submitted pursuant to ECOSOC resolution 2000/3. This followed the submission of his previous report E/CN.4/2000/14 and Corr.1 to the Commission on Human Rights on 22 March 2000. The Special Rapporteur submitted his report (A/55/334) to the General Assembly on 18 October 2000.

9. Ibid., para. 50.

10. See paras. 31, 44, 34, 39, 42, 45, 49, and 60: 'Mercenaries are hired as pilots, co-pilots or flight engineers for the transport of weapons, as arms salesmen in the field or as instructors in the use of the weapons and military material that have been sold, and to train troops or paramilitary groups, which in many cases comprise raw recruits, persons with little training or knowledge or ad hoc combatants.' (para. 60).

11. Ibid., para. 52.

12. Ibid., paras. 53 and 54, 57.

13. Ibid., para. 49. See also para. 74.

14. See ibid., paras. 62-64.

activity in the area of security and military advice and assistance should be monitored by a specialized public international institution'.[15] '[C]lear legal norms are required which specify the areas in which private military and security companies can legitimately operate and those in which their intervention should be prohibited. Such regulations should be established at the national, regional and international levels.'[16] The report also called for the requirement to be a non-national of the country in which the mercenary becomes involved to be reviewed and analysed more carefully, 'so as to give greater weight in the definition to the nature and purpose of the illicit act with which an agent is paid to be associated'.[17]

The Special Rapporteur recommended, *inter alia*, that the Commission hold consultations, working meetings and solicit expert opinions with a view to obtaining, as rapidly as possible, suggestions and proposals for a better legal definition of mercenarism and proposals for updating international instruments on the subject.[18] The Commission should also call for the establishment of international machinery to monitor the diamond trade.[19]

The interim report of the Special Rapporteur to the General Assembly[20] addressed many of the same issues as the above-mentioned report, including most importantly, the legal definition of mercenary; the current status of mercenary activities and private security and military assistance companies operating internationally. In addition, the Special Rapporteur included in his interim report summaries of his correspondence with several governments. He made several recommendations, including that the GA address the myriad manifestations of mercenarism and its link with international criminality, including arms trafficking, illegal exploitation of natural resources and terrorism; that greater effort be made to develop legal instruments to facilitate prosecution of mercenary activities; and that the GA direct him to propose a new, more contemporary, definition of mercenarism and a procedure for its international adoption.

Nine experts, from different geographical regions, met from 29 January to 2 February 2001 to consider traditional and new types of mercenarism as a means of violating human rights and impeding the exercise of the right of peoples to self-determination. The report of the meeting contained summaries of the papers presented by the Special Rapporteur and the experts and the discussions that followed, as well as conclusions and recommendations.[21] In particular, it identified weaknesses in the Mercenaries Convention, which does not include any enforcement or control mechanism. The definition of mercenarism contained therein suffers from the same shortcomings as that found in Additional Protocol I. The Convention is also concerned with extraterritorial rather than internal deployment

15. Ibid., para. 65.
16. Ibid., para. 67.
17. Ibid., para. 76.
18. Ibid., para. 91.
19. Ibid., para. 93.
20. 'Use of mercenaries as a means of violating human rights and impeding the exercise of the right of peoples to self-determination', A/56/224, 27 July 2001.
21. The meeting's report, E/CN.4/2001/18, was issued on 14 February 2001.

of mercenaries, whereas the latter is a growing problem. The experts' meeting stressed the need for states to enact legislation to deal with the new manifestations of mercenary activities, as well as to sign up to the Mercenaries Convention. Another major shortcoming with current international law is that it does not regulate private security companies. Given the relative lack of support by states for current international law concerning mercenaries, and the likely difficulties in amending existing international law, the experts suggested that the best way forward in regulating mercenaries lay in the adoption of tighter regulations at the national level.

They also made several recommendations for moving the issue forward, in particular, that 'a systematic and comprehensive review of the legal definition of mercenary be considered as a matter of urgency and include, *inter alia*, the elements of motive, purpose, payment, type of action and nationality; particular attention be given to the purpose for which a mercenary is hired; a distinction be made between new forms of mercenaries and related crimes such as terrorism, arms trafficking and organised crime in which mercenaries might be involved', that states implement IHL and human rights treaties which aim to curb mercenarism; that, given that mercenarism is not a crime under the ICC Statute, 'consideration be given to the extent to which mercenarism could be considered an aggravating circumstance in the event of liability for genocide, crimes against humanity and war crimes'; that the problem be addressed by all UN treaty monitoring bodies; and that the Special Rapporteur's mandate be expanded to include private security firms.

On 6 April 2001 the UN Commission on Human Rights adopted resolution 2001/3 on the use of mercenaries. As well as expressing its concern at the widespread use of mercenaries and the implications for peace and security and human rights, and acknowledging the link identified by Mr Ballesteros between mercenarism and terrorism and organised crime, including arms trafficking, the Commission reiterated the importance of a clearer legal definition of mercenaries that would make for more efficient prevention and punishment of mercenary activities, and urged all states to adopt legislation to ensure that their territories and nationals are not used for mercenary activities and to investigate the links between mercenarism and international and national criminality.

The General Assembly adopted resolution A/RES/56/2[22] on 24 December 2001 in which it, *inter alia*, expressed its alarm about the impact of mercenarism on peace and security, particularly in Africa and small states, and stated that mercenaries and mercenarism constitute a threat to peace and security and to the enjoyment of human rights, including self-determination. It also recognised that 'armed conflict, terrorism, arms trafficking and covert operations by third powers, among other things, encourage the demand for mercenaries on the global market'

22. Entitled, 'Use of mercenaries as a means of violating human rights and impeding the exercise of the right of peoples to self-determination'. This followed its adoption on 26 October 2000 of resolution 55/86 entitled 'Use of mercenaries as a means of violating human rights and impeding the exercise of the right of peoples to self-determination'.

and 'urged all states to take the necessary steps and to exercise the utmost vigilance against the menace posed by the activities of mercenaries'. It also called on states 'to investigate the possibility of mercenary involvement whenever and wherever criminal acts of a terrorist nature occur and to hold those responsible to account', and requested the UN Special Rapporteur to propose 'a clearer definition of mercenaries, including clear nationality criteria, and to make suggestions on the procedure to be followed for the international adoption of a new definition'.

The Third Committee of the GA also devoted its meeting of 15 November to the subject, and here also addressed the connection between mercenarism and terrorism, and other criminal activities, including the financing of terrorism. Addressing the meeting, the Special Rapporteur said that when terrorist attacks are investigated, it is imperative to explore whether mercenaries are involved, and to address mercenarism in any counter-terrorism initiatives. They are also frequently involved in fights for self-determination.[23]

3. PROTECTED PERSONS

3.1 Civilians generally

On 30 March 2001, the UN Secretary-General published his second Report of the Secretary-General to the Security Council on the protection of civilians in armed conflict.[24] In it he noted that the majority of suggestions he had made in his first report had not yet been implemented.[25] Most of the problems identified in the first report – the use of child soldiers; the indiscriminate use of landmines, large-scale forced displacement and ethnic cleansing, the targeting of women and children, the denial of the most basic human rights, and widespread impunity – are still characteristic features of armed conflict. Another feature is increasing attacks on the staff of international organisations.[26]

The report's focus was on identifying 'additional steps which Member States can take to strengthen their own capacity to protect the civilian victims of war more effectively, and on initiatives that the Security Council and other organs of the United Nations can take to complement these efforts'.[27] The Secretary-General emphasised the need to establish a 'culture of protection', and set out suggestions for how this might be achieved. But he also stressed that the protection of civilians

23. See 'Right of people to self-determination', Report of the Third Committee, A/56/582, 7 December 2001. For an overview of the work of the UN Special Rapporteur, see 'The mercenary issue at the UN Commission on Human Rights: the need for a new approach', International Alert, http://www.international-alert.org/pdf/pubsec/unhr.pdf.

24. S/2001/331, 30 March 2001. The first report, S/1999/957, was submitted to the Security Council on 8 September 1999. See 2 *YIHL* (1999) pp. 214-215.

25. Ibid., para. 2.

26. Ibid.

27. Ibid., para. 4.

is most effectively achieved through conflict prevention.[28] Measures to enhance protection of the civilian population include: prosecuting those who violate international criminal law and denying amnesties for serious crimes.[29] The Secretary-General urged the SC and the GA 'to provide, from the outset, reliable, sufficient and sustained funding for international efforts, whether existing or future international tribunals, arrangements established in the context of United Nations peace operations, or initiatives undertaken in concert with individual Member States, to bring to justice perpetrators of grave violations of international humanitarian and human rights law.'[30] Further, he recommend that the SC consider addressing the issue of impunity, and truth and reconciliation as appropriate, during the crafting of peacekeeping mandates, 'in particular where this response has been triggered by widespread and systematic violations of international humanitarian and human rights law'.[31]

3.2 Children

On 7 September 2001, the UN Secretary-General issued his second report entitled 'Children and Armed Conflict', pursuant to resolution 1314 (2000).[32] It reported on the progress made in implementing the 55 recommendations set out in his first report and highlighted key steps that should be taken in the short-term, and set out some measures or 'action points' to ensure better protection of children during and following armed conflict. His report indicated that while significant progress had been made in many aspects of child protection, the challenges ahead remained overwhelming. Particular problems highlighted include the continuing widespread abduction and forced recruitment of children; the connection between the illegal exploitation of natural resources by armed groups and exploitation of minors; the particular needs of children in any demobilisation and reintegration process; and the problem of HIV and AIDS as it affects children. The report also addressed the need to punish serious violations of international humanitarian law, particularly those directed against children. It pointed out that all the relevant players – states, international and non-governmental organisations and the UN bodies – all agreed that prosecution and if necessary punishment of those who commit such crimes is essential in order to construct the foundations for post-conflict peace and security. When children are involved as victims or witnesses of such crimes, very special consideration must be given to the manner in which their experiences are portrayed and documented, and what redress the processes established to deal with such criminality bring for children and their families and societies.

On 20 November 2001, the UN Security Council again turned its attention to the

---

28. See ibid., paras. 6-8.
29. Ibid., paras. 9-10.
30. Recommendation 1.
31. Recommendation 2.
32. A/56/342-S/200/852, 7 September 2001. For a discussion of his first report, see 3 *YIHL* (2000) p. 174.

subject of children and armed conflict, specifically, the effect of armed conflict on children. Resolution 1379 was a long resolution, which set out the intentions of the Security Council with respect to this issue, as well as addressing the parties to armed conflicts; states and regional and sub-regional organisations and arrangements; UN agencies, funds and programme; international and regional financial and development institutions; and the UN Secretary-General.

Alluding to the Secretary-General's report, and expressing its commitment to addressing the impact of armed conflict on children, it expressed 'its determination to give the fullest attention to the question of the protection of children in armed conflict when considering the matters of which it is seized' (para. 1). It further expressed its 'readiness to explicitly include provisions for the protection of children, when considering the mandates of peacekeeping operations', and reaffirmed 'its readiness to continue to include, where appropriate, children protection advisers in peacekeeping operations'.

It called on all parties to armed conflicts to fully respect the relevant provisions of applicable international law relating to the rights of children in armed conflict.[33] After further addressing the steps that financial and development and regional institutions should take, it requested the SG to take the protection of children into account in peacekeeping plans; to ensure that all peacekeeping personnel receive and follow appropriate guidance on HIV/AIDS and training in human rights, humanitarian and refugee law relevant to children; and to intensify monitoring and reporting by peacekeeping operations on the situation of children in armed conflict. It further requested him to submit a report to the Council by 31 October 2002 on the implementation of the resolution as well as resolutions 1261 (1999) and 1314 (2000), and to attach to it a list of parties to armed conflicts that recruit or use children, in situations that are on the SC's agenda or that may be brought to its attention under Article 99 of the Charter where he thinks they may threaten international peace and security.

4. TRUTH AND RECONCILIATION COMMISSIONS

4.1 Truth and Reconciliation Commission for Bosnia and Herzegovina

The President of the International Criminal Tribunal for the Former Yugoslavia, Claude Jorda, and a representative of the OTP attended a conference held in Bosnia in May on the establishment of a truth and reconciliation commission for Bosnia and Herzegovina. In his presentation, President Jorda stressed the ICTY's support

33. In particular, the 1949 Geneva Conventions and Additional Protocol, the 1989 Child's Convention and its Additional Protocol of 2000, Amended Protocol II to the Certain Convention Weapons Convention, ILO Convention No. 182 on the Elimination of the Worst Forms of Child Labour, the 1997 Landmine Convention. The SG also noted the inclusion as a war crime in the ICC Statute of the conscription or enlistment of children under the age of 15 years into the Armed Forces or using them to actively participate in hostilities.

for the initiative to establish a TRC for Bosnia.[34] He acknowledged the limitations of the ICTY, in particular, *vis-à-vis* victims, in establishing the causes of the conflicts, and in reconstructing a national identity.[35] The President expressed some reservations about the draft law to establish the TRC, however, including the fact that it appeared 'to grant to the commission functions and powers similar in many ways to those of the International Tribunal', and further that it failed 'to define clearly the commission's obligations to the International Tribunal'. He suggested 'a redefinition of the objectives, mandate and tasks of the commission so that they will be more in keeping with the conception' he articulated in his address, to ensure that 'the commission is an organ truly *complementary* to the International Tribunal'.

5. INTERNATIONAL CRIMINAL LAW

5.1 Ad Hoc International Criminal Tribunals

By 2001 both Tribunals worked at full capacity and, in the words of Carla Del Ponte, Chief Prosecutor for both Tribunals, began 'to consider what has been called "our exit strategy"'.[36] In line with the policy of streamlining the prosecutorial strategy, investigations and prosecutions focused almost exclusively on those in a leadership position or 'notorious individuals'.[37]

On 20 September, the Registrars of the ICTY and ICTR signed a 'joint statement on co-operation' aimed at improving the work of both Tribunals. It signalled that the two Tribunals would work more closely together in the areas of court management; judicial matters; chambers, including the Appeals Chamber; legal aid and defence matters; legal advisory matters; library; victims and witnesses issues; outreach programmes; administrative matters; communications, public information and press relations; and translation. At a joint press conference, the two Registrars stated that they were 'striving to achieve the common goal of completing the respective mandates of the two Tribunals by the year 2008, or as soon as possible thereafter'.[38]

---

34. See 'The ICTY and the Truth and Reconciliation Commission in Bosnia and Herzegovina', Press Release of the President, JL/P.I.S./591-e/The Hague, 17 May 2001.

35. Ibid.

36. For details see 'Address by the Prosecutor of the International Criminal Tribunal for the Former Yugoslavia, Carla Del Ponte, to the UN Security Council', Press Release of the Office of the Prosecutor, GR/P.I.S./642-e, The Hague, 27 November 2001.

37. Ibid.

38. 'Registrars of ICTY and ICTR sign statement on co-operation', Press Release of the Registry, TK/ICTR/621-e, The Hague, 21 September 2001.

5.1.1 *International Criminal Tribunal for the Former Yugoslavia*

5.1.1.1 Appointment of new judges

With the implementation of the various reforms initiated in 1999 and 2000, the Tribunal was able to shift into top gear.[39] A major contributing factor was the election and taking up of office of the *ad litem* judges.[40] On 12 June 2001, the General Assembly elected 27 *ad litem* judges to serve on the ICTY. The first six to serve were appointed by UN Secretary-General Kofi Annan, and took up their new posts as of 3 September,[41] coincident with a significant increase in trial activity beginning in September. President Jorda hailed their appointment as 'a significant turning point in the history of the Tribunal in that it will allow the Trial Chambers to double their judgement capacity to six simultaneous trials by the end of January 2002'.[42] Six new permanent judges were appointed on 22 November 2001.[43]

5.1.1.2 State cooperation

Cooperation with the states of the former Yugoslavia improved, particularly with Serbia. The turning point was the overthrow and arrest by the new government of President Slobodan Milošević. His handover to the Tribunal by Prime Minister Zoran Dindjić indicated a new spirit of cooperation, but that cooperation was equally influenced by the threat by the United States *inter alia* to withhold economic aid to Serbia. Moreover, the handover itself exposed sharp differences of opinion and attitudes towards the ICTY within the new government, with President Kostunica an outspoken opponent of the handover and Prime Minister Dindjić adopting a more pragmatic position. In his address to the General Assembly on 26 November, President Jorda said that while there was enhanced cooperation of all UN Member States, there was still some way to go.[44]

5.1.1.3 Changes to the Rules

On the procedural side, important changes to the Rules of Procedure and Evidence were made by the Judges at their 12 April Plenary. According to President Jorda,

---

39. For details see 'Address by His Excellency, Judge Claude Jorda, President of the International Criminal Tribunal for the Former Yugoslavia, to the UN General Assembly', Press Release of the President, JD/P.I.S./640-e, The Hague, 27 November 2001.

40. See to 3 *YIHL* (2000) p. 180.

41. 'The first six ad-litem judges appointed by United Nations Secretary-General, Kofi Annan, Press Release of the President, SB/P.I.S./607-e, The Hague, 31 July 2001.

42. 'The first six *ad litem* judges to make their solemn declarations at the ICTY on Thursday 6 September 2001', Press Release of the President, JL/P.I.S./614-e, The Hague, 4 September 2001.

43. 'Events to mark the beginning of ICTY Judges' third term of office', Press Release of the Chambers, JL/P.I.S./636-e, The Hague, 21 November 2001.

44. 'Address by His Excellency, Judge Claude Jorda, President of the International Criminal Tribunal for the Former Yugoslavia, to the UN General Assembly', Press Release of the President, JD/P.I.S./640-e, The Hague, 27 November 2001.

they were 'aimed at allowing Judges to exercise better control over trials, thus reducing their length without infringing on the fundamental rights of the accused'. They included changes arising from the appointment of *ad litem* judges which delineated the differences of functions and duties between them and the permanent judges; changes which streamlined and enhanced pre-trial procedures, including allowing Senior Legal Officers a limited role in pre-trial preparations; changes designed to enhance and improve the contents of prosecution and defence pre-trial briefs to enable judges to assess the relevance of proposed witnesses and their number; changes to allow judges, after hearing from the prosecution and defence, to set the number of witnesses that could be called and determine the time available to the parties for presenting evidence; changes to allow judges to impose sanctions on the parties when they failed to respect their commitments by refusing to hear witnesses whose names do not appear on the witness lists that were agreed on; and changes to allow judges to prevent a trial from being interrupted by untimely interlocutory appeals.[45]

5.1.1.4 Arrests and surrenders

A number of accused either surrendered to the Tribunal or were apprehended. On 12 March, Blagoje Simić, jointly accused in the Bosanski Samac indictment, along with five others, with crimes against humanity committed during 1992, voluntarily and unconditionally surrendered. His surrender meant that a trial of all of the accused (all of whom were now in ICTY custody, except for one, Slobodan Miljković, who had died) could go ahead.[46]

On 23 March, Milomir Stakić, former head of the Crisis Staff of the Prijedor Municipality in Bosnia, and charged with both individual and command responsibility for genocide, was transferred to the Tribunal following his arrest on 22 March.[47]

On 15 April, Dragan Obrenović, the former commander of the Zvornik Brigade, and accused under Article 7(1) and (3) of genocide, crimes against humanity and war crimes committed in Srebrencia, was transferred to the Tribunal, following his arrest earlier that day by SFOR.

On 29 June, the Tribunal took custody of its most senior accused, former Yugoslav President Slobodan Milošević. President Jorda hailed Milošević's handover as 'a turning point and the beginning of a new era in the development of international criminal justice. The forthcoming trial of a former Head of State is a new and irreversible step in relation to the international community's resolve to

45. See 'Results of Extraordinary Plenary held on 12 April, 2001', Press Release of the Plenary, SB/P.I.S./587e, The Hague, 17 April 2001.

46. See Press Release of the Office of the Prosecutor, FH/P.I.S./574e, The Hague, 12 March 2001.

47. See 'Milomir Stakić transferred to the ICTY', Press Release of the Tribunal, JL/FH/P.I.S./581e, The Hague, 23 March 2001.

fight against impunity.'[48] Carla Del Ponte called it 'an important milestone for international criminal justice'.[49] The handover of Milošević also presented the Tribunal with new challenges, as the accused quickly made clear his refusal to recognise the court, which he dubbed 'a false' and illegal tribunal. He also indicated his intention not to appoint defence counsel, despite there being no shortage of lawyers eager to represent the world's most infamous defendant. The Tribunal's solution was to appoint three *amicus curiae* 'not to represent the accused but to assist in the proper determination of the case'.[50]

Originally accused under Article 7(1) and (3) with crimes against humanity and war crimes committed in Kosovo,[51] on 8 October 2001 a second indictment against Milošević charging him with crimes against humanity and war crimes committed in Croatia, was confirmed.[52] Then, on 22 November, a third indictment, concerning Bosnia, and most importantly charging him with genocide, as well as with crimes against humanity and war crimes, was confirmed.[53] On 27 November, the Prosecutor filed a motion requesting joinder of the three indictments.[54] On 11 December, Trial Chamber III rendered an oral decision on the Prosecutor's Motion for Joinder of the indictments, followed on 13 December by a written decision. It held that while Croatia and Bosnia could be joined, the Kosovo Indictment should be tried separately, and that case should commence first.[55] It reasoned that while it accepted the Prosecutor's argument that the crimes charged in the Croatia and Bosnia indictments formed part of a common scheme, strategy or plan, the crimes committed in Kosovo did not form part of this 'joint criminal enterprise'. The Prosecutor appealed. No decision had been rendered by the end of the year. Earlier, on 8 November, the Trial Chamber issued its Decision on Preliminary Motions, which, *inter alia*, rejected the accused's arguments concerning the illegality and independence of the Tribunal and its inability to grant him a fair and impartial trial.[56]

48. 'Slobodan Milošević transferred into the custody of the International Criminal Tribunal for the Former Yugoslavia', Press Release of the Registry, CC/P.I.S./597e, The Hague, 29 June 2001.

49. Ibid. See also 'Statement of the Prosecutor, Carla Del Ponte', Press Release of the Office of the Prosecutor, F.H./P.I.S./598e, The Hague, 29 June 2001.

50. 'Milošević case: The Registrar appoints a team of experienced international lawyers as *amicus curiae* to assist the Trial Chamber', Press Release of the Registry, CC/P.I.S./617e, The Hague, 6 September 2001.

51. *Prosecutor* v. *Slobodan Milošević et al*, Case No. IT-99-37-PT. Originally confirmed on 24 May 1999 and subsequently confirmed in an amended form on 29 June 2001.

52. *Prosecutor* v. *Slobodan Milošević et al*, Case No. IT-01-50-PT. 8 October 2001. 'Judge Rodrigues confirms indictment charging Slobodan Milošević with crimes committed in Croatia', Press Release of the Chambers, JL/P.I.S./627e, The Hague, 9 October 2001.

53. *Prosecutor* v. *Slobodan Milošević et al*, Case No. IT-01-51-PT, 22 November 2001.

54. *Prosecutor* v. *Slobodan Milošević et al*, Prosecutor's Motion for Joinder, filed 27 November 2001, and Prosecutor's Corrigendum to Motion for Joinder filed 27 November 2001, filed 10 December 2001.

55. *Prosecutor* v. *Slobodan Milošević*, Case No. IT-99-37-PT; IT-01-50-PT; IT-01-51-PT. Decision on Prosecution's Motion for Joinder, 13 December 2001.

56. *Prosecutor* v. *Slobodan Milošević et al*, Decision on Preliminary Motions, 8 November 2001.

On 25 July, Major-General Rahim Ademi, Acting Commander of the Gospić Military District during the Medak Pocket operation, and charged under Article 7(1) and (3) with crimes against humanity and war crimes allegedly committed against Serb civilians in the so-called Republika Srpska Krajina in 1993, voluntarily surrendered.

On 2 August, Bosnia and Herzegovina arrested three senior Bosnian commanders who had been indicted by the Tribunal. General Enver Hadzihasanović, General Mehmed Alagić and Colonel Amir Kubura were indicted under Article 7(3) on 13 July for grave breaches and violations of the laws or customs of war. Controversially, most of the crimes of which they were accused were perpetrated by foreign Muslim fighters or so-called 'Mujahedin'.[57]

On 15 August, Dragan Jokić, former Chief of Engineering of the 1st Zvornik Brigade, with the rank of Major and accused under Article 7(1) of crimes against humanity and war crimes carried out against the civilian population of Srebrenica, surrendered and was transferred to the Tribunal.[58] On 25 September, Sefer Halilović, at various times Deputy Commander of the Supreme Command Staff of the Army of Bosnia and Herzegovina and Chief of the Supreme Command Staff, and charged under Article 7(3) with violations of the laws and customs of war with respect to the killing of Bosnian Croat civilians during the Neretva-93 Operation,[59] voluntarily surrendered to the Tribunal.

On 12 November, Miodrag Jokić was transferred to the ICTY following his voluntary surrender earlier that day. He was accused with several others of war crimes for launching an attack on the Croatian town of Dubrovnik.[60]

On 21 November, Pasko Ljubicić, the former commander of the 4th Military Police Battalion of the HVO Military Police and later the Assistant Chief of Military Police Administration for the Central Bosnia Operative Zone, and accused under Article 7(1) and (3) of crimes against humanity and violations of the law or customs of war committed in the course of attacks by the HVO on the Bosnian Muslim towns of Ahmići, Nadioći, Pirići and Santići in 1993, voluntarily surrendered and was transferred to the Tribunal.[61]

A number of those detained were subsequently granted provisional release, signalling a shift in the Tribunal's policy on this matter. The fact that those accused who were granted provisional release had all surrendered seems to have been a relevant factor.

57. 'Arrest of General Enver Hadzihasanovic, General Mehmed Alagic and Colonel Amir Kubura', Press Release of the Office of the Prosecutor, GB/P.I.S./610e, The Hague, 3 August 2001.

58. 'Surrender of Dragan Jokić to the International Criminal Tribunal for the Former Yugoslavia', Press Release of the Registry, JL/P.I.S./612e, The Hague, 15 August 2001.

59. 'Voluntary surrender of Sefer Halilović to the International Criminal Tribunal for the Former Yugoslavia', Press Release of the Registry, JL/P.I.S./622e, The Hague, 25 September 2001.

60. See 'Voluntary surrender of Miodrag Jokić to the International Criminal Tribunal for the Former Yugoslavia', Press Release of the Registry, JL/P.I.S./634e, The Hague, 12 November 2001. See also 'Full contents of the Dubrovnik indictment made public', Press Release of the Registry, JL/P.I.S./625e, The Hague, 2 October 2001.

61. See 'Voluntary surrender of Pasko Ljubicić to the International Criminal Tribunal for the Former Yugoslavia', Press Release of the Registry, JL/P.I.S./637e, The Hague, 21 November 2001.

Notwithstanding these arrests and surrenders, by the end of 2001 a number of important accused remained at large, most notably, Radovan Karadžić and Ratko Mladić.[62]

5.1.1.5 New trials

Several new trials commenced. That of Dusko Sikirica, Damir Dosen and Dragan Kolundžija began on 19 March. The 10th of September represented a milestone of sorts, with an unprecedented three trials commencing simultaneously: the Bosanski Samac trial, involving Milan and Blagoje Simić, Miroslav Tadić and Simo Zarić, the Martinović and Naletilić ('Stela' and 'Tuta') trial and the Mitar Viseljević trial.[63]

The trial began on 3 December of Major General Stanislav Galić, commander of the Sarajevo Romanija corps during the siege of Sarajevo.[64] He was charged under Article 7(1) and (3) with crimes against humanity and war crimes perpetrated against the citizens of Sarajevo.

5.1.1.6 Judgements[65]

5.1.1.6.1 *Prosecutor v. Zejnil Delalić, Zdravko Mucić, Hazim Delić and Esad Landžo*, Appeals Judgement, 20 February 2001

Three of the four accused had filed appeals against their convictions (Delalić had been acquitted) and sentences. The Prosecutor had filed a cross appeal, including against Delalić's acquittal. A total of 48 grounds of appeals were filed. The Judgement was significant as it was the first of the ICTY Appeals Chamber to pronounce on several issues, including that of command responsibility and cumulative convictions.

The Appeals Chamber upheld the ninth and tenth grounds of appeal filed by Delić[66] and entered a verdict of not-guilty on counts one and two of the indictment.[67]

---

62. See 'Address by His Excellency, Judge Claude Jorda, President of the International Criminal Tribunal for the Former Yugoslavia, to the UN General Assembly', Press Release of the Presidency, JD/P.I.S./640-e, The Hague, 27 November 2001.

63. 'Three trials to begin on Monday 10 September before newly composed Trial Chambers', Press Release of the Presidency, CC/P.I.S./618-e, The Hague, 7 September 2001.

64. 'The trial of Stanislav Galić will begin on Monday 3 December 2001', JL/P.I.S./643-e, The Hague, 30 November 2001.

65. The following case summaries are not intended to be comprehensive. The aim is to give a broad overview of the legal and factual findings, and to highlight any original jurisprudence and significant divergences from earlier cases.

66. Whether the evidence was (9) legally and (10) factually sufficient to sustain a conviction on counts one and two of the indictment.

67. Charging him with the murder of Šcepo Gotovac. See para. 460.

5.1.1.6.1.1 Cumulative convictions

Concerning the appeals relating to the issue of cumulative convictions, the Chamber upheld the twenty-first ground of appeal by Delić[68] and the seventh ground of appeal by Mucić,[69] and accordingly dismissed their convictions under Article 3 of the Statute,[70] notwithstanding that in earlier jurisprudence of the ICTY, including of the Appeals Chamber itself, multiple convictions based on the same acts had been upheld.[71] It found that reasons of fairness to the accused, and the consideration that only distinct crimes justify cumulative convictions, require that cumulative convictions are permissible only if each statutory provision involved has a materially distinct element not contained in the other. 'An element is materially distinct from another if it requires proof of a fact not required by the other.'[72]

A majority of the Chamber found that this assessment of the elements of the offences must take into account all of the elements of the offences, including the *chapeaux* requirements. Where this test is not met, a decision must be made in relation to which offence it will enter a conviction, on the basis that the conviction must be for the offence containing the more specific provision. In this case, that should have been Article 2.[73] Judges Hunt and Bennouna, dissenting, agreed with the view that cumulative convictions should be permissible only where each offence has a materially different element not contained in the other, but proposed a different test of determining whether this was so in particular cases.

The Appeals Chamber remitted to a newly constituted Trial Chamber the issue of whether their sentences should be adjusted in light of the dismissal of these war crimes charges.[74]

Notwithstanding the fact that Landžo had not appealed on the question of cumulative convictions, the Appeals Chamber dismissed the less specific (war crimes) convictions against him.

5.1.1.6.1.2 Sentences

Concerning Mucić's eleventh ground of appeal, as to whether the Trial Chamber

---

68. Whether the Trial Chamber erred in entering a guilty verdict for grave breaches and for violations of the laws or customs of war based on the same acts.

69. Ibid.

70. I.e., Counts 4, 12, 19, 22, 43 and 47 against Delić and Counts 14, 34, 39, 45 and 47 against Mucić. See para. para. 431.

71. See *Tadić* Appeals Judgement. Here, however, the problem of multiple convictions was not as such addressed by the Chamber. Multiple convictions were also allowed in *Akayesu*. Under the *Tadić/Akayesu* test, the accused can be charged with and convicted of as many crimes as the facts of the case disclose if there is ideal concurrence. Ideal concurrence describes the situation where a single act of an accused contravenes more than one provision of the criminal law. In *Kupreškić*, conversely, the Trial Chamber held that the primary applicable test is whether each offence contains an element not required by the other. An additional test, which ascertains whether the various provisions at issue protect different values, can be used in conjunction with and in support of the primary test. At para. 682 of the *Kupreškić* Judgement, 14 January 2000. See 3 *YIHL* (2000) pp. 186 at 190-192.

72. Ibid., para. 412.

73. Ibid., para. 413.

74. Ibid., para. 431.

had given him an appropriate sentence, the Appeals Chamber found that the Trial Chamber erred in making adverse reference when imposing sentence to the fact that he had not given oral evidence in the trial, and directed the reconstituted Trial Chamber to consider the effect, if any, of that error on the sentence to be imposed on Mucić. All other grounds of appeal by the appellants were dismissed.

The Appeals Chamber upheld the Prosecutor's fourth ground of appeal, that the seven year sentence imposed on Mucić was inadequate, and remitted to the new Trial Chamber the question of an appropriate revised sentence. All other grounds of appeal by the cross-appellant, including the acquittal of Delalić, were dismissed.

5.1.1.6.1.3 Command responsibility

The Appeals Chamber in particular confirmed that command responsibility under Article 7(3) of the Statute is not limited to *de jure* but extends to *de facto* commanders. The critical thing is that the superior has the power to prevent or punish, and that this 'power or authority to prevent or to punish does not solely arise from *de jure* authority conferred through official appointment'.[75]

The Chamber found that a position of de facto command may be sufficient to establish the necessary superior-subordinate relationship, as long as the relevant degree of control is established, specifically, where the superior has effective control over the persons committing the underlying violations of international humanitarian law, in the sense of having the material ability to prevent or punish the commission of these offences. This showing of effective control must be established both in cases of military and civilian, and de jure as well as de facto superiors,[76] and is more important than a formal title. In fact, 'the possession of *de jure* power in itself may not suffice for the finding of command responsibility if it does not manifest in effective control, although a court may presume that possession of such power *prima facie* results in effective control unless proof to the contrary is produced'.[77] The Chamber specifically rejected the argument of the prosecution that substantial influence is a sufficient basis for a finding of superior responsibility.

The Chamber also looked in detail at the question of the mental element, and particularly at the meaning of the term 'knew or had reason to know', given its importance to the jurisprudence of the Tribunal. In particular, it rejected the Prosecutor's contention that there is a separate duty on the commander, not specified in Article 7(3), to acquire knowledge. 'The point here should not be that knowledge may be presumed if a person fails in his *duty* to obtain the relevant information of a crime, but that it may be presumed if he had the *means* to obtain the knowledge but deliberately refrained from doing so. ... It is however noted that although a commander's failure to remain apprised of his subordinates' action, or to set up a monitoring system may constitute a neglect of duty which results in liability within the military disciplinary framework, it will not necessarily result in criminal

75. Ibid., para. 193.
76. Ibid., para. 196.
77. Ibid., paras. 197, 198.

liability.'[78] 'In the Appeals Chamber's view, an assessment of the mental element required by Article 7(3) of the Statute should be conducted in the specific circumstances of each case, taking into account the specific situation of the superior concerned at the time in question. ... The Appeals Chamber would not describe superior responsibility as a vicarious liability doctrine, insofar as vicarious liability may suggest a form of *strict* imputed liability.'[79]

As for civilian superiors, 'a superior will be criminally responsible through the principles of superior responsibility only if information was available to him which would have put him on notice of offences committed by subordinates. This is consistent with the customary law standard of *mens rea* as existing at the time of the offences charged in the Indictment.'[80]

5.1.1.6.2 *Prosecutor* v. *Dragoljub Kunarac, Radomir Kovac and Zoran Vuković (Foča)*, Judgement, 22 February 2001

In a groundbreaking judgement in the so-called 'rape camp case', the Trial Chamber convicted all three accused on charges of orchestrated sexual offences carried out in the town of Foča between early-1992 and mid-1993. Most notably, the Chamber handed down the first convictions by the ICTY for rape and enslavement as crimes against humanity. While denying that the systematic rape of women and girls in the town of Foča was used by VRS troops as a 'weapon of war', in the sense of a concerted approach as part of combat activities, the Chamber found that rape was used by the VRS as an instrument of terror, which they were given free rein to apply whenever and against whomsoever they wished. It was part of a systematic attack against Muslim civilians.

Dragoljub Kunarac was convicted of 11 counts and acquitted of five. He was convicted of torture as a crime against humanity, of rape as a crime against humanity, of torture as a violation of the laws or customs or war and of rape as a violation of the laws or customs of war perpetrated against various victims. He was acquitted of the same charges with respect to other victims. He was also acquitted of outrages upon personal dignity as a violation of the laws or customs of war. He was sentenced to a single sentence of 28 years' imprisonment.

Radomir Kovac was convicted on the four counts with which he was charged: enslavement as a crime against humanity, rape as a crime against humanity, rape as a violation of the laws or customs of war, and outrages upon personal dignity as a violation of the laws or customs of war. He received a single sentence of 20 years.

Zoran Vuković was acquitted of four counts: rape as a crime against humanity, torture as a crime against humanity, rape as a violation of the laws or customs of war and torture as a violation of the laws or customs of war, on the grounds that these charges had not been proven beyond reasonable doubt. He was convicted of four other counts of rape as a crime against humanity, torture as a crime against

78. Ibid., para. 226.
79. Ibid., para. 239.
80. Ibid., para. 241.

humanity, rape as a violation of the laws or customs of war and torture as a violation of the laws or customs of war. He received a single sentence of 12 years' imprisonment.

The main contribution of this judgement to the jurisprudence is on the question of rape and enslavement as crimes against humanity and torture.

5.1.1.6.2.1 Responsibility under Article 7(1) and 7(3)

On this question, the Judgement reaffirmed earlier jurisprudence of the Tribunal in *Furundžija, Tadić, Aleksovski* and *Čelebići.*

5.1.1.6.2.2 Common Article 3

The Trial Chamber mainly reiterated earlier jurisprudence on the crimes under Article 3 of the Statute, but did make one interesting statement *obiter* on the question of general requirements for both the application of common Article 3 of the Geneva Conventions and the specific offences charged under common Article 3. It set out the list of requirement identified in *Čelebići*,[81] then found: 'It would appear to the Trial Chamber that common Article 3 may also require some relationship to exist between a perpetrator and a party to the conflict.'[82] However, a determination on this question was not necessary in this case as all of the accused fought on behalf of parties to the conflict.

5.1.1.6.2.3 Article 5 Crimes Against Humanity

On the common elements of the crimes under Article 5, the judgement confirmed earlier jurisprudence, mainly *Tadić* and *Kupreskić.*

On the question of rape as a crime against humanity, the Chamber by and large concurred with the approach taken in the *Furundžija* case, which adopted a more narrow definition of the *actus reus* of rape[83] than that adopted in the *Akayesu* case.[84] However, it registered one clarification. With regard to its understanding of the element in the *Furundžija* definition that the act be committed 'by coercion or force or threat of force against the victim or the third person', it considered that

> 'the *Furundžija* definition, although appropriate to the circumstances of that case, is in one respect more narrowly stated than is required by international law. In stating that the relevant act of sexual penetration will constitute rape only if accompanied by coercion or force or threat of force against the will of the victim of a third person, the *Furundžija* definition does not refer to other factors which would render an act of sexual penetration *non-consensual or non-voluntary* on the part of the victim, which, as foreshadowed in the

81. *Čelebići* Judgement, 20 February 2000, para. 420.

82. *Kunarac*, para. 407. For the subsequent response to this finding by the Appeals Chamber in the *Akayesu* case, see *infra*, p. 297.

83. See 2 *YIHL* (1999) pp. 224 at 225.

84. See 1 *YIHL* (1998) pp. 126-127.

> hearing ... is in the opinion of this Trial Chamber the accurate scope of this aspect of the definition in international law.'[85]
>
> 'Given that it is evident from the *Furundžija* case that the terms coercion, force, or threat of force were not be interpreted narrowly and that coercion in particular would encompass *most* conduct which negates consent, this understanding of the international law on the subject does not differ substantially from the *Furundžija* definition.'[86]

The Chamber then offered a third definition of rape (following those given in *Akayesu/Čelebići* and *Furundžija*), a modified version of the *Furundžija* one:

> '... the Trial Chamber understands that the *actus reus* of the crime of rape in international law is constituted by: the sexual penetration, however slight, (a) of the vagina or anus by the penis of the perpetrator or any other object used by the perpetrator; or (b) of the mouth of the victim by the penis of the perpetrator; where such sexual penetration occurs without the consent of the victim. Consent for this purpose must be given voluntary, as a result of the victim's free will, assessed in the context of the surrounding circumstances. The *mens rea* is the intention to effect this sexual penetration, and the knowledge that it occurs without the consent of the victim.'[87]

5.1.1.6.2.4 Torture as war crimes and crimes against humanity

As regards torture as a war crime and crime against humanity, the Chamber first undertook to provide a definition of the crime of torture under international humanitarian law. It noted its view that 'notions developed in the field of human rights can be transposed in international humanitarian law only if they take into consideration the specificities of the latter body of law'.[88] It stated that the definition of torture set out in Article 1 of the Torture Convention could not be considered as the definition under customary international law, and that therefore the Convention could only serve as an interpretational aid.[89] It found to be customary the following prohibited purposes: '(a) obtaining information or a confession, (b) punishing, intimidating or coercing the victim or a third person, (c) discriminating, on any ground, against the victim or a third person. There are some doubts as to whether other purposes have come to be recognised under customary international law. The issue does not need to be resolved here, because the conduct of the accused is appropriately subsumable under the above-mentioned purposes.'[90]

The Chamber concurred with the *Čelebići* Decision of 16 November 1998 that 'there is no requirement under customary international law that the conduct must be solely perpetrated for one of the prohibited purposes'.[91] 'Secondly, the nature of the relationship between the underlying offence – torture – and the armed conflict

85. Kunarac, para. 438.
86. Ibid., para. 459.
87. Ibid., para. 460.
88. Ibid., para. 471.
89. Ibid., para. 482.
90. Ibid., para. 485.
91. Ibid., para. 468.

depends, under the Tribunal's Statute, on the qualification of the offence, as a grave breach, a war crime or a crime against humanity.'[92] 'Thirdly, the Torture Convention requires that the pain or suffering be inflicted by or at the instigation of or with the consent or acquiescence of a public official or other person acting in an official capacity.'[93]

The Trial Chamber concluded that

> '... the definition of torture under international humanitarian law does not comprise the same elements as the definition of torture generally applied under human rights law. In particular, the Trial Chamber is of the view that the presence of a state official or of any other authority-wielding person in the torture process is not necessary for the offence to be regarded as torture under international humanitarian law.'[94]

The Trial Chamber therefore held that,

> '... in the field of international humanitarian law, the elements of the offence of torture, under customary international law are as follows:
> (i)The infliction, by act or omission, of severe pain or suffering, whether physical or mental.
> (ii)The act or omission must be intentional.
> (iii)The act or omission must aim at obtaining information or a confession, or at punishing, intimidating or coercing the victim of a third person, or at discriminating, on any ground, against the victim or a third person.'[95]

5.1.1.6.2.5 Outrages upon personal dignity

While both the Trial and Appeals Chambers had in earlier jurisprudence recognised outrages upon personal dignity as constituting an offence recognised by Article 3 of the Statute, the precise elements of the offence had not previously been set out by the Appeals Chamber, although some of the elements of the offence had earlier been set out by the Trial Chamber in *Alekovski*.[96] Both the Trial and Appeals Decisions in the *Aleksovski* case had noted that outrages upon personal dignity is a category of the crime of inhuman treatment.[97] As noted in that case, the key aspect of the *actus reus* of the offence is that there is *serious* suffering or humiliation, measured objectively, although there is no requirement that the suffering or humiliation be long-lasting.[98] The Appeals Chamber in *Kunarac* found that the Trial Chamber in *Aleksovski* had not, however, clearly identified the *mens rea*

92. Ibid., para. 487.
93. Ibid., para. 488.
94. Ibid., para. 496.
95. Ibid., para. 496.
96. See *Prosecutor* v. *Aleksovski*, Judgement, case No. 95-14/1-T, 28 June 1999, paras. 51, 54, 56.
97. Ibid., para. 54, and the decision of the Appeals Chamber, 24 March 2000, para. 26
98. Aleksovski, Trial Chamber, para. 54; Appeals Chamber, para. 37.

elements.[99] The Appeals Chamber in *Aleksovski* had, however, decided that specific intent to humiliate, ridicule or degrade the victim was not required,[100] but left open the question whether there is any requirement of knowledge of the foreseeable consequences.[101]

Having reviewed the applicable jurisprudence, the Trial Chamber in *Kunarac* stated that it was of the view that

> 'the requirement of an intent to commit the specific act or omission which gives rise to criminal liability in this context involves a requirement that the perpetrator be aware of the objective character of the relevant act or omission. It is a necessary aspect of a true intention to undertake a particular action that there is an awareness of the nature of that act. As the relevant act or omission for an outrage upon personal dignity is an act or omission which would be generally considered to cause serious humiliation, degradation or otherwise be a serious attack on human dignity, an accused must know that his act or omission is of that character - ie., that it could cause serious humiliation, degradation or affront to human dignity. This is not the same as requiring that the accused knew of the *actual* consequences of the act.'[102]

The Chamber concluded:

> 'In the view of the Trial Chamber, the offence of outrages upon personal dignity requires (i) that the accused intentionally committed or participated in an act or omission which would be generally considered to cause serious humiliation, degradation or otherwise be a serious attack on human dignity, and
> (ii) that he knew that the act or omission could have that effect.'[103]

5.1.1.6.2.6 Enslavement as a crime against humanity

The Chamber made clear that its pronouncement on enslavement as a crime against humanity was not meant to be an exhaustive treatment of the subject 'as the enslavement charges in the present case relate solely to the treatment of women and children and certain allegations of forced or compulsory labour or service'.[104]

Since this was the first case to decide on charges of enslavement, and since the crime is not defined in the ICTY Statute, it fell to the Trial Chamber to try and define the crime, by reference to relevant sources of law, including IHL and human rights law. While many of these sources prohibit slavery and the slave trade, as well as compulsory or forced labour, only a few define these crimes, in particular, the 1956 Supplementary Slavery Convention and the 1930 Forced Labour and Compulsory Labour Convention and 1957 Forced Labour Convention. After a

---

99. Kunarac, para. 509.
100. Ibid.
101. Ibid., para. 510.
102. Ibid., para. 512.
103. Ibid., para. 513.
104. Ibid., para. 516.

thorough review of the relevant sources, the Trial Chamber found that, at the time relevant to the indictment, enslavement as a crime against humanity in customary international law consisted of 'the exercise of any or all of the powers attaching to the right of ownership over a person'.[105] 'Thus, the Trial Chamber finds that the *actus reus* of the violation is the exercise of any or all of the powers attaching to the right of ownership over a person. The *mens rea* of the violation consists in the intentional exercise of such powers.'[106] It recognised that this definition 'may be broader than the traditional and sometimes apparently distinct definitions of either slavery, the slave trade and servitude or forced or compulsory labour found in other areas of international law'.[107] After setting out some indicators of enslavement, it concluded:

> 'The Trial Chamber is therefore in general agreement with the factors put forward by the Prosecutor, to be taken into consideration in determining whether enslavement was committed. These are the control of someone's movement, control of physical environment, psychological control, measures taken to prevent or deter escape, force, threat of force or coercion, duration, assertion of exclusivity, subjection to cruel treatment and abuse, control of sexuality and forced labour. The Prosecutor also submitted that the mere ability to buy, sell, trade or inherit a person or his or her labours or services could be a relevant factor. The Trial Chamber considers that the *mere ability* to do so is insufficient, such actions actually occurring could be a relevant factor.'[108]

5.1.1.6.3 *Prosecutor* v. *Dario Kordić and Mario Čerkez*, 26 February 2001

On 26 February, Trial Chamber III convicted Dario Kordić and Mario Čerkez of grave breaches of the Geneva Conventions, violations of the laws or customs of war and crimes against humanity, committed in the Lašva River Valley area of Bosnia in 1992 and 1993.

Dario Kordić, the first high-ranking politician to be convicted by the Tribunal, was at the relevant time Vice-President of the HZ H-B, a branch of the Croatian Democratic Union political party in Bosnia. Mario Čerkez was one of the founders of the HVO (Croatian Defence Council) and commander of its Viteska Brigade.

Kordić was convicted of 12 counts (four crimes against humanity, five violations of the laws or customs of war and three grave breaches) and acquitted of ten (five violations of the laws or customs of war and five grave breaches). He received a single sentence of 25 years. Čerkez was convicted of 15 counts (four crimes against humanity, five violations of the laws or customs of war and six grave breaches) and acquitted of seven (five violations of the laws or customs of war and two grave breaches). He was sentenced to 15 years' imprisonment.

---

105. Ibid., para. 539.
106. Ibid., para. 540.
107. Ibid., para. 541.
108. Ibid., para. 543.

The Chamber found that while command responsibility under Article 7(3) may attach to civilians provided the requisite level of power to prevent or punish crimes exists, Kordić possessed neither authority to prevent the crimes nor punish the perpetrators and so could not be found guilty of superior responsibility. However, it found that Čerkez did possess authority over the troops under his command.[109] He failed to take the necessary steps to prevent attacks by those troops or punish the perpetrators. He was therefore found guilty under Article 7(3).[110]

5.1.1.6.3.1 The character of the conflict

The judgement found that there was an armed conflict in Central Bosnia at the relevant time, which was internationalised by the intervention of the Republic of Croatia.[111]

5.1.1.6.3.2 Persecution as a crime against humanity

The judgement concurred with the Trial Chamber in *Kupreskić* in finding that persecution may include conduct not specifically enumerated as a crime against humanity in Article 5 of the ICTY Statute,[112] but that such conduct must reach the same level of gravity as the other crimes that are listed.[113] It also agreed with the *Kupreskić* finding that 'a single act may constitute persecution', provided there is 'clear evidence of the discriminatory intent'.[114] The Trial Chamber noted that the Indictment against Kordić was the first in the history of the International Tribunal to allege encouraging and promoting hatred on political grounds, *inter alia*, as a crime against humanity. But it found that this act, as alleged in the Indictment, did not by itself constitute persecution as a crime against humanity.

> 'It is not enumerated as a crime elsewhere in the International Tribunal Statute, but most importantly, it does not rise to the same level of gravity as the other acts enumerated in Article 5. Furthermore, the criminal prohibition of this act has not attained the status of customary international law. Thus to convict the accused for such an act as is alleged as persecution would violate the principle of legality.'[115]

The Chamber also found that dismissing and removing Bosnian Muslims from government etc. was not of sufficient gravity as to constitute a crime against humanity.[116]

The Chamber found that there was a campaign of persecution in Central Bosnia during the period covered by the indictment, directed against the Bosnian Muslim

109. Ibid., paras. 840-841.
110. Ibid., paras. 842-843.
111. See in particular paras. 109 and 145.
112. Para. 194.
113. Para. 195.
114. Para. 199.
115. Para. 209.
116. Para. 210.

community and with the aim of subjugating that population.[117] However, it found that the evidence did not support the prosecution assertion that Dario Kordić was in the top echelons of the Bosnian Croat leadership or that he conceived of the campaign of persecution.[118]

5.1.1.6.4 *Prosecutor* v. *Goran Jelisić*, Appeal Judgement, 5 July 2001[119]

The Appeals Chamber upheld almost all of the prosecution's three grounds of appeal, in particular, Jelisić's acquittal by the Trial Chamber on the genocide charge,[120] but it declined its request to remit the case for further proceedings or to reverse the acquittal. The defendant's grounds of appeals were for the most part dismissed and his 40-year sentence was affirmed.

5.1.1.6.4.1 The prosecution's appeals

The prosecution's first ground of appeal asserted that the Trial Chamber had made an error of law under Article 25 of the Statute by not giving it an opportunity to be heard on a *proprio motu* decision of the Trial Chamber under Rule 98*bis*. Acting under Rule 98*bis*(B), in an oral judgement of 19 October 1999, the Trial Chamber had acquitted the accused of genocide, *proprio motu*, at the end of the prosecution case without first hearing from the prosecution on the question of substance as to whether the evidence was insufficient to sustain a conviction.

The prosecution's second ground of appeal asserted that the Trial Chamber had made an error of law in adopting the beyond a reasonable doubt standard of guilt for the purposes of a Rule 98*bis* determination of the sufficiency of the evidence to sustain a conviction on the genocide charge.

Finally, the prosecution claimed an error in law by the Trial Chamber (i) to the extent that it proposed that the requisite mental state for genocide in Article 4 of the Statute includes the *dolus specialis* standard, and not the broader notion of genocidal intent; (ii) when it decided that the evidence did not establish beyond a reasonable doubt that there was a plan to destroy all the Muslims in Brčko and elsewhere within which encompassed the murders committed by Jelisić; and (iii) when it decided that Jelisić's acts were not the physical expression of an affirmed resolve to destroy, in whole or in part a group as such, but rather, were arbitrary acts of killing resulting from a disturbed personality.

The remedy sought by the Prosecutor was a remittal of the case to a different Trial Chamber for a new trial.

Jelisić filed a cross-appeal in which he appealed against the imposition of cumulative convictions by the Trial Chamber and the 40-year sentence imposed on him.

---

117. Para. 520.

118. Ibid., para. 829.

119. *The Prosecutor* v. *Goran Jelisić*, Case No. IT-95-10-A, 5 July 2001.

120. *The Prosecutor* v. *Goran Jelisić*, Case No. IT-95-10-I, Judgement, 19 October 1999. See 2 *YIHL* (1999) pp. 229-230.

In unanimously upholding the prosecution's first ground of appeal, the Appeals Chamber noted that while a party has the right to be heard, the hearing need not always be oral.[121] In this case, however, 'the Trial Chamber considered that, where it was acting *proprio motu*, the prosecution had no right to be heard at all; such a right was not accorded by the Rules and could not be based upon the principle *audi alteram partem*'.[122] The Appeals Chamber found that the fact that a Trial Chamber has a right to take a decision *proprio motu* 'does not relieve it of the normal duty of a judicial body first to hear a party whose rights can be affected by the decisions to be made. Failure to hear a party against whom the Trial Chamber is provisonally inclined is not consistent with the requirement to hold a fair trial'.[123] The prosecution had been denied its right to be heard.

By a majority (Judge Pocar dissenting), the Chamber upheld the prosecution's second ground of appeal. The question turned on an interpretation of the meaning of the words 'the evidence is insufficient to sustain a conviction' contained in Rule 98*bis*(B). According to the Appeals Chamber, 'those words must of necessity import the concept of guilt beyond reasonable doubt, for it is only if the evidence is not capable of satisfying the reasonable doubt test that it can be described as "insufficient to sustain a convention" within the meaning of Rule 98*bis*(B). Rule 87(A), confirms this interpretation ...'.[124] 'Consequently, the notion of guilt beyond reasonable doubt must be retained in the operation of Rule 98*bis*(B).'[125] (See also the decision of the Trial Chambers in *Kunarac* and *Kvočka.*)

'The Appeals Chamber considers that the reference in Rule 98*bis* to a situation in which "the evidence is insufficient to sustain a conviction" means a case in which, in the opinion of the Trial Chamber, the prosecution evidence, if believed, is insufficient for any reasonable trier of fact to find that guilt has been proved beyond reasonable doubt.' Following its holding in the *Delalić* appeals judgement, it said that: 'The capacity of the prosecution evidence (if accepted) to sustain a conviction beyond reasonable doubt by a reasonable trier of fact is the key concept; thus the test is not whether the trier would in fact arrive at a conviction beyond reasonable doubt on the prosecution evidence (if accepted) but whether it could.'[126]

The Chamber found that 'the Trial Chamber's application of an erroneous standard in making its determination under Rule 98*bis* led it to incorrectly assess evidence'.[127]

As to the prosecution's third ground, on the first question of the requisite *mens rea* the Chamber unanimously dismissed the appeal as not well-founded, 'being based on a misunderstanding of the Judgement'.[128] The requisite *mens rea* is set out in Article 4 of the Statute, which largely reflects the Genocide Convention. It is, in

---

121. *The Prosecutor* v. *Goran Jelisić*, Case No. IT-95-10-A, 5 July 2001, para. 25.
122. Ibid., para. 26.
123. Ibid., para. 27.
124. Ibid., para. 35.
125. Ibid., para. 36.
126. Ibid., para. 37.
127. Ibid., para. 39.
128. Ibid., para. 52.

the words of the Appeals Chamber a '"specific intent" ... to destroy in whole or in part, a national, ethnical, racial or religious group, as such.'[129] Proof of specific intent may, 'in the absence of direct explicit evidence, be inferred from a number of facts and circumstances, such as the general context, the perpetration of other culpable acts systematically directed against the same group, the scale of atrocities committed, the systematic targeting of victims on account of their membership of a particular group, or the repetition of destructive and discriminatory acts.'[130] The Chamber found that 'the existence of a plan or policy is not a legal ingredient of the crime. However, in the context of proving specific intent, the existence of a plan or policy may become an important factor in most cases.'[131] Recalling the need to distinguish between specific intent and personal motive, the Chamber noted that '[t]he existence of a personal motive does not preclude the perpetrator from also having the specific intent to commit genocide' (see also *Tadić* Appeals decision, para. 269). 'Read in context, the question with which the Judgement was concerned in referring to *dolus specialis* was whether destruction of a group was intended. The Appeals Chamber finds that the Trial Chamber only used the Latin phrase to express specific intent as defined above.'[132]

On the second part of the third ground of appeal, the Appeals Chamber found that the Trial Chamber's erroneous application of the standard under Rule 98 *bis*(B) led it to make an incorrect assessment of the evidence, and it upheld the Prosecutor's appeal on this ground.[133] However, the Appeals Chamber decided that it was not appropriate in this case to reverse the acquittal on the genocide charge and to remit the case to a new Trial Chamber.[134]

5.1.1.6.4.2 Jelisić's appeals

Regarding Jelisić's grounds of appeals, the Chamber, dismissed the first ground which argued that, following the appeals decision in *Čelebići*, some convictions should be quashed as they were cumulative.[135] The Chamber found that, in this case, cumulative convictions under both Articles 3 and 5 are permissible as each crime had a special ingredient not possessed by the other.[136]

> 'Article 5 requires proof that the act occurred as part of a widespread or systematic attack against a civilian population; that element is not required by Article 3. Thus each Article has an element requiring proof of a fact not required by the other. As a result, cumulative convictions under both Articles 3 and 5 are permissible. In such a situation, it is not

129. Ibid., para. 45.
130. Ibid., para. 47.
131. Ibid., para. 48.
132. Ibid., para. 51.
133. Ibid., para. 72.
134. Ibid., para. 77.
135. Ibid., paras. 78-80.
136. Ibid., para. 82.

> possible to hold, as is submitted by the cross-appellant, that either offence is a "lesser included offence" of the other.'[137]

As to the second ground, that the Trial Chamber erred in fact and in the exercise of its discretion when imposing sentence, the Chamber rejected it in part and upheld it in part.

First, regarding the appellant's claim that the Trial Chamber erred in taking into account during sentencing evidence presented during his genocide trial, it found that it was open to the Trial Chamber when imposing sentence 'to take into account evidence presented during the genocide trial, insofar as that evidence was presented to demonstrate facts or conduct to which the cross-appellant had pleaded guilty'. The important point is that in considering evidence for the purpose of sentencing, the Trial Chamber should afford the cross-appellant an opportunity to test the evidence in cross-examination and/or by way of evidence adduced by the cross-appellant himself.[138] It accordingly dismissed this part of the second ground of appeal.

The second part of the second ground of his appeal was partially upheld. The Chamber held that the appellant had been wrongly convicted of murdering both of the *Zahirović* brothers, when he had only pleaded guilty to killing one, and that his sentence should be reduced.[139] It thus quashed the conviction for the murder of one of the brothers.[140] 'The Appeals Chamber is of the opinion that the additional murder of which the cross-appellant was convicted does not substantially influence the totality of his criminal conduct'.[141]

As the third part of the second ground, the Appeals Chamber found that he had failed to show that the Trial Chamber had erred in exercising its discretion in the sentence it imposed on him.[142]

As to the fourth part of the second ground, where the cross-appellant argued that the Trial Chamber had failed to have regard to the sentencing practice of the former Yugoslavia and to that of the separate entities, the Appeals Chamber dismissed it.[143] It dismissed his argument that the Trial Chamber had not given due credit to his guilty plea in determining sentence.[144] It dismissed his argument that the Trial Chamber failed to take due account of his cooperation with the Prosecutor.[145] It also dismissed his argument that the Trial Chamber failed to properly take into account his youth at the time of the commission of the crimes as a mitigating factor, finding that the appellant had not shown that the Trial Chamber erred in the exercise of its discretion in this respect.[146]

---

137. Ibid., paras. 82, 83.
138. Ibid., para. 87.
139. Ibid., para. 91.
140. Ibid., paras. 91, 95.
141. Ibid., para. 94.
142. Ibid., para. 96.
143. Ibid., paras. 114, 116.
144. Ibid., paras. 112, 113, 119.
145. Ibid., paras. 124-127.
146. Ibid., paras. 131 and 132.

5.1.1.6.5 *Prosecutor* v. *Radislav Krštić*, Judgement, 2 August 2001

In a landmark judgement, on 2 August 2001 Radislav Krštić became the first person to be convicted and sentenced for genocide by the ICTY. In delivering its guilty verdict, the Trial Chamber, Judge Rodrigues presiding, said that it was 'convinced beyond any reasonable doubt that a crime of genocide was committed in Srebrenica' and that General Radislav Krštić was guilty of this crime.[147]

General Krštić, who was, at the time of the attack on the town of Srebrenica by Bosnian Serb forces (VRS), the deputy commander of the Drina Corps and who later became the commander, was found guilty of genocide and the crimes against humanity of persecution and murder and sentenced to 46 years' imprisonment, the longest sentence rendered by the Tribunal up to that point. The Chamber stated that although the elements of his responsibility under Article 7(3) had been fulfilled, it would not enter a conviction to that effect because in its view General Krštić's responsibility for the participation of his troops in the killings is sufficiently expressed in a finding of guilt under Article 7(1).[148]

The judgement described at length the events of July 1995, when Bosnian Serb (VRS) forces carried out the planned attack on the so-called 'safe haven' of Srebrenica, and found that 'following the take-over of Srebrenica, Bosnian Serb forces executed several thousand Bosnian Muslim men. The total number is likely to be within the range of 7,000 -8,000 men.'[149] 'A concerted effort was made to capture all Muslim men of military age.'[150] The Chamber held that while there was no evidence that the Drina Corps had devised the plan to commit atrocities, including the execution of the men and boys, and that the plan seemed to be the brainchild and was directed by the VRS Mainstaff, under the direction of General Mladić, the corps became increasingly involved in and aware of the situation, and between 14 and 17 July was involved in the mass executions.[151] While there was no evidence that General Krštić was personally present at any of the execution sites,[152] '[g]iven his position in the Drina Corps Command, first as Chief of Staff and then as Commander from the evening of 13 July 1995, General Krštić must have also known about these matters. By 14 July 1995, General Krštić, in his role as Corps Commander, must have been informed about the participation of his subordinate units in the executions commencing on that date.'[153]

While the Chamber found that the following crimes were committed: genocide, persecution, extermination, murder as a violation of the laws or customs of war, murder as a crime against humanity, and forced transfer (i.e., displacement within a

147. See 'Radislav Krštić becomes the first person to be convicted of genocide at the ICTY and is sentenced to 46 years imprisonment', Press Release of the Trial Chamber, OF/P.I.S./609e, The Hague, 2 August 2001.

148. *Prosecutor* v. *Radislav Krštić*, Case No. IT-98-33-T, 2 August 2001, para. 652.

149. Ibid., paras. 84, 426, 427.

150. Ibid., para. 85.

151. Ibid., paras. 294-295.

152. Ibid., para. 378.

153. Ibid., paras. 379, 423, 472,

state's borders[154]), because of the rules on cumulative charging, only the crimes of genocide, persecution and murder as a violation of the laws or customs of war were retained.

5.1.1.6.5.1 Genocide

As the first ICTY conviction and sentencing on charges of genocide, and its first finding that genocide was committed in Srebrenica, the court's findings on this point are the most significant aspect of the judgement.

As far as serious mental harm as a genocidal crime is concerned, the Chamber distinguished between 'serious mental harm and emotional or psychological damage or attacks on the dignity of the human person not causing lasting impairment'.[155] It found that serious bodily or mental harm for purposes of Article 4 *actus reus* is an intentional act or omission causing serious bodily or mental suffering. The gravity of the suffering must be assessed on a case by case basis and with due regard for the particular circumstances.'[156] It agreed with the *Akayesu* Judgement that 'serious harm need not cause permanent and irremediable harm, but it must involve harm that goes beyond temporary unhappiness, embarrassment or humiliation. It must be harm that results in a grave and long-term disadvantage to a person's ability to lead a normal and constructive life'.[157]

The Chamber emphasised 'the need to distinguish between the individual intent of the accused and the intent involved in the conception and commission of the crime. On the question of the necessary intent, the Chamber adhered 'to the characterisation of genocide which encompass only acts committed with the *goal* of destroying all or part of a group'.[158] The plan to commit genocide does not have to be devised long in advance of the commission of the acts. 'It is conceivable that, although the intention at the outset of an operation was not the destruction of a group, it may become the goal at some later point during the implementation of the operation. For instance, an armed force could decide to destroy a protected group during a military operation whose primary objective was totally unrelated to the fate of the group.'[159]

The Chamber was not able to determine precisely when the decision to kill all the military aged men was taken. 'Hence, it cannot find that the killings committed in Potočari on12 and 13 July 1995 formed part of the plan to kill all the military aged men. Nevertheless, the Trial Chamber is confident that the mass executions and other killings committed from 13 July onwards were part of this plan.'[160]

The Chamber stated that the existence of the principle *nullum crimen sine lege* compelled it to recognise that:

154. Ibid., para. 521.
155. Ibid., para. 510.
156. Ibid., para. 513.
157. Ibid.
158. Ibid., para. 571.
159. Ibid., para. 572.
160. Ibid., para. 576.

> 'despite recent developments, customary international law limits the definition of genocide to those acts seeking the physical or biological destruction of all or part of the group. Hence, an enterprise attacking only the cultural or sociological characteristics of a human group in order to annihilate these elements which give to that group its own identity distinct from the rest of the community would not fall under the definition of genocide. The Trial Chamber however points out that where there is physical or biological destruction there are often simultaneous attacks on the cultural and religious property and symbols of the targeted group as well, attacks which may legitimately be considered as evidence of an intent to physically destroy the group. In this case, the Trial Chamber will thus take into account as evidence of intent to destroy the group the deliberate destruction of mosques and houses belonging to members of the group.'[161]

As far as the meaning of the term 'in part' is concerned, the Chamber found that 'any act committed with the intent to destroy a part of a group, as such, constitutes an act of genocide within the meaning of the Convention'.[162] It had a margin of discretion in assessing what is meant by destruction 'in part' of the group. The Trial Chamber stated that

> 'the intent to destroy a group, even if only in part, means seeking to destroy a distinct part of the group as opposed to an accumulation of isolated individuals within it. Although the perpetrators of genocide need not seek to destroy the entire group protected by the Convention, they must view the part of the group they wish to destroy as a distinct entity which must be eliminated as such. A campaign resulting in the killings, in different places spread over a broad geographical area, of a finite number of members of a protected group might not thus qualify as genocide, despite the high total number of casualties, because it would not show an intent by the perpetrators to target the very existence of the group as such. Conversely, the killing of all members of the part of a group located within a small geographical area, although resulting in a lesser number of victims, would qualify as genocide if carried out with the intent to destroy the part of the group as such located in this small geographical area. Indeed, the physical destruction may target only a part of the geographically limited part of the larger group because the perpetrators of the genocide regard the intended destruction as sufficient to annihilate the group as a distinct entity in the geographic area at issue. In this regard, it is important to bear in mind the total context in which the physical destruction is carried out.'[163]

161. Ibid., para. 580.
162. Ibid., para. 583.
163. Ibid., para. 590.

5.1.1.6.5.2 Extermination

Another major contribution of the judgement was to define the crime of extermination (a crime against humanity), the first time that an ICTY Chamber had done so.[164]

The Chamber stated that the crimes of murder and extermination have the same *mens rea,* which is 'the intention to kill or the intention to cause serious bodily injury to the victim which the perpetrator must have reasonably foreseen was likely to result in death'.[165]

The Chamber distinguished between extermination and genocide and noted that in the case of extermination there need be 'no discriminatory intent nor intention to destroy the group as such on national, ethnical, racial or religious grounds', nor need the targeted population share common national, ethnical, racial or religious characteristics.[166]

> 'The very term "extermination" strongly suggests the commission of a massive crime, which in turn assumes a substantial degree of preparation and organisation. It should be noted, though, that "extermination" could also, theoretically, be applied to the commission of a crime which is not "widespread" but nonetheless consists in eradicating an entire population, distinguishable by some characteristic(s) not covered by the Genocide Convention, but made up of only a relatively small number of people. In other words, while extermination generally involves a large number of victims, it may be constituted even where the number of victims is limited.'[167]
>
> 'In sum, the Trial Chamber finds that for the crime of extermination to be established, in addition to the general requirements for a crime against humanity, there must be evidence that a particular population was targeted and that its members were killed or otherwise subjected to conditions of life calculated to bring about the destruction of a numerically significant part of the population.'[168]

It found that, in this case, the crime of extermination was committed at Srebrenica.[169]

---

164. Although the elements of the crime of extermination had been defined by the ICTR. See *The* Prosecutor v. *Jean-Paul Akayesu,* Case No. ICTR-96-4-T, Judgement, 2 September 1998, paras. 591-592; *The Prosecutor* v. *Kambanda,* Case No. ICTR-97-23, Judgement, 4 September 1998; *The Prosecutor* v. *Kayishema/Ruzindana,* Case No. ICTR-95-1-T, Judgement, 21 May 1999, paras. 141-147; *The Prosecutor* v. *Rutaganda,* Case No. ICTR-96-3-T, Judgement, 6 December 1999, paras. 82-84; *The Prosecutor* v. *Musema,* Case No. ICTR-96-13-T, Judgement, 27 January 2000.

165. *Krštić,* para. 495.

166. Ibid., para. 500.

167. Ibid., para. 501.

168. Ibid., para. 503

169. Ibid., para. 505.

5.1.1.6.6 *Prosecutor* v. *Stevan Todorović*, Sentencing Judgement, 31 July 2001

Following the plea agreement reached between the accused and the prosecution, which Todorović, the former Chief of Police of Bosanski Samac, pleaded guilty to one count of persecution (crime against humanity) in return for all other 14 charges (of grave breaches of the Geneva Conventions, violations of the law or customs of war and crimes against humanity) against him being dropped.[170] On 24 January 2001 the accused confirmed his guilty plea before the full Trial Chamber, which entered a finding of guilt on that date.[171]

On 31 July 2001, the Trial Chamber sentenced him to ten years' imprisonment. The Chamber said that it had taken into account the aggravating circumstances, namely, the accused's superior authority as Chief of Police of Bosanski Samac and the manner in which the crimes were perpetrated[172] (demonstrating particular cruelty and of lengthy duration[173]). It concluded that Todorović's crimes were particularly grave.[174]

It considered as mitigating factors his guilty plea,[175] his agreement to cooperate with the Prosecutor (although here it noted that it was not bound by the plea agreement[176]), and his actual assistance in this regard[177] and his remorse.[178] It did not accept his alleged diminished responsibility as a relevant factor in this case.[179]

5.1.1.6.7 *Prosecutor* v. *Zejnil Delalić, Zdravko Mucić, Hazim Delić and Esad Landžo*, Sentencing Judgement, 9 October 2001

Following the decision of the Appeals Chamber of 20 February 2001 and the remission of the case to a new Trial Chamber for a new decision on sentencing, Trial Chamber III, Judge May presiding, rendered its decision on sentencing of the three convicted persons.

The sentence of Zdravko Mucić was increased from seven to nine years. The sentence of Hazim Delić was reduced from 20 to 18 years, and the sentence of Esad Landžo was confirmed at 15 years.

The Chamber departed from the practice of the earlier Chamber that had sentenced the convicted by issuing global rather than cumulative sentences in respect of all three, which it said reflected, in this case, the total criminality and culpability of the accused.

---

170. 3 *YIHL* (2000) p. 185.
171. Ibid., para. 5.
172. Ibid., para. 59.
173. Ibid., paras. 63 and 65.
174. Ibid., para. 66.
175. Ibid., para. 82.
176. Ibid., para. 86.
177. Ibid., para. 88.
178. Ibid., paras. 91 and 92.
179. Ibid., para. 95.

5.1.1.6.8 *Prosecutor* v. *Zoran Kupreskić, Mirjan Kupreskić, Vlatko Kupreskić, Drago Josipovic and Vladimir Santić*, Appeals Judgement, 23 October 2001

In an unprecented move, the Appeals Chamber overturned the convictions of three of the accused: Zoran Kupreskić, Mirjan Kupreskić and Vlatko Kupreskić, and reduced the sentences of the other two accused.

Zoran Kupreskić, Mirjan Kupreskić and Vlatko Kupreskić were ordered to be immediately released from the custody of the Tribunal. The appeal of Drago Josipović was partly allowed, and his sentence was reduced from 15 to 12 years. Vladimir Santić's appeal was also partially allowed, and his sentence reduced from 18 to 15 years' imprisonment.

All of the accused had appealed both their convictions and sentences, with the vast majority of the grounds concerning errors of fact. The Prosecutor had appealed the acquittal by the Trial Chamber of Drago Josipović and Vladimir Santić for violations of the laws or customs of war for reasons based on its rejection of cumulative convictions.

In its Judgement, the Appeals Chamber alluded to the complexity of the appeals process, which involved 26 motions to introduce new evidence.[180] The indictment was defective because it failed to properly plead the prosecution's case. The Chamber had 'been confronted with an issue that domestic jurisdictions have struggled with over centuries: the circumstances in which it is reasonable for a finder of fact to rely upon identification given by a single witness'. In this case, it found that the main witness to most of the crimes, H, was not a reliable witness, and that: 'In the absence of Witness H's testimony, the cases against Zoran and Mirjan Kupreskić cannot stand. The other evidence submitted does not sustain the convictions of the two Defendants. Having decided that the Trial Chamber erred in relying upon the evidence of Witness H, the Appeals Chamber must conclude that a miscarriage of justice has occurred in the present case.'[181]

Regarding Vlatko Kupreskić, it found, based on the additional evidence submitted to it, that the circumstantial evidence relied upon by the Trial Chamber could not support his conviction, and that a miscarriage of justice had been occasioned.[182]

It found that the indictment against Drago Josipović was partly defective because it failed to plead all of the material facts of the prosecution case. Further, the evidence presented at trial did not disclose a sufficient basis for the Trial Chamber's finding that he was in a position of command during the attack on the village of Ahmići.[183]

Finally, it rejected the finding of the Trial Chamber that Vladimir Santić had assisted in the strategic planning of the attack on Ahmići. It also took into account

180. Ibid., para. 42.
181. Ibid., para. 245.
182. Ibid., paras. 303-304.
183. Ibid., para. 361.

his partial acceptance of responsibility for his role in the attack on Ahmići, and his substantial cooperation with the prosecution since his conviction. It dismissed his other grounds of appeal.[184]

It allowed the prosecution's appeal on the question of cumulative charging and cumulative convictions. Therefore, the acquittal of Drago Josipović and Vladimir Santić for violations of the laws or customs of war were reversed.[185] However, because the Prosecutor had not requested any consequent increase in their sentences, it did not take these additional convictions into account for sentencing purposes.

5.1.1.6.9 *Prosecutor* v. *Dusko Sikirica, Damir Dosen and Dragan Kolundžija*, Sentencing Judgement, 13 November 2001

On 21 June, Trial Chamber III, hearing the case, rendered an oral decision on the Defence Motions to Acquit in which it dismissed, *inter alia*, counts 1 (genocide) and 2 (complicity in genocide) against Sikirica and counts 12 to 15 (torture, inhuman acts and cruel treatment) against Dosen, finding that there was no case to answer to on these charges. A written judgement on the motion followed on 3 September.[186] On 4 September, Dragan Kolundžija pleaded guilty to one count of persecution (a crime against humanity) as part of a plea agreement with the Prosecutor, who, in return, agreed to drop the other four counts against him and to seek a sentence of not more than five years and not less than three years. On 19 September the other two accused entered guilty pleas to one count of persecution (crime against humanity) pursuant to an agreement entered into by the accused and the Prosecutor on 7 September. Under this agreement, the Prosecutor agreed to drop the other charges against the accused and seek sentences of no more than 17 and no less than 10 years' imprisonment for Sikirica and no more than seven and no less than five years' imprisonment for Dosen. In addition, both the defendants and the Prosecutor agreed not to appeal the sentences provided they fell within this range.[187]

5.1.2 *International Criminal Tribunal for Rwanda*

2001 was a difficult year for the ICTR, as it came in for considerable criticism, including by victims' groups and the Rwandan government, over tardiness, remoteness and inappropriate practices.

A report of the International Crisis Group of 7 June 2001 entitled 'International Criminal Tribunal for Rwanda: Justice Delayed', accused the Tribunal of having a

---

184. Ibid., para. 378.

185. Ibid., para. 396.

186. *Prosecutor* v. *Dusko Sikirica, Damir Dosen and Dragan Kolundžija*, case No. IT-95-8-T, Judgement on Defence Motions to Acquit, 3 September 2001.

187. 'Dusko Sikirica and Damir Dosen enter guilty pleas', Press Release of the Trial Chamber, SP/P.I.S./620-e, The Hague, 19 September 2001.

'lamentable record' and of 'failing to meet its basic mandate: to deliver justice to the people of Rwanda and to provide a record of events'. It said that the majority of Rwandans regarded the Tribunal as 'a useless institution' and found the Tribunal distant and indifferent to their situations.[188]

The inappropriate practices included fee-splitting, whereby an accused person gets a cut of his counsel's fees in exchange for hiring him, and the fact that persons indicted for genocide by Rwanda were known to be working as ICTR defence investigators. The Tribunal responded robustly to these criticisms.[189] But in a statement of 13 June, the Registrar noted that the report of the United Nations Office of Internal Oversight Services (OIOS) had found evidence of abuse of the legal aid system of both the ICTY and the ICTR. Friends and relatives had been hired as defence investigators, defence counsel had given gifts to the accused's relatives; and several defence counsel had been solicited and had accepted requests for fee-splitting between them and their clients. He described steps that had been taken to address these problems.[190] In July, a statement of the Registrar declared that the contracts of certain investigators working for defence counsel would not be renewed or would be suspended.[191] In October, the Tribunal addressed the practice of fee-splitting in its jurisprudence, in the case of *Prosecutor* v. *Joseph Nzirorera*. The Trial Chamber II directed the Registry to look into the matter and to take all necessary measures to inform all accused and counsel that fee-splitting is unacceptable and merits sanctions under the Rules.[192]

Addressing the issue of tardiness, in November the President of the Tribunal told the UN General Assembly that the Prosecutor anticipated indicting up to 136 new accused by the year 2005. That is why she had submitted a proposal to the SC for the creation of *ad litem* judges, as had been done for the ICTY.[193]

---

188. http://www.intl-crisis-group.org/projects/africa/rwanda/reports/A400442_02102001.pdf.

189. 'Statement by the Registar, Mr. Adama Dieng, on the Report of the International Crisis Group', ICTR/INFO-9-3-01.EN, Arusha, 11 June 2001.

190. 'Statement by the Registrar, Mr. Adama Dieng, on some issues relating to the defence of accused persons', ICTR/INFO-9-2-02.EN, Arusha, 13 June 2001. The GA's Report of the Office of Internal Oversight Services on the investigation into possible fee-splitting arrangements between defence counsel and indigent detainees at the International Criminal Tribunal for Rwanda and the International Tribunal for the Former Yugoslavia, A/RES/55/250, was issued on 12 April 2001.

191. 'Statement of the Registar concerning the Contract of Employment of a defence investigator', ICTR/INFO-3-04.EN, Arusha, 17 August 2001.

192. Decision on Nzirorera's Motion for Withdrawal of Counsel, *Prosecutor* v. *Joseph Nzirorera*, 3 October 2001. 'Statement by the Registrar, Mr. Adama Dieng, on Allegations of Fee Splitting between a Detainee of the ICTR and his Defence Counsel.' ICTR/INFO-9-3-06.EN, Arusha, 29 October 2001.

193. 'ICTR President addresses General Assembly', ICTR/INFO-9-2-295.EN, Arusha, 26 November 2001.

5.1.2.1 New appointments

A new Registrar, Mr Adama Dieng of Senegal, was sworn in on 1 March 2001.[194] Judge Navanethem Pillay of South Africa was reelected as President of the ICTR for a second term on 31 May.[195]

5.1.2.2 Arrests

On 26 April, Bishop Samuel Musabyimana was arrested in Kenya and immediately transferred to the ICTR detention facility in Arusha. At his initial appearance on 2 May, he pleaded not guilty to four counts of genocide, conspiracy to commit genocide and crimes against humanity (extermination).[196]

On 19 May, Simeon Nshamihigo was arrested in Arusha and transferred to the Tribunal's detention facilities on 25 May. He pleaded not guilty to three counts of genocide and crimes against humanity at his initial appearance on 29 June.[197]

On 20 June, Sylvestre Gacumbitsi was arrested in Mukungwa refugee camp in Tanzania and transferred on the same day to the ICTR. At his initial appearance on 26 June, he pleaded not guilty to five counts of genocide and crimes against humanity.[198]

Jean Mpambara was arrested in Mukungwa refugee camp in Tanzania on 21 June and was transferred to Arusha on 23 June. At his initial appearance on 27 July, he pleaded not guilty to one count of genocide.[199]

On 12 July, three arrests in Europe were made. Emmanuel Ndindabahizi, indicted for genocide and crimes against humanity, was arrested in Belgium. He was transferred to the ICTR on 25 September.[200] He pleaded not guilty at his initial appearance on 19 October 2001.[201] Emmanuel Rukundo, indicted for genocide and crimes against humanity, was arrested in Geneva. He was transferred to the Tribunal on 20 September.[202] And Simon Bikindi was arrested in the Netherlands.

---

194. 'Mr. Adama Dieng sworn in as new Tribunal Registrar', ICTR/INFO-9-2-258.EN, Arusha, 1 March 2001.

195. ICTR/INFO-9-2-268.EN, Arusha, 1 June 2001.

196. ICTR/INFO-9-2-263.EN, Arusha, 27 April 2001; ICTR/INFO-9-2-264.EN, Arusha, 2 May 2001.

197. 'Nshamihigo pleads not guilty to three counts', ICTR/INFO-9-2-275.EN, Arusha, 29 June 2001.

198. 'Former Bourgmestre of Rusumo pleads not guilty to five counts', ICTR/INFO-9-2-274.EN, Arusha, 26 June 2001.

199. 'Former Bourgmestre of Rukara pleads not-guilty', ICTR/INFO-9-2-270.EN, Arusha, 27 July 2001.

200. 'Minister transferred, Chaplain pleads not guilty', ICTR/INFO-9-2-285, Arusha, 26 September 2001.

201. 'Emmanuel Ndindabahizi pleads not guilty', ICTR/INFO-9-2-290.EN, Arusha, 19 October 2001.

202. 'Former Military Chaplain transferred to Arusha', ICTR/INFO-9-2-282.EN, Arusha, 21 September 2001.

On 26 July, Protais Zigiranyirazo, indicted for crimes against humanity, was arrested in Belgium. He was transferred to the ICTR on 3 October.[203] He pleaded not guilty at his initial appearance on 10 October.[204]

On 20 October, François Karera was arrested in Nairobi, Kenya, and immediately transferred to the ICTR.[205] At his initial appearance on 26 October, he pleaded not guilty to charges of crimes against humanity.[206]

On 21 December, Joseph Nzabirinda, indicted for genocide and crimes against humanity, was arrested in Belgium[207]

5.1.2.3 New trials

The trial of Juvenal Kajelijeli, former Mayor of Mukingo Commune, Ruhengeri Prefecture, began on 13 April. He is accused of genocide, conspiracy to commit genocide, direct and public incitement to commit genocide, crimes against humanity, including rape and extermination and war crimes.[208]

The trial of Jean de Dieu Kamuhanda, former Minister of Higher Education, Research and Culture in the Interim Government of Rwanda in 1994, opened on 17 April [209] but was adjourned following the death of Presiding Judge Laity Kama on 6 May. It reopened before a reconstituted Trial Chamber II on 3 September. Kamuhanda is charged with genocide and crimes against humanity.

On 12 June, the trial began of the 'Butare Group', six persons indicted for genocide, crimes against humanity and war crimes.[210]

On 18 September, the joint trial of Elizaphan Ntakirutimana, the former Senior Paster of the Seventh Day Adventist Church in Kibuye, and his son Gerard Ntakirutimana, former doctor in Kibuye, commenced.[211]

By the end of 2001, seven trials involving 17 accused were underway, with all three Trial Chambers engaged in hearing simultaneous trials on a twin or multi-track system. Twenty-six detainees awaited trial and 22 indicted suspects remained at large. On 9 December, Jean Kambanda, Jean-Paul Akayesu, Clement Kayishema, Obed Ruzindana, Alfred Musema and Omar Serushago became the first Tribunal indictees to begin serving their sentences when they were transferred to Mali.[212]

---

203. 'Akazu member transferred, Deputy Registrar Sworn In', ICTR/INFO-9-2-287.EN, Arusha, 4 October 2001.

204. 'Zigiranyirazo pleads not guilty', ICTR/INFO-9-2-289.EN, Arusha, 10 October 2001.

205. 'Prefect arrested for genocide', ICTR/INFO-9-2-291.EN, Arusha, 22 October 2001.

206. 'Former Prefect pleads not-guilty', ICTR/INFO-9-293.EN, Arusha, 26 October 2001.

207. ICTR/INFO-9-2-297.EN, Arusha, 21 December 2001.

208. 'Kajelijeli trial begins', ICTR/INFO-9-2-259.EN, Arusha, 13 March 2001.

209. ICTR/INFO-9-2-261.EN, Arusha, 17 April 2001.

210. 'Trial of the 'Butare Group' begins', ICTR/INFO-9-2-273.EN, Arusha, 12 June 2001.

211. 'Genocide trial of Pastor and Doctor opens', ICTR/INFO-9-2-281.EN, Arusha, 18 September 2001.

212. 'Former Prime Minister and five other convicts sent to prison in Mali', ICTR/INFO-9-2-296.EN, Arusha, 11 December 2001.

5.1.2.4 Judgements

5.1.2.4.1 *Akayesu* Appeals Decision, 1 June 2001

On 1 June, the Appeal Chamber rendered its judgement in the case of *Prosecutor* v. *Akayesu.*[213] It unanimously dismissed each of the grounds of appeal raised by Jean-Paul Akayesu and reaffirmed his conviction and life sentence. As a result, it found that there was no need for it to consider the Other Issues and the 'eighty Ground of Appeal'.[214]

Akayesu's grounds of appeal against the judgement were that he had been denied the right to counsel of his choice and the right to competent counsel; that the Tribunal was biased and lacked independence; and various arguments concerning absence of the rule of law/errors invalidating the finding of guilty. Regarding the sentence, he appealed on grounds that he had been denied the right to counsel during two hearings, and against the unreasonable and unwarranted sentence.

5.1.2.4.1.1 Grounds relating to counsel

The Chamber dismissed Akayesu's ground of appeal respecting choice of counsel. The right to choose counsel applies only to those accused who can financially 'bear the costs of counsel'.[215] It found that 'the rights of the Accused as provided under Article 2(4) of the Statute were indeed complied with'.

The Chamber rejected Akayesu's ground of appeal concerning the right to conduct one's own defence, finding that his attitude, including his insistence on counsel of his own choosing, did not indicate a wish to defend himself, despite expressing such a desire on occasion.[216] The Chamber found that while indigent accused have the right to competent assigned counsel, the competence of the counsel is presumed and the burden of proving the contrary lies with the accused. The Appeals Chamber found that 'Akayesu has failed to prove incompetence of his Counsel (as understood by the Tribunal): he failed to provide any tangible example of gross professional misconduct by his Counsel such as resulted in a miscarriage of justice,'[217] and dismissed this ground of appeal.[218]

5.1.2.4.1.2 Grounds relating to the impartiality of the Tribunal

The Chamber rejected all the grounds of appeal relating to the impartiality of the Tribunal.[219] The Chamber also dismissed Akayesu's argument that the Tribunal

---

213. *The Prosecutor* v. *Jean-Paul Akayesu,* Judgement, 1 June 2001. http://www.ictr.org/ENGLISH/cases/judgement/Arret/index.htm.

214. Ibid., para. 423.

215. Ibid., para. 61.

216. Ibid., paras. 65 and 66.

217. Ibid., para. 80

218. Ibid., para. 84.

219. Ibid., paras. 91 and 92.

pursued a partisan prosecution strategy because it had not prosecuted the perpetrators of 'crimes of extermination of the Hutu'.[220] The Chamber also dismissed his argument that he could not have a fair trial because of the very functioning of the Tribunal, and the problems in conducting investigations.[221]

5.1.2.3.1.3 Grounds relating to amendment of the indictment and evidence

The Chamber rejected all of Akayesu's arguments that the Trial Chamber erred in law in allowing the Prosecutor to amend the indictment to include three counts of sexual crimes. As to his allegations of improper treatment of prior witness statements, the Appeals Chamber rejected his allegation that there was a policy by 'the Trial Chamber to give precedence to testimonies over prior witness statements, and found that the Trial Chamber did not err in any way in its general reasoning regarding the overall evaluation and assessment of the credibility of witness testimony and the factors to be taken into account'.[222] Nor had Akayesu shown that the Trial Chamber adopted an improper policy as to the treatment of prior statements.[223] It rejected his arguments relating to disclosure of evidence and extrinsic evidence.

The Chamber also rejected all arguments regarding non-application of the reasonable doubt standard and substantial factual errors.

Regarding his argument that the Trial Chamber erred in law by relying on out-of-court evidence to pass on a central issue of the trial, the Chamber rejected the submission. It also rejected his assertion that it had relied on the evidence of the expert witness in the *Rutaganda* case in reaching its conclusions in his case, and found that there was no violation of the right to cross-examination.[224]

The Chamber also rejected his appeal on the grounds that the Trial Chamber erred in the way it handled hearsay evidence, finding that the Trial Chamber had fulfilled the requirement to treat hearsay evidence with caution.[225] The evidence challenged by *Akayesu* in this case fell 'in principle within the Trial Chamber's discretion to find that such evidence is sufficiently reliable to warrant admission under the general principle governing admissibility of hearsay evidence before the Tribunal'.[226]

The Chamber rejected all the grounds of appeal against the cross-examination, finding that Akayesu had failed to show any prejudice such as would invalidate the judgement.[227]

The Chamber also rejected his submission that a letter allegedly by Witness DAAX to the judges following his testimony constituted a violation of his right to

---

220. Ibid., paras. 95-96.
221. Ibid., para. 100.
222. Ibid., para. 146.
223. Ibid., para. 169.
224. Ibid., paras. 266, 267 and 268.
225. Ibid., para. 289.
226. Ibid., para. 290.
227. Ibid., paras. 326, 325.

cross-examine prosecution witnesses.[228] Since he could not show prejudice, this ground was dismissed. It also rejected his submission that the testimony of Witness DAAX rendered his trial unfair.

5.1.2.4.1.4 Grounds relating to detention and sentence

The Chamber rejected his tenth ground of appeal challenging the lawfulness of his detention. By not raising the issue of an alleged violation of the right to be promptly charged and a violation of the right to be informed of the nature of the charges against him before the Trial Chamber, Akayesu had waived his right to have these matters heard on appeal.[229]

It also dismissed his eleventh ground of appeal, wherein he challenged his sentence, and also submitted that his right to be represented by counsel during the sentencing procedure was violated.[230] It also rejected his submission that he had been unlawfully deprived of his right to address the Trial Chamber at the delivery of the Sentencing Judgment.[231]

As to Akayesu's argument that his sentence was unreasonable and unjustified and should be reduced, the Chamber, in deciding to exercise its discretion to consider this ground of appeal on the merits, gave the matter considered judgement. It reiterated the test set out in the *Kambanda* and the *Furundžija* Appeals Judgements that 'before the Appeals Chamber is able to revise a sentence or substitute its own sentence for the one imposed by the Trial Chamber, it must be shown that the Trial Chamber ventured outside discretion in imposing the sentence'.[232] 'The Appeals Chamber finds that the sentence imposed is proportionate to the gravity of the offences committed, and, consequently, remains within the discretion of the Trial Chamber.'[233]

While it had found that the torture of one victim had not been shown, this was not such as to justify a reduction in sentence.[234]

5.1.2.4.1.5 The prosecution appeal

The Prosecutor had four grounds of appeal. First, that the Trial Chamber had erred in law in applying a 'public agent of government representative test' in determining who can be held responsible for serious violations of common Article 3 and Additional Protocol II, or second, in the alternative, that having applied the 'public agent or government representative test', the Trial Chamber erred in fact in finding that Jean-Paul Akayesu did not fall within the category of persons who could be responsible under Article 4; third, the Trial Chamber erred in law in finding that discriminatory intent is required for a crime mentioned in Article 3 to constitute a crime against humanity by holding that 'The victim must have been murdered

228. Ibid., para. 344.
229. Ibid., paras. 370 and 375.
230. Ibid., para. 391.
231. Ibid., paras. 400, 401.
232. Ibid., para. 409.
233. Ibid., para. 417.
234. Ibid., para. 419.

because he was discriminated against on national, ethnic, racial, political or religious grounds'; and fourth, the Trial Chamber erred in law in holding that instigation in Article 6(1) must be direct and public.

5.1.2.4.1.6 First and second grounds - responsibility for violations of Article 4 of the Statute (common Article 3 and Additional Protocol II)

This ground of appeal provided important jurisprudence, given that it was the first time that the Appeals Chamber clearly described who can be held criminally responsible under common Article 3.

The Appeals Chamber confirmed that the Trial Chamber had used the public agent test in interpreting Article 4 of the Statute. It then questioned whether this had been the right approach. It noted that 'there is no explicit provision in the Statute that individual criminal responsibility is restricted to a particular class of people'.[235] Neither does common Article 3 clearly identify the persons covered by its provisions nor contain any explicit reference to the perpetrator's criminal liability for violations of its provision.

> 'The chapeau of Common Article 3 only provides that "each party to the conflict shall be bound to apply, as a minimum, the following provisions". The primary object of this provision is to highlight the "unconditional" character of the duty imposed on each party to afford minimum protection to persons covered under Common Article 3. In the Opinion of the Appeals Chamber, it does not follow that the perpetrator of a violation of Article 3 must of necessity have specific link with one of the above-mentioned Parties.'[236]

The Chamber noted that it had never before been necessary for it to circumscribe the category of persons who may be prosecuted under Article 3, and that the only jurisprudence on this question of the ICTY, the decision in *Kunarac*, where the Trial Chamber found that 'common Article 3 may also require some relationship to exist between a perpetrator and a party to the conflict',[237] had no support either in statute or case-law.

The Appeals Chamber found that

> 'common Article 3 requires a close nexus between violations and the armed conflict. This nexus between violations and the armed conflict implies that, in most cases, the perpetrator of the crime will probably have a special relationship with one party to the conflict. However, such a special relationship is not a condition precedent to the application of common Article 3 and, hence of Article 4 of the Statute. In the opinion of the Appeals Chamber, the Trial Chamber erred in requiring that a special relationship should be a separate condition for triggering criminal responsibility for a violation of Article 4 of the Statute.'[238]

235. Ibid., para. 436.
236. Ibid., para. 437.
237. *Kunarac* Judgement, para. 407.
238. *Akayesu*, para. 444.

> 'Accordingly, the Appeals Chamber finds that the Trial Chamber erred on point of law in restricting the application of common Article 3 to a certain category of persons, as defined by the Trial Chamber.'[239]

In entertaining this ground of appeal, the Chamber found that it was not necessary to rule on the prosecution's alternative ground.

5.1.2.4.1.7 Third ground - Article 3 crimes against humanity

The Chamber held that the Trial Chamber had erred in its reasoning and findings on the question of discriminatory intent in the context of crimes against humanity.

> '... the Appeals Chamber is of the view that any interpretation of the chapeau of Article 2 of the Statute such as would add a requirement for a showing of a discriminatory intent with respect to all crimes against humanity would likely render redundant the express if more succinct reference to discrimination – contained in Article 3 of the Statute (Persecutions), which reference is understood as a requirement of a discriminatory intent.'[240]
>
> '... the Appeals Chamber considers the present ground of appeal and finds that: (1) Article 3 of the Statute does no [sic] require that all crimes against humanity enumerated therein be committed with a discriminatory intent. (2) Article 3 restricts the jurisdiction of the Tribunal to crimes against humanity committed in a specific situation, that is, "as part of a widespread or systematic attack against any civilian population" on discriminatory grounds.'[241]

5.1.2.4.1.8 Fourth ground - meaning of 'direct and public' instigation

As to the Prosecutor's Fourth Ground of Appeal, the Appeals Chamber considered whether the Trial Chamber had erred in requiring that instigation under Article 6(1) must be direct and public. It stated that neither the French nor English texts of the Statute 'contains any suggestion or recommendation that incitement must be direct and public. Consequently, by interpreting this provision "in accordance with [its] ordinary meaning", the Appeals Chamber holds that, although an instigation may, in certain circumstances be direct and public, this does not, however, constitute a requirement.'[242]

5.1.2.4.2 *The Prosecutor* v. *Ignace Bagilishema*, Judgement, 7 June 2001

On 7 June 2001, Ignace Bagilishema became the first person to be acquitted by the ICTR. The Trial Chamber unanimously found him not guilty of one count of genocide and two counts of violations of Article 3 of the Geneva Conventions and Additional Protocol II (Art. 4(a) and (e) of the Statute), and, by a majority (Judge Güney dissenting), not guilty of complicity in genocide and three counts of crimes against humanity (murder, extermination and other inhumane acts). The Chamber found that the testimonies of the prosecution witnesses were inconsistent and

239. Ibid., para. 445.
240. Ibid., para. 468
241. Ibid., para. 469.
242. Ibid., para. 478.

contradictory, and that the Prosecution had failed to prove its case beyond a reasonable doubt.[243]

Jurisprudentially, the Judgement provided little that was new, confining itself to confirming early findings of the ICTR and ICTY.

On 8 June, Trial Chamber I ordered Bagilishema's conditional release.[244] On 8 October 2001, he left for France, where he will reside by agreement with the Tribunal, pending the prosecutor's appeal.[245]

5.1.2.4.3 *Prosecutor* v. *Alfred Musema*, Appeals Decision, 16 November 2001

The Appeals Chamber confirmed the conviction of Alfred Musema for genocide and for extermination as a crime against humanity, and upheld his life sentence.[246] However, it quashed his conviction for rape as a crime against humanity on the basis of the evidence of two new witnesses.

The Appeals Chamber rejected the argument relating to the credibility of certain prosecution witnesses to massacres or sexual crimes, that the Trial Chamber had erred in its evaluation of the evidence. However, it found that although the Trial Chamber could not be said to have erred in its assessment of the evidence before it, it would have reached a different conclusion had the evidence of the two new witnesses been available to it.

The Appeals Chamber rejected Musema's argument that the Trial Chamber had reversed the burden of proof by requiring him to prove his innocence.

It also rejected his argument that the Trial Chamber had erred in law in convicting him of both genocide and extermination on the basis of the same facts. For the Appeals Chamber, the test was whether the relevant provisions of the Statute for one of the crimes included a significantly distinct constitutive element which was absent in the other provisions.[247] A constitutive element was to be considered as significantly distinct if it required the proof of a fact which was not required in the case of the other crime. In this case, while genocide required evidence of *dolus specialis*, the crime against humanity of extermination requires that it be committed as part of a widespread or systematic attack against any civilian population. Consequently, the criterion for a double conviction was satisfied in this case, and both convictions were upheld.[248]

The Chamber upheld his life sentence despite overturning the rape conviction. The Chamber observed that the quashing of his conviction for rape did not affect the exceptional gravity of the crimes of which he had been convicted.[249]

---

243. 'Tribunal acquits Bagilishema', ICTR/INFO-9-2-271.EN, Arusha, 7 June 2001.

244. 'Tribunal releases Bagilishema on conditions', ICTR/INFO-9-2-272.EN, Arusha, 8 June 2001.

245. 'Bagilishema to reside in France pending appeal', ICTR/INFO-9-2-284, 21 September 2001; 'Bagilishema leaves for France', ICTR/INFO-9-2-288.EN, Arusha, 9 October 2001.

246. *Prosecutor* v. *Alfred Musema*, Judgement, 7 June 2001, para. 399.

247. Ibid., paras. 362, 365.

248. Ibid., para. 367.

249. Ibid., para. 373. See also 'Musema's genocide conviction upheld', ICTR/INFO-9-2-294.EN, Arusha, 16 November 2001.

6. FACT-FINDING, INCLUDING THE INTERNATIONAL FACT-FINDING COMMISSION

6.1 The International Fact-Finding Commission

The five-yearly meeting of representatives of the High Contracting Parties to Article 90 of Additional Protocol I was convened by Switzerland on 9 November 2001 in Berne.

The meeting elected nine new members of the International Fact-Finding Committee: Ambassador Juan Antonio Yañez-Barnuevo, 2nd vice-president (Spain); Dr Elzbieta Mikos-Skuza, 3rd vice-president (Poland); Professor Michael Bothe (Germany); Professor Ove Bring (Sweden); Dr Jeannette Irigoin Barrenne (Chile); Lieutenant-colonel Hugo Corujo Sanseviero (Uruguay); Professor Flavia Lattanzi (Italy); Professor Stelios Perrakis (Greece); and Major-General Anthony Rogers (UK).[250]

2001 also saw the publication of the second five-year report of the Commission, covering 1997 to 2001.[251] The report noted that, 'in spite of numerous efforts both by and on behalf of the Commission, including those in the second five-year period, it has not been approached with any concrete enquiries nor been involved in any good offices'. While the Commission had been approached on a number of occasions, it was mainly by members of armed opposition groups and never with regard to an international armed conflict or in a situation in which both parties had recognised the Commission's competence. 'Once they had become aware of the required procedure, including the necessary consent of both parties (and with it, the probability of a counter-request), they did not pursue the matter.'

The only situation where the Commission had become actively involved was Colombia. 'Between 1995 and 1999, repeated contacts with the government and one armed opposition group led to a stage in which the two parties were on the verge of signing an agreement to submit selected cases to the Commission. A change in the political landscape brought the process to an end.'

The Commission participated in a fictional training exercise in September 1998 in Sweden. 'The experience gained from the very realistic practice provided the basis for seminars that the Commission held in February 2000 and February 2001, both times within the context of its annual meeting. The seminars focused on the methodology and techniques of enquiry, including practical matters such as the definition of the mandate of a Chamber, the logistics of a mission, relations with the parties and with the media, and, finally, the principles to be respected in interrogation and the protection of witnesses. On the basis of these activities, the Commission has prepared a draft set of operational rules.' The Commission also engaged in a number of promotional activities.

---

250. For a complete list of members of the Fact-Finding Committee see http://www.ihffc.org/en/members.html.

251. http://www.ihffc.org/en/documents/Report-2001-en.pdf.

Two states recognised the Fact-Finding Commission during the year, Trinidad and Tobago on 20 July and Yugoslavia on 16 October, bringing the total number by the end of the year to 60.

7. INTERNATIONAL ORGANISATIONS

7.1 **United Nations Organization**

7.1.1 *The Security Council*[252]

7.1.1.1 Afghanistan

By resolution 1378 of 14 November 2001, the Security Council condemned the Taliban 'for allowing Afghanistan to be used as a base for the export of terrorism by the Al-Qaida network and other terrorist groups and for providing safe haven to Usama Bin Laden, Al-Qaida and others associated with them, and supporting the efforts of the Afghan people to replace the Taliban regime', expressed its deep concern by the 'grave humanitarian situation and the continuing serious violations by the Taliban of human rights and international humanitarian law'. It called on all Afghan forces 'to refrain from acts of reprisal, to adhere strictly to their obligations under human rights and international humanitarian law, and to ensure the safety and security and freedom of movement of United Nations and associated personnel, as well as personnel of humanitarian organization' (para. 2).

By resolution 1383 of 6 December, the Council expressed its determination to help the people of Afghanistan bring an end to conflict and promote reconciliation, lasting peace, stability and respect for human rights, as well as to cooperate with the international community to put an end to the use of Afghanistan as a base for terrorism. It welcomed the signing in Bonn on 5 December 2001 of an Agreement on provisional arrangements in Afghanistan, pending the reestablishment of permanent government institutions, and called on all Afghan groups to implement the Agreement in full, in particular through full cooperation with the Interim Authority, which was due to take office on 22 December 2001.

By resolution 1386 of 20 December, the SC reaffirmed the above resolutions and other previous resolutions on Afghanistan, and took note of the request to the SC in the Bonn Agreement to consider authorising the early deployment to Afghanistan of an international security force. It determined to ensure the full implementation of the mandate of the International Security Assistance Force, in

252. The intention is not to allude to all SC resolutions and Presidential Statements of 2000, but only those concerned with armed conflicts and/or violations of international humanitarian law. Even then, the aim is not to comprehensively summarise and to analyse all relevant resolutions, but merely to draw attention to their key, and especially humanitarian, aspects, and particularly to specific references to international humanitarian law or breaches of the law, even where the resolution does not itself use the language of the law.

consultation with the Interim Authority. It took note of a letter from the UK offering to organise and command the force. The resolution again stressed that all Afghan forces 'must adhere strictly to their obligations under human rights law, including respect for the rights of women, and under international humanitarian law'.

7.1.1.2 Angola

On 23 January 2001, the Council passed resolution 1336 (2001) which expressed its continuing concern about the humanitarian effects of the situation and determined that the situation still constituted a threat to international peace and security. Acting under Chapter VII of the Charter, it took note of the final report (S/2000/1225) of the monitoring mechanism established pursuant to resolution 1295 (2000) and expressed its intention to give it its full consideration. Extending the monitoring mechanism's mandate for three months, it requested it to periodically report to the Committee established pursuant to SC resolution 864 (1993), and to provide a written addendum to the final report by 19 April 2001. It also requested the SG to reappoint five of the experts appointed by him pursuant to resolution 1295 to serve on the monitoring mechanism.

By resolution 1348 of 23 April, which was adopted by the SC on 19 April, the SC took note of an addendum to the final report (S/2000/1225) of the monitoring mechanism established pursuant to resolution 1295 (2000).[253] It further requested the Secretary-General to appoint up to five experts to serve on the monitoring mechanism, and ordered all states to cooperate fully with it in the discharge of its mandate.

By resolution 1374 of 19 October, the Council again expressed its concern at the humanitarian situation and further extended the monitoring mechanism's mandate for six months, till 19 April 2002.

7.1.1.3 Burundi

In a Statement made on its behalf by the President of the SC, on 2 March 2001,[254] the SC condemned the recent attacks by armed groups in Burundi, particularly those launched on Bujambura by the Forces for National Liberation (FNL). It condemned 'the deliberate targeting of the civilian population by the armed groups and called upon all parties to abide by international humanitarian law and in particular to refrain from any further attacks or any other military action that endangers the civilian population'. It called on the FNL and the Forces for the Defence of Democracy (FDD) to cease hostilities immediately and to join the peace process. It stressed the importance of providing urgent humanitarian assistance to the civilians displaced by the hostilities, and called upon all parties to guarantee safe and unhindered access by humanitarian personnel to those in need. By resolution

---

253. See 'Year in Review', 3 *YIHL* (2000) pp. 169 at 204.
254. S/PRST/2001/6, 2 March 2001.

1375 of 29 October 2001, the Council expressed its deep concern at the ongoing violence and insecurity in Burundi and its belief that the Arusha Peace and Reconciliation Agreement of 28 August 2000 remained the most viable basis for a resolution of the conflict together with efforts to build an internal political partnership. It reaffirmed its strong support for the installation of the transitional government in Burundi on 1 November 2001 and called on all parties to the Arusha Agreement and the armed groups to immediately cease all violence against civilians. It called on the FDD and FNL to immediately cease hostilities, to enter into negotiations and join the peace process, and called on all states in the region to fully support the process.

7.1.1.4 Croatia

Resolution 1335 of 12 January, concerning the disputed issue of Prevlaka, authorised the UN military observers (UNMOP) to continue to monitor the demilitarisation of the Prevlaka Peninsula, in accordance with earlier resolutions, until 15 July 2001. It also urged the parties to resume talks on the issue. By resolution 1362 of 11 July, the SC further authorised UNMOP to continue to monitor the demilitarisation of the Prevlaka Peninsula.

7.1.1.5 Cyprus

By resolution 1384 of 14 December 2001, the Council extended the mandate of the UN Peacekeeping Force in Cyprus (UNFICYP) until 15 June 2002.

7.1.1.6 Democratic Republic of the Congo

The DRC was again a particularly active item on the Council's agenda. By resolution 1341 of 22 February, acting under Chapter VII, it called on the parties to the Lusaka Ceasefire Agreement not to resume hostilities and to implement the Agreement. Further, it called on Uganda and Rwanda and other states to withdraw their forces from DRC. The resolution made a couple of direct references to humanitarian law. In its Preamble, it expressed its 'deep concern at all violations of human rights and international humanitarian law, including atrocities against civilian populations, especially in the eastern provinces'. In paragraph 9, it condemned the 'massacres and atrocities committed in the territory of the Democratic Republic of the Congo and demand[ed] once again that all the parties concerned put an immediate end to violations of human rights and international humanitarian law'. In paragraph 14, it reminded 'all parties of their obligations with respect to the security of civilian populations under the Fourth Geneva Convention relative to the Protection of Civilian Persons in Times of War of 12 August 1949 and *stress[ed]* that occupying forces should be held responsible for human rights violations in the territory under their control'.

The comprehensive resolution also dealt with other aspects of the conflict, including exploitation of natural resources, the use of child soldiers and the increased spread of HIV and AIDS as a result of the conflict, and clearly linked the conflict in DRC with other regional conflicts, including in Burundi.

Resolution 1355 of 15 June, adopted under Chapter VII, noted the Council's satisfaction that the parties to the Lusaka Ceasefire Agreement were respecting it and urged all parties to implement it and other relevant agreements and SC resolutions. It welcomed progress on disengagement and redeployment. It demanded that the Front de Libération du Congo disengage and redeploy in accordance with the Harare sub-plans and the commitment it made to the Security Council mission to the Great Lakes region. It repeated many of the Council's earlier demands, including that the forces of Uganda and Rwanda and other states withdraw from Congolese territory. The resolution also extended the mandate of the United Nations Organization Mission in the Democratic Republic of the Congo (MONUC) for another year.

Resolution 1355 made several direct references to humanitarian law. In the preamble, it expressed its deep concern at all violations of human rights and international humanitarian law, including atrocities against civilian populations, especially in the eastern provinces. In paragraph 15, it condemned the massacres and atrocities committed in the territory of the DRC, demanded that all parties to the conflict cease immediately all violations of human rights and humanitarian law and stressed that those responsible would be held accountable. Paragraph 16 reminded all parties of their obligations with respect to the security of civilian populations under the Fourth Geneva Convention and stressed that all forces present on Congolese territory are responsible for preventing violations of international humanitarian law in the territory under their control. Paragraph 35 called on the SG to ensure sufficient deployment of child protection advisers to ensure consistent and systematic monitoring and reporting on the conduct of the parties to the conflict as concerned their child protection obligations under humanitarian and human rights law.

This detailed resolution also addressed many other aspects of the conflict, including the use of child soldiers and the need for safe and unhindered access for relief workers, as well as the exploitation of Congo's natural resources by parties to the conflict, and the link between this exploitation and the continuation of the conflict. Moreover, it recognised that the cessation of support to the ex-forces of the Rwandan Army and the Interahamwe forces was essential to the settlement of the conflict in Congo.

Resolution 1376 of 9 November welcomed the general respect for the ceasefire among the parties to the Lusaka Ceasefire Agreement, but expressed its concern at the hostilities in areas of the eastern Democratic Republic of the Congo and called on the parties to cease any form of support to the armed groups, particularly in the east of the country. It welcomed the withdrawal of some foreign troops and called on all others to withdraw. It expressed its grave concern at the repeated human rights violations throughout the Democratic Republic of the Congo, in particular in the territories under the control of the rebel groups party to the Lusaka Ceasefire Agreement, and called on all parties to put an end to such violations.

In a Statement of the President of the SC on its behalf of 19 December, the President of the Security Council expressed the Council's concern about the plundering of natural resources and other forms of wealth from the DRC and strongly condemned these activities, which perpetuate the conflict. The Security Council requested the SG to renew the mandate of the Expert Panel for six months, when the panel should report to it, following the submission of an interim report after three months. It urged governments named in previous reports to conduct their own inquiries, cooperate fully with the Expert Panel and take, on an urgent basis, the necessary steps to end all illegal exploitation of the natural resources of Congo.

7.1.1.7 East Timor

Resolution 1338 of 31 January 2001 extended the mandate of the United Nations Transitional Administration in East Timor (UNTAET) for a year, until 31 January 2002, bearing in mind the need to make adjustments related to the independence timetable. At the same time, it requested the Special Representative of the Secretary-General to continue to take steps to delegate further authority to the East Timorese people until authority is fully transferred to the government of an independent state of East Timor. It emphasised the need for measures to address shortcomings in the administration of justice in East Timor, particularly with a view to bringing to justice those responsible for serious crimes in 1999.

7.1.1.8 Ethiopia and Eritrea

Following the deployment by the SC of a UN Mission in Ethiopia and Eritrea (UNMEE) to the contested border area between Ethiopia and Eritrea in late-2000,[255] and the signing in Algiers on 12 December 2000 of the Peace Agreements between Ethiopia and Eritrea (the Algiers Agreements), the UN Secretary-General proposed the creation of a Boundary and Claims Commission to decide on demarcation and delineation of the contested border.

On 9 February 2001, in a Statement by the President of the Security Council on its behalf, the Council expressed its strong support for the peace process and called on the parties to work towards the prompt and full implementation of the Algiers Agreement. It called on all parties to, *inter alia*, guarantee the safety and security of all UNMEE, ICRC and other humanitarian personnel and to respect strictly the relevant provisions of international humanitarian law'.[256] It also encouraged them to continue the release and voluntary and orderly return under the auspices of the ICRC of interned civilians and to release remaining POWs and facilitate their return, and to fulfill their commitments under the Algiers Agreement to afford humane treatment to each other's nationals.

On 15 March, by resolution 1344, the SC extended the mandate of UNMEE for six months until 7 September. It further called upon the parties to work towards a full and prompt implementation of the Peace Agreements. UNMEE's mandate should terminate once the work to delimit and demark the border has taken place. The preamble reaffirmed the need for both parties 'to fulfill all of their obligations under international humanitarian law, human rights and refugee law'.

---

255. See 3 *YIHL* (2000) p. 209.
256. S/PRST/2001/4, 9 February 2001.

Resolution 1369 of 14 September 2001 further reaffirmed the need for both parties to fulfill their obligations under international law, international humanitarian law, human rights law and refugee law, and to ensure the safety of all UN staff and personnel of the ICRC and other humanitarian organisations. It also reaffirmed the Council's strong support for the Comprehensive Peace Agreement and its strong support for the UNMEE, whose mandate, at the troop and military observer levels, it extended until 15 March 2002. It called on both parties to the conflict to urgently resolve outstanding issues. In a particular reference to IHL, it called on the parties to unconditionally and without delay and in accordance with the Geneva Conventions, release and return the remaining prisoners of war and detainees.

7.1.1.9 Georgia

Resolution 1364 of 31 July addressed the unstable security situation in the Georgian state of Abkhazia. It expressed the Council's regret of the situation in the conflict zone due to ongoing violence, hostage-taking, the rise in criminality and the activities of illegal armed groups, which threatened the peace process. It further expressed the Council's support for all efforts to stabilise the situation and to achieve a comprehensive political settlement, including of the political status of Abkhazia.

7.1.1.10 Lebanon

Resolution 1337 of 30 January 2001 extended the mandate of the United Nations Interim Force in Lebanon for six months, until 31 July 2001, while recognising the interim nature of the mission. By resolution 1365 of 31 July, the Council further extended UNIFIL's mandate by six months.

7.1.1.11 Liberia

Resolution 1343 of 7 March concerned the support by the government of Liberia for the illicit trade in conflict diamonds originating from Sierra Leone and for the main rebel group in Sierra Leone, the Revolutionary United Front. In this highly detailed resolution, adopted under Chapter VII, the Council condemned such support and set out concrete steps for the cessation of Liberian support for rebel factions and for illegal smuggling activities, finding the Liberian activities to constitute a threat to international peace and security. It noted with deep concern the 'unequivocal and overwhelming evidence' of the Panel of Experts[257] that the Liberian government supported the RUF at all levels. Among other measures, the Security Council called on all other states in the region to take appropriate action to prevent their territory from being used for the preparation or commission of armed

257. Report of the Panel of Experts Established pursuant to Resolution 1306 (2000), S/2000/1195, 19 December 2000.

attacks against neighbouring countries and to refrain from any activities that might further destabilise the regional situation. All states should also take measures to prevent the direct or indirect import of all rough diamonds from Liberia.

7.1.1.12 Macedonia

Resolution 1345 of 21 March expressed the Council's concern at the outbreak of violence in the Former Yugoslav Republic of Macedonia, including terrorist activities. It strongly condemned such extremist violence and demanded that all those involved immediately cease such activities, lay down their weapons and return home.

The resolution made a direct reference to humanitarian law in paragraph 7, which underlined 'the requirement for all parties to act with restraint and full respect for international humanitarian law'.

7.1.1.13 Sierra Leone

Resolution 1346 of 30 March extended the mandate of the United Nations Mission in Sierra Leone (UNAMSIL) for a further six months, and extended the mission's size to 17,500, including 120 military observers. It also requested the Secretary-General to keep it informed as to progress made by UNAMSIL in the implementation of key aspects of its concept of operations, and called on all parties to fully implement the Abuja Ceasefire Agreement.

While not condemning violations of humanitarian law explicitly (perhaps because technically, the conflict had ended at this point), the resolution expressed the Council's 'deep concern at the reports of human rights abuses committed by the Revolutionary United Front ... and others, including other military groups, against the civilian population, in particular the harassment and forced recruitment of adults and children for fighting and forced labour ... (para. 6).'

In resolution 1370 of 18 September, the SC further extended UNAMSIL's mandate until 30 September 2001. Among many other issues addressed, it expressed the Council's 'deep concern at the reports of human rights abuses and attacks committed by the RUF, the Civil Defence Forces and other armed groups and individuals against the civilian population, in particular, widespread violations of the human rights of women and children, including sexual violence and demanded that they cease immediately' (para. 4).

On 19 December, by resolution 1385 (2001), the Council addressed the illicit diamond trade in Sierra Leone. It welcomed the establishment of the Kimberly Process and other efforts 'to break the link between illicit trade in rough diamonds and armed conflict'. Acting under Chapter VII, it welcomed the establishment and implementation of the Certificate of Origin regime for trade in diamonds in Sierra Leone and welcomed reports that the regime was helping to curb the flow of conflict diamonds out of the country.

7.1.1.14 Somalia

Somalia was not the subject of a SC resolution during 2001, but the President of the SC did issue a Statement on its behalf on 11 January 2001.[258] In it, he emphasised 'the importance of respect for human rights and international humanitarian law', and noted concern that the humanitarian and security situation remained fragile in several parts of Somalia, including Mogadishu. It strongly condemned attacks by armed groups on civilians and humanitarian personnel and called on all Somalis to respect fully the security and safety of the UN, the ICRC and NGOs (but not specifically civilians), and to guarantee their complete freedom of movement and safe access throughout Somalia. It reiterated the obligation on all states to ensure full implementation and enforcement of the arms embargo and to report to it on possible violations. It insisted that all states should refrain from any military intervention in the internal situation of Somalia and that its territory should not be used to undermine regional stability. It welcomed the SG's intention to establish a trust fund for peace-building in Somalia and invited him to prepare a proposal for a peace-building mission for Somalia. Such a proposal should, with specific attention to the security situation in the country, outline possible ways to advance the peace process further.

7.1.1.15 Western Sahara

Resolution 1349 of 27 April extended the mandate of the UN Mission for the Referendum in Western Sahara (MINURSO) until 30 June 2001, to enable the parties to continue to resolve the multiple disputes relating to the implementation of the Settlement Plan. Resolution 1359 of 29 June further extended the mandate of MINURSO until 30 November. It made a direct reference to humanitarian law in paragraph 5, where it urged 'the parties to solve the problem of the fate of people unaccounted for, and call[ed] on the parties to abide by their obligations under international humanitarian law to release without further delay all those held since the start of the conflict'. Resolution 1380 of 27 November further extended the mandate until 28 February 2002.

7.2 The International Court of Justice

On 31 January 2001, the ICJ removed from its List the cases concerning Armed Activities on the Territory of the Congo (*Democratic Republic of the Congo* v. *Burundi*) and (*Democratic Republic of the Congo* v. *Rwanda*), at the request of the DRC,[259] following the conclusion of an agreement between the parties. The cases, which had been brought by the DRC on 23 June 1999, alleged acts of armed aggression by Rwanda and Burundi against the DRC. A third case, against Uganda, remained on the Court's list.

---

258. S/PRST/2001/1, 11 January 2001.
259. Made in a letter dated 15 January 2001.

On 24 April 2001, the Federal Republic of Yugoslavia (FRY) filed an Application for revision of the Judgment delivered by the International Court of Justice on 11 July 1996 in the case concerning the Application of the Convention on the Prevention and Punishment of the Crime of Genocide (*Bosnia and Herzegovina* v. *Yugoslavia*), Preliminary Objections.

The FRY claimed that a revision was justified on the grounds that a 'new fact' had emerged, that being its becoming a member of the United Nations on 1 November 2000. It argued that before 1 November 2000, it did not continue the international legal and political personality of the Socialist Federal Republic of Yugoslavia, was not a Member of the United Nations, was not a State Party to the Statute of the Court, and was not a State Party to the Genocide Convention (which is only open to United Nations Member States or to non-Member States to which an invitation to sign or accede has been addressed by the General Assembly). '[S]ince membership in the United Nations, combined with the status of a party to the Statute [of the Court] and to the Genocide Convention represent the only basis on which jurisdiction over the FRY was assumed, and could be assumed, the disappearance of this assumption . . . [is] clearly of such a nature [as] to be a decisive factor.'[260]

8. INTERNATIONAL ACTIONS

8.1 Peacekeeping and peace-enforcement

On 16 January, the Security Council held a debate on the subject of 'Strengthening cooperation with troop-contributing countries'.

On 31 January, the President of the SC issued a Statement on its behalf in which it stressed the importance of the full implementation of resolution 1327 (2000). It took note of the interventions of Member States at the 16 January meeting, and noted its recognition of the view of the increasing complexity of peacekeeping operations, and the need for a transparent three-way relationship between the Security Council, the Secretariat, and the troop contributing countries that will foster a new spirit of partnership, cooperation and confidence. It acknowledged that the Secretariat must be able to rely on sufficient human and financial resources to respond to the demands placed on it, and underlined the importance of strengthening the Department of Peacekeeping Operations and other relevant departments. It decided to establish a Working Group of the Whole on United Nations peacekeeping operations, which would, however, not replace the private meetings with the troop-contributing countries.[261]

On 20 April, the SG issued his Report entitled, 'No exit without strategy: Security Council decision-making and the closure or transition of United Nations

260. The full text of Yugoslavia's Application for revision is available on the Court's website at the following address: http://www.icj-cij.org.

261. S/PRST/2001/3 of 31 January 2001.

peacekeeping operations',[262] pursuant to the request of the SC. It followed on an open debate in the SC on 15 November 2000. The key question was what factors the SC should consider in deciding to launch, close or significantly alter a UN peacekeeping mission. The report concluded that the UN needs to tailor its strategy to the prevailing conditions. 'Given the potentially large challenges and costs such comprehensive peace-building often encompasses, it is essential to ensure that all key parts of the United Nations system are fully engaged in a collaborative and constructive fashion.'[263]

On 13 June, the Council introduced by resolution 1353 a comprehensive resolution dealing with the subject of cooperation between it and the SG and troop-contributing countries.

On 24 December 2001, the UN General Assembly issued its 'Comprehensive review of the whole question of peacekeeping operations in all their aspects'.[264]

8.2 Peace-building

In a Statement on 20 February, the President recalled the SC's open debate on 5 February on 'Peace-building: towards a comprehensive approach'. It welcomed the convening by the SG of the fourth high-level United Nations Regional Organizations Meeting and noted with interest its results, in particular the Framework for cooperation in peace-building', as conveyed by the SG to the President of the SC in his letter of 12 February 2001. It further stated the Council's understanding of its own responsibilities with respect to international peace and security, the link between peacemaking, peacekeeping and peace-building, and the fact that this relationship requires a comprehensive approach in order to preserve the results achieved and prevent the reoccurrence of conflict. To this end, it reiterated the value of including, as appropriate, peace-building elements in the mandates of peacekeeping operations. The SC recognised that peace-building is aimed at preventing the outbreak, the reoccurrence or continuation of armed conflict and therefore encompasses a wide range of political, developmental, humanitarian and human rights programmes and mechanisms, and requires both short- and long-term actions to achieve it. It affirmed that a comprehensive and integrated strategy in peace-building must involve all the relevant actors in this field, taking into account the unique circumstances of each conflict situation.

8.3 Prevention of armed conflict

The SG issued a detailed Report on Prevention of armed conflict on 7 June.[265] In it he reviewed the progress that had been made by the UN in developing its conflict prevention strategy and made 29 recommendations for how the UN's efforts in this

262. S/2001/394, 20 April 2001.
263. Ibid., para. 21.
264. A/RES/56/24, 24 December 2001.
265. S/2001/574, 7 June 2001.

area could be improved, with the cooperation of Member States. The SG said that conflict prevention lies at the heart of the UN mandate in the maintenance of international peace and security. According to the SG, the primary responsibility lies with states, and the role of the UN and the international community is to support national efforts for conflict prevention and assist in building national capacity in this field. Preventative action should be initiated at the earliest possible stage of a conflict in order to be most effective. One of its principal aims should be to address the socio-economic, cultural, environmental, institutional and other structural causes that often underlie the immediate political symptoms of conflicts.

8.4 Humanitarian and other interventions

An interesting article prepared by the Legal Division of the ICRC and published in the June 2001 issue of the *International Review of the Red Cross* set out the ICRC's position on the controversial subject of humanitarian intervention.[266] The purpose of the article was to 'aid in internal discussions intended to clarify the organization's position in this topical debate'. It stated that it is not for the ICRC to pronounce on the legality or otherwise of such interventions,[267] particularly since such interventions are not governed by IHL but by UN Charter law. The article stated further that: 'The ICRC seeks to promote the term 'armed intervention in response to grave violations of human rights and of international humanitarian law', in place of the term 'humanitarian intervention'.[268] It stated that 'it is not currently possible to say that there is any right to take unilateral action or use force against a State that commits abuses of human rights or breaches of humanitarian law. In our view, international custom in this field has yet to be established.'[269] As to what the ICRC should do in the face of extremely serious violations of IHL or genocide, it 'must sound the alarm and inform the States that humanitarian action has reached its limits. However, it is not the business of the ICRC to specify the means (such as armed force) that should be employed to bring an end to the violations. The ICRC does not express an opinion regarding the legitimacy of operations carried out in response to breaches of human rights or humanitarian law.'[270] It warned that while armed intervention in response to serious violations of IHL or human rights may in some extreme situations be unavoidable, the international community should not view it as inevitable. 'To systematically use armed intervention for humanitarian purposes would amount to an abdication by the international community of its true responsibilities: preventing conflict and promoting the basic values expressed in international humanitarian law.'

---

266. A. Ryniker, 'The ICRC's position on "humanitarian intervention"', 83 *IRRC* (2001) p. 527.
267. Ibid.
268. Ibid.
269. Ibid., p. 530.
270. Ibid., p. 531.

In December 2001, the International Commission on Intervention and State Sovereignty presented its Report entitled *The Responsibility to Protect* and dealing with 'the so-called "right of humanitarian intervention": the question of when, if ever, it is appropriate for states to take coercive - and in particular military - action, against another state for the purposes of protecting people at risk in that other state'. The Commission, co-chaired by Gareth Evans and Mohamed Sahnoun, was launched on 14 September 2000 by the Canadian government 'as a response to Secretary-General Kofi Annan's challenge to the international community to endeavour to build a new international consensus on how to respond in the face of massive violations of human rights and humanitarian law'.[271] It concluded, *inter alia*, that 'State sovereignty implies responsibility, and the primary responsibility for the protection of its people lies with the state itself' and that 'Where a population is suffering serious harm, as a result of internal war, insurgency, repression or state failure, and the state in question is unwilling or unable to halt or avert it, the principle of non-intervention yields to the international responsibility to protect.'[272]

8.5 Counter-terrorism

On 30 January 2001, the GA passed resolution 55/158 on Measures to eliminate international terrorism, reaffirming and reiterating much of what it had already said in previous resolutions.[273] The resolution strongly condemned 'all acts, methods and practices of terrorism as criminal and unjustifiable, wherever and by whomsoever committed' (para. 1) and, *inter alia*, reiterated that 'criminal acts intended or calculated to provoke a state of terror in the general public, a group of persons for political purposes are in any circumstances unjustifiable, whatever the considerations of a political, philosophical, ideological, racial, ethnic, religious or other nature that may be invoked to justify them' (para. 2); and its call to all states to adopt further measures to prevent terrorism and strengthen international cooperation in combating terrorism (para. 3). It also called on all states to refrain from financing, encouraging, providing training for or otherwise supporting terrorist activities (para. 5) and, where they are not already parties, to accede to international conventions relating to terrorism (para. 7). It decided that the Ad Hoc Committee established by GA resolution 51/210 of 17 December 1996 should continue to elaborate a comprehensive convention on international terrorism, as well as continue to try and resolve the outstanding issues relating to the elaboration of a draft international convention relating to the suppression of acts of nuclear terrorism. It should also keep on its agenda the question of convening a high-level conference under UN auspices to formulate a joint-organised response of the inter-

---

271. Report, p. 81.
272. Report, p. XI.
273. Including resolution 51/210 of 17 December 1996; the Declaration on Measures to Eliminate International Terrorism contained in the annex to resolution 49/60 of 9 December 1994; and resolution 54/110 of 9 December 1999.

national community to terrorism in all its forms and manifestations (paras. 13 and 14).

On 12 September 2001, following the 11 September 2001 terrorist attacks on the US, the UN Security Council, by resolution 1368, expressed its condemnation of those attacks, and qualified those acts, like any acts of international terrorism, as threats to international peace and security. It expressed also its readiness to take all necessary steps to respond to the attacks and to combat all forms of terrorism, in accordance with its responsibilities under the Charter. It called on all states to 'redouble their efforts to prevent and suppress terrorist acts including by increased cooperation and full implementation of the relevant international anti-terrorist conventions and Security Council Resolution, in particular resolution 1269 of 19 October 1999' (para. 4).[274] Unlike resolution 1269, however, resolution 1368 did not include the additional phrase, 'based on respect for humanitarian law and human rights'. Deciding to remain seized of the matter, the resolution also called on 'all states to work together urgently to bring to justice the perpetrators, organizers and sponsors of these terrorist attacks' and stressed that 'those responsible for aiding, supporting or harbouring the perpetrators, organizers and sponsors of these acts will be held responsible' (para. 3).

The General Assembly passed resolution 56/1 on 18 September condemning the terrorist attacks on the USA. It called for international cooperation to bring the perpetrators and organisers to justice and to eradicate acts of terrorism, and stressed that 'those responsible for aiding, supporting or harbouring the perpetrators, organizers and sponsors of such acts will be held accountable'.

SC resolution 1373 followed on 28 September. Again acting under Chapter VII, it decided, *inter alia*, that all states shall prevent and suppress the financing of terrorist acts; refrain from providing any support whatsoever, active or passive, to entitities involved in terrorist acts, including by suppressing recruitment of members of terrorist groups and eliminating the supply of weapons to terrorists; take the necessary steps to prevent the commission of terrorist acts, including by provision of early warning to other states; deny safe haven to those who plan, support or commit terrorist acts or provide safe havens; ensure that any person who participates in the financing, planning or perpetration of terrorist acts or in supporting terrorist acts is brought to justice and that their punishment reflects the seriousness of the crime; cooperate to the fullest extent in connection with criminal investigations or criminal proceedings relating to the financing or support of terrorist acts; become parties to the relevant conventions; take appropriate steps to ensure before granting refugee status that asylum seekers have not planned, facilitated or participated in the commission of terrorist acts, and ensure that refugee status is not abused by terrorists and that claims of political motivation are not grounds for denial of extradition of alleged terrorists. It noted the connection between terrorism and transnational organised crime, including the trafficking in nuclear, chemical and biological weapons, arms trafficking, drugs and money-

274. Regarding resolution 1269, see Year in Review in 2 *YIHL* (1999) pp. 248-249.

laundering, and emphasised the need to enhance coordination of efforts at the national, sub-regional, regional and international levels in order to strengthen a global response to this serious challenge and threat to international security. Illustrating its seriousness in the matter, it decided to establish, in accordance with Rule 28 of its provisional rules of procedure, a SC committee to monitor compliance with the resolution and called on all states to report to the Committee within 90 days on the steps they have taken to implement the resolution. Finally, it expressed the Council's determination to take all necessary steps in order to ensure the full implementation of the resolution. Both resolutions 1368 and 1373 reaffirmed the right of individual and collective self-defence.

On 12 November 2001, the Council took the unusual step of issuing a declaration on the global effort to combat terrorism, which was attached to its resolution 1377. Noting that the Council had met at ministerial level, it declared that 'acts of international terrorism constitute one of the most serious threats to international peace and security in the twenty-first century' and that 'acts of international terrorism constitute a challenge to all States and to all of humanity'. It reaffirmed its unequivocal condemnation of all acts, methods and practices of terrorism as criminal and unjustifiable, regardless of their motivation, in all their manifestations, wherever and by whomever committed'. It stressed that 'acts of international terrorism are contrary to the purposes and principles of the United Nations, and that the financing, planning and preparation of, as well as any other form of support for acts of international terrorism are similarly contrary to the purposes and principles of the United Nations. It underlined that 'acts of terrorism endanger innocent lives and the dignity and security of human beings everywhere, threaten the social and economic development of all States and undermine global stability and prosperity'. It affirmed its belief that a sustained, comprehensive approach involving the active participation and collaboration of all Member States, and in accordance with the Charter, is essential to combat the scourge of international terrorism. It called on all Member States to accede to international conventions and protocols relating to terrorism, to take urgent steps to implement fully resolution 1373 (2001) and to assist each other in this respect, and underlined the obligation on states to deny financial and all other forms of support and safe haven to terrorism and those who support it. The resolution further expressed the Council's determination to proceed with the implementation of that resolution in full cooperation with the whole membership of the UN, and welcomed the progress made by the Counter-Terrorism Committee established by paragraph 6 of resolution 1373 to monitor its implementation. Finally, it called on all states to intensify their efforts to eliminate international terrorism.

9. REGIONAL ORGANISATIONS AND ACTIONS

9.1 European Court of Human Rights

9.1.1 *Banković case*

The Admissibility Decision in the case of *Banković and Others* v. *Belgium and 16 Other Contracting States*[275] considered whether the European Court should hear a case brought by a survivor of NATO's air strikes of 23 April 1999 on the headquarters of Radio Televizije Srbije (RTS) and the relatives of others who died in the raid. The applicants claimed that each of the named respondent states was individually and severally liable, even though the strikes were executed under the NATO umbrella. They alleged violations of Articles 2 (right to life), 10 (freedom of expression) and 13 (right to an effective remedy) of the European Convention on Human Rights.

Although the Grand Chamber declared the case inadmissible, its decision is interesting to humanitarian lawyers because it deals with the extra-territorial effects of air strikes. It is also interesting for the comments the Court made, *obiter,* on the obligations of Occupying Powers under human rights law.

A key question for the Court concerned jurisdiction: could the applicants bring a case before the European Court of Human Rights even though technically they did not fall within the jurisdiction of any of the respondent states?[276] In other words, could the applicants and their relatives fall within the jurisdiction of the respondent states as a result of 'extra-territorial acts', in this case, air strikes? Another relevant issue for humanitarian lawyers was whether the actions of NATO forces could be imputed to the governments of the Member States of the Alliance.

For persons resident in non-Council of Europe states who are on the receiving ends of air strikes by a Member State, the decision is undoubtedly a disappointment. The Court found that Article 1 of the European Convention must be interpreted in such a way as to reflect the ordinary and essential territorial notion of jurisdiction, with other bases of jurisdiction being exceptional and requiring special justification in the particular circumstances of each case.[277] Its examination of state practice in the application of the Convention found it to show a lack of any apprehension by States Parties of any extra-territorial responsibility of a type claimed in this case.[278]

While States Parties to the ECHR have been involved in various military missions, on no occasion has a state indicated its belief that its extra-territorial actions involved an exercise of jurisdiction within the meaning of Article 1 by

---

275. Application No. 52207/99. The decision is reprinted in this volume of the yearbook at p. 748. For commentary on the decision, see M. Happold, 'Bankovic *v* Belgium and The Territorial Scope of the European Convention', 3 *Human Rights* Law Review (2003) p. 77.

276. See para. 54.

277. See paras. 59-61.

278. See paras. 62-63.

making a derogation pursuant to Article 15 (derogation in time of emergency) of the Convention.[279]

The Court noted that in its previous jurisdiction it had only exceptionally recognised extra-territorial acts as constituting exercises of jurisdiction by States Parties.[280] Referring to the first *Loizidou* judgment (*preliminary objections*), the Court noted that 'the responsibility of a Contracting Party was capable of being engaged when as a consequence of military action (lawful or unlawful) it exercised effective control of an area outside its national territory. The obligation to secure, in such an area, the Convention rights and freedoms was found to derive from the fact of such control whether it was exercised directly, through the respondent State's armed forces, or through a subordinate local administration.'[281]

The Court refused to accept the applicants' claim that a state's extra-territorial obligations under Article 1 of the European Convention are linked to the level of control it exercises, finding that this would mean that anyone who was adversely affected by an act attributable to a State Party would fall within that state's jurisdiction. Had the drafters of the Convention wished to ensure jurisdiction as extensive as that advocated by the applicants, they could have adopted a text the same as or similar to the common Article 1 of the 1949 Geneva Conventions. It also pointed out that the applicants' notion of jurisdiction would assimilate jurisdiction with victimisation, which are two distinct concepts, with different admissibility criteria under the Convention.[282]

The Court stated that the Convention was not designed to apply throughout the world, even in respect of the conduct of its States Parties. It was not convinced that there was any jurisdictional link between the persons who were victims of the act complained of and the respondent states. Accordingly, it was not satisfied that the applicants and their deceased relatives were capable of coming within the jurisdiction of the respondent states on account of the extra-territorial act in question.[283]

9.2 Organization of American States

A Governmental Expert's Meeting on 'The Implementation of International Humanitarian Law and Related Inter-American Conventions' was held under OAS auspices, in cooperation with the ICRC and the National Commission for the Improvement of the Administration of Justice of the Republic of Costa Rica, from 6-8 March 2001 in San José, Costa Rica. It aimed to promote the implementation of IHL treaties, *inter alia*, within Member States; examine and evaluate the measures already taken by Member States to implement these treaties and disseminate their contents; faciliate the exchange of relevant information inter state; provide information on recent developments concerning international criminal justice and the

279. Para. 62.
280. See paras. 67, 71, 73.
281. Para. 70.
282. Ibid., para. 75.
283. Ibid., para. 80.

ICC; and prepare a document on its findings to present to the next General Assembly of the OAS.[284]

During its third plenary session on 5 June, the General Assembly of the OAS passed several resolutions concerning international humanitarian law.

By resolution 1770 concerning the International Criminal Court,[285] the GA, recalling its earlier relevant resolutions,[286] urged those OAS Member States that had not already done so to consider the possibility of ratifying or acceding to, as applicable, the Rome Statute of the International Criminal Court.

By resolution 1771[287] regarding Promotion of and Respect for International Humanitarian Law, the GA resolved to increase the number of States Parties to the various IHL treaties, including weapons conventions and the ICC Statute, and drew states' attention to the need to adopt the necessary national implementing legislation, including criminal law to punish breaches; to their obligations under Article 36 of Additional Protocol I concerning new weapons; to the need for the widest possible dissemination of the law throughout the population but particularly amongst the armed forces; and to the need to establish national commissions, where they had not already done so. It recalled its previous resolutions concerning IHL,[288] and the obligation on all states to observe and enforce the law and the need to punish serious violations.

By resolution 1791 (XXXI-O/O1), the General Assembly expressed inter-American support for the Comprehensive Test Ban Treaty.[289] The resolution noted the General Assembly's recognition that a nuclear-weapons' free zone is an effective and concrete mechanism that contributes to the safeguarding of international peace and security, and urged states of the region to sign or ratify the CTBT and facilitate its entry into force.

Resolution 1794, entitled the Western Hemisphere as an Antipersonnel-Land-Mine-Free Zone,[290] reaffirmed the goals of the global elimination of antipersonnel landmines and the conversion of the Western Hemisphere into an antipersonnel landmine-free zone, and urged OAS Member States that had not already done so to ratify or accede to the Ottawa Treaty and to the Certain Conventional Weapons Convention and its four additional protocols. Those states already party to the Landmines Treaty were challenged to destroy their stockpiles of the weapons by

284. http://www.oas.org/juridico/english/governmental_experts_meeting_dlci.htm.

285. AG/RES. 1770 (XXXI-O/01).

286. AG/RES. 1619 (XXIX-O/99), AG/RES. 1706 (XXX-O/00), and AG/RES. 1709 (XXX-O/00); the recommendation of the Inter-American Commission on Human Rights (OEA/Ser.L/V/II.102, Doc. 6 rev., April 16, 1999, Chap. VII, 21.3.B); and the document 'Framework for OAS Action on the International Criminal Court' (AG/INF.248/00).

287. OEA/Ser.P, AG/RES. 1771 (XXXI-O/01).

288. AG/RES. 1270 (XXIV-O/94), AG/RES. 1335 (XXV-O/95), AG/RES. 1408 (XXVI-O/96), AG/RES. 1503 (XXVII-O/97), AG/RES. 1565 (XXVIII-O/98), AG/RES. 1619 (XXIX-O/99), and AG/RES. 1706 (XXX-O/00).

289. See also at p. 325 of this review.

290. AG/RES. 1794 (XXXI-O/01).

September 2001. Recalling its earlier resolutions on the subject,[291] it noted with satisfaction the efforts being made the Governments of Colombia, Costa Rica, Ecuador, Guatemala, Honduras, Nicaragua, and Peru to complete mine-clearing activities and the destruction of stockpiles, as well as programs of those countries and El Salvador aimed at the physical and psychological rehabilitation of victims and the socio-economic reclamation of demined areas in their countries and the important coordination work of the OAS General Secretariat, through the Unit for the Promotion of Democracy's Mine Action Team. It encouraged Member States either to request or to provide assistance, as appropriate, to the OAS Mine Action Team through its programs on mine clearance, stockpile destruction, mine awareness, and victim assistance, in order to advance mine action in the region, and requested the SG to continue to consider the possibility of developing new demining programs in the Americas to assist affected member states, upon request, in fulfilling their commitment to convert the Western Hemisphere into an anti-personnel landmine-free zone.

9.3 African Union

Several decisions of the African Union taken at the Seventy-Fourth Ordinary Session of the Council of Ministers, held from 5 to 8 July 2001 in Lusaka, Zambia, made direct reference to humanitarian law.[292]

CM/Decision 10 on the Situation in Burundi, *inter alia*, appealed 'to the belligerents to scrupulously adhere to the international humanitarian law' (para. 11). Decision 12 on the Situation in the Democratic Republic of Congo, *inter alia*, expressed 'grave concern at the humanitarian situation and the repeated violations of the international humanitarian law perpetrated in the DCR', and exhorted 'the parties to respect the international humanitarian law' (para. 19). Decision 16 on the Situation in Angola, *inter alia*, expressed the Ministers' 'grave concern over the repeated violations of the International Humanitarian Law', and urged 'UNITA to comply with this Law and put an immediate end to its indiscriminate attacks against civilian populations and the personnel of humanitarian agencies'. Decision 20 on the Question of Palestine condemned 'Israel for using internationally prohibited weapons and excessive force against unarmed Palestinian civilians' and, *inter alia*, urged it to 'respect all international humanitarian laws in the Palestinian lands occupied since 1967, including Jerusalem, as provided for, by the Fourth Geneva Convention of 1949.'

---

291. 'The Western Hemisphere as an Antipersonnel-Land-Mine-Free Zone' [AG/RES. 1644 (XXIX-O/99), AG/RES. 1569 (XXVIII-O/98), AG/RES. 1496 (XXVII-O/97), and AG/RES. 1411 (XXVI-O/96)] and 'Cooperation for Security in the Hemisphere' [AG/RES. 1744 (XXX-O/00)], which reaffirmed the goals of the global elimination of antipersonnel landmines and the conversion of the Western Hemisphere into an antipersonnel landmine-free zone.

292. See Council of Ministers, Seventy-fourth Ordinary Session/Ninth Ordinary Session of the AEC, 5-6 July 2001, Lusaka, Zambia, CM/Dec. 1-46) LXXIX). http://www.au2002.gov.za/docs/summit_council/cm.pdf.

Other relevant decisions included No. 19, on the Illicit Proliferation, Circulation and Trafficking of Small Arms and Light Weapons, and Decision 21 on the Situation in the Middle East.

10. ARMS CONTROL AND DISARMAMENT

10.1 Conventional weapons

10.1.1 *RevCon of the 1980 Certain Conventional Weapons Convention*

In December 2001, States Parties to the 1980 Convention on Prohibitions or Restriction on the Use of Certain Conventional Weapons Which May be Deemed to be Excessively Injurious or to Have Indiscriminate Effects of 10 October 1980 gathered for only the second time to review the Convention. The meeting, held between 11 and 21 December in Geneva, proved to be very fruitful. It resulted in the extension of its application to non-international armed conflicts. Moreover, it established a Group of Government Experts to address the contentious issue of explosive remnants of war, in particular, cluster bombs. The RevCon also addressed the issue of small calibre weapons, and adopted a Final Declaration which makes reference to multipurpose explosive bullets, legal reviews of new weapons, means or methods of warfare and blinding laser weapons.

By an amendment to the Convention's Article 1, the applicability of the Convention and all of its annexed Protocols was extended from international armed conflicts to common Article 3 conflicts (although notably not Protocol II conflicts).[293] Previously, only Amended Protocol II to the Convention, concerning landmines, booby traps and similar devices, applied during common Article 3 conflicts. While amended Article 1 makes the existing protocols applicable during common Article 3 situations once the amendment comes into force following its adoption by 20 states, it does not make any future protocol adopted automatically applicable in such situations. Instead, by virtue of Article 1, the nature of the armed conflicts to which future protocols will be applicable will be determined on a case-by-case basis, during the course of negotiations on each protocol. 'Protocols adopted after 1 January 2002 may apply, exclude or modify this new scope of application.'[294]

The other big agenda item was explosive remnants of war. These are munitions which did not explode when they were delivered or lain, but which lay dormant but live. Switzerland proposed that a new protocol be adopted which would aim to set technical specifications in order to prevent submunitions from becoming explosive remnants of war. 'This proposal would require all submunitions to have a 98% reliability through the combination of the primary fusing mechanism and a back-up

293. The amendment is reproduced at p. 766 of this volume.

294. L. Maresca, 'Second Review Conference of the Convention on Certain Conventional Weapons', *International Review of the Red Cross*, No. 845 (2002) pp. 255-262.

self-destruct feature, thereby ensuring that *if the weapon does fail to explode as intended against a military target, it would self-destruct soon after*'.[295]

The USA pushed for the introduction of a new protocol to the 1980 Convention to reduce the impact of anti-vehicle mines. 'All anti-vehicle mines would have to be detectable by commonly available mine detectors, and only remotely delivered anti-vehicle mines would be required to contain self-destruct or self-neutralization features. Like the requirements proposed by Switzerland for submunitions, these characteristics would help ensure that anti-vehicle mines no longer pose a threat once the military purpose for the weapons has ended.'[296]

The ICRC also pushed for new responses to the problems of explosive remnants of war. 'In its view, measures to reduce the consequences of such remnants should cover all types of explosive munitions which threaten civilian populations in a post-conflict environment. The main emphasis in addressing the problem would be placed on general rules to ensure rapid and safe clearance, plus warnings to civilian populations living in affected areas. The ICRC has also called for a prohibition on the use of submunitions against any military objective situated within a concentration of civilians.'[297] The Conference also addressed efforts to update the Hague Declaration of 1899 on Expanding Bullets in order cover small-calibre weapons systems.

10.1.2 *Firearms*

On 2 March 2001, an international Protocol against the Illicit Manufacturing of and Trafficking in Firearms, Their Parts and Components and Ammunition was adopted. It is designed to supplement the 2000 UN Convention against Transnational Organized Crime.

10.1.3 *Small arms*

From 9 to 20 July 2001, the United Nations Conference on the Illicit Trade in Small Arms and Light Weapons in All Its Aspects convened in New York. Presided over by Camilo Reyes Rodriguez of Colombia, the Conference – the first meeting of its kind – brought together world leaders, politicians and experts to discuss the problems and threat to human security caused by small arms and the illegal trade in these weapons, and how the current situation can be ameliorated.[298] The Conference heard that there are an estimated 500 million small arms and light weapons in circulation, and that many of these end up in the hands of irregular forces, criminals

295. Ibid.
296. Ibid.
297. Ibid.
298. The subject of small arms and light weapons has been on the General Assembly's agenda since the mid-1990s. By resolution 54/54 of 15 December 1999, it resolved to convene the Conference, and established a preparatory committee for this purpose, which was also charged with recommending a draft final document for the conference. See further 'Conference on small arms set to convene at headquarters, 9-20 July', UN Press Release DC/2782, 05/07/2001.

and terrorists, fueling armed conflicts. 'Small arms and light weapons are currently responsible for nearly 90 percent of the deaths in conflicts around the world', in total, about 4 million deaths. 'Even in societies not torn by conflict, the proliferation of small arms had contributed to a culture of violence and crime. Their illicit proliferation eroded the authority of legitimate but weak governments; undermined respect for international humanitarian law and the rule of law; contributed to the displacement of innocent civilians; and made peacekeeping that much more difficult.'[299] Among the background documents submitted for the Conference's consideration was the Report of the Group of Governmental Experts established pursuant to General Assembly resolution 54/54 V of 15 December 1999, entitled 'Small arms'.[300]

The meeting concluded with the adoption without a vote by 140 nations on 21 July of a Programme for Action to Prevent, Combat and Eradicate the Illicit Trade in Small Arms and Light Weapons in All Its Aspects.[301] The Programme of Action is motivated by concern about the humanitarian and socio-economic consequences of the illicit manufacture, transfer and circulation of small arms and light weapons, which it recognises 'sustains conflicts, exacerbates violence, contributes to the displacement of civilians, undermines respect for humanitarian law, impedes the provision of humanitarian assistance to victims and armed conflict and fuels crime and terrorism' as well as by concern about the devastating consequences on children and negative impact on women and the elderly.

The 86-paragraph Programme of Action requires member states to make illicit gun possession or production a criminal offence; to put in place adequate laws, regulations and administrative procedures to exercise effective control over the production of small arms and light weapons within their areas of jurisdiction, and over the export, import, transit or retransfer of such weapons in order to prevent illegal manufacture of and illicit trafficking in such weapons or their diversion to unauthorised recipients; to establish a national coordination agency on small arms responsible for policy guidance, research monitoring of efforts to prevent, combat and eradicate the illicit trade, as well as tracing, finance, collection and destruction of small arms and light weapons; to identify and destroy stocks of surplus weapons; to identify groups and individuals engaged in the illegal manufacture, trade, stockpiling, transfer, possession, as well as financing for acquisition, of illicit small arms and light weapons, and to take action under appropriate national law against such groups and individuals; to keep track of officially-held guns; to issue end-user certificates for exports/transit; to notify the original supplier nation of re-export; to engage in the disarmament, demobilisation and re-integration of ex-combatants,

---

299. 'Small Arms Conference Urged to Forge Comprehensive Action Plan: Fifteen speakers address opening session', United Nations Conference on the Illicit Trade in Small Arms, 1st Meeting, Press Release DC/2783, 09/07/2001.

300. Submitted by the Secretary-General, A/CONF/192.2, 11 May 2001.

301. Report of the United Nations Conference on the Illicit Trade in Small Arms and Light Weapons in All Its Aspects, New York, 9-20 July 2001, A/CONF.192/15; 'Small Arms Conference Concludes with Consensus Adoption of Action Programme', United Nations Conference on the Illicit Trade in Small Arms, 10th Meeting and Round-up, Press Release DC/2795, 21/07/2001.

including the collection and destruction of their weapons; to support regional small arms control agreements, and encourage moratoria on the sale or use of small arms; to maintain records of gun manufacture; to ensure better enforcement of arms embargoes; and to include civil society organisations in efforts to prevent small arms proliferation, *inter alia*. However, the Programme of Action is not legally binding: it merely provides a framework for curtailing illicit arms sales.

The Programme has been criticised for not addressing key aspects of the problem. In particular, it does not contain any provisions for maintaining and controlling private ownership of small arms and their transfer to non-state actors. Despite almost universal consensus on the desirability of including such provisions, the unwillingness of the US to agree to such provisions meant that they could not be included. Many states 'expressed dismay that the view of the overwhelming majority, on issues related to the control of arms used by citizens and the transfer of such weapons to non-State actors, had been held hostage by the "singular interest" of one delegation'.[302]

The Conference President reminded the delegates that the Conference and its outcome must be understood as only first steps in a process. A follow-up conference should be convened by the General Assembly no later than 2006, to review progress made in the implementation of the Programme for Action. Further, the Conference recommended that 'a United Nations study be undertaken, within existing resources, for examining the feasibility of developing an international instrument to enable States to identify and trace in a timely and reliable manner illicit small arms and light weapons'.[303]

A problem is that there is no universally accepted definition of which weapons constitute small arms or light weapons, although a UN study in 1997 proposed working definitions which are broadly supported. 'A small arm is one that can be fired, maintained and transported by one person, while a light weapon is used by a small crew and transported on a light vehicle or pack animal. The two categories include such weapons as pistols, assault rifles, machine guns, grenade launchers and shoulder-fired anti-tank and anti-aircraft missiles.'[304]

As much as half of the trade in small arms and light weapons may be illegal. Moreover, legally exported weapons may find their way into the illicit market. The fact that they are cheap and easily available makes them very popular in particular to non-state actors, especially young people and children.

Following the Conference on Small Arms, on 2 August 2001, the UN Security Council held a day-long open debate on the subject of small arms and light weapons. The meeting's objectives, as outlined by chairman Guillermo Fernandez de Soto, Minister for Foreign Affairs of Colombia, included a critical examination

302. 'Small Arms Conference Concludes with Consensus Adoption of Action Programme', United Nations Conference on the Illicit Trade in Small Arms, 10th Meeting and Round-up, Press Release DC/2795, 21/07/2001.

303. Ibid.

304. 'Conference on small arms set to convene at headquarters, 9-20 July', UN Press Release DC/2782, 05/07/2001.

of how the Security Council had addressed the subject in conflicts engaging its attention since September 1999 (when small arms had first appeared on its agenda). Addressing the meeting, the Secretary-General expressed his concern about the absence of any framework of binding norms and standards concerning small arms and light weapons, and his belief that the SC has a major role to play in making small arms the focus of urgent global attention.[305]

In its intervention to the meeting, the delegate for the United States expressed that state's rather different view of the role of the SC. In his view, the Security Council has only a limited, albeit important, role to play and should not seek a more elaborate role beyond the limits of its competence. 'The focus of the Conference, as reflected in the Programme of Action, was properly on Member States and their obligations to eliminate the illicit small arms trade. . . . Thus, the Security Council's role was circumscribed.'[306]

10.1.4 *Landmines*

On 12 January 2001, the UN General Assembly adopted resolution A/RES/55/33 on the Implementation of the Convention on the Prohibition of the Use, Stockpiling, Production and Transfer of Anti-Personnel Mines and on Their Destruction, in which, *inter alia*, it reaffirmed its determination to put an end to the suffering and casualties caused by anti-personnel mines and invited all states that were not yet parties to accede to the treaty.

On 6 September 2001, the European Parliament adopted a resolution on measures to promote a commitment by non-state actors to a total ban on anti-personnel landmines.[307] *Inter alia*, it called for the elimination of the use, production, stockpiling and transfer of anti-personnel landmines by non-state actors; requested the European Union to consider all possible means of putting pressure on those non-state actors openly reluctant to undertake to adhere to a total ban on anti-personnel landmines; urged the Council and the Commission to identify the sources of supply of anti-personnel landmines to non-state actors; and called for increased resources for humanitarian demining and mine awareness and landmine victim rehabilitation and assistance programmes.

The Third Annual Meeting of States Parties to the Convention on the Prohibition of the Use, Stockpiling, Production and Transfer of Anti-Personnel Mines and on Their Destruction, was held from 18 to 21 September in Managua, Nicaragua.

The meeting heard that 28 countries had already completely destroyed their stockpiles of anti-personnel landmines, while a further 28 were in the process of doing so. One hundred and eighteen states had signed and ratified the Ottawa Convention, including 20 mine-affected states, and a further 21 had signed but not

---

305. 'In Wake of Assembly Conference on Small Arms, Security Council Examines its Role in Implementation of Action Programme', Security Council, 4355th Meeting, Press Release SC/7114, 02/08/01.

306. Ibid.

307. http://www.icbl.org/wg/nsa/library/eu%20res%20nsa.html.

yet ratified. Non-participating states were urged to join the Convention.

The meeting closed on 21 September with the adoption of the Managua Declaration in which the States Parties to the Ottawa Convention welcomed the progress made so far in destroying landmines stockpiles, and in clearing land of mines, but expressed their continuing concern at the indiscriminate and lingering effects of landmines in countries throughout the world. They expressed their commitment to the total eradication of landmines and to addressing the insidious and inhumane effects of these weapons. The meeting also approved the establishment of an implementation unit for the Convention within the Geneva International Centre for Humanitarian Demining.

10.1.5 *Depleted uranium*

Depleted uranium-tipped munitions were the subject of considerable attention in 2001, following their use by NATO[308] against the Federal Republic of Yugoslavia in 1999, and subsequent concerns about their potential impact on the health of soldiers and peacekeepers, and – almost incidentally – the local population, and their effect on the environment.

The impact of DU weapons on human health and the natural environment invited extravagant claims both by persons favouring and opposed to their use. In the polarised atmosphere that characterised debate on these weapons, it was difficult to separate fact from fiction, and clear that not enough is known about the effects of DU weapons to be able to reach definitive conclusions.

Several countries that sent soldiers to Kosovo on a peacekeeping mission following the war initiated their own reports into the effects of DU on human health and the environment, and a number of important reports were published by national and international organisations, most notably, Britain's Royal Society[309] and the World Health Organization.[310]

The WHO study concluded that '[p]otentially depleted uranium has both chemical and radiological toxicity with the two important target organs being the kidneys and the lungs. Health consequences are determined by the physical and chemical nature of the depleted uranium to which an individual is exposed, and to the level and duration of exposure.'[311] 'Only military use of depleted uranium is likely to have any significant impact on environmental levels.'[312] Still, it acknowledged that '[g]aps in knowledge exist and further research is recommended in key areas that would allow better health risk assessments to be made.'[313]

---

308. To the end of 2001, only one state, the USA, had admitted to using DU weapons in combat.

309. The Royal Society, *The Health Hazards of Depleted Uranium Munitions*, Part I (London, 2001).

310. World Health Organization, Depleted Uranium: Sources, Exposure and Health Effects, (WHO/SDE/PHE/01.1) (Geneva, 2001). The complete report can be found and downloaded in parts at http://www.who.int/ionizing_radiation/pub_meet/ir_pub/en/.

311. Ibid., p. iv.

312. Ibid., p. vi.

313. Ibid., p. vii.

The WHO also published several other reports in 2001 concerning DU weapons, namely, *WHO Guidance on Exposure to Depleted Uranium For Medical Officers and Programme Administrators*, prepared in collaboration with United Nations Joint Medical Staff,[314] a report by the WHO Secretariat entitled *Health Effects of Depleted Uranium*,[315] and a Report entitled *Depleted Uranium Mission to Kosovo Undertaken at the request of the Special Representative of the Secretary-General and Head of the United Nations Interim Administration Mission in Kosovo* (UNMIK) 22 to 31 January 2001.[316]

The Royal Society Report found that 'the radiological risks from the use of DU in munitions are for the most part low, but that for small numbers of soldiers there might be circumstances in which risks are higher, and it is for that reason that further work should be undertaken to clarify their extent.'[317]

10.2 Weapons of mass destruction

10.2.1 *Nuclear weapons*

With 41 nuclear-capable states having ratified the Comprehensive Test Ban Treaty and only three more ratifications outstanding in order to trigger its entry into force, the second 'Conference on Facilitating the Entry into Force of the Comprehensive Nuclear-Test-Ban Treaty' took place at UN headquarters in New York from 11 to 13 November.[318] Opening the meeting, UN Secretary General Kofi Annan, said: 'If anyone thinks that [the CTBT and the Conference] have been overshadowed or marginalised by the events of 11 September and their aftermath ... those events should have made it clear to everyone that we cannot afford further proliferation of nuclear weapons.' The meeting adopted a Final Declaration, which highlighted the importance of the CTBT for non-proliferation and international security, and called on states to ratify or sign the Treaty as soon as possible, in order to facilitate the swift entry into force of the Treaty.[319] The meeting was attended by 108 state signatories to the treaty and a number of NGOs and international observers. The meeting was not attended by the USA, itself a signatory.[320] A week before the meeting, the US forced a vote at the First Committee (Security and Disarmament) of the UN on what had been considered to be a mere formality: whether to retain

314. http://www.who.int/ionizing_radiation/en/Recommend_Med_Officers_final.pdf.
315. http://www.who.int/ionizing_radiation/pub_meet/en/WHA54report.pdf.
316. http://www.who.int/ionizing_radiation/pub_meet/en/Report_WHO_depleted_uranium_Eng.pdf.
317. *Supra* n. 309.
318. http://disarmament2.un.org:8080/wmd/ctbt/article_IV/index.html, http://pws.ctbto.org/.
319. http://disarmament2.un.org:8080/wmd/ctbt/article_IV/ctbt%20final%20declarationE.pdf.
320. President Clinton was the first world leader to sign the CTBT on 24 September 1996. http://www.nawcwpns.navy.mil/~treaty/CTBT.html.

the CTBT on the GA's active agenda in 2002.[321] After forcing the vote, the USA was the only country to oppose.

The controversy over low-yield precision nuclear weapons, otherwise known as mini- or smart-nukes, heated up during the year.[322] The US has been developing these weapons, such as the B61-11, not for defensive purposes, but with a view to using them in conventional conflicts, against hard and deeply buried targets. The DOE and the weapons labs have consistently argued, however, that the B61-11 is merely a 'modification' of an older delivery system, because it uses an existing 'physics package'.[323]

Refuting the claim that the effects of these weapons can be limited, one scientist wrote:

> 'The use of any nuclear weapon capable of destroying a buried target that is otherwise immune to conventional attack will necessarily produce enormous numbers of civilian casualties. No earth-burrowing missile can penetrate deep enough into the earth to contain an explosion with a nuclear yield even as small as 1 percent of the 15 kiloton bomb dropped on Hiroshima. The explosion simply blows out a massive crater of radioactive dirt, which rains down on the local region with an especially intense and deadly fallout.'[324]

10.2.2 *Biological weapons*

The great flaw in the 1972 Convention on the Prohibition of the Development, Production and Stockpiling of Bacteriological (Biological) and Toxin Weapons and on Their Destruction is its lack of any verification mechanism. For several years, attention focused on the need to adopt a verification regime for the Convention which would ensure its better observance.

It was hoped that a compliance protocol would be adopted during the Fifth RevCon of the Convention, scheduled to be held at the end of 2001. In advance of that RevCon, three meetings of the Preparatory Committee were held between 25 and 27 April.[325]

On 14 June, the European Parliament adopted almost unanimously a resolution on the Compliance Protocol for the Biological and Toxin Weapons Convention,[326] in which it expressed the EU's strong support for the adoption of a Protocol introducing the strongest possible compliance regime, and its belief that such a Protocol would increase confidence in the Convention.

---

321. R. Johnson, 'High Level CTBT Meeting "Successful" despite US Boycott', The Acronym Institute for Disarmament Diplomacy, Disarmament Diplomacy. http://www.acronym.org.uk/ctbt/2001xiv.htm.

322. H. Josef Hebert, 'Low-Yield Nuclear Device Considered', AP, 19 December 2001.

323. R.W. Nelson, 'Low-Yield Earth Penetrating Nuclear Weapons', FAS Public Interest Report, Vol. 1, 2001.

324. Ibid.

325. Its report was issued on 27 October. BWC/CONF.V/PC/1.

326. http://projects.sipri.se/cbw/research/BWC-euro.PDF.

With expectations high, the Fifth Review Conference of the States Parties to the Convention on the Prohibition of the Development, Production and Stockpiling of Bacteriological (Biological) and Toxin Weapons and on Their Destruction was convened in Geneva from 19 November to 7 December, following three meetings of the Preparatory Committee held between 25 and 27 April. Unfortunately, the RevCon ended as it began, in acrimony and disarray.[327] The main source of conflict was the proposed verification regime. The US in particular was strongly opposed to compulsory inspections. Indeed, it had indicated its opposition well in advance of the meeting.[328]

On the other hand, the US retained the element of surprise. At the sixth plenary meeting on 7 December, it proposed to terminate the Ad Hoc Group which was responsible for negotiating the proposed verification Protocol during the preceding six years, a suggestion that was roundly condemned.[329] With complete failure looming, it was decided by consensus to adjourn proceedings and reconvene at Geneva from 11 to 22 November 2002. It was felt was that a 'cooling off' period might concentrate minds and help avoid the torpedoing of the verification protocol. The RevCon adopted an Interim Report[330] recording the results of the work achieved during the 2001 meeting.[331]

---

327. See BWC Rev.Con. Bulletin, 19 November, 2001.

328. The US policy review on the Compliance Protocol had recommended that the US government reject the current draft compromise proposal. See S. Brugger, 'U.S. BWC Protocol Policy Still Unclear With Talks Short on Time', *Arms Control Today*, July/August 2001. http://www.armscontrol.org/act/2001_07-08/bwcjul_aug01.asp.

329. See J. Rissanen, 'Anger after the ambush: Review Conference suspended after US asks for AHG's termination', BWC Review Conference Bulletin, 9 December 2001. http://www.acronym.org.uk/bwc/revcon8.htm.

330. BWC/CONF.V/12, 7 December 2001.

331. See further the article by B. Matthews in this volume at p. 406. To read a full analysis of the Fifth Review Conference, please see Disarmament Diplomacy No. 62, January 2002. http://www.acronym.org.uk/dd/dd62/index.htm

INTERNATIONAL HUMANITARIAN LAW, THE PROHIBITION OF TERRORIST ACTS AND THE FIGHT AGAINST TERRORISM[1]

Hans-Peter Gasser[2]

1. INTRODUCTION

Terrorism is said to be a substitute for conventional – or classic – warfare. And the response to terrorism is now called a 'war on terrorism'. Acts of terrorism have always been with us and so has war. Since time immemorial, warfare has been subject to legal regulations: the laws of war. Their foundations can be retraced to age-old practices established to mitigate the effects of recourse to violence when conflicts could not be resolved by peaceful means. These rules used to belong to customs observed by belligerents as a matter of course. Today, international treaties are the main source of the rules governing humanitarian aspects of the conduct of war: the Geneva Conventions for the protection of war victims of 12 August 1949[3] and their two Additional Protocols of 1977.[4] Is international humanitarian law relevant to the horrors of modern warfare and, in particular, to terrorism? And does it sufficiently take into account the interest of states in combating terrorism?

From the outset, two basic points should be noted. First, the Geneva Conventions and the other treaties of international humanitarian law have nothing to say on the right of a state to use force against another state or its own population. They are no source for justifying violence. The only direct contact between *jus in bello* and

2. Hans-Peter Gasser, Dr. jur. is former Senior Legal Advisor, International Committee of the Red Cross, Geneva. An original version of this paper was prepared for a Conference organized by the International Peace Academy in New York on 'Responding to Terrorism: What role for the United Nations', 25-26 October 2002.

3. Convention (I) for the Amelioration of the Condition of the Wounded and Sick in Armed Forces in the Field, Geneva, 12 August 1949; Convention (II) for the Amelioration of the Condition of Wounded, Sick and Shipwrecked Members of Armed Forces at Sea. Geneva, 12 August 1949; Convention (III) relative to the Treatment of Prisoners of War, Geneva, 12 August 1949; Convention (IV) relative to the Protection of Civilian Persons in Time of War, Geneva, 12 August 1949. The Conventions had 190 States Parties as of 31 January 2003.

4. Protocol Additional to the Geneva Conventions of 12 August 1949, and relating to the Protection of Victims of International Armed Conflicts (Protocol I), 8 June 1977, and Protocol Additional to the Geneva Conventions of 12 August 1949, and relating to the Protection of Victims of Non-International Armed Conflicts (Protocol II), 8 June 1977. Respectively, 160 and 153 States Parties at 31 January 2003.

Yearbook of International Humanitarian Law
Volume 4 – 2001 – pp. 329-347

jus ad bellum occurs when a third state, or the international community as a whole, intends to react against a belligerent guilty of serious violations of international humanitarian law in an ongoing armed conflict. Can force be used to establish or restore compliance with the Geneva Conventions? Again, these treaties do not answer the question. But the law laid down in the UN Charter does.[5] Second, international humanitarian law applies in armed conflict only. The Geneva Conventions are special law geared to the specific conditions of warfare. While human rights guaranteed by international treaties can be suspended in times of public emergency, including war, international humanitarian law adapts human rights concerns to the conditions of armed conflict, especially to belligerent occupation. In peacetime, international and domestic human rights law exclusively governs the relations between state and citizens.

2. THE RESPONSE OF INTERNATIONAL HUMANITARIAN LAW TO TERRORISM[6]

The 1949 Geneva Conventions deal with humanitarian problems arising primarily in conventional, or classic, warfare in which the armed forces of one state clash with the armed forces of another state. In addition, however, those original treaties of international humanitarian law already include rules for hostilities involving forces other than governmental armies.[7] Since then, the law's concern for such groups other than official armed forces, groups which may also use different methods of combat, has been developed by 1977 Protocol I.[8] These new rules by no means only strengthen the 'privileges' of these fighters, but make the whole body of law applicable to them, thus together with the obligations it entails. Finally, it should be remembered that during negotiation of the 1899/1907 Hague Conventions, the Martens Clause was first of all intended to establish a legal 'safety net' for 'unlawful combatants'.[9] It is therefore simply erroneous to say that international humanitarian law ignores the phenomenon of unconventional warfare.

Violence against persons and destruction of property are inherent in warfare. The use of deadly force against persons and objects is contrary to international

5. Chapter VII of the UN Charter. See also the ongoing debate on a right to 'humanitarian intervention'.

6. This section draws on the author's article: 'Acts of terror, 'terrorism' and international humanitarian law', 84 *IRRC* (September 2002) pp. 547-570.

7. Under the name of 'militias', 'volunteer corps' or 'resistance movements'. See Third Geneva Convention, Art. 4A (1) and (2).

8. See in particular, Protocol I, Arts. 1(4) on the status of national liberation movements, and 44(3), on guerrilla warfare.

9. Hague Convention respecting the Laws and Customs of War on Land, 18 October 1907, preamble. The Martens Clause says that, in the absence of a specific prohibition 'civilians and combatants remain under the protection and authority of the principles of international law derived from established custom, from the principles of humanity and from the dictates of public conscience', in the wording of Art. 1(2), Protocol I.

humanitarian law only if such acts transgress the limits established by the international rules. Violence is also one of the salient features of terrorism. International law must therefore draw a line to distinguish the violence which is legitimate in war from acts of terrorism, which violate international humanitarian law. How is this distinction achieved?

International humanitarian law approaches the problem from two angles. First, the right to use force and commit acts of violence is restricted to the armed forces of each party to an armed conflict. As a rule, only members of such armed forces[10] have the 'privilege' to use force against other armed forces, but their choice of methods or means of warfare is subject to certain constraints. On the other hand, only members of armed forces and military objectives may be the target of acts of violence. Second, other categories of persons, in particular the civilian population, or of objects, primarily the civilian infrastructure, are not legitimate targets for military attacks – they are, in the words of the Geneva Conventions, 'protected' and must in all circumstances be spared.

International humanitarian law does not grant unfettered licence to use any conceivable form of violence against the other party to an armed conflict. Indeed, '... the right of the parties to the conflict to choose methods or means of warfare is not unlimited'.[11] For ages past, international rules have drawn a line between acceptable methods of warfare and others, such as the assassination of civilians not taking part in the hostilities or, more recently, the use of chemical weapons. To resort to illegal methods and means violates the legal order and, in aggravated circumstances, can be prosecuted as a crime under domestic law or as a war crime. Consequently, members of armed forces, though entitled to commit acts of violence, may be held responsible for violations of rules protecting persons or civilian property. In other words, any officer or ordinary soldier must be put on trial if he has committed a violation of the laws of war, including acts of terrorism.

Modern international humanitarian law prohibits terrorist acts in all circumstances and, in serious cases, such acts must be punished as grave breaches of the Conventions or the Protocols. However, none of the international humanitarian law treaties has established a definition of 'terrorism' or 'terrorist acts'.

2.1 A definition of a legal concept 'terrorism'?

Terrorism is a social phenomenon with many aspects which vary from case to case. Neither experts in international law nor government representatives have yet agreed on a comprehensive and widely acceptable definition. The only agreed text dates back to the 1937 Convention for the Prevention and Punishment of Terrorism adopted by the League of Nations,[12] which defined acts of terrorism as 'criminal acts directed against a State or intended to create a state of terror in the minds of

---

10. For the exception, see *supra* nn. 7 and 8.
11. Protocol I, Art. 35(1).
12. B.B. Ferencz, 'International Criminal Court', in R. Bernhardt, ed., 2 *Encyclopedia of Public International Law* (Amsterdam, Elsevier 1995) p. 1124.

particular persons, or a group of persons or the general public'. This definition is not very explicit, as the text refers only to 'criminal acts' and does not specify which acts are illegal in the context of terrorism. It is, however, interesting to note that at the same time a Convention for an International Criminal Court was adopted (but never ratified by a sufficient number of states). The link between justice and the ban on terrorism was understood by that generation of international lawyers and diplomats.

The draft UN Comprehensive Convention on International Terrorism, as formulated by the ad hoc Committee established by the UN General Assembly and its Working Group, ventures the following definition of terrorist acts (Art. 2):

> 'Any person commits an offence within the meaning of this Convention if that person, by any means, unlawfully and intentionally, causes
> — death or serious bodily injury to any person; or
> — serious damage to public or private property, including a place of public use, a State or government facility, a public transportation system, an infrastructure facility or the environment; or
> — damage to property, places, facilities, or systems referred to in paragraph 1(b) of this article, resulting or likely to result in major economic loss,
> when the purpose of the conduct, by its nature or context, is to intimidate a population, or to compel a government or an international organization to do or abstain from doing any act.'[13]

Whether this text will become a universally accepted reference for coming to grips with the phenomenon of terrorism remains to be seen.

There is no intention in this paper to work out a definition of terrorism or terrorist acts. The many attempts to do just that have shown that the issue is fraught with political considerations which do not lend themselves to workable and broadly acceptable legal definitions. Moreover, the notion of terrorism is changing with the passage of time. It has been broadened of late to cover such phenomena as cyber terrorism or illegal financial transactions across national borders. As long as there is no consensus on how to respond to the phenomenon, agreement on definitions is unlikely to emerge. The often heard slogan that one person's terrorist is another person's freedom fighter may well be an 'insurmountable difficulty' for any definition.[14]

Yet we all know more or less what is meant by the notion, even in the absence of a clear-cut definition. It can be assumed that this common perception of terrorism is made up of the following elements:

— terrorism is violence or the threat of violence against ordinary civilians, against their life, their property, their well-being;

---

13. UNGA Res. 51/210, 17 December 1996, and 'Measures to Eliminate International Terrorism', Report of the Working Group, UN Doc. A/C.6/56/L.9, 29 October 2001.

14. R.A. Friedländer, 'Terrorism', in R. Bernhardt, ed., 4 *Encyclopedia of Public International Law* (Amsterdam, Elsevier 2000) p. 846.

—terrorist acts do not distinguish between the intended target and bystanders, or between different groups of bystanders: terrorists strike indiscriminately;
—terrorism has a cause: terrorist acts are a means to attain political goals which allegedly could not be attained by ordinary, lawful means, i.e., within the context of the established constitutional order;
—terrorist acts are usually part of a strategy: they are carried out by organized groups over a longer period of time;
—the purpose of terrorist acts is to create fear in order to establish conditions which, in the perpetrators' opinion, should further their cause;
—terrorism always humiliates fellow human beings.

Acts of terrorism are perceived as crimes by the large majority of people. In certain circumstances, however, some persons may attempt to justify such acts as allegedly helping to achieve a goal which, in their view, is more important than the prohibition of indiscriminate violence against civilians.

2.2 Rules applicable to international armed conflict

Under the heading 'Protection of the civilian population', Chapter IV of 1977 Protocol I codifies the basic rules to be respected in military operations. After a reminder of the obligation to protect the civilian population against dangers arising from military operations, an obligation firmly anchored in customary law, paragraph 2 of Article 51 reads:

> 'The civilian population as such, as well as individual civilians, shall not be the object of attack. Acts or threats of violence the primary purpose of which is to spread terror among the civilian population are prohibited.'

Paragraph 4 of the same provision prohibits indiscriminate attacks in warfare.[15] This provision covers military operations (or any act of violence) which
—are not directed at a specific military objective;
—employ a method or means of combat which cannot be directed at a specific military objective; or
—employ a method or means of combat the effects of which cannot be limited as required by the law;

and consequently are of a nature to strike military objectives and civilians or civilian objects without distinction. In other words, attacks or acts of violence are prohibited if, though intended to hit a military target, they disproportionately kill or wound civilians or destroy civilian objects, including the civilian infrastructure.

Beyond all doubt, these rules ban terrorist activities insofar as they are directed against civilians. By definition, terrorist acts *are* acts 'the primary purpose of which is to spread terror among the civilian population' (Art. 51(2)). Acts of terrorism are always either attacks against civilians or indiscriminate attacks which

15. '"Attacks" means acts of violence against the adversary ...', Art. 49 of Protocol I.

also strike civilians. However, terrorist acts, to qualify as such, must not necessarily or exclusively strike civilians or the civilian infrastructure. *Threats* of violence intended to spread terror among the civilian population are also prohibited. This intention to spread terror among civilians is a necessary element for defining acts of terrorism, for the simple reason that in war any use of deadly force may create fear among bystanders, even though the attack may be directed at a lawful target (e.g., aerial bombardment of a military target close to a civilian area).

In addition to the general prohibitions established by Articles 51 and 52 (on the protection of civilian objects), the main parts of which give expression to customary law rules, several other provisions of humanitarian law are also relevant in a discussion on the response of international humanitarian law to terrorism. They usually cover specific needs for protection, such as the rules on the protection of cultural property from any hostile act,[16] or the legal protection given to installations containing dangerous forces (such as dams, dykes and nuclear power plants).[17]

While we have hitherto examined the protection afforded by international humanitarian law to civilians and civilian property in times of armed conflict, we now turn to the question whether international rules also confer protection upon members of armed forces. The answer is not self-evident, because in accordance with the laws of war soldiers are allowed to shoot and can be shot at. They are active participants in, and simultaneously a legitimate target of, military operations. And what appears to be a terrorist act in a civilian context may well be a legitimate act of war if carried out against enemy personnel. However, 'the right of parties to the conflict to choose methods or means of warfare is not unlimited', says the above-mentioned fundamental rule of the laws of war. As codified by Article 35(1) of Protocol I, this rule imposes upon warfare limits for the benefit of those who participate in the war effort, i.e., members of the armed forces. Article 35 goes on to state in its second paragraph that 'it is prohibited to employ weapons, projectiles and material and methods of warfare of a nature to cause superfluous injury or unnecessary suffering'. Perfidy is an example of such illegal behaviour against combatants.[18] The use of violence against a combatant while feigning civilian status is a perfidious act.

Serious violations of international humanitarian law committed in the course of an international armed conflict are, in the words of the Geneva Conventions, 'grave breaches'. Protocol I calls them war crimes. Serious individual terrorist acts constitute such grave breaches.[19] Humanitarian law treaties do not make terrorism as such a crime, but rather its individual components. Is this satisfactory? For

16. Convention for the Protection of Cultural Property in the Event of Armed Conflict, 14 May 1954, Art. 4. See also Protocol I, Art. 53.

17. Protocol I, Art. 56.

18. Protocol I, Art. 37.

19. In particular, First Geneva Convention, Art. 50; Third Geneva Convention, Art. 130; Fourth Geneva Convention, Art. 147; and Protocol I, Art. 85. The International Criminal Tribunal for the former Yugoslavia has found that serious violations of the law on non-international armed conflicts are also international crimes. See n. 21.

terrorism as such to constitute a crime, a definition of the behaviour deemed criminal would be required. As we have already shown, the international community is far from reaching a consensus on what constitutes 'terrorism'. Since all conceivable, individual acts of a terrorist nature are already an international crime, the need to look for new law in such a controversial area is hardly urgent. Moreover, prosecuting somebody for 'terrorism' (and not for specific terrorist acts) could well turn out to be a politically motivated judicial procedure.

2.3 International rules applicable to non-international armed conflict

International humanitarian law applicable in non-international armed conflict is the result of a compromise between the concept of sovereignty and humanitarian concern about the effects of armed conflict. In an internal armed conflict, at least one party is not a state but an insurgent group determined to change the political system and/or to overthrow the government, or a rebel movement fighting for autonomy or secession. Today, the great majority of armed conflicts worldwide are of a non-international character.

Civil wars have the same devastating effects as armed conflict between states. It is at present generally accepted that internal conflicts where violence has reached a certain level of intensity cannot remain beyond the reach of international law protecting persons from the effects of hostilities, whether those persons are actively involved in acts of violence or not. Article 3 common to the four 1949 Geneva Conventions and, in particular, the 15 substantive provisions of Additional Protocol II of 8 June 1977, have set the basic standards intended to limit violence and suffering in non-international armed conflict. Customary law confirms and supplements these standards.

It is not our intention to blur the dissimilarities between the two types of armed conflict. But in this case the norms prohibiting acts of terrorism in non-international armed conflict are basically identical with those applicable in international armed conflict. Article 3 common to the four Geneva Conventions prohibits acts of terrorism with the following words, though without explicitly using the word 'terrorism':

> 'Persons taking no active part in the hostilities, including members of armed forces who have laid down their arms and those placed *hors de combat* by sickness, wounds, detention, or any other cause, shall in all circumstances be treated humanely, without any adverse distinction founded on race, colour, religion or faith, sex, birth or wealth, or any other similar criteria.
>
> To this end, the following acts are and shall remain prohibited at any time and in any place whatsoever with respect to the above-mentioned persons:
>
> (a) violence to life and person, in particular murder of all kinds, mutilation, cruel treatment and torture;
>
> (b) taking of hostages;
>
> (c) outrages upon personal dignity, in particular humiliating and degrading treatment; (...).'

Protocol II reaffirms and develops these rules. Under the heading 'Humane treatment' of those who do not, or no longer, take part in military operations, Article 4(2)(d), even condemns 'acts of terrorism' outright as contrary to the law. Moreover, Protocol II – and in this respect it breaks new ground – also codifies standards for the conduct of military operations in internal conflicts. The basic provision is, of course, the obligation to distinguish between those who take an active part in hostilities and those who do not, in particular civilians, the wounded and the sick. Article 13 specifically prohibits attacks on the civilian population as well as on individual civilians. It furthermore states in paragraph 2 that '[a]cts or threats of violence the primary purpose of which is to spread terror among the civilian population are prohibited'. These are the same words as those to be found in Article 52(2) of Protocol I, which deals with international armed conflict.

Neither common Article 3 nor Protocol II have a provision similar to Article 35 of Protocol I which, for international armed conflict, codifies the long-established principle that parties to an armed conflict are not free to choose methods or means of combat to their liking and, in particular, that weapons which cause superfluous injury or unnecessary suffering are outlawed. However, the fourth preambular paragraph of Protocol II restates the message of the Martens Clause for non-international armed conflict: that, in the absence of a specific prohibition, a rule must be found which is compatible with 'the principles of humanity and the dictates of the public conscience'.[20]

Common Article 3 and Protocol II of 1977 do not have any provision on criminal responsibility for (mis)behaviour in an internal armed conflict. It is up to domestic jurisdictions to deal with persons who have committed a crime in such a context. However, in an important decision, the International Criminal Tribunal for the former Yugoslavia (ICTY) has concluded that the more egregious crimes committed in a non-international armed conflict are to be considered as crimes of an international character. Therefore, international rules do apply to crimes committed in a non-international armed conflict.[21] This means that acts of terrorism committed in a non-international armed conflict may indeed be equated with grave breaches as defined by the 1949 Geneva Conventions, and the same rules regarding the jurisdiction of states are applicable. But, again, terrorism as such is not a crime under any of the humanitarian law treaties.[22]

What distinguishes non-international armed conflict from armed conflict between states is the fact that on one side there is a state and on the other there are one or more groups of individuals who oppose the government's authority. While it is no surprise to learn that the state (or its government) is under an obligation to comply with its international commitments (*pacta sunt servanda*), Article 3 and Protocol II also impose obligations on the dissident forces and their members, which are non-state parties. Thus members of those forces must heed the ban on

---

20. Protocol I, Art. 1(2). See also *supra* n. 9.

21. Decision on the Defence Motion for Interlocutory Appeal on Jurisdiction, *The Prosecutor* v. *Duško Tadić*, case No. IT-94-1-AR 72, ICTY Appeals Chamber, 2 October 1995.

22. Ibid.

terrorist acts, and commanders of dissident forces are under an obligation to enforce compliance with the international rules. In other words, they must take all necessary steps to enforce the prohibition of terrorist acts, including appropriate sanctions if that prohibition is violated by members of their group.

To sum up, it can safely be said that the prohibition of recourse to terrorist acts is as firmly anchored in the law applicable in non-international armed conflict as it is in the rules governing international armed conflict. Acts of terrorism are banned, without exception. This conclusion is important, as non-international armed conflicts are particularly prone to wanton violence.

2.4 Rules for wars of national liberation and guerrilla warfare: weakening the ban on acts of terrorism?

While negotiating Protocol I, delegates at the Diplomatic Conference in Geneva (1974-1977) had to find solutions for two particularly controversial issues, namely, the legal status of wars of national liberation, and the legal regime applicable to guerrilla warfare. Acceptable solutions were found for both, and on 8 June 1977 the conference adopted Protocol I by consensus. The two issues have a certain importance for the debate on the law applicable to terrorism.

Article 1(4) of Protocol I declares wars of national liberation to be international armed conflicts. This means that the whole body of law elaborated for international armed conflict also applies to a war in which a people fight against a colonial power, in the exercise of their right of self-determination. International humanitarian law must consequently be respected in its entirety by any group which claims to be a liberation movement in the sense of Articles 1(4) and 96(3). Thus, the ban on terrorist acts applies without any doubt to wars of national liberation.

Article 44 of Protocol I slightly modifies one of the time-honoured conditions a combatant must fulfil in order to be recognized by international law as a member of an armed force. That condition requires a combatant to be identifiable as such, i.e., he must distinguish himself from his civilian surroundings. According to the new law of 1977, a member of an armed force will, however, not necessarily lose his status as a combatant if, in narrowly defined circumstances of combat, he does not distinguish himself from the civilian environment. Any combatant who chooses to engage in guerrilla warfare nonetheless remains bound to respect all rules on the conduct of military operations and the protection of civilians. So this new rule does not weaken the ban on terrorism, which remains unchanged. There will be no legal justification for acts of terrorism in guerrilla warfare.

Controversy over these two issues subsided after the end of the Diplomatic Conference in 1977. It is interesting to note that no party to any armed conflict has ever invoked either of these two provisions. In 1987, however, the President of the United States submitted Protocol II, on non-international armed conflict, to the Senate 'for [its] advice and consent' with a view to ratification.[23] In the same *Letter*

23. Text of the Letter of Transmittal published in 'AGORA: The U.S. decision not to ratify Protocol I to the Geneva Conventions on the protection of war victims', 81 *AJIL* (1987) p. 910. See also

of Transmittal President Reagan spelled out the reasons for rejecting Protocol I, though this latter treaty had been signed in 1977.

During the same period, the main architects of the US Administration's negative position on Protocol I published their views in various journals. All specific arguments used to demolish Protocol I revolved around Article 1(4) – on wars of national liberation, – and Article 44 – on guerrilla warfare. Douglas J. Feith, at that time Deputy Assistant Secretary in the Department of Defense, came to the somewhat astonishing if not nonsensical conclusion that the new law of Protocol I was in the service of terror, and that it 'lays waste the legal and moral achievement of ages'.[24] For his part, Abraham D. Sofaer, then Legal Advisor at the State Department, equated a people's armed struggle for self-determination with terrorism.[25] Hence his refusal to accept Protocol I which, he claimed, by including a clause on wars of national liberation justifies such wars – an argument which has no merits, as neither Protocol I nor any other treaty on international humanitarian law ever justifies recourse to force.

3. INTERNATIONAL HUMANITARIAN LAW AND 'WAR ON TERROR'

3.1 Some preliminary remarks

Acts of terrorism violate commonly accepted international standards and must be punished as crimes of an international character. Like any other serious violation of the 1949 Geneva Conventions and their Additional Protocols, of other humanitarian law treaties or of international customary law, such acts call for action by States Parties to those treaties to redress the situation. These not only have a legitimate interest in stopping criminal behaviour and thereby protecting their own citizens, they are also legally obliged to monitor compliance with the law, to prosecute and where appropriate punish offenders and to prevent any further act contrary to humanitarian law.[26]

The Geneva Conventions and their Additional Protocols of 1977 have laid down a number of measures and procedures to ensure compliance with their provisions. In particular, serious violations of the more important provisions are crimes of an international character, i.e., 'grave breaches', in the words of the Geneva Conventions, or war crimes. All States Parties have jurisdiction to prosecute offenders

a commentary by the author of the present paper: H.-P. Gasser, 'An appeal for ratification by the United States', ibid., p. 912.

24. D.J. Feith, 'Law in the service of terror: The strange case of the Additional Protocol', *The National Interest*, No. 1 (Fall 1985). At the time of writing this paper Feith was Under Secretary of Defense for Policy in the Bush Administration.

25. A.D. Sofaer, 'Terrorism and the law', *Foreign Affairs* (Summer 1986) p. 901.

26. Art. 1 common to the four 1949 Geneva Conventions recalls this basic truth with the following words: 'The High Contracting Parties undertake to respect and to ensure respect for the present Convention in all circumstances.'

(universal jurisdiction) for, as has been abundantly shown in this paper, serious acts of terrorism are grave breaches of international humanitarian law. Those who have committed such acts must be brought before domestic courts or any special international criminal court.[27] The newly established International Criminal Court (ICC)[28] has jurisdiction over war crimes (Art. 8) and crimes against humanity (Art. 7). As long as terrorist acts are 'most serious crimes of concern to the international community as a whole',[29] they fall under the Court's jurisdiction if the precise conditions set out by the Statute are met, in particular if the state concerned is unwilling or unable to prosecute.[30] The ICC is called upon to make a limited but significant contribution to the enforcement of criminal law at the international level, including legal action against crimes of a terrorist nature. It must, however, be borne in mind that the ICC does not serve as a substitute for domestic courts. Domestic criminal jurisdiction will always play the major part in prosecuting war and other criminals. The decision to establish an international tribunal is a signal to domestic jurisdiction to keep up with its task of bringing criminals to court.

The Geneva Conventions provide for action by third states with a view to responding to grave breaches or preventing further violations,[31] in particular if the state concerned does not or cannot take appropriate action to that effect. Whether action against such a state includes the right to use force is not a question for international humanitarian law but for the law of the United Nations Charter.[32]

Under the grim impression of the events of 11 September 2001, a number of states have taken action to prevent terrorist acts from being committed on their territory. The measures taken include, *inter alia*:

—tightening of police surveillance, particularly of foreign residents;
—adopting more 'robust' interrogation procedures, which may amount to inhumane treatment or even to torture;
—curtailing the right of alleged terrorists to a fair trial by, for e.g., imposing limits upon access to counsel and witnesses and the exercise of other rights of the defendant;
—detention without trial for an unlimited in time;
—toughening the attitude *vis-à-vis* asylum-seekers, refugees and migrants, among other things by ignoring the prohibition on returning such persons against their will to a country where they have to fear for their lives (*non-refoulement*).

Certain fundamental and inalienable human rights must be respected in *all* circumstances. The right to life or the prohibition of torture (to take two examples) are such rights; they cannot simply be set aside by those who have to fight terrorism.

---

27. Such as the *Ad Hoc* Tribunals for the former Yugoslavia and for Rwanda.

28. Rome Statute of the International Criminal Court, 17 July 1998.

29. ICC Statute, Art. 5(1).

30. ICC Statute, Art. 17. 'The Statute does not include a 'crime of terrorism' (as was the case in early drafts), partly because of US opposition.

31. *Supra* n. 26.

32. H.-P. Gasser, 'Ensuring respect for the Geneva Conventions and Protocols: The role of third States and the United Nations', in H. Fox and M.A. Meyer, eds., *Effecting Compliance* (London, The British Institute of International and Comparative Law 1993) pp. 15-49, esp. pp. 27 et seq.

Those of the above measures which are not illegal as such may, if applied disproportionately with regard to the purpose, amount to violations of a government's commitment to respect international human rights and humanitarian law obligations.

The 'wars on terrorism' in Afghanistan and the Middle East have been presented to the world as legitimate measures to 'eliminate' terrorists and terrorism. Yet the operations of the occupying power in the West Bank and the military intervention in Afghanistan raise disturbing questions as to the legitimacy of the use of force (*jus ad bellum*) and, on the other hand, about the way in which force is being used (*jus in bello*). It would be beyond the scope of this study to examine whether, in the prevailing circumstances, the use of force against a foreign state or an occupied territory is compatible with the law of the United Nations Charter. Only those issues which are relevant under international humanitarian law, in particular its rules governing the way force may be used in a counter-terrorist operation, are of interest here.

Adam Roberts has the following to say about the difficulties international humanitarian law has to face in counter-terrorist operations:

> 'In military operations with the purpose of stopping terrorist activities, there has been a tendency for counter-terrorist forces to violate basic legal restraints. There have been many instances in which prisoners were subjected to mistreatment or torture. In some cases, excesses by the government or by intervening forces may have contributed to the growth of a terrorist campaign against it. External states supporting the government have sometimes contributed to such excesses. Applying pressure on a government or army to change its approach to anti-terrorism, to bring it more into line with the laws of war and human-rights law, can be a difficult task.'[33]

Two issues require consideration at this point: the situation of detained persons and the rule of proportionality in anti-terrorist campaigns.

3.2 The status of detainees in a campaign against terrorism

The US government's decision on the status and treatment to be given to prisoners captured during the military campaign in Afghanistan and held at the US base of Guantanamo and elsewhere sparked controversy worldwide.[34] The main issue was the legal status to be given to various categories of detained persons, some of whom arguably were members of the Afghan armed forces ('the Taliban'), while others were not (members of Al-Qaeda or other groups). The US government decided to consider none of these detainees as POWs: they were just 'terrorists'. As they have allegedly resorted to violence, they are referred to as 'unlawful combat-

33. A. Roberts, 'Counter-terrorism, armed force and the laws of war', 44 *Survival* (Spring 2002) p. 13.

34. 'Decision not to regard persons detained in Afghanistan as POWs: Contemporary Practice of the United States', 96 *AJIL* (2002) p. 475.

ants', a non-existent concept in international humanitarian law. In this way it has been possible to avoid reference to any international protection regime. It seems that, in the view of the US government, persons detained in connection with the Afghan military campaign are not entitled to any international protection at all.

This is not the place to determine the legal status of Afghan and other detainees captured during the 2002 Afghan war. It should, however, be remembered that the Third Geneva Convention recognizes that doubts may arise as to the status of a detained person. According to its Article 5, a 'competent tribunal' must in that case examine the situation and decide on the status to be given to the person concerned. According to the information available, the United States has not complied with that procedure. This clear violation of the Third Geneva Convention is not in the interest of military personnel who may have to endure captivity, including American soldiers in the hands of a foreign authority.

It may be of some interest to recall that the United States had to solve similar problems during the Vietnam War, where captured enemy personnel either belonged to the North Vietnamese Armed Forces or were members of the Vietcong and were thus not recognized as combatants within the meaning of the laws of war. The US Military Command in Vietnam adopted and applied the following guidelines: captured military personnel belonging to the North Vietnamese Armed Forces were to be granted POW status, in accordance with the Third Geneva Convention. Members of Vietcong guerrilla units were to be treated as if they were POWs, provided they were caught while actually engaged in a military operation and, at the same time, were carrying their arms openly. Thus they were considered to be 'illegal fighters' – but who were recognizable as persons taking part in hostilities, and were therefore treated as POWs without being given actual POW status. The wearing of a uniform was not a condition laid down by the US guidelines. A Vietcong arrested while throwing a grenade into a downtown Saigon café was handed over to the Vietnamese authorities for prosecution as a criminal or 'terrorist'.[35]

This policy seems to have worked to the satisfaction of the US military authorities. Criminal proceedings for war crimes against any prisoner or detainee, of whatever category, were not precluded. This fine-tuned attitude by the US Military Command toward a highly sensitive issue was no doubt also influenced by the fact that North Vietnam held a number of American servicemen, especially pilots. There were no US prisoners in the hands of any adverse party during the Afghan campaign, and hence no reciprocity considerations to serve as an inducement to respect the law.

In view of some statements made in the heat of the Afghan campaign, even at the highest level of government, it must be stressed again and again that to recognize the POW status of a captured member of the enemy forces is not tantamount to granting him impunity. Under the Geneva Conventions, a POW suspected of

---

35. United States Military Assistance Command, Vietnam, 'Criteria for classification and disposition of detainees', Annex A of Directive No. 381-46 (Dec. 27. 1967), reprinted in 62 *AJIL* (1968) p. 766. See also Gasser, op. cit. n. 23, p. 921.

having committed terrorist acts can and even must be put on trial. Yet the defendant is entitled to a fair trial, in accordance with the Third Geneva Convention – the provisions of which correspond to the general standards for fair trial as codified by human rights treaties. The proposal made by the White House to set up ad hoc military commissions to try 'terrorists' (as long as they are not US citizens) was not a positive contribution to the rule of law.[36]

Moreover, the denial of POW status to a captured enemy 'fighter' does not make him a legal pariah. Such a person remains under the protection of international law. If he is not a national of the adverse party but a citizen of a third state, he retains the status of a foreign national. A civilian detainee must be treated according to the rules set out in the Fourth Geneva Convention.[37] That treaty does not grant any immunity from prosecution for acts of terrorism, but does establish the requirement for a fair trial.

Whatever the legal qualification of a detainee's status – and the controversy over that issue – he always benefits by a set of fundamental guarantees as recognized by the international legal system. Article 75 of Protocol I has codified these fundamental guarantees for armed conflicts. Since the drafting of the Martens Clause there has been no 'no man's land'[38] in the international protection of human dignity.[39]

The Third Geneva Convention with its comprehensive set of rules determining the fate of members of the armed forces taken prisoner is perhaps the best known and strongest pillar of the international legal system which protects victims of warfare. The POW Convention best serves the interests of armed forces and of their members, officers and men, and to weaken it would be a tragedy for members of armed forces who have to fight in future conflicts.

3.3 Proportionality of the use of force in an anti-terrorist campaign

The use of force against the Palestinian population and against civilian property is probably the most disturbing aspect of Israel's so-called war against the 'infrastructure of terrorism'. The extent of the death and destruction wrought on several towns in the West Bank and on densely populated Gaza by the Israeli armed forces

---

36. Military Order of 13 November 2001. See J.J. Paust, 'Antiterrorism military commissions: Courting illegality', 23 *Michigan JIL* (Fall 2001) p. 1. In response to harsh criticism the rights of the accused have been better brought in line with accepted notions of a fair trial. See 'Contemporary practice of the United States relating to international law: U.S. Department of Defense rules on military commissions', 96 *AJIL* (2002) p. 731.

37. Convention relative to the Protection of Civilian Persons in Time of War, 12 August 1949. Art. 5 of the Fourth Geneva Convention curtails the rights of a person who 'is definitely suspected of or engaged in activities hostile to the security' of the state concerned. The right to be treated with humanity and to be given a fair trial is, however, absolute (or, in human rights terminology, non-derogable).

38. In the *Abbasi & Anor* case (of two UK citizens held in Guantánamo), the UK Court of Appeal held on 6 November 2002 that 'Mr Abbashi is at present arbitrarily detained in a "legal black-hole"'. Case [2002] EWCA Civ. 1598.

39. Protocol I, Art. 1(2).

in 2002 has become a matter of international concern. Was the amount of force used proportional to the objective of the military campaign, presented as a 'war against terrorism'? Was the absolute prohibition on using force against civilians and civilian property heeded? Only a thorough and impartial analysis of the facts can lead to a fair judgment on what has happened and determine whether the acts in question are compatible with international law or not.[40] Within the scope of this paper, however, consideration must be limited to a brief comment on the meaning of the rule of proportionality.

The question is as follows: the amount of force exerted to achieve a military objective must be proportionate to what? As a result of lengthy debates and intensive negotiations during the Diplomatic Conference of 1974-1977, Protocol I of 1977 now authoritatively states that attacks must not be 'excessive in relation to the concrete and direct military advantage anticipated'.[41] It is the anticipated military gain brought about by a military operation which counts. Disproportionate force is not acceptable. Thus, the use of force to fight terrorism must be proportionate to what the military operation is intended to achieve, i.e., to stop terrorist behaviour. The proportionality of retaliatory measures must not be weighed against the number of casualties or the scale of the damage caused by the original terrorist attack. The survivors' grief, however understandable and legitimate, is not a factor for determining the size or number of bombs to be dropped on 'enemy' territory. Nor is the call for revenge made by politicians or the media an acceptable yardstick.

A war against terrorism carries a particular danger that the force used will exceed what the principle of proportionality actually requires – and authorizes. In other words, violence gradually escalates and attains a level which far exceeds what is morally acceptable, and sometimes also what is militarily necessary. Those who suffer are the civilians, in particular women, children and the elderly.

3.4 More on the dangers of anti-terrorist campaigns

Both in Afghanistan and in the Middle East, particularly cruel acts have been committed in the course of the campaign to 'eradicate' terrorism. They have often been 'justified' as reprisal actions. How is restraint by government forces to be justified if the 'terrorists' commit such atrocious crimes? The answer is, of course, that the obligation to respect the life and dignity of war victims is not built on reciprocity. Persistent reliance on the creed of 'an eye for an eye and a tooth for a tooth' destroys the delicate fabric of international humanitarian law. Moreover, insisting on reciprocity introduces the idea of punishment into military campaigns to

---

40. Israel refused to cooperate with a UN-appointed commission to establish the facts about the events in Jenin refugee camp. SC Res. 1405(2002) of 19 April 2002. See also the Report of the Secretary-General prepared pursuant to General Assembly Resolution GS-10/10 of 7 May 2002.

41. Protocol I, Art. 57.2(a)(iii), and also Art. 51.5(b). On these provisions see Y. Sandoz, C. Swinarski and B. Zimmermann, eds., *Commentary to the Additional Protocols of 8 June 1977 to the Geneva Conventions of 12 August 1949* (Geneva, International Committee of the Red Cross/The Hague, Martinus Nijhoff Publishers 1987).

eradicate terrorism. But 'punishment' through military operations hits the guilty and the innocent alike, without discrimination. The rule of law requires that guilt be determined and punishment meted out by courts, and not by the armed forces.

One of the more disturbing aspects of the 'war against terrorism' is the persistent tendency to dehumanize and demonize the 'enemy', the 'terrorists'. Some of those who decide or legitimize the use of force 'against terrorism' seem convinced that they are defending good against attack by evil, right against wrong. At the same time, it is not understood why responding to 'terrorism' should ever be the object of debate or even criticism. Such an attitude is reminiscent of the battle cry of medieval crusaders approaching Jerusalem and killing virtually everybody on their way – 'the infidels' – convinced that in a campaign for a just cause everything is allowed. The ICRC President is right to voice a warning:

> 'One line of reasoning appears to suggest that certain individuals are undeserving of the protection of the law because of the heinous nature of their criminal acts. Such an assumption should be rejected. Human beings, by virtue of being human, are entitled to the protection of the law.'[42]

The right of humanitarian organizations to have free access to victims of military operations, in particular the civilian population, is a cornerstone of international humanitarian law. The 1949 Geneva Conventions have given the International Committee of the Red Cross (ICRC) the mandate 'to protect and assist' victims of warfare, and the ICRC has been doing this ever since its foundation in 1863. ICRC delegates have occasionally been denied access in the past to civilians in occupied territory, to other victims of military operations or to detained persons, military or civilian. But since the end of the Cold War and the emergence of a multipolarized world, parties to armed conflicts, whether international or non-international, have accepted the ICRC's presence and humanitarian activities. Regrettably, both in the present conflict in the Middle East and in the aftermath of the military campaign in Afghanistan the ICRC has encountered unusual difficulties in seeking to fulfil its humanitarian mandate, for instance, in visiting captured military personnel, providing medical assistance and distributing relief to the civilian population.[43] It would be wholly unacceptable and inexcusable if the activities of humanitarian organizations in crisis situations caused by war were a – probably unintended – casualty of the 'war against terrorism'.

The most alarming aspect of any 'war against terror' is, however, the fact that the objective of such operations intentionally or inadvertently tends to shift. In the

---

42. Statement made at the 58th Annual Session of the UN Commission on Human Rights, Geneva, 26 March 2002.

43. Quotations from ICRC statements on its activities in the Middle East: '... security incidents involving Israel Defense Forces soldiers and directed at Red Cross staff, and attacks on its vehicles and premises ...', *ICRC Press Release*, 5 April 2002; '... frequent and often serious instances in which medical personnel were prevented from performing their life-saving duties ...', '... sudden degradation of the usual lines of communication between [ICRC delegates] and the Israeli authorities', *ICRC News and Communications*, 2 April 2002.

Middle East, the declared objective of Israel's military campaigns and partial reoccupation of territory is to catch suspected 'terrorists' and to destroy the infrastructure of 'terrorism'. But the government's objective is also to secure the Israeli presence in the West Bank and Gaza, *inter alia*, by defending the settlements and colonies built on Palestinian territory. In other words, the Israeli armed forces are not only fighting to eliminate terrorism but also for territorial control, a classic objective of power politics. And the United States' military campaign in Afghanistan to eliminate terrorism has also resulted in the establishment of military bases in Afghanistan itself and in neighbouring countries of Central Asia, i.e., in a strategically and economically important and very sensitive part of the world. It would seem that (arguably legitimate) counter-terrorist operations have been used in both cases to achieve results which have little to do with combating terrorism to protect one's own citizens. The legitimacy of military interventions to fight terrorism and to establish security is the first victim of such a policy.

4. CONCLUDING REMARKS: IS INTERNATIONAL HUMANITARIAN LAW ADEQUATE FOR COMBATING TERRORISM?

The 1949 Geneva Conventions, their 1977 Additional Protocols, other international treaties and customary law prohibit, without any exception, terrorist acts committed in the course of an international or non-international armed conflict. Treaty law has established procedures which enjoin states to take measures to prevent and repress violations, and allows the international community to react, especially within the framework of the United Nations. In particular, terrorist acts are serious violations of international humanitarian law, or crimes of an international character, which entail the obligation of states to bring the alleged offender to justice, either before their own courts, the courts of another State Party or an international criminal jurisdiction.

Measures to combat terrorism and to bring alleged terrorists to justice must comply with international humanitarian law. In view of the increased danger of even fundamental humanitarian obligations being disregarded in any 'war on terrorism', there is a special need to emphasize that all those who, in the context of an armed conflict, are involved in the fight against terrorism have a duty to respect international humanitarian law. Only scrupulous respect for international humanitarian law in military campaigns to eradicate terrorism helps to strengthen the determination of all members of the international community to abide by the law in all circumstances. Recourse to indiscriminate violence is illegitimate and reprehensible – and ultimately useless or even counterproductive. Armed forces and law enforcement agencies must be made aware that full respect for international humanitarian law in counter-terrorist operations is a positive contribution to the eradication of terrorism.

Various provisions of international law guarantee humane treatment for persons (be they military or civilian) who have committed even the most atrocious crimes. These rules do not obstruct criminal justice in the accomplishment of its task. It is quite simply wrong to maintain that humanitarian law provisions are obstacles in the fight against impunity, and particularly the attempt to eradicate terrorism.[44] Bringing suspected criminals to justice is an essential part of ensuring respect for humanitarian commitments, be it in time of war or peace. By establishing the International Criminal Court, the international community has made an important contribution both to the policy of prosecuting and punishing alleged terrorists and to the prevention of acts of terrorism. At the same time, the Statute of Rome of 1998 and the Geneva Conventions of 1949 enshrine the right of all persons to a fair trial – hardly an unacceptable claim for 'civilized' nations at the beginning of the Twenty-First century.

In the author's opinion, the 1949 Geneva Conventions and their Additional Protocols are equipped for any international 'war on terrorism' that is conducted to eradicate terrorism.

Immediately after the atrocious events of 11 September 2001 the question was raised, particularly in the United States, whether international humanitarian law is up to the task of combating terrorism or whether it should be amended. No law is perfect and immutable, and international humanitarian law in particular has to adapt to changes in the conduct of armed conflicts. Constant evaluation of the law's ability to respond to the real problems of war is therefore necessary to determine whether the rules are adequate or not, and any ideas to enhance the protection of war victims must be taken seriously. However, before launching new initiatives to amend the Geneva Conventions and their Additional Protocols, the law as it stands must be properly understood. Some statements made in the debate on the alleged need to amend the Geneva Conventions reveal a clear ignorance of the present law. Moreover, it does not make much sense to amend the law if the last improvement of it has not yet been fully accepted: the 1977 Additional Protocols, which strengthen the ban on terrorism, must still be ratified by *all* states, thus also and in particular by the United States.

International humanitarian law does not stand alone. It is part of international law in general, of which the Universal Declaration of Human Rights is one of the most fundamental expressions. Denying 'terrorists', in an armed conflict, any protection under the Geneva Conventions, allowing indefinite detention without a trial, refusing access to legal counsel or legitimizing 'unconventional' interrogation techniques are challenges that could undermine not only international humanitarian law but the international legal system as a whole.

To the author's knowledge, no specific proposal has yet been made to amend the Geneva Conventions or their Additional Protocols with a view to making international law more effective in the fight against terrorism. It may therefore be concluded that, as this paper has attempted to show, international humanitarian law is well developed to confront terrorism. The painful problem lies elsewhere: humanitarian commitments must be fully respected – in any armed conflict and by all States- and non-State Parties involved in such conflict – as a matter of interna-

44. Whether the organization of the domestic criminal system is itself an obstacle is another question.

tional law, which is the ultimate expression of the combined national interests of all members of the international community. In the end, however, international humanitarian law cannot eradicate terrorism, only civil society can attain that goal by concerted efforts and patient action abroad and at home. Conflicts which foster violence and terror must be settled by political means and not perpetuated by terrorist acts, in such a way that the door to more justice for all will be opened.

THE MOSCOW HOSTAGE CRISIS IN THE LIGHT OF THE ARMED CONFLICT IN CHECHNYA[1]

Noëlle Quénivet[2]

1. INTRODUCTION

On 23 October 2002, a group of about 50 Chechens seized a Moscow theatre and held hundreds of people hostage, threatening to shoot their captives and blow up the building if Russian security amassed outside the theatre attacked. Their demand, that the operations mounted by the Russian army in Chechnya cease, was not taken into account by the authorities who, from the outset, declared that they would not negotiate. The crisis was brought to an end when special troops stormed the theatre, using gas in order to incapacitate the hostage-takers, and averted the detonation of a massive explosion that might have killed all the hostages. Up to 40 Chechens were killed as well as 129 theatregoers.[3]

Most comments following the hostage seizure concentrated on the raid of the Alpha Team, an elite unit of special troops within the Spetznas. The use of an unidentified sleep-inducing gas during the raid that caused the death of many hostages was strongly criticised by the international community. On the Russian side, the complaints, notably relating to compensation to the victims of the raid,[4] focused on the seemingly disproportionate effects of the gas.

Few commentators have analysed the Moscow tragedy in the light of the armed conflict raging in the Republic of Chechnya. Yet, it is of utmost importance to relate this act to the conflict, because it may reveal and underline a new war tactic employed by the Chechen insurgents, or simply prove that the Chechen rebel leadership is unable to maintain its troops under a single command. In both cases, it undoubtedly begs the question of the nature of the armed conflict on the territory of Chechnya as well as the legal qualification of the protagonists. 'The general view is

---

2. Research Associate, Institute for International Law of Peace and Armed Conflict, University of Bochum; Ph.D Candidate, University of Essex. I would like to thank Prof. Frits Kalshoven for his invaluable comments on reprisals. I would also like to thank Ivan Gololobov for helping to find materials in Russian and Bernard Dougherty for his useful comments.

3. R. Philippe, 'La prise d'otages de Moscou vue par la presse russe; Pour la première fois, des victimes du terrorisme ont porté plainte contre les autorités', *Le Monde* (20 December 2002).

4. A. Jack, 'Curtain Rises Again on Moscow Siege Musical', *Financial Times* (10 February 2003) p. 5.

Yearbook of International Humanitarian Law
Volume 4 – 2001 – pp. 348-372

that "guerrilla" is used popularly as a synonym for "good guy", while "terrorism" refers to the actions of the "bad guys". This distinction depends on the side with which one sympathizes.'[5]

It should briefly be recalled that the Chechen population has suffered from two armed conflicts. The first started in mid-1994 when Russia began moving troops into Chechnya in a covert war to overthrow then-Chechen President Dzhokhar Dudayev and reintegrate Chechnya – otherwise known as the Republic of Ichkeria – which had declared independence from Russia in 1991. Shortly before the outbreak of the hostilities, the *Economist* already noted that 'Chechnya has gained an international reputation, not as a gallant little nation struggling against Kremlin imperialism, but as a tinpot dictatorship with gun-mad gangsters prone to vendettas and shining sport cars.'[6] After a war against Chechen separatists that lasted for less than two years, the Russian Federation withdrew all forces and signed a peace agreement, the Khasavyurt Accords, on 31 August 1996.

The ceasefire agreement, while postponing the definition of Chechnya's status until 31 December 2001, conspicuously failed to determine the governing authorities of Chechnya. This lack of definition appeared to be fatal as it allowed both sides to continue to promote their own interests: Chechnya continued to assert its independence while Russia maintained its influence over the territory. 'Personal and ideological/religious conflicts projected an image of a bandit republic with no one in charge. Law and order collapsed, and kidnapping and extortion became widespread. Various Islamic factions produced further splits among the Chechen leadership.'[7]

Eventually, Russian troops moved in anew in August 1999, thereby recommencing the hostilities, on the basis that the forces of the Chechen government, led by Maskhadov,[8] had made incursions in Daghestan, a federal entity of Russia; had promoted an Islamic revolution against the Russian authorities; and had instigated a series of bomb attacks in Moscow and southern Russia. Preying on the fear of Islamic fundamentalism in the Russian psyche, the authorities gained wide approval of their military activities in the Chechen Republic.[9]

---

5. F. Kalshoven, '"Guerrilla" and "Terrorism" in Internal Armed Conflict', 33 *Amer. Univ. LR* (1983) p. 67.

6. *The Economist* (24 October 1994) p. 48.

7. W.G. Lester and J.W. Kipp, 'Chechen Nationalism and the Tragedy of the Struggle for Independence', 10 *National Strategy Forum Review* (2000). http://call.army.mil/fmso/fmsopubs/issues/chechnatism.htm, 17 February 2003.

8. Colonel Aslan Maskhadov, who engineered the victory in Grozny, was elected President of Chechnya in early-1997, but at this time his power base was already quite limited.

9. For a view on how Russians perceive Chechens, see J. Russell, 'Mujahedeen, Mafia, Madmen: Russian Perceptions of Chechens During the Wars in Chechnya, 1994-1996 and 1999-2001', 18 *Journal of Communist Studies and Transition Politics* (2001) pp. 73-96.

2. WHAT LAWS ARE APPLICABLE TO THE ARMED CONFLICT IN CHECHNYA?

The situation in Chechnya has generated much debate around the world, mostly because of the death toll and the violations of the most basic principles of humanity by both parties to the conflict. Dissension appears not only as to the means of resolving the conflict but also as to its legal characterisation. This lack of agreement as to which laws are applicable led both parties, to varying degrees,[10] to implement different sets of international rules, in turn sparking friction regarding which acts were in violation of human rights and humanitarian law provisions. The immediate consequence was a general mistrust of the other party to the conflict and the voluntary infringement of applicable humanitarian law and human rights. Yet, however the situation is defined, international human rights law is applicable and all rules encapsulated in the European Convention on Human Rights, to which the Russian Federation is a Party, are to be respected at all times. The contentious point is whether humanitarian law is applicable, and if so, which rules.

While the Russian government has continuously claimed that it has been carrying out a police operation in Chechnya, the Chechen government,[11] at least at the inception of the conflict, stressed that the Republic of Ichkeria was an independent state, and hence that the conflict was of an international character. In addition to legal scholars, international organisations and foreign governments expressed views ranging from considering the situation in Chechnya as an international armed conflict involving two states to a counter-terrorist operation led by the Russian Federation against terrorists, to a common Article 3 or Protocol II internal armed conflict.[12]

To determine whether there is currently an armed conflict in Chechnya is more than problematic as it involves a knowledge not only of the law but also of the situation on the ground. In addition, '[t]he process of classifying conflicts can appear at first sight a simple one, but manifold difficulties start arising when one starts to consider the dynamics of conflict situations.'[13] Despite the new trend towards extending the rules enshrined in treaties covering international armed

---

10. As O'Brien notes, '[b]elligerents in these wars are seldom inclined to respect the laws of war'. W. O'Brien, 'The Rule of Law in Small Wars', 541 *Annals of the American Academy of Political and Social Science* (1995) p. 37.

11. In 1991, the Chechen authorities adopted a constitution proclaiming the independence and sovereignty of the Chechen Republic, that many call the Chechen Republic of Ichkeria. Its President is Maskhadov and Ahmed Zakaev is Vice-Premier. In parallel exists a pro-Russian government, headed by Akhmad Kadyrov.

12. F. Hampson, A.P.V. Rogers, H. Wayne Elliott and B. Tuzmukhamedov, M.C. Bassiouni, D. Turns http://www.crimesofwar.org/expert/chechnya.html, 27 January 2003.

13. C. Swinarski, 'On the Classification of Conflicts as a Factor of their Dynamics', Actes du Colloque de Bruges, Current Challenges in International Humanitarian Law, *Collegium n° 21 – IX-2001* (27-28 October 2000) p. 29.

conflicts to internal conflicts,[14] there still remains a difference in the law applicable in the two situations,[15] a legal distinction perpetuated in the ICC Statute.

2.1 An international armed conflict?

So far no legal author, except Professor Francis Boyle,[16] has argued that the conflict that takes place on the territory of Chechnya is an international armed conflict between two states. A first legal argument is that, since the Republic of Ichkeria is not a High Contracting Party to the Geneva Conventions, it cannot be sustained that the conflict is of an international nature.

While under customary international humanitarian law, it does not matter whether the Republic of Ichkeria is a party to the conventions or not, one of the major hurdles in this case relates to Chechnya's lack of statehood. Although it declared independence in 1991, this was not recognised by the international community. International humanitarian law asserts that recognition between the parties to the conflict is not necessary for that body of law to apply.[17] On the other hand, practice shows that some sort of recognition – usually by other states and not by entities such as the then-Taliban-government of Afghanistan that recognised the Republic of Ichkeria[18] – is necessary. While that unequivocal gesture of recognition from an outside power endowed the Chechen Republic with more political weight, the problem remained that the Taliban were very far from being a fully recognised government themselves. Another idea entertained by Professor Boyle is that the Treaty on Peace and the Principles of Interrelations Between the Russian Federation and the Chechen Republic of Ichkeria of 12 May 1997 provides for a *de facto* recognition of the State of Ichkeria,[19] thereby validating the claim that the conflict that is raging on the territory of Chechnya is of international nature. Nonetheless, one must stress that Professor Boyle is the sole author defending that position, and that he has been widely criticised for his comments on the legal

14. The *Tadić* Interlocutory Appeal Decision has been instrumental in this regard as well as the Rome Statute of the International Criminal Court. *The Prosecutor* v. *Tadić*, case No. IT-94-1-AR72, Decision on the Defence Motion for Interlocutory Appeal on Jurisdiction, 2 October 1995, paras. 96-127 (hereinafter, *Tadić* jurisdiction Decision). Rome Statute of the International Criminal Court, 17 July 1998, UN Doc. A/CONF.183/9, 37 *ILM* (1998) p. 999 (hereinafter, ICC Statute).

15. 'In the field of international humanitarian law, a clear distinction as to the thresholds of application has been made between situations of international armed conflicts, in which the law of armed conflicts is applicable as a whole, situations of non-international (internal) armed conflicts, where Common Article 3 and Additional Protocol II are applicable, and non-international armed conflicts where only Common Article 3 is applicable.' *Prosecutor* v. *Akayesu*, Judgement, No. ICTR-96-4-T, 2 September 1998, para. 602.

16. F.A. Boyle, 'Independent Chechnya: Treaty of Peace with Russia of 12 May 1997', http://www.amina.com/article/peace_tret.html, 18 February 2003.

17. See Art. 2 of the Geneva Conventions.

18. The Taliban government recognised on 16 January 2000 Chechnya's independence. See T.D. Grant, 'Afghanistan Recognises Chechnya', 15 Amer. Univ. ILR (2000) pp. 869-894.

19. F.A. Boyle, 'Independent Chechnya: Treaty of Peace with Russia of 12 May 1997', http://www.amina.com/article/peace_tret.html, 18 February 2003.

regime in Chechnya. His stance may be explained by his position as the legal advisor of the Republic of Chechnya, notably in the case submitted to the International Court of Justice regarding the alleged acts of genocide committed by the Russian authorities. 'Multilateral organisations have also viewed the conflict with Russia cautiously to avoid suggesting that it is an international conflict.'[20] Further, a panel of legal and historical experts patronised by President Maskhadov came to the conclusion that 'it is likely that Russia legally acquired Chechnya' and hence Chechnya could not be considered as an independent state.[21] Indeed, 'it must be recognised that conquest was a valid basis for the acquisition of territory until 1945, and accordingly this is not a productive exercise'.[22]

Nevertheless, a conflict can become internationalised on other grounds, for example, if the military forces of another state intervene or if 'some of the participants in the internal armed conflict act on behalf of that other State',[23] two hypotheses not applicable to the instant case. In this regard, the varying tests adopted by the International Criminal Tribunal for the former Yugoslavia (hereinafter, ICTY) to distinguish international from non-international armed conflicts are also of little help to support the view that the conflict in Chechnya is of an international nature.[24]

It may be argued that the conflict is a war of national liberation, thus triggering the applicability of Additional Protocol I (hereinafter, AP I) to the Geneva Conventions and granting the conflict the characterisation of 'international'. It must be stressed that having a conflict classified in a particular way (e.g., international v. non-international) constitutes one of the main objective of some warring factions, amongst them the Chechen armed opposition group. This is undoubtedly because qualifying a conflict in a given way has the effect of attributing legal benefits to the armed groups involved.

In pursuance of Article 96(3) of AP I, the authority representing the people engaged in such an armed conflict needs to issue a declaration whereby it undertakes to abide by the rules enshrined in the Geneva Conventions as well as in AP I. This article has led to much criticism, probably one of the sharpest being expressed by Professor Dinstein in the following terms:

> '[o]ne of the more preposterous innovations of the Protocol is that, in accordance with Article 96, para. 3, combined with Article 1, para. 4, a group of terrorists proclaiming itself to be a national liberation movement fighting for the right to self-determination

---

20. T.D. Grant, 'A Panel of Experts for Chechnya: Purposes and Prospects in Light of International Law', 40 *Virginia JIL* (1999) at p. 118.

21. Ibid., at p. 186.

22. C. Hare, 'External Assistance to Secession Struggles: Could Afghan Recognition of Chechnya Legally Have Gone Further?', http://www.ca-c.org/dataeng/hare.shtml, 18 February 2003.

23. *The Prosecutor* v. *Tadić*, case No. IT-94-1, Appeal Chamber Judgement, 15 July 1999, para. 84.

24. For an excellent review of the different tests adopted by the ICTY, see C. Byron, 'Armed Conflicts: International or Non-International?', 6 *Journal of Conflict and Security Law* (2001) pp. 63-90.

may make a unilateral declaration whereby it assumes all the rights and obligations of a Contracting Party, despite the fact that the terrorists themselves fail to observe the laws of armed conflict'.[25]

Several organisations have submitted informal declarations addressed to the Swiss government, as depositary of the Geneva Conventions, stating their intent to abide by the laws of armed conflicts to the extent possible, but none has ever utilised the procedure of Article 96(3). The Chechen insurgents issued a declaration but their statement was not accepted by the Swiss government.

Article 1(4) of AP I clearly states that such conflicts are confined to struggles against 'colonial domination', 'alien occupation' and 'racist regimes'. Professor Cassese, already in 1984, lamented that 'the basic deficiency [of this rule] is [...] that it is 'dated', in that it only refers to three situations that are bound to disappear in the near future.'[26] At the Diplomatic Conference, it was agreed that these were special types of armed conflicts linked with the process of decolonisation.[27] It is the view of the author that neither the Soviet nor the Russian regime can be regarded as colonial especially in the light of General Assembly resolution 1541 that declares that the threshold requirement for colonial status is that the territory in question (1) be geographically separate from the metropole and (2) be inhabited by a people.[28] However, the author agrees with Professor Kovács that

'[t]oday, the Chechen perception of the reasons and solutions of the Chechen conflict obviously challenges the assumption that colonialism should be exclusively limited to the traditional relationship between a European country and its overseas dependency, The Chechen perception calls for an expansion of the concept of colonialism to include the relationship between the Soviet Union and its former republics.'[29]

As for being an alien or racist power, one would need to prove that the Russian Federation was in the past more or less akin to an occupying power in the Republic of Chechnya which it is not, or blatantly discriminated against persons of Chechen origin. 'All other kinds of wars of liberation are excluded, such as wars of secession

25. Y. Dinstein, 'Comments on Protocol I', 37 *IRRC* No. 320 (1997) pp. 517-518.

26. A. Cassese, 'Wars of National Liberation and Humanitarian Law', in C. Swinarski, ed, *Studies and Essays on International Humanitarian Law and Red Cross Principles in Honour of Jean Pictet* (Dordrecht, Martinus Nijhoff Publishers 1984) p. 319. A position also shared by H.-J. Heintze, 'Ächtung des Terrorismus durch das Völkerrecht', in H. Frank and K. Hirschmann, eds., *Die weltweite Gefahr: Terrorismus als internationale Herausforderung* (Berlin, Berlin Verlag 2002) p. 78.

27. D. Schindler, 'The Different Types of Conflicts according to the Geneva Conventions and Protocols', 163 *Hague Recueil* (1979) p. 138.

28. UN GAOR, 15th Sess. Supp. No. 16, 948th plen. mtg. at 153, UN Doc. A/4684 (1960). For an analysis of whether Chechnya is a Russian colony, see C. Hare, 'External Assistance to Secession Struggles: Could Afghan Recognition of Chechnya Legally Have Gone Further?', http://www.ca-c.org/dataeng/hare.shtml, 18 February 2003.

29. P. Kovács, 'Authority and weakness of the 1977 Geneva Protocol II in the light of the conflict in Chechnya', 6 *International Peacekeeping* (2000) p. 138.

and struggles against oppressive regimes.'[30] The reply by the Federal Government of Germany to the written question submitted by the Parliamentary Social Democratic Party concerning the Chechen conflict in 1995 buttresses this viewpoint. It plainly states that 'Protocol I applies only to international armed conflicts arising between the contracting parties thereto. Therefore it cannot apply to an internal conflict within the borders of a contracting State.'[31]

The Chechen people could be said to be entitled to the right to secession on the basis of the principle of self-determination[32] all the more as 'there has been no real acceptance by Chechnya of Russian sovereignty'.[33] Nevertheless one needs to bear in mind that the definition adopted in AP I is more restrictive than the one offered by international law in several resolutions of the General Assembly of the United Nations. Only a liberal construction of article 1(4) of AP I might warrant the conclusion that the armed conflict in Chechnya amounted to a war of national liberation covered by that Protocol.[34] And as far as the armed opposition group has not been recognised either by a significant number of states or by inter-governmental organisations (universal or regional), such a liberal approach can not be applied to the given case.

30. Schindler, loc. cit. n. 27, at p. 137. That the Russian regime may be (or was) oppressive for the Chechens is a matter of discussion that is best left to the specialists of the North Caucasus region and to peace research specialists. Some argue that '[t]here is little doubt, for example, that the Russo-Chechen wars of the 1990s are characterised by a deep, clear and bitter sense of ethnic identity on the Chechen side, as well as by an all too widespread Russian racism against the Chechens. For over 200 years, Chechen movements have resisted Russian control'. D. Smith, 'Trends and Causes of Armed Conflicts', in N. Ropers, M. Fischer, A. Austin and C.-D. Wild, eds., *The Berghof Handbook for Conflict Transformation* (Berlin, Berghof Foundation 2000).

31. Reply by the Federal Government to the written question submitted by the Parliamentary Social Democratic Party. Document 12/437. The Federal Government's position on Russian action in the Chechen conflict. German Bundestag, Document 13/718, 13th legislative period, 9 March 1995. English translation in M. Sassòli and A.A. Bouvier, *How Does Law Protect in War? Cases, Documents and Teaching Materials on Contemporary Practice in International Humanitarian Law*, (Geneva, ICRC 1999) p. 1404.

32. This idea is entertained by several authors. See e.g., E.S. Berke, 'The Chechnya Inquiry: Constitutional Commitment or Abandonment?', 10 *EILR* (1996) pp. 879-918. http://www.law.emory.edu/EILR/volumes/win96/berke.html, 18 February 2003 and P.D. DiPaola, 'A Noble Sacrifice? Jus ad Bellum and the International Community's Gamble in Chechnya', 4 *IJGLS* (1997) p. 435.

33. Hare, loc. cit. n. 22.

34. Some commentators, such as Abi-Saab, assert that the enumeration of the specific types of situations as described in Art. 1(4) of AP I is illustrative and not exhaustive. A humanitarian point of view would favour such an approach. G. Abi-Saab, 'Wars of national liberation in the Geneva Conventions and Protocols', 165 *Hague Recueil* (1979-IV), pp. 397-398. See also the declaration made by the Australian delegate at the 1977-1979 Conference and quoted in A. Cassese, 'Wars of national liberation and humanitarian law', in C. Swinarski, ed., *Studies and Essays on International Humanitarian Law and Red Cross principles in Honour of Jean Pictet*, (Dodrecht, Martinus, Nijhoff Publishers 1984) p. 318.

2.2 A non-international armed conflict?

Having come to the conclusion that the conflict that rages in the Russian Republic of Chechnya is not of international nature, one needs to assess whether it is a non-international armed conflict within the meaning of the Geneva Conventions and their second Additional Protocol.

2.2.1 *The situation in Chechnya*

The first Chechen armed conflict (1994-1996) was deemed non-international within the meaning of Article 1 of AP II, a position confirmed by the Constitutional Court of Russia.[35] Since a general cessation of hostilities was agreed upon in 1996, it can be said that this body of law is not automatically applicable now and hence a new assessment of the characterisation of the conflict needs to be undertaken. The Appeals Chamber of the ICTY correctly declared that international humanitarian law applies from the initiation of an armed conflict until, 'in the case of internal conflicts, a peaceful settlement is achieved'.[36]

Years later, the Russian troops moved anew into Chechnya while, repeatedly, Moscow insisted that the conflict was not over Chechen independence, but a war against terrorism and Chechen attempts to spread subversion through the North Caucasus on Russian territory.[37] As a consequence, the classification of the second armed conflict was less unanimous, with some authors proposing that it was a low-intensity armed conflict and with only common Article 3 being applicable[38] and others maintaining that, like the first conflict, it had reached the threshold entrenched in Article 1 of AP II.[39]

2.2.2 *The applicability of AP II*

The threshold of applicability of AP II is fairly demanding in comparison to Article 3 as it postulates that the dissidents 'must exercise such control over a part of the

---

35. 'постановление конституционного суда российской федерации', 31 июля 1995 года; http://ks.rfnet.ru/pos/p10_95.html, 11 April 2001. An unofficial English translation of this judgement has been published by the European Commission for Democracy through Law of the Council of Europe, CDL-INF (96) p. 1.

36. *Tadić* jurisdiction Decision, *supra* n. 14, para. 70.

37. 'To us it is absolutely of no fundamental importance as of now, the question of Chechnya's dependence or independence from Russia. Only one matter is fundamental to us. We will no longer allow this territory to be used as a bridgehead for attack on Russia. We won't allow!' Statement of the President of the Russian Federation on the occasion of the 10th Anniversary of the signing of the Treaty on Conventional Armed Forces in Europe. *Press Bulletin of the Permanent Mission of the Russian Federation to the United Nations*, No. 65 (3225) Special Issue, 21 November 2000.

38. F. Hampson, A.P.V. Rogers, H. Wayne Elliott and B. Tuzmukhamedov, http://www.crimesofwar.org/expert/chechnya.html, 27 January 2003.

39. F.L. Kirgis, 'Russian Use of Force in Grozny, 39 *Asil Insights* (1999), http://www.asil.org/insights/insigh39.htm, 12 January 2003, M.C. Bassiouni, D. Turns, http://www.crimesofwar.org/expert/chechnya.html, 27 January 2003.

territory as to enable them to carry out sustained and concerted military operations and to implement this Protocol'.

A first criterion is that they are able to carry out sustained and concerted military operations against the State Party to AP II. Looking at the conflict in El Salvador, the Swiss Directorate for Public International Law remarked that although an advanced degree of integration is not necessary, it must be shown that the armed opposition group is able to exercise 'a degree of control which enables it to successfully counter the operations launched by government forces'.[40] To talk of concerted conduct of operations in the sense of joint preparation and execution of military actions is not possible. The current situation on the ground shows that, unlike in 2000-2001, the Russian armed forces are in full control of the territory of the Russian Republic of Chechnya and not launching operations against the insurgents. They are nonetheless compelled, from time to time, to exert military power to come to terms with isolated attacks carried out by the insurgents. In this regard, it is crucial to note that President Maskhadov's lack of centralised control does not allow for coordinated action. The insurgents have thereby demonstrated that the attacks they have been carrying out for some time have fallen outside the purview of AP II. Conspicuously, Article 1(2) of AP II indicates that the Protocol does not apply to situations of internal disturbances, a stance reiterated by the Inter-American Commission on Human Rights in the *Tablada* case.[41]

In order for AP II to apply, another requirement enunciated in Article 1 needs to be fulfilled: the dissident armed forces or other organised armed groups must be under a responsible command and able to implement the provisions encapsulated in AP II; the question whether or not they do so effectively is of little importance. As the Commentary explains, this

> 'does not necessarily mean that there is a hierarchical system of military organisation similar to that of regular armed forces. It means an organisation capable, on the one hand, of planning and carrying out sustained and concerted military operations, and on the other, of imposing discipline in the name of a de facto authority'.[42]

---

40. Law of armed conflicts: conditions governing the application of Protocol II Additional to the 1949 Geneva Conventions (case of El Salvador), 43 *Annuaire Suisse de Droit International* (1987) p. 186, translation in M. Sassòli and A.A. Bouvier, op. cit. n. 31, p. 917.

41. *IACHR Report No. 55/97*, case No. 11.137, Argentina, OEA/Ser/L/V/II.97, Doc. 38, 30 October 1997, para. 151.

42. C. Pilloud, Y. Sandoz, C. Swinarski and B. Zimmermann, eds., *Commentary on the Additional Protocols of 8 June 1977 to the Geneva Conventions of 12 August 1949* (Geneva, ICRC/ Dordrecht, Martinus Nijhoff Publishers 1987) para. 4463. However Professor Hampson claims that '[i]t is not clear whether the dissident armed forces must manifest the ability to apply the Protocol by doing so or if it is sufficient that they have the capacity or ability to do so'. F. Hampson, 'Human rights and humanitarian law in internal conflicts', in M.A. Meyer, ed., *Armed conflict and the New Law: Aspects of the 1977 Protocols and 1981 Weapons Convention* (London, British Institute of International and Comparative Law 1989) p. 67.

President Maskhadov's long-standing inability to control the different war factions and his equal inability to punish humanitarian law offenders proves the inapplicability of AP II in the current state of affairs.[43]

As noted by Schindler[44] and by the Appeals Chamber in the *Tadić* case,[45] the applicability of AP II very much hinges upon the prevailing circumstances since the protocol can become inapplicable if, in the course of a conflict, the dissidents lose the ability to exercise control over a part of the territory and are unable to carry out concerted military operations. The events of the last few months have proved that the insurgents have lost this ability and hence Protocol II is not applicable in Chechnya.

2.2.3 *The applicability of common Article 3*

As the threshold of applicability of Common Article 3 is lower than that of AP II, it seems expedient to determine whether common Article 3 is applicable in principle and in actual fact given the particular circumstances. Although common Article 3 does not offer a clear definition of the notion of non-international armed conflict, i.e., of the minimum level of violence required, practice has established some criteria to delineate internal armed conflicts from internal disturbances. It was always the position of the Russian government to consider the conflict in Chechnya as a policing operation and an anti-terrorist campaign. Accordingly, 'the restoration of democracy and the safeguarding of Russia's territorial integrity from Chechen terrorism was the major objective of the offensive in the Republic'.[46]

Examining the Commentary's criteria for common Article 3 to be applicable, firstly, the Russian government is compelled to employ its armed forces rather than mere police forces; second, the hostilities are of a collective character and the insurgents exhibit a minimum amount of organisation, as a government exists; third, until recently, it seemed that the insurgents were under some kind of responsible command and capable of meeting minimal humanitarian requirements, although they prefer not to. Although these criteria appear to be similar to those embodied in Additional Protocol II, their interpretation is less stringent. As Professor Hampson stresses: 'Nothing in Common Article 3 requires that the

---

43. 'Представитель лидера чеченских сепаратистов Аслана Масхадова Ахмед Закаев косвенно признает, что Масхадов уже не контролирует ситуацию' [...] 'Глава администрации Чечни Ахмад Кадыров также заявил, что Масхадов не управляет боевиками, находящимися на чеченской территории. По его словам, 'и Басаев, и Хаттаб никогда не подчинялись Масхадову, между ними всегда был раздрай'. 'За Масхадовым стоят 3-4 человека, которые его прячут', – заявил Кадыров. Об этом сообщает агентство 'Интерфакс'.' Масходов уже не контролирует ситуацию в Чечне, считает Ахмед Закаев, 26-11-2001, izvestia http://main.izv.info/community/2, 23 January 2003.

44. Schindler, loc. cit. n. 27, p. 148.

45. *Tadić* jurisdiction Decision, *supra* n. 14.

46. E.S. Berke, 'The Chechnya Inquiry: Constitutional Commitment or Abandonment?', 10 *EILR* (1996) http://www.law.emory.edu/EILR/volumes/win96/berke.html, 18 February 2003.

dissident armed forces satisfy organisational requirements or hold territory'.[47] Maskhadov appears to be the head of the insurgency and more or less able to direct hostilities of a collective character. Furthermore, a state of belligerency must be recognised between the parties to the conflict. There is no doubt that, although the Russian government has claimed that it was conducting a policing operation in Chechnya, it has likewise claimed that it refused to negotiate with President Maskhadov not only because he was a criminal but because he did not appropriately represent all the factions involved in the conflict in Chechnya.[48] Another way to argue that some sort of belligerency has been recognised is to show the amount of documents produced by international organisations calling for the resolution of the conflict in Chechnya.[49]

Although the compliance with humanitarian legal obligations is not strictly required, it can have an impact on the application of the conditions of applicability of common Article 3. The Commentary indeed explains that 'if an insurgent party applies article 3, so much the better for the victims of the conflict. No one will complain. If it does not apply it, it will prove that those who regard its actions are mere facts of anarchy or brigandage are right.'[50]

An additional hint is the presence of the ICRC on the ground, as common Article 3 provides a legal basis for the ICRC to offer its services to parties of non-international armed conflicts.[51] At first sight, the facts seem to support the view that the military operations undertaken by both the Russian Armed Forces and the Chechens are more than mere internal disturbances and that common Article 3 is applicable.

3. THE HOSTAGE CRISIS IN MOSCOW AS AN ACT OF REPRISAL IN A NON-INTERNATIONAL ARMED CONFLICT

Having determined that the armed conflict in Chechnya is covered by common Article 3 of the Geneva Conventions, one needs to examine whether the hostage seizure that took place from 23 to 26 October 2002 in Moscow was carried out in

47. F. Hampson, loc. cit. n. 42, p. 67.

48. 'По сообщениям агентств "Интерфакс" и Страна.Ру, на заседании комиссии Государственной Думы РФ по нормализации ситуации в Чеченской Республике, которое проходит в Грозном, в своем выступлении Глава администрации Чеченской Республики Ахмад Кадыров призвал не вступать ни в какие переговоры с Асланом Масхадовым. [...] Он также отметил, что сейчас Масхадов не представляет интересы чеченского народа.' Аслаханов выступает за переговоры с Масхадовым, Кадыров не согласен, 2 July 2001, http://news.ng.ru/2001/07/02/994079275.html, 25 January 2003.

49. Usually, international organisations do not pay much attention to internal disturbances unless they lead to a high level of civilian casualties, in which case Common Article 3 is applicable.

50. J. Pictet, *Commentary on Geneva I* (Geneva, ICRC 1952) p. 52.

51. Yet, 'the mere fact that the ICRC offers its services in a country does not necessarily imply that serious humanitarian problems have been observed there [...]; other parameters also have a bearing on the decision'. M. Harroff-Tavel, 'Internal Violence', *IRRC* No. 294 (1993) p. 201.

pursuance of the armed conflict in Chechnya as it *prima facie* appeared to the world community. From the inception of the hostage seizure, some organisations, such as Amnesty International, argued that international humanitarian law was applicable to the given circumstances. For example, it 'reiterate[d] its fullest condemnation of the taking of hostages, which is a violation of Article 3 of the Geneva Conventions' and requested '[t]hose responsible for the terrifying ordeal in the Moscow theatre [to] be held accountable for these violations of international humanitarian law [...].'[52]

The real question is, how does the incident relate to the armed conflict in Chechnya? Arguably, the most suitable way to connect the two events is to argue that the hostage crisis was an act of reprisal performed by an armed opposition group against the Russian Federation.

3.1 Armed reprisals must be carried out during an armed conflict

If one accepts that the rebel group led by Movsar Barayev, nephew of the infamous warlord Arbi Barayev, took over the theatre in Moscow is linked to Maskhadov, then it may be possible to argue that the act was a reprisal for the violations of humanitarian law committed by the Russian Armed Forces in Chechnya. Indeed, reprisals must occur in the context of an existing armed conflict. It does not mean that the act must occur on the territory where the armed conflict takes place, though, for the application of international humanitarian law extends beyond the realm of the hostilities.[53]

The ICTY declared in the *Kupreskić* case that reprisals are lawful provided they fulfil some requirements, one of them being 'the obligation to take special precautions before implementing them (they may be taken only after a decision to this effect has been made at the highest political or military level; in other words, they may not be decided by local commanders)'.[54] Therefore, it must be demonstrated that there was a clear line of hierarchy between Maskhadov and the leader of the hostage takers, Barayev, and that the latter was acting on behalf of the Chechen president. An indirect link my be drawn via Shamil Basayev who, it is alleged, was giving orders to Barayev.[55] However, given the complexities of the Chechen political hierarchy, it is difficult to gauge the level of connection between

52. Amnesty International Expresses Condolences, EUR 46/052/2002, 26 October 2002, http://www.amnestyusa.org/news/2002/russia10262002.html, 13 February 2002. &&&

53. *Prosecutor* v. *Akayesu*, *supra* n. 15, para. 635: AP II and common Article 3 are applicable 'irrespective of the exact location of the affected person in the territory of the State engaged in the conflict'. A similar conclusion was drawn by the Appeals Chamber in its decision on jurisdiction in *Tadić* where the Court held that the rules contained in Common Article 3 apply beyond the narrow geographical context of the actual theatre of combat operations. *Supra* n. 14, para. 69.

54. *Prosecutor* v. *Kupreskić et al*, No. ICTY-IT-95-16, 14 January 2000, para. 535.

55. In an interview with NTV, Barayev stated that 'We are acting on the orders of the supreme military emir', [...] 'Our military emir is Shamil Basayev, you all know him well'. A. Vernidoub, 'FSB Says Barayev Acted on Orders From Above', 1 November 2002, http://www.gazeta.ru/2002/11/01/FSBsaysBaray.shtml.

Maskhadov and Basayev, the latter who claimed entire responsibility for the hostage siege,[56] and therefore evaluate whether the operation took place within the framework of the internal strife in Chechnya.

A first view is that there was no link, as facts have established that there are, in Chechnya, individual groups that have elements of internal structure and discipline and hence could be able to mount such an operation independently. Further, the Chechen President condemned the Moscow hostage taking. To bolster this position, one may add that shortly after the raid on the Moscow theatre, Basayev claimed the attack was planned without the knowledge of President Maskhadov, publicly apologised and resigned from all posts in the rebel hierarchy. The phone record of the hostage takers gives some insight into the names and status of the organisers of the act. Namely, phone calls could be traced to Saudi Arabia, to the Emirates, and to Qatar.[57]

On the other hand, 'Kremlin officials, who have said Maskhadov was a chief organizer of the hostage attack, called Basayev's statement a smoke screen designed to divert attention from the rebel leader'.[58] It is indeed difficult to believe that President Maskhadov was not informed of at least the decision to take hostages in Moscow, as the interview with Barayev proves.[59]

The Russian authorities also believe that there is a link between President Maskhadov and the hostage crisis via Ahmed Zakayev, one of his top aides. They suspect that Zakayev took part in the planning of the hostage seizure and consequently requested the Danish authorities to arrest him while he was participating in a conference in Copenhagen. Though arrested on 29 October 2002, Zakayev was subsequently freed as the Danish authorities found the evidence submitted by the Russian Federation for his extradition to be weak. He then made his way to the United Kingdom where he was served with a warrant by officers from the Metropolitan Police's Extradition Unit, and on 29 January 2003, British Home Secretary David Blunkett signed an order authorising the launch of Zakayev's extradition proceedings. [60]

Since there might be a link between the armed conflict in Chechnya and the hostage crisis, it appears expedient to address the issue whether the former was a lawful act of reprisal.

---

56. 'Warlord Admits Moscow Hostage Siege', CBS News, 1 November 2002.

57. N.P. Walsh, 'Chechen rebels phoned Gulf during siege. Moscow says theatre hostage takers were funded from Saudi Arabia', *The Guardian* (5 December 2002).

58. 'Warlord Admits Moscow Hostage Siege', CBS News, 1 November 2002.

59. Interviewed, Barayev declared the following 'Maskhadov – he is our president ... And though we have repeatedly heard that nobody reports to Maskhadov, nobody recognises him, this – I do not know how to say it your way – this, as they say, is lies and libel. We do report to him and do recognise him. And our talks with Maskhadov...' *Supra* n. 55.

60. 'The Russian Prosecutor's Office accuses Zakayev of forming illegal bandit formations, killing 302 people, including two clergymen, captivity and mutilation, any of which could have been subjects of his camp lectures.' Russian Information Centre, 'Bad News for Akhmed Zakayev', 31 January 2003.

3.2 The law of armed reprisals in non-international armed conflicts

The use of illegal means of warfare by a belligerent in response to violations of the laws of war by its adversary is considered as belligerent reprisals. In this sense, they are distinctive from retorsion or retaliation measures. One could hence argue that the Chechens, by taking hostages and thereby committing an unlawful act,[61] may have acted lawfully if they were acting in reprisal for prior international humanitarian law violations and provided they abide by the rules regulating reprisals in non-international armed conflicts.

'When it comes to the matter of reprisals in situations of internal armed conflict, the treaties in force are simply silent.'[62] As rightly established by the Commission of Experts, '[t]here is no ban on reprisals contained in common Article 3 and Additional Protocol II applicable to internal armed conflict.'[63]

Even if reprisals in times of intra-state conflicts are not precluded by treaty, they might be by customary international humanitarian law. As the ICTY asserted:

> '[t]he emergence of international rules governing internal strife has occurred at two different levels: at the level of customary law and at that of treaty law. Two bodies of rules have thus crystallised, which are by no means conflicting or inconsistent, but instead mutually support and supplement each other.'[64]

It is indeed into this body of law that the ICTY plunged when trying to determine in the *Martić* decision whether reprisals were allowed in non-international armed conflicts. Unfortunately, the *Martić* decision, while investigating whether reprisals aimed at a civilian population are lawful, does not examine the legality of reprisals in non-international armed conflicts *per se*.[65] Similarly, the *Kupreskić* Judgement only addresses reprisals directed against civilians in the context of an international armed conflict.[66]

As for scholarly writings, it must be noted that, whereas the legality of reprisals in international armed conflicts is well discussed in the literature, reprisals in non-international armed conflicts have received little attention from the academic sphere.

Since there is no ready-made answer in either the jurisprudence or scholarly articles, one is compelled to try to apply the rules applicable to international armed conflicts by analogy, bearing in mind that this always needs to be done with great

---

61. There is no doubt that 'the ban on hostage-taking is one of the most firmly established rules of international humanitarian law, dating back to articles 46 and 50 of the Regulations annexed to the 1907 Hague Convention concerning the Laws and Customs of War on Land'. H. Salinas Burgos, 'The Taking of Hostages and International Humanitarian Law', *IRRC* No. 270 (1989) p. 201.

62. F. Kalshoven, 'Belligerent reprisals revisited', 21 *NYIL* (1990) p. 75.

63. Final Report of the United Nations Commission of Experts Established Pursuant to Security Council Resolution 780 (1992), UN Doc. S/1994/674, 27 May 1994.

64. *Tadić* jurisdiction Decision, *supra* n. 14, para. 98.

65. *Prosecutor* v. *Martić*, Decision No. IT-95-11-R61, T, 8 March 1996, para. 11.

66. *Prosecutor* v. *Kupreskić et al.*, No. ICTY-IT-95-16, 14 January 2000.

caution. Assuredly, it is not possible to bluntly transpose the rules of international armed conflicts to situations of internal conflicts. A way of arguing that analogy can be made is that

> '[t]here exists, at present, a corpus of customary international law applicable to all armed conflicts irrespective of their characterisation as international or non-international armed conflicts. This corpus includes general rules or principles designed to protect the civilian population as well as rules governing means and methods of warfare'.[67]

As hostage seizure is without a shadow of doubt a means of warfare, and in the particular case of the act committed in the Moscow theatre, civilians were the targets of that attack, it may be argued that the rules applicable in international armed conflicts may be applicable in the instant case.

3.3 Requirements for the lawfulness of armed reprisals

Taking into account the ever-growing assimilation of the rules concerning inter-state and intra-state armed conflicts, one may argue that reprisals in non-international armed conflicts, if allowed, should at least meet the same requirements as those imposed in the *Naulilaa Incident Arbitration*,[68] in which the Court declared that

> '[t]he State seeking to invoke a right to take reprisal action must show that it has been the victim of a prior unlawful act, that it has made an unsatisfied demand for reparation and that the action it has taken in response was proportionate to the original wrong'.[69]

Let us suppose for the sake of argument that such criteria need to be met.

First, it must be a response to a prior violation of international law imputable to the state against which the reprisal is directed. There is no doubt that the Russian armed forces have, on numerous occasions, violated the rules of humanitarian law while operating in Chechnya[70] and these violations are to be attributed to the Russian State that has often failed to prevent and/or punish them.[71] Maskhadov, for example, explained that the tragedy in Moscow was a direct consequence of

---

67. *Prosecutor* v. *Martić*, *supra* n. 65, para. 11.

68. Naulilaa Incident Arbitration, *Portugal* v. *Germany* 2 *RIAA* (1928) p. 1012.

69. F. Hampson, 'Belligerent Reprisals and the 1977 Protocols to the Geneva Conventions of 1949', 37 *ICLQ* (1988) p. 822.

70. See the numerous reports written by Human Rights Watch or resolutions adopted by the UN Sub-Commission on the Promotion and Protection of Human Rights.

71. In a report on the situation in the Chechen Republic of the Russian Federation, the High Commissioner for Human Rights concludes that an independent, wide-ranging inquiry commensurate with the scale of allegations of serious human rights abuses in the region has not been carried out, although the Government of the Russian Federation has established a number of constructive mechanisms. UN High Commissioner for Human Rights, Situation in the Republic of Chechnya of the Russian Federation, UN Doc. E/CN.4/2002/38, 26 February 2002.

Russia's war in Chechnya that pushed a group of desperate Chechens to extreme actions. A parallel can be drawn with earlier hostage seizures by the Chechens. Wilkinson stresses that in these times the

> 'brutality of the Russian armed forces' assault on Chechnya only served to strengthen the determination of the militants who in 1996 achieved the withdrawal of Russia following further acts of political violence, including mass hostage-taking, against the Russians'.[72]

In a similar vein to the Moscow hostage tragedy, during the hostage crisis of June 1995 in Budennovsk, the 'Chechen gunmen [...] stuck to their key demands: an end to Russian military operations in Chechnya and negotiations to discuss the withdrawal of forces',[73] demands renewed in January 1996 in Kizlyar where the Chechens took over a hospital.

Second, since reprisals are a subsidiary means of redress, it must be demonstrated that no other effective method of redress was available to the rebels. As the Russian government has refused to negotiate with the Chechen insurgents, on the basis that Maskhadov is not in control of all the parties to the conflict, it may be argued that the rebels saw no other means to publicly articulate their wish to stop the conflict. Various calls for peace made by the Chechen government have been left unanswered as have their requests to the international community that it should put an end to violations of human rights and humanitarian law perpetrated by the Russian forces.[74]

Third, and this is probably the trickiest criterion to meet, the reprisal must be proportionate. Despite the merit of the *lex talionis*, the proportionality principle that 'envisages the possibility of an equivalent but not identical response'[75] was adopted to gauge the lawfulness of an act of reprisal. As Professor Kalshoven suggests, 'proportionality in this context means the absence of obvious disproportionality, as opposed to strict proportionality. In other words, belligerents are left with a certain freedom of appreciation'.[76] Additionally, '[t]he proportionality is not strict, for if the reprisal is to be effective, it will often be greater than the original wrongdoing.'[77] Another hot topic is whether proportionality should be measured against past violations or in the light of the purpose of the reprisal, which is the vow that violations of humanitarian law will not recur.[78] A classical view is that reprisals should be proportionate to the initial violation of international law. It is argued that the taking of about 700 hostages may be proportionate to both viola-

---

72. P. Wilkinson, *Terrorism Versus Democracy: The Liberal State Response* (London, Frank Cass 2001) p. 103.

73. Ibid., p. 145.

74. See for example the appeal of the Ministry of Foreign Affairs of the Chechen Republic to the Secretary General of the Council of Europe on 20 April 2000.

75. Hampson, loc. cit. n. 69, p. 823.

76. Kalshoven, loc. cit. n. 62, pp. 341-342.

77. Final Report of the United Nations Commission of Experts Established Pursuant to Security Council Resolution 780 (1992), UN Doc. S/1994/674, 27 May 1994, # F.

78. C. Greenwood, 'The Twilight of the Law of Belligerent Reprisals', 20 *NYIL* (1989) p. 44.

tions of humanitarian law committed by Russian armed forces[79] and as a means of precipitating the end of the armed conflict in Chechnya. Seven hundred hostages may be the price to pay for the withdrawal of the Russian troops from Chechnya, although that, in the opinion of the author, would probably not lead to the restoration of peace in that region as Chechen authorities have proved to be unable to run an independent and viable entity.

According to Professor Greenwood, for an act to constitute a lawful belligerent reprisal, it must satisfy one more requirement, which is that the act must have law enforcement purposes, i.e., request the end of the enemy's unlawful conduct and also deflect future illegalities.[80] It is, however, not too clear whether this requirement is additional to the three aforementioned or whether it has been elaborated upon the basis of the second. Since one of the first demands of the hostage-takers was that the Russian Federation stop its operations on the territory of the Republic of Chechnya,[81] it may be contended that this requirement was met.

3.4 Reprisals against civilians are unlawful *per se*

As of now, it appears that the hostage crisis in Moscow was a lawful reprisal. Still, two additional requirements are sometimes mentioned in the literature, one of which is that belligerent reprisals must not violate basic principles of humanity.[82] This question is inextricably bound up with the issue of reprisals against civilians, which means that the Moscow tragedy does fall within one of the greyest areas of international humanitarian law, concerning reprisals in Common Article 3 conflicts. Thanks to the *Martić* decision and the *Kupreskić* judgement, some light has been shed on the debate.

In fact, there is considerable disagreement as to whether reprisals against the enemy's civilian population are prohibited in an international armed conflict under customary international law. Whereas AP I precludes such an attack, state practice as well as declarations of state delegations prove that such a ban is still not ingrained, at least in customary humanitarian law pertaining to international armed conflicts.[83] This would support the view that under customary law, reprisals against civilians and civilian objects are allowed in international armed conflicts. Since the body of law pertaining to non-international armed conflicts is less developed than that pertaining to international armed conflicts, it is difficult to see how reprisals

79. See the numerous reports written by Human Rights Watch (http://www.hrw.org/campaigns/russia/chechnya/) and by Amnesty International (http://www.amnesty.org/ailib/intcam/chechnya/).

80. Greenwood, loc. cit. n. 78, p. 40.

81. 'Они требуют прекращения войны в Чечне и вывода российских войск из республики', Британец взял интервью у Бараева, BBC Russian, 25 October 2002.

82. See *Prosecutor* v. *Kupreskić supra* n. 54, para. 535.

83. 'Countries making reservations in respect to the articles addressing reprisals include Germany and the United Kingdom. Although worded differently, both countries have reserved the right to take reprisals against countries making serious and deliberate attacks against their: civilians, civilian population, or civilian objects.' Y. Dinstein, *War, Aggression and Self-Defence* (Cambridge, Cambridge University Press 2001) 3rd edn., p. 197.

against civilians in humanitarian law pertaining to non-international armed conflicts could be prohibited under customary law. However, this step was (too?) easily made by the ICTY in the *Kupreskić* and more particularly in the *Martić* decision.

After rightly asserting and confirming the *Tadić* jurisdiction jurisprudence that there are minimum rules to be abided by in all armed conflicts, the Tribunal in the *Martić* decision declared that one fundamental rule relates to the protection of civilians. The Tribunal argued that such a rule can be derived from common Article 3 as an attack on civilians would automatically 'lead to an infringement of the mandatory minimum norms applicable to all armed conflicts',[84] of the Martens clause, and of two General Assembly resolutions 2444 (XXIII) and 2675 (XXV). To bolster its argument, the Chamber adduced that a similar comment had already been made by the ICRC which, in its Commentary on Article 4 of AP II, took the position that 'there is in fact no room left at all for carrying out reprisals against protected persons'.[85] Yet, the statement that recourse to such acts by way of reprisals was impliedly precluded is, as Professor Kalshoven remarks, mistaken since

> '[t]he comment at article 4 must [...] be understood to be restricted to "humane treatment" provisions of that article, and has no bearing on the provisions in article 13 on general protection of the civilian population against the effects of hostilities or on the issue of reprisals in that context in particular'.[86]

It is more likely that Article 4 should be understood as a clause belonging to the realm of Geneva law rather than of Hague law.

Instead of delving into the depth of the legality of reprisals against civilians, the ICTY succinctly affirmed that '[t]he prohibition against attacking the civilian population as such as well as individual civilians must be respected in all circumstances regardless of the behaviour of the other party'.[87] This means that reprisals, a means of enforcement of international humanitarian law, cannot target civilians.[88] The Court wrongly bases its argumentation on Article 1 common to all Geneva Conventions that, in its opinion, confirms the view that the Conventions must be respected in all circumstances, even when the behaviour of the other party might be

---

84. *Prosecutor* v. *Martić*, *supra* n. 65, para. 17.

85. J. Pictet, *Commentary on the Fourth Geneva Convention* (Geneva, ICRC 1958) p. 39. It should also be noted that the International Law Commission took a similar position in 1995. *ILC Yearbook* (1995) Vol. II, Part Two, A/CN.4/SER.A/1995/Add.1 (Part 2) (State responsibility), para. 18, p. 72.

86. F. Kalshoven, 'Reprisals and the protection of civilians: two recent decisions of the Yugoslavia Tribunal', to be published (on file with author).

87. *Prosecutor* v. *Martić*, *supra* n. 65, para. 15.

88. In the background of this assertion, one needs to keep in mind the statement of the Court in the *Kupreskic* case where the Court declared that '[i]t cannot be denied that reprisals against civilians are inherently a barbarous means of seeking compliance with international law.' *Kupreskić*, *supra* n. 54, para. 528.

considered wrongful. Such a statement in fact is tantamount to asserting that reprisals are prohibited *per se*. This comment is even more irrelevant as the case dealt with a non-international armed conflict to which Article 1 is not applicable. In 1989, Professor Greenwood came to the conclusion that, as of that date, customary international law was not as restrictive as Articles 51-56 of AP I relating to reprisals[89] and hence civilians could be the targets of lawful reprisals. The Court in the *Kupreskić* case, on the other hand, finds that there is enough State practice and *opinio juris* to support the view that reprisals against civilians are precluded in international armed conflicts. As pointed out by Prof. Greenwood and Prof. Kalshoven, no reference is made in the *Martić* and *Kupreskić* jurisprudence to all the declarations and practice running against the conclusions of the Court.[90]

Additionally, the Court mentions Article 51(6) of AP I which states that, in all circumstances, attacks against the civilian population are prohibited. However, the Court fails to recognise that 'in all circumstances' needs to be interpreted in the context of a treaty that pertains to international armed conflicts and does not, in fact, relate to non-international armed conflicts. Another basis for the ban of reprisals on civilians is Article 4 of AP II that spells out absolute and non-derogable prohibitions. Another unhappy link which proves the confusion of the court as to the distinction between reprisals and retorsion is made in paragraph 17 of *Martić*, where it considers the prohibition of collective punishments as an additional proof of the ban on reprisals against civilians. A similar stance is found in the *Kupreskić* case where, when examining the legality of reprisals against civilians, the court states '[t]hese retaliatory [sic] measures are aimed instead at other more vulnerable individuals or groups.'[91] While there is no doubt that a rule 61 decision such as *Martić* is usually less elaborated in terms of law, much more clarification is needed to confirm the view that reprisals against civilians are unlawful in internal armed conflicts. The author has trouble subscribing to the view articulated by the ICTY but obviously, if one follows this jurisprudence, the Moscow hostage seizure was an illegal act of reprisal.

Unfortunately, the analysis does not yield the expected outcome, which was to prove that the Chechen hostage-takers were pursuing the armed conflict. Had the act been considered as lawful under international law, then one may have argued that the armed opposition group was only taking the conflict to the capital, and, as mentioned, nothing prevents international humanitarian law from applying elsewhere than in the actual place of hostilities.[92] Alas, the illegality of the hostage seizure in the light of international humanitarian law does not give credit to the

---

89. Greenwood, loc. cit. n. 78, p. 64.

90. C. Greenwood, 'Belligerent reprisals in the jurisprudence of the International Criminal Tribunal for the Former Yugoslavia', in H. Fischer, C. Kreß and S.R. Lüder, eds., *International and National Prosecution of Crimes under International Law: Current Developments* (Berlin, Arno Spitz 2001) pp. 546-556. For an analysis of state practice and *opinio juris*, see Kalshoven, loc. cit. n. 62, p. 53 and Kalshoven, loc. cit. n. 87.

91. *Kupreskić*, *supra* n. 54, para. 528

92. See the aforementioned *Tadić* jurisprudence.

Chechens' claim that they are fighting an armed conflict against the Russian authorities. On the contrary, by attacking the theatre in Moscow, they only bolstered the Russian government's claim that they are using terrorist methods.

4. THE HOSTAGE CRISIS AS A CLASSICAL 'TERRORIST' ACT

Another possibility is that the armed opposition group has opened a new front in Moscow in the sense that the hostage seizure was an armed conflict in itself. Yet, the majority of commentators viewed the act as terrorism and possibly a change in tactics.

4.1 The hostage crisis as an armed conflict *per se*

Notwithstanding the above conclusion that the armed conflict in Chechnya appears to be covered by common Article 3, it is doubtful whether the Moscow hostage crisis can be considered as part of the armed conflict that is covered by common Article 3 because there is no assurance that there is a link between the insurgents in Chechnya and the hostage-takers in Moscow. If there was a link, the act was in contravention of international humanitarian law, and one needs to investigate whether the hostage operation was an armed conflict of itself. If it was, it shows that a second front was temporarily opened by the armed opposition group against the Russian authorities, this time in the capital.

Whereas it is clear when international humanitarian law pertaining to international armed conflicts starts to be applicable, it is difficult to pinpoint the precise moment when a non-international armed conflict begins. Common Article 3 does not set a distinctive threshold while the test spelled out in Article 1 of Additional Protocol II is one related to the characterisation of the armed opposition group.[93] As discussed earlier, 'the threshold of application entailed in Protocol II is so high that only full scale civil wars qualify for protection'[94] and it cannot be reached in a single attack. However 'Article 3 does not require the existence of large-scale and generalised hostilities or a situation comparable to a civil war in which dissident armed groups exercise control over parts of national territory.'[95] We then need to assess whether the hostage seizure triggered the applicability of Common Article 3.

---

93. As noted in the commentary, 'the criteria of duration and intensity were not retained as such in the definition because they would have introduced a subjective element'. Y. Sandoz, C. Swinarski and B. Zimmermann, eds., *Commentary on the Additional Protocols of 8 June 1977 to the Geneva Conventions of 12 August 1949* (Geneva, ICRC/Dordrecht, Martinus Nijhoff 1987) para. 4469.

94. H. Salinas Burgos, 'The application of international humanitarian law as compared to human rights law in situations qualified as internal armed conflict, internal disturbances and tensions, or public emergency, with special reference to war crimes and political crimes', in F. Kalshoven and Y. Sandoz, *Implementation of International Humanitarian Law* (Dordrecht, Martinus Nijhoff 1989) p. 9.

95. *Tablada* case, *supra* n. 41, para. 152.

Since Professor Forsythe's remark that '[n]o-one has been completely sure as to what factual situations the article applies, and no one has been totally sure exactly what is prohibited in whatever situation it is that is regulated',[96] much has been written and decided on the applicability of common Article 3. As the Commentary explains, state delegations to the Diplomatic Conference refused to envisage the applicability of common Article 3 to any form of anarchy, rebellion, or even plain banditry. The initial idea that the word 'conflict' should be defined or that certain conditions should be enumerated was finally abandoned. The commentators on common Article 3 nevertheless believe that these criteria may be convenient to gauge the applicability of humanitarian law to such low levels conflicts.

To start with, the rebels – in the given case the hostage-takers – must possess 'an organised military force, an authority responsible for its acts, acting within a determinate territory and having the means of respecting and ensuring respect for the Convention'.[97] It is clear from the facts that the hostage-takers were organised and answered to a responsible person or to a group of people as they were constantly in touch by phone with some external companions-in-arms. The hostage operation can qualify as a military operation, though unlawful under humanitarian law, that took place within a determinate territory, the theatre in the instant case. The hostage-takers also had the means of respecting and ensuring respect for the Convention.

The second criterion mentioned in the Commentary, that the legal government uses armed forces and is in possession of a part of the national territory, is fulfilled. The third criterion, that the armed opposition group be under a responsible command and capable of meeting minimum humanitarian standards, is rather tricky because it requires a certain amount of recognition of belligerency between the parties. Having regard to the attitude of the Russian government during the hostage crisis, there is no doubt that it did not consider the hostage-takers as anything but criminals, and that although they claimed to be linked to the party to the Chechen conflict, it refused to see them as belligerents. The Commentary also mentions a fourth requirement, composed of four subparts: First, that 'the insurgents have an organisation purporting to have the characteristics of a State';[98] second, the rebels exercise *de facto* authority over persons within a determinate territory; third, 'the armed forces act under the direction of the organised civil authority and are prepared to observe the ordinary laws of war';[99] and fourth, it must also be shown that the insurgents agree to be bound by the provisions of the Convention. As for the first requirement, although the government of President Maskhadov may claim such a nature, it is doubtful that the direct brains behind the hostage-taking fulfil such a criterion. As for the second, while undeniably the hostage-takers were sovereign in the theatre, some commentators believe that more

---

96. D.P. Forsythe, 'Legal management of internal war: the 1977 Protocol on non-international armed conflicts', 72 *AJIL* (1978) p. 273.

97. Pictet, op. cit. n. 85, p. 49.

98. Ibid., p. 50.

99. Ibid., p. 50.

is needed to meet the 'territory requirement'. As for the third, it is hard to say that the hostage takers qualify as an armed force and even more difficult to ascertain that they acted under the direction of an organised civil authority as it appears that the lead was taken by an independent warlord. Finally, there is no recording of the hostage-takers expressing their wish to be bound by the Conventions.

Although the Commentary clearly states that these are only indicators and that a conflict may fall within the purview of common Article 3 without fulfilling all the requirements, checking their relevance in the light of the hostage seizure helps in identifying the nature of the hostage crisis according to international humanitarian law. Given the number of unfulfilled requirements, it may be argued that the crisis did not reach the level of applicability of common Article 3.

Turning towards jurisprudence, one notes with surprise that there is little help besides the *Tablada* case.[100] The Inter-American Commission for Human Rights, after examining the facts, declared that common Article 3 was applicable despite the brief duration (30 hours) of the events. It based its arguments on the fact that 'the attackers involved carefully planned, co-ordinated and executed an armed attack, i.e., a military operation, against a quintessential military objective – a military base.'[101] Applying this argument to the hostage crisis in Moscow does not yield much of a result because, although it appears that the attack was carefully planned, it was directed against a non-military target, a civilian building containing civilians. Terrorist acts do not fall within the purview of humanitarian law because they aim at destabilising a country using psychological means whereas guerrilla tactics are of military nature since they principally target armed forces and 'military objects'.[102] There is no doubt that the hostage seizure was of no military value and that it was intended to make the demands of a part of the armed opposition group public. From the wording of paragraph 155 of the *Tablada* decision, it is not possible to detect whether the principal criterion is the planning, coordination and execution of the act as an armed attack or the military target. In the instant case, we are compelled to admit that it is unlikely that common Article 3 was applicable to the hostage seizure in Moscow as such.

4.2 The hostage crisis as a classical terrorist act

From the analysis, two things are clear: first, the hostage-taking is not a lawful act of reprisal and there is no support for the view that the Chechen hostage-takers were carrying on the armed conflict on a second front, and second, the hostage-taking was not an armed conflict as such. It may even be submitted that by their

---

100. The Inter-American Court of Human Rights was requested by the applicant in the *Las Palmeras* case to gauge the legality of the killing of a Colombian national in the light of Common Article 3 of the Geneva Conventions. However, the Court did not rule on humanitarian law and restricted itself to the application of Article 4 of the Inter-American Convention on Human Rights. *Las Palmeras*, IACHR, Ser. C No. 90, Judgement of 6 December 2001.

101. *Supra* n. 41.

102. Heintze, loc. cit. n. 26, p. 76.

actions, the hostage-takers have proven President Putin's assertion that the situation in Chechnya does not amount to an armed conflict and that the Russian armed forces are involved in an anti-terrorist operation.

From that, a legal consequence can be drawn: either the Moscow hostage crisis was an act of terrorism committed in an armed conflict, in which case international humanitarian law is applicable, or it was a purely criminal act falling within the purview of what is commonly known and referred to as 'terrorism'.[103] In both cases, the hostage seizure contravened widely accepted norms of international law.

Both in armed conflicts and in situations falling outside the purview of humanitarian law, hostage-taking is a common tactic in the repertoire of modern terrorism. The crime involves three elements: '(a) seizure or detention of the hostage; (b) the threat to kill, to injure or to continue to detain the hostage; (c) the attempt to compel a third party to act in a given way.'[104] According to Resolution 31/103 of the United Nations General Assembly, it is an act which places innocent human lives in danger and violates human dignity.[105]

The deliberate use of terror as a means of warfare is strictly banned by international humanitarian law, both by the texts as well as by custom. Article 4 of AP II clearly stipulates that terrorist means and hostage-taking are prohibited acts in non-international armed conflict. Even if only common Article 3 is applicable to the conflict in Chechnya, hostage-taking is banned under its subparagraph (1)(b). From these rules, it is crystal clear that if the hostage seizure in Moscow is part of the armed conflict that rages in Chechnya and if not a lawful reprisal as earlier demonstrated, it is an unlawful act of terror prohibited both in conventional and customary international law.

The way the hostage crisis was engineered and developed is classical of that type of terrorist activity in the sense that the police surrounded the premises in overwhelming force, adding to the high level of tension and imminent danger, and then had the initiative as to the means employed to put an end to the situation. It should be underlined that 'the only thing left for [the hostage-takers] to gain is publicity. They probably knew this all the time, so that is usually their primary aim'.[106] In the instant case, it is not a mistake to assert that the hostage-takers wished publicity, as a camera that shot the entire scene was found on the premises and the Russian authorities believed that it was the intention of the hostage-takers to send that videotape to Muslim organisations that would have been able to provide for more funding for the conflict in Chechnya.

---

103. For example, Art. 12 of the Convention on Terrorism clearly states that it is not applicable if the hostage situation takes place in the framework of an armed conflict and that only humanitarian law is then applicable, thereby delineating the scope of application of both sets of rules, human rights/criminal law and humanitarian law. One should nonetheless bear in mind that this Convention is not applicable in the given case as there is no transborder element.

104. Salinas Burgos, loc. cit. n. 61, p. 198.

105. UN General Assembly, Drafting Of An International Convention Against The Taking Of Hostages, Resolution 31/103, UN Doc. A/RES/31/103, 15 December 1976.

106. R.L. Clutterbuck, *Terrorism in an Unstable World* (London, Routledge 1994) p. 176.

Looking at the following definition of terrorism that focuses on tactics,

> '[t]errorism is normally considered to be a coercive mechanism, part of a guerrilla strategy [sic], in that actions create threats of worse to come if political demands are not met, and these demands (until recently at least) tended to be geared to ending foreign occupation or a secessionist movement',[107]

one immediately notices the analogy with reprisals. Indeed, both acts aim at posing demands to the government but while reprisals may be lawful, terrorism can never fall within the purview of legality. The request formulated by the hostage-takers, that the conflict in Chechnya end, can be considered as both a demand that the violations of international law perpetrated by the Russian army stop (reprisals) or a classical terrorist demand that the government cease its brutal policy against a particular group. This distinction is of some importance because if the Moscow tragedy was an act of reprisal, then it was a legitimate manner of enforcing international humanitarian law. On the other hand, if it was an act of terrorism, the government could be seen entitled to enunciate a 'no concessions to terrorists' policy.[108] The fact that the Russian government immediately after the seizure uttered their refusal to talk to the hostage-takers signifies that the authorities considered from the very beginning that it was a terrorist operation.

Another way of arguing that the Moscow hostage crisis is a classical terrorist act is to show that previous well-known terrorist groups have employed and developed similar strategies which aim to delocalise the theatre of conflict and bring it to the capital, in the hope that their activities will have more resonance on the authorities, especially via the population. Indeed, '[t]raditional terrorist groups, such as the Basque ETA and the Provisional IRA have taken the fight to their opponents' capitals, and in the case of the PIRA this strategy was arguably successful in helping to persuade the British government to seek a settlement.'[109]

Hostage-taking obviously belongs to a category of acts commonly perceived and legally coined 'terrorism'. Yet, because hostage situations can also occur in the framework of an armed conflict, one needs to be careful when automatically claiming that it is an act of pure terrorism. In this regard, it is enlightening to consider Heintze's claim that the yardstick to distinguish between terrorism and guerrilla activity is the different value given to the use of force by the perpetrators.[110] Phrased differently, it means that '[t]errorism is distinguished from guerrillaism by its attacks upon the innocent and the separation of its victims from

---

107. L. Freedman, 'A new type of war', in K. Booth and T. Dunne, eds., *Worlds in Collision: Terror and the Future of Global Order* (Basingstoke, Palgrave 2002) p. 37.

108. G. Wardlaw, *Political Terrorism: Theory, Tactics and Counter-measure*, 2nd edn. (Cambridge, Cambridge University Press 1989) p. 155.

109. Freedman, loc. cit. n. 116, p. 39.

110. H.-J. Heintze, loc. cit. n. 26, p. 76.

the ultimate target.'[111] As hostage operations are more likely to be viewed as terrorist tactics than unlawful military operations in an armed conflict, it is possible to argue that the group who organised the hostage seizure has a different view of the use of force than the group led by President Maskhadov.

5. CONCLUSION

The analysis has demonstrated that there are serious doubts as to whether the hostage-takers were connected to the head of the Chechen armed opposition group, which means that there might be several groups involved in the 'armed conflict' in Chechnya. While it seems that one group would prefer to conduct military operations although it is factually not able to do so, another group has decided to have recourse to terrorist methods. The legal consequence is that, due to the lack of responsible command and the inability to launch concerted (military) operations, even common Article 3 may not be applicable to the conflict in Chechnya unless one accepts that there is a sharp split in the Chechen armed opposition and that President Maskhadov continues to be the leader acting on the territory of the Republic of Chechnya and Basayev is a terrorist. Still one would need to prove that, Basayev's group aside, President Maskhadov is still in command of the armed opposition group and able to launch military operations against the Russian armed forces.

However, the most recent bombing of the headquarters of the pro-Moscow government of Chechnya[112] blurs that distinction, and one may wonder whether the Chechen insurgents have not completely altered their tactics and engaged in classical terrorism, thereby buttressing the statements of the Russian authorities. According to the Chechen Minister of Internal Affairs, suicide bombers detonated two explosives-packed vehicles after driving through security cordons surrounding the building. Also, as noted by Human Rights Watch, 'rebels have also pursued a vicious assassination campaign against Chechen civil servants, policemen and religious clergymen co-operating with the Russian authorities, killing dozens each year'.[113] In fact, after two massive hostage-takings in 1995-1996, the Chechen militants were able to convince the Russian authorities to leave the territory of Chechnya. What appears to be a change of tactics in the second Chechen war may in fact be nothing more than a repetition of the first armed conflict. Only future events will be able to properly answer this question.

---

111. R.A. Friedlander, 'Terrorism and national liberation movements: can rights derive from wrongs?', 13 *Case Western Reserve JIL* (1981) p. 282.

112. On 27 December 2002, Chechen suicide bombers detonated two explosives-packed vehicle near the Chechen Government headquarters in Grozny. As a result 46 people died and another 76 were wounded.

113. 'Chechen Rebels Must Stop Targeting Civilians', Human Rights Watch, 27 December 2002.

THE ICJ'S JUDGMENT IN THE CASE CONCERNING THE ARREST WARRANT OF 11 APRIL 2000: SOME CRITICAL OBSERVATIONS[1]

Jan Wouters[2] and Leen De Smet[3]

1. INTRODUCTION

On 14 February 2002, the International Court of Justice (the Court) delivered its judgment in the case concerning the Arrest Warrant of 11 April 2000.[4] In this case, the Court had the opportunity to take an authoritative stance on, and to contribute to the development of, two major questions in the field of immunities and jurisdiction of contemporary international law: do Ministers for Foreign Affairs enjoy immunity against prosecution by national courts of another state for crimes under international law, and how far can a state go in granting universal jurisdiction to its domestic courts?

The case rose out of the application *in absentia* of the controversial Belgian Law of 16 June 1993, as amended by the Law of 10 February 1999, concerning the punishment of grave breaches of international humanitarian law (the Law) against Yerodia Ndombasi (Yerodia).[5] With this Law, Belgium took a rather progressive stance regarding the prosecution of genocide, crimes against humanity and war crimes[6]: it gives the Belgian courts jurisdiction over those crimes (Art. 7) irrespec-

---

2. Professor Dr. Jan Wouters is Professor of International Law and the Law of International Organisations at the Catholic University of Leuven.

3. Leen De Smet is academic assistent at the Institute for International Law of the Catholic University of Leuven. She is preparing a Ph.D. on the legal position of multinational enterprises in public international law.

4. International Court of Justice, case concerning the arrest warrant of 11 April 2000, available at http://www.icj-cij.org/ ('*Arrest Warrant* case').

5. Law concerning the punishment of grave breaches of international humanitarian Law of 16 June 1993, as amended by Law of 10 February 1999 (Wet van 16 juni 1993 betreffende de bestraffing van ernstige schendingen van het internationaal humanitair recht zoals geamendeerd bij wet van 10 februari 1999, 38 *ILM* (1999) at p. 918 (English translation by S. Smis and K. Van der Borght); *Belgian Official Gazette*, 5 August 1993 and 23 March 1999. Both the 1993 and 1999 Laws are also reproduced in 2 *YIHL* (1999) at pp. 539 and 541, respectively.

6. See on this law especially P. d'Argent, 'La loi du 10 février 1999 relative à la répression des violations graves du droit international humanitaire', 118 *Journal des Tribunaux* (1999) pp. 549-555; L. De Smet and F. Naert, 'Making or breaking international law? An international law analysis of Belgiums Act concerning the punishment of grave breaches of international humanitarian law', forthcoming in 35 *Revue belge de Droit International* (2002) Vol. 1-2 and the contributions in J. Wouters and H. Panken, eds., *De Genocidewet in Internationaal Perspectief* (Ghent, Larcier 2002).

Yearbook of International Humanitarian Law
Volume 4 – 2001 – pp. 373-388

tive of where, by whom and against whom the crime was committed (universal jurisdiction) and even irrespective of the presence of the alleged perpetrator on Belgian territory[7] (i.e., universal jurisdiction *in absentia*, unconditional or absolute universal jurisdiction). It furthermore contains a provision denying any immunity attached to an official position (Art. 5, para. 3).

Based on those two rather progressive provisions of the Law, a Belgian investigating judge issued on 11 April 2000 an international arrest warrant against Yerodia, who was at that time Minister for Foreign Affairs of the Democratic Republic of the Congo (the Congo) for violations of international humanitarian law that Yerodia allegedly committed in 1998 in his capacity of Principal Private Secretary to the late-President Laurent Kabila.

On 17 October 2000, the Congo filed a request for the indication of provisional measures. This was rejected by the Court in an Order of 8 December 2000.[8] On the same date, Congo filed an application instituting proceedings against Belgium.[9] In that application it challenged the legality of the arrest warrant under international law.

Initially the Congo requested the Court to declare that 'Belgium shall annul the international warrant issued on 11 April 2000 (...)'. It based this claim on two legal grounds.[10] Firstly, the Congo held that Belgium, by issuing the arrest warrant against Yerodia, violated the principle that a state may not exercise its authority on the territory of another state and the principle of sovereign equality among all members of the United Nations, as laid down in Article 2(1) of the United Nations Charter. Thereby, the Congo indirectly challenged the legality of Article 7 of the Law in which the principle of universal jurisdiction is embedded. Secondly, it argued that the arrest warrant violated international law because it failed to respect the diplomatic immunity of Yerodia as Minister for Foreign Affairs. It thereby in essence challenged Article 5(3) of the Law.

In its final submission, however, the Congo pursued only the latter claim, i.e., that the arrest warrant was unlawful because it violated the rule of customary international law concerning the absolute inviolability and immunity from criminal process of incumbent Ministers for Foreign Affairs.[11]

---

7. Parliamentary Documents of the Senate, 1990-91, No. 1317/1, 16. See, however, the three judgments of the Brussels Court of Appeal, *infra* nn. 81, 82 and 83 and the discussion thereof below.

8. International Court of Justice, case concerning the *Arrest Warrant* of 11 April 2000, Order of 8 December 2000, available at http://www.icj-cij.org.

9. International Court of Justice, case concerning the *Arrest Warrant* of 11 April 2000, application instituting proceedings, filed in the Registry of the Court on 17 October 2000, available at http://www.icj-cij.org ('The application').

10. Application, at pp. 7-13.

11. *Arrest Warrant* case, at paras. 11-12.

2. THE ISSUE OF IMMUNITY

The central legal questions the Court had to examine with regard to immunities were (1) to what extent a Minister for Foreign Affairs is entitled to immunity under international law, and (2) whether that immunity extends to universally condemned international crimes such as war crimes and crimes against humanity.

2.1 The general rule

On the issue of immunities, the Congo maintained that, during his term of office, a Minister for Foreign Affairs enjoys absolute inviolability and immunity for all his acts,[12] while Belgium for its part submitted that the immunity accorded to a Minister for Foreign Affairs in office is limited to the so-called 'official acts', and in no way can be upheld when the Minister is alleged to have committed international crimes like war crimes or crimes against humanity.[13]

The Court first recalled that, since no specific treaty provisions with regard to Ministers for Foreign Affairs exist, it had to decide on their immunities on the basis of customary international law. It then proceeded to state that, in customary international law, immunities are granted to Ministers for Foreign Affairs not for their personal benefit but to guarantee the effective performance of their functions on behalf of the state. Therefore, the extent of the immunity should be determined in relation to the nature of their functions and their position. According to the Court, a Minister for Foreign Affairs occupies a position comparable to that of a Head of State or a Head of Government. His functions are such that, throughout the duration of his office, when abroad he enjoys full immunity from criminal jurisdiction and inviolability, both for acts performed in a 'private capacity' and for acts performed in an 'official capacity', regardless of whether he is present in the territory of the arresting state on an 'official' or a 'private' visit. This immunity and inviolability protect the Minister against any act of authority that would hinder him in the performance of his duties.[14] No exception to this rule is recognized.[15]

The Court's judgment raises a number of questions both with regard to its motivation (i) and its scope of application (ii).

2.1.1 *The rule of customary international law*

As to the motivation of the rule of 'full and absolute immunity', it should first be emphasized that the mere fact that there may be good political or pragmatic reasons for granting or not granting immunities of itself in no way implies the existence of a legally binding norm of customary international law. It is remarkable that, although the Court refers to customary international law, it does not bother to

12. Ibid., at para. 47.
13. Ibid., at para. 49.
14. Ibid., at paras. 51-55.
15. Ibid., at para. 58.

establish proof of *opinio juris* and state practice, two essential components of a rule of customary law. This is all the more regrettable since the customary character of the rule is far from being generally acknowledged, especially with regard to acts performed in a private capacity. Judge ad hoc Van den Wyngaert, and to a lesser extent, Judge Al-Khasawneh, emphasized that, in their view, no rule of customary international law exists since the proposition of a 'full' immunity of Ministers for Foreign Affairs is not supported by *opinio juris* or state practice.[16]

We can subscribe to the Court's decision that an incumbent Minister for Foreign Affairs, in order to safeguard the unhindered exercise of his functions, enjoys an absolute functional immunity when he is on an official visit. First of all, this is nothing more than an application of the generally accepted idea that a Minister for Foreign Affairs is at all times entitled to immunity *ratione materiae* for the acts that he performs in his official capacity. As a matter of fact, to the extent that a Minister for Foreign Affairs acts on behalf of the state, those acts are legally attributable to the state, and not to the Minister.[17] Secondly, the idea of granting immunities to a Minister for Foreign Affairs when on an official visit is clearly supported by state practice and *opinio juris*. This principle was not challenged by the Congo or Belgium in this case.[18] Moreover, the disputed arrest warrant clearly mentioned an exception for official visits.[19] It is expressly confirmed in case-law[20] and indirectly by Article 21 of the 1969 UN Convention on Special Missions.[21]

The Court's view that this rule of customary international law also extends to private acts is less evident.[22] First of all, there is some case law indicating that a

---

16. Ibid. Dissenting opinion, Judge ad hoc Van den Wyngaert, at paras. 11-23 and Dissenting Opinion, Judge Al-Khasawneh, at para. 8.

17. A. Cassese, 'When may senior state officials be tried for international crimes? Some comments on the *Congo v. Belgium* case,' 13 *EJIL* (2002) pp. 853 at 862, F. Naert, 'Immuniteit voor internationale misdaden?' in Wouters and Panken, op. cit. n. 6.

18. *Arrest Warrant* case, at paras. 47 and 49.

19. 'Pursuant to the general principle of fairness in judicial proceedings, immunity from enforcement must, in our view, be accorded to all State representatives welcomed as such on the territory of Belgium (on 'official visits'). Welcoming such foreign dignitaries as official representatives of sovereign States involves not only relations between individuals but also relations between States. This implies that such welcome includes an undertaking by the host State and its various components to refrain from taking any coercive measures against its guest and the invitation cannot become a pretext for ensnaring the individual concerned in what would then have to be labelled a trap. In the contrary case, failure to respect this undertaking could give rise to the host State's international responsibility.'

20. State of Hawaii, *Chong Boon Kim* v. *Kim Yong Shik and David Kim*, Civil No. 12565, Cir. Ct., 1st Cir., Hawaii, 1963, 81 *ILR* (1990) p. 604. Cf., *Kilroy* v. *Windsor and Others*, Civil Action No. C-78-291, United States District Court for the Northern District of Ohio, Eastern Division, 81 *ILR* (1990) pp. 605-607, granting immunity to the Prince of Wales while on an 'official visit'. See also A. Cassese, *International Law* (Oxford, Oxford University Press 2001) p. 423, n. 29.

21. United Nations Convention on Special Missions, New York, 16 December 1969, 1400 *UNTS* 23. See also M. Ruffert, 48 *NILR* (2001) pp. 171 at 180-181 and the references therein. The principle of immunity in the event of an official visit is also adhered to in legal doctrine: see e.g., A. Cassese, ibid., at p. 96; J. Salmon, *Manuel de droit diplomatique* (Brussels, Bruylant 1994) p. 539.

22. See, however, J. Verhoeven, 'Mandat d'arrêt international et statut de ministre', Actualité et droit international 2002 available at http://www.ridi.org/adi; also published in 435 *Journal des Procès* (2002) p. 20 at 20, who considers the Court's view 'très classique'.

minister who is not on an official visit is not entitled to full immunity under customary international law.[23] Although limited in number, those cases make it difficult to support unreservedly the Court's view; at the very least, they should have been properly addressed by the Court.[24] Furthermore, the question whether incumbent Ministers for Foreign Affairs are entitled to immunities during private travel and for acts committed in their private capacity is the subject of serious controversy in legal writings. A number of prominent scholars state that this question probably should be answered negatively.[25] In addition, the Court's argument of the assimilation of the position of Ministers for Foreign Affairs with that of Heads of State or other high officials in this regard has been rejected in legal doctrine.[26] We can refer to the dissenting Judges Van den Wyngaert[27] and Al-Khasawneh[28] and Judges Higgins, Kooijmans and Buergenthal in their joint separate opinion[29] and the arguments they made in this regard. It has also been argued that the mere fact that a Minister for Foreign Affairs will be limited in his freedom to undertake private travel because he might expose himself to legal proceedings, for example, because an arrest warrant has been issued against him, does not put the effective exercise of his functions at jeopardy.[30] On the other hand, it must be granted that this argument is not an absolute one since, for instance, the detention or arrest of a Minister for Foreign Affairs while on a private visit, obviously also has a negative effect on the effective performance of his functions. However, this does not necessarily make the 'full' immunity from criminal jurisdiction and inviolability of a Minister for Foreign Affairs a rule under customary international law.[31]

Even if one holds the view that there is a rule of customary international law in this respect, it remains disturbing that the Court, rather uncharacteristically, did not bother to give any evidence of *opinio juris* and state practice. This was recognized

---

23. See M. Bothe, 'Die strafrechtliche Immunität fremder Staatsorgane', 31 *ZaöRV* (1971) pp. 246 at 264 (mentioning a French case against the Moroccan Minister for Internal Affairs). In Germany, an arrest warrant was issued against an Iranian Minister (See Naert, op. cit. n. 17, at n. 116).

24. See on this *Arrest Warrant* case, Dissenting Opinion Judge ad hoc Van den Wyngaert, at para. 13.

25. Bothe, loc. cit. n. 23, at pp. 264-265; H.-E. Folz and M. Soppe, 'Zur Frage der Völkerrechtmäßigkeit von Haftbefehlen gegen Regierungsmitglieder anderer Staaten', *Neue Zeitschrift für Strafrecht* (1996) pp. 576 at 577; Ruffert, loc. cit. n. 21, at pp. 180-181; A. Watts, 'The legal position in international law of Heads of States, Heads of Governments and Foreign Ministers', *Recueil Cours* 1994/III, pp. 9 at 109. See also Naert, op. cit. n. 17.

26. Ruffert, loc. cit. n. 21, at p. 180; Watts, ibid., at pp. 102-103. One should also note in this regard that whereas the draft Resolution on the immunities of Heads of State and Government of the Institut de droit international did assimilate the position of Ministers for Foreign Affairs with that of Heads of State, this can no longer be found in the final text: see on this Resolution Lady Hazel Fox, 'The Resolution of the Institute of International Law on the Immunities of Heads of State and Government,' 51 *ICLQ* (2002) pp. 119 at 120.

27. Ibid., Dissenting Opinion Judge ad hoc Van den Wyngaert, at paras. 20-21.

28. Ibid., Dissenting Opinion Judge Al-Khasawneh, at paras. 1-2.

29. Ibid., Joint Opinion, at paras. 81-83.

30. Ibid., Dissenting Opinion Judge Al-Khasawneh, at para. 4.

31. Ibid., at para. 54.

by Judge Koroma who, although he fully subscribed to the Court's ruling, stated that 'while it would have been interesting if the Court had done so, the Court did not consider it necessary to undertake a disquisition of the law in order to reach its decision'.[32] We might also refer to Judge Oda's observation that the answer to the question as to what privileges foreign ministers are entitled to might not be clear under customary international law.[33] This unorthodox way of establishing a rule of customary international law by the Court is highly regrettable. Such an approach not only endangers the legitimacy of the principle embedded in the rule but also weakens the position of customary international law in international law as such.[34]

2.1.2 *The scope of the immunity rule*

As to exactly which acts of authority of a state are precluded because of the immunity from criminal jurisdiction and inviolability of an incumbent Minister for Foreign Affairs of another state, some ambiguity remains. It is the Court's view that 'that immunity and that inviolability protect the individual concerned against any act of authority of another State which would hinder him or her in the performance of his or her duties'.[35]

Sensu stricto, however, the Court only pronounced itself in this case on the issuing and the circulation of an arrest warrant. It more precisely declared that '... given the nature and purpose of the warrant, its mere issue violated the immunity which Mr. Yerodia enjoyed as the Congo's incumbent Minister for Foreign Affairs',[36] and that the 'circulation of the warrant, whether or not it significantly interfered with Mr. Yerodia's diplomatic activity, ... infringed the immunity from criminal jurisdiction and the inviolability then enjoyed by him under international law'.[37] The fact that the arrest warrant had not yet been enforced or the fact that further steps were needed by Belgium to enforce the arrest warrant in third states did not prevent the Court from reaching this conclusion. From this, one can deduce that in case of an enforcement measure, the mere risk that a Minister for Foreign Affairs might be hindered in the exercise of his functions is sufficient to violate his or her immunity; a real impediment is not required. Again, the Court opts for a very broad 'functionality' concept. However, several judges and legal scholars[38] have

---

32. Ibid., Separate Opinion Judge Koroma, at para. 6.

33. Ibid., Dissenting Opinion Judge Oda, at para. 14.

34. See A. Nollkaemper, 'The legitimacy of international law in the case law of the International Criminal Tribunal for the Former Yugoslavia', in T. Vandamme and J.-H. Reestman, eds., *Ambiguity in the Rule of Law. The Interface between National and International Legal Systems* (Groningen, Europa Law Publishing 2001) pp. 13-23.

35. *Arrest Warrant* case, at para. 54.

36. Ibid., para. 70.

37. Ibid., para. 71.

38. Amnesty International, 'Universal Jurisdiction: Belgian Court has jurisdiction in Sharon case to investigate 1982 Sabra and Chatila killings', AI Index: IOR 53/001/2002; E. David, 'La loi belge de 1993/1999: conforme ou contraire au droit international?' in Wouters and Panken, op. cit. n. 6; S. Vandeginste, 'Uitspraak van het Internationaal Gerechtshof in de zaak Yerodia: veel vragen, weinig antwoorden', 11 *Zoeklicht* (2002) pp. 26 at 27; A. Winants, 'Kanttekeningen bij de toepassing van de

defended the idea that the mere act of investigating criminal charges against a Minister for Foreign Affairs should pass the functionality criterion that the Court upholds. Judges Higgins, Kooijmans and Buergenthal, for example, came to the conclusion that, although the scope of immunities during private travels is not clear, it is certain that a Minister for Foreign Affairs may not be subjected to measures which would prevent effective performance of his functions.[39] On the other hand, they also stated that the commencement of an investigation does not violate the inviolability or immunities of the person concerned.[40] Judge Al-Khasani shares this position in his dissenting opinion:

> 'A Minister for Foreign Affairs is entitled to immunity from enforcement when on official mission ... but the mere opening of criminal investigations against him can hardly be said by any objective criteria to constitute interference with the conduct of diplomacy. A faint-hearted or ultra-sensitive Minister may restrict his private travels or feel discomfort but this is a subjective element that must be discarded.'[41]

It can indeed be argued that the mere opening of a criminal investigation will hardly have any effect on the effective performance of a Minister's functions. It remains controversial, though, exactly how far one can go in this regard.[42] What about investigating acts, for example? Whereas the mere interrogation of a witness might constitute no problem for the performance of ministerial functions, this is obviously different from the interrogation of the Minister himself. According to Judge ad hoc Van den Wyngaert, the solution might be found in the rules developed in this regard based on the 1961 Vienna Convention on Diplomatic Relations.[43] This would mean, in her view, that the complaint as such can be examined, but that the Minister involved cannot be interrogated or ordered to appear.[44]

2.2 An exception for international crimes?

Having established this customary rule of full immunity from criminal jurisdiction of incumbent Ministers for Foreign Affairs, the Court turned to the examination of Belgium's argument that 'immunities accordéd to incumbent Ministers for Foreign Affairs can in no way protect them where they are suspected of having committed war crimes or crimes against humanity'. Belgium supported this view by referring

---

wet in de praktijk', in Wouters and Panken, op. cit. n. 6. See on this also J. d'Aspremont Lynden and F. Dopagne, 'Cour Internationale de Justice, 14 février 2002, Observations', 121 *Journal des Tribunaux* (2002) pp. 282 at 286.

39. *Arrest Warrant* case, Joint opinion, at para. 84.
40. Ibid., Joint opinion, at para. 59.
41. Ibid., Dissenting opinion Judge Al-Khasawneh, at para. 4.
42. See on this d'Aspremont Lynden and Dopagne, loc. cit. n. 38, at p. 286.
43. *Arrest Warrant* case, Dissenting opinion Judge ad hoc Van den Wyngaert, at para. 75.
44. See further with regard to persons enjoying diplomatic immunity, Salmon, op. cit. n. 21, at p. 303.

amongst others to the legal instruments creating international criminal tribunals and to the *Pinochet* and *Qaddafi* cases.[45]

The Court brushed aside those arguments by stating, without further explanation, that it could not deduce any exception to the rule according absolute immunity from jurisdiction and inviolability to incumbent Ministers for Foreign Affairs from the cases mentioned. It likewise rejected the relevance of the Statutes of International Criminal Tribunals for national courts. For a number of reasons, we are, with all due respect, unable to share the Court's view on this.

As to the Court's argument that the non-application of immunities only exists with regard to international courts, we can refer to several instruments indicating the opposite.[46] Reference can be made, for example, to the ILC's Draft Code of Crimes against the Peace and Security of Mankind.[47] This is also the case in the Statute of the Special Court for Sierra Leone[48] and it likewise appears in the draft Statute of the Extraordinary Court for Cambodia (which both have a mixed national-international character).[49] The ICTY qualified it as a rule of customary international law,[50] and it has also been stated in legal doctrine that the principle embedded in Article 7(2) of the ICTY Statute, which provides for the non-application of immunities, also applies in proceedings before domestic courts.[51]

The *Quaddafi* case also pointed in this direction. The statement of the French Cour de Cassation that

> 'la coutume internationale s'oppose à ce que chefs d'Etat en exercise puissent en l'absence de dispositions internationales contraires s'imposant aux parties concernées, faire l'objet de poursuites devant les jurisdictions pénales d'un Etat étranger'

---

45. *Arrest Warrant* case, at para. 56.

46. De Smet and Naert, op. cit. n. 6. See also Amnesty International, *supra* n. 38, at pp. 5-11.

47. Art. 7 *juncto* 8, International Law Commission, Draft Code of Crimes against the peace and security of mankind, *Yb ILC* (1996) Vol. II: 'The official position of an individual who commits a crime against the peace and security of mankind, even if he acted as head of State or Government, does not relieve him of criminal responsibility or mitigate punishment', *juncto* 'Without prejudice to the jurisdiction of an international criminal court, each State Party shall take such measures as may be necessary to establish its jurisdiction over the crimes [...] irrespective of where or by whom those crimes were committed ...'

48. Art. 6(2) Statute of the Special Court for Sierra Leone, available at http://www.un.org/Docs/sc/letters/2002/ (246): 'The official position of any accused persons, whether as Head of State or Government or as a responsible government official, shall not relieve such person of criminal responsibility nor mitigate punishment'.

49. Art. 29 draft Law on the establishment of extraordinary chambers in the courts of Cambodia for the prosecution of crimes committed during the period of Democratic Kampuchea, available at http://www.diplomatiejudiciaire.com/Cambodge/LoiCambodge.htm: 'Any Suspect who planned, instigated, ordered, aided and abetted, or committed the crimes referred to in Articles 3, 4, 5, 6, 7 and 8 of this law shall be individually responsible for the crime. The position or rank of any Suspect shall not relieve such person of criminal responsibility or mitigate punishment'.

50. *Prosecutor* v. *Furundžija,* case No. ICTY-95-17/1, 10 December 1998, at para. 140, 38 *ILM* (1999) at p. 346.

51. International Law Association, 'Final Report on the exercise of universal jurisdiction in respect of gross human rights offences' (2000) at p. 13.

and that terrorism

> 'ne relève pas des exceptions au principe de l'immunité de jurisdiction des chefs d'Etat étrangers en excercice'

implies that there might exist an exception to the immunities before national courts for international crimes, on the basis of international law. The fact that the *Quaddafi* case concerned an incumbent Head of State and not an incumbent Minister for Foreign Affairs should not make a difference. Actually, the Court itself assimilates in its judgment the position of a Minister with that of a Head of State with regard to the immunity issue.[52]

Furthermore, the Rome Statute of the International Criminal Court (ICC Statute) might be particularly relevant.[53] Pursuant to Article 27(2) of the ICC Statute, immunities or special procedural rules which may attach to the official capacity of a person, whether under national or international law, shall not bar the Court from exercising its jurisdiction over such a person. Thus, although it is clear that a claim of immunity before the ICC is not possible, it is not clear what this provision means for prosecutions before national courts. It is unlikely, however, that it would imply an obligation to exclude the application of immunities before national courts. Nevertheless, in light of the complementary principle and the purpose of the Statute – namely, putting an end to impunity for the perpetrators of the crimes involved – it could be submitted that, by ratifying the ICC Statute, states implicitly agree to forego the right to invoke immunity for their officials before the domestic courts of other State Parties for the crimes covered by the ICC Statute.[54] Any other interpretation would create the risk that an official would escape trial. Hence, if he or she enjoys immunity at the national level, it is not unlikely that the ICC will have to declare the case inadmissible according to Article 17 of the ICC Statute, which states that a case is inadmissible where it 'has been investigated by a State which has jurisdiction over it and the State has decided not to prosecute the person concerned, unless the decision resulted from the unwillingness or inability of the State genuinely to prosecute'. From paragraphs 2 and 3 of this Article it can be inferred that it is rather unlikely that an investigation which is ended because of a bona fide determination that there is immunity falls under the scope of unwillingness or inability. It must be granted, though, that this situation could be avoided if the ICC would opt for a broad and flexible interpretation of the aforementioned concepts.

In sum, it is submitted that the Court in its judgment fails to place the issue in the broader context of international criminal law and the undeniable developments in this area. In essence, the Court has considered the importance of the prosecution of

---

52. *Arrest Warrant* case, at para. 53.

53. See on this De Smet and Naert, loc. cit. n. 6; see also Ongena and Van Daele, 'De zaak COBE voor het Internationaal Gerechtshof: gaat onze Wet Oorlogsmisdaden te ver?', 2 *Tijdschrift voor Strafrecht* (2001) pp. 178 at 191.

54. See David, loc. cit. n. 38, and Ongena and Van Daele, ibid., at pp. 191-192.

international crimes that are of concern to the international community as a whole to be inferior to the importance of an unhindered conduct of international relations. It thereby regrettably ignores the fact that since 1945 the international community has increasingly evolved towards an international legal order in which the traditional limits on criminal prosecution are no longer applicable with regard to the most serious international crimes and in which individual criminal responsibility increasingly gains the upper hand over immunity. The Court's approach has rightly been criticized by several judges[55] and regretted by prominent scholars[56] and NGOs.[57]

2.3 Does immunity not mean impunity?

In its judgment, the Court takes great pains to stress that 'immunity from jurisdiction enjoyed by incumbent Ministers for Foreign Affairs does not mean that they enjoy impunity'[58] since the immunities do not prohibit criminal prosecution in certain circumstances. It supports this view by stating, in paragraph 61 of the judgment, that Ministers for Foreign Affairs can still be prosecuted for their acts in their own countries or in foreign countries if the state which they represent or have represented waives their immunity. The Court adds that former Ministers for Foreign affairs no longer enjoy immunities for acts committed prior or subsequent to their period of office or for acts committed during that period of office in a private capacity. Finally, they can be prosecuted before international criminal courts where these have jurisdiction.

With all due respect, it can seriously be questioned whether the circumstances described in paragraph 61 have any practical relevance.

In the first place, trial by the home country's courts or a waiver of immunity by the home country seems unrealistic, especially in the case of international crimes, since those crimes are typically committed with the knowledge or involvement of that state. In her dissenting opinion, Judge ad hoc Van den Wyngaert rightly points out that, ironically enough, the *Yerodia* case itself constitutes an illustration hereof.[59]

Furthermore, prosecution by international courts does not constitute a decisive solution. The few international criminal tribunals in operation at the time of the Court's judgment have a very specific scope of jurisdiction, and the jurisdiction of the International Criminal Court is subject to several constraints.

Finally, the Court observes that former Ministers for Foreign Affairs can be brought before a court of another state for 'acts committed prior or subsequent to his or her period of office, as well as in respect of acts committed during that period

55. *Arrest Warrant* case, Dissenting Opinion Judge ad hoc Van den Wyngaert, at para. 27; *Arrest Warrant* case, Joint Opinion, at para. 75.

56. Cassese, loc. cit. n. 17, at pp. 874-875.

57. J. Lobe, 'International Court ruling seen as major setback on impunity', *Inter Press Service*, 15 February 2002 (available at http://www.commondreams.org/headlines02/0215-04.htm).

58. *Arrest Warrant* case, at para. 60.

59. *Arrest Warrant* case, Dissenting Opinion Judge ad hoc Van den Wyngaert, at para. 35.

of office in a private capacity'.[60] This is probably the most controversial statement of the whole judgement. Whether former Ministers can be prosecuted for international crimes committed during their period of office thus depends, according to the Court, on the question whether such international crimes can ever be qualified as 'private acts' rather than as 'official acts'. Unfortunately, the Court does not answer this crucial question. In legal writings it has often been argued that international crimes such as genocide, crimes against humanity and war crimes can never be part of the official functions, and therefore cannot be considered as official acts.[61] In the *Pinochet* case, this view was taken by several Lords.[62] This argument, however, is not waterproof since it ignores the sad reality that in most cases those crimes are precisely committed by or with the support of high-ranking officials as part of a state's policy, and thus can fall within the scope of official acts.[63] In a strict reading, the Court's view could confront us with the peculiar and unacceptable fact that precisely the most serious crimes would not be subject to prosecution even after a person has ceased to hold office, and that immunity would indeed lead to impunity. Therefore, we cannot but regret that the Court used the ambiguous and controversial criterion of 'official/private acts' instead of recognizing an exception to the granting of immunities to former Ministers in case of international crimes.[64] Moreover, the argument of the importance of the unhindered conduct of international relations - the main reason, according to the Court in its judgment, to grant immunities - can no longer be invoked in the case of former Ministers. Finally, it is interesting to note that four of the Judges, while voting with the majority, express serious reservations concerning this paragraph.[65]

3. THE ISSUE OF UNIVERSAL JURISDICTION

The Court decided not to address the issue of universal jurisdiction. It thereby missed a great opportunity to clarify a very controversial but increasingly important issue of international law. It justified this decision by reference to the request of both parties to limit its decision to the question of immunity. Although

60. Ibid., Judgement, at para. 61.

61. See e.g., A. Bianchi, 'State immunity to violations of human rights', 46 *Austrian JPIL* (1994) at p. 229, cited in *Arrest Warrant* case, Joint Opinion, at para. 85; D. Sarooshi, 'The Statute of the International Criminal Court', 48 *ICLQ* (1999) pp. 387 at 392.

62. Lord Browne-Wilkinson and Lord Hutton in *Regina* v. *Bartle and the Commissioner for the Metropolis and others*, ex parte *Pinochet*, 38 *ILM* (1999) [Pinochet III].

63. Bothe, loc. cit. n. 23, at p. 262; Lord Goff of Chievely in Pinochet III, ibid., and Naert, op. cit. n. 17.

64. Compare the resolution of the Institut de droit international on the immunities of Heads of State and Government, drawing a distinction between serving Heads of State and Government and former Heads of State and Government in respect of immunities for international crimes (Lady Hazel Fox, loc. cit. n. 26, at p. 120).

65. *Arrest Warrant* case, Joint opinion, at para. 78; ibid., Dissenting Opinion Judge Al-Khasawneh, at paras. 5-8; and ibid., Dissenting Opinion Judge ad hoc Van den Wyngaert, at paras. 34-38.

the Congo claimed that Article 7 of the Law, granting universal jurisdiction *in absentia* to the national courts, and the arrest warrant issued on the basis of that provision, breached international law, this claim cannot be found in its final submissions. Therefore, Belgium argued, herein followed by the Court, that according to the *non ultra petita* rule, the Court was precluded to rule on this issue. This argumentation is not entirely convincing, however. Although the *non ultra petita* rule indeed prevented the Court from ruling on the matter in the operative part of its judgment, it did not preclude it from addressing certain aspects of it as part of its reasoning. Why the Court did not do so is hard to understand, especially since the Court itself stated that it would be no more than logical that the question of immunities should be addressed only once the question of jurisdiction had been determined.[66]

The real reason may be that the judges were very much divided on this controversial issue. No fewer than ten judges found it necessary to address it in a separate or dissenting opinion, and although most of them were of the view that the Court should have ruled on the issue of jurisdiction, they did not agree on the way that the Court should have pronounced itself.

Judge ad hoc Van den Wyngaert, for example, favoured universal jurisdiction even *in absentia* over genocide, crimes against humanity and war crimes.[67] Judges Higgins, Kooijmans and Buergenthal seemed to accept that universal jurisdiction *in absentia* for the most heinous international crimes is permitted under international law, provided certain safeguards are met:[68] (i) the exercise of universal jurisdiction may in no way infringe the inviolability or immunity of the person involved; (ii) the national state of the accused person should first have the opportunity to act upon the charges concerned; and (iii) charges based on universal jurisdiction may only be brought by a prosecutor who acts in full independence. Judge Koroma likewise seemed to be in favour of universal jurisdiction, but remained silent on the modalities.[69] Judges Rezek[70] and Ranjeva,[71] on the other hand, accepted universal jurisdiction over some international crimes but rejected universal jurisdiction *in absentia*. Judge ad hoc Bula Bula also took a stand against universal jurisdiction *in absentia*.[72] President Guillaume stated that universal jurisdiction *in absentia* is unknown to international law. In his view, the exceptional cases in which an international convention provides for universal jurisdiction apply only if the offender is present on the territory.[73] Judge Oda, finally, limited his view to a reference to the existing uncertainty on the issue in contemporary international law.[74]

66. Ibid., at para. 46.
67. Ibid., Dissenting Opinion Judge ad hoc Van den Wyngaert, at paras. 48-67.
68. Ibid., Joint Opinion, at para. 59.
69. Ibid., Separate Opinion Judge Koroma, at paras. 7-9.
70. Ibid., Individual Opinion Judge Rezek, at paras. 4 -10.
71. Ibid., Declaration Judge Ranjeva, at paras. 5-11.
72. Ibid., Individual Opinion Judge ad hoc Bula Bula, at para. 74.
73. Ibid., Separate Opinion President Guillaume, at paras. 4 -17.
74. Ibid., Dissenting Opinion Judge Oda, at para. 12.

In sum, although most judges seemed to recognise the admissibility of universal jurisdiction under international law, it remains uncertain how far states are allowed to go in this respect. In this respect, the Court's judgment is, again, a sadly missed opportunity.

4. THE IMPACT OF THE ICJ'S JUDGMENT ON THE LAW AND THE CURRENT PROCEEDINGS BASED ON THE LAW

According to Article 59 of the Court's Statute, a decision of the Court has no binding force except between the parties and in respect of that particular case. So, theoretically, the only legal consequences flowing from the decision of the Court in this case were the cancelling of the arrest warrant against Yerodia by Belgium[75] and the forwarding of the judgement by Belgium to those to whom the warrant was circulated.

It goes without saying, however, that in practice the impact of the Court's judgment as a precedent or leading case with regard to the issue of immunities is much broader than the mere withdrawal of this particular arrest warrant. The Court's decision will seriously affect the way Belgium and other states deal with the issue of immunities in pending and future cases.

First of all, an amendment of the Law seems inevitable. Article 5(3) of the Law, recognizing no immunities attached to official capacities, needs to be amended. How far should the amendment go? It is clear that it should at least make clear that incumbent Ministers for Foreign Affairs enjoy immunity from criminal jurisdiction and inviolability before the Belgian courts. Uncertainties remain, however: should the respect for immunity go as far as to prohibit the mere opening of a criminal investigation or any act of investigation? How to apply the reasoning of the Court to other cabinet ministers and to other persons enjoying an international immunity, such as diplomats and officials of international organizations?[76]

As far as the latter question is concerned, it is not unlikely that the judgment, although strictly speaking concerning only Ministers for Foreign Affairs, will have an impact on the way the international community deals more generally with immunities of other 'high officials'. The general tone of the judgment gives the impression that the Court would be reluctant to accept any exception to the rule of absolute immunity of other high officials.[77] Judge ad hoc Van den Wyngaert warned in this regard that the Court, by recognizing immunities to incumbent Foreign Ministers, might have opened the door to 'other sorts of abuse'.[78]

---

75. Belga (Official Belgian Press Agency), 'Yerodia: KI oordeelt klacht onontvankelijk', 16 April 2002, available at http://www.belga.be/.

76. As to the latter, some guidance can be found in the Court's 1999 *Opinion on Difference Relating to Immunity from Legal Process of a Special Rapporteur of the Commission on Human Rights*, available at http://www.icj-cij.org/.

77. See *Arrest Warrant* case, at paras. 51 and 53-55. See also D'Aspremont Lynden and Dopagne, loc. cit. n. 38, at p. 285; J. Verhoeven, loc. cit. n. 22, at p. 21.

78. *Arrest Warrant* case, Dissenting Opinion Judge ad hoc Van den Wyngaert, at para. 87.

Those ambiguities and considerations might explain the rather general and pragmatic approach of a recent legislative proposal of some Belgian senators to amend Article 5(3).[79] This proposal maintains the rule that immunities attached to an official position in principle do not affect the application of the Law but subjects it to 'the limitations laid down in international law'.[80]

On the basis of the judgment, no amendment of the provision on universal jurisdiction in the Law is required. However, for practical and political reasons an amendment would be appropriate.[81]

It may be interesting in this regard to point out that the Brussels Court of Appeal in three recent judgments, respectively, in the cases of *Yerodia*,[82] *Sharon*[83] and *Gbagbo*,[84] decided, based on a Belgian provision of criminal procedure,[85] in favour of conditional universal jurisdiction: only if the alleged perpetrator can be found on Belgian territory can a criminal prosecution take place in Belgium. It is remarkable that, in the *Sharon* case in particular, the Court of Appeal did not declare the prosecution inadmissible because of Sharon's immunity as Prime Minister, as the Attorney General had suggested based on the Court's judgment.[86] A possible explanation for this approach could be that this case could be distinguished from the *Yerodia* case as the investigation against Sharon is based on genocide, and not

---

79. Legislative proposal amending the Law of 16 June 1993 concerning the grave breaches of international humanitarian law, 18 July 2002, Senate, 2-1256/1.

80. See on this proposal J. Wouters and H. Panken, 'Waar naartoe met de genocidewet?', *Rechtskundig Weekblad* (2002-2003) pp. 241, at 253-255.

81. See on this De Smet and Naert, loc. cit. n. 6.

82. Cour d'appel de Bruxelles, 16 April 2002, reproduced in Wouters and Panken, op. cit. n. 6, p. 317. In this case the Brussels Court of Appeal decided on the admissibility of the prosecution in Belgium of Yerodia for violations of international humanitarian law that he allegedly committed in 1998 (see also *supra*). The Brussels Court of Appeal declared the prosecution inadmissable because Yerodia was not present on Belgian territory. See also B. Spriet,'Genocidewet vereist aanwezigheid verdachte niet', 50 *Juristenkrant* (2002) p. 15. See the critical consideration of this judgment in J. Wouters and H. Panken, "Waar naartoe met de Genocidewet?", *Rechtskundig Weekblad* (2002) pp. 241, at 249-250. The judgment has meanwhile been quashed, on procedural grounds, by the Belgian Supreme Court in a judgment of 20 November 2002, not yet published.

83. Cour d'appel de Bruxelles, 26 June 2002, reproduced in Wouters and Panken, op. cit. n. 6, p. 323. This case dealt with the admissibility of the prosecution in Belgium of the present Prime Minister of Israel, Ariel Sharon, for acts of genocide, crimes against humanity and war crimes that he allegedly committed during to the 1982 killings in the Sabra and Chatila refugee camps (see on this case Amnesty International, supra n. 38).

84. Cour d'Appel de Bruxelles, 26 June 2002, not yet published. This case dealt with the admissibility of the prosecution against Laurent Gbagbo, president of the Ivory Coast for crimes against humanity that he allegedly committed in October and December 2000. Again, the prosecution was declared inadmissible because the alleged perpetrator could not be found on Belgian territory.

85. The Court of Appeal based its decision on Art. 12 of the Preliminary Title of the Code of Criminal Procdedure of 1878. This article states that the crimes envisaged in the article can only be prosecuted in Belgium when the accused is present in Belgium (with the exception of those cases specifically mentioned in the article). According to the recent judgments, this article, as a common rule of criminal procedure, also applies to the crimes envisaged in the Act since the Act does not expressly deviate from it.

86. Openbaar Ministerie roept immuniteit Sharon in, *De Standaard online*, 15 May 2002, available at http:// www.destandaard.be.

on war crimes or crimes against humanity. This difference might have its importance. Indeed, the argument of an exception to immunity before national courts is even stronger in case of genocide, because it is based on an international convention. A combined reading of Articles IV and VI of the 1948 Genocide Convention shows us that no immunity can be invoked before the national courts of the state where the genocide took place. However, legal doctrine, national legislation and the case law of the Court[87] have affirmed that, as a rule of customary international law, the latter article has a universal character. It is submitted, therefore, that no immunity can be invoked before national courts in case of genocide.[88]

It must be said, however, that the approach chosen by the Brussels Court of Appeal will have a negative effect on a larger number of cases than the 'immunity-based approach' since it affects not only the admissibility of complaints against a person enjoying immunity, but also more generally the admissibility of any other complaint based on the Law wherein the alleged perpetrator cannot be found in Belgium.[89] This interpretation of the Brussels Court of Appeal is, however, subject to appeals before Belgium's Supreme Court. Meanwhile, two legislative initiatives were taken in this regard.[90]

5. CONCLUSION

Although it is not yet possible to assess the full implications of the judgment, we can already make some general observations.

First of all, it is clear that the judgment will have a tremendous impact on the future possibilities for national judges to prosecute incumbent Ministers for Foreign Affairs and probably also senior officials. The judgment makes it 'clear' that incumbent Ministers for Foreign Affairs are, under customary international law, entitled to 'full' immunity of criminal jurisdiction and inviolability before the national courts of other states, both for acts performed in an 'official capacity' and in a 'private capacity'. No exception to this rule is accepted for international crimes. The Court thus favours the unhindered conduct of international relations above the interest the international community has in the prosecution of international crimes. But there is more. The Court's judgment can unfortunately also be read to the effect that persons may still be immune for prosecution for international crimes after ceasing their ministerial post. Such an ambiguity, even if not deliberately created, is simply unacceptable. To this it should be added that, although strictly speaking the judgment only deals with Ministers for Foreign Affairs, it will

87. International Court of Justice, *ICJ Rep.* (1996) pp. 595 at 616, para. 31.

88. Amnesty International, *supra* n. 38, at p. 14.

89. So the prosecution against Amos Yaron, an ex-general who was not entitled to any immunities, was declared inadmissible because he could not be found in Belgium.

90. Legislative proposal amending the Law of 16 June 1993 concerning the grave breaches of international humanitarian law, 18 July 2002, Senate, 2-1256/1 and Legislative proposal interpreting Art. 7 paragraph of the Law of 16 June 1993 concerning the grave breaches of international humanitarian law, 18 July 2002, Senate, 2-1255/1, both available at http://www.senaat.be/home/home.html.

probably be applied more broadly. In a worst case scenario, the door to impunity for a great number of 'officials', even for the most heinous crimes, may have been opened rather than closed, in spite of the Court's specifications in paragraphs 60 and 61 of the judgment.

Why the Court decided not to address the question of universal jurisdiction is hard to understand. Here again, the Court missed a great opportunity to end the uncertainty that exists in this regard. For all these reasons it may be said that the Court took a rather conservative stand in its judgment, which fails to reflect important developments that have taken place in international (criminal) law during the last decades. It is, in this and other respects, anything but a forward-looking judgment.

THE CONFERENCE OF HIGH CONTRACTING PARTIES TO THE FOURTH GENEVA CONVENTION[1]

Matthew Happold[2]

1. THE ORIGINS OF THE CONFERENCE

On 5 December 2001, a conference of High Contracting Parties to the Fourth Geneva Convention concerning the application of international humanitarian law in the occupied Palestinian territories, including East Jerusalem, took place in Geneva.

The meeting of the Conference was the culmination of a long political process. Since the 1967 Six Day War, Israel has been in occupation of the West Bank, East Jerusalem and the Gaza Strip (hereafter, the Occupied Territories).[3] Israel acknowledges that it is in occupation of the West Bank and the Gaza Strip (although not of East Jerusalem, which it has purportedly annexed), but claims that the Fourth Geneva Convention Relative to the Protection of Civilian Persons in Time of War[4] is not applicable to its activities as occupier. Other states have disagreed. By Resolution 681 of 2 December 1990 on the situation in the territories occupied by Israel, the Security Council decided, *inter alia*, to request the Secretary-General, 'in cooperation with the International Committee of the Red Cross, to develop further the idea ... of convening a meeting of the high Contracting Parties to the [Fourth] Geneva Convention to discuss possible measures that might be taken by them under the Convention'. The Secretary-General duly reported[5] but the proposal never materialised.[6] A number of states considered the holding of such a meeting inappropriate and inopportune.

---

2. Lecturer in Law, University of Nottingham. I am grateful to Robert Cryer for his comments on a draft of this article. The usual disclaimer applies.

3. For background, the most recent histories are B. Morris, *Righteous Victims: A History of the Zionist Arab Conflict 1881-1999* (London, John Murray 2000);Y. Sayigh, *Armed Struggle and the Search for State: The Palestinian National Struggle 1949-1993* (Oxford, OUP 1999), and A. Shlaim, *The Iron Wall: Israel and the Arab World* (London, Allen Lane 2000).

4. 75 *UNTS* 297 (1950).

5. SC Doc. 22472 of 9 April 1991.

6. See H.-P. Gasser, 'Ensuring Respect for the Geneva Conventions and Protocols: The Role of Third States and the United Nations', in H. Fox and M.A. Meyer, eds., *Armed Conflict and the New Law Volume II; Ensuring Compliance* (London, BIICL 1993) at p. 43.

The idea of convening such a conference did not, however, go away. Since 1997 the United Nations General Assembly has been in periodic emergency special session in relation to Israel's activities in the Occupied Territories.[7] On a number of occasions[8] the General Assembly recommended that the High Contracting Parties to the Fourth Geneva Convention convene a conference on measures to enforce the Convention in the Occupied Territories. By Resolution ES-10/6 of 9 February 1999, the General Assembly[9] reiterated its recommendation and further recommended that the conference be convened on 15 July 1999 in Geneva.

The Conference duly took place and reaffirmed the applicability of the Fourth Geneva Convention to the Occupied Territories, but was adjourned on the understanding that it would convene again the light of consultations on the development of the humanitarian situation in the field. It did so '[t]aking into consideration the improved atmosphere in the Middle East'.[10] Nineteen ninety-nine had seen the defeat of Benjamin Netanyahu (Likud) by Ehud Barak (Labour) in the Israeli elections in May, the formation of a new, Labour-led coalition government, and the revival of the Israeli-Palestinian peace process.[11] September 1999 saw the signing of the Sharm el-Sheikh Memorandum. However, the peace process broke down in 2000-1, with the failure of the Israeli-Palestinian negotiations at Camp David and Taba,[12] and the election of Ariel Sharon (Likud) as Israeli prime minister. Renewed violence culminated in the Israeli army's invasion of areas of the West Bank under the control of Palestinian Authority in April 2002.

---

7. Under the 'Uniting for Peace' resolution (GA Res. 377(V)), an emergency special session can be convened within 24 hours. The tenth special session was convened upon the request of the Arab Group of States, following the beginning of construction of a new settlement at Har Homa/Jabal Abu Ghneim and the failure of the Security Council, due to the US veto, to adopt a resolution calling on Israel to cease building.

8. Starting with GA Res. ES-10/3 of 15 July 1997. Resolution ES-10/3 requested the Secretary-General to present a report on the matter within three months. The Secretary-General then requested Switzerland, as depositary, to provide him with the necessary information. Switzerland duly circulated a note verbale to the High Contracting Parties to the Convention, requesting their views. Most responses received were broadly in favour of the convening of a conference. See the Report of the Secretary-General submitted in accordance with GA Res. ES-10/3, UN Docs. A/ES-10/16, 14 October 1997, and A/ES-10/16/Add.1, 10 November 1997. GA Res. ES-10/4 of 13 November 1997 consequently reiterated the General Assembly's recommendation and requested Switzerland to undertake the necessary steps, including the convening of a meeting of experts, to follow up on the recommendation, with a target date not later than the end of February 1998. GA Res. ES-10/5 of 17 March 1998 extended the target date for the convening of the meeting of experts until the end of April 1998. The Expert Meeting on the Fourth Geneva Convention was eventually held in Geneva on 27-28 October 1998.

9. By a vote of 115 in favour, two against and five abstentions.

10. Statement, Conference of High Contracting Parties to the Fourth Geneva Convention, Geneva, 15 July 1999.

11. For discussion and analysis, see G.R. Watson, *The Oslo Accords: International Law and the Israeli-Palestinian Peace Agreements* (Oxford, OUP 2000).

12. See H. Agha and R. Malley, 'Camp David: The Tragedy of Errors', *New York Review of Books* (9 August 2001); B. Morris, 'Camp David and After: An Exchange (1. An Interview with Ehud Barak)', *New York Review of Books* (13 June 2002); and H. Agha and R. Malley, 'Camp David and After: An Exchange (2. A Reply to Ehud Barak)', *New York Review of Books* (13 June 2002).

Following the resumption of violence resulting from Mr Sharon's pre-election visit to the Temple Mount/Al-Haram al-Sharif on 28 September 2000, General Assembly Resolution ES-10/7 of 20 October 2000 invited Switzerland, as the depositary of the Fourth Geneva Convention, 'to consult on the development of the humanitarian situation in the field, in accordance with the statement adopted on 15 July 1999 by the ... Conference of High Contracting Parties to the Convention'. In response to this invitation, Switzerland engaged in extensive negotiations and consultations culminating in the reconvening of the Conference.

2. THE CONFERENCE OF HIGH CONTRACTING PARTIES

The conference, which was hosted by the Swiss Federal Department of Foreign Affairs (the DFA), was attended by 122 participants, 114 of which were High Contracting Parties to the Convention and the remaining eight other participants and observers. Very substantial informal consultations had taken place before the conference and a declaration for adoption by the conference had been discussed and drafted. The conference itself was merely the occasion for the formal adoption of an already agreed statement.

The conference itself took place *in camera*. It was chaired by Ambassador Peter Maurer, Head of the Political Affairs Division 'Human Security' of the DFA. Following an opening statement by the Chair, the participants heard from Mr François Bugnion, Director of International Law and Communications, the International Committee of the Red Cross; Mrs Mary Robinson, the UN High Commissioner for Human Rights, and Mr Peter Hanson, Commissioner-General of the United Nations Relief and Works Agency for Palestinian Refugees in the Near East (UNRWA). The Conference was also addressed by the representatives of a number of the High Contracting Parties: Jordan, on behalf of the Arab League; Belgium on behalf of the European Union and others; South Africa, on behalf of the Non-Aligned Movement; Malaysia, on behalf of the Organisation of the Islamic Conference; China; Canada, from the western countries and others, and Russia, from the countries of Eastern and Central Europe. The speeches having been concluded, the Conference adopted a Declaration reaffirming the applicability of the Fourth Geneva Convention to the Occupied Territories. The Declaration having been adopted, the Conference was closed.

3. REACTIONS TO THE CONFERENCE

Three states boycotted the conference: Israel, the United States of America and Australia.[13]

---

13. Most of the other non-attending states did not have permanent missions in Geneva.

The United States' attitude to the conference can be seen from the statement of Mr C. David Welsh, then Assistant Secretary for International Organisation Affairs before the US House of Representatives International Relations Committee in July 1999.[14] In respect of General Assembly Resolution ES-10/6 and the decision to call a meeting of the parties to the Fourth Geneva Convention, Mr Welsh stated:

> 'The US voted against this resolution. We have worked strenuously in the days since its adoption – up to and including today – to cancel or delay this ill-conceived conference. We strongly oppose convening this conference on legal and policy grounds. We have conveyed these objections to a number of other governments at the highest levels. President Clinton has raised this issue personally with the presidents of Switzerland and France. Secretary Albright has had a number of conversations with her counterpart ministers to underscore the approaches we have made in capitals and with other UN delegations. We have also addressed this issue with senior Palestinian and other Arab leaders. We have informed Switzerland (in its role as depositary of the Convention) and others that the US would not attend the conference.'

The US policy objection to the convening of the conference was stated to be that it would have a negative effect on the Israeli-Palestinian peace process, in particular in the light of the recent election of a new Israeli government. The legal objection was that the Fourth Geneva Convention did not contain any provision for such a meeting of the High Contracting Parties. Mr Welsh stated that the Convention did contain certain provisions regarding enforcement;[15] *a contrario*, what was not included was excluded. He also stated that the establishment of such a mechanism was specifically rejected during the negotiations of Additional Protocol I to the Geneva Conventions. Consequently, Mr Welsh argued: 'The negotiating record demonstrates clearly that the High Contracting Parties discussed and rejected precisely this sort of conference.' The attitude of the Clinton Administration was maintained by the Bush Administration.

Israel's objections to the conference were on similar grounds.[16] Reacting to the convening of the conference, an Israeli Foreign Ministry spokesperson stated that: 'There was no legal basis in the Convention for the holding of such a conference, which could have no positive effect and might undermine the delicate situation in

---

14. C. David Welsh, Assistant Secretary for International Organisation Affairs, US Department of State, Testimony Before the House International Relations Committee, Washington, DC, 14 July 1999. Available at <www.state.gov/www/policy_remarks/1999/990714_welsh_un-israel.html> (visited 11 December 2001).

15. He cited Arts. 12 (conciliation procedure) and 149 (enquiry procedure).

16. As were Australia's. See its response to the Secretary-General's note verbale of 14 May 1997, in which Australia stated that it had abstained on GA Res. ES-10/2 because it did not consider it would advance the Middle East peace process: Report of the Secretary-General submitted in accordance with GA Res. ES-10/2, UN Doc. A/ES-10/6, 26 June 1997. See also United Nations General Assembly 54th Session, Item 43: the Situation in the Middle East, Statement by HE Ms Penny Wensley, Ambassador and Permanent Representative, 30 November 1999, which stated that Australia was 'concerned about the dangers of politicisation of one of the most effective humanitarian instruments the international community has been able to devise'.

the region.'[17] The spokesperson did not, however, go into further detail about why the Convention did not permit such a conference.

4. THE CONFERENCE AND THE LAW OF MILITARY OCCUPATION

The Israeli position regarding the inapplicability of the Fourth Geneva Convention to its conduct as occupier of the Occupied Territories has remained consistent throughout the duration of its occupation.[18] The *locus classicus* of its position is in a 1970 article by the then-Israeli Attorney-General Meir Shamgar.[19] According to Shamgar:

> 'Territory conquered does not always become occupied territory to which the rules of the Fourth Convention apply ... The whole idea of the restriction of military government powers is based on the assumption that there has been a sovereign who was ousted and that he had been a legitimate sovereign.'[20]

Neither Egypt, in respect of the Gaza Strip, nor Jordan, in respect of the West Bank, was the legitimate sovereign of those territories. Both areas had been part of the British mandate of Palestine. From 1948 Egypt held the Gaza Strip under military occupation. Although Jordan purported to annex the West Bank in 1950, its annexation was recognised by only two states: the United Kingdom and Pakistan. In actual fact, Jordan was in military occupation from 1948. In particular, Israel never recognised the rights of Egypt and Jordan to the territories occupied by them until 1967.[21]

The Israeli position is, consequently, based upon the wording of the second paragraph of Article 2 of the Fourth Geneva Convention. The first paragraph provides that the Convention shall apply in situations of armed conflict. Paragraph two continues that: 'The Convention shall also apply to all cases of partial or total occupation of the territory of a High Contracting Party'. The West Bank and Gaza Strip not being territory belonging to any of the parties to the Convention, the Convention does not apply. Only the relevant provisions of the Hague Regula-

---

17. Israel's reaction to the convening of the High Contracting Parties to the Fourth Geneva Convention (Communicated by the Foreign Ministry Spokesperson, 5 December 2001). Available on <www.israel-mfa.gov.il/mfa/go.asp?MFAH0kv10> (visited 11 December 2001).

18. For a full examination of the official Israeli view, see A. Roberts, 'Prolonged Military Occupation: The Israeli Occupied Territories 1967-1988', in E. Playfair, ed., *International Law and the Administration of Occupied Territories: Two Decades of Israeli Occupation of the West Bank and Gaza Strip* (Oxford, Clarendon Press 1992) at pp. 44-49.

19. M. Shamgar, 'The Observance of International Law in the Administered Territories', 1 *Israel YB HR* (1971) p. 262. See also Y. Blum, 'The Missing Reversioner: Reflections on the Status of Judea and Samaria', 3 *Israel LR* (1968) p. 279.

20. Ibid., at p. 263.

21. Ibid., pp. 263-265.

tions,[22] having been incorporated into customary international law, are applicable.[23] Israel asserts, however, that although the Fourth Geneva Convention is not applicable *de jure*, it nevertheless acts *de facto* in accordance with the 'humanitarian provisions' of the Convention.[24]

The Israeli position differs, however, from the view held by other states and the vast majority of commentators.[25] As Adam Roberts has said: 'a remarkable degree of unanimity prevails on this matter'.[26] Within the United Nations, both the General Assembly and the Security Council have consistently taken the view that the Fourth Geneva Convention applies to the Occupied Territories. Indeed, since 1975 Israel has completely lacked positive support within the General Assembly. And, although the United States has abstained from supporting such resolutions, on other occasions it has stated that it considers that the Convention applies.[27] The International Committee of the Red Cross has also taken the position that the Convention applies.

The Israeli view has been criticised on a number of grounds. The general view is that the second paragraph of Article 2 of the Convention is subordinate to the first. That is, the Convention applies in 'all cases of declared war or of any other armed conflict which may arise between two or more of the High Contracting Parties'. Article 2 then has to be read in conjunction with Article 6, which sets out when the application of the Convention begins and ends.

> The present Convention shall apply from the outset of any conflict or occupation mentioned in Article 2.
>
> ...
>
> In the case of occupied territory, the application of the present convention shall cease one year after the general close of military operations; however, the Occupying Power shall be bound, for the duration of the occupation, to the extent that such Power exercises the functions of government in such territory, by the provisions of the following Articles of the present Convention: 1 to 12, 27, 29 to 34, 47, 49, 51, 52, 53, 59, 61 to 77, 143.

---

22. Regulations Respecting the Laws and Customs of War on Land annexed to the 1907 Hague Convention IV Respecting the Laws and Customs of War on Land, UKTS 9 (1910). The Convention is widely viewed as being reflective of customary international law. See, in particular, *Trial of the Major War Criminals before the International Military Tribunal*, Nuremberg 22 (1948) at 497. Indeed, Israel not being a party to the Convention, its provisions could only apply as part of customary law.

23. See *Ayub* v. *Minister of Defence*, 33(2) *Piskei Din* 113 (Supreme Court of Israel), summarised and partly translated in 9 *Israel YB HR* (1979) p. 337.

24. Op. cit. n. 19, at p. 266.

25. For commentary, see Roberts and other contributors in Playfair, op. cit. n. 18; Y. Dinstein, 'The International law of Belligerent Occupation and Human Rights', 8 *Israel YB HR* (1978) and N. Bar-Yaacov, 'The Applicability of the Laws of War to Judea and Samaria (the West Bank) and the Gaza Strip', 24 *Israel LR* (1990) p. 5.

26. Loc. cit. n. 18, at p. 52.

27. See for example, letter from State Department Legal Adviser concerning the legality of Israeli settlements in the Occupied Territories, 21 April 1978, reproduced in 17 *ILM* (1978) p. 777.

In other words, the Israeli occupation having commenced during a period of armed conflict (the Six Day War), at the least the provisions of the Convention listed in Article 6 continue to apply regardless of the status of the territories occupied for as long as Israel continues its occupation.[28] The listed provisions are mainly about the treatment of protected persons, that is, those inhabitants of the occupied territory who are not nationals of the occupying state.[29] By contrast, the older Hague Regulations concentrate on the protection of state rather than individual interests. Fundamentally, the Israeli view is overly state-centred. It emphasises the ousted sovereign's reversionary rights over the protections afforded by the Convention for the population of the occupied territory. The conclusion must be that Israel has advocated such a position because there is no such reversioner, whereas there is a large and militant Palestinian population living under occupation.[30]

5. THE LEGAL STATUS OF THE DECLARATION

The Conference reiterated the common understanding of the applicability of the Fourth Geneva Convention to the Occupied Territories. Paragraph 3 of the Declaration states that:

> Taking into account Art. 1 of the Fourth Geneva Convention of 1949 and bearing in mind the United Nations' General Assembly resolution ES-10/7, the participating High Contracting Parties reaffirm the applicability of the Convention to the Occupied Palestinian Territory, including East Jerusalem and reiterate the need for full respect for the provisions of the said Convention to that Territory. Through the present Declaration, they recall in particular the respective obligations under the Convention of all High Contracting Parties, of the parties to the conflict and of the State of Israel as the Occupying Power.[31]

The Declaration also 'reaffirmed' the illegality of Israeli settlements in the Occupied Territories.[32] However, with that rather uncontentious exception, the Declaration did not explicitly condemn Israeli activities in the Occupied Territories, restricting itself to general exhortations directed not only at Israeli as the occupying power, but also to 'the parties to the conflict'. Nor did it outline any

---

28. Although it might be asked, particularly in the light of recent events, whether there has in fact been a 'general close of military operations'. Roberts, however, considers the 'one year after' provision as having been effectively rescinded. See loc. cit. n. 18, at p. 55.

29. See Art. 4 (definition of protected persons), GC IV.

30. Although Israel must be given credit for having admitted that it is in occupation of the West Bank and the Gaza Trip. The tendency in the post-war period has been for occupying states to deny they are in occupation. See E. Benvenisti, *The International Law of Occupation* (Princeton N.J., Princeton University Press 1993) at p. 107.

31. Conference of High Contracting Parties to the Fourth Geneva Convention, Geneva, 5 December 2001, Declaration (paragraph references omitted).

32. Ibid., para. 12.

concrete measures to ensure respect for the Fourth Geneva Convention in the Occupied Territories in future. This was a disappointment to a number of states and NGOs.[33]

But what force, if any, does the Declaration have? Here, it might be thought, the provisions of the Vienna Convention on the Law of Treaties[34] on treaty interpretation are of relevance. The basic rule is that a treaty is to be interpreted 'in good faith in accordance with the ordinary meaning to be given to the terms of the treaty in their context and in the light of its object and purpose'.[35] In addition, however, Article 31(3) provides that:

> There shall be taken into account, together with the context:
> (a) any subsequent agreement between the parties regarding the interpretation of the treaty or the application of its provisions;
> (b) any subsequent practice in the application of the treaty which establishes the agreement of the parties regarding its interpretation.

Article 31(3)(a) refers to subsequent agreements rather than subsequent treaties. The parties to a treaty can always modify it by an amending treaty, so the provision would be meaningless if it only referred to treaties. As Anthony Aust states: 'The agreement can take various forms, including a decision adopted by a meeting of the parties, provided the purpose is clear.'[36] Little attention has, however, been paid to the scope of Article 31(3)(a), as such agreements are uncommon. As Sir Ian Sinclair has stated: 'it is rarely that one comes across subsequent agreements between the parties bearing upon the interpretation of a treaty which they have concluded'.[37] Looking at the work of the various commentators on the law of treaties, it can be seen, firstly, that they view the issue as one arising between parties to bilateral treaties, and, secondly, that the presumption on which their comments are based is that such agreements require the consent of both parties to the treaty.[38] This latter point, however, would seem to apply with equal force to

33. See for example, Amnesty International, 'Israeli: Respect of Fourth Geneva Convention must be ensured by High Contracting parties meeting in Geneva', AI Index MDE 15/108/2001, 4 December 2001: 'Reaffirmation of the principles defined for the protection of civilian populations in time of war is an important move but it is not enough'.

34. 1115 *UNTS* 331 (1969).

35. Ibid., Art. 31(1).

36. A. Aust, *Modern Treaty Law and Practice* (Cambridge, CUP 2000) p. 191. See also, M. Kamil Yasseen, 'L'interprétation des traités d'après la convention de Vienne sur le droit des traités', 151 *Recueil des cours* (1976-III) pp. 1 at p. 45. Yasseen states that it is unnecessary that the interpretative agreement take the same form as the treaty; it can be in simplified form, by an exchange of notes, or by concordant oral declarations.

37. I. Sinclair, *The Vienna Convention on the Law of Treaties*, 2nd edn. (Manchester, MUP 1984) p. 137. For a possible explanation for this, see Yasseen, ibid., at p. 44.

38. See Sinclair, ibid., p. 136; Lord McNair, *The Law of Treaties* (Oxford, Clarendon Press 1961) pp. 427-429; P. Reuter, *Introduction to the Law of Treaties*, transl. J. Mico and P. Haggenmacher, 2nd edn. (London, Kegan Paul 1995) pp. 96-97; and T.O. Elias, *The Modern Law of Treaties* (Dobbs Ferry, Oceana 1974) pp. 75-76.

multilateral treaties. Such was the view of Professor Yasseen, chair of the drafting committee at the Vienna Conference, who stated that:

> 'Un accord interprétatif d'un traité est *res inter alios acta* à l'égard de toutes les parties à ce traité qui n'ont pas accepté cet accord. Ce n'est que l'application d'un principle général. Mais cela n'empéche pas que l'accord interprétatif produise ses effets dans les relations de ceux qui l'ont conclu. Dans un différend qui n'implique que ceux-ci seulement ou certains d'entre eux, une jurisdiction internationale n'hesiterait pas, a notre sens, à appliquer cet accord. L'application *inter se* d'un accord interprétatif ne semble soumis à aucune restriction.'[39]

In other words, parties to a treaty will only be bound by an interpretative agreement if in addition to being parties to the original treaty they are parties also to the subsequent agreement. The same applies with respect to Article 31(3)(b). For subsequent practice to fall within the scope of the provision it must be of a particular form: concordant, common and consistent.[40] The commentators are agreed that although not all parties should have engaged in the practice, all must have accepted it.[41] The practice must evidence, in Yasseen's words, a tacit agreement between (all) the parties to the treaty.[42]

In the instant case, it cannot be said that the purpose of the Conference was unclear. However, not all of the parties to the Convention participated in the Conference. It might be argued that the Conference was open to all and that parties that did not attend choose not to do so. Such arguments are unconvincing. Had Israel, the USA and Australia attended, it can be presumed that they would have voted against the Declaration. Could it then have been argued that they would have been bound by the Declaration and, if so, how? If it cannot, then how does their absence affect matters? The requirement of consent is a basic principle of international law; it cannot lightly be presumed to have been discarded.[43]

This, however, is not to say that the Declaration wholly lacks legal effect. Article 31(3)(b) of the Vienna Convention only refers to a specific form of subsequent practice. Subsequent practice not falling within its terms can be utilised as a supplementary means of interpretation under Article 32 of the Convention.[44]

39. Loc. cit. n. 36, at p. 46.

40. Yasseen, loc. cit. n. 36, p. 48.

41. See Yasseen, loc. cit. n. 36 pp. 48-52; Sinclair, op. cit. n. 37, at pp. 137-38; Elias, op. cit. n. 38, at p. 76; and Aust, op. cit. n. 36, at p. 195. See also *Legal Consequences for States of the Continued Presence of South Africa in Namibia (South West Africa) notwithstanding Security Council Resolution 276 (1970), ICJ Rep.* (1971) pp. 16 at 22; and the *United States-United Kingdom Arbitration concerning Heathrow Airport User Charges*, 102 *ILR* (1992) 216, at p. 353, in which the tribunal referred to 'consensual subsequent practice' by the parties.

42. Yasseen, loc. cit. n. 36 at p. 48.

43. The same view was taken by Gasser when discussing the Security Council's 1990 proposal. See Gasser, loc. cit. n. 4, at p. 43.

44. See Yasseen, loc. cit. n. 36, pp. 52 and 79-80. NcNair, writing before the adoption of the Vienna Convention, would seem to agree: see op. cit. n. 38, at p. 431. For McNair, such practice,

Recourse may be had to supplementary means of interpretation, *inter alia*, to determine the meaning when the interpretation according to Article 31 leaves the meaning ambiguous or obscure. Such might be thought to be the situation with regard to the scope of the Fourth Geneva Convention, given that neither side's interpretation lacks textual support.

Such a view gains some support from a series of articles written by Sir Gerald Fitzmaurice on the law and procedure of the International Court of Justice.[45] For Fitzmaurice, subsequent practice was evidence of what a treaty meant. As the International Court of Justice said in the *South-West Africa* case: 'Interpretations placed upon legal instruments by the parties to them, though not conclusive as to their meaning, have considerable probative value when they contain a recognition by a party of their own obligations under an instrument.'[46]

Nor did Fitzmaurice consider that such practice had always to be unanimous. As he wrote: 'It is, of course, axiomatic that the conduct in question must have been that of both or all – or, in the case of general multilateral conventions, of the great majority of the parties, and not merely of one.'[47]

The Fourth Geneva Convention is a general multilateral treaty; it is open to accession by all states and has some 188 parties. However, the reason Fitzmaurice considered subsequent practice a useful aid to treaty interpretation was that he thought conduct a more reliable guide to states' intentions and purposes than mere verbal or paper assertions such as those found in the *travaux préparatoires* to a treaty.[48] The Declaration is precisely such an assertion. It is submitted, however, that one should not be too dogmatic in this regard. With regard to the formation of customary international law, it is generally agreed that declarations and other statements can amount to state practice.[49] There seems no reason why such an approach should not be taken with regard to treaty interpretation. The real issue is simply what weight should be given to the particular practice.

The Declaration says nothing that has not been said previously in any of a number of General Assembly resolutions. A distinction might be drawn, however, between the practice of states acting as members of the United Nations and acting as High Contracting Parties to the Fourth Geneva Convention. It was as the latter that they met and issued the Declaration. The Declaration reflects the vast majority of the parties to the Convention's understanding of its application and, indeed, its

---

although relevant evidence, cannot be conclusive. Aust, however, does not include subsequent practice in his list of other supplementary means of interpretation: see op. cit. n. 36, at pp. 200-201.

45. G.G. Fitzmaurice, 'The Law and Procedure of the International Court of Justice: Treaty Interpretation and Certain Other Treaty Points', 28 *BYIL* (1951) p. 1; G. Fitzmaurice, 'The Law and Procedure of the International Court of Justice, 1951-54: General Principles, and Sources of Law', 30 *BYIL* (1953) p. 1, and G. Fitzmaurice,' The Law and Procedure of the International Court of Justice, 1951-54: Treaty Interpretation and Other Treaty Points', 34 *BYIL* (1957) p. 203. The articles, of course, predate the Vienna Convention.

46. *International Status of South-West Africa, ICJ Rep.* (1950) p. 128, at pp. 135-136.

47. Fitzmaurice (1957) op. cit. n. 47, at p. 223.

48. Ibid.

49. See in particular, M. Akehurst, 'Custom as a Source of International Law', 47 *BYIL* (1974-75) pp. 1 at pp. 4-9.

interpretation. As shown above, whether the Fourth Geneva Convention is applicable to the Occupied Territories is a consequence of how its provisions are interpreted. The issue is one of law, not of fact. And, although the Declaration was made following the crystallisation of the dispute as to the interpretation of the Fourth Geneva Convention, which would generally reduce its evidential weight, it is difficult to see it as a self-serving statement. It can hardly be said that the majority of states participating in the meeting had any material interest in the application of the Convention in the Occupied Territories.[50]

In addition, two out of the three non-attenders have, in other contexts, stated that the Convention does apply to the Occupied Territories.[51] Their absence, it appears, was for other reasons: their belief that the Conference could not be legally convened; that Israel should not be singled out as being in breach of the Convention, and that such action would only hinder resolution of the underlying dispute. Accordingly, the Declaration can be said to be highly persuasive evidence as to the proper interpretation of the scope of the Fourth Geneva Convention and its application to the Occupied Territories.

6. THE CONFERENCE AND THE OBLIGATION TO ENSURE RESPECT FOR INTERNATIONAL HUMANITARIAN LAW

Common Article 1 of the Geneva Conventions provides that: 'The High Contracting Parties undertake to respect and to ensure respect for the present Convention in all circumstances.' For a number of years there has been discussion as to the extent of States' obligations under Common Article 1, in particular as to the breath of the obligation 'to ensure respect ... in all circumstances'.

By the obligation 'to ensure respect' was originally meant simply that Contracting Parties to the Geneva Conventions had to take especial measures to ensure compliance with the Conventions by all persons under their authority. It is not enough to have ratified the conventions and incorporated them into domestic law; it is also necessary to ensure their dissemination among the armed forces and, indeed, the population generally, and to construct and maintain effective mechanisms for their enforcement. However, as early as the 1950s, arguments developed that the obligation went further. Pictet's *Commentary* stated that:

> 'The use of the words "and to ensure respect" was ... deliberate: they were intended to emphasise and strengthen the responsibility of the Contracting Parties. ... It follows, therefore, that in the event of a Power failing to fulfil its obligations, the other

50. Their interest was solely a legal one, that of ensuring that other parties apply the Convention.

51. In respect of the USA, see *supra* n. 27. Australia has on a number of occasions voted for General Assembly resolutions reaffirming the applicability of the Fourth Geneva Convention to the Occupied Territories.

Contracting Parties (neutral, allied or enemy) may, and should, endeavour to bring it back to an attitude of respect for the Convention.'[52]

This view has been followed and expanded by a number of commentators.[53] It has been argued that the provision means that Contracting States not party to a conflict between other Contracting States have an obligation to attempt to ensure those latter states' compliance with the Geneva Conventions, through diplomatic means, retorsion or even reprisals. This is the favoured interpretation of the provision by the International Red Cross/Crescent Movement. It has not, however, been without its doubters. Professor Adam Roberts, for example, has pointed out that such an interpretation has no basis in the negotiating history of the Geneva Conventions.[54]

The content of Common Article 1 and the obligation to 'ensure respect' was addressed by the International Court of Justice in the *Nicaragua* case.[55] Although excluded from ruling on the USA's compliance with the Geneva Conventions directly, due to the US multilateral treaties reservation, the Court found that Common Article 1 reflected customary international law. It stated that:

'The Court considers that there is an obligation on the United States Government, in the terms of Article 1 of the Geneva conventions, to "respect" the Conventions and even "to ensure respect" for them "in all circumstances", since such an obligation does not derive only from the Conventions themselves, but from the general principles of humanitarian law to which the Conventions merely give specific expression. The United States is thus under an obligation not to encourage persons or groups engaged in the conflict in Nicaragua to act in violation of the provisions of Article 3 common to the four 1944 Geneva Conventions.'[56]

---

52. J. Pictet, ed., *Commentary on the Geneva Conventions of 12 August 1949* (Geneva, International Committee of the Red Cross 1952-59) Vol. I, at p. 226.

53. See L. Condorelli and L. Boisson de Chazournes, 'Quelques remarques á propos de l'obligation des Etats de "respecter et faire respecter" le droit international humanitaire "en toutes circonstances"', in Ch. Swinarski, ed., *Studies and Essays on International Humanitarian and Red Cross Principles in Honour of Jean Pictet* (Geneva ICRC 1984); N. Levrat, 'Les conséquences de l'engagement pris par les Hautes parties contractantes de 'fair respecter' les Conventions humanitaires', in F. Kalshoven and Y. Sandoz, eds., *Implementation of International Humanitarian Law* (Dordrecht, Nijhoff 1989); H-P. Gasser, loc. cit. n. 4; U. Palwankar, 'Measures Available to States for Fulfilling Their Obligation to Ensure Respect for International Humanitarian Law', *IRRC* No. 298 (1994) p. 9; and L. Boisson de Chazournes and Luigi Condorelli, 'Common Article 1 of the Geneva Conventions Revisited: Protecting Collective Interests', *IRRC* No. 837 (2000) p. 67.

54. A. Roberts, 'The Laws of War: Problems of Implementation in Contemporary Conflicts', in *Law in Humanitarian Crises* (European Commission, Luxembourg, OOPEC 1995) at pp. 31-32. It may, however, be doubted whether the *travaux préparatoires* of a multilateral treaty negotiated between 58 states over 50 years ago should prevail over the subsequent practice of the far larger number of parties to the treaty.

55. *Case Concerning Military and Paramilitary Activities in and Against Nicaragua* (Nicaragua v. USA), Merits, *ICJ Rep.* (1986) p. 14.

56. Ibid., at p. 104. The Court also considered common Article 3 to reflect customary international law.

However, these comments were made in the context of the publication and dissemination of a CIA manual on psychological guerrilla warfare which recommended the use by insurgents of a variety of acts contrary to Common Article 3. It was the distribution of this manual to the Contras at a time when, at the least, the United States was aware of allegations that they were violating international humanitarian law that was the basis for the Court's ruling that the US had breached its international obligations.[57] In the circumstances, the Court's comments can only be read as providing that Common Article 1 requires that a state does not encourage or incite other persons to breach international humanitarian law. It does not include any positive obligation to ensure that such persons do not do so.

Even some of the advocates of an expansive reading of Common Article 1 admit that their preferred interpretation lacks firm support in State practice. As Hans-Peter Gasser wrote in 1993:

> 'It is difficult to draw conclusions from the practice of governments ... and to prove it with hard evidence. The reasons are obvious when we refer to confidential transactions between governments ... Although no clear evidence is available, we have reason to believe that governments actually do act in support of better respect for humanitarian law by states parties to an armed conflict, confidentially and on a bilateral level.'[58]

Developments since show that states do indeed make such interventions, although there are no indications that they do so because they consider themselves required to act in such a manner.[59] Accordingly, it can be said the obligation to 'ensure respect' permits (but does not oblige) states to attempt by diplomatic means to ensure other states respect international humanitarian law. Such actions do not amount to illegal interference into other states' internal affairs. There seems little evidence, however, to support the view that the obligation permits states not party to a conflict to use (non-forcible) reprisals to ensure compliance with the Conventions.[60] And arguments that Common Article 1 permits forcible intervention to repress violations of international humanitarian law are even less sustainable.

If states are entitled by individual diplomatic *démarche* to attempt to ensure other states respect the Geneva Conventions, there seems no reason why they should not be able to do so collectively. What one state can do alone, a number of

57. Ibid., at p. 120.

58. Gasser, loc. cit. n. 4, at p. 31.

59. Gasser, ibid., p. 32.

60. It is noteworthy, for example, that in 1998, when suspending flights by Yugoslav carriers to the United Kingdom in response to the activities of the Yugoslav security forces in Kosovo, the UK did not provide any legal justification for doing so without giving the twelve months notice required under the 1959 UK/Yugoslavia Air Services Agreement. The decision to do so was simply said to be on moral and political grounds. See letter of Mr Robin Cook, Secretary of State for Foreign and Commonwealth Affairs, to the Chairman of the House of Commons Foreign Affairs Committee, dated 30 November 1998, reproduced in G. Marston, 'United Kingdom Materials on International Law 1999', 70 *BYIL* (1999) pp. 368 at 555-556. The United Kingdom, as a party to the Geneva Conventions, has an obligation to 'ensure respect' for Common Article 3, which is applicable in internal armed conflicts.

states can do together.[61] Given this, the Declaration is legally unobjectionable. Indeed, taking into account the number of participating states, its issue would seem to be good evidence that Common Article 1 does permit such behaviour, particularly as the Declaration expressly states that it was adopted to 'ensure respect', as mandated by that provision, for the Fourth Geneva Convention. Certainly, no state which participated in the adoption of the Declaration can from now on complain about diplomatic representations concerning its compliance with humanitarian law. What is more contentious is whether the states subscribing to the Declaration were entitled to convene together as a meeting of High Contracting Parties to the Fourth Geneva Convention.

7. THE CONVENTION, THE CONFERENCE AND THE ROLE OF THE DEPOSITARY

One of the objections to the convening of the Conference was that there was no legal basis in the Fourth Geneva Convention for it. The Convention provides no mechanism for the convening of any type of meeting of the Contracting Parties. Additional Protocol I,[62] however, does. Article 7 provides that:

> The depository of this Protocol shall convene a meeting of the High Contracting Parties, at the request of one or more of the said Parties and upon the approval of the majority of the said Parties, to consider general problems concerning the application of the Conventions and Protocol.

The Swiss Federal Council (i.e., Switzerland) is the depositary of Additional Protocol I.[63] Article 7 cannot, however, justify Switzerland's actions in the instant case.[64] Although Article 7 purports to permit the convening of meetings to consider problems concerning the application of the 1949 Conventions, as a treaty provision it can only bind parties to the treaty. Not all States Parties to the Geneva Conventions are parties to Additional Protocol I.[65] The legal basis for the Conference must be sought elsewhere.

The Declaration itself did not specifically address the issue. It was, however, dealt with in Ambassador Maurer's opening statement. He spoke as follows.

'The legal basis of this Conference is provided by the first article of the Geneva Conventions: Common Article 1 of the Geneva Conventions states that all High Contracting Parties must not only undertake to *respect* their obligations but must

---

61. See e.g., International Military Tribunal (Nuremberg), Judgment and Sentences, 1 October 1946, reprinted in 41 *AJIL* (1947) pp. 172 at 216.

62. Protocol Additional to the Geneva Conventions of 12 August 1949, and Relating to the Protection of Victims of International Armed Conflicts (Protocol I), 1125 *UNTS* 3 (1979).

63. Art. 93.

64. Nor has there been any attempt to use it to do so. What has been notable is the absence of any mention of the provision.

65. In particular, in this context, neither Israel nor the USA are parties to Additional Protocol I.

also *ensure respect* for them *in all circumstances*. This is the reason why, and with the protection of civilian victims primarily in mind, we are here today.'[66]

In the Fourth Geneva Convention, as in the other three 1949 Geneva Conventions and the two 1977 Additional Protocols, Switzerland is designated as the depositary of the treaty.[67] The role of a depositary is dealt with in Articles 76 to 80 of the Vienna Convention on the Law of Treaties.[68] Article 76(2) provides, *inter alia*, that: 'The functions of a depositary of a treaty are international in character and the depositary is under an obligation to act impartially in their performance.' Article 77(1) then sets out the various functions of depositaries.[69] The list does not include the convening of meetings of the parties to the treaty. From the wording of the *chapeau* it might be thought that such a function has to be expressly conferred on the depositary by the treaty itself. However, perhaps the better reading is simply that the list of functions is not exhaustive. Nevertheless, the Vienna Convention cannot be seen to support the proposition that depositaries, in general, have the authority to convene meetings of the parties to treaties.

Discussing the earlier Security Council proposal that a meeting of the High Contracting Parties to the Fourth Geneva Convention be convened, Gasser stated that the United Nations Secretary-General (from whom the idea originated) must have made his proposal on the basis that either the Security Council or he himself had the competence to convene such a conference. Gasser found no reasons not to endorse this position.[70] It is difficult, however, to see on what basis he came to this conclusion. In any case, the Conference was not convened on such a basis. The operative paragraph of Resolution ES-10/6 stated that the General Assembly:

---

66. Conference of the High Contracting Parties to the Fourth Geneva Convention, Geneva, 5 December 2001, Opening Statement by the Chair read by Ambassador Peter Maurer (emphasis and underlining in the original).

67. Although the term itself is not used: see Arts. 150, 152 and 156-159.

68. For commentary, see Aust, op. cit. n. 36, at pp. 261-274.

69. '1. The functions of a depositary, unless otherwise provided in the treaty or agreed by the contracting States, comprise in particular:
(a) keeping custody of the original text of the treaty and of any full powers delivered to the depositary;
(b) preparing certified copies of the original text and preparing any further text of the treaty in such additional languages as may be required by the treaty and transmitting them to the parties and the States entitled to become parties to the treaty;
(c) receiving any signatures to the treaty and receiving and keeping custody of any instruments, notifications and communications relating to it;
(d) examining whether the signature or any instrument, notification or communication relating to the treaty is in due and proper form and, if need be, bringing the matter to the attention of the State in question;
(e) informing the parties and the States entitled to become parties to the treaty of the acts, notifications and communications relating to the treaty;
(f) informing the States entitled to become parties to the treaty when the number of signatures or of instruments of ratification, acceptance, approval or accession required for the entry into force of the treaty has been received or deposited;
(g) registering the treaty with the Secretariat of the United Nations;
(h) performing the functions specified in other provisions of the present Convention.'

70. H-P. Gasser, loc. cit. n. 4, at p. 43.

> *Reiterates* its recommendation that the High Contracting Parties to the Fourth Geneva Convention convene a conference on measures to enforce the Convention in the Occupied Palestinian Territory, including Jerusalem, and to ensure respect thereof in accordance with common Article 1, …

The General Assembly merely recommended the convening of a conference. It did not purport to convene the conference itself. And, as in the Conference Declaration, convening the conference was stated to be a measure in fulfilment of the Contracting Parties' obligations under Common Article 1.

Switzerland, as depositary, convened the conference in 1999, but only after extensive consultations with the High Contracting Parties and having determined that a majority of them were in favour of it doing so. Similarly, it only reconvened the conference in 2001 after General Assembly Resolution ES-10/7 invited it to do so and after similarly extensive negotiations and consultations. There seems to be no rule that states parties to a treaty cannot meet together to discuss the application and interpretation of the treaty if they agree to do so,[71] subject, of course, to the proviso that no State Party has to attend and that any agreement reached is not binding on states which do not consent to its adoption. The conclusion must be that the Conference, like the Declaration, was an expression of what the participating states considered to be their obligation to 'ensure respect' for the Convention. The widespread participation in the Conference is strong evidence for such an interpretation.

The US objections[72] miss the point. International law is a largely permissive system. Provided the Convention does not prohibit a conference of High Contracting Parties, it is difficult to see why one cannot be convened if the parties want to do so. Given that, as has already been shown, acts of the Conference cannot bind non-attenders, whether it is a meeting 'of High Contracting Parties' or not is simply an issue of semantics.[73]

8. CONCLUSION

Discussion of the political implications of the Conference is beyond the scope of this note. Nevertheless, it is only stating the obvious to say that it has had no immediate effect in amending Israeli (or Palestinian) behaviour. Given this, it is perhaps the legal implications of the conference that are of more significance. The Declaration's reiteration that the Fourth Geneva Convention did apply to Israel's

---

71. In its capacity of depositary of the Geneva Conventions and their Additional Protocols, Switzerland had previously convened the 1993 International Conference for the Protection of War Victims and the 1995 Meeting of the Intergovernmental Group of Experts for the Protection of War Victims. See Th. Meron, 'The Continuing Role of Custom in the Formation of International Humanitarian Law', 90 *AJIL* (1996) pp. 238 at 244.

72. See p. 391 above.

73. And, on that level, it might be noted that the Conference was billed as being one 'of High Contracting Parties', not 'of *the* High Contracting Parties', to the Convention.

activities in the Occupied Territories was hardly novel. The convening of the Conference and the issuing of the Declaration on the basis of Common Article 1 was, and provides clarification of the extent of the obligation 'to ensure respect for the ... Convention in all circumstances'. The most cogent criticism of the Conference was that it singled out Israel as a violator of international humanitarian law when there are many other states who are equally, if not more, guilty. It is probably naïve to hope that similar conferences will be convened to discuss other notorious cases, but the Conference's expansive reading of Common Article 1 may provide support for future endeavours at the individual and regional levels to promote compliance with international humanitarian law.

THE SECOND REVIEW CONFERENCE OF THE 1980 CONVENTION ON CERTAIN CONVENTIONAL WEAPONS[1]

Robert J. Mathews[2]

1. INTRODUCTION

The 1980 Convention on Certain Conventional Weapons (CCW)[3] was opened for signature on 10 October 1980 and entered into force on 2 December 1983 (six months after the deposit of the twentieth ratification). Following several years of virtual obscurity, interest in the CCW increased in the early 1990s, partly as a consequence of greater interest in the potential of the CCW in reducing the inhumane consequences of anti-personnel landmines (APLs). This led to the convening of the First Review Conference (Revcon) in 1995/6.[4] One of the decisions taken by the first Revcon was that a second Revcon should be convened within five years to review the operation of the CCW. This indicated that for many states the CCW had come to assume a greater importance than they had accorded it during the preceding 15 years, as well as their acceptance that APLs and other weapons covered by the CCW warranted closer attention.[5] In the lead-up to the

2. Principal Fellow, Faculty of Law, University of Melbourne. The author is very grateful to Mr Todd Mercer (Department of Foreign Affairs and Trade, Canberra), Ms Sonja Litz (Department of Defence, Canberra) Professor Timothy McCormack (University of Melbourne) and Dr Peter Herby (ICRC, Geneva) for helpful comments on an earlier draft of this document, and Ms Sharon Pimm (Resource Centre, Australian Red Cross) for providing relevant documents.

3. Convention on Prohibitions or Restrictions on the Use of Certain Conventional Weapons Which May be Deemed to be Excessively Injurious or to Have Indiscriminate Effects and Protocols I-III (1980 Convention on Certain Conventional Weapons), 1342 *UNTS* 137; 19 *ILM* 1523. Opened for signature 10 October 1980, entered into force 2 December 1983.

4. Art. 8 of the CCW (Review and Amendments) specified that a Review Conference could be convened, if agreed by a majority of States Parties, to consider proposals for amendments to the CCW or for additional protocols relating to categories of other weapons. Further, if no such Conference had been convened in the first ten years following entry into force, then a Conference could be convened to review the scope and operation of the CCW.

5. Art. 8 of the Final Declaration of the first Revcon stated that 'The Conference agrees that future Review Conferences should be held more frequently, with consideration to holding a Review Conference every five years. The Conference decides, consistent with Article 8(c) to convene a further Conference ... not later than 2001, with preparatory expert meetings starting as early as 2000, as necessary'. Agreement on the five year interval between the first and second Revcon for the CCW also brought the CCW in line with a number of other arms controls treaties, including the Chemical

second Revcon, which was convened in December 2001, major issues under consideration included the scope of the CCW and Explosive Remnants of War (ERW), including cluster bombs and other forms of unexploded ordnance not covered by existing international law, and strengthened provisions relating to anti-vehicle landmines (AVMs).[6]

This report discusses developments in the relevant weapons-related issues following the first Revcon, and the various issues that were considered in the lead-up to the second Revcon. The outcomes of the second Revcon are then discussed, followed by an assessment of the current status of the CCW and consideration of the potential of the Convention to achieve its original objectives.

2. CCW-RELATED ACTIVITIES FOLLOWING THE FIRST REVIEW CONFERENCE (1995/1956)

2.1 Anti-personnel landmines

The First Revcon produced some useful improvements to Protocol II.[7] The twentieth ratification of Amended Protocol II was deposited on 3 June 1998, resulting in its entry into force on 3 December 1998. The First Annual Conference of States Parties (CSP) of Amended Protocol II was convened in Geneva from 15 to 17 December 1999, the Second CSP from 11 to 13 December 2000, and the Third on 10 December 2001. These Conferences reviewed the operation and status of Amended Protocol II,[8] which by December 2001 had 63 States Parties.

While the outcomes of the First Revcon were seen as useful by some States

---

Weapons Convention (CWC) and Comprehensive Test Ban Treaty (CTBT) (which specified five yearly intervals between Review Conferences in the treaty texts), and the Nuclear Non-Proliferation Treaty (NPT) and Biological Weapons Convention (BWC) (for which five yearly intervals between Review Conferences has become the accepted practice).

6. For a detailed discussion of the negotiation of the CCW, the first Revcon, and developments leading up to the second Revcon, see R.J. Mathews, 'The 1980 Convention on Certain Conventional Weapons: A Useful Framework Despite Earlier Disappointments', 83 *IRRC* (December 2001) pp. 991-1012. (Available at http://www.icrc.org/eng/review).

7. Protocol on Prohibitions or Restrictions on the Use of Mines, Booby-Traps and Other Devices as Amended on 3 May 1996 (1996), 35 *ILM* 1209 (Amended Protocol II to the UN Convention on Certain Conventional Weapons). Opened for signature 3 May 1996. Amended Protocol II (APII) included: the scope extended to internal armed conflicts; strengthened general humanitarian restrictions on use of APLs; bans on non-detectable APLs; bans on anti-sensing devices on APLs; enhanced rules on mine laying (e.g., long-lived mines may only be used if properly fenced, marked and monitored); stronger restrictions on use of remotely-delivered APLs (including a ban on remotely-delivering long-lived mines); and transfer restrictions.

8. These meetings were well attended and generally regarded as successful. For example, 47 of the (then) 58 States Parties participated in the Second CSP and an additional 27 states not parties to Amended Protocol II participated as observers. However, concerns were expressed at the Second CSP that only 29 of the 58 States Parties had submitted their National Annual Report in accordance with para. 4 of Art. 13 of Amended Protocol II. (See Report of the Second Annual Conference of States Parties to Amended Protocol II, CCW/AP.II/CONF.2/1, dated 3 February 2001).

Parties, the failure of the first Revcon to agree on a total prohibition of APLs caused considerable disappointment in some quarters. This led to a very strong humanitarian quest, driven by the NGO community and a number of governments, most notably Canada, which resulted in the negotiation of a disarmament treaty (the 1997 Ottawa Treaty).[9]

In the late 1990s, some states proposed that the UN Conference on Disarmament (CD) should be given a mandate to negotiate a transfer ban on APLs. This proposal was stalled because of broader problems in the CD and because many states considered that the issue of APLs was adequately addressed by the Ottawa Treaty.[10] For these reasons, and the assessment that the situation with APLs was seen to be improving (see section 5), the issue of APLs, which had been the major issue considered during the first Revcon, did not become an issue for consideration in the lead up to the second Revcon.

2.2 Blinding laser weapons

A protocol prohibiting the use of blinding laser weapons (Protocol IV) was agreed during the first formal session of the first Revcon in November 1995.[11] The twentieth ratification of Protocol IV was deposited on 30 January 1998, resulting in its entry into force on 30 July 1998. By December 2001, there were 60 States parties to Protocol IV.

2.3 Other weapons issues

In the late 1990s, the severe consequences of explosive remnants of war (including unexploded cluster bomblets) were highlighted by the ICRC. One study commissioned by the ICRC provided an overview of the high levels of civilian casualties caused by ERW after the conflict had ended, including a case study of the situation

---

9. The 1997 Ottawa Treaty was negotiated, in record time, externally to the UN-based arms control negotiation machinery. For more details see L. Maresca and S. Maslen, *The Banning of Anti-personnel Landmines: The Legal Contribution of the International Committee of the Red Cross 1955-1999*, (Cambridge, Cambridge University Press 2000). Convention on the Prohibition of the Use, Stockpiling, Production and Transfer of Anti-Personnel Mines and on Their Destruction, opened for signature 18 September 1997, 36 *ILM* p. 1507 (The Ottawa Landmines Convention) (entered into force on 1 March 1999).

10. For example, see Z. Lachowski, 'The Ban on anti-personnel mines', *SIPRI Yearbook* (1999) pp. 658-659.

11. Additional Protocol to the Convention on Prohibitions or Restrictions on the Use of Certain Conventional Weapons which may be Deemed to be Excessively Injurious or to have Indiscriminate Effects (Protocol on Blinding Laser Weapons), (Protocol IV to the 1980 Convention on Certain Conventional Weapons), 35 *ILM* 1218. Opened for signature 13 October 1995, entered into force 30 July 1998. This agreement was particularly noteworthy because it was the first time since the conclusion of the negotiation of the CCW in 1980 that a new protocol was added to the CCW, and was also unique in arms control history because the prohibition was negotiated before the weapons were actually used in battle.

in Laos.[12] Another study focussed on the situation following the Kosovo conflict. According to data collected by the ICRC, in the year following the end of the conflict in the Kosovo region, 492 people were killed or injured in unexploded ordnance accidents, with approximately one third killed or injured by APLs, one third by cluster bomb submunitions and one third by other ordnance.[13]

Major problems are also caused by anti-vehicle mines, including preventing the delivery of humanitarian assistance, limiting the movement of people and slowing the rebuilding of affected countries once conflict has ended.[14] The ICRC prepared a number of reports[15] and conducted a meeting of experts to consider these ERW issues in the lead up to the second Revcon.[16]

2.4 Timing of the second Review Conference

As discussed above, the first CCW Revcon agreed that the second Revcon would be held no later than 2001, with preparatory work beginning as early as 2000. The UN General Assembly subsequently agreed that the second Revcon would be held in December 2001, and that in the lead up to the second Revcon, Preparatory Committee sessions would be held on 14 December 2000 and from 2 to 6 April and 24 to 28 September 2001.[17]

3. PREPARATORY SESSIONS OF THE SECOND REVCON

The first session of the Preparatory Committee on 14 December 2000[18] covered mainly procedural issues, including the provisional agenda, cost estimates of the preparatory sessions and the Conference, nomination of the President, and the organisation of work of the Conference and its subsidiary bodies. The Committee also agreed to recommend that the Conference adopt the same rules of Procedure as those of the first Revcon, with emphasis that the decision-making would be by consensus.[19] The

---

12. *Submunitions and other Unexploded Ordnance: A Study: Explosive Remnants of War* (Geneva, ICRC 2000).

13. *Cluster Bombs and Landmines in Kosovo: Explosive Renmants of War* (Geneva, ICRC 2000).

14. Ibid. pp. 19-24.

15. P. Herby and A. Nuiten, 'Explosive Remnants of War: Protecting civilians through an additional protocol to the 1980 Convention on Certain Conventional Weapons', 83 *IRRC* (March 2001) pp. 195-205.

16. 'Expert Meeting on Explosive Remnants of War'. Report of meeting held on 18-19 September 2000 in Nyon, Switzerland (Geneva, ICRC 2000).

17. UN GA Res. 55/37, of 20 November 2000.

18. This meeting was chaired by Ambassador Henrik Salander of Sweden. Fifty-three States Parties participated, and six states not parties participated as observers. The ICRC participated in the work of the Committee. In addition, representatives of the ICBL attended this meeting.

19. The Committee recommended that the President of the Second Revcon make the following statement: 'With regard to Rules of Procedure, it is affirmed that, in the deliberation and negotiations relating to the Convention and its annexed Protocols, High Contracting Parties have proceeded on the basis of consensus and no decisions have been taken by vote'. (See CCW/CONF.II/PC.2, dated 6 April 2001).

Committee also decided that the second Revcon would be held in Geneva from 11 to 21 December 2001.

At the second Preparatory Committee session held in April 2001, the then-Australian Ambassador for Disarmament (Ambassador Les Luck) was appointed President-designate of the Revcon and chaired the remaining preparatory meetings and the Revcon.

A number of formal proposals were developed in the lead up to the Revcon including:

—Scope: To extend the scope of the CCW and each of its annexed protocols to include non-international armed conflicts;[20]

—Compliance-monitoring: For the whole CCW to be covered by compliance-monitoring procedures, or alternatively that amended Protocol II be covered by compliance-monitoring;[21]

—Explosive Remnants of War: A protocol for ERW, including cluster bombs and other forms of unexploded ordnance not covered by existing international law. This proposal from the ICRC included: users to be responsible for clearance; sharing technical information on munitions to facilitate clearance; users to warn civilians; and prohibition on use of submunitions against military objects co-located with civilians;[22]

—Anti-Vehicle Mines: A protocol containing provisions that all AVMs be detectable, and that remotely deliverable AVMs be self-destructing and self deactivating;[23]

—Small calibre weapons and ammunition: A protocol incorporating certain design standards for small calibre bullets to minimise the extent of wounding.[24]

Four ambassadors were appointed as Friends of the Chair to assist with consultations on various issues: Ambassador Sood of India (scope and compliance issues); Ambassador Sanders of the Netherlands (ERW); Ambassador Draganov of Bulgaria (AVM); and Ambassador Jakubowski of Poland (small calibre weapons and ammunition).[25]

In addition to the three formal sessions of the Preparatory Committee, a week of informal consultations was held in August 2001 in Geneva, and there was an active

---

20. Proposals had been provided by the ICRC, through adopting a new protocol which would extend the scope of the whole CCW (CCW/CONF.II/PC.1/WP.1) and the USA, through amendment of Article I on the Framework Convention (CCW/CONF.II/PC.1/WP.2). For details of this and other USA proposals see http://www3.itu.missions/US/CCW/.

21. There were proposals by France (Non-paper titled 'Compliance', dated 2 April 2001, presented to the Second Preparatory Committee) and USA (CCW/CONF.II/PC.1/WP.7).

22. Loc. cit. n. 15.

23. Working paper presented by Denmark, Finland, Germany, Japan, Poland, United Kingdom and USA, 'Protocol on mines other than anti-personnel mines'. (CCW/CONF.II/PC.3/WP.11).

24. Working paper presented by Switzerland, 'Restrictions on Small Calibre Ammunition which cause excessive wounding and unnecessary injuries'. (CCW/CONF.II/PC.3/WP.3).

25. It is interesting to note that these proposals were similar to some of the proposals that had first been considered during the negotiation of the CCW during the 1970s, and some of these issues were also considered at the First Revcon in 1995/6.

process of informal consultations on CCW issues in Geneva and many capitals during 2001. A number of workshops and seminars were also conducted by States Parties and the ICRC in the months preceding the second Revcon.[26]

4. THE CCW SECOND REVIEW CONFERENCE (2001)

The second Revcon of the CCW took place in Geneva from 11 to 21 December 2001.[27] Sixty-five of the 88 States Parties participated. In addition, representatives from four signatory states and 18 observer states attended, as well as representatives from the ICRC and several non-government organisations, including the International Campaign to Ban Landmines (ICBL).

4.1 **Scope**

The Revcon agreed to extend the Convention's scope so that it and all existing protocols will apply to non-international, as well as international, armed conflicts.[28] This was achieved through amendment of Article I of the framework convention. The only contentious issue was how this expanded scope would apply to future protocols, with several States Parties calling for a safeguard so that it would not automatically apply. Despite some initial resistance, in the interests of achieving consensus, these States Parties agreed to the language (developed by the USA) clarifying that the provisions of paragraphs 2 to 6 of Article I of the Convention 'shall not prejudice additional protocols adopted after 1 January 2002, which may apply, exclude or modify the scope of their application in relation to this Article'.

4.2 **Follow-up procedures**

It had become clear in the lead up to the Revcon that the other proposals, including compliance, ERW, AVMs, and small calibre bullets would not achieve consensus support at the Revcon and would require further consideration. Thus, a key issue which needed to be addressed during the Revcon was how the follow-up work would be managed.

In recognition of the potential benefits of annual formal meetings to enable States Parties to monitor follow-up activities agreed by the Revcon (as well as the demonstrated value of the Annual Conference of States Parties of Amended

26. In particular, a workshop on small calibre weapon effects was hosted by Switzerland and the Netherlands hosted a workshop on ERW.

27. The 2nd CCW Revcon followed immediately after the third annual Conference of States Parties of Amended Protocol II, which took place on 10 December 2001.

28. Indeed, it would have been difficult to argue against broadening the scope to include non-international armed conflicts, as most injuries (especially to civilians) in recent conflicts have been caused during non-international armed conflicts (for example, recent conflicts involving insurgents and rebels, and civil wars).

Protocol II in fostering closer consultation and cooperation), a number of States Parties proposed that there should be annual meetings of States Parties of the CCW.[29] However, a number of other States Parties were reluctant. As a compromise, the Revcon agreed that a meeting of States Parties would be held in December 2002, on the understanding that further meetings of States Parties (in advance of the third Revcon) could be considered if and when necessary.

The second Revcon also agreed that the third CCW Revcon would be held no later than 2006, with preparatory work beginning as early as 2005.[30]

4.3 Compliance monitoring

Following opposition from several States Parties to proposals for compliance-monitoring provisions (either for Amended Protocol II or for the CCW as a whole),[31] the Revcon decided that 'the Chairman-Designate shall undertake consultations during the intersessional period on possible options to promote compliance', and that the Chairman-Designate would submit a report on this issue to States Parties.[32]

4.4 Small calibre weapons and ammunition

There was very limited support from delegations for the specific details of the Swiss proposal on small calibre weapons, with few delegations being convinced of the technical merits of the proposal. However, there was some support for exploring the general approach proposed by the Swiss. It was eventually agreed that the Final Declaration would invite 'interested States Parties to convene experts to consider possible issues related to small calibre weapons and ammunition' and 'report on their work to the States Parties of the Convention'.[33]

---

29. Indeed, in South Africa's national statement, the Ambassador stated that 'South Africa believes that the absence of regular meetings of States Parties since entry into force of the CCW in 1983 until the First Review Conference in October 1995 created a climate of near obscurity of the CCW thereby contributing to its restricted impact' and was convinced that a decision to include annual meetings of States Parties of the CCW should be taken at the Revcon.

30. Second Review Conference of the States Parties to the CCW, Final Document, CCW/CONF.II/2, Art. 8 (Review and amendments), p. 16 (Geneva 2001).

31. It has been reported that a number of CCW States Parties from the Non-Aligned Movement (NAM) have opposed inclusion of compliance measures in the CCW because of concerns that such measures could be applied in times of armed conflicts and subject ongoing military operations to scrutiny. See M.J Matheson, 'Filling the Gaps in the Conventional Weapons Convention', *Arms Control Today* (November 2002) (available at http://www.armscontrol.org/act/2001_11/).

32. Second Review Conference of the States Parties to the CCW, Final Document, CCW/CONF.II/2,), p. 13 (Geneva 2001).

33. Ibid.

4.5 Explosive remnants of war/anti-vehicle mines

On the issues of ERW and AVMs, the Revcon agreed to establish a group of governmental experts which will meet on three occasions during 2002, for a total of five weeks.[34] The Revcon mandated the group of governmental experts to discuss ways and means of addressing the problems posed by ERW and AVMs.

The mandate with respect to ERW tasks the experts to look at a broad range of relevant issues, including: technical improvements; the adequacy of international humanitarian law; clearance of ERW; assistance; and cooperation. It specifically calls on the group of governmental experts to report to States Parties on whether to proceed with negotiating a legally-binding instrument, i.e., a new protocol dealing with particular weapons which generate ERW.

The same group of governmental experts has also been tasked to study measures which might be taken to address the humanitarian impact of mines other than anti-personnel mines, i.e., AVMs. In addition to considering USA proposals on detectability and self-destruction/self-deactivation features for remotely delivered AVMs, the broad nature of the mandate on AVMs will open the way for consideration of a range of other issues related to AVMs.[35]

The expectation of most delegations, and certainly the NGO community, was that the bulk of the expert group's time would be dedicated to consideration of ERW. The work of the expert group will culminate in the meeting of States Parties which will be held on 12-13 December 2002,[36] with the objective that the coordinators on ERW and AVMs[37] will report to the meeting on their findings.[38] The key decision of States Parties will be whether to adopt a mandate to begin negotiation of a protocol on ERW and/or AVMs.

---

34. The dates agreed for the three sessions are as follows: 20-24 May, 8-19 July or 22 July-2 August 2002, and 2-10 December 2002. (The dates for the second period will be finalised once dates for the UN Disarmament Commission are confirmed for July, so as to avoid any overlap).

35. For example, South Africa expressed the view that the group of government experts should cover issues such as AVMs with sensitive fuses or with sensitive handling devices. (CCW/CONF.II/2, p. 77). Concerns have been expressed by some developing countries that they depend to a greater degree on AVMs than developed countries, and that any further restrictions on the use of AVMs could seriously harm their security interests. See for example, 'Position of the Chinese Delegation on the Issue of Anti-Vehicle Mines', Document CCW/CONF.II/PC.3/WP.15 (presented at the Third Preparatory Committee, 24-28 September 2001).

36. This will follow immediately after the fourth Annual Conference of States Parties to Amended Protocol II, which will be held on 11 December 2002.

37. Ambassador Sood of India was appointed Chairman-Designate of the December 2002 meeting of States Parties and will oversee the inter-sessional work program, with Ambassador Sanders of the Netherlands appointed coordinator on ERW and Peter Kolarov, Deputy Permanent Representative of Bulgaria, coordinator for AVMs.

38. The general view was that the group should aim to complete its work in time to present its findings to the December 2002 meeting of States Parties. However, a small number of delegations argued that the Revcon should not set 'artificial deadlines' as there was no way of knowing how long it would take for the group to conclude its work. A number of delegations intervened to acknowledge this concern but noted that the group should at the very least be in a position to submit an interim report.

4.6 Weapons reviews

In response to proposals by Sweden and the ICRC,[39] the Final Declaration of the Revcon also urged states that do not already do so to conduct reviews of new weapons, means and methods of warfare (as specified in Article 36 of Additional Protocol I to the Geneva Conventions[40]) to ensure that they are in conformity with the rules of international humanitarian law or other applicable rules of international law.[41]

4.7 General atmosphere during the second Revcon

Overall, delegations considered that the Second CCW Revcon had been a successful conference at the end of a difficult year for multilateralism.[42] At the final session, many delegations spoke of the spirit of cooperation that had been evident throughout the conference and the role of the Australian President, the officers of the Conference and the secretariat staff in achieving these outcomes.[43]

The high level of cooperation among the States Parties during the 12 months of negotiations associated with the second Revcon was in marked contrast to the 27 months of tortuous negotiations that took place during the first Revcon. However, the issues being considered in 2001 were less controversial and there were lower expectations from the second Revcon. In particular, the issue of APLs, which was the most difficult issue addressed during the first Revcon process, was regarded as adequately covered (annual meetings of States Parties to Amended Protocol II and the Ottawa Treaty), and was not a contentious issue at the second Revcon.

---

39. ICRC, 'Ensuring Respect for the 1868 St. Petersburg Declaration Prohibiting the Use of Certain Explosive Projectiles', Document CCW/CONF.II/PC.3/WP.6 (presented at the Third Preparatory Committee, 24-28 September 2001).

40. Protocol Additional to the Geneva Convention of 12 August 1949, and Relating to the Protection of Victims of International Armed Conflict, 1125 *UNTS* 3; 16 *ILM* 1391 (Additional Protocol I) (entered into force 7 December 1978).

41. This exemplifies the link between coverage of weapons issues in Additional Protocol I of the Geneva Conventions and the CCW. The third preambular paragraph of the CCW contains a very similar objective to Art. 35 of Additional Protocol I (In any armed conflict, the right of the Parties to the conflict to choose methods or means of warfare is not unlimited. It is prohibited to employ weapons, projectiles and material and methods of warfare of a nature to cause superfluous injury or unnecessary suffering).

42. For example, the fifth Review Conference of the Biological Weapons Convention, which took place in Geneva in the three weeks prior to the CCW Revcon, was eventually suspended until November 2002 after a rather unpleasant debate. See S. Brugger, 'BWC Conference Suspended after Controversial End', *Arms Control Today* (January/February 2002). (http://www.armscontrol.org/act/2002_01-02/).

43. For example, at the closing session, the representative of Pakistan stated: 'the successful outcome of the Conference was largely due to the leadership and diplomatic skills of its President and the dedication and diligence of the Australian delegation and the secretariat'. The representative of USA 'credited the extraordinary leadership of the President and officers of the Conference with the fact that the session had been a success in many respects. It had made a lasting contribution to international humanitarian law ...'. Several other speakers, including representatives of regional groups, echoed sentiments similar to those expressed by Pakistan and USA. (See Summary Record of the Fourth Meeting, CCW/CONF.II/SR4, dated 31 December 2001).

The ICRC continued to make a substantial contribution in the lead up and during the second Revcon, playing a creative and constructive role in highlighting issues of humanitarian concern and in developing proposals.[44] The support of the ICBL for the negotiation of regulations on ERW and AVMs through the CCW was also a useful contribution.[45]

5. ASSESSMENT OF THE CCW

Before assessing the status of the CCW at the conclusion of the second Revcon, it is useful to briefly consider the evolution of the CCW since the negotiation of the Convention in the 1970s. The CCW, as agreed in 1980, was seen as a very modest achievement. Indeed, the final outcome was a major disappointment for its proponents (primarily smaller neutral European countries and developing countries), who felt that military considerations had been given much greater priority than humanitarian concerns.[46] Further disappointments were the absence of compliance-monitoring provisions in the CCW, the fact that the application of the CCW was limited to international armed conflict, and the minimal implementation-related obligations for States Parties. As a consequence, very limited attention was paid to the CCW during the 1980s. It was a neglected treaty, with many smaller developing countries considering it not worth ratifying and a number of militarily significant states not wishing to be bound by its provisions.[47] And, based on the widespread use of APLs in various conflicts in the 1980s and on the amount of suffering and devastation caused by their use, the CCW was clearly ineffective in reducing the inhumane deployment of APLs during that timeframe.

There has been considerably greater interest by the international community in the CCW since the early 1990s, resulting in the convening of the first Revcon and the second Revcon. Most of the militarily significant states which opposed the more ambitious proposals for the CCW in the 1970s have now ratified/acceded.[48]

The CCW was designed to be a dynamic treaty, with the facility to evolve in response to weapons developments, and within the changing international climate.

---

44. This was a role the ICRC had played since the 1950s. See for example, ICRC, 'Draft Rules for the Limitation of the Dangers Incurred by the Civilian Population in Time of War' (Published with commentary, Geneva 1958).

45. In the ICBL statement to the second Preparatory Meeting in April 2001, the ICBL expressed its support for the prohibition of AVMs with anti-handling devices that function like APLs, and in the ICBL statement to the final plenary of the Revcon in December 2001, the ICBL expressed support for the urgent negotiation of a new protocol on explosive remnants of war in the CCW. (Available at http://www.icbl.org/statements/2001_ccw_apr.php and http://www.icbl.org/statements/2001/137.php)

46. R.J. Mathews, 'The 1980 Convention on Certain Conventional Weapons: A Useful Framework Despite Earlier Disappointments', 83 *IRRC* (December 2001) pp. 991-1012. (Available at http://www.icrc.org/eng/review).

47. Indeed, Preambular Para. 6 of the CCW referred specifically to the importance of ratification by 'militarily significant States'.

48. However, there are still approximately 90 states that have yet to ratify or accede to the CCW, including many small developing states.

The outcomes from the first and second Revcons would suggest that this intention of the original drafters of the CCW is now 'working'. There is a changed reality with respect to the availability and use of the weapons covered by the CCW. It has become clear in recent years that the CCW is no longer regarded as a treaty primarily for the protection of civilians in developing countries, which was the view taken by a number of militarily significant states during the negotiation of the CCW in the late 1970s. For example, more recent consideration of weapons such as APLs and blinding laser weapons has resulted in recognition of the potential benefits of the CCW in protecting combatants, including those from militarily significant states, during military operations.[49] Moreover, the experience of the past 20 years, exemplified by the APL problem, is that 'inhumane' weapons are readily available and used by developing countries and various non-state groups in internal armed conflict.

Another significant outcome from the second Revcon is that the CCW has now developed an agreed pattern of Review Conferences at five yearly intervals. Likewise, there is agreement to conduct inter-sessional work and to have meetings of States Parties between the Revcons.[50] With the greater interest and respect for the CCW in recent years comes greater recognition for the role of the CCW as an instrument for the regulation of the use of specific weapons which may cause excessive injuries to combatants and indiscriminate effects to non-combatants. More states are regarding the CCW as a complement to the Ottawa Treaty, with respect to APLs, and a part of the 'tapestry of treaties', including the 1949 Geneva Conventions and their Additional Protocols, and other treaties which have been negotiated within the international humanitarian law/arms control framework.

However, despite these positive trends and developments, it is still not a straightforward task to make an assessment of the effectiveness of the CCW at the end of 2001. On the issue of reducing the inhumane effects of APLs, there have recently been encouraging reports. The ICBL 2001 annual report includes findings of decreased use of APLs, an almost complete halt in trade of APLs and fewer new

---

49. For example, in a letter sent to the US Secretary of Defense dated 31 July 1995 by 51 members of the US Congress who supported the prohibition of blinding laser weapons, it was stated: 'We dread the day when hundreds or thousands of American service men and women return home from combat to face the rest of their lives without eyesight.' (Letter to Secretary of Defense William Perry from 51 US Members of Congress, 31 July 1995. (Appendix G in 'Blinding Laser Weapons: The need to ban a cruel and inhumane weapon', Human Rights Watch Project, Vol. 7, No. 1, September 1995). This line of reasoning, that changed the US position from initially being opposed to Protocol IV on Blinding Laser Weapons to being a strong supporter at the CCW Revcon in 1995, was also echoed by eight high-ranking retired US Generals, including those who commanded in Korea, in a letter they recently sent to President Bush urging that the USA accede to the Ottawa Treaty. In their letter, the retired Generals stated that their recommendation was 'motivated by a deep concern for the welfare of the men and women of our armed services' and '... most importantly, to protect our nation's sons and daughters when we send them into harm's way'. (The letter to President Bush, dated 19 May 2001, may be viewed at http://www.banminesusa/).

50. Although there was not agreement on annual meetings of States Parties, *per se*, there was a sense that States Parties would not oppose a meeting of States Parties each year provided there were substantial issues that needed to be discussed.

APL casualties,[51] and the ICRC has also reported a significant decrease in the number of landmine casualties.[52] The extent of the contribution of the CCW to the improving situation is difficult to judge.[53] After all, membership of Amended Protocol II remains low, especially when compared to the Ottawa Treaty.[54] That said, the three Annual Conferences of States Parties to Amended Protocol II that have been held so far do appear to be playing a useful role in fostering cooperation and consultation among States Parties.[55] In the author's view, the encouraging recent developments are due to a combination of factors including: the increased membership of the CCW; the strengthened provisions in Amended Protocol II; the strong support shown by many states for the Ottawa Treaty; and the increased resources allocated to mine clearance in recent years.

The extent of adherence to the provisions of Protocols I, III and IV of the CCW is unclear.[56] The absence of concerns about compliance being expressed at the second Revcon provides some reassurance that States Parties are complying with their obligations.[57] However, the situation would be more reassuring if the CCW was amended to make it mandatory for States Parties to provide information on their relevant activities (including implementation procedures) and contained compliance-monitoring provisions.

---

51. On 12 September 2001, the ICBL released its third annual report on the global landmine situation, detailing substantial results in implementation of the Ottawa Treaty. The major findings of the 2001 report included: decreased use of APLs; a dramatic drop in production of APLs; an almost complete halt in trade of APLs; destruction of millions of stockpiled APLs; increased funding for humanitarian mine action; more land cleared of mines; and most importantly, fewer new APL casualties. (http://www.icbl.org/lm/2001/findings/).

52. For example, the ICRC recently stated that: 'Although a global assessment may be premature, statistics gathered by the ICRC and mine action organizations show that the average number of monthly casualties due to landmines and unexploded ordnance has decreased significantly in several affected countries.' (Statement by the ICRC, United Nations General Assembly, 55th Session, November 2000).

53. Although it would be reasonable to conclude that adherence by APL producers to the transfer restrictions in Amended Protocol II would be a major factor in the almost complete halt in trade of APLs.

54. It is interesting to note that 122 states have now ratified the Ottawa Treaty, whereas only 63 states have ratified Amended Protocol II (as of 31 December 2001).

55. For example, at the second annual meeting of States Parties of Amended Protocol II, Canada sought clarification of Russia's compliance with Protocol II, and Russia provided explanations to the effect that it was in full compliance with Protocol II obligations. See CCW/AP.II/CONF.1, pp. 26 and 41(Geneva, 2000).

56. With respect to Protocol IV, there have been unofficial reports that the small number of states which were developing laser blinding weapons in the mid 1990s are no longer doing so, and that the blinding laser weapon system which was being advertised in the mid 1990s is no longer available.

57. This was in contrast to the fifth Review Conference of the Convention on the Prohibition of the Development, Production and Stockpiling of Bacteriological (Biological) and Toxin Weapons and on Their Destruction, opened for signature 10 April 1972, 1015 *UNTS* 163; 11 *ILM* 109 (entered into force 26 March 1975) (Biological Weapons Convention), which took place in Geneva in the three weeks prior to the CCW Revcon. In its national statement at the BWC Revcon, the USA accused several countries of non-compliance with their BWC obligations. See S. Brugger, 'BWC Conference Suspended after Controversial End', *Arms Control Today* (Washington DC, USA) January/February 2002 (Available at http://www.armscontrol.org/act/2002_01-02/bwcjanfeb02.asp).

6. CONCLUDING COMMENTS

It is interesting to reflect on the efforts that have been expended over many years, by many states, the ICRC and various NGOs, ranging from expert group meetings to long and tortuous negotiations, in order to conclude and strengthen the Convention. Despite the earlier disappointments, the CCW is now regarded as a valuable part of the various treaties that have been negotiated within the international humanitarian law/arms control framework.

There is currently a sense of optimism that the CCW will realise the early objective of becoming an effective instrument for the regulation of the use of specific weapons which may cause excessive injuries to combatants and indiscriminate effects to non-combatants. Further, following the efforts since the early 1990s, the CCW is finally fulfilling its intended design as a dynamic treaty, with the facility to evolve in response to specific weapons developments, and within the changing international climate.

However, as a cautionary note, while the second Revcon was regarded as a success, in a very real sense, the jury is still out. At the conclusion of the Revcon, there appeared to be a strong sense of goodwill among the States Parties, and an apparent willingness to consider seriously the issue of ERWs, and to a lesser extent AVMs, with the objective of developing regulations aimed at reducing excessive injuries to combatants and indiscriminate effects to non-combatants. However, the international community will have to wait until the meeting of States Parties scheduled for December 2002 to see what can be achieved by the group of governmental experts, and in particular, whether States Parties will agree to adopt a mandate to begin negotiation of a protocol on ERW and/or AVMs.

As a final comment, it is clear that the CCW needs strengthening through greater universality, measures to encourage and monitor adherence to the provisions (including compliance-monitoring procedures), as well as coverage of other weapons by specific protocols. It is to be hoped that States Parties to the CCW will look beyond the various proposals that have been earmarked for further consideration as follow-up actions flowing from the Second Revcon, and will also adequately address the key issues of increased membership and greater respect for and adherence to the provisions of the CCW.[58] Unless these latter objectives are achieved, only limited benefit may be achieved in adding new protocols to cover other types of weapons.

---

58. This view accords with a recent statement by the ICRC, which, with reference to international humanitarian law, stated: 'The effective implementation of existing law, including the obligation to ensure its respect, is indeed the most pressing matter, rather than the development of new rules.' Statement by the ICRC, United Nations General Assembly, 53rd session, Sixth Committee, 17 November 1998.

THE CONTROL SYSTEM UNDER THE HAGUE CONVENTION FOR THE PROTECTION OF CULTURAL PROPERTY IN THE EVENT OF ARMED CONFLICT 1954 AND ITS SECOND PROTOCOL[1]

Jan Hladik[2]

This article examines the control system under the Hague Convention for the Protection of Cultural Property in the Event of Armed Conflict 1954 (the Convention) and its Second Protocol (the Protocol). It is divided into three parts. Part 1 introduces the control system and provides some examples of its implementation; Part 2 focuses on the evaluation of the control system during a recent review of the Convention; and Part 3 compares the control system under the Convention with that under the Second Protocol to the Convention.

1. THE CONTROL SYSTEM OF THE CONVENTION

The control system is set forth in Chapter VII and in the Regulations for the Execution of the Convention (the Regulations). It is based on three elements: representatives of the High Contracting Parties engaged in a conflict, Protecting Powers and Commissioners-General for Cultural Property (Commissioners-General) appointed to Parties to the conflict. In addition, there is a fourth element which is not formally included in the control system but which in reality plays a very important role: the UNESCO Secretariat.

Article 2 of the Regulations provides for the obligation of any High Contracting Party engaged in an armed conflict to which Article 18[3] of the Convention applies

2. Jan Hladik is Programme Specialist, International Standards Section, Division of Cultural Heritage, UNESCO. The author is responsible for the choice and the presentation of the facts contained in this article and for the opinions expressed therein, which are not necessarily those of UNESCO and do not commit the Organization. This article is partly based on a presentation entitled 'UNESCO's Ability to Intervene in Crises and Conflicts' made at the NATO/Partnership for Peace Seminar 'Protection of Cultural Property in the Event of Armed Conflict – a Challenge in Peace Support Operations' (Bregenz, Austria, 24-28 September 2001).

3. Art. 18 reads as follows:
'1. Apart from the provisions which shall take effect in time of peace, the present Convention shall apply in the event of declared war or of any other armed conflict which may arise between two or more of the High Contracting Parties, even if the state of war is not recognized by one or more of them.
2. The Convention shall also apply to all cases of partial or total occupation of the territory of a High Contracting Party, even if the said occupation meets with no armed resistance.

Yearbook of International Humanitarian Law
Volume 4 – 2001 – pp. 419-431

to appoint a representative for cultural property situated in its territory or, if it occupies another territory, to appoint a representative for cultural property in the occupied territory as well. The commentary on the Convention provides the reader with two cases of the appointment of such delegates: during the Cambodian conflict and in the aftermath of the Six-Day War.[4]

The second element of the control system is comprised of the delegates of Protecting Powers. Before analysing the system of Protecting Powers under the Convention, it may be helpful to provide a definition of a Protecting Power in international humanitarian law.

> 'For purposes of the Geneva Conventions on the Protection of War Victims and Protocol I of 8 April 1977 "Protecting Power" means a neutral or other State not a Party to the conflict which has been designated by a Party to the conflict and accepted by the adverse Party and has agreed to carry out the functions assigned to a Protecting Power under the Conventions and Protocol.'[5]

The institution of Protecting Powers is set forth in Articles 21 and 22 of the Convention and further developed in Chapter I of the Regulations. Their main role is to 'lend their good offices in all cases where they may deem it useful in the interest of cultural property, particularly if there is disagreement between the Parties to the conflict as to the application or interpretation of the provisions of the present Convention or the Regulations for its execution'.[6] In particular, under Article 5 of the Regulations, the delegates of the Protecting Powers take note of violations of the Convention, investigate with the approval of the Party to which they are accredited the circumstances in which they have occurred, make representations locally to secure their cessation and, if necessary, notify the Commissioner-General of such violation and keep him informed of their activities.

The system of Protecting Powers was inspired mainly by and is closely based on the relevant provisions of the four 1949 Geneva Conventions for the Protection of War Victims (Arts. 8/8/8/9). The Convention does not contain a provision on the appointment of Protecting Powers, thus leaving this issue to public international law in general.

---

3. If one of the Powers in conflict is not a Party to the present Convention, the Powers which are Parties thereto shall nevertheless remain bound by it in their mutual relations. They shall furthermore be bound by the Convention, in relation to the said Power, if the latter has declared that it accepts the provisions thereof and so long as it applies them.'
From the above text it follows that this Article is applicable only in international armed conflicts. Thus, the Regulations and the control system based on them are not applicable in non-international armed conflicts or conflicts of mixed character.

4. J. Toman, *The Protection of Cultural Property in the Event of Armed Conflict* (Commentary on the Convention for the Protection of Cultural Property in the Event of Armed Conflict and its Protocol, signed on 14 May 1954 in The Hague, and on other instruments of international law concerning such protection) (Aldershot, Dartmouth /Paris, UNESCO 1996) pp. 231-232.

5. C. Parry and J.P. Grant, *Encyclopaedic Dictionary of International Law* (New York, Oceana Publications 1986) p. 308.

6. Art. 22(1) of the Convention.

> 'In international law, the Protecting Powers may be appointed either in accordance with the Vienna Convention on Diplomatic Relations of 18 April 1961 (Article 46) or in conformity with the provisions of the Geneva Conventions and Additional Protocol I. The Protecting Power thus appointed must act in accordance with the requirements laid down in the articles of these international conventions.'[7]

The system of Protecting Powers has been applied only once since the adoption of the Convention, following the 1967 Middle East conflict. In January 1978, the Permanent Delegates to UNESCO of Egypt, Jordan, Lebanon and the Syrian Arab Republic expressed their collective desire that Switzerland assume the functions of Protecting Power, and in February 1978 the Permanent Delegate of Switzerland to UNESCO informed the Director-General of Switzerland's readiness to do so. This information was forwarded to the Permanent Delegates of the four Arab States concerned as well as to the Permanent Delegate of Israel to UNESCO. The Permanent Delegate of Israel to UNESCO informed the Secretariat in April 1978 of the decision of his government to select Switzerland to assume the functions of the Protecting Power. In May 1978, the Permanent Delegate of Switzerland to UNESCO informed the Secretariat of Switzerland's readiness to assume those functions.[8]

The third element of the control system is the institution of Commissioners-General. A Commissioner-General is a person appointed from a special international list of persons nominated by the High Contracting Parties as qualified to carry out this function. Such a list is compiled by the Director-General of UNESCO.

The Commissioner-General is selected by joint agreement between the Party to which he/she will be accredited and the Protecting Powers acting on behalf of the opposing Parties. In accordance with Article 6(1) of the Regulations, he/she must deal with all the matters referred to him/her in connection with the application of the Convention, in conjunction with the representative of the Party to which he/she is accredited and with the delegates of Protecting Powers. His/her functions include carrying out investigations, making representations to the Parties to the conflict or to their Protecting Powers and drawing up reports on the implementation of the Convention. He/she exercises the function of the Protecting Power if there is no Protecting Power. In addition, following Chapters II and III of the Regulations, the Commissioner-General plays a role in the granting of special protection and in the transport under special protection of cultural property. The latest version of the list is dated 31 March 1983. It was revised on several occasions, most recently in 1986.

---

7. Toman, op. cit. n. 4, at p. 224.

8. For detailed information concerning the designation of Protecting Powers as well as Commissioners-General, see 'Information on the Implementation of the Convention for the Protection of Cultural Property in Case of Armed Conflict', The Hague 1954, UNESCO Doc. CC/MD/41, Paris, 25 June 1979, p. 7.

As with the system of Protecting Powers, the system of Commissioners-General has been applied only once since the adoption of the Convention, following the 1967 Middle East conflict.[9] The nomination process failed because it was impossible to obtain the agreement of all the Parties to the conflict on the choice of the future Commissioner-General to be accredited to the Arab governments concerned.[10]

There are mainly two reasons for the failure of the system of Protecting Powers and Commissioners-General. Originally, the system was conceived to be of assistance during classical interstate wars lasting months or even years. However, the majority of contemporary armed conflicts do not correspond to such a profile. Second, its successful implementation depends on the agreement of all parties to the conflict, which is extremely difficult to accomplish. For this reason, in recent conflicts, such as the Middle East conflict, the Iran-Iraq war and during the break-up of the former Yugoslavia, the Director-General preferred to use the services of his personal representative(s) to conduct quiet diplomacy between the states concerned, with a view to improving the protection of cultural property.

Turning to the role of the UNESCO Secretariat in the implementation of the Convention, in case of conflict among Parties to the Convention, UNESCO's main ability to intervene for the protection of cultural property is based upon Article 23 of the Convention. This important provision allows UNESCO to take a flexible approach to providing assistance according to the nature of the conflict, its territorial and temporal scope and its specific circumstances. This approach may vary – from a letter addressed to the Permanent Delegate to UNESCO of the state(s) concerned, drawing attention to the need to protect cultural property, through the despatch of a personal representative of the Director-General to the conflict area to assess the damage to cultural property caused by armed conflict and to propose concrete ways of restoring it, to a special appeal made by the Director-General to warring Parties to comply with the provisions of the Convention.

This Article has been applied on several occasions, for example, during the evaluation of the archaeological site of the city of Tyre in Lebanon in 1982, the Iran-Iraq war, the Gulf War and the conflict in the former Yugoslavia.[11]

Article 19(3) of the Convention,[12] concerning conflicts not of an international character provides the Secretariat with the possibility of providing assistance in non-international armed conflicts. Such assistance does not affect the legal status of the parties to the conflict (Art. 19(4)). One example should be mentioned – a letter of the Director-General to the Nigerian authorities during the conflict there, dated 11 April 1968, proposing UNESCO's services under this Article. The

---

9. Ibid., p. 7

10. For the detailed information concerning the selection of the Commissioners-General, see 'Information on the Implementation of the Convention for the Protection of Cultural Property in the Event of Armed Conflict', The Hague 1954, 1989 Reports, UNESCO Doc. CC/MD-11, Paris, December 1989, p. 6.

11. Toman, op. cit. n. 4, pp. 264-267.

12. 'The United Nations Educational, Scientific and Cultural Organization may offer its services to the parties to the conflict.'

Nigerian authorities declined this offer by stating, among other things, that the Federal Military Government and its agencies had scrupulously observed the provisions of the Convention.[13]

Finally, the Director-General has one other option available: he/she may use his/her general mandate for the protection of the world's cultural property under Article 1*(2)(c)* of the UNESCO Constitution.[14] His/her actions may include public appeals, as was done in case of the destruction of Afghan cultural heritage in 2001,[15] diplomatic negotiations, or despatch of his/her personal representatives to the conflict area to prevent damage to or destruction of cultural heritage or, if such damage or destruction has already taken place, to prevent the repetition of such acts and to restore cultural heritage which may still be restored. The use of the general mandate has two main advantages: (i) it may be used in conflicts where one or more states involved are not bound by the provisions of the Convention and; (ii) when the character of the conflict is not determined and the reference to the general mandate under the UNESCO Constitution would avoid the need to refer to Article 19(3) of the Convention.

2. EVALUATION OF THE CONTROL SYSTEM DURING THE REVIEW OF THE CONVENTION

One of the issues raised at the outset of the review of the Convention in the 1990s concerned the efficiency of the control system under the Convention.[16]

The report by the Director-General on the reinforcement of UNESCO's action for the protection of the world cultural and natural heritage,[17] submitted for the 140th session of the Executive Board of UNESCO pointed out that 'the procedure for appointing Commissioners-General is complex, slow and often impracticable

---

13. 'Information on the Implementation of the Convention for the Protection of Cultural Property in the Event of Armed Conflict', The Hague 1954, 1970, UNESCO Doc. SHC/MD/6, Paris, 30 April 1970, p. 8.

14. Constitution of the United Nations Educational, Scientific and Cultural Organization, *Basic Texts* (Paris UNESCO 2000) p. 8.

15. For more detailed information concerning UNESCO's action for the protection of Afghan cultural heritage, visit http://www.unesco.org/opi2/afghan-crisis/.

16. The scope of destruction of cultural property in the last decade both in international and non-international armed conflicts and the practice of the implementation of the Convention showed certain deficiencies. For this reason, in 1991 the Secretariat undertook a review of the Convention with a view to elaborating a new supplementary legal instrument to fill in existing gaps, such as the lack of clarity in the interpretation of the clause of 'military necessity', the application of special protection and of the control system of the Convention, and the reinforcement of penal provisions, as well as the lack of an institutional body to monitor the implementation of the Convention. The review of the Convention resulted in the adoption of the Second Protocol to the Hague Convention by the March 1999 Hague Diplomatic Conference. For more detailed information on different issues raised during the review of the Convention, see J. Hladík, 'The Review Process of the 1954 Hague Convention for the Protection of Cultural Property in the Event of Armed Conflict and its Impact on International Humanitarian Law', 1 *YIHL* (1998) pp. 313-322.

17. UNESCO Doc. 140 EX/13, Paris, 4 September 1992.

in cases of limited conflict' and that 'the provision for "Assistance of UNESCO" is too weak'.[18] The Netherlands position paper on the review of the Convention[19] proposed to discuss

> '... whether UNESCO should be given greater powers of initiative and more adequate means of intervention in the event of cultural property being destroyed during an armed conflict. If, on the basis of a general evaluation, this is deemed necessary and appropriate, the development of new legal mechanisms and competences directed towards an improvement of the effectiveness of the protection and safeguarding regime must be studied. One might in this respect also consider the development of new fact-finding and new conciliation mechanisms and/or the development of some sort of institutional arrangement. Furthermore, the system of Protecting Powers ('borrowed' from the Geneva Conventions of 1949) as this has been laid down in the 1954 Convention must be reappraised in the light of a possible new role for UNESCO and/or knowledgeable non-governmental organizations like, for example, ICOMOS.'[20]

The paper went on to discuss the efficiency of the system of Protecting Powers and the adequacy of the Regulations.[21]

The Dutch proposal has considerably influenced further discussions on the advisability of establishing a supervisory body in charge of the monitoring of the implementation of a new instrument. Those discussions have resulted in the creation of a 12-member Intergovernmental Committee for the Protection of Cultural Property in the Event of Armed Conflict.

Professor Boylan, in his study of the review of the Convention,[22] also provided critical assessment of the system of Protecting Powers and Commissioners-General,[23] and stressed the importance of the practice established under Article 23 of the Convention of despatching personal representatives of the Director-General to conflict areas.[24] Professor Boylan recommended that 'in any revision of the 1954 Convention, or any Additional Protocol to it, the legal provisions and arrangements for the appointing of Commissioners-General be reviewed, in order to make these more effective',[25] and pleaded in favour of establishing an Intergovernmental Advisory Committee on the Protection of Cultural Property in the Event of Armed Conflict, modelled on the World Heritage Committee.[26]

---

18. Ibid., p. 3.
19. 'Review of the application of the Convention for the Protection of Cultural Property in the Event of Armed Conflict, (The Hague, 14 May 1954)', UNESCO Doc. 140 EX/26, Paris, 11 September 1992.
20. Ibid., p. 5. ICOMOS is the International Council on Monuments and Sites.
21. *Idem.*
22. P.J. Boylan, *Review of the Convention for the Protection of Cultural Property in the Event of Armed Conflict (The Hague Convention of 1954)*, UNESCO Doc. CLT-93/WS/12, Paris, 1993.
23. Ibid., pp. 17 and 85-88.
24. Ibid., p. 87.
25. *Idem.*
26. Ibid., p. 18.

To facilitate the review of the Convention, the Netherlands authorities convened a meeting of experts from 9 to 11 February 1994 in Lauswolt which resulted in the elaboration of the so-called Lauswolt document, a draft set of detailed legal provisions complementing the Convention. The Lauswolt document included Chapter 4 on Commissioners-General/Protecting Powers, containing only one single article, Article 13 on the *Substitute for the organization of control*, which reads as follows:

> '1. In addition to the provisions of the Convention the States Parties are invited to encourage the Director-General of UNESCO to perform the mission of control according to the Regulations for the execution of the Convention in coordination with the Committee.
> 2. The Committee may also invite the Director-General of UNESCO to fulfil those functions.'[27]

The Lauswolt document also included a chapter on Institutional Issues, which provided for the establishment of an Intergovernmental Committee and the role of the UNESCO Secretariat servicing the Committee.[28] The provisions on the Committee are close to those contained in Chapter 6 of the Second Protocol. When preparing its working paper for the first meeting of experts following the elaboration of the Lauswolt document and commenting on different provisions of that document, the UNESCO Secretariat expressed its reservations about the establishment of this Committee. In particular, the Secretariat's commentary noted three problems: political (States Parties to the Convention may be reluctant to cede their sovereignty to a body over which they may exercise only limited control), financial (the functioning of the Committee could be quite costly and would require additional financial and human resources) and operational (convening the Committee in time of crisis may require some time). In addition, the obligation to contribute to the functioning of the Committee could deter some states not yet party to the Convention from joining it.[29]

The Secretariat's working paper proposed an alternative consisting of the creation by election of an *ad hoc* Bureau during a meeting of States Parties to the Convention, held on the occasion of the session of the General Conference of UNESCO, and an advisory committee to be composed of representatives of the International Committee of Museums (ICOM), International Council on Monuments and Sites (ICOMOS) and the International Centre for the Study of the Preservation and Restoration of Cultural Property (ICCROM). The main advantage of this structure would have been its flexibility.[30]

---

27. Document 'The Second Expert meeting on the 1954 Hague Convention for the Protection of Cultural Property in the Event of Armed Conflict', Lauswolt, The Netherlands, 9-11 February 1994, p. 7.

28. Ibid., pp. 8-10.

29. Expert meeting on the 'Review of the 1954 Hague Convention for the Protection of Cultural Property in the Event of Armed Conflict – a working document prepared by the Secretariat', UNESCO Doc. CLT/94/608/1, 28 November 1994, Paris, p. 20.

30. Ibid., p. 21.

The meeting of experts reviewing the Convention, which took place in Paris in March 1997, resulted in a redrafting of the Lauswolt document. The redrafted version[31] contained two options. Option I proposed an Intergovernmental Committee assisted by several international entities: the International Committee of the Blue Shield (ICBS), a coordinating umbrella body, composed of representatives of the International Council on Archives (ICA), the International Council of Museums (ICOM), the International Council on Monuments and Sites (ICOMOS) and the International Federation of Library Associations and Institutions (IFLA), as well as by the International Centre for the Study of the Preservation and Restoration of Cultural Property (ICCROM). The Intergovernmental Committee under Option I was very close to the current version of the Committee under the relevant provisions of Chapter 6 on the Institutional Issues of the Second Protocol. Option II proposed as the alternative a Bureau of six States Parties to the Convention elected during a meeting of States Parties to the Convention, held on the occasion of the session of the General Conference of UNESCO, assisted by the ICBS and ICCROM. Neither the November-December 1994 meeting of experts, nor the second meeting of States Parties to the Convention (Paris, 13 November 1995), nor the March 1997 meeting, nor the third meeting of States Parties to the Convention (Paris, 13 November 1997) revealed any unanimous position of States Parties to the Convention with respect to a supervisory body to monitor the implementation of the Convention. The turning point was the Vienna expert meeting on the revision of the Convention. The following quote from the final report is instructive.

> 'Although several delegates spoke in favour of Option II (election of a non-permanent bureau of States Parties), most delegates were in favour of the creation of an intergovernmental committee inspired by the proposal contained in Option I of the revised Lauswolt document. A number of important concerns were expressed regarding the composition, the function and the financial implications of such a committee. It was considered that it should not have more than 12 members and that it should be based on an equitable geographical distribution. Reference was also made to the useful precedent of Article 90 (International Fact-Finding Commission) of Protocol I to the Geneva Conventions. The professional expertise of specialized international non-governmental organizations was recognized and it was unanimously felt important that their role be clearly mentioned in the text of Option I. Two particular concerns were expressed: first that the functions of the committee should be further elaborated and second that careful attention be given to financial implications in order to allow the committee to perform its functions.'[32]

31. 'Draft provisions for the revision of the 1954 Hague Convention and commentary from the UNESCO Secretariat', UNESCO Doc. CLT-97/CONF.208/2, Paris, October 1997, pp. 18-26.

32. Annex to 'Report by the Director-General on the results of the meeting of governmental experts on the revision of the Hague Convention for the Protection of Cultural Property in the Event of Armed Conflict 1954 (Vienna, 11-13 May 1998)', UNESCO Doc. 155 EX/51, Paris, 17 August 1998, p. 4.

The Preliminary Draft Second Protocol to the 1954 Hague Convention[33] contained in its Chapter 6 on Institutional Issues only Option I related to the Intergovernmental Committee. However, Article 18 on the Committee was accompanied by a footnote stating that 'UNESCO proposed an alternative institutional mechanism which would consist of a Bureau of States Parties and the Advisory bodies (International Committee of the Blue Shield and ICCROM)'.[34] The final Draft Second Protocol to the 1954 Convention for the protection of cultural property in the event of armed conflict[35] included both Options in its Chapter 6 on Institutional Issues.[36]

The Diplomatic Conference on the Second Protocol to the Convention which took place at The Hague from 15 to 26 March 1999 and resulted in the elaboration and adoption of the Second Protocol to the Convention considered both Options.[37]

> 'Discussion of Chapter 6 (Institutional issues) revealed two options for Parties to the new Protocol: an Intergovernmental Committee or a Bureau. Some doubted that whether an intergovernmental body because of its political character was the best forum for taking decisions on the protection of cultural property of importance to all humankind and preferred an impartial, expert body. Others favoured the political weight and representative character of an Intergovernmental Committee for such decisions. The financial and institutional implications for the administration of the new Protocol made others prefer a Bureau, perhaps with some simplification of its functions.'[38]

The Conference set up an informal Working Group to work on Chapter 6.

> 'This Group reported back to the Plenary that the revised text of Chapter 6 represented a compromise between the two options proposed. The Plenary meeting decided that this body should be called an intergovernmental committee. ... The Working Group also added other professional non-governmental organizations which might advise the new supervisory body.'[39]

Thus, in addition to Articles 34 and 35 of the Second Protocol on the Protecting Powers and the Conciliation Procedure, respectively, which are almost identical to Articles 21 and 22 of the Convention on the same subject, the Second Protocol contains Article 36 on Conciliation in the absence of Protecting Powers, providing

---

33. Doc. HC/1999/1, October 1998, pp. 7-10.

34. Ibid., p. 7.

35. Doc. HC/1999/1/rev. 1, February 1999.

36. Ibid., pp. 16-23.

37. For a more detailed account of the Conference, see J. Hladík, 'Diplomatic Conference on the Second Protocol to the Hague Convention for the Protection of Cultural Property in the Event of Armed Conflict, The Hague, Netherlands (15-26 March 1999)', 8 *International Journal of Cultural Property* (1999) pp. 526-529.

38. 'Diplomatic Conference on the Second Protocol to the Hague Convention for the Protection of Cultural Property in the Event of Armed Conflict (The Hague, 1-26 March 1999) – summary report', UNESCO Doc. Paris, June 1999, p. 5.

39. Ibid., p. 8.

the Director-General or the Chairperson of the Committee with additional means of settling a disagreement among the Parties. Article 36 is inspired partly by Article 11 of the First Geneva Convention.[40]

One of the most important achievements of the Second Protocol is the establishment of the 12-member Committee for the Protection of Cultural Property in the Event of Armed Conflict (the Committee) in Chapter 6 of the Second Protocol (Art. 24(1)).

The Committee meets once a year in ordinary session and, if necessary, may meet in extraordinary session (Art. 24(2)). It must reflect an equitable geographic distribution of the different regions and cultures of the world (Art. 24(3)). Its members must be selected from professionals in the field of cultural heritage, defence or international law (Art. 24(4)) by the meeting of States Parties to the Protocol (Art. 23(3)(a)). Their mandate is for four years and they are eligible for re-election only once (Art. 25(1)). However, the term of office of half of the members designated at the first election will cease at the end of the first ordinary session of the meeting of States Parties to the Protocol following that at which they were elected (Art. 25(2)).

The functions of the Committee are laid down in Article 27 on Functions, and may be summarized as follows:

—elaboration of the Guidelines of the Committee;
—granting, suspension or cancellation of enhanced protection;
—assistance in the identification of cultural property under enhanced protection;
—supervision of the implementation of the Protocol;
—consideration of reports of Parties to the Protocol and elaboration of its own report for submission to the meeting of States Parties to the Protocol; and
—consideration and distribution of international assistance and the use of the Fund for the Protection of Cultural Property in the Event of Armed Conflict.

The Committee will cooperate with international and national governmental and non-governmental organizations having objectives similar to those of the Convention and its two Protocols, and it may invite to its meetings eminent professional organizations such as the ICBS and its components, ICCROM and ICRC (Art. 27(3)).

The Committee is prevented from a possible procedural paralysis, which is important, in particular, in case of granting, suspending or cancelling enhanced protection, by Article 26(3), stipulating *expressis verbis* that the Committee's

40. The relevant part of Art. 11 of the 1949 First Geneva Convention on the Amelioration of the Condition of the Wounded and Sick in Armed Forces in the Field reads as follows: '... For this purpose, each of the Protecting Powers may, either at the invitation of one Party or on its own initiative, propose to the Parties to the Conflict a meeting of their representatives, in particular of the authorities responsible for the wounded and sick, members of medical personnel and chaplains, possibly on neutral territory suitably chosen ...' Thus, Art. 36 provides for a solution of the situation where there is no Protecting Power. If such a situation occurred under the Convention, it would be settled under Art. 9 of the Regulations.

members 'shall not participate in the voting on any decision relating to cultural property affected by an armed conflict to which they are parties'.

The new system of enhanced protection combines aspects of the special protection under the Convention[41] with criteria for listing of outstanding cultural property in the World Heritage List under the 1972 UNESCO Convention concerning the Protection of the World Cultural and Natural Heritage. To qualify for enhanced protection, three conditions must be met: the cultural property in question must be of the greatest importance for humanity; it must be protected by adequate domestic legal and administrative measures; and it may not be used for military purposes or to shield military sites. A declaration to this end must be provided by the state concerned. Enhanced protection is granted by the entry of the cultural property in question onto the List of Cultural Property under Enhanced Protection. In contrast to the system of special protection under the Convention, the new system provides for the granting of enhanced protection by the Committee. As in the case of special protection, objections to the granting of enhanced protection may be made but they must be based on one of the three criteria noted above. This prevents States Parties to the Second Protocol from making objections based purely on political animosity or mutual non-recognition, thus avoiding cases such as that of Cambodia. In 1972 it requested the entry of several sites in the Register but because of opposition of four States Parties to the Convention, which did not recognize the Government of Cambodia at that time, the entry was not made. Finally, unlike the granting of special protection, which requires unanimity of all States Parties to the Hague Convention, enhanced protection may be granted by a majority of four-fifths of members of the Committee.

41. In addition to the general protection available to all categories of cultural property listed in Art. 1 of the Convention, the Convention also provides for special protection which may be granted to three categories of property: (a) refuges intended to shelter movable cultural property in the event of armed conflict; (b) centres containing monuments; and (c) other immovable cultural property of very great importance (Art. 8(1)). The granting of special protection is essentially subject to two conditions: the cultural property in question must be situated at an adequate distance from any large industrial centre or from any important military objective constituting a vulnerable point; and secondly, such property may not be used for military purposes (Art. 8(1)(a) and 8(1)(b)). However, in case of proximity of the cultural property to an important military objective, such property may be placed under special protection if the state on whose territory the property in question is located undertakes not to use the military objective (Art. 8(5)). Special protection is not granted automatically; it is granted upon a special request of the state on whose territory the cultural property in question is situated (Art. 13(1) of the Regulations). Such a request is addressed to the Director-General of UNESCO (Art. 13(1) of the Regulations. Finally, it should be pointed out that in order to obtain special protection for its cultural property, the state requesting special protection is requested to obtain consent of all other States Parties; otherwise special protection will not be granted (Art. 14 of the Regulations).

Cultural property under special protection is listed in the *International Register of Cultural Property under Special Protection*, a special register maintained by the Director-General of UNESCO (Art. 8(6) of the Convention). To date, cultural property in three High Contracting Parties (Germany, the Holy See and the Netherlands) has been entered in the Register at the request of those states (a total number of four refuges as well as the whole of the Vatican City State).

It should be noted that the concept of special protection has never fully developed its potential, given that only three States Parties have placed five sites under special protection and the last entry in the Register took place in 1978.

Finally, the Second Protocol includes Article 33 on the Assistance of UNESCO (applicable to international armed conflicts), closely based on Article 23 of the Convention on the same subject and Article 22(7) (applicable to non-international armed conflicts) identical in its content to Article 19(3) of the Convention.

The Committee is not yet operational because, as of December 2002, the Second Protocol had not yet entered into force.[42]

3. COMPARISON OF THE CONTROL SYSTEM UNDER THE CONVENTION WITH THE NEW SYSTEM ESTABLISHED BY THE SECOND PROTOCOL TO THE CONVENTION

The adoption of the Second Protocol has created a two-tier level of protection: basic protection under the Convention for states wishing to obtain a first-level protection, and advanced protection under the Second Protocol for those states wishing to benefit from it. In this connection, it should be pointed out that the new Protocol is a complementary instrument which does not replace the original Convention *vis-à-vis* its States Parties. The original Convention is legally binding for its States Parties and is still open to non-States Parties for accession, ratification or succession. Consequently, the original control system of the Convention has not been formally abolished and may be still used in conflicts involving its States Parties.

The new system under the Second Protocol, based almost exclusively on the Committee, represents an advance because it involves its States Parties more actively in the implementation of the Protocol through the new institutional body whose principal functions were described above. Compared to the original Convention, the Committee will mainly contribute to better protection of cultural property in the event of armed conflict by two aspects: the granting of enhanced protection and the disbursement of international assistance. However, the Committee may also play the less formal role of a negotiating forum, facilitating background negotiations. This is also an important role because experience shows that background negotiations and patient dialogue are more effective (at least, at the beginning of the conflict) than trading of public accusations and finger-pointing. Finally, the existence of the Committee does not formally exclude the use of Protecting Powers in international armed conflicts for those states not wishing to entrust the negotiations to the Committee. To conclude, the new control system under the Second Protocol represents a considerable advance. It shows the willingness of the drafters of the Second Protocol to increase the protection of cultural

---

42. In conformity with Art. 43 of the Second Protocol, for entry into force, the deposition with UNESCO's Director-General of 20 instruments of ratification, acceptance, approval or accession is required. To date, seven states (Austria, Belarus, Bulgaria, Cyprus, the former Yugoslav Republic of Macedonia, Qatar and Spain) have deposited their instruments of ratification and Argentina, Azerbaijan, Libyan Arab Jamahiriya, Lithuania, Nicaragua and Panama have deposited their instruments of accession. Thus, five additional instruments of acceptance, accession, approval or ratification are needed for its entry into force.

heritage during hostilities by providing an institutional framework for such protection. Its efficiency, however, will depend on the participation of major military powers in the Second Protocol.

CORRESPONDENTS' REPORTS

A guide to state practice concerning International Humanitarian Law

CORRESPONDENTS' REPORTS [1]

A Guide to State Practice
Concerning International Humanitarian Law

1. Correspondents' Reports is compiled and edited by Avril McDonald, Managing Editor of the *YIHL*, primarily from information provided to the *YIHL* by its correspondents but also drawing on other sources. The assistance of Maria Nybondas, Anna Danieli and Jann Kleffner is very gratefully acknowledged. The section does not purport to be a fully inclusive compilation of all international humanitarian law-related developments in every state, reporting in this volume mainly developments since the beginning of 2000 until the end of 2001 that have come to the Yearbook's attention. Developments from early-2002 that are part of a sequence of events starting in 2001 or earlier are noted in brief. Readers are thus advised to consult this section in conjunction with Correspondents' Reports in volume 3. Some pre-2000 humanitarian law-related developments came to our attention after volume 3 went to press and could not be noted there. For the sake of completeness we have included them here. Reference is also included to a number of legal developments which are not strictly-speaking related to IHL but which are nonetheless interesting and relevant for our readers, in particular, relating to justice issues, jurisdictional questions, *jus ad bellum*, state security, human rights, refugee law and terrorism. Presentation of subject matter roughly follows the sequence in the Classification of Documents at pp. 645-648, with the exception that all cases are grouped together at the end of each report, followed by news of pending developments. Where citations or dates have not been provided, they were not available or obtainable. Where not otherwise specified, comments are prepared by Avril McDonald, Maria Nybondas and Anna Danieli, mainly based on reports of NGOs and IGOs and news media, *inter alia*. The *YIHL* is actively seeking correspondents, particularly in Africa, Asia and Latin America. Interested persons and anyone who is willing to contribute information should contact the Managing Editor at A.McDonald@asser.nl.

Editor's Note: The Yearbook has decided not to include information concerning signings or ratifications of treaties. This information, constantly updated and referring to over 91 IHL treaties, is provided by the ICRC at its IHL database: http://www.icrc.org. Current information regarding ratifications, as well as full texts of reservations and declarations, is also available from the UN Treaty Website at http://untreaty.un.org/.

AFGHANISTAN

Cultural Property

☛ Destruction of the Buddahs of Bamiyan, March 2001

After recapturing the town of Bamiyan from the Northern Alliance, the Taleban government announced that it would destroy all statutes, including the world famous Buddahs of Bamiyan, the world's tallest standing Buddahs, claiming that they were unislamic. The statutes were reduced to rubble during a 21-day demolition operation. Their destruction was widely condemned, including by UNESCO and the UN Secretary-General.[2]

Peace Process

☛ Agreement on provisional arrangements in Afghanistan pending the re-establishment of permanent government institutions (the 'Bonn Agreement'), UN Doc. S/2001/1154, 5 December 2001

The Bonn Agreement, signed on 5 December 2001, provided for the transfer of power in Afghanistan from Burhanuddin Rabbani, whom the UN officially recognised as the head of state,[3] to an Interim Authority, established on 22 December 2001, and set out the composition and functions of the Interim Authority. The Agreement also provided for the convening of an Emergency Loya Jirga six months following the establishment of the Interim Authority, which would elect the Transitional Authority. The Transitional Authority would rule until free and fair elections could be held no later than two years after the convening of the Emergency Loya Jirga. The Agreement also provided for the convening of a Constitutional Loya Jirga within 18 months of the establishment of the Transitional Authority in order to adopt a new constitution for Afghanistan.

The Ageement made a direct reference to international humanitarian law in part V, paragraph 2, which provided that: 'The Interim Authority and the Emergency Loya Jirga shall act in accordance with basic principles and provisions contained in international instruments on human rights and international humanitarian law to which Afghanistan is a party.'

ANGOLA[4]

POWs

☛ Implementation of the 2000 Amnesty Law

---

2. For a comprehensive index of articles on the destruction of the Buddahs of Bamiyan, go to http://www.tamu.edu/anthropology/Buddhas.html.

3. The Taleban government was never officially recognised by the UN.

4. Information provided by Dr Jose Doria, formerly Professor of International Law, Peoples' Friendship University of Russia, Moscow, currently Legal Adviser, Office of the Prosecutor, International Criminal Tribunal for the Former Yugoslavia in The Hague. The views expressed are solely those of the author and do not necessarily coincide with those of the Office of the Prosecutor or the United Nations.

Independent sources confirmed that in the first half of 2001, 'thousands of prisoners of war, including those accused of crimes against the security of the state, were released', under the terms of the November 2000 amnesty law.[5]

However, despite this, the civil war, which entered a guerrilla phase in 2000, after government forces expelled UNITA from its strongholds, continued to devastate the country. The government continued to control an estimated 90 percent of the country. There were increased attacks by UNITA forces on villages and roads, killing thousands of defenceless civilians.

JOSE DORIA

ARGENTINA[6]

Implementation and Dissemination

☛ Update of the 1968 Joint Regulation of the Laws of War [Reglamento Conjunto de Leyes de Guerra de 1968]

An expert group constituted by the Joint General Staff of the Argentine Armed Forces finished the update of the 'Joint Regulation of the Laws of War' and submitted it to the Commission for the Application of International Humanitarian Law (CADIH).[7] A pronouncement was expected by the end of 2002.

☛ National Information Office

CADIH and the Ministry of Foreign Relations started to design the National Information Office required by Articles 122-124 of the Third Geneva Convention of 1949 and Articles 136-141 of the Fourth Convention.

Pending

☛ Revision of the Penal Law to conform with the provisions of the ICC Statute

On 8 February 2001, Argentina ratified the ICC Statute without reservations. The Interministry Study Commission[8] established to analyze and to evaluate the adaptation of Argentine legislation to the Statute worked throughout 2001. Opinions were requested from NGO experts, international organizations and independent experts. Concerning IHL, the Commission considered that the crimes included in Article 8 of the Rome Statute do not encompass all the major breaches mentioned in the Geneva Conventions and Protocol I. It was decided to take advantage of the opportunity to include these crimes in the Argentine

---

5. See Report on Angola of Amnesty International, 2001 at www.ai.org. For a detailed overview of the 2000 Amnesty Law, see 3 *YIHL* (2000) pp. 411-412.

6. Information and commentaries by Professor José Alejandro Consigli, Head of the Rectorate of the Austral University, Buenos Aires, and Gabriel Pablo Valladares, Legal Advisor of the ICRC Office for Argentina, Bolivia, Brazil, Chile, Paraguay and Uruguay (Advisory Service on IHL of the International Committee of the Red Cross) and former Assistant Professor of IHL at Buenos Aires University.

7. See 3 *YIHL* (2000) p. 414.

8. See ibid., p. 413.

Penal Code. In this way, Argentina would abide by its international commitments. The Commission's report was expected in early-2002.

- Project for the modification of the Code of Military Justice, including the specific crimes that constitute major breaches of international humanitarian law. The project is now under the examination of the Defense Commission of the Deputy Chamber.

- Law on the emblem of the Red Cross[9]

- Project of Law to include some articles related to the 1997 Landmines Treaty and the 1980 Certain Conventional Weapons Convention in the Penal Law[10]

JOSÉ CONSIGLI and GABRIEL VALLADARES

ARMENIA

The Emblem

- According to the ICRC, 'draft legislation on the use and protection of the red cross and red crescent emblem, ... was adopted by the National Assembly at first reading in November 2001'.[11]

AUSTRALIA[12]

Compensation

- The Compensation (Japanese Internment) Act, 2001, No. 41 of 2001. Assented to on 25 May 2001 [http://www.austlii.edu.au/]

This Act made a provision for a once only payment of A$25,000 to certain widows and widowers of veteran prisoners of war and to civilians interned by Japan or their widows or widowers.

Conventional Weapons

- Media Release by the Foreign Minister, 'Australia to Chair Major International Conference on Arms Control', 11 April 2001 [http://www.dfat.gov.au/media/releases/foreign/2001/fa044_01.html]
- Media Release by the Foreign Minister, 'Australia Leads Efforts to Reduce the Humanitarian Impact of War', 24 December 2001 [http://www.dfat.gov.au/media/releases/foreign/2001/fa189_01.html]

9. See ibid., p. 414.
10. Ibid.
11. ICRC Advisory Service, *National Implementation of International Humanitarian Law*: Biennial report 2000-2001 (Geneva, ICRC 2002) p. 13.
12. Information provided by Professor Tim McCormack, Australian Red Cross Professor of International Humanitarian Law and Foundation Director of the Asia-Pacific Centre for Military Law, University of Melbourne; member of the Board of Editors, *Yearbook of International Humanitarian Law*.

From the announcement of the timing of the Review Conference of the 1980 Certain Conventional Weapons Convention (CCWC), the Australian government was committed to strengthening the Convention. However, the appointment of Ambassador Les Luck as President-Designate of the Conference, eight months before the commencement of the conference on 10 December 2001, ensured that the attention of senior levels of government in Canberra was more focussed on the Review Conference than might have otherwise been the case. Ambassador Luck worked with Geneva-based delegations in the lead up to December 2001 to ensure positive outcomes from the Review Conference. At the Conference itself, the Australian Government Delegation supported the initiative to extend the scope of application of each of the Protocols to the Convention to internal as well as international armed conflicts and the decision to establish expert working groups throughout 2002 on the issues of Explosive Remnants of War and Anti-Vehicle Mines (AVMs).

In the lead up to the Review Conference, the Australian Foreign Minister, Alexander Downer, wrote to 104 other Foreign Ministers of states not yet party to the CCWC. The government was pleased that some signatory sates attended the Conference as observers and has indicated that it will work to encourage greater levels of participation in the Convention.[13]

Cases (Application of Article 1(F) of the Refugee Convention)

☛ *'VAB' and Minister for Immigration and Multicultural Affairs* [2001] *AATA* 990 (5 December 2001) [http://www.austlii.edu.au/cgibin/disp.pl/au/cases/cth/aat/2001/990.html]

Consistent with its practice in 2000,[14] the Administrative Appeals Tribunal of Australia in 2001 again decided a case involving an appeal against the application of Article 1(F) of the Refugee Convention by an administrative representative of the Department of Immigration and Multicultural Affairs.

In this particular case, VAB (real name suppressed for anonymity) had arrived in Australia from Afganistan and applied for refugee status. He had joined the KHAD (Khedamat-e Etela'are Dawlati), Afghanistan's Secret Police, in 1980 as a non-military intelligence officer. After a period of only six weeks, VAB was promoted to the position of Director of L35 Department, a position he maintained for 12 years until the demise of KHAD in 1992. In his capacity as Director of the Department, VAB had an intimate understanding of the work of each of the three Divisions within the Department and knew the place of his own Department within the overall work and structure of the organisation. VAB's Department handled files pertaining to people under 65 years of age of interest to KHAD, including those who died in detention as a result of ill-treatment and/or torture.

In applying Article 1(F) of the Convention as the basis for denying VAB refugee status, the representative of the Department of Immigration and Multicultural Affairs did not have evidence that VAB had personally committed a war crime or crime against humanity. Instead, the argument was that VAB's senior position within the organisation meant that he was well aware of its work and the atrocities it routinely committed. VAB made no attempt

---

13. For a discussion of the work of the Review Conference, see Year in Review in this volume, p. 319 and, specifically on the question of explosive remnants of war, see Matthews in this volume at p. 406.

14. See Correspondents' Report for Australia in Vol. 3 of the Yearbook at pp. 416-419.

to protest any of those practices or to leave the organisation when he became fully aware of its *modus operandi*. His sustained involvement at such a senior level of responsibility made him complicit in the work and the crimes of KHAD.

Deputy President Estcourt upheld the decision of the Departmental Representative. He reaffirmed the position of the Tribunal that the Department is not required to prove a crime but only needs to show reasonable grounds for believing that a war crime or crime against humanity have been committed. VAB was voluntarily involved in a process that he knew would often end in serious human rights abuses. He shared the purposes of the organisation for which he worked and he knowingly and voluntarily participated in the chain of operation. The fact that his position was administrative rather than operational made him no less complicit in the crimes against humanity routinely perpetrated by KHAD.

Cases (Extradition)

☛ *Magistrate's Decision In the Matter of a Request for the Extradition of Konrads Alfreds Kalejs*, Magistrates' Court of Victoria, 29 May 2001. The magistrate's decision is unreported and so unavailable in electronic form.

Latvia's lodgement of a formal request for extradition of Konrads Kalejs from Australia was communicated on 13 December 2000.[15] According to the Australian Federal Extradition Act 1988, a magistrate in the jurisdiction of any of Australia's States or Territories is a 'designated person' for the purposes of decision-making in respect of requests for extradition of persons in Australia. Accordingly, the magistrate, Ms Lisa Hannan, operating in Melbourne in the State of Victoria, handed down her decision in relation to Latvia's request for the extradition of Konrads Kalejs on 29 May 2001. The case was heard in Melbourne because Kalejs had taken up residency there.

The magistrate was called upon to decide, *inter alia,* whether or not Kalejs' alleged conduct constituted an extraditable offence. In other words, the magistrate had to be satisfied that if Kalejs' alleged conduct had been perpetrated in Victoria it would have constituted an offence under its criminal law. Section 19(2)(c) of the Extradition Act 1988 specifies that the date for the determination of the 'dual criminality' rule is the date of the extradition request and not the date of the alleged conduct in question. This legislative specification of the latter date was important to the magistrate's decision because it enabled her to review the specific offences of grave breaches of the 1949 Geneva Conventions pursuant to the Australian Federal Geneva Conventions Act 1957 – legislation that did not exist at the time of Kalejs' alleged acts (the magistrate also considered a list of 'ordinary' domestic crimes pursuant to the Victorian Crimes Act 1958). This decision appears to be the first Australian judicial consideration of the Geneva Conventions Act 1957, as there has never been a prosecution under the terms of that Act nor any earlier extradition proceedings based on the legislation.

The magistrate decided that persons in Victoria who found themselves in the hands of an occupying power in relation to which they were not nationals were protected persons for the purposes of Article 4 of Geneva Convention IV and, consequently, covered by the grave breaches regime of that Convention and the Australian Geneva Conventions Act 1957. Counsel for Kalejs presented an interesting argument to the effect that as many of the

15. See 3 *YIHL* (2000), pp. 414-415, for details of the extradition case history of Kalejs.

inmates of the Salspils camp in Latvia were Austrian, and Germany had annexed Austria and extended German nationality to Austrians, the inmates of the camp were not of a different nationality to the German forces occupying Latvia at the time of the alleged acts. Consequently, so the argument ran, the inmates of the Camp were not 'protected persons' for the purposes of the application of Geneva Convention IV. Counsel for the Australian government representing Latvia countered the argument with the fact that even if some of the camp inmates were of the same nationality as the occupying forces, not all inmates fell into that category. In any case, irrespective of the relative proportion of Austrians and those of Latvian or other nationality in the camp, the argument was that the magistrate should follow the ICTY Appeals Chamber in its judgment in the *Tadić* case.[16] According to the Appeals Chamber, even in 1949 the intention of the drafters of the Convention was not to narrow the scope of protection of the Convention on strictly formalistic notions of 'nationality'. Notions of allegiance to one party or another to the conflict (whether that allegiance be based on ethnicity, religion, nationality or some other ground) ought to be the determinative factor for the purposes of the protection of Geneva Convention IV.

Although the Victorian magistrate avoided engaging in the complexities of this particular argument, she did indicate her decision that inmates of a camp in Australia in a similar situation to those inmates in Salspils would be 'protected persons' for the purposes of Geneva Convention IV 'bearing in mind the sort of definition of nationals as referred to in *Dusko Tadić*.'[17]

The magistrate went on to decide that the necessary elements of the following grave breaches of Geneva Convention IV are alleged in Latvia's Statement of Conduct (here the role of the magistrate in deciding whether to grant the extradition request is not to be satisfied that the evidence is sufficient to prove each of the elements beyond reasonable doubt – only that the elements of each offence exist on the alleged facts): wilful killing; torture; inhuman treatment; wilfully causing great suffering to body or health; wilfully causing serious injury to body or health; unlawful transfer; and unlawful confinement.

Following the delivery of the magistrate's decision, counsel for Kalejs announced his client's intention to appeal it. On 23 October 2001, Kalejs was wheeled on a stretcher into the Federal Court of Australia. Kalejs was excused from Court by Justice Susan Kenny on the grounds of poor health and argument proceeded in his absence. On 8 November 2001, Kalejs died at the age of 88 years, after argument in the appeal case had concluded but before judgment was delivered.

Pending (International Criminal Court)

- International Criminal Court Bill 2001
- International Criminal Court (Consequential Amendments) Bill 2001 [http://www.ag.gov.au/intcrimcourt/welcome.html]

Throughout the Rome Diplomatic Conference for an International Criminal Court in 1998, the Australian Government Delegation played a high profile leadership role as Chair of the

16. *Prosecutor* v. *Duško Tadić*, Case No. IT-94-1-A, Judgement, 15 July 1999.

17. At p. 25 of the magistrate's decision. Note that while the decision cited the Trial Chamber Judgment in *Tadić*, it was clearly referring to paras. 164-166 of the Appeals Chamber Judgment of 15 July 1999.

so-called 'Like Minded Group'. Many, including members of the Australian Delegation itself, assumed that Australia would be one of the first group of states to ratify the Statute and certainly amongst the first 60 states to ratify to help trigger its entry into force. On 31 December 2001, the number of States Parties to the Rome Statute stood at 50 and to the disappointment of many people, Australia was not among them. In fact, by the end of 2001 it seemed a distinct possibility that Australia might not deposit its instrument of ratification before entry into force of the Statute, then anticipated sometime in the latter half of 2002. What were the reasons for this delay in ratification?

Following the conclusion of the Rome Diplomatic Conference in July 1998, there were no substantive developments in Canberra regarding domestic preparation for implementation of the Rome Statute until October 2000. There has never been any official explanation for this lapse of time and it seems as though the bureaucracy was simply preoccupied with other, more pressing issues. In retrospect though, this 27-month hiatus seems costly because if preparatory work towards ratification had commenced earlier, Australia may well have deposited its instrument of ratification before the end of 2001.

On 15 October 2000, the Attorney-General and Foreign Minister issued a joint press release announcing their intention to introduce implementing legislation into Federal Parliament early in 2001 and to make ratification of the Rome Statute a high priority after the enactment of that implementing legislation. In response to the issuance of this press release, the then-Chair of the Joint Parliamentary Standing Committee on Treaties (JSCOT), the Parliamentary Committee tasked to report to Parliament on the desirability or otherwise of all proposed treaty action, claimed that the joint ministerial press release constituted an attempt to usurp the role of JSCOT by assuming that ratification was in Australia's national interests. The then-Chair, Andrew Thomson MP, then embarked on a public campaign against the International Criminal Court and Australian participation in the Rome Statute.

Mr Thomson called a public inquiry by JSCOT into the implications of Australian participation in the Rome Statute and received in excess of 250 written submissions.[18]

He also held meetings of the Committee in several Australian cities at which some of those providing written submissions to the Committee were invited to appear in person to present their views. While this common Parliamentary Committee process was underway, Mr Thomson appeared on popular radio to speak out against the Court and Australian participation in it and made no attempt to present a public impression of impartiality on the issue. He even delivered a speech to the Annual Meeting of the Australian and New Zealand Society of International Law in June 2001 in Canberra in which he openly expressed his opposition to the Court and his hope that under his chairmanship JSCOT would prevent Australian ratification of the Rome Statute.

Prior to the Australian Federal Parliamentary elections in November 2001, Mr Thomson lost his political party's pre-selection for his safely held seat and, consequently, he was precluded from contesting the election. One of his final acts as Chair of JSCOT prior to the election was to issue a second call for written submissions in relation to the International Criminal Court, this time into the government's draft implementing legislation (see commentary below). This call for submissions ensured that JSCOT would not table its report on Australian participation in the Rome Statute prior to the Federal election and, as a

18. For the text of most of the written submissions see: http://www.aph.gov.au/house/committee/jsct/icc/subs.htm.

consequence, not until some months into 2002 – after the new Parliament was assembled, JSCOT reconstituted and the new Committee in a position to complete the inquiry.

Two draft Bills for the domestic implementation of Australia's international obligations in anticipation of ratification of the Rome Statute were tabled in mid-2001. The first of the two draft Bills, the International Criminal Court Bill 2001, established the legislative framework for the practicalities of Australia's legal relationship with the new Court. The rationale for this Bill was similar to that behind the enactment of the International War Crimes Tribunals Act 1995 although, in relation to the ICC, the legislative detail is much more extensive than was enacted in respect of the two *ad hoc* International Criminal Tribunals. In the common law domestic legal system of Australia, international obligations, regardless of their source (UN Security Council resolutions in respect of the establishment of the two International Criminal Tribunals and a multilateral treaty in the case of the International Criminal Court), only become enforceable before Australian courts once implementing legislation has been adopted.[19] Consequently, for example, a person in Australia will only be surrendered upon request to the International Criminal Court once the International Criminal Court Bill 2001 is enacted because that legislation will provide legislative authorisation to an Australian magistrate to order the issuance of a warrant of arrest to enable that surrender to occur. The same magistrate will not be empowered to order the surrender merely on the basis that Australia has become a State Party to the Rome Statute and so has the international legal obligations to issue such an order.

The first draft Bill includes 119 pages incorporating 149 provisions (referred to in Australia as 'sections') in 12 distinct Parts, including 'Requests by the ICC for Co-operation'; 'Requests by the ICC for Arrest and Surrender of Persons'; 'Investigations or Sittings of the ICC in Australia'; 'Search, Seizure and Powers of Arrest'; 'Protection of Australia's National Security Interests'; and 'Enforcement in Australia of Sentences Imposed by the ICC'. The provisions of the Bill include minute details envisaging as many contingencies as possible. These are not esoteric details for their own sake but represent a serious attempt to deal with practical issues. Some specific examples help to illustrate this point.

The draft legislation, for example, does not simply detail the test a magistrate is to apply in deciding whether or not to issue a warrant for the arrest of a person the subject of a request for surrender by the ICC. The draft Bill also covers the much more complex issue of competing requests in respect of the same person – for surrender by the ICC and for extradition by another state. In such situations, the proposed legislation enumerates a list of factors the Attorney-General must take into account in weighing up the decision as to whether the request should be granted. This list of factors is slightly different for situations where the foreign state requesting extradition is a party to the Rome Statute and where that state is not. In this respect, the draft legislation mirrors the provisions in Article 90 of the Rome Statute. The draft Bill also details the requirements for the issuance of a warrant for search of a person, of premises, or for the seizure of goods or property and goes on to provide limita-

---

19. For a summary of the Australian domestic legal approach in the context of international criminal law see K.L. Doherty and T.L.H. McCormack, 'Complementarity as a Catalyst for Comprehensive Domestic Penal Legislation', 5 *University of California, Davis Journal of International Law and Policy* (1999) pp. 147 at 156-161. For a more detailed analysis generally of the implementation of international legal obligations into Australian law see R. Balkin, 'International Law and Domestic Law', in S. Blay, R. Piotrowicz and M. Tsamenyi, eds., *Public International Law: An Australian Perspective* (Melbourne, Oxford University Press 1997) pp. 119-145.

tions on the powers for search and seizure. Some additional provisions go as far as to specify the circumstances as well as the precise limitations on the extent of different types of search of a person – including, in certain specified circumstances, strip searches. Finally by way of illustration, the draft legislation proposes a mechanism for resolution of a dispute between the ICC and the Australian government in relation to the revelation of requested information with the potential to damage Australia's national interests.[20] The draft Bill even specifies the process to be followed if a dispute of this nature cannot be resolved.

The second of the two draft Bills, the International Criminal Court (Consequential Amendments) Bill 2001, will, if and when enacted, result in amendments to a number of existing Acts of the Australian Federal Parliament for the criminalisation in Australian Law of the offences within the subject matter jurisdiction of the International Criminal Court. The proposed legislation involves 87 pages of text with a total of three prefatory sections and 173 additional provisions in eight separate annexed schedules. Each of these schedules contains the provisions to amend a different existing Act of Parliament. Schedules 2-8 contain a combined total of 20 provisions and all the other 153 provisions – the overwhelming bulk of the draft Bill – are contained in Schedule 1. Schedule 1 proposes amendments to the Criminal Code Act 1995 with an entire new Division (No. 268) to be added to the Criminal Code Act 1995. That new Division is tentatively entitled 'Genocide, Crimes Against Humanity, War Crimes and Crimes Against the Administration of the Justice of the International Criminal Court'. The proposed Schedule includes 129 new sections in 11 different subdivisions of the new Division.

The approach of the draft legislation is to include a separate section for each of the distinct offences provided for in Articles 6, 7 and 8 of the Statute, similar to the approach adopted in the Elements of Crimes. So, for example, Subdivision B of the new Division 268 includes five separate offences (268.3-268.7) of genocide, mirroring the five separate offences included in the Elements of the Crimes: i.e., genocide by killing; by causing serious bodily or mental harm; by deliberately inflicting conditions of life calculated to bring about physical destruction; by imposing measures intended to prevent births; and by forcibly transferring children. The same approach is replicated in Subdivision C with 16 separate offences of crimes against humanity and in Subdivisions D, E, F and G, with 70 separate offences for war crimes.

This unique approach of a separate section for each individual offence specifying the precise elements of each offence is entirely consistent with the overall approach already adopted in the Criminal Code Act 1995. The most recent substantial amendment to the Criminal Code Act 1995 prior to the proposed legislation was the Criminal Code Amendment (United Nations and Associated Personnel) Act 2000, implementing Australia's obligations as a State Party to the 1994 Convention on the Safety of United Nations and Associated Personnel into Australian Domestic Law. The newly added Division 71 of the Criminal Code Act 1995 entitled 'Offences Against United Nations and Associated Personnel' reflects exactly the same approach as that adopted in Schedule 1 of the International Criminal Court (Consequential Amendments) Act 2002. Although it creates an unwieldy and complicated impression, the approach does have the advantage of introducing certainty into the criminal trial process for all the parties involved – prosecution, defence and the judiciary. The approach involves the enumeration of the precise elements which must be

20. See Art. 72 of the Rome Statute.

proved beyond reasonable doubt as well as facilitating the identification of a maximum penalty for each separate offence.

It is worth noting that, unlike a number of other states that have already ratified the Statute, the Australian Government has indicated that it will not deposit its instrument of ratification prior to the formal enactment of its implementing legislation, even though no obligations arise until after entry into force of the Statute. The Australian Government has consistently maintained that it will not ratify a treaty unless it has passed any domestic legislation that is required for compliance with its obligations under that treaty. Although there is no express constitutional requirement to take this approach, ratification prior to enactment of implementing legislation would presume parliamentary approval for that legislation. In Australia, ratification of treaties is an Executive Act not requiring parliamentary approval. If the Executive ratified a treaty prior to the enactment of implementing legislation and Parliament subsequently refused to support the enactment of the draft legislation, Australia could find itself in breach of its international obligations.

TIM MCCORMACK

AUSTRIA[21]

International Criminal Tribunals

☛ Memorandum of Understanding between the Federal Government of Austria and the United Nations on the Extension and Amendment of the Memorandum of Understanding between the Federal Government of Austria and the United Nations for the Loan of Prison Staff to the International Criminal Tribunal for the former Yugoslavia[22] [Vereinbarung zwischen der Österreichischen Bundesregierung und den Vereinten Nationen über die Verlängerung und Abänderung der Vereinbarung zwischen der Österreichischen Bundesregierung und den Vereinten Nationen zur leihweisen Beistellung von Gefängnispersonal an den Internationalen Strafgerichtshof für das ehemalige Jugoslawien]. This Agreement is laid up for insight at the Federal Ministry for Foreign Affairs (cf.,, Austrian Federal Law Gazette, *BGBl. [Bundesgesetzblatt]*[23] III Nr. 142/2001). Entered into force on 1 June 2001.

Counter-terrorism

☛ International Convention for the Suppression of Terrorist Bombings [Internationales Übereinkommen zur Bekämpfung terroristischer Bombenanschläge], *BGBl* III Nr. 168/2001

This Convention, which expressly stipulates that it does not affect other rights, obligations and responsibilities of states and individuals under international humanitarian law, and it does not govern the activities of armed forces during an armed conflict (cf.,, Art. 19), was ratified by Austria on 6 September 2000. It entered into force on 23 May 2001. For the text, draft translation into German and Explanatory Memorandum see *RV [Regierungsvorlage]*

21. Information and commentaries by Dr Thomas Desch, Federal Ministry of Defence, Vienna, and Mag. Peter Kustor, Federal Chancellery, Vienna.

22. For the original version of the agreement cf., 3 *YIHL* (2000) p. 422.

23. The Federal Law Gazette is also available via Internet: http://www.ris.bka.gv.at.

47 *BlgNR [Beilagen zu den Stenographischen Protokollen des Nationalrates]*[24] 21. *GP [Gesetzgebungsperiode].*

Safety of UN Personnel

☛ Convention on the Safety of United Nations and Associated Personnel [Übereinkommen über die Sicherheit von Personal der Vereinten Nationen und beigeordnetem Personal], *BGBl* III Nr. 180/2000

This Convention contains 'savings clauses', which *inter alia* stipulate that nothing in this Convention shall affect the applicability of international humanitarian law (cf., Art. 20). Austria acceded to this Convention on 6 September 2000. The Convention entered into force for Austria on 6 October 2000. For the text, draft translation into German and Explanatory Memorandum see *RV* 50 *BlgNR* 21. *GP*

Reparations and War Damages

☛ Agreement between the government of the United States of America and the Austrian Federal government concerning the Austrian Fund 'Reconciliation, Peace and Cooperation' (Reconciliation Fund) ('Agreement'), signed 24 October 2000. Reproduced in ILM (2001) p. 565

☛ Exchange of Notes between the Austrian Federal government and the government of the United States of America Concerning Matters of Compensation of and Restitution for Victims of National Socialism [Abkommen zwischen der Österreichischen Bundesregierung und der Regierung der Vereinigten Staaten von Amerika zur Regelung von Fragen der Entschädigung und Restitution für Opfer des Nationalsozialsmus], *BGBl.* III Nr. 121/2001

Although Austria cannot be held legally responsible for crimes that were organized and carried out by the Nazi regime of the 'German Reich', it reaffirmed its moral responsibility in this context and took measures to supplement the numerous Austrian restitution measures of the past. In the years 2000-2001, based on an agreement between the Austrian Federal Government and the US Government, as well as the Conference on Jewish Material Claims, the Austrian Jewish Community, representatives of Austrian companies and, for a large number of plaintiffs, attorneys, a package of measures to resolve all remaining claims against Austria and/or Austrian companies arising out of or related to the National Socialist Era or World War II were agreed upon. The main elements of this agreement are:

1. Immediate compensation for survivors
2. Establishment of a General Settlement Fund
3. Arbitration panel for *In Rem* restitution of publicly owned property
4. Additional social benefits to survivors
5. Restitution of works of art
6. Hakoah sports club
7. State archives
8. Jewish cemeteries

---

24. Parliamentary documents are also available via Internet: http://www.parlament.gv.at.

9. Subsidies to the Annual Holocaust Education Program at the Salzburg Seminar
10. Legal closure

☛ Federal Law amending the Federal Law to Establish the National Fund of the Republic of Austria for Victims of National Socialism [Bundesgesetz, mit dem das Bundesgesetz über den Nationalfonds der Republik Österreich für Opfer des Nationalsozialismus geändert wird], (BGBl. I Nr. 11/2001). Entered into force on 23 February 2001 (*BGBl.* I Nr. 14/2001)

This Federal Law provides for the immediate compensation for Holocaust survivors originating from or living in Austria and having lost apartment and small business leases, household property or personal valuables and effects.

☛ Federal Law on the Establishment of a General Settlement Fund for Victims of National Socialism and on Restitution Measures (General Settlement Fund Law), as well as on an Amendment to the General Social Security Law and the Victims Assistance Act [Bundesgesetz über die Einrichtung eines Allgemeinen Entschädigungsfonds für Opfer des Nationalsozialismus und über Restitutionsmaßnahmen (Entschädigungsfondsgesetz) sowie zur Änderung des Allgemeinen Sozialversicherungsgesetzes und des Opferfürsorgegesetzes], *BGBl* I Nr. 12/2001. For the draft text and the Explanatory Memorandum see 476 *BlgNR* 21. *GP*. For further information and details see http://www.nationalfonds.org/aef/english/index.htm; http://www.bmaa.gv.at/oesterreich/entns.html.en ('Payments to NS Victims')

The Austrian Parliament (the Austrian National Council on 31 January 2001 and the Federal Council on 15 February 2001) unanimously adopted this Federal Law, which was initiated by all four parties represented in the Austrian Parliament. The law creates the legal basis for the establishment of a General Settlement Fund for Victims of National Socialism (GSF). The GSF is a voluntary fund that will provide *ex gratia* payments to certain applicants. Persons (in the claims-based process also associations) who/which were persecuted by the National Socialist regime on political grounds, on grounds of origin, religion, nationality, sexual orientation, or of physical or mental handicap or of accusations of so-called asociality, or who left the country to escape such persecution, and who suffered losses or damages as a result of or in connection with events having occurred on the territory of the present-day Republic of Austria during the National Socialist era shall be eligible to file an application and, additionally, heirs of eligible claimants. After all contributions to the GSF had been made available, this Federal Law entered into force on 28 May 2001 (*BGBl.* I Nr. 58/2001).

Claims for forced and slave labour were excluded from the above-mentioned package as they were covered by the Austrian Reconciliation Fund set up in 2000.[25] After the signing of bilateral agreements between Austria and six Central and Eastern European countries, namely Belarus (*BGBl.* III Nr. 44/2001), the Czech Republic (*BGBl.* III Nr. 19/2001), Hungary (*BGBl.* III Nr. 21/2001), Poland (*BGBl.* III Nr. 20/2001), the Russian Federation (*BGBl.* III Nr. 17/2001), Ukraine (*BGBl.* III Nr. 18/2001) as well as the United States (*BGBl.* III Nr. 221/2000), and after the necessary financial resources were made available to the

25. Cf., 3 *YIHL* (2000) p. 422.

Fund, the Reconciliation Fund Law was brought into force on 27 November 2000 (cf., *BGBl.* I Nr. 122/2000).[26]

Claims for *in rem* restitution of works of art were also excluded from the above-mentioned package as they were covered by proceedings conducted under the Austrian Art Restitution Law [Kunstrückgabegesetz], *BGBl.* I Nr. 181/1998.

THOMAS DESCHand PETER KUSTOR

AZERBAIJAN

Criminal Law

☛ (The new Criminal Code of Azerbaijan was adopted by the Parliament on 30 September 30 1999 and came into force 1 September 2000

'It includes an entire section on the repression of war crimes commited in both international and internal armed conflicts, and sets forth general principles for their repression, such as universal jurisdiction and the non-application of statutory limitations to perpetrators of war crimes. The Code already refers to a number of war crimes listed in the Rome Statute of the International Criminal Court.'[27]

BANGLADESH

International Criminal Court

☛ Establishment of Inter-Ministerial Committee on the ICC

Following its signature of the ICC Statute on 16 September 1999, attention focussed on ratification and the steps that are necessary to harmonise national criminal law with the terms of the Statute. An inter-ministerial committee was established with the task of studying the Statute and determining its implications for domestic legislation. No constitutional or other legal barriers are envisaged. With the change of government in 2001, however, the impetus towards ratification suffered a setback.[28]

BELARUS[29]

The Emblem

☛ Law on the Belarusian Society of the Red Cross. Adopted on 24 October 2000. Entered into force 11 November 2000. Published *in Национальный реестр правовых актов Республики Беларусь* [National Register of Legal Acts of the Republic of Belarus], 9 November 2000, No. 103, 2/212

26. For further details see: http://www.reconciliationfund.at/.

27. ICRC Advisory Service, *National Implementation of International Humanitarian Law*: Biennial report 2000-2001 (Geneva, ICRC 2002) p. 16.

28. http://www.iccnow.org/countryinfo/asia/bangladesh.html.

29. Oleg Starovoitov is a Lecturer in Public International Law at the Faculty of International Relations of the Belarusian State University, Minsk, Belarus.

According to the Law, the Belarusian Society of the Red Cross is a voluntary organization created to provide assistance in the realization of tasks mandated by the 1949 Geneva Conventions and the 1977 Additional Protocols, for the promotion of international humanitarian law and the principles of the International Movement of the Red Cross and Red Crescent, and for enlightenment in the sphere of public health.

Geneva Law

☛ Law of the Republic of Belarus concerning the withdrawal of the Republic of Belarus reservations to the 1949 Geneva Conventions, 14 May 2001, No. 15-3. Published in *Национальный реестр правовых актов Республики Беларусь* [National Register of Legal Acts of the Republic of Belarus], 24 May 2001, No. 48, 2/758

On 14 May 2001, Belarus withdrew reservations made by the Belorussian Soviet Socialist Republic (BSSR) when signing the four Geneva Conventions of 1949 on 12 December 1949 and maintained upon their ratification of 5 June 1954. These reservations concerned Article 10 of Geneva Convention I; Article 10 of Geneva Convention II; Articles 10, 12 and 85 of Geneva Convention III; and Articles 11 and 45 of Geneva Convention IV.

Peace and security

☛ President Decree No. 390 of 17 July 2001, adopting the National Security Concept of the Republic of Belarus. Entered into force on 18 July 2001. Published in *Национальный реестр правовых актов Республики Беларусь* [National Register of Legal Acts of the Republic of Belarus], 27 July 2001, No. 69, 1/2852

☛ Law on the Military Doctrine of the Republic of Belarus. Adopted on 3 January 2002. Entered into force on 17 January 2002. Published in *Национальный реестр правовых актов Республики Беларусь* [National Register of Legal Acts of the Republic of Belarus], 17 January 2002, No. 6, 2/826

According to these documents, the most important aspect of Belarus' external security is strengthening the union with the Russian Federation and maintaining close cooperation with other Member States of the Commonwealth of Independent States (CIC) in political and military areas, in particular within the framework of the 1992 CIS Treaty on Collective Security. Currently, Belarus does not consider any state as a potential enemy, and Belarusian Military Doctrine has a purely defensive character. Belarussian Armed Forces are excluded from participation in armed conflicts of any kind outside of the country, and the Belarussian Armed Forces must be under the control of the civilian authorities.

Children

☛ Law of the Republic of Belarus on amendments and supplements to the Law of the Republic of Belarus on Child's Rights, 25 October 2000, No. 440-3. Entered into force on 3 November 2000. Published in *Национальный реестр правовых актов Республики Беларусь* [National Register of Legal Acts of the Republic of Belarus], 9 November 2000, No. 103, 2/215

The Law of the Republic of Belarus on Children's Rights of 25 October 2000 (adopted on 19 November 1993 and revised in October 2000) prohibits the involvement of children in any military operations, armed conflicts, propaganda of war and violence directed towards children, and the establishment of children's military formations. The age of conscription to military service is 18. Admission of minors to special military institutions shall be governed by regulations of these institutions (Art. 33). Refugee children without homes or private property as a result of military operations, armed national or international conflicts, shall have rights of protection. State bodies of protection of childhood shall take measures to search for the parents or relatives of a child, provide material, medical or other aid and assistance and, if necessary, put the child in a medical, boarding or other educational institution (Art. 34).

Cultural Property

☛ Law of the Republic of Belarus on the ratification of the Second Protocol to the 1954 Hague Convention for the Protection of Cultural Property in the Event of Armed Conflict. No. 434-3. Adopted on 24 October 2000. Published in *Национальный реестр правовых актов Республики Беларусь* [National Register of Legal Acts of the Republic of Belarus], 9 November 2000, No. 103, 2/209

The law contains two articles and the text of the Second Protocol. Article 1 prescribes ratification of the Second Protocol to the 1954 Hague Convention. Article 2 provides that: 'The Council of Ministers has to take necessary measures for implementation of provisions of the Second Protocol to the 1954 Hague Convention ...'

☛ Resolution No. 1930 of the Council of Ministers on appointment of an organ responsible for the implementation of the Second Protocol to the 1954 Hague Convention for the Protection of Cultural Property in the Event of Armed Conflict. Adopted on 18 December 2000

On 24 October 2000, Belarus ratified the 1999 Second Protocol to the 1954 Hague Convention for the Protection of Cultural Property in the Event of Armed Conflict. According to the 1998 Law on International Treaties of Belarus, legislative norms contained in international treaties of the Republic of Belarus, which have entered into force in Belarus, are part of Belarus legislation, and are subject to direct application, except where it follows from the international treaty that for application of such norms it is necessary to issue an inter-state act (Art. 15(3)).

On 18 December 2000, the Council of Ministers appointed the Ministry of Culture as the governmental organ responsible for implementation of the Second Protocol.

Implementation and Dissemination

☛ Resolution No. 1242 of the Council of Ministers on the establishment of the Commission on the Implementation of International Humanitarian Law. Adopted on 19 September 1997. Published in *Собрание декретов, указов Президента и постановлений Совета Министров Республики Беларусь* [Collection of Decrees and Ukases of the President and Resolutions of the Council of Ministers of the Republic of Belarus] 1997, No. 26, st. 887

☛ Regulation on the Commission on the Implementation of International Humanitarian Law. Adopted by the Council of Ministers' Resolution No. 104 on 26 January 1998. Published in *Собрание декретов, указов Президента и постановлений Совета Министров Республики Беларусь* [Collection of Decrees and Ukases of the President and Resolutions of the Council of Ministers of the Republic of Belarus] 1998, No. 3, st. 65

On 19 September 1997, the National Commission on the Implementation of International Humanitarian Law was created in Belarus. In accordance with Resolution No. 104 of the Council of Ministers of 26 January 1998, the Commission is the Council of Ministers' permanent consultative organ, which takes upon itself the following tasks:

— To assist in adopting Belarusian legislation in accordance with the Geneva Conventions and other agreements in the area of international humanitarian law in which Belarus takes part;
— To assist Belarus in concluding treaties in the sphere of international humanitarian law;
— To study and assess Belarusian legislation to determine its compatibility with international humanitarian law;
— To examine and prepare consultative remarks on international treaty projects and Belarusian legislative acts in the area of international humanitarian law;
— To coordinate appropriate national organs for the implementation of international humanitarian law in Belarusian legislation;
— To assist in the dissemination of international humanitarian law and assemble information on this issue;
— To prepare and present an annual report to the Council of Ministers of the Republic of Belarus on its activities; To conduct research and prepare reports and proposals in the area of international humanitarian legal achievements;
— To establish cooperation with the International Committee of the Red Cross and other international organisations conducting activities in the area of international humanitarian law.

OLEG STAROVOITOV

BELGIUM[30]

Cases

☛ Proceedings against *Vincent Ntezimana, Alphonse Higaniro, Consolata Mukangango (Sister Gertrude)* and *Julienne Mukabutera (Sister Maria Kisito)*. Decisions of 8 and 9 June 2001 by the Court of Assizes (Cour d'assises) of Brussels; Decision of 9 January 2002 by Cour de Cassation

After a public trial which began on 17 April 2001 before the Court of Assizes of Brussels, the four accused were found guilty, on 8 June 2001, of war crimes and/or complicity in war crimes for their participation in the 1994 Rwandan genocide. The accused were prosecuted on the basis of the Law of 16 June 1993 relating to the repression of grave breaches of the Geneva Conventions of 1949 and their Additional Protocols of 1977. The sentences given on 9 June 2001 were as follows:

30. Information and commentaries by Eric David, Professeur ordinaire, Brussels Free University.

— A. Hinganiro: found guilty of all six counts attributed to him, including incitement to commit war crimes, and sentenced to 20 years' imprisonment;
— V. Ntezimana: found guilty of three of the five counts attributed to him and sentenced to 12 years' imprisonment;
— Consolata Mukangango (Sister Gertrude) and Julienne Mukabutera (Sister Maria Kisito): found guilty of having helped Hutu militias to kill thousands of refugees in their convent and sentenced to 15 and 12 years' imprisonment respectively.[31]

An appeal (*pourvoi*) filed before the Court of Cassation by A. Hinganiro, C. Mukangango and J. Mukabutera was dismissed on 9 January 2002. Most grounds for the appeal related to procedural questions. For Hinganiro, the ground of the appeal was founded on the *ne bis in idem* rule. As already stated in this Yearbook,[32] the appellant – who had been transferred to the ICTR in 1996 – contended that the dismissal of the Prosecutor's indictment by the confirming judge of the ICTR at the time was tantamount to a final decision for lack of evidence. This ground of appeal had already been dismissed in Belgium by the Chamber of Council (28 March 2000) and by the Indictments Chamber (27 June 2001).[33] The Court of Cassation also ruled that the decision of the ICTR's confirming judge did not amount to a decision on the merits.[34]

☛ Criminal complaints under the 1993 Law

During the reporting period, a number of complaints founded on the Law of 16 June 1993, as amended on 10 February 1999, concerning the punishment of grave breaches of international humanitarian law[35] were lodged by private individuals before Belgian investigating judges (*juges d'instruction*) against various actual and former foreign heads of state and government. The complaints were directed, among others, against:
— *Hissène Habré*, former President of Chad, for his involvement in crimes against humanity committed between 1982 and 1990. The complaint was brought by a Belgian citizen of Chadian origin on 30 November 2000;[36]
— *Ariel Sharon*, Prime Minister of Israel, General *Amos Yaron* and other Israeli and Lebanese people for their involvement in the massacres of Sabra and Shatila committed on 16-18 November 1982 in Lebanon at the time of the occupation of Beruit by Israel. The complaint was brought by 23 Palestinian and Lebanese citizens on 18 June 2001;[37]

---

31. See the international press of the time. As the decisions on the merits given by the Court of assizes only consist of 'yes' or 'no' answers to questions asked to the jury by the Court, they are almost never published.

32. See 3 *YIHL* (2000) pp. 429-430.

33. Ibid.

34. Not published at the time of writing. However, the decision should be available on the Court's website (www.cass.be) by the time of the publication of this Yearbook.

35. The text of the 1993 Law is reproduced in English in 2 *YIHL* (1999) pp. 541-555; text of the amendments, ibid., pp. 539-541; for a text of the law as amended, *ILM* (1999) pp. 921-925.

36. *Le Soir*, 21 March 2001.

37. Ibid., 18 June 2001.

— *Saddam Hussein*, President of Iraq, and other Iraqi ministers, for their involvement in crimes against humanity committed in 1991 against the Kurdish population in Iraq. The complaint was brought on 26 June 2001 by five persons of Kurdish origin living in Belgium;[38]
— *Laurent Gbagbo*, President of Ivory Coast, the former President, *Robert Gueï*, and the ministers of Defence and Interior for their involvement in a massacre committed on 27 October 2000 against people of the Dioula ethnic group. The complaint was brought on 30 June 2001 by a citizen of Ivory Coast living in Belgium, on behalf of 150 persons;[39]
— *Fidel Castro*, President of Cuba, for his involvement in crimes against humanity, and in particular, for his responsibility in the destruction of two small civilian airplanes in 1996. The complaint was brought on 5 October 2001 by nine Cuban citizens living in the USA and two Cuban citizens living in Belgium;[40]
— *Denis Sassou Nguesso*, President of the Republic of Congo-Brazzaville, and the oil company Total-Fina, for their involvement in war crimes and crimes against humanity committed in 1998-1999. The complaint was brought on 12 October 2001 by three persons of Congolese origin, one Belgian citizen, one UN refugee living in Belgium and one Congolese citizen;[41]
— *Ange-Félix Patasse*, President of the Central-African Republic, and 26 members of his government for their involvement in crimes against humanity committed after a coup which failed on 28 May 2001 against members of the Yakoma ethnic group: the complaint was brought, on 14 November 2001, by nine members of this group;[42]
— *Paul Biya*, President of Cameroon, and 11 members of his regime, for their involvement in crimes against humanity, and more especially for the forced disappearance of nine young people which occurred in January 2001. The complaint was brought on 18 December 2001 by the President of a Cameroonian association, the 'Collectif national contre l'impunité', and by Cameroonian citizens living in Belgium.[43]

☛ Proceedings against *Ariel Sharon* et al[44]

Among the various complaints mentioned above, the complaint against Ariel Sharon gave rise to some proceedings. On 2 August 2001, counsel for the State of Israel raised a number of objections to the admissibility of the complaint.

On 7 September 2001, the investigating judge in charge of the case, Mr P. Collignon, gave an order according some weight to two Israeli arguments disputing the legality of the prosecution of A. Sharon in Belgium: firstly, Lebanon had adopted an amnesty law which would prevent any criminal prosecution for the Sabra and Shatila massacres, and secondly,

38. Ibid., 26 June 2001.
39. Ibid., 30 June 2001.
40. Ibid., 5 October 2001.
41. Ibid., 12 October 2001.
42. *De Standaard*, 14 November 2001.
43. Ibid., 19 December 2001.
44. The information relating to this case has not been published, with the exception of a number of newspaper articles. Most of the following information is based on the present writer's personal knowledge of the case.

Article 12 of the Preliminary Title of the Belgian Code of Criminal Procedure of 1878[45] states that prosecution for any extraterritorial crime provided for in this Title would require the presence of the accused on the Belgian soil.

Another investigating judge, Mr D. Vandermeersch, who is responsible for a number of similar cases, gave an opinion asserting the jurisdiction of the Belgian judge even when the accused is not in Belgium. One of his main arguments is that the 1993/1999 Law which provides for the extraterritorial jurisdiction is not covered by Article 12 of the Preliminary Title above-mentioned. This provision only deals with offences stipulated in the Preliminary Title and these offences do not include the crimes provided for in the 1993/1999 Law.

On 21 September, the Public Prosecutor also concluded that the Belgian investigating judge had jurisdiction in the absence of the accused. Among various arguments in favour of the jurisdiction of the Belgian judge, the Public Prosecutor stated in particular that the rule appeared in other Belgian criminal laws which were also not dealt with by Article 12, and Parliament never required that Article 12 be applied to these laws; the text of Article 7 of the 1993/1999 Law did not require the presence of the accused in Belgium; the *travaux préparatoires* of Article 12 showed that the crimes contemplated by this provision (mainly common crimes committed against persons) were incomparable with crimes of the magnitude of those provided for by the 1993/1999 law; international law did not prevent states from prosecuting people *in absentia*; the Israeli jurisprudence in the *Eichmann* case supported such a conclusion; *a fortiori* should it be the case at the stage of a simple investigation.

On 29 November 2001, at the time of the pleadings before the Chamber of indictments (*Chambre des mises en accusation*), counsel for A. Sharon developed numerous arguments to dispute the jurisdiction of the Belgian court and the admissibility of the complain. In particular, he contended that:

— universal jurisdiction could not apply *in absentia*;
— A. Sharon, as a foreign head of state, was entitled to an absolute criminal immunity;
— the decision of Israel not to prosecute the accused prevented prosecution in Belgium according to the *ne bis in idem* rule;
— the amnesty law in Lebanon also prevented prosecution in Belgium;
— the acts had been committed in 1982 and the 1993/1999 Law could not be retroactive;
— the 1982 acts were covered by prescription (statutory limitations);
— the prosecution was barred by the reasonable time or undue delay rule.

All of these arguments were refuted by counsels for complainants who showed that:

— neither Belgian law, nor international law prohibited prosecution *in absentia*;
— criminal immunity did not apply to foreign officials, according to Belgian and to international law, in case of war crimes, crimes against humanity or genocide;
— *ne bis in idem* did not prevent prosecution in Belgium since there had never been any judicial decision in Israel in this respect;
— a Lebanese amnesty law had no effect abroad and could not prevent prosecution in Belgium, especially for crimes such as war crimes, crimes against humanity and genocide;

45. Law of 17 April 1878.

— the 1993/1999 law was not retroactive since war crimes, crimes against humanity and genocide were already part of Belgian criminal law in 1982 as they were provided for in international instruments and in international customary law which bound Belgium for than a half-century;
— international law excluded any statute of limitations for these kind of crimes;
— the reasonable time rule only applied from the beginning of the proceedings, not from the time of the crimes.

Counsel for A. Sharon made another argument which deserves some examination. He showed that the 1993/1999 Law was discriminatory in as much as a foreign head of state or minister would be subject to ordinary proceedings whereas a Belgian minister would benefit from special proceedings.[46] Some examples: firstly, anybody could complain against a foreign head of state or minister and trigger public prosecution (Code of Criminal Procedure, Art. 63) while prosecution against a Belgian minister can only be triggered by a General Prosecutor (Constitution, Arts. 103 and 125); secondly, a foreign head of state or minister indicted on the basis of the 1993/1999 Law would be prosecuted before a Court of Assizes like any ordinary criminal (1993/1999 Law, Arts. 2 and 7 combined with the Constitution, Art. 150) whereas a Belgian minister can only be prosecuted before a Court of Appeals (Law of 25 June 1998 relating to the criminal responsibility of ministers, Art. 2(1); Special Law of 25 June 1998 relating to the criminal responsibility of community and regional ministers, Art. 2(2); thirdly, enforcement measures could be taken against a foreign head of state or minister prosecuted on the basis of the 1993/1999 law (Art. 5(3)) while the same measures against a Belgian minister require a special authorisation from the competent (federal or federate) parliament (Law of 25 June 1998, Arts. 7 and 17; Special Law of 25 June 1998, Arts. 7 and 17). For these various reasons, counsel for Sharon considered that this inequality between the persons subject to trial should lead the Chamber of indictments to request the Court of Arbitration to give a ruling thereon. This court has been established to settle conflicts, on the one hand, between federal and federate laws or between federate laws themselves, and, on the other hand, between any law and some constitutional provisions relating more especially to the equality of Belgians (and foreigners present on the Belgian soil) between themselves (Constitution, Arts. 142 and 191; Special Law of 6 January 1989, Art. 1).

Counsels for the complainants considered that this kind of *renvoi* to the Court of Arbitration did not precisely square with the legal hypothesis that this Court had jurisdiction, e.g., the mere fact that Sharon was not in Belgium. Concerning the merits of the argument, they explained why it was justified to subject the waiver of enforcement immunity to some conditions for Belgian ministers and not for foreign ministers. He added that, in any case, this *renvoi* to the Court of Arbitration, if accepted by the Chamber, would certainly not prevent the investigation from going on for the other accused, who were not foreign ministers.

A decision of the Chamber of Indictments was expected on 6 March 2002.

☛ Proceedings against *Abdulaye Yerodia Ndombasi*, warrant of arrest of 11 April 2000 (not published) and proceedings before the ICJ[47]

46. *De Standaard*, 29 November 2001.
47. For analysis of the case, see J. Wouters and L. DeSmet, in this volume at p. 373.

According to the order of 8 December 2000 and to the orders of 14 March and 12 April 2001 granting new time limits for the submissions of the memorials, the DRC filed its Memorial on 15 May and Belgium filed its Counter-Memorial on 28 September 2001. The oral pleadings took place in The Hague from 15 to 19 October 2001.[48] As the Court decided in its order of 8 December 2000, for the first time in the history of the Court, the Parties had to plead at the same time the jurisdiction and admissibility issues and the merits.

Belgium argued that the Congolese application was not admissible since Mr Yerodia was no longer minister, and therefore could no longer avail of any immunity. Therefore, the case was moot. In addition, the case had changed and appeared now as an example of diplomatic protection exercised by the DRC in favour of one of its citizens. Such an application was not admissible either since the domestic remedies in Belgium had not been exhausted. The DRC answered that the case was not moot: the immunity of a foreign minister had been violated and this violation had not disappeared; in the *Northern Cameroon* and the *Nuclear Tests* precedents, the object of the dispute had disappeared whereas in the present case, the subject of the dispute – the warrant of arrest – continued to exist. Thus, the question did not become a problem of diplomatic protection but remained a problem of immunity from criminal process.

As to the merits of the case, the DRC claimed that Belgium did not respect the criminal immunity of a foreign minister. According to Belgium, there was no breach of immunity as long as Mr Yerodia did not come to Belgium. From this point of view, the case remained quite theoretical. Anyway, international law did not grant any kind of immunity to somebody accused of incitement to commit war crimes and crimes against humanity. Belgium was nevertheless prepared to recognise the immunity of Mr Yerodia in the case of him being officially invited to Belgium by the Belgian government or by an international organisation of which Belgium was a member. Consequently, the immunity was refused only in the case Mr Yerodia would come to Belgium outside the framework of an official invitation.

Interestingly, the DRC refrained from making any final submission relating to the exercise of universal jurisdiction *in absentia* while this claim appeared in its initial application.[49] The DRC confined itself to requesting the Court to declare that Belgium had violated international law by not respecting the absolute inviolability and immunity from criminal process of incumbent foreign ministers.

Pending

☛ Law to adapt Belgian Law to the ICC Statute

Belgium having ratified the ICC Statute on 28 June 2000,[50] the government considered that the Constitution should be modified (chiefly, because of the absolute inviolability of the king or queen) and that a draft law should be adopted in order to adapt Belgian law to the

---

48. See www.icj-cij.org/.
49. See in this volume at pp. 373 at 374.
50. See 3 *YIHL* (2000) pp. 426-428.

ICC Statute.[51] Such a draft was submitted to the Government at the beginning of 2002.[52] The general idea of the draft is to modify the law of 22 March 1996 relating to the cooperation of Belgium with the International Criminal Tribunals in order to establish a single act regulating Belgium's relations with all international criminal courts.

ERIC DAVID

BENIN

International Criminal Court

☛ Parliamentary Approval of Bill of Ratification

On 7 August 2001, the Parliament unanimously approved the bill of ratification and authorized President Mathieu Kerekou to ratify the Rome Statute. Benin signed the ICC Statute on 24 September 1999.[53]

BOLIVIA

International Criminal Court

☛ In July 2001, the Ministry of Foreign Affairs established a governmental working group, consisting of the Ministries of Foreign Affairs, Justice, Defense, the Ombudsman Office and civil society organisations (in the role of observers) to explore possible ratification of the ICC Statute and implementing legislation.[54]

Implementation and Dissemination

☛ The Comisión Nacional Permanente para la Aplicaction del DIH (CNPADIH) conducted a study in 2000 and 2001 to ascertain the extent to which Bolivia's Penal Code incorporates provisions of international humanitarian law, and prepared draft amendments providing for the punishment of breaches of the law. Moreover, the Ministry of Defence announced its intention to revise the Military Justice Code in order to comprehensively incriminate and penalise war crimes.[55]

Pending

☛ A draft law authorising Bolivia's ratification of the 1954 Cultural Property Convention and its two Protocols was presented to the House of Representatives in 2001.[56]

---

51. *Doc. parl.*, Sénat, 1999-2000, *Projet de loi portant assentiment au Statut de Rome de la Cour pénale internationale*, 3 février 2000, n° 2-329/1, pp. 7 ff. See E. David, 'Les conséquences du Statut de la Cour pénale internationale pour la répression en droit belge', *in Actualité du droit international humanitaire* (Bruxelles, La Charte 2001) pp. 73-92.

52. Not yet published.

53. http://www.iccnow.org/countryinfo/africa/benin.html.

54. Source: http://iccnow.org/countryinfo/theamericas/bolivia.html.

55. ICRC Advisory Service, *National Implementation of International Humanitarian Law*: Biennial report 2000-2001 (Geneva, ICRC 2002) p. 20.

56. Ibid.

BOSNIA AND HERZEGOVINA[57]

International Criminal Tribunals

- RS Law on Cooperation with the ICTY. Adopted 2 October 2001. Gazetted on 17 October 2001. Entered into force on 25 October 2001. Published in *Official Gazette RS* No. 52/01[58]
- Establishment of Bureau of Government of Republic of Srpska for relations with International Tribunal for War Crimes in Den Haag. Published in *Official Gazette* RS No. 52/01

On 2 October 2001, the People's Assembly of Republika Srpska finally passed a bill on cooperation with the International Criminal Tribunal for the former Yugoslavia.

Debates on the proposed legislation had been delayed twice. Eventually, the bill was adopted by a vote of 42 to nine with 25 abstentions. According to the Law on Cooperation with the ICTY, the Repulika Srpska Justice Department has the authority to act upon the ICTY requests and to forward them to the bodies that the requests pertain to.[59] Most international observers, including the ICTY, pointed out that such a bill was not actually necessary, given that the requirement to cooperate with the ICTY is specified in the Dayton Agreement.

The Bureau of the Government of Republic of Srpska for relations with International Tribunal for War Crimes in Den Haag was set up following the passage of the Law on Cooperation with International Tribunal. Within the authorisations provided by this Law, the Bureau is the conduit for cooperation between the Government of the Republic of Srpska and the Tribunal.

Cases

- *Golubović* case (*Miralem Macić, Jusuf Potur* and *Adem Landžo*), Mostar Cantonal Court, 25 July 2000

On 25 July 2000, the Cantonal Court in Mostar, the multi-ethnic court that held Mostar's first war crimes trial, convicted three Bosniak policemen – Miralem Macić, Adem Landžo and Jusuf Potur – of war crimes against the civilian population, for having killed the four members of the Golubović family in July 1992.

Originally, six defendants were arrested in April 1994 after an investigation into the murder of the ethnic Serb Golubović family but were declared mentally incompetent and released the following month.

Three of the original six defendants – Macić, Landžo and Potur – were then indicted on 8 December 1995 for war crimes against the civilian population (Article 154 of the 1998 FBiH Criminal Code),[60] but the charges were later reduced to murder. The remaining three –

---

57. Information provided by the Office of the High Representative, Sarajevo. Commentaries by Jann K. Kleffner, University of Amsterdam.

58. See 'U.S. notes Bosnian Serb Parliament's adoption of warcrimes law', AFP, 5 October 2001; 'RS finally passes bill on cooperation with ICTY', AIM Banja Luka, 4 October 2001. http://www.aimpress.org/dyn/trae/archive/data/200110/11020-002-trae-sar.htm.

59. OHR media roundup, 31 October 2001.

60. War Crimes against Civilians: Art. 154

(1) Whoever in violation of rules of international law applicable in time of war, armed conflict or occupation, orders attack at civilian population, settlement, individual civilians or persons unable to fight, which results in the death, grave bodily injuries or serious damaging of people's health; an attack

Hadzo Macić, Drazen Marković and Halil Tucaković – were indicted for failing to report the crime. The trial started on 16 October 1996, but no hearings took place in 1997 or 1998.

On 7 January 1999, the prosecutor filed a request for detention of the three main defendants on charges of murder. They were subsequently rearrested on 18 January 1999 and detained in Mostar. Commencement of the trial was further delayed due to the Office of the High Representative's insistence on sending the file for ICTY review under the 'Rules of the Road'. On 26 April 1999, the ICTY concluded that there was sufficient evidence for indictment for either murder or war crimes.

The trial on war crimes charges officially commenced on 24 May 1999 but was again delayed on numerous occasions due to the ill-health of the judge and non-appearance of some of the defendants. In the judgment of 25 July 2000, the Court sentenced Miralem Macić and Adem Landžo to 12 years and Jusuf Potur to nine years imprisonment.[61]

☛ *Momir Cović* case, Sarajevo Cantonal Court, 18 October 2000

Momir Cović was arrested in Bosnia on 29 March 1996 and charged with war crimes against the civilian population under Article 142 of the Inherited Criminal Law.[62]

---

without selecting a target, by which civilian population gets hurt; that civilian population be subject to killings, torture, inhuman treatment, biological, medical or other scientific experiments, taking of tissue or organs for the purpose of transplantation, immense suffering or violation of bodily integrity or health; dislocation or displacement or forced conversion to another nationality or religion; forcible prostitution or rape; application of measures of intimidation and terror, taking hostages, pronouncing collective punishment, unlawful bringing in concentration camps and other illegal arrests and detention, deprivation of rights to fair and impartial trial; forcible service in the armed forces of enemy's army or in its intelligence service or administration; forced labor, starvation of the population, property confiscation, pillaging, illegal and self-willed destruction and stealing on large scale of a property that is not justified by military needs, taking an illegal and disproportionate contribution or requisition, devaluation of domestic currency or the unlawful issuance of currency, or who commits one of the foregoing acts, shall be punished with a sentence of imprisonment for not less than five years or long term imprisonment.
(2) Punishment defined under paragraph 1 of this Article shall be pronounced also on those who in violation of rules of international law applicable in the time of war, armed conflict or occupation, order: that an attack be launched against objects specifically protected by the international law, as well as objects and facilities with dangerous power, such as dams, embankments and nuclear power stations; that civilian objects which are under specific protection of the international law, non-defended places and demilitarized zones be indiscriminately targeted; long-lasting and large-scale environment devastation which may be detrimental to the health or survival of the population, or whoever commits some of the aforementioned acts.
(3) Whoever in violation of rules of international law applicable in the time of war, armed conflict or occupation, orders or carries out as an occupier the resettlement of parts of his/her civilian population into the occupied territory, shall be punished with a sentence of imprisonment for not less than five years; or by long term imprisonment.

61. Source OHR War Crimes Chart October 2002 on file with author. http://www.ohr.int/print/?content_id=1815.

62. The 1977 Inherited Criminal Law (which is the Penal Code of the Socialist Federal Republic of Yugoslavia) predated the 1998 Bosnian Criminal Code. Therefore, Article 142 ICL is the equivalent of Art. 154 BiH CC. Art. 142 provides: War crime against the civilian population:
'Whoever in violation of rules of international law effective at the time of war, armed conflict or occupation, orders that civilian population be subject to killings, torture, inhuman treatment, biological experiments, immense suffering or violation of bodily integrity or health; dislocation or displacement

After the ICTY reviewed the indictment in accordance with the 'Rules of the Road' and decided that there was sufficient evidence to proceed, his trial commenced in September 1996. On 6 March 1997, the accused was acquitted for lack of evidence. The prosecution subsequently filed an appeal with the Federation Supreme Court and a hearing was held on 9 June 1998. After confirming the prosecutor's appeal relating to war crimes against the civilian population under Article 142 of the Inherited Criminal Law, the Federation Supreme Court ordered a retrial regarding the criminal act of destruction of cultural and historic monuments under Article 164 of the Criminal Code of Bosnia and Herzegovina (Art. 151 of the ICL).

The retrial began on 15 December 1998. On 18 October 2000, the Sarajevo Cantonal Court, Judge Amira Rizvić presiding, acquitted Momir Ćović of charges of war crimes against the civilian population under Article 142 of the Criminal Code of the Federal Republic of Yugoslavia due to lack of evidence.[63]

☛ *Dervo Dziho, Refik Tule* and *Kasim Colić* case, Mostar Cantonal Court, 23 March 2001

On 23 March 2001, the Mostar Cantonal Court acquitted Dervo Dziho, Refik Tule and Kasim Colić, three former soldiers of the Bosnian Army, of war crimes against ethnic Croats during the 1992-1995 war. They were accused of the maltreatment of 18 Croat civilians who were kept prisoners in a house in Gnojnice, near Mostar, in 1993.

The trial, which was approved by the ICTY under the 'Rules of the Road', opened in February 2001.

Court president Nurko Pobrić said the charges against them were not corroborated during the trial. Colić had been tried *in absentia*, while Tule and Dziho had surrendered to the court.[64]

☛ *Hanefija Prijić* case, Travnik County Court, 6 July 2001

On 6 July 2001, the Travnik County Court found Hanefija Prijić 'guilty of war crimes committed against civilians resulting from his command responsibility at the time of the event'. He was sentenced to 15 years imprisonment for ordering the killing of five Italian aid workers, two of whom managed to escape.[65]

☛ *Dragan Stanković* case, Sarajevo Cantonal Court, 24 October 2001

---

or forcible conversion to another nationality or religion; forcible prostitution or rape; application of measures of intimidation and terror, taking hostages, imposing collective punishment, unlawful bringing in concentration camps and other illegal arrests and detention, deprivation of rights to fair and impartial trial; forcible service in the armed forces of enemy's army or in its intelligence service or administration; forcible labour, starvation of the population, property confiscation, pillaging, illegal and self-willed destruction and stealing on large scale of a property that is not justified by military needs, taking an illegal and disproportionate contribution or requisition, devaluation of domestic currency or the unlawful issuance of currency, or who commits one of the foregoing acts, shall be punished by imprisonment for not less than five years or by the death penalty.'

63. Information provided by the Office of the High Representative, Sarajevo.
64. 'Bosnian court acquits three Bosnian Muslims of war crimes', AFP, 23 March 2001.
65. 'Bosnian Muslim gets 15 years for ordering killings of aid workers', AFP, 6 July 2001.

On 24 October 2001, the Sarajevo Cantonal Court sentenced an ethnic Serb to ten years imprisonment for crimes against humanity committed during the Bosnian war. Dragan Stanković was found guilty of raping Bosnian Muslim women and taking part in the expulsion of non-Serb civilians. Because of the nature of the accusations, the trial was closed to the public and no further details were given. The ICTY had approved the case being heard locally under the 'Rules of the Road'.[66]

Ongoing cases

☛ *Zeljko Dzidić, Erhard Poznić, Zoran Soldo, Mato Anicić* and *Ivan Skutor* case, Mostar Cantonal Court

In November 2000, the trial against the five defendants, all former members of the Bosnian Croat militia, HVO, began. The five are charged with murdering four civilians and 20 soldiers from the Muslim-dominated Bosnian army. The list of victims allegedly includes 12 soldiers captured in early-May 1993. The captives mysteriously vanished, after being paraded on Croatian state television. As the trial commenced, two of the indictees, Anicić and Skutor, were still at large.[67]

☛ *Zikrija Ljevo, Vernes Zehirović, Becir Omanović, Meho Kaminić, Habib Copelj* and *Husnija Orucević* case, Mostar Cantonal Court

The trial against the six Bosnian Muslims opened on 23 January 2001 in Mostar. The trial, which was approved by the ICTY, involves six former members of the Bosnian Army who were indicted by the Mostar regional court in October 2000. The six are charged with killing two and torturing five ethnic Croat prisoners of war in 1993, in Potoci, near Mostar. The indictment against the six was one of three collective indictments handed down by the Mostar court and approved by the ICTY. The indictments concern a total of 21 Bosnian Muslims suspected of committing war crimes against ethnic Croat civilians and prisoners of war in 1993.[68]

☛ Trial of 13 Bosnian Muslims, Mostar Cantonal Court

In another case pursuant to a collective indictment handed down by the Mostar court, in April 2001, the trial of 13 Muslims accused of murdering and torturing Bosnian Croat prisoners during fighting around Mostar in 1993-94 commenced. According to the indictment, the accused were responsible for the deaths of 17 prisoners during forced labour at the front line, and another who was tortured at a local prison. Ten of the accused turned themselves in. Three, who fled to the United States, are being tried *in absentia*.

---

66. 'Bosnia sentences Serb for war crimes', BBC World Europe, 24 October 2001; Helsinki Committee of Human Rights in Bosnia and Herzegovina, FaxLetter No. 123 at http://www.bh-hchr.org/faxlett/1998/no123.htm.

67. http://www.mladi-most.org/newsletter/newsletterfeb01.htm.

68. 'Bosnian Muslims on trial for war crimes against Croats', AFP, 23 January 2001.

☛ *Goran Vasić* case, Sarajevo Cantonal Court

The second retrial of Goran Vasić, accused of war crimes against the civilian population and war crimes against prisoners of war (Arts. 142 and 144[69] Inherited Criminal Law/FRY Criminal Code), allegedly committed in 1992 and 1993, commenced in May 2001 before the Sarajevo Cantonal Court, Judge Amira Rizvić presiding.

Goran Vasić was arrested on 6 February 1998 and imprisoned in Sarajevo (Centar) prison after the ICTY reviewed the charges and concluded on 13 February 1998 that there was sufficient evidence for detention. After an indictment was brought on 1 July 1998, the trial commenced on 31 August 1998. In the first instance judgment of 13 April 1999, the defendant was convicted of war crimes against the civilian population and war crimes against prisoners of war and sentenced to ten years imprisonment. He was acquitted of the murder of Hakija Turajlić, former vice president of the Bosnian government, who was shot in an UNPROFOR vehicle at a Serb checkpoint in Sarajevo on 8 January 1993. After an appeal was lodged on 9 September 1999, the Supreme Court of the Federation of Bosnia and Herzegovina ordered a retrial, which commenced on 25 October 1999 and resulted in a conviction and sentence of seven years imprisonment on 9 October 2000. After another appeal by the defense lawyer, the Supreme Court of the Federation of Bosnia and Herzegovina ordered another retrial. The concerns expressed by the Office of the High Representative, which monitored the trials, included the expansion of the charges against Goran Vasić by the Court after the ICTY had reviewed the file, thus involving a potential breach of the 'Rules of the Road', and the fact that the judge ruled in favour of hearing Republika Srpska (RS) witnesses in the RS. The prosecutor had objected to their statements being read out in the Sarajevo Court after they had been taken, but a decision was taken by the judge on 16 December 1998 to read the statements into the evidence.[70]

On 2 January 2002, Judge Davorin Jukić of the Sarajevo Canton Court announced that Goran Vasić has been sentenced to four and a half years in jail for was crimes committed against civilians and prisoners of war. In consideration of the time Vasić had spent in custody, the court decided to release him immediately.[71]

☛ *Miroslav Pandurević* case, FBiH Supreme Court

The BiH Federation police arrested Miroslav Pandurević on 6 June 2000. According to the indictment, on 22 August 1992, Pandurević, as a member of Serb Army, together with two other persons, took part in setting fire to houses in the Sarajevan settlement of Grbavica, in which Bosniaks Mustafa Trnka, Zulejha Trnka and Jasminka Trnka, who was pregnant,

---

69. War crime against prisoners of war: Art. 144:
'Whoever, in violation of the rules of international law, orders murders, tortures or inhuman treatment of prisoners of war, including therein biological experiments, causing of great sufferings or serious injury to the bodily integrity or health, compulsive enlistment into the armed forces of an enemy power, or deprivation of the right to a fair and impartial trial, or who commits some of the foregoing acts, shall be punished by imprisonment for not less than five years or by the death penalty.'

70. *Supra* n. 63. See also A. Kebo, 'Regional Report: Local Justice, Bosnian-Style', IWPR's Tribunal Update No. 220, 7-12 May 2001.

71. Source: BiH Media Round-up: 2/1/2002. http://www.ohr.int/ohr-dept/presso/bh-media-rep/round-ups/default.asp?content_id=6677.

were burned to ashes.[72] His trial commenced on 26 September 2000 before the Cantonal Court in Sarajevo,[73] Judge Saban Maksumić presiding. Following the defendant's acquittal on the charges of war crimes against civilians (Art. 154, in conjunction with Art. 23[74] of the FBiH Criminal Code) on 15 March 2001, the Prosecutor appealed against the decision. The appeal was still pending before the FBiH Supreme Court by the end of the year.

☛ *Dominik 'Como' Ilijasević* case, Zenica Cantonal Court

On 20 February 2001, the Cantonal Prosecutor's Office in Zenica issued an indictment against Dominik 'Como' Ilijasević, charging him with war crimes against the civilian population in central Bosnia, pursuant to Article 154(1) of the FBiH Criminal Code. The accused was arrested on 28 August 2000 by a special police unit of the BiH Federation, pursuant to a warrant issued on 9 August. His trial on the war crimes charges awaited completion of his trial on charges of murder against the former FBiH Minister of Interior Jozo Leutar.[75]

☛ *Vlatko Buzuk* case, Sarajevo Cantonal Court

On 16 May 2001, the Cantonal Prosecutor's Office in Sarajevo issued an indictment against Vlatko Buzuk for genocide and war crimes under Articles 153[76] and 154 of the FBiH Criminal Code. During the armed conflict he was a member of the Croatian Defence Council for Kreševo. According to his indictment, during 1993 he participated in the ethnic cleansing, frightening, persecution, maltreatment, robbery of property, forced labour of citizens, hostage-taking and illegal imprisonment of Bosniaks. The accused was arrested on 1 September 2000. The trial began before the Sarajevo Cantonal Court on 30 August 2001, before Trial Judge Muhamed Podrug.[77] On 17 January 2002, he was acquitted of all charges and released.[78]

---

72. Source: Helsinki Committee for Human Rights in Bosnia and Herzegovina. http://www.bh-hchr.org/faxlett/1998/no86.htm.

73. Source: Source OHR War Crimes Chart October 2002 on file with author. http://www.ohr.int/print/?content_id=1815.

74. Accomplices: Art. 23: 'Several persons who have jointly committed a criminal offense by participating in the act of commission or in some other way, shall each be punished as prescribed for the act.'

75. Source OHR War Crimes Chart October 2002 on file with author. http://www.ohr.int/print/?content_id=1815.

76. Genocide: Art. 153:
'Whoever, with the intention of destroying a national, ethnic, racial or religious group in whole or in part, orders killings or inflicting serious bodily injuries or serious disturbance of physical or mental health of the group members, or a forced dislocation of the population, or that the group be put under such living conditions which are created to bring about its physical destruction in whole or in part, or that measures be pronounced intended to prevent births within the group, or that children of the group be forcibly moved to another group, or whoever with the same intent commits one of the foregoing acts, shall be punished with a sentence of imprisonment for not less than five years or long term imprisonment.'

77. OHR War Crimes Chart October 2002 on file with author. http://www.ohr.int/print/?content_id=1815.

78. Human Rights Chamber for Bosnia and Herzegovina, Annual Report 2002. http://www.hrc.ba/ENGLISH/annual_report/2002/ANNEX/a11.htm.

☛ *Tibor Prajo* case, Travnik Cantonal Court

After the Sarajevo Cantonal Court conducted an investigation against Tibor Prajo regarding war crimes against the civilian population in central Bosnia, the FBiH Supreme Court, at the request of Tibor Prajo's defense counsel, transferred the case to the Cantonal Court in Travnik for the reason of territorial jurisdiction. The trial was scheduled to commence on 25 October 2001. Prajo was arrested on 24 November 2000, and the indictment was issued on 23 May 2001.[79]

☛ *Sretko Damjanović* case, Sarajevo Cantonal Court

A retrial of Sretko Damjanović took place before the Cantonal Court in Sarajevo. The defendant was originally sentenced to death in 1993 by a District Army Court for genocide and war crimes against the civilian population. Sretko Damjanović, who claimed he had been coerced into making a confession, was convicted largely on the testimony of a fellow soldier who had confessed to genocide and crimes against civilians while fighting for Serb forces around Sarajevo in 1992.[80]

On 30 July 1993, the High Court in Sarajevo altered the factual basis of the conviction but upheld the death sentence. The conviction, as upheld by the High Court, was for the murder of two brothers named Blekić and also for the murder of a third person, named Ramiz Krso. In December 1996, Damjanović filed a request for a retrial after it was discovered that the brothers are alive and living in the Sarajevo suburb of Vogosca.

☛ *Alia Izetbegović* indictment

In late-2001, the Republika Srpska authorities submitted an indictment accusing former Bosnian President Alija Izetbegović of criminal responsibility for war crimes against Serbs during the 1992-95 Bosnian war to the ICTY for review in accordance with the 'Rules of the Road'.[81]

☛ Dismissal of Police Officers due to War Crimes Allegations

On two occasions in late-2001 the UN administration dismissed local police officers for their alleged involvement in war crimes.

On the first occasion, three Bosnian Serb police officers, Brane Cosović, Miodrag Koprivica and Zoran Vladicić, who worked in Foča were dismissed. UN spokesman Stefo Lehmann said the UN Human Rights Unit collected evidence that Cosović was the commander of the Foča military police in 1992 and suspected to be liable for violations and counts of serious crimes committed by the Foča military police officers under his command. Koprivica and Vladicić were identified by witnesses as having served as interrogators in the

---

79. OHR War Crimes Chart October 2002 on file with author. http://www.ohr.int/print/?content_id=1815.

80. Death Penalty News March 1997. Amnesty International: AI Index Act 53/002/1997, 1 March 1997. http://web.amnesty.org/library/Index/ENGACT530021997?open&of=ENG-PRI.

81. 'Izetbegovic's party attacks his indictment by Bosnian Serbs', AFP, 7 November 2001.

KP-Dom detention facility in 1992. Possible evidence against the three was passed on to the ICTY, and the UN authorities urged the Bosnian Serb interior ministry to launch a criminal investigation into the three.[82]

The second occasion concerned two Bosnian Muslim policemen, Enver Dupovac and Mensur Ćović, who were allegedly involved in the detention and abuse of non-Muslim civilians in an army facility near Sarajevo during the 1992-95 war. Prior to their dismissal, Dupovac was a police chief while Ćović was a police officer in Hadzici, near Tarcin. The records on the two were also shared with the ICTY.[83]

JANN K. KLEFFNER

BRAZIL

Landmines

☛ Law No. 10.300 of 31 October 2001 on the Prohibition of the Use, Stockpiling, Production and Transfer, directly or indirectly, of Anti-personnel Mines [Lei No. 10.300, de 31 outubro de 2001, Proíbe o emprego, o desenvolvimento, a fabricação, a comercialização, a importação, a exportação, a acquisiçao, a estocagem, a rentção ou a transerência, direta ou indirectamente, de minas terrestres antipessoal]. Entered into force on 1 November 2001. Published in *Diario Oficial* of 1 November 2001[84]

International Criminal Court

☛ Establishment of working group on the International Criminal Court

At the end of 2001, the Minister of Justice appointed a working group of legal experts whose task is to study what Brazil must do in order to comply with the provisions contained in the Rome Statute, which Brazil signed on 7 February 2000.[85]

BURKINA FASO

Landmines

☛ Decree on the prohibition of anti-personnel mines and other implementing measures for the 1977 Ottawa Convention [Décret No. 2001-180/PRES/PM/SECU du 2 mai 2001]. Published in *Journal Officiel du Burkina Faso*, No. 20, 2001[86]

'This decree was adopted to implement the 1997 Ottawa Treaty on Landmines. It prohibits the development, manufacturing, production, acquisition, stockpiling, retention, offer, import, export and transfer of anti-personnel mines. It stipulates the maximum number of mines (500) that may be held by State services for training in detection, demining and destruction techniques. It also includes provisions for the operation of a fact-finding mission

---

82. 'U.N. officials fire three police officers for their wartime roles', AP, 27 November 2001.
83. 'UN sacks two Bosnian Muslim policemen for serving in war-time camp', AFP, 4 December 2001.
84. ICRC Advisory Service, *National Implementation of International Humanitarian Law*: Biennial report 2000-2001 (Geneva, ICRC 2002) p. 23.
85. Ibid.
86. Ibid., p. 25.

in Burkina Faso, in accordance with Article 8 of the treaty. This decree refers to the penal code and stipulates sentences of 1 to 5 years imprisonment and/or a fine for breaches of its provisions.'[87]

CAMBODIA

Internationalised Tribunals

☛ Draft Law on the Establishment of Extraordinary Chambers in the Courts of Cambodia for the Prosecution of Crimes Committed During the Period of Democratic Kampuchea [http://csf.colorado.edu/bcas/main-cas/camb-law.htm]

The bill was debated by the National Assembly from 29 December 2000 to 2 January 2001 and was adopted unanimously by all members present. On 2 January 2001, the Cambodian National Assembly, the lower house of parliament, approved the draft Law on the Establishment of Extraordinary Chambers in the Courts of Cambodia for the Prosecution of Crimes Committed During the Period of Democratic Kampuchea, which, once it is ratified by the king, would establish an internationalised Cambodian court to prosecute senior leaders of Democratic Kampuchea responsible for serious violations of Cambodian and international law committed between 17 April 1975 and 6 January 1979. Under the draft Law, the Tribunal would be composed of both Cambodian and international judges. While the legislation largely met UN demands, critics said that it gave the Cambodian judiciary too much influence.[88]

The passage of the law followed two years of difficult negotiations between the UN and the Cambodian government on the establishment of the mixed court. The National Assembly approved the draft after two days of discussion, with all 92 legislators present backing it. Thirty members were absent from the vote. On 15 January, 51 of the 61 Senators sitting in the Senate passed the law. Before becoming law, the legislation still had to attain the approval of the Constitutional Council before being signed by King Norodom Sihanouk, but its smooth passage was confidently expected, and it was officially announced that the King would be signing the law into force by the third week of January. Then, an Agreement between the Cambodian Government and the United Nations regarding the Extraordinary Chambers could be signed.[89]

On 12 February, the process ran into difficulties, however, when the Constitutional Council objected to references to the 1956 penal law, which refers to the death penalty, which was abolished a decade ago. On 23 February 2001, the Prime Minister, Hun Sen, said

---

87. Source: ICRC Database on IHL. Implementing Laws and Regulations. http://www.icrc.org/Web/eng/siteeng0.nsf/html/57KL22?OpenDocument.

88. Ibid.

89. C. Sotheacheath, 'Cambodia to try Khmer Rouge leaders', AP, 2 January 2001; C. Sophal, 'Cambodia parliament approves Khmer Rouge trial', Reuters, 2 January 2001; 'UN welcomes steps to try Khmer Rouge', *South China Morning Post*, 3 January 2001; K. Johnson, 'Lawmakers approve setting up of 'killing fields' tribunal', *South China Morning Post*, 3 January 2001; Statement by the Press Secretary/Director-General for Press and Public Relations, Ministry of Foreign Affairs, on the Passage of the 'Law on the Establishment of Extraordinary Chambers in the Courts of Cambodia for the Prosecution of Crimes Committed during the Period of Democratic Kampuchea' in the Senate of the Kingdom of Cambodia. http://www.mofa.go.jp/announce/announce/2001/1/0115.html.

that there were inconsistencies in the draft law and that it would need to be revised and approved by Parliament a second time.[90]

On 28 June, the Council of Ministers approved a revision of the draft law to establish the tribunal. The revision consisted of adding one sentence to Article 3 of the law, stating: 'Punishment under article 209, 500, 506, and 507 of the 1956 Penal Code are determined that the maximum penalty is life time imprisonment pursuant to article 32 of the Constitution of the Kingdom of Cambodia and is additionally emphasized under article 38 and 39 of this law'. Some thought that the revision was unnecessary given that Article 38 of the draft law states that all sentences shall be limited to life imprisonment. Prime Minister Hun Sen said that it was important to move quickly to establish the Court, given that the only two suspects currently in custoy, Ta Mok, the former Khmer Rouge military chief, and Kaing Kek lev, aka, Duch, the director its secret police, must be tried before March 2002. Under a special law, they can remain in custody for a maximum of three years without trial.[91]

The National Assembly and Senate passed the revised legislation in July. On 7 August, the Constitutional Council also approved the draft law.[92]

On 10 August 2001, King Norodom Sihanouk promulgated a Law on the Establishment of Extraordinary Chambers in the Courts of Cambodia for the Prosecution of Crimes Committed during the Period of Democratic Kampuchea. In October, the UN received an invitation from Cambodia to begin final negotiations to establish the Tribunal. In the letter, Cabinet Minister Sok An, who led the government's talks with the UN, told UN Under-Secretary-General Hans Corell that no serious obstacles remained to the signing of a memorandum of understanding on the conduct of the trials.[93]

However, by the end of the year, the Tribunal had still not been established.

CANADA[94]

The Armed Forces

☛ Annual Report of the Judge Advocate General to the Minister of National Defence on the administration of military justice in the Canadian Forces: a review from 1 April 2000 to 31 March 2001
[http://www.forces.gc.ca/jag/office/publications/annual_reports/2001annualreport_e.pdf]

This is the second annual report by the Judge Advocate General (JAG) on the administration of justice in the Canadian Armed Forces, with the aim of increasing the public accountability and transparency of military justice. The report describes the function of the JAG and

90. 'Further negotiations needed for Cambodian war crimes tribunal', AFP, 28 June 2002; 'Genocide and international crimes in domestic courts'. A survey by Prevent Genocide International, available at its website: http://www.preventgenocide.org/punish/domestic/.

91. 'Draft law for Khmer Rouge trial amended: No death penalty', AP, 22 June 2001.

92. B. Crossette, 'Pact sought on Khmer Rouge trials', *New York Times*, 28 June 2001.

93. 'Cambodia set for Khmer Rouge trials', BBC, 7 August 2001; 'Khmer Rouge tribunal talks expected to be; tough', AP, 11 August 2001; 'King Norodom Sihanouk signs Khmer Rouge legislation', AFP, 10 August 2001. 'Invitation sent U.N. for negotiation on Khmer Rouge trials', UNWire, 10 October 2001.

94. Information and commentaries by René Provost, Associate Professor and Associate Dean, Faculty of Law and Institute of Comparative Law, McGill University. Thanks to Guillaume Beaupré for his excellent research assistance.

its links with other institutions, and explains the Canadian military justice system measures that have been taken to improve its administration. It also reviews summary charges, proceedings and court martial decisions from April 2000 to March 2001. According to the report, no charges were made during that period for violations of humanitarian law of armed conflict.

POWs

☛ Canada's position on the status of Afghan prisoners held by the United States

Following the arrest by Canadian special forces of suspected terrorists in Afghanistan and their handing over to the United States, a debate emerged in Canada on the legality and morality of such action, since there was no guarantee that the Americans would grant captives prisoner of war status. In response to the criticisms and concerns expressed by many members of Parliament, especially from the opposition parties, the Canadian government adopted a relatively mixed position on the issue. First prudently asserting that the United States would follow international law and bring the detainees before a competent tribunal to determine their formal status, the Canadian government then gradually moved to a stricter position, urging the US to clarify its intentions and the process by which the status of captured fighters would be determined. Canada did not go as far as to clearly state its position on whether the prisoners should be granted prisoner of war status or be declared unlawful combatants, but it always emphasized the need to respect the Geneva Conventions and give the captives fair and humane treatment. Canadian troops in Afghanistan received the order to treat all captives as prisoners of war.[95]

Military Manuals

☛ Collection of documents on the Law of Armed Conflict, Office of the Judge Advocate General, Directorate of Law Training, B-GG-005-027/AF-021. Published on 21 February 2001 [http://www.forces.gc.ca/jag/training/publications/law_of_armed_conflict/loac_collection_e.pdf]

This document is an updated version of the Draft Collection of Documents on the Law of Armed Conflict, 1999 Edition, and completes The Law of Armed Conflict at the Operational and Tactical Levels (B-GG-005-027/AF-021), published in 2000.[96] It consists of a collection of treaties and other international texts and instruments relating to the Law of Armed Conflict (from the 1868 St. Petersburg Declaration to the 1998 Rome Statute of the International Criminal Court), and includes some Canadian Acts of Parliament relevant to the implementation of the Law of Armed Conflict into Canadian Law, such as the Crimes against Humanity and War Crimes Act (2000) and the Anti-Personnel Mines Convention Implementation Act (1997).

---

95. See 'Canada presses U.S. on status of Afghan prisoners', by R. Palmer, Canadian Press, 1 February 2002. http://ca.news.yahoo.com/020201/5/i90i.html.

96. See the comment of R. Provost in 3 *YIHL* (2000) at pp. 440-441.

Landmines

☛ Launch of 'virtual classroom' on landmines [http://webapps.dfait-maeci.gc.ca/minpub/listpublications.asp?pubtypeid=100001&year=2001&language=e]

Marking the second anniversary of the entry into force of the Ottawa Convention banning anti-personnel mines, the Minister of Foreign Affairs launched a 'Virtual Classroom' on landmines for Canadian students. This project will give students across the country the opportunity to participate in a number of interactive video conference sessions designed to promote learning about the global landmine program. The Minister also announced further mine action funding ($475,000) in Thailand, southeastern Europe and Uganda. Since 1998, Canada has disbursed approximately $50 million from the five-year Canadian Landmine Fund to support mine clearance, victim assistance, mine awareness and other mine action initiatives in more than 25 countries throughout the world.

War Crimes

☛ Canada's War Crimes Program, 4th Annual Report 2000-2001. Published in June 2001. [http://www.cic.gc.ca/english/pub/war2001.html]

Based on the premise that 'Canada will not become a safe haven for those individuals who have committed war crimes, crimes against humanity or any other reprehensible acts during armed conflict', Canada's War Crimes Program provides a financial and operational framework to ensure that appropriate enforcement action is taken against suspected war criminals. The program works through a special partnership between the Department of Justice Canada, the Department of Citizenship and Immigration and the RCMP (Royal Canadian Mounted Police), who, in 1998, were allocated $46.8 million over three years to investigate and litigate new cases, expand capacity for interdiction abroad, improve case processing in Canada and provide enhanced infrastructure for the War Crimes Program.

This fourth report, covering the fiscal year 2000-2001, details the government's progress in bringing to justice those involved in war crimes during World War II and more recent wars, and provides information concerning Canada's war crimes strategy, international cooperation, partnerships and the resources set aside to achieve the Government's objectives. The report reveals that 644 people were prevented from entering Canada in 2000-2001 (bringing the total to 1,556 for the last ten years) and that 42 people were removed from Canada for war crimes-related allegations (bringing the total to 187 since the inception of the program). There are approximately 82 active World War II files and 172 modern war crimes files on which the Department of Justice War Crimes Section and the RCMP are currently working, some of them being presently subject to judicial proceedings before the Federal Court of Canada.

Counter-Terrorism

☛ The Anti-Terrorism Act, S.C. 2001, c. 41. (An Act to amend the Criminal Code, the Official Secrets Act, the Canada Evidence Act, the Proceeds of Crime (Money Laundering) Act and other Acts, and to enact measures respecting the registration of charities, in order to combat terrorism). Passed by Parliament on 28 November 2001. Received Royal Assent on 18 December 2001 [http://www.parl.gc.ca/37/1/parlbus/chambus/house/bills/government/C-36/C-36_4/C-36_cover-E.html]

In response to the terrorist attacks on the United States on 11 September 2001 and the alleged possibility of Canada harbouring presumed terrorists, the Canadian Government announced it would set up an Anti-Terrorism Plan designed to protect the population and prevent terrorist activities in Canada. As a part of this plan, the Canadian Parliament passed the Anti-Terrorism Act (Bill C-36) on 28 November 2001, introducing a series of provisions to detect, deter and disable terrorist groups. The Act also establishes a process for identifying terrorist organizations and creates new and specialized criminal offences that both prevent and punish terrorist acts. This piece of legislation is multi-dimensional, in the sense that it modifies a series of existing statutes in different fields of activity, such as the Criminal Code, the Canada Evidence Act, the Security of Information Act, the Firearms Act, the National Defence Act and the Federal Court Act.

Most importantly, the Anti-Terrorism Act enabled Canada to ratify the remaining two (of 12) UN counter-terrorism conventions: the Suppression of Terrorist Financing Convention – which will allow a Federal Court judge to order the seizure and forfeiture of property used in or related to terrorist activity (ratified on 15 February 2002) – and the Suppression of Terrorist Bombings Convention – which contains provisions relating to the targeting of public places, government or infrastructure facilities and transportation systems with explosives or other lethal devices, including chemical or biological agents. The Canadian Government also indicated its will to ratify the 1994 Safety of United Nations and Associated Personnel Convention, which relates to ensuring the safety of UN personnel from attacks against their person, official premises and modes of transport. The Anti-Terrorism Act received Royal Assent on 18 December 2001.

Immigration

☛ The Immigration and Refugee Protection Act, S.C. 2001, c.27. (An Act respecting immigration to Canada and the granting of refugee protection to persons who are displaced, persecuted or in danger) [http://www.parl.gc.ca/37/1/parlbus/chambus/house/bills/government/C-11/C-11_3/C-11_cover-E.html. Legislative summary: http://www. parl. gc.ca/common/Bills_ls.asp?lang=E&Parl=37&Ses=1&ls=C11&source=Bills_Individual]

The Immigration and Refugee Protection Act, which replaced the former Immigration Act, was passed by the House of Commons on 13 June and received Royal Assent on 1 November 2001. This new Act ensues from Bill C-11, which itself resumed the legislative works of previous Bill C-31, of the same title, that had been abolished following the dissolution of Parliament on 22 October 2000 and the call for elections (any bill of a previous Parliament, in order to be proceeded with, must be introduced again as a new bill).[97] The differences between Bill C-11 and Bill C-31 were largely organizational and technical, but some substantive changes were also made in response to the alleged weaknesses of Bill C-31.

In many respects, the Immigration and Refugee Protection Act Bill mirrors the former Immigration Act but also consolidates some of its provisions by introducing key measures to strengthen the integrity of the refugee determination system. Such measures include front-end security screening for all claimants; clearer grounds for detention; fewer appeals and opportunities for judicial review to delay the removal of serious criminals; and suspen-

97. See the comment of R. Provost in 3 *YIHL* (2000) at pp. 446-447.

sion of refugee claims for people charged with serious crimes until the courts have rendered a decision. Its main purpose is thus to provide public authorities with a more simple and coherent operational framework in order to facilitate the entering and integration of genuine refugees and immigrants while 'denying access to foreign nationals, including refugee claimants, who are serious criminals or security risks'. The Act is also designed to maintain Canada's humanitarian tradition of providing safe haven to people in need of protection.

The Act contains very important sections that apply to suspected war criminals as well as to other categories of persons involved in serious criminality, such as organised crime and terrorism. They include inadmissibility clauses. One of the grounds for inadmissibility is what is referred to in the bill as 'Human or International Rights Violations', that is, the prohibition against admitting war criminals and senior officials of regimes that violate human or international rights norms. Originally, a new provision would also have made inadmissible representatives of a government against which Canada has imposed sanctions, or had the intention to do so. The House Committee, however, has broadened this provision to encompass all persons, other than permanent residents, whose entry into or stay in Canada has been restricted by sanctions imposed by an international organization or association of states of which Canada is a member. This reflects one of the declared objectives of the Immigration and Refugee Protection Act, that is, to promote international justice and security, as well as respect for human rights. The intent of this amendment was also to ensure that the government would be able to fully implement sanctions imposed by the international community and supported by Canada.

Internationalised Tribunals

☛ Canadian support for the Special Court for Sierra Leone [http://webapps.dfait-maeci.gc.ca/minpub/Publication.asp?FileSpec=/Min_Pub_Docs/104439.htm&bPrint=False&Year=&ID=&Language=E]

Canada will contribute $2.25 million over three years to the Sierra Leone Special Court, which is established to try those suspected of having committed serious violations of international humanitarian law in Sierra Leone since 1996. This contribution includes $1.5 million over three years from the Canadian International Development Agency, as well as $750,000 over two years from the Department of Foreign Affairs and International Trade. A portion of these funds will be used to send Canadian experts to the Special Court to contribute to rebuilding the rule of law in Sierra Leone.

Cases

☛ *Borojević* et al v. *Canada*, Ontario High Court, 10 January 2001

In what is considered a precedent-setting ruling, a High Court of Ontario judge held in January 2001 that a group of mostly expatriate Serbs could sue the Canadian government over NATO's bombing of their homeland. The claim was launched by 50 Canadians of Serbian origin and seven Serb nationals. It alleged that Canada violated both international law and the Canadian Charter of Rights and Freedoms[98] by taking part in the air strikes. The group demands $75 million in compensation for deaths, injuries and property damage

98. http://www.laurentia.com/ccrf/ccrf.htm.

suffered by them and their relatives in Serbia. The judge gave them 60 days to update their statement of claim to establish exactly how each of them was directly affected by the bombing. By the end of the year, no trial date had been set.

☛ *The Minister of Citizenship and Immigration* v. *Odynsky*, Federal Court of Canada, Trial Division, 2 March 2001. Reported at (2001) 196 F.T.R. 1; (2001) 14 Imm.L.R. (3d) 3 [http://www.cmf.gc.ca/fc/2001/ori/2001fc28294.html]

Mr Odynsky was found to have concealed his service as a guard at the SS forced labour camps of Trawniki and Poniatowa. Consequently, the Court ordered and declared that Mr Odynski 'obtained citizenship by false representation or by knowingly concealing material circumstances' within the meaning of s.18(1)(b) of the Citizenship Act, with the consequence that the Minister of Citizenship and Immigration could now recommend to the Cabinet that Mr Odynsky be denaturalized and deported. The judge recognized, however, that Mr Odynsky did not voluntarily join the SS auxiliary forces, and that there was no evidence of any incident in which he was involved that could be considered as directed wrongfully at any other individual. Furthermore, no evidence was presented of any wrongdoing by Mr Odynsky since he came to Canada in 1949. The decision was thus solely based on Mr Odynsky's false representation to the Canadian immigration authorities. No information is available regarding actions taken by the Government in the wake of this decision.

☛ *Mugesera* v. *The Minister of Citizenship and Immigration*, Federal Court of Canada, Trial Division, 12 April 2001. Reported at [2001] 4 F.C. 421 [http://reports.fja.gc.ca/fc/2001/pub/v4/2001fc28726.html]

Leon Mugesera, an adviser to a Rwandan cabinet minister, was alleged to have incited a massacre in Rwanda following a 1992 speech in which he told Hutus to kill Tutsis. Two immigration board tribunals, which held that his speech amounted to counseling to murder, incitement to genocide and crimes against humanity, ordered that he be deported. In a long-awaited ruling, the Federal Court found that Leon Mugesera was not a war criminal and could therefore remain in Canada, and urged a review of his deportation case. In its decision, the court declared that one of the tribunals erred in its ruling that Mugesera should face charges of crimes against humanity, and also asked the lower tribunal of the immigration board to review its claim that the accused helped incite hatred and genocide. The court concluded that no evidence was given as to potential links between the speech and the 800,000 murders committed in the spring of 1994.

☛ *The Minister of Citizenship and Immigration* v. *Baumgartner*, Federal Court of Canada, Trial Division, 31 August 2001. Reported at (2001) 17 Imm. L.R. (3d) 85; (2001) 211 F.T.R. 197 [http://decisions.fct-cf.,gc.ca/cf/2001/2001cfpi970.html]

Pursuant to s. 18.1(a) of the Citizenship Act, the Minister of Citizenship and Immigration undertook procedures to revoke Mr Baumgartner's citizenship on the ground that he had been admitted to Canada 'by false representations or fraud or by knowingly concealing material circumstances'. Mr Baumgartner failed to divulge his service during the Second World War in the Waffen SS and his collaboration with German authorities while engaged in activities connected with forced labour and concentration camps during the period 1942-

1943. In his ruling, the judge stated that Mr Baumgartner, in not disclosing that he served as a concentration camp guard, circumvented an inquiry that may have uncovered information rendering him ineligible to apply for Canadian citizenship. The court thus concluded that Mr Baumgartner was not lawfully admitted to Canada and therefore did not acquire Canadian domicile. He now faces deportation. No information is available regarding actions taken by the Government in the wake of this decision.

☛ *The Minister of Citizenship and Immigration* v. *Fast*, Federal Court of Canada, 5 June 2001, 19 November and 29 November 2001. Reported at [2001] 3 F.C. 373 [http://decisions.fct-cf.,gc.ca/fct/2001/2001fct594.html] (5 June 2001); [http://decisions.fct-cf.,gc.ca/fct/2001/2001fct1269.html] (19 November 2001); [http://decisions.fct-cf.,gc.ca/fct/2001/2001fca373.html] (29 November 2001)]

Jacob Fast, a 89-year-old Canadian citizen born in the Ukraine, was suspected of having been admitted to Canada by false representations in failing to divulge certain information to Canadian officials concerning his activities during the Second World War, including his collaboration with the German occupation authorities in Ukraine and other wartime activities which would have rendered him inadmissible at the time. In 1999, the accused launched a judicial review application, seeking to quash the citizenship revocation notice and prohibit the Minister from referring the case to the Court, on the grounds that it was void, ineffective and unfair. The Minister and Attorney General then moved to have the application for judicial review dismissed, a motion that was allowed by the Federal Court in July 2000. In June 2001 the Federal Court ordered the setting up of a special Commission in Ukraine in order to gather the relevant evidence and question key witnesses. In the meantime, Mr Fast brought a new motion seeking a stay of the proceedings with respect to his citizenship, an application that was dismissed by the Federal Court on 19 November 2001. The appeal of this decision was also dismissed on 29 November 2001.

Pending

☛ The Public Safety Act, Bill C-42, 37th Parliament, 1st Session, 49 Eliz. II, 2001 (An Act to amend certain Acts of Canada, and to enact measures for implementing the Biological and Toxin Weapons Convention, in order to enhance public safety) [http://www.parl.gc.ca/37/1/parlbus/chambus/house/bills/government/C-42/C-42_1/C-42_cover-E.html. Legislative summary: http://www.parl.gc.ca/common/Bills_ls.asp?lang=E&ls=C42&source=Bills_House_Government&Parl=37&Ses=1]

The Public Safety Act (Bill C-42) is also part of the government's Anti-Terrorism Plan (see supra). The Bill was introduced in the House of Commons on 22 November 2001 for a first reading and was debated on 3 December 2001 in a second reading. As is the case for the Anti-Terrorism Act, the Public Safety Act would amend a series of federal laws (19 in all) in order to strengthen the Government's ability to improve the safety of Canadians, to prevent terrorist attacks and to respond swiftly if a significant threat should arise.

One of the statutes that the Public Safety Act would amend is the current Immigration Act, scheduled to be replaced by the new Immigration and Refugee Protection Act on 28 June 2002. One of the effects of Bill C-42 would be precisely to implement some provisions of the Immigration and Refugee Protection Act long before this new Act comes into force. A first amendment would ensure that suspected terrorists, members of groups engaging in organized crime, war criminals, security risks, or senior members of governments that have seriously violated human rights will have their Immigration and Refugee Board proceedings suspended if negative information comes to light following their referral. If the information is confirmed, the refugee claim would then simply not proceed. Currently, the law provides for the suspension of a refugee claim only for cases of serious criminality. Another amendment would permit the Minister, in all removal cases, to direct a person to a particular country, should circumstances require. Thus, individuals wanted in that country could not avoid justice. Presently, a person subject to a departure order can choose which country to go to on leaving Canada. These proposed amendments are consistent with provisions found in the Immigration and Refugee Protection Act.

Bill C-42 also enacts the Biological and Toxin Weapons Convention Implementation Act whose stated purpose is 'to fulfill Canada's obligations under the Convention on the Prohibition of the Development, Production and Stockpiling of Bacteriological (Biological) and Toxin Weapons and on their Destruction', a Convention that supplements the prohibition on the use of biological weapons contained in the 1925 Geneva Protocol. Canada was one of the original signatories of the Convention (10 April 1972), and ratified it on 18 September 1972, but the implementation of the Convention in Canada never resulted in any new domestic legislation. Thus, the Convention has now been fully implemented under federal legislation. In particular, it will prohibit the development, production, stockpiling, use or transfer of any biological agent or toxin for any non-peaceful purposes, as well as of any weapon, equipment and other means of delivery of agents or toxins for use in armed conflict. The proposed Act would also allow for the establishment of a National Authority, to ensure compliance with the Convention or with Canada's other related international obligations.

☛ The Holocaust Memorial Day Act, Bill C-214, 37th Parliament, 1st Session, 49 Eliz. II, 2001(An Act to establish the Holocaust Memorial Day) [http://www.parl.gc.ca/37/1/parlbus/chambus/house/bills/private/C-214/C-214_1/C-214_cover-E.html]

Introduced in the House of Commons on 5 February 2001 by a member of the opposition, Bill C-214 is primarily intended to proclaim an annual Holocaust Memorial Day – Yom ha-Shoah. Its preamble also recognizes that systematic violence, genocide, persecution, racism and hatred continue to occur throughout the world, and it reiterates the House of Commons' commitment to use legislation, education and example to uphold human rights and to protect Canadians from violence. By the end of the year, the Bill awaited a second reading.

☛ The Ukrainian Canadian Restitution Act, Bill C-331, 37th Parliament, 1st Session, 49 Eliz, 2001 (An Act to recognize the injustice that was done to persons of Ukrainian descent and other Europeans who were interned at the time of the First World War and to provide for public commemoration and for restitution which is to be devoted to education and the promotion of tolerance) [http://www.parl.gc.ca/37/1/parlbus/chambus/house/bills/private/C-331/C-331_1/C-331_cover-E.html]

This Bill was introduced in the House of Commons on 4 April 2001 for a first reading, but by the end of the year still awaited a second reading. The purpose of this Act is to provide for redress for the injustice done to persons of Ukrainian descent and other Europeans during the First World War, to commemorate this event in Canadian history and to provide for restitution to be made. The restitution is to be devoted mainly to educational materials dealing with Canada's past internment policies and activities, as well as the payment of a certain amount to Ukrainian Canadians for the confiscation of their property and other assets during the First World War. The Bill was introduced by the Canadian Alliance chief opposition critic for Citizenship and Immigration.

RENÉ PROVOST

CAPE VERDE

Implementation and Dissemination

☛ Decree No. 19/2001 of 24 September 2001 establishing a national committee for human rights [Comité national para los Direitos humanos]

'The Committee is chaired by the Ministry of Justice and has a mandate to promote human rights and humanitarian law and to advise the authorities on the national implementation thereof.'[99]

CHILE[100]

Cases

☛ Santiago Court of Appeals No. 28.075-2001 admitting the temporary stay in favour of Augusto Pinochet and suspending the process against him, 9 July 2001 [www.upaz.edu.uy/informes/Pinochet/sentencia.htm]

Senator Pinochet's lawyer had requested the Court of Appeals to annul Judge's Guzman resolution of 29 January 2001 that disregarded the health considerations raised by Senator Pinochet's defence and indicted him as the author of 57 homicides and 16 kidnappings. At the same time, counsel requested a 'temporary stay' or a stay of proceedings so long as Mr Pinochet's state of health does not improve.

The petition was based on his constitutional rights of due process (Art. 19(3) of the Chilean Constitution) and to life (Art. 19(1)), as recognised in Articles 14 and 6 of the International Covenant on Civil and Political Rights and Articles 8(2) and 4 of the American Convention on Human Rights.

The Court of Appeal deciding this matter examined: a) The state of health of Mr Pinochet according to the medical test brought before the Court, b) If Pinochet suffered from 'insanity', according to Article 409(3) of the Chilean Criminal Procedure Code,[101] c) If Pinochet's state of health really constrained his prosecution because it would violate the due process principle, and d) The law applicable to the case, specifically the new Chilean Criminal Procedure Code.

The Court ruled that former dictator Augusto Pinochet is not mentally fit to stand trial on charges of concealing political killings, effectively ending attempts to prosecute him.

---

99. ICRC Advisory Service, *National Implementation of International Humanitarian Law*: Biennial report 2000-2001 (Geneva, ICRC 2002) p. 28.

100. Information and commentaries by Hernán Salinas Burgos, Professor of Public International Law at the University of Chile and the University of Los Andes, and Carlos Dettleff Beros, Professor of Public International Law at the University of Chile.

101. Código Procesal Penal, Ley No. 19.696. Published in *Diario Oficial*, 12 October 2000.

Concerning Mr Pinochet's state of health, the Court found that, taking into account the neurological, psychiatric and psychological evaluations, Mr Pinochet suffers from a moderate vascular sub-cortical insanity caused by brain injuries. According to the medical reports, this injury is permanent and progressive, and for that reason, Mr. Pinochet lacks all the requirements for a finding of criminal responsibility under Chilean criminal law.

According to the Court's interpretation of Article 409(3) of the Chilean Criminal Procedure, a finding of 'insanity' does not require a complete absence of his faculty of reasoning. As a consequence, the current situation of Mr Pinochet falls within the meaning and purpose of the above article and a 'temporary stay' could be granted in this case.

In relation to the third issue, the Court found that, because of his illness, Pinochet did not have the capacity to efficiently exercise the rights and judicial guarantees granted to him under international human rights law in all the procedural stages. Regarding the final question, the Court stated that it had granted a 'temporary stay' in Pinochet's favour based on the nature of the facts investigated in the case, the new development of constitutional and procedural law recognized in the new Chilean procedural law and, in particular, Article 29 of the new Criminal Procedural Code, that stated that at any stage of the proceedings, if the judge considers that the accused cannot exercise his or her constitutional rights, he or she can *proprio motu* or by petition, take the necessary measures to allow the complete exercise of those rights.

To conclude, the Court, by two votes to one, annulled the decision of 29 January 2001, thus admitting the temporary stay in favour of Mr Pinochet and suspending the process against the accused.

The decision was appealed to the Supreme Court by the plaintiffs Graciela Alvarez and others, all of them members of the families of persons kidnapped and killed by a military group during the 1973 'Caravan of Death'.

☛ Order to submit questions to *Henry Kissinger*, Supreme Court, 31 July 2000

On 31 July 2001, Chile's highest court authorized investigating judge Juan Guzman to submit questions to former US Secretary of State Henry Kissinger about the assassination of the American filmmaker Charles Horman, who was killed shortly after Pinochet seized power.[102] The 17 questions would be relayed through diplomatic channels. Lawyers in the case said they were prompted by CIA and US State Department documents declassified by the Clinton administration, which center on any knowledge US officials may have had about the case. Washington reacted furiously to the request.[103]

---

102. E. Gallardo, 'Chilean court authorizes submitting questions to Kissinger about slaying of U.S. filmmaker', AP, 31 July 2001.

103. T. Harnden, 'US angry as Chile asks Kissinger about death', *The Daily Telegraph* (London), 1 August 2001.

Pending

- The National Commission for the Implementation of International Humanitarian Law, a governmental institution created in 1994,[104] is studying legislative measures specifically a law for the repression and punishment of war crimes and genocide. A draft has been prepared by the Commission with the technical assistance of the Faculty of Law of the University of Chile. Its presentation is pending before the Parliament.
- The Rome Statute, which was signed by Chile on 11 September 1998, has been submitted to the Parliament for its approval before ratification.

HERNÁN SALINAS BURGOS AND CARLOS DETTLEFF BEROS

Pending

- 'An interministerial working group was mandated to prepare draft legislation providing for the repression of breaches of humanitarian law for inclusion in the revised ordinary and military Penal Codes. A study on the topic was requested of the University of Chile's Department of Criminal Law.'[105]
- In 2001, the Comision Nacional de Derecho Humanitario launched a study to pave the way for Chile's ratification of the 1980 Convention on Certain Conventional Weapons and its Protocols.[106]

COLOMBIA[107]

The Armed Forces

- Permanent Directive No. 011 of April 2000 of the Ministry of Defence
- Permanent Directive No. 80010/2000 of the General Command of the Military Forces
- Transitory Directive No. 014/2000 of the Navy

'By Permanent Directive No. 011 of April 2000, the Ministry of Defence established human rights and humanitarian law policies for the armed forces and the police. The latter were supplemented with Permanent Directive No. 80010/2000 of the General Command of the Military Forces and Transitory Directive No. 014/2000 of the Navy.'[108]

---

104. The National Commission for the Implementation of International Humanitarian Law was created by Decree No. 1.229 of 1994, Ministry of Foreign Relations. Published in *Diario Oficial*, 27 October 1994.

105. ICRC Advisory Service, *National Implementation of International Humanitarian Law*: Biennial report 2000-2001 (Geneva, ICRC 2002) p. 29.

106. Ibid.

107. Information and commentaries by Professor Rafael A. Prieto Sanjuán (Paris II), Consultant and Professor of Public International Law and International Relations at Externado University of Colombia, Bogotá, D.C.

108. ICRC Advisory Service, *National Implementation of International Humanitarian Law*: Biennial report 2000-2001 (Geneva, ICRC 2002) p. 30.

Landmines

- Presidential decree No. 2113 of 8 October 2001 creating a Nacional Inter-Agency Commission against Anti-Personnel Mines [Departamento administrativo de la presidencia de la República. Decreto No. 2113 de 2001 (8 de octubre) por el cual se crea la Comisión Intersectorial Nacional para la Acción contra las Minas Antipersonal]. Published in *Diario Oficial* (*D.O.*) No. 44580, 12 October de 2001, p. 1
- Special report of the Presidential Program for Human Rights and IHL – Observations on Human Rights and IHL and on Anti-personnel Mines [Minas antipersonal en Colombia], Office of the Vice President – International Organisation for Migration, Bogotá. Published by Peace Investment Fund, December 2001. Bilingual (span/eng.) edition of 12 pp. [http://www.derechoshumanos.gov.co/http://www.humanrights.gov.co]

Colombia ratified the Ottawa Convention on 6 September 2000 (after Constitutional Judgment C-991 of 2 August 2000 of Approval Law 554 of 14 January 2000).[109] As a country still experiencing a long-running internal armed conflict, which has resulted in a large number of landmines being scattered, dealing with the obligations arising under that treaty is of particular relevance to Colombia, and well as posing difficult challenges.[110] Therefore, Decree 2113 of 2001 has created a special Commission to deal with these arms,[111] that strengthens the Program for Prevention and Care of Victims and on Sign-posting, Mapping and Mine Removal (Programa de Prevención de Accidentes por Minas Antipersonal y Atención a las Víctimas y de Señalización, Mapeo y Desminado).

Although the government intends to renounce the production, use and trade of antipersonnel mines – with certain exceptions – given that the Colombian armed conflict is of a guerrilla type, armed opposition groups will continue to use them for strategic purposes. Even assuming the end of the internal conflict within ten years, and with adequate funds to clear existing mines, a study has considered that eradication would still take 20 years.[112]

International Criminal Court

- Constitutional Reform by Legislative Act No. 02 of 27 December 2001 adding a second paragraph to Article 93 of the Constitution (1st art.). [Acto Legislativo No. 02 de 2001 (diciembre 27) por medio del cual se adiciona el artículo 93 de la Constitución]. Published in *D.O.* No. 44663 of 31 December 2001, p. 2

RAFAEL A. PRIETO SANJUÁN

Implementation and Dissemination

- Decree No. 321 of 25 October 2000 establishing the Comisión Intersectorial Permanente para los Derechos Humanos y el Derecho Internacional Humanitario

---

109. See 3 *YIHL* (2000) p. 453.

110. For an overview of this problem, see the special report of the Presidential Program for Human Rights and IHL.

111. This Commission is composed by represents of the Republic's Vice-presidency, the Ministries of Foreign Affairs, Defense, Health, Interior, the Department of National Planning and the Presidential Program on Human Rights and IHL, as well as Technical Sub-Commissions or Committees.

112. See Observatory on Anti-personnel Mines, Minas antipersonal en Colombia, p. 10.

This decree established the Permanent Intersectorial Commission for Human Rights and International Humanitarian Law. 'The Committee is in charge of preparing and proposing policy on human rights and IHL, in order to facilitate the government's decision-making process. It is assisted by a technical intersectorial committee.'[113]

Education and training

☛ Postgraduate course on IHL

☛ Resolution No. 391 of October 2001 of the General Santandar Police School

'A postgraduate course on IHL developed by the *Universidad Externado de Colombia* was held for the first time in 2001. University professors from around the country were trained in 2001 with a view to making humanitarian law part of the university curriculum nationwide.'[114]

The General Santandar Police School adopted resolution No. 391 of October 2001, establishing a committee in charge of drawing up a teaching model for instruction in human rights and humanitarian law within the police force.

(THE REPUBLIC OF THE) CONGO

Education and Training

☛ Training of the military

'In 2001, IHL was incorporated into the curricula of the Military Academy, armed forces' military schools, and training institutes run by the police and the security forces. Training programs for military units and regions run by the Ministry of Defence Training Directorate of Schools also included instruction in IHL. At the Law Faculty of Marien Ngouabi University, IHL was an option in the third-year master's programme. The Faculty also proposed to include IHL in the curriculum of the third year of the second cycle. IHL was also incorporated into the 2000-2001 curriculum of the diplomatic stream at the *École nationale d'Administration et de Magistrature (ENAM).*'[115]

Cases

☛ In an unprecedented move, in February 2001, a court sent an Army General to jail for failing to prevent a parliamentary massacre. The Attorney General filed kidnapping and murder charges against Carlos Castano, the leader of the right-wing paramilitary group United Self-Defense Forces of Colombia, for an incident in 1997.[116]

---

113. ICRC Advisory Service, *National Implementation of International Humanitarian Law*: Biennial report 2000-2001 (Geneva, ICRC 2002) p. 30.

114. Ibid.

115. Ibid., p. 31.

116. 'News Monitor for February 2001'. Prevent Genocide International. http://www.preventgenocide.org/prevent/news-monitor/2001feb.htm.

Pending

- A draft law to replace Presidental Decree No. 860 of May 1998 concerning the use of the red cross name and emblems [Por el cual se reglamenta lo relative a la protección y el uso que debe dares al nombre y el emblema de la Cruz Roja, se protegen sus actividades y se facilita la prestación de los servicios humanitario en Colombia] was prepared during 2001 by the Colombia Red Cross Society with the assistance of the ICRC Advisory Service.[117]

COSTA RICA

The Emblems

- Law No. 8031 concerning the use and protection of the emblems of the red cross and the red crescent [Ley No. 8031, Uso y protección de los emblemas de la cruz roja y de la media luna roja]. Adopted 19 October September 2000. Entered into force 2 November 2000. Published in Alcance No. 75 de *La Gaceta* No. 210, 2 November 2000 [Published online in Spanish at http://www.icrc.org/ihl-nat.nsf/6fa4d35e5e302539 4125673e00508143/ee02988f032f1aedc1256b18003a64d9?OpenDocument][118]

Education and Training

- 'IHL was incorporated into university curricula and the programme of instruction of the *Instituo del Servicio Exterior Manuel María de Peralta.*'

Pending

- Moves to reform the penal law are underway. 'Two draft revisions of the Penal Code were prepared, one by the judiciary and the other by the Legislative Assembly. Further to consultations between the Advisory Service and the executive and legislative branches of government, a further project for Penal Code reform that included sanctions for war crimes was prepared in 2001 and submitted to the Legislative Assembly for approval.'[119]
- Costa Rica is preparing to implement the Landmines Treaty. In 2001, draft legislation was submitted to the Legislative Assembly for its approval.[120]

CROATIA

Cultural Property

- Protocol on the transport of objects of art, cultural assets and other exhibits from the museum of Vojvodina and the Novi Sad city museum (in Yugoslavia) to the Vukovar city museum, signed on 7 December 2001 in Belgrade[121]

---

117. ICRC Advisory Service, *National Implementation of International Humanitarian Law*: Biennial report 2000-2001 (Geneva, ICRC 2002) p. 30.

118. Ibid., p. 33.

119. Ibid.

120. Ibid.

121. '10 years on stolen art works return to Croatian town', AFP, 12 December 2001; 'Art collection of war-torn Croatian town of Vukovar returns home', Deutsche Presse-Agentur, 12 December 2001; 'Croatia's precious artwork returned', BBC News, 12 December 2001.

Thousands of pieces of arts were removed by the JNA from the municipal museum in Vukovar during the 1991 war between Croatia and the Federal Republic of Yugoslavia after the town was overrun. The collection had been stored at the museum in Novi Sad, in the Yugoslavia's northern province of Vojvodina. Under the terms of this agreement, it was returned to Vukovar.

Pardon

☛ Pardon of five Serbs convicted for crimes against humanity and genocide

In a statement issued on 26 March 2001, Croatian President Stipe Mesić announced that he had pardoned five Croatian citizens of Serb nationality in accordance with Article 98 of the constitution and Article 1 of the amnesty law,[122] and at the motion of the amnesty commission dating 23 March 2001. Vaso Graovac, Milenko Milanković, Milos Horvat, Bogdan Banić and Djuro Kuzmanović had submitted appeals for pardon, and had already served the majority of their sentences. All of them were sentenced for committing war crimes against civilians and genocide. The amnesty commission had suggested that the President grant pardon to the five Serbs in exchange for the release of five Croatians imprisoned in Serbia.[123]

International Criminal Tribunals

☛ Resolution to confirm cooperation with the ICTY, 17 July 2001

In an emergency meeting on 7 July 2001, the Croatian cabinet gave the green light to the extradition to the International Criminal Tribunal for the former Yugoslavia of any Croatian citizen indicted by the Tribunal. Four liberal ministers in the 23-member cabinet offered their resignations in protest. The ICTY revealed that it had indicted two retired Croat Generals, Ante Gotovina and Rahim Ademi. The Croatian government plunged into crisis over the decision to hand them over.[124]

By Resolution to confirm cooperation with the ICTY of 17 July 2001, Croatia reaffirmed its intention to cooperate with the ICTY.[125] The measure won the support of 71 lawmakers in the 151-seat legislature. Forty deputies, largely hardliners of the late-President Franjo Tudman's nationalist party, opposed the vote.

The debate over Croatia's relations with the Tribunal was prompted by nationalists in a renewed effort to discredit the government's decision to surrender to the ICTY two Croat generals suspected of atrocities in Croatia's war for independence from Yugoslavia from 1991-1995.

---

122. 'Law on General Amnesty', 20 September 1996, published in *Narodne novine*, no. 27/1996, Art. 3. 3. See also M. Seršić, 1 *YIHL* (1998) p. 427.

123. 'Croatian president pardons five Serbs imprisoned for war crimes', BBC Monitoring European - Political, 26 March 2001.

124. Stabilization Force (SFOR) Chronology of Event, January 1, 2001. http://home.wanadoo.nl/tcc/balkan/sfor_chron_2e.html.

125. 'Defying nationalists again, Croatia reaffirms cooperation with war crimes tribunal', AP, 17 July 2001.

Implementation and Dissemination

☛ Government Decision to establish National Committee on International Humanitarian Law, July 2000

By a government decision of July 2000, signed by the Deputy Minister of Foreign Affairs, Croatia established the Croatian National Committee on International Humanitarian Law. The Committee is chaired by the President of the Croatian Red Cross, and its members comprise representatives of the National Society and the Ministries of Foreign Affairs, Defence, the Interior, Justice, Health and Education and Sports, local authorities, the government human rights office and academic experts.[126]

Cases

☛ *Momcilo Draca* case, Zadar District Attorney's Office, 20 December 2001

Momcilo Draca, an ethnic Serb arrested by Hungarian border guards in May 2001 and extradited to Croatia in September to face war crimes charges, was acquitted by the Zadar district attorney's office for lack of evidence and released on 20 December 2001. Draca was accused of taking part in the killing of 43 Croatian people, including elderly people, women and children, in the village of Skabrnje. Croatian radio reported that, according to the DA's office, none of ten witnesses to the massacre recognized Draca as one of the perpetrators.[127] The only remaining charge, armed rebellion, was dismissed pursuant to Croatia's 1996 amnesty law.[128]

☛ Acquittal of four Croatian police officers, Bjelovar, December 2001

'In December 2001, four Croatian police officers were acquitted of war crimes charges for killing six prisoners of war in 1991 in Bjelovar. A key prosecution witness changed his testimony at the trial, and the presiding judge accepted the changed testimony without question. There was widespread speculation that the witness was pressured to change his testimony.'[129]

Ongoing Cases

☛ Arrest of *Natasa Janković*, 3 February 2001

On 3 February 2001, Croatian authorities arrested a Bosnian woman who had been sentenced *in absentia* to eight years imprisonment in 1996 by a court in Pozega, Croatia. Nataša Janković had been found guilty of inhumane treatment, allegedly committed on

---

126. ICRC Advisory Service, *National Implementation of International Humanitarian Law*: Biennial report 2000-2001 (Geneva, ICRC 2002) p. 35.

127. 'Croatian court acquits ethnic Serb of war crimes charges', AP, 20 December 2001.

128. Regarding the Amnesty Law, see 1 *YIHL* (1998) p. 427.

129. US Department of State: 'Croatia: Country Reports on Human Rights Practices 2002. 31 March 2003. http://www.state.gov/g/drl/rls/hrrpt/2002/18359.htm.

civilians detained in a prison camp in Nova Gradiska,[130] where she supposedly worked as a guard. Due to lack of evidence, she was released in June.[131]

☛ Request for the extradition of *Josip Budimcić*, 3 March 2001

On 3 March 2001, Croatia requested the extradition of Josip Budimcić, an ethnic Serb who was granted Canadian citizenship in 1997. Budimcić worked as a mechanic for Canadian military forces in Croatia as part of the UN peacekeeping contingent. He emigrated to Canada in 1995. Shortly after he left Croatia, a Croatian court found him guilty of war crimes relating to the killing of Croat prisoners of war during the 1991 fighting in the eastern region of Vukovar. He was sentenced *in absentia* to 15 years in prison. The judgement was revoked by the Supreme Court following a defence appeal. In a repeat trial in 1996, he was again found guilty of the execution and disappearance of Croatian soldiers in Eastern Slavonia in 1991, and was again sentenced to 15 years in prison.

☛ *Gospić five/Norac case*, Rejeka County Court

On 5 March 2001, the Rijeka County Court issued an indictment against Croatian Army General Mirko Norac and four others, namely, Tihomor Oresković, Stjepan Grandić, Ivica Rozić and Milan Canić, for war crimes and crimes against humanity, following a six-month investigation. They were accused of having executed at least 24 civilians, including women and elderly citizens, in the Croatian town of Gospić, northeast of Rijeka, between 14 and 25 October 1991, during the war between the Croatian Army and the rebel Croatian Serb forces.[132]

The indictment of Norac, the first Croatian army general to be indicted for such crimes by a Croatian court, and his co-accused, whom many Croatians considered as war heroes who fought for their country against the aggressing Yugoslav Army, aroused great passion amongst the population.[133] If found guilty, Norac and the others would face 20 years in prison. After being charged, Norac went into hiding for two weeks. He turned himself into the national authorities after ICTY Prosecutor Carla del Ponte allowed Croatian authorities to try Norac under the 'Rules of the Road'.

The accused were arrested on 14 September 2000 after war veteran Milan Levar was killed in a bomb explosion in Gospić, on 2 August 2000. Before he died, Levar told ICTY investigators and made public statements, including before the Rejeka County Court, that Norac and Oresković were involved in war crimes against Croatian Serb civilians in the Gospić area at the beginning of the 1991-95 Serb-Croat war.

The five defendants submitted a plea that the prosecuting lawyer, Doris Harst, should be

---

130. 'Bosnian suspected of war crimes arrested in Croatia', AFP, 3 February 2001.

131. 'Croatia – Country Reports on Human Rights Practices- 2001', US Department of State: http://www.state.gov/g/drl/rls/hrrpt/2001/eur/8240.htm.

132. 'Croatia indicts general on war crimes', CNN.com/World. 5 March 2001. http://www.cnn.com/2001/WORLD/europe/03/05/croatia.norac/.

133. For a flavour of the pro-Gospić Five press, see J. Jović, 'Head of John the Baptist', *Slobadna Dalmacija,* 9 February 2001. http://voiceofcroatia.net/Manolic.htm. See also I. Traynor, 'Croats turn on leaders for hunting 'war criminals', *The Guardian*, 12 February 2001, describing a demonstration of 100,000 persons in Split in support of General Norac.

dismissed and the case moved to Gospić, but on 14 September, the Rijeka Supreme Court decided that the case should be heard in Rijeka.

The trial of the Gospić five began on 25 June 2001 but was adjourned after two weeks.[134]

☛ Arrest of *Miroslav Anić*

On 31 March 2001, Croatian police arrested Bosnian Croat Miroslav Anić, indicted by the ICTY in a sealed indictment for the 1993 murder of 16 Muslim civilians in the central Bosnian village of Stupni Do. The investigation of his case commenced in Croatia after the ICTY had declined to ask for his surrender.[135]

☛ Trial of nine Serbs for genocide, Ojijek County Court

The trial of nine Serbs for genocide committed during the rebellion by Croatian Serbs opened on 4 June 2001. Luka Milisavljević, Radovan Brdjan, Stojan Zivković, Milan Miljković, Zoran Stojcić, Srecko Radovanović, Rajko and Rade Kojcinović, and Vlado Simić are accused of expelling local residents from Sodolovci, Koprivna, Ernestinovo and Paulin Dvor while they were members or commanders of the so-called Serbian Volunteer Guard under the command of Zeljko Raznjatović, aka, Arkan. Luka Milisavljević and Radovan Brdjan are defending themselves outside of custody, while the other seven remain at large, probably hiding outside of Croatian territory.[136]

☛ *Fikret Abdić* case, Karlovac County Court

Fikret Abdić, the former Bosnian warlord, who ruled the small breakaway fiefdom of Bihac in northwestern Bosnia from his headquarters in Velika Kladusa during the 1992-95 war in Bosnia, went on trial before Karlovac County Court on 19 July 2001, accused of 'ordering, planning and organising the formation of transit and detention camps' for opponents of his self-proclaimed autonomous region, causing the death of 121 civilians and three prisoners of war and wounding over 400 civilians. Although the alleged crimes were committed in Bosnia, the trial was held in Croatia because Abdić is a Croatian national, and Croatian law does not permit the extradition of Croatian citizens to a foreign country.[137]

The trial was adjourned until 23 October 2001 to give the judges time to consider the huge volume of evidence and to allow witnesses from Bosnia to travel to Croatia.

☛ Arrest of four war crimes suspects

On 5 September 2001, four men were arrested on suspicion of war crimes against ethnic Serb civilians in 1995, committed during Croatia's military operation to regain territories

---

134. 'Croatian general indicted for crimes against humanity', Deutsche Presse-Agentur, 5 March 2001; 'Norac's trial adjourned after he punched other war crimes indictee', Deutsche Presse-Agentur, 18 September 2001.

135. 'Croatian cops arrest war suspect', AP, 31 March 2001.

136. Foreign Press Bureau Zagreb, *Daily Bulletin* – No. 122/2001, 26 June 2001.

137. 'Bosnian Muslim rebel leader on trial for war crimes in Croatia', AFP, 19 July 2001; G. Partos, 'Warlord on trial in Croatia', BBC World Europe, 20 July 2001.

occupied by rebel Serbs. One of the four was a junior officer and the others were conscripts in the Croatian army during the war.[138]

☛ Arrest of seven war crimes suspects

In late-September 2001, Croatian police arrested seven former military policemen suspected of crimes against humanity and war crimes against civilians at the Croatian military police base of Lora in Split during Croatia's 1991-95 war for independence. By the end of the year, police were reportedly still hunting for the former chief warden of Lora military prison.[139]

☛ *Luka Markesić, Zdenko Radić, Zoran Maras* and *Ivan Orlović* case, Bjelovar County Court

On 15 December 2001, the trial of four former police officers, charged with the attempted killing by firing squad of a man and the killing of six others during the 1991 war against the FRY, commenced before the Bjelovar County Court. Former police chief, Luka Markesić, and three former members of the special police, Zdenko Radić, Zoran Maras and Ivan Orlović, were accused of capturing six Yugoslav army reservists and killing them in a woods on the outskirts of Bjelovar, 45 miles east of Zagreb in October 1991. They were also accused of attempting to murder a Serb civilian. The suspects were arrested in August 2001.[140]

AVRIL MCDONALDand JANN K. KLEFFNER

CUBA

Education and Training

☛ Training of the military and civilians

In 2000 and 2001, the Study Centre for International Humanitarian Law of the Cuban Red Cross [Centro de Estudio del Derecho Internacional Humanitario de la Cruz Roja Cubana] was involved in the training of civil and military experts in IHL, the preparation of teaching material for different target groups and levels, and dissemination to the armed forces, the police and civil authorities.[141]

---

138. 'Croatian police arrest four war crimes suspects', AFP, 5 September 2001.

139. 'Croatia authorities arrest seven on war crimes charges', RFE/RL Newsline Vol. 5, No. 185, Part II, 1 October 2001.

140. 'Croatia opens war crimes trial', AP, 15 December 2001; Foreign Press Bureau Zagreb, Daily Bulletin No. 168/2001, available at http://www.hic.hr/hrvatski/vijesti/archiv/latest/DAILY_BULLETIN_168_2001.

141. ICRC Advisory Service, *National Implementation of International Humanitarian Law*: Biennial report 2000-2001 (Geneva, ICRC 2002) p. 36.

CZECH REPUBLIC[142]

Geneva Law

☛ Withdrawal of Reservations to the Geneva Conventions

On 27 September 2001, the Czech Republic deposited its instrument of withdrawal of all reservations to the Geneva Conventions made by the former Czechoslovakia.

International Criminal Court

☛ Government Bill on the Constitutional Law Concerning the Rome Statute

'In September 2001, the Czech government adopted the Government Bill on the Constitutional Law Concerning the Rome Statute and submitted it to the Chamber of Deputies for further consideration. The Czech Parliament vetoed the Bill, which the Government had to withdraw.'[143]

Education and Training

☛ Protocol to the Agreement between the Ministry of Defence of the Czech Republic and the Ministry of National Defence of the Hellenic Republic on Co-operation in the Military Field

Following the conclusion of the above Agreement in Prague on 27 January 1998, on 30 May 2001, both Ministries concluded a Protocol to this Agreement providing for modalities of exchange of military personnel, with a view to providing them with military education.

JAN HLADIK

DENMARK[144]

International Criminal Court

☛ Law No. 342 of 16 May 2001 on the International Criminal Court. Entered into force on 1 July 2002. Published in *Lovtidende* A (2001) pp. 2137-38 [www.retsinfo.dk][145]

As reported in *YIHL* Vol. 3 (p. 470), a Draft Bill on the International Criminal Court, intending to make ratification of the ICC possible, was put before the Danish Parliament in October 2000. After adoption of the Draft Bill in May 2001, Denmark ratified the Statute on 21 June 2001 becoming the 35th state to do so.

Article 1 states that the Statute of the ICC has legal effect in Denmark. The primary effect of this statement, which copies the wording of the ICTY Implementation Act from 1994, is that the ICC Statute is made part of Danish law. Thus is established authority for legal action in Denmark by the ICC in order to prosecute crimes covered by the Statute. This implies that

---

142. Information and commentaries provided by Jan Hladik, Programme Specialist, International Standards Section, Division of Cultural Heritage, UNESCO.

143. ICRC Advisory Service, *National Implementation of International Humanitarian Law*: Biennial report 2000-2001 (Geneva, ICRC 2002) p. 37.

144. Information and commentaries provided by Peter Otken, LL.M., Special Assistant to the Judge Advocate General, Copenhagen.

145. Reprinted in this volume at p. 728.

Danish authorities are also authorised to cooperate with the ICC in accordance with the Statute, including the provision of assistance to the ICC in the form of criminal investigation by Danish authorities in support of the ICC, and the surrender of persons to the ICC. Making the Statute part of Danish law, however, has significance only so far as Danish authorities are required by the Statute to act in support of the ICC. Article 1 also includes a provision authorising the Minister of Foreign Affairs to make the ICC Rules of Procedure, the Elements of Crimes and possible future amendments to the Statute made in accordance with Article 121-123 of the Statute part of Danish law as well.

Article 2 authorises the Minister of Justice to make decisions on the surrender of persons to the ICC. The Minister of Justice is authorised to surrender persons when the ICC has initiated criminal proceedings against such persons and for the purpose of serving sentences imposed by the ICC. The Danish law uses the term 'extradition in order to be consistent with other Danish legislation regulating the extradition of persons to other states. Chapter 3 and 4 of the Extradition Act, Consolidated Act No. 110 of 18 February 1998, with later amendments, concerning the procedures for extradition, are made applicable to situations where persons are surrendered to the ICC.

The Minister of Justice is also authorised by Article 3 to make decisions regarding the service in Denmark of sentences imposed by the ICC. Like other situations where a sentence has been imposed by a foreign court and the sentence shall be served in Denmark, such decisions are subject to review by the Danish Courts.

Article 4 specifically states that persons sentenced or acquitted by the ICC cannot be tried again for the same acts in Denmark. Article 5 makes the provisions in the Penal Code relating to false statements in Court applicable to statements relating to the ICC. Article 6 provides for Government payment of expenses related to the provision of defense attorney assistance during interrogations in Denmark required by the ICC. Article 7 authorises the Minister of Justice to issue administrative regulations necessary to further implement the Statute in Danish law if necessary, including such specific measures made necessary after entering into specific agreements with the ICC. The last two Articles of the Act deals with the entry into force of the Act.

The Danish ICC Implementation Act of only nine articles may appear short in comparison with the rather more elaborate legislation enacted by some other states in order to enable ratification or adoption of the ICC Statute. However, first, it must be remembered that ratification of the ICC does not entail any *new* obligations to make possible under national law the punishment of the crimes of genocide, crimes against humanity or war crimes covered by the Statute. On the contrary, the purpose of the ICC is to ensure criminal investigation and adjudication in situations where no national possibility or will to prosecute exists. However, such obligations to prosecute in a national forum already follows from a number of international agreements that have been in force for a number of years, such as, for instance, the Genocide Convention and the 1949 Geneva Conventions. For that reason, if a nation has already made possible the national investigation and punishment of such international crimes where nations are under an obligation to do so, there is no legal requirement to criminalise those same crimes again in connection with ratification of the ICC.

Some of the very elaborate legislation seen in other countries can be explained by the wish of those countries to make certain that they are able to exercise the primary, national jurisdiction envisaged in Article 17 of the ICC Statute. It is the opinion of the Danish authorities that such primary jurisdiction can be exercised in accordance with such criminalisation of international crimes that is already in existence under Danish law. For that reason, the

Danish ICC Implementation Act does not include any new criminalisation of crimes mentioned in the Statute, nor does it reproduce the description or definition of crimes from the Statute. In addition, under Danish law Danish authorities have for a number of years been able to prosecute non-nationals present in Denmark for international crimes committed abroad, provided the crime is covered by an international agreement that obligates Denmark to exercise jurisdiction. The primary example of such obligations are the grave breaches provisions of the 1949 Geneva Conventions. Authority to prosecute such crimes follows from Article 8(5) of the Danish Penal Code, and has been evidenced in the prosecution and sentencing in 1995 of a Bosnian citizen for war crimes committed against Bosnian Muslims in Bosnia.[146]

Implementation and Dissemination

☛ Government Committee Report No. 1407 (2001) by the Incorporation Committee on the Incorporation of Human Rights Conventions in Danish Law. With a Summary in English [www.jm.dk/publikationer/bet1407]

During the ratification process, a Convention subject to ratification is normally reviewed in order to establish whether Danish law is in compliance with the obligations arising from ratification. If that is not so, Danish law is amended accordingly. However, a special Implementation Act such as the ICC Implementation Act making an international convention 'part of Danish law' is the exception to the rule. The question whether a number of Human Rights Conventions formerly ratified by Denmark should also be made the subject of such a special Implementation Act is the subject of an analysis by the Incorporation Committee.

In 1992, the European Convention of Human Rights (ECHR) was made part of Danish law by a special Implementation Act. Based on the experience from that particular implementation and the implementation of other Human Rights Conventions, the Incorporation Committee has concluded that those other conventions not specifically made 'part of Danish Law', although certainly also directly applicable in Denmark, are not so often invoked for the Danish Courts or in administrative practice as is the ECHR. For that reason, the Committee has examined a number of particularly important conventions (namely, the International Covenant on Civil and Political Rights, the International Covenant on Economic, Social and Cultural Rights, the International Convention on the Elimination of All Forms of Racial Discrimination, the Convention Against Torture and other Cruel, Inhuman or Degrading Treatment or Punishment, the Convention on the Rights of the Child, and the Convention on the Elimination of All Forms of Discrimination against Women) with the purpose of investigating whether to recommend making them part of Danish law by special Implementation Acts as well.

The Incorporation Committee has recommended the specific implementation only of the International Covenant on Civil and Political Rights, the Racial Discrimination Convention and the Torture Convention. Although all conventions are found to be 'central to protection of fundamental human rights', this recommendation is partly based on finding the contents of these three conventions more 'specific' and thus more suitable for providing solutions to actual legal problems. The decision is also based on a wish to implement a limited number of

146. Reported in 1 *YIHL* (1998) at p. 431.

conventions first in order to gain more experience from such implementation. A Draft Bill with comments is included in the Committee's Report.

Apart from reviewing and making comments on the above-mentioned conventions, the Incorporation Committee has provided interesting comments on the general implementation in Denmark of international law, including international humanitarian and human rights law.

Cases

- Investigation of possible war crimes committed in 1988 by an Iraqi General now living in Denmark

A person described by the press as a 62-year old former Chief of the Iraqi General Staff, not qualifying for refugee status but nevertheless allowed to stay in Denmark after having escaped from Iraq, has been made the object of a criminal investigation by Danish authorities. He is alleged to have been responsible for war crimes committed by the Iraqi army during the Iraqi campaign against the Kurds in Northern Iraq in the late 1980s, including such crimes carried out during the Iraq-Iran War. According to information in the press, this might include the poison gas attack against the city of Halabja in March 1988 where several thousand people, mainly civilians, are thought to have been killed.

In November 2001, the Danish Solicitor General confirmed that Danish authorities have jurisdiction over such a crime and directed the local Commissioner of Police to proceed with the investigation. By the end of the year, no decision as to the formal indictment of the General had been made public.

PETER OKTEN

DOMINICAN REPUBLIC

Pending

- In 2000 and 2001, the Comision Nacional Permanente para la Aplicacion y el Seguimiento del DIH[147] prepared draft legislation governing the use of the red cross and red crescent emblems and designations and submitted it to the National Congress for approval.[148]

---

147. The Commission was established by Executive Decree No. 131-99 of 30 March 1999. 'Its functions include recommending measures for the national implementation of humanitarian law treaties, spreading knowledge of the law among the authorities and proposing draft implementing legislation.' ICRC Advisory Service, *National Implementation of International Humanitarian Law*: Biennial report 2000-2001 (Geneva, ICRC 2002) p. 39.

148. Ibid.

EAST TIMOR[149]

☛ *Investigation and Prosecution of Serious Crimes*

2001 saw 33 indictments filed against 83 individuals and a busy schedule for the Special Panel of the District Court of Dili. In November 2001 a second panel was constituted. Amid the many trials for murder, only one trial for crimes against humanity (*Lospalos*, see below at p. 494) was held and concluded over six months, resulting in delays for other cases. Indonesia's refusal to extradite indictees to East Timor meant that no accused person of any hierarchical significance was tried by the Special Panels.[150] By year's end, approximately half the persons held in detention had been charged with crimes against humanity rather than domestic crimes, marking an important shift from the earlier tendency to charge nearly all accused under the Indonesian Penal Code.

Despite considerable achievements in the face of tremendous obstacles, the Serious Crimes project came under the spotlight during the course of 2001 for all the wrong reasons.[151] After a year of sustained and serious criticism from NGOs, East Timorese and even the Security Council and the UN High Commissioner for Human Rights, UNTAET finally took remedial action. The changes began after the 30 August 2001 elections and the arrival of a new Deputy Special Representative of the Secretary-General (SRSG). The Serious Crimes Unit was removed from the control of the Ministry of Justice and placed under the supervision of the Deputy SRSG's office. Meaningful resources were finally made available and offices were opened in the rural districts of East Timor. Prosecutors began to supervise investigations directly. By the end of the year, there was new leadership at the Ministry of Justice and in the Office of the General Prosecutor, including the Serious Crimes Unit.

Reception, Truth and Reconciliation Commission

☛ UNTAET REGULATION 2001/10 on the Establishment of a Commission for Reception, Truth and Reconciliation, 13 July 2001 [http://www.jsmp.minihub.org]

---

149. Information and commentaries by Suzannah Linton, Visiting Fellow, Center for Civil and Human Rights, Law School, University of Notre Dame. Readers seeking more detailed analysis are referred to the author's article 'The Evolving Jurisprudence and Practice of East Timor's Special Panels For Serious Crimes on Admissions Of Guilt, Duress And Superior Orders' at p. 169 of this volume.

150. The most senior were two local commanders of the Team Alfa Militia in Lospalos, Joni Marques and Manuel da Costa.

151. See Report of the Security Council Mission to East Timor and Indonesia, UN Doc. S/2000/1105 (2000) para. 8, and concerns voiced by the Security Council when extending UNTAET's mandate to 31 January 2002. UN Doc. S/RES/1338 (2001) and Report of the High Commissioner for Human Rights on the situation of human rights in East Timor, UN Doc. E/CN.4/2001/37, para. 13. Also see Amnesty International, 'East Timor: Building a New Country based on Human Rights, 2000', http://www.amnesty.org/ailib/aipub/2000/SUM/35700500.htm, and 'East Timor: Justice Past, Present and Future, 2001', http://web.amnesty.org/library/Index/engASA570012001; 'Judicial System Monitoring Programme, Justice in Practice: Human Rights in Court Administration', November 2001, http://www.jsmp.minihub.org/Reports/JSMP1.pdf; 'UK Groups in Solidarity with East Timor, Petition for International Tribunal on East Timor', http://www.pcug.og.au/~wildwood/01maytribunalpetition.htm; 'Nobel Laureate appeals For East Timor tribunal', AP, 23 April 2001; 'International court must be set up in Timor Lorosae as fast as possible', *Suara Timor Lorosae,* 11 April 2001.

The Reception, Truth and Reconciliation (RTR) Commission was established after extensive grassroots discussions and consultations which took over a year. East Timor's RTR Commission has a two-year mandate, which can be extended for six months. It is comprised of seven commissioners (nominated in December 2001 and sworn in on 21 January 2002) and has two main functions. The first is to investigate the period before and during the Indonesian occupation, in order to establish the facts, pattern and scope of human rights violations from 1974 to 1999. Both individual incidents and the wider context in which they took place and the reasons for them will be examined. The commission will be able to conduct its own investigations by questioning witnesses and holding public hearings. Findings will be published in a comprehensive report.

The second function is to facilitate community acceptance of those who committed lesser crimes. This involves a mechanism for community – based reconciliation which draws on traditional practices – where there are ceremonies enabling perpetrators of less serious crimes to confess and apologise for what they did-the testimony of witnesses and victims and the perpetrator's agreement to perform an act of contrition as recommended by the commissioners (Community Reconciliation Process). By law criminal acts that appear to be Serious Crimes are referred to the General Prosecutor for review, as such offences cannot be processed through the Community Reconciliation Process and may not be amnestied. The agreement whereby the perpetrator agrees to make amends in the form suggested by the commissioners will be registered at the relevant District Court, which is required to ensure that the punishment is proportionate to the crime and that rights are not violated.

One of the recognised motivations behind the RTR Commission is its intended use as a means of persuading pro-Indonesian East Timorese who are still in the refugee camps of Indonesia to return. Those who demonstrate the necessary contrition and willingness to reconcile and to be accountable for their acts, whether through the courts or the Community Reconciliation Process, are welcomed back. The RTR Commission is also meant to complement the judicial mechanism. East Timor's commission is therefore part of a wider vision for achieving reconciliation and justice. Concerns about the RTR Commission in 2001 centred around the possible use of this mechanism to provide immunity to those militia members who 'embrace' the philosophy and means of reconciliation.[152] 2001 saw considerable controversy about UNTAET's push for reconciliation by wooing militia leaders in West Timor, with a view to getting the approximately 100,000 refugees there to return to East Timor. Many observers noted that a number of notorious individuals were not being indicted (UNTAET was thus able to deny negotiating with persons 'accused' of committing Serious Crimes), leading to suspicions about politics influencing prosecutorial decisions.[153] East Timor's leading political leader, Xanana Gusmao, made clear his preference for amnestying all crimes as a means of achieving reconciliation, leading to concerns about how the impunity issue will develop when East Timor becomes an independent state on 20 May 2002. Another potential problem was that the relevant legislation provides guidance governing the relationship between Serious Crimes and the Community Reconciliation Process,

---

152. UNTAET has strenuously denied this, and the legislation specifically prohibits Serious Crimes from being dealt with by the Community Reconciliation Process.

153. See M. Dodd, 'Timor's crime fighters in crisis', *The Age*, 1 May 2001; 'UN in Secret Parleys with East Timor Militia Leaders', *Times of India*, 18 November 2000; 'East Timor: UN lets Indonesian military off the hook', *Green Left Weekly*, Issue 447, 9 May 2001.

but is virtually silent on how the Commission and the criminal justice mechanisms are to interact in relation to the Commission's investigations into incidents from 1974 to 1999.

Cases[154]

- *General Prosecutor of UNTAET* v. *Joni Marques, Manuel da Costa, Joao da Costa alias Lemorai, Paulo da Costa, Amelio da Costa, Hilario da Silva, Gonsalo dos Santos, Alarico Fernandes, Mautersa Monis, Gilberto Fernandes and Syaful Anwar*, Case No. 9/2000 ('Lospalos'), Judgement, 11 December 2001

On 9 July 2001, the trial commenced with all accused except Lt. Syaful Anwar of Indonesia being present. The judgement was issued on 11 December 2001. It was East Timor's first crimes against humanity trial and conviction: all of the accused bar the one absentee were convicted and received sentences ranging from four to 33 years and four months.

Despite being a lengthy document and the first to deal with international crimes, the judgement contains no analysis of the content of international law on crimes against humanity or the rules governing individual criminal responsibility under Section 14 of UNTAET Regulation 2000/15, both of which follow the Rome Statute of the International Criminal Court. It simply reiterates the submissions of the parties and accepts findings of fact made by other institutions, notably the Report of the International Commission of Inquiry on East Timor,[155] the Report of the Special Rapporteurs[156] and the Indonesian KPP-HAM Report.[157] In its reference to these documents, the panel seemed to have considered that the existence of an armed conflict is a prerequisite for crimes against humanity and that there must be a link between an armed conflict and the crime for there to be a crime against humanity.

Although the case revolved around the actions of a militia group, the panel did not examine any of the linkages between that group and the Indonesian authorities, nor did it examine the structure and workings of the group.

On the status of East Timor, the Special Panel found that

> 'during 24 years of Indonesian rule in East Timor, there was an armed conflict between para-military groups openly supported by Jakarta and others dedicated to the independence of this half-island territory since the Portuguese colonial period. That conflict heightened in the second half of the late-1990s with the persecution against civilian population when the inter-

154. All of the judgements and indictments mentioned in this segment are available online at http://www.jsmp.minihub.org.

155. See Report of the International Commission of Inquiry on East Timor to the Secretary-General, UN Doc. A/54/726, S/2000/59, 31 January 2000. http://193.194.138.190/huridocda/huridoca.nsf/(Symbol)/A.54.726,+S.2000.59.En?OpenDocument.

156. Report submitted by the Secretary General to the General Assembly on the Situation on Human Rights in East Timor, Doc. A/54/660 of 10 December 1999.

157. KPP-HAM, Report on the Investigation of Human Rights Violations in East Timor (2000). Only an Executive Summary of this Report has been officially released: see http://www.indonesia-ottawa.org/news/Issue/HumanRights/ham-kpp-timtim-01312000.htm.

national community addressed its concerns about the autonomy or independence of this territory.'[158]

The panel noted that the parties were agreed that at least some months before and after the popular consultation on 30 August 1999, there was an armed conflict in East Timor, and was therefore satisfied that an armed conflict existed during the times relevant to the indictment (April 1999 and September 1999).

Indictments for Crimes against Humanity

☛ *General Prosecutor of UNTAET* v. *2nd Lt. Bambang Indra, Joao Franca Da Silva aka Jhoni Franca, Jose Cardoso Fereira aka Mouzinho, Francisco Noronha, Sabino Gouvia Leite*, Case No. 4/2001 ('Lolotoe'), 25 May 2001

The Lolotoe indictment, filed on 6 February 2001, concerned the activities of the Kaer Metin Merah Putih militia and the local TNI (Tentara Nasional Indonesia or Indonesian National Army) leadership in the Lolotoe sub-district of Bobonaro District between May and October 1999. The accused were charged with the crimes against humanity of torture, murder, persecution, rape, inhumane acts and unlawful deprivation of liberty and in the alternative, with violations of the Indonesian Penal Code, namely murder, serious maltreatment, unlawful deprivation of liberty and rape. These offences allegedly arose in the course of concerted acts of violence directed against members of the civilian population of Lolotoe Sub-District who were considered to be pro-independence, linked to or sympathetic to the independence cause. Included within the indictment was the targeting of a number of women whose husbands were suspected of involvement with the independence movement; the indictment charged the accused with their abduction, enslavement and rape whilst in captivity. It also accused them of persecuting the civilian population in the Lolotoe area 'because of their opinion on the future political status of East Timor, because they supported Falintil or were sympathetic to it or its members'.

Only two of the accused were in custody; one of them, Jose Cardoso Fereira, aka Mouzinho, was alleged to be the commander of the Kaer Metin Merah Putih militia. The most senior accused was 2nd Lt. Bambang Indra, the former Sub-District Military Commander (Danramil) of the TNI in Lolotoe Sub-District. Both Mouzinho and 2nd Lt. Bambang Indra were charged with command responsibility for the acts of their subordinates. Indonesia has not surrendered the wanted accused under the Memorandum of Understanding from April 2000 (see 2 *YIHL* (2000) pp. 524-525).

☛ *General Prosecutor of UNTAET* v. *Anastacio Martins and Domingos Goncalves*, Case No. 11/2001

☛ *General Prosecutor of UNTAET* v. *Armando dos Santos*, Case No. 16/2001

☛ *General Prosecutor of UNTAET* v. *Leoneto Martens and 19 others*, Case No. 21/2001

Three crimes against humanity indictments were filed in relation to atrocities committed in the district of Liquiça, where the Besi Merah Putih militia were active.

---

158. Materials directed cited in support of this proposition (two popular books) do not appear to have been submitted as evidence in the course of proceedings.

Anastacio Martins and Domingos Goncalves, both in custody, were charged on 1 May 2001 with the crimes against humanity of murder and deportation or forcible transfer of the civilian population. These charges arose in relation to incidents in September 1999.

The second indictment, filed on 5 June 2001, was against Armando Dos Santos. Dos Santos was in custody and was charged with the crimes against humanity of murder and inhumane acts. The indictment alleged that he participated in Besi Merah Putih violence in Liquiça district in March and April 1999, and that he took part in the massacre of civilians sheltering at the João Britto church in Liquiça on 6 April 1999. He was also charged with participating in the attack on the house of pro-independence leader Manuel Carrascalão in Dili on 17 April 1999.

On 22 November 2001, the most high level indictment to date was filed against 20 persons, among them the Bupati (Regent) of Liquiça (Leoneto Martens), five TNI officers and members of the Besi Merah Putih militia. They were accused of the crimes against humanity of murder, torture, persecution, inhumane acts, forced deportation and extermination arising from the massacre at the João Britto church in Liquiça.

None of the accused was in custody; they were all believed to be in Indonesia, which had not responded to warrants of arrest. Several, including Leoneto Martens and Lt. Col. Asep Kuswani, were due to stand trial before the Ad Hoc Human Rights Court in Jakarta in relation to their role in the Liquiça Church massacre.

☛ *General Prosecutor* v. *Lino de Carvalho*, Case No. 10/2001

Lino de Carvalho was originally charged with murder and maltreatment. On 19 October 2001, the Court of Appeal granted leave for a new indictment to be issued charging him with murder and inhumane acts.

☛ *General Prosecutor of UNTAET* v. *Benjamin Sarmento, Romeiro Tilman, Joao Sarmento and Domingos Mendonca* ('Same'*)*, Case No. 18/2001

The Same indictment was filed on 7 August 2001, and focused on the activities of members of the Tim Sasurut Ablai militia in Same Sub-District. This militia group belonged to the larger Ablai militia which operated throughout Manufahi District.

Between April and October 1999, members of the Tim Sasurut Ablai Militia, including the accused, allegedly committed the crimes against humanity of murder, severe deprivation of physical liberty, deportation or forcible transfer of population and persecution. These crimes were said to have been directed against those members of the civilian population suspected of being linked to or sympathetic with the pro-independence movement. The most significant feature of the Same indictment was the charge of deportation or forcible transfer of population in September 1999, when commanders of the Tim Sasurut Ablai militia were alleged to have violently and coercively displaced over 15,000 villagers from Same Sub-District from their homes and forcibly moved them to West Timor in trucks and ships belonging to the Indonesian navy.

Three of the accused were in custody. Benjamin Sarmento and Romeiro Tilman were charged with command responsibility for the acts of their subordinates.

☛ *General Prosecutor of UNTAET* v. *Simao Lopes, Laurentio Soares (alias 'Moko'), Gabriel Kolo, Bonifacio Bobo (alias 'Bone'), Andre Ulan, Anton Sabraka, Florenco Tacaqui, Tomas Bubun, Elvis Lopes, Domingos Obe and Julio da Costa*, Case No. 20/2001 ('Passabe')

On 27 September 2001, the Passabe indictment was filed charging 11 accused for their alleged role in the crimes against humanity of imprisonment, inhumane acts, deportation, persecution, murder and extermination.

This indictment revolved around the actions of the Sakunar militia and TNI in the remote enclave of Oecussi-Ambeno in April, August and September 1999. Simao Lopes was the supreme commander of the Sakunar Militia and his commanders were Laurentio Soares (Moko) and Passabe village chief Gabriel Kolo. Two TNI officers were also charged: Sergeants Andre Ulan and Anton Sabraka.

On 8 September 1999, there was a concerted attack on the villages of Tumin, Nibin and Kiobiselo. Eighteen people were killed and the surviving villagers were rounded up and taken across the border to West Timor where a selection process identified young men with education and pro-independence leanings. On 10 September 1999, the group of captured men, with their arms bound, was marched back over the border to East Timor to Passabe where they were attacked with machetes, swords and guns. Forty-seven were killed.

Only Florenco Tacqui, a 'footsoldier' of the Sakunar Militia, was in custody. All others were believed to be in Indonesia, which failed to respond to warrants of arrest.

SUZANNAH LINTON

ECUADOR

Criminal Law

☛ Code of Penal Procedure, 2000 [Código de Procedimiento Penal]. Entered into force 13 July 2001. Published in, *Registro Oficial*, 13 de enero del 2000

Cases

☛ Case No. 0005-2000-Cl on the 'Rome Statute of the International Criminal Court', Constitutional Court, 21 Februrary 2001

EGYPT

Implementation and Dissemination

☛ Prime Ministerial Decree No. 149/2000 establishing the National Committee on International Humanitarian Law [http://www.icrc.org/ihl-nat.nsf/6fa4d35e5e3025394125673e00508143/6054d615d1d1022dc1256af4004e0b7f?OpenDocument]

☛ Regional meeting of Arab experts on IHL

'Pursuant to the recommendations of the Cairo Declaration, the National Committee on International Humanitarian Law was established by Prime Ministerial Decree No. 149/

2000.'[159] 'In May 2001 the National Committee, in cooperation with the League of Arab States and the ICRC, convened a regional meeting of Arab experts pursuant to the Cairo Declaration (November 1999). Representatives of 16 Arab States adopted a regional plan of action on the implementation of IHL. The plan of action urges Arab countries to implement the law and to set up national committees with that objective in mind. It also aims to facilitate the harmonization of national legislation on humanitarian law issues and on dissemination. A coordinator's office, made up of representatives from the League of Arab States and the ICRC, was established to ensure the plan's application.'[160]

Pending

- In 2000 and 2001, the National Committee drafted a bill on the emblem to be submitted to the Council of Ministers.[161]

EL SALVADOR

Education and Training

- Training of the military and civilians

'Efforts were pursued in 2000 and 2001 to include humanitarian law in the curricula of university law faculties throughout the country. The Law Faculty of the University of El Salvador offered a mandatory course on the law within the framework of its Master's Programme on Human Rights and Education for Peace. On the basis of an order issued by the Chief of Staff, IHL ws taught in 2000 and 2001 as part of armed and security forces' training programmes.'[162]

Pending

- Draft amendments of the Criminal Code and the Code of Criminal Procedure
- Draft legislation to ban landmines

During 2000 and 2001, the Inter-Institutional Committee on International Humanitarian Law [Comité interstitucional de Derecho Internacional Humanitario] 'prepared draft amendments of the Criminal Code and the Code of Criminal Procedure that included punishment for breaches of IHL and brought them in line with the requirements of the law; it submitted the drafts to its member institutions for further study. ... In addition the CIDIH-ES prepared draft legislation to ban landmines and undertook to supplement the study of national law from the standpoint of IHL that had been prepared by a team of legal experts from the *Universidad centroamericano José Simeón Cañas.*'

159. ICRC Advisory Service, *National Implementation of International Humanitarian Law*: Biennial report 2000-2001 (Geneva, ICRC 2002) p. 41.

160. Ibid.

161. Ibid.

162. Ibid.

ETHIOPIA

Cases

☛ Trials of the Dergue

Since 1994, trials of members of the former Dergue[163] regime have been ongoing in Ethiopia, based on charges of genocide under Article 281 of the Ethiopian Penal Code of 1957,[164] and other crimes. Originally, 66 persons were charged and their trial opened in 1994, with 21 defendants being tried *in absentia*. The 269-page indictment against them charges that the crimes include the killing of 1,823 identified victims, including the former Emperor Haile Selassie), bodily harm to 99 identified victims, enforced disappearances of 194 identified victims, and forced relocation, causing the deaths of 100,000 by famine. Since then, many thousands of others have been charged and put on trial, with the result being great pressure on the Ethiopian judicial system and protracted trials. Violations of defendants' right to due process have been alleged.

On 8 May 2001, it was announced in the Ethiopian press that in the previous six months, 222 persons had been sentenced to between two years and life imprisonment, in verdicts rendered between early-November 2001 and the end of April 2001. It was also mentioned that the sixth criminal chamber of Ethiopia's federal high court had acquitted 122 defendants for lack of evidence.

In June 2001, a court in Addis Ababa acquitted a further 27 former officers, 15 of whom had been tried *in absentia*, of genocide and crimes against humanity charges. They were ordered to be immediately released.[165]

FEDERAL REPUBLIC OF YUGOSLAVIA

A. Kosovo[166]

Reparations and Compensation

☛ UNMIK Regulation No. 2000/66 of 21 December 2000 on Benefits for War Invalids of Kosovo and for the Next of Kin of those Who Died as a Result of the Armed Conflict in Kosovo

---

163. That is, the 108-member body known as the Dergue Coordinating Committee of the Armed Forces, which ruled Ethiopia from 12 September 1974 until 28 May 1991, when it was overthrown in a military coup.

164. Art. 281, Genocide; Crimes against Humanity, provides: 'Whosoever, with intent to destroy, in whole or in part, a national, ethnic, racial, religious or political group, organizes, orders or engages in, be it in time of war or in time of peace: (a) killings, bodily harm or serious injury to the physical or mental health of members of the group, in any way whatsoever; or (b) measures to prevent the propagation or continued survival of its members or their progeny; or (c) the compulsory movement or dispersion of peoples or children, or their placing under living conditions calculated to result in their death or disappearance, is punishable with rigorous imprisonment from five years to life, or, in cases of exceptional gravity, with death.'

165. Source: 'Genocide and international crimes in domestic courts'. Published on the website of Prevent Genocide International. http://www.preventgenocide.org/punish/domestic/.

166. Information and commentaries by Michael Hartman, International Prosecutor, Kosovo. The author can be reached at Intprosecutor@yahoo.com. Lynne Madnick, Research Assistant and American University law student, contributed to this report.

Any person who has received physical injury as a direct result of the armed conflict in Kosovo (Section) may be entitled to receive benefits under Regulation 2000/66. It provides for financial payments for war invalids, free access to medical care; exemption from tax on special vehicles; and financial benefits for next of kin who those who died as a result of the armed conflict (Section 2). A Special Fund is established to provide special benefits for eligible war invalids (Section 3).

Internationalised Courts and Prosecutors[167]

- UNMIK Regulation 2000/6 on the Appointment and Removal from Office of International Judges and International Prosecutors, 15 February 2000 [http://www.un.org/peace/kosovo/pages/regulations/reg06.html]
- UNMIK Regulation 2000/34 amending UNMIK Regulation No. 2000-6 on the Appointment and Removal from Office of International Judges and International Prosecutors, 27 May 2000 [http://www.un.org/peace/kosovo/pages/regulations/reg034.html]
- UNMIK Regulation 2000/64 on Assignment of International Judges and Prosecutors and Change of Venue, 15 December 2000 [http://www.un.org/peace/kosovo/pages/regulations/reg063.html]
- Regulation 2001/2 Amending UNMIK Regulation No. 2000/6, as Amended, on the Appointment and Removal from Office of International Judges and International Prosecutors, 12 January 2001 [http://www.un.org/peace/kosovo/pages/regulations/reg01.02.html]

Chapter VII of the UN Charter provides the authority for the unprecedented United Nations 'Executive Mission' civil administration in Kosovo under Security Council Resolution 1244. Resolution 1244, in turn, authorized issuance of UNMIK Regulations, which are the laws promulgated by the Special Representative of the Secretary-General (SRSG).[168]

UNMIK Regulation 1999/24 established that the applicable procedure and law within Kosovo would be that applicable in 1989, when Kosovo was still an 'autonomous province' within the Yugoslav Republic of Serbia, with its own legislature, before the Milošević regime abolished its autonomous status.

International humanitarian law protecting civilians is incorporated in the Federal Republic of Yugoslavia (FRY) Criminal Code (which was part of the law applicable in Kosovo in 1989) in Articles 141 (genocide), 142 (war crimes) and 143 (attacks on sick and wounded).[169] The death penalty provided for in those provisions was abolished by Regulation 1999/24, leaving either 15 or 20 years as the maximum sentence for these crimes,

167. There are a number of sources upon which this report relied, in addition to the author's presence in Kosovo as an International Prosecutor with UNMIK from February 2000. Among others, the OSCE's Legal System Assessment Section has done an extensive evaluation of war crimes cases reflecting their views. See
http://www.osce.org/kosovo/documents/human_rights/10_WarCrimesReport_eng.pdf.

168. See especially Regulations 1999/1 and 1999/24, which establish the Adminstration's competencies and the applicable law.

169. FRY CC: Genocide, Art. 141. 'Whoever, with the intention of destroying a national, ethnic, racial or religious group in whole or in part, orders the commission of killings or the inflicting of serious bodily injuries or serious disturbance of physical or mental health of the group members, or a forcible dislocation of the population, or that the group be inflicted conditions of life calculated to bring about its physical destruction in whole or in part, or that measures be imposed intended to prevent

depending upon the court's interpretation of several other articles in the FRY Criminal Code (FRYCC).

By the end of January 2000, there was an international consensus – among the UN, OSCE and NGOs – that the justice system had significant and inherent problems. Some were due to a lack of sufficiently qualified, experienced and trained local judges and prosecutors, caused by a boycott by ethnic Serbian judges of the UNMIK judicial positions because of both political reasons and safety concerns. Other problems originated in what was regarded as bias and discrimination by the Albanian-Kosovar judiciary against Serbian accused and victims of crimes, including war crimes. This bias could be seen in the local judiciary's detention, prosecution and conviction of ethnic Serbs on the basis of insufficient evidence. Furthermore, similar crimes, such as possession of one gun or grenade, resulted in disparate treatment whereby an ethnic Albanian would be released from detention but an Albanian Serb would remain in detention. UNMIK police cases where ethnic Albanians were arrested for crimes against ethnic Serbs were often abandoned.

The final impetus for the introduction of international judges and prosecutors into the Kosovo criminal justice system came in the form of death and chaos. In the first week of February 2000, massive riots, inter-ethnic mob violence and murders involving both ethnicities took place in the divided city of Mitrovica.[170]

---

births within the group, or that children of the group be forcibly transferred to another group, or whoever with the same intent commits one of the foregoing acts, shall be punished by imprisonment for not less than five years or by the death penalty.'

War crime against the civilian population, Art. 142. Whoever in violation of rules of international law effective at the time of war, armed conflict or occupation, orders that civilian population be subject to killings, torture, inhuman treatment, biological experiments, immense suffering or violation of bodily integrity or health; dislocation or displacement or forcible conversion to another nationality or religion; forcible prostitution or rape; application of measures of intimidation and terror, taking hostages, imposing collective punishment, unlawful bringing in concentration camps and other illegal arrests and detention, deprivation of rights to fair and impartial trial; forcible service in the armed forces of enemy's army or in its intelligence service or administration; forcible labour, starvation of the population, property confiscation, pillaging, illegal and self-willed destruction and stealing on large scale of a property that is not justified by military needs, taking an illegal and disproportionate contribution or requisition, devaluation of domestic currency or the unlawful issuance of currency, or who commits one of the foregoing acts, shall be punished by imprisonment for not less than five years or by the death penalty.

War crime against the wounded and sick, Art. 143. Whoever, in violation of the rules of international law at the time of war or armed conflict, orders murders, tortures, inhuman treatment of the wounded, sick, the shipwrecked persons or medical personnel, including therein biological experiments, causing of great sufferings or serious injury to the bodily integrity or health; or whoever orders unlawful and arbitrary destruction or large-scale appropriation of material and stocks of medical facilities or units which is not justified by military needs, or whoever commits some of the foregoing acts, shall be punished by imprisonment for not less than five years or by the death penalty.

170. The Ibar River divides the city, and north of Mitrovica are primarily ethnic Serbian villages and towns up to the Serbian administrative boundary. Now, after the conflict, the northern section of the city is primarily ethnic Serbian, with a small enclave of ethnic Albanian and Bosniak, and the southern section of the city is almost all ethnic Albanian.

After KFOR and the UNMIK Police reestablished order, the SRSG enacted Regulation 2000/6 on the Appointment and Removal from Office of International Judges and International Prosecutors, which states in part:[171]

> '1.2 International judges shall have the authority and responsibility to perform the functions of their office, including the authority to select and take responsibility for new and pending criminal cases within the jurisdiction of the court to which he or she is appointed.
> 1.3 International prosecutors shall have the authority and responsibility to perform the functions of their office, including the authority and responsibility to conduct criminal investigations and to select and take responsibility for new and pending criminal investigations or proceedings within the jurisdiction of the office of the prosecutor to which he or she is appointed.'

The international judges and prosecutors are selected through an UNMIK staff recruiting process, sometimes through recommendations by states or IGOs, such as the Council of Europe. They are appointed by the SRSG for six-month renewable terms, which is the standard term for all UN Department of Peacekeeping Operations Mission personnel. While some NGOs and the Ombudsperson (which is also an UNMIK appointment under Regulation 2000/38) have raised the issue of whether such short terms infringe upon judicial and prosecutorial independence and allow implicit executive control – as the threat of non-renewal could cause jurists to favor the SRSG's position on cases – by the end of 2001, there had not yet been a change in the normal bureaucratic rules for all personnel in order to treat the newly established judiciary differently than any other Mission personnel.

Regulation 2000/6 also establishes criteria for dismissing international judges and prosecutors by the SRSG, such as physical or mental incapacity, serious misconduct and failure in the due execution of office (Sec. 4.1). However, given the short contract term, it is not surprising that these methods have not yet been used, although at least one judge has not had his contracted renewed.

Regulation 6 was limited to the Mitrovica District, which is only one of the five judicial districts of Kosovo, thus omitting Pristina – the capital District, with approximately 40 percent of total crimes in Kosovo – Prizern, Gjilan, and Pec/Peje, and did not include the Supreme Court. Significantly, the regulation did not alter in any way the traditional composition of court panels. In Kosovo, in a trial for genocide or war crimes under Articles 141 or 142, respectively, of the FRYCC, five judges sit on the panel, of which only two are professional and three are lay, in a system similar to the German trial system. This meant that international judges (IJ) could never make up the voting majority, given the presence of three lay judges, even if both professional judge places were occupied by internationals. Moreover, it was unlikely that both professional judges would be IJs because there were a maximum of

---

171. Regulation 6 was limited to Mitrovica. Section 1 is entitled: Appointment and Removal from Office of International Judges and International Prosecutors, and provides:
1.1 The Special Representative of the Secretary-General may appoint and remove from office international judges and international prosecutors, taking into account the criteria set forth under sections 2 and 4 of the present regulation. Such appointments shall be made to the District Court of Mitrovica, other courts within the territorial jurisdiction of the District Court of Mitrovica and offices of the prosecutor with corresponding jurisdiction.

two IJs appointed per District, and an IJ's previous role as an investigating judge or in deciding a motion challenging the indictment would disqualify him or her for the main trial hearing panel.

On 27 May 2000, Regulation 2000/34 was enacted, expanding the scope of the international judges and prosecutors (IJP) program to all courts and prosecutor's offices in Kosovo. The UNMIK Administration announced plans to appoint IJs to the Supreme Court of Kosovo, which hears the second instance appeals as well as providing a review of some detention decisions. IJP [11]subject matter jurisdiction remained restricted to criminal cases and investigations. The expansion was encouraged by the results of the Mitrovica IJP program and also because ethnic Serbians accused of war crimes and genocide started hunger strikes in May to publicize their being held in custody without trial for as long as ten months. Accordingly, by the end of 2000, IJ were appointed to each of the five district courts throughout Kosovo with one appointed to the Supreme Court, totalling ten IJ. By the end of 2000, however, only two other IP joined the Mitrovica IP appointment, in Pristina and Prizern, bringing the number of IP to three. Through the end of 2000, by IJP choice and consensus, they dealt primarily with cases of war crime and inter-ethnic violence.

This minimalist approach to international intervention – inserting the IJP into the local criminal justice system, and having them apply the existing applicable law, without otherwise changing the criminal procedure or panel size and composition – meant that the IJ could be used for 'window dressing', to justify an unjust decision which was controlled by local judge voting,[172] given that the IJ could never be a majority of the trial panel[12]. Moreover, the assignment of only one IJ to the Supreme Court resulted in local judge voting control of the three professional judge appeals panels. Finally, throughout 2000 and the first half of 2001 there was an insufficient number of international prosecutors [13]to assign one to the Provincial Prosecutor's Office before the Supreme Court to deal with appeals.

With the expansion of the IJP program, the experiences of the IJP convinced the UNMIK Administration that there were three critical problems inherent in the minimalist international intervention concept. First, the international judges were being outvoted by both lay and professional local judges, resulting in local voting control and verdicts of guilt against Serbian defendants in war crimes and genocide cases, as well as those dealing with interethnic violence and terrorism crimes.[173] Second, the local prosecutors consistently 'overcharged' Serbs, and would initiate criminal investigations and propose detentions based on insufficient evidence that did not meet the standard of being a 'grounded suspicion'.[174] Finally, the lack of any limitation of IJP subject matter jurisdiction, through no limits on IJP case selection under Regulation 34, resulted in increasing case volume beyond the capacity of the IJP, which negatively affected their ability to spend appropriate time on case and verdict preparation, research and drafting.

---

172. The law does not allow any judge to reveal to the public or parties the results of judicial voting, including whether a decision is unanimous or had dissenting votes.

173. This also occurred in some cases where Serbs were accused of crimes committed after the war against Albanians. In addition, the Albanian-Kosovar prosecutors and judges would at times favor Albanian suspects accused of crimes against Serbs by either releasing them when Serbs in like crimes would be detained, or by under-charging their crimes or finding them guilty of lesser crimes than the evidence supported.

174. In inter-ethnic cases with Albanian-Kosovar accused, local prosecutors sometimes proposed releasing the suspects, or abandoned a case, presenting an international prosecutor with a *fait accompli*.

The international judges being outvoted by the local judges became a serious issue, especially in the war crimes cases. While the local criminal procedural law does not allow any individual judge on the panel to publicly state his or her vote, it became clear to observers, both within UNMIK and outside, that the international judges, using accepted legal standards of proof, were often overruled on determinations of guilt. This situation meant that persons were being convicted without substantial evidence and in the face of violations of the rights of the accused. International NGOs and the Legal System Monitoring Section (LSMS) of OSCE's Department of Human Rights and Rule of Law have reported that the decisions on detention and guilt by the virtually monoethnic Albanian Kosovar judiciary were in some cases not impartial, and in others had the appearance of partiality. Since Regulation 2000/6, as amended by 2000/34, only allowed internationals to be professional judges, the ethnic Albanian local judges could always outvote the international judges, because no ethnic Serbs were selected by the majority ethnic court presidents to sit on war crimes trial panels in 2000 or 2001. This resulted in what were seen as injustices, and indeed, those local majority panel genocide and war crimes case convictions were almost all reversed by international judges-majority Supreme Court Panels, as advised by the international prosecutor appointed to the Provincial Prosecutor's Office, later renamed as the Office of the Public Prosecutor of Kosovo (OPPK). The Public Prosecutor of Kosovo appears before the Supreme Court, and has the duty to give written recommendations (Opinions) to the Court and appear during oral argument representing the interests of justice, rather than representing the District Public Prosecutor, who files appeals and responds to appeals by the defense.[175]

The second problem: local prosecutors filed a number of genocide and war crimes cases, in Requests to Initiate a (Criminal) Prosecution and through Indictments, that were 'overcharged'. According to International NGOs, OSCE's LSMS and the later decisions of IJP, these cases were based upon insufficient evidence in the records upon which the law requires that they be based – police reports and complaints and testimony before an investigative judge, respectively.[176] Conversely, in some of the cases where ethnic Albanians were accused of committing serious violent non-war crimes against ethnic Serbs in Kosovo, or in cases where socially and politically powerful ethnic Albanian Kosovars, such as former UCK (KLA) and current TMK (the new civil corps, the Kosovo Protection Force) were accused of any crimes against Albanian Kosovars, the local prosecutors and judges would sometimes release the accused, or find lesser charges, in the face of evidence that called for detention.

The third problem of unrestricted case selection under Regulations 2000/6 and 2000/34 in 2000, later exacerbated by the unlimited case assignment under Regulation 2000/64[177] in

---

175. See the applicable law on criminal procedure, which in Kosovo was the 1989 criminal law and procedure, Art. 370, per Regulation 1999/24.

176. Where locally-tried cases were reversed by IJ majority Supreme Court, and retried by IJP and convicted of more severe war crimes offenses, the higher charges second-time around can be attributed to IJP efforts to locate and hear new witnesses, and to reexamine prior witnesses thoroughly.

177. Ironically, Regulation 2000/64 solved the first two problems but contributed to the expansion of the third. The societal, victim and political pressures upon the SRSG, and the desire to respond to public desires and minority cries for protection of an international panel, resulted in increased IJP assignments, which were now also decided by administrators, rather than by just the individual IJPs who were more familiar to their workload burdens and time needs. The administration set

2001, resulted in a growing problem of 'overbooking' the IJP. This resulted in some trials being stretched out over four months or more, but with only several trial days per month, and IJP being forced to simultaneously prepare for three or four different trials per month. This resulted in IJP having very little time to prepare for trials, in IJ having insufficient time to write the verdict and reasoning,[178] and in IP not being able to adequately advise police and screen their cases.

The first two problems, being the most urgent, resulted in two significant regulations being enacted. On 15 December 2000, Regulation 2000/64 on Assignment of International Judges and Prosecutors and Change of Venue was enacted, which gave UNMIK and the SRSG a method to ensure majority international control of voting. The Regulation also allowed the assignment of international judicial personnel to different Districts than those to which they were appointed. When the SRSG approved a '64 petition', what would have been a five judge trial panel with two professional and three lay judges became a three professional judge panel with a minimum of two international judges.

Regulation 2001/2, enacted on 12 January 2001, not coincidentally within a month of the *Afrim Zeqiri* Supreme Court decision (see below), allowed international prosecutors to resume cases abandoned by local prosecutors, without having to do so through the arcane and burdensome procedures and burdens of proof required by local law.

Ironically, however, these procedural changes were not only opposed in 2000 and 2001 by the local judiciary as illegal, improper and creating a 'parallel system of justice' but also, in effect, did create a separate trial procedure, with the Department of Judicial Affairs, later renamed the Department of Justice, scheduling international judges and international prosecutors for the '64' Panel trials, with international judges presiding. Some local judges were assigned to some 64 panels, but it had been demonstrated that for war crimes, the previous 'insertion into the local structures without majority voting control' was not effective, and that this was the new paradigm: international control of voting and the result.

In August 2001, the first international prosecutor was appointed to the Office of the Public Prosecutor of Kosovo before the Supreme Court, bringing the total of international prosecutors to six. During 2001, the number of international judicial personnel varied due to recruitment and departures, with 17 IJ and 11 IP being the high-water mark. By the end of 2001, approximately 80 ongoing court cases were being handled by IJP. These numbers did not include an additional and significant number of cases that were being investigated by the police and being supervised by the IP.[179] The need for careful IP scrutiny of police investigation and case facts before initiating a request for a judicial investigation is especially

---

up meticulous scheduling processes to take judicial commitments into account as a result, with some success.

178. In the applicable civil law judicial panel system, unlike the common law jury system, the written verdict and reasons must be quite detailed and very precise, usually tens of pages, or the verdict risks reversal.

179. Under the applicable Law on Criminal Procedure, Arts. 45 and 155, the prosecutor has the authority to guide and direct all police operations. Over 4,000 UN Police, and more KPS officers, are currently in Kosovo, along with such specialized units as CCIU [Complex Criminal Investigations Unit], Kosovo Organized Crime Bureau [KOCB], Trafficking and Prostitution Investigation Unit [TPIU], and several Task Forces on such things as Terrorism, Organized Crime, Corruption, and the like. Only 12 international prosecutors are insufficient to properly supervise all such cases, so the international prosecutors try to concentrate on war crimes, terrorism, and the most important organized crime and inter-ethnic violence cases.

important given the complexity of the legal elements and requirements, and factual determinations, in the war crimes cases. Where IJP are assigned to multiple and disparate court appearances and cases, it inevitably impacts upon the time which can be budgeted by them for preparation, legal research and careful investigation of their top priority: war crimes cases.

The eventual issue, given the growing caseload, will be whether there will be a limit imposed by Regulation or under current applicable law that restricts the ability to select/assign any case, or that enables a review process of which cases are selected by/assigned to international judicial personnel.

Cases

The first genocide and war crimes trials did not start until early-2000, and the trial panels were either completely or majority local judges, with at most one international judge on the panel. They resulted in convictions on all of the war crimes and genocide charges, which were then reversed by a majority international judge Supreme Court on appeal.[180] All such trials to date involved either ethnic Serbs, or in one case, an ethnic Albanian who allegedly collaborated with the Serbian paramilitary forces.[181]

Before discussing particular cases it is first necessary to clarify some of the terminology of the applicable procedure, which is based upon the 1989 Yugoslav Criminal Procedure Code, with modifications by UNMIK Regulations and the application of the European Convention of Human Rights. The 'Indictment' in these cases is not filed until after a judicial investigation, which is initiated by a formal filing of the charges and supporting reports by the prosecutor. The Investigating Judge rules on whether the investigation should then proceed. Based on a proposal by the prosecutor and defense, the Investigating Judge examines witnesses and evidence. When the judge completes the investigation, she or he then returns the court file and evidence to the prosecutor, who then decides whether or not to file an indictment. Thus, the date of the Indictment has been months, and sometimes up to the allowable maximum of a year, after the initial arrest and prosecutorial Request to Initiate an Investigation.[182]

This report concerns only that small minority of war crimes cases that reached a court trial. Many more cases were under investigation by the Complex Criminal Investigative Unit of the UNMIK Police, with guidance from International Prosecutors, and other cases were selected by International Prosecutors and Judges at the judicial investigation stage and resulted in no indictment being filed.

☛ *Juvenile V* case, District Court of Mitrovica/Mitrovicë, Juvenile Panel under FRY LCP Arts. 476 and 480 et seq and Supreme Court

Juvenile V was a 16-year-old ethnic Serbian boy who on 23 December 1999 was charged with genocide by a local prosecutor, under Article 141 of the FRYCC, for allegedly burning

180. The conviction of Zvezdan Simić, and in another case the conviction of Zoran Stanojević, each for murder, were affirmed by Supreme Court international judge majority panels.

181. Lulzim Ademi was convicted of war crimes under Art. 142 of the Criminal Code of the FRY in August 2000, by a majority local panel with one international judge.

182. See FRY Law of Criminal Procedure, Arts. 158 et seq.

down 100 houses. He was 15 and 1/2 years old at the time the criminal acts were alleged to have taken place between March and May 1999. The prosecutor's recommendation (a juvenile equivalent of what would be an indictment against an adult) alleged that, in complicity with an adult, Juvenile V had 'the intent of forcefully purging the Albanian population ... with the intent of partially or completely destroying the Albanian community, ... They had come to the said township in the evening, with fire arms, and threatening to kill and purge forced the inhabitants from their homes...'.[183] There was no evidence in the record or brought before the court of the intent or *dolus specialis* of genocide. Rather, evidence showed that Juvenile V had a below-normal intelligence, as well as what bordered on 'hero worship' and watched the adult (an escapee from the Mitrovica Detention Center) perpetrator start fires. The juvenile had admitted to starting only three fires himself, and those only upon the urging of the adult. The juvenile procedure under local law required that there be only three judges, with only one professional judge under the FRY Law of Criminal Procedure (LCP) Articles 463(1), 476 and 480 et seq. Given that they were inexperienced with Yugoslav juvenile procedure, no international judge selected the case, allowing an experienced juvenile specialist to be the presiding judge in this trial.

The juvenile appeared before a wholly-local panel, but with an international prosecutor, who amended the Article 141 genocide charge drastically to allege instead the crime of causing general danger (through arson) under Kosovo Criminal Code (KCC) Article 157, as well as of grave acts against general security under KCC Article 164, and further reduced the count of 100 houses to only three houses. Those amended charges carry a maximum sentence of five years in a locked juvenile 'educational' facility. The international prosecutor then argued in closing for the lesser punishment of education and counseling out of custody, based on testimony proposed and presented by psychologists and teachers who had worked with, and were willing to supervise, Juvenile V. The local panel instead sentenced the juvenile to one to five years in custody on 13 September 2000. The Supreme Court, local panel, affirmed that decision on 8 March 2001, as recommended by the local Public Prosecutor of Kosovo.

☛ *Lulzim Ademi* case, District Court Mitrovica/ Mitrovicë and Supreme Court

Lulzim Ademi, a Kosovar Albanian who allegedly collaborated and was complicit with ethnic Serbian paramilitaries, was charged with war crimes under the applicable law, Article 142 of the FRYCC. The local majority five-judge panel, with a local presiding judge and one international judge on the panel, convicted him of Article 142 war crimes on 30 August 2000.

---

183. There were no specifics alleged regarding the intent of the accused juvenile other than the second paragraph of the prosecutor's recommendation:
'During the war activities and the NATO bombing of the FR of Yugoslavia, he committed the crime of burning of houses with the intent of forcefully purging the Albanian population and with the intent of partially or completely destroying the Albanian community, and he jointly with the also accused Dragan Jovanovic burned about 100 houses in the 'Bosniak Town', among them houses of Redzo Karakasi, Veton Grdovci, Enver Pazari, and Maso Grudic. They had come to the said township in the evening, with fire arms, and threatening to kill and purge forced the inhabitants from their homes. The residents obeyed in fear. Following this they entered the houses and set them on fire.'

The verdict did not make any specific findings on the existence of the armed conflict or its character, other than a general preamble or *chapeau.*[184] The verdict and later written reasons, published on 30 August 2000, convicted him of committing seven murders constituting war crimes under Article 142. However, this was an *in absentia* conviction, as Ademi escaped from the UNMIK Mitrovica Detention facilities on 24 February 2000, before the trial started. Regardless, the trial court decided on 3 July 2000 to try Ademi *in absentia.* The defense counsel appealed this decision, and on 12 July 2000 the Supreme Court, in a local three-judge panel, approved the commencement of the trial. The defense counsel filed an appeal of the verdict, and by the end of 2001 the case remained under consideration by the Supreme Court, which will sit as a '64' Panel international majority. The Supreme Court has been advised by the written Opinion of the International Prosecutor of the Office of the Public Prosecutor of Kosovo[185] that it should reverse the conviction due to the effect of Regulation 2001/1, which prohibits *in absentia* war crimes proceedings, both trials and appeals, in combination with the International Covenant on Civil and Political Rights, Article 15(2).

☛ *Dragan Nikolić* case, District Court of Gjilan/Gnjilane and Supreme Court

The first conviction in a murder case within the context of armed conflict was of Dragan Nikolić, who was indicted on 5 November 1999 for murder in complicity with Serbian military and police forces, after attempting to rob an ethnic Albanian family on 5 April 1999. While the indictment could have alleged, and the prosecution could have proposed evidence to prove, that the murder was a war crime, committed during the conflict and with a nexus to it, the local prosecutor chose not to do so. After a trial before the local majority panel District Court of Gjilan/Gnjilane, Nikolić was convicted on 3 July 2000. On 9 April 2001 an international majority Supreme Court reversed the conviction due to incorrect and insufficient findings of fact and the refusal of the trial court to hear proposed defense witnesses. His retrial began in September 2001, prosecuted by an IP before a '64' Panel of IJ, and was ongoing as of the end of the year.

☛ *Milos Jokić* case, District Court of Gjilan/Gnjilane and Supreme Court

Milos Jokić was indicted for genocide under Article 141 of the FRYCC, and his trial began on 15 May 2000 before a local panel with a local presiding judge and with one international judge. During closing argument, the local prosecutor amended the indictment down to war crimes under Article 142.[186] After only seven days of trial stretched over five months, Jokić was found guilty on 20 September 2000 of war crimes under Article 142 FRYCC for

---

184. 'By violating the rules of the International Law during the time of the war - armed conflict, against the civil population, by murders, inhumane behavior, forced displacement, intimidation, property looting, and by causing grave sufferings, as member - employee of the local security in Mitrovica, together with a group comprising members of the Yugoslavian Army, Ministry of Internal Affairs of Serbia, and the Serb paramilitary organizations, armed with fire weapons and other weapons, during the military intervention of the NATO air forces in Yugoslavia, ...'.

185. Aka, International Public Prosecutor of Kosovo.

186. Pursuant to LCP Art. 337.

shooting one, and ordering the killing of another, ethnic Albanian. He was additionally found guilty of rape as a war crime:

> '(After robbing her of jewellery) ... under the threat of the machine gun and the knife has constrained her to sexual relation by violence, and after 5 hours of confinement and ill-treatment has ordered her to go to Albania declaring to her that 'this is Serb land'.'

The reasoning also made reference to the lack of sufficient evidence of intent to commit genocide:

> 'in order to commit the criminal act of genocide, the author of such criminal act should have aimed the destruction of an ethnic and racial group and such act has not been supported with any evidence in this concrete case.'

On appeal, the Supreme Court, with a '64' Panel international judge majority, reversed the verdict on 26 April 2001 due to insufficient facts in the record and a failure to hear witnesses proposed by the defense. An international prosecutor and '64' Panel of international judges retried the case. A decision had not been rendered as of the end of 2001.

☛ *Igor Simić et al.* case, District Court of Mitrovica/Mitrovicë

Although six men were initially charged in connection with the 14 April 1999, Mitrovica 'Popović Street' war crimes murders, five escaped from UNMIK custody,[187] so that only Igor Simić, a Serbian law student, remained in this case. The other five members were severed from the case by the motion of the international prosecutor due to the same considerations that later resulted in Regulation 2001/1. The indictment of 20 June 2000, filed by a local prosecutor before being superceded by the international prosecutor, alleged that he committed genocide by killing, in complicity with others, 26 Kosovo Albanian civilians and burning houses, all with the intent to completely or partially destroy or displace the Albanian community from Mitrovica and from Kosovo.

The trial began on 5 December 2000, before a local majority panel, with a local presiding judge and one international judge, and with an international prosecutor. After all significant witnesses were heard and extensively examined, some over several days, the international prosecutor abandoned the prosecution on 10 April 2001, because as a matter of law there was no specific intent to destroy all or part of the ethnic Albanian people, and because there was no credible evidence that Simić was guilty of any of the lesser crimes of war crimes, murder or any other crimes covered by the facts alleged in the indictment.

During the trial, the significantly contradictory testimony among witnesses, and witness testimony discredited by documentary evidence, demonstrated a willingness by some witnesses to testify falsely in order to identify Simić as one of the perpetrators. While the injured party's attorney attempted to reinstitute the case as an injured party prosecution under Kosovo criminal procedure,[188] Simić has since been released from detention and has fled Kosovo.

---

187. On 2 September 2000, 13 Serbs successfully escaped from custody at the UNMIK Detention Center in Mitrovica.

188. See LCP Arts. 61 et seq.

☛ *Miroslav Vucković* case, District Court of Mitrovica/Mitrovicë and Supreme Court

The case of Miroslav Vucković presented the only deliberation on genocide under Article 141 of the Yugoslav Criminal Code by a first instance court and later by the Supreme Court. The indictment by a local prosecutor alleged that Vucković and an *in absentia* co-accused,[189] with the intention of forcefully displacing the Albanian population and of completely or partially destroying the Albanian community, shot at villagers to force them to flee, burned houses and confiscated property.[190] One murder was alleged due to arson. The majority local panel, with a local presiding judge and one international judge, convicted Vucković for genocide, but the presiding judge[191] specifically stated in the verdict that he was not guilty of the arson-murder. The court held that Vucković committed or was an accomplice to genocide within the meaning of Article 141 of the Yugoslav Penal Code through the 'forcible expulsion of the population in the special circumstances that would bring total or partial destruction of that population'.[192]

The Court also stated that:

> 'the incriminating act of the accused during the consequent period of time, convinced the court, that in complicity with his group the accused manifested the will of the strong intensity to forcefully expel population from their houses, homes, and brought the population to the unbearable living conditions, without food, clothes in the heavy weather conditions without shelter, and in that way the perpetrators were ready to accept the consequence that the part or entire group of Albanian population of these three villages will be exterminated.'[193]

---

189. Bozur Bizevac, who escaped from custody in August 2000. With the passage of Regulation 2001/1, his case was abandoned.

190. 'In the period from 22 March until early May 1999, in the villages of Gusavac and Gornji Suvi Do, Mitrovica Municipality, with the intention of forcefully displacing Albanian population and with the intention of completely or partially destroying the Albanian community, together with to date unidentified persons, dressed in different military, police and paramilitary uniforms out of which majority were wearing masks and all of them were armed with firearms, came to the above stated villages, shooting from firearms, with threats of murder created such an atmosphere of fear and intimidation amongst the Albanian population from these village that these inhabitants, including women, children and elderly were forced to flee into the surrounding villages and a forest following which they, by illegal and ruthless confiscation of personal property of Albanians, entered the houses and took all valuable items which they took away in tractors and other means of transportation and distributed among themselves, in order to by illegal destruction of personal property and houses achieve the goal that the inhabitants of these villages of Albanian ethnicity can no longer return to their homes, set on fire the houses of: Ismet, Jakup, Haljit, Jonuz, Miran, Ajet, Husnija, Dzevat, Hamit, Bajram, Sinan, Murselj, Sevelj, Agim, Bejtulah, Sokolj, Seljim, Adem, Ragip, Dibran, Tafilja, Sadik, Fadilj, Hetem, Fehmija, Dzeljadin, Nedzmedin, Abit, Safet, Naim and Agron Sahitim as well as houses of other villagers of the village of Gusavac and the houses of Bedri Hajra, Veselj Hasani, Ekrem Beka, Sadije Seljimi and other houses in the village of Gornji Suvi Do, and in the houses of Seljim Sahiti in the village of Gusavac an immobile, old and weak now deceased Hazire Sahiti burned to death, even though the accused were aware, when setting the house on fire, that the mentioned person was in the premises of the house.'

191. Under applicable law and judicial custom, the Presiding Judge will write the reasons after orally announcing the verdict.

192. See Verdict, para. 30 of section 'Reasoning'.

193. See Verdict, para. 35 of section 'Reasoning'.

However, there was never any quantification or specific evidence during the trial as to severe weather, starvation, or the number of people who died due to such conditions. Upon his review of the defense appeal and record, the International Prosecutor submitted an extensive Opinion to the Supreme Court that recommended that the conviction should be reversed as a matter of law and of fact.

Subsequently, the Supreme Court '64' panel reversed the conviction. In controversial dicta, however, the Supreme Court Panel's presiding judge, an international judge from France, overlooking the limited scope of the trial and its evidence, wrote:

> 'More generally, according to the [this] Supreme Court, the exactions committed by the Milosevic's regime in 1999 cannot be qualified as criminal acts of genocide, since their purpose was not the destruction of the Albanian ethnic group in whole or in part, but its forcefully departure from Kosovo as a result of systematic campaign of terror including murders, rapes, arsons and severe maltreatments. Such criminal acts correspond to the definition of crimes against humanity given by international laws (widespread or systematic plan of attack against civilian population during the war) or can be qualified war crimes as per Article 142 of the CLY [FRYCC].' [p. 2 of Verdict]

This language would have been called *dicta* in any common law system, and was heavily criticized by local jurists and press, as well as the ICTY, as there was absolutely no evidence before the first or second instance court as to the purpose of the Milošević regime in Kosovo; rather, the entire testimony concerned the alleged criminal acts of a group of paramilitary and ethnic Serb residents against ethnic Albanians in three small villages. Certainly, no expert or even government/NGO general statements regarding the overall plan or purpose of the Milošević regime was before the court.[194] The Kosovo Supreme Court (local judges) called a general assembly within itself, and then a five-member informal commission proceeded to give a press conference stating that the remarks must be limited to the facts of that particular case, and do not bind or reflect the Supreme Court's opinion on future cases.

Moreover, the Supreme Court's *dicta* regarding crimes against humanity seemed to imply direct application to a domestic system of international crimes without any domestic legislation (since the 1989 applicable law only criminalizes genocide in Article 141, and war crimes in Article 142).[195]

☛ *Sava Matić* case, District Court of Prizren and Supreme Court

Sava Matić was indicted on 11 September 2000 for war crimes under Article 142 of the FRYCC. He was alleged to have obeyed orders to take part in the murders of 42 civilians from one village. The trial began on 22 January 2001, a month after the enactment of Regulation 64, with a local prosecutor. On 29 January 2001, the majority international judge '64' Panel found him guilty only of light bodily injury in connection with an incident that had not been in the indictment. Both the prosecutor and the defense appealed. The Supreme Court,

---

194. This was the stated position of the International Prosecutor of the Office of the Public Prosecutor of Kosovo, who had presented the case on behalf of the prosecution in the Supreme Court.

195. International Judge Patrice de Charette was also the IJ for the first instance court hearing the *Trajković* case, discussed *infra*.

composed of an international majority panel, reversed the conviction on 13 June 2001, as it was for a crime different from that alleged in the indictment.

The retrial began on 22 November 2001, again with a local prosecutor.

☛ *Momcilo Trajković* case, District Court of Gjilan/Gnjilane and Supreme Court

Perhaps the most significant verdict, from a legal standpoint of setting precedents, was the conviction of Momcilo Trajković, a Serb police commander, under a legal liability theory of command responsibility. He was indicted on 3 April 2000 for war crimes under Article 142 of the FRYCC, for attempted murder under KCC Article 30 (murder) in relation to FRYCC Article 19 (attempt), and various other crimes, including murder, that were based primarily upon command responsibility, because he was the Chief of Police of the Kamenica Office for Internal Affairs. A local prosecutor filed the charges and later indictment.

During the trial, which took place between 23 November 2000 and 6 March 2001, the accused denied any involvement in the crimes committed, and stated to the court that his functions as Chief were only administrative in nature, or dealt with the plainclothes police functions, without any control over uniformed police. However, the witnesses at the trial testified, without giving any specifics, that the competencies of the accused were not limited to administrative matters during the time of the war and that this fact was well-known to the people of the Kamenica area.

On 6 March 2001,[196] the local majority trial panel of the District Court of Gjilan/Gnjilane, with one international judge who wrote the reasoning and verdict, found him guilty of attempted murder based on shooting at ethnic Albanians, raising an Albanian national flag over the police station, weapons violations for weapons found inside his house, and war crimes under Article 142 of the Yugoslav Criminal Code, based upon a finding of command responsibility. However, these war crimes were confusingly qualified as crimes against humanity, apparently based upon the 'violation of international law' provision contained in Article 142 of the Yugoslav Criminal Code. There was no discussion of whether this was an attempt to apply the international proscription of a crime against humanity directly in a domestic court, which would be difficult without any specific penal provision, or whether the court was simply finding that a violation of the crime against humanity fulfilled the element of 'violation of international law' that was one of the necessary elements of an Article 142 war crimes. In any event, the Defendant was sentenced to 20 years' imprisonment.

The defense appealed to the Supreme Court, each defense attorney filing an appeal, on 29 March and 2 April 2001. In his Opinion, the international prosecutor recommended that the Supreme Court reverse the conviction because both as a matter of law and fact, command responsibility and direct action and ordering were not proven. In particular, the lengthy IP Opinion reviewed the lack of any specifics to support the defendant's authority and control over the unidentified Serb police who committed murders, as well as the absence of necessary and thorough examination of witnesses and victims.[197] The Supreme Court '64'

---

196. Verdict number P.nr.68/2000.

197. The Opinion of the IP, as well as the District Court and Supreme Court's judgements, can be viewed on the Internet at http://www.ridi.org/adi/dip/des20010315.htm.

panel, with a presiding international judge and one local judge, came to the same conclusion in reversing the conviction on 30 November 2001.[198]

☛ *Cedomir Jovanović* and *Andjelko Kolasinac* case, District Court of Prizren and Supreme Court

Jovanović and Kolasinac were the two remaining accused from a group of eight, the other six of whom escaped. The original indictment had been filed on 7 August 2000, and on 1 May 2001 the international prosecutor amended the indictment to strike the six escapees, as per the requirements of Regulation 2001/1. Their trial was jointly held before an all international '64' panel with an international prosecutor. The trial began 2 May 2001 and concluded on 14 June 2001. Jovanović was found guilty of war crimes under Article 142 of FRYCC for participating in a massacre of 62 civilians on 25 March 1999, as well as ordering deportation of civilians and burning and looting houses.

Kolasinac, the President of the Municipal Assembly and Head of the Civil Defence Unit, the highest ranking civilian Serb government employee in Kosovo, who had been charged with seven counts of war crimes, was found guilty only of the crime of Assisting an Offender after Commission of a Criminal Act, under Article 174 KCC, the destroying of traces of a crime, which was committed by ordering the ethnic Albanian Kosovars to clean up the evidence of the forced deportation of Albanians from Kosovo, such as family goods left behind. He was sentenced to five years imprisonment.

On 2 November 2001, the Supreme Court affirmed Jovanović's conviction. This was the first affirmed conviction by the Supreme Court in an international majority of any war crimes or genocide conviction in Kosovo's UNMIK courts. The written reasons took pains to analyze and discuss the legal elements of Article 142 FRYCC, including the existence and nature of an armed conflict,[199] and found that 'an internal armed conflict existed in the municipality of Orahovac/Rahovec itself during the summer of 1998' and through Spring 1999. The court found that Jovanović

> 'as a uniformed paramilitary member, participated in the execution of sixty-two people on the morning of 25 March 1999. According to the indictment, these murders occurred at a place known as "Ura e Bellajes" near the village of Bela Crkva. The indictment also states that on the same day, Jovanovic participated in the killing of an additional thirteen people near the village of Celina.'

He received a sentence of 20 years. The Supreme Court reversed the conviction of Kolasinac, finding that the trial court had performed an incorrect assessment of the evidence, and an incorrect evaluation of his acts' connection to the criminal acts.

---

198. The case was subsequently returned to the District Court for retrial on 27 May 2002, with the trial continuing through 2002. See 5 *YIHL* (2002) for further details.

199. The judges cited in their decision, for example, ICTY jurisprudence as well as reports of the OSCE.

☛ *Radovan Apostolić* case, District Court of Mitrovicë/Mitrovica

Radovan Apostolić was originally indicted on 8 September 2000 by a local prosecutor for war crimes, under Article 142 of FRYCC, along with four others who later escaped from UNMIK custody. Apostolić was accused of looting and burning houses, and an attempted murder as a war crimes act – which consisted of shooting at an Albanian Kosovar with the intent to kill. A '64 panel' was appointed. On 10 April 2001, the absent accused were severed from the indictment by an amendment of the international prosecutor, and the trial began. After the main injured party and some supporting witnesses testified, on 13 July 2001 the international prosecutor reduced the charges to causing general danger by arson under KCC Article 157, looting [aggravated theft] under KCC Article 135, as well as attempted murder under KCC Article 30 related to FRYCC Article 19. The case lasted ten months, due to the conflicting schedules of parties and jurists, and efforts to follow-up on discoveries in trial hearings of potential relevant evidence. Finally, on 28 January 2002, just before delivering his closing argument, the international prosecutor amended the indictment once again to reduce the charges to aggravated theft, based on conflicting and inconsistent witness testimony in contradiction with prior statements. Further, the prosecutor argued in closing to the court that the main witness, the injured party and the owner of the looted property, had lied to the court numerous times, so that at most the court might believe that the accused took only candles and tea, not the hundreds of thousands of Deutsche Marks claimed by the victims. The verdict was expected in early-2002.

MICHAEL HARTMANN

FINLAND

Counter-terrorism

☛ Statement by H.E. Rasi, Permanent Representative of Finland to the United Nations, UNGA 56th Session, New York, 3 October 2001

☛ Act 989/2001 to implement the 1991 Convention on the Marking of Plastic Explosives for the Purpose of Identification

☛ Finnish security and defence policy 2001, Report by the Government to Parliament on 13 June 2001, VNS 2/2001 vp

On 3 October 2001, Ambassador Marjatta Rasi gave an address in New York in which she stated that Finland subscribes to the Plan of Action of the European Union to eliminate international terrorism. The statement made clear Finland's intention to ratify all 12 conventions elaborated under UN auspices to prevent and suppress terrorist acts. At the time of the statement, Finland had ratified nine of the 12 Conventions and intended to ratify the Convention on the Marking of Plastic Explosives for the Purpose of Identification of 1991 by the end of 2001. Preparations for the ratification of the 1997 International Convention for the Suppression of Terrorist Bombings and the 1999 International Convention for the Suppression of the Financing of Terrorism were carried out.

In its report to Parliament regarding the Finnish security and defence policy of 2001, the Government addressed the issue of ratification by Finland of the 1997 Ottawa Convention on the Prohibition of the Use, Stockpiling, Production and Transfer of Anti-Personnel Mines and on their Destruction. Finland is not a party to the Convention, the reasons being the lack of economic and technical possibilities to bind itself to destroy the mines as mentioned in the agreement within the timeframe laid down in the Convention. Without a system replacing the anti-personnel mines that now make part of the Finnish defence, the ability to defend the country would be significantly reduced.[200] However, it should be noted that Finland neither produces nor exports anti-personnel mines. The report also states that Finland is working on realising adherence to the Ottawa Convention in 2006, meaning destruction of the mines before 2010, in accordance with the four-year period mentioned in the Convention.

MARIA NYBONDAS

FRANCE[201]

Geneva Law

- Law No. 2001-79 of 30 January 2001 authorising accession to the Protocol Additional to the Geneva Conventions of 12 August 1949, and relating to the protection of victims of international armed conflicts (Protocol I) [Loi no 2001-79 du 30 janvier 2001 autorisant l'adhésion au protocole additionnel aux conventions de Genève du 12 août 1949 relatif à la protection des victimes des conflits armés internationaux (protocole I)]. Published in Journal officiel de la République française, No. 26 of 31 January 2001, p. 1650
- Decree No. 2001-565 of 25 June 2001 publishing the Protocol Additional to the Geneva Conventions of 12 August 1949, and relating to the protection of victims of international armed conflicts (Protocol I), adopted at Geneva, 8 June 1977. Added are the French reservations and declarations [Décret No. 2001-565 du 25 juin 2001 portant publication du protocole additionnel aux conventions de Genève du 12 août 1949 relatif à la protection des victimes des conflits armés internationaux (protocole I), adopté à Genève le 8 juin 1977, réserves et déclarations de la France]. Published in *Journal Officiel de la République Française*, 30 June 2001, p. 10409

France declares that Protocol I does not interfere with her right to self-defence under Article 51 of the UN Charter, and considers that the use of nuclear weapons is not covered by this Protocol. Otherwise, French reservations and declarations (18 paragraphs) concern various clauses of the Protocol.

- Opinion adopted on 6 July 2001 by the Plenary session of the National Advisory Commission on Human Rights on the French accession to the Protocol Additional to the Geneva Conventions of 12 August 1949, and relating to the protection of victims of international armed conflict (Protocol I) [Commission nationale consultative des droits de l'homme (C.N.C.D.H.), Avis sur l'adhésion française au Protocole additionnel aux Conventions de Genève du 12 août 1949 relatif à la protection des victimes de conflits armés internationaux (Protocole I) (Adopté par l'assemblée plénière du 6 juillet 2001)] [http://www.commission-droits-homme.fr/]

---

200. For commentary on Finland's position on anti-personnel landmines, see L. Hannikainen, 1 *YIHL* (1998) pp. 436-438.

201. Information and commentaries provided by Professor Paul Tavernier, Professor Paris-Sud University, Director, Centre de Recherches et d'Etudes sur les droits de l'Homme et le droit humanitaire (Credho), with the assistance of Alexandre Balguy-Gallois, Credho and Catholic Law Faculty, Paris.

In this opinion, the French Commission regrets France's belated accession to Protocol I with numerous reservations and declarations and that the French government did not seek advice from the Commission before this accession. The Commission emphasizes that humanitarian law's rules and principles are applicable to nuclear weapons and that the protection of the civilian population is essential.

Landmines

- 2000 Report of National Commission for suppression of anti-personnel mines [Commission nationale pour l'élimination des mines antipersonnel, *Rapport 2000*] (Paris, *La Documentation française* 2001, 152 pp.)

This second report was prepared for the French Government and will be transmitted to the Parliament.

- France's action in implementing the Ottawa Treaty and in the fight against anti-personnel mines, Ministry of Foreign Affairs, Archive files, August 2001, 9 pp. [L'action de la France pour la mise en œuvre de la Convention d'Ottawa et dans la lutte contre les mines antipersonnel, Ministère des Affaires étrangères, dossiers d'archive, août 2001, 9 pp.] [http://www.france.diplomatie.fr/actual/dossiers/mines/mines7.html]
Chemical Weapons
- Decree No. 2001-269 of 26 March 2001 concerning challenge inspections as foreseen in sect. III of the Law No. 98-467 of 17 June 1998 concerning enforcement of the 13 January 1993 Convention on the Prohibition of the Development, Production, Stockpiling and Use of Chemical Weapons and on Their Destruction (A/RES/47/39). [Décret, 2001-269, 2001-03-26, concernant les inspections par mise en demeure prévues par le titre III de la loi n° 98-467 du 17 juin 1998 relative à l'application de la convention du 13 janvier 1993 sur l'interdiction de la mise au point, de la fabrication, du stockage et de l'emploi des armes chimiques et sur leur destruction. Published in Journal officiel de la République française, 31 March 2001, p. 5040 [http://www.legifrance.gouv.fr]
- Decree No. 2001-143 of 15 February 2001, concerning implementation of section II clauses of Law No. 98-467 of 17 June 1998 concerning enforcement of the 13 January 1993 Convention on the Prohibition of the Development, Production, Stockpiling and Use of Chemical Weapons and on Their Destruction [Décret, 2001-143, 2001-02-15, concernant la mise en oeuvre des dispositions du titre II de la loi n° 98-467 du 17 juin 1998 relative à l'application de la convention du 13 janvier 1993 sur l'interdiction de la mise au point, de la fabrication, du stockage et de l'emploi des armes chimiques et sur leur destruction. Published in Journal officiel de la République française, 17 February 2001, p. 2648 [http://www.legifrance.gouv.fr]
- Decree No. 2001-144 of 15 February 2001, specifying conditions for sampling of chemicals as provided in Article 51 of Law No. 98-467 of 17 June 1998 concerning enforcement of the 13 January 1993 Convention on the Prohibition of the Development, Production, Stockpiling and Use of Chemical Weapons and on Their Destruction [Décret, 2001-144, 2001-02-15, définissant les conditions du prélèvement d'échantillons de produits chimiques prévu par l'article 51 de la loi n° 98-467 du 17 juin 1998 relative à l'application de la convention du 13 janvier 1993 sur l'interdiction de la mise au point, de la fabrication, du stockage et de l'emploi des armes chimiques et sur leur destruction.

Published in Journal officiel de la République française, 17 February 2001, p. 2653 [http://www.legifrance.gouv.fr]

☛ Decree No. 2001-145 of 15 February 2001, concerning national investigations and administrative sanctions as provided by Law No. 98-467 of 17 June 1998 concerning enforcement of the 13 January 1993 Convention on the prohibition of the development, production, stockpiling and use of chemical weapons and to their destruction Décret, 2001-145, 2001-02-15, relatif aux investigations nationales et aux sanctions administratives prévues par la loi n° 98-467 du 17 juin 1998 relative à l'application de la convention du 13 janvier 1993 sur l'interdiction de la mise au point, de la fabrication, du stockage et de l'emploi des armes chimiques et sur leur destruction. Published in Journal officiel de la République française, 17 February 2001, p. 2654 [http://www.legifrance.gouv.fr]

These four decrees contain very precise and accurate provisions for implementing, at the national level, the clauses of the 1993 Convention on Chemical Weapons, especially clauses concerning verification.

Specific Conflicts

AFGHANISTAN

☛ Government's Statement on the situation in Afghanistan by Mr. Lionel Jospin, Prime Minister. Registered by Presidency of the National Assembly on 21 November 2001, Parliamentary Papers, National Assembly, No. 3402 [Déclaration du Gouvernement sur la situation en Afghanistan, par M. Lionel JOSPIN, Premier ministre, Enregistré à la Présidence de l'Assemblée nationale le 21 novembre 2001, N° 3402, Assemblée nationale]

☛ Senate, 23 August 2001 – No. 34858 – Situation of humanitarian personnel accused by Kabul's Rulers of proselytizing for Christian faith. M.P's Written Questions, Senate, question N°34858, 23 August 2001, Government's Answer published in JORF of 22 November 2001 [Situation des travailleurs humanitaires accusés de propagation du Christianisme par le pouvoir à Kaboul].

CONGO-BRAZZAVILLE

☛ Information Report registered as provided in Article 145 of the Rules of Procedure by the Committee for Foreign Affairs on the mission carried out by a delegation of the Committee in the Democratic Republic of the Congo and set out by Mr Gérard Charasse, Mrs Monique Collange and Michel Terrot, deputies. Registered by the Presidency of the National Assembly on 7 February 2001, Parliamentary Papers, National Assembly, No. 2918 [Rapport d'information déposé en application de l'article 145 du règlement par la Commission des Affaires étrangères sur la mission effectuée par une délégation de la Commission en République du Congo et présenté par M. Gérard Charasse, Mme Monique Collange et Michel Terrot, Députés, Enregistré à la Présidence de l'Assemblée nationale le 7 février 2001, N° 2918 Assemblée nationale]

MACEDONIA

☛ Hearing of Mr. François Leotard, European Union's Representative in Macedonia. Committee for Foreign Affairs, National Assembly, Tuesday 23 October 2001, Compte-Rendu No. 8 [Audition de M. François Léotard, représentant de l'Union européenne en Macédoine, Commission des affaires étrangères, Assemblée Nationale, Mardi 23 octobre 2001, Compte rendu N° 8]

THE OCCUPIED TERRORITIES

☛ Opinion of the National Advisory Commission on Human Rights on the situation of human rights and humanitarian law in Israel and the Palestinian territories. Adopted 6 July 2001 [Commission Nationale Consultative des Droits de l'Homme (CNCDH). Avis sur la situation des droits de l'homme et du droit humanitaire en Israël et les territoires palestiniens. Adopté le 06 juillet 2001] [http://www.commission-droits-homme.fr/]

☛ Senate, Written question No. 33317 of 24 May 2001 (p. 1727) (Implementing the measures regarding the improvement of the Israeli-Palestinian situation) from/de Gilbert Chabroux, (Sénateur du Rhône), Groupe Socialiste [SÉNAT, Question écrite n° 33317 du 24 Mai 2001 (p. 1727) (Mise en œuvre de mesures relatives à l'amélioration de la situation israélo-palestinienne)] With responses/Avec réponse

Genocide

☛ Law No. 2001-70 of 29 January 2001 concerning the recognition of the Armenian genocide of 1915 [Loi N° 2001-70 du 29 janvier 2001 relative à la reconnaissance du génocide arménien de 1915]. Published in *Journal officiel de la République française,* N° 25 of 30 janvier 2001, p. 1590 [Cf., 3 *YIHL* (2000) p. 505]

On 29 January 2001, both houses of the French Parliament voted unanimously to proclaim that the massacre of up to 1.5 million Armenians during the period of the Ottoman Empire constituted genocide.[202]

The text of the law is extremely short: 'France publicly recognizes the Armenian genocide of 1915' ['La France reconnaît publiquement le genocide arménien de 1915.']

Turkey reacted furiously with a raft of economic and diplomatic reprisals against France and French companies, and threatened sanctions against any country that accused it of carrying out a deliberate policy of genocide. It scapped a $US259 million ($A477.2 million) spy satellite deal with the French firm Alacatel and barred French companies from tendering for a $US7 billion defence contract. It also recalled its ambassador from Paris. Several Turkish universities threatened to close their French-language departments. The Turkish Parliament would be asked to vote on a declaration accusing France of genocide during Algeria's 1955-62 independence war.

Turkey has refused to accept responsibility for the genocide and apologise to the descendents of the victims. On 10 May 2001, however, Turkey announced the return of its Ambassador to Paris and the normalisation of relations with France.

---

202. S. Tisdall, 'Turkish fury over genocide claims', *The Age*, 26 January 2001; G. Parmentier, 'French-Turkish rift puts NATO at risk', *Los Angeles Times*, 12 February 2001.

Counter-Terrorism

- National Advisory Commission on Human Rights, Opinion on law provisions proposed by the government for strengthening the struggle against terrorism. Adopted on 29 October 2001 [Commission nationale consultative des droits de l'homme (CNCDH), Avis sur les dispositions législatives proposées par le gouvernement en vue de renforcer la lutte contre le terrorisme (Adopté le 29 octobre 2001] [http://www.commission-droits-homme.fr/]

In this opinion, the National Advisory Commission on Human Rights declared that every democratic state has the right and duty to protect itself, but measures taken for that purpose must be adequate and proportionate. The struggle against terrorism should not impose non-justified restrictions on human rights and liberties. The Commission suggested amendments to provisions laid down by the French government after the terrorist attack of 11 September 2001.

- A special meeting of the Senate was held on 10 October 2001 on the situation after the terrorist attacks perpetrated on 11 September 2001 in the USA [Senate, Séance du 10 octobre 2001: séance exceptionnelle sur la situation consécutive aux attentats perpétrés le 11 septembre 2001 aux Etats-Unis]
- On 11 October 2001 the French Senate adopted a bill authorizing ratification of the International Convention for the Suppression of the Financing of Terrorism, signed in New York on 10 January 2000 [Senate, adoption d'un projet de loi autorisant la ratification de la Convention internationale pour la répression du financement du terrorisme, le 11 octobre 2001]

Compensation

- Retirement pensions and invalidity grants for war veterans who are natives of Overseas Territories. State Council, No. 212179, 212211, Judgment of 30 November 2001, *Defence Minister and Minister for Economy, Finance and Industry* v. *Mr Diop* [Pensions de retraite et d'invalidité des anciens combattants de l'outre-mer. Conseil d'État, n°s 212179, 212211, arrêt, 30 novembre 2001, Ministre de la Défense et Ministre de l'Économie, des Finances et de l'Industrie c. M. Diop] [http://www.conseil-etat.fr/ce/jurispd/index_ac_ld0112.shtml]

This judgment is very important because it rules on questions disputed for a long time. After the former French colonies became independent, the French Parliament decided to freeze the amount of retirement pensions and invalidity grants and not to apply to war veterans who are natives of these territories the increase scale applicable to French nationals. The problem was examined by the United Nations Human Rights Committee, which criticized France for so doing. The Human Rights Committee found there was a violation of Article 26 of the International Covenant on Civil and Political Rights.[203] In spite of this ruling, the French State Council delivered an opinion on 15 April 1996 which contended that Article 26 ICCPR is not applicable to pensions, because it's not covered by this treaty (implicitly, it's

---

203. *Ibrahima Gueye* v. *France*, Communication No. 196/1983, 3 April 1989, UN Doc., A/44/40 at 189.

an economic right). In the Diop Judgment, the State Council found that French legislation is discriminatory and violates Article 14 ECHR. New legislation should be passed and probably agreements shall be negotiated with the states concerned.[204]

☛ Agreement between the government of France and the government of the United States of America concerning payments for certain losses suffered during World War II [Accord entre le Gouvernement de la République française et le Gouvernement des Etats-Unis d'Amérique relatif à l'indemnisation de certaines spoliations intervenues pendant la seconde guerre mondiale]. Signed by France on 18 January 2001. Entered into force on 5 February 2001 (exchange of notes of the same day) [Mis en vigueur par l'accord par échange de notes du 05.02.2001 depuis le 5.02.2001]. Published by decree No. 2001-243 of 21 March 2001, J.O.R.F. 23 March 2001, p. 4561 [décret de publication n° 2001-243 du 21 mars 2001)] [http://www.civs.gouv.fr/index.htm or http://www.civs.gouv.fr/uk/autre/index.htm]

First, a Commission for the compensation of victims of spoliations[205] resulting from anti-semitic legislation in force during the German Occupation was established by decree of 10 September 1999 and is attached to the Office of the Prime Minister. Establishment of this Commission was recommended by the Study Mission on the spoliations of Jews in France (Matteoli Mission), established by the Prime Minister on 5 February 1997. It does not handle compensation for the orphans of Jewish Deportees who died during deportation or in the concentration camps, for which there are special provisions (Decree No. 2000-657 of 13 July 2000, instituting reparations for orphans whose parents where victims of anti-semitic persecutions, J.O.R.F. No. 162 of 14 July 2000, p. 16838).

Secondly, Charters and by-laws concerning the establishment of a Foundation for the Memory of the Shoah were approved by decree of 26 December 1999. Its main task is to develop research and further public knowledge about anti-semitic persecutions and human rights violations during World War II, and about the victims of these persecutions.

Thirdly, a Fund to compensate persons who were deprived of their bank assets under anti-semitic legislation in force during the German Occupation has been started by the Banks concerned with US $22.5 million.

The 2001 Agreement recognizes that the Commission, the Fund and the Foundation cover any and all claims against Banks for the spoliation of property resulting from anti-semitic legislation in force during this period.

International Criminal Court

☛ Opinion of the National Advisory Commission on Human Rights on the adaptation of national legislation to the ICC Statute [Avis de la Commission Nationale consultative des droits de l'Homme (CNCDH) sur l'adaptation du droit interne au Statut de la Cour pénale internationale]. Adopted 23 November 2001 [http://www.commission-droits-homme.fr/]

---

204. See excerpts of the judgement and a commentary by A. Geslin, 'Jurisprudence français en matière de droit international public', 106 *RGDIP* (2002) pp. 207-224.

205. That is, people or their heirs who were stripped of assets (goods or real estate, financial assets) as a result of anti-Semitic legislation passed during the Occupation, whether by the occupying power or the Vichy authorities.

This advisory opinion contains some critical remarks concerning the inclusion in French legislation of the definition of crimes as provided in the Rome Statute. It also deals with war crimes, although France applied the opt out clause (Art. 124). In the opinion of the Commission, it is quite necessary to include in the Criminal Code clauses like those of Article 8 of the Rome Statute, as there is no definition of war crimes in French legislation, although France is a Party to the 1949 Geneva Conventions and to the 1977 Additional Protocols.

Humanitarian Assistance

☛ Opinion of the National Advisory Commission on Human Rights on the evolution of ECHO within the context [cadre] of the reform of European foreign aid. Adopted 25 January 2001 [Commission Nationale consultative des droits de l'Homme (CNCDH): Avis sur l'évolution d'ECHO dans le cadre de la réforme de l'aide exterieure européenne. Adopté le 25 janvier 2001 [http://www.commission-droits-homme.fr/]

Education and Training

☛ Ministry of Defence Directive relating to the dissemination of IHL within the Armed Forces, 4 January 2000

☛ New Military Manual 2001[206]

Cases (compensation)

☛ Rejection of case No. 224945, 224951, 225012, 225705, 225950, 226039, 226853, 228837 against the Decree of indemnification of the orphans of deportees jews. State Council, decision of 6 April 2001 [Rejet du recours contre le décret d'indemnisation des orphelins de déportés juifs du 13 juillet 2000, Conseil d'État, décision du 6 avril 2001, State Council [http://www.conseil-etat.fr/ce/jurispd/index_ac_ld0155.shtml]

The cases brought against the decree concerning compensation for the orphan children of Jewish prisoner in concentration camp of 13 July 2000, J.O.R.F. No. 162 of 14 July 2000, p. 16838 [décret d'indemnisation des orphelins de déportés juifs du 13 juillet 2000] before the State Council was dismissed on 6 April 2001.

☛ State Council, 7 November 2001, Madame Elser. Published in Tables du Recueil Lebon [http://www.legifrance.gouv.fr/]

This Judgment concerns the immediate application of Article 15 of the Convention against torture and other cruel, inhuman or degrading treatment or punishment. This clause was invoked by a German citizen in an extradition case.[207]

---

206. ICRC Advisory Service, *National Implementation of International Humanitarian Law*: Biennial report 2000-2001 (Geneva, ICRC 2002) p. 45.

207. See also commentary by F. Poirat and A. Geslin, 106 *Revue Générale de Droit international Public* (2002) pp. 459-463.

Pending

- Senate, Bill authorizing ratification of the Optional Protocol to the Convention on the rights of the child on the involvement of children in armed conflicts, 12 September 2001 [Senat, Projet de Loi autorisant la ratification du protocole facultatif à la convention relative aux droits de l'enfant concernant l'implication d'enfants dans les conflits armés, 12 septembre 2001]
- Bill examined by Senate. Bill concerning rules for authorizing intermediary and purchase for reselling operations and amending statutory order of 18 April 1939 setting rules for war equipments, weapons and ammunitions. Parliamentary Papers, Senate No. 137 (2001-2002), registered on 12 December 2001 [Projet de loi en instance au Sénat. Projet de loi relatif au régime d'autorisation des opérations d'intermédiation et d'achat pour revendre et modifiant le décret-loi du 18 avril 1939 fixant le régime des matériels de guerre, armes et munitions, N° 137 (2001-2002), déposé le 12 décembre 2001]
- Report by Mr Michel Caldaguès, on behalf of the Committee for Foreign Affairs [Rapport de M. Michel Caldaguès, au nom de la commission des affaires étrangères (2001-2002)]. [http://www.assemblee-nationale.fr/dossiers/armes.asp]

PAUL TAVENIER

GEORGIA

Criminal Law

- New Criminal Code
- Presidential Decree No. 177 of March 2001 establishing a commission of experts to study implementation of the Rome Statute

'The new Criminal Code, adopted in 1999, entered into force on 1 June 2000. It includes an entire section on the repression of war crimes committed in both international and non-international armed conflicts, and sets forth the general principles for their repression, such as universal jurisdiction and the non-application of statutory limitations to perpetrators of war crimes. The Code already takes into consideration a number of war crimes enumerated in the Rome Statute.'[208] 'The study of the compatibility of national law with the Rome Statute, conducted by a national expert, was completed in November 2001. A commission of experts was established by Presidential Decree No. 177 in March 2001 to study the compatibility of Georgian legislation with the Rome Statute and certain other treaties pertaining to criminal law. The Commission, which is chaired by the Minister of Justice, will put forward concrete proposals for bringing national legislation in line with international criminal law instruments, including the Rome Statute.' The Interministerial Committee on International Humanitarian Law met in November 2001 to discuss the draft study of the compatibility of national law with the Rome Statute and to draw up its plan of action for 2002.[209]

---

208. ICRC Advisory Service, *National Implementation of International Humanitarian Law*: Biennial report 2000-2001 (Geneva, ICRC 2002) p. 46.

209. Ibid.

Education and Training

- Advanced course on IHL, October 2000, Tbilisi, organised by the ICRC and the European Law Students' Association (ELSA)
- Seminar on IHL, January, 2001, Likani

The seminar in Likani was attended by representatives of the ministries concerned, NGOs and the Georgian Red Cross Society. 'Its objective was to provide intense training in IHL, with particular regard to the repression of war crimes at national and international levels and protection of the emblem.'[210]

GERMANY[211]

Humanitarian Assistance

- Speech of the Federal Minister for Foreign Affairs at the 56th Session of the United Nations General Assembly. Permanent Mission of Germany to the United Nations, Press Release 12 November 2001
- Safety and Security of Humanitarian Personnel and Protection of United Nations Personnel. United Nations General Assembly, Draft Resolution, 18 December 2001, UN Doc. A/56/L.64
- Situation of Human Rights in the Democratic Republic of the Congo, United Nations General Assembly. Draft Resolution, 10 December 2001, UN Doc. A/56/583/Add.3
- Emergency International Assistance for Peace, Normalcy and Reconstruction of Warstricken Afghanistan. United Nations General Assembly, Draft Resolution, 14 December 2001, UN Doc. A/56/L.62

Before the 56th Session of the United Nations General Assembly, the Federal Minister for Foreign Affairs emphasized the need to support refugees and the civilian population in Afghanistan. He said that it could not be tolerated that the Taliban were hindering humanitarian access and were using the civilian population as a shield. In particular, with a view to the approaching winter, everything possible had to be done to provide people with at least the most basic necessities and to alleviate their despair and hardship.

In December 2001, Germany co-sponsored a draft resolution on the 'Situation of Human Rights in the Democratic Republic of the Congo'. The resolution condemns the killing of six humanitarian workers of the International Committee of the Red Cross in the eastern part of the Democratic Republic of the Congo and stresses that those responsible had to be brought to justice. The resolution urges all parties to the conflict to ensure the safety and freedom of movement of UN and associated personnel and to ensure full, safe and unhindered access of humanitarian personnel to all affected populations throughout the territory of the Democratic Republic of Congo.

Also in December 2001, Germany co-sponsored a draft resolution on 'Safety and

210. Ibid.

211. Information and commentaries provided by Sascha Rolf Lüder, Counsellor at the General Representative of the Johanniter Order to the European Union, Brussels, and Gregor Schotten, Research Associate at the Institute for International Law of Peace and Armed Conflict (IFHV), Ruhr-Universität Bochum. The views expressed in this report are those of the authors alone.

Security of Humanitarian Personnel and Protection of United Nations Personnel'. The resolution urges all states to take the necessary measures to ensure the safety and security of humanitarian personnel and the UN and its associated personnel and to respect and ensure respect for the inviolability of UN premises, which are essential to the continuation and successful implementation of UN operations. Furthermore, the resolution calls upon all governments and parties in complex humanitarian emergencies to ensure the safe and unhindered access of humanitarian personnel in order to allow them to perform efficiently their task of assisting the affected population, including refugees and internally displaced persons. Finally, the resolution strongly condemns any act or failure to act, contrary to international law which obstructs or prevents humanitarian personnel and UN personnel from discharging their humanitarian functions or which entails their being subjected to threats, the use of force or physical attack, which frequently result in injury or death, and affirms the need to hold accountable those who commit such acts.

Finally, mention should be made of a draft resolution concerning Afghanistan which was also co-sponsored by Germany. The resolution strongly condemns all acts of violence and intimidation directed against UN and other humanitarian personnel, and regrets the loss of life and physical harm suffered among their Afghan staff. Moreover, the resolution urges all Afghan groups to respect international humanitarian law, to ensure the safety, security and free movement of all UN and humanitarian personnel as well as their safe and unimpeded access to all affected populations, and to protect the property of the UN and of humanitarian organizations, including non-governmental organizations, against, *inter alia*, looting and theft, so as to facilitate their work.

Biological Weapons

☛ Speech of the Federal Minister for Foreign Affairs at the 56th Session of the United Nations General Assembly. Permanent Mission of Germany to the United Nations, Press Release, 12 November 2001

The Federal Foreign Minister stressed before the 56th Session of the UN General Assembly that in view of the acute threat, effective global control mechanisms had finally to be created.

Chemical Weapons

☛ Speech of the Federal Minister for Foreign Affairs at the 56th Session of the United Nations General Assembly. Permanent Mission of Germany to the United Nations, Press Release, 12 November 2001

The Federal Foreign Minister underlined at the 56th Session of the UN General Assembly that the Chemical Weapons Convention had to be more rigorously implemented.

International Criminal Court

☛ Draft Act of Implementation of the Rome Statute of the International Criminal Court [*Entwurf eines Gesetzes zur Ausführung des Römischen Statutes des Internationalen Strafgerichtshofes*]. Published in *Bundesrats-Drucksache* 30/02

☛ Expert Working Group Hands Over Draft International Criminal Code [*Expertenarbeitsgruppe übergibt Entwurf eines Völkerstrafgesetzbuches*]. Federal Ministry of Justice, Press Release of 2 May 2001

☛ Draft International Criminal Code [*Entwurf eines Gesetzes zur Einführung des Völkerstrafgesetzbuches*]. Published in *Bundesrats-Drucksache* 29/02

The Rome Statute of the International Criminal Court contains numerous provisions in respect of which there is a need to make adjustments in the existing domestic legal order.[212]

In the first place, this relates to the area of all forms of cooperation between Germany and the International Criminal Court in criminal matters: surrender and transit of persons, execution of the Court's decisions, rendering other forms of legal assistance, and acquiescence in acts undertaken on national territory in the proceedings concerned.

After participation on the part of the relevant institutions in 2001, a Draft Act of Implementation of the Rome Statute of the International Criminal Court was tabled in the German Parliament on 18 January 2002. With the object of implementing the obligations ensuing from the Statute, this draft embodies a coherent regulation of the Law relating to cooperation with the Court in criminal matters. Since the provisions on cooperation with the Court contained in the Statute diverge from German mutual assistance in criminal matters with foreign countries in many respects, cooperation in criminal matters with the Court is to be dealt with by a separate law. This is also in line with the approach taken in respect of regulation of cooperation with the International Criminal Tribunals for the Former Yugoslavia and for Rwanda.

The provisions on jurisdiction and procedure for the surrender of persons to the Court, which for the greater part implement Articles 89 to 92 of the ICC Statute, are of the main importance. When a request for surrender is received, Court proceedings are usually instituted to determine admissibility. Surrender without a Court decision is possible in the cases of simplified surrender (Art. 92(3) of the Statute). Surrender is made on the basis of approval granted by the competent authority. The Law will further contain provisions concerning the relationship between a request for surrender and national proceedings as well as the relationship between a request for surrender and competing requests (Art. 90 of the Statute).

Further provisions of the draft cover, *inter alia*, questions on transit and taking over enforcement of sentences.[213]

In the second place, Germany resolved to create, in an International Criminal Code, a new and improved legal basis for the prosecution of crimes defined in the Statute by German courts. The important objectives of this project are to cover, appropriately, the specific wrongfulness of international crimes; to simplify the application of the law; to achieve greater legal clarity and certainty; and to help disseminate international humanitarian law.

On 2 May 2001, a working group made up of prominent scholars from the fields of criminal law and international law, in particular international humanitarian law, as well as experts from the Federal Foreign Office, the Federal Ministry of Justice and the Federal Ministry of Defence, handed over a working draft to the Federal Minister of Justice.[214] On 16 June 2001, the Federal Ministry of Justice submitted a draft which was almost exactly based on the expert working group's proceedings. On 18 January 2002, the draft was tabled in the German Parliament.

---

212. H.-P. Kaul, 'Die Entwicklung des Völkerstrafrechts: Auf dem Weg zur Herrschaft des Rechts in den internationalen Beziehungen?', 14 *Humanitäres Völkerrecht - Informationsschriften* (2001) pp. 251 et seq.; C. Kreß, 'Völkerstrafrecht in Deutschland: Gedanken aus Anlaß der Ratifikation des Statuts des Internationalen Strafgerichtshofs', 20 *Neue Zeitschrift für Strafrecht* (2000) pp. 617 et seq.

213. See in detail, J. Meißner, 'Die Zusammenarbeit Deutschlands mit dem Internationalen Strafgerichtshof: Anmerkungen zum Regierungsentwurf eines IStGH-Gesetzes', 15 *Humanitäres Völkerrecht - Informationsschriften* (2002) pp. 35 et seq.

214. Bundesministerium der Justiz. ed., *Arbeitsentwurf eines Gesetzes zur Einführung des Völkerstrafgesetzbuches* (Baden-Baden, Nomos Verlagsgesellschaft 2001).

Implementation of the crimes defined in the Statute is the primary focus of attention. With regard to individual items regulated therein, customary international law, however, already goes beyond what is laid down in the Statute. Hence the International Criminal Code also contains individual provisions extending criminal liability compared with the Statute. In some instances, norms of customary international law with a wider scope of application are taken into consideration, particularly under Additional Protocol I of 1977 to the Geneva Conventions of 1949 and under Additional Protocol II of 1999 to the Convention for the Protection of Cultural Property in the Event of Armed Conflict of 1954. In this respect, the International Criminal Code does justice to Article 10 of the Statute.

In the General Part, the draft dispenses as far as possible with special provisions in relation to existing criminal law so as to ensure legal clarity and certainty. Special rules are only in place where this is necessary, e.g., for self-defence, the responsibility of superiors and the statute of limitations.

A Special Part then contains definitions of the individual offences under international criminal law. The contents of the provisions of the International Criminal Code are kept as closely as possible to the offences described in the Statute and the corresponding Elements of Crimes. Furthermore, offences not covered by the Statute are included from international treaties binding Germany so far as they can claim validity in terms of customary international law. Account is also taken of the judgments of the International Criminal Tribunals as well as of general state practice.

Compared to the Statute, a new systematisation and tightening up has been undertaken in respect of war crimes, through bringing together parallel provisions. The state of customary international law so permitting, the individual offences, therefore, apply to all kinds of armed conflict. The distinction between international and non-international armed conflicts now only becomes relevant in exceptional cases where special offences have been established.[215]

Prisoners of War

☛ Statement by the Federal Minister for Foreign Affairs on the Guantanamo Detainees [*Erklärung von Bundesaußenminister Fischer zur Frage der in Guantanamo Inhaftierten*]. Federal Foreign Office, Press Release of 22 January 2002

The fight against international terrorism raised various questions in the field of international law of peace as well as in humanitarian law. In Germany, the discussion also covered the participation of the German armed forces in Operation 'Enduring Freedom'.[216]

With regard to the detainees in Guantanamo, the Federal Minister for Foreign Affairs stated that he believed that these persons should be treated as prisoners of war, regardless of

---

215. H.-P. Kaul, 'The International Criminal Court', in E. Riedel, ed., *Stocktaking in German Public Law: German Reports on Public Law - Presented to the XVI. International Congress on Comparative Law, Brisbane, 14 to 20 July 2002* (Baden-Baden, Nomos Verlagsgesellschaft 2002) pp. 9 et seq. at pp. 25 et seq.; G. Werle, 'Konturen eines deutschen Völkerstrafrechts: Zum Arbeitsentwurf eines Völkerstrafgesetzbuchs', 18 *Juristenzeitung* (2001) pp. 885 et seq.; A. Zimmermann, 'Auf dem Weg zu einem deutschen Völkerstrafgesetzbuch: Entstehung, völkerrechtlicher Rahmen und wesentliche Inhalte', 35 *Zeitschrift für Rechtspolitik* (2002) pp. 97 et seq.

216. See in this respect, the Freiburg Declaration on Respecting International Law [*Freiburger Juristen-Erklärung zur Achtung des Völkerrechts*] in Th. Vormbaum, ed., *Jahrbuch für Juristische Zeitgeschichte 3 (2001/2002)* (Baden-Baden, Nomos Verlagsgesellschaft 2002) pp. 99 et seq.

their subsequent final status. In accordance with the Fourth Geneva Convention that meant humane treatment; respect for the person and his honor; protection against acts of violence and intimidation; a right to medical treatment; and guarantees in keeping with the rule of law during trial proceedings.

The ICRC, which the United States of America had granted full access and inspection rights in Guantanamo detainee camp, was monitoring the full compliance with these standards under international law. Of course, the prisoners had to be called to account individually for any crimes they might have committed.

Cases

- *Jorgić* case. Federal Constitutional Court, Chamber's Decision of 16 January 2001 [*Bundesverfassungsgericht, Kammerbeschluß vom 16. Januar 2001* – 2 BvR 1290/99]
- *Sokolović* case. Federal Supreme Court, Judgment of 21 February 2001 [*Bundesgerichtshof, Urteil vom 21. Februar 2001* – 3 StR 372/00]
- *Kusljić* case. Federal Supreme Court, Decision of 21 February 2001 [*Bundesgerichtshof, Beschluß vom 21. Februar 2001* – 3 StR 244/00]
- *Grbić* case. Department of Public Prosecution at Celle, Preliminary Proceedings [*Staatsanwaltschaft Celle, Ermittlungsverfahren*], *Agence France-Press*, Press Release of 17 August 2001

On 26 September 1997, Nikolai Jorgić was convicted of 30 counts of murder in Bosnia and Herzegovina amounting to grave breaches of the Fourth Geneva Convention of 1949 and eleven counts of genocide by the *Oberlandesgericht Düsseldorf* (OLG Düsseldorf),[217] and sentenced to life imprisonment. The conviction was upheld on appeal by the *Bundesgerichtshof* (BGH).[218]

A subsequent constitutional challenge arguing that customary international law and Article VI of the Genocide Convention prohibited the exercise of universal jurisdiction over genocide was rejected by the *Bundesverfassungsgericht* (BVerfG). First, the Court held that a customary international law prohibition on the exercise of universal jurisdiction would be contrary to the obligations of Germany under Article I of the Genocide Convention, a derogation that would be impermissible since the prohibition of genocide is part of *ius cogens*. Second, it reaffirmed the conclusion of the BGH that Article VI did not prohibit States Parties from exercising universal jurisdiction over genocide.

The universality principle applies to certain acts that endanger the legal interests of the international community of states. It differs from the representation principle codified in s. 7(2) of the German Penal Code (StGB) in that it does not require double criminality and non-extradition. Whether the Genocide Convention contains a provision on universal jurisdiction has to be examined through interpretation. International treaties are to be interpreted from their text in accordance with their object and purpose with due regard to general international law. The lower Courts' interpretation of s. 6(1) of the StGB, in conjunction with Article VI of the Genocide Convention, regarding the scope of application of German law,

---

217. Higher Regional Court at Düsseldorf, Judgment, 30 April 1999 [*Oberlandesgericht Düsseldorf, Urteil vom 30 April 1999* – 2 StR 215/98].

218. Federal Supreme Court, Judgment, 21 February 2000 [*Bundesgerichtshof, Urteil vom 21. Februar 2000* – 3 StR 372/00].

is, at any rate, neither manifestly untenable nor impossible to maintain under no imaginable circumstances, and hence arbitrary.

According to a textual interpretation, the lower courts have constitutionally correctly determined that Article VI of the Genocide Convention, in any event, does not contain a prohibition on German criminal jurisdiction. On the other hand, the Convention clearly does not regulate the question of jurisdiction exclusively, because, for example, the active or passive universality principles are not mentioned. The courts have thereupon interpreted Article I of the Genocide Convention according to its object and purpose that the Convention intended effective punishment; consequently, the fact that there is no mention of the universality principle only means that the contracting Parties are not obliged to prosecute, although they are competent on the basis of this principle. It does not invite objections to prefer in some cases a 'systematic-teleological' interpretation above a textual interpretation of treaties. This applies in particular in the field of criminal jurisdiction over extraterritorial conduct on the basis of international conventions, because they are often vague on the issue of jurisdiction. Genocide, the most grave violation of human rights, is the classical example of the universality principle, whose function precisely is to close all loopholes in the prosecution of crimes against the fundamental legal interests of the community of States.

Yet the drafting history of the Genocide Convention indicates that was deliberately not included. Article VII of the initial draft contained the universality principle. In the draft of the Ad Hoc Committee, however, the universality principle was abandoned in favour of the territoriality principle. Sovereignty concerns and considerations of accession influenced that decision. There are, however, no constitutional objections against the decision of the lower courts not to attribute decisive importance to the drafting history. The preparatory work of a treaty is, according to Article 32 of the Vienna Convention of the Law of Treaties, only a 'supplementary means of interpretation', to which recourse may only be had when the interpretation according to Article 31 leaves the meaning ambiguous or obscure or leads to a result which is manifestly absurd or unreasonable. None of these alternatives is present in this case. The interpretation according to Article 31 clearly leads the courts the conclusion that the Convention allows prosecution on the basis of the universality principle. This result is not manifestly absurd or unreasonable.

However, the Court left open the question whether a link to Germany was required in universal jurisdiction cases.[219]

On 15 December 1999, the *Bayerisches Oberstes Landesgericht* (BayObLG)[220] convicted *Djuradj Kusljić* of inflicting physical injuries on Muslim civilians in five cases in May 1992 in Bosnia and Herzegovina and unlawfully detaining Muslim civilians in 56 cases, conduct amounting to grave breaches of the Fourth Geneva Convention, and genocide and abetting genocide in these cases and sentenced him to nine years in prison. On 21

219. See in particular, St. Kadelbach, 'Anmerkung zu BVerfG, Kammerbeschluß v. 12.12.2000 – BvR 1290/99', 56 *Juristenzeitung* (2001) pp. 981 et seq.

220. Bavarian Supreme Court, Judgment, 15 December 1999 [*Bayerisches Oberstes Landesgericht, Urteil vom 15. Dezember 1999* – 6 St 1/99].

February 2001, the BGH confirmed the judgment as well as the decision of the OLG Düsseldorf[221] against *Maksim Sokolović*of 29 November 1999.[222]

On 14 August 2001, German police arrested *Mile Grbić*, wanted for murder in Croatia, acting on an international arrest warrant issued by a Court in Gospić on 21 November 2000. *Mile Grbić*, a Croat citizen, was arrested at Bremervoerde where he had been working as a waiter. He was remanded in custody by a German Court pending proceedings for his extradition. *Mile Grbić* is accused of joining a Serbian terror organization in the second half of 1991 at the beginning of the 1991-1995 Serb-Croat war. The group has been linked with the massacre of Croatian civilians and *Mile Grbić* is accused of murdering some 30 people personally. He is also said to have taken part in armed attacks in Poljanak, Sertić, Poljana, Korana and Smoljanac. *Mile Grbić* and his accomplices shot at, looted and burned down commercial premises and homes, according to the indictment. Croatian civilians from these locations were taken to a camp at Knin and 30 people were said to have been killed in actions in which *Mile Grbić* allegedly participated.

In Zagreb, the Ministry of the Interior said, Croatia would request the extradition of *Mile Grbić* within one month. The *Landgericht Celle* (LG Celle) said Croatia had 40 days to issue a formal request. The extradition decision would be made by the foreign ministry unless it decides to delegate authority to the Ministry of Justice in the State of Lower Saxony.

SASCHA ROLF LÜDER and GREGOR SCHOTTEN

GREECE

Implementation and Dissemination

- ☛ Establishment of the Committee on the Implementation and Dissemination of International Humanitarian Law, Ministerial Decision of 20 March 2000 [http://www.icrc.org/ihl-nat.nsf/6fa4d35e5e3025394125673e00508143/997591b893b33d20c1256a9d002deac1?OpenDocument]
- ☛ Implementation of the Rome Statute

The Committee was officially established by decision of the Ministry of Foreign Affairs. Its members include representatives of the Ministries of Foreign Affairs, National Defence, Public Order, Education, Justice, Health, the Interior, and Culture, the General Secretariat of Youth and Emergency Civil Defence Planning, and academic experts.

In September 2000, the Ministries of Foreign Affairs and Defence, together with the Institute of International Relations, organized an international colloquium in Santorini on the national implementation of the Rome Statute.[223]

---

221. Higher Regional Court at Düsseldorf, Judgment, 29 November 1999 [*Oberlandesgericht Düsseldorf, Urteil vom 29. November 1999* – 2 StE 6/97].

222. See K. Ambos, 'Immer mehr Fragen im internationalen Strafrecht', 21 *Neue Zeitschrift für Strafrecht* (2001) pp. 628 et seq.; K. Ambos and St. Wirth, 'Genocide and War Crimes in the Former Yugoslavia Before German Criminal Courts', in H. Fischer, C. Kreß and S.R. Lüder, eds., *International and National Prosecution of Crimes Under International Law: Current Developments* (Berlin, Berlin Verlag Arno Spitz 2001) pp. 769 et seq.

223. ICRC Advisory Service, *National Implementation of International Humanitarian Law*: Biennial report 2000-2001 (Geneva, ICRC 2002) p. 49.

GUATEMALA

Education and Training

☛ Education and training of the military, police and civilians

'In 2000 and 2001, the international law of armed conflict formed part of the instruction programmes for the armed forces and the *Centro de Estudios Militares*. The Armed Forces of Guatemala also organized their own training courses for instructors in the law. In January 2001, police officers started participating in IHL training courses on the basis of the cooperation agreement between the ICRC and the Presidential Commission of Human Rights (COPREDEH).' 'In 2001, Rafael Landívar University started to teach humanitarian law as part of the law faculty's courses on human rights and international public law and as a regular course at the master's level; at the University of San Carols humanitarian law remained an option.'[224]

Cases

☛ *García* case

General Romeo Lucas García was accused, together with his brother and former Army Chief of Staff Benedicto Lucas García and former Minister of Defence Luís Mendoza Palomo, of genocide, crimes against humanity and war crimes, as provided for in the Guatemalan Penal code (respectively, Arts. 376 and 378) on 3 May 2000. The Association for Justice and Reconciliation (*Asociación Justicia y Reconciliación-AJR)* filed a criminal complaint against the former dictator before a court in Guatemala City for the facts related to ten massacres committed between October 1981 and March 1982 against Mayan civilians. These crimes were allegedly perpetrated by a special Task Force (Iximché Task Force) that was under the authority of the accused. In June 2001 the investigative stage of the trial began with the appointment of an investigating judge (Judge Marco Antonio Pichillá).[225]

☛ Decision in the case of *Byron Lima Disrael Estrada, Byron Lima Oliva, Jose Obdulio Villanueva, Mario Orantes* Nájera and *Margarita Lopez* (*Bishop Geraldi* case), 8 June 2001, Third Trial Court (Tribunal Tercero de Sentencia Penal, Guatemala City) [http://www.odhag.org.gt/Caso%20Gerardi/default.htm]. Appeal rendered on 9 October 2002

On 8 June 2001, four men were convicted of the 1998 murder of Roman Catholic Bishop Juan Gerardi Conedera.

A three-judge tribunal found retired Army Colonel Byron Disrael Lima Estrada, his Army Captain son Byron Lima Oliva and former presidential bodyguard Jose Obdulio Villanueva guilty of murder and sentenced them each to 30 years in prison. Roman Catholic priest Mario Orantes Nájera was sentenced to 20 years as an accessory to the murder while housemaid Margarita López was acquitted. The panel recognised the murder as politically

224. Ibid., p. 50.

225. See http://www.justiceforgenocide.org/document1.html. The complaint against General Luca García is available at: http://www.justiceforgenocide.org/pdf/complaintlucas.pdf .

motivated and committed in retaliation for the activities of Bishop Juan Gerardi Conedera, in particular for his leading role in the investigations into violations of human rights.[226]

Gerardi was found bludgeoned to death in his Guatemala City residence on 26 April 1998, shortly after releasing a report blaming the military for most of the 200,000 deaths during the Central American nation's 36-year civil war.[227] The trial, delayed for three years as prosecutors, witnesses and a judge fled the country amid death threats, began on 23 March, two days after a grenade attack on one judge's house.[228]

☛ Complaint against *Ríos Montt* and the military high command, 6 June 2001

On 6 June 2001, the Association for Justice and Reconciliation together with the Guatemala City-based Centre for Legal Action on Human Rights (Centro de Acción Legal en Derechos Humanos-CALDH), representing 12 Mayan communities, filed a genocide complaint against the current President of the Congress, and former President of the Republic, General José Efraín Ríos Montt, and the military high command for the deaths of 1,200 highland villagers occurred between 1982 and 1983.

The General was initially accused, together with other 23 members of the Guatemalan Revolutionary Front (Frente Republicano Guatemalteco) of corruption in relation to the modification of a tax on liquors. For this purpose, in March 2001 the Supreme Court of Guatemala lifted the immunity they benefit from as members of the Congress. However, on 25 April 2001, Ríos Montt was eventually freed.

The evidence against Ríos Montt relies heavily on the concept of the chain of command. A report sponsored by the United Nations and commissioned to the Guatemalan Historical Clarification Commission[229] described this country's civil war and showed that nearly half of the documented massacres in Guatemala took place from 1980 to 1983, when Generals Lucas Garcia and Ríos Montt were in power.[230]

Anna Danieli

---

226. Misión de Verificación de las Naciones Unidas en Guatemala (MINUGUA), Publicaciones-Oficina del Portavoz, Crónicas de Minugua No. 26. Available at: http://www.minugua.guate.net/PUBLICACIONES/CRONIC2001/CRONICAS01.htm.

227. The Report 'Guatemala: Nunca Más', issued by the REMHI (Recuperación de la Memoria Histórica) is available at: http://www.odhag.org.gt/INFREMHI/Default.htm.

228. 'Verdict buoys Guatemala human rights activists', Reuters, 13 June 2001; 'Four convicted in murder of Guatemalan bishop', CNN Online News Report, 8 June 2001; United Nations Verification Mission in Guatemala, A/56/273, 8 August 2001.

229. The Guatemalan Historical Clarification Commission was set up after the Accord of Oslo, signed as part of the Peace Process in 1994. In September 1997, the Commission began receiving testimonies of human rights violations committed during the 36-year armed conflict.

230. See the Report of the Commission for Historical Clarification, Conclusions and Recommendations 'Guatemala-Memory of Silence', available at http://shr.aaas.org/guatemala/ceh/report/english/conc2.html; in May 2000 the AJR filed a complaint for the massacres committed between 1978 and 1982 against officials of the administration of General Fernando Romeo Lucas García. See Amnesty Reports 'Guatemala-Human Rights Community Under Siege' at http://web.amnesty.org/ai.nsf/Recent/AMR340222001!Open, and 'Guatemala: Submission to Param Cumaraswamy, Special Rapporteur of the UN Commission on Human Rights on the independence of judges and lawyers' at http://web.amnesty.org/ai.nsf/Recent/AMR340322001!Open.

HONDURAS[231]

Landmines

- Law No. 60-2000 prohibiting the production, acquisition, sale, import, export, transit, use, possession and transfer of anti-personnel landmines and of anti-detection devices or mines or parts thereof. Adopted 20 May 2000 [http://www.icrc.org/ihl-nat.nsf/6fa4d35e5e3025394125673e00508143/11cf0fb3a8edf42ec1256cdf005e11c7?OpenDocument]

Cultural Property

- Decree-Law No. 54-2001 approving the 1954 Cultural Property Convention. Published in *La Gaceta* No. 29 511 on 23 June 2001

Education and Training

- In 2001, IHL was an option in the Master's Course on Human Rights at the Universidad Nacional Autónoma de Honduras

HUNGARY[232]

International Criminal Court

- Parliamentary Resolution 72/2001 (XI.7) enabling ratification of the ICC Statute, 30 November 2001
- Act CXXI/2001 modifying the Penal Code

Hungary ratified the ICC Statute without any special reservation or declaration. On the basis of parliamentary resolution 72/2001(XI.7), the instrument of ratification was submitted and took effect on 30 November 2001. Some changes to the Hungarian Penal Code (Act IV/1978) will be necessary in order to properly reflect the following crimes of the ICC Statute and to exclude their prescription, namely: enslavement; rape; sexual slavery; enforced prostitution; forced pregnancy; enforced sterilization, or any other form of sexual violence of comparable gravity; as well as enforced disappearance of persons.

The preparation of the necessary legal modifications is in progress, as part of a comprehensive reform of the Penal Code.

One of the necessary modifications was already made by Act CXXI/2001 modifying the Penal Code. Its Article 6 (international judicial co-operation and aid) now provides

> '(6) Under foreign judgment is understood also a res judicata judgment of an international criminal tribunal acting on the basis of an international treaty duly promulgated or of a mandatory resolution adopted by the UN Security Council.'

PÉTER KOVÁCS

231. ICRC Advisory Service, *National Implementation of International Humanitarian Law*: Biennial report 2000-2001 (Geneva, ICRC 2002) p. 51.

232. Information and commentaries by Professor Péter Kovaćs, Professor of International Law, Péter Pázmány Catholic University of Budapest and Miskolc University.

Implementation and Dissemination

- Government Resolution No. 2095/2000 (V.9), March 2000 establishing the National Committee for the Dissemination and Implementation of International Humanitarian Law[233] [http://www.icrc.org/ihl-nat.nsf/6fa4d35e5e3025394125673e00508143/f722d00a833b4826c1256b210037f06b?OpenDocument]
- Study on Hungarian legislation

A national study on the compatibility of Hungarian legislation and practice with IHL was completed in January 2001.[234]

INDIA

Chemical Weapons

- Chemical Weapons Act, 2000. Adopted on 26 August 2000. Published in the *Gazette of India*, Extraordinary, Part II-Sec. 1, dt. 28.08.2000, S. No. 42; reprinted in *Chemical Weapons Convention Act, 2000 (Act No. 34 of 2000)*, Akalank Publications, Delhi, 2001 [http://chemicals.nic.in/cwc-act2000.pdf]

'India's national legislation to implement the Chemical Weapons Convention ... establishes a National Authority to implement the Convention, prohibits the production of chemical weapons and toxic chemicals and penalizes violations of the Convention.'[235]

Education and Training

- Inclusion of IHL in military manuals
- Web-based post-graduate distance education
- University education

'Further to the recommendations made by a national seminar on the implementation of IHL, organized by the ICRC and the Ministry of External Affairs in 2001, the Department of the Judge Advocate General of the Indian Army took steps to incorporate IHL into India's military manuals. The seminar also recommended that the Legal and Treaty Division of the Ministry of External Affairs examine, with the ICRC's support, the possibility of establishing a national interministerial working group on IHL, a matter the ICRC was pursuing with the Legal and Treaties Division.'

'In 2001, the University of Law in Hyderbad, working with ICRC support, launched a web-based postgraduate distance education programme in IHL. The programme will be open to students from South Asia.'

'In cooperation with the National Law Schools of India, the ICRC organized the Second and Third South East Asian Teaching Sessions in IHL in 2000 and 2001 respectively in Bangalore. Thirty participants from various South Asian countries took part in the eight-day teaching session. Further to recommendations made by the Association of Indian Universi-

233. ICRC Advisory Service, *National Implementation of International Humanitarian Law*: Biennial report 2000-2001 (Geneva, ICRC 2002) p. 51.

234. Ibid., p. 52.

235. Ibid. p. 53.

ties at the ICRC's prompting, IHL was incorporated into the syllabuses of the undergraduate law courses, postgraduate courses in defence studies and courses in human rights of most Indian universities.'[236]

INDONESIA[237]

Military Operations

- Aceh: Presidential Instruction (Instruksi Presiden, INPRES) No. 4 of 2001 on Comprehensive Steps in the Matter of the Aceh problem, 11 April 2001 [Instruksi Presiden Republik Indonesia Nomor 4 Tahun 2001 Tentang Langkah-Langkah Komprehensif Dalam Rangka Penyelesaian Masalah Aceh, 11 April 2001] [http://www.geocities.com/nanggroe2001/inpres.htm]

Introduced parallel to peace negotiations and the introduction of autonomy legislation for Aceh (see below), INPRES No. 4/2001 outlined six 'comprehensive' steps to deal with Aceh and the separatist movement known as GAM (Gerakan Aceh Merdeka, Free Aceh Movement). Of greatest importance was the renewed authorisation of stronger security and law enforcement measures. INPRES No. 4/2001 gave the military (Tentara Nasional Indonesia, TNI) a free hand in its attempt to solve the conflict by force. Over 20,000 additional troops were deployed. Aceh came to be officially in the throes of a 'limited security operation', and a special military command structure, the KOLAKOPS was established to implement Opslihkan (Operation for the Restoration of Order) for the purpose of waging all-out war to destroy GAM. Aceh's leading independent human rights watchdog, the Commission for Missing Persons and Victims of Violence (Kontras), reported 544 deaths in the first six months of the implementation of INPRES 4/2001.[238]

Regional Autonomy

- Law No. 22/1999 on Regional Administration, promulgated 9 May 1999, *Official Gazette of the Republic of Indonesia* 1999 No. 60 [Undang-Undang Republik Indonesia Nomor 22 Tahun 1999 Tentang Pemerintahan Daerah, 7 Mei 1999, Lembaran Negara Republik Indonesia Tahun 1999 Nomor 60] [http://www.landpolicy.org/lawsregs/ind/UU-22-1999.pdf]
- Law No. 25/1999 on Fiscal Balance between Central and Local Government, promulgated 19 May 1999, Official Gazette of the Republic of Indonesia 1999 No. 72 [Undang-Undang Republik Indonesia Nomor 25 Tahun 1999 Tentang Perimbangan Keuangan Antara Pemerintah Pusat Dan Daerah, 19 Mei 1999, Lembaran Negara Republik Indonesia Tahun 1999 Nomor 72] [http://fisip-unmul.hypermart.net/uuperimbangan.html]

---

236. Ibid.

237. Information and commentaries by Suzannah Linton, Visiting Fellow, Center for Civil and Human Rights, Law School, University of Notre Dame. This report is limited in its coverage of the many IHL issues in Indonesia in 2000 and 2001 by spatial demands.

238. '544 die despite Aceh Presidential Instruction', Laksamana.Net, 27 October 2001.

- Law No. 18/2001 on Special Autonomy for the Special District of Aceh, promulgated 9 August 2001, *Official Gazette of the Republic of Indonesia 2001* No. 114 [Undang-Undang Republik Indonesia Nomor 18 Tahun 2001 Tentang Otonomi Khusus Bagi Provinsi Daerah Istimewa Aceh Sebagai Provinsi Nanggroe Aceh Darussalam, 9 Ogos 2001, Lembaran Negara Republik Indonesia Tahun 2001 Nomor 114] [www.gtzsfdm.or.id/documents/laws_n_regs/ laws/2001/UU18_2001.pdf]
- Law 21/2001 on Special Autonomy for Papua Province, 21 November 2001, *Official Gazette of the Republic of Indonesia* 2001 No. 114 Undang-Undang Republik Indonesia Nomor 21 Tahun 2001 Tentang Otonomi Khusus Bagi Provinsi Papua, 21 November 2001, Lembaran Negara Republik Indonesia Tahun 2001 Nomor 135 [http://theceli.cltc-online.com/UU/2001/21-2001.htm]

The use of autonomy as a strategy for the containment and prevention of armed conflict was initiated during the presidency of B.J. Habibie. Hoping to assuage the armed struggles in East Timor, Papua/Irian Jaya and Aceh and facilitate the decentralization process, Habibie presented two proposals which were approved by the DPR (People's Consultative Assembly) in May 1999. Both laws were designed to maintain the territorial integrity of Indonesia by granting greater power and autonomy to all regions, but most importantly to Aceh and Papua/Irian Jaya which would receive 'special autonomy' status. The laws divide power between the central and regional authorities. The real 'sweetener' is the increased share of local government in central government's revenues, which is particularly significant in the cases of resource-rich Aceh and Papua/Irian Jaya. However, the central government's offer prohibits any referenda on independence; autonomy within Indonesia is as far as the government will go and it will not tolerate threats to the sovereignty and territorial integrity of the Indonesian state.

On 20 July 2001, a special autonomy plan was adopted for Aceh, designed as a means of ending the armed conflict without loss of sovereignty. On 1 January 2002, a similar law came into force in Papua/Irian Jaya, which also made it clear that despite the increased control over its own resources, the territory would always be an integral part of the Indonesian Republic.

Peace negotiations and processes

- Aceh: Joint Understanding on Humanitarian Pause between GAM and the Indonesian Government, signed on 12 May 2000 [http://www.indonesia-ottawa.org/news/Issue/Aceh/aceh-ptri-geneva-051200.htm]

Under the terms of this agreement brokered by the Henri Dunant Institute in Switzerland, both the government and the GAM agreed not to undertake offensive operations or maneuvers in Aceh (a period to be know as the 'humanitarian pause') for a period of three months commencing three weeks from 12 May 2000. The objectives of the 'humanitarian pause' as stated in the Joint Understanding were to ensure the delivery of humanitarian assistance to the population of Aceh affected by the conflict situation; provide security modalities with a view to supporting the delivery of humanitarian assistance and reducing tension and violence which may cause further suffering; and promote confidence building measures towards a peaceful solution to the conflict situation in Aceh.

Initially, the humanitarian pause greatly reduced violence in Aceh but by September 2000 violence had returned to roughly pre-pause levels. Nevertheless, the Joint Understanding was extended from September 2000 to January 2001. The government later announced it would not engage in further negotiations with the GAM after the expiration of the 'humanitarian pause' on 15 January 2001 and peace talks with provincial leaders broke down in June 2001 following the arrest of six negotiators on charges of subversion.

☛ Sulawesi: The Malino Declaration, 20 December 2001 [www.embassyofindonesia.org/releases/press/poso.htm]

On 20 December 2001, representatives of the Moslem and Christian communities involved in the religious conflict in Poso, Sulawesi signed a ten-point peace agreement brokered by the government at Malino. It was the fifth such attempt to bring an end to the conflict, which has claimed thousands of lives since violence first erupted in late-1998. As part of the agreement, the parties agreed to stop fighting and to work towards restoration of normal life in Sulawesi. The government pledged to introduce a series of short-term programs to restore peace and order to Central Sulawesi by allowing the return of displaced persons through disarming warring locals, rehabilitating and rebuilding destroyed homes, schools and places of worship and removing 'outsiders who had entered the area during the conflicts', i.e., the Laskar Jihad. The government was to allocate some Rp100 billion (US$10 million) to rebuild at least 10,000 houses, several schools and places of worship, and to return IDPs to their places of origin.

Human Rights Courts

☛ Presidential Decree No. 53/2001 establishing an Ad Hoc Human Rights Court at the Central Jakarta District Court, issued 23 April 2001, *Official Gazette of the Republic of Indonesia* 2001 No. 38 [Keputusan Presiden Republik Indonesia Nomor 53 Tahun 2001 Tentang Pembentukan Pengadilan Hak Asasi Manusia Ad Hoc Pada Pengadilan Negeri Jakarta Pusat, 23 April 2001, Lembaran Negara Republik Indonesia Tahun 2001 Nomor 38] [http://www.ri.go.id/produk_uu/isi/keppres2001/kp-53-01.html]

☛ Presidential Decree No. 96/2001 amending Presidential Decree No. 53/2001 establishing an Ad Hoc Human Rights Court at the Central Jakarta District Court, issued 2 August 2001 [Keputusan Presiden Republik Indonesia Nomor 96 Tahun 2001 Tentang Perubahan Atas Keputusan Presiden Nomor 53 Tahun 2001 Tentang Pembentukan Pengadilan Hak Asasi Manusia Ad Hoc Pada Pengadilan Negeri Jakarta Pusat, 1 August 2001, Lembaran Negara Republik Indonesia Tahun 2001 Nomor 111] [http://www.ri.go.id/produk_uu/isi/keppres2001/kp962701.html]

On 24 April 2001, President Wahid issued the long-awaited decree establishing an *ad hoc* human rights court to hear the cases arising from East Timor and Tanjung Priok (see below). It was greatly criticised for limiting the temporal jurisdiction of the court as the jurisdiction for East Timor was limited to cases arising after the 30 August 1999 referendum, ruling out several of the major atrocities of 1999. The Attorney General's office dropped six out of the 18 cases it was investigating, among them the Liquiça Church massacre of 6 April 1999 and the attack on the house of pro-independence leader Manuel Carrascalão of 17 April 1999 and a variety of serious attacks on civilians that took place between April and September 1999.

In what was initially seen as a highly symbolic move, the first official act of newly appointed President Megawati Sukarnoputri was to issue a decree widening the temporal jurisdiction of the *ad hoc* Human Rights Court for East Timor. Issued on 2 August 2001, Presidential Decree No. 96/2001 amended the decree of her predecessor, and provided that the *ad hoc* court would have jurisdiction over cases of human rights violations in East Timor which took place in April 1999 and September 1999. However, the new decree did not open up the period from April to September 1999 to the jurisdiction of the court but simply the month of April 1999, and the jurisdiction was expressly limited to incidents in Dili, Suai and Liquiça.

By the end of the year, the workload of the Attorney General's office was limited to just five East Timorese cases: the massacre at the João Britto church in Liquiça on 6 April 1999, the killings in the house of Manuel Carrascalão in Dili on 17 April 1999, the attack on the Diocese of Dili on 5 September 1999, the attack on the residence of Bishop Carlos Belo in Dili on 6 September 1999 and the massacre at the Ave Maria church in Suai on 6 September 1999. And by the end of the year, not a single one of the five planned Human Rights Courts nor the one *ad hoc* court, was operational.[239]

Human Rights Commission (Komisi Nasional Hak Asasi Manusia, or Komnas HAM)

☛ Investigatory Commission for Tanjung Priok, Komnas HAM decision SK No. 012/ KOMNAS HAM/VII/200, 12 July 2000

On 12 September 1984, hundreds of Muslims in Tanjung Priok, the port near Jakarta, took part in a march to demand the release of four mosque officials, who had been arrested following a dispute over a group of soldiers who had entered a mosque without removing their shoes. Troops fired on the protesters, many were arrested and abused whilst in custody, and many more 'disappeared'.

The political climate of the New Order meant that this case was never properly investigated in the Suharto years. Komnas HAM established a commission of investigation on 7 March 2000, and on 6 July 2000 presented its confidential report to President Abdurrahman Wahid. Its official statement summarised the findings and the recommendation of further investigations.[240] It made vague statements about the need for the state to apologise and seek forgiveness and while accepting the doctrine of command responsibility and the need for further investigation, did not name any suspects. The commission came under severe NGO criticism for this as well as an alleged lack of transparency and for having clandestine meetings with senior military officials.[241]

The perceived weaknesses in the report were supplemented by further investigations at the request of the Attorney General, and on 11 October 2000 the commission found that there had been unlawful arrest and detention, torture and enforced or involuntary disappear-

239. The first judges were appointed in January 2002 and the first indictments were filed one month later. 'Government unveils names of rights tribunal judges', *Jakarta Post*, 15 January 2002. See http://www.jsmp.minihub.org/Indonesia/judges.htm for a list of the judges.

240. Ringkasan Eksekutif, Hasil Penyelidikan Komisi Penyelidikan Dan Pemeriksaan Pelanggaran Hak Asasi Manusia Di Tanjung Priok (KP3T), 12 June 2000.

241. 'Indonesia's Tanjong Priok inquiry: a safe harbour for human rights abuses?', Human Rights Feature, Asia-Pacific Human Rights Network, 20 July 2000, at http://www.hrdc.net/sahrdc/hrfeatures/ hrf23.htm.

ances.[242] At least 24 people had been summarily executed by the military and nine persons of Chinese ethnicity burnt in the course of the ensuing riots. In addition to recommendations for social justice and improvement of military professionalism, it also called for the prosecution of 14 low-ranking soldiers and nine officers, including three Captains, one Major, one Major General, one Lieutenant Colonel, one Colonel, one Brigadier General and a General (Benny Moerdani, former head of the Armed Forces).

☛ Investigatory commission for Abepura, Komnas HAM Decision SK No. 020/ KomnasHAM/II/2001

On 5 February 2001, Komnas HAM established a Commission of Inquiry to investigate events in the Papuan capital, Abepura, on 7 December 2000.[243] The Abepura case centred around excessive use of force during police raids on student hostels and other locations in search of those responsible for a separatist (Organisasi Papua Merdeka, OPM, otherwise Free Papua Movement] attack on a police station earlier on 7 December 2000 which left three dead. Regular police and BRIMOB (Brigade Mobil, Mobile Brigade, i.e., riot police) detained over 100 people during the raids. One person was shot dead and two persons died in police custody in circumstances which indicated they had been tortured. The treatment of the detainees received international attention due to the active campaigning of NGOs and a Swiss journalist, Oswald Iten, who witnessed police violence while in police custody in Jayapura for an alleged visa offence.

Komnas HAM reported on 20 April 2001.[244] The team found that the police had followed a systematic plan, that is, the attacks on the hostels and the detentions were organized and followed the same pattern. The patterns of abuse became particularly obvious when one looked back at how the police had been dealing with flag raisings in the district since 1998,[245] which indicated to the investigators that the police had been trigger-happy and too quick to arrest and detain, and had been torturing protesters and those categorized as separatists. The team found that the torture, summary executions, assault on the basis of gender, race and religion, arbitrary detention and violation of property rights had been committed in Abepura as part of a systematic and widespread attack. The perpetrators were not directly named in the Executive Summary, although a total of 25 Police and BRIMOB officers were recommended for investigation and prosecution by the Attorney General for gross violation of human rights under Law 26/2000 in the confidential complete report.

The national chief of police condemned the commission, alleging that it had prejudged the case.[246] In July 2001, the Attorney General's office returned the file to Komnas HAM,

---

242. Ringkasan Eksekutif, Laporan Tim Tindak Lanjut Hasil Komisi Penyelidik Dan Pemeriksaan Pelanggaran Hak Asasi Manusia Di Tanjung Priok (KP3T), 11 October 2000.

243. Ringkasan Eksekutif, Komisi Penyelidikan Pelanggaran Hak Asasi Manusia (KPP-Ham) Papua/Irian Jaya, 8 May 2001.

244. Ringkasan Eksekutif, Komisi Penyelidikan Hak Asasi Manusia (KPP HAM) Papua/Irian Jaya, 8 Mei 2001.

245. The raising of the Papuan flag (the 'Morning Star' flag), is an act of indigenous Papuan nationalism that is perceived as particularly threatening by the Indonesian authorities.

246. 'Polri Protes KPP HAM Abepura', *Antara*, 24 April 2001.

claiming the case was incomplete.[247] The file has since been completed but no charges have been laid.[248]

☛ Investigatory Commission for Sampit/Kalteng, Komnas HAM decision SK No. 24/KOMNAS HAM/V/2001, 5 May 2001

On 3 April 2001, Komnas HAM approved the establishment of a commission of inquiry to investigate serious ethnic fighting in Kalimantan (Borneo). On 17 February 2001, long simmering tensions between Dayaks and Madurese exploded in the town of Sampit, Central Kalimantan and spread to other areas such as Kualakayan and Palangkaraya. By early-March 2001, the death toll reportedly reached 469, among whom 456 were Madurese.[249] Virtually the entire Madurese population had fled; Sampit and Central Kalimantan had been ethnically cleansed. Another estimate is that indigenous Dayaks killed some five hundred Madurese and that the fighting displaced more than 150,000 people.[250]

The KPP-HAM for Sampit/Kalteng came into existence on 5 May 2001. It was tasked to analyse the causes of the conflict to find alternative ways to achieve peace and reconciliation and examine the role of state forces or other groups in the perpetration of gross violations of human rights that occurred since the passing of Law No. 26/2000 on Human Rights Courts.

The team gathered materials on serious violations of human rights perpetrated during and after the ethnic clashes in Sampit and Palangkaraya; its report was issued nine months after its establishment and came under fierce NGO fire. The team found that weak internal police coordination contributed to the social factors which led to the violence and found no evidence of a widespread systematic attack on the civilian population and thus no gross violations of human rights as defined in Article 9 of Law 26/2000. Komnas HAM nevertheless recommended that seven persons be prosecuted for ordinary crimes.[251]

☛ Investigatory Commission for Trisakti and Semanggi I and II, Komnas HAM decision SK No. 34/KOMNAS-HAM/VII/2001 of 27 August 2001

On 5 June 2001, KOMNAS-HAM approved the establishment of a commission of inquiry to examine several apparently linked incidents in Jakarta connected to the chaos and political turmoil of the months preceding and following the fall of President Suharto in 1998. One of the pivotal incidents in the chain of events was the fatal shooting by armed riot police (BRIMOB) on 12 May 1998 of six unarmed student demonstrators from the Trisakti University and the wounding of many others (known as the Trisakti attack). The students had been demonstrating against Suharto and were attempting to march on Parliament. The

---

247. 'Abepura case returned to Komnas HAM, Attorney-General's office says: documents incomplete', *Papua Post*, 28 July 2001.

248. This case would, if prosecuted, have been the first to be heard before a permanent Human Rights Court. The relevant court for Papua is meant to sit at Makassar. However, not one of the five Human Rights Courts was operational by the end of 2001.

249. 'Communal Violene in Indonesia: lessons from Kalimantan', International Crisis Group, Jakarta/Brussels, 27 June 2001, ICG Asia Report N° 19.

250. Human Rights Watch, *Annual World Report 2001.*

251. Kompas, 'KPP HAM Sampit: Tidak Ada Pelanggaran Berat HAM di Sampit', 28 November 2001; Kompas 'Kontras: Tidak Sulit Buktikan Pelanggaran Berat Ham di Sampit', 30 November 2001.

shootings led to massive rioting and loss of life in Jakarta, forcing the resignation of President Suharto on 21 May 1998. On 14 November 1998, TNI and BRIMOB troops opened fire on a demonstration in front of the Atma Jaya University in Semanggi, Jakarta. This occurred in connection with the 1998 MPR (People's Consultative Assembly) meeting and calls for fundamental reform. Five students were killed and many wounded (this incident is referred to as Semanggi I). On 24 September 1999, five students were killed by the armed forces in the Semanggi district while protesting increases in military power through new security laws (Semanggi II).

On 27 May 2002, a special committee of the DPR (House of Representatives) concluded its own investigations into the incidents, controversially finding that there was no evidence of gross violations of human rights.[252] It recommended against processing the cases through a special ad-hoc court; any suspects should instead be tried in the regular justice system, i.e., civilian or military courts as relevant.[253] In June 2001, a military tribunal began hearing the case of ten army personnel charged in relation to the Trisakti killings.[254]

Undeterred, on 27 August 2001, Komnas HAM established a single commission to investigate both Trisakti and Semanggi I and II, with a mandate to investigate and examine the incidents and related cases, interview witnesses, call and examine suspects, collect evidence, visit relevant sites and carry out any other activities necessary for the completion of their tasks.[255]

Investigations and hearings continued through to the end of 2001. Key TNI personnel refused to attend before the KPP HAM on the grounds that the DPR had already determined that there were no grounds for further investigation or prosecution. KPP-HAM Trisakti-Semanggi's three-month mandate (27/8/2001 to 27/11/2001) was extended in November 2001 for a further 90 days.

☛ Committee on Investigation of Human Rights Violations and Mediation in Maluku (Komisi Penyelidik Pelanggaran Hak Asasi Manusia dan Mediasi di Maluku or KPMM)

The Committee was established to 'anticipate' problems of gross violations of human rights in the Malukan communal violence, with a focus on mediation and conflict prevention. This focus caused the committee and its parent, Komnas HAM, to come under fire for not acting on the ongoing gross violations of human rights.[256]

On 2 July 2000, Komnas HAM conceded that after 19 months of conflict, the 'State has failed to overcome the situation and conflict that has occurred in this region'. It called for the government to place its resolution at the very top of the national agenda and reminded the

---

252. 'Rekomendasi 'Telur Busuk' DPR dan Sikap Bisu Pemerintah', Kompas Cyber Media, 15 May 2002 at http://www.kompas.com/utama/news/0205/15/010101.htm.

253. Kompas Online, 10 July 2001, 'Students Protest Decision of Parliament' at www.kompas.com/kompas-cetak/0107/10/ENGLISH/stud.htm; Forum Cybernews, 10 July 2001, 'Dengarlah Jeritan Rakyat' at www.forum.co.id/terkini/07-01/pansus.htm.

254. 'Peradilan HAM Ad Hoc Trisakti/Semanggi Harus Tetap Digelar', Radio Nederland, 18 June 2001, transcript at http://www.rnw.nl. There was an earlier trial in August 1998, where two police officers were tried by a military tribunal (the police was then part of the armed forces). Ten and four month sentences were imposed.

255. See http://www.komnasham.or.id.

256. G. Corputty, 'Kasus Pelanggaran HAM Yang Terjadi Di Maluku', Yayasan Baileo Maluku, at www.infid.be/infidforum2001-corputty-maluku-ind.html.

government of its obligation to 'take steps which are concrete and humane and which do not distinguish between religious, group or cultural backgrounds to help overcome the turmoil in Maluku'.[257] The most striking finding was the fourth:

> 'As the government is not able to overcome this conflict, we are concerned that the international community will force an intervention which will only widen the conflict. Therefore, the time has come for the Indonesian government to consider international cooperation, with a preference for assistance from ASEAN nations, to overcome the humanitarian problem in Maluku.'[258]

The Secretary General of Komnas HAM called for UN peacekeepers, given the public's deep mistrust of the Indonesian security forces.[259] The commission also made general recommendations for steps to be taken by the Civilian Emergency authorities against alleged provocateurs of the violence, and called for thorough investigation of a number of matters that it considered key to the conflict.[260]

☛ Fact-finding mission in Maluku (Kebun Cengkih)
Komnas HAM decision No. 030/KOMNAS HAM/VII/2001

On 25 June 2001, Komnas HAM approved the setting up of a fact-finding team to investigate a TNI attack on a medical centre run by the Laskar Jihad at Kebun Cengkih in Ambon.[261] On 14 June 2001, Yon Gab (Batalyon Gabungan, Joint Battalion), along with infantry battalions 408 and 407 of the Central Java Military Command, were involved in a 'sweeping' raid on Laskar Jihad camps in the predominantly Moslem areas of Galunggung and Kebon Cengkih, Ambon.[262] It was alleged that during the assault the military fired on patients and paramedics at a Laskar Jihad clinic. The attacks claimed at least 17 lives. Some 30 others, including members of the battalion, were injured during three consecutive days of gunfights with the group.

No public summary or report has been issued, but on 5 September 2001 the team's head reported that Yon Gab had committed a gross violation of human rights that met the definition of section 104 of Law No. 39/1999 Concerning Human Rights.[263] According to the Chair of Komnas HAM, Yon Gab had attacked the clinic and its occupants in violation of the

257. 'Indonesia: Statement by Komnas HAM on turmoil in Maluku', 2 July 2000 at www.ahrchk.net/hrsolid/mainfile.php/2000vol10no09/691/.

258. Ibid.

259. See Interview with Asmara Nababan, Secretary General of Komnas HAM, Radio Nederland, 'PBB Dan Pasukan Internasional Harus Segera Masuk Maluku', 17 juli 2000, at http://www.ranesi.nl.

260. Laporan Komisi Penyelidik Pelanggaran Hak Asasi Manusia Dan Mediasi Di Maluku, 18 December 2000.

261. Komnas HAM Decision No. SK 030/KOMNAS HAM/VII/2001, 12 July 2001. Komnas HAM, Laporan Kegiatan Sub Komisi Pemantauan Pelaksanaan Hak Asasi Manusia, available at http://www.komnasham.or.id/berita/sub komisi pemantauan.html. See also transcript, 'Human rights team to visit Ambon', ABC News/Radio Australia, 26 June 2001.

262. 'Indonesia: The Search for Truth in Maluku', International Crisis Group, 8 February 2002.

263. See www.komnasham/or.id/berita_komnasham.html.

Geneva Conventions.[264] The team reported to Komnas HAM on 23 November 2001 with findings that there had been violations of human rights amounting to extrajudicial killings and torture.[265] Komnas HAM has referred the case to the authorities, recommending trial in either a military or civilian court rather than the recommended processing before the relevant Human Rights Court.[266] No charges have been filed.

Education and Training

☛ Education and training of the military, police and civilians

'In November 2000, the ICRC manual on humanitarian law and human rights for police and security forces, *To Serve and to Protect*, was translated into Bahasa Indonesian and approved for use within the education and training programme of the Indonesian National Police.'

'In 2001, the Legal Services of the Indonesian Army (TNI) approved the ICRC's *Model Manual on the Law of Armed Conflict* for use in Indonesian military education and training.'

During the same year, the ICRC translated into Bahasa Indonesia and published, in association with the Indonesian delegation to the Inter-Parliamentary Union (IPU), the IPU handbook for parliamentarians, *Respect for International Humanitarian Law*.'[267]

Cases

☛ Decision in the trial of 24 army personnel and a civilian in relation to the killing of civilians at the Teungku Bantaqiah religious school in Beutong Ateuh, Banda Aceh, 17 May 2000, unreported

After five postponements, the trial of 25 low-ranking TNI soldiers began on 19 April 2000 before a 'koneksitas' court[268] comprised of two military officers and three civilians.[269] The accused were one civilian and 24 soldiers from the local territorial command and from the army's strategic command, Kostrad (a captain and two lieutenants plus 21 NCOs and privates).[270] One of the main suspects, Kasi Intel 011/Lilawangsa Lt. Col. Inf. Sudjono disappeared from his military base along with a number of relevant documents before the trial. He had given preliminary testimony to investigators in Jakarta, and was considered to

264. 'Yon Gab TNI Lakukan Kekerasan Di Klinik Laskar Jihad Di Ambon', Media Indonesia Online, 29 June 2001, at http://www.infomaluku.net/arc/01/010629mio.html. Note that war crimes are not recognized in Indonesian law as a gross violation of human rights under Law 26/2000 or an ordinary crime.

265. Komnas Ham, Laporan Kegiatan Sub Komisi Pemantauan Pelaksanaan Hak Asasi Manusia, available at http://www.komnasham.or.id/berita/sub komisi pemantauan.html.

266. Ibid.

267. ICRC Advisory Service, *National Implementation of International Humanitarian Law*: Biennial report 2000-2001 (Geneva, ICRC 2002) p. 54.

268. Crimes that are committed by a combination of military and civilian actors are tried in a general court of justice by a mixed panel of civilian and military judges (koneksitas court) unless the Chief Justice of the Supreme Court decides that the case should be tried in a military court of justice (Art. 40, Law 35 of 1999).

269. 'Human rights trial gets underway in Aceh province', first broadcast 19 April 2000, transcript at http://www.abc.net.au/ra/asiapac/archive/2000/apr/raap-20apr2000-1.htm.

270. 'Bantaqiah trial: an examination of the indictment by Tapol', Tapol Report, 25 April 2000.

be the lynchpin that would deliver irrefutable evidence linking senior officers to military abuses.[271]

The indictment alleged that the 25 accused had taken part in an attack on a religious school run by Teungku Bantaqiah in Beutong Ateuh, leading to 56 civilian fatalities.[272] On 17 May 2000, all 25 accused were convicted and sentenced to verdicts ranging from eight and a half to ten years.[273] Amnesty International and Human Rights Watch expressed serious misgivings about the trial process and emphasized the failure to prosecute commanding officers and the absence of key witnesses, such as the missing Lt. Col. Sudjono and victims who were eyewitnesses.[274]

☛ Decision in the case of *Eurico Guterres*, North Jakarta District Court, 31 April 2001, unreported

On 31 April 2001, Eurico Guterres, former commander of the East Timorese Aitarak militia, was convicted of incitement to violence in violation of section 160 of the Indonesian Penal Code, illegal possession of firearms in violation of section 1 of Emergency Regulation no. 2 of 1951 and interfering with government officers in the conduct of their duties in violation of section 212 of the Penal Code. The charges arose during the Indonesian government's efforts to disarm the East Timorese militias in West Timor, in the course of which Guterres had attempted to recover arms that had been surrendered to authorities in Atambua and incite his followers to do the same. Guterres was sentenced to six months imprisonment (he had faced up to six years imprisonment for his role in incitement and 16 months for his role in obstructing government officers in the conduct of their duties). Much international outrage followed the verdict and when Guterres was released on 23 May 2001 after serving just 23 days. However his time under house arrest since October 2000 was taken into consideration and his service of the sentence was accordingly reduced.

☛ Decision in the case of Julius Naisama, Jose Francisco, Joao Alvez da Cruz, Xisto Pereira, Joao Martins and Serafin Ximenes, North Jakarta District Court, 4 May 2001, unreported.

On 4 May 2001, the North Jakarta District Court convicted six men accused of the killing of three UNHCR workers in Atambua, West Timor, on 6 September 2000. The six men received sentences ranging from ten to 20 months imprisonment for violence against persons or property.[275] The case had been moved from West Timor amid fears that pro-Jakarta East Timorese militias might disrupt the hearings. Although of East Timorese

---

271. 'Human rights trial gets underway in Aceh province', first broadcast 19 April 2000, transcript at http://www.abc.net.au/ra/asiapac/archive/2000/apr/raap-20apr2000-1.htm.

272. See further L. Murdoch, 'The enemy within: shoot first ... Indonesian troops on the move in Aceh', *Sydney Morning Herald*, 14 August 1999; 'Indonesian Army massacred unarmed civilians in Aceh: probe team', AFP, 31 October 1999.

273. 'Indonesia: Aceh trial - Amnesty International and Human Rights Watch call for full accountability', Amnesty International and Human Rights Watch, 17 May 2000.

274. Ibid.

275. Despite confessions from the accused, the prosecution claimed that there was a lack of evidence to justify murder/manslaughter charges and sought a maximum of three years in jail.

ethnicity, the militiamen, as with Guterres above, had Indonesian nationality and so the court was able to exercise jurisdiction.

Media coverage reported that Judge Anak Agung Gede Dalem concluded that 'the elements that caused the U.N. officers' deaths cannot be proved to be (linked to the defendants) ... because the action was perpetrated by a mob'.[276] Although some of the defendants had admitted taking part in hacking the victims to death before the bodies were burned, '[t]he attack was carried out not only by them but by a mob which makes it difficult to determine the perpetrators of the deaths'.[277] Furthermore, the autopsy results showed the victims' bodies were badly damaged by fire and it was not possible to identify who committed the manslaughter.[278]

The verdicts were widely condemned. The UN Secretary General expressed his shock and said the ruling appeared to be 'incommensurate with what is known to have been deliberate and brutal killings'.[279] The United States said it was 'extremely disappointed' with the lenient sentences. The UNHCR called the sentences a 'mockery' of the judicial process.[280] In response to the outcry, the Attorney General's office appealed on sentence and on 18 January 2002, the Supreme Court revealed that it had on 15 November 2001 increased the sentences for Perreira (to five years), Martin (to five years) and Ximenes (to seven years).[281]

SUZANNAH LINTON

Pending

☛ New law on the emblem

A new draft law on the use and protection of the emblem was completed and awaiting the approval of the Council of Ministers before being submitted for adoption to the Indonesian Parliament.[282]

IRELAND[283]

International Criminal Court, and the Death Penalty

☛ Amendments to the Irish Constitution of 1937 to prohibit the death penalty, and to facilitate ratification of the Rome Statute of the International Criminal Court

There were two important constitutional amendments during 2001, the adoption of which required a national referendum. Both amendments were carried by a comfortable majority.

---

276. 'Outrage at Indonesia court's Timor murder sentences', Reuters, 4 May 2001; 'Legal experts decry Atambua sentences', *Jakarta Post*, 8 May 2001.

277. Ibid.

278. Ibid.

279. 'Secretary-General shocked by light sentences handed down in Indonesian court case concerning killing of UNHCR staff', UN News Update, SG/SM/7793, 7 May 2001.

280. 'UN refugee body blasts Timor verdicts as "mockery"', Reuters, 4 May 2001; 'Sentences for Timor killings deeply disturbing', UNHCR Press Release, 4 May 2001.

281. 'Convicted UN staff killers get heavier sentences', *Jakarta Post*, 19 January 2002.

282. ICRC Advisory Service, *National Implementation of International Humanitarian Law*: Biennial report 2000-2001 (Geneva, ICRC 2002) p. 54.

283. Information and commentaries by Ray Murphy, Irish Centre for Human Rights, School of Law, National University of Ireland, Galway.

The first amendment (formally referred to as the twenty-first Amendment to the Constitution) concerned the abolition of the death penalty. It is now expressly prohibited under the Irish Constitution for the legislature to enact any law providing for the imposition of the death penalty. This prohibition is absolute and includes laws enacted during time of war, armed rebellion or other national emergency.

The second amendment (formally referred to as the twenty-third Amendment of the Constitution) was intended to facilitate ratification of the Rome Statute of the International Criminal Court and remove any constitutional impediments that existed before ratification by Ireland can take place. The referendum was only the first step. Ratification of the Statute still required the introduction of national legislation to comply with the complex international criminal law (the proposed International Criminal Court Bill, not yet published) and judicial cooperation requirements of the Statute.

☛ Extradition (European Union Conventions) Act 2001, No. 49/2001 [www.irlgov.ie/ag]

The purpose of the Act is to give effect to two European Union Conventions on Extradition (the 1995 and 1996 Conventions) by amending, *inter alia*, the principal legislation governing extradition in Ireland, i.e., the Extradition Act, 1965. The 1995 Convention provides for a simplified procedure where the person sought consents to his or her surrender. Once consent is given, and where the person claimed is a citizen of Ireland, the Minister for Justice, Equality and Law Reform agrees, the person will be extradited. Such persons may also renounce their right to the Speciality Rule (the rule whereby a person extradited for one offence may not be tried for other offences committed before his or her extradition).

The 1996 Convention relating to extradition between the Members States of the European Union, as well as extending the range of extraditable offences, also provides for the improvement and simplification of procedures in a number of respects. Extradition requests, documents and correspondence may be sent by facsimile transmission provided that the facsimile machine is fitted with a cryptographic device to ensure authenticity and confidentiality. The Convention also requires all states to designate a Central Authority to be responsible for transmitting and receiving extradition requests and supporting documents. In Ireland, this role will be fulfilled by the Office of the Minister for Justice, Equality and Law Reform.

It should be noted that the position in Irish law in relation to the political offence exception remains unchanged by this legislation. Since all the European Union states are parties to the Suppression of Terrorism Convention, and orders applying Part II of the Extradition Act, 1965 have been made in relation to all European Union states, the Irish Extradition (European Convention on Suppression of Terrorism) Act, 1987 as amended, will apply (without more) to all European Union states and there is therefore no need to include any 'political offence' provision in this Act.

Pending

☛ European Convention on Human Rights Bill, 2001

In April 2001, the Minister for Justice, Equality and Law Reform in Ireland introduced the European Convention on Human Rights Bill, 2001, with the intention of incorporating the ECHR into domestic law. The proposed Act was quite controversial as it adopted a minimalist approach, and it has not yet been passed into Irish law. Ireland was among the first states to ratify the ECHR and citizens have had the right to appeal to the European Court of Human Rights for a decision on those rights, provided that they have exhausted local remedies. It is the generally accepted view that, because of the dualist nature of the Irish legal system, prior to incorporation the Convention did not form part of domestic law. While the question of incorporation of the ECHR into Irish domestic law has been considered for some time, the conclusion of the Belfast Agreement in 1998 added urgency to the issue.[284]

Ireland has ratified both the ECHR and the International Covenant on Civil and Political Rights, but until recently it has been reluctant to incorporate either of them into domestic law, citing the Constitution as the primary reason for not doing so. After the passing of the Human Rights Act, 1998 (HRA) in the United Kingdom, Ireland found itself in the embarrassing position of being the only state in the Council of Europe not to have incorporated the ECHR into its domestic law.

The possible options for incorporation available to the Irish government could be placed in two general broad categories, constitutional and legislative. At no stage in the debate did it seem likely that a constitutional option would be given serious consideration.

The current proposals indicate that Ireland has decided to follow the example set by the United Kingdom and adopt an interpretive model. The crucial provisions in the proposed Irish legislation are Sections 2, 3 and 4. Section 2 establishes the framework through which further effect is to be given to the provisions of the Convention. It provides that any statutory provision (defined in Section 1) and any rule of law shall be interpreted, in so far as possible, in a manner compatible with the State's obligations under the Convention.[285]

The Act provides a wide margin of discretion to an Irish court in taking cognisance of the jurisprudence of the European Court of Human Rights, and Irish courts are neither bound to follow or apply a precedent of the Court or related bodies. The Act will require a court to interpret and apply any statutory provision or rule of law, in so far as possible, in a manner compatible with the obligations under the ECHR. Similar to the HRA in the United Kingdom, where there is a declaration of incompatibility, the proposed Act confers no power to strike down the offending legislation. In this way, the declaration of incompatibility should not be seen as a potential remedy, but as a device to alert the legislature to inconsistent legislation. This leaves the ultimate responsibility for ensuring legislation is compatible with the ECHR with the parliament. An obvious disadvantage is that the courts are powerless should the parliament decide to ignore any inconsistency or violation brought to its attention.

Unfortunately, the linkage of the incorporation of the ECHR with the Belfast Agreement has meant that the wider debate regarding incorporation of other international treaties has largely been ignored. Although the Act does have a number of positive aspects it is unlikely that incorporation will have a profound impact on the daily routine and decisions of the Irish courts. The Act will require organs of state to perform their functions in a manner compatible with ECHR provisions, though the express exclusion of the courts from the definition of organs of state is a serious deficiency. Nonetheless, people will now enjoy a right of due

---

284. British-Irish Agreement done at Belfast on 10 April 1998. http://www.gov.ie/iveagh/angloirish/goodfriday/default.htm]. Belfast Agreement, Rights, Safeguards and Equality of Opportunity, para. 1. See generally R. Murphy, 'The Incorporation of the ECHR into Irish Domestic Law', *European Human Rights Law Review*, Issue 6 (2001) pp. 640-656.

285. The European Convention on Human Rights Bill, 2001, sect. 2(1). The section will apply retrospectively and prospectively.

process in the determination of their entitlements by local and state officials; this will include a right to a fair hearing and a reasoned decision that will be open to challenge in the courts. In fact, Article 6 has the most potential for influencing procedural issues in the conduct of criminal and civil cases in Ireland. It is to be hoped that the deferment of the proposed Act to allow for 'further consultation' will provide the opportunity to expand its minimalist provisions.

RAY MURPHY

ISRAEL[286]

Geneva Law

☛ Declaration of the States Parties to the Geneva Conventions present at the Conference of High Contracting Parties to the Geneva Convention, 5 December 2001

On 5 December 2001, a Conference of the High Contracting Parties to the Fourth Geneva Convention was convened in Geneva. The Conference reaffirmed the applicability of the Fourth Geneva Convention to the Occupied Territories (including East Jerusalem) and called upon Israel to cease all violations of the Convention.[287] The participants in the Conference were presented, *inter alia*, with an ICRC statement criticizing certain Israeli practices in the West Bank and Gaza Strip.[288]

Israel denounced the meeting as an abusive act of politicizing the mechanisms of international humanitarian law. It also challenged the declaration adopted by the Conference as one-sided and unsubstantiated.[289] See further the article of M. Happold in this volume at p. 389, and the report on the Occupied Palestinian Territories, at p. 603.

International Criminal Tribunals

☛ Amendment No. 7 to the Extradition Law 1954, adopted on 9 May 2001, entered into force on 24 May 2001, published in *Official Gazette* vol. 1790, p. 384 [www.knesset.gov.il/privatelaw/data/2940_3.rtf (in Hebrew)]

Article 2A to the amended Law provides that the term 'Applicant State', a state that is entitled to request extradition under the Law, also encompasses the ICTY and the ICTR. This Amendment will facilitate extradition proceedings in the State of Israel of fugitives,

---

286. Information and commentaries by Dr Yuval Shany, School of Law, Academic College of Management, Israel. The reporter would like to thank the Research Foundation of the Law School of the Academic College of Management for their financial support of this research. Additional thanks are due to Ms Matat Gutterman, who assisted in the research for this report. See also the report on the Occupied Territories at p. 548 of this volume.

287. Declaration of the Conference of the Parties to the Fourth Geneva Convention, 5 December 2001. Available online at http://www.eda.admin.ch/eda/e/home/foreign/hupol/4gc/docum2.Par.0006.UpFile.pdf/mg_011205_4gcdeclarn_e.pdf. Reprinted at p. 664 of this volume.

288. Statement by the International Committee of the Red Cross, Geneva, 5 December 2001. Available at http://www.icrc.org/Web/eng/siteeng0.nsf/ 322bdba384116a00412566480050a932/64ef7fe0fc58b5ebc1256b660060bcf0?OpenDocument. Reprinted at p. 667 of this volume.

289. Ministry of Foreign Affairs, Israel's reaction to the convening of the High Contracting Parties to the Fourth Geneva Convention, 5 December 2001. Available online at http://www.mfa.gov.il/mfa/go.asp?MFAH0kv10. Reprinted at p. 667 of this volume.

which were indicted by the two *ad hoc* Tribunals.

The Situation in the Occupied Territories
☛ Report of the UN Human Rights Commission, 16 March 2001

A Commission of Inquiry established by the UN Human Rights Commission, and comprised of three eminent international scholars (Prof. John Dugard, Dr. Kamal Hossain and Prof. Richard Falk), published a report on the Question of Violations of Human Rights in the Occupied Arab Territories, including Palestine, on 16 March 2001.[290] The report was critical of certain Israeli policies – most notably, the excessive use of force, extrajudicial killings, the maintenance of settlements and severe restrictions upon Palestinian's freedom of movement.

One of the most controversial measures employed by Israel in an attempt to suppress the Palestinians *intifadah* has been the policy of 'targeted killings' (sometimes referred to as the policy of 'liquidations'). In pursuance of this policy, Israeli soldiers have killed several dozen Palestinians[291] suspected by Israel of involvement in terrorism, mainly by way of pinpoint missile attacks, sniper shots and detonation of car bombs. It is uncontested that a number of innocent bystanders have been also killed as result of the Israeli strikes.

The Palestinian Authority and several Israeli and international human rights NGOs have insisted that 'targeted killings' are a form of extra-judicial execution, which is unlawful under international humanitarian law.[292] One of the Israeli NGOs – the Public Committee Against Torture – has even petitioned the Israeli Supreme Court, challenging the legality of 'targeted killings' (the case is still pending before the Court).

The Report makes an important contribution to the discussion of the legal dimensions of the policy of 'targeted killings'. It outlined the legal situation existing in the Occupied Territories and, on the basis of its analysis, reached the conclusion that Israel's use of 'targeted killings' is inconsistent with international law. Still, the Commission did implicitly accept one of Israel's central submissions with respect to the lawfulness of its practices.

The controversy surrounding the policy of 'targeted killings' concerns several different aspects of the policy. First, there are serious questions pertaining to the sufficiency of the evidence implicating targeted persons in terrorist activity, which serves as the basis for targeting actions. Second, there are grave doubts, whether the policy, as applied by Israel, is in conformity with the basic humanitarian law principles of distinction and proportionality (given the high rate of collateral loss of life of innocent bystanders as result of this policy). However, the first and foremost legal issue associated with determining the legality of the policy is the question of the applicable law. Here, one can find, at first sight, two irreconcil-

---

290. Human Rights Inquiry Commission, Report on the Question of Violations of Human Rights in the Occupied Arab Territories, including Palestine, UN Doc. E/CN.4/2001/121 (2001).

291. According to Amnesty International, 32 Palestinians were targeted under this policy throughout 2001. The targeted killings also resulted in the death of 15 innocent bystanders.

292. 'Palestinian Authority condemns acts of assassination, liquidation', Arabic News.Com, 18 Oct. 2001. http://www.arabicnews.com/ansub/Daily/Day/011018/2001101810.html; Human Rights Inquiry Commission, 'Report on the Question of Violation of Human Rights in the Occupied Arab Territories, including Palestine', UN Doc. E/CN.4/2001/121 (2001), paras. 53-64. See also B'teselem Israel's 'Assassination Policy: Extra-judicial Executions' (2001) URL?; Amnesty International, Israel and the Occupied Territories: 'State assassinations and other unlawful killings' (2001).

able positions. While Israel claims that the relevant law governing measures taken against persons involved in armed hostilities against it (including terrorist attacks) is the law of warfare (i.e., customary law, as reflected in the 1907 Hague Regulations, Part IV of the First Additional Protocol 1977 and Part IV of the Second Additional Protocols), the Commission seemed to have held that the governing law is the law of occupation:

> 'Because the law of occupation also applies, provisions of this *lex specialis* take precedence over human rights... Thus, whether a particular loss of life is to be considered an arbitrary loss of life contrary to article 6 of the International Covenant on Civil and Political Rights can only be decided by reference to the law of occupation in the Fourth Geneva Convention.'[293]

Since the Commission held that the Fourth Geneva Convention prohibits the extra-judicial killing of protected persons, even if there are suspicions that they are involved in hostile acts against the Occupying Power, it concluded that the practice constitutes a grave breach of the Fourth Convention.[294]

However, on closer inspection, one cannot but conclude that the Commission did accept the legal position of Israel in one key aspect. The report acknowledges that: 'Civilians lose the protection under the Fourth Geneva Convention when they become combatants by taking a direct part in hostilities (Art. 51(3) of the Additional Protocol I).'

In other words, deviating from its earlier pronouncement upholding the supremacy of the law of occupation with respect to protected civilians, the Commission did seem to accept the proposition that the *lex specialis* with regard to civilians directly engaged in armed hostilities is indeed the law of warfare (or the law governing the conduct of hostilities). Indeed, this position finds support in the text of Article 5 of the Fourth Geneva Convention – which permits, under certain conditions, derogation from some of the rights of protected persons, if they are involved in hostilities – and in the text of Article 13(3) of the Second Additional Protocol, which removes protection from civilians directly involved in hostilities in the context of a non-international armed conflict (such as the Israeli-Palestinian conflict).[295] A point, which needs to be emphasized, however, is that the law of warfare can only become applicable if there exists an armed conflict of an international or non-international nature. Although the Commission was not convinced at the time of the preparation of the report (early-2001) that the situation in the West Bank and the Gaza Strip reached the requisite level of intensity so as to qualify as a non-international armed conflict, it seems that the subsequent deterioration on the ground (including the high number of causalities and the use of heavy weaponry by both parties to the conflict) leaves little doubt that a high-intensity and protracted conflict between armed and organized Palestinian and Israel groups is now taking place in the region.[296]

The crux of the matter is therefore whether Palestinians targeted by Israel's policies have taken 'direct part' in the hostilities, as provided by Article 51(3) of the First Additional

---

293. Human Rights Inquiry Commission Report. Ibid., para. 62.

294. Ibid. paras. 63-64.

295. Ibid., para. 39. 'Clearly, there is no international armed conflict in the region, as Palestine ... still falls short of the accepted criteria of statehood.'

296. *Prosecutor* v. *Tadić*, Decision of the Appeals Chamber on the Interlocutory Appeal on Jurisdiction, Case IT-94-1-AR72, 35 *ILM* (1996) p. 32; Art. 8(2)(d) and (f) of the Rome Statute of the International Criminal Court, 17 July 1998, UN Doc. A/Conf.183/9, 37 *ILM* (1998) p. 999.

Protocol (which arguably reflects customary law on the matter).[297] While it seems that the Commission rightfully criticized Israel for its failure to produce evidence supporting its allegations that persons targeted were actually involved in armed hostilities, its legal position, according to which the targeting of irregular armed activists can only take place if they are involved in hostilities at that *very same time* at which they were targeted, is more problematic. Although the Commission's view on the matter is certainly in line with the official ICRC Commentary to Article 51 of the First Additional Protocol,[298] it seems detached from the complexities of the situation on the ground in the Occupied Territories and should merit reexamination.

In reality, Israel evacuated its military forces in 1995-96 from all major Palestinian towns and submitted virtually all of its authorities and powers of control *vis-à-vis* these areas, including the power to maintain law and order, to the newly established Palestinian Authority (PA). While the Commission held that the Fourth Geneva Convention is still applicable to the areas controlled by the PA, by virtue of Article 47 of the Convention and because of the *de jure* powers of legal control remaining in Israeli hands,[299] it would seem artificial to expect Israel to limit itself only to self-defense measures permissible under the Fourth Convention. This is because the most effective measure authorized by the Fourth Convention – the arrest and trial of persons involved in hostilities – is often impractical in the ruling circumstances, given Israel's lack of *de facto* control over PA-controlled areas (with the exception of the control exercised by Israel during its incursions into Palestinian areas).

Thus, restricting the right to use force against civilians engaged in hostilities, in areas outside Israel's *de facto effective* control, to the actual duration of the perpetration of the hostile acts seriously undermines Israel's ability to effectively thwart military operations carried out against it (for instance, it would entitle it to target a suicide bomber only while on route to carry out his or her deadly mission, a temporal limitation which significantly reduces the chances of successful interception). This is especially so since targeting civilians while they are actively engaged in hostilities might be undesirable from a humanitarian point of view, because it might conflict with other prescriptions of international humanitarian law, such as the principles of distinction and proportionality (e.g., if a bomb maker operates from a densely populated center, it is tenuous to maintain that he can be targeted only while on the job, but not after 'working hours' in his remote home). Thus, the proposed restrictive reading of Article 51(3), in the circumstances faced by Israel, might result in a grant of *de facto* immunity (and in the case of Palestinian activists perpetrating international crimes, also grant of impunity) to armed militants in the Occupied Territories.

Consequently, it would seem that a more realistic construction of the applicable law is needed. Indeed, it is possible to construe Article 51(3) of the First Additional Protocol in a broader temporal manner, so as to encompass civilians directly involved in hostilities, as long as they meet the definition of a legitimate military objective under Article 52(2) of the

---

297. This is supported, *inter alia*, by the introduction of a similar requirement in Art. 13(3) of the Second Additional Protocol to the Geneva Conventions and in Arts. 8(2)(b)(1) and (8)(2)(e)(1) of the Rome Statute.

298. C. Pilloud, Y. Sandoz, Ch. Swinarski and B. Zimmerman, eds., *Commentary on the Additional Protocols of 8 June 1977 to the Geneva Conventions of 12 August 1949* (Geneva, ICRC 1987) pp. 618-619, at paras. 1943-1945; M. Bothe, K. Josef Partsch, W. Solf, *New Rules for Victims of Armed Conflict* (The Hague, Boston, Martinus Nijhoff 1982) pp. 302-304 at paras. 2.4.2-2.4.2.2.

299. Human Rights Commission Inquiry Report, *supra* n. 292, paras. 36, 44.

First Additional Protocol (i.e., they continue to provide an effective contribution to military action and to offer a definite military advantage in their destruction or neutralization). Such a construction, would equate, in effect, the status of civilians who take direct part in hostilities to that of regular members of enemy military forces (who are, in the event of an armed conflict, legitimate targets for the duration of their active service – that is, even while they are asleep in their barracks). Both categories of persons could thus be the legitimate target of attack for the duration of their regular or irregular military service. This construction would justify the targeting of persons involved in hostilities during short intermissions between active military assignments, but would exclude the punitive targeting of persons after their retirement from an active role in the hostilities.

Still, in line with Article 5 of the Fourth Geneva Convention, it seems prudent to maintain that the targeting of civilians taking direct part in the hostilities can only be permissible if and when no other measures of neutralizing them (such as arrest and trial) are reasonably possible. In other words, it is submitted that civilians engaged in hostilities *do* remain under the protection of the Fourth Geneva Convention to the degree that there exists no military necessity which entitles the Occupying Power to derogate from their rights. This would mean that the targeting of a person when there exists a reasonable alternative for his arrest is impermissible. Indeed, the Commission held that at least in one prominent case of a 'targeted killing', Israel could have easily arrested the targeted individual and thus failed to meet the burden of pursuing the least injurious feasible measure.[300]

In sum, the position of the Commission that the policy of 'selected targeting' as actually practiced by Israel raises serious legal concerns seems to be justified. However, it should also be noted that the report implicitly embraces the view that civilians directly involved in hostilities can be the legitimate targets of an attack under certain circumstances, notwithstanding the terms of the Fourth Geneva Convention. While the Commission was of the view that Israel failed to meet the necessary conditions for lawfully pursuing such attacks, it could be argued that some of the legal criteria applied by it *vis-à-vis* Israel were too stringent and out of touch with the complexity of the challenges faced by Israel.

☛ Final Report of the Sharm El Sheikh Fact Finding Committee, 30 April 2001 [http://usinfo.state.gov/ regional/nea/mitchell.htm]

The Sharm El Sheikh Fact Finding Committee (chaired by former US Senator George Mitchell) submitted its report to US President George W. Bush on 30 April 2001. The report expressed certain concerns relating, *inter alia,* to what it considered excessive use of force by the Israeli Defence Forces (IDF) and Israel's controversial policy of 'selective killing' of Palestinians activists. While the Israeli Ministry of Foreign Affairs welcomed the report, it insisted that Israeli policies were consistent with international law.[301]

---

300. This is the case of Dr Thabat, who was killed on 9 December 2000, when, according to the Commission, he could easily have been arrested by the IDF. Human Rights Commission Report, ibid., para. 64.

301. Ministry of Foreign Affairs, Israel's Comments on the Mitchell Committee Report, 15 May 2001. http://www.mfa.gov.il/mfa/go.asp?MFAH0jyg0.

☛ Reports by Israeli and international NGOs regarding human rights violations in the Occupied Territories

Israeli and international NGOs investigating human rights violations in the Occupied Territories, such as B'tselem,[302] Amnesty International[303] and Human Rights Watch[304] issued several reports in 2001, alleging, *inter alia*, that Israeli forces committed the following violations of IHL:

1. Excessive use of force against Palestinian stone-throwing demonstrators, including the use of live ammunition against children.
2. Engagement in a policy of assassinations of Palestinian armed activists, which entailed, among other things, the incidental killing of innocent civilians, hit by reason of erroneous identification of targets or the imprecise nature of the attacks, which have been undertaken in civilian settings.
3. Routine beatings and abusive treatment of Palestinians detained by the Israeli General Security Service. In particular, it had been alleged that torture of Palestinian children took place while they were held in police custody by police investigators at the Gush-E'tzion police station, in the Occupied Territories.
4. Prolonged restrictions of Palestinian's freedom of movement through roadblocks scattered throughout the Occupied Territories. Closures, resulting in the exclusion of Palestinians from the territory of Israel proper, and the encirclement of Palestinian cities, led to severe restrictions upon the mobility of Palestinians, hampered their economic life and resulted, on a number of occasions, in critical delays in access of patients to medical facilities.
5. In a number of instances, IDF soldiers have demolished without prior warning Palestinian houses and crops. As result of these activities, thousands of Palestinians have been left without a place to live and work.

---

302. B'teselem, 'Excessive Force: Human Rights Violations during IDF Actions in Area A (2001)', B'teselem, 'Whitewash: Office of the Military Advocate General's Investigation into the Death of Khalil al-Mughrabi, age 11, on July 7, 2001 (2001)'; B'teselem, 'Beit Rima, 24 October, 2001: Human Rights Violations during the IDF Action in Beit Rima (2001)'; B'teselem Free Rein: 'Vigilante Settlers and Israel's Non-Enforcement of the Law' (2001); B'teselem, 'In Broad Daylight: Abuse of Palestinians by IDF soldiers on July 23, 2001' (2001); B'teselem, 'Not even a Drop: Water Crisis in Palestinian Villages' (2001); B'teselem, 'Torture of Palestinian Minors in the Gush Etzion Police Station' (2001); B'teselem, 'No Way Out: Medical Implications of Israel's Siege Policy' (2001); B'teselem, 'Excessive Force: Analysis of the events of 6 May 2001 in Beit Jala' (2001); B'teselem, 'On Human Rights in the Occupied Territories' (2001); B'teselem, 'Standard Routine: Beatings and Abuse of Palestinians by Israeli Security Forces during the Al Aqsa Intifadah' (2001); B'teselem, 'Tacit Consent: Law Enforcement towards Israeli Settlers in the West Bank' (2001); B'teselem, 'Civilians under Siege: Restrictions on Freedom of Movement as Collective Punishment' (2001), B'teselem, 'Israel's Assassination Policy: Extra-judicial Executions' (2001). All reports are available online at http://www.btselem.org.

303. Amnesty International, Report 2002: 'Israel and the Occupied Territories (2002); Amnesty International, 'Israel and the Occupied Territories: State assassinations and other unlawful killings' (2001); Amnesty International, 'Israel and the Occupied Territories: Broken lives – a year of intifada' (2001).

304. See e.g., Human Rights Watch, Center of the Storm: A Case Study of Human Rights Abuses in Hebron District (2001); Human Rights Watch, World Report 2002: 'Israel, the Occupied West Bank and Gaza Strip, and Palestinian Authority Territories' (2002).

The official position of the State of Israel with respect to these allegations, as reflected in media accounts and official position papers[305] is that:

1. The IDF has generally acted with restraint in difficult situations presented before it in the current uprising. Soldiers were generally instructed not to open fire, unless placed in a life-threatening situation or in order foil terror attacks. Still, specific allegations of excessive use of force are being investigated.
2. The policy of 'selective targeting' is a legitimate act of self-defense against legitimate military objectives. The persons targeted under this type of warfare are armed terrorists who operate from densely populated civilian centers, in breach of their duty to distinguish themselves from the civilian population. In all cases, persons targeted were involved in the perpetration of homicidal and/or suicidal attacks against Israelis, and in some cases were targeted while being on their way to commit such an attack. The IDF states that the killings have taken place in areas where Israel does not have effective control, and consequently cannot arrest and bring these terrorists to trial. Since the Palestinian Authority has refused to arrest these terrorists who were operating in areas subject to its jurisdiction and control or to otherwise halt their hostile activities, Israel is entitled to neutralize them itself. The IDF has undertaken precautionary measures to minimize the incidental loss of life of innocent civilian and regrets any such occurrence.
3. All accusations of maltreatment of detained Palestinians are routinely investigated and have, in most cases, been found to be baseless.
4. Movement restrictions are an indispensable measure in the war against terrorism, and are designed to prevent infiltration of terrorists into Israel proper and to other military and civilian targets throughout the Territories.
5. House demolitions take place in the Territories only where military conditions so require. Whenever operationally possible, prior notice is given to the owners of the relevant property.

Cases[306]

1. The Right of Administrative detainees to receive ICRC visits

☛ *Sheikh Abed al-Karim Obeid and Mustafa al-Dirani* v. *Minister of Defense,* H.C. 794/98, Supreme Court of Israel, Judgment of 23 August 2001[307]

The applicants, two Lebanese citizens affiliated with the Hizbullah organization, have been held by Israel in administrative detention since 1989 (Obeid) and 1994 (Dirani). In their petition to the Supreme Court, they complained against the refusal of the Israeli authorities to grant ICRC representatives access to them. The state attorneys argued that it would be

---

305. See Ministry of Foreign Affairs, Second Statement of the Government of Israel submitted to the Sharm El Sheikh Fact Finding Committee, 20 March 2001, available online at http://www.mfa.gov.il/mfa/ go.asp?MFAH0jrb0#e; Ministry of Foreign Affairs, Targetting Terrorists - Background Paper, 1 August 2001, available online at http://www.mfa.gov.il/mfa/go.asp?MFAH0k9d0. Reprinted in this volume at p. 663.

306. Unless noted otherwise, the cases discussed herein have not been officially published but are available at the Supreme Court's website: http://www.court.gov.il.

307. H.C. 794/98 *Obeid* v. *Minister of Defence*, 55 (5) P.D. 769. A request by family members of Ron Arad for reexamination of the decision by the Supreme Court was rejected on 23 April 2002. H.C.R. 7060/01 *Arad* v. *Dirani* (not yet published).

counter-productive to facilitate such visits as long as no information had been made available to Israel regarding the fate of four Israeli citizens (three soldiers and one civilian) who were captured by the Hizbullah and regarding the fate of Ron Arad, an Israeli Missing in Action, who was held captive at some point in time by a Hizbullah affiliated organization.

The Court rejected the state's position and ruled that Obeid and Dirani are entitled to receive ICRC visits. While the Court was willing to accept the government's position that Article 142 of the Fourth Geneva Convention might not be fully applicable to the applicants, by virtue of Article 5 (inapplicability of visitation privileges to persons engaged in hostile activities), it held that such derogation could only be relied upon in a reasonable manner. In this case, the Court held that the long duration of the applicants' detention creates a strong presumption in favor of upholding their humanitarian rights and privileges. In addition, the Court was not persuaded that the exclusion of ICRC visits contributed in any meaningful manner to Israel's efforts to ascertain the fate of its captured nationals.

2. Right of Administrative Detainees to meet with Attorneys

- *Muna* v. *General Secret Service*, H.C. 970/01, Judgment of 15 February 2001
- *Kfarna* v. *General Security Service*, H.C. 1392/01, Judgment of 21 February 2001
- *Taha* v. *General Security Service*, H.C. 3330/01, Judgment of 2 May 2001
- *Abu Mussa* v. *General Security Service*, H.C. 3814/01, Judgment of 15 May 2001
- *Alhashi* v. *General Security Service*, H.C. 4092/01, Judgment of 24 May 2001
- *Rabia* v. *General Security Service*, H.C. 4490/01, Judgment of 7 June 2001
- *Ibrahim* v. *Minister of Defense* H.C. 3425/01, (Judgment of 26 June 2001)

In all cases, the applicants, Palestinians residing in the Occupied Territories, who were at the time administrative detainees, petitioned the Supreme Court for enforcement of their right to meet with their attorneys, without delay. The Supreme Court rejected all of these applications, citing confidential intelligence reports which justified the postponement of attorney-client meetings, in accordance with the applicable Military Order governing security-related detention of suspects in the Occupied Territories, in order to facilitate investigation of the detainees.

In the *Muna* case, the applicant also complained that while being investigated by the ISA she had been deprived of sleep, in contravention of the Court's decision in *Public Committee against Torture in Israel* v. *Government of Israel*, H.C. 5100/94.[308] The Court held that in light of information brought to its attention, it was convinced that any extension of the investigation which might have occurred served a legitimate investigative purpose and was not designed to break the applicant's spirit.

3. Allegations of Torture and Maltreatment of Protected Persons

- *Al-Ahmar* v. *Minister of Defense*, H.C. 4592/01, Judgment of 12 June 2001

The applicant, detained for investigation in the Israel Security Agency (ISA; formally known as the General Security Service – GSS) facilities, petitioned the Supreme Court of

---

308. *Public Committee against Torture in Israel* v. *Government of Israel*, H.C. 5100/94, 53(4) P.D. 817.

Israel requesting it to order the ISA to cease torturing him and provide him with medical treatment, without delay. The Court rejected the petition. In doing so, it accepted statements made by the responsible ISA interrogator and by a physician employed by the ISA to the effect that no maltreatment had taken place and that adequate medical treatment was provided to the detainee for his pre-existing health problems.

4. Passage of Medical Patients through Road blocks in the Occupied Territories

☛ *Doctors Association for Human Rights* v. *Minister of Defense*, H.C. 9242/00, Judgment of 21 March 2001

The applicant, a human rights NGO, requested the Supreme Court of Israel to order the military to refrain from delaying or preventing the movement of Palestinian medical patients in roadblocks scattered throughout the Occupied Territories. The Court rejected the petition, for reasons of its general nature and lack of factual substantiation. Given the IDF position that soldiers positioned in roadblocks have been instructed to permit passage of people with medical needs, even at times of movement restrictions (such as closures and blockades), the Court held that no evidence was introduced that the IDF soldiers were not acting, as a rule, in conformity with this policy. It further suggested that any specific breach of the said instructions should be brought to the attention of the military authorities.

5. Military use of land seizures in Occupied Territories

☛ *Kna'an* v. *IDF West Bank Commander*, H.C. 2461/01, Judgment of 19 March 2001

The applicants challenged before the Supreme Court of Israel the seizing of 9500 m^2 of their land by the IDF for the purpose of creating truck loading areas in proximity to a military roadblock, separating Israeli and Palestinian controlled areas. According to the military, the purpose of the confiscation was to facilitate the transfer of goods between Israel proper and the Palestinian areas, through a system of 'back to back' loading and unloading of Israeli and Palestinian trucks (the latter are not permitted to travel into Israel because of security concerns). The Court accepted the position of the respondents that valid military considerations justified the confiscation. However, the Court recommended that compensation be awarded to the landowners.

☛ *Tsabih* v. *Minister of Defense*, h.c. 3950/99, Judgment of 27 June 2001

The applicants, residents of a village situated in the Jenin district of the West Bank, requested the Supreme Court of Israel to order the IDF to cease using the village lands as soldiers' training grounds. According to the petition, military drills in the area create a nuisance, endanger the lives of the villagers and obstruct the agricultural use of the lands. The Court rejected the claim and held that the use of the land by the IDF clearly serves a legitimate military purpose. However, it noted that the IDF has recently issued a new set of orders, designed to minimise any inconvenience caused to the villagers (including the appointment of a liaison officer, whose task would be to handle villagers' complaints), and that preparations to move the training grounds to a different location (inside Israel proper) have been initiated.

Pending

- Draft Law on Imprisonment of Combatants not Entitled to Prisoners of War 2000

This law remained pending before a Knesset Committee throughout 2001. During the year, the Knesset Committee for Foreign Relations and Defense reconsidered several of the Draft's key provisions with a view to preparing a revised text for second and third reading. This reconsideration has been spurred by severe criticism leveled by academia and NGOs against the original text of the Draft Law, and by an undisclosed legal opinion issued by the Knesset legal division questioning the constitutionality of the draft legislation, *inter alia,* in light of its potential incompatibility with international humanitarian law. As explained in volume 3 of the Yearbook, the first reading of the Draft Law, which passed in the Knesset on 21 June 2000,[309] authorized the Israel Defense Force (IDF) Chief of Staff to order the detention of members of enemy organizations, not entitled to POW status, for the entire duration of the hostilities.

The main changes upon which the Committee members seemed to agree were a change in the law's title to the 'Incarceration of Unlawful Combatants Law' and the introduction of a 'personal risk' element into the grounds for detention, i.e., a requirement that the detaining authorities should demonstrate that the detained individual threatens the security of the State of Israel. However, this element would be subject to a refutable presumption that membership in a force perpetrating hostile acts against the State of Israel, which has been designated by the Minister of Defense as such, or the fact that a person actually participated in hostile acts, would be considered as creating a security risk. The Committee then proceeded to prepare the Draft Law for passage in the Knesset in early-2002.

- Draft Law for the Punishment of Perpetrators of Conflict-Related Crimes and Their Families
- Draft Amendment of the Terror Prevention Ordinance (Deprivation of Insurance Benefits from Members of Terror Organization)

Two new draft bills, which seek to introduce new sanctions against terrorists and other perpetrators of nationally-motivated crimes, were presented during 2001 before the Knesset by private Members of Parliament. The first bill, the Draft Law for the Punishment of Perpetrators of Conflict-Related Crimes and Their Families (Legislative Amendments) 2001, seeks to reimpose the death penalty on murderers operating out of nationalistic motives (related to the Israeli-Arab conflict) and provides for the deprivation of certain health and social security benefits from all perpetrators of conflict-related crimes and their family members.[310] The second bill would withhold social security benefits from convicted and suspect terrorists (unless they are acquitted).[311]

YUVAL SHANY

309. 3 *YIHL* (2000) pp. 532-533.

310. Draft Law for the Punishment of Perpetrators of Conflict-Related Crimes and Their Families (Legislative Amendments, 2001 (presented on 17 December 2001).

311. Draft Amendment of the Terror Prevention Ordinance 1948 (Deprivation of Insurance Benefits from Members in Terror Organization), 2001 (presented on 28 March 2001).

ITALY[312]

Children

☛ Law No. 2 of 8 January 2001, abrogation of Article 3 of Law No. 191 of 31 May 1975, regarding conscription of minors [www.parlamento.it//leg/ldl/sldlelenco/012001ordcron.htm]

With this Act, the Italian Parliament removed from domestic law the possibility of recruitment of minors.

Before this law entered into force, Italy was one of only 49 countries in the world that permitted a minor to join the military. Article 3 of Law No. 191 of 31 May 1975 lowered the minimum age of compulsory military service to 17 years. Law No. 2 of 2001 abrogated that provision, thus eliminating the possibility of the presence of minors in the military. The importance of the law in question is predominantly political as, in Italy, under Law No. 331 of 2000, compulsory military service was abolished for men born after January 1985 anyway.

GIULIANO SALBERINI[313]

Landmines

☛ Law No. 58 of 7 March 2001 concerning the Institution of the Fund for humanitarian mine clearance. Published in the Italian Official Journal (Gazzetta Ufficiale della Repubblica italiana) of 20 March 2001, No. 66 [http://www.parlamento.it/parlam/leggi/010581.htm]

The Italian Parliament, by Law No. 58 of 7 March 2001, created a fund to finance the clearing of landmines and the social recovery of their victims.

The Fund aims to support programs for the elimination of landmines, including educational campaigns on the presence of mines and the reduction of their associated risks; census, mapping and demarcation of the mined fields; care of the victims, including psycho-physical and social-economic rehabilitation; promoting the development of the communities that live with the presence of mines; training local operators in mine clearance; supporting acquisition and transfer of the relevant clearance technology; and, finally, promotion of campaigns against the use of landmines.[314]

The Law establishes, moreover, that the programs of humanitarian mine clearance, financed by the Fund, must be carried out in conformity with three main criteria: the participation of the population involved; the integration of the activity into plans for the reconstruction and development of the affected areas; the performance of the humanitarian action in a spirit of solidarity with the people involved.

Law No. 58 of 2001 establishes that the Fund will be endowed with about 15 million euro

312. Information and commentaries by Professor Sergio Marchisio and the team of researchers at the Institute for Legal International Studies, National Research Council (CNR), Rome.

313. Giuliano Salberini is a researcher at the Institute for Legal International Studies, National Research Council (CNR), Rome.

314. See the Guidelines approved on July 1999 by the Italian Committee for humanitarian actions against anti-personnel landmines (*Le azioni umanitarie contro le mine antipersona nell'ambito della cooperazione internazionale dell'Italia. Linee-guida*, Roma, 14 luglio 1999). http://www.esteri.it/polestera/cooperaz/quadro/mina.htm.

for the first three years.[315] Those resources could be used also for urgent interventions and for activities of environmental decontamination in territories affected by recent armed conflicts (such as the Balkans). In addition to public resources, the Law also provides for the acceptance of financial contributions from international organisations and private donations only in support of the purposes the Fund pursues.

VALENTINA DELLA FINA[316]

Depleted Uranium

- Reports of the Ministerial Commission of 19 March 2001 and 28 May 2001 on the use of depleted uranium during military operations in Bosnia and Kosovo [http://www.difesa.it/approfondimenti/pdf/relazione_preliminare.pdf http://www.difesa.it/approfondimenti/pdf/seconda_relazione.pdf]

Following the suspicious deaths of Italian soldiers who participated in the NATO operations in Bosnia and Kosovo, the Italian Ministry of Defence, by a decree of 22 December 2000, instituted a Commission of Enquiry to verify all medical-scientific aspects of the cases of pathological tumours found in Italian military personnel deployed there.

The technical committee worked to establish the incidence of pathological tumours amongst military personnel who had served at least one tour of duty in Bosnia and/or Kosovo between December 1995 and January 2001 and compare the data with that contained in the various national Italian Registers of Tumours.

The aim of the enquiry was to establish whether there was a connection between the depleted uranium munitions used in the area and the pathologies found in some subjects and to determine the chances of identifying the different aetiologies of the pathologies.

The committee was concerned with 28 cases of confirmed diagnoses and with 58 cases where there existed suspect pathologies. This limitation was imposed by the Minister of Defence who wished to limit research to those cases already found.

On 19 March 2001, the committee produced its preliminary report on the incidence of neoplastic malignancies among soldiers deployed in Bosnia and Kosovo.

The report excluded a link between lymphomas and depleted uranium. However, it noted a 'not significant' increase in the number of cases of Hodgkin's lymphoma and acute lymphatic leukaemia, necessitating further investigation with the aim of confirming results and preparing a new report by May.

On 28 May 2001, the Committee presented a second report containing revised data and the results of a sample analysis of the soldiers to establish the effects of exposure to depleted uranium.

The conclusions of the second report confirmed that the incidence of tumoral pathologies was less than expected. It also affirmed, however, that there was a statistically significant excess of cases of Hodgkins's lymphoma. The committee requested to be allowed to conduct further investigations. The Ministry authorized the continuation of the enquiry, whose final report is expected during 2002.

---

315. In 2001, 2.5 million euros were donated to victims' assistance programs in Afghanistan.

316. Valentina Della Fina is a researcher at the Institute for International Legal Studies, National Research Council (CNR), Rome.

On the basis of this report, it should be possible to evaluate the Italian situation and the government will be able to decide on its position at the international level.

Currently, the report excludes a direct causal link between the onset of tumoral pathologies and the use of weapons containing depleted uranium.

It should be noted that the work of the Ministerial Commission was heavily criticized by the Associazione nazionale assistenza vittime arruolate nelle forze armate e famiglie dei caduti, which denounced the results as unreliable. The statistical validity of the revelations was denied and the association complained of the undue influence of the Minister of Defence on some choices relating to the sample, which might render the report unobjective.

GIULIANO SALBERINI[317]

Peacekeeping

- Decree-Law No. 294 of 19 July 2001 entitled 'Extension of the Italian military participation in international peace missions' [www.parlamento.it/leg/ldl/sldlelenco072001ordcron.htm]
- Law No. 339 of 28 August 2001 concerning the Italian participation in Operation 'Essential Harvest' [in the Former Yugoslav Republic of Macedonia]. Published in the Italian Official Journal [*Gazzetta Ufficiale della Repubblica italiana*] No. 201 of 30 August 2001 [www. parlamento.it/parlam/leggi/013391.htm]
- Decree-Law No. 348 of 18 September 2001 setting 'Urgent measures for the Italian military participation in the International Peace-Keeping Mission in Macedonia' [www.parlamento.it/leg/ldl/sldlelenco092001ordcron.htm]
- Law No. 406 of 16 November 2001 concerning the Italian participation in Operation 'Amber Fox' [in the Former Yugoslav Republic of Macedonia]. Published in the Italian Official Journal [*Gazzetta Ufficiale della Repubblica italiana*] No. 268 of 17 November 2001 [www. parlamento.it/parlam/leggi/014061.htm]
- Decree-Law No. 451 of 28 December 2001. Published in the Italian Official Journal [*Gazzetta Ufficiale della Repubblica italiana*] No. 301 of 29 December 2001 [www.parlamento.it/leg/ldl/sldlelenco122001ordcron.htm]

Following the signature of the Ohrid Peace Agreement between the Macedonian Government and the Albanian Liberation Army (NLA) on 13 August 2001, which provided for a ceasefire and decided the dissolution of the NLA, NATO agreed, at the request of the Macedonian authorities, to deploy a multinational force in charge of collecting and destroy NLA's weapons on 22 August (effectively started on 27 August).

On 29 June 2001, the North Atlantic Council approved the operational plan named 'Essential Harvest'. On 22 August, the Task Force Harvest (THF) was constituted, with the participation of 13 states. The Operation began on 27 August and ended on 6 October 2001.

The Italian participation, with a personnel of 700 military units, was authorised by Law No. 339 of 28 August 2001, which embodied Decree-Law No. 294 of 19 July 2001 entitled: 'Extension of the Italian military participation in international peace missions'.

The TFH's intervention did not envisage military actions involving fighting other than in

317. Giuliano Salberini is a researcher at the Institute for Legal International Studies, National Research Council (CNR), Rome.

case of self-defence, necessity to protect the contingent (force protection) and when the use of force is essential to the accomplishment of the mission (mission accomplishment).

Accordingly, the application of the Military Penal Code of Peace to the Italian personnel operating in the TFH was therefore established, in accordance with Italian practice relating to participation in peacekeeping operations.

The operation was carried out, in fact, in a non-hostile environment, in which the parties were engaged to achieve a peaceful solution of the crisis.

The Italian participation in the new Mission called 'Amber Fox' was authorised by Decree-Law No. 348 of 18 September 2001 setting 'Urgent measures for the Italian military participation in the International Peace-Keeping Mission in Macedonia', which was embodied by Law No. 406 of 16 November 2001. Article 1 of such Law authorised, starting from 23 August 2001 and until 31 December 2001, the participation of a military contingent in the Peace Operation in Macedonia.

The Italian participation in the Task Force Fox was further extended until 31 March 2002, by Decree-Law No. 451 of 28 December 2001, setting urgent provisions for the extension of the Italian participation in international military operations. Article 1 of the above-mentioned Decree-Law establishes the application of the Military Penal Code of War to the Italian military personnel participating in peace operations in Macedonia. In fact, the task of each national contingent taking part in Amber Fox was, basically, to carry out 'evacuation operations' of the international observers in case of threat and to ensure the Force protection.

To accomplish its mandate, Task Force Fox was organised in several operative units, such as the extraction forces, with the task of intervening in case of danger for the members of the international organisations and to rescue these personnel, including by the use of military force.

In legislative sitting, during the process of conversion into law of Decree-Law No. 451 of 2001, by means of a parliamentary amendment of the draft law (Law No. 15 of 27 February 2002), it was specified that, for the purpose of the military criminal law of war, an armed conflict is 'the conflict in which at least one of the parties makes a protracted and militarily organised use of arms against the other party, with the purpose to carry out military operations'.[318]

Such reform of the Italian Penal Code of War was motivated by the participation of Italy in the multinational operation carried out in Afghanistan and in the so-called 'war against terrorism' which began at the end of 2001.

Therefore, it was decided in legislative sitting to emphasise the distinction between the Italian participation in peacekeeping operations (such as those conducted in FYROM and

318. Art. 2 of Law No. 15 of 27 February 2002 in fact provides that: 'Article 165 of the Military Penal Code of War as replaced by Art. 2, paragraph 1 (d) of Law No. 6 of 31 January 2002, is modified by adding the two following paragraphs: "for the purpose of the Military Criminal Law of War, an armed conflict is a conflict in which at least one of the parties makes a protracted and military organised use of arms against the other party for the conduct of military operations. Awaiting the issuing of an organic regulation of this subject, the provisions of such title are to be applied to the armed military operations carried out abroad by the Italian armed forces".'

Albania) and in enforcement operations. The latter presents different characters and issues, especially in relation to the use of force and its legal regulation.

NAZZARENA FERRARO[319]

Sanctions

☛ Law No. 415 of 27 November 2001, 'converting into law, with amendments, the law decree of 28 September, 2001, No. 353, with sanctioning provisions for violations of the measures adopted against the Afghan faction of the Taliban'. Published in the Italian Official Journal [*Gazzetta Ufficiale della Repubblica italiana*] No. 277 of 28 November 2001

On 27 November 2001, the Italian Parliament adopted Law No. 415 with sanctioning provisions for violations of the measures adopted against the Afghan faction of the Taliban. Law No. 415 was issued in order to bring Italian law in conformity with obligations imposed by EC Council Regulation No. 467/2001 adopted, in turn, to bring about Security Council resolution 1333 (2000) of 19 December 2000, by means of which the UN Security Council, acting under Chapter VII of the Charter of the United Nations, decided on sanctioning measures against the Taliban.

Law No. 415 imposes sanctions for the violation of the Council Regulation (Art. 1); it indicates the subjects bound to give information about the forbidden behaviour (Art. 2); it defines the practice for establishing and imposing sanctions (Art. 3); and it contains rules to bring about the Council Regulation No. 1334/2000 of 22 June 2000, concerning the export of products and technologies that can be also utilized for military purposes (Art. 4).

Among the above-mentioned provisions, those stating the sanctions framework are of particular interest.

Article 1(1) of the Law establishes that all the adopted acts violating the regulation are null and void. Then, the next paragraphs of Article 1 set both administrative and penal sanctions. On this subject, however, the Decree-Law issued by the Government provided only administrative sanctions, but during the conversion into Law by the Parliament, penal sanctions concerning the most serious cases were introduced. The firm engagement of Italy in fighting those governments supporting international terrorism deserves particular mention. Paragraph 2-*bis* of Article 1 provides that in case of violation of Article 4 of the regulation, concerning the supply of acetic anhydride, Article 250 of the penal code (trade with the enemy) shall be applied. Paragraph 2-ter of Article 1 decrees that in case of violation of the prohibition of technical advice, assistance or training related to military activities, as stated by Article 5 of the regulation, the penalty set forth in Article 247 of the penal code (war aiding and abetting) shall be applied.

The introduction of penal sanctions was criticised during the approval of the Law from two different points of view. The first opposition, of a systematic nature, criticised the introduction of penal sanctions into a regulation aiming at condemning, by means of administrative rules, wrong behaviour related to finance and trade.

The second opposition, of a substantial nature, prescribes that the two penal rules, as clearly shown, shall be applied in wartime only; that was not the situation with respect to the

---

319. Nazzarena Ferraro is a consultant at the Institute for International Legal Studies, National Research Council (CNR), Rome.

Taliban in Afghanistan.

Some considerations are necessary. Article 78 of the Italian Constitution provides that the resolution of a state of war is adopted by the two Chambers, while its declaration is made by the Head of the State (as established by Article 87(2) of the Italian Constitution). On the other hand, referring to the Constitution praxis, the preeminent publicists assert that the Constitution provisions related to the state of war shall not be applied to contemporary wars, whose nature comes from the international law and from the Charter of the United Nations.[320]

In the Parliament praxis, in order for the Italian forces to take part in the operations undertaken or authorized by the UN, the government shall be empowered by the Parliament; in this case, it issues atypical acts, usually resolutions.

This is not the place to discuss if a favourable pronouncement by the Parliament concerning Italian participation in military operations underUN aegis or with its permission implies the beginning of a state of war.[321] Yet, referring to Law No. 415, one can consider the provision of regulations that can be applied in wartime as scarcely convincing. This Law was in fact adopted to permit Italy to comply with EU Council regulation No. 467/2001 and in particular with the obligations arising from UN Security Council resolution 1333/2000. As explicitly affirmed in this resolution, this resolution was enacted by the UN Security Council under Chapter VII of the UN Charter and can be considered as a decision issued pursuant to Article 41 of the Charter. This disposition permits the Security Council to impose on the Member States the adoption of measures not involving the use of armed force.

With regard to this disposition, war actions have to be avoided, except when the Security Council expressly states that military measures shall be adopted for the compulsory application of economic sanctions[322] (that is not the case regarding the resolution in point). On the basis of Article 41 of the Charter, states are called to apply sanctioning measures of a commercial, financial and diplomatic, but not military, nature. Thus it is difficult to assert that the simple adoption of Security Council resolution 1333/2000 has precipitated an international armed conflict and the application of the laws of war.

The delay related to the adoption of Law No. 415 is in favour of the Italian legislator's choice of recourse to provisions applicable in wartime. More than eight months had elapsed since the issue of the UE regulation and two years since the issuance of Security Council resolution 1333/2000. This delay caused the Italian Law to enter into force in a completely changed international context. During the approbation of the Italian Law, the terrorist attack

---

320. See R. Pannain, 'Personalità dello Stato (disposizioni comuni ai delitti contro la personalità dello Stato e delitti complementari)', XII *Novissimo Digesto Italiano* (1976) pp. 1132-; G.Ferrari, 'Stato di guerra (diritto costituzionale)', XIX *Enciclopedia giuridica* (1970) pp. 816; P.G.Grasso, 'Guerra (disciplina costituzionale della guerra)', XV *Enciclopedia Giuridica Treccani* (1989) p. 1; P.Pinna, 'Guerra (stato di)', in *Digesto delle Discipline Pubblicistiche*, p. 50; D.Cabras, *Il controllo parlamentare nazionale nell'impiego delle truppe impegnate in missioni di pace*, in N.Ronzitti,*(a cura di), Comando e controllo nelle forze armate di pace e nelle coalizioni militari* (Milano, Franco Angeli 1999) p. 61.

321. Law No. 6 of 31 January 2002 concerning the Italian participation in Operation Enduring Freedom removed certain doubts regarding this subject. Art. 2(*d*), modified Art. 165 of the Penal Code of War by applying the rules relating to the crimes against the law and uses of war 'in any case of armed conflict, independently from the declaration of a state of war'. See N. Ronzitti, 'Una legge organica per l'invio di corpi all'estero?', in *Rivista di diritto internazionale* (2002) p. 139.

322. See S. Marchisio, *L'ONU, Il diritto delle Nazioni Unite* (Bologna, Il Mulino 2000) p. 235.

of 11 September 2001 against the World Trade Centre took place, and resolution 1368/2001 of 12 September 2001, by which the Security Council reasserted the right to both individual and collective self-defence to fight international terrorism, was adopted. On 7 November 2001, the Italian Chamber of Deputies adopted a resolution aiming at supporting the Italian intervention in Operation *Enduring Freedom* against the Taliban in Afghanistan.[323]

Recalling the mentioned acts, the Italian legislator had to refer to the above-cited Acts that would provide a stronger legal basis for the reference to the penal rules of Law No. 415 that can be applied in wartime.

FABIO RASPADORI[324]

Military Cooperation in International Operations

- ☛ Decree-law No. 421 of 1 December 2001, concerning urgent dispositions for the participation of military staff in the multifunctional operation called 'Enduring Freedom'. Published in the Italian Official Journal [*Gazzetta Ufficiale della Repubblica italiana*] No. 282 of 4 December 2001
- ☛ Law No. 6 of 31 January 2002, 'Conversion in law, with modifications, of Decree-law No. 421 of 1 December 2001, concerning urgent dispositions for the participation of military staff in the multifunctional operation called 'Enduring Freedom'. Amendments to the Military Penal Code of War, approved by Royal Decree No. 303 of 20 February 1941. Published in the Italian Official Journal [*Gazzetta Ufficiale della Repubblica italiana*] No. 28 of 2 February 2002 [http://www.parlamento.it/parlam/leggi/020061.htm]

Currently, the Italian legal system lacks a comprehensive law governing military contingents engaged in international missions abroad. In particular, the question whether to apply the Military Penal Code of Peace or the Military Penal Code of War (both approved by Royal Decree No. 303 of 20 February 1941) to such missions is still open. In fact, Article 9 of the Military Penal Code of War states that the Code is to be applied not only in cases of war but also in peace time for contingents engaged in military operations abroad.

Italian practice, starting in the early-1980s with Italy's participation in the multinational Force in Lebanon, was orientated, however, toward the application of the Military Penal Code of Peace for military contingents that take part in peacekeeping operations of the United Nations or regional organisations such as NATO. The legislator generally inserted a specific norm into the law concerning the individual mission, with the aim of avoiding the application of the Military Penal Code of War.

With Decree-Law No. 421 of 1 December 2001, the Italian Government established that the Military Penal Code of War applies to military contingents engaged in the operation for the restoration and maintenance of international law in Afghanistan, i.e., Operation Enduring Freedom.[325] The change in practice followed for this operation is justified by the

---

323. Camera dei deputati, Atti parlamentari, Seduta n. 57 del 7/11/2001, Allegato A (Sezione 1 – Risoluzioni), comunicazioni del Governo sull'impiego di contingenti militari italiani all'estero in relazione alla crisi internazionale in atto, p. 7.

324. Associate Professor of European Union Law at Perugia University, Faculty of Political Sciences.

325. Operation Enduring Freedom is the military response to the 11 September 2001 terrorist attacks on the United States. The objectives of the Operation, which commenced on 7 October 2001, included the destruction of terrorist training camps and infrastructure in Afghanistan, the capture of Al-

need to guarantee a greater protection for prisoners of war and the civilian population, since the operation involves the use of armed force.

The Law converting Decree-Law No. 421 of 1 December 2001 (Law No. 6 of 31 January 2002) introduced some important amendments to the Military Penal Code of War, in compliance with obligations deriving from the 1949 Geneva Conventions and the Additional Protocols of 1977.[326]

It should be noted that Law No. 6 of 2001 does not have the form of a temporary legislative provision; according to Article 9, the modifications to the Code have been introduced on a permanent basis 'until such time as a new organic law on military penal matter shall come into effect'.

In particular, Article 9(1) of the Code has been amended with the introduction of the adjective 'armed' to military operations. The Military Penal Code of War applies, therefore, also in time of peace, 'to contingents engaged in armed military operations abroad'. Such specification aims to limit the application of military penal law to those operations involving the use of armed force, and exclude those characterised by purely humanitarian goals.

In consideration of modern technologies, a new paragraph has been inserted into Article 9 allowing for the extension of the Code's regulations to command, control and support staff, whether in Italy or abroad, from the moment of notification of duty, and limited to those actions committed while on duty.

In order to make the Code conform to international humanitarian law, Article 165 has also been modified, eliminating the two conditions (reciprocity and appropriate action by the commander-in-chief) to which disciplinary actions on the military staff were subordinated. The same Article then specifies that Title IV of the Code, concerning breaches of the laws and customs of war, shall be applied in any case 'of armed conflict, independently from the declaration of the state of war'.

Such reformulation reflects the evolution of the international law of war and the fact that the term 'war' has been replaced by the expression 'armed conflict'; a broader notion. The modification, moreover, takes into account the most recent developments of international criminal law and the circumstance that war crimes can also be committed in cases of non-international armed conflicts.

In addition, Article 184*bis* concerns the punishment of soldiers who breach the norms 'on international conflicts' prohibiting the capture of hostages. With regard to this Article, it must be noted that international humanitarian law extends the prohibition to cases of non-international conflict as well. Therefore, the new provision of the Code needs further modification.

It is noteworthy that Article 185*bis* introduces the prohibition of acts of torture and other cruel treatment, illegal transfers and all other acts forbidden by international conventions. These include the performance of biological experiments or medical treatment that are not justified by their state of health, on prisoners of war, civilians or other persons protected by the same Conventions. Finally, the Law, in Article 2(h) repealed a series of regulations of

Qaeda leaders and the cessation of their terrorist activities. The Italian participation in the Operation was approved by the Parliament on 7 November 2001, after a debate at the Chamber of Deputies and at the Senate. The Security Council, in Resolution No. 1368 (2001) of 12 September 2001, affirmed that the terrorist attacks were a 'threat to international peace and security' and called on 'all States to work together urgently to bring to justice the perpetrators, organisers and sponsors of these terrorist attacks'.

326. Italy ratified the 1949 Geneva Conventions by Law No. 1739 of 27 October 1951, and the Additional Protocols of 1977 by Law No. 438 of 4 June 1982.

the Code which conflicted with international humanitarian law, such as Article 183 which permitted, in certain cases, the immediate execution of those who breached the laws and the customs of war as well as any individual caught in the act of espionage.

VALENTINA DELLA FINA[327]

Cases

☛ Tribunal of Milan Judge for the Preliminary Hearing, Decree of dismissal in proceedings against *Franco Carlini*, 21 March 2001

This decree states the dismissal of criminal proceedings against Major Franco Carlini, commanding officer of the Italian detachment at Mogadishu during the IBIS II Mission,[328] charged, pursuant to Articles 519, 575 and 576(5) of the Italian Penal Code, with the rape and murder of a Somali child, presumed killed in the Italian embassy on 6 March 1994.

Proceedings against Major Carlini were initiated by the Public Prosecutor's office of Milan on 1 June 1997 as a consequence of accusations made by Abdi Hassan, a former interpreter to the Italian contingent in Somalia, present when the event was presumed to have occurred and who, for these accusations, was himself charged with false allegations to the detriment of the Major. Pre-trial investigations carried out by the Public Prosecutor ended inconclusively, due to the numerous difficulties that emerged during the collection of evidence, which was hampered not only by the almost total lack of cooperation from the Somalian judicial authorities but also because of the Italian military authorities' negligence in promptly sending the documents which the Italian magistrates had requested. In light of the scanty evidence collected, insufficient to request the committal for trial of the accused soldier, the Public Prosecutor, on 7 September 1999, presented to the Judge for the Preliminary Hearing a request for dismissal of the case which, however, did not include a full discharge of the parties concerned. For this reason, Major Carlini's defence opposed the request for dismissal as it had been formulated and asked that the decree of dismissal state the absolute groundlessness of the accusation so that all suspicions surrounding the Major be permanently laid to rest. At the same time, Major Carlini's attorney asked that the Somali interpreter be committed for trial for false allegations.

Following the filing of the petition by Carlini's defence, the Judge for the Preliminary Hearing, in an order dated 28 April 2000, rejected the request for dismissal presented by the Public Prosecutor on 7 September 1999 and ordered further investigation. The Judge for the Preliminary Hearing ordered not only the collection of all of SISMI's (Information and Military Security Service) documentation on this matter-as this agency is in charge of military security and counter-intelligence feedback gathering-but also a new hearing involving the soldiers present at the embassy at the time of the presumed crime who were considered to be important witnesses for the verification of truthfulness of the events in question.[329]

---

327. Valentina Della Fina is a researcher at the Institute for International Legal Studies, National Research Council (CNR), Rome.

328. In this regard, one must remember that Italy took part in two successive missions, 'IBIS I' and 'IBIS II', in the United Nations Operations in Somalia, UNOSOM I and UNOSOM II, established, respectively, by Security Council Resolutions 751 (1992) and 814 (1993).

329. See Tribunal of Milan, Judge for the Preliminary Hearing, *Order rejecting the request of dismissal and, at the same time, requesting further investigations*, 28 April 2000. Not published.

Following the supplemental investigation and in light of the new evidence collected, the Judge for the Preliminary Hearing ordered the complete dismissal of proceedings against Major Carlini. The grounds for the decree in question provide that, on the basis of the documentation and evidence collected, the Somali interpreter's charges, made long after the event and probably motivated by interest or grudge, are not reliable and that the events described seem to be baseless and unsubstantiated by any facts whatsoever.

Nevertheless, the Judge for the Preliminary Hearing rejected the defence's petition to proceed against the interpreter for the crime of false allegations, pursuant to Article 368(2) of the Italian Penal Code, because of the lack of legal conditions for the commencement of the criminal action stated by Article 10 of the above-mentioned code. The Judge did in fact emphasize that, according to this article, the crime of false allegations committed abroad by a foreigner against an Italian citizen can be prosecuted in Italy, but only on two conditions: the first is the petition by the victim, contained, in this case, in the first memoranda and declarations of Major Carlini; the second condition requires that the person indicted for the crime committed abroad be within the state's borders. This last condition is not satisfied, as the interpreter is not at present within the state's territory nor indeed has he ever been on Italian soil.

Therefore, on the basis of the present decree issued by the Tribunal, proceedings ended with a full dismissal, thus overcoming the impasse which distinguished the first request for dismissal by the Public Prosecutor and putting an end to the 'dubious formula' in which the proceedings would have otherwise terminated.

ROSA DINUZZI[330]

☛ Military Court of Appeal of Verona, Judgement No. 252, 18 October 2001, in proceedings against *Michael Seifert*

This judgement of the Military Court of Appeal of Verona confirmed the sentence of life imprisonment delivered on 24 November 2000 by the Military Tribunal of Verona against Michael Seifert, charged with acts of violence and murder against civilian enemies according to Articles 81(2), 110, 575, 577(3), 61(4) of the Italian Penal Code and Articles 13, 185 of the Italian Military Penal Code of War.

Seifert, convicted *in absentia*, was accused of killing 18 Italian prisoners between December 1944 and April 1945, while he was on active service in the German Armed Forces as a guard at the Bolzano concentration camp during the state of war between Italy and Germany.

The Court of Appeal denied all the defence's motions, which raised doubts and objections, particularly on procedural points. In this regard, the defence alleged the lack of jurisdiction of the Italian military judge, affirming that Seifert, as a member of the S.D. (*Sicherheitsdienst*) and not of the Nazi Special Corps 'SS' (*Schutz-Staffeln*), did not have military status and that the crimes had been committed only for reasons of politics or racial persecution and that these reasons were in no way related to the war. According to the defence, therefore, of which Seifert was accused, being crimes committed by a civilian in

330. Rosa Dinuzzi is a consultant at the Institute for International Legal Studies, National Research Council (CNR), Rome.

wartime, are not punishable under Article 185 of the Military Penal Code of War.[331] Consequently, the Court having jurisdiction over them would be the ordinary judge, and in this case, the Bolzano Court of Assizes.

The Court of Appeal, on the contrary, sharing the observations made on this point by the Military Tribunal of Verona, reaffirmed the defendant's military status, as not only a member of an organized corps in the German armed forces, notorious as a branch of the 'SS', but also as being assigned to a territory under German occupation (*the Alpenvorland*) and conducting an activity closely linked to the military goals of the Third Reich.

That being stated, the Court of Appeal, on the basis of current legislation[332] and following the well-established caselaw of the Court of Cassation,[333] reaffirmed the jurisdiction of Italian military tribunals, in peacetime, over crimes against the rules and conventions of war committed in wartime by members of the enemy armed forces against the Italian state or Italian citizens.

Furthermore, Seifert's defence alleged the voidness of his service abroad, as regulated by Article 169(3) of the Italian Criminal Procedural Code,[334] since it had been drawn up in English and not, as provided for by Article 63 of the supplemental rules of the Criminal Procedural Code, in the official language of defendant's birth state (Ukraine, in this case). In this context, the defence also alleged the violation of the defendant's right to a fair trial, guaranteed by Article 6 of the European Convention of Human Rights.

The Court of Appeal denied this plea, stating that the *ratio* of the rules referred to by Seifert's defence is to assure that the accused be promptly informed, in a language which he understands and in detail, of the nature and cause of the accusations made against him. According to the Court of Appeal, the fact that the accused had lived for 40 years in Canada, an Anglophone country, where he had based his business, is well-grounded evidence that the act, translated into English, gave the defendant specific knowledge of the nature of the crime which the above-mentioned rules aim to assure, and therefore, that no rights had been infringed.

The Court of Appeal also refused to accept the generic mitigating circumstances, provided for by Article 62 *bis* of the Italian Penal Code, which had already been denied by the Tribunal of Verona, and which would have brought about the discharge of the accused under the statute of limitations.[335] The Tribunal of Verona explained its decision for not

---

331. See Art. 185(1) of the current Military Penal Code of War, which punishes 'the serviceman who unnecessarily or, in any case, unjustifiably, for motives not extraneous to war, commits acts of violence against civilian enemies, who are not involved in military operations'.

332. See Legislative Decree No. 144, 21 March 1946, which laid down the regulations on the transition from the application of wartime military penal law to peacetime military penal law. In particular, Art. 6 assigned temporary jurisdiction over military crimes to peacetime military tribunals according to the military penal code of war, as well as over crimes against the rules and conventions of war committed in wartime by members of the enemy armed forces.

333. See Court of Cassation, Criminal Section I, Judgment of 10 February 1997, 'Conflict of jurisdiction in the Priebke case', in *La Giustizia Penale* (1998), Vol. III, p. 148.

334. It is an act notified by the judge to the defendant living abroad which specifies the proceeding judge, the crime which the defendant is accused of, the date when and place where it was presumably committed and the request to declare or choose domicile in the state's territory.

335. In particular, Seifert's defence alleged, as generic mitigating circumstances, the amount of time that had passed since the event without his committing new crimes and the defendant's advanced age.

having granted mitigating circumstances by comparing their marginal importance to the extraordinarily hideous crimes committed by Seifert, who was accused of cruelty to and torture of individuals and of having acted with premeditation under Articles 577(3) and 61(4) of the Italian Penal Code. On this point, the Court of Appeal reaffirmed the observations made by the Tribunal of Verona and emphasized once again the accused's deplorable criminal persistence in planning the murders and his absolute lack of respect not only for his victims but also for life and humanity in general. In addition, in the opinion of the Court of Appeal, no relevance could be given to the youthfulness of the accused at the time the crimes occurred, when the incredible criminal capacity in committing them was taken into consideration.

The Court of Appeal also rejected a petition filed by the defence to grant the accused amnesty in accordance with the D.P.R. (Presidential Decree) No. 332 of 4 June 1966. The Court of Appeal specified that the military crime Seifert is accused of is punishable with life imprisonment and is therefore not regulated by Article 1 of the aforesaid decree, which provides that the amnesty may be granted 'only for those crimes punished by a custodial sentence with a maximum term of not more than three years'.

ROSA DINUZZI[336]

JAPAN[337]

Counter-terrorism

☛ Anti-Terrorism Special Measures Law (Law No. 113 of 2 November 2001). Published in Japanese Official Gazette [*kanpou*], No. 3234 of 2 November 2001, pp. 4-6

This new law allows the Self-Defense Forces (SDF) to conduct: (1) rear-area logistic support for US-led forces; (2) search and rescue operations for downed pilots and other US military personnel in need of assistance; and (3) provide humanitarian relief for refugees, including medical care and the transport of emergency supplies (tents and blankets). This law limits the area of SDF support operations for the US-led coalition to non-combat areas. During the operations, SDF personnel can use weapons to protect not only themselves but also those under their care, such as refugees and wounded soldiers. The SDF troops can operate anywhere as long as the assisted nation consents.

This is the first law since World War II that allows SDF troops to be sent overseas during wartime. There was a strong argument that providing logistic support to combat operations is tantamount to engaging in collective defense. As the government has long interpreted the Constitution as banning the nation from engaging in collective defense, the constitutional validity of this law had been discussed in the Diet. The Cabinet's interpretation passed in the Diet was that those logistic support operations in non-combat areas are not involved in the use of force and do not violate the Constitution. The legislation expires in two years but can be extended.

---

336. Rosa Dinuzzi is a consultant at the Institute for International Legal Studies, National Research Council (CNR), Rome.

337. Information and commentaries provided by Professor Hideyuki Kasutani, Professor of International Law, Setsunan University, Japan, and Professor Seigo Iwamoto, Professor of International Law, Suzuka International University, Japan.

On 9 November 2001, two Maritime Self-Defense Force destroyers and a supply ship left Japan for an intelligence-gathering mission in the Indian Ocean as part of Japan's non-combat support of the US-led attacks on Afghanistan. According to the basic plan approved by the Cabinet under the law, Japan sent a destroyer, a supply ship and a minesweeper tender to the Indian Ocean for logistic support on 25 November.

The minesweeper tender carried relief supplies (tents and blankets) for Afghan refugees to the port of Karachi in Pakistan and returned to Japan on 31 December. Another five ships will continue the operations (the intelligence gathering, provision of fuel and other supplies) in the Indian Ocean until 31 March 2002.

☛ Amendment to the Self-Defense Forces Law, Law No. 165 of 1954 (Law No. 115 of 2 November 2001). Published in Japanese Official Gazette [*kanpou*], No. 3234 of 2 November 2001, pp. 7-8

This revised law allows SDF units to guard US bases in Japan and SDF facilities, including SDF barracks, ports and airfields, when terrorist attacks against them are anticipated. The amendment adds the new SDF mission of intelligence gathering, on the order of internal security operations. SDF personnel can use weapons in those guarding and intelligence gathering operations. Before the revision, SDF personnel could only use arms to protect themselves, weapons, ammunition, vehicles and aircraft.

☛ Amendment to the Japan Coast Guard Law, Law No. 28 of 27 April 1948 (Law No. 114 of 2 November 2001). Published in Japanese Official Gazette [*kanpou*], No. 3234 of 2 November 2001), pp. 6-7

In March 1999, two suspicious ships, thought to be from North Korea, turned up in Japanese territorial waters then fled, pursued by Japanese Coast Guard and Maritime Self-Defense Force vessels. At that time, in order to stop the suspicious ships, the Japanese patrol vessels could only use weapons for firing warning shots without harm, except to protect themselves (legitimate self-defense). Japanese vessels were in fact unable to fire shots directly at them. Therefore, the amendment to the Japan Coast Guard Law makes it possible for Japanese patrol vessels to fire direct warning shots, even if that would cause harm, if the ships are in Japan's territorial waters and are suspected of involvement in a serious crime.

☛ Legislation pursuant to the ratification of Japan's ratification of the 1997 International Convention for the Suppression of Terrorist Bombings adopted on 15 December 1997 and enacted on 23 May 2001 (Treaty No. 10 of 21 November 2001). Published in Japanese Official Gazette [*kanpou*], No. 3247 of 21 November 2001, pp. 3-13

In line with this treaty, Japan revised seven domestic laws, including those covering the handling of explosives, chemical weapons and nuclear reactors.

Peacekeeping

☛ Amendment to the International Peace Cooperation Law, Law No. 79 of 19 June 1992 (Law No. 157 of 14 December 2001). Published in Japanese Official Gazette [*kanpou*], No. 3263 of 14 December 2001, p. 4

Since 1992, the Self Defense Forces have taken part in UN peacekeeping operations, such as building infrastructure, providing transportation and medical support. The amendment lifts a ban on SDF participation in activities such as monitoring ceasefires, disarming local forces, patrolling demilitarized zones, inspecting the transport of weapons, and collecting and disposing of abandoned weapons.

The amendment also eases restrictions on the use of weapons by SDF units during peacekeeping missions. The 1992 law only allowed SDF personnel to use weapons to protect themselves but the amendment allows them to use weapons to protect those 'under their control', such as troops from other countries, refugees, government officials and personnel from the United Nations and other international organizations. Furthermore, the amendment lifts a ban on the application of Article 95 of the SDF law, which stipulates that weapons may be used to protect weapons stores.

☛ Amendment to the Law concerning the dispatch of SDF personnel to international organizations, Law No. 122 of 1995 (Law No. 125 of 28 November 2001). Published in Japanese Official Gazette [*kanpou*], Extra No. 252 of 28 November 2001, pp. 6-7

The revision allows SDF personnel to be dispatched to the United Nations Secretariat, especially its peacekeeping division.

Ongoing Cases

☛ The *Kanpu ex-'comfort women's* case (*Korean ex-'comfort women'* v. *Japanese Government*).[338] Hiroshima High Court, Judgment of 29 March 2001, *Hanrei Jiho*, No. 1759, pp. 42-58

On 29 March 2001, the Hiroshima High Court overturned a Yamaguchi District Court ruling of 27 April 1998 that had ordered the government to pay 300,000 yen each to three former sex slaves for its failure to introduce a law on state compensation. The court, however, did not award any compensation to seven forced laborers, saying that it was not such a major human rights violation. The 1998 ruling was the only one to have ordered compensation in the approximately ten similar suits being heard in Japan.

The plaintiffs had appealed the ruling as the amount of compensation was far below what they are seeking. They had sought a total of 396 million yen in damages from the Japanese government and had been also demanding a public apology for their physical and mental suffering during the war.

The Japanese government had also appealed the case, arguing that it is not the government's duty to make public apologies and offer compensation under the Constitution.[339] The government maintains issues concerning war-related compensation have been settled through government treaties signed after World War II.

The Court rejected the plaintiffs' appeal, but upheld the Japanese government's appeal. The Court held that the frustration of the plaintiffs at the government's failure to enact a law

---

338. See 3 *YIHL* (2000) p. 543.

339. The plaintiffs had argued that the Japanese government is obliged to enact a law to compensate the war victims under the provisions of the Constitution, such as the preamble, Arts. 9, 13, 14, 17, 29(1), 29(3), 40 and 92(2).

to fully compensate victims of Japan's war effort can be imagined; however, the Constitution does not clearly state that the government is obligated to introduce such a law.

☛ The *Dutch Former POWs* case.[340] Tokyo High Court, Judgment of 11 October 2001, *Hanrei Jiho*, No. 1769, pp. 61-73

On 11 October 2001, the Tokyo High Court rejected an appeal by eight Dutch former prisoners of war, who sought 22,000 dollars each in compensation from the Japanese government for abuse they suffered at the hands of the former Imperial Japanese Army while interned in POW camps.

Plaintiffs claimed compensation on the ground that some members of the Japanese military abused plaintiffs in the camps during WWII in breach of international humanitarian law, especially Article 3 of the 1907 Hague Convention respecting the Laws and Customs of War on Land and as well as the 1929 Geneva Convention.

The plaintiffs had appealed a November 1998 ruling by the Tokyo District Court, which acknowledged that the plaintiffs had been abused but pointed out that Article 3 of the 1907 Hague Convention only clarifies the responsibilities of the aggressor nation to the victim nation.

The Tokyo High Court reaffirmed that Article 3 of the Hague Convention does not allow individuals to directly demand compensation from the state, but only admits the state responsibility of the offending state to the victim state. The Court also upheld the defendant's appeal that all rights by the Allied Powers (which did not include Holland) and their citizens to demand compensation from Japan were relinquished with the signing of the San Francisco Peace Treaty in September 1951 (Holland became a signatory to the treaty in June 1952).

Pending

☛ The *So Shinto* case,[341] in which plaintiffs' appeal was dismissed by the Tokyo High Court on 30 November 2000, is pending before the Supreme Court.

☛ The *Filipino* case,[342] in which plaintiffs' appeal was dismissed by the Tokyo High Court on 6 December 2000, is pending before the Supreme Court.

HIDEYUKI KASUTANI and SEIGO IWAMOTO

JORDAN

Pending

A proposal is being studied to amend the 1952 Penal Code on the basis of a draft submitted by the military judiciary in 1997 and providing for the repression of grave breaches of international humanitarian law.[343]

---

340. As to the Judgment of 30 November 1998 by the Tokyo District Court, see *Hanrei Taimuzu*, No. 991, pp. 262-277 and 2 *YIHL* (1999) pp. 389-390.

341. 2 *YIHL* (1999) pp. 543-544.

342. Ibid., p. 544.

343. ICRC Advisory Service, *National Implementation of International Humanitarian Law*: Biennial report 2000-2001 (Geneva, ICRC 2002) p. 56.

KAZAKHSTAN

The Emblem

☛ Law on the emblem and the distinctive sign of the armed forces medical service. Signed by the President on 14 December 2001. Entered into force on 20 December 2001 following its publication in the official gazette.

'The law provides for the withdrawal of the reservations relating to the use of the double emblem made by Kazakhstan when it succeeded to the 1949 Geneva Conventions, and for the use henceforth of the red crescent emblem as the sole distinctive sign by the armed forces medical service. The draft presidential decree prepared following the adoption of the law charges the government *inter alia* to draft a law on the Red Crescent Society of Kazakhstan and on the use and protection of the red crescent and red cross emblems, to be submitted to parliament in 2002.'[344]

Implementation and Dissemination

☛ National Seminar on the Implementation of IHL in Kazakstan, 19 April 2000

☛ Government Decree No. 1794 establishing the Interdepartmental Committtee for International Humanitarian Law, 1 December 2000

☛ Seminar for the members of the Interdepartmental Committee for International Humanitarian Law, 27 June 2001

A national seminar was held in Astana on 19 April 2000 with the aim of presenting the results of a study on the compatibility of national legislation with IHL. Organised by the Advisory Service of the ICRC and the Ministry of Foreign Affairs, it 'was attended was representatives of the relevant ministries, universities and the National Society. The participants adopted recommendations encouraging the authorities to establish a national structure for implementation, to revise the Penal Code and to translate the Geneva Conventions and their Additional Protocols into Kazakh.'

The Interdepartmental Committtee for International Humanitarian Law, established on 1 December 2000 'is in charge of drawing up proposals for the national implementation of IHL. Its priorities include penal law reform to provide for effective repression of war crimes, the adoption of comprehensive legislation on the use and protection of the red cross and red crescent emblems, the dissemination of humanitarian rules and the possibility of Kazakhstan's accession to other humanitarian law treaties.'

'Another seminar on the implementation of humanitarian law in Kazakhstan was held in Astana on 27 June 2001 for the members of the Interdepartmental Committee for International Humanitarian Law. The discussion focused on the major issues of concern to the Committee, namely the withdrawal of Kazakhstan's reservations to the 1949 Geneva Conventions relating to the use of the double emblem, the adoption of comprehensive legislation on the use and protection of the emblem, the incorporation in the Penal Code of a complete system for the repression of war crimes, the strengthening of dissemination and Kazakhstan's accession to major humanitarian law treaties, such as the Rome Statute of the International Criminal Code and the Ottawa Convention.'[345]

---

344. Ibid., p. 57.
345. Ibid.

KENYA[346]

Implementation and Dissemination

☛ Legal Notice No 489/2002 of 28 January 2002 establishing the National Committee on the Implementation of International Humanitarian Law. Published in *the Kenya Gazette* of 1 February 2002 p. 401

The National Committee on the Implementation of International Humanitarian Law (hereunder the 'Committee') was officially launched by the Attorney-General, Mr Amos Wako, on 5 October 2001. The appointments to the Committee were later published in Legal Notice No 489/2002. They are Julius Kandie (the Solicitor General of the Republic of Kenya, Chairman), Brigadier Titus K. Githiora, T.O. Nyangeri, Winnie Ngugi, N.E. Bodo, Dola Indidis, Jane Chokaa, Richard Wa mwenje, Maurice B. Otungar, Dr Mohamud Said, Alfred Langat, T. Mwenda Karani, Francis Masika, P.L.O. Lumumba, Beatrice Karago and Wabua Nzioka.

The main task of the Committee is to coordinate efforts by different government ministries, civil society organisations and the ICRC relating to the implementation of IHL in Kenya. According to Legal Notice No 489/2002, the specific terms of reference of the Committee are to:

— Advise the Government on international humanitarian law instruments that need to be ratified;

— Advise and assist on reporting obligations, and advise on administrative measures that need to be taken to harmonise domestic law with international obligations;

— To review the existing national legislation of relevance to international humanitarian law, and recommend amendments where necessary;

— To recommend adoption of new national legislation, as the Committee may deem necessary;

— To coordinate, monitor, evaluate, disseminate, and undertake or commission research on development in international humanitarian law and make appropriate recommendations to the Government.

The Committee held its inaugural meeting on 24 November 2001.

Education and Training

☛ Parliamentarians' Handbook. Published by ICRC & Inter-Parliamentary Union, both in Geneva

On the same day that the National Committee was launched (5 October 2001), the Handbook for Parliamentarians on Respect for International Humanitarian Law was launched in Kenya at the Serena Hotel, Nairobi. The handbook is a guide for Members of Parliament on frequently asked questions about IHL, and the need to harmonise domestic law with international humanitarian law. The occasion was attended by Dr Astrid Heiberg, President of the International Federation of Red Cross and Red Crescent Societies; Jacob Kellenberger, President of the ICRC; David Musila, Deputy Speaker of the Kenyan Parliament; David Sunkuli, Minister for Defence; and Amos Wako, Attorney-General.

---

346. Information and commentaries by Kithure Kindiki, Lecturer in Law, Moi University, Kenya.

Pending

- The National Committee on Implementation of IHL is considering proposals to review or amend the following laws that are relevant to IHL:
  —The Kenya Red Cross Act (Chapter 25 c, Laws of Kenya;
  —The Geneva Conventions Act (Chapter 198, Laws of Kenya);
  —The College of Arms (Chapter 98, Laws of Kenya);
  —National Flags, Emblems and Names Act (Chapter 99, Laws of Kenya).
- The National Committee on IHL has formed a sub-committee on dissemination of IHL. The sub-committee came up with the proposal to launch a newsletter which would address IHL issues. The newsletter is forthcoming, though the exact launch date was not indicated by the Committee's Secretariat.
- The Police Training Manual on Human Rights and IHL Issues is to be launched in 2002. It proposes several approaches to policing methods, which would incorporate IHL and human rights.

KITHURE KINDIKI

(REPUBLIC OF) KOREA

Conventional Weapons

- Act on the Regulation of the Use and Transfer of Certain Conventional Weapons including Mines. Adopted on 24 May 2001. Entered into force 9 October 2001

The Act 'prohibits the use and transfer of mines, booby traps and other devices and stipulates penal sanctions for violations, the maximum being the death penalty'.[347]

Implementation and Dissemination

- Seminar of the Consultative Committee on International Humanitarian Law, November 2001

'In November 2001, the Committee held a symposium on humanitarian law and its relevance to the budding relationship between the two Koreas. The ICRC initiated a dialogue with the Consultative Committee with a view to strengthening the Committee's role as an advisor to the government on the national implementation of IHL.'[348]

KYRGYZSTAN

The Emblems

- Law on the Use and Protection of the Red Crescent and Red Cross Emblems. Entered into force 10 October 2000.

The Law 'governs the use and protection of the emblems in accordance with Kyrgyzstan's international obligations, distinguishing between the indicative and protective uses, attrib-

347. ICRC Advisory Service, *National Implementation of International Humanitarian Law*: Biennial report 2000-2001 (Geneva, ICRC 2002) p. 59.

348. Ibid.

uting rights in this respect to specific entities, providing for control over use of the emblems by the Red Crescent Society of Kyrgyzstan and the relevant State bodies, and referring to national legislation regarding punishment for non-compliance'.[349]

Pending
☛ Reform of the Criminal Code

'In 2000 and 2001 the Interdepartmental Committee on the Implementation of International Humanitarian Law and the [ICRC] Advisory Service pursued their consultations on modifications to the Criminal Code aimed at aligning the Code with the requirements of the 1949 Geneva Conventions and the Additional Protocol I and with the Rome Statute of the International Criminal Court. The issue of repression of violations of IHL was addressed during a seminar on humanitarian law which was organized jointly by the ICRC and the Secretariat of the Interdepartmental Committee and held in Bishkek on 13 November 2001. The seminar was attended by newly nominated Committee members. Issues pertaining to the ratification and implementation of the Rome Statute were also discussed.'[350]

LATVIA

National Defence
☛ The National Defence Concept of the Republic of Latvia. Confirmed at the Saeima on 20 September 2001 [http://www.mod.gov.lv/english/08akti/02defence.php]
☛ National Security Law. Adopted by the Saeima on 14 December 2000. Amendments up to 18 December 2001 [http://www.mod.gov.lv/english/08akti/01_06ndl.php]

In 2001, the Latvian Saeima (Parliament) either adopted or amended a number of documents related to national defence and the armed forces. One of these is the National Defence Concept, which was confirmed by the Saeima in September 2001. This document aims to specify the basic principles of the Latvian national defence. It also sets out the guidelines for the implementation of these principles. The National Defence Concept is also the basis for the National Defence Plan, which is mentioned in Article 31 of the National Security Law, adopted in December 2000 and amended in 2001.

The National Security Law determines what should be understood by the national security system and what kind of tasks it should fulfill. The competences of the persons and institutions responsible for the national security system are also described. Accordingly, the Law includes a list of the competences of the President and the Prime Minister of Latvia, with regard to the National Armed Forces. The tasks of the President include the performance of the duties of the Commander-in-Chief of the armed forces. He is also to appoint the Supreme Commander of the armed forces in wartime. The role of the Prime Minister is to take measures to prevent situations that could endanger the security of the state. Furthermore, the Law describes the powers of these persons and various institutions in the case of a war or military aggression.

MARIA NYBONDAS

349. Ibid., p. 60.
350. Ibid.

LESOTHO

Implementation and Dissemination

☛ Establishment of the Lesotho National Committee for International Humanitarian Law, March 2001

A national seminar held in Maseru on 1 March 2001 recommended the establishment of a national committee on IHL.

'[T]he Lesotho National Committee for International Humanitarian Law was founded in March 2001 pursuant to a memorandum of understanding between the Ministries of Defence, Foreign Affairs, Law and Constitutional Affairs, Home Affairs, Health and Education, the Lesotho Defence Force, the Lesotho Mounted Police Force, the University of Lesotho and the Lesotho Red Cross Society. The Committee is chaired by the Principal Secretary of the Ministry of Defence and held its inaugural meeting on 8 June 2001. A bill was drafted to enshrine the Committee's existence in law.' 'Lesotho was in the process of drafting legislation to implement the Geneva Conventions and their Additional Protocols, a task in which it was assisted by the [ICRC] Advisory Service.'[351]

LITHUANIA[352]

Declaration of War and Military Defence

☛ Law On the State of War. Published in *Valstybes Śinios* No. 52, 28 June 2000, Publ. No. 1482 [Lietuvos Respublikos karo padeties istatymas. Priimtas 2000 m. birželio 8 d. (Skelbta: *Valstybes Śinios*, 2000.06.28, Nr.: 52, Publ. Nr.: 1482]

The Law sets forth the order for proclamation of and revocation of proclamation of the state of war, limitations of freedoms of residents and foreigners, competence of state authorities, peculiarities of activities of business entities, institutions and organizations. The Law seeks to guarantee public safety and maintenance of public order during war. The Law also provides (Art. 38) that institutions of the Republic of Lithuania have to abide by and in the sphere of their competence have to ensure that all persons who are under the jurisdiction of the Republic of Lithuania abide by provisions of international humanitarian law.

☛ Law on the Armed Defense and Resistance to Aggression. Published in *Valstybes Śinios* No. 64, 31 July 2000, Publ. No. 1927; *Valstybes Žinios* No. 86, 13 October 2000 [Lietuvos Respublikos ginkluotos gynybos ir pasipriešinimo agresijai istatymas. Priimtas 2000 m. liepos 17 d. (Skelbta: Valstybes Śinios, 2000.07.31, Nr.: 64, Publ. Nr.: 1927, 2000-10-13, Nr. 86) Isigalioja po paskelbimo *Valstybes Žiniose* (The first date is the date of the primary source, whilst the second date is the date of the proclamation and enforcement of the law.)

351. ICRC Advisory Service, *National Implementation of International Humanitarian Law*: Biennial report 2000-2001 (Geneva, ICRC 2002) p. 61.

352. Information and commentaries by Gediminas Mesonis, Associate Professor in Constitutional Law, Law University of Lithuania, Vilnius, Head of the Center for the Development of the Rule of the Law, and Rytis Satkauskas, First Secretary, Legal and International Treaties Department, Ministry of Foreign Affairs of the Republic of Lithuania.

The law sets forth principles and foundations of military defense and resistance in the Republic of Lithuania. Apart from other significant aspects, the law (Article 13) provides that 'Participants of military defense and resistance must abide by internationally recognized norms of humanitarian law'. It is a crucial provision, which sets limits for the appropriate resistance against aggression.

☛ Law on the Organization of the System of Homeland Defense and Military Service. Published in *Valstybes Žinios* No. 49, 27 May 1998, Publ. Nr.: 1325 [Lietuvos Respublikos krašto apsaugos sistemos organizavimo ir karo tarnybos istatymas. Priimtas 1998 m. gegužes 5 d. (Skelbta: *Valstybes Žinios*, 1998.05.27, Nr. 49, Publ. Nr.: 1325)]

This Law establishes the fundamentals of organization, management and control, the order of execution of military service and maintenance of soldiers as well as niceties of service of civilians in the system of homeland defense. Crucially, this Act provides for a possibility to refuse to carry out orders which of their nature contradict international humanitarian law and Lithuanian law.

Occupation

☛ Decision of the Parliament No. IX-294 on 24 April 2001 setting up the Commission on rights and matters of participants of the movement against occupational regimes and those injured by the occupational regimes.

The Parliament of Lithuania is authorized to set up various commissions to investigate infringements of international humanitarian law. Currently active is a commission set up by the Parliament of Lithuania on Rights and matters of participants of the movement against occupational regimes and the aggrieved by the occupational regimes, which is competent to investigate crimes of World War II (the Holocaust, genocide, mass executions, etc.)

The work of the commission is based on the 26 June 1996 Decision No. VIII-340 'On the approval of rules of the commission of the Parliament of the Republic of Lithuania on rights and matters of persons who took part in the resistance against occupational regimes and aggrieved in the course of occupation'. The commission supervises and controls the activities of the Center for Investigation of Genocide and Resistance; supervises and controls the activities of other governmental institutions related to the implementation of the rights of participants in the resistance movements; supervises and controls the order of recognition of the status of soldiers volunteers and fighters of freedom, examines laws.

The Center for the investigation of Genocide and Resistance, whose Special Investigation Department collects and works with material on crimes committed by occupation regimes, discloses the essence of totalitarian crimes and the system of committing the crimes of genocide and crimes against humanity, and establishes who were the organizers of genocide and provides references on them.

GEDIMINAS MESONIS

Reparations for War Damages

☛ Law of 13 June 2000 on compensation of damage resulting from the occupation by the USSR (Law on compensation), No. VIII – 1727. Adopted on 13 June 2000 [English text at http://www3.lrs.lt/cgi-bin/getfmt?C1=w&C2=104885]

The Law of 13 June 2000 on compensation of damage resulting from the occupation by the USSR (Law on compensation), which obliges the Lithuanian government to submit an estimate of damage inflicted by the Soviet occupation and to form a delegation for negotiations with Russia for compensation, attracted controversy from the first day of its adoption.[353]

As of the end of 2001, all attempts to change the Law had failed.[354] Therefore, at least for the time being, the Lithuanian position could be best illustrated by the words of deputy foreign minister Evaldas Ignatavicius: 'We are obliged to [raise the compensation issue] by a referendum held and by legislation adopted, and Russia has certain obligations in these matters as well.'[355]

As for the position of Russian Federation, it was clearly reaffirmed by the Russian Minister of Foreign Affairs, Mr. Igor Ivanov: 'Lithuanian parliamentarians should review the Law'.[356] At the same time, Russian Ministry of Foreign Affairs spokesman Alexander Yakovenko called the Lithuanian Law on compensation 'an anachronism [...] in which financial claims against Russia, groundless from the legal point of view, are formulated'.[357]

RYTIS SATKAUSKAS

Criminal Law

☛ New Criminal Code [Lietuvos Respublikos baudžiamasis kodeksas]. Adopted on 26 September 2000. Enters into force 1 January 2003. (The date of coming into force shall be established by a separate law of 26 September 2000, namely, the Law of Approval and Coming into Force of the Criminal Code, published in *Valstybes Žinios* Nr. 89-2741, 25 October 2000.). Published in *Valstybes Žinios* No. 89-2741, 2000

The new Criminal Code of the Republic of Lithuania was adopted in 2000, and comes into effect at the beginning of January 2003.

---

353. For details about Baltic claims for the compensation of damages caused by Soviet occupation see R. Satkauskas, 'A claim for the occupant or an issue to negotiate?', 14 *Finnish Yearbook of International Law* (2003) forthcoming.

354. See 'Lithuanian lawmakers include revoking of Soviet Compensation bill into spring agenda', *BNS report* of 20 March 2002.

355. See 'Deputy foreign minister says Lithuania to expand bilateral ties', *BNS report* of 18 January 2001.

356. 'Transcript of Russian Foreign Minister Igor Ivanov Press Conference on Outcomes of Meeting with Lithuanian President Valdas Adamkus (Vilnius, 7 March 2002)', *Daily News Bulletin of Ministry of Foreign Affairs of the Russian Federation Information and Press Department*, 12 March 2002. Text at the Internet site of the Russian Foreign Ministry at www.mid.ru.

357. 'Interview to Russian News Agency RIA Novosti in Relation to the Upcoming Visit of Russian Minister of Foreign Affairs Igor Ivanov to Lithuania', *Daily News Bulletin of Ministry of Foreign Affairs of the Russian Federation Information and Press Department*, 6 March 2002. Text at the Internet site of the Russian Foreign Ministry at www.mid.ru.

The new Criminal Code covers such crimes as violations of international humanitarian law,[358] genocide,[359] crimes against humanity as well as crimes under international treaties to which Lithuania is a party. Violations of humanitarian law that are specifically prohibited include murder and manslaughter of those protected under international humanitarian law; deportation of civilians of an occupied territory; degrading behavior; infringement of international humanitarian law concerning the protection of civilians and their property; exploitation of civilians and prisoners of war in the armed forces of the enemy; destruction of protected objects and looting of national assets; delay in the repatriation of prisoners of war; delay in the release of civilians internees or impeding the repatriation of any other civilians; illegal usage of the emblem of the Red Cross and Red Crescent or of the United Nations; aggression; the usage of prohibited methods and means of warfare; and marauding. The new Criminal Code also provides for criminal responsibility for crimes such as people trafficking; acts of terror; seizure of aircraft; etc.

The Code introduces criminal responsibility for aliens for violations of humanitarian law committed against Lithuanians abroad. Further, the Code stipulates that persons are answerable according to this Code irrespective of their citizenship and place of residence regardless whether the crime is punishable according to the laws of the actual place of crime, in other words, it introduces universal jurisdiction for IHL violations into Lithuanian law.

A key progressive element of the Criminal Code is the introduction of a new and more humane system of criminal punishment. The new Code provides for a wider range of alternative sanctions. The system of punishment in the new Criminal Code was structured in accordance with provisions of the European Convention for the Protection of Human Rights and Fundamental Freedoms and other international treaties.

The new Criminal Code establishes and regulates the conditions and the process of extradition. It provides that (a) a citizen of the Republic of Lithuania who has committed a crime in the Republic of Lithuania or the territory of any other state may only be extradited to a foreign state or surrendered to the International Criminal Court on the basis of an international treaty of the Republic of Lithuania; (b) A foreign national who has committed a crime in the territory of Republic of Lithuania or any other state shall be surrendered to the appropriate state or the International Criminal Court only on the basis of an international treaty of the Republic of Lithuania. It also provides for cases when Lithuanian and foreign nationals may not be surrendered.

---

358. However, this is not the first incrimination of war crimes under Lithuanian law. Criminal acts infringing humanitarian law were regulated in the old Criminal Code since 9 June 1998 (the relevant amendments came into force on 9 June 1998 by Law No. VIII-776. Published in Śin, Nr. 57-1580, 1998). In fact, most of these criminal activities were transferred to the Criminal Code with regard to international documents ratified by Lithuania. The crimes are incorporated into the national legal system of Lithuania with regard to international conventions and agreements and responsibility and definitions of crimes provided therein.

359. The crime of genocide had earlier been incorporated into the old Criminal Code by means of an amendment adopted on 21 April 1998.

Asylum

☛ Law On Refugee Status in the Republic of Lithuania. Published in *Valstybes Śinios*, No. 63, 2 August 1995, Publ. No. 1578; *Valstybes Śinios*, No. 56, 12 July 2000, Publ. No. 1651. [The law was replaced with the law on the replacement of the law. The first date is the date of the primary source, and the second date is the date of the proclamation and enforcement of the original law.]

The Law establishes the conditions and procedure for the provision or denial of refugee status to asylum seekers in the Republic of Lithuania; refugee's rights and duties; the basis for entry and deportation; and basis for social integration of refugees.

The law also covers those refugees who apply for refuge in Lithuania because of violations of humanitarian law in other states.

☛ The Law 'On the Legal Status of Aliens', the arrival and departure, temporary and permanent residence, legal responsibility and other issues relating to the legal status of aliens in the Republic of Lithuania, No. VIII-978, amended on 12 June 2001. Published in *Valstybes Śinio*s, 1998, Nr. 115-3237
[http://www3.lrs.lt/cgi-bin/getfmt?c1=w&c2=151227]

Foreign nationals coming to Lithuania because of war or infringements of humanitarian law have a certain legal status, regulated by this law, except for the cases when they apply for refuge and the status of a refugee.

☛ Government Act of the Republic of Lithuania 'The Confirmation of the Order of Social Integration for Successful Asylum Applicants'. Published in *Valstybes Śinios*, Nr. 43, 23 May 2001, Publ. Nr. 1518

This order regulates conditions of the integration into Lithuanian society of (1) foreign nationals to whom a permit for permanent residence has been issued following the granting the refugee status, in accordance with Lithuanian law, and their family members who have come to Lithuania on the grounds of family reunion; (2) foreign nationals to whom a permit for temporary residence has been issued on humanitarian grounds and in accordance with Lithuanian law, if the foreign national cannot be returned to the country of origin after he/she has been granted refugee status due to natural disaster or acts of war in the country of origin. The Law provides such foreign nationals with equal opportunities to maintain themselves and participate in public life.

The law reflects social policy of the state in relation to refugees. If they come from a country where humanitarian law violations are being committed, it is necessary to ensure their safety, integrate them into society and, as to the local residents, to ensure their rights in critical situations.

☛ Government Act of the Republic of Lithuania 'On the Approval of the Order of Preparation and Submission of Reports in Accordance with UN Conventions, of which Lithuania is a Party and Establishment of Commissions'. Published in *Valstybes Žinios*, Nr. 107, 2001, Publ. Nr. 3874

- The Order of the Ministry of the Interior of the Republic of Lithuania 'On the Approval of the Order of Examination of Applications to Grant the Refugee Status and Issuance of Personal Documents'. Published in *Valstybes Žinios*, Nr. 87, 12 October 2001, Publ. Nr. 3057

The above-mentioned legislation serves as the basis for the activities of the Foreigner National Registration Center ((FNRC) www.pasienis.lt), and provides that Lithuania must take care of refugees who may be victims of war. Established in 1996 by the government, the Center is now in its fifth year of activity. The FNRC is located in Pabrade and is the only center in the country where, following court decisions, illegal entrants are provided with temporary accommodation.

Following the decision of the Department of Migration, foreign nationals who ask to be granted refugee status in Lithuania are accommodated in FNRC, which also organizes the transfer of foreign nationals who have been granted temporary asylum to the Refugee Center in Rukla. FNRC facilitates voluntary return of foreign nationals to the country of origin and deportation of foreigners.

Peacekeeping and Overseas Missions

- Memorandum of Understanding between the United Nations and the Government of the Republic of Lithuania on standby arrangements to identify resources which the Government could allocate to the United Nations peace-keeping operations, Published in *Valstybes Žinios* No. 101, 30 November 2001, Publ. No. 3600 [Jungtiniu Tautu ir Lietuvos Respublikos Vyriausybes tarpusavio supratimo memorandumas del dalyvavimo Jungtiniu Tautu nuolatines parengties sistemoje.1998 m. sausio 13 d. (Skelbta: *Valstybes Žinios*, No. 101, 30 November 2001, Publ. No. 3600). Isigalioja kita diena po paskelbimo *Valstybes Žiniose*]
- Statement by the President of Lithuania on Lithuanian participation in international missions, 2 April 2002 [2002 m. balandžio 2 d. pranešimas Seimui] [www.president.lt/en/pmp2002.phtml]
- Declaration by Parliament on US Military action [Lietuvos Respublikos Seimas, 2001 m. spalio 9 d.] Published in *Valstybes Žinios* No. 87-3034, 2001

In his annual address to the Parliament, the President of Lithuania stated that:

> 'Our security in the modern world depends on our contribution to the defense of Western civilization. By participating in different multinational missions such as peacekeeping, humanitarian aid and military operations, we strengthen global security and, hence, the security of our nation.'

The Parliament of Lithuania in the declaration 'On the Military Actions by the US and its Allies against terrorists' stated that it approves of steps taken by the allies but expresses the hope that the attacks will not claim lives of innocent people. With this declaration, Lithuania undertook to participate in international humanitarian missions.

Implementation and Dissemination

- Establishment of the Commission on the Implementation of International Humanitarian Law, 30 August 2001

'A national study on the compatibility of Lithuanian legislation and practice with IHL was completed, submitted to the authorities and published in 2000.'

On 30 August 2001, the government established the Commission on the Implementation of International Humanitarian Law. 'The Commission focuses on providing assistance to the Ministry and on the overall coordination of activities related to the adoption of national measures of implementation in Lithuania.'[360]

In its programme for 2001-2004, the government of the Lithuania expressed its willingness to facilitate speedy implementation of norms of international humanitarian law and seeking to achieve this end to become a party to the following relevant multilateral agreements: Second Protocol to the Hague Convention for the Protection of Cultural Property in the Event of Armed Conflict; the Optional Protocol to the Convention on the Rights of the Child on the Involvement of Children in Armed Conflict 2000; the Convention on the Prohibition of Military or any Hostile Use of Environmental Modification Techniques, and International Convention against the Recruitment, Use, Financing and Training of Mercenaries. The government committed itself to analyze current national legislation which needs to be amended to secure swift accession to the above-mentioned treaties.

Education and Training

By signing and ratifying the 1949 Geneva Conventions and 1977 Additional Protocols, Lithuania undertook to acquaint society – the military and civilians – with their texts. Educational programmes are carried out by state institutions (universities, institutes, societies) and NGOs.

Principles of international humanitarian law are promoted by the Lithuanian Red Cross Society, which, since April 1998, in cooperation with the ICRC, has conducted international humanitarian law programmes in Lithuania. The programmes aim to disseminate key principles of the Red Cross and Red Crescent; promote humanitarian law; stimulate humanitarian action; and to contribute to the prevention of violations of humanitarian law and general prevention of violence in Lithuanian society.

Implementation of the programmes consists of several aspects: (a) seminars, training courses, summer schools and other events related to humanitarian law, relevant training of the military, police and civil servants, etc.; (b) Dissemination of information about humanitarian law in the Lithuanian press; (c) publishing of literature and rendition of consultations on humanitarian law; (d) cooperation with state institutions and NGOs in implementation of humanitarian law.

Special courses on international humanitarian law are conducted in Lithuanian universities. The courses are held at the Law University of Lithuania, the Lithuanian War Academy and Vilnius University. For example, the Law University of Lithuania has developed a programme and gives lectures on international humanitarian law.

Cases

☛ *Kazys Gimzauskas* case, Vilnius District Court, 14 February 2001

---

360. ICRC Advisory Service, *National Implementation of International Humanitarian Law*: Biennial report 2000-2001 (Geneva, ICRC 2002) p. 62.

The genocide trial of Kazys Gimzauskas, 92, a former senior commander of Saugumas, the Nazi-sponsored Lithuanian security police, resumed on 25 April 2000, pursuant to a law that allows trials to proceed even if the accused is too ill to appear in court. According to his indictment, while he was an officer in the Vilnius security police during the 1941-1944 Nazi occupation Gimzauskas sent Jews to their deaths. 'Documents signed by Gimzauskas and found in the Lithuanian Central State Archives show that he ordered the arrest, interrogation, incarceration and turnover to the German Security Police for execution of civilians, including many Jews.'[361]

On 14 February 2001, Gimzauskas became the first ever person to be convicted of genocide by a Lithuanian court. The District Court in Vilnius found Gimzauskas guilty of collaborating in the genocide of Jews in Lithuania during the Nazi occupation. However, Gimzauskas could not be sentenced as he suffers from Alzheimer's disease.[362] Doctors said that he was too ill to go to prison. The Prosecutor, Rimvydas Valentukevicius, said: 'It's unfortunate he's too ill to serve any sentence. Nevertheless, historical justice has been done.'[363]

☛ Warrant against *Anton Gecas*, 19 February 2001

On 19 February 2001, a court in Vilnius issued a warrant for the arrest of Mr Anton Gecas, 84. Gecas, a former lieutenant in the 12th auxiliary police service battalion, was charged with 13 crimes relating to the genocide of Jews and the mass murder of other civilians in Lithuania and what is today Belarus.[364] A formal request for his extradition from Scotland, where he lives, followed on 26 March 2001.[365] Extradition proceedings began in Scotland on 27 July, after Jim Wallace, the Scottish Justice Minister, authorised the move and a sheriff ordered the arrest of the octogenarian.[366] However, the warrant was not served on Mr Gecas because he had suffered a stroke. The UK authorities indicated that they would follow medical advice on the matter.[367]

More than 90 percent of Lithuania's 220,000 Jews were murdered during the Holocaust.[368]

---

361. Source: 'Genocide and international crimes in domestic courts'. A survey by Prevent Genocide International. Available at its website at http://www.preventgenocide.org/punish/domestic/.

362. Source: Ministry of Foreign Affairs Republic of Lithuania, Fact Sheets, August 2002. Online at http://www.ltembassyus.org/press/fact-sheets/August.html.

363. L. Dapkus, 'Nazi Suspect Said Too Ill for Jail', AP, 14 February 2001.

364. Source: 'February 2001 News Monitor'. Prevent Genocide International. http://www.preventgenocide.org/prevent/news-monitor/2001feb.htm.

365. 'Lithuania Asks UK to Extradite War Crimes Suspect', Union of Council for Jews in the Former Soviet Union, 28 March 2001; 'Wiesenthal Center Welcomes Lithuanian Extradition Request For Gecas; Urges Additional Prosecutions', Press Information, Simon Wiesenthal Center, 27 March 2001.

366. 'War crimes extradition begins', The Telegraph, 28 July 2001. Online at http://www.telegraph.co.uk/news/main.jhtml?xml=/news/2001/07/28/nbul28.xml.

367. 'War crime suspect 'unfit' to face extradition', Basis, Archives breaking news, 4 September 2001. Online at http://archives.tcm.ie/breakingnews/2001/09/04/story22576.asp.

368. 'Lithuania Orders Arrest of UK Genocide Suspect', Union of Council for Jews in the Former Soviet Union, 20 February 2001.

Pending

- New Code of Criminal Procedure
- New Code of Execution of Penalties

GEDIMINAS MESONIS

LUXEMBOURG

Landmines and Laser Weapons

- Law of 29 April 1999 approving the Protocol on Prohibitions or Restrictions on the Use of Mines, Booby Traps and Other Devices as amended on 3 May 1996 (Protocol II) and the Protocol on Blinding Laser Weapons (Protocol IV) to the 1980 Convention on Conventional Weapons [Loi du 29 avril 1999 portant approbation du Protocole II, tel qu'il a été modifié le 3 mai 1996:... du Protocole IV intitulé Protocole relative aux armes à laser aveuglantes...][369]

International Criminal Court

- Law of 8 August 2000 revising Article 118 of the Constitution [Loi du 8 aout 2000 portant revision de l'article 118 de la Constitution]. Adopted on 8 August 2000

This law amends the Constitution to permit Luxembourg to ratify the 1988 Rome Statute of the International Criminal Court.[370]

MACEDONIA

Peace Process

- Framework Agreement, 13 August 2001 [http://www.president.gov.mk/eng/info/soopstenija.asp?id=90]

MALAWI

Implementation and Dissemination

- Establishment of the Malawi National Committee on International Humanitarian Law, March 2001

The Committee was established 'on the basis of a memorandum of understanding between the Ministries of Defence, Foreign Affairs, Justice and Home Affairs, the judiciary, the police, the Human Rights Commission, and the Malawi Red Cross Society. The Committee can also co-opt other bodies. Its role is to advise the government on implementing legislation, to consider the adoption of measures for the punishment of war criminals, respect for the emblem and the protection of civilians during armed conflicts, and to spread knowledge of humanitarian law.'[371]

---

369. ICRC Advisory Service, *National Implementation of International Humanitarian Law*: Biennial report 2000-2001 (Geneva, ICRC 2002) p. 63.

370. Ibid.

371. Ibid., p. 64.

MALAYSIA

Landmines

☛ Anti-Personnel Mines Convention Implementation Act 2000, Act No. 603 of 2000. Adopted on 30 May 2000. Published in *Gazette,* 15 June 2000 [http://www.icrc.org/ihl-nat.nsf/6fa4d35e5e3025394125673e00508143/b249d5211959ecebc1256a22002a4bdd?OpenDocument]

'The purpose of the Act is to implement the Ottawa treaty on landmines of 1997, which entered into force for Malaysia on 1 October 1999. The Act prohibits the use, development, production, possession, acquisition, stockpiling, retention and transfer of anti-personnel mines. Prohibited activities, including assistance, encouragement or inducement to engage in a prohibited activity, are punished by fine and/or imprisonment. The Act also requires marking and mine clearance in mined areas of Malaysia. The minister responsible for defence may require any person to furnish the necessary information for the enforcement of the Act and for the fulfilment of the reporting obligations under the treaty. The Act recognizes the right of fact-finding missions to conduct inspections and secures access to places in accordance with the treaty.'[372]

MALI

Landmines

☛ Anti-Personnel Mines Order (2000). Adopted on 27 September 2000. Entered into force on 27 September 2000. [Ordonnance N° 00-049/P-MR du 27 septembre 2000 portant mise en oeuvre de la Convention sur l'interdiction de l'emploi, du stockage, de la production et du transfert des mines antipersonnel et sur leur destruction, signée à Ottawa le 3 décembre 1997]. Published in the *Official Journal of Mali*, No. 32, 20 November 2000, pp. 1255-1257

'The purpose of this Order is to implement the Ottawa treaty. It creates prohibitions and offences relating to the use, development, production, acquisition, stockpiling, retention, import, export and transfer of anti-personnel mines, as defined in the treaty, and of their components. Penalties are forced labour for life and a fine, and, optionally, a ban on remaining in the country. State agents, however, are entitled to acquire, possess or transfer mines, provided that this is with a view to their destruction or to the development of detection, clearance and destruction techniques. The Order, supplemented in that respect by Decree No.00/569/P-RM relating to the application of the Anti-Personnel Mines Order (2000), confirms the right of members of fact-finding missions to conduct inspections on the territory of Mali. The Order also establishes a National Commission to ensure its application.'[373]

---

372. Source: ICRC National Implementation Database. http://www.icrc.org/ihl-nat.nsf/6fa4d35e5e3025394125673e00508143/22e1c80ab8abe975c1256a1c002d7038?OpenDocument.

373. Ibid.

- Decree relating to the application of the Anti-Personnel Mines Order (2000) [Décret N° 00-569/P-RM du 15 novembre 2000 fixant les modalités d'application de Ordonnance N° 00-049/P-MR du 27 septembre 2000 portant mise en oeuvre de la Convention sur l'interdiction de l'emploi, du stockage, de la production et du transfert des mines antipersonnel et sur leur destruction, signée à Ottawa le 3 décembre 1997]. Adopted on 15 November 2000. Entered into force on 15 November 2000

'This Decree supplements Anti-Personnel Mines Order (2000) with regard to the rights of the members of fact-finding missions when conducting inspections.'[374]

- Law No. 88-86 of 26 December 2000 pertaining to the ratification of ordonance No. 00-049/P-RM of 27 December 2000 pertaining to the adoption of the Convention of the Prohibition of the Use, Stockpiling, production of transfer of antipersonnel mines and on their destruction. Adopted by the National Assembly on 14 December 2000 and promulgated by the President of the Republic on 26 December 2000[375]

Criminal Law

- New Penal Code [Loi No. 01-079/ANRM du 20 août 2001 portant Code pénal au Mali]. Adopted by the National Assembly on 30 June 2001 and promulgated by the President of the Republic on 20 August 2001

'The first section of the code ("crimes against humanity") includes articles on genocide, crimes against humanity and war crimes. The text of the provisions defining these crimes (Articles 29 to 31) is essentially based on Articles 6 to 8 of the Rome Statute of the International Criminal Court with, however, some important differences as far as war crimes are concerned. Article 32 of the code provides for the inadmissibility of statutory limitations and for the death penalty to be used against violators.'[376] 'Article 31 provides for the repression of war crimes as defined in humanitarian law treaties.'[377]

MAURITIUS

Landmines

- (Anti-Personnel Mines (Prohibition) Act, 2001. No. 1 of 2001. Adopted by the Mauritian National Assembly on 27 March 2001. Assented to by the President on 10 April 2001. Entered into force on the day of its publication in the *Government Gazette of Mauritius* on 28 April 2001

The Act 'gives effect to the Ottawa Convention. The Act provides for the prohibition of the use, development, acquisition, stockpiling, retention or transfer or anti-personnel mines other than for the development of and training in mine detection, clearance and destruction.

374. Ibid.
375. Ibid.
376. Ibid.
377. Ibid.

It provides for the punishment of offenders and gives the Defence Minister the power to prescribe the manner in which the mines are to be destroyed'.[378]

Pending

- Efforts are underway to amend the Geneva Conventions Act 1970 in order to implement the Additional Protocols.[379]

MEXICO[380]

The Peace Process in Chiapas

- Reform of the Constitution

In early-2001, an attempt was made to restart the Chiapas peace negotiations, which have been stalled since 1996.

Following a 12-day armed conflict in the Southeastern Mexican State of Chiapas, between the Zapatista Army of National Liberation (Ejército Zapatista de Liberación Nacional (EZLN) and the Federal Government, on 12 January 1994, the Mexican government declared a ceasefire, which the EZLN agreed to honour. Peace negotiations began on 29 August 1996 but were interrupted when EZLN's participation was suspended[381] due to the government's failure to comply with one of the three preconditions for peace talks, namely the reform of the Constitution to incorporate the San Andres Accords on indigenous rights and culture (the other two, which were fulfilled by the Mexican government, were the demilitarisation of seven areas in Chiapas and the release of EZLN political prisoners).

The San Andres Accords were appropriated by President Vicente Fox and presented to the Mexican Congress on 5 December 2000, as a proposal to amend the Constitution.[382] As a result of the debates in both Chambers but particularly the Senate, a Constitutional Reform was approved. However, this reform did not respond to EZLN's demands nor did it reflect President's Fox proposal. Nevertheless, the reform was completed by the approval of the majority of the Mexican states. Therefore, EZLN rejected the amendment and considers that the condition for their return to the peace process remains unfulfilled.[383]

Criminal Code

- Criminalisation of forced disappearance of persons as a federal offence by including Articles 215-A, 215-B, 215-C and 215-D in new Chapter 3 bis of Title X of the Federal Criminal Code. Reform published in the *Diario Oficial de la Federación* (DOF), 1 June 2001, p. 2

---

378. *Supra* n. 11 at p. 440.

379. Ibid.

380. Information and commentaries by José A. Guevara, Researcher at the Human Rights Programme of the Iberoamericana University and Lecturer in International Human Rights Law at the Law Faculty of Iberoamericana University.

381. See the web page of the EZLN: http://www.ezln.org.

382. Iniciativa de Reforma Constitucional en materia indígena. Presidencia de la República. Documento: 05/12/2000 (001205). http://www.presidencia.gob.mx.

383. http://www.ezln.org.

Education and Training

☛ Training of the police

'Efforts were pursued in 2001 to incorporate the principles of humanitarian law and human rights law into police practice, specifically with regard to the use of force and firearms and detention matters. Courses comprising theoretical and practical training were given to members of the *Políca Federal Preventiva* (PFR), police agents of the Procuraduría General de la República (PGR) and police officers of the Secretaria de Seguridad Pública of the government of Chiapas state.

'In 2000 and 2001 training workshops on humanitarian law continued to be organized throughout the country for university professors teaching international law and/or international relations, the aim being to make IHL part of official teaching programme. IHL was included in several postgraduate university programmes.'[384]

Cases

☛ Recommendation 26/2001 regarding crimes against humanity of the 1970s and 1980s, 27 November 2001

On 27 November 2001, the President of the National Commission for Human Rights (CNDH)[385] issued Recommendation 26/2001 to the Mexican Executive in connection with the cases of enforced disappearances presented to the CNDH.[386] Among the concrete recommendations were the designation of a special prosecutor by the Attorney General to investigate more than 500 cases of enforced disappearances of persons during the 1970s and early-1980s.[387] Following the recommendation, President Fox instructed the Attorney General to designate a special prosecutor to investigate the crimes committed by public officials against persons involved with social and political movements.[388] By 31 December 2001, such designation had not been given.

☛ Decision to extradite *Ricardo Cavallo* to Spain, 12 January 2001

On 12 January 2001, a Mexican court[389] ruled in favour of extraditing former military general, Ricardo Cavallo, to Spain, to face charges there of genocide and terrorism. Spanish magistrate Baltasar Garzón Real indicted Cavallo on 1 September 2000[390] for genocide, torture and terrorism, for crimes allegedly committed during Argentina's 'dirty war' of the 1970s and 1980s. On 2 February 2001, the decision was confirmed by Foreign Minister

384. ICRC Advisory Service, *National Implementation of International Humanitarian Law*: Biennial report 2000-2001 (Geneva, ICRC 2002) p. 67.

385. Comisión Nacional de Derechos Humanos.

386. See the report at http://www.cndh.org.mx/Principal/document/recomen/2001/fr_rec01.htm.

387. Informe especial sobre las quejas en materia de desapariciones forzadas ocurridas en la década de los 70 y principios de los 80. http://www.cndh.org.mx/.

388. Acuerdo por el que se Disponen Diversas Medidas para la Procuración de Justicia por Delitos Cometidos contra Personas Vinculadas con Movimientos Sociales y Políticos del Pasado. Presidencia de la República. Documento 27/11/2001. http://www.presidencia.gob.mx/.

389. Juez Sexto de Distrito de Procesos Penales Federales en el Distrito Federal.

390. J. Watson, 'Mexico to extradite former soldier', AP, 3 February 2001; A. Trejo, 'Mexico judge rules on extradition', AP, 12 January 2001.

Jorge Castaneda, who extended the charges for which Cavallo could be extradited to include torture.

Cavallo was detained in Mexico on 25 August 2000, and extradition proceedings began. His extradition is legally regulated by the Extradition and Mutual Cooperation in Criminal Matters Convention[391] entered into by and between Mexico and Spain and its 1996 Protocol,[392] and subsidiarily by the International Extradition Law of 1975.[393]

The extradition process in Mexico has two phases: the first one consists of the issuance of a legal opinion by the judiciary and the second of an issuance of a resolution of the Ministry of Foreign Affairs (MFA),[394] granting or denying the extradition request. Extradition file 5/2000 was opened by Judge Jesus Gudalupe Luna Altamirano at the Judge Number 6 of District of Federal Criminal Procedures in Mexico City, responsible for the formulation of the non-binding legal opinion to the MFA. This opinion was issued on 11 January 2001. Judge Luna Altamirano recognised the *sui generis* nature of the extradition procedure of Cavallo. For him, it was a particular procedure as there was no traditional exemption to the territoriality principle (active or passive) applicable for this case between the requesting state (Spain) and the country where the crimes were presumably committed (Argentina). Therefore, he explicitly recognised the universal jurisdiction established by the Spanish Law (Art. 24.3 of the Organic Law of the Spanish Judiciary), which confers jurisdiction on the Audiencia Nacional to try the crimes of genocide, torture and terrorism, regardless of where they were committed. Notwithstanding, he determined the legality of the extradition of Cavallo to Spain only for the crimes of genocide and terrorism, excluding torture due to its statutory limitations derived from the Mexican legislation applicable at the time the crimes were presumably committed. The ratification of the Convention on the Non-Applicability of Statutory Limitations to War Crimes and Crimes Against Humanity was not concluded on the date of issuance of the Opinion. It is important to point out that Judge Luna did not consider enforced disappearances as a form of torture for the determination of the statutory limitations.

According to the applicable laws, in particular the International Extradition Law, the final determination as to Cavallo's extradition is the responsibility of the MFA, which rendered its conclusion on 2 February 2001. The MFA concluded that the request from Spain for Cavallo's extradition from Mexico is authorised and that the Spanish tribunals can try Cavallo for genocide, torture and terrorism. The MFA reviewed the legal analysis of the statutory limitations applicable under Mexican criminal law during the period from 1976 to 1983 and found that Judge Luna did not take into consideration certain elements in finding that the crime of torture was not subject to prescription on the date of the initiation of the criminal procedure before Judge Garzón. Thus, the Minister found that extradition on the torture charge was also permitted.[395]

---

391. Tratado de Extradición y Asistencia Mutua en Materia Penal, de 21 de noviembre de 1978.

392. Protocolo por el que se Modifica el Tratado de Extradición y Asistencia Mutua en Materia Penal entre los Estados Unidos Mexicanos y el Reino de España.

393. Ley de Extradición Internacional. Published in the Official Gazette on 29 December 1975. http://www.cddhcu.gob.mx/leyinfo/pdf/36.pdf.

394. Secretaría de Relaciones Exteriores.

395. 'Acuerdo que concede la extradición del reclamado RICARDO MIGUEL CAVALLO, conocido como MIGUEL ANGEL CAVALLO, solicitada por el Gobierno de España, por conducto de su Embajada en México para que sea procesado por los delitos de genocidio, terrorismo y tortura.' File

Following this decision, Cavallo requested the protection of the *amparo*[396] before the Judiciary,[397] by arguing violations of the Mexican Constitution by the executive and the Senate in the process of ratifying the Extradition Convention and its Protocol, and the Genocide Convention, and the application of such instruments in the Extradition procedure. Cavallo also argued that the crimes imputed to him are of a political nature, and that, under the Mexican Constitution and jurisprudence, extradition in respect of political crimes is restricted.

A group of Mexican and Argentinean NGOs,[398] coordinated by the victims organisation Genocidio Nunca Mas[399] prepared an amicus curiae brief which discussed the legal matters alleged by Cavallo in his *amparo* proceeding before Judge García Orzco. Their brief was submitted to the Attorney General to provide additional support for his position in the process as part of the *amparo* proceeding. It is important to mention that Mexican criminal procedure does not contemplate the participation of *amici*; thus the Attorney General's Office received it on informal basis and the brief was not included in the case file at the *amparo* tribunal.

Pending

☛ Constitutional Amendment concerning ratification of the ICC Statute

Before the ICC Statute can be submitted by the Executive to the Senate for its approval, the Constitution must be amended.[400] The Executive Branch considers that Mexico will be able to fully comply with the obligations arising under the Statute once the Constitutional reform is completed. Therefore, on 6 December 2001, an amendment to Article 21 of the Constitution[401] was proposed to the Congress, but it was not included in the agenda for discussion under the ordinary period,[402] which concluded on 15 December due its late submission to

---

number VII/230/1324/2000 of the General Direction of Legal Affairs of the Ministry of Foreign Affairs.

396. Amparo is a legal procedure which seeks the protection of constitutional rights from the appropriate authority (judicial, executive, legislative) before the federal tribunals.

397. Judge García Orozco, Amparo Tribunal 1st B.

398. Mexican NGOs: Acción de Cristianos para la Abolición de la Tortura, Comisión Mexicana de Defensa y Promoción de los Derechos Humanos, Genocidio Nunca Mas and José A. Guevara. Argentinan NGOs: Centro de Estudios Legales y Sociales and Liga Argentina por los Derechos del Hombre.

399. http://www.laneta.apc.org/cavalloentrerejas/.

400. Joint press conference of Jorge Castañeda, Head of the Ministry of Foreign Affairs and Santiago Creel, Head of the Ministry of the Interior, by means of which they communicated the proposal submitted by the Executive to reform Art. 21 of the Constitution, 6 December 2001. http://www.sre.gob.mx. See also the speech of President Vicente Fox at the Eleventh National Conference on Administration of Justice on 12 December 2001. Discurso: 07/12/2002. http://www.presidencia.gob.mx.

401. According to which punishments can exclusively be established by the judiciary, and the investigation and prosecution of crimes can only be performed by the Ministerio Publico – Attorney General – which can be assisted by the police under its command. The Article also establishes the public security responsibilities of the federation, the states and the municipalities.

402. Based on the Constitution, the Mexican Congress celebrates two ordinary periods of meetings, one from 1 September to 15 December and the other from February till the beginning of May.

the Senate. The amendment, in general terms, consists of the recognition of the binding nature of all decisions of international tribunals whose jurisdiction Mexico has recognised. Such amendment would bind the legislative, judicial and executive branches by any decision issued by any international tribunal, namely, the Inter-American Court of Human Rights, the International Court of Justice and the International Criminal Court. The procedure to amend the Constitution consists of the approval of the proposal by a qualified majority of the Congress (composed of the two chambers, Representatives and Senate) and by the approval of the majority of the legislatures of the federated states.[403]

☛ 'Humanitarian package'

On 9 October 2001, the Executive Branch presented for the approval by the Senate a 'humanitarian package',[404] which included a considerable number of international human rights and humanitarian law agreements, the recognition of the individual complaints procedures of human rights treaty bodies and withdrawals of certain reservations of human rights treaties. Within the package was also included the Host Country Agreement for the Establishment of a Regional Delegation of the International Committee of the Red Cross, but this was not discussed during the parliamentary period which concluded on 15 December 2001. It was expected to be discussed during the first ordinary period of 2002.

JOSÉ A. GUEVARA

MOLDOVA

Criminal Law

☛ The Penal Code of 1999 and the Penal Procedural Code of 1999.[405] Enacted on 12 June 1999. Promulgated by the President by decree No. 873-III on 6 September 2002. Published on 13 September 2002 in the *Official Monitor of the Republic of Moldova.* Penal Code of the Republic of Moldova (Will come into effect 12 June 2003)

'The Penal Code of 1999 provides for the punishment of a number of serious violations of IHL.'[406]

☛ Establishment in 2001 of working group under the auspices of the Ministry of Justice to study the compatibility of national legislation with the Statute of the International Criminal Court[407]

The Movement

☛ Law on the Red Cross Society. Adopted 10 May 2001. Entered into force 22 June 2001

'The National Society was officially recognized by the ICRC on 24 October 2001, thus

403. Art. 135 of the Constitution.
404. http://www.senado.gob.mx.
405. Replacing the 1961 Penal Code.
406. *Supra* n. 11 at p. 440.
407. Ibid.

becoming the 178th member of the International Red Cross and Red Crescent Movement.'[408]

Implementation

☛ Establishment of the Association of Humanitarian Law

In 2000, the Ministry of Justice registered the Association of Humanitarian Law, a public body. Its objective is to promote IHL and the implementation process in Moldova.

☛ Conference on current problems of implementation and dissemination of IHL in the Republic of Moldova

Held in February 2000, the Conference was jointly organized by the National Committee on Consultation and Coordination of Implementation of International Humanitarian Law and the Armed Forces' General Staff.[409]

☛ Round Table on the problems of and outlook for the implementation of IHL in Moldova

The Round Table was organised jointly by the National Committee and the Association of Humanitarian Law, and was attended by about 40 participants from all major ministries, academic institutions, the ICRC, the National Red Cross Society and UNHRC.[410]

Education and Training

☛ Teaching guide on international humanitarian law

'A teaching guide on IHL was published in the national language on the initiative and with the support of the National Committee.'[411]

Pending

☛ Draft Criminal Code

The National Committe, with the assistance and legal advice of the Advisory Service, prepared amendments to the draft Criminal Code adopted at first reading, providing for a complete system of repression of war crimes.[412]

MONGOLIA

The Emblem

☛ Law on the Legal Status of the Mongolian Red Cross Society, 28 April 2000

---

408. Ibid.
409. Ibid.
410. Ibid.
411. Ibid.
412. Ibid.

This law 'governs the mandate and operating procedure of the Mongolian Red Cross as an auxiliary to the national authorities in humanitarian societies. A section on the name and emblem of the Mongolian Red Cross Society defines the conditions of use of the red cross emblem by the National Society and prohibits unauthorized use of the emblem by citizens and bodies corporate'.[413]

THE NETHERLANDS[414]

Cases

☛ *Milošević* v. *The Netherlands* (Slobodan Milošević tegen de Staat der Nederlanden), The Hague District Court, 31 August 2001, LJN: AD3266, KG 01/975 [http://www.rechtspraak.nl/flashed.asp]

The plaintiff, Slobodan Milošević, former president of the FRY, detained in the detention center made available by the Netherlands to the ICTY, brought summary civil proceedings (*kort geding*) against the State of the Netherlands before the President of the District Court (*arrondissementsrechtbank*) of The Hague. He sought an order directed against the state for his unconditional release; alternatively, for the state to make representations to the 'so-called Tribunal' (i.e., the ICTY) and other competent international bodies and institutions for his release; alternatively, for the state to make representations to 'the alleged Tribunal' and other competent international bodies and institutions for his return to the FRY.

In support of his claims, the plaintiff argued that his transfer to the ICTY was illegal under the domestic law of the FRY; that the ICTY itself lacked a basis in international law, having been set up by a resolution of the Security Council of the United Nations (by Resolution 827 of 25 May 1993) and not by a multilateral treaty; that the ICTY was the handmaiden of NATO and can therefore not be considered independent and impartial in the sense of Article 6 of the European Convention of Human Rights. He further contended that the actions of the Security Council and the ICTY were discriminatory and that he was entitled to immunity as a former head of state. In view of these considerations the defendant, the State of The Netherlands, was acting unlawfully by allowing him to be detained on its territory. The plaintiff further submitted that the Dutch courts were competent to rule on the legal protection of persons within the territory of The Netherlands and this applied to the plaintiff in the same way as to anyone else.

The respondent's principal line of argument was that national and international law expressly acknowledge that the Tribunal possesses exclusive competence within the Dutch legal order to decide on the deprivation of liberty facing charges before the Tribunal. It is not a matter for The Netherlands to decide on the plaintiff's appeal for release.

The Court first addressed the plaintiff's contentions relating to the Tribunal's legal basis. It found that the ICTY did in fact have sufficient legal basis as was correctly determined in the Appeals Chamber Decision in *Tadić* on 2 October 1995. Despite the plaintiff's objections to the latter decision, the Court upheld it. As to the plaintiff's contention that the

413. Ibid., p. 69.

414. Information and commentaries by Professor emeritus Nico Keijzer, Professor of Criminal Law, University of Tilburg; Advocate-General at the Supreme Court of the Netherlands and Elies van Sliedregt, researcher at T.M.C. Asser Institute and Tilburg University.

Tribunal is not an independent and impartial tribunal within the meaning of Article 6 of the European Convention on Human Rights, the Court dismissed it by pointing to the Tribunal's procedural guarantees and detailed rules on the protection of the rights of the accused. In supporting its view the President referred to the European Court of Human Rights in *Naletelić* v. *Croatia* (No. 51891/99, 4 May 2000, ttp://hudoc.echr.coe.int/hudoc.

The Court then proceeded to consider the exclusive competence of the Tribunal. It held that as the Kingdom of the Netherlands had lawfully transferred its jurisdiction over the ICTY detainees to the ICTY,[415] the courts of the Netherlands were not competent to consider the applicant's request for release.

The President declared he had no jurisdiction to hear the plaintiff's principal claim and alternative claims. The applicant lodged an appeal against this judgement, but withdrew it on 17 January 2002.

Bearing in mind the usually brief reasoning of decisions in summary proceedings, this judgement stands out as a well-motivated decision. Part of the Court's reasoning is based on the jurisdiction decision in *Prosecutor* v. *Duško Tadić* of the ICTY Appeals Chamber.[416] The latter ruled that the Security Council's competence to establish the Tribunal can be based on Chapter VII of the UN Charter and can be considered to be within the scope of Article 41 of the UN Charter.[417] The ICTY Trial Chamber had ruled along the same lines when the issue of the illegal foundation of the Tribunal was raised at the start of the actual trial. The *Tadić* decision was again instrumental in the Trial Chamber's decision:

> 'In the Chamber's view, the establishment of the International Tribunal with power to prosecute persons responsible for serious violations of international humanitarian law in the former Yugoslavia, and with the obligation to guarantee fully the rights of the accused, is, in the context of the conflict in the country at that time, pre-eminently a measure to restore international peace and security. Indeed, the role of the International Tribunal in promoting peace and reconciliation in the former Yugoslavia is highlighted in Security Council resolution 827 which established it. The Appeals Chamber in the *Tadić Jurisdiction Appeal* arrived at the same conclusion and concluded that "the establishment of the International Tribunal falls squarely within the powers of the Security Council under Article 41".'[418]

ELIES VAN SLIEDREGT

☛ Decision of the Hoge Raad der Nederlanden (Supreme Court) in the Case of *Desi Bouterse*, 18 September 2001

---

415. Support was found in the Headquarters Agreement and the Act implementing it, Art. 9(2) of the ICTY Statute and Art. 103 of the UN Charter.

416. Decision on the Defence Motion for Interlocutory Appeal on Jurisdiction, 2 October 1995.

417. Art. 41: 'The Security Council may decide what measures not involving the use of armed force are to be employed to give effect to its decisions, and it may call upon the Members of the United Nations to apply such measures. These may include complete or partial interruption of economic relations and or rail, sea, air, postal telegraphic, radio, and other means of communication, and the severance of diplomatic relations.'

418. *Prosecutor* v. *Slobodan Milošević*, Decision on Preliminary Motions, 8 November 2001.

On 18 September 2001, the Supreme Court of the Netherlands quashed the injunction, given by the Amsterdam Appeals Court on 20 November 2000, to prosecute Desi D. Bouterse for his probable role in the so-called 'December murders' in Surinam (see 3 *YIHL* (2000) pp. 548-550). This refers to the killing, on the night of 8-9 December 1982, in Paramaribo, Surinam, of 15 persons. All were political opponents of Bouterse, who, at the time, was the leader of the Surinamese government.

Prosecution of Bouterse in Surinam not being feasible for political reasons, next of kin had asked the Dutch prosecutor to initiate proceedings against him. After the Dutch prosecutor had refused, the next of kin applied to the Amsterdam Appeals Court, which, acting on the basis of Article 12 of the Dutch Code of Criminal Procedure, issued its Decree of 20 November 2000 ordering the prosecutor to demand a preliminary inquiry. Dutch law not providing for extraterritorial jurisdiction concerning murders committed by foreigners on foreign territory, the Amsterdam Appeals Court had based its Decree on the theory that the murders in question had constituted acts of torture, for which crime Article 5 of the Dutch Torture Act, taken to the letter, provides for universal jurisdiction.

Because this Decree raised many interesting questions of law for which it was important to find authoritative answers at an early stage of the proceedings, and the Dutch Code of Criminal Procedure not providing defendants or the prosecution with a legal remedy against decrees of this kind, the Procurator-General of the Supreme Court, making use of his power to lodge an extraordinary appeal against any lower court's decision, requested the Supreme Court to shed light on those questions and set aside the Decree. This is what the Supreme Court did by its ruling of 18 September 2001.

The Procurator-General had challenged the Decree on five points: (1) By ordering prosecution for acts which had taken place in 1982, the Amsterdam Appeals Court had given retroactive application to the Torture Act, which came into force in 1989. (2) By applying the Torture Act to what apparently had been premeditated murders, the Appeals Court had misinterpreted the Torture Act, murder by itself not amounting to torture. (3) By assuming that the Netherlands had established jurisdiction for acts of torture which occurred in 1982, the Appeals Court had again given retroactive application to the Torture Act. (4) The Appeals Court seemed to have overlooked that, when the Decree was given, Bouterse had already, through lapse of time, become immune for prosecution for torture. (5) Given that most of the victims were not Dutch nationals, the Appeals Court had failed to take into account that customary international law does not permit a state to apply universal jurisdiction to a person who is not present on its territory.

The Supreme Court, in its ruling of 18 September 2001, agreed with the first four of those challenges. As concerns the fifth, it took a different line. Without dealing with the general question of whether customary international law does or does not permit a state to apply universal jurisdiction in the absence of the suspect, the Supreme Court ruled that Article 5 of the Dutch Torture Act must be construed as not establishing any wider jurisdiction than is mentioned in Article 5(1) and (2) of the 1984 Torture Convention.

For these five reasons, the Decree of the Amsterdam Appeals Court was quashed.

☛ *Lawyers for Peace et al.* v. *the State*, Supreme Court of the Netherlands. Decision of 21 December 2001. Published in *Militair Rechtelijk Tijdschrift* (Netherlands Military Law Review) 2002, pp. 243-248 (with annotation by F.F. Langemeijer)

In 1989, the Dutch Supreme Court had ruled on a request by certain opposition groups to declare unlawful and to prohibit any Dutch cooperation in the employment of American nuclear-headed cruise missiles on Dutch territory. The request had been refused. The Supreme Court had rejected the appeal against that decision, ruling that the allegation that the mere presence of such missiles on Dutch territory was contrary to international law was unfounded.[419]

In 1992, a new attempt was made. This time, the plaintiffs (the Association 'Lawyers for Peace', the Foundation 'Millions Oppose' and several others) requested the District Court of The Hague to declare unlawful and to prohibit any Dutch cooperation in or preparation for the actual employment of nuclear weapons, or, alternatively, to declare unlawful and to prohibit any first use of such weapons, being an employment or use in conflict with the principles of international humanitarian law.

On appeal against an interlocutory judgement of the District Court, the Court of Appeal at The Hague refused the request on the formal ground that it is a requirement for such an injunction that the plaintiffs are subject to an actual and concrete danger, which requirement had not been met in the present case. The plaintiffs appealed this decision to the Supreme Court.

The Supreme Court based its reasoning on the following premises:

A. At issue is whether the request is admissible; the merits of the request are at present not under discussion.

B. The International Court of Justice, in its advisory opinion on the legality of the threat or use of nuclear weapons, of 8 July 1996, has taken the view, *inter alia*, that:

> 'in view of the current state of international law, and of the elements of fact at its disposal, the Court cannot conclude definitively whether the threat or use of nuclear weapons would be lawful or unlawful in an extreme circumstance of self-defense, in which the very survival of a State would be at stake'.

C. The request concerns the foreign and defence policy of the state, regarding which courts must take a reticent attitude.

D. A request for an injunction against future action can only be admissible if the plaintiff is subject to an actual and concrete danger. Whether or not this requirement has been met in the present case was for the lower court to determine; the Supreme Court can only check whether that Court's decision is understandable and adequately reasoned.

The Appeals Court's judgement that the request is inadmissible because it cannot in advance be determined that the acts by the state that the plaintiffs wanted to be prohibited would under all circumstances be unlawful, was considered to be understandable and adequately reasoned by the Supreme Court. Whether or not the use of nuclear weapons, even in a densely populated area, will be lawful, can only be determined, according to the Supreme Court, with an eye on the concrete circumstances of the case.

By ruling that the plaintiffs' allegation that nuclear weapons will possibly be used (instead of: will be used) is an insufficiently concrete cause for the requested prohibition, the Appeals Court applied the right criterion, according to the Supreme Court.

---

419. Hoge Raad der Nederlanden 10 November 1989, *Nederlandse Jurisprudentie* 1001, p. 248 (with annotation by P.H. Kooijmans). See also XII *NYIL* (1991) p. 453.

For those reasons, the Supreme Court, in its decision of 21 December 2001, has rejected the appeal.

☛ Transfer of suspect to Rwanda Tribunal, District Court of The Hague, Decision of 16 October 2001. Published in *Nederlandse Jurisprudentie* (Netherlands Law Reports) 2002, No. 20 C

The Registrar of the Rwanda Tribunal had requested the Dutch authorities to transfer Simon Bikindi to the Tribunal for prosecution on the basis of an indictment accusing him of having between 1 January and 31 December 1994 committed in Rwanda: conspiracy to commit genocide, genocide, direct and public incitement to commit genocide, and crimes against humanity (murder and persecution). In conformity with the Netherlands' 1997 Rwanda Tribunal Implementation Act, the Dutch prosecutor at The Hague had submitted this request to the Hague District Court for a decision whether there were any legal objections to the transfer.

Before the court, Bikindi declared that even if he is the requested person, he is not guilty of the alleged crimes.

Taking into account that the request related to crimes under the jurisdiction of the Rwanda Tribunal, the court found no legal objections to the requested transfer.

The court judged inadmissible Bikindi's plea of not guilty, and refused his counsel the opportunity to bring evidence proving his innocence. The Court reasoned that, apart from cases of mistake of identity (but Bikindi had admitted to being the person requested), any defence concerning the proof of the *actus reus* or of the *mens rea* or blameworthiness of the accused is exclusively a matter for the Tribunal to determine. Because of Article 103 of the United Nations Charter, a request from the Rwanda Tribunal supersedes any conflicting obligations under international or domestic law.

Bikindi's counsel further argued that, because of the considerable danger that after his transfer he would be killed by persons belonging to a hostile tribe, the Tribunal should be asked to guarantee that following any conviction he would be returned to the Netherlands. For this reason, the court advised the Minister of Justice to enter an enforcement of sentences agreement to that effect with the Tribunal.

A few comments are necessary to explain the court's decision. The Extradition Act (1967), to which the Yugoslavia Tribunal Implementation Act (1994) and the Rwanda Tribunal Implementation Act (1997) refer, by its Article 26(3) explicitly gives a requested person the right to immediately prove his innocence.[420] This provision is normally applied in such a way that only a plea of mistaken identity or of a convincing alibi (e.g., the requested person was on the day of the crime in hospital or in prison elsewhere) is admissible. In relation to the Yugoslavia or the Rwanda Tribunals, however, a refusal of a requested transfer on the ground of the apparent innocence of the requested person would conflict with Articles 29/28 of the Statutes of those Tribunals. Unlike the Extradition Act, the Yugoslavia Tribunal Implementation Act and the Rwanda Tribunal Implementation Act for this reason do not empower the Court to prohibit a requested transfer on the ground that the requested person cannot possibly have committed the offence. Consequently, if a

420. A similar right has not been given to a requested person by the International Criminal Court Implementation Act (2002).

requested person immediately proves his innocence, the Court cannot block the transfer, but it can of course advise the Minister of Justice to inform (the Prosecutor of) the Tribunal of its findings.

In the present case, the District Court has (apart from the defence of mistaken identity) ruled out the admissibility of any plea of innocence. The Court seems to be right in its judgement that a state's obligation under the Statute to cooperate with the Tribunal not only supersedes its obligations under any other international agreement but also its domestic legislation implementing such an agreement, as far as this domestic legislation would conflict with that obligation. That same view had earlier been taken by the Minister of Justice during the Parliamentary discussions concerning the Bill that has produced the Rwanda Tribunal Implementation Act (1997).[421] However, the Court failed to make clear why application of the domestic provision which gives a requested person the right to immediately prove his innocence would conflict with that obligation.

NICO KEIJZER

NEW ZEALAND[422]

Children

☛ Defence Amendment Act 2001, commenced 27 September 2001
[http://rangi.knowledge-basket.co.nz/gpacts/public/text/2001/an/062.html]

New Zealand deposited its instrument of ratification of the 2000 Optional Protocol to the Convention on the Rights of the Child on the Involvement of Children in Armed Conflict on 12 November 2001. Some minor statutory amendments were required to comply with the Protocol's limit of 18 years for active service.[423] By virtue of the Defence Act 1990, no person serving in the Army or Air Force was liable for active service outside New Zealand while under 18 years.[424] For the Navy, the minimum age for active service was 16 years and six months.[425] In fact, New Zealand Defence Force policy restricted posting of all those on active or operational service to 18 years and over.[426] This policy has now been given statutory effect whereby the Defence Act, as amended by the Defence Amendment Act 2001, specifies that no person under 18 years is liable for active service.[427] The Act, as amended, also specifies that no person under 17 years can be enlisted.[428]

---

421. Kamerstukken I (Printed matter, Senate) 1997-1998, 24818, nr. 68b.

422. Information and commentaries by Treasa Dunworth, Lecturer in Law, Faculty of Law, University of Auckland.

423. Optional Protocol, Art. 1. See M. Happold, 'The Optional Protocol to the Convention on the Rights of the Child on the Involvement of Children in Armed Conflict', 3 *YIHL* (2000) pp. 226-244.

424. S. 37(1) Defence Act 1990.

425. S. 37(2) Defence Act 1990.

426. Report of the Foreign Affairs, Defence and Trade Committee on the United Nations Convention on the Rights of the Child Optional Protocol on the Involvement of Children in Armed Conflict, 18 October 2001.

427. S. 37 Defence Act, as amended by Defence Amendment Act 2001. The original provision referred to 'active service outside New Zealand' whereas the amended section simply refers to 'active service'.

428. S. 33, Defence Act 1990, as amended by Defence Amendment Act 2001.

Because New Zealand currently does not have conscription, no legislation was necessary to comply with Article 2 of the Protocol.

Education and Training[429]

The New Zealand Defence Force completed its first full year of training under a revised Law of Armed Conflict training package. The package uses multi-media presentations, drawing on examples from New Zealand's military history to illustrate principles of the Law of Armed Conflict.

Every member of the Defence Forces, from the newest recruit through to the Chief of the Defence Forces, must attend a basic four-hour presentation. Service members whose duties are likely to require a higher level of knowledge, especially those involved in combat roles or those who are likely to be involved in dealing with prisoners of war or detainees, receive a more indepth package tailored to their speciality. All Service members about to be deployed on operations, including peace support operations, receive refresher training. New Zealand Service members are currently deployed throughout the world, including East Timor, Africa, the Middle East and the Balkans.

The programme is taught as an integral part of operational preparedness, not simply as an academic subject. The presentations can therefore be delivered in the camps and bases, in the field and on board warships at sea.

The Defence Force has also produced a plasticised code of conduct card which is carried by every deployed Service member. It contains 11 basic rules and sets out the obligations and rights of a Service member who becomes a POW or detainee. The card is being studied by other armed forces in the Asia Pacific region as a possible model.

Pending

☛ New Zealand Nuclear Free Zone Extension Bill 2000, No. 32-1

Following its consideration of the New Zealand Nuclear Free Zone Extension Bill 2000, the Foreign Affairs, Defence and Trade Committee of the House of Representatives reported back to Parliament on 31 August 2001.[430] As expected, the majority of the Committee recommended that the Bill not proceed on the basis that it would be inconsistent with the current state of international law.[431] A minority report, tabled by the Green member of the Committee, supported the Bill's passage into law. The Bill currently awaits its second reading in Parliament.

TREASA DUNWORTH

---

429. Information supplied by Colonel K.J. Riordan, Director of Legal Services, HQ NZ Defence Force, Wellington, New Zealand.

430. The purpose of the Bill was to extend the existing New Zealand Nuclear Free Zone up to 200 nautical miles and prohibit the passage within that area of nuclear-propelled ships or ships carrying radioactive waste or reprocessed nuclear fuel. See 3 *YIHL* (2000) pp. 555-556.

431. 24 TCL, pp. 33, 14.

NIGERIA

Pending

- Rome Statute of the International Criminal Court (Ratification and Jurisdiction) Bill 2001

Nigeria ratified the Rome Statute on 27 September 2001. The first reading of the bill took place on 27 September, followed by the Debate on General Principles on 9 October 2001. The bill was referred to a Committee of the Whole that same day.[432]

NORWAY

International Criminal Court

- Act No. 65 of 15 June 2001 relating to the implementation of the Statute of the International Criminal Court of 17 July 1998 (the Rome Statute) in Norwegian law [LOV 2001-06-15 nr 65: Lov om gjennomføring i norsk rett av Den internasjonale straffedomstols vedtekter 17. juli 1998 (Roma-vedtektene), Avd I 2001 hefte 7] [http://www.icrc.org/ihl-nat.nsf/6fa4d35e5e3025394125673e00508143/328c47a0efe19411c1256b36005d3165?OpenDocument]

Pending

- Proposal to change the Penal Code and the Procedural Code provisions concerning terrorism

As a consequence of the adoption of Resolution 1373 by the UN Security Council on 28 September 2001, the international obligations included in the Resolution were provisionally implemented in Norwegian law on 5 October 2001. As Norway almost at the same time, on 1 October, signed the 1999 Convention on the Suppression of the Financing of Terrorism,[433] the implementation of provisional rules was done in the context of both of these events.

At the end of 2001, the Norwegian Ministry of Justice made a proposal for several new changes in those parts of the Norwegian legislation that can have an effect on the prevention of terrorist attacks. The term terrorism has not been defined or used in Norwegian criminal law. The main goal of the proposal was to clearly have it pointed out in the law that terrorist acts cause serious damage to society and must be severely punished. Among other things, the new legislation is to make planning and preparation of terrorist acts punishable. Some provisions are to cover the financing of and cooperation in the financing of terrorism. The new provisions will also change the authority of the police to use non-traditional investigation methods. As regards procedural law, the proposal suggests that the possibilities to broaden the scope of the rules dealing with anonymous witnesses in court should be looked into. The work on changing the legislation was done having regard to changes in the legislation in this field in other countries, especially the European countries and the United States of America.

MARIA NYBONDAS

432. Source: http://iccnow.org/countryinfo/africa/nigeria.html.

433. Adopted by the General Assembly of the United Nations in resolution 54/109 of 9 December 1999.

OCCUPIED PALESTINIAN TERRITORIES[434]

The Peace Process

- Palestinian – Israeli security implementation work plan (Tenet Cease-Fire Plan), 14 June 2001 [thttp://www.mfa.gov.il/mfa/go.asp?MFAH0khz0; http://www.jmcc.org/documents/tenet.htm]
- Israeli-Palestinian Joint Communiqué, 26 September 2001 [http://www.israel-mfa.gov.il/mfa/go.asp?MFAH0kim0]
- Work Plan for Implementation of the Cease-Fire, 26 September 2001 [www.mfa.gov.il/mfa/go.asp?MFAH0kin0]

2001 witnessed only a minimal level of Israeli-Palestinian contacts on both the diplomatic and operational levels. The lack of progress on the political level was represented in the failure of the parties to conclude further agreements, notably, on permanent status issues, including the issues of refugees, Israeli settlements and borders and Jerusalem.

The only agreements reached were the above security-related ceasefire documents. However, none was carried out. Instead, the level of violence in the Occupied Palestinian Territories (OPTs) increased to unprecedented levels, with the Israeli army invading most Palestinian towns, villages and refugee camps, including those areas in the OPTs which have been under Palestinian National Authority (PNA) control in accordance with the many previous Israeli-Palestinian agreements.[435] As the UN High Commissioner for Human Rights rightly emphasized in her address to the Conference of High Contracting Parties to the Fourth Geneva Convention, 'neither the Israeli policy of targeted assassination of Palestinian civilians, nor Palestinian attacks against Israeli civilians, can be reconciled with provisions of international humanitarian law, including the Fourth Geneva Convention'.[436]

Many cases involving violations of various rights of civilians protected under international humanitarian law were documented by the many human rights groups active in the OPTS, including Amnesty International, Human Rights Watch, the Israeli human rights organization B'Tselem, and the Palestinian organizations Al-Haq, Palestinian Center for Human Rights, LAW, and the Palestinian Independent Commission for Citizens' Rights.[437]

---

434. Information and commentaries provided by Dr Mustafa Mari, Lecturer at the School of Graduate Studies at the Bir Zeit University, Bir Zeit, Palestine, formerly, Head of the Legal Department of the Palestinian Independent Commission for Citizens' Rights (PICCR), Head of the Legal Department of al-Haq, West Bank affiliate of the Geneva-based International Commission of Jurists.

435. For details and listing of previous Israeli-Palestinian agreements, see Vols. 1 and 3 *YHIL* at p. 467 and p. 532, respectively. See also www.pna.net, www.mofa.gov.il.

436. Statement by Mary Robinson, United Nations High Commissioner for Human Rights to the Conference of High Contracting Parties of the Fourth Geneva Convention, Geneva, 5 December 2001. http://www.unhchr.ch/huricane/huricane.nsf/view01/
2775EBBA0EF8B4AFC1256B1900312F6C?opendocument.

437. On this generally see Amnesty International's Report 2002, section on Israel and the Occupied Territories, available online at www.amnesty.org; Human Rights Watch World Report 2002, section on Israel, the Occupied West Bank and Gaza Strip, and Palestinian Authority Territories, pp. 440-452, available online at www.hrw.org; Palestinian Independent Commission for Citizens' Rights, *Israeli Violations of Palestinian Citizen's Rights During 2001* (2002) (Arabic), available online at www.piccr.org; 'International humanitarian law is being flouted, says Poul Nielson', European Commission – Humanitarian Aid Office (ECHO), 16 April 2002, available online at http://wwww.reliefweb.int/w/Rwb.nsf/s/A7649925D0A8C8EBC1256B9D0040AEBE.
See also www.lawsociety.org, www.alhaq.org, www.piccr.org, and www.btselem.org.

Palestinian individuals, including those belonging to organizations committed to violent resistance to the Israeli occupation, carried out operations targeting Israeli troops in the OPTs, but on many occasions also targeted Israeli civilians, both inside and outside the OPTs, in violation of the IHL prohibition on targeting civilians.[438]

According to Amnesty International 'more than 460 Palestinians were killed during 2001 by the Israeli security forces; most were unlawfully killed. Among the victims were 79 children.'[439] Amnesty reported that many of these killings occurred 'when the lives of others were not in imminent danger, during demonstrations, during shelling of residential areas and at checkpoints'.[440] Concern was also expressed that the Israeli authorities continued to use Palestinian civilians as human shields during raids on Palestinian towns and villages, thus endangering their lives.[441]

Among the more than 460 Palestinians killed by Israeli forces in 2001 were 32 individuals targeted for assassination.[442] During a 7 November visit to Ramallah in the OPTs, the Director-General of the ICRC described the Israeli assassination of three Palestinians the day before as 'a barbaric act', and 'one of the worst human rights violations that one could possibly imagine'.[443] Despite the clear prohibition in IHL of summary executions, and calls both abroad and at home on the Israeli government to abandon such practice, the Israeli Government remained committed to the policy and its Military Judge Advocate General spelled out the conditions for assassinations.[444] Moreover, on 29 January 2002, the Israeli Supreme Court rejected an application brought before it by Member of Israel's parliament Muhammad Barakeh asking the Court to order the authorities to refrain from carrying out such assassinations in the future. The Court found that the investigation of operational methods employed by the State of Israel in order to prevent anti-Israel activities is not amongst the matters the Court finds appropriate to intervene in.[445]

Human rights organizations also documented hundreds of cases involving trials of Palestinians by Israeli military courts, in trials which did not meet international standards for fair trial. Israeli authorities also resorted to administrative detention, without charges or trial, in many cases. According to the Israeli human rights organization, B'Tselem, dozens of Pales-

438. On this see Amnesty International Report 2002, section on Palestinian Authority, Amnesty International, 2002, available online at www.amnesty.org.

439. Ibid. See also Human Rights Watch World Report 2002.

440. Amnesty International Report 2002.

441. See 'In a Dark Hour: The Use of Civilians During IDF Arrest Operations', Human Rights Watch, April 2002.

442. Amnesty International Report 2002. See also Human Rights Watch World Report 2002.

443. See 'International Committee of the Red Cross condemns Israel's inhumane measures against the Palestinian people, Palestine Media Center, 8 November 2001.

444. See 'IDF lawyers step in with 'conditions' for assassination policy', *Haaretz*, 4 February 2002. On the legal debate pertaining to Israeli assassinations see 'Easier to kill, harder to judge', *Haaretz*, 31 January 2002.

445. See for example 'Easier to kill, harder to judge', *Haaretz*, 31 January 2002. See also *Muhammad Barakeh, MP* v. *Prime Minister and Minister of Defense*, HCJ case number 5872/01, 29 January 2002.

tinians were placed under administrative detention during the year following the outbreak of the Palestinian uprising, a number which has recently reached over a 1000.[446]

The treatment of the thousands of Palestinians detained by Israeli authorities remained a source of concern, as human rights groups, including the Israeli Public Committee against Torture, reported that Israeli authorities employed various torture techniques.[447] The UN Committee against Torture, on 23 November 2001, expressed its concern that a 1999 Israeli Supreme Court decision banning certain practices employed by Israeli authorities during the interrogation of Palestinians did not definitely prohibit torture, and that Israel's policies of closure and house demolitions might, in some cases, constitute cruel, inhuman or degrading treatment or punishment.[448] The location of detention facilities outside of the OPTs also makes family and lawyer visits almost impossible. According to HRW, '[t]he ICRC reported that its family visits program to prisoners was severely hampered by Israeli closures and administrative requirements.'[449]

Other punitive measures employed during the year by the Israeli authorities included intensification of the destruction of homes and other property,[450] prohibited under humanitarian law as collective punishments. The period September 2000-October 2001 witnessed the destruction by Israeli authorities of more than 300 homes and the uprooting of 385,000 fruit and olive trees.[451]

2001 also witnessed the imposition of severe limitations on the freedom of ambulance crews and other personnel providing humanitarian services to the population of the OPTs.[452]

Geneva Law

☛ Declaration of the Conference of High Contracting Parties to the Fourth Geneva Convention, 5 December 2001[453]

The Conference, which took place on 5 December in Geneva, Switzerland, was held upon the invitation of the government of Switzerland, the depository of the Geneva Conventions,

---

446. According to B'Tselem, Israeli authorities currently hold 1,007 Palestinians under administrative detention, the largest number at any given date since 1991. See 'For the first time since 1991 – over 1000 administrative detainees', press statement by B'Tselem, 1 January 2003. Available online at http://www.btselem.org/English/Press_Releases/2003/030102.asp. See also *Human Rights Watch World Report 2002*, pp. 443-44. For administrative detention updates, check http://btselem.org/English/Administrative_Detention/Statistics.asp.

447. *Human Rights Watch World Report 2002*, p. 443.

448. Ibid. See also 'UN: Israel torture ban has loopholes', AP, 23 November 2001.

449. *Human Rights Watch World Report 2002*, p. 444.

450. See, for example, 'Israel and the autonomous/occupied territories: House destruction in Khan Younis. ICRC assists 62 families', ICRC News 02/01, 11 January 2002. See also 'Israel's policy of house demolitions and destruction of agricultural land in the Gaza Strip, Jerusalem, B'Tselem, 2002.

451. *Human Rights Watch World Report 2002*, p. 443.

452. For details on this see, for example, 'Multiple violations of International Humanitarian law by the Israeli Defense Forces in the Palestinian Occupied Territories and measures taken against international humanitarian workers', Médecins du Monde, 12 April 2002. Available online at http://wwww.reliefweb.int/w/Rwb.nsf/s/D8EEDA7EEB8F2EEDC1256B9C002E544E.

453. Full text of the declaration available online at http://wwww.reliefweb.int/w/Rwb.nsf/s/E7FC889EFA54AB1EC1256B190048CDE6.

following a call by the UN General Assembly.[454] It was attended by representatives of 114 states and delegates representing international and non-governmental organizations, including the UN and the ICRC.

However, the Conference did not live up to the expectations of many human rights and other concerned organizations. While its aim was to discuss 'measures to enforce the Convention in the Occupied Palestinian Territory, including Jerusalem, and to ensure respect thereof in accordance with common article 1', it ended with a general Declaration affirming its applicability to the OPTs, including East Jerusalem, without dealing with enforcement measures of any kind.[455] The Conference also stressed 'that the Fourth Geneva Convention, which takes fully into account imperative military necessity, has to be respected in all circumstances'.

Compensation

☛ Civil Wrongs (State Liability) Law (Amendment No. 4), 24 July 2002[456]

On 24 July 2002, the Israeli parliament passed an amendment of the Civil Wrongs (State Responsibility) law, which makes the State of Israel exempt from paying compensation to Palestinian civilians, even in cases where they have acted illegally, and therefore renders the Israeli security forces immune from almost all civil suits.[457]

MUSTAFA MARI

PANAMA

The Emblem

☛ Law No. 32 concerning the use of the red cross and red crescent emblems and designations [Ley No. 32 de 4 de julio de 2001 que dicta disposiciones para la protección y el uso del emblema de la Cruz Roja y el de la Media Luna Roja]. Adopted on 4 July 2001. Entered into force on 6 July 2001, the day of its publication in *Gaceta Oficial* No. 24.339 of 6 July 2001, pp. 21-26[458]

454. The Conference was boycotted by the US, Israel and Australia. See 'Geneva parley delegates blast Israel', *Jerusalem Post*, 6 December 2001.

455. *PCHR and LAW condemn High Contracting Parties farce*, 22 November 2001. Available online at www.lawsociety.org. See also Declaration of the NGO parallel meeting concerning the Fourth Geneva Convention, 4-5 December 2001, Geneva. Available online at http://wwww.reliefweb.int/w/Rwb.nsf/s/34D82A8C0B950F5B85256B1A005A76ED.

456. Copy of the approved amendment, in Hebrew, is available online at http://www.knesset.gov.il/provatelaw/data/2645_3_1.rtf. Translation of an earlier draft is available online at http://www.btselem.org.

457. See the press statement four leading Israeli human rights organizations issued following the adoption of this law entitled 'Human rights organizations call law a black stain on Israel's Statutes', 24 July 2002. Available online at http://www.btselem.org/english/special/020724_compensation.asp. See also M. Mari and M. Pujara, 'In Light of the Israeli Draft Law on Denying Compensation to Palestinians: Accountability of the Israeli Occupier for Violations of Palestinian Rights', Ramallah, Al-Haq 1998.

458. ICRC Advisory Service, *National Implementation of International Humanitarian Law*: Biennial report 2000-2001 (Geneva, ICRC 2002) p. 76.

'Law No. 32 of 4 July 2001, passed by the Legislative Assembly and published in Official Gazette No. 24.339, provides for the protection and use of the red cross and red crescent emblems. It is an excellent example of how to implement the provisions of the Geneva Convention of 1949 and the Additional Protocols of 1977. It covers all aspects of this protection regime: definitions, protective and indicative use, civil and military personnel addressed, special use by the Panamanian Red Cross Society, use by the components of the International Red Cross Movement, monitoring and penalties.'[459]

Truth Commission

☛ Establishment of Truth Commission, 18 January 2001
[http://www.comisiondelaverdad.org.pa/index.htm]

On 18 January 2001, Panamanian President Mireya Moscoso established a truth commission to investigate human rights violations perpetrated during the military dictatorships of Generals Omar Torrijos and Manuel Noriega between 1968 and 1989. Led by lawyer Alberto Santiago Almanza Henriquez, committee members include Bishop Julio Murray, lawyer Juan Antonio Tejada, Dr Osvaldo Velasquez, businessman and president of the Panama branch of International Transparency Fernando Berguido, human rights activist Otilia Tejeira de Coster and Rosa Maria Britton. The commission was given six months to present a report to the Attorney-General, with the possibility of a three-month extension if deemed necessary by commissioners to complete their work.

Pending

☛ Criminal law reform

'[I]n 2000 and 2001 the *Comisión Nacional Permanente para la Aplicación de Derecho Internacional Humanitario* (CPDIH) prepared draft amendments to introduce sanctions for violations of IHL into the Criminal Code and bring its provisions in line with the requirements of the law, and submitted them for approval to the Legislative Assembly. The CPDIH also endeavoured to promote ratification of the 1998 Rome Statute of the International Criminal Court.'[460]

PARAGUAY

Implementation and Dissemination

☛ Establishment of the Department of Human Rights and International Humanitarian Law by the General Secretariat of the Ministry of Defence, December 1999

☛ Launch of study by the Human Rights Department of the Ministry of Foreign Affairs concerning Paraguay's ratification of the 1954 Cultural Property Convention and the 1980 Certain Conventional Weapons Convention and its Protocols, 2001[461]

---

459. Source: ICRC National Implementation Database. http://www.icrc.org/ihl-nat.nsf/6fa4d35e5e3025394125673e00508143/30f98ff18183cdaac1256d1f0053a932?OpenDocument.

460. Ibid.

461. Ibid., p. 77.

- Presidential Decree No. 15 926 of 28 December 2001 modifying the 1995 Presidential Decree establishing the Comisión Interministerial de Aplicacion del Derecho Internacional Humanitario (CIADIH),[462] with a view to reorganising the Committee.

Training and Education

- In 2001, IHL was taught at the law faculties of most of the universities of Paraguay, as part of public international law.
- In 2001, the armed forces underwent training in IHL as part of their programme of instruction at military academies and other institutions.[463]

PERU

Truth and Reconciliation Commission

- Law of 9 December 2000. Resolutión Suprema No. 304-2000-Jus of 9 December 2000 Establece Grupo de Trabajo Interinstitucional Encargado de Elaborar Propuestas Legislativas y Administrativas Necesarisas para el Establecimiento de una Comision de la Verda
- Supreme Decree [Resolución Suprema] Nº 065-2001-PCM, 4 June 2001

In December 2000, the government of Valentin Paniagua agreed to the establishment of a truth commission to investigate violations of human rights and humanitarian law committed between 1980 and 2000.

The Commission's objectives were set out in Supreme Decreee No. 065-2001-PCM of 4 June 2001:

—To determine the causes of the conflict Peru experienced between May 1980 and November 2000;
—To contribute to the clarification of the crimes and human rights violations perpetrated during this period;
—To identify, to the best of its abilities, those responsible for violent acts;
—To elaborate proposals for the reparation and dignification of the victims of their families;
—To recommend the implementation of reforms as preventive measures;
—To establish follow up mechanisms for its recommendations.

The Commission, presided over by Salomon Lerner Fresnes, was inaugurated on 13 July 2001 and began work later that month. In September 2001, at the request of the Catholic Church, the name of the commission was changed to the Truth and Reconciliation Commission, and the Commission began its work. Once its work is completed in 2003, it will publish a detailed report of its findings.

The Commission operates from five regional offices. The Central South Regional Office, based in Huamanga, covers the departments of Ayacucho, Apurímac and Huancavelica; the

462. The Committee's mandate is to spread knowledge of the rules contained in the 1949 Geneva Conventions and their Additional Protocols and to promote their implementation through the adoption of legislative and other administrative measures.' Ibid.

463. Ibid.

Northeast Regional Office, based in Huanuco, covers the departments of Huánuco, San Martín and Ucayali; the Regional Office of the Southern Andes, based in Abancay (it moved from Sicunai/Cusco), covers the departments of Cusco, Puno, Apurímac and Madre de Dios; the Central Regional Office, based in Huancayo (Junín), covers the departments of Junín, Pasco and Huancavelica; and finally, the Regional Office of Lima North East and South, based in Lima, covers the departments of Lima, Tumbes, Piura, Lambayeque, La Libertad, Ancash, Ica, Arequipa, Moquegua, Tacna, Cajamarca, Amazonas and Loreto. The role of these regional offices is to collect testimonies from persons affected by the violence during the period covered by the TRC.

International Criminal Court

- Supreme Resolution Resolución Suprema] authorising the ratification of the Rome Statute. Published in *El Peruano* on 14 February 2001

The Foreign Affairs Commission of the Peruvian Congress unanimously approved the ratification of the Rome Statute by Peru on 29 May 2001, following a favourable decision by the Commission of Justice. The resulting resolutions were submitted to Congress and a final vote on the Statute took place in Congress at a Plenary. On 13 September 2001, by 84 votes to one, Congress authorised President Toledo to ratify the Rome Statute.[464]

Implementation and Dissemination

- Supreme Resolution No. 234-2001-JUS, 1 June 2001 establishing the Comisión Nacional de Estudio y Aplicación del DIH (CONADIH).

'The Commission's mandate is to propose national legislation for the implementation of humanitarian law. The ICRC acted as an observer on the CONADIH and provided it in 2001 with technical expertise and documentation. The CONDADIH adopted rules of procedure and a plan of action.'[465]

Education and Training

- Directives No. 005 MD/I of June 2001
- Directive No. 026-CCFFAA-FI/DAACC-DDHH of July 2001
- Directive No. 011 M-4/DIRAC/23

The first and second directives renew the requirement of Directive No. 017 CCFFAA-EM-FI/DDHH of August 1998, issued by the Armed Forces Joint Chiefs of Staff, that all military and police institutes include IHL and human rights law as part of their training program. The third directive refers to a plan to incorporate the law of armed conflict into armed forces training programs.[466]

464. http://iccnow.org/countryinfo/theamericas/peru.html.

465. ICRC Advisory Service, *National Implementation of International Humanitarian Law*: Biennial report 2000-2001 (Geneva, ICRC 2002) p. 78.

466. Ibid.

- The University of Lima offered IHL as an optional course in 2001 and in the same year, the University of San Marcos also introduced an optional course on IHL. The Catholic University included it in its public law seminar.[467]

THE PHILIPPINES

Implementation and Dissemination

- Establishment of the Philippine National Red Cross International Humanitarian Law National Committee, April 2000
- 'The Committee's main responsibilities and activities include advocacy, campaigning and dissemination. It is made up of members of the Philippine National Red Cross Board of Governors, representatives of a wide range of national governmental authorities, including the Departments of Foreign Affairs, National Defence, the Interior and Local Government, Education, Culture and Sports, the Philippine National Police, the National Commission on Human Rights, the National Commission on Education, and members of the local NGO community and academic circles. The ICRC participates in the Committee's work as an observer.'[468]

Pending

- Bill to ratify Statute of the International Criminal Court

Following a recommendation by the Philippine Commission on Human Rights that the 1998 Rome Statute of the International Criminal Court be ratified by the Philippines, a draft ratification bill was prepared by the Department of Foreign Affairs and submitted for consideration to the Office of the President of the Republic.[469]

POLAND

International Criminal Court

- ICC Ratification Bill

The Bill of Ratification of the Rome Statute was referred by the Polish Government to Parliament in December 2000. The Parliament adopted the Draft Bill on 5 July 2001 and referred it to the Senate, which adopted it on 2 August. The Bill was signed by the President on 27 August 2001, giving effect to the domestic legislation.

A few issues were raised by Parliament before it adopted the Draft Bill. The question was considered whether a ratification of the Rome Statute would require a change of the Polish Constitution. One point of concern was related to the surrender of Polish citizens to the ICC. Under Article 55 of the Constitution, extradition of Polish citizens is prohibited. It was, however, concluded that surrender to the Court is not identical to the meaning of extradition according to Article 55 and that no conflict, therefore, existed. The Parliament also concluded that in the case of surrender of a person protected by immunity, there would not

467. Ibid.
468. Ibid., p. 79.
469. Ibid.

be a conflict with Polish law. It was further held that the ratification of the Rome Statute could be done in accordance with the normal ratification procedure, as opposed to a proposed special procedure, applied for example in situations where competence of the State was to be referred to an international organization (also applied for the accession of Poland to the European Union).

The Statute of the ICC was ratified by Poland on 21 November 2001. Legislative work related to the implementation of the Rome Statute in national law was to be done after ratification. In 2001 proposals were already made for changes both to the Penal Code and the Code of Criminal Procedure.[470]

Education and Training

☛ Establishment of the Regional Centre of Education for Middle-East States of Europe on the Protection of Cultural Heritage in Case of Emergency in Cracow, July 2001

Ongoing cases

☛ *Czeslaw Geborski* case, Regional court of Opole

The trial opened on 26 January 2001 before the regional court in Opole of former prison camp commander Czeslaw Geborski, accused of crimes against humanity for committing atrocities against German detainees following WWII.[471] Geborski, 76, from the Silesian city of Katowice, is accused of ordering guards to set fire to a prison barracks and shoot inmates who fled. Prosecutors say at least 48 prisoners died on 4 October 1945 in the Lambinowice camp he commanded in southwestern Poland. Geborski denies the charges. He contends that the prisoners set fire to the barracks themselves during an escape attempt, and only three were killed by guards trying to stop them.

PORTUGAL

International Criminal Court

☛ Constitutional Law No. 1/2001 [Ley Constitucional No. 1/2001] enabling Portugal to accept the jurisdiction of the International Criminal Court. The Law was promulgated on 20 November 2001[472]

ROMANIA

Pending

☛ ICC ratification bill. On 18 December 2001, the President submitted the draft ratification bill to the Legislative Committee of the Parliament for review.

---

470. 'The Implications for Council of Europe Member States of the Ratification of the Rome Statute of the International Criminal Court', Progress Report by Poland and Appendix, Council of Europe, Strasbourg, 7 August 2001, Consult/ICC (2001) p. 22.

471. B. Pasek, 'Geborski accused of atrocities', AP, 26 January 2001.

472. ICRC Advisory Service, *National Implementation of International Humanitarian Law*: Biennial report 2000-2001 (Geneva, ICRC 2002) p. 81.

- The Ministry of Foreign Affairs approved the withdrawal of reservations made by Romania to the Geneva Conventions. The parliament was expected to adopt the new law in early-2001

RUSSIAN FEDERATION

Education and Training

- Order No. 360 of 8 August 2001 adopted by the Ministry of Defence on measures of observance of international humanitarian law in the armed forces of the Russian Federation

'Pursuant thereto, the Ministry of Defence published a manual on IHL for the armed forces, in cooperation with the ICRC.'[473]

RWANDA

Cases

- Trials in connection with the 1994 genocide

According to NGO sources, by January 2000, more than 2,500 persons of the 120,000 originally detained, have been tried for genocide and other crimes committed in 1994 during the genocide in Rwanda. Of these, about 370 have received death sentences, 800 sentences of life imprisonment, 500 acquitted, and the remainder various sentences of imprisonment. It is difficult to get precise information about the ongoing trials and their outcomes, and available information is incomplete. Many decisions are rendered orally, and there is no trial record. The following is based on NGO and press reports.

- *Theoneste Rukeratabar and 27 others* case, Cyangugu commune, 31 March 2000

On 31 March 2000, Theoneste Rukeratabar, the former mayor of Gisuma in Cyangugu Prefecture and 14 others, were found guilty for their role in the 1994 genocide.[474] Rukeratabar and seven others received the death penalty, seven defendants received sentences of life imprisonment; three received 20-year sentences, two received sentences of 15 years; two received sentences of 11 years, and six were acquitted. According to a radio report of the sentencing, the court in the south-western commune of Cynangugu also ordered the defendants to pay a total of $500,000 to 30 families of victims who sought compensation.[475]

- Case against 14 people for genocide and crimes against humanity, Taba Commune, 17 December 2000

---

473. ICRC Advisory Service, *National Implementation of International Humanitarian Law*: Biennial report 2000-2001 (Geneva, ICRC 2002) p. 83.

474. 'Genocide and international crimes in domestic courts'. A survey undertaken by Prevent Genocide International. Available at its website: http://www.preventgenocide.org/punish/domestic.

475. 'Rwanda Court Sentences 8 To Death', AP, 2 April 2000; 'Rwanda genocide death sentences', BBC News, 1 April 2000. Online at http://news.bbc.co.uk/2/hi/africa/698249.stm.

On 17 December 2000, a court in Taba Commune sentenced 14 persons to life imprisonment for genocide and crimes against humanity.

☛ *Paul Kadogi et al.* case, 6 February 2001

On 6 February 2001, Paul Kadogi, the former mayor of Nshili municipality in Gikongoro province, and three others were sentenced to death for their involvement in the 1994 genocide.[476]

☛ *Wellars Benzi* and 33 others case, 26 May 2001

On 26 May 2001, a court in Gisenyi sentenced Wellars Benzi, former member of the Rwandan Parliament and former president of the National Revolutionary Movement of Rwanda (MRND) and ten others to death for having organised the militias that carried out the genocide against the Tutsi population and moderate Hutus, and for having published anti-Tutsi propaganda in the *Kangura* newspaper. Twenty-three others received sentences of life imprisonment.

☛ Case against 126 genocide suspects, 16 June 2001

A mass trial of 126 persons accused of involvement in the 1994 genocide ended with a verdict on 16 June 2001. Nine persons were sentenced to death, 30 received sentences of life imprisonment, 25 were acquitted and the remainder were sentenced to between four and 20 years in prison.[477] Several dozen accused escaped harsher sentences by admitting their crimes during the trial. The seven-month long trial was held in a makeshift courtroom, built in order to accommodate the large number of defendants.[478]

Gacaca

☛ Preliminary session of the gacaca courts, 28 May 2001

☛ Presidentiel order No. 12/01 of 26/06/2001 establishing modalities for organizing elections of members of Gacaca jurisdictions organs, 26 June 2001 [Arrêté présidentiel No. 12/01 du 26/06/2001 fixant les modalités d'organisation des élections des membres des organes des "Juridictions Gacaca"]. Published in *Journal officiel de la République rwandaise*, 40th Year 40, No. 14, 15 July 2001

☛ Election of Gacaca Judges, 4 and 5 October 2001

---

476. Source: 'News Monitor for February 2001'. Prevent Genocide International. http://www.preventgenocide.org/prevent/news-monitor/2001feb.htm.

477. Source: 'Genocide and international crimes in domestic courts'. A survey undertaken by Prevent Genocide International. Available at its website: http://www.preventgenocide.org/punish/domestic. See also 'Nine sentenced to die at Rwanda genocide trial', CNN News Online, 16 June 2001.

478. 'Nine sentenced to death over Rwandan genocide', *The Namibian*, 18 June 2001.

A preliminary session of the 'gacaca' courts, that is, traditional local and provincial courts,[479] established under the Law on Gacaca[480] was held on 28 May 2001 in Nogwe commune, Gitarama province. Under 'gacaca', judges chosen from the community accompany the accused to the scenes of their alleged crimes in the hope that the guilty will confess and ask for forgiveness. The traditional system applies only to people accused of local killings or of collaboration with the killers.

Seven cases were heard by the preliminary session, which sat on a grass patch on a small hill next to a road. 'Each detainee stood before approximately 2000 local residents while Jean Barushinana, the region's prosecutor, read out their names, age and asked the community if anyone knew of any reason why the person should be detained.' Four suspects who had been detained for more than four years in Gitarama prison on genocide charges were released because nobody had any evidence against them.[481]

Presidential order No. 12/01 of 26/06/2001 establishing modalities for organizing elections of members of Gacaca jurisdictions organs 'states that Gacaca jurisdictions are to be established in Rwanda at all levels of local authority ("cellules", "secteurs", districts, cities and provinces). It further specifies who is entitled to vote for members of those jurisdictions, who is eligible to become a member, who, how, when and through which body elections are to be organized, the way the voting is to proceed, and also provides for cases where the outcome of those elections is unsatisfactory.'[482]

On 4 and 5 October 2001, Rwanda elected 260,000 lay judges to serve on its 'gacaca' courts. Nineteen judges will be assigned to each 'cell' or group of 50 households, which will judge less serious crimes. More serious crimes will be judged at the provincial level, while those charged with the most serious 'category 1' offences will continue to be tried by the ordinary courts.

The 'gacaca' courts were expected to start operating in early-2002.

SENEGAL

Cases

☛ Decision of the Cour de Cassation in the case of Hissène Habré, Arrêt n' 14 du 20-3-2001 Pénal, 20 March 2001[483] [http://www.hrw.org/french/themes/habre-cour_de_cass.html]

---

479. J. Baptiste Kayigamba, 'Rwanda elects 260,000 judges for genocide trials', Reuters, 4 October 2001; R. Ngowi, 'Rwandans use traditional justice', AP, 6 October 2001.

480. Organic Law No. 40/2000 of 26/01/2001 Setting Up "Gacacca Jurisdictions" and Organizing Prosecutions for Offences Constituting the Crime of Genocide or Crimes Against Humanity Committed between October 1, 1990 and December 31, 1994, 26 January 2001. Reprinted in 3 *YIHL* (2001) pp. 739 et seq. For commentary see J.K. Kleffner, Correspondents' Reports, in the same volume at pp. 569-570.

481. Source: 'Genocide and international crimes in domestic courts'. A survey undertaken by Prevent Genocide International. Available at its website: http://www.preventgenocide.org/punish/domestic. See also M. Kimani, 'Community frees four Genocide suspects during pilot Gacaca Justice Process', Internews, 20 May 2001.

482. Source: ICRC National Implementation Database. http://www.icrc.org/ihl-nat.nsf/6fa4d35e5e3025394125673e00508143/6e7e5d91a76ba8e5c1256b2700321e54?OpenDocument.

483. For background to the case, see I. Sansani, 'The Pinochet precedent in Africa: Prosecution of Hissene Habre', 8 *Human Rights Brief*, Issue 2. Online at http://www.wcl.american.edu/hrbrief/08/

On 20 March 2001, the Cour de Cassation upheld a ruling of the Indictment Chamber of 4 July 2000[484] that the former President of Chad, Hissène Habré, who has lived in Senegal since 1990, when he was deposed in a military coup, should not stand trial there on charges of torture committed while in office, as the alleged offences had been committed elsewhere. It found that 'Senegalese courts do not have competence over acts of torture committed by a foreigner outside of Senegalese territory regardless of the nationality of the victims'.[485]

SEYCHELLES

Implementation and Dissemination

☛ Establishment of the National Committee on Humanitarian Affairs, 2001

The Committee's mandate covers IHL and human rights.[486]

SIERRA LEONE[487]

Truth and Reconciliation

☛ The Truth and Reconciliation Commission Act 2000 of 22 February 2000 [http://www.sierra-leone.org/trcact2000.html]

Following the adoption of the Truth and Reconciliation Act on 22 February 2000, Sierra Leone took the first steps to establish a Truth and Reconciliation Commission. It is the first time that an international court, even a quasi one such as the Special Court, will function simultaneously with a TRC and offers an interesting experiment in how criminal prosecutions can complement other processes aiming at providing justice and promoting reconciliation.

The Commission shall be composed of seven members, four of whom shall be Sierra Leoneans and the remaining three non-nationals (Art. 3(1)). The Commission's mandate is for one year (Art. 5(1)), to be preceded by a preparatory period of three months (Art. 5(2)). The Commission's purpose is clearly set out in Article 6(1):

> 'The object for which the Commission is established is to create an impartial historical record of violations and abuses of human rights and international humanitarian law related to the armed conflict in Sierra Leone, from the beginning of the conflict in 1991 to the signing of the Lome Peace Agreement; to address impunity; to respond to the needs of the victims; to promote healing and reconciliation and to prevent a repetition of the violations and abuses suffered.'

2Pinochet.cfm; R. Brody, 'The prosecution of Hissene Habre - An "African Pinochet"', 35 *New England Law Review* (2001). Online at http://www.hrw.org/editorials/2001/habre0515.htm.

484. See 3 *YIHL* (2000) p. 570, and Brody, ibid.

485. Translation by Brody, ibid.

486. ICRC Advisory Service, *National Implementation of International Humanitarian Law*: Biennial report 2000-2001 (Geneva, ICRC 2002) p. 84.

487. Information and commentaries by Avril McDonald, Managing Editor of the Yearbook, and Abdul Tejan Cole, Lecturer in Law at the University of Sierra Leone.

What this means in practice is that the Commission's functions are (Art. 6(2)):

> (a) 'to investigate and report on the causes, nature and extent of the violations and abuses . . . to the fullest degreee possible, including their antecedents, the context in which the violations and abuses occurred, the question of, whether those violations and abuses were the result of deliberate planning, policy or authorisation by any government, group or individual, and the role of both internal and external factors in the conflict;
> (b) to work to restore the human dignity of victims and promote reconciliation by providing an opportunity for victims to give an account of the violations and abuses suffered and for perpetrators to relate their experiences, and by creating a climate which fosters constructive interchange between victims and perpetrators, giving special attention to the subject of sexual abuse and to the experiences of children within the armed conflict;
> ....'

The Commission shall carry out its work by means of undertaking research and investigations, holding sessions, some of which may be public, to hear from the victims and perpetrators and other interested parties, and taking individual statements and gathering additional information (Art. 7(1)).

The Commission shall take into consideration the interests of victims and witnesses when inviting them to give statements (Art. 7(4)).

At the end of its work, it shall submit its report to the President (Art. 15(1)).

By the end of the year, the Commission had not yet been inaugurated or commenced its work.

Special Court for Sierra Leone

- Letter from the Secretary-General addressed to the President of the Security Council, S/2001/40, 12 January 2001
- Letter from the President of the Security Council addressed to the Secretary-General, S/2001/9, 31 January 2001
- Letter from the Government of Sierra Leone to the Legal Counsel, 9 February 2001
- Letter dated 9 February 2001 from the Secretary-General to the President of the Security Council
- Letter dated 12 July 2001 from the Secretary-General to the President of the Security Council, UN Doc. S/2001/693, 13 July 2001
- Agreement between the United Nations and the Government of Sierra Leone on the Establishment of a Special Court for Sierra Leone, 16 January 2002 [http://www.sierra-leone.org/specialcourtagreement.html]
- Statute of the Special Court for Sierra Leone [http://www.sierra-leone.org/specialcourtstatute.html]

Negotiations to establish a Special Court for Sierra Leone by agreement between the government of Sierra Leone and the UN continued throughout 2001. Agreement on the Statute and Rules was reached in January 2001. By a letter of 9 February 2001 to the UN Legal Counsel, Sierra Leone expressed its willingness to accept the Statute and Agreement proposed by the SG.[488] However, as the year closed, the final agreement to establish the court had not yet been signed, mainly due to difficulty in finding sufficient funds to set up the Special Court.

The Council recommended that the court be funded by voluntary contributions from member states and rejected the idea of assessed contributions as a way of funding the court suggested by the Secretary-General. The Secretary-General warned of the risks involved in establishing the court without sufficient funds to support its first three years of operation and proposed that the process of establishing the court should not commence until the United Nations Secretariat has obtained sufficient contributions in hand to finance the establishment of the court for 12 months of its operation, as well as pledges equal to the anticipated expenses of the following 24 months.

As the year progressed, it became clear that the Secretary-General's original estimates for the establishment of a Special Court could not be met.[489] The SG therefore convened a meeting of Security Council members on 1 June 2001, in order to address the question of the financing of the Court. This was followed by a meeting on 14 June, at which 'the Secretariat presented to the group of interested States revised budget estimates amounting to approximately $57 million for the first three years of operation of the Court, with $6.5 milllion of the first year'. Despite deciding to push ahead with the creation of the Court, the Secretary-General, cognisant of its financial precariousness, reserved 'the right to revert to the Council at any time in the course of the operation of the Special Court and ask it to reconsider alternative means of financing the Court'.[490] Once the minimum funds necessary to launch the court had been secured, the UN and the government of Sierra Leone were able to sign, on 16 January 2002, the Agreeement setting up the Special Court to prosecute persons bearing the 'greatest responsibility' for crimes committed in that county'.

AVRIL MCDONALD and ABDUL TEJAN COLE

SINGAPORE

Chemical Weapons

- The Chemical Weapons (Prohibition) Act 2000, An Act to give effect to the Convention on the prohibition of the development, production, stockpiling and use of chemical weapons and on their destruction concluded at Paris on 13th January 1993, No. 17 of 2000. Adopted on 8 May 2000. Published in *Government Gazette (Acts Supplement)*, 2 June 2000, p. 343

---

488. See Report of the Secretary-General on the establishment of a Special Court for Sierra Leone, S/2000/915, 4 October 2000 and the annexed Agreement and Statute. For commentary, see A. Tejan Cole, Correspondents' Reports, 3 *YIHL* (2000) pp. 574 to 576. See also A. McDonald, 'Sierra Leone's Shoestring Special Court', 84 *IRRC* (March 2002) p. 121; M. Frulli, 'The Special Court for Sierra Leone: Some Preliminary Comments', 11 *EJIL* (2000) p. 859; R. Cryer, 'A Special Court for Sierra Leone', 50 *ICLQ* (2001) p. 443.

489. The Secretary-General's original estimates for the establishment and first year operation of the Court and for the following 24 months were $30.2 and $84.4 million, respectively, a total of $114.6 million. Letter dated 12 July 2001 from the Secretary-General addressed to the President of the Security Council, UN Doc. S/2001/693/13 July 2001.

490. Ibid.

SLOVAKIA[491]

International Criminal Court

☛ Modification of the Constitution to enable ratification of the ICC Statute

The modification of the Slovak Constitution in 2001 created preconditions for the ratification of the Rome Statute of the International Criminal Court, signed by the Slovak Republic on 23 December 1998.

In conformity with the new Article 7(5) of the Slovak Constitution, certain categories of international treaties (international treaties on human rights and fundamental freedoms and those creating direct rights and obligations for physical or legal persons) shall prevail over national laws. Accordingly to Article 86(d) of the Slovak Constitution, a decision as to whether a particular treaty belongs to such category is left to the discretion of the Slovak National Council. In addition, the modification of Article 23(4) of the Slovak Constitution repealed the prohibition of extradition of Slovak citizens to another state. The accompanying report specified that one of the main aims of this modification was to allow for transfer of Slovak citizens to the International Criminal Court. On 6 December 2001, the Slovak Government expressed its consent to proceed with the ratification. The Slovak National Council was expected to consider the Rome Statute at the beginning of 2002, with subsequent ratification by the President.

Implementation

☛ Statute of the National Committee on Humanitarian Law. Decision of the Ministry of Foreign Affairs, November 2001. Entered into force on 1 January 2002

Further to the advice of the International Committee of the Red Cross, the Slovak authorities are preparing the establishment of a national committee on the implementation of international humanitarian law as a permanent inter-ministerial advisory body of the Ministry of Foreign Affairs of the Slovak Republic. The Committee's main role will consist in analysing the implementation of international humanitarian law in Slovak national legislation. The Committee will have up to 15 members.

JAN HLADIK

SOUTH AFRICA[492]

Peacekeeping

☛ Decision of the Military Technical Committee of 11 October 2001 regarding the involvement of South African troops in peacekeeping in Burundi

After 1994, South Africa was reluctant to contribute troops to peacekeeping missions, despite on it pressure from the international community to play a leading role in conflict resolution, especially on the African continent. Initially, South Africa only contributed

491. Information provided by Jan Hladik, Programme Specialist, International Standards Section, Division of Cultural Heritage, UNESCO.

492. Information provided by Phenyo Keiseng Rakate, Senior Researcher, South African Human Rights Commission, Johannesburg, South Africa.

technical and logistical support to two UN peacekeeping missions, in the Democratic Republic of the Congo (MONUC) and the United Nations Mission in Ethiopia and Eritrea (UNMEE).

Immediately after the death of the original facilitator of the Burundi peace process, former Tanzania president the late Dr Julius Nyerere, Nelson Mandela, former South African president was appointed as the new facilitator. In July 2001, the Ministers of Defence of Ghana, Senegal, Nigeria and South Africa decided to establish a Military Technical Committee, whose purpose is to ensure the implementation of the 1993 Arusha Reconciliation and Peace Agreement. The government of Burundi accepted the Technical Committee's decision of 11 October 2001 to deploy South African troops. A Memorandum of Understanding was signed between the two countries on 26 October 2001, and the deployment was further endorsed by UN Security Council Resolution 1375 of 29 October 2001. This marked the first time that South Africa actually participated in a peacekeeping mission. By the end of the year, South Africa has already deployed a total of 230 troops as part of the 700-member Special Protection Unit. The objective of the military operation was to protect returning opposition leaders for the next three years to enable them to participate in the transitional government.

Conflict Diamonds

☛ The Kimberly Process [http://www.kimberleyprocess.com/]

The Kimberley Process, a South African-led diplomatic effort, is a system of international standards and certification schemes on the import and export of rough diamonds, intended to stem the flow of illegal diamonds from conflict areas. Begun in May 2000, it aimed to develop proposals for an international diamond certification system before the 56th session of the United Nations (UN) General Assembly in December 2001.

The Kimberley Process seeks to create an international certification system that will remove conflict diamonds from legitimate channels of commerce by ensuring a clean stream of diamonds from point of extraction to retail sale.

Pending

☛ International Criminal Court Bill

South Africa ratified the Rome Statute of the International Court on 27 November 2000. In the meantime, it has played an important role in coordinating efforts in partnership with other Southern African Development Community countries to have the Rome Statute ratified by as many African states as possible.

Draft legislation incorporating provisions of the Rome Statute was before Parliament as 2001 closed. The purpose and objective of the International Criminal Court Bill is firstly to introduce substantive international humanitarian law as part of South African municipal law in order to fulfil its obligation to investigate and prosecute international crimes nationally. In the second place, it aims to provide for international legal assistance to the International Criminal Court.[493] The draft law incorporates the core ICC crimes of genocide, crimes

493. S. 3(a) &(b) of the Bill.

against humanity and war crimes (but not aggression) as punishable offences under South African criminal law.[494]

PHENYO RAKATE

SRI LANKA

Implementation and Dissemination

☛ Establishment of the National Committee on International Humanitarian Law, 2000

During 2001, the Committee worked with the ICRC Advisory Service on draft legislation to incorporate the Geneva Conventions in the domestic law of Sri Lanka.[495]

SPAIN[496]

International Criminal Tribunals

☛ Agreement between the Kingdom of Spain and the United Nations on the Enforcement of Sentences Imposed by the International Criminal Tribunal for the Former Yugoslavia, signed on 28 March 2000, entered into force on 16 January 2001. Published in issue 54 of the *BOE,* Boletín Oficial del Estad*o* (The Official State Gazette) on 3 March 2001

On 28 March 2000 in The Hague, the Kingdom of Spain and the United Nations signed the Agreement on the enforcement of sentences imposed by the International Criminal Tribunal for the Former Yugoslavia. After the corresponding parliamentary procedure and notification of Spain's ratification, the Agreement came into force on 16 January 2001. The ratification procedure, following the indications of the State Council's Consultative Opinion of 3 February 2000 (file 3733/1999), first had to be authorized by Parliament, as stipulated by Article 94.1 of the Spanish Constitution of 1978, for two reasons. First, because, in accordance with section c), it affects the fundamental rights and duties established in Title 1 of the Constitution, particularly Article 25.2, which deals with sentences of imprisonment. Second, because, according to section e), it affects the General Penitentiary Organic Law 1/1979 of 26 September.

The government's authorization of the ratification met with no opposition and was passed unanimously, which was hardly surprising since this agreement culminated a process during which Spain had voluntarily collaborated with the ICTY, and the various political groups represented in Parliament had clearly expressed their wishes and opinions to this effect.

As is well known, the ICTY has drawn up a list of states that expressed their desire to accept convicted persons, including Finland, Italy, Norway, Sweden, Austria, France, Germany and Spain, and is now drawing up agreements, such as the one that concerns us here, with these states. In accordance with its Rules of Procedure and Evidence,[497] the ICTY

494. The Criminal Procedure Act 51 of 1977 (18) (g)(as amended).

495. ICRC Advisory Service, *National Implementation of International Humanitarian Law*: Biennial report 2000-2001 (Geneva, ICRC 2002) p. 90.

496. Information and commentaries by Antoni Pigrau, Professor of International Law, Rovira i Virgili University, Tarragona.

497. ICTY Doc. IT/32/REV.24, 5 August 2002.

Presidency chooses a state from this list in which the convicted persons shall serve their sentence, in the light of the document Practice Direction on the Procedure for the International Tribunal's Designation of the State in which a Convicted Person Is to Serve his/her Sentence of Imprisonment (ICTY, Doc. IT/137, 9 July 1998).

A hypothetical Spanish declaration, in the terms of Article 27 of the Statute, was bound by Article 8 of Organic Law 15/1994 of 1 June 1994 on cooperation with the ICTY,[498] which was related to the serving of sentences, to specify that a sentence served in Spain could in no case 'exceed the maximum envisaged for imprisonment sentences in Spain'. It also established that the National Court (*Audiencia Nacional*) and the Ministry of Justice would be the competent judicial and political authorities. Likewise, it accepted the primacy of the ICTY in questions relating to pardons or commutation of the sentence.

As is well known, the ICTY 'shall have recourse to the general practice regarding prison sentences in the courts of the former Yugoslavia' (Statute, Article 24), which allows sentences to be imposed that are longer than the maximum allowed by Spanish law. These include life sentences, which clearly contradicts the constitutional obligation of orienting sentences of imprisonment towards the reeducation and reintegration into society of the convicted person.[499]

For all these reasons, Article 3.2 of the Agreement establishes that 'Spain shall only consider the enforcement of a sentence imposed by the International Criminal Tribunal in those cases in which the duration does not exceed the maximum envisaged for any crime prescribed by Spanish law'.

The conditions of imprisonment are governed by Spanish laws, although under the exclusive authority of the ICTY, which shall decide on all aspects regarding early releases (Articles 3.4 and 3.5), pardons or commutation of sentences (Article 8). If under Spanish law a convicted person can benefit from one of the grounds for early release, Spain should notify the ICTY, who shall then determine whether to apply these benefits to the convicted person. Any decision by the ICTY not to apply the benefits would mean that Spanish law could not be applied. Spain would therefore refuse to continue enforcing the sentence and would return the convicted person to the direct custody of the ICTY for transfer to another collaborating state where he or she would serve out the sentence imposed. Accordingly, the only grounds that Article 9 envisages for terminating a sentence in Spain, apart from the impossibility of applying Spanish penitentiary legislation mentioned above, are: a) the serving of the whole sentence; b) the death of the prisoner; c) the granting of a pardon by the ICTY; and d) the decision by the ICTY to transfer the convict to another state.

Pursuant to the present Agreement, of unlimited duration, the ICTY has so far determined that three people should serve their sentences in Spanish prisons. They are Stevan Todorović (ten years imprisonment, from 1 December 2001), Drago Josipović (12 years imprisonment, from 9 April 2002) and Vladimir Santić (18 years imprisonment, from 11 April 2002).

☛ Indictment against six suspected Al Quaeda members, Central Court of Instruction No. Five, Audiencia Nacional, Madrid, Sumario 35/01, 18 November 2001

ANTONI PIGRAU

498. Published in *BOE*, issue 131, 2 June 1994.

499. See the Comment to the Spanish State Council Consultative Opinion on the Rome Statute of the International Criminal Court of 22 July 1999 (No. 1374/99), in 3 *YIHL* (2000) pp. 581-586.

SUDAN

Peace Process

- The Nairobi Peace Accord between Uganda and Sudan, 8 December 1999. [See below under Uganda]

SWEDEN[500]

The Armed Forces

- Ordinance concerning the Status of Total Defence Personnel according to International Law [Totalförsvarets folkrättsförordning], *Svensk Författningssamling (SFS)* 1990:12. [http://www.icrc.org/ihl-nat.nsf/WebLAW?OpenView&Start=78.6.1.3&Count=150&Expand=81.5.1#81.5.1]
- (Swedish Government Official Report regarding surveillance and control of Swedish borders during increased emergency preparedness [Gränsövervakning under höjd beredskap], *Statens Offentliga Utredningar (SOU)* 2002:4, concluded in December 2001

The Swedish Total Defence system reflects a unified view of military and civilian defence. According to the Ordinance concerning the Status of Total Defence Personnel according to International Law, officers of the Police Forces and Customs personnel may acquire combatant status when Sweden is at war, depending on their duties. These personnel have been referred to as having a 'temporary combatant status'.

A Swedish Government Official Report regarding surveillance and control of Swedish borders during increased emergency preparedness, proposes a new law on the organisation of that surveillance and control, allowing only personnel from the Armed Forces to carry out tasks requiring combatant status. The matter is currently under review by the government.

Conventional Weapons

- Speech of the State Secretary for Foreign Affairs at the Review Conference of the Certain Conventional Weapons Convention, Geneva, 12 December 2001 [http://www.utrikes.regeringen.se/inenglish/pressinfo/other_speeches/20011212.htm]

A resolution presented by Sweden regarding the strengthening of the Convention on Certain Conventional Weapons[501] (CCW) was unanimously adopted by the United Nations General Assembly on 5 November 2001.[502] The resolution contained different proposals to be discussed during the review conference in Geneva in December 2001. At the Conference, the State Secretary for Foreign Affairs, Mr Hans Dahlgren, explained the Swedish position. The dangers of Explosive Remnants of War were emphasised and that the delegations needed 'to pave the way for a CCW protocol on the matter, and to find an effective and efficient way to ease this humanitarian problem'. Moreover, it was maintained, taking the perspective of the victims, that the scope of the convention obviously should be extended.

---

500. Information and commentaries by Ola Engdahl, Doctoral Candidate in International Law at the Stockholm University and the Swedish National Defence College.

501. Convention on the Prohibition or Restriction on the Use of Certain Conventional Weapons Which May Be Deemed to be Excessively Injurious or to Have Indiscriminate Effects (1980) 19 *ILM* (1980) p. 1523.

502. A/RES/56/28.

According to the Swedish view 'all present and future protocols of the CCW should apply also in non-international conflicts'.

Extradition

☛ Amendment (*SFS 2001:612*) to the Swedish Act on Extradition of Offenders (*SFS* 1957:668). The Amendment came into force 2001-10-01

Sweden's ratification of the 1996 Convention Relating to Extradition between the Member States of the European Union[503] and the 1997 International Convention for the Suppression of Terrorist Bombings[504] has prompted changes to the 1957 Swedish Act on Extradition of Offenders. The Amendment has, *inter alia*, made extradition possible also for political crimes. The general prohibition of extraditing persons accused of political crimes is not applicable if it is contrary to an international agreement between Sweden and the requesting state.

Pending

☛ Legislative measures regarding the International Criminal Court

Sweden ratified the statute of the International Criminal Court on 28 June 2001. Certain legislative measures were found to be necessary in order for Sweden to fulfil its obligations as a State Party.[505] Amendment of Swedish legislation is primarily found to be required with regard to matters of international cooperation and judicial assistance with the ICC, *ne bis in idem,* enforcement measures, offences against the ICC, and privileges and immunities of the Court. It is moreover suggested that Sweden should accept sentenced persons to serve their sentences in Swedish prisons. Sweden already accepts persons sentenced by the International Criminal Tribunals for the former Yugoslavia and Rwanda. A Government Bill on the extent of new legislation with regard to the above-mentioned matters is expected in 2002.

Member states are not required to incorporate the penal provisions of the ICC statute in their national legislation. According to the Government Bill, the complementary principle suggests, however, a moral obligation to bring national penal law in conformity with that of the Statute. A Commission of Inquiry is currently reviewing national penal legislation regarding, *inter alia*, genocide, crimes against humanity and war crimes.[506] Moreover, the Commission is to review questions of Swedish jurisdiction for such crimes committed abroad as well as questions related to statute of limitations. The results will be presented in October 2002.

☛ Government Bill 2001/02:60 regarding peace support operations

The Swedish government proposed that the Parliament should authorize the government to

---

503. Convention drawn up on the basis of Article K.3 of the Treaty on European Union, relating to extradition between the Member States of the European Union, Official Journal C 313, 23/10/1996. Not yet in force.

504. A/RES/52/164. In force 23 May 2001.

505. Government Bill 2000/01:122.

506. Committee terms of references (2000:76).

contribute military personnel to the multinational security force in Afghanistan.[507] The Swedish component will be an intelligence platoon, consisting of a maximum of 45 persons with command and logistics functions, whose tasks will include reconnaissance.

OLA ENGDAHL

SWITZERLAND

International Criminal Court and International Tribunals

- Federal Law on Cooperation with the International Criminal Court [Loi fédérale sur la cooperation avec la Cour pénale internationale]. Adopted on 22 June 2001. Published on 3 July 2001 in *Feuille fédérale* 2001 2748[508]
- Federal Law Modifying the Ordinary and Military Penal Codes [Loi fédérale portent modification du code pénal et du code pénal militaire]. Adopted on 22 June 2001. Published on 3 July 2001 in *Feuille fédérale* 2001 2748

The Federal Law on Cooperation with the International Criminal Court 'sets out the procedure for Switzerland's assistance to the International Criminal Court and for enforcement in Switzerland of sentences handed down by the Court. It establishes a central service for cooperation with the Court within the Federal Office of Justice, cooperation comprising *inter alia* the arrest and surrender of persons and the communication of evidence to the Court. The central service is also empowered to challenge the Court's jurisdiction and case admissibility. However, the decision to refer a situation to the Court or to waive immunity falls to the Swiss Federal Council. The law also grants judicial guarantees to any person being questioned under its provisions.'[509]

The Federal Law Modifying the Ordinary and Military Penal Codes permits Switzerland to cooperate with the ICC, while the Federal Law Modifying the Ordinary and Military Penal Codes extends the application of offences against the administration of justice to procedures before international tribunals. Switzerland ratified the Rome Statute on 12 October 2001.[510]

Cases

- *Fulgence Niyonteze* case, Appeals Court, 25 May 2000

Following his conviction by the military court of Lausanne on 29 April 1999 for murder, incitement to murder and war crimes, committed during the 1994 genocide in Rwanda,[511] Fulgence Niyonteze, the former mayor of Mushubati, central Rwanda, during the Rwandan genocide, was sentenced to life imprisonment. On 25 May 2000, that was reduced to 14

---

507. Government Bill 2001/02:60.

508. Reprinted in the documents section of this volume at p. 732.

509. Source: ICRC National Implementation Database. http://www.icrc.org/ihl-nat.nsf/6fa4d35e5e3025394125673e00508143/adcfceb02b0260f2c1256b0200566903?OpenDocument.

510. ICRC Advisory Service, *National Implementation of International Humanitarian Law*: Biennial report 2000-2001 (Geneva, ICRC 2002) p. 92.

511. Prosecutors had initially tried to charge him with the crime of genocide but the judge refused to entertain this charge because at the time the crime of genocide had not been incorporate into Swiss law.

years.[512] The appeals court found Niyonteze guilty of war crimes for participation in massacres in Rwanda in 1994. He was found guilty of having convened a public meeting where he called on people to kill Tutsis and of having told refugees at a camp (Kabgayi) to go home, thus sending them to their deaths. However, the Appeals Court rejected the murder count.

☛ *Niyontezev* v. *Public Prosecutor*, Tribunal militaire de cassation, 27 April 2001 [http://www.vbs.admin.ch/internet/OA/d/urteile.htm][513]

On 27 April 2001, the Swiss military court of final appeal upheld the 14-year sentence handed down to Fulgence Niyonteze by the military court of Lausanne.

The tribunal rejected all of the prosecution and most of the defence arguments, and revised the decision of the appeals court on one point only, relating to Niyonteze's expulsion from Switzerland after serving his sentence. While he may still risk deportation, that matter will now have to be referred back to the appeals court.

It is interesting that the court found that ICTR jurisprudence was relevant to this case. Concerning the applicability of the 1949 Geneva Conventions, the military tribunal found that the criteria developed by the ICTR apropos war crimes were applicable in the case of Niyonteze.

The prosecutor had argued that the 14-year sentence was excessively light considering the gravity of the crimes. However, the court found that the sentence was in line with applicable law and could not be compared with those pronounced by the ICTR, such as in the Akayesu case.

The court ordered that Niyonteze's time in detention since arrest in 1996 be subtracted from his sentence. It ordered that the sentence be implemented by the canton of Fribourg, where the convict's family has been living since they obtained asylum. Under Swiss law, the ex-mayor could be eligible for conditional semi-release in 2002 and could request conditional release for good conduct as of 2005.[514]

TAJIKISTAN[515]

Geneva Law

☛ Order No. 218 of the Minister of Defence, 3 August 2000 establishing the National Information Bureau and Grave Registration Service

This order established the National Information Bureau and Grave Registration Service prescribed by Articles 122 of the Third Geneva Convention and 136 of the Fourth Convention and Articles 17 of the First Convention and 120 of the Third Convention, respectively.

---

512. Source: 'Genocide and international crimes in domestic courts'. A survey by Prevent Genocide International. Available at its website at http://www.preventgenocide.org/punish/domestic/.

513. For commentary on the case, see L. Reydams, 'Niyonteze v. Public Prosecutor', 96 *AJIL* (2002) p. 231.

514. '14-year sentence confirmed for former Rwandan mayor', Hirondelle, 27 April 2001.

515. ICRC Advisory Service, *National Implementation of International Humanitarian Law*: Biennial report 2000-2001 (Geneva, ICRC 2002) p. 93.

The Emblem

- Law on the use and protection of the emblems and designations of the red cross and red crescent. Entered into force on 2 June 2001

Education and Training

- Establishment of a national humanitarian law training centre at the Tajik High Military College, 2001
- Order No. 815 of the Minister of Education on the incorporation of a compulsory course on IHL into the curricula of higher education institute law faculties and journalism faculties. Adopted on 4 December 2001

TRINIDAD AND TOBAGO[516]

Anti-personnel Mines

- Anti-Personnel Mines Act, 2001. An Act to give effect to the Convention on the Prohibition of the Use, Stockpiling, Production and Transfer of Anti-Personnel Mines and on their Destruction in Trinidad and Tobago [http://www.icrc.org/ihl-nat.nsf/6fa4d35e5e3025394125673e00508143/fe075f7c789bbc7cc1256b250044f383?OpenDocument]

'The Act prohibits and characterizes as criminal offences the use, development, production, acquisition, stockpiling, retention and transfer of antipersonnel mines.'

Implementation and Dissemnation

- In 2001, an ad hoc interministerial committee was constituted in order to examine the 1954 Cultural Property Convention and the 1980 Certain Conventional Weapons and its Protocols, with a view to their ratification.

TURKMENISTAN

The Emblem

- Law on the use and protection of the red cross and red crescent emblems. Adopted on 7 July 2001. Entered into force on 6 August 2001.

'The law governs the use and protection of the red crescent and red cross emblems, their designations and distinctive signals, in compliance with Turkmenistan's international obligations. It distinguishes between the indicative and protective uses of the emblems, attributes rights in this respect to specific entities, provides for control over use of the emblems by the Red Crescent Society of Turkmenistan and the relevant State bodies, and refers to national legislation regarding punishment for non-compliance.'[517]

---

516. ICRC Advisory Service, *supra* n. 11, at p. 440.
517. Ibid., p. 96.

UGANDA[518]

Peace Process

☛ The Nairobi Peace Accord between Uganda and Sudan, 8 December 1999

The poor relations between Uganda and Sudan have long contributed to the continuance of insecurity in northern Uganda. While Uganda accuses Sudan of supporting the Lord's Resistance Army (LRA) rebellion on one hand, Sudan accuses Uganda for supporting the Sudan People's Liberation army (SPLA) on the other. In 1999, efforts to promote peace between the two countries were more visible and intensive. As a result, in December 1999 an agreement was signed between President Yoweri Museveni of Uganda and President Omara-el- Bashir of Sudan committing the two countries to normalize relations. The accord was based on the following conditions: release of children abducted by the LRA and kept in Sudan; exchange of all prisoners of war; respect for international law on refugees; facilitation of cross border activities; restoration of diplomatic relations; and resettlement and rehabilitation of combatants who renounce rebellion.

This accord has been implemented to some extent. Uganda has released all Sudanese prisoners of war; Uganda has enacted the Amnesty Law granting amnesty to all rebels fighting the government (see below); and Sudan repatriated some children through UNICEF.

Amnesty

☛ The Amnesty Act of Uganda 2000 (The Act of Forgiveness). Adopted 17 January 2000; entered into force 21 January 2000. Published in *Uganda Gazette* No. 5 Volume XCIII 21 January, 2000

In January 2000, the Amnesty Act became law. The Act represents for many ordinary Ugandans the hope that the 16-year-old conflict in the country can be ended peacefully.

The Act owes its origins to the determination of the people of Uganda to seek reconciliation with those who have inflicted so much pain and suffering through conflict. Because of the hope and effort invested by ordinary people in the Act, there is interest in the country to see that the amnesty is implemented. Since the law was introduced, a growing number of people have taken advantage of the amnesty and have received certificates.

The Act has several important provisions bearing on humanitarian law. It uses two words to describe amnesty: 'pardon' and 'forgiveness'. It provides an offer from government to reconcile with the insurgents.[519] All forms of insurgency are covered. A blanket amnesty is offered to any Ugandan who has at any time since 26 January 1986 engaged in or is engaging in insurgency against the Government of Uganda.[520] This implies that former and current insurgents are entitled to amnesty. Thus, all those who have never claimed amnesty for rebel activities in the past may therefore come forward in the same way as those who are currently fighting the government.

The Law specifically provides that the amnesty is extended to all Ugandans who have been in insurgency through: actual participating in combat; collaborating with insurgents;

---

518. Information and commentaries by Emmanuel Kasimbazi, Lecturer, Faculty of Law, Makerere University, Uganda.

519. S. 2 of the Amnesty Act 2000.

520. 26 January 1986 is when the National Resistance Movement (NRM) took power in Uganda.

committing other crimes to support insurgency; or in any other way assisting others involved in insurgency.[521]

A person seeking amnesty under the Act is termed 'a reporter'.[522] There are three types of reporters. The first are those who are within the country but who are not facing criminal charges, the second are those who are already facing charges, and the third are those who are currently living outside Uganda.[523] The reporter must hand over his weapons, and after reporting and taking all the necessary steps he will be issued with a certificate of amnesty.[524]

The Act establishes the Amnesty Commission as the main body to oversee the granting of amnesty.[525] It should consist of seven persons who are appointed by the President with the approval of Parliament. The chairperson should be a judge of the High Court, or someone qualified to be a judge. All members must be people of high moral integrity.[526] The Commission has several functions. Some are very practical, while others involve making and overseeing policies. The Commissioners should coordinate with others to ensure that amnesty is achieved, including non-government organizations, community-based organizations, traditional chiefs and religious and other community leaders. The Commission supervises the practical work of a Demobilization and Resettlement Team, whose functions are to demobilize, reintegrate and resettle reporters.[527] The Commission is also supposed to educate the public about the amnesty, promote dialogue and reconciliation.[528]

The Act is to be extended every six months by the Minister of Internal Affairs.[529]

The Amnesty Commission commenced its work in the middle of 2001. However, by the end of the year it was still not effective because of inadequate funding.

EMMANUEL KASIMBAZI

UKRAINE

The Emblem

☛ Resolution No. 939 of the Cabinet of Ministers of 12 June 2000 establishing the procedure for the production, use and registration of the identify cards issued to medical personnel authorized to use the emblem[530]

International Criminal Court

☛ Decision of the Constitutional Court of Ukraine, 11 July 2001

'... the Constitutional Court of Ukraine, whose opinion in the matter had been requested by the country's President, found that the 1998 Rome Statute of the International Criminal Court, which provides that "the International Criminal Court [...] shall be complementary to

521. S. 3(1).
522. S. 4.
523. Ibid.
524. Ibid.
525. S. 7.
526. S. 8.
527. S. 9.
528. Ibid.
529. S. 17.
530. ICRC Advisory Service, *supra* n. 11, at p. 440.

national jurisdictions", did not correspond to the Constitution. According to the Constitutional Court, most of the Statute's provisions did correspond, paragraph 10 of the Preamble and Article 1 being the only execeptions. The Court considered that these provisions were at variance with Article 124 of the Constitution, which provides that justice in Ukraine can be administered only by the courts and that the latter cannot delegate their powers to other bodies or officials. As the Constitution does not allow for the conclusion of international treaties that contradict its provisions, Ukraine will be able to ratify the Rome Statute only once it has modified the Constitution. ... Further to the Constitutional Court's decision ... a working group was set up under the auspices of the Ministry of Justice to consider the legal consequences of that decision and to draft proposals for resolving the contradiction between the Ukrainian Constitution and the Rome Statute. It identified two ways of resolving the matter: modifying the Constitution or adopting a new constitutional provision.'[531]

Criminal Law

☛ Criminal Code of Ukraine N°2341-14. Adopted by the Rada [Ukrainian Parliament] on 5 April 2001. Entered into force on 1 September 2001. Published in the Newsletter of *Verkhovna Rada*, 2001, N° 25-26 [http://www.hri.ca/fortherecord2001/euro2001/documentation/parassembly/pa12622001.htm[532]/http://www.icrc.org/ihl-nat.nsf/WebLAW?OpenView&Start=86.2.1.1&Count=150&Expand=88.3.1#88.3.1]

The new Criminal Code 'attributes responsibility for a number of acts which can be qualified as war crimes under the terms of the Geneva Conventions and Additional Protocol I, including ill-treatment of prisoners of war, the transfer of civilians for forced labor and misuse of the red cross and red crescent emblems.'[533]

The new Criminal Code formally abolishes the death penalty, and thereby changing the maximum form of punishment into life imprisonment. The new Code also excludes people under the age of 18 and older than 65 years, as well as women who at the time of the commission of the crime were pregnant, from life imprisonment. The adoption of a law abolishing the death penalty was the result of a promise made by Ukraine when joining the Council of Europe in 1995. Before the abolishment was included in a new Code and thereby formalized, the Ukrainian Constitutional Court in 1999 ruled that the death penalty was illegal.[534]

Implementation and Dissemination

☛ Resolution No. 1157 of 21 July 2000 of the Cabinet of Ministers establishing the Interdepartmental Committee for Implementation of International Humanitarian Law in Ukraine [http://www.icrc.org/ihl-nat.nsf/6fa4d35e5e3025394125673e00508143/f3de5602eab1d4784125698100053cf3a?OpenDocument]

531. Ibid.

532. Council of Europe, Parliamentary Assembly, Resolution 1262 (2001).

533. ICRC Advisory Service, *National Implementation of International Humanitarian Law*: Biennial report 2000-2001 (Geneva, ICRC 2002) p. 97.

534. *Las Vegas Sun*, 21 May 2000. Available online at http://www.againstdp.org/ukraine.html.

'The Committee is a permanent body acting under the auspices of the Cabinet of Ministers and responsible for the coordination of national implementation. It consists of 16 members representing the relevant Ministries and the Ukrainian Red Cross Society. At its first session in June 2001, the Committee addressed mainly organizational issues and drew up its plan of action.'[535]

Pending

☛ New Code of Criminal Procedure

The final draft of a new Code of Criminal Procedure was submitted to the Rada on 1 September 2001.[536]

UNITED KINGDOM[537]

Landmines

☛ The Landmines Act 1998 (Overseas Territories) Order 2001, Statutory Instruments, 2001 No. 3499. Entered into force on 14 November 2001

This extends the Landmines Act 1998 (the national enabling legislation for the Ottawa Convention 1997), with exceptions, adaptations and modifications, to Anguilla, Bermuda, British Antarctic Territory, British Indian Ocean Territory, the Cayman Islands, the Falkland Islands, Montserrat, Pitcairn Island, St Helena and Dependencies, South Georgia and the South Sandwich Islands, the Sovereign Base Areas of Akrotiri and Dhekelia, Turks and Caicos Islands and the Virgin Islands.

International Criminal Tribunals

☛ The United Nations (International Tribunals) (Former Yugoslavia and Rwanda) (Amendment) (No. 2) Order 2000, Statutory Instruments, 2000 No. 3243. Entered into force on 1 April 2001

This was a technical amendment to reflect changes in national terminology.

☛ The United Nations (International Tribunals) (Former Yugoslavia and Rwanda) (Amendment) Order 2001, Statutory Instruments, 2001 No. 412. Entered into force 12 March 2001

This was a technical amendment to reflect changes to the Statutes of the Yugoslav and Rwanda tribunals introduced by United Nations Security Council resolution 1329 (2000).

---

535. ICRC Advisory Service, *National Implementation of International Humanitarian Law*: Biennial report 2000-2001 (Geneva, ICRC 2002) p. 97.

536. Council of Europe, Parliamentary Assembly, Resolution 1262 (2001). http://www.hri.ca/fortherecord2001/euro2001/documentation/parassembly/pa12622001.htm.

537. Information and commentaries provided by A.P.V. Rogers, Fellow of the Lauterpacht Research Centre for International Law, University of Cambridge. Thanks to Ms Helen Upton and Mr Gavin Watson, Assistant Legal Advisers, Foreign and Commonwealth Office, London.

International Criminal Court

☛ International Criminal Court Act 2001. Entered into force 1 September 2001 [http://www.hmso.gov.uk/acts/acts2001/20010017.htm]

☛ International Criminal Court (Scotland) Act 2001 Entered into force 17 December 2001 [http://www.icrc.org/ihl-nat.nsf/WebLAW?OpenView&Start=89.11.1.8&Count=150&Expand=89.12.1#89.12.1]

These Orders brought the International Criminal Court Act 2001 into force on 1 September 2001 and the corresponding Scottish legislation on 17 December 2001.

These are substantial pieces of legislation with, between them, 114 sections and 16 schedules. They provide the legal basis for the UK to provide support and cooperation to the ICC insofar as this was not already possible under UK law. This includes provisions on arrest of suspects and their surrender to the ICC; taking of evidence; provision of information; freezing and forfeiture of assets; and service of sentences in domestic prisons. They also establish in UK law the same criminal offences that the ICC will be dealing with. This means that any UK national or resident or person subject to UK service jurisdiction accused of committing war crimes, crimes against humanity or genocide under UK law can be tried by the UK courts for these specific crimes, wherever in the world they have been committed. Individuals who are not within the criminal jurisdiction of the UK courts can be extradited to stand trial for these crimes in states with such jurisdiction. The publication *United Kingdom and International Humanitarian Law*, referred to below, states: '... the UK is not a place where war criminals can consider a quiet retirement.'

☛ The International Criminal Court Act 2001 (Elements of Crime) Regulations 2001, Statutory Instruments, 2001 No. 2505. Entered into force on 1 September 2001

Section 50(2) of the International Criminal Court Act 2001 provides that in interpreting and applying Articles 6, 7 and 8(2) of the ICC Statute, a court shall take into account any relevant elements of crimes adopted in accordance with Article 9 of the ICC Statute and, pending that, any elements of crimes contained in the report of the Preparatory Commission for the ICC adopted on 30 June 2000. The regulations set out the text of the elements of crimes as contained in the commission's report.

☛ The International Criminal Court Act 2001 (Reservations and Declarations) Order 2001, Statutory Instruments, 2001 No. 2559. Entered into force on 1 September 2001

Section 50(4)(a) of the International Criminal Court Act 2001 provides that in relation to the criminal offences of genocide, crimes against humanity and war crimes in UK domestic law under the Act, the ICC Statute is to be construed subject to any relevant reservation or declaration made by the UK when ratifying any relevant treaty. The order sets out the text of the statements made by the UK on ratification of Additional Protocol I of 1977,[538] on the

538. For the text of the declaration, see 1 *YIHL* (1998) p. 640.

Convention on Certain Conventional Weapons of 1980 and its Protocols II and III,[539] on Protocol IV to that Convention,[540] on Amended Protocol II to that Convention,[541] and on the Ottawa Convention 1997.[542]

- The International Criminal Court Act 2001 (Commencement) Order 2001, Statutory Instruments, 2001 No. 2161. Made 13 June 2001
- The International Criminal Court (Scotland) Act 2001 (Commencement) Order 2001, Statutory Instruments No. 456. Entered into force 17 December 2001

These Orders brought the International Criminal Court Act 2001 into force on 1 September 2001 and the corresponding Scottish legislation on 17 December 2001.

- Declaration regarding the Rome Statute of the International Criminal Court of 17 July 1998, 3 October 2001

The UK made the following declaration on depositing its instrument of ratification of the ICC Statute on 3 October 2001:

> 'The United Kingdom understands the term 'the established framework of international law', used in article 8(2)(b) and (e),[543] to include customary international law as established by State practice and opinio juris. In that context the United Kingdom confirms and draws to the attention of the Court its views as expressed, inter alia, in its statements made on ratification of relevant instruments of international law, including the Protocol Additional to the Geneva Conventions of 12th August 1949, and relating to the Protection of Victims of International Armed Conflicts (Protocol I) of 8th June 1997.'

The United Kingdom declares, pursuant to article 87(2) of the Statute, that requests for co-operation, and any documents supporting the request, must be made in the English language.'

---

539. See 3 *YIHL* (2000) p. 597, n. 396. For completeness it should be noted that the UK also made a declaration on ratification of the Convention of 1980 that: 'The terms "civilian" and "civilian population" have the same meaning as in Article 50 of the 1st Additional Protocol of 1977 to the 1949 Geneva Conventions. Civilians shall enjoy the protection afforded by this Convention unless and for such time as they take a direct part in hostilities.' In relation to Protocol III, Art. 2, the UK declared that: 'The United Kingdom accepts the provisions of Article 2(2) and (3) on the understanding that the terms of those paragraphs of that Article do not imply that air-delivery of incendiary weapons, or of any other weapons, projectiles or munitions, is less accurate or less capable of being carried out discriminately than all or any other means of delivery.'

540. For the text of the declaration, see 3 *YIHL* (2000) p. 597.

541. For the text of the declaration, see ibid.

542. For the text of the declaration, see 1 *YIHL* (1998) p. 516.

543. Art. 8(2)(b) and (e) lists offences, other than grave breaches, that amount to war crimes being other serious violations of the laws and customs of war 'within the established framework of international law'.

International Fact-Finding Commission

☛ On 9 November 2001, the United Kingdom correspondent of the Yearbook, A.P.V. Rogers, was elected a member of the International Fact-Finding Commission established under Article 90 of Additional Protocol I 1977

Implementation and Dissemination

☛ The National Committee for International Humanitarian Law held its third meeting on 16 October 2002. A meeting of the Sub-Committee on dissemination was held on 14 February 2001

☛ The Foreign and Commonwealth Office published the illustrated booklet, *United Kingdom and International Humanitarian Law*, in September 2001. It contains chapters on the origins, basic principles and implementation within the United Kingdom of international humanitarian law; the role of the ICRC and British Red Cross Society; the *ad hoc* International Criminal Tribunals for the Former Yugoslavia and Rwanda; and the International Criminal Court; with some shorter contributions on cultural property, the Ottawa Convention of 1997 and on women and armed conflict. The booklet has been widely distributed both within and outside the Government. It is available from: Foreign and Commonwealth Office, United Nations Department, King Charles Street, London SW1A 2AH quoting order number 0248D.

A.P.V. ROGERS

Counter-terrorism

☛ Anti-terrorism, Crime and Security Act, 2001. Received Royal Assent on 14 December 2001 [http://www.hmso.gov.uk/acts/acts2001/20010024.htm]

☛ Explanatory Notes to Anti-Terrorism, Crime And Security Act 2001 [http://www.legislation.hmso.gov.uk/acts/en/2001en24.htm]

☛ Human Rights Act 1998 (Designated Derogation) Order 2001

A controversial bill that, *inter alia*, that allows Britain to detain indefinitely without trial non-citizens accused of terrorist offences passed into law on 14 December 2001. 'The Bill was processed as an emergency measure. It had its first reading in the House of Commons on 12 November 2001 and received Royal Assent on 14 December 2001.'[544] Members of Parliament voted overwhelmingly in favour of the legislation, although the Bill faced strenuous opposition in the House of Lords, which curtailed some of its more draconian provisions.[545]

The Human Rights Act 1998 (Designated Derogation) Order 2001 amended the 1998 Human Rights Act to allow the UK to derogate from Article 5 of the European Convention on Human Rights regarding liberty and security of person.

The Anti-terrorism, Crime and Security Act, 2001 purports to build on existing legisla-

544. House of Lords-House of Commons Joint Committee on Human Rights, 'Continuance in force of sections 21 to 23 of the Anti-Terrorism, Crime and Security Act 2001', Fifth Report of Session 2002-2003. HL Paper 59, HC 462, para. 1.

545. 'Anti-terror bill clears first hurdle. Blunkett: "Proposals could have been more Draconian"', BBC News UK Online, 19 November 2001; H. Young, 'The terror threat is being used to attack civil rights here and in the US', *The Guardian*, 11 December 2001.

tion to ensure that the government, 'in light of the new situation arising from the September 11 terrorist attacks on New York and Washington, have the necessary powers to counter the threat to the UK'.[546] These measures are intended to, *inter alia*: cut off terrorist funding; ensure that government departments and agencies can collect and share information, streamline immigration procedures; improve the security of the nuclear and aviation industries; extend police powers available to relevant forces; and update part of the UK's anti-terrorist threats. Among other things, it strengths existing law controlling chemical, nuclear and biological weapons.

According to the Explanatory Notes, Part 4, sections 21 to 23 ("Suspected international terrorists"), allows 'the detention of those the Secretary of State has certified as threats to national security and who are suspected of being international terrorists where their removal is not possible at the present time. Such detention would be subject to regular independent review by the Special Immigration Appeals Commission (SIAC). These provisions change the current law, which allows the detention with a view to removal only where removal is a realistic option within a reasonable period of time. The detention powers will cease to have effect on 10 November 2006.'

Cases

☛ *R.* v. *Secretary of State ex parte Thring, Court of Appeal* (Civil Division), 20 July 2000[547]

Thring had sought an order quashing the order of the Secretary of State for Defence to the Royal Air Force to fly over Iraqi territory and attack targets inside Iraq. Alternatively, an order was sought quashing the order of the Secretary of State for Defence to finance the operation of the Royal Air Force over Iraq from the revenue provided by taxpayers. In the alternative, declarations of illegality were sought by the applicant.

The application was refused on the grounds that it was not appropriate for the court to intervene upon judicial review in the deployment of the armed forces abroad. According to Lord Scarman: 'His application would involve consideration of the policy and the nature of the operations of the armed services abroad, and particularly of the Royal Air Force. In my judgment, those are not matters which can be the subject of judicial review, because the courts are not equipped so to do.'

UNITED STATES OF AMERICA[548]

The Armed Forces and Combatant Status

☛ Military Extraterritorial Jurisdiction Act of 2000[549]

'The Military Extraterritorial Jurisdiction Act of 2000, establishes federal jurisdiction over offenses committed overseas by US civilians employed by or accompanying the armed

546. Explanatory notes to the Act.

547. Reprinted in this volume at p. 723.

548. Information and commentaries by Burrus M. Carnahan, Professarial Lecturer in Law, the George Washingon University, Washington D.C.

549. Reprinted in this volume at p. 650.

forces as well as certain military service members. ... Previously, civilians could not be tried in the United States for many different offenses committed overseas.'[550]

Counter-terrorism

- Presidential Military Order 13 November 2001, relating to Detention, Treatment, and Trial of Certain Non-Citizens in the War Against Terrorism[551]
- Department of Defense News Briefing – Secretary Rumsfeld and Gen. Myers, 11 January 2002, 2:10 PM EST, the Pentagon, Arlington, Virginia
- (Department of Defense News Briefing – Assistant Secretary of Defense for Public Affairs Clarke, 14 January 2002 – 12:30 p.m. EST, the Pentagon, Arlington, Virginia

The United States Government caused both domestic and international controversy when, shortly after the 11 September 2001 Al Qaida attacks on the New York World Trade Center and the Pentagon, it announced plans to regard captured terrorists as 'unlawful combatants' and try them before *ad hoc* military tribunals called 'military commissions'.

The roots of these tribunals lie deep in American legal and political history. These criminal tribunals are unique in the United States' constitutional order in that they owe their existence directly to the President's authority as commander-in-chief of the Armed Forces, and not to any statute enacted by Congress. The penal law they apply is derived directly from the law of war, both customary and treaty-based.

In the late-Eighteenth Century, the United States Congress first enacted a military penal code in the form of the 'Articles of War', and authorized courts-martial to enforce the Articles. At that time, Congress apparently assumed that the United States Army would rarely operate outside the territory of the United States. The Articles of War did not include provisions for governing occupied territory or punishing acts of unlawful belligerency against US forces. Malicious destruction of civilian property was only punishable if it belonged to inhabitants of the United States. Most common law crimes, including murder, rape and theft, were omitted from the Articles of War; it was apparently assumed that a soldier committing such offenses would be turned over to the local civil authorities for trial and punishment. In enemy territory, of course, this solution would be impractical since the local courts would almost certainly be hostile to the enemy forces in their midst. Finally, the Articles of War did not provide for court-martial jurisdiction over prisoners of war.

These defects did not become fully apparent until the war between the United States and Mexico from 1846 to 1848. The commanding general of the US Army, Winfield Scott, had studied law before entering the Army and foresaw the problems to come as war approached. He brought them to the attention of the Congress, but without result. By the end of the war, the United States Army occupied an immense area of northern Mexico, including the present states of California, Arizona and New Mexico. In central Mexico, an army personally led by Lt. General Scott also occupied the enemy capital, Mexico City, and the port of Vera Cruz. The occupying forces had to deal with the guerrilla attacks from local resistance

550. See W. Specht, 'New law closes civilians' legal loophole on crimes committed abroad', Stars and Stripes, 25 June 2001. For the House Committee debates on the law see http://commdocs.house.gov/committees/judiciary/hju64399.000/hju64399_0.HTM. For an analysis of the law see J.R. Perlak, 'The Military Extraterritorial Jurisdiction Act of 2000: Implications for contractor personnel', 169 *Military Law Review* (2001) p. 92.

551. Reprinted in this volume at p. 654.

forces, who fought without uniforms or regular organization, and were thus not entitled to prisoner of war status.

General Scott reasoned that dealing with these problems was an inherent part of waging war, just as much as engaging in combat against enemy forces. When the US Constitution made the President the commander-in-chief of the army and navy of the United States, it necessarily granted him (and officers acting under his authority) all powers necessary to wage war, including the power to adjudicate and punish violations of the laws of war. To exercise this power, General Scott, taking a term from French military law of the Napoleonic era, appointed informal courts he referred to as 'military commissions'. Originally consisting of at least three officers plus a Recorder or Judge Advocate to act as prosecutor, military commissions in Mexico tried unlawful enemy belligerents for 'violations of the laws of war' and also dealt with common law crimes by US soldiers and local civilians in occupied territory. The procedures used in military commission trials generally followed those in US Army courts martial, *mutatis mutandis*. The Presidential Military Order of 13 November 2001 indicate that this custom will be followed in any military commission proceedings during the War on Terrorism.

During the American Civil War of 1861-1865, military commissions were used even more extensively by the United States government, both to punish acts of illegal belligerency as well as alleged sedition and disloyalty. The most famous case of that period involving illegal belligerency was the 1865 trial of several co-conspirators of John Wilkes Booth for the assassination of President Lincoln. The accused were tried by military commission, rather than a civil court, on the theory that they had carried out acts of belligerency in wartime by killing the commander-in-chief of the US armed forces, while holding themselves out as ordinary civilians.

Following the Civil War, the US Supreme Court, in the case of *Ex pare* Milligan,[552] severely limited the power of the government to use military commissions to punish sedition and disloyalty by US citizens, while leaving in doubt their jurisdiction over violations of the law of war and unlawful belligerency. Early in World War II, the Supreme Court clarified matters in *Ex parte* Quirin,[553] which upheld the government's power to try unlawful belligerents by military commission. The defendants in *Quirin* were German agents who had entered the United States clandestinely to sabotage war industries. One of the accused had at least some claim to American citizenship, but the Court dismissed this claim as immaterial, since he had in fact become an enemy belligerent.

While no hostile acts had been committed at the time of their arrest, the Court stressed that their clandestine crossing of US military lines, with hostile intent, made them subject to punishment under the laws of war. In fact the only 'military line' crossed by the defendants was the ordinary maritime boundary of the United States (they were landed on the Atlantic coast from submarines).

After World War II, army military commissions were widely used to try war crimes allegedly committed by German and Japanese personnel. (The US Navy also convened at least one military commission to try war crimes in the Pacific Theater.) These trials marked an innovation in the procedure of military commissions, which had, up until this time, generally followed those of courts-martial. In light of the unique difficulties of gathering

552. 4 Wall. 2 (1866).
553. 317 U.S. 1 (1942).

and presenting evidence in war crimes cases, the post-World War II commissions were allowed to deviate from the strict requirements of the Anglo-American hearsay rule, and admit affidavits and other extra-judicial statements where the accused might not have had the opportunity to cross-examine and confront the person giving evidence.

Since most of the post-World War II defendants were captured military personnel, they were considered prisoners of war under the 1929 Geneva Convention on that subject. That Geneva Convention required that prisoners of war be tried by the same courts and according to the same procedure as for members of the Armed Forces of the Detaining Power. If applied to war crimes prosecutions, this provision would mean that prisoners of war would have to be tried by courts martial, which fully applied the hearsay rule and the right to confrontation. The US Supreme Court rejected this argument, however, holding that the Geneva Convention provision only referred to trials for offenses committed after capture, not pre-capture offenses like war crimes.[554] The International Military Tribunals at Nuremburg and Tokyo later adopted this reasoning.

It was largely to reverse these decisions that Article 85 of the Third 1949 Geneva Convention on Prisoners of War makes clear that its provisions on trial and punishment of prisoners apply both to pre-capture and post-capture offenses. As a result of Article 85, the United States Government now generally recognizes that prisoners of war cannot be tried by military commissions, but must be tried by courts-martial (a somewhat ironic conclusion, since military commissions were initially created in the 1840s to try offenses by US military personnel).

In the War on Terrorism, Department of Defense Military Commission Order No. 1 makes it clear that in at least some cases the full rigor of the hearsay and confrontation rules would not apply. It is undoubtedly to preserve the option of military commission trial that the United States has sought to categorize captured Taliban and Al Qaida forces as unlawful combatants, who do not meet the requirements of Article 4 of the 1949 Geneva Convention on Prisoners of War (see statement of Secretary Rumsfeld, 11 January 2002). While the detainees are not, in the US view, technically prisoners of war, as a matter of policy the government claims to be granting them treatment equivalent in most respects to that required by the 1949 Convention (see statement of Assistant Secretary Clarke, 14 January 2002).

In this respect, the United States seems to be following in part the provisions of Article 44(4) of 1977 Protocol I Additional to the Geneva Conventions, even though it is not a party to that Protocol. Paragraph 4 of Article 44 recognizes that a combatant who fails to meet the requirement to distinguish himself from the civilian population (i.e., an unlawful belligerent) 'shall forfeit his right to be a prisoner of war, but he shall, nevertheless, be given protections equivalent in all respects to those accorded to prisoners of war by the Third Convention and by this Protocol'. The last sentence of the paragraph, however, goes on to state that this 'includes protections equivalent to those accorded to prisoners of war by the Third Convention in the case where such a person is tried and punished for any offences he has committed'. This sentence would appear to prohibit the trial of most unlawful combatants before military commissions. This far the United States government is not yet prepared to go.

BURRUS M. CARNAHAN

554. See *Hirota* v. *MacArthur*, 338 U.S. 197 (1948); *In re* Yamashita, 327 U.S. 1 (1947).

Nuclear Weapons

- Nuclear Posture Review Report. 8 January 2002. Submitted to Congress 31 December 2001

The controversial Nuclear Posture Review Report presents the results of a review by the Department of Defense at the request of Congress into the direction for American nuclear forces over the next five to ten years. The Report 'puts in motion a major change in our approach to the role of nuclear offensive forces in our deterrent strategy and presents the blueprint for transforming our strategic posture'. It established a 'New Triad', consisting of: '(i) offensive strike systems (both nuclear and non-nuclear); (ii) defenses (both active and passive); and (iii) a revitalized defense infrastructure that will provide new capabilities in a timely fashion to meet emerging threats'.[555]

The Report stated that: 'Nuclear weapons play a critical role in the defense capabilities of the United States, its allies and friends. They provide credible military options to deter a wide range of threats, including WMD and large-scale conventional military force. These nuclear capabilities possess unique properties that give the United States options to hold at risk classes of targets [that are] important to achieve strategic and political objectives.'[556]

The Report envisaged the use of nuclear weapons against 'targets able to withstand non-nuclear attack, (for example, deep underground bunkers or bio-weapon facilities)'.[557] It said that: 'New capabilities must be developed to defeat emerging threats such as hard and deeply buried targets (HDBT), to find and attack mobile and relocatable targets, to defeat chemical or biological agents, and to improve accuracy and limit collateral damage. Development of these capabilities, to include extensive research and timely fielding of new systems to address these challenges, are imperative to make the New Triad a reality.'[558]

Counter-terrorism

- Uniting and Strengthening America by Providing Appropriate Tools Required to Intercept and Obstruct Terrorism (USA Patriot Act) of 2001, Public Law 107-56, page 115 STAT. 272. Approved 26 October 2001

This voluminous Act, which was adopted following the September 11 terrorist attacks on the US, is concerned with several aspects of counter-terrorism. It is avowedly 'An Act [t]o deter and punish terrorist acts in the United States and around the world, to enhance law enforcement and investigatory tools, and for other purposes'. Consisting of ten Titles (parts), it aims to enhance domestic security against terrorism (Title I); enhance surveillance procedures (Title II); reduce international money laundering (Title III); protect US borders (Title IV); remove obstacles to investigating terrorism (Title V); provide for victims of terrorism, public safety officers and their families (Title VI); increase information sharing for critical infrastructure protection (Title VII); strengthen criminal laws against terrorism (Title VIII); improve intelligence (Title IX); and other miscellaneous matters (Title X).

---

555. Nuclear Posture Review Report, Forward.
556. Ibid., p. 7.
557. Ibid., pp. 12-13.
558. Ibid., pp. 46 et seq.

The Act gives the US authorities broad powers, particularly in the area of surveillance and detention of aliens considered to be suspected terrorist, by amending a number of pre-existing laws, and curbs the powers of the courts to review the exercise of such powers.

Title VII – Strengthening the criminal laws against terrorism – is particularly interesting for these purposes. Section 801 amends the United States Code, Chapter 97, Title 18, by adding the crime of terrorist attacks and other acts of violence against mass transportation systems. The acts included under the general prohibition include placing or causing to be placed any biological weapon or toxin for use as a weapon or destructive device in, upon or near any mass transportation vehicle or ferry and the use of dangerous weapons with the intention of causing death or serious bodily injury to an employee or passenger of a mass transportation provider. Section 802 amends the definition of domestic terrorism to include mass destruction. 'Domestic terrorism' is defined to mean activities that '(A) involve acts dangerous to human life that are a violation of the criminal laws of the United State or of any State; (B) appear to be intended-(i) to intimidate or coerce a civilian population; (ii) to influence the policy of a government by intimidation or coercion; or (iii) to affect the conduct of a government by mass destruction, assassination, or kidnapping; and (C) occur primarily within the territorial jurisdiction of the United States'. The Law further defines an act of terrorism as an act of domestic or international terrorism. Section 808 amends the definition of the federal crime of terrorism contained in Section 233b of Title 18 of the United States Code.

Foreign Assistance

☛ Foreign Operations Appropriations Act for Fiscal Year 2001, Section 563, P.L. 104-208

The provision prohibits the US from giving funds 'to any unit of the security forces of a foreign country if the Secretary of State has credible evidence that such unit has committed gross violations of human rights, unless the Secretary determines that . . . the government of such country is taking effective measures to bring the responsible members of the security forces unit to justice'.

Conflict Diamonds

☛ House and Senate legislation, introduced before 11 September 2001 requiring certification of origin for rough diamonds imported into the United States, has now received bipartisan support; a vote is expected in the week of 12 November 2001.[559] [http://www.amnesty-usa.org/news/2001/sierraleone09072001.html]

AVRIL MCDONALD

Cases

☛ *Jane Doe and John Does I, II, III, IV and V v. Lumintang,* Civil Action No. 00-674 (GK), United States District Court for the District of Columbia, Findings of Fact and Conclusions of Law, 10 September 2001 [http://www.etan.org/news/2001a/10lumjudg.htm]

On 10 September 2001, Judge Alan Kay of the District Court of Columbia awarded a total of $66 million in damages to five unnamed East Timorese plaintiffs against a senior TNI

559. 'Congress may act on "blood diamonds" next week', Reuters, 8 November 2001.

officer, Johny Lumintang. Major General Johny Lumintang was Vice Chief of Staff of the Indonesian military (TNI) at the time of the alleged violations.

The plaintiffs complained of individual acts that included torture, wrongful killing, summary execution, assault, battery, intentional infliction of emotional distress and other harms done to them in East Timor. The claims were made under the Alien Tort Claims Act, Torture Victim Protection Act and 'principles of supplemental jurisdiction'.

The large award comprised three types of damages intended to restore the status quo ante: monetary damages in compensation for all pecuniary and non-pecuniary injuries; compensatory damages for tort claims under Portuguese law; punitive damages both to punish and deter such egregious violations of international law (which require a showing of evidence of similar acts or a pattern of similar activity not directed specifically against the plaintiffs).

The award of 10 September 2001 follows an earlier default judgement against Lumintang, entered by US District Judge Gladys Kessler on 8 November 2000. In the absence of any challenge from Lumintang, who had been served on 30 March 2000, the court accepted the plaintiff's allegations as true and uncontrovertable. The judgement contains striking findings about Indonesia's role in East Timor, including that played by Lumintang. In the absence of litigation, the judgement's findings of fact must, however, be viewed with caution. With that caveat, it is of interest that the following findings of fact were made:

1. In August 1998, the militias became effectively part of the Indonesian armed forces. They were instructed, supported and guided by the TNI and received arms directly from the KODAM (Military Area Resort Command);
2. Lt.Col. Sudrajat, the head of the Combined Intelligence Task Force (part of KOPASSUS – Special Forces Command) gave an order on 16 February 1999 that independence leaders and their families be wiped out. Lumintang was responsible for ensuring the implementation of the order;
3. On 26 March 1999, at a meeting of senior Indonesian civil and military leaders, the Governor of East Timor, Abilio Soares, directed militias to prepare for the 'liquidation' of all senior pro-independence people and their families. Those who sought shelter in the churches would be killed along with the nuns and priests. This led directly to the massacre of 54 people including clergy at the Liquica church in April 1999;
4. On 5 May 1999, the day of the tripartite agreement between the UN, Indonesia and Portugal on a referendum for East Timor, Lumintang issued a telegram alerting commanders to prepare a security plan with the aim of 'preventing a possible civil war' and directing the military to prepare for 'evacuation';
5. On 18 June 1999, Major General Zacky Anwar, Col. Tono Suratman and militia leaders met in Dili to create a plan to disrupt the referendum, and if the vote went for independence, to partition East Timor into an Indonesian and independent part. The plan included forced relocation of civilians and repopulation and transmigration into emptied East Timor.

Judge Kay found that Lumintang had direct responsibility for the acts complained of by the five plaintiffs. It held that he and other high-ranking members of the Indonesian military planned, ordered and instigated acts carried out by military subordinates to terrorise and displace the civilian population, repress supporters of independence and destroy East Timor's infrastructure following the vote for independence. The documents submitted as evidence showed that Lumintang ordered, instigated or planned acts which led to the plaintiffs' injuries. Lumintang was found to have participated in a pattern of conduct that supported, aided, abetted, armed, encouraged and directed the militias, and also participated directly in their chain of command. Lumintang's indirect command responsibility arose from his position as Vice Chief of Staff of the TNI which made him the legal commander of those who injured the plaintiffs. He failed to act to prevent or punish the violations despite the fact that he knew or should have known that subordinates were committing, about to commit or had committed widespread and systematic human rights violations. He was found have responsibility for the massacre of 54 persons at the Liquica church in April 1999. According to the judgement, Lumintang issued instructions on military tactics and techniques that included abducting, killing, kidnapping and terror and those instructions were put into effect, causing the harm complained of by the plaintiffs.

This civil judgement confirmed that command responsibility requires proof that: (1) A relationship of subordination existed between the commander and perpetrator; (2) The commander knew or should have known that troops under his command were committing, were about to commit or had committed international law violations (*mens rea*); (3) The commander failed to prevent or punish abuses (*actus reus*). Judge Kay cited previous jurisprudence in the *Hilao* v. *Estate of Marcos*[560] case that a commander who knew of the involvement of subordinates in torture, summary execution and disappearance and failed to use his power to prevent it could be found civilly liable. Also cited was *Xuncax* v. *Gramajo*,[561] where the court entered a default judgement against a former military ruler of Haiti because of acts committed by those members of the military acting under his instructions, authority and control and acting within the scope of the authority granted by him. *Forti* v. *Suarez-Mason*[562] indicated to Judge Kay that a policy, pattern or practice of human rights violations committed by subordinates under a defendant's command is relevant to both a defendant's knowledge of such acts and his failure to exercise an affirmative duty to control his subordinates. By failing to intervene to prevent or punish a policy, pattern or practice of abuses, a commander may be found to have essentially ratified the abuses.

Finally, Judge Kay also found that '[t]he law that currently applies in East Timor is Portuguese law' and therefore used Portuguese municipal law to determine Lumintang's liability in tort.[563] Since the judgement, Johny Lumintang has denied that as Deputy Chief of Staff he had any role or influence over what happened in East Timor.[564]

SUZANNAH LINTON

---

560. *Hilao* v. *Estate of Marcos*, 103 F.3d 767 (9th Cir. 1996).

561. *Xuncax* v. *Gramajo*, 886 F. Supp. 162 (D. Mass 1995).

562. *Forti* v. *Suarez-Mason*, No. 87-2058-DLJ (N.D.Cal. Apr. 25, 1990).

563. The imposition of Indonesian law upon occupied East Timor was probably in violation of Article 64 of the Geneva Convention Relative to the Protection of Civilian Persons in Time of War which prohibits the replacement of local law with the law of the Occupying Power unless such law constitutes a threat to its security or to implementation of the convention. However, the reality is that for 24 years, Indonesian law applied and was enforced in occupied East Timor. It continues to apply in East Timor through UNTAET Regulation 1999/1, which preserves the applicable laws of East Timor (Indonesian law) unless amended by later UNTAET regulations and to the extent consistent with international standards. This is evidenced, for example, by the continued use of the Indonesian Penal Code in East Timor. Portuguese law has not been applied in East Timor under UN administration, and was not applied during the 24-years of Indonesian occupation.

564. 'Johny denies responsibility over mayhem in East Timor', *The Jakarta Post*, 6 October 2001.

URUGUAY

Military Criminal Law

☛ Review of the military criminal law

'The *Institutio Jurídico para la Defensa* assessed the Military Justice Code from the standpoint of humanitarian law, with a view to proposig the amendments required to allow for the punishment of breaches of the law.'[565]

Education and Training

☛ 'Pursuant to Executive Decree 678/992 (*Cométese la instrumentación de cursos en coordinación con la Comisión Nacional de Derecho Humanitario*), IHL was taught in 2000 and 2001 at the Military Institute of Superior Studies where it was a mandatory subject in the Courses of High National Studies, and at the Instituto Artigas de Relacionnes Exteriores – Escuela Diplómatica'[566]

UZBEKISTAN

Civil Defence

☛ Law on civil defence. Entered into force on 26 May 2000

'It establishes a comprehensive system of civil defence, designed to cope with emergency situations resulting, *inter alia*, from armed conflicts.'[567]

VENEZUELA

Criminal Law

☛ Penal Code [Codigo Penal]. Published in *Gaceta Oficial* Nº 5.494 Extraordinario de fecha 20 de octubre de 2000

ZIMBABWE

Anti-personnel Mines

☛ Anti-Personnel Mines (Prohibition Act) (To enable effect to be given within Zimbabwe to the Convention on the Prohibition of the Use, Stockpiling, Production and Transfer of Anti-Personnel Mines and on their Destruction, signed at Oslo, Norway, on the 18th September, 1997). Adopted March 2001. Entered into force on 2 November 2000. Published in *Government Gazette*, 2000, No. 17

'The Act provides for the punishment of the use, stockpiling, transfer or possession of anti-personnel mines other than for the development of and training in mine detection, clearance,

565. ICRC Advisory Service, *National Implementation of International Humanitarian Law*: Biennial report 2000-2001 (Geneva, ICRC 2002) p. 99.

566. Ibid.

567. ICRC Advisory Service, *National Implementation of International Humanitarian Law*: Biennial report 2000-2001 (Geneva, ICRC 2002) p. 100.

or destruction. It also provides for the destruction of all mines not used for the above purposes'.[568]

568. Ibid., p. 104.

DOCUMENTATION[1]

1. The Documentation section has been prepared by Avril McDonald, Managing Editor of the *YIHL*, from materials provided to the *YIHL* by its correspondents, *inter alia*. Restricted space forces us to be selective in the documents included. The *YIHL's* general policy is to prefer documents to which access might otherwise be difficult, in particular regarding state practice. In general, we will tend not to publish documents that are easily and widely available, although we may make exceptions, particularly where the material supports an article in the yearbook. The documents are reproduced as we have received them, although some may be in a slightly condensed form. All spelling, grammatical and layout irregularities are therefore in the original. The source of the document and translation, where applicable, is indicated alongside each document. The titles of documents listed in the table of contents *infra* at p. 649 are not the exact titles. The latter appear alongside the particular documents.

Yearbook of International Humanitarian Law
Volume 4 – 2001 – pp. 643-775

CLASSIFICATION OF DOCUMENTS

0.	**Zero:**	**INTERNATIONAL HUMANITARIAN LAW IN GENERAL**
1.	**One:**	**SOURCES AND GENERAL PRINCIPLES**
1.1	I	SOURCES
1.11		A. Pre-Hague
1.12		B. Hague Law
1.13		C. Geneva Law
1.14		D. Post-1977 Developments
1.15		E. Customary Law
1.2	II	GENERAL PRINCIPLES
1.21		A. Martens Clause
1.22		B. Superfluous Injury and Unnecessary Suffering
1.23		C. Principle of Distinction
1.24		D. Principle of Proportionality
1.25		E. Military Necessity
2.	**Two:**	**CONFLICTS, ARMED FORCES AND COMBATANTS**
2.1	I	TYPES OF CONFLICTS
2.11		A. International
2.12		B. Non-international
2.13		C. Other
2.2	II	TYPES OF ACTOR(S)
2.21		A. Armed Forces and Combatant Status
2.22		B. Non-State Actors
2.23		C. Specific Groups
2.231		1. Mercenaries
2.232		2. Spies
2.233		3. Other
3.	**Three:**	**PROTECTED PERSONS**
3.1	I	TYPES OF PROTECTED PERSONS
3.11		A. Wounded, Sick and Shipwrecked
3.12		B. Prisoners of War
3.13		C. Civilian Population
3.131		1. Civilians Generally
3.132		2. Women and Children
3.133		3. Medical and Religious Personnel
3.134		4. Journalists
3.135		5. Other
3.2	II	SPECIFIC SITUATIONS AND PROHIBITIONS
3.21		A. Internment
3.22		B. Occupation
3.23		C. Prohibition of Collective Punishment
3.24		D. Prohibition of Deportation and Transfer
3.25		E. Reprisals

4.	**Four:**	**METHODS, MEANS AND TYPES OF WARFARE**
4.1	I	METHODS AND MEANS OF WARFARE
4.11		A. Basic Rules
4.111		1. Existing Weapons
4.1111		a. Conventional Weapons
4.11111		i. Mines
4.11112		ii. Small Weapons and Others
4.1112		b. Weapons of Mass Destruction
4.11121		i. Nuclear Weapons
4.11122		ii. Chemical and Biological Weapons
4.112		2. New Weapons
4.113		3. Prohibition of Perfidy
4.114		4. Emblems and Safeguards of Persons *hors de combat*
4.12		B. Direct and Indiscriminate Attacks
4.13		C. Precautionary Measures
4.14		D. Protection of Civilian and Other Specified Objects
4.141		1. Specifically Protected Objects
4.142		2. Cultural Property and Places of Worship
4.143		3. Works and Installations Containing Dangerous Forces
4.144		4. The Natural Environment
4.145		5. Localities and Zones
4.146		6. Civil Defence
4.15		E. Medical Assistance
4.16		F. Humanitarian Assistance Operations
4.2	II	SPECIFIC TYPES OF WARFARE
4.21		A. Land Warfare
4.22		B. Air and Missile Warfare
4.23		C. Naval Warfare
5.	**Five:**	**TERMINATION OF ARMED CONFLICTS**
5.1	I	CEASEFIRE, ARMISTICES AND PEACE AGREEMENTS
5.2	II	WAR CRIMES COMMISSIONS
5.3	III	AMNESTIES, TRUTH AND RECONCILIATION COMMISSIONS
5.4	IV	REPARATIONS/COMPENSATION
6.	**Six:**	**INTERNATIONAL CRIMINAL LAW**
6.1	I	THE CRIMES
6.11		A. War Crimes
6.12		B. Genocide
6.13		C. Crimes Against Humanity
6.14		D. Aggression
6.2	II	GENERAL PRINCIPLES, INCLUDING DEFENCES
6.21		A. Nullum Crimen Sine Lege and Nulla Poena Sine Lege
6.22		B. Individual Criminal Responsibility
6.23		C. Superior/Command Responsibility
6.24		D. Irrelevance of Official Capacity

10.	**Ten:**	**REGIONAL ORGANIZATIONS AND ACTIONS**
10.1	I	EUROPEAN
10.2	II	AMERICAN
10.3	III	ASIAN
10.4	IV	AFRICAN
11.	**Eleven:**	**ARMS CONTROL AND DISARMAMENT**
11.1	I	CONVENTIONAL WEAPONS
11.11		A. Mines
11.12		B. Small Weapons and Others
11.13		C. Production and Transfer
11.2	II	WEAPONS OF MASS DESTRUCTION
11.21		A. Nuclear Weapons
11.22		B. Chemical and Biological Weapons
11.23		C. New Types
12.	**Twelve:**	**CONFLICT PREVENTION AND RESOLUTION**
12.1	I	CONFLICT PREVENTION
12.2	II	CONFLICT RESOLUTION
12.3	III	THE PEACE MOVEMENT
13.	**Thirteen:**	**RELATED FIELDS**
13.1	I	JUS AD BELLUM
13.2	II	THE LAW RELATING TO TERRORISM AND COUNTER-TERRORISM
13.3	III	MILITARY LAW
13.4	IV	HUMAN RIGHTS LAW
13.5	V	REFUGEE LAW

NOTE: Many international and national documents related to international humanitarian law are available on the Internet through an on-line access to the ICRC IHL database (ICRC website: http://www.icrc.org). This database now contains almost 100 treaties and texts on the conduct of hostilities and the protection of victims of war (dating from 1856 to the present); the commentaries on the four Geneva Conventions and their Additional Protocols; an up-to-date list of signatures, ratifications, accessions or successions to IHL treaties; and, the full text of reservations. Constantly updated, this data is also regularly replicated on a D-ROM that can be obtained from the ICRC (Public Information Division, 19, av. de la Paix, CH-1202 GENEVA; e-mail: webmaster.gva@icrc.org; Fax: ++ 41 22 733 20 57; CHF 49.- or USD 39,-). National implementing legislation (Geneva Conventions Acts, extracts from Penal Codes, laws related to the protection of the emblem, laws on cooperation with the international Tribunals, etc.) and jurisprudence are also available for an increasing number of countries.

DOCUMENTS

2.21 ARMED FORCES AND COMBATANT STATUS

☛ USA: Military Extraterritorial Jurisdiction Act of 2000

S.768
One Hundred Sixth Congress of the United States of America
At the Second Session
Begun and held at the City of Washington on Monday,
the twenty-fourth day of January, two thousand
An Act
To amend title 18, United States Code, to establish Federal jurisdiction over offenses committed outside the United States by persons employed by or accompanying the Armed Forces, or by members of the Armed Forces who are released or separated from active duty prior to being identified and prosecuted for the commission of such offenses, and for other purposes.
Be it enacted by the Senate and House of Representatives of the United States of America in Congress assembled,

Section 1: Short Title

This Act may be cited as the 'Military Extraterritorial Jurisdiction Act of 2000'.

Sec. 2. Federal Jurisdiction.

(a) Certain Criminal Offenses Committee Outside the United States- Title 18, United States Code, is amended by inserting after chapter 211 the following new chapter:

Chapter 212-Military Extraterritorial Jurisdiction

'Sec.

'3261. Criminal offenses committed by certain members of the Armed Forces and by persons employed by or accompanying the Armed Forces outside the United States.
'3262. Arrest and commitment.
'3263. Delivery to authorities of foreign countries.
'3264. Limitation on removal.
'3265. Initial proceedings.
'3266. Regulations.
'3267. Definitions.

'Sec. 3261. Criminal offenses committed by certain members of the Armed Forces and by persons employed by or accompanying the Armed Forces outside the United States

'(a) Whoever engages in conduct outside the United States that would constitute an offense punishable by imprisonment for more than 1 year if the conduct had been engaged in within the special maritime and territorial jurisdiction of the United States—
'(1) while employed by or accompanying the Armed Forces outside the United States; or

'(2) while a member of the Armed Forces subject to chapter 47 of title 10 (the Uniform Code of Military Justice),
shall be punished as provided for that offense.
'(b) No prosecution may be commenced against a person under this section if a foreign government, in accordance with jurisdiction recognized by the United States, has prosecuted or is prosecuting such person for the conduct constituting such offense, except upon the approval of the Attorney General or the Deputy Attorney General (or a person acting in either such capacity), which function of approval may not be delegated.
'(c) Nothing in this chapter may be construed to deprive a court-martial, military commission, provost court, or other military tribunal of concurrent jurisdiction with respect to offenders or offenses that by statute or by the law of war may be tried by a court-martial, military commission, provost court, or other military tribunal.
'(d) No prosecution may be commenced against a member of the Armed Forces subject to chapter 47 of title 10 (the Uniform Code of Military Justice) under this section unless—
'(1) such member ceases to be subject to such chapter; or
'(2) an indictment or information charges that the member committed the offense with one or more other defendants, at least one of whom is not subject to such chapter.

'Sec. 3262. Arrest and commitment

'(a) The Secretary of Defense may designate and authorize any person serving in a law enforcement position in the Department of Defense to arrest, in accordance with applicable international agreements, outside the United States any person described in section 3261(a) if there is probable cause to believe that such person violated section 3261(a).
'(b) Except as provided in sections 3263 and 3264, a person arrested under subsection (a) shall be delivered as soon as practicable to the custody of civilian law enforcement authorities of the United States for removal to the United States for judicial proceedings in relation to conduct referred to in such subsection unless such person has had charges brought against him or her under chapter 47 of title 10 for such conduct.

'Sec. 3263. Delivery to authorities of foreign countries

'(a) Any person designated and authorized under section 3262(a) may deliver a person described in section 3261(a) to the appropriate authorities of a foreign country in which such person is alleged to have violated section 3261(a) if—
'(1) appropriate authorities of that country request the delivery of the person to such country for trial for such conduct as an offense under the laws of that country; and
'(2) the delivery of such person to that country is authorized by a treaty or other international agreement to which the United States is a party.
'(b) The Secretary of Defense, in consultation with the Secretary of State, shall determine which officials of a foreign country constitute appropriate authorities for purposes of this section.

'Sec. 3264. Limitation on removal

'(a) Except as provided in subsection (b), and except for a person delivered to authorities of a foreign country under section 3263, a person arrested for or charged with a violation of

section 3261(a) shall not be removed—
'(1) to the United States; or
'(2) to any foreign country other than a country in which such person is believed to have violated section 3261(a).
'(b) The limitation in subsection (a) does not apply if—
'(1) a Federal magistrate judge orders the person to be removed to the United States to be present at a detention hearing held pursuant to section 3142(f);
'(2) a Federal magistrate judge orders the detention of the person before trial pursuant to section 3142(e), in which case the person shall be promptly removed to the United States for purposes of such detention;
'(3) the person is entitled to, and does not waive, a preliminary examination under the Federal Rules of Criminal Procedure, in which case the person shall be removed to the United States in time for such examination;
'(4) a Federal magistrate judge otherwise orders the person to be removed to the United States; or
'(5) the Secretary of Defense determines that military necessity requires that the limitations in subsection (a) be waived, in which case the person shall be removed to the nearest United States military installation outside the United States adequate to detain the person and to facilitate the initial appearance described in section 3265(a).

'Sec. 3265. Initial proceedings

'(a)(1) In the case of any person arrested for or charged with a violation of section 3261(a) who is not delivered to authorities of a foreign country under section 3263, the initial appearance of that person under the Federal Rules of Criminal Procedure—
'(A) shall be conducted by a Federal magistrate judge; and
'(B) may be carried out by telephony or such other means that enables voice communication among the participants, including any counsel representing the person.
'(2) In conducting the initial appearance, the Federal magistrate judge shall also determine whether there is probable cause to believe that an offense under section 3261(a) was committed and that the person committed it.
'(3) If the Federal magistrate judge determines that probable cause exists that the person committed an offense under section 3261(a), and if no motion is made seeking the person's detention before trial, the Federal magistrate judge shall also determine at the initial appearance the conditions of the person's release before trial under chapter 207 of this title.
'(b) In the case of any person described in subsection (a), any detention hearing of that person under section 3142(f)—
'(1) shall be conducted by a Federal magistrate judge; and
'(2) at the request of the person, may be carried out by telephony or such other means that enables voice communication among the participants, including any counsel representing the person.
'(c)(1) If any initial proceeding under this section with respect to any such person is conducted while the person is outside the United States, and the person is entitled to have counsel appointed for purposes of such proceeding, the Federal magistrate judge may appoint as such counsel for purposes of such hearing a qualified military counsel.

'(2) For purposes of this subsection, the term 'qualified military counsel' means a judge advocate made available by the Secretary of Defense for purposes of such proceedings, who—
'(A) is a graduate of an accredited law school or is a member of the bar of a Federal court or of the highest court of a State; and
'(B) is certified as competent to perform such duties by the Judge Advocate General of the armed force of which he is a member.

'Sec. 3266. Regulations

'(a) The Secretary of Defense, after consultation with the Secretary of State and the Attorney General, shall prescribe regulations governing the apprehension, detention, delivery, and removal of persons under this chapter and the facilitation of proceedings under section 3265. Such regulations shall be uniform throughout the Department of Defense.
'(b)(1) The Secretary of Defense, after consultation with the Secretary of State and the Attorney General, shall prescribe regulations requiring that, to the maximum extent practicable, notice shall be provided to any person employed by or accompanying the Armed Forces outside the United States who is not a national of the United States that such person is potentially subject to the criminal jurisdiction of the United States under this chapter.
'(2) A failure to provide notice in accordance with the regulations prescribed under paragraph (1) shall not defeat the jurisdiction of a court of the United States or provide a defense in any judicial proceeding arising under this chapter.
'(c) The regulations prescribed under this section, and any amendments to those regulations, shall not take effect before the date that is 90 days after the date on which the Secretary of Defense submits a report containing those regulations or amendments (as the case may be) to the Committee on the Judiciary of the House of Representatives and the Committee on the Judiciary of the Senate.

'Sec. 3267. Definitions

'As used in this chapter:
'(1) The term 'employed by the Armed Forces outside the United States' means—
'(A) employed as a civilian employee of the Department of Defense (including a nonappropriated fund instrumentality of the Department), as a Department of Defense contractor (including a subcontractor at any tier), or as an employee of a Department of Defense contractor (including a subcontractor at any tier);
'(B) present or residing outside the United States in connection with such employment; and
'(C) not a national of or ordinarily resident in the host nation.
'(2) The term 'accompanying the Armed Forces outside the United States' means—
'(A) a dependent of—
'(i) a member of the Armed Forces;
'(ii) a civilian employee of the Department of Defense (including a nonappropriated fund instrumentality of the Department); or
'(iii) a Department of Defense contractor (including a subcontractor at any tier) or an employee of a Department of Defense contractor (including a subcontractor at any tier);
'(B) residing with such member, civilian employee, contractor, or contractor employee outside the United States; and

'(C) not a national of or ordinarily resident in the host nation.
'(3) The term 'Armed Forces' has the meaning given the term 'armed forces' in section 101(a)(4) of title 10.
'(4) The terms 'Judge Advocate General' and 'judge advocate' have the meanings given such terms in section 801 of title 10.'.
(b) Clerical Amendment – The table of chapters for part II of title 18, United States Code, is amended by inserting after the item relating to chapter 211 the following new item:

3261'.

Speaker of the House of Representatives.
Vice President of the United States and
President of the Senate.

3.21 INTERNMENT

☛ USA: Military Order: Detention, Treatment, and Trial of Certain Non-Citizens in the War Against Terrorism, 13 November 2001

By the authority vested in me as President and as Commander in Chief of the Armed Forces of the United States by the Constitution and the laws of the United States of America, including the Authorization for Use of Military Force Joint Resolution (Public Law 107-40, 115 Stat. 224) and sections 821 and 836 of title 10, United States Code, it is hereby ordered as follows:

Section 1. Findings.

(a) International terrorists, including members of al Qaida, have carried out attacks on United States diplomatic and military personnel and facilities abroad and on citizens and property within the United States on a scale that has created a state of armed conflict that requires the use of the United States Armed Forces.
(b) In light of grave acts of terrorism and threats of terrorism, including the terrorist attacks on September 11, 2001, on the headquarters of the United States Department of Defense in the national capital region, on the World Trade Center in New York, and on civilian aircraft such as in Pennsylvania, I proclaimed a national emergency on September 14, 2001 (Proc. 7463, Declaration of National Emergency by Reason of Certain Terrorist Attacks).
(c) Individuals acting alone and in concert involved in international terrorism possess both the capability and the intention to undertake further terrorist attacks against the United States that, if not detected and prevented, will cause mass deaths, mass injuries, and massive destruction of property, and may place at risk the continuity of the operations of the United States Government.
(d) The ability of the United States to protect the United States and its citizens, and to help its allies and other cooperating nations protect their nations and their citizens, from such further terrorist attacks depends in significant part upon using the United States Armed Forces to identify terrorists and those who support them, to disrupt their activities, and to eliminate their ability to conduct or support such attacks.

(e) To protect the United States and its citizens, and for the effective conduct of military operations and prevention of terrorist attacks, it is necessary for individuals subject to this order pursuant to section 2 hereof to be detained, and, when tried, to be tried for violations of the laws of war and other applicable laws by military tribunals.
(f) Given the danger to the safety of the United States and the nature of international terrorism, and to the extent provided by and under this order, I find consistent with section 836 of title 10, United States Code, that it is not practicable to apply in military commissions under this order the principles of law and the rules of evidence generally recognized in the trial of criminal cases in the United States district courts.
(g) Having fully considered the magnitude of the potential deaths, injuries, and property destruction that would result from potential acts of terrorism against the United States, and the probability that such acts will occur, I have determined that an extraordinary emergency exists for national defense purposes, that this emergency constitutes an urgent and compelling government interest, and that issuance of this order is necessary to meet the emergency.

Sec. 2. Definition and Policy.

(a) The term "individual subject to this order" shall mean any individual who is not a United States citizen with respect to whom I determine from time to time in writing that:
(1) there is reason to believe that such individual, at the relevant times,
(i) is or was a member of the organization known as al Qaida;
(ii) has engaged in, aided or abetted, or conspired to commit, acts of international terrorism, or acts in preparation therefor, that have caused, threaten to cause, or have as their aim to cause, injury to or adverse effects on the United States, its citizens, national security, foreign policy, or economy; or
(iii) has knowingly harbored one or more individuals described in subparagraphs (i) or (ii) of subsection 2(a)(1) of this order;
and
(2) it is in the interest of the United States that such individual be subject to this order.
(b) It is the policy of the United States that the Secretary of Defense shall take all necessary measures to ensure that any individual subject to this order is detained in accordance with section 3, and, if the individual is to be tried, that such individual is tried only in accordance with section 4.
(c) It is further the policy of the United States that any individual subject to this order who is not already under the control of the Secretary of Defense but who is under the control of any other officer or agent of the United States or any State shall, upon delivery of a copy of such written determination to such officer or agent, forthwith be placed under the control of the Secretary of Defense.

Sec. 3. Detention Authority of the Secretary of Defense. Any individual subject to this order shall be —

(a) detained at an appropriate location designated by the Secretary of Defense outside or within the United States;
(b) treated humanely, without any adverse distinction based on race, color, religion, gender, birth, wealth, or any similar criteria;
(c) afforded adequate food, drinking water, shelter, clothing, and medical treatment;

(d) allowed the free exercise of religion consistent with the requirements of such detention; and
(e) detained in accordance with such other conditions as the Secretary of Defense may prescribe.

Sec. 4. Authority of the Secretary of Defense Regarding Trials of Individuals Subject to this Order.

(a) Any individual subject to this order shall, when tried, be tried by military commission for any and all offenses triable by military commission that such individual is alleged to have committed, and may be punished in accordance with the penalties provided under applicable law, including life imprisonment or death.
(b) As a military function and in light of the findings in section 1, including subsection (f) thereof, the Secretary of Defense shall issue such orders and regulations, including orders for the appointment of one or more military commissions, as may be necessary to carry out subsection (a) of this section.
(c) Orders and regulations issued under subsection (b) of this section shall include, but not be limited to, rules for the conduct of the proceedings of military commissions, including pretrial, trial, and post-trial procedures, modes of proof, issuance of process, and qualifications of attorneys, which shall at a minimum provide for —
(1) military commissions to sit at any time and any place, consistent with such guidance regarding time and place as the Secretary of Defense may provide;
(2) a full and fair trial, with the military commission sitting as the triers of both fact and law;
(3) admission of such evidence as would, in the opinion of the presiding officer of the military commission (or instead, if any other member of the commission so requests at the time the presiding officer renders that opinion, the opinion of the commission rendered at that time by a majority of the commission), have probative value to a reasonable person;
(4) in a manner consistent with the protection of information classified or classifiable under Executive Order 12958 of April 17, 1995, as amended, or any successor Executive Order, protected by statute or rule from unauthorized disclosure, or otherwise protected by law, (A) the handling of, admission into evidence of, and access to materials and information, and (B) the conduct, closure of, and access to proceedings;
(5) conduct of the prosecution by one or more attorneys designated by the Secretary of Defense and conduct of the defense by attorneys for the individual subject to this order;
(6) conviction only upon the concurrence of two-thirds of the members of the commission present at the time of the vote, a majority being present;
(7) sentencing only upon the concurrence of two-thirds of the members of the commission present at the time of the vote, a majority being present; and
(8) submission of the record of the trial, including any conviction or sentence, for review and final decision by me or by the Secretary of Defense if so designated by me for that purpose.

Sec. 5. Obligation of Other Agencies to Assist the Secretary of Defense.

Departments, agencies, entities, and officers of the United States shall, to the maximum extent permitted by law, provide to the Secretary of Defense such assistance as he may request to implement this order.

Sec. 6. Additional Authorities of the Secretary of Defense.

(a) As a military function and in light of the findings in section 1, the Secretary of Defense shall issue such orders and regulations as may be necessary to carry out any of the provisions of this order.
(b) The Secretary of Defense may perform any of his functions or duties, and may exercise any of the powers provided to him under this order (other than under section 4(c)(8) hereof) in accordance with section 113(d) of title 10, United States Code.

Sec. 7. Relationship to Other Law and Forums.

(a) Nothing in this order shall be construed to —
(1) authorize the disclosure of state secrets to any person not otherwise authorized to have access to them;
(2) limit the authority of the President as Commander in Chief of the Armed Forces or the power of the President to grant reprieves and pardons; or
(3) limit the lawful authority of the Secretary of Defense, any military commander, or any other officer or agent of the United States or of any State to detain or try any person who is not an individual subject to this order.
(b) With respect to any individual subject to this order —
(1) military tribunals shall have exclusive jurisdiction with respect to offenses by the individual; and
(2) the individual shall not be privileged to seek any remedy or maintain any proceeding, directly or indirectly, or to have any such remedy or proceeding sought on the individual's behalf, in (i) any court of the United States, or any State thereof, (ii) any court of any foreign nation, or (iii) any international tribunal.
(c) This order is not intended to and does not create any right, benefit, or privilege, substantive or procedural, enforceable at law or equity by any party, against the United States, its departments, agencies, or other entities, its officers or employees, or any other person.
(d) For purposes of this order, the term "State" includes any State, district, territory, or possession of the United States.
(e) I reserve the authority to direct the Secretary of Defense, at any time hereafter, to transfer to a governmental authority control of any individual subject to this order. Nothing in this order shall be construed to limit the authority of any such governmental authority to prosecute any individual for whom control is transferred.

Sec. 8. Publication.

This order shall be published in the Federal Register.
George W. Bush
The White House
November 13, 2001.

☛ **DoD News Briefing – Secretary Rumsfeld and Gen. Myers**
11 January 2002, 2:10 PM EST (Pentagon)

Sec. Rumsfeld: (in answer to question about treatment of Al Qaeda detainees under U.S. control)

They will be handled not as prisoners of wars, because they're not, but as unlawful combatants. [A]s I understand it, technically unlawful combatants do not have any rights under the Geneva Convention. We have indicated that we do plan to, for the most part, treat them in a manner that is reasonably consistent with the Geneva Conventions, to the extent they are appropriate, and that is exactly what we have been doing.

☛ **DoD News Briefing – ASD PA Clarke**
14 January 2002 – 12:30 p.m. EST

A couple of things on detainees. As of today, there are 414 detainees in Afghanistan; there are 20 in Guantanamo. When additional detainees arrive there, we will tell you. When the procedures for the questioning of the detainees has been worked through, we'll also talk to you about that. And there have been a lot of questions, obviously, about the treatment of the detainees. So I just wanted to give you – share with you a few of the details of what is going on there. Each day the detainees are given three culturally appropriate meals. They have daily opportunities to shower, exercise and receive medical attention. So in keeping with – in accordance with the Geneva Convention, they are receiving very humane treatment, and we expect representatives from the ICRC to visit with them later this week.

3.22 OCCUPATION

☛ **Israel: Second statement of the government of Israel to the Sharm e-Sheikh Fact-Finding Committee, 20 March 2001/25 Adar 5761**

...

D. Allegations of excessive use of force

41. Israel is accused of the excessive use of force against Palestinian civilians. It is alleged that Israel is acting in violation of the *Fourth Geneva Convention* in that it is acting against civilians protected by that Convention. It is alleged that Israel has failed to comply with the *Code of Conduct for Law Enforcement Officials* ("Law Enforcement Code") and the *Basic Principles on the Use of Force and Firearms by Law Enforcement Officials* ("Firearms Principles") in that Israeli forces are using firearms in response to demonstrations and stone throwing. It is alleged that Israel has failed to use alternative means to disperse demonstrations and that it has been too quick to resort to force. It is alleged that Israel has been using force indiscriminately.
42. The allegations trip easily off the page. Little attempt is made, however, to address the essential underlying issues of substance. They do not bear scrutiny.

1. The applicability of the Fourth Geneva Convention

43. The applicability of the *Fourth Geneva Convention* to events in the West Bank and the Gaza Strip has been the subject of considerable debate over the years. The position is complicated by the status of these territories prior to the 1967 Middle East war. It is further complicated now by the reality of progressive Israeli redeployment from significant parts of the West Bank and virtually all of the Gaza Strip in favour of almost complete Palestinian civil competence and extensive, and in some cases complete, Palestinian security competence over these areas. Almost 100% of the Palestinian

population of these areas now come under the jurisdiction of the Palestinian Authority. The *Fourth Geneva Convention* is, however, intended in large measure to address circumstances in which civilians are subject to enemy authority in times of armed conflict.

44. Issues relating to the applicability of the Convention notwithstanding, Israel has long made it clear that it applies the Convention on a *de facto* basis, affording such protection to the civilian population as is required by its terms. The law relating to the conduct of hostilities more generally also requires that civilians are immune from attack.

45. Those who take a direct part in hostilities forfeit the immunity that attaches to civilians. This point is clear. There is, however, no recognition of this principle in the Palestinian submissions. By way of elaboration of the basic proposition, the character and status of civilians in armed conflict is addressed in unambiguous terms in the *Model Manual on the Law of Armed Conflict for Armed Forces* of 1999, prepared by the International Committee of the Red Cross ("ICRC Model Manual"), as follows:

   "Civilians are not permitted to take a direct part in hostilities and are immune from attack. If they take a direct part in hostilities they forfeit this immunity."

46. "Taking a direct part in hostilities" is defined in the *ICRC Model Manual* as "engaging in hostile action against enemy armed forces". Civilians who take a direct part in hostilities become combatants and become the legitimate object of attack (subject to the relevant principles relating to such action). It is furthermore equally clear that "[p]ersons cannot acquire and divest themselves of combatant status at will. Once they have become combatants, they remain combatants until the close of hostilities ..."

47. In addition to these accepted principles relating to civilians in times of armed conflict, it is also well established in the law of armed conflict that combatants are required to distinguish themselves from the civilian population. The commentary to this provision in the *ICRC Model Manual* elaborates on this principle in the following terms:

   "Since combatants are entitled to engage in hostilities and are subject to attack they need to be distinguishable from the civilian population who are protected from attack. Members of the armed forces distinguish themselves by wearing *military uniform...*

   Combatants who take part in hostilities without distinguishing themselves from civilians lose their combatant status ... That means that on capture they may be tried for the war crime of unlawfully taking part in hostilities ..."

48. As was discussed in detail in Israel's *First Statement*, the reality of the circumstances under consideration is that Israeli civilians and armed forces have come under violent attack, frequently involving a live fire dimension, by persons who do not wear uniforms or other distinguishing insignia. Often, these attacks are initiated from within crowded civilian areas. Often, they take place from behind or within groups of unarmed participants. The perpetrators of such attacks are acting in violation of accepted rules relating to the conduct of hostilities. They cannot claim to be civilians. They are not entitled to the protection afforded to civilians in time of armed conflict. Indeed, they may be prosecuted for the war crime of unlawfully taking part in hostilities.

49. In this regard, it is worth recalling the Statement by the US Central Command addressing the circumstances faced by UN peacekeeping troops in Somalia in 1993:

   "[The Somali] gunmen do not wear uniforms or distinctive insignia; they do not carry arms openly; they are not led by accountable military leadership; they are not subject to military discipline and they do not comply with international law. It is they who initiated the firefight and who bear ultimate responsibility for this tragic loss of life."

50. As noted in Israel's *First Statement*, the United Nations Military Spokesman at the time defended action by the UN forces in which "civilians" had been killed and injured in the following terms:

 "Everyone on the ground in the vicinity was a combatant, because they meant to do us harm."

51. Israel has been restrained in its response to Palestinian attacks. Israeli troops have acted in self-defence and in the defence of others. In doing so, they have responded to those who have initiated the attacks. The attacks have had lethal intent. There have been around 3,500 such attacks involving a live fire dimension against Israelis since the violence began involving automatic weapons, assault rifles, pistols, hand grenades, explosives and, most recently, mortars. Many more attacks have involved the use of molotov cocktails. This is an armed conflict. Those perpetrating the attacks against Israelis are not civilians. They cannot claim immunity from Israeli response.

E. Allegations of "assassination"

67. The PLO alleges that Israel has a policy of "assassinations". The allegation is made in passing in the Palestinian *Second Submission*. It is addressed further in the *Palestinian Assassinations Paper* of 12 January 2001. Various other documents produced by the Palestinian side which have no doubt found, or will find, their way to the Committee touch upon this matter further. Elements of these allegations have already been addressed in the preceding paragraphs. The issue nevertheless calls for further comment.
68. As with its references to the *Fourth Geneva Convention*, the *Law Enforcement Code* and the *Firearms Principles*, the PLO endeavours to give its allegations of assassinations credibility by citing various provisions of law – notably Articles 27, 32 and 33 of the *Fourth Geneva Convention*, Articles 51, 75 and 85 of the *Protocol Additional to the Geneva Conventions of 12 August 1949, and Relating to the Protection of Victims of International Armed Conflicts (Protocol I) of 8 June 1977* ("Geneva Protocol I), and Article 23(b) of the 1907 *Hague Regulations respecting the laws and customs of war on land* ("Hague Regulations"). It does not, however, address the interpretation of these provisions or their application to the factual circumstances alleged. These shortcomings are fundamental.
69. The subject of "assassinations" is controversial within the law of armed conflict. Some argue that there is no bar on "assassinations" *per se*. Others argue that, while the law may at one point have prohibited "assassinations", the nature of the threat posed by terrorist activities justifies the targeting of such individuals in covert operations and that the law has evolved to permit such action. Others still, and this is probably where majority opinion coalesces, argue that the relevant issue is not whether a particular act is characterised as an "assassination" or as some other type of action but whether the attack comes within the bounds of permissible military action under the law of armed conflict. In particular, it is argued that the question of whether the targeting of any given individual is permissible will depend on whether that individual is a combatant and the methods and means of the attack.
70. Before addressing this issue further, it will be useful to recall a number of basic and uncontroversial principles relating to the conduct of hostilities:

- *first*, all combat activity must be justified on military grounds. Combat activity which is not militarily necessary is prohibited;
- *second*, attacks must not be indiscriminate and must be proportionate to the military objective to be achieved;
- *third*, a distinction must be made between combatants and non-combatants. Combatants are permitted to take a direct part in hostilities; non-combatants are not. Combatants may be attacked. Non-combatants are protected from attack but lose their protection if they take part in hostilities;
- *fourth*, civilians who take a direct part in hostilities – including engaging in hostile action against enemy forces – forfeit their immunity from attack;
- *fifth*, persons cannot acquire and divest themselves of combatant status at will. Once they have become combatants, they remain combatants until the close of hostilities;
- *sixth*, combatants are required to distinguish themselves from the civilian population. Combatants who do not so distinguish themselves may be tried for the war crime of unlawfully taking a direct part in hostilities. Combatants who do not distinguish themselves from the civilian population remain the legitimate target of attack.

71. Within this framework, there is further elaboration on what is permissible by way of military action in pursuit of legitimate military objectives. Thus, even if a person, object or location is the legitimate target of attack, the means and method of that attack must come within the bounds of legally permissible action.
72. The targeting of individual enemy combatants is permitted. The matter is addressed in the *ICRC Model Manual* in the following terms:

    "There is nothing in law to prevent the attacking of an enemy individual provided he is a combatant, the attack is carried out by combatants, who distinguish themselves as such, or at least carry their weapons openly, and it is not done perfidiously."
73. As this makes clear, the targeting of individual enemy combatants – ie, those who take a direct part in hostilities – is permissible. Such action also accords with the basic principle that military activity must not be indiscriminate. The targeting of an individual combatant using permissible means is thus lawful.
74. How does this apply to the facts as alleged in the Palestinian submissions? A number of general observations are warranted.
75. First, persons who take, or have taken, a direct part in the hostilities are, by reference to accepted principles of the law of armed conflict, to be considered as combatants. They remain combatants until such time as the hostilities come to an end. They cannot acquire and divest themselves of combatant status at will. While Israel makes no comment here on the specific Palestinian allegations of Israeli action, it may be observed that the targeting of individual Palestinian combatants would come within the scope of permissible means of response to on-going Palestinian attacks.
76. Second, as a matter of general proposition, Israel has only targeted those Palestinians who, because they have taken a direct part in the hostilities through the active planning and perpetration of attacks of intended lethal effect against Israelis, are properly to be regarded as combatants.
77. Third, on the question of the method and means of attack, it is evident, simply on the basis of the facts as alleged in the Palestinian submissions, that many of the cases cited would not in principle come within the scope of acts prohibited by the law of armed

conflict. This applies notably to allegations of attacks by Israeli helicopter gunships, fire from Israeli tanks, or actions involving exchanges of fire between Israeli troops and Palestinian militia.

78. Fourth, as a matter of general proposition, Israel rejects the allegation that it has a policy of "assassinations" of Palestinians. Whatever action Israel has taken has been taken firmly within the bounds of the relevant and accepted principles relating to the conduct of hostilities.

79. Fifth, it ought also to be observed that those Palestinians who take, or have taken, a direct part in hostilities in circumstances in which they do not distinguish, or have not distinguished, themselves from the civilian population, have themselves acted in violation of the law of armed conflict and may be tried for the war crime of unlawfully taking a direct part in the hostilities.

80. For completeness, it should also be observed that none of the various provisions of law cited in the Palestinian submissions in support of their allegations on this matter prohibit the targeting of individual combatants using permissible methods and means of attack.

H. Allegations of collective punishment

103. There are a number of other allegations raised by the Palestinian side under the heading of collective punishment measures said to be in violation of Article 33 of the *Fourth Geneva Convention.* These allegations, which in many cases simply paraphrase unsubstantiated observations made in reports published by other organisations, refer to a number of alleged practices – demolition of homes, laying siege to Palestinian centres, indiscriminate shooting, shelling, mass arrests, etc. A number of observations on these allegations are warranted.

104. First, Israel repeats that it has not taken action against Palestinians except for reasons of security to avert or respond to attacks against Israeli civilians or armed forces. Second, there is a confusion, no doubt intended, in the Palestinian allegations under this heading in that they address, by reference to Article 33 of the *Fourth Geneva Convention*, allegations of collective punishment against "protected persons" – in this case civilians – as well as allegations concerning other action such as the shelling of strategic targets. As has already been observed, however, those who take a direct part in hostilities, are not immune from attack. The same is true of objects or locations that, for reasons of military necessity, are legitimate targets of attack. Such objects or locations include

> "not only things of a military nature such as tanks and military aircraft but also things of a civilian nature which make an effective contribution to military action ...

A civilian building becomes a military objective if it is used for military purposes, for example, if an office block is used as a military headquarters or a house is used as a sniper post or a barn is used to park military vehicles under cover."

105. Third, in a number of cases the subject-matter of the Palestinian allegations has been raised in proceedings before Israeli courts. The lawfulness of an order to close a number of schools was, for example, raised in Petition No. 8286/00, *League for Human Rights in Israel v. IDF Forces Commander in the West Bank* before the High Court of Justice. In this case, the Court concluded, taking relevant provisions of international law into account, that the order closing the schools was justified on security grounds.

106. In another case, Petition No. 76/01, *Afuna v. Minister of Defence and the West Bank Military Commander* concerning the intended removal of a number of the Petitioner's

olive trees bordering a road, the High Court of Justice dismissed the Petition. From the observations of one of the Judges in the case, it is evident that the Court considered that the removal of the trees on grounds of military necessity was permissible in the circumstances. A number of other cases on related questions are pending.

107. In this regard, it should be noted that the Israeli Supreme Court and High Court of Justice has an established reputation of fairness and balance in the protection of human rights. There is also a practice of legal assistance by both Israeli and Palestinian NGOs testing Israeli policies and practices in this field before the courts. Decisions of the courts bind the Government. The decisions of the High Court of Justice referred to above cannot therefore be taken as partisan support for IDF practices.

108. Fourth, the Palestinian allegations in respect of these submissions are littered with errors of fact. For example, it is simply factually incorrect to allege that "Israel has cut off electricity and water to a number of Palestinian towns at various intervals including Bethlehem, Tulkarem, and Seilat". What is accurate is that electricity installations and installations of the joint water infrastructure have been damaged by Palestinian action on around 20 separate occasions since the outbreak of violence. So, for example, on 4 October 2000, an electricity transformer near Rachel's Tomb on the outskirts of Bethlehem was damaged by Palestinian gunfire causing an electricity blackout in part of Bethlehem. Similarly, on 15 October 2000, electricity was again cut off to Bethlehem as a result of Palestinian action damaging a high-voltage electricity pylon in the area of Hosen-Batir. There is no basis at all to the allegations of Israeli action affecting supplies of water or electricity to Palestinian areas.

109. Another example of factual inaccuracy concerns the use of so-called dum-dum bullets. Israel does not use dum-dum bullets. Palestinian allegations to this effect have been expressly rejected by forensic pathologists who have examined injuries said to have been caused by such projectiles. The motivation behind the allegation is clear – dum-dum bullets are generally regarded as unlawful. Allegations of the use of such projectiles by Israel is therefore both emotive and prejudicial. The only casualty in this case, however, is truth.

110. More recently, in similar vein, there have been allegations of the use by Israel of depleted uranium and of nerve gas. Israel does not use depleted uranium. It does not use nerve gas. These allegations are unequivocally false. They are made in the absence of any foundation of fact simply to create prejudice.

111. For the avoidance of doubt, in respect of all of the allegations advanced by the Palestinians under the heading of collective punishments, Israel has either not acted in the manner alleged at all or, where it has taken action, it has done so for reasons of security within the parameters of permissible action under the law of armed conflict.

☛ Israel: 'Targeting Terrorists' – Background. Statement of Ministry of Foreign Affairs, 1 August 2001

...

Currently, Israel is engaged in a situation best defined as an armed conflict. International law in general and the law of armed conflict in particular recognize that individuals who directly take part in hostilities cannot claim immunity from attack or protection as innocent civilians. Such individuals have, by their own actions, by taking part in armed attacks against Israeli civilians or security personnel, designated themselves as combatants in the

conflict, and therefore have forfeited such legal protection.
An individual who becomes a combatant is considered to remain a combatant until such time as the hostilities come to an end and not merely during that exact instant when the individual is instigating, carrying out, or organizing an attack. They are therefore to be considered legitimate military targets both when planning attacks, and after their attacks have been carried out.
The inaction of the Palestinian Authority in the face of widespread terrorism in its areas, coupled with the PA's tacit support for this violence, have left Israel with no alternative but to take the necessary action itself to prevent continued attacks. Therefore, Israel must undertake preventive, precisely-targeted operations which would bring about a cessation of these clearly lethal threats.
Whenever possible, Israeli operations are directed toward arresting terrorists and their accomplices. In recent months, over 1000 terrorists have been arrested by the IDF and brought to justice. In a small minority of cases, when arrests are impossible, and when an clear, specific and imminent terrorist threat must be countered, Israel is forced to carry out other types of preventative operations. All civilized nations would act in a similar fashion.
Israel does not condone or take part in 'assassinations' or 'extra-judicial killings'. These terms are derived from spheres unrelated to armed conflict and cannot properly be used to describe Israel's counter-terrorist operations. Use of these terms by Palestinian spokespeople is intended to portray Israel and its actions in a pejorative light, and does not reflect the legal reality.
Israel only acts in a manner which is in compliance with the principles and practice of armed conflict, and makes every effort to avoid involvement of innocent civilians, taking action only in conditions where inaction by Israel would result in additional loss of innocent lives.

☛ Declaration of the Conference of High Contracting Parties to the Fourth Geneva Convention, 5 December 2001

Conference of High Contracting Parties to the Fourth Geneva Convention
Geneva, 5 December 2001

Declaration

1. This Declaration reflects the common understanding reached by the participating High Contracting Parties to the reconvened Conference of High Contracting Parties to the Fourth Geneva Convention. The Conference of 15 July 1999, recommended by United Nations' General Assembly Resolution ES-10/6 in an Emergency Special Session, issued a statement as follows:
'...The participating High Contracting Parties reaffirmed the applicability of the Fourth Geneva Convention to the Occupied Palestinian Territory, including East Jerusalem. Furthermore, they reiterated the need for full respect for the provisions of the said Convention in that Territory. Taking into consideration the improved atmosphere in the Middle East as a whole, the Conference was adjourned on the understanding that it will convene again in the light of consultations on the development of the humanitarian situation in the field.'
2. The participating High Contracting Parties express deep concern about the deterioration of the humanitarian situation in the field. They deplore the great number of civilian victims,

in particular children and other vulnerable groups, due to indiscriminate or disproportionate use of force and due to lack of respect for international humanitarian law.

3. Taking into account art. 1 of the Fourth Geneva Convention of 1949 and bearing in mind the United Nations' General Assembly Resolution ES-10/7, the participating High Contracting Parties reaffirm the applicability of the Convention to the Occupied Palestinian Territory, including East Jerusalem and reiterate the need for full respect for the provisions of the said Convention in that Territory. Through the present Declaration, they recall in particular the respective obligations under the Convention of all High Contracting Parties (para 4-7), of the parties to the conflict (para 8-11) and of the State of Israel as the Occupying Power (para 12-15).

4. The participating High Contracting Parties call upon all parties, directly involved in the conflict or not, to respect and to ensure respect for the Geneva Conventions in all circumstances, to disseminate and take measures necessary for the prevention and suppression of breaches of the Conventions. They reaffirm the obligations of the High Contracting Parties under articles 146, 147 and 148 of the Fourth Geneva Convention with regard to penal sanctions, grave breaches and responsibilities of the High Contracting Parties.

5. The participating High Contracting Parties stress that the Fourth Geneva Convention, which takes fully into account imperative military necessity, has to be respected in all circumstances.

6. The participating High Contracting Parties see the need to recall basic humanitarian rules with regard to persons taking no active part in the hostilities, which shall be treated humanely without any discrimination, and to recall the prohibition at any time and in any place whatsoever of acts of violence to life and person, torture, outrages upon personal dignity and of arbitrary or extra-judiciary executions.

7. The participating High Contracting Parties express their support for the endeavours of the humanitarian relief societies in the field in ensuring that the wounded and sick receive assistance, and for the activities of the International Committee of the Red Cross (ICRC), the United Nations Relief and Works Agency in the Near East (UNRWA) and of other impartial humanitarian organisations. They also express their support for the efforts of the United Nations High Commissioner for Human Rights and of UN Special Rapporteurs in order to assess the situation in the field and they take note of the reports and recommendations of the High Commissioner for Human Rights (E/CN/4/2001/114) and of the Commission of Inquiry (E/CN/4/2001/121).

8. The participating High Contracting Parties call upon the parties to the conflict to ensure respect for and protection of the civilian population and civilian objects and to distinguish at all times between the civilian population and combatants and between civilian objects and military objectives. They also call upon the parties to abstain from any measures of brutality and violence against the civilian population whether applied by civilian or military agents and to abstain from exposing the civilian population to military operations.

9. The participating High Contracting Parties call upon the parties to the conflict to respect and to protect at all times the fixed establishments and mobile medical units of the Medical Services and to facilitate the operations of the humanitarian relief societies in the field, including the free passage of their ambulances and medical personnel, and to guarantee their protection.

10. The participating High Contracting Parties call upon the parties to the conflict to facilitate the activities of the ICRC, within its particular role conferred upon it by the Geneva Conventions, the UNRWA and of other impartial humanitarian organisations. They

recognise and support their efforts to assess and to improve the humanitarian situation in the field. They invite the parties to the conflict to co-operate with independent and impartial observers such as the Temporary International Presence in the City of Hebron (TIPH).

11. The participating High Contracting Parties call upon the parties to the conflict to consider anew suggestions made at the meeting of experts of High Contracting Parties in 1998 to resolve problems of implementation of the Fourth Geneva Convention and to respect and to ensure respect in all circumstances for the rules of international humanitarian law and to co-operate within the framework of direct contacts, including procedures of inquiry and of conciliation. They encourage any arrangements and agreements supported by the parties to the conflict on the deployment of independent and impartial observers to monitor, inter alia, breaches of the Fourth Geneva Convention as a protection and confidence building measure, with the aim to ensure effectiveness of humanitarian rules.

12. The participating High Contracting Parties call upon the Occupying Power to fully and effectively respect the Fourth Geneva Convention in the Occupied Palestinian Territory, including East Jerusalem, and to refrain from perpetrating any violation of the Convention. They reaffirm the illegality of the settlements in the said territories and of the extension thereof. They recall the need to safeguard and guarantee the rights and access of all inhabitants to the Holy Places.

13. The participating High Contracting Parties call upon the Occupying Power to immediately refrain from committing grave breaches involving any of the acts mentioned in art. 147 of the Fourth Geneva Convention, such as wilful killing, torture, unlawful deportation, wilful depriving of the rights of fair and regular trial, extensive destruction and appropriation of property not justified by military necessity and carried out unlawfully and wantonly. The participating High Contracting Parties recall that according to art. 148 no High Contracting Party shall be allowed to absolve itself of any liability incurred by itself in respect to grave breaches. The participating High Contracting Parties also recall the responsibilities of the Occupying Power according to art. 29 of the Fourth Geneva Convention for the treatment of protected persons.

14. The participating High Contracting Parties also call upon the Occupying Power to refrain from perpetrating any other violation of the Convention, in particular reprisals against protected persons and their property, collective penalties, unjustified restrictions of free movement, and to treat the protected persons humanely, without any adverse distinction founded on race, colour, religion or faith, sex, birth or wealth, or any other similar criteria.

15. The participating High Contracting Parties call upon the Occupying Power to facilitate the relief operations and free passage of the ICRC, UNRWA, as well as any other impartial humanitarian organisation, to guarantee their protection and, where applicable, to refrain from levying taxes and imposing undue financial burdens on these organisations.

16. The participating High Contracting Parties stress that respect for the Fourth Geneva Convention and international humanitarian law in general is essential to improve the humanitarian situation in the field and to achieve a just and lasting peace. The participating High Contracting Parties invite the parties concerned to bring the conflict to an end by means of negotiation and to settle their disputes in accordance with applicable international law.

17. The participating High Contracting Parties welcome and encourage the initiatives by States Parties, both individually and collectively, according to art. 1 of the Convention and aimed at ensuring the respect of the Convention, and they underline the need for the Parties, to follow up on the implementation of the present Declaration.

18. The participating High Contracting Parties express their gratitude to the Depositary of the Fourth Geneva Convention for its good services and offices.

☛ Israel: Israel's reaction to the convening of the High Contracting Parties to the Fourth Geneva Convention, 5 December 2001

(Communicated by the Foreign Ministry Spokesperson December 5, 2001)

Reacting to High Contracting Parties to the Fourth Geneva Convention meeting held in Geneva today, Israel termed the meeting a futile exercise and an abuse of a humanitarian instrument.

There is no legal basis in the Convention for holding such a conference, which could have no positive humanitarian effect and might undermine the delicate situation in the region.
This Conference will neither solve the humanitarian concerns on the ground, nor contribute to the welfare of the Palestinian population. Furthermore, the declaration contains no reference to the conscious Palestinian decision to resort to violence rather than continue negotiations, nor to the many thousands of acts of terrorism against Israelis, which have resulted in the death of 230 Israelis and the wounding of more than a thousand. Convening the meeting just days after 28 Israeli civilians were massacred in Jerusalem and in Haifa by Palestinian terrorists without any reference to these horrendous terrorist acts render it meaningless. Nor does the declaration make a reference to the constant fraudulent misuse of ambulances by the Palestinian side and to the attacks on ambulances of the Israeli Red Magen David Society.
The statement adopted at the meeting is clearly one-sided and contains sections with unsubstantiated allegations against Israel. The declaration ignores entirely the continuous and vicious incitement against Israel in the Palestinian media and in school textbooks, which together with actions by organs of the Palestinian Authority contribute to creating a cult of suicide bombers who have wreaked havoc in Israeli towns and villages, killing and maiming innocent civilians in discotheques, restaurants and markets.
Israel expressed regret the convening of the Conference risks turning a humanitarian instrument with the highest aspirations into a tool for political attacks against one party, thus rewarding a deliberate policy of instigating violence. It could also encourage the Palestinian leadership to believe that the path to political gains is not through the implementation of the Mitchell Report and consequently at the negotiating table but rather through other means.

☛ ICRC: Statement by the International Committee of the Red Cross, Geneva, 5 December 2001

1. Pursuant to the relevant provisions of international humanitarian law and to the mandate conferred on it by the States party to the 1949 Geneva Conventions, the International Committee of the Red Cross (ICRC) established a permanent presence in Israel, the neighbouring Arab countries and the occupied territories in 1967 with a view to carrying out its humanitarian tasks in the region and to working for the faithful application of international humanitarian law.

2. In accordance with a number of resolutions adopted by the United Nations General

Assembly and Security Council and by the International Conference of the Red Cross and Red Crescent, which reflect the view of the international community, the ICRC has always affirmed the *de jure* applicability of the Fourth Geneva Convention to the territories occupied since 1967 by the State of Israel, including East Jerusalem. This Convention, ratified by Israel in 1951, remains fully applicable and relevant in the current context of violence. As an Occupying Power, Israel is also bound by other customary rules relating to occupation, expressed in the Regulations annexed to the Hague Convention respecting the Laws and Customs of War on Land of 18 October 1907.

3. In general terms, the Fourth Geneva Convention protects the civilian population of occupied territories against abuses on the part of an Occupying Power, in particular by ensuring that it is not discriminated against, that it is protected against all forms of violence, and that despite occupation and war it is allowed to live as normal a life as possible, in accordance with its own laws, culture and traditions. While humanitarian law confers certain rights on the Occupying Power, it also imposes limits on the scope of its powers. Being only a temporary administrator of occupied territory, the Occupying Power must not interfere with its original economic and social structures, organization, legal system or demography. It must ensure the protection, security and welfare of the population living under occupation. This also implies allowing the normal development of the territory, if the occupation lasts for a prolonged period of time.

4. More precisely, the Fourth Geneva Convention sets out rules aimed at safeguarding the dignity and physical integrity of persons living under occupation, including detainees. It prohibits all forms of physical and mental ill-treatment and coercion, collective punishment, and reprisals against protected persons or property. It also prohibits the transfer of parts of the Occupying Power's civilian population into the occupied territory, forcible transfer or deportation of protected persons from the occupied territory, and destruction of real or personal property, except when such destruction is rendered absolutely necessary by military operations.

5. In the course of its activities in the territories occupied by Israel, the ICRC has repeatedly noted breaches of various provisions of international humanitarian law, such as the transfer by Israel of parts of its population into the occupied territories, the destruction of houses, failure to respect medical activities, and detention of protected persons outside the occupied territories. Certain practices which contravene the Fourth Geneva Convention have been incorporated into laws and administrative guidelines and have been sanctioned by the highest judicial authorities. While acknowledging the facilities it has been granted for the conduct of its humanitarian tasks, the ICRC has regularly drawn the attention of the Israeli authorities to the suffering and the heavy burden borne by the Palestinian population owing to the occupation policy and, in line with its standard practice, has increasingly expressed its concern through bilateral and multilateral representations and in public appeals. In particular, the ICRC has expressed growing concern about the consequences in humanitarian terms of the establishment of Israeli settlements in the occupied territories, in violation of the Fourth Geneva Convention. The settlement policy has often meant the destruction of Palestinian homes, the confiscation of land and water resources and the parcelling out of the territories. Measures taken to extend the settlements and to protect the settlers, entailing the destruction of houses, land requisitions, the sealing-off of areas, roadblocks and the imposi-

tion of long curfews, have also seriously hindered the daily life of the Palestinian population. However, the fact that settlements have been established in violation of the provisions of the Fourth Geneva Convention does not mean that civilians residing in those settlements can be the object of attack. They are protected by humanitarian law as civilians as long as they do not take an active part in fighting.

6. The ICRC has also drawn the attention of the Israeli authorities to the effects of prolonged curfews and the sealing-off of certain areas by the Israel Defense Forces. The resulting restrictions on movements have disastrous consequences for the entire Palestinian population. They hamper the activities of emergency medical services as well as access to health care, workplaces, schools and places of worship, and have a devastating effect on the economy. They also prevent, for months on end, Palestinian families from visiting relatives detained in Israel. The concern caused by these practices has grown considerably during the past 14 months as measures taken to contain the upsurge of violence have led to a further deterioration in the living conditions of the population under occupation.

7. The ICRC has reminded all those taking part in the violence that whenever armed force is used the choice of means and methods employed is not unlimited. Today, in view of the sharp increase in armed confrontations, the ICRC has to stress that Palestinian armed groups operating within or outside the occupied territories are also bound by the principles of international humanitarian law. Apart from the Fourth Geneva Convention, which relates to the protection of the civilian population, there are other universally accepted rules and principles of international humanitarian law that deal with the conduct of military operations. They stipulate in particular that only military objectives may be attacked. Thus indiscriminate attacks, such as bomb attacks by Palestinian individuals or armed groups against Israeli civilians, and acts intended to spread terror among the civilian population are absolutely and unconditionally prohibited. The same applies to targeted attacks on and the killing of Palestinian individuals by the Israeli authorities while those individuals are not directly taking part in the hostilities or immediately endangering human life. Reprisals against civilians and their property are also prohibited. When a military objective is targeted, all feasible precautions must be taken to minimize civilian casualties and damage to civilian property. To avoid endangering the civilian population, those bearing weapons and those taking part in armed violence must distinguish themselves from civilians.

8. Demonstrations against the occupying forces by the civilian population under occupation or stand-offs between them are not acts of war. They should therefore not be dealt with by military methods and means. When faced with the civilian population, Israeli forces must exercise restraint: any use of force must be proportionate, all necessary precautions must be taken to avoid casualties, and the lethal use of firearms must be strictly limited to what is unavoidable as an immediate measure to protect life.

9. Access to emergency medical services for all those in need is also of paramount importance in the current situation. Such access must not be unduly delayed or denied. Ambulances and medical personnel must be allowed to move about unharmed and must not be prevented from discharging their medical duties. All those taking part in the violence must respect and assist the medical services, whether deployed by the armed forces, civilian organizations, the Palestine Red Crescent Society, the Magen David Adom, the ICRC, the Inter-

national Federation of Red Cross and Red Crescent Societies or other humanitarian organizations.

10. Article 1 common to the four Geneva Conventions stipulates that the "High Contracting Parties undertake to respect and ensure respect for the present Convention in all circumstances". This conference is to be viewed within that context. The ICRC has always welcomed all individual and joint efforts made by States party to the Geneva Conventions to fulfil this obligation and ensure respect for international humanitarian law. These efforts are all the more vital as violations of humanitarian law are far too common around the globe.

11. The means used to meet these legal and political responsibilities are naturally a matter to be decided upon by States. Whatever the means chosen, however, the ICRC wishes to emphasize that any action States may decide to take at international level must be aimed at achieving practical results and at ensuring application of and compliance with international humanitarian law, in the interests of the protected population.

12. Beyond all legal considerations and in view of the current humanitarian situation, the ICRC again calls upon all parties concerned to make every possible effort to spare civilian lives and preserve a measure of humanity.

13. For its part, the ICRC will continue to do its utmost to assist and protect all victims in accordance with its mandate and with the principles of neutrality, impartiality and independence which govern its humanitarian work. It counts on the full support of the parties concerned in promoting compliance with the humanitarian rules and facilitating humanitarian activities, which may also help pave the way towards the establishment of peace between all
peoples and nations in the region.

14. The steady deterioration of the humanitarian situation over the last few months and, in particular, the tragic events of the past few days have highlighted the need to break the spiral of violence and restore respect for international humanitarian law

4.112 NEW WEAPONS

☛ **USA: Instruction No. 5000.2 of the Department of Defense on the operation of the Defense Acquisition System, 23 October 2000**

Department of Defense Instruction Number 5000.2, October 23, 2000

Subject: Operation of the Defense Acquisition System

References:
(a) DoD Directive 5000.1, "The Defense Acquisition System," October 23, 2000
(b) OMB Circular A-11, Part 3, July 1999 and "Supplemental Capital Programming Guide: Planning, Budgeting, and Acquisition of Capital Assets," July 1997

(c) USD(AT&L), ASD(C3I), and DOT&E Memorandum, "Mandatory Procedures for Major Defense Acquisition Programs (MDAPs) and Major Automated Information System (MAIS) Acquisition Programs," October 23, 2000
(d) DoD Directive 5025.1, "DoD Directives System," July 27, 2000
(e) through (zz), see enclosure 1

1. Purpose

This Instruction:

1.1. Establishes a simplified and flexible management framework for translating mission needs and technological opportunities, based on validated mission needs and requirements, into stable, affordable, and well-managed acquisition programs that include weapon systems and automated information systems.
1.2. Establishes a general approach for managing acquisition programs while acknowledging that every technology project and acquisition program is unique and that any particular project or program, particularly non-major programs, may not need to follow the entire process.
1.3. Consistent with statutory requirements and reference (a), authorizes Milestone Decision Authorities (MDAs) to tailor procedures in order to achieve cost, schedule, and performance goals.
1.4. Implements reference (a), the guidelines of OMB Circular A-11, Part 3 (reference (b)), and current laws, and the procedures in reference (c).
1.5. Authorizes the publication of DoD 5000.2-R, which establishes procedures to be followed for Major Defense Acquisition Programs (MDAPs), Major Automated Information Systems (MAISs), and those non-major systems specifically identified in the Regulation in accordance with DoD Directive 5025.1 (reference (d)).

2. Applicability and Scope

This Instruction applies to:

2.1. The Office of the Secretary of Defense, the Military Departments, the Chairman of the Joint Chiefs of Staff, the Combatant Commands, the Office of the Inspector General of the Department of Defense, the Defense Agencies, DoD Field Activities, and all other organizational entities within the Department of Defense (hereafter referred to collectively as "the DoD Components").
2.2. All defense technology projects and acquisition programs. Some requirements, where stated, apply only to MDAPs and MAISs.
2.3. In general, highly sensitive classified, cryptologic, and intelligence projects and programs shall follow the guidance in this Instruction and reference (c) for technology projects and acquisition programs of equivalent acquisition category. The MDA shall approve proposed tailoring of the systems acquisition process for these projects and programs.

3. Definitions

Terms used in this Instruction are defined in enclosure 2.

4. Procedures

4.1. MDAs shall establish mandatory procedures for assigned programs. These procedures shall not exceed the requirements for MDAPs and MAIS acquisition programs established in this Instruction or in reference (c). The Heads of the DoD Components shall keep the issuance of any directives, instructions, policy memorandums, or regulations necessary to implement the mandatory procedures contained in this Instruction and reference (c) to a minimum. The Heads of the DoD Components shall provide copies of all such documents to the Under Secretary of Defense for Acquisition, Technology, and Logistics (USD(AT&L)) PRIOR TO publication. Waivers or requests for exceptions to the provisions of this Instruction shall be submitted to the USD(AT&L), Assistant Secretary of Defense for Command, Control, Communications, and Intelligence (ASD(C3I)), or Director of Operational Test and Evaluation (DOT&E), as appropriate via the Component Acquisition Executive (CAE). Statutory requirements cannot be waived unless the statute specifically provides for waiver of the stated requirements.
4.2. The DoD Components (including Office of the Secretary of Defense (OSD) staff offices) shall coordinate proposed policy memorandums and changes to individual sections of this Instruction or reference (c) with the Executive Secretary of the Defense Acquisition Policy Steering Group (DAPSG) (reference (e)) prior to Department-wide staffing of the change. The purpose of this policy is to maintain administrative control of this Instruction and is not intended to imply any approval authority on the part of the Executive Secretary.
4.3. The DAPSG shall submit proposed changes to the USD(AT&L), ASD(C3I), and DOT&E, who jointly have the authority to change this Instruction. All three officials shall jointly sign future changes. Proposed changes shall be considered annually by the Defense Acquisition Policy Working Group (DAPWG) (see reference
(e)).
4.4. This Instruction and references (a) and (c) are located in the Reference Library of the Defense Acquisition Deskbook (reference (f)). Mandatory and discretionary acquisition information, practical advice, and lessons learned are also located in the Deskbook.
4.5. Implementation of the New Acquisition Process
4.5.1. New Milestones. Programs planned in accordance with the 1996 version of DoD Directive 5000.1 (reference (g)) and the 1996 version of DoD 5000.2-R (reference (h)) shall be executed in accordance with approved program documentation. That documentation shall not be updated solely to satisfy the requirements of this Instruction. Unless otherwise directed by the MDA, the new decision points and phases in this Instruction shall be applied to efforts that have not yet been approved as acquisition programs (usually pre-Milestone I), and to acquisition programs that are pre-Milestone II. Unless otherwise directed by the MDA, the new decision points and phases shall not be applied to acquisition programs that are post-Milestone II.
4.5.2. Policies and Procedures. The new policies and procedures in this Instruction shall be applied to efforts that have not yet been approved as acquisition programs, and to all acquisition programs, including those planned in accordance with the 1996 version of DoD Directive 5000.1 (reference (g)) and DoD 5000.2-R (reference (h)).
4.5.3. Compliance with Statutes. For purposes of complying with applicable laws, Milestone A will serve as Milestone 0; Program Initiation, when it occurs at or during

Component Advanced Development, will serve as Milestone I; Milestone B will serve as Milestone II; Milestone C will serve as the Low-Rate Initial Production decision point; and the Full-Rate Production Decision Review will serve as Milestone III. In addition, System Development and Demonstration will serve as Engineering and Manufacturing Development.

[...]

4.7. The Defense Acquisition Management Framework

4.7.1. General

[...]

4.7.2. Pre-Systems Acquisition

[...]

4.7.3. Systems Acquisition

4.7.3.1. General

4.7.3.1.1. Systems acquisition is the process of developing concepts into producible and deployable products that provide capability to the user. The concept to exploit in systems acquisition is based on an analysis of alternative ways to meet the military need (done either in Concept Exploration or technological opportunities development), including commercial and non-developmental technologies and products and services determined through market analysis. The DoD Component (or appropriate principal staff office for MAIS programs) responsible for the mission area in which a deficiency or opportunity has been identified, but not the PM, shall normally prepare the analysis of alternatives (although the PM or PM's representative may participate in the analysis).

4.7.3.1.2. The goal is to develop the best overall value solution over the system's life cycle that meets the user's operational requirements. Generally, use or modification of systems or equipment that the DoD Components already own is more cost and schedule-effective than acquiring new materiel. If existing U.S. military systems or other on-hand materiel cannot be economically used or modified to meet the operational requirement, an acquisition program may be justified and acquisition decision-makers shall follow the following hierarchy of alternatives: the procurement (including modification) of commercially available domestic or international technologies, systems or equipment, or the additional production (including modification) of previously-developed U.S. military systems or equipment, or Allied systems or equipment; cooperative development program with one or more Allied nations; new joint Component or Government Agency development program; and a new Component-unique development program. Important in this evaluation process for new or modified systems are considerations for interoperability and supportability with existing and planned future components or systems.

4.7.3.1.3. The use of Allied systems and equipment is a preferred source of meeting user requirements. The Department of Defense places great weight on interoperability of equipment with Allied governments and coalition partners and on Allied participation in DoD acquisition programs through cooperative development and production and through sales of U.S. equipment. Accordingly, potential foreign participation shall be considered as part of the acquisition strategy approved for Milestone B, to be reviewed at each subsequent major decision point. In addition, the PM shall specifically consider and be responsible for proposing program disclosure guidance at each major decision point. The PM shall ensure that appropriate measures are in place to protect Critical Program Information and that appropriate anti-tampering measures are taken, at all times.

4.7.3.1.4. DoD acquisition and procurement of weapons and weapon systems shall be

consistent with all applicable domestic law and all applicable treaties, customary international law, and the law of armed conflict (also known as the laws and customs of war). The Head of each DoD Component shall ensure that all Component activities that could reasonably generate questions concerning compliance with obligations under arms control agreements to which the United States is a party shall have clearance from the USD(AT&L), in coordination with the General Counsel, DoD, and the Under Secretary of Defense (Policy), before such activity is undertaken. The Head of each DoD Component shall ensure that the Component's General Counsel or Judge Advocate General, as appropriate, conducts a legal review of the intended acquisition of a potential weapon or weapon system to determine that it is consistent with U.S. obligations. The review shall be conducted again before the award of a system development and demonstration contract for the weapon or weapon system and before the award of the initial production contract. Files shall be kept permanently. Additionally, legal reviews of new, advanced or emerging technologies that may lead to development of weapons or weapon systems are encouraged.
[...]

5. Effective Date

This Instruction is effective immediately.

E1. Enclosure
References, continued

(e) Under Secretary of Defense (AT&L), Assistant Secretary of Defense (C3I), and Director, Operational Test and Evaluation, "Defense Acquisition Policy Steering Group and Defense Acquisition Policy Working Group Charter," August 5, 1999
(f) Defense Acquisition Deskbook, www.deskbook.osd.mil
(g) DoD Directive 5000.1, "Defense Acquisition," March 15, 1996 (canceled)
(h) DoD 5000.2-R, "Mandatory Procedures for Major Defense Acquisition Programs and Major Automated Information Systems," March 1996 (canceled)
(i) CJCS Instruction 3170.01A, "Requirements Generation System," August 10, 1999
(j) DoD 7000.14-R, "DoD Financial Management Regulation," Volumes 2A and 2B, "Budget Presentation and Formation," July 1998
(k) DoD Directive 5200.39, "Security, Intelligence, and Counterintelligence Support to Acquisition Program Protection," September 10, 1997
(l) DoD Directive 5230.11, "Disclosure of Classified Military Information to Foreign Governments and International Organizations," June 16, 1992
(m) Section 1401 et seq. of title 40, United States Code, "Clinger-Cohen Act of 1996"
(n) DoD Directive 8000.1, "Defense Information Management (IM) Program," October 27, 1992
(o) DoD Directive 8320.1, "DoD Data Administration," September 26, 1991
(p) DoD Directive 4630.5, "Compatibility, Interoperability, and Integration of Command, Control, Communications, and Intelligence (C3I) Systems," November 12, 1992
(q) DoD Instruction 4630.8, "Procedures for Compatibility, Interoperability, and Integration of Command, Control, Communications, and Intelligence (C3I) Systems," November 18, 1992

(r) CJCS Instruction 6212.01B, "Interoperability and Supportability on National Security Systems, and Information Technology Systems," May 14, 2000
(s) Federal Acquisition Regulation, Part 15.404-1, "Proposal Analysis Techniques"
(t) Section 2350a of title 10, United States Code, "Cooperative Research and Development Programs: Allied Countries"
(u) Fiscal Year 2001 DoD Appropriations Act, Section 8102 (Pub. L. 106-259)
(v) Section 794 of title 29, United States Code, "Rehabilitation Act"
(w) Section 2364 of title 10, United States Code, "Coordination and Communication of Defense Research Activities"
(x) Government Performance and Results Act (Pub. L. 103-62)
(y) Section 2366 of title 10, United States Code, "Major Systems and Munitions Programs: Survivability and Lethality Testing Required Before Full-scale Production"
(z) Section 306 of title 5, United States Code, "Strategic Plans" (part of the Government Performance and Results Act)
(aa) Section 4321 et seq. of title 42, United States Code, "National Environmental Policy Act"
(bb) DoD 7000.14-R, " DoD Financial Management Regulation," Volume 2A, "Budget Presentation and Formation," Chapter 1, "General Information," Section 010212, "Research, Development, Test, and Evaluation-Selection and Criteria" (cc) Section 139 of title 10, United States Code, "Director of Operational Test and Evaluation"
(dd) Section 2400 of title 10, United States Code, "Low-rate Initial Production of New Systems"
(ee) Section 3501 et seq. of title 44, United States Code, "Paperwork Reduction Act of 1980"
(ff) Section 1734 of title 10, United States Code, "Career Development"
(gg) Section 2430 of title 10, United States Code, "Major Defense Acquisition Program Defined"
(hh) Section 2302d of title 10, United States Code, "Major System: Definitional Threshold Amounts"
(ii) DoD 5000.4-M, "Cost Analysis Guidance and Procedures," December 1992
(jj) Section 2377 of title 10, United States Code, "Preference for Acquisition of Commercial Items"
(kk) Section 2435 of title 10, United States Code, "Baseline Description"
(ll) Section 2432 of title 10, United States Code, "Selected Acquisition Reports"
(mm) Section 2433 of title 10, United States Code, "Unit Cost Reports"
(nn) Section 2440 of title 10, United States Code, "Technology and Industrial Base Plans"
(oo) Section 2434 of title 10, United States Code, "Independent Cost Estimates; Operational Manpower Requirements"
(pp) Section 2399 of title 10, United States Code, "Operational Test and Evaluation of Defense Acquisition Programs"
(qq) Section 811 of the National Defense Authorization Act for Fiscal Year 2001 (Pub. L. 106-398)
(rr) Section 305 of title 47, United States Code, "Government-Owned Stations"
(ss) Section 104 of the National Telecommunications and Information Organization Act, "Spectrum Management Activities" (Pub. L. 102-538)
(tt) Sections 901, 902, 903, and 904 of title 47, United States Code
(uu) Section 2464 of title 10, United States Code, "Core "Logistics Functions"

(vv) Section 2460 of title 10, United States Code, "Definition of Depot-Level Maintenance and Repair"
(ww) Section 2466 of title 10, United States Code, "Limitations on the Performance of Depot-Level Maintenance of Material"
(xx) Section 2469 of title 10, United States Code, "Contracts to Perform Workloads Previously Performed by Depot-Level Activities of the Department of Defense: Requirement of Competition"
(yy) DoD Directive 5105.21, "Defense Intelligence Agency," February 18, 1997
(zz) DoD 5200.1-M, "Acquisition System Program Protection," March 16, 1994

E2. Enclosure 2
Definitions

E2.1.1. Acquisition Executive. The individual within the Department and Components charged with overall acquisition management responsibilities within his or her respective organization. The Under Secretary of Defense for Acquisition, Technology, and Logistics is the Defense Acquisition Executive (DAE) responsible for all acquisition matters within the Department or Defense. The Component Acquisition Executives (CAEs) for each of the Components are the Secretary of the Military Departments or the Heads of Agencies with power of redelegation. The CAEs are responsible for all acquisition matters within their respective Component.
E2.1.2. Acquisition Program. A directed, funded effort designed to provide a new, improved, or continuing materiel, weapon, or information system or service capability in response to a validated operational or business need. Acquisition programs are divided into different categories that are established to facilitate decentralized decision-making, execution, and compliance with statutory requirements. Technology projects are not acquisition programs.
[...]
E2.1.9. Major Defense Acquisition Program (MDAP)
E2.1.9.1. An acquisition program that is not a highly sensitive classified program (as determined by the Secretary of Defense) and that is designated by the Under Secretary of Defense (Acquisition, Technology, and Logistics) (USD(AT&L)) as an MDAP, or estimated by the USD(AT&L) to require an eventual total expenditure for research, development, test and evaluation of more than $365 million in fiscal year (FY) 2000 constant dollars or, for procurement, of more than $2.190 billion in FY 2000 constant dollars.
E2.1.9.2. The estimate shall consider all blocks that will make up an evolutionary acquisition program (to the extent that subsequent blocks can be defined).
E2.1.9.3. This definition is from 10 U.S.C. 2430 (reference (gg)). The dollar requirements are established in statute in FY 1990 dollars. The dollar amounts have been updated in accordance with procedures identified in the statute.
[...]
E2.1.16. Program Executive Officer (PEO). A military or civilian official who has primary responsibility for directing several MDAPs and for assigned major system and non-major system acquisition programs. A PEO has no other command or staff responsibilities within the Component, and only reports to and receives guidance and direction from the DoD Component Acquisition Executive.

E2.1.17. Program Manager (PM). The individual designated in accordance with criteria established by the appropriate Component Acquisition Executive to manage an acquisition program and is appropriately certified under the provisions of the DAWIA (reference (ff)). A PM has no other command or staff responsibilities within the Component.
E2.1.18. Requirements Authority. The individual within the DoD Components charged with overall requirements definition and validation. The Vice-Chairman of the Joint Chiefs of Staff, in the role as Chairman of the JROC, is the requirements authority for all potential major defense acquisition programs and is responsible for all requirements policy and procedures, including MNSs, CRDs, and ORDs. The Requirements Authority for other acquisition category programs is specified in reference (i).
E2.1.19. Technology Project. A directed, incrementally funded effort designed to provide new capability in response to technological opportunities or an operational or business (e.g., accounting, inventory cataloging, etc.) need. Technology projects are "pre-systems acquisition," do not have an acquisition category, and precede program initiation. Technology is the output of the science and technology program that is used in systems acquisition. The decision authority and information necessary for decision-making on each project shall be specified by the appropriate S&T Executive (for projects not yet approved for Milestone A) or by the MDA (for projects past Milestone A).
[...]
E2.1.21. Weapon System. An item or set of items that can be used directly by warfighters to carry out combat or combat support missions to include tactical communication systems.

4.11122 CHEMICAL AND BIOLOGICAL WEAPONS

☛ India: The Chemical Weapons Convention Act, 2000

An Act to give effect to the Convention on the Prohibition of the Development, Production, Stockpiling and Use of Chemical Weapons and on their Destruction and to provide for matters connected therewith or incidental to their Destruction and to provide for matters connected therewith or incidental thereto.
Whereas a Convention on the Prohibition of the Development, Production, Stockpiling and Use of Chemical Weapons and on their Destruction was signed on behalf of the Government of India at Paris on the14th day of January, 1993; and Whereas India, having ratified the said Convention, has to make provisions for giving effect thereto and for matters connected therewith or incidental thereto.
Be it enacted by Parliament in the Fifty-first Year of the Republic of India as follows:-

Chapter 1
Preliminary

1. (*1*) This act may be called the Chemical Weapons Convention Act, 2000.
(*2*) It extends to the whole of India, and it shall apply to -
(*a*) citizens of India outside India; and
(*b*) associates, branches or subsidiaries, outside India of companies or bodies corporate, registered or incorporated in India.
(*3*) It shall come into force on such date as the Central Government may, by notification in

the Official Gazette, appoint; and different dates may be appointed for different provisions of this Act.

2. In this Act, unless the context otherwise requires, -
(*a*)"Article" means an Article of the Convention;
(*b*)"Chemical Weapons" means,-
(*i*) the Toxic Chemicals and their precursors, except where intended for purposes not prohibited under the Convention, as long as the types and quantities are consistent with such purposes;
(*ii*) the munitions and devices, specifically designed to cause death or other harm through the toxic properties of those Toxic Chemicals specified in subclause (i), which would be released as a result of the employment of such munitions and devices;
(*iii*) any equipment specifically designed for use directly in connection with the employment of munitions and devices specified in sub-clause (*ii*), together or separately;
(*c*) "Convention" means the Convention on the Prohibition of the Development, Production, Stockpiling and Use of Chemical Weapons and on their Destruction signed on behalf of the Government of India at Paris on the 14th day of January, 1993;
(*d*) "enforcement officer" means a person appointed as such by the Central Government under sub-section (*1*) of section 9 or by the State Government under sub-section (*2*) of that section;
(*e*) "goods", in relation to Toxic Chemicals, Precursors or Discrete Organic Chemicals including those Discrete Organic Chemicals containing elements of phosphorous, sulphur or fluorine, means any material, commodity, article or compound consisting of such Toxic Chemicals, Precursors or Discrete Organic Chemicals including those Discrete Organic Chemicals containing elements of phosphorous, sulphur or fluorine and includes materials, commodities, articles, compounds or apparatus used in the production, processing or storing of Toxic Chemicals, Precursors or Discrete Organic Chemicals including those Discrete Organic Chemicals containing elements of phosphorous, sulphur or fluorine;
(*f*) "industry" includes a Facility;
(*g*) "Inspector" means an individual designated by the Technical Secretariat, according to the procedures as set forth in Part II, Section A, of the Verification Annex to the Convention, to carry out an inspection or visit in accordance with the convention;
(*h*) "National Authority" means the National Authority for the Chemical Weapons Convention established under sub-section (1) of section 6;
(*i*) "Organisation" means the Organisation for the prohibition of Chemical Weapons established pursuant to Article VIII;
(*j*) "prescribed" means prescribed by rules made under this Act;
(*k*) "purposes not prohibited under the Convention" means -
(*i*) industrial, agricultural, research, medical, pharmaceutical or other peaceful purposes;
(*ii*) protective purposes namely those purposes directly related to protection against Toxic Chemicals and to protection against Chemical Weapons;
(*iii*) military purposes not connected with the use of Chemical Weapons and not dependant on the use of the Toxic Properties of Chemicals as a method of warfare; and
(*iv*) law enforcement including domestic riot control purposes;
(*l*) "State Party" means a signatory or acceding State to the Convention whose instrument of ratification or accession has been deposited with the Depository of the Convention;

(*m*) words and expressions used in this Act and not defined but defined in the Convention, or the Code of Criminal Procedure, 1973, shall have the meanings respectively assigned to them in that Convention or Code.

3. (*1*) Notwithstanding anything to the contrary contained in any other law, the provisions of the Convention set out in the Schedule to this Act shall have the force of law in India.
(*2*) The Central Government may, from time to time and by notification in the Official Gazette, amend the Schedule in conformity with any amendments, duly made and adopted, of the provisions of the said Convention set out therein.

4. Where the Central Government considers any inspection of a Chemical Weapons Production Facility in India under this act to be against the interest of national security or economic interests of India, it may deny the request for such inspection.

5. The Central Government may, by notification in the Official Gazette, declare that this Act shall cease to be in force in case the Government of India withdraws from the Convention in accordance with the provisions of Article XVI, and on such declaration this Act shall cease to be in force, but its expiry under the operation of this Section shall not affect -
(*a*) the previous operation of, or anything duly done or suffered under, this Act or rule made thereunder or any order made under any such rule, or
(*b*) any right privilege, obligation or liability acquired, accrued or incurred under this Act or any rule made thereunder or any order made under any such rule, or
(*c*) any penalty, forfeiture or punishment incurred in respect of any offence under this act, or
(*d*) any investigation, legal proceeding or remedy in respect of any such right, privilege, obligation, liability penalty, forfeiture or punishment as aforesaid, and any such investigation, legal proceeding or remedy may be instituted, continued or enforced and any such penalty, forfeiture or punishment may be imposed as if this Act had not expired.

Chapter II
Establishment of the National Authority and its Powers and Functions

6. (*1*) For the purposes of this Act, the Central Government shall establish, by notification in the Official Gazette, an Authority to be known as the National Authority for implementing the provisions of the Convention which shall consist of a Chairperson and such number of Directors as may be appointed by the Central Government.
(*2*) The Central Government may appoint officers and such other employees to the National Authority as it thinks fit for the purposes of this Act.
(*3*) The salary and allowances payable to, and other terms and conditions of service of, the chairperson and the Directors shall be such as may be prescribed.
(*4*) The salary and allowances payable to, and other terms and conditions of service of, officers and other employees of the National Authority shall be such as may be prescribed.
(*5*) In the exercise of its powers and performance of its functions under this Act, the National Authority shall be subject to the control of the Central Government.

7. (*1*) Subject to the provisions of this Act,–
(*a*) it shall be the general duty of the National Authority to fulfil, on behalf of the Government of India, the obligations under the Convention;

(*b*) it shall be incumbent on the National Authority to act as the national focal point for effective liaison with the Organisation and other States Parties on matters relating to the Convention;

(*2*) Subject to the provisions of sub-section (*1*), the functions of the National Authority shall be to -

(*a*) interact with the Organisation and other States Parties for the purpose of fulfilling the obligations of the Government of India under the Convention;

(*b*) monitor compliance with the provisions of the Convention;

(*c*) regulate and monitor the development, production, processing, consumption, transfer or use of Toxic Chemicals or Precursors as specified in the Convention;

(*d*) make request to, or to receive request from, a State Party for assistance and protection under Article X, against the use or threat of use of Chemical Weapons;

(*e*) manage routine inspection or Challenge Inspection managing investigation, in case a complaint of use of Chemical Weapons or riot control agents as a method of warfare is received from the Organisation;

(*f*) conduct inspections for the purposes of this act;

(*g*) interact with the Organisation in respect of acceptance of request of India for Challenge Inspection or to counter any frivolous or defamatory request made by any State Party against India to the Organisation;

(*h*) scrutinise and accept list of Inspectors and to verify the Approved Equipment brought by an Inspection Team on to the Inspection Site;

(*i*) provide escort to the Inspection Team and the Observer within the territory of India;

Powers and functions of National Authority

(*j*) identify and oversee the closure and destruction of Chemical Weapons, Chemical Weapons Production Facilities, Old Chemical Weapons or Abandoned Chemical Weapons;

(*k*) negotiate Managed Access during the Challenge Inspection;

(*l*) ensure decontamination of Approved Equipment after completion of an Inspection;

(*m*) advise Central Government for laying down safeguards for transportation, sampling or storage of Chemical Weapons and fixation of standards for emission or discharge of environmental pollutants arising out of the destruction of Chemical Weapons, Old Chemical Weapons, Abandoned Chemical Weapons or Chemical Weapons Production Facility;

(*n*) ensure data base confidentiality and maintain secrecy of confidential information and technology collected or received by the National Authority under this Act;

(*o*) facilitate exchange of scientific and technological information relating to developments in chemicals amongst the States Parties;

(*p*) call for such information from any person which the National Authority has reasonable cause to believe that such information may be required for complying with the provisions of the Convention;

(*q*) approve and declare, on behalf of the Government of India, a single small-scale facility for production of Toxic Chemicals listed in Schedule 1 in the Annex on Chemicals to the Convention for purposes not prohibited under the Convention;

(*r*) provide training to enforcement officers;

(*s*) ensure protection of environment, health and safety of the people during transportation, sampling, storage or destruction of Chemical Weapons, Chemical Weapons Production Facilities, Old Chemical Weapons or Abandoned Chemical Weapons;

(*t*) co-ordinate exchange of scientific and technological information among laboratories handling Toxic Chemicals or Precursors;

(*u*) determine, from time to time, the quantity limit that a person at any time may produce, otherwise acquire, retain, transfer or use any Toxic Chemical or Precursor listed in any of the Schedules 1 to 3 in the Annex on Chemicals to the Convention, any Discrete Organic Chemical including Chemicals to the Convention, any Discrete Organic Chemical including Discrete Organic Chemical containing elements of phosphorous, sulphur or fluorine for purposes not prohibited under the Convention;
(*v*) such other functions as may be prescribed.

8. The National Authority shall prepare such initial, annual and other periodical declarations regarding Toxic Chemicals or Precursors listed in any of the Schedules 1 to 3 in the Annex on Chemicals to the Convention, Discrete Organic Chemicals including those Discrete Organic Chemicals containing elements of phosphorous, sulphur or fluorine Chemical Weapons, Old Chemical Weapons, Abandoned Chemical Weapons, riot control agents, Chemical Weapons Production Facilities, past transfers of Chemical Weapons or their production equipments or any other declaration required to be made under the Convention and shall submit such declarations to the Organization at such time as are specified under the Convention.

9. (*1*) The Central Government may, by notification in the Official Gazette, appoint such of the officers of the National Authority as it thinks fit to be enforcement officers for the purposes of this Act.
(*2*) The State Government may, as and when so directed by the Central Government and by notification in the Official Gazette, appoint such of its officers of gazetted rank as it thinks fit to be enforcement officer for the purposes of this Act and assign to them such local limits as it may think fit.
(*3*) Every officer appointed as enforcement officer under sub-section (*1*) or under sub-section (*2*) shall be furnished by the Central Government or by the State Government, as the case may be, with a certificate of appointment as an enforcement officer and the certificate shall, on demand, be produced by such enforcement officer.

10. Notwithstanding anything contained in any other law but subject to the provisions of this Act, the National Authority may, in the exercise of its powers and performance of its functions under this Act, issue directions in writing to any person, officer or authority and such person, officer or authority shall be bound to comply with such directions.

Explanation.– For the avoidance of doubts, it is hereby declared that the power to issue direction under this Section includes the power to direct –
(*a*) the closure, prohibition or regulation of any company, firm or industry engaged in the development, production, processing, consumption or use of any Toxic Chemical or Precursor listed in the Annex on Chemicals to the Convention or, the production of any Discrete Organic Chemical including Discrete Organic Chemical containing elements of phosphorous, sulphur or fluorine; or (*b*) the stoppage or regulation of the supply of electricity or water or any other service to such company, firm or industry.

11.The Central Government may, if it considers it necessary or expedient so to do for the purposes of this Act, by order, published in the Official Gazette, constitute a Committee by such name as may be specified in the order for the purpose of overseeing the functions of the

National Authority and exercising and performing such of the powers and functions of the Central Government under this Act (except the power to make rules under section 56) as may be specified in the order and subject to the supervision and control of the Central Government and the provisions of such order, such Committee may exercise the powers or perform the functions so specified in the order as if such Committee had been empowered by this Act to exercise those powers or perform those functions.

12. (*1*) Notwithstanding anything contained in any other law for the time being in force, the National Authority may, by general or special order, call upon a person, to furnish to that Authority periodically or as and when required any information, declaration or return concerning Toxic Chemicals or Precursors listed in any of the Schedules 1 to 3 in the Annex on Chemicals to the Convention, Chemical Weapons, Old Chemical Weapons, Abandoned Chemical Weapons, Chemical Weapons Production Facilities, riot control agents, single small-scale facility or Discrete Organic Chemicals including those Discrete Organic Chemicals containing elements of phosphorous, sulphur or fluorine with such particulars as may be specified by the National Authority.
(*2*) No person shall, when complying with any requisition made under subsection (*1*), give any information or furnish any declaration, return or statement which he knows, or has reasonable cause to believe to be false or not true in any material particular.

14. Any person having knowledge about the possession or location of Old Chemical Weapons or Abandoned Chemical Weapons shall inform the National Authority of such possession and the precise location of such Old Chemical .Weapons or Abandoned Chemical Weapons within seven days from the commencement of this Act:

Provided that where the knowledge about the possession or location of Old Chemical Weapons or Abandoned Chemical Weapons is obtained after the commencement of this Act, an information about knowledge of such possession or location shall be given to the National Authority within seven days from the occurrence of such knowledge.

15. No person shall -
(*a*) produce, acquire, retain or use Toxic Chemicals or Precursors listed in Schedule 1 in the Annex on Chemicals to the Convention, outside the territories of States Parties, and shall not transfer such Chemicals or Precursors outside the territory of India except to another State Party;
(*b*) produce, acquire, retain, transfer or use Toxic Chemicals or Precursors listed in Schedule 1 in the Annex on Chemicals to the Convention without permission from the National Authority and unless -
(*i*) the Toxic Chemicals or Precursors listed in Schedule 1 in the Annex on Chemicals to the Convention are for the purposes to be applied to research, medical, pharmaceutical or protective purposes; and
(*ii*) the types of Toxic Chemicals or Precursors are strictly limited to those that can be justified with reference to the purposes specified in sub-clause (*i*) and the quantities of such Toxic Chemicals or Precursors for such purposes at any time do not exceed the limits fixed by the National Authority;
(*c*) transfer the Toxic Chemicals or Precursors listed in Schedule 1 in the Annex on Chemicals to the Convention to another State Party outside India except-

(*i*) for the purposes specified in sub-clause (*i*) of clause (*b*); and
(*ii*) in accordance with the procedure set out in Part VI of the Verification Annex to the Convention:
Provided that no Toxic Chemicals or Precursors referred to in clause (*c*) shall be retransferred to any third State.

16. No person shall, three years after the 29th day of April, 1997, transfer to or receive from any person, who is not a citizen of a State Party, any Toxic Chemical or Precursor listed in Schedule 2 in the Annex on Chemicals to the Convention.

17. No person shall export from, or import into, India a Toxic Chemical or Precursor listed in any of the Schedules 1 to 3 in the Annex on Chemicals to the Convention except in accordance with the provisions of the Export and Import Policy determined by the Central Government from time to time under the Foreign Trade (Development and Regulation) Act, 1992 and the Orders issued thereunder.

Chapter IV
Registration of Persons as producers, Users, Etc.

18 (*1*) Every person who is engaged in the production, processing, acquisition, consumption, transfer, import, export or use of any Toxic Chemical or Precursor listed in any of the Schedules 1 to 3 in the Annex on Chemicals to the Convention or, engaged in the production of any Discrete Organic Chemical including Discrete Organic Chemical containing elements of phosphorous, sulphur or fluorine shall make, within thirty days from the commencement of this Act, an application for registration of his name, as a producer, processor, acquirer, consumer, transferor, importer, exporter or user of any Toxic Chemical or Precursor or, as the case may be, as a producer of any Discrete Organic Chemical including Discrete Organic Chemicals containing elements of phosphorous, sulphur or fluorine, to such registration authority as the Central Government may, by notification in the Official Gazette, specify in this behalf.
(*2*) No person, who after the commencement of this Act, desires to produce, process, acquire, consume, transfer, import, export or use any Toxic Chemical or precursor listed in any of the Schedules 1 to 3 in the Annex on Chemicals to the Convention or, desires to produce any Discrete Organic Chemical including Discrete Organic Chemicals containing elements of phosphorous, sulphur or fluorine, shall commence business unless such person has applied to the registration authority specified under sub-section (*1*) for registration of his name as a producer, processor, acquirer, consumer, transferor, importer, exporter or user of any Toxic Chemical or Precursor or, as the case may be as a producer of any Discrete Organic Chemical including Discrete Organic Chemicals containing elements of phosphorus, sulphur or fluorine.
(*3*) The form of application to be made to the registration authority under subsection
(*1*) or sub-section (*2*), the particulars to be contained in such application form, the manner in which such application shall be made, the fee payable on such application, the form of certificate of registration, the procedure to be followed in granting or cancelling certificate of registration shall be such as may be prescribed.
(*4*) On receipt of the application referred to in sub-section (*1*) or sub-section
(*2*), the registration authority shall, if the application is in the prescribed form, register the

name of the applicant and grant him a certificate of registration.
(*5*) The certificate of registration granted in pursuance of this section shall be valid for a period specified therein and may be renewed from time to time for such further period and on payment of such fee as may be prescribed.

Chapter V
Inspection, Search, Seizure and Forfeiture

19. (*1*) An Inspector may inspect -
(*a*) any person who is engaged in -
(*i*) the production, processing, acquisition, consumption, transfer, import, export or use of any Toxic Chemical or Precursor listed in any of the Schedules 1 to 3 in the Annex on Chemicals to the Convention; or
(*ii*) the production of any Discrete Organic Chemical including those Discrete Organic Chemicals containing elements of phosphorous, sulphur or fluorine;
(*b*) any place where any Chemical Weapon, Old Chemical Weapon or Abandoned Chemical Weapon is located or Chemical Weapon Production Facility exists, for the purposes specified in the Verification Annex to the Convention.
(*2*) An Inspection Team may undertake a Challenge Inspection of any Facility or location pursuant to Article IX and such inspection shall be undertaken in accordance with the provisions of the Verification Annex to the Convention.
(*3*) The Inspection Team may, while carrying out a Challenge Inspection, be accompanied by an Observer to observe the conduct of the Challenge Inspection.
(*4*) An enforcement officer shall accompany the Inspector or Inspection Team to observe all verification activities carried out by the Inspector or Inspection Team and to provide the Inspector or Inspection Team, during the inspection, with such clarifications in connection with an ambiguity that may arise during an inspection as may be necessary to remove such ambiguity.
(*5*) Every Inspector or Inspection Team shall have -
(*a*) the right to interview any Facility personnel in the presence of enforcement officer for the purpose of establishing relevant facts;
(*b*) the right to request clarifications in connection with ambiguities that may arise during inspection;
(*c*) the right to demand production of such documentation and records which are relevant and necessary for the purpose of inspection;
(*d*) the right to take photographs of an object or a building located within the Inspection Site if question relating to that object or building is not resolved;
(*e*) the right to draw samples, perform on site analysis of such samples; and
(*f*) such other rights as are provided under the Convention.
(*6*) An Inspector or Inspection Team shall, during the conduct of verification activities or Challenge Inspection, enjoy the privileges and immunities referred to in Part II of the Verification Annex to the Convention.
(*7*) No sample drawn under clause (*e*) of sub-section (*5*) by an Inspector or Inspection Team shall be sent for analysis in any laboratory situated outside the territory of India.

20. (*1*) Any enforcement Officer shall have the right to enter with such assistance as he consider necessary, any building or place for the purpose of -

(*a*) verifying the correctness of any information, declaration or return furnished under sub-section (*1*)of section 12;
(*b*) performing any of the functions of the National Authority entrusted to him;
(*c*) determining whether any provisions of this Act or the rules made thereunder or any direction given under this Act is being complied with any person engaged in the production, processing, acquisition, consumption, transfer, import, export or use of any Toxic Chemical or Precursor listed in any of the Schedules 1 to 3 in the Annex on Chemicals to the Convention or engaged in the production of any Discrete Organic Chemical including Discrete Organic Chemical containing elements of phosphorous, sulphur or fluorine; Enforcement officer to enter into any place for examining and testing facility or to conduct search.
(*d*) examining or testing any facility, record, document or any other material object, as the case may be, or conducting a search of any place or person;
(*e*) Conducting a search where a warrant under sub-section (*1*) of section 22 is addressed to such enforcement officer or he is so authorized under subsection (2) of that section.
(2) Any enforcement officer shall have a right to accompany the Inspector or Inspection Team as a representative of India during inspection in India.

21. If any person wilfully -
(*a*) refuses without reasonable excuse to comply with the request made by the Inspector or Inspection Team for the purpose of facilitating the conduct of that inspection in accordance with the Verification Annex to the Convention;
(*b*) delays or obstructs any member of the Inspection Team , Inspector, enforcement officer or the Observer in the conduct of inspection;
(*c*) removes or tampers with any on-site instrument or Approved Equipment installed by the enforcement officer , Inspector or Inspection Team with the intention of adversely affecting the operation of such instrument or Equipment, he shall be guilty of an offence punishable under this Act.

22. (*1*) A Metropolitan Magistrate or a Judicial Magistrate of the first class or any Magistrate of the second class specially empowered by the State Government in this behalf, may issue a warrant for the arrest of any person whom he has reason to believe to have committed any offence punishable under Chapter VI or for the search, whether by day or by night, of any industry, building, conveyance or place in which he has reason to believe that any goods in relation to which an offence punishable under Chapter VI has been committed or any document or other goods which may furnish evidence of the commission of such offence is kept or concealed.
(*2*) Any enforcement officer or such other officer of the National Authority as is empowered in this behalf by general or special order by the Central Government or any such officer of a State Government as is empowered in this behalf by general or special order of the State Government, if he has reason to believe from personal knowledge or information given by any person and taken down in writing that any person has committed an offence punishable under Chapter VI or any goods in relation to which an offence punishable under Chapter VI has been committed or any document or other goods which may furnish evidence of the commission of such offence has been kept or concealed in any industry, building, conveyance or place, may authorise any officer subordinate to him to arrest such person or search an industry or a building , conveyance or place, whether by day or by night, or himself arrest a person or search an industry or a building, conveyance or place.

(*3*) The officer to whom a warrant under sub-section (*1*) is addressed and the officer who authorised the arrest or search or such subordinate officer who is so authorised under sub-section (*2*) shall have all the powers of an officer acting under section 23.

23. (*1*) Any such subordinate officer to the enforcement officer as is authorised in this behalf by general or special order by the Central Government or any such subordinate officer to the enforcement officer as is authorised in this behalf by general or special order of the State Government, if he has reason to believe from personal knowledge or information given by any person and taken down in writing, that any goods in relation to which an offence punishable under Chapter VI has been committed or any document or goods which may furnish evidence of the commission of such offence is kept or concealed in any industry, building, conveyance or place, may, between sunrise and sunset,–
(*a*) enter into and search any such industry, building, conveyance or place;
(*b*) in case of resistance ,break open any door and remove any obstacle to such entry;
(*c*) seize such Chemical Weapons, Chemical Weapons Production Facilities, riot control agents, Old Chemical Weapons, Abandoned Chemical Weapons, Toxic Chemicals or Precursors or Discrete Organic Chemicals including those Discrete Organic Chemicals containing elements of phosphorous, sulphur or fluorine ,all goods and any conveyance which he has reason to believe to be liable to confiscation under this Act and any document or other goods which he has reason to believe may furnish evidence of the commission of any offence punishable under Chapter VI relating to such Chemical Weapons, Chemical Weapons Production Facilities, riot control agents, Old Chemical Weapons, Abandoned Chemical Weapons, Toxic Chemicals or Precursors or Discrete Organic Chemicals including those Discrete Organic Chemicals containing elements of phosphorous, sulphur or fluorine; and
(*d*) detain and search, if he thinks proper, arrest any person whom he has reason to believe to have committed any offence punishable under Chapter VI relating to such Chemical Weapons, Chemical Weapons Production Facilities, riot control agents, Old Chemical Weapons, Abandoned Chemical Weapons ,Toxic Chemicals or Precursors or Discrete Organic Chemicals including those Discrete Organic Chemicals containing elements of phosphorous, sulphur or fluorine: Provided that if such subordinate officer has reason to believe that search warrant or authorisation cannot be obtained without affording opportunity for the concealment of evidence or facility for the escape of an offender, he may enter and search such industry, building, conveyance or place, at any time between sunrise and sunset after recording the grounds of his belief.
(*2*) Where an officer takes down any information in writing under subsection (*1*) or records grounds for his belief under the proviso thereto, he shall forthwith send a copy thereof to his immediate superior officer.

24. Any subordinate officer to the enforcement officer as is authorised in section 23 may –
(*a*) seize, in any pubic place or in transit, any goods, in relation to which he has reason to believe an offence punishable under Chapter VI has been committed , and, along with such goods, any conveyance liable to confiscation under this Act, and any document or goods which he has reason to believe may furnish evidence of the commission of an offence punishable under Chapter VI relating to such goods;

(*b*) detain and search any person whom he has reason to believe to have committed an offence punishable under Chapter VI , and, if such person has any Toxic Chemical or Precursor or any Discrete Organic Chemical containing elements of phosphorous, sulphur or fluorine in his possession and such possession appears to him to be unlawful, arrest him and any other person in his company.

Explanation.– For the purpose of this section, the expression "public place" includes any public conveyance, shop, hotel or other place intended for use by, or accessible to, the public.

25. (*1*) Where it is not practicable to seize any goods which are liable to confiscation under this Act, any officer authorised under Section 23 may serve on the owner or person in possession of the goods, an order that he shall not remove, part with or otherwise deal with the goods except with the previous permission of such officer.
(*2*) For effecting seizure and confiscation, the owner, the plant operator, and other officials of the facility shall provide all assistance with regard to safety in handling of goods.

26. Any subordinate officer authorised under section 23 may, if he has reason to suspect that any conveyance is , or is likely to be, used for the transport of any goods in respect of which he suspects that any provision of this Act has been, or is being, or is likely to be , contravened at any time, stop such conveyance, or in the case of an aircraft compel it to land and -
(*a*) rummage and search the conveyance or part thereof;
(*b*) examine and search any goods in the conveyance;
(*c*) if it becomes necessary to stop the conveyance , he may use all lawful means for stopping it.

27. (*1*) When any subordinate officer authorised under section 23 or any subordinate officer exercising power in pursuance of sub-section (*3*) of section 22 is about to search any person under the provisions of section 22 or section 23 or section 24, he shall, if such person so requires, take such person without unnecessary delay to the nearest enforcement officer or the officer authorising such search or the nearest Magistrate.
(*2*) If such requisition is made, the officer may detain the person until he can bring him before the officer or the Magistrate referred to in sub-section (*1*).
(*3*) The officer or the Magistrate before whom any such person is brought shall, if he sees no reasonable ground for search, forthwith discharge the person but otherwise shall direct that search be made.
(*4*) No female shall be searched by anyone excepting a female.

28. The provisions of the Code of Criminal Procedure, 1973 shall apply, in so far as they are not inconsistent with the provisions of this Act, to all warrants issued and arrests, searches and seizures made under this Act.

29. (*1*) Any Officer arresting a person under Section 22 or section 23 or section 24 shall, as soon as may be, inform him of the grounds for such arrest.
(*2*) Every person arrested and goods seized under warrant issued under sub-section (*1*) of section 22 shall be forwarded without unnecessary delay to Magistrate by whom the warrant was issued.

(*3*) Every person arrested and goods seized under sub-section (*2*) of section 22 or section 23 or section 24 shall be forwarded without unnecessary delay to -
(*a*) the officer in charge of the nearest police station; or
(*b*) the officer empowered under section 30.
(*4*) The authority or officer to whom any person or goods is forwarded under sub-section (*2*) or sub-section (*3*) shall, with all convenient dispatch, take such measures as may be necessary for the disposal according to law of such persons or goods.

30. (*1*) The Central Government may, after consultation with the State Government, by notification published in the Official Gazette, invest any officer of the National Authority with the powers of an officer in charge of a police station for the investigation of the offences under this Act.
(*2*) The State Government may, by notification published in the Official Gazette, invest any officer of gazetted rank or any class of such officers with the powers of an officer in charge of a police station for the investigation of the offences under this Act.

31. An officer in charge of a police station shall take charge of and keep in safe custody, pending the orders of the Magistrate, all goods seized under this Act within the local area of that police station and which may be delivered to him, and shall allow any officer who may accompany such goods to the police station or who may be deputed for the purpose, to affix his seal to such goods or to take samples of and from them and all samples so taken shall also be sealed with a seal of the officer in charge of the police station.

32. Whenever any person makes any arrest or seizure under this Act, he shall, within forty – eight hours next after such arrest or seizure, make a full report of all the particulars of such arrest or seizure to his immediate superior.

33. (*1*) Whenever any offence punishable under Chapter VI has been committed, the goods or in respect of which or by means of which such offence has been committed, shall be liable to confiscation.
(*2*) Any Toxic Chemical or Precursor lawfully produced, imported into India, transported, used, purchased or sold along with, or in addition to, any goods which is liable to confiscation under sub-section (*1*) and the receptacles, packages and coverings in which any goods liable to confiscation under sub-section (*1*) is found, and the other contents, if any, of such receptacles or packages shall likewise be liable to confiscation.
(*3*) Any conveyance used in carrying any goods liable to confiscation under sub-section (*1*) or sub-section (2) shall be liable to confiscation, unless the owner of the conveyance proves that it was used without the knowledge or connivance of the owner himself, his agent, if any, and the person in charge of the conveyance and that each of them had taken all reasonable precautions against such use.

34. Any goods used for concealing any goods which is liable to confiscation under this Act shall also be liable to confiscation.

Explanation.- In this section, "Goods" includes conveyance as a means of transport.

35. Where any goods is sold by a person having knowledge or reason to believe that the goods is liable to confiscation under this Act, the sale proceeds thereof shall also be liable to confiscation.

36. (*1*) In the trail of offences under this Act, whether the accused is convicted or acquitted or discharged, the court shall decide whether any goods seized under this Act is liable to confiscation and, if it decides that the goods is so liable, it may order confiscation accordingly.
(*2*) Where any goods seized under this Act appears to be liable to confiscation under section 33 or section 34 or section 35, but the person who committed the offence therewith is not known or cannot be found, the court may inquiry into and decide such liability, and may order confiscation accordingly:
Provided that no order of confiscation of any goods shall be made until the expiry of one month from the date of seizure, or without hearing any person who may claim any right thereto and the evidence, if any, which he produces in respect of his claim.
(*3*) Any person not convicted who claims any right to property which has been confiscated under this section may appeal to the Court of Session against the order of confiscation.

37. Any subordinate officer authorized under section 23 may, during the course of any inquiry in connection with the contravention of any provision of this Act,–
(*a*) call for information from any person for the purpose of satisfying himself whether there has been any contravention of the provisions of this Act or any rule or order made or direction issued thereunder;
(*b*) require any person to produce or deliver any document or thing useful or relevant to the enquiry;
(*c*) examine any person acquainted with the facts and circumstances of the case.

38. No enforcement officer, subordinate officer to enforcement officer or officer of the National Authority or the State Government or officer subordinate to such officer as is mentioned in sub-section (*2*) of section 22 acting in exercise of powers vested in him under any provision of this Act or any such order made thereunder shall be compelled to say when he got any information as to the commission of any offence.

Chapter VI
Offences and Penalties

39. Whoever–
(*a*) before the commencement of this Act had been engaged in development, production, processing, acquisition, consumption, transfer, import, export or use of any Toxic Chemical or Precursor listed in any of the Schedules 1 to 3 in the Annex on chemicals to the Convention or engaged in the production of any Discrete Organic Chemical including Discrete Organic Chemical containing elements of phosphorous, sulphur or fluorine and continues to be, after such commencement, so engaged; or
(*b*) after the commencement of this Act produces, processes, acquires, consumes, transfers, imports, exports or uses any Toxic Chemical or Precursor listed in any of the Schedules 1 to 3 in the Annex on Chemicals to the Convention or produces any Discrete Organic Chemical including Discrete Organic chemical containing elements of phosphorous, sulphur or

fluorine, without complying with the provisions of sub-section (*1*) or, as the case may be, sub-section (*2*) of section 18 shall, unless his name is registered in accordance with the provisions of that section, be punishable with fine which may extend to one lakh rupees, and in the case of continuing default, with a further fine which may extend to one lakh rupees every day during which such default continues after conviction for the first default or with imprisonment for a term which may extend to three years, or with both.

40. Whoever, in contravention of any provision of this Act, develops, produces, otherwise acquires, stockpiles, retains or uses Chemical Weapons, transfers, directly or indirectly, any Chemical Weapon to any person, uses any riot control agent as a method of warfare, engages in any military preparations to use Chemical Weapons, assists, encourages or induces in any manner any person to engage in the use of any riot control agent as a method of warfare or any other activity prohibited to a State Party under the Convention, shall be punishable with imprisonment for a term which shall not be less than one year but which may extend to term of life and shall also be liable to fine which may extend to one lakh rupees.

41. Whoever, in contravention of any provision of this Act, produces, acquires, retains, transfers or uses any Toxic Chemical or Precursor listed in Scheduled 1 in the Annex on Chemicals to the Convention for the purposes prohibited to a State Party under the Convention or transfers any Toxic Chemical or Precursor listed in Scheduled 1 in the Annex on Chemicals to the Convention outside India, shall be punishable with imprisonment for a term which shall not be less than one year but which may extend to term of life and shall also be liable to fine which may extend to one lakh rupees.

42. Whoever, in contravention of any provision of this Act transfers to or receives from any person who is not a citizen of a State Party any Toxic Chemical or Precursor listed in Schedule 2 in the Annex on Chemicals to the Convention, shall be punishable with imprisonment for a term which shall not be less than one year but which may extend to term of life and shall also be liable to fine which may extend to one lakh rupees.

43. Whoever, in contravention of any provision of this Act, exports from or imports into India any Toxic Chemical or Precursor listed in any of the Schedules 1 to 3 in the Annex on Chemicals to the Convention, shall be punishable with imprisonment for a term which shall not be less than one year but which may extend to term of life and shall also be liable to fine which may extend to one lakh rupees

44. Whoever, in contravention of any provision of this Act, divulges any confidential information obtained by the National Authority from any declaration or return furnished or any statement made, information supplied to, or obtained by, an enforcement officer during the course of any inspection carried out under the provisions of this Act to any other person, shall be punishable with imprisonment for a term which shall not be less than one year but which may extend to term of life and shall also be liable to fine which may extend to one lakh rupees.

45. Whoever does not comply with the obligations related to inspection activity under the Convention or delays or obstructs any Inspection Team or Inspector, enforcement officer or Observer in performance of his functions or willfully removes or tampers with any installed

on site instrument or any Approved Equipment shall be punishable with imprisonment for a term which shall not be less than one year but which may extend to term of life and shall also be liable to fine which may extend to one lakh rupees.

46. Any person who being required by or under this Act to furnish any–
(*a*) information;
(*b*) declaration; or
(*c*) return,
fails to furnish such information, declaration or return shall be punishable with fine which may extend to one lakh rupees, and in the case of continuing default, with a further fine which may extend to one lakh rupees for every day during which such default continues after conviction for the first such default, or with imprisonment for a term which may extend to three years, or with both.

47. Notwithstanding anything contained in the Code of Criminal Procedure, 1973, the offence punishable under section 46 shall be cognizable.

48. (*1*) Where any offence under Chapter VI has been committed by a company, every person who at the time the offence was committed was in charge of, or was responsible to, the company for the conduct of the business of the company as well as the company, shall be deemed to be guilty of the offence and shall be liable to be proceeded against and punished accordingly:
Provided that nothing contained in this sub-section shall render any such person liable to any punishment if he proves that the offence was committed without his knowledge or that he had exercised all due diligence to prevent the commission of such offence.
(2) Notwithstanding anything contained in sub-section (*1*), where any offence under Chapter VI has been committed by a company and it is proved that the offence has been committed with the consent or connivance of, or is attributable to any neglect on the part of, any director, manager, secretary or other officer of the company, such director, manager, secretary or other officer shall be deemed to be guilty of that offence and shall be liable to be proceeded against and punished accordingly.

Explanation.- For the purposes of this section, -
(*a*) "company" means any body corporate, and includes a firm or other association of individuals; and
(*b*) "director", in relation to a firm, means a partner of the firm.

49. No court shall take cognizance of any offence punishable under this Act except with the previous sanction of the Central Government or the authority notified by the Central Government, in the Official Gazette, to be competent to sanction prosecution of the offences under this Act.

50. (*1*) Any person aggrieved by any direction of the National Authority issued under section 10 may prefer an appeal to the Central Government within such time as may be prescribed.
(2) No appeal shall be admitted if it is preferred after the expiry of the period prescribed therefor:

Provided that an appeal may be admitted after the expiry of the period prescribed therefor if the appellant satisfies the Central Government that he had sufficient cause for not preferring the appeal within the prescribed period.
(*3*) Every appeal made under this section shall be made in such form and shall be accompanied by a copy of the direction appealed against and by such fee as may be prescribed.
(*4*) The procedure for disposing of an appeal shall be such as may be prescribed:
Provided that before disposing of an appeal, the appellant shall be given a reasonable opportunity of being heard.

51. Notwithstanding anything contained in this Act, the provisions of the Convention in so far as they relate to-
(*a*) restriction or reporting;
(*b*) inspection; or
(*c*) declaration and verification,
shall not apply to any mixtures containing such concentration of any Chemical specified in Schedule 2 or Schedule 3 in the Annex on Chemicals to the Convention as the Central Government may, by notification in the Official Gazette, specify.

Chapter VII
Miscellaneous

52. No suit, prosecution or other legal proceeding shall lie against the Central Government or a State Government or any officer of the Central Government or of a State Government or the Chairperson, Directors, officers and other employees of the National Authority or any other person exercising any powers or discharging any functions or performing any duties under this Act, for anything in good faith done or intended to be done under this Act or any rule or order made thereunder.

53. (*1*) The Central Government may, by notification in the Official Gazette, delegate, subject to such conditions and limitations as may be specified in the notification, such of its powers and functions under this Act (except the power to make rules under section 56) as it may deem necessary or expedient, to the National Authority or the Committee referred to in section 11.
(2) The State Government may, by notification in the Official Gazette, delegate, subject to such conditions and limitations as may be specified in the notification, such of its powers and functions under this Act, as it may deem necessary or expedient, to any authority or officer of that Government.

54. The Chairperson, Directors, officers and other employees of the National Authority or any other person exercising any powers or discharging any functions under this Act shall be deemed to be the public servant within the meaning of section 21 of the Indian Penal Code.

55. If any difficulty arises in giving effect to the provisions of this Act, the Central Government may, by order published in the Official Gazette, make such provisions not inconsistent with the provisions of this Act, as appear to it to be necessary or expedient for removing the difficulty: Provided that no such order shall be made after the expiry of a period of three years from the date on which this Act receives the assent of the President.

56. (*1*) The Central Government may, by notification in the Official Gazette, make rules for carrying out the purposes of this Act.
(*2*) In particular, and without prejudice to the generality of the foregoing power, such rules may provide for all or any of the following matters, namely:-
(*a*) the salary and allowances payable to, and other terms and conditions of service of, the Chairperson and the Directors under sub-section (*3*) of section 6, and the salary and allowances payable to and other terms and conditions of service of officers and other employees of the National Authority under sub-section (*4*) of that section;
(*b*) other functions of the National Authority that may be prescribed under clause (v) of sub-section (*2*) of section 7;
(*c*) the form of application, the particulars to be contained in the application form, the form of certificate of registration, the manner of making application, the amount of fee payable, the procedure to be followed in granting or cancelling certificate of registration under sub-section(*3*) of section 18 and the period for which a renewed certificate of registration may be issued and the amount of fee payable therefor under sub-section (*5*) of that section;
(*d*) the time within which appeal may be preferred under sub-section (*1*) of section 50;
(*e*) the form for making appeal and the fee to be accompanied therewith under sub-section (*3*) of section 50;
(*f*) the procedure for disposing of appeal under sub-section (*4*) of section 50;
(*g*) any other matter which is to be, or may be prescribed.
(*3*) Every notification issued under sub-section (*2*) of section 3, any declaration made under section 5, every order made under section 55 and every rule made under section 56 shall be laid, as soon as may be after it is issued or made, before each House of Parliament, while it is in session, for a total period of thirty days which may be comprised in one session or in two or more successive sessions, and if, before the expiry of the session immediately following the session or the successive sessions aforesaid, both Houses agree in making any modification in the notification, order or rule or both Houses agree that the notification, order or rule should not be issued or made, the notification, order or rule shall thereafter have effect only in such modified form or be of no effect, as the case may be; so, however, that any such modification or annulment shall be without prejudice to the validity of anything previously done under that notification, order or rule.

5.3 AMNESTIES, TRUTH AND RECONCILIATION COMMISSIONS

☛ Uganda: The Amnesty Act 2000 17 Jauary 2000

An Act to provide for an Amnesty for Ugandans involved in acts of a war-like nature in various parts of the country and for other connected purposes.
Whereas it is common knowledge that hostilities directed at the Government of Uganda continue to persist in some parts of the country, thereby causing unnecessary suffering to the people of those areas;
And Whereas it is the expressed desire of the people of Uganda to end armed hostilities, reconcile with those who have caused suffering and rebuild their communities;
And Whereas it is the desire and determination of the Government to genuinely implement its policy of reconciliation in order to establish peace, security and tranquillity throughout the whole country:

Now Therefore, be it enacted by Parliament as follows –

Part I – Preliminary

1. This Act may be cited as the Amnesty Act, 2000.

2. In this Act, unless the context otherwise requires –

"Amnesty" means a pardon, forgiveness, exemption or discharge from criminal prosecution or any other form of punishment by the State;

"Commission" means the Amnesty Commission established under Part II of this Act;

"DRT" means the Demobilization and Resettlement Team;

"Minister" means the Minister responsible for internal affairs;

"Reporter" means a person seeking to be granted Amnesty under this Act.

Part II – Declaration of Amnesty, Etc.

3. (1) An Amnesty is declared in respect of any Ugandan who has at any time since the 26th day of January, 1986 engaged in or is engaging in war or armed rebellion against the government of the Republic of Uganda by –

(a) actual participation in combat;

(b) collaborating with the perpetrators of the war or armed rebellion;

(c) committing any other crime in the furtherance of the war or armed rebellion; or

(d) assisting or aiding the conduct or prosecution of the war or armed rebellion.

(2) A person referred to under subsection (1) shall not be prosecuted or subjected to any form of punishment for the participation in the war or rebellion for any crime committed in the cause of the war or armed rebellion.

4. (1) A reporter shall be taken to be granted the amnesty declared under section 3 if the reporter – 1. reports to the nearest Army or Police Unit, a Chief, a member of the Executive Committee of a local government unit, a magistrate or a religious leader within the locality; 2. renounces and abandons involvement in the war or armed rebellion; 3. surrenders at any such place or to any such authority or person any weapons in his or her possession; and 4. is issued with a Certificate of Amnesty as shall be prescribed in regulations to be made by the Minister.

(2) Where a reporter is a person charged with or is under lawful detention in relation to any offence mentioned in section 3 of this Act, the reporter shall also be deemed to be granted the amnesty if the reporter –

(a) declares to a prison officer or to a Judge or Magistrate before whom he or she is being tried that he or she has renounced the activity referred to in Section 3 of this Act; and

(b) declared his or her intention to apply for the amnesty under this Act.

(3) A reporter to whom subsection (2) applies shall not be released from custody until the Director of Public Prosecutions has certified that he or she is satisfied that –

(a) the person falls within the provisions of section 3 of this Act; and

(b) he or she is not charged or detained to be prosecuted for any offence not falling under section 3 of this Act.

(4) Subject to subsection (3), the Director of Public Prosecutions shall investigate the cases of all persons charged with or held in custody for criminal offences and shall take steps to cause to be released all persons involved in such cases who qualify for grant of amnesty under this Act, if those persons renounce all activity mentioned in section 3, in which they have been involved.

(5) Persons to whom section 3 applies and who are living outside Uganda shall be deemed to have been granted the amnesty if –

(a) they renounce all activities described in section 3; and

(b) report to any Ugandan diplomatic mission, consulate or any international organisation which has agreed with the Government of Uganda to receive such persons.

(6) A reporter who has complied with any of the provisions of subsections (1), (2), (3), (4) and (5) applicable to him or her shall be granted a certificate to be specified by regulations as evidence of the grant of the Amnesty.

5. An official or authority specified in section 4 of this Act who receives a reporter under section 4 shall hand over the reporter and weapons, if any, to the Sub-county Chief of the area.

6. The Sub-county Chief on receiving a reporter seeking amnesty, shall hand over that reporter to the Demobilization and Resettlement Team established under section 11.

Part III – Amnesty Commission

7. An Amnesty Commission is hereby established.

8. The Amnesty Commission shall be composed of the following persons appointed by the President with the approval of Parliament –

(a) a Chairperson who shall be a judge of the High Court or a person qualified to be a judge of the High Court; and

(b) six other members who shall be persons of high moral integrity.

9. The Commission shall have the following functions –

(a) to monitor programmes of –

(i) demobilization;

(ii) reintegration; and

(iii) resettlement of reporters;

(b) to co-ordinate a programme of sensitization of the general public on the amnesty law;

(c) to consider and promote appropriate reconciliation mechanisms in the affected areas;

(d) to promote dialogue and reconciliation within the spirit of this Act;

(e) to perform any other function that is associated or connected with the execution of the functions stipulated in this Act.

10. (1) The Commission shall have a Secretary who shall be a public officer appointed by the Commission acting in consultation with the Public Service Commission, upon such terms and conditions as may be determined by the Commission in consultation with the Public Service Commission and specified in his or her instrument of appointment.

(2) The Secretary shall be a person of high moral character and proven integrity, possessing the relevant qualifications and proven ability in the field of public administration.

(3) The Secretary shall perform such functions as may be assigned to him or her by the Commission.

(4) The Secretary may be removed by the Commission only for –

(a) inability to perform the functions of his or her office arising out of physical or mental incapacity;

(b) misbehaviour or misconduct; or

(c) incompetence.

(5) The Commission shall also have such other officers and employees as may be necessary for the discharge of its functions.

(6) The officers and employees referred to in subsection (5) shall be appointed by the Commission acting in consultation with the Public Service Commission, and shall hold office upon such terms and conditions as shall be determined by the Commission in consultation with the Public Service Commission.

11. A Demobilization and Resettlement Team is hereby established.
12. The DRT shall be composed of not more than seven members to be appointed by the President with the approval of the Sectoral Committee on Defence and Internal Security of Parliament.
13. The functions of the DRT shall be to draw programmes for –
    (a) de-commissioning of arms;
    (b) demobilization;
    (c) re-settlement; and
    (d) reintegration of reporters.
14. (1) Subject to this Act, the DRT shall carry out its functions in accordance with Regulations made by the Minister.
    (2) The DRT shall, in its day to day functions, be under the direct supervision of the Commission.
15. The Minister in consultation with the Minister responsible for finance shall determine the salaries and emoluments of the members of the Commission and the DRT which shall be charged on the Consolidated Fund.
16. All monies required to defray all expenses that may be incurred in the discharge of the functions of the Commission or the DRT in the carrying out of the purposes of this Act are charged on the Consolidated Fund.

Part IV – General

17. This Act will remain in force for a period not exceeding six months and on expiry, the Minister may be statutory instrument extend that period.
18. The Minister may make regulations for the settlement of persons under this Act and generally for the better carrying out of the provisions and principles of this Act.

6.315 EAST TIMOR'S SPECIAL PANELS FOR SERIOUS CRIMES

☛ ***Prosecutor* v. *Joni Marques, Manuel da Costa, João da Costa, Paulo da Costa, Amélio da Costa, Hilário da Silva, Gonsala dos Santos, Alarico Fernandes, Mautersa Monis and Gilberto Fernandes (Los Palos)*, 11 December 2001**

Case No. 09/2000
Date: 11 December 2001
Original: English and Bahasa Indonesia

In the Trial Chamber

Before: Judge Marcelo Dolzany da Costa, Presiding
Judge Sylver Ntukamazina

Judge Maria Natércia Gusmão Pereira
Registrar: Mr. João Nauro

Judgment

...

V. Applicable Law

634. The applicable law for the offences alleged to have been committed by the Defendants are provided for in Sect. 5.1. of UR-2000/15.[2] The acts foreseen in that provision of law are deemed as crimes against humanity insofar as they are committed as part of a widespread or systematic attack and directed against any civilian population, with knowledge of the attack. The parties agreed on the applicable law. As specified by the parties, Sect. 5 of UR-2000/15 embodies the words which are contained in Art. 7 of the Finalized Draft Text of the Elements of Crimes, issued by the Preparatory Commission for the International Criminal Court.
635. In accordance with this view and pursuant to many precedents from the International Tribunals, the contents of the context element are:
636. The requirement of a widespread attack: an attack as the multiple commission of acts with the requirement of inhumane acts 54 as provided in Sect. 5 of UR-2000/15; or
637. The requirement of a systematic attack: an attack "carried out pursuant to a preconceived policy or plan"55
638. The concept of "any population" as the victims implies a multiplicity of civilians attacked in a widespread or a systematic approach. Those hostilities may entail as victims both the members of a resistance movement and/or former combatants, regardless of whether they were in uniform or not, as well as those who were no longer involved in the fighting at the time the crimes were perpetrated 56.
639. In conjunction with the aforementioned context element, a crime against humanity is bound to a policy context, which requires that a widespread or systematic attack results from a state or *de facto* power by means of the policy of that entity. It is required that a State or organization which exercises the highest *de facto* authority in a given territory at the relevant time control all the other holders of power and all individuals 57.
640. About the individual act and the context element (widespread or systematic attack), it has already been stated that "it is sufficient to know how the act took place in the context of an accumulation of acts of violence which, individually, may vary greatly in nature and gravity" 58. The perpetrator needs to have knowledge of the attack.
641. The mental element required *(mens re*a) is that the perpetrator, or aider, or abettor or contributor knowingly took the risk of participating in the implementation of that context 59. The perpetrator *knowingly* performed his acts in the context of a widespread or systematic attack 60. The perpetrator needs only to be aware of the risk of the existence of an attack and the risk of the existence of some circumstances of the attack, regardless of his or her knowledge about the details.
642. His or her knowledge about the policy behind the attack must exist in the perpetrator's

---

2. UNTAET Regulation No. 15/2000.

mind, at least taking the risk that he may be performing his conduct in the context of a policy upheld by a State or organization 61. The individual inhumane acts as defined in Section 5.1 of UR-2000/15 Section 5.1.a: murder as crime against humanity

643. The Panel, having assessed the shortcomings in the definition of murder as a crime against the humanity in Sect. 5.1(a) of UR-2000/15, is persuaded of the benefit of the guidance provided by the Preparatory Committee for the Rome Statute of the International Court 62 and the precedents from the International Tribunals 63, with the remarks foreseen in Sect. 18 of UR-2000/15.

54 ICTY: Prosecutor v. Blaskic, Judgement, ICTY Case n. IT-95-14-T, TCh. I (, 3 Mar. 2000, paragraph 202).

55 ICTR: The Prosecutor v. Bagilishema, Judgement, Case n. ICTR-95-1A-T, T. Ch.I, 7 June 2001, paragraph 77.

56 ICTY: Blaskic Trial Judgment, supra, paragraph 214.

57 ICTY: Tadic Trial Judgment, Case IT-94-I, 27 Feb. 2001, para. 655. ICTR: Kayishema Trial Judgment, Case 95-1-T, Ch. I, para. 126; Kupreskic Trial Judgement, Case IT-95-16, TCh. II, 14 Jan. 2000, para. 551-552, Blaskic Trial Judgment, supra, para. 205; Bagilishema Trial Judgment, supra, para. 78.

58 ICTY: Kunarac Trial Judgment, Case IT-96-23 and IT-96-23/1, T.Ch II, 22 Feb. 2001, para. 419.

59 ICTY: Blaskic Trial Judgment, supra, para. 251.

60 ICTY: Kordic Trial Judgment, IT-95-14/2, TCh. III, 26 Feb. 2001, para. 185-187.

61 ICTY: Kupreskic Trial Judgment, supra, para. 556.

62 Under (Sect. 7.1.a) of ICC Statute under the explanation by the Preparatory Commission, these are the elements of murder as a crime against humanity: (a) the perpetrator killed one or more persons; (b) the conduct was committed as part of a widespread or.Case 9-PID.C.G/ 2000 206 11 December 2001

644. The Panel accepts the opinion of the parties in relation to the general *mens rea* provided by Sect. 18 of UR-2000/15. For this reason, an accused charged with murder as a crime against humanity shall have his or her *mens rea* deemed by this Panel insofar as he or she has shown intent to cause the death of the victim or be aware that it will occur in the ordinary course of events. Accordingly, the Panel lists the four requisite elements of murder as a crime against humanity:

645. The victim is dead.

646. The death of the victim is the result of the perpetrator's act.

647. The act must be a substantial cause of the death of the victim.

648. At the time of the killing, the accused must have meant to cause the death of the victim or was aware that it would occur in the ordinary course of events.

649. In summary, in a murder, as a crime against humanity, there is no requirement of premeditation as the mental element for murder as a crime pursuant to Sect. 340 of Penal Code of Indonesia (KUHP). The *mens rea* is restricted to the deliberate intent to cause the death of the victim or that such result would occur in the ordinary course of events. Section 5.1.d: deportation or forcible transfer of population

650. The Panel reiterates the shortcomings in UR-2000/15 about the definition of the requisite elements for the crime of deportation or forcible transfer. Accordingly, the Panel accepts the rules of the draft of the ICC Statute, which are substantially grounded on the Additional Protocol to the Geneva Conventions of 12 August 1949, and Relating to the Protection of Victims of Non-International Armed Conflicts), as follows:

651. The perpetrator deported or forcibly transferred, without grounds permitted under international law, one or more persons to another State or location, by expulsion or other coercive acts.
652. Such person or persons were lawfully present in the area from which they were so deported or transferred.
653. The perpetrator was aware of the factual circumstances that established the lawfulness of such presence.
654. The conduct was committed as part of a widespread or systematic attack directed against a civilian population.
655. The perpetrator knew that the conduct was part of or intended the conduct to be part of a widespread or systematic attack directed against a civilian population.
Section 5.1.f: torture
656. The Panel is satisfied with the definition of torture as a crime against humanity provided by Sect. 5.2 (d) of UR-2000/15, which is the same as Art. 7.2.e of the ICC Statute. These are the elements:
657. The perpetrator inflicted severe physical or mental pain or suffering upon one or more persons.
658. Such person or persons were in the custody or under the control of the perpetrator.
659. Such pain or suffering did not arise only from, and was not inherent in or incidental to, lawful sanctions.
660. The conduct was committed as part of a widespread or systematic attack directed against a civilian population.
661. The perpetrator knew that the conduct was part of or intended the conduct to be part of a widespread or systematic attack directed against a civilian population.
Section 5.1.h: persecution
662. Lastly, the Panel is also satisfied with the definition of persecution as a crime against humanity provided by Sect. 5.1. (h) and 5.2(f) of UR-2000/15, which is the same as Art. 7.1(e) and (2) (g) of the ICC Statute. These are the elements: systematic attack directed against a civilian population; (c) the perpetrator knew that the conduct was part of or intended the conduct to be part of a widespread or systematic attack against a civilian population.
63 ICTR, in the Rutaganda Trial Judgement *(Case ICTR-96-3-T, T.Ch. I, 6 Dec. 1999, para. 80)*, *inter alia*, established the following elements: (a) the victim is dead; (b) the death resulted from an unlawful act or omission of the accused or a subordinate; (c) at the time of the killing the accused or a subordinate had the intention to kill or inflict grievous bodily harm on the deceased having known that such bodily harm is likely to cause the victim's death, and is reckless whether death ensues or not. Case 9-PID.C.G/2000 207 11 December 2001.
663. The perpetrator severely deprived, contrary to international law, one or more persons of fundamental rights.
664. The perpetrator targeted such person or persons by reason of identity of a group or collectivity or targeted the group or collectivity as such.
665. Such targeting was based on political, racial, national, ethnic, cultural, religious, gender (as defined in article 7, paragraph 3, of the Statute), or other grounds that are universally recognized as impermissible under international law.
666. The conduct was committed in connection with any act referred to in article 7, paragraph 1, of the Statute or any crime within the jurisdiction of the Court.

667. The conduct was committed as part of a widespread or systematic attack directed against a civilian population.
668. The perpetrator knew that the conduct was part of or intended the conduct to be part of a widespread or systematic attack directed against a civilian population.
669. Furthermore, the mental element of a discriminatory intent, which is assessed as that the reason for singling out the victim, has to be grounded on a particular characteristic of the identity of the group or collectivity. Case 9-PID.C.G/2000 208 11 December 2001

6.316 KOSOVO'S INTERNATIONALISED COURTS

☛ Federal Republic of Yugoslavia (Kosovo): *Prosecutor* v. *Momcilo Trajković*, District Court of Gjilan, 6 March 2001

District Court of Gjilan
P Nr 68/2000
06.03.2001

In the Name of the People

The District Court of Gjilan, as a court of first instance, composed of Patrice de Charette, presiding judge, Hasan Sadiku, judge, and Halit Gashi, Elfete Shala and Tefik Muji, lay judges, assisted with minute taker Igballe Azemi, in a penal case against the accused Momcilo TRAJKOVIĆ, of father Lazar and mother Lubica born Zhivkovic, born on 03.05.1947 in the village of Carakove, permanent resident of Kamenica, M. Pijade street, Serb, married , father of three children, with a University degree, completed regular military service, of medium economic status, no criminal record, in custody since 07.09.1999

For criminal acts of:
— war crimes against civilian population from 24.03.1999 until the day of the entry of the International Forces in Kosovo, under Article 142 of Criminal Law of Yugoslavia, according to the indictment of the Public Prosecutor of Gjilan No 115/2000 of 21.09.2000
— attempted murder on 27 June 1999 in Kamenica, under Article 30 par. 1 in connection with Article 19 of Criminal Law of Yugoslavia and illegal possession of weapons and explosive material in Kamenica until 7 September 1999, under Article 199 par. 3 in relation with par. 1 of Criminal Law of Kosovo, according to the indictment of the Public Prosecutor of Gjilan No 84/2000 of 3 April 2000,

After the main hearing was held in public on 23, 24, 27, 30 November, 01, 04, 05, 06, 07, 08 December 2000, 09, 10, 15, 26 January, 08, 13, February and 01 March 2001 in the presence of the parties, the Deputy Public Prosecutor of Gjilan Vaxhid Idrizi, the accused and his attorneys Zhivojin Jokanovic and Stoja Gjurishic
And the aggrieved parties:
— Mehmet Ramnabaja, M. Nicolic street no 57, Kamenica
— Ibrahim Berisha, M. Nicolic street no 36, Kamenica
— Avdullah Berisha, Z. Hajdini no 40, Kamenica
— Hadjar Ramnabaja, Malesia str, Kamenica

— Xhemail Limani, A. Presheva str no 65, Kamenica
— Taibe Isufi, Kamenica
— Fatmire Kastrati, " 29 Nentori " str, Kamenica
— Rexhep Mehmeti, Blendit str no 33, Pristina
— Bahtije Sinani, Village Leshtar, Kamenica
— Avdyl Demolli, Village Krileve, Kamenica
— Eqir Demolli, Village Krileve, Kamenica
— Latif Latifi, Village Petrovc, Kamenica
— Arif Krasniqi, Malesia str no 74, Kamenica
— Fetije Thaqi, Village Karaqeve e Ullet, Kamenica
— Ferije Sabedinaj, Ulpiana P-4/1, Pristina
— Selatin Ismajli, Village Matiqan, Pristina
— Bejtije Kryeziu, Village Ragacice, Kamenica
— Musa Keka, Village Karaqeve Ulet, Kamenica
— Sabri Dermaku, Village Shipashnice e Eperme, Kamenica
— Harje Shurdani, Village Policke, Kamenica
— Shefki Berisha, Vilage Honodeve, Kamenica
— Halime Haxhiu, Village Koretin, Kamenica
— Sinan Selishta, 7 Korriku no 7, Kamenica
— Xhavit Ramadani, Village Koretin, Kamenica
— Raif Ramadani, Village Koretin, Kamenica
— Mevlud Fazliu, M Nikolic str no 49, Kamenica
— Gezim Limoni, A. Presheva str no 65, Kamenica

On the hearing held on 06 March 2001 publicly announced this

Verdict

The accused Momcilo Trajkovic

I

Is Guilty

Of attempted murder on 27 June 1999 in Kamenica, according to the indictment of 3 April 2000, under Article 30 par. 1 in connection with Article 19 of the Criminal Law of Yugoslavia.

Reasons:

The facticity of the act is established on the basis of the injuries suffered by Mevlud Fazliu who received a treatment in the Medical Center in Gjilan and produced the medical certificate.
The statement of the latter and of his friend Arif Pireva describe precisely what happened when they were shot by the accused from his apartment with an automatic rifle, after they hoisted an Albanian flag on the former building of Internal Affairs.
These statements were checked during the reconstruction on the spot which proved that it

was possible to shoot from the window of the Trajkovic's apartment towards the victims located close to the fence of the yard, trying to flee after having heard the accused screaming.
They are confirmed by the witness Xhevdet Krasniqi, neighbour of the accused who stated that, standing on his balcony, on the floor under the apartment of the accused, he heard Momcilo Trajkovic shouting in a loud voice in Serbian language: "I can't imagine how it's possible that someone can put up an Albanian flag in the middle of the day", then heard him shooting several times.
In face of this evidence, the testimony produced by the defense about the presence of the accused in another place at the time of the incident cannot be considered as reliable.
Thus, Momcilo Trajkovic is declared guilty of this crime, with the correction that the shots came from the window above the street and not from the balcony.

II

Is Guilty

Of illegal possession of weapons and explosive material in Kamenica until 7 September 1999, according to the indictment of 3 April 2000, under Article 199 par. 3 in relation with par. 1 of Criminal Law of Kosovo

Reasons:

One AK 47 rifle, 300 bullets and two hand grenades were discovered in the apartment of the accused by KFOR soldiers on 7 September 1999 during a search. The explanations of Momcilo Trajkovic, stating he found them just prior to that in another apartment that was broken into are illogical and not convincing, since it's clear that an unknown person having broken the door would have taken these weapons and ammunition.
Besides, according to the witness Bryan Hunlock, US-KFOR soldier, the accused gave a false statement before the search, telling that he didn't have any weapon in his flat, but at the beginning of the search, suddenly said that he had something to give to the soldiers.
Thus, there is enough evidence that the accused committed this offence.

III

Is Acquitted

According to Article 350 par. 3 of Criminal Procedure Law of Yugoslavia,
For the following crimes, qualified war crimes under Article 142 of Criminal Law of Yugoslavia according to the indictment of 21 September 2000
— on 1 April 1999, in Kamenica, injuries of Raif Ramabaja with firearms. Reason: Raif Ramabaja stated before the investigating judge and during the trial that he was not wounded
— on 3 April 1999, in Kamenica, injuries of Ibrahim Berisha and Abdullah Berisha, with a hand grenade thrown in their backyard. Reason: the victims didn't see the perpetrators of the crime. There is no proof it was an organized act
— on 17 April 1999, in Kamenica, injuries with firearms of Gezil Limani and Vlera Shabani. Reason: there is no proof they were wounded.

— on 1 May 1999 at the place named Qafa and Kopernices, murder of Emin Jerliu and Ramadan Sijarina. Reason: the exact circumstances of the death of Ramadan Sijarina, disappeared on the road are unknown and there were no witnesses. There are no information on the death of Emin Jerliu.
— on 11 May 1999 in the village Hodonovc, injuries of Shefki Berisha and Hajrije Shurdani while the were traveling in their vehicle. Reasons: there is no proof it was an organized act.
— on 20 May in the village Koretin, injuries of Sinan Selishta, Halime Hazliu and Xhavit Ramadani. Reason: there is no proof it was an organized act.

And for these general reasons:
— Article 35 of the Law on Internal Affairs (Official Gazette of Kosovo 46/1987 foresees that the Head of Internal Affairs is in charge of administrative matters
— but:
= 1) the Federal Republic of Yugoslavia's Constitution (Article 78 par 3 and Art 99 par 1) and the Republic of Serbia's Constitution (Article 83 par 1) provide for the possibility of derogations of the ordinary provisions concerning the work and organization of State agencies and Ministries after the proclamation of state of war
= 2) the Law on Defense of the Federal Republic of Yugoslavia (Official Gazette 27 May 1994), Articles 15 and 17, allows the use of units and bodies of Ministry of Internal Affairs in combat tasks, fighting or conducting armed resistance particularly in case of declaration of state of war
= 3) the state of war was declared by the Yugoslavian government on 24 March 1999
= 4) a Decree on the powers of the Internal Affairs during the state of war (Official Gazette of Republic of Serbia, 7 April 1999), Article 8, allowed the Minister of Interior to relocate any employee if the interests of the service require
= 5) the ordinary Law on Internal Affairs, Article 38, foresees a specific Act on War Organization and Systematization of the Working Positions establishing that during the state of war, units and positions can merge and group together creating a new list of duties and allocation plan.

Therefore, it's obvious that the competences of Momcilo Trajkovic were not limited to administrative matters during the time of the war. The precise competences of the accused were perfectly known by the people of the Kamenica area. It's remarkable to notice that, when they wanted to get news of their relatives disappeared, they came directly to Momcilo Trajkovic, to his office and sometimes to his private house, and not to the Head of Police (in particular, Hazir Thaqi about the disappearance of Asslan Thaqi, Naime Keka and the brothers of Ramadan Kastrati about the disappearance of the latter, Zenan Jerliu about the disappearance of his brother Emin Jerliu, according to the testimony of Haqif Jerliu).
Besides, according to several testimonies, the accused acted personally in preparation or execution of some crimes.
Thus, Ramadan Morina, examined on 10.07.2000 by the investigating judge and on 08.12.2000 by the Court, stated that on 23 March 1999, several policemen from Kamenica came to his house to take his buses and his car "Mercedes", which was taken by Momcilo Trajkovic himself. He added that, on 27 April 1999 at the Police Station of Kamenica, he was interrogated and punched by the accused who told him in Serbian language: "Serbs will fight until the last Albanian will die".
The witness Taip Mala, heard by the Court on 09.01.2001, stated that he saw Momcilo

Trajkovic on 09 May 1999 on the road close to Bujanovc, in a black car "Golf", talking in Serbian language with policemen Ahmet Ameti and Krana about preparation of a planed action. He added that, after 11 May, when several villages were surrounded, he found a list with names of several persons to be killed. In this list were in particular the names of Ramadan Latifaj and Mehmet Sabedinaj, who had been killed on that day.
These different elements constitute the proof that Momcilo Trajkovic is personally responsible of the criminal acts committed in the Kamenica area against civilian population, but only for organized actions and not for isolated ones.

IV

Is Guilty

Of the following crimes, qualified war crimes under Article 142 of Criminal Law of Yugoslavia according to the indictment of 21 September 2000:
— on 1 April 1999, in Kamenica, injuries with firearms of Mehmet Ramabaja. Reason: the victim identified the shooter, Dragan, who declared that he did it acting upon the order of Momcilo Trajkovic.
— on 11 April 1999 in Kamenica, arson of a house and a bus of Hajdar Ramabaja.
Reason: few hours before, with other policemen, Momcilo Trajkovic came to the driving school of the later and threatened to put on fire the house and the bus if they didn't get the keys.
— on 17 April in Kamenica, injuries with firearms of Xhemail Limani. Reason: one of the shooter, named Streqka, from the police station of Kamenice, was recognized by the witnesses
— on 17 April 1999 in village Krileve, kidnapping and maltreatment of Haqif Demolli.
Reason: the victim identified two policemen from Kamenica, Vlado Trajkovic and Nenad Trajkovic
— on 18 April 1999, creation of panic and terror and eviction of civilian population in villages of Strezovc, Leshtar, Rahovice, Krileve, and murder of Ahmet Mehmeti, Arsim Isufi, Shemsi Isufi and Ramadan Kastrati. Reason: it was a planned and organized action, committed by a number of forces, especially police forces
— on 18 April 1999 in village Krileve, injuries with firearms of Zeqir Demolli, Avdyl Demolli and Bahtije Sinani. Reason: the action was undertaken on the same day, particularly by police forces.
— on 19 April 1999, in Petrovc, eviction by force of civilian population, arson of houses and disappearance (and not murder, as indicated in the indictment) of Murtez Sherifi and Fadil Sherifi.
Reason: it was a planed action, undertaken by police forces.
— on 4 May 1999 in Kamenice, injuries of Arif Kraniqi. Reason: this action was undertaken by policemen from Kamenica, especially by five identified by the victim.
— on 11 May 1999, surrounding of Hoghost, Kopernice, Shispanice, Kranidell, Upper Karaqeve, Lower Karaqeve, Rogocice, Hodonovc, Topanice and Koretin villages, with lists of names already compiled, murder of Ramadan Latifaj, Mehmet Sabedinaj, Ismail Ismajli, Nevzat Kryeziu, Asslan Thaqi. Reason: it was a planed and organized action, undertaken in particular by police forces, with lists of names prepared in advance.

— on 17 May 1999, in village Topanice and in Kamenice, kidnapping, maltreatments and torture of Rexhep Morina. Reason: these acts were committed by policemen from Kamenica, inside the police station.

And for the general reasons mentioned above.

These crimes will be qualified *crimes against humanity.*

Reasons:

War crimes against civilian population:

This crime, envisaged in Article 142 of the Criminal Law of Yugoslavia, concerns attacks against civilian populations during the war or armed conflict resulting in death, grievous bodily harms or inhuman treatment or displacement of populations.

This qualification doesn't include an essential element, characteristic of the treatment inflicted to Kosovo: the existence of widespread or systematic attack against civilian population. This circumstance is one of the components of the crime against humanity defined by international laws.

Then, it is necessary to seek if Article 142 allows to retain against the accused the elements of this crime.

Crime against humanity:

The crimes against humanity are explicitly mentioned in Article 37 dealing with crimes punishable by death. Article 37 par. 4 quotes among these crimes the "criminal acts against humanity and international law".

On the other hand, Article 142 is located in a Chapter 16, named "Criminal acts against humanity and international law".

Besides, Article 142 refers expressly to "violation of the rules of the international law ". The international law doesn't include only international texts in the applicable codes or international treaties regularly signed by the State concerned. It must also be taken firstly as *general principles of international law* recognized by all the nations.

This principle was expressed in the " Martens clause " stated in the Preamble to Convention II of the Hague of 1899: " Until a more complete code of the laws of the war is issued, the High Contracting Parties think that it is right to declare that, in case not included in the Regulations adopted by them, populations and the belligerents remain under the protection and the empire of the principles of international law, such as they result from the usages established between civilized nations, from the laws of humanity and the requirements of the public conscience".

Each of the 1949 Geneva Conventions on protection of civilians during the war draws upon the text of the Martens Clause: I (article 63), II (article 62), III (article 142), IV (article 158). This reference appears also in article 1 of the additional Protocol I of 1977 and in the preamble to the additional Protocol II.

The international law includes as well the *Customary International Law.* Article 38 of the Statute of the International Court of Justice, established in the Hague for the settlement of litigations involving States, defines these rules as follows: " International custom as evidence of a general practices accepted as law". According to the Customary International Law, it is possible to refer in particular to the rules included in the *statute* of the International Courts, as well as with the *jurisprudence* of these courts.

The London Agreement of 8 August 1945 (article 6 c) foresees the existence of crime against humanity, as well as article 10 of the Control Council Law and the statute the International Military Tribunal of Nuremberg. The statute of the Tokyo International Tribunal (article 5 c) also envisages the existence of this crime.

Article 5 of the Statute of the International Criminal Tribunal for the former Yugoslavia (ICTY) includes a precise definition of the crime against humanity, taken up in article 7 of the Statute of the future International Criminal Court created by the Treaty of Rome on 17 July 1998: constitutes a crime against humanity one of the acts taken again essentially by article 142 of Criminal Law of Yugoslavia, when it is committed within a " widespread or systematic attack against any civilian population, with knowledge of the attack".
In the Tadic decision, ICTY worked out the conditions required for the existence of the crime against humanity by analyzing in a precise way particularly the concepts of war or armed conflict and civilian population, by deciding that a discriminatory intent was required only for racial persecution crimes and by estimating that, insofar as the other conditions were in addition met, an act carried out for purely personal motives could constitute a crime against humanity (ICTY Appeal Chamber, Tadic, 15 July 1999, IT-94-1-T).
According to Article 16 of the Federal Republic of Yugoslavia Constitution, these "generally accepted rules of international law shall be a constituent part of the internal legal order".
As a result of the whole of these elements, it is appropriate to decide that the reference in article 142 of the Criminal Law of Yugoslavia to the violation of the rules of the international law makes it possible to charge the author of the acts aimed by this text with crimes against humanity, when theses acts were committed within a widespread or systematic plan of attack against the civilian population.
According to the facts pointed out previously, there are sufficient evidences that Momcilo Trajkovic committed the acts that he is charged with, in time of war (characterized by going in the conflict of the international NATO armed forces), against the civilian population and within a concerted plan aiming systematic atrocities of which he had a complete knowledge.
As a result, it is necessary to declare the accused guilty of crimes against humanity, on the grounds of Article 142 of Criminal Law of Yugoslavia.

V

Sentence

Determination of the sentence for crimes against humanity
It is necessary to apply the 1990 amended article 142.
Indeed, the Regulation 1999/24 states that the applicable laws in Kosovo are those in force on 22 March 1999, but adds that post 1989 laws apply if they address a subject matter that is not already covered (Section 1.2) or if they contain provisions more favorable to a criminal defendant (Section 1.4).

The 1990 amended article foresees 20 years imprisonment as a maximum sentence. It is thus more favorable to the defendant than the previous version of the same text, which contained the death penalty. Anyway, after the abolition of the death penalty by the Regulation 1999/24, the maximum penalty applicable in Kosovo to authors of crimes previously punished by death is now twenty years of prison.
Indeed, when a supreme penalty is abolished without being replaced, it's necessary to refer to the penalty immediately underneath when it was applicable. In this regard, Article 38 par. 2 of Criminal Law of Yugoslavia stipulated that the court might impose a punishment for 20 years or imprisonment for a criminal act eligible for the death penalty.

This Article was not expressly repealed by the Regulation 1999/24 and cannot be considered as included in the general abolition of death penalty by this Regulation.
Indeed, Article 38 par. 3, which is without connection with death penalty, is still in force. As an exception to Article 38 par. 1, which foresees a general maximum of fifteen years of prison, this text allows to impose a punishment of twenty years of imprisonment for the offences punished with a term of fifteen years, if they were committed with intent and particular aggravating circumstances or caused grave consequences, when it is provided by the Law.
Then, such a twenty years penalty can be imposed for grave case of plunder (Art. 141.2 KCL), special grave acts against general security (Art. 164-3 KCL), counterfeiting money of falsifying representative of values with consequent upset in the national economy (Art. 168-3 and 169-2 YCL), grave case of robbery in office (Art. 177-2 YCL), grave case of hijack of aircraft (Art. 240 YCL) or jeopardizing the safety of an aircraft's flight (Art. 241-2 YCC).
Therefore, the thesis of the abrogation of Art. 38-2 would create a paradoxical situation of an inversion of the hierarchy of penalties, since a less severe maximum punishment (15 years) could be imposed for the most serious offences.
Then, it is established that 20 years of prison are now the penalty incurred by the authors of crimes previously punishable by death.
It follows that the sentence incurred by the accused is 20 years imprisonment. The extreme gravity of the committed acts, in the circumstances detailed previously, justifies to sentence Momcilo Trajkovic to the maximum of this penalty.
Determination of the sentence for the other offences
For the other offences, the Court defines:
— for illegal possession of weapons and explosive materials, 4 months of prison
— for attempted murder, 3 years of prison

Global sentence
According to Article 42 of Criminal Law of Yugoslavia, when a sentence of 20 years of prison is defined for one type of crimes, only this sentence is pronounced.
Thus the Court sentences Momcilo Trajkovic to 20 years of imprisonment.
This time includes the pre trial detention, from 7 September 1999.
The detention of the accused shall continue until the omnipotence of this decision, according to a separate decision based on article 353 par. 1 and 6 of Criminal Procedure Law of Yugoslavia.
The Court decides on the confiscation of the AK 47 rifle, the 300 bullets and the two hand grenades, according to article 69 of Criminal Law of Yugoslavia.
The costs of the criminal proceedings will be paid by the accused.
The injured parties can present their compensatory claim in a new trial before the competent civil Court.
From what was said above, it was decided as in the enacting clause of this decision act.

District Court of Gjilan
ON 06.03.2001

6.32 NATIONAL COURTS

☛ France: *Gaddafi* case, 13 March 2001

N° Z 00-87.215 FS-P + F N° 1414

DF
March 13, 2001

M. Cottee Chief Judge,

Republic of France

In the Name of the French People

At a public hearing held in the Paris municipal court building *(Palais de justice à Paris)*, the Court of Cassation, Criminal Division, rendered the following judgment:

Ruling in the appeal by:
— The District Attorney – Paris Court of Appeals
of the judgment by the Indictment Division of that Court of Appeals handed down on October 20, 2000 which affirmed the investigating magistrate's order ruling that there were grounds to investigate the complaint filed by S.O.S. Attentats, an association, and Béatrice Boëry, against Muammar Gaddafi, for aiding and abetting in the destruction of property by an explosive substance which caused the death of another, in connection with a terrorist enterprise,

This Court, ruling following oral argument in open court on February 27, 2001, at which the following individuals were present: Mr. Cotte, Chief Judge, Mrs. Chanet, Reporting Judge, Mr. Joly, Mr. Le Gall, Mr. Farge, Mrs. Anzani, Mr. Pelletier, Mrs. Mazars, Mr. Palisse, Mr. Arnould, Mrs. Koering-Joulin, and Mr. Corneloup, Divisional Judges, Mr. Desportes, Mrs. Karsenty, Mr. Sassoust and Mrs. Caron, Auxiliary Judges,

District Attorney: Mr. Launay,

Divisional Clerk: Mrs. Nicolas,

On the report by Judge Chanet, the comments filed by Me. Bouthors and Piwnica et Molinié, a professional partnership of attorneys admitted to practice before the Court of Cassation, and the brief filed by District Attorney Launay,

In view of the order made by the Chief Judge of the Criminal Division on November 22, 2000, ordering immediate review of the appeal,

In view of the briefs submitted by appellants and respondents,

On the sole ground of appeal, based on a violation of the customary international criminal law on the jurisdictional immunity of foreign heads of state,

In view of the basic principles of international law,

Whereas, absent contrary provisions binding on the parties concerned, international custom holds that incumbent heads of state are not subject to prosecution in the criminal courts of a foreign state.

Whereas, S.O.S. Attentats, an association, and Béatrice Boëry filed a summons and complaint seeking civil damages for the offence of aiding and abetting in the destruction of property by an explosive substance that resulted in the death of another, in connection with a terrorist enterprise, from Muammar Gaddafi, the incumbent head of state of the Libyan Arab Jamahiriya, whom they accuse of being implicated in the attack on September 19, 1989 on a UTA DC 10 which, when it blew up over Niger, caused the death of 170 persons, many of whom were French citizens.

Whereas, in affirming the order by the investigating magistrate, who held that there were grounds to investigate, notwithstanding the district attorney's arguments to the contrary, the court of appeals held that although the international community, including France, had always recognized the immunity of foreign heads of state, the act of aiding and abetting in the destruction of property by an explosive substance resulting in the death of another, in connection with a terrorist enterprise, was not covered by immunity.

However, in so ruling, despite the fact that, regardless of how serious it is, under international law the offense charged is not one of the exceptions to the rule that incumbent foreign heads of state are immune from jurisdiction, the Indictment Division disregarded the above-mentioned rule.

It follows that the judgment must be vacated. It will be vacated without a remand, as the Court of Cassation is able to apply the applicable rule of law and thereby put an end to the dispute as permitted by article L. 131-5 of the Code of Judicial Organization.

Wherefore,

[This Court] hereby vacates and reverses the judgment of the Paris Court of Appeals, Indictment Division dated October 20, 2000, in its entirety,

Decrees that there are no grounds to conduct an investigation,

Decrees that there are no grounds for a remand,

Orders that this judgment be printed and entered in the records of the Clerk of the Investigating Division of the Paris Court of Appeals and that it be referenced either as a marginal notation to the judgment, or appended to the reversed judgment.

So done and adjudicated by the Court of Cassation, Criminal Division, as pronounced by the

Chief Judge on the thirteenth day of March, in the year two thousand and one.

In witness whereof, this judgment was signed by the Chief Judge, the Reporter and the Divisional Clerk.

☛ The Netherlands: Decision of the Supreme Court on Appeal in cassation in the interests of the law,[3] Supreme Court, 18 September 2001

The Facts: On 20 November 2000 the Court of Appeal of Amsterdam upheld the complaint made by R. Wijngaarde and R.A. Hoost under Article 12 of the Code of Criminal Procedure against the decision not to prosecute Desi Bouterse.[4] The Procurator General at the Supreme Court appealed against this judgment to the Supreme Court in the interests of the law.[5]

Held: '...1. The disputed decision.
1.1. According to the disputed decision, the applicants objected to the refusal of the Public Prosecutor in the District of Amsterdam to prosecute Desiré Delano Bouterse for the offence of 'having given orders to a group of military personnel acting under his control to execute fifteen people, including [victim A] (the brother of [complainant A]) and [victim B] (the nephew of [complainant B]) in Fort Zeelandia in Paramaribo, Surinam, on 8 or 9 December 1982'.
1.2. According to the disputed decision, the purpose of the complaint lodged by the applicants is to ensure that: (a) the criminal courts examine whether Bouterse himself took part in the executions, and (b) Bouterse will be prosecuted for the torture to which the fifteen people concerned were subjected before they were killed.
1.3. The rulings of the Court of Appeal in the disputed decision, in so far as relevant here, are as follows:
"— orders the public prosecutor in the district of Amsterdam to prosecute Desiré Delano Bouterse, born in the District of Surinam, Surinam, on 13 October 1945 for the offences to which the complaints relate and which were committed in Paramaribo, Surinam, on or about 8/9 December 1982;

---

3. Under Art. 95 of the Judiciary (Organisation) Act, the Procurator General of the Supreme Court may 'in the interests of the law' appeal in cassation to the Supreme Court against decrees and decisions of Courts of Appeal, District Courts and Sub-District Courts (known as 'cassation in the interests of the law'). The aim of such appeal is to ensure the uniform application of the law. Such a decision of the Supreme Court does not affect the rights of the parties in the particular case (Art. 98 of the Judiciary (Organisation) Act).

4. The decision is reprinted in 3 *YIHL* (2000) p. 677.

5. The grounds of appeal in cassation and the explanatory notes of acting Advocate General N. Keijzer can also be found on-line in the source referred to in note 1.

— directs the public prosecutor to file an application with the examining magistrate responsible for dealing with criminal cases in the District Court of Amsterdam for the institution of a preliminary judicial examination into the offences concerned."[6]
1.4. The disputed decision is attached to this judgment and forms part of it.

2. Proceedings in cassation
The purpose of the recommendation and the application in cassation by the Procurator General at the Supreme Court in the interests of the law is to have the decision of the Court of Appeal set aside. The recommendation and application are attached to this judgment and form part of it.
The Supreme Court has taken cognizance of the written comments of the applicants' counsel with regard to the recommendation and application, which they were given the opportunity to make at their request. In addition, the Supreme Court has taken cognizance of the written comments of Bouterse's counsel.

3. The legislative context
3.1. The Convention against Torture and Other Cruel, Inhuman or Degrading Treatment or Punishment (Convention of 10 December 1984, Trb. 1985, 69) reads, in so far as relevant, as follows:[7]
"*Article 1*
1. For the purpose of this Convention, the term "torture" means any act by which severe pain or suffering, whether physical or mental, is intentionally inflicted on a person for such purposes as obtaining from him or a third person information or a confession, punishing him for an act he or a third person has committed or is suspected of having committed, or intimidating or coercing him or a third person, or for any reason based on discrimination of any kind, when such pain or suffering is inflicted by or at the instigation of or with the consent or acquiescence of a public official or other person acting in an official capacity. It does not include pain or suffering arising only from, inherent in or incidental to lawful sanctions.
2. This article is without prejudice to any international instrument or national legislation which does or may contain provisions of wider application.
Article 2
1. Each State Party shall take effective legislative, administrative, judicial or other
2. No exceptional circumstances whatsoever, whether a state of war or a threat of war, measures to prevent acts of torture in any territory under its jurisdiction internal political

6. The examining magistrate at the District Court of Amsterdam then granted the application for the institution of a preliminary judicial examination by the Public Prosecution Service on 30 January 2001 (Institute's Collection No. 5026). He adopted the opinion of the Court of Appeal that the claim could be based on the Implementation Act. He rejected the claim in so far as it was based on the Wartime Criminal Law Act. Application was also made to the examining magistrate in Arnhem because the Military Judge of the District Court of Arnhem had jurisdiction in respect of the prosecution of war crimes as defined in the Wartime Criminal Law Act. The examining magistrate too considered that the Wartime Criminal Law Act did not apply. Unlike the examining magistrate in Amsterdam, however, he also rejected the claim that the Implementation Act had retroactive effect. He thus dismissed the application for the institution of a preliminary judicial investigation (decision of 22 December 2000, Institute's Collection No. 5025).

7. The Supreme Court used the Dutch translation.

instability or any other public emergency, may be invoked as a justification of torture.
3. An order from a superior officer or a public authority may not be invoked as a justification of torture.

Article 4

1. Each State Party shall ensure that all acts of torture are offences under its criminal law. The same shall apply to an attempt to commit torture and to an act by any person which constitutes complicity or participation in torture.
2. Each State Party shall make these offences punishable by appropriate penalties which take into account their grave nature.

Article 5

1. Each State Party shall take such measures as may be necessary to establish its jurisdiction over the offences referred to in Article 4 in the following cases:
(a) when the offences are committed in any territory under its jurisdiction or on board a ship or aircraft registered in that State;
(b) when the alleged offender is a national of that State;
(c) when the victim is a national of that State if that State considers it appropriate.
2. Each State Party shall likewise take such measures as may be necessary to establish its jurisdiction over such offences in cases where the alleged offender is present in any territory under its jurisdiction and it does not extradite him pursuant to Article 8 to any of the States mentioned in paragraph 1 of this Article.
3. This Convention does not exclude any criminal jurisdiction exercised in accordance with internal law.

Article 6

1. Upon being satisfied, after an examination of information available to it, that the circumstances so warrant, any State Party in whose territory a person alleged to have committed any offence referred to in Article 4 is present shall take him into custody or take other legal measures to ensure his presence. The custody and other legal measures shall be as provided in the law of that State but may be continued only for such time as is necessary to enable any criminal or extradition proceedings to be instituted.
2. Such State shall immediately make a preliminary inquiry into the facts.
3. Any person in custody pursuant to paragraph 1 of this Article shall be assisted in communicating immediately with the nearest appropriate representative of the State of which he is a national, or, if he is a stateless person, with the representative of the State where he usually resides.
4. When a State, pursuant to this Article, has taken a person into custody, it shall immediately notify the States referred to in Article 5, paragraph 1, of the fact that such person is in custody and of the circumstances which warrant his detention. The State which makes the preliminary inquiry contemplated in paragraph 2 of this Article shall promptly report its findings to the said States and shall indicate whether it intends to exercise jurisdiction.

Article 7

1. The State Party in the territory under whose jurisdiction a person alleged to have committed any offence referred to in Article 4 is found shall, in the cases contemplated in Article 5, if it does not extradite him, submit the case to its competent authorities for the purpose of prosecution.
2. These authorities shall take their decision in the same manner as in the case of any ordinary offence of a serious nature under the law of that State. In the cases referred to in Article 5, paragraph 2, the standards of evidence required for prosecution and conviction

shall in no way be less stringent than those which apply in the cases referred to in Article 5, paragraph 1.
3. Any person regarding whom proceedings are brought in connection with any of the offences referred to in Article 4 shall be guaranteed fair treatment at all stages of the proceedings."
3.2. The Torture Convention Implementation Act (Act of 29 September 1988, Stb. 478, to implement the Convention against Torture and Other Cruel, Inhuman or Degrading Treatment or Punishment) came into force on 20 January 1989.[8] The relevant provisions of this Act read as follows:
"*Article 1*
1. Assault committed by a public official, or by any other person in the employ of the authorities, in the course of his duties on someone who has been deprived of his liberty, with a view to extracting information or a confession from him, punishing him, or intimidating or coercing him or a third person to do or permit something, or an assault committed in contemptuous disregard of his entitlement to human dignity, shall be punished as torture if the conduct is conducive to promoting the intended aim and shall carry a term of imprisonment not exceeding 15 years or a fine of the fifth category.
2. Conduct which deliberately brings about a condition of extreme fear or any other form of serious mental distress shall be treated as equivalent to assault.
3. If the offence results in death, the guilty person shall be liable to a sentence of life imprisonment or to a term of imprisonment not exceeding 20 years or a fine of the fifth category.
Article 2
The following persons shall be liable to the same sentences as those for the offences referred to in the previous article:
(a) a public official or any other person in the employ of the authorities who, by one of the means referred to in Article 47, paragraph 1 (2) of the Criminal Code, incites or deliberately permits the commission by another person of a form of assault referred to in Article 1;
(b) any person who commits the form of assault referred to in Article 1 if such assault has been incited or deliberately permitted by a public official, or any other person in the employ of the authorities, in the course of his duties, by one of the means referred to in Article 47, paragraph 1 (2) of the Criminal Code.
Article 4
The offences made punishable in Articles 1 and 2 are indictable offences.
Article 5
Dutch criminal law is applicable to any person who is guilty of committing outside the Netherlands one of the indictable offences defined in Articles 1 and 2 of this Act."

4. Assessment of the first ground of appeal
4.1. The ground of appeal raises the question of whether Articles 1 and 2 of the Torture Convention Implementation Act can be applied to offences committed before the entry into force of that Act.
4.2. Article 16 of the Constitution (and Article 1, paragraph 1, of the Criminal Code) and Article 94 of the Constitution are relevant to assessment of the point of law raised in this connection.

---

8. See 20 *NYIL* (1989) pp. 274-275.

4.3.1. Article 16 of the Constitution and Article 1, paragraph 1, of the Criminal Code contain an unreserved prohibition on the trial and punishment of a person for an offence that did not constitute an offence under Dutch law at the time it was committed.
4.3.2. In this connection reference may be made to the parliamentary history of Article 16 of the Constitution and in particular to:
(a) the Explanatory Memorandum to the Bill that resulted in the present Article 16 of the Constitution, which provides as follows with regard to Article 1.15 (subsequently renumbered as Article 16), and with regard to the present additional Article IX of the Constitution: "This article, the text of which is the same as Article 11 of the State Committee and Article 9e of Bill 11 051, contains the principle that no act whatever may be made punishable with retroactive effect. This principle is currently laid down in Article 1, paragraph 1, of the Criminal Code. A similar provision is contained in Article 7 (1) of the European Convention for the Protection of Human Rights and Fundamental Freedoms and Article 15 (1) of the International Covenant on Civil and Political Rights. These treaty provisions mean that no one may be convicted for an act or omission which did not constitute a criminal offence under national or international law at the time the act or omission occurred. Both treaties make an exception to this principle for an act or omission which was criminal according to the general principles of law recognised by the community of nations. We do not consider it necessary to include in the Constitution the exception contained in these treaties relating to such crimes. The commission of such offences in the future is now punishable under the Wartime Criminal Offences Act and the Genocide Convention Implementation Act. As regards the past, however, reference should be made to the Wartimes Offences Decree (*Besluit Buitengewoon Strafrecht*)(Stb. D 61), which was later amended by Act of 10 July 1947 (Stb. H 233). Pursuant to the Act of 8 April 1971 (Stb. 210) containing further rules on the limitation period for the right to prosecute and enforce sentences for war crimes and crimes against humanity[9], the only provision of the Wartimes Offences Decree which is still of importance is Article 27a, under which war crimes and crimes against humanity committed during the last war may still be prosecuted or the pronounced sentence may still be enforced.
Article 27a of the Wartime Offences Decree provides that the definitions contained in the Charter of the International Military Tribunal of Nuremberg of 1945 are applicable to these offences. Although the legal force of this provision of the Decree, which has the effect of an Act of Parliament, would, owing to the inviolability of statute law, be maintained on the inclusion of the proposed article 1.15 in the Constitution, there would nonetheless be a rule in conflict with this constitutional provision. It therefore seems to us to be desirable to introduce another constitutional rule as an additional provision offsetting the constitutional rule of Article 1.15 with regard to offences made punishable under the Wartime Offences Decree. This is why the additional article A 1.15 was included.
Finally, it should be noted that the expression 'statutory criminal provision', as now contained in Article 1, paragraph 1, of the Criminal Code, covers every criminal provision

9. See 4 *NYIL* (1973) pp. 433-435.

which has been introduced by provisions of 'substantive law' [wet in materiele zin]".[10] (Parliamentary Documents II 1975-1976, 13 872, no. 3, p. 51).
(b) the explanatory notes to the said Article 11 of the State Committee, which include the following passage: "Article 1 of the Criminal Code records the principle that criminal provisions do not have retroactive effect. A similar provision is contained in Article 7 of the Rome Convention; an exception is made in this Article for crimes against humanity, as tried in Nuremberg after the Second World War. The great majority of the members of the State Committee would wish to enshrine in the Constitution the principle of *nulla poena sine praevia lege poenali*, as now laid down in the Criminal Code. The review of statutory regulations by reference to this principle (already possible under the provisions of the said Article 7 of the Rome Convention) would thus be given a statutory basis. These members consider it unnecessary to adopt the exception contained in the Treaty of Rome relating to crimes against humanity. As a result, the safeguard to be included in the Constitution will be of wider scope than the provision in the Treaty.
It should be noted that under Article 15 of the Convention no derogation from the *nulla poena* principle, as defined in Article 7, is permissible even in emergency situations.[11] A few members of the Committee see no clear advantages in the present proposal. Under the law as it stands, criminal provisions introduced by lower-tier public bodies are assessed by reference to Article 1 of the Criminal Code, and all criminal provisions (including those contained in an Act of Parliament) can be reviewed by reference to Article 7 of the Convention. This provides an adequate guarantee. These members therefore consider that there is no need for inclusion in the Constitution of the article in the Convention." (Second report of the State Advisory Committee for the Constitution and the Franchise Act, 1969, pp. 81-82).
(c) the Explanatory Memorandum in relation to the said Article 9e of Bill 11 051, which was submitted on 27 November 1970 but later withdrawn, includes the following passage: "Some members of the State Committee see no clear advantages in the present proposal. Under the law as it stands criminal provisions introduced by lower-tier public bodies are assessed by reference to Article 1 of the Criminal Code, and all criminal provisions (including those contained in an Act of Parliament) can be reviewed by reference to Article

---

10. The term 'wet in materiele zin' means general binding provision (in stead of binding on one person only) and includes not only Acts of Parliament, but also Royal Decrees, Ministerial Orders, Provincial and Municipal Decrees and in the view of some commentators, Treaties.

11. Art. 7 reads: '1. No one shall be held guilty of any criminal offence on account of any act or omission which did not constitute a criminal offence under national or international law at the time it was committed. Nor shall a heavier penalty be imposed than the one that was applicable at the time the criminal offence was committed. 2. This Article shall not prejudice the trial and punishment of any person for any act or omission which, at the time when it was committed, was criminal according to the general principles of law recognised by civilised nations.'
Art. 15 reads: '1. In time of war or other public emergency threatening the life of the nation any High Contracting Party may take measures derogating from its obligations under this Convention to the extent strictly required by the exigencies of the situation, provided that such measures are not inconsistent with its other obligations under international law. 2. No derogation from Article 2, except in respect of deaths resulting from lawful acts of war, or from Articles 3, 4 (para. 1) and 7 shall be made under this provision. 3. Any High Contracting Party availing itself of this right of derogation shall keep the Secretary General of the Council of Europe fully informed of the measures which it has taken and the reasons therefor. It shall also inform the Secretary General of the Council of Europe when such measures have ceased to operate and the provisions of the Convention are again being fully executed.

7 of the Convention. In the opinion of these members this provides an adequate guarantee. The undersigned are not convinced by these members' argument that such an important principle need not be included in the Constitution. It is also evident from the above that the safeguard to be included in the constitutional provision, which does not include the exception relating to crimes against humanity, will be of wider scope than the corresponding provision in the Rome Convention.

On the basis of the above, the undersigned have adopted the wording recommended for the article by the State Committee, with the above-mentioned addition relating to the applicability of the Wartime Offences Decree. (Parliamentary Documents II 1970-1971, 11 051, no. 3, p. 20).

4.4.1. Article 94 of the Constitution means that statutory regulations in force within the Kingdom are not applicable if such application is in conflict with provisions of treaties that are binding on any person or of resolutions by international institutions. In so far as it is relevant here, this provision stipulates that the courts should review the prohibition on granting retroactive effect, as contained in Article 16 of the Constitution and Article 1, paragraph 1, of the Criminal Code, by reference to treaties and resolutions of international organisations, but may not do so by reference to unwritten international law.

4.4.2. This interpretation is in keeping with the parliamentary history of Article 94 of the Constitution. Reference may be made in this connection to the Explanatory Memorandum to the Bill which resulted in this provision. This provides as follows:

'Article 5.2.2b (Article 73, State Committee). The purpose of this Article is to replace the present Articles 66 and part of 67 of the Constitution. The present Article 66 resolves the difficulty that arises if the application of provisions of a treaty binding on all persons conflicts with national statutory regulations. According to the Constitution, application of the national regulations must then be omitted. This rule has been maintained in the proposed new article. [...]

[We should] also devote attention to the application of unwritten rules of international law within the Dutch legal system, in particular the question of whether they should, like treaty provisions binding on all persons, prevail over municipal law. In its [...] advisory opinion on the proposal, the Advisory Committee on Issues of Public International Law recommended this expansion of the rule of what is now Article 66 of the Constitution on wide-ranging grounds.

Although we can understand the conviction of the Advisory Committee that in a constantly developing international legal order a similar prevalent position for unwritten international law has a certain attraction and could, theoretically, be defended in a Constitution, we agree with the Cals/Donner State Commission that this is not the right course to take. To avoid misunderstanding it should be added that there is no difference of opinion on the fact that rules of international customary law have been applied by judicial bodies in the Netherlands ever since the last century. These rules should also be observed by the legislature and executive. Unwritten international law can be regarded as binding in the Dutch legal system. The internal operation of international law was recognised in Dutch legislation in 1963 when the ground of cassation in Article 99 (2) of the Judiciary (Organisation) Act, previously reading 'on the grounds of faulty application or violation of the law [*wet*]' was changed to 'on the grounds of violation of the law [*recht*], except the law of foreign States'. As appears from the written and oral explanations in the States-General, this amendment was intended, inter alia, to make it possible for cassation to be based on grounds of unwritten international law.

However, opinions differ on the question whether it is desirable to apply unwritten international law if this application would be incompatible with municipal statutory regulations. Before the 1953 revision [of the Constitution] it was impossible to establish with certainty whether this application of unwritten international law would be compatible with the Constitution. The Supreme Court could not pronounce on the question since it had never been submitted to the Court up to 1953. Since the 1953 and 1956 revisions, however, it may be assumed, on the basis of the parliamentary history, that the present Constitution rules out the primacy of unwritten international law over municipal statutory regulations.

We consider that the course taken in 1953 and 1956 in respect of unwritten international law should be pursued in the new Constitution. Deviation therefrom in the manner advocated by the Advisory Committee on Issues of Public International Law would encounter objections both fundamental and practical, which we would describe as follows. In this description we also deal with the main arguments adduced by the Advisory Committee in favour of the primacy of the unwritten rules of international law. The fundamental objection is that a constitutional bar to the application of statutory regulations on the ground of incompatibility with unwritten international law would imply an extension of the judge's power of review of constitutionality under Article 66 of the Constitution. It is the same objection that would arise if the words 'binding on all persons' of Article 66 were left out, a subject already dealt with above. Extension of such judicial review to include the sphere of unwritten international law would, in our opinion, also encounter practical difficulties, since there is often much uncertainty as to the substance of the law.

A further serious objection to the primacy of unwritten international law over Dutch municipal law seems to us to be the risk of a court being under an obligation not to apply Dutch statutory regulations on the basis of a treaty that is not (yet) in force within the Kingdom. Primacy of unwritten international law over municipal statutory regulations is, in our view, only desirable to the extent of the present Constitution (Articles 65 and 66), viz., a priority limited to the rules of operative agreements and decisions of international organisations. A different system might frustrate the constitutional powers of the Government and Parliament.

None of this is outweighed by the main argument of Advisory Committee on Issues of Public International Law, namely that, in a Constitution purporting to be defensible in the field of legal theory with regard to the internal operation of international law, a distinction between written and unwritten international law is hardly acceptable. In our view, a system for the internal operation of international law that takes account of our constitutional arrangements, and provides a sound basis for the courts, the administration and the citizen is more important than the aspect of legal theory.

We are convinced that, from an international point of view, the regulation proposed by us in line with the present Convention meets reasonable standards.

We certainly do not endorse the statement of the Advisory Committee on Issues of Public International Law that the Netherlands, as compared with other States, scores low by neglecting unwritten international law in favour of written international law. Article 25 of the 1949 Constitution of the German Federal Republic which is cited in this connection by the Advisory Committee and which gives priority to the general rules of international law even over national laws – a priority which in this Constitution is not given to treaties – therefore possesses little attraction for us.

For the sake of completeness, it may be pointed out that Dutch statutory regulations, which under the proposed Article must give way before written international law, include provisions of the Constitution. (Parliamentary Documents II 1977-1978, 15 049 (R1100), no. 3, p. 11 et seq.).'

4.5. The findings at 4.4 above mean that the unreserved prohibition of Article 16 of the Constitution and the Article 1, paragraph 1, of the Criminal Code, as referred to at 4.3 above, should not be applicable in cases where this would be incompatible with provisions of treaties or decisions of international organisations binding on all persons. However, neither the Convention against Torture and Other Cruel, Inhuman or Degrading Treatment or Punishment nor any other treaties or decisions of an international organisation applicable here contains a provision entailing an obligation to treat acts as referred to in the Torture Convention Implementation Act as punishable with retroactive effect.

4.6. It follows that the provisions of the Criminal Code applicable at the time when the offences that are the subject of the complaint were committed in 1982 may be applied to the offences in so far as they were envisaged and made punishable at the time, but also that Articles 1 and 2 of the Implementation Act may not be applied to such offences since this legislation did not come into force until 20 January 1989. It also follows from the above that in so far as the obligation to declare such offences as punishable with retroactive effect results from unwritten international law, the courts are not free to decide not to apply the Torture Convention Implementation Act (which does not provide for this) on account of the fact that it is contrary to unwritten international law. According to the parliamentary history of Article 94 of the Constitution, as recounted at 4.4 above, the framers of the Constitution did not wish to accept the application of unwritten international law if such application would conflict with national legal regulations.

4.7. In view of the above findings, it is not necessary to answer the question of whether the offences referred to by the Court of Appeal can be deemed to be offences within the meaning of Article 7 of the European Convention on Human Rights and Article 15 of the International Covenant on Civil and Political Rights, which provide that the rule referred to in the first paragraph of these provisions, namely that no one may be held guilty of any criminal offence on account of any act or omission which did not constitute a criminal offence under national or international law at the time when it was committed, does not prevent the trial and punishment of anyone who commits an act or omission that constituted a criminal offence at the time of the act or omission in accordance with the general principles of law recognised by the community of nations.

4.8. It may be concluded from the above that the Court of Appeal infringed Article 16 of the Constitution and Article 1, paragraph 1, of the Criminal Code and that the disputed decision cannot be upheld.

4.9. Nonetheless, the Supreme Court considers that there are grounds for discussing the legal issues raised in the other grounds of appeal.[12] The Supreme Court will deal with the matters in the order in which they are raised in the application.

5. Assessment of the second ground of appeal

5.1. This ground of appeal means that it is necessary to answer the question of whether 'killing independently', i.e. without any preceding torture, comes within the scope of the Torture Convention Implementation Act.

12. This was the express request of the Procurator General.

5.2. Article 1 of the Torture Convention Implementation Act provides that assault committed by the persons and for the motives referred to therein constitutes torture. The text of this provision leaves no scope for the view that the killing of a person without this being preceded by or accompanied by assault within the meaning of Article 1 can be treated as torture.

6. Assessment of the third ground of appeal
6.1. This ground of appeal raises the question of whether the Netherlands has jurisdiction in relation to the relevant acts committed before the entry into force of the Torture Convention Implementation Act, in so far as such acts constituted criminal offences under the Criminal Code at the time when they were committed.
6.2. As regards the relevant offences of the Criminal Code, the jurisdiction rules of Articles 2-8 of the Criminal Code are applicable. These rules do not provide for jurisdiction in a case such as the present one, which involves – as it has been submitted – offences committed outside the Netherlands by a person not having Dutch nationality.
6.3. Neither in the Torture Convention Implementation Act nor elsewhere is retroactive effect given to the expansion in Article 5 of the Torture Convention Implementation Act of the jurisdiction rules as regards criminal offences under the Criminal Code, which also fulfil the definition of torture now provided for in the Torture Convention Implementation Act. Nor does the parliamentary history of this provision contain any basis for the granting of retroactive effect to the said Article 5, and indeed the parliamentary history as set out in the explanatory notes to the ground of appeal, at 59, could much more easily be interpreted as an indication to the contrary.
6.4. It is not necessary to answer whether a rule of unwritten international law exists on the basis of which the Netherlands has jurisdiction with retroactive effect with regard to the offences referred to in 6.3 because the courts, in accordance with the findings at 4.4-4.6 above, are not free to decide not to apply the national jurisdiction rules on account of conflict with unwritten international law.

7. Assessment of the fourth ground of appeal
7.1. This ground of appeal raises the question of whether the right to prosecute for the present offences has been barred by expiry of the limitation period, in so far as the offences constitute assault within the meaning of Article 300 et seq. of the Criminal Code.
7.2.1. According to the provisions of Title XX of Book 2 of the Criminal Code the term of imprisonment for the offences described therein runs from two years for assault (Article 300, paragraph 1, Criminal Code) to fifteen years for premeditated grave assault that results in death (Article 303, paragraph 2, Criminal Code).
7.2.2. In December 1982 Article 72 of the Criminal Code, in so far as relevant here, read as follows: 'The right to prosecute lapses upon the expiry of the period of limitation: [...] (2) after six years for indictable offences punishable by [...] a term of imprisonment of not more than three years; (3) after twelve years for indictable offences punishable by a term of imprisonment of more than three years; (4) after eighteen years for indictable offences punishable by life imprisonment.'
7.2.3. The Act of 19 January 1989 (Stb. 1989, 7), which entered into force on 1 March 1989, added a provision to Article 70 of the Criminal Code, namely that the right to prosecute for offences punishable by a term of imprisonment of more than ten years is barred by expiry of the period of limitation after 15 years. Under Article VI of this Act, this amendment does

not, however, have any consequences for offences committed before its entry into force, with the result that the limitation period in this case does not exceed twelve years.
7.2.4. Under Article 71 of the Criminal Code this limitation period runs from the day after that on which the offence was committed.
7.2.5. Article 72, paragraph 1, of the Criminal Code provides that the limitation period is interrupted by an act of prosecution, provided that this act is notified to or served on the prosecuted person.
7.3. It follows from the above that the right to prosecute in respect of the offences committed on 8 or 9 December 1982, in so far as they constitute any form of assault within the meaning of Title XX, lapsed at the latest on 9 December 1984 owing to expiry of the period of limitation, unless the period was interrupted by an act of prosecution, of which there is, incidentally, no evidence in this case.
7.4. As a consequence of the entry into force of Article 1, paragraph 3, of the Torture Convention Implementation Act, the offence of torture resulting in death has carried a sentence of life imprisonment since 20 January 1989. Since that date this offence has therefore been subject to a limitation period of eighteen years.
7.5. There is no support either in the Torture Convention Implementation Act or elsewhere for the view that this limitation period of eighteen years is also applicable in a case where the offence was committed before the entry into effect of the Torture Convention Implementation Act and at the time of the commission of the offence (if that offence were also to come within the definition of torture as provided for in that Act) a shorter limitation period applied which had not yet expired at the time of the entry into force of the Torture Convention Implementation Act.
7.6. There is therefore no need to consider whether a rule of unwritten international law exists on the basis of which the right to prosecute in respect of torture cannot be barred by passage of time and to which priority should be given over national limitation period rules, because the courts are not free, in accordance with the above provisions at 4.4-4.6, to decide not to apply an Act of Parliament on account of conflict with an unwritten rule of international law.

8. Assessment of the fifth ground of appeal
8.1. The ground of appeal makes it necessary to answer the question whether the suspected perpetrator of an offence within the meaning of Articles 1 and 2 of the Torture Convention Implementation Act committed abroad can be prosecuted and tried in the Netherlands if he is not in the Netherlands. According to the explanatory memorandum the question focuses on the case in which neither the suspected perpetrator nor the victim has Dutch nationality.
8.2. Under Article 5 of the Torture Convention Implementation Act Dutch criminal law is applicable to anyone who is guilty outside the Netherlands of one of the offences described in Articles 1 and 2 of this Act. It follows that the text of this provision does not of itself prevent prosecution and trial in the Netherlands of a person who does not possess Dutch nationality and is suspected of having committed such offence outside the Netherlands against another person who does not possess Dutch nationality. The following points should, however, be taken into account when interpreting this provision.
8.3.1. The title of the Torture Convention Implementation Act means 'that some statutory provisions must be made to implement the [...] Convention against Torture and other Cruel, Inhuman or Degrading Treatment or Punishment'.

8.3.2. The Explanatory Memorandum to the Bill which resulted in the Torture Convention Implementation Act contains the observation that the proposers consider 'the treaty obligations to be fair' for the reasons stated therein (Parliamentary Documents II 1986-1987, 20 042, no. 3, p. 5).[13]

8.3.3 In addition, the Explanatory Memorandum to the Bill introducing the Kingdom Act to approve the Convention against Torture and other Cruel, Inhuman or Degrading Treatment or Punishment (Kingdom Act of 29 September 1988, Stb. 477) includes the following passage: "Articles 4-7. These articles concern the criminal prosecution of torture, attempted torture and complicity or participation in torture. The main aspect of the rule contained herein is the system of universal jurisdiction [...]. Article 5, paragraph 2, obliges each party to the Convention to establish criminal jurisdiction even for cases in which the offences have been committed by aliens outside the territory of the contracting party; Article 7 obliges the contracting party to take steps to prosecute even in such cases if the suspect is found in its territory and it does not extradite him. The wording of these articles follows the example of similar provisions in the Convention for the Suppression of Unlawful Seizure of Aircraft (The Hague, 16 December 1970), the Convention for the Suppression of Unlawful Acts against the Safety of Civil Aviation (Montreal, 23 September 1971) [...]. During the discussions in the working group various members observed that this wording was not satisfactory because it contained a number of imperfections. A few suggestions were made for a better wording of the relevant provisions. Other members argued that the same imperfections appear in the treaties that served as a model and that it would be very difficult to design a better system and this would seriously delay the entry into force of the Convention against Torture. Various delegations also had objections in principle to derogating from the systems of the Conventions of The Hague, Montreal and New York, since such a derogation might have unforeseen consequences for the interpretation of these conventions. The working group therefore decided to maintain this system in the articles referred to here." (Parliamentary Documents II 1985-1986, 19 617 (R1312), no. 3, p. 21).

8.3.4. The Act implementing the Conventions of The Hague and Montreal referred to in the Explanatory Memorandum described above (Act of 10 May 1973, Stb. 228) inserts a provision in Article 4, at 7, of the Criminal Code to the effect that Dutch criminal law is applicable, inter alia, to any person who commits one of the specified offences outside the Netherlands in cases 'where the suspect is in the Netherlands'. This jurisdiction provision is explained in the Explanatory Memorandum to the Bill introducing the Act in the following way: "The undersigned cannot share the view that the system adopted in the Bill for implementation of the two Conventions is unnecessarily complicated, in any event on the basis of the text of the Conventions themselves. The chosen system [...] is a consequence of the principle already discussed at length upon the entry into force of the Act of 31 March 1971, Stb. 167, namely that so-called universal jurisdiction should have a basis in international law. This principle is based not only on dogmatic arguments but also and above all on grounds of efficiency. It would, in general, be harmful to the international legal order if countries were to prosecute offences over which they have no jurisdiction on the basis of the territoriality, personality or protective principle. If this were to happen it could frustrate prosecution in countries which do have a connection. Only in a comparatively small number

13. See 19 *NYIL* (1988) p. 341.

of cases has international law considered the possibility of prosecution and conviction anywhere in the world to be of greater importance. The Conventions of The Hague and Montreal are, subject to certain limitations, examples of this. It is therefore no more than logical – and also in accordance with the intention of the conventions – that the States should observe the limits imposed by the conventions when expanding their normal jurisdiction. [...] although it could, admittedly, be said that the courts should, having regard to Article 8 of the Criminal Code, observe these limits, the legislator should not make things more difficult for the courts than is strictly necessary. It is, however, possible to give examples of cases of air piracy not covered by the universality principle, in which the Dutch courts could not therefore act if the case were to take place outside the Dutch legal sphere. This is, however, a consequence not of the chosen system of implementation, but of the conventions themselves. The undersigned consider the system of implementation chosen in the Bill to be correct, even after further consideration, and are not therefore prepared to propose a different system'. (Parliamentary Documents II 1972, 11 865 (R859) 11 866, no. 9, p. 3).
8.3.5. In addition, it should be noted that according to the Explanatory Memorandum referred to above (page 3) at 8.3.2, the Genocide Convention Implementation Act (Act of 2 July 1964, Stb. 243) 'has served to an important extent as a model' for the drafting of the Torture Convention Implementation Act. In the Genocide Convention Implementation Act acts are made punishable which the legislator evidently considered, judging by the sentences imposed, to be more serious than torture within the meaning of Article 1, paragraphs 1 and 2, of the Torture Convention Implementation Act. However, Article 5 of the Genocide Convention Implementation Act contains a jurisdiction arrangement which is considerably more limited than that of Article 5 of the Torture Convention Implementation Act.[14]
8.4. On the basis of what is said above at 8.3 – when viewed in its overall context – it must be assumed that the legislator, when introducing the jurisdiction rule of Article 5 of the Torture Convention Implementation Act did not wish to go further than the obligation to which the Netherlands is subject under Article 5, paragraphs 1 and 2, of the Convention against Torture and other Cruel, Inhuman or Degrading Treatment or Punishment.
8.5. It follows that the prosecution and trial in the Netherlands of the suspected perpetrator of an offence within the meaning of Articles 1 and 2 of the Torture Convention Implementation Act, which was committed abroad, is possible only if a connection mentioned in that Convention for the establishment of jurisdiction is present, for example because the suspected perpetrator or the victim is of Dutch nationality or must be equated with a Dutch national, or because the suspected perpetrator is in the Netherlands at the time of his arrest.

9. Conclusion
It follows from the above findings that the disputed decision cannot be upheld and that the following decision must be taken.

10. Decision
The Supreme Court quashes the disputed decision in the interests of the law...'

---

14. See 4 *NYIL* (1973) pp. 429-430.

☛ United Kingdom: *R.* v. *Secretary of State ex parte Thring*, Court of Appeal (Civil Division), 20 July 2000

Panel: Pill, Clarke and Bennett, LJJ

Pill LJ: This is an application by Mr James P Thring, who is a United Kingdom taxpayer and elector, to quash decisions of the United Kingdom government. It is a renewed application. Permission to apply for judicial review was refused on paper by Latham J., and was refused following an oral hearing on 23 March 2000 by Hidden J. Latham J. refused on the ground that it was not arguable that Mr Thring, whom I will describe as the applicant, had standing. Before Hidden J., it was held that it was not arguable that the applicant would not be defeated by delay.

The applicant seeks an order quashing the order of the Secretary of State for Defence to the Royal Air Force to fly over Iraqi territory and attack targets inside Iraq. Alternatively, an order is sought quashing the order of the Secretary of State for Defence to finance the operation of the Royal Air Force over Iraq from the revenue provided by taxpayers. In the alternative, declarations of illegality are sought by the applicant.

At page 11 of the bundle it is put in this way; what it is sought to quash is:

'The decision by the Secretary of State for Defence to over-fly the sovereign State of Iraq by military Air Forces in cooperation with United States Air Forces and to attack Iraqi Air Forces and ground defences including communications equipment and dual-use facilities.'

Reference has been made to operation Desert Storm which was conducted by governments, including the British and United States governments, in Iraq about ten years ago. Reference has been made to a subsequent resolution of the United Nations' security council. It is accepted that there are military operations by the Royal Air Force over the territory of Iraq, which is a sovereign state.

I can say at once that I would not refuse permission to apply by reason of any lack of standing of the applicant or by reason of delay on his part. If, upon the merits of the application, there were to be an arguable case, then I would not prevent it being put forward upon a full application for either of those reasons. That is not to say that upon the full hearing the questions of standing and of delay could not be argued by the respondent and considered by the court.

It is in my judgment at this stage appropriate to look at the merits of the application.

The grounds on which relief is sought are set out on page 7 of the principal bundle. It is recited that the Gulf war ended on 6 April 1991 and that the government of Iraq subsequently accepted United Nations security resolution 687 of 1991, which has been included with the papers. The applicant submits that there is no express approval of the imposition of a no-fly zone over parts of Iraq in that resolution. The grounds conclude by stating at para (7):

'These activities of the British Air Force, [that is flying over Iraq and conducting bombing operations there] are being unlawfully financed by the tax payer in the UK. There is no war declared by the UK on the Republic of Iraq and Parliament has not authorised such spending.'

I say in parenthesis that, as presented to this court, Mr Thring's application does not depend upon whether or not there is a state of war in existence. He submits that whether or not that is the position, the action of the government in instructing the Royal Air Force to conduct operations over Iraq is unlawful.

The applicant puts it in this way: these attacks damage the reputation of the United Kingdom for justice, they damage the concept of the peaceful resolution of conflicts and undermine the credibility of the government's policy in seeking to pronounce on moral and humanitarian issues. He submits that the government is spending £4.5m a month on the operations over Iraq.

In support of the application that delay should not deprive him of permission, the applicant has referred to notes of an interview which he conducted with Mr Hans von Sponeck, who is a former United Nations representative in Iraq. The object of the reference to it is to establish that there has been an escalation of the activity of the Royal Air Force over Iraq and since there is, in the submission of the applicant, a continuing operation, he should not be defeated on grounds of delay. In any event, he submits, the escalation introduces a new factor which means that he should not be defeated by delay. I have already indicated my view on the question of delay.

The aspect of his submission which has this morning gained prominence is by reference to the Geneva Convention. That has been adopted by the United Kingdom and appears as a schedule to the Geneva Conventions Act 1957, as amended by the Geneva Conventions (Amendment) Act 1995. The applicant has included with his bundle of papers extracts from the Convention, and he submits that there is sufficient evidence of a breach of the Convention, by reason of the operations of the Royal Air Force, to ensure that permission to apply for judicial review should be given.

The applicant refers to art 51 of the Convention, headed 'Protection of the civilian population'. That provides in para 4 that:

'Indiscriminate attacks are prohibited.'

There is then a definition of indiscriminate attacks and at para 5, the paragraph upon which the applicant relies, it is stated:

'Among others, the following types of attacks are to be considered as indiscriminate. . .

(b) an attack which may be expected to cause incidental loss of civilian life, injury to civilians, damage to civilian objects, or a combination thereof, which would be excessive in relation to the concrete and direct military advantage anticipated.'

The suggestion that in the absence of a state of war there could be no direct military advantage was understandably abandoned by the applicant, and I approach the case on the basis that the Geneva Convention does apply, without deciding whether the Geneva Convention does cover operations of the Royal Air Force and the United States Air Force in Iraq.

The submission is that there is sufficient evidence in the papers, including the notes of interview with Mr Hans von Sponeck, to establish that it is arguable that there is a breach of that paragraph. It is submitted that there is a breach which constitutes a crime committed by the United Kingdom government and the court upon this application should address that crime. It is submitted that, even if the operations are lawful, taxpayers' money is being wasted. There is no evidence of any positive results being achieved by the operations of the Royal Air Force and it follows, at least as an arguable case, that there is a waste of money which the court should intervene to prevent.

The applicant further submits that he has established at least an arguable case that the court should not refuse permission. If such an arguable case is established as to the test, the applicant has referred to statements by Lord Donaldson and Lord Diplock.

In my judgment no arguable case has been established to justify the grant of permission in this case. I deal first with the case specifically put upon the Geneva Conventions Act, though it does in my view overlap with the more general case which has been put forward as to the duty of the court to intervene in operations abroad of the armed forces.

I note first that s 1 of the 1957 Act, headed 'Punishment of offenders against conventions' and 'Grave breaches of scheduled conventions' provides that (and I paraphrase) any person who whether in or outside the United Kingdom permits, aids, abets or procures the commission by any person of any grave breach of the scheduled conventions as referred to in the following articles shall be guilty of felony. Provision is made for punishment. The articles set out include art 51, on which the applicant relies. The precise wording of s 1 (1) has been amended in the 1995 Act, s 1, but for present purposes I need not consider that amendment in detail. What the Act provides is for the punishment of a criminal offence by an individual. That is a wholly different matter from an application by way of judicial review. Criminal matters are dealt with in the criminal courts, not by way of challenge to government action, which is what is the applicant seeks to achieve in this case. That is not a mere technicality. The courts have developed remedies for particular purposes, and the remedy of judicial review is a wholly different one from the criminal sanction which is enacted in the 1957 Act, as amended.

Moreover, the factual difficulties involved are not appropriate for consideration by way of judicial review. I have read the relevant paragraph of art 51. As Mr Justice Bennett has pointed out in the course of argument, it involves complex factual issues with which, in my judgment, upon judicial review it is quite inappropriate to deal. Courts are not deterred by complexities or difficulties in evidence from discharging their duty, but the issues which arise under art 51 confirm and demonstrate the fact that judicial review is not an appropriate remedy in the present circumstances.

In my view, that also applies to the more general submission which is made. The applicant accepts that it is not the duty of the courts to intervene in the activities of the forces of the Crown world-wide. He accepts, as he has to, that an ordered system of government cannot require the courts of a country to conduct in detail the operations of its armed forces abroad. The constitution of the United Kingdom, as developed by Parliament and the courts, certainly does not operate on that footing.

What the applicant does submit, by reference to the Geneva Convention and to the material which he has provided, is that the courts should intervene in this particular case. Moreover, he submits that it is for the Ministry of Defence to come to court and persuade the court that what it is doing is legal. I say at once that I find that submission to be a misconception. The courts do not operate on the principle that whenever anyone makes an accusation against a government body, he is entitled to a remedy in court unless that government body comes along to satisfy the court that the action taken is a lawful one. It is for an applicant to show on a permission application that it is arguable that an act is unlawful by the law of England.

In my judgment it is not appropriate for the court to intervene upon judicial review in the deployment of the armed forces abroad. Parliament has authorised a defence budget. The Secretary of State for Defence is answerable to Parliament and not to the courts for the conduct of military operations abroad. The court has no power to control how money is spent by the executive arm of government on overseas operations. Any remedy must be political remedy. The applicant and those who take the same view as he has and he has many supporters in court today have sought a political remedy and have not achieved one which satisfies them.

The applicant has provided us with notes of the official record in Hansard of debates in the House of Commons where the then Secretary of State for Defence set out the policies of the government towards Iraq. He is answerable for the conduct of those policies to Parliament. I refer to the statement of Sir William Wade in the 7th edition of Administrative Law, Wade & Forsyth, at page 841 :

'. . . acts of force committed by the Crown in foreign countries are no concern of the English courts. In the time of the naval campaign against the slave trade, for example, a Spanish slave trader failed in an action for damages against a British naval commander who destroyed one of his establishments in West Africa (Buron v Denman (1848) 2 Ex 167). It is by this fundamental rule that acts of violence in foreign affairs, including acts of war, if committed abroad, cannot be questioned in English courts.'

I respectfully adopt that statement as an accurate one.

Mr Thring has addressed us courteously and, if I may say so, forcefully. He has produced documents for the court's consideration. In my judgment he has not shown an arguable case that the relief he seeks should be granted by the courts and for the reasons I have given I would refuse this application.

Clarke LJ: The decision or decisions which it is sought judicially to review are described in the material before us in this way:

'The decision by the Secretary of State for Defence to over-fly the sovereign State of Iraq by military Air Forces in cooperation with United States Air Forces and to attack Iraqi Air Forces and ground defences including communications equipment and dual-use facilities.'

The relief sought is put in this way:

'(1) An order of certiorari to quash the order of the Secretary of State for Defence to the British Air Force to fly over Iraqi territory and attack targets inside Iraq,

(2) Alternatively an order of certiorari to quash the order of the Secretary of State for Defence to finance the operation of the British Air Force over Iraq from the taxpayer revenue,

(3) Alternatively for a declaration that the orders of the Secretary of State for Defence to the British Air Forces to fly over Iraqi territory and attack targets within Iraq and finance these operations from taxpayer revenue are unlawful.'

It appears to me that those decisions as so defined are not susceptible to judicial review. None of those orders involves an unlawful act contrary to any provision of English domestic law.

However, it is said that the policy has involved indiscriminate bombing of civilians which is unlawful under art 51 of the Geneva Convention 1957. The problem is that the Geneva Convention is not itself part of English domestic or municipal law. As my Lord has indicated, the Geneva Conventions Act 1957, as amended by the Geneva Conventions (Amendment) Act 1995, provides in essence that a person who commits certain breaches of the Convention, including breaches of art 51, is guilty of a criminal offence.

However, as I read the Acts, neither the Crown nor the United Kingdom government could be prosecuted under either of those statutes. In these circumstances I do not think that the 1957 or the 1995 Act provide a sufficient basis upon which the court could entertain an application for judicial review of this kind.

This is highlighted by a further consideration, to which my Lord has referred. The court would face what seems to me to be an almost insuperable problem. In order to determine whether an attack was indiscriminate within art 51 (5)(b) of the Geneva Convention, it would be necessary to consider whether an attack or attacks might be expected to cause:

'. . . incidental loss of civilian life, injury to civilians, damage to civilian objects, or a combination thereof, which would be excessive in relation to the concrete and direct military advantage anticipated.'

This would involve a consideration of the military advantages concerned. For my part, while I see the force of the submissions made by the applicant, I do not think that the court could sensibly carry out an analysis of such a military advantages or disadvantages, which would involve a consideration of the activities of United Kingdom military operations over Iraq.

In these circumstances, I would not for my part grant permission to move for judicial review. Nor do I think that this is a case in which it would be appropriate to adjourn the application for the respondent to be represented, although I recognise that there are many cases in which such a course would be appropriate. For these reasons, I agree that the application should be refused.

Bennett J: I agree with both judgments and wish to add only a few words. In my judgment, the issue is whether or not the subject matter raised in Mr Thring's application is amenable to the process of judicial review. In the fifth edition of *Judicial Review of Administrative Action*, De Smith Woolf & Jowell, it is said at para 6-042, page 319:

'However, the question of whether or not prerogative powers could be reviewed was authoritatively determined in favour of their being reviewable by the House of Lords in the GCHQ case. The majority of their Lordships were of the opinion that the exercise of powers authorised by the prerogative may be reviewable when their exercise is open to judicial review. It depended on the subject-matter. The minority preferred to leave open the question as to whether prerogative powers were reviewable until it had to be determined. Prerogative powers may, however, relate to areas which because of their nature are not justiciable. As Lord Roskill said in the course of his speech in the GCHQ case: "Prerogative powers such as those relating to the making of treaties, the defence of the realm, the prerogative of mercy, the grant of honours, the dissolution of Parliament and the appointment of Ministers as well as others are not, I think, susceptible to judicial review because their nature and subject matter is such as not to be amendable to the judicial process".'

Lord Scarman considered that:

'The controlling factor in determining whether the exercise of prerogative power is subjected to judicial review is not its source but its subject matter.'

I do not rest my decision on whether or not the policy and operations of the armed services in Iraq are the exercise of prerogative powers, but I derive considerable assistance from the passages that I have quoted. In my judgment the nature and subject-matter of Mr Thring's application is not amenable to the process of judicial review. His application would involve consideration of the policy and the nature of the operations of the armed services abroad, and particularly of the Royal Air Force. In my judgment, those are not matters which can be the subject of judicial review, because the courts are not equipped so to do.

The fact that the courts are ill-equipped in these matters is graphically shown by the terms of para (5) of art 51 of the Geneva Convention, now in the Geneva Conventions (Amendment) Act 1995, which my Lord has quoted. During the course of Mr Thring's concise, courteous and moderate submissions, he accepted that it would be necessary to go into what happened on the occasions upon which the Royal Air Force used either missiles or bombs. It would then be necessary for the court to have evidence about the 'concrete and direct military advantage anticipated'; and, having had that, it would then be necessary for the court to exercise its judgment, as I read the paragraph, as to whether or not that advantage was excessive in relation to the incidental loss of civilian life, injury to civilians or damage to

civilian objects, or a combination thereof. In my judgment, the resolution of such issues is not susceptible to judicial review.
Thus, for those reasons and the reasons given by my Lords, Lord Justice Pill and Lord Justice Clarke, I would refuse the application.
Disposition
Application refused.

7.22 LEGISLATION TO IMPLEMENT OBLIGATIONS *VIS-À-VIS* THE INTERNATIONAL CRIMINAL COURT

☛ Denmark: Act No. 342 of 16 May 2001 on the International Criminal Court

We Margrethe The Second, Queen of Denmark by the Grace of God, proclaim:
The Folketing has passed and We by Our consent have ratified the following law:

§ 1. The Statute of the International Criminal Court, cf. the annex to this law, shall apply in this country.
Para. 2. The Minister for Foreign Affairs may decide that the following provisions shall apply in this country:
1) The Rules of procedure and amendments thereto, cf. article 51 of the Statute.
2) The recommended descriptions of the content of crimes and amendments thereto, cf. article 9 of the Statute.
3) Amendments to the Statute provided they are adopted in accordance with articles 121-123 of the Statute.

§ 2. The Minister for Justice shall decide upon a request from the International Criminal Court on the extradition of persons against whom the Court has initiated criminal proceedings.
Para. 2. The Minister for Justice shall decide moreover upon a request on extradition for execution of the Court's judgement.
Para. 3. Chapters 3 and 4 of the law on the extradition of offenders shall apply *mutatis mutandis.*
Para. 4. The court shall determine upon a request from a person who has been remanded in custody with a view to being extradited to the International Criminal Court whether the requirements for provisional release pursuant to article 59, paras. 3-5, have been met.

§ 3. The Minister for Justice may determine that sentences etc. that are handed down by the International Criminal Court can be executed in this country in accordance with the rules in Chapter 10 of the Statute.
Para. 2. Execution shall as far as possible be in accordance with Danish rules and may not result in a worsening of the convicted person's situation under criminal law.
Para. 3. The decision by the Minister for Justice shall be submitted to a court for approval. The court's decision shall be reached by verdict. The provisions of the Law on the administration of justice on out-of-court decisions on fines or confiscation shall however apply as appropriate.

Para. 4. No alternative punishment may be imposed in this country for a fine imposed by the International Criminal Court.
Para. 5. Compensation to a victim decreed by the International Criminal Court pursuant to article 75 of the Statute can be recovered by the Minister for Justice by distrainment and by withholding of the income of the person concerned in accordance with the rules for the recovery of personal taxes in the law on tax deducted at source and the rules in the law on The Common Register of Pay Retention. The rules on the recovery of fines shall also be applicable as appropriate.
Para. 6. The Minister for Justice may establish more precise rules for the execution in this country of sentences etc. handed down by the International Criminal Court including those based on an agreement with the Court.

§ 4. A person who has been found guilty or acquitted by the International Criminal Court may not be tried in this country for the same act.

§ 5. The provisions of Chapter 14 of the Criminal Code on offences against public authorities or Chapter 17 on perjury and false accusations shall also apply when the matter relates to the International Criminal Court.

§ 6. The costs of appointed defence counsel in connection with hearings in this country upon a request from the International Criminal Court shall be paid by the State, unless the court decides under particular circumstances that they shall be paid by the person being heard.

§ 7. The Minister for Justice may establish other provisions for the implementation of the Statute of the International Criminal Court, including those based on an agreement with the Court.

§ 8. The Minister for Foreign Affairs shall establish the time at which the law shall come into force.

§ 9. The law shall not apply for the Faeroe Islands or Greenland, but may be given effect in whole or in part by Royal Decree for those parts of the country with such differences as the particular circumstances of the Faeroes and Greenland dictate.
Done at Christiansborg Castle, on 16 May 2001

Under Our Royal Hand and Seal

Margrethe R.

☛ **Norway: Act No. 65 of 15 June 2001 relating to the implementation of the Statute of the International Criminal Court of 17 July 1998 (the Rome Statute) in Norwegian law**

§ 1. *Scope etc. of the Act*
Any request for the surrender of a person sought and other forms of assistance submitted by the International Criminal Court (the Court) in accordance with the Court's Statute of 17 July 1998 (the Rome Statute) shall be dealt with in accordance with the provisions of this

Act.
Such requests shall be submitted to the Ministry.
Requests from the Court shall be complied with in so far as the Rome Statute so provides.

§ 2. *Surrender*
At the request of the Court any person who is suspected, accused or convicted of a crime that falls within the jurisdiction of the Court and who is present in the realm may be surrendered to the Court.
When dealing with a request for surrender, the provisions of Chapter II of the Act of 13 June 1975 No. 39 relating to the surrender of offenders apply in so far as they are appropriate.
The Ministry may consent to the transportation through Norwegian territory of a person who is being surrendered to the Court by a foreign state.

§ 3. *Other assistance*
Norwegian courts and other authorities may on request provide the Court with such assistance as is mentioned in Article 93 of the Rome Statute.
Such requests shall be dealt with and executed in accordance with Norwegian law in so far as it is appropriate. If the Court has requested that a particular procedure be followed, this shall be complied with unless the procedure is prohibited by Norwegian law.
The Ministry may on request authorize the Court to examine witnesses and carry out other investigations in the realm.

§ 4. *Compulsory measures*
Compulsory measures may be used at the request of the Court. The provisions of sections 15, 20 and 24 of the Act of 13 June 1975 No. 39 relating to the surrender of offenders apply correspondingly in so far as they are appropriate. If the use of a compulsory measure is conditional on there being just cause to suspect that an offence has been committed, the Court's finding on this point shall be adopted. A person may be arrested and remanded in custody on the application of the Court, even if the conditions set out in sections 170a and 171 of the Criminal Procedure Act are not fulfilled.
A person who has been arrested has the right to apply for interim release pending surrender. The said person may be granted interim release if the Rome Statute's conditions for so doing are fulfilled. Before the court releases the said person, the Court shall be notified and given the opportunity to make recommendations.

§ 5. *The suspect's right to a defence counsel*
A person who is suspected or accused of offences that come within the jurisdiction of the Court is entitled to the assistance of a defence counsel of his own choice at every stage of the case. The said person shall be informed of this prior to being questioned.
If the Court has requested surrender of a person sought or other assistance from the Norwegian authorities, an official defence counsel shall be appointed for him on the same terms as provided by section 16, first paragraph, first sentence, and section 20 of the Act relating to the surrender of offenders, and sections 97, 98, 100, second paragraph, and 100a of the Criminal Procedure Act.

§ 6. *The aggrieved person's right to counsel*

A counsel may on application be appointed for the aggrieved person in cases being dealt with by the Court if there is reason to believe that as a result of the offence the said person will suffer considerable harm to body or health and there is deemed to be a need for a counsel. The provisions of Chapter 9a of the Criminal Procedure Act apply correspondingly in so far as they are appropriate.

§ 7. *Exemption from the duty of secrecy in connection with testimony and the submission of other evidence before the Court*
The King may grant leave for the Court to receive testimony about a matter that is being kept secret in the interests of national security or relations with a foreign state.
The duty of secrecy or other legislation or instructions shall not preclude a person from testifying before the Court in so far as the Court so orders.
The provisions of the first and second paragraphs apply correspondingly to the surrender of documents or other objects that contain information that is subject to a duty of secrecy.

§ 8. *Anonymous testimony*
At the request of or with the consent of the Court, the court may allow anonymous testimony before the court or the police to the same degree as in cases concerning crimes of a similar nature that are prosecuted in the realm. Sections 130a and 234a of the Criminal Procedure Act apply correspondingly in so far as they are appropriate.

§ 9. *Ne bis in idem*
No person may be prosecuted or convicted in the realm for conduct for which the said person has been convicted or acquitted by the Court.

§ 10. *Enforcement of a sentence of imprisonment in Norway*
The Ministry may consent to a sentence of imprisonment imposed by the Court being served in Norway, and may request the prosecuting authority to commence enforcement. Enforcement is to be effected in accordance with the provisions of Part 10 of the Statute of Rome and the conditions attached by the Ministry to accepting the sentenced person for serving the sentence.

§ 11. *Enforcement of other sanctions in Norway*
Payment of fines ordered by the Court may be enforced in Norway. The same applies to forfeitures and reparations to aggrieved persons that have been ordered by the Court. In so far as they are appropriate, sections 456 and 457 of the Criminal Procedure Act apply correspondingly to the enforcement of pecuniary claims.

§ 12. *Penalties for offences against the Court etc.*
Sections 163 to 167 of the Penal Code apply correspondingly to criminal liability for giving false testimony before the Court.
Sections 127, 128, 132 and 132a of the Penal Code apply correspondingly to criminal liability for offences against an official of the Court.
Sections 112 to 114 of the Penal Code apply correspondingly to judges and other employees of the Court.
This section also applies to offences committed abroad by Norwegian nationals.

§ 13. *Prosecution in the realm*
Section 13, first paragraph, of the Penal Code does not apply to prosecution in the realm of offences that come within the jurisdiction of the Court.

§ 14. *Regulations*
The King may issue further regulations to supplement and for the implementation of this Act.

§ 15. *Entry into force*
This Act enters into force on the date on which the Statute of Rome enters into force for Norway.

§ 16. *Amendments to other Acts*
The Act of 13 June 1975 No. 39 relating to the surrender of offenders etc. is amended as follows:
§15, first sentence, shall read:
In order to further the investigation and ensure surrender of the person sought, such coercive measures as are mentioned in chapters 14, 15, 15a, 16, 16a and 16b of the Criminal Procedure Act may be applied to the same degree as in cases concerning crimes of a similar nature that are prosecuted in the realm.
§20, subsection 1, first sentence, shall read:
When a person in a foreign state is charged, indicted or convicted of an offence that could justify surrender pursuant to this Act, coercive measures pursuant to chapters 14, 15, 15a, 16, 16a and 16b of the Criminal Procedure Act may be applied to the same degree as in cases concerning crimes of a similar nature that are prosecuted in the realm, provided that a competent authority in the foreign state so requests before an application for surrender has been submitted.
§ 24, subsection 1, shall read:
For the purpose of criminal proceedings in a foreign country, it may on application be decided that such coercive measures as are mentioned in chapters 15, 15a , 16, 16a, 16b and 17 of the Criminal Procedure Act may be applied in the same way as in cases concerning crimes of a similar nature that are prosecuted in the realm.

☛ Switzerland: Federal Law on Cooperation with the International Criminal Court of 22 June 2001

The Federal Assembly of the Swiss Confederation,
based on article 123 paragraph 1 of the Federal Constitution ,after examining the message of the Federal Council of 15 November 2000 ,
decides:

Chapter 1: General provisions

Art. 1 Object

1 This law shall govern cooperation with the International Criminal Court (Court),

established by the Rome Statute of the International Criminal Court of 17 July 1998 (Statute).
2 It shall regulate in particular:
a. the surrender of persons being prosecuted and of persons convicted by the Court (Chapter 3);
b. other forms of cooperation (Chapter 4);
c. the enforcement of penalties of the Court (Chapter 5).

Art. 2 Applicable law

Cooperation with the Court shall be rendered exclusively in accordance with the provisions of this law and the provisions of the Statute.

Chapter 2: Cooperation with the Court

Section 1: Principles of cooperation

Art. 3 Central Authority

1 The Federal Office of Justice shall administer a Central Authority for cooperation with the Court.
2 The Central Authority shall have the following responsibilities in particular:
a. It shall receive the requests of the Court.
b. It shall decide on the admissibility of cooperation, on cooperation procedures, and, if applicable, challenge the jurisdiction of the Court.
c. It shall order necessary measures, the scope of these measures, and the manner of execution of the request, and it shall designate the federal authorities or the canton responsible for the execution of the request.
d. It shall appoint, where necessary, an official counsel.
e. It shall surrender to the Court persons being prosecuted and shall transmit to the Court the results of the execution of the request.
f. It shall forward to the competent authorities requests of the Court to undertake prosecutions in accordance with article 70 paragraph 4 subparagraph b of the Statute.
g. It shall decide on requests of the Court for enforcement of penalties.
h. It shall enforce fines and forfeitures.

Art. 4 Consultations

The Central Authority shall conduct consultations as indicated in article 97 of the Statute, in particular when the execution of a request:
a. would conflict with an existing fundamental legal principle (art. 93 para. 3 of the Statute);
b. would prejudice national security interests (art. 72 and art. 93 para. 4 of the Statute);
c. would interfere with an ongoing investigation or prosecution of a different case (art. 94 para. 1 of the Statute);
d. could violate State or diplomatic immunity (art. 98 in connection with art. 27 of the Statute).

Art. 5 Executing authorities

1 The cantonal and federal authorities designated to execute requests of the Court shall execute the measures ordered by the Central Authority expeditiously and without taking their own procedural steps of substantive nature.
2 Acts of the executing authorities cannot be appealed.

Art. 6 Immunities

1 On application by the Federal Department of Justice and Police (Department), the Federal Council shall decide on questions of immunity relating to article 98 in conjunction with article 27 of the Statute which arise in the course of the execution of requests..
2 Where paragraph 1 applies, the Department may order arrest or other preventive measures.
Section 2: Jurisdiction of the Court

Art. 7 Determination of jurisdiction

1 If the Court claims jurisdiction over proceedings, the Central Authority may, in agreement with the competent authorities in the Swiss proceedings, assert Swiss jurisdiction as indicated in article 18 of the Statute or may, if necessary, challenge the jurisdiction of the Court in accordance with article 19 of the Statute.
2 If the Central Authority does not challenge the jurisdiction of the Court or if the Court, upon consideration, reaches the conclusion that its jurisdiction takes precedence, then all documents pertaining to the proceedings shall be transmitted to the Court. The competent Swiss authorities shall suspend the proceedings.
3 Decisions on challenges to jurisdiction cannot be appealed.

Art. 8 Reporting of a crime and spontaneous transmittal of evidence and information

1 The Central Authority may, without a request from the Court, transmit to the Court evidence and information gathered by Swiss prosecution authorities for their own investigations, if criminal proceedings may be initiated or a pending investigation may be facilitated due to the transmission.
2 The transmission cannot be appealed.

Art. 9 Referral of a situation

1 The Federal Council shall decide whether a situation shall be referred to the Court as provided in article 14 of the Statute.
2 The Central Authority shall transmit the corresponding request to the Court.

Section 3: Communication with the Court

Art. 10 Form and transmission of requests of the Court
1 Requests of the Court shall be made in writing. The Central Authority may receive requests directly from organs of the Court.

2 Requests and supporting documentation shall be submitted in German, French, or Italian, or shall be accompanied by an officially certified translation into one of these languages.
3 Subject to subsequent confirmation through ordinary channels, requests for provisional measures, searches, arrests, and other urgent requests may be transmitted:
a. through the International Criminal Police Organization (Interpol); or
b. by any medium capable of delivering a written record.
4 The Central Authority shall immediately inform the Court of the inadmissibility or denial of a request and shall explain its decision. The Central Authority shall consult with the Court before the definite denial of a request.

Art. 11 Swiss requests

1 Cantonal or federal prosecution authorities may request the cooperation of the Court in the case of serious crimes. The Central Authority shall forward such requests to the Court.
2 The documents shall be transmitted in French or English, or be accompanied by a translation into one of these languages. For the rest, the conditions for requests of the Court shall apply by analogy to Swiss requests.
3 Conditions placed by the Court on the execution of a request shall be respected by the Swiss authorities.

Art. 12 Costs

1 Requests of the Court shall as a rule be executed free of charge. Exceptions are:
a. costs associated with the travel and security of witnesses and experts or the transfer of persons in custody under article 93 of the Statute ;
b. costs of translation, interpretation, and transcription;
c. travel and subsistence costs of the Judges, the Prosecutor, the Deputy Prosecutors, the Registrar, the Deputy Registrar, and staff of any organ of the Court;
d. costs of expert opinions or reports requested by the Court;
e. costs associated with the transport of a person being surrendered to the Court;
f. following consultations, any extraordinary costs that may result from the execution of a request.
2 Federal and cantonal authorities shall not bill each other for charges or compensation for labor arising from the execution of a request of the Court.
3 Costs associated with detention ordered by the Central Authority and, if applicable, costs of the public defender are charged to the Confederation . The corresponding rates of the Court for compensation of the host State (art. 3 para. 1 of the Statute) are used as the basis of assessment.

Section 4: Further provisions

Art. 13 Transit

1 Upon request of the Court, the Central Authority may authorize the transit of a person in detention and the measures necessary for transit, without hearing the views of the affected person.
2 No authorization is required if the person in detention is to be transported by air over Swiss

territory and no landing is scheduled.
3 If an unscheduled landing occurs, the person in transit shall be kept in custody . The Central Authority shall immediately ask the Court to make a request for transit. If the request is not received within 96 hours, the person shall be released. If the request is received after this period of time has elapsed, the person may again be arrested and the transit of the person may be authorized.
4 An authorization of transit cannot be appealed.

Art. 14 Competing requests

1 If Switzerland receives a request from the Court for the surrender of a person and a request from another State for the extradition of the same person, the Central Authority shall decide in accordance with article 90 of the Statute.
2 If Switzerland receives competing requests from the Court and from another State for a purpose other than arrest or surrender, the Central Authority shall decide in accordance with article 93 paragraph 9 of the Statute.
3 If the Central Authority has given priority to the request from the State, but if the request is then denied, the Central Authority shall notify the Court without delay.

Art. 15 Compensation

1 Provisions of federal law governing the compensation for unjustified detention and other disadvantages shall apply by analogy to proceedings against persons pursuant to a request of the Court that are conducted in Switzerland in accordance with this law.
2 Compensation may be reduced or denied if the person has provoked the investigation or detention through his fault or has, without reason obstructed or delayed the proceedings.
3 Compensation for detention in Switzerland pending surrender may also be reduced if the Court:
a. withdraws its request for arrest for the purpose of surrender; or
b. does not submit its request for surrender with supporting documentation within the deadline set.
4 Compensation shall be refused to the extent that the Court has awarded or denied compensation in accordance with article 85 of the Statute.

Chapter 3: Surrender of persons being prosecuted and of persons convicted by the Court

Section 1: Conditions

Art. 16 Principle

1 A person shall be surrendered to the Court if the request and supporting documentation indicate that the act is within the jurisdiction of the Court.
2 If the Court is considering a challenge to its jurisdiction in accordance with articles 17-19 of the Statute, the Central Authority may postpone the execution of a request until the Court has decided.
3 If a Swiss citizen is surrendered to the Court, the Central Authority shall request the repatriation of the citizen upon completion of the proceedings.

Art. 17 Content and documentation of the request

1 A request for arrest and surrender of a person for whom the Court has issued a warrant of arrest shall include:
a. a description of the person, sufficient to identify the person, and information as to that person's probable location;
b. a copy of the warrant of arrest;
c. the reason for arrest.
2 A request for the arrest and surrender of a person already convicted shall include:
a. a copy of the warrant of arrest;
b. a copy of the judgment of conviction;
c. if the person has been sentenced, a copy of the sentence imposed and, in the case of a sentence of imprisonment, a statement of any time already served and the time remaining to be served.
3 The request shall be accompanied by:
a. a concise statement of the relevant facts sufficient for a legal assessment of the act;
b. the applicable provisions of the Statute and of the Rules of Procedure and Evidence of the Court.

Section 2: Detention pending surrender and seizure

Art. 18 Search, arrest and seizure

1 Requests for search and arrest shall contain:
a. information as accurate and complete as possible describing the person sought, including information as to the person's probable location;
b. a short statement of the facts including, where possible, the date and place of the act;
c. a statement of the existence of a valid warrant of arrest or a judgment of conviction against the person;
d. a statement that a request for surrender will follow.
2 If the Central Authority honors the request, it shall initiate a search for the person and order the arrest and, if necessary, search of the person.
3 Upon arrest, objects and assets shall be seized that may serve as evidence in proceedings before the Court or that derive from the criminal act.
4 Arrest and seizure shall be reported to the Central Authority . The Central Authority shall inform the Court immediately and ask the Court to make a request for surrender.

Art. 19 Warrant for arrest pending surrender

1 In anticipation of arrest or immediately after arrest the Central Authority shall issue a warrant for arrest pending surrender. The warrant shall include:
a. information concerning the person being prosecuted and the alleged act;
b. notification that the Court is asking for the surrender of the person;
c. notice of the right to appeal as provided in paragraph 4 and of the right to counsel.
2 If the person is not fit to remain in detention or if otherwise justified, the Central Authority may, after informing the Court and giving full consideration to the Court's recommendations, order security measures other than detention.

3 Upon presentation of the warrant for detention pending surrender, the executing authorities shall ascertain whether the person is identical to the person designated in the request. The authorities shall explain to the person the conditions for surrender and for simplified surrender (art. 23). The person shall be questioned briefly regarding personal circumstances and whether and for what reasons the person objects to the warrant or to the surrender; the person's counsel may assist at this hearing.
4 The warrant for detention pending surrender may be appealed within ten days of written presentation of the warrant; appeals must be lodged with the Federal Supreme Court. Articles 214 et seq. of the Federal Law of 15 June 1934 on Federal Criminal Procedure shall apply by analogy .

Art. 20 Detention pending surrender

1 Detention pending surrender generally shall be maintained throughout the proceedings.
2 Detention may exceptionally be lifted at any stage of the proceedings if it appears justified under the circumstances. The person may at any time submit an application for interim release. Before reaching a decision, the Central Authority shall inform the Court and give full consideration to the Court's recommendations. The decision of the Central Authority may be appealed within ten days of written presentation of the decision; appeals must be lodged with the Federal Supreme Court. Articles 214 et seq. of the Federal Law of 15 June 1934 on Federal Criminal Procedure shall apply by analogy.
3 If the person already is being held in pre-trial detention or is serving a prison sentence, the warrant for detention pending surrender shall have the following effects in particular, subject to other instructions of the Court:
a. Without approval of the Central Authority, the person may neither be released nor deported from Switzerland.
b. Approval of the Central Authority shall be necessary for alleviation of the conditions of detention.
c. Visitation rights may only be granted and correspondence may only be censored in agreement with the Central Authority.

Art. 21 Release from detention pending surrender

1 If the request for surrender and supporting documentation are not received by the Central Authority, the Central Authority shall release from the detention pending surrender at the latest 60 days after the arrest.
2 If the person already is being held in pre-trial detention or is serving a prison sentence, the period of time in paragraph 1 shall begin upon transfer into detention pending surrender.
3 A release from detention as provided in paragraph 1 shall not prejudice subsequent arrest and surrender, if the request for surrender and supporting documentation are transmitted at a later time.
4 Articles 53-60 of the Federal Law of 15 June 1934 on Federal Criminal Procedure shall further apply by analogy to suspension of detention.

Section 3: Decision to surrender

Art. 22 Right to be heard

1 The request for surrender and supporting documentation shall be submitted to the person being prosecuted and, if applicable , to the person's counsel.
2 The executing authorities shall explain to the person the conditions for surrender and for simplified surrender; the executing authorities shall also inform the person of the right:
a. to challenge the jurisdiction of the Court;
b. to be defended by counsel of the person's choosing or, if the person does not have counsel, to have the Central Authority assign counsel or, if applicable, an official counsel.
3 The person shall be questioned briefly regarding personal circumstances and whether and for what reasons the person objects to the surrender; the person's counsel may assist at this hearing .

Art. 23 Simplified surrender

1 If the person being prosecuted waives the right to surrender proceedings and has the waiver put on record, the Central Authority shall authorize the surrender, unless there are exceptional misgivings.
2 The Central Authority may request the Court to supply the documentation specified in article 17, if the Central Authority deems this documentation necessary for authorization of the surrender.
3 The person may revoke the waiver in paragraph 1, as long as the Central Authority has not authorized the surrender.

Art. 24 Authorization of surrender

1 The Central Authority shall authorize the surrender of the person being prosecuted and the transmission of the seized objects and assets.
2 If the person or the Central Authority challenges the jurisdiction of the Court, the authorization shall be postponed until the Court has decided.
3 If third parties who have acquired rights in good faith, authorities, or victims whose usual residence is in Switzerland assert rights with regard to the seized objects or assets that may serve as evidence, their handing over shall be subject to the condition that the Court gives the guarantee to return them without cost after conclusion of the proceedings.

Art. 25 Execution of the surrender

1 The surrender shall be executed immediately. The Central Authority shall issue the necessary orders in agreement with the Court.
2 The Central Authority may postpone the execution of the surrender by a period of time agreed upon with the Court, if the person to be surrendered is being prosecuted in Switzerland for another criminal act or if the person is in detention.
3 If the surrender is denied, the Central Authority shall lift the detention pending surrender.

Art. 26 Temporary transfer

1 When article 24 paragraph 2 or article 25 paragraph 2 applies, the Central Authority may authorize temporary transfer of the person, if consultations with the Court indicate:
a. how long the Court requires the person;

b. that the person will remain in detention for the entire duration;
c. which proceedings the imprisonment will be counted toward;
d. that the person will be returned after completion of the proceedings, upon request of the Central Authority.
2 Until the Central Authority has decided on surrender, temporary transfer may only be undertaken in agreement with the person to be transferred.

Art. 27 Rule of speciality

A person surrendered to the Court may be prosecuted, punished, or detained by the Court for any act within its jurisdiction.

Art. 28 Costs

Personal property of the person being prosecuted may be used to cover Swiss costs, to the extent the property is not to be transmitted to the Court.

Chapter 4: Other forms of cooperation

Section 1: Conditions

Art. 29 Principle

1 Cooperation as provided in article 30 shall be granted to the Court if the request and supporting documentation indicate that the act is within the jurisdiction of the Court.
2 If the Court is considering a challenge to its jurisdiction in accordance with articles 17- 19 of the Statute, the Central Authority may postpone execution of a request until the Court has decided; this shall not affect orders of preventive measures.

Art. 30 Forms of cooperation

Cooperation according to this chapter may include any procedural acts not prohibited by Swiss law that facilitate the investigation and prosecution of crimes within the jurisdiction of the Court or that serve to produce the proceeds of such crimes, in particular:
a. the identification and determination of the whereabouts of persons not being prosecuted by the Court or the location of objects;
b. the taking of evidence, including testimony under oath, and the production of evidence, including expert opinions and reports necessary to the Court;
c. the questioning of any person being investigated or prosecuted;
d. the service of documents, including judicial documents;
e. the temporary transfer of persons in detention as provided in article 39;
f. the examination of places or sites, including the exhumation and examination of grave sites;
g. the execution of searches and seizures;
h. the provision of records and documents, including official records and documents;
i. the protection of victims and witnesses and the preservation of evidence;

j. the identification, tracing and freezing or seizure of proceeds, property and assets and instrumentalities of crimes for the purpose of eventual forfeiture.

Art. 31 Preserving measures

1 Upon the explicit request of the Court, the Central Authority may take preventive measures to maintain existing conditions, to protect threatened legal interests, or to preserve endangered evidence.
2 If delay was to jeopardize the proceedings , the Central Authority may order preventive measures as soon as a request is announced and sufficient information is available to assess the conditions. The preserving measures shall be lifted if the Court does not make the request within the period of time specified by the Central Authority.

Art. 32 Application of the procedures of the Court

Upon the explicit request of the Court, requests shall be executed in the manner specified by the Court, in particular:
a. The statements of witnesses and experts shall be substantiated in the manner prescribed by the Statute or the Rules of Procedure and Evidence of the Court.
b. The procedures necessary for judicial admissibility of other evidence may be taken into account.
c. Measures may be taken to ensure the safety or physical or psychological well-being of victims, any witnesses, and their families.
d. Persons involved in the proceedings before the Court may be allowed to participate in the execution of requests and to examine the records.

Art. 33 Handing over of evidence to another State

If the Court requests the consent of the Central Authority to forward evidence to another State that was transmitted to the Court by Switzerland, then:
a. the Central Authority shall grant the request in accordance with the provisions of this chapter if the act is within the jurisdiction of the Court;
b. proceedings in accordance with the provisions of the Federal Law of 20 March 1981 on Mutual Legal Assistance shall be undertaken, if the act is a serious crime under the domestic law of the requesting State.

Section 2: Specific forms of cooperation

Art. 34 Principles for questioning

1 If a person is questioned in a language other than a language the person fully understands and speaks, a competent interpreter and such translations as are necessary to meet the requirements of fairness shall be provided.
2 The person may refuse to make a statement if:
a. the person would thereby incriminate himself or herself or a person named in this regard in the Rules of Procedure and Evidence of the Court, or if the person would thereby confess guilt; or

b. by refusing to make the statement, the person intends to prevent the disclosure of confidential information pertaining to national security in accordance with article 72 of the Statute.
3 The person shall be informed, prior to being questioned, of the rights provided in paragraph 2.
4 If the person asserts a ground specified in paragraph 2, the Central Authority shall decide on the admissibility of the questioning.

Art. 35 Questioning of a suspect

1 Where there are grounds to believe that a person has committed a crime within the jurisdiction of the Court, the person shall also have the following rights in addition to those provided in article 34:
a. to be informed, prior to being questioned, that there are grounds to believe that he or she has committed a crime within the jurisdiction of the Court;
b. to remain silent, without such silence being a consideration in the determination of guilt or innocence;
c. to be defended by counsel of the person's choosing or, if the person does not have counsel, to have the Central Authority assign counsel or, if applicable, a public defender;
d. to be questioned in the presence of counsel, unless the person has voluntarily waived the right to counsel.
2 The person shall be informed, prior to being questioned, of the rights provided in paragraph 1.

Art. 36 Service of records

The Court may serve its decisions and other records or documents upon recipients in Switzerland directly by mail.

Art. 37 Summons

1 A summons to appear before the Court as a witness or expert shall be accompanied by the Rule of Procedure and Evidence of the Court on self-incrimination. The Rule shall be given to the person in a language that the person understands.
2 The person summoned is under no obligation to comply with the summons. If so requested, the Central Authority shall obtain written assurances from the Court guaranteeing the safe-conduct of the witness or expert.

Art. 38 Investigative measures on Swiss territory

1 Upon request of the Prosecutor, the Central Authority may authorize the Prosecutor to conduct investigative measures on Swiss territory as indicated in article 99 paragraph 4 of the Statute.
2 The Central Authority shall inform the authorities which would be responsible for the investigative acts according to Swiss law.

Art. 39 Temporary transfer of persons in detention

1 Persons not accused by the Court who are in detention in Switzerland may be transferred temporarily to the Court for purposes of identification, questioning, confrontation, or other investigative acts, if the person consents in full knowledge of the circumstances.
2 The Court shall grant the transferred person safe-conduct, keep the person in detention, and give assurances that the person will be returned once the purpose of the transfer is satisfied.

Art. 40 Handing over of evidence

1 Objects, documents, or assets that have been seized as evidence, as well as records and decisions shall be provided to the Court upon the request of the Court.
2 If third parties who have acquired rights in good faith, authorities, or victims whose usual residence is in Switzerland claim rights with regard to objects, documents, or assets as described in paragraph 1, their handing over shall be subject to the condition that the Court gives the guarantee to return them without cost after conclusion of the proceedings.
3 Transmission may be postponed as long as the objects, documents, or assets are required for criminal proceedings pending in Switzerland and if the Court consents upon consultation.

Art. 41 Handing over for forfeiture, transfer to the Trust Fund, or restitution

1 Objects or assets subject to a precautionary seizure may at any time, upon request, be transmitted to the Court for the purpose of forfeiture, transfer to the Trust Fund (art. 79 of the Statute), or restitution.
2 Objects and assets referred to in paragraph 1 include:
a. instruments which served to commit the crime;
b. the product or proceeds of a criminal act, their replacement value, and illicit advantages;
c. gifts and other contributions that served as or that were intended as an inducement or reward for the criminal act, as well as their replacement value.
3 Objects and assets shall remain seized until they have been transmitted to the Court or until the Court notifies the Central Authority that it waives transmission.
4 Objects and assets may be retained in Switzerland if:
a. the victim's usual residence is in Switzerland and the objects and assets are to be returned to the victim;
b. authorities assert rights over them;
c. a person not involved in the criminal act claims that he or she acquired rights to the objects and assets in good faith in Switzerland or, provided that the person's usual residence is in Switzerland, in a foreign country;
d. the objects or assets are required for criminal proceedings pending in Switzerland or they could be forfeited in Switzerland.
5 If a person asserts a claim provided for in paragraph 4, the handing over of the objects or assets to the Court is suspended until the legal situation is clarified. The contested objects or assets may only be handed over to the person if:
a. the Court consents;
b. the authorities consent in the case of paragraph 4 subparagraph b; or
c. Swiss authorities recognize the validity of the claim.

Section 3: Procedure

Art. 42 Content of a request

1 A request shall contain:
a. a concise statement of the essential facts underlying the request, as well as the legal description of the act;
b. information as accurate and complete as possible about the person against whom the criminal proceedings are being conducted;
c. a concise statement of the purpose of the request and the cooperation sought, including the legal basis and the grounds for the request;
d. if applicable, as much detailed information as possible about the location or identification of any person or about any place or site that must be found or identified in order for the cooperation sought to be provided;
e. if applicable, the reasons for and details of any procedure or condition to be followed.
2 If a request does not satisfy the requirements of paragraph 1, the Central Authority may ask that the request be improved or supplemented; this shall not affect orders of preserving measures.

Art. 43 Decision to proceed and execution of request

1 Upon considering the request, the Central Authority shall issue a decision to proceed containing a summary explanation that cannot be appealed. The Central Authority shall designate the federal authorities or the canton responsible for the execution of the request and shall order the measures admissible for cooperation.
2 If the immediate execution of a request would interfere with an ongoing investigation or prosecution of a case different from that to which the request refers, the Central Authority may postpone the execution of the request for a period of time agreed upon with the Court.

Art. 44 National security

1 If the Central Authority has serious grounds to believe that the execution of a request could prejudice national security interests, it shall immediately inform the Department.
2 Where paragraph 1 applies, the Department may suspend execution measures.
3 Upon request of the Department, the Federal Council shall deny the request of the Court for cooperation, to the extent that granting the request would prejudice national security.

Art. 45 Notification of decisions

1 The executing authorities and the Central Authority shall notify their decisions upon the persons who, as provided in article 50, have a right to appeal and whose usual residence or service address is in Switzerland.
2 The right to notification shall expire once the order terminating the proceedings is executory.

Art. 46 Assistance at the proceedings and access to the files

1 To the extent necessary to protect their interests, persons may assist at the proceedings and examine the records.
2 The rights provided in paragraph 1 may, to the extent necessary, be restricted:
a. in the interest of the proceedings before the Court;
b. to protect an essential legal interest, provided that the Court asks for such protection;
c. due to the nature or the urgency of the measures to be taken;
d. to protect essential private interests;
e. in the interest of Swiss proceedings.
3 The holders of documents have the right to inform their clients of the existence of a request and of all facts related to it, provided this has not expressly been prohibited by the Central Authority either in exceptional circumstances or upon request of the Court and under menace of sanctions as provided in article 292 of the Criminal Code.

Art. 47 Simplified procedure

1 Persons who, as provided in article 50, have a right to appeal, in particular the holders of objects, documents, information, or assets, may consent to the handing over thereof to the Court until completion of the proceedings. Such consent shall be irrevocable.
2 If all persons entitled according to paragraph 1 give their consent, the executing authorities shall record this consent in writing and notify the Central Authority. The Central Authority shall complete the proceedings without issuing a final order.
3 If the handing over includes only part of the requested objects, documents, information, or assets, the regular procedure shall be followed for the remainder.

Art. 48 Final decision

When the Central Authority considers a request to be entirely or partially completed, it shall issue an decision, with reasons on whether cooperation is granted and to what extent.

Section 4: Appeals

Art. 49 Administrative court appeal

The final order of the Central Authority shall be subject to administrative court appeal to the Federal Supreme Court.

Art. 50 Right to appeal

Shall be entitled to appeal whoever :
a. is not accused in the proceedings before the Court;
b. is personally and directly affected by a measure;
c. has an interest worthy of protection in the modification or suspension of the decision; and
d. cannot assert his or her rights before the Court or cannot reasonably be expected to do so.

Art. 51 Grounds and deadline for appeal

1 Appeals may be lodged to allege violations of federal law, including excess or abuse of discretion.
2 If the appellant asserts grounds which, according to the provisions of the Statute, may only be adjudicated by the Court, then the Central Authority shall forward the appeal to the Court, unless the Court has already decided.
3 Appeals against a final order must be lodged within ten days of notification of the order.
4 The person entitled who intervenes in a pending proceeding may no longer challenge decisions that have become executory.

Art. 52 Postponement of proceedings

1 Appeals have suspensive effect.
2 In urgent cases as indicated in article 99 paragraph 2 of the Statute, the Central Authority may apply to the Federal Supreme Court for annulment of the suspension.
3 If the Federal Supreme Court annuls the suspension, it may join this decision with the condition specified in article 93 paragraph 8 subparagraph b of the Statute.

Chapter 5: Enforcement of penalties of the Court

Section 1: Sentencing decisions

Art. 53 Conditions

1 Upon the request of the Court, Switzerland may accept the enforcement of a final and executable sentencing decision, if:
a. the convicted person is a Swiss citizen; or
b. if the person's usual residence is in Switzerland.
2 Fines may also be executed if the convicted person's usual residence is outside of Switzerland, but the person has assets in Switzerland.

Art. 54 Decision on the request of the Court for executing a sentence of imprisonment

1 Upon consultation with the authorities to be designated to execute sentences of imprisonment, the Central Authority shall decide on a request of the Court for executing a sentence of imprisonment.
2 If the Central Authority accepts the request, it shall notify the Court and transmit all relevant information regarding the execution of the sentence.

Art. 55 Execution of the sentence of imprisonment

1 Upon acceptance of the request by the Central Authority, the sentence of imprisonment imposed by the Court shall become executable in Switzerland. The sentence shall be binding; only the Court shall have the right to decide on any reduction of the term of imprisonment.
2 The sentence shall be executed in accordance with Swiss law, subject to paragraph 1.
3 Upon the request of the Court, the Central Authority shall transmit all relevant information concerning the execution of the sentence to the Court. The Court may at any time send one

of its members to verify the conditions of imprisonment and meet unaccompanied with the convicted person.
4 Communications between the Court and the convicted person shall be confidential.

Art. 56 Requests of the convicted person

If the convicted person submits a request for conditional release, pardon, appeal, or retrial, the request shall be transmitted to the Central Authority. The Central Authority shall immediately forward the request with all useful documentation to the Court.

Art. 57 Costs

1 The Court shall be responsible for transportation costs as well as the costs specified in article 100 paragraph 1 subparagraphs c-e of the Statute.
2 The federal government shall be responsible for the remaining costs of the execution of sentences. The costs of detention shall be calculated on the basis of the rates for enforcement agreed upon between the Court and the host State in accordance with article 103 paragraph 4 of the Statute.

Section 2: Orders of forfeiture

Art. 58

Article 41 shall apply by analogy to the enforcement of orders of forfeiture, if the Court has already decided on the disposition of objects or assets in accordance with article 75 or 79 of the Statute and if the Court asks Switzerland for enforcement.

Chapter 6: Final provisions

Art. 59 Amendments to existing law

Existing legislation shall be amended as follows:
1. Federal Law of 20 March1981 on Mutual Legal Assistance
Preamble
pursuant to articles 103 and 114bis of the Federal Constitution ,
...
Art. 1 para. 1 Introduction
1 This law shall regulate all procedures pertaining to international cooperation in criminal matters, to the extent that other laws or international agreements do not determine otherwise,
in particular:
2. Federal Decree of 21 December 1995 on Cooperation with the International Tribunals for the Prosecution of Serious Violations of International Humanitarian Law
Preamble
pursuant to the competence of the Confederation in foreign affairs ,
...
Art. 34 para. 4 (new)

4 The validity of this decree shall be extended until 31 December 2008.

Art. 60 Referendum and entry into force

1 This law shall be subject to a facultative referendum.
2 The Federal Council shall determine entry into force.

National Council, 22 June 2001 Council of States, 22 June 2001
The President: Peter Hess The President: Françoise Saudan
The Secretary: Ueli Anliker The Secretary: Christoph Lanz
Date of publication: 3 July 2001
Deadline for a referendum: 11 October 2001

10.1 EUROPEAN

☛ European Court of Human Rights: Banković Case (admissibility), 12 December 2001

Grand Chamber

Decision

As to Admissibility of

Application no. 52207/99
by Vlastimir and Borka BANKOVIĆ, Śivana STOJANOVIĆ, Mirjana STOIMENOVSKI, Dragana JOKSIMOVIĆ and Dragan SUKOVIĆ
against
Belgium, the Czech Republic, Denmark, France, Germany, Greece, Hungary, Iceland, Italy, Luxembourg, the Netherlands, Norway, Poland, Portugal, Spain, Turkey and the United Kingdom
The European Court of Human Rights, sitting as a Grand Chamber composed of
Mr L. Wildhaber, *President*,
Mrs E. Palm,
Mr C.L. Rozakis,
Mr G. Ress,
Mr J.-P. Costa,
Mr Gaukur Jörundsson,
Mr L. Caflisch,
Mr P. Kuris,
Mr I. Cabral Barreto,
Mr R. Türmen,
Mrs V. StráŽnická,
Mr C. Bîrsan,
Mr J. Casadevall,
Mr J. Hedigan,

Mrs W. Thomassen,
Mr A.B. Baka,
Mr K. Traja, *Judges*,
and Mr P.J. Mahoney, *Registrar*,
Having regard to the above application lodged on 20 October 1999 and registered on 28 October 1999,
Having regard to the decision of 14 November 2000 by which the Chamber of the First Section to which the case had originally been assigned relinquished its jurisdiction in favour of the Grand Chamber (Article 30 of the Convention),
Having regard to the observations submitted by the respondent Governments and the observations in reply submitted by the applicants,
Having regard to the parties' oral submissions on 24 October 2001 and their subsequent written comments in reply to Judges' questions,
Having deliberated on 24 October and 12 December 2001, decides, on the last-mentioned date, as follows:

The Facts

1. The applicants are all citizens of the Federal Republic of Yugoslavia ("FRY"). The first and second applicants, Vlastimir and Borka Banković, were born in 1942 and 1945, respectively and they apply to the Court on their own behalf and on behalf of their deceased daughter, Ksenija Banković. The third applicant, Śivana Stojanović, was born in 1937 and she applies on her own behalf and on behalf of her deceased son, Nebojsa Stojanović. The fourth applicant, Mirjana Stoimenovski, applies on her own behalf and on behalf of her deceased son, Darko Stoimenovski. The fifth applicant, Dragana Joksimović, was born in 1956 and she applies on her own behalf and on behalf of her deceased husband, Milan Joksimović. The sixth applicant, Dragan Suković, applies in his own right.
2. The applicants are represented before the Court by Mr Anthony Fisher, a solicitor practising in Essex, by Mr Vojin Dimitrijević, Director of the Belgrade Centre for Human Rights, by Mr Hurst Hannum, Professor of International Law at Tufts University, Medford, MA, the United States and by Ms Françoise Hampson, barrister and Professor of International Law at the University of Essex. Those representatives attended the oral hearing before the Court together with their advisers, Mr Rick Lawson, Ms Tatjana Papić and Mr Vladan Joksimović. The third applicant, Ms Śivana Stojanović, also attended the hearing.
3. The Governments are represented before the Court by their Agents. At the oral hearing the following Governments were represented as follows: the United Kingdom (whose submissions were made on behalf of all respondents) by Mr Christopher Greenwood Q.C. and Professor of International Law, by Mr James Eadie, Counsel, by Mr Martin Eaton, Agent, Foreign and Commonwealth Office and by Mr Martin Hemming, Adviser; Belgium by Mr Jan Lathouwers, Deputy Agent; France by Mr Pierre Boussaroque, Counsel; Germany by Mr Christoph Blosen, Deputy to the German Permanent Representative to the Council of Europe; Greece by Mr Michael Apessos, Advisor; Hungary by Mr Lipót Höltzl and Ms Monika Weller, Agent and Co-Agent, respectively; Italy by Mr Francesco Crisafulli, Deputy Co-Agent; Luxembourg by Mr Nicolas Mackel, Agent; The Netherlands by Ms Jolien Schukking, Agent; Norway by Mr Frode Elgesem, Acting Agent; Poland by Mr Krysztof Drzewicki, Agent and Ms Renata Kowalska, Counsel; and Turkey by Ms Deniz Akçay, Co-Agent.

A. The circumstances of the case

4. The facts of the case, as submitted by the parties, may be summarised as follows.
5. The respondent Governments considered the application inadmissible without any need to address the facts of the case and submitted that any failure on their part to expressly dispute a fact should not be held against them. The Court has not, in summarising the circumstances of the case below, interpreted any failure expressly to contest a fact as any party's acceptance of it.

1. Background

6. The conflict in Kosovo between Serbian and Kosovar Albanian forces during 1998 and 1999 is well documented. Against the background of the escalating conflict, together with the growing concerns and unsuccessful diplomatic initiatives of the international community, the six-nation Contact Group (established in 1992 by the London Conference) met and agreed to convene negotiations between the parties to the conflict.
7. On 30 January 1999, and following a decision of its North Atlantic Council ("NAC"), the North Atlantic Treaty Organisation ("NATO") announced air strikes on the territory of the FRY in the case of non-compliance with the demands of the international community. Negotiations consequently took place between the parties to the conflict from 6 to 23 February 1999 in Rambouillet and from 15 to 18 March 1999 in Paris. The resulting proposed peace agreement was signed by the Kosovar Albanian delegation but not by the Serbian delegation.
8. Considering that all efforts to achieve a negotiated, political solution to the Kosovo crisis had failed, the NAC decided on, and on 23 March 1999 the Secretary General of NATO announced, the beginning of air strikes (Operation Allied Force) against the FRY. The air strikes lasted from 24 March to 8 June 1999.

2. The bombing of Radio Televizije Srbije ("RTS")

9. Three television channels and four radio stations operated from the RTS facilities in Belgrade. The main production facilities were housed in three buildings at Takovska Street. The master control room was housed on the first floor of one of the buildings and was staffed mainly by technical staff.
10. On 23 April 1999, just after 2.00 am approximately, one of the RTS buildings at Takovska Street was hit by a missile launched from a NATO forces' aircraft. Two of the four floors of the building collapsed and the master control room was destroyed.
11. The daughter of the first and second applicants, the sons of the third and fourth applicants and the husband of the fifth applicant were killed and the sixth applicant was injured. Sixteen persons were killed and another sixteen were seriously injured in the bombing of the RTS. Twenty-four targets were hit in the FRY that night, including three in Belgrade.

3. Relevant proceedings before other international tribunals

12. On 26 April 1999 the FRY deposited with the Secretary General of the United Nations ("UN") its declaration recognising the compulsory jurisdiction of the International Court of Justice ("ICJ"). On 29 April 1999 the FRY instituted proceedings against Belgium and nine

other States concerning their participation in Operation Allied Force and submitted a request for the indication of provisional measures pursuant to Article 73 of the Rules of Court of the ICJ. By order dated 2 June 1999 the ICJ rejected that request. The remaining issues in the case are pending.
13. In June 2000 the Committee established to review Operation Allied Force reported to the Prosecutor of the International Criminal Tribunal for the Former Yugoslavia ("ICTY"). An investigation was not recommended. On 2 June 2000 the Prosecutor informed the UN Security Council of her decision not to open an investigation.

B. Relevant international legal materials

1. The Treaty of Washington 1949

14. The Treaty of Washington came into force on 24 August 1949 ("the 1949 Treaty") and created an alliance called the North Atlantic Treaty Organisation ("NATO") of ten European states (Belgium, France, Luxembourg, the Netherlands, the United Kingdom, Denmark, Iceland, Italy, Norway, Portugal) with Canada and the United States. In 1952 Greece and Turkey acceded to the 1949 Treaty, the Federal Republic of Germany joined in 1955 and Spain also became a member in 1982. These countries were joined on 12 March 1999 by the Czech Republic, Hungary and Poland.
15. The essential purpose of NATO is to safeguard the freedom and security of all its members by political and military means in accordance with the principles of the UN Charter. Its fundamental operating principle is that of a common commitment to mutual co-operation among sovereign states based on the indivisibility of the security of its members.

2. The Vienna Convention on the Law of Treaties 1969 ("the Vienna Convention 1969")

16. Article 31 of the Vienna Convention 1969 is entitled "General rule of interpretation" and reads, in so far as relevant, as follows:

> "1. A treaty shall be interpreted in good faith in accordance with the ordinary meaning to be given to the terms of the treaty in their context and in light of its object and purpose.
> ...
> 3. There shall be taken into account, together with the context:
> ...
> (b) any subsequent practice in the application of the treaty which establishes the agreement of the parties regarding its interpretation;
> (c) any relevant rules of international law applicable in the relations between the parties."

17. Article 32 is entitled "Supplementary means of interpretation" and reads as follows:

> "Recourse may be had to supplementary means of interpretation, including the preparatory work of the treaty and the circumstances of its conclusion, in order to confirm the meaning resulting from the application of article 31, or to determine the meaning when the interpretation according to article 31:
> (a) leaves the meaning ambiguous or obscure;
> (b) leads to a result which is manifestly absurd."

18. In its commentary on these Articles, the International Law Commission noted that Articles 31 and 32 should operate in conjunction, and would not have the effect of drawing a rigid line between the "general rule" and the "supplementary means" of interpretation. At the same time the distinction itself was justified since the elements of interpretation in Article 31 all relate to the agreement between the parties at the time when or after it received authentic expression in the text. Preparatory work did not have the same authentic character "however valuable it may sometimes be in throwing light on the expression of agreement in the text" (Yrbk. ILC (1966), ii. 219-220).

3. The drafting history of Article 1 of the Convention

19. The text prepared by the Committee of the Consultative Assembly of the Council of Europe on legal and administrative questions provided, in what became Article 1 of the Convention, that the "member States shall undertake to ensure to all persons residing within their territories the rights...". The Expert Intergovernmental Committee, which considered the Consultative Assembly's draft, decided to replace the reference to "all persons residing within their territories" with a reference to persons "within their jurisdiction". The reasons were noted in the following extract from the *Collected Edition of the* Travaux Préparatoires *of the European Convention on Human Rights* (Vol. III, p. 260):

> "The Assembly draft had extended the benefits of the Convention to 'all persons residing within the territories of the signatory States'. It seemed to the Committee that the term 'residing' might be considered too restrictive. It was felt that there were good grounds for extending the benefits of the Convention to all persons in the territories of the signatory States, even those who could not be considered as residing there in the legal sense of the word. The Committee therefore replaced the term 'residing' by the words 'within their jurisdiction' which are also contained in Article 2 of the Draft Covenant of the United Nations Commission."

20. The next relevant comment prior to the adoption of Article 1 of the Convention, made by the Belgian representative on 25 August 1950 during the plenary sitting of the Consultative Assembly, was to the effect that

> "henceforth the right of protection by our States, by virtue of a formal clause of the Convention, may be exercised with full force, and without any differentiation or distinction, in favour of individuals of whatever nationality, who on the territory of any one of our States, may have had reason to complain that [their] rights have been violated".

21. The *travaux préparatoires* go on to note that the wording of Article 1 including "within their jurisdiction", did not give rise to any further discussion and the text as it was (and is now) was adopted by the Consultative Assembly on 25 August 1950 without further amendment (the above-cited Collected Edition (Vol. VI, p. 132).

4. The American Declaration on the Rights and Duties of Man 1948

22. Article 2 of this declaration reads as follows:

"All persons are equal before the law and have the rights and duties established in this Declaration, without distinction as to race, sex, language, creed or any other factor."

23. In its report in the *Coard* case (Report No. 109/99, case No. 10.951, *Coard et al. v. the United States*, 29 September 1999, §§ 37, 39, 41 and 43), the Inter-American Commission of Human Rights examined complaints about the applicants' detention and treatment by United States' forces in the first days of the military operation in Grenada and commented:

"While the extraterritorial application of the American Declaration has not been placed at issue by the parties, the Commission finds it pertinent to note that, under certain circumstances, the exercise of its jurisdiction over acts with an extra-territorial locus will not only be consistent with, but required by, the norms which pertain. The fundamental rights of the individual are proclaimed in the Americas on the basis of the principles of equality and non-discrimination – 'without distinction as to race, nationality, creed or sex'. ... Given that individual rights inhere simply by virtue of a person's humanity, each American State is obliged to uphold the protected rights of any person subject to its jurisdiction. While this most commonly refers to persons within a state's territory, it may, under given circumstances, refer to conduct with an extraterritorial locus where the person concerned is present in the territory of one state, but subject to the control of another state – usually through the acts of the latter's agents abroad. In principle, the inquiry turns not on the presumed victim's nationality or presence within a particular geographic area, but on whether, under the specific circumstances, the State observed the rights of a person subject to its authority and control."

24. Article 1 of the American Convention on Human Rights 1978, on which the substantive jurisdiction of the Inter-American Court of Human Rights is based, reads, in so far as relevant, as follows:

"The States Parties to this Convention undertake to respect the rights and freedoms recognised herein and to ensure to all persons subject to their jurisdiction the free and full exercise of those rights and freedoms, without any discrimination..."

5. The four Geneva Conventions on the Protection of War Victims 1949

25. Article 1 of each of these Conventions ("the Geneva Conventions 1949") requires the Contracting Parties to undertake "to respect and to ensure respect for the present Convention in all circumstances".

6. Covenant on Civil and Political Rights 1966 ("CCPR 1966") and its Optional Protocol 1966

26. Article 2 § 1 of CCPR 1966 reads, in so far as relevant, as follows:

"Each State Party to the present Convention undertakes to respect and to ensure to all individuals within its territory and subject to its jurisdiction the rights recognised in the present Covenant ..."

The Commission on Human Rights approved during its sixth session in 1950 a motion to include the words "within its territory and subject to its" in Article 2 § 1 of the draft Covenant. Subsequent proposals to exclude those words were defeated in 1952 and 1963. Subsequently, the Human Rights Committee has sought to develop, in certain limited contexts, the Contracting States' responsibility for the acts of their agents abroad.
27. Article 1 of the Optional Protocol 1966 reads, in so far as relevant, as follows:

> "A State Party to the Covenant that becomes a Party to the present Protocol recognises the competence of the Committee to receive and consider communications from individuals subject to its jurisdiction who claim to be victims of a violation by that State Party of any of the rights set forth in the Covenant. ..."

Complaints

28. The applicants complain about the bombing of the RTS building on 23 April 1999 by NATO forces and they invoke the following provisions of the Convention: Article 2 (the right to life), Article 10 (freedom of expression) and Article 13 (the right to an effective remedy).

The Law

29. The first to the fifth applicants rely on Articles 2, 10 and 13 on their own behalf and on behalf of their deceased close relatives. The sixth applicant, injured during the strike, relies on these Articles on his own behalf. With the consent of the Court, the parties' written and oral submissions were limited to the admissibility issues, the Governments' further accepting that they would not be arguing that the complaints were manifestly ill-founded.
30. As to the admissibility of the case, the applicants submit that the application is compatible *ratione loci* with the provisions of the Convention because the impugned acts of the respondent States, which were either in the FRY or on their own territories but producing effects in the FRY, brought them and their deceased relatives within the jurisdiction of those States. They also suggest that the respondent States are severally liable for the strike despite its having been carried out by NATO forces, and that they had no effective remedies to exhaust.
31. The Governments dispute the admissibility of the case. They mainly contend that the application is incompatible *ratione personae* with the provisions of the Convention because the applicants did not fall within the jurisdiction of the respondent States within the meaning of Article 1 of the Convention. They also maintain that, in accordance with the "*Monetary Gold* principle" of the ICJ, this Court cannot decide the merits of the case as it would be determining the rights and obligations of the United States, of Canada and of NATO itself, none of whom are Contracting Parties to the Convention or, therefore, parties to the present application (*Monetary Gold Removed from Rome in 1943*, ICJ Reports 1954, p. 19 as applied in *East Timor*, ICJ Reports 1995, p. 90).
32. The French Government further argue that the bombardment was not imputable to the respondent States but to NATO, an organisation with an international legal personality separate from that of the respondent States. The Turkish Government made certain submissions as regards their view of the position in northern Cyprus.

33. Finally, the Hungarian, Italian and Polish Governments submit that the applicants have failed to exhaust effective remedies available in those States as required by Article 35 § 1 of the Convention.

A. Whether the applicants and their deceased relatives came within the "jurisdiction" of the respondent States within the meaning of Article 1 of the Convention

34. This is the principal basis upon which the Governments contest the admissibility of the application and the Court will consider first this question. Article 1 of the Convention reads as follows:

> "The High Contracting Parties shall secure to everyone within their jurisdiction the rights and freedoms defined in Section I of [the] Convention."

1. The submissions of the respondent Governments

35. The Governments contend that the applicants and their deceased relatives were not, at the relevant time, within the "jurisdiction" of the respondent States and that the application is therefore incompatible *ratione personae* with the provisions of the Convention.
36. As to the precise meaning of "jurisdiction", they suggest that it should be interpreted in accordance with the ordinary and well-established meaning of that term in public international law. The exercise of "jurisdiction" therefore involves the assertion or exercise of legal authority, actual or purported, over persons owing some form of allegiance to that State or who have been brought within that State's control. They also suggest that the term "jurisdiction" generally entails some form of structured relationship normally existing over a period of time.
37. They maintain that they are supported in this respect by the jurisprudence of the Court which has applied this notion of jurisdiction to confirm that certain individuals affected by acts of a respondent State outside of its territory can be considered to fall within its jurisdiction because there was an exercise of some form of legal authority by the relevant State over them. The arrest and detention of the applicants outside of the territory of the respondent State in the *Issa* and *Öcalan* cases (*Issa and Others v. Turkey*, (dec.), no. 31821/96, 30 May 2000, unreported and *Öcalan v. Turkey*, (dec.), no. 46221/99, 14 December 2000, unreported) constituted, according to the Governments, a classic exercise of such legal authority or jurisdiction over those persons by military forces on foreign soil. Jurisdiction in the *Xhavara* case which concerned the alleged deliberate striking of an Albanian ship by an Italian naval vessel 35 nautical miles off the coast of Italy (*Xhavara and Others v. Italy and Albania*, (dec.), no. 39473/98, 11 January 2001, unreported) was shared by written agreement between the respondent States. The Governments consider that they are also supported in their interpretation of jurisdiction by the *travaux préparatoires* and by State practice in applying the Convention since its ratification by them. They refer, in this latter respect, to the lack of derogations under Article 15 of the Convention in respect of military operations in which the Contracting States participated outside of their territories.
38. The Governments conclude that it is clear that the conduct of which the applicants complain could not be described as the exercise of such legal authority or competence.
39. Moreover, the Governments go on to take issue with the applicants' principal submissions as to the meaning of jurisdiction in Article 1 of the Convention namely, that the

positive obligation to protect in Article 1 of the Convention applies proportionately to the control exercised.

40. In the first place, the Governments consider that the very text of Article 1 does not support this interpretation. Had the drafters wished for what is effectively a "cause-and-effect" type of responsibility, they could have adopted wording similar to that of Article 1 of the Geneva Conventions 1949 (cited above at § 25). In any event, the applicants' interpretation of jurisdiction would invert and divide the positive obligation on Contracting States to secure the substantive rights in a manner never contemplated by Article 1 of the Convention.

41. Secondly, they consider the applicants' reliance on Article 15 in support of their expansive interpretation of Article 1 to be mistaken and that Article 15, in fact, supports the Governments' own position. The Governments argue that there is nothing in the text or application of Article
15 of the Convention to imply, as the applicants wrongly assume, that Article 15 § 2 refers to "war" or "public emergency" situations outside as well as inside the territories of the Contracting States. Accordingly, Article 15 § 2 does not strengthen the applicants' broad interpretation of Article 1 of the Convention.

42. Thirdly, and as to the applicants' suggestion that the citizens of the FRY would be left without a Convention remedy, the Governments recall that a finding that Turkey was not responsible under the Convention in the northern Cyprus cases would have deprived the inhabitants of that territory of the benefit of the Convention rights they would otherwise have enjoyed (see, Loizidou v. Turkey judgment of 23 March 1995 (*preliminary objections*), Series A no. 310, Loizidou v. Turkey judgment of 18 December 1996 (*Merits*), *Reports of Judgments and Decisions* 1996-VI, no. 26 and *Cyprus v. Turkey* [GC], no. 25781/94, ECHR 2001). In the present case, the Governments note that the FRY was not and is not a party to the Convention and its inhabitants had no existing rights under the Convention.

43. Fourthly, the Governments strongly dispute the applicants' assertions as to the risk involved in not rendering respondent States participating in such military missions accountable under the Convention. The Governments contend that it is rather the applicants' novel "cause-and-effect" theory of extra-territorial jurisdiction that would have serious international consequences. Such a theory would, when added to the applicants' assertion concerning the several liability of all respondent States as members of NATO, seriously distort the purpose and scheme of the Convention. In particular, it would have serious consequences for international military collective action as it would render the Court competent to review the participation of Contracting States in military missions all over the world in circumstances when it would be impossible for those States to secure any of the Convention rights to the inhabitants of those territories and even in situations where a Contracting State had no active part in the relevant mission. The resulting Convention exposure would, according to the Governments, risk undermining significantly the States' participation in such missions and would, in any event, result in far more protective derogations under Article 15 of the Convention. In addition, they suggest that international humanitarian law, the ICTY and, most recently, the International Criminal Court ("ICC") exist to regulate such State conduct.

44. Finally, the Governments also contest the applicants' alternative theories of State responsibility under Article 1 of the Convention. As to their argument concerning the alleged control of the airspace over Belgrade by NATO forces, the Governments deny such control and, in any event, dispute that any such control could be equated with the territorial control of the nature and extent, identified in the above-cited judgments concerning northern

Cyprus, which results in the exercise of effective control or of legal authority. The Governments further consider the applicants' comparison of the present case with the Soering case to be fundamentally flawed (Soering v. the United Kingdom judgment of 7 July 1989, Series A no. 161). At the time the impugned decision was to be taken in respect of Mr Soering's extradition, he was detained on the territory of the respondent State, a situation constituting a classic exercise of legal authority over an individual to whom the State could secure the full range of Convention rights.

45. In sum, the Governments submit that the applicants and their deceased relatives did not fall within the jurisdiction of the respondent States and that their application is, therefore, incompatible *ratione personae* with the provisions of the Convention.

2. The submissions of the applicants

46. The applicants consider the application to be compatible *ratione loci* with the provisions of the Convention because they were brought within the jurisdiction of the respondent States by the RTS strike. In particular, they suggest that the determination of "jurisdiction" can be done by adapting the "effective control" criteria developed in the above-cited Loizidou judgments (*preliminary objections* and *merits*) so that the extent of the positive obligation under Article 1 of the Convention to secure Convention rights would be proportionate to the level of control in fact exercised. They consider that this approach to jurisdiction in Article 1 would provide manageable criteria by which the Court could deal with future complaints arising out of comparable circumstances.

47. Accordingly, when, as in the above-noted Loizidou judgments (*preliminary objections* and *merits*), the Turkish forces were found to have had effective control of northern Cyprus, it was appropriate to consider Turkey obliged to vindicate the full range of Convention rights in that area. However, when the respondent States strike a target outside their territory, they are not obliged to do the impossible (secure the full range of Convention rights) but rather are held accountable for those Convention rights within their control in the situation in question.

48. The applicants maintain that this approach is entirely consistent with the Convention jurisprudence to date, and they rely, in particular, on the admissibility decisions in the above-cited cases of *Issa*, *Xhavara* and *Öcalan* together with the admissibility decision in the *Ilascu* case (*Ilascu v. Moldova and the Russian Federation*, (dec.), no. 48787/99, 4 July 2001, unreported). They consider it also consistent with the interpretation of similar phrases by the Inter-American Commission of Human Rights (the Report in the *Coard* case, at § 23 above). Citing one case of the Human Rights Committee, they contend that that Committee has reached consistent conclusions as regards Article 2 § 1 of the CCPR 1966 and Article 1 of its Optional Protocol.

49. They further suggest that support for their approach to the concept of "jurisdiction" is to be found in the text and structure of the Convention and, in particular, in Article 15. They argue that Article 15 would be rendered meaningless if it did not also apply to extra-territorial war or emergencies. A State is therefore required to make a derogation under Article 15 because, without that derogation, the Convention applies even during such conflicts.

50. As to the Governments' reliance on the *travaux préparatoires*, they point out that this is not a source of primary or definitive evidence as to the meaning to be accorded to the use of jurisdiction in Article 1 of the Convention. Indeed, they note that the "legal authority" and "structured relationship" which the Governments submit are essential elements of jurisdic-

tion are not mentioned in the *travaux préparatoires.*

51. They reject the Governments' suggestion that their interpretation of Article 1 would be a dangerous development. The present case is not about an accident or omission during a UN peace-keeping mission or about rogue soldiers. Rather it concerns a deliberate act approved by each of the respondent States and executed as planned. Indeed, the applicants suggest that it would be dangerous not to render States accountable for the violations of the Convention arising from this type of State action. In emphasising the pre-eminence of the right to life and the role of the Convention as an instrument for European public order, they stress that a failure to find the respondent States responsible would leave these applicants without a remedy and the respondent States' armies free to act with impunity. The ICJ is not open to an application from individuals, the ICTY adjudicates on the responsibility of individuals for serious war crimes and the ICC has not yet been established.

52. Alternatively, the applicants argue that, given the size of the air operation and the relatively few air casualties, NATO's control over the airspace was nearly as complete as Turkey's control over the territory of northern Cyprus. While it was a control limited in scope (airspace only), the

Article 1 positive obligation could be similarly limited. They consider that the concepts of "effective control" and "jurisdiction" must be flexible enough to take account of the availability and use of modern precision weapons which allow extra-territorial action of great precision and impact without the need for ground troops. Given such modern advances, reliance on the difference between air attacks and ground troops has become unrealistic.

53. Alternatively, the applicants compare the circumstances of the present case to those of the above-cited Soering case, arguing that the impugned act was, in fact, the extra-territorial effect of prior decisions, to strike RTS and to launch the missile, which decisions had been taken on the territory of the respondent State or States. They suggest therefore that jurisdiction can be established for the same reasons it was in the Soering case.

3. The Court's assessment

54. The Court notes that the real connection between the applicants and the respondent States is the impugned act which, wherever decided, was performed, or had effects, outside of the territory of those States ("the extra-territorial act"). It considers that the essential question to be examined therefore is whether the applicants and their deceased relatives were, as a result of that extra-territorial act, capable of falling within the jurisdiction of the respondent States (Drozd and Janousek v. France and Spain, judgment of 26 June 1992, Series A no. 240, § 91, the above-cited Loizidou judgments (*preliminary objections* and *merits*), at § 64 and § 56 respectively, and the *Cyprus v. Turkey* judgment, cited above, at § 80).

(a) The applicable rules of interpretation

55. The Court recalls that the Convention must be interpreted in the light of the rules set out in the Vienna Convention 1969 (Golder v. the United Kingdom judgment of 21 February 1975, Series A no. 18, § 29).

56. It will, therefore, seek to ascertain the ordinary meaning to be given to the phrase "within their jurisdiction" in its context and in the light of the object and purpose of the Convention (Article 31 § 1 of the Vienna Convention 1969 and, amongst other authorities, Johnston and

Others v. Ireland judgment of 18 December 1986, Series A no. 112, § 51). The Court will also consider "any subsequent practice in the application of the treaty which establishes the agreement of the parties regarding its interpretation" (Article 31 § 3 (b) of the Vienna Convention 1969 and the above-cited Loizidou judgment (*preliminary objections*), at § 73).
57. Moreover, Article 31 § 3 (c) indicates that account is to be taken of "any relevant rules of international law applicable in the relations between the parties". More generally, the Court recalls that the principles underlying the Convention cannot be interpreted and applied in a vacuum. The Court must also take into account any relevant rules of international law when examining questions concerning its jurisdiction and, consequently, determine State responsibility in conformity with the governing principles of international law, although it must remain mindful of the Convention's special character as a human rights treaty (the above-cited Loizidou judgment (*merits*), at §§ 43 and 52). The Convention should be interpreted as far as possible in harmony with other principles of international law of which it forms part (*Al-Adsani v. the United Kingdom*, [GC], no. 35763, § 60, to be reported in ECHR 2001).
58. It is further recalled that the *travaux préparatoires* can also be consulted with a view to confirming any meaning resulting from the application of Article 31 of the Vienna Convention 1969 or to determining the meaning when the interpretation under Article 31 of the Vienna Convention 1969 leaves the meaning "ambiguous or obscure" or leads to a result which is "manifestly absurd or unreasonable" (Article 32). The Court has also noted the ILC commentary on the relationship between the rules of interpretation codified in those Articles 31 and 32 (the text of those Articles and a summary of the ILC commentary is set out above at §§ 16-18 above).

(b) The meaning of the words "within their jurisdiction"

59. As to the "ordinary meaning" of the relevant term in Article 1 of the Convention, the Court is satisfied that, from the standpoint of public international law, the jurisdictional competence of a State is primarily territorial. While international law does not exclude a State's exercise of jurisdiction extra-territorially, the suggested bases of such jurisdiction (including nationality, flag, diplomatic and consular relations, effect, protection, passive personality and universality) are, as a general rule, defined and limited by the sovereign territorial rights of the other relevant States (Mann, *"The Doctrine of Jurisdiction in International Law"*, RdC, 1964, Vol. 1; Mann, *"The Doctrine of Jurisdiction in International Law, Twenty Years Later"*, RdC, 1984, Vol. 1; Bernhardt, *Encyclopaedia of Public International Law*, Edition 1997, Vol. 3, pp. 55-59 *"Jurisdiction of States"* and Edition 1995, Vol. 2, pp. 337-343 *"Extra-territorial Effects of Administrative, Judicial and Legislative Acts"*; Oppenheim's *International Law*, 9th Edition 1992 (Jennings and Watts), Vol. 1, § 137; P.M. Dupuy, *Droit International Public*, 4th Edition 1998, p. 61; and Brownlie, *Principles of International Law*, 5th Edition 1998, pp. 287, 301 and 312-314).
60. Accordingly, for example, a State's competence to exercise jurisdiction over its own nationals abroad is subordinate to that State's and other States' territorial competence (Higgins, *Problems and Process* (1994), at p. 73; and Nguyen Quoc Dinh, *Droit International Public*, 6th Edition 1999 (Daillier and Pellet), p. 500). In addition, a State may not actually exercise jurisdiction on the territory of another without the latter's consent, invitation or acquiescence, unless the former is an occupying State in which case it can be found to exercise jurisdiction in that territory, at least in certain respects (Bernhardt, cited above, Vol. 3 at p. 59 and Vol. 2 at pp. 338-340; Oppenheim, cited above, at § 137; P.M. Dupuy, cited

above, at pp. 64-65; Brownlie, cited above, at p. 313; Cassese, *International Law*, 2001, p. 89; and, most recently, the "*Report on the Preferential Treatment of National Minorities by their Kin-States*" adopted by the Venice Commission at its 48th Plenary Meeting, Venice, 19-20 October 2001).

61. The Court is of the view, therefore, that Article 1 of the Convention must be considered to reflect this ordinary and essentially territorial notion of jurisdiction, other bases of jurisdiction being exceptional and requiring special justification in the particular circumstances of each case (see, *mutatis mutandis* and in general, Select Committee of Experts on Extraterritorial Criminal Jurisdiction, European Committee on Crime Problems, Council of Europe, "*Extraterritorial Criminal Jurisdiction*", Report published in 1990, at pp. 8-30).

62. The Court finds State practice in the application of the Convention since its ratification to be indicative of a lack of any apprehension on the part of the Contracting States of their extra-territorial responsibility in contexts similar to the present case. Although there have been a number of military missions involving Contracting States acting extra-territorially since their ratification of the Convention (*inter alia*, in the Gulf, in Bosnia and Herzegovina and in the FRY), no State has indicated a belief that its extra-territorial actions involved an exercise of jurisdiction within the meaning of Article 1 of the Convention by making a derogation pursuant to Article 15 of the Convention. The existing derogations were lodged by Turkey and the United Kingdom[15] in respect of certain internal conflicts (in south-east Turkey and Northern Ireland, respectively) and the Court does not find any basis upon which to accept the applicants' suggestion that Article 15 covers all "war" and "public emergency" situations generally, whether obtaining inside or outside the territory of the Contracting State. Indeed, Article 15 itself is to be read subject to the "jurisdiction" limitation enumerated in Article 1 of the Convention.

63. Finally, the Court finds clear confirmation of this essentially territorial notion of jurisdiction in the *travaux préparatoires* which demonstrate that the Expert Intergovernmental Committee replaced the words "all persons residing within their territories" with a reference to persons "within their jurisdiction" with a view to expanding the Convention's application to others who may not reside, in a legal sense, but who are, nevertheless, on the territory of the Contracting States (§ 19 above).

64. It is true that the notion of the Convention being a living instrument to be interpreted in light of present-day conditions is firmly rooted in the Court's case-law. The Court has applied that approach not only to the Convention's substantive provisions (for example, the Soering judgment cited above, at § 102; the Dudgeon v. the United Kingdom judgment of 22 October 1981, Series A no. 45; the X, Y and Z v. the United Kingdom judgment of 22 April 1997, *Reports* 1997-II; *V. v. the United Kingdom* [GC], no. 24888/94, § 72, ECHR 1999-IX; and *Matthews v. the United Kingdom* [GC], no. 24833/94, § 39, ECHR 1999-I) but more relevantly to its interpretation of former Articles 25 and 46 concerning the recognition by a Contracting State of the competence of the Convention organs (the above-cited Loizidou judgment (*preliminary objections*), at § 71). The Court concluded in the latter judgment that former Articles 25 and 46 of the Convention could not be interpreted solely in accordance with the intentions of their authors expressed more than forty years previously to the extent

---

15. The United Kingdom has withdrawn its derogation as of 26 February 2001, except in relation to Crown Dependencies. Turkey reduced the scope of its derogation by communication to the Secretary General of the Council of Europe dated 5 May 1992.

that, even if it had been established that the restrictions at issue were considered permissible under Articles 25 and 46 when the Convention was adopted by a minority of the then Contracting Parties, such evidence "could not be decisive".

65. However, the scope of Article 1, at issue in the present case, is determinative of the very scope of the Contracting Parties' positive obligations and, as such, of the scope and reach of the entire Convention system of human rights' protection as opposed to the question, under discussion in the Loizidou case (*preliminary objections*), of the competence of the Convention organs to examine a case. In any event, the extracts from the *travaux préparatoires* detailed above constitute a clear indication of the intended meaning of Article 1 of the Convention which cannot be ignored. The Court would emphasise that it is not interpreting Article 1 "solely" in accordance with the *travaux préparatoires* or finding those *travaux* "decisive"; rather this preparatory material constitutes clear confirmatory evidence of the ordinary meaning of Article 1 of the Convention as already identified by the Court (Article 32 of the Vienna Convention 1969).

66. Accordingly, and as the Court stated in the Soering case:

> "Article 1 sets a limit, notably territorial, on the reach of the Convention. In particular, the engagement undertaken by a Contracting State is confined to 'securing' ('*reconnaître*' in the French text) the listed rights and freedoms to persons within its own 'jurisdiction'. Further, the Convention does not govern the actions of States not Parties to it, nor does it purport to be a means of requiring the Contracting States to impose Convention standards on other States."

(c) Extra-territorial acts recognised as constituting an exercise of jurisdiction

67. In keeping with the essentially territorial notion of jurisdiction, the Court has accepted only in exceptional cases that acts of the Contracting States performed, or producing effects, outside their territories can constitute an exercise of jurisdiction by them within the meaning of Article 1 of the Convention.

68. Reference has been made in the Court's case-law, as an example of jurisdiction "not restricted to the national territory" of the respondent State (the Loizidou judgment (*preliminary objections*), at § 62), to situations where the extradition or expulsion of a person by a Contracting State may give rise to an issue under Articles 2 and/or 3 (or, exceptionally, under Articles 5 and or 6) and hence engage the responsibility of that State under the Convention (the above-cited Soering case, at § 91, Cruz Varas and Others v. Sweden judgment of 20 March 1991, Series A no. 201, §§ 69 and 70, and the Vilvarajah and Others v. the United Kingdom judgment of 30 October 1991, Series A no. 215, § 103).
However, the Court notes that liability is incurred in such cases by an action of the respondent State concerning a person while he or she is on its territory, clearly within its jurisdiction, and that such cases do not concern the actual exercise of a State's competence or jurisdiction abroad (see also, the above-cited *Al-Adsani judgment, at* § 39).

69. In addition, a further example noted at paragraph 62 of the Loizidou judgment (*preliminary objections*) was the Drozd and Janousek case where, citing a number of admissibility decisions by the Commission, the Court accepted that the responsibility of Contracting Parties (France and Spain) could, in principle, be engaged because of acts of their authorities (judges) which produced effects or were performed outside their own territory (the above-cited Drozd and Janousek judgment, at § 91). In that case, the impugned acts could not, in

the circumstances, be attributed to the respondent States because the judges in question were not acting in their capacity as French or Spanish judges and as the Andorran courts functioned independently of the respondent States.

70. Moreover, in that first Loizidou judgment (*preliminary objections*), the Court found that, bearing in mind the object and purpose of the Convention, the responsibility of a Contracting Party was capable of being engaged when as a consequence of military action (lawful or unlawful) it exercised effective control of an area outside its national territory. The obligation to secure, in such an area, the Convention rights and freedoms was found to derive from the fact of such control whether it was exercised directly, through the respondent State's armed forces, or through a subordinate local administration. The Court concluded that the acts of which the applicant complained were capable of falling within Turkish jurisdiction within the meaning of Article 1 of the Convention.

On the merits, the Court found that it was not necessary to determine whether Turkey actually exercised detailed control over the policies and actions of the authorities of the "Turkish Republic of Northern Cyprus" ("TRNC"). It was obvious from the large number of troops engaged in active duties in northern Cyprus that Turkey's army exercised "effective overall control over that part of the island". Such control, according to the relevant test and in the circumstances of the case, was found to entail the responsibility of Turkey for the policies and actions of the "TRNC". The Court concluded that those affected by such policies or actions therefore came within the "jurisdiction" of Turkey for the purposes of Article 1 of the Convention. Turkey's obligation to secure the rights and freedoms set out in the Convention was found therefore to extend to northern Cyprus.

In its subsequent *Cyprus v. Turkey* judgment (cited above), the Court added that since Turkey had such "effective control", its responsibility could not be confined to the acts of its own agents therein but was engaged by the acts of the local administration which survived by virtue of Turkish support. Turkey's "jurisdiction" under Article 1 was therefore considered to extend to securing the entire range of substantive Convention rights in northern Cyprus.

71. In sum, the case-law of the Court demonstrates that its recognition of the exercise of extra-territorial jurisdiction by a Contracting State is exceptional: it has done so when the respondent State, through the effective control of the relevant territory and its inhabitants abroad as a consequence of military occupation or through the consent, invitation or acquiescence of the Government of that territory, exercises all or some of the public powers normally to be exercised by that Government.

72. In line with this approach, the Court has recently found that the participation of a State in the defence of proceedings against it in another State does not, without more, amount to an exercise of extra-territorial jurisdiction (*McElhinney v. Ireland and the United Kingdom* (dec.), no. 31253/96, p. 7, 9 February 2000, unpublished). The Court said:

> "In so far as the applicant complains under Article 6 ... about the stance taken by the Government of the United Kingdom in the Irish proceedings, the Court does not consider it necessary to address in the abstract the question of whether the actions of a Government as a litigant before the courts of another Contracting State can engage their responsibility under Article 6 ... The Court considers that, in the particular circumstances of the case, the fact that the United Kingdom Government raised the defence of sovereign immunity before the Irish courts, where the applicant had decided to sue, does not suffice to bring

him within the jurisdiction of the United Kingdom within the meaning of Article 1 of the Convention."

73. Additionally, the Court notes that other recognised instances of the extra-territorial exercise of jurisdiction by a State include cases involving the activities of its diplomatic or consular agents abroad and on board craft and vessels registered in, or flying the flag of, that State. In these specific situations, customary international law and treaty provisions have recognised the extra-territorial exercise of jurisdiction by the relevant State.

(d) Were the present applicants therefore capable of coming within the "jurisdiction" of the respondent States?

74. The applicants maintain that the bombing of RTS by the respondent States constitutes yet a further example of an extra-territorial act which can be accommodated by the notion of "jurisdiction" in Article 1 of the Convention, and are thereby proposing a further specification of the ordinary meaning of the term "jurisdiction" in Article 1 of the Convention. The Court must be satisfied that equally exceptional circumstances exist in the present case which could amount to the extra-territorial exercise of jurisdiction by a Contracting State.
75. In the first place, the applicants suggest a specific application of the "effective control" criteria developed in the northern Cyprus cases. They claim that the positive obligation under Article 1 extends to securing the Convention rights in a manner proportionate to the level of control exercised in any given extra-territorial situation. The Governments contend that this amounts to a "cause-and-effect" notion of jurisdiction not contemplated by or appropriate to Article 1 of the Convention. The Court considers that the applicants' submission is tantamount to arguing that anyone adversely affected by an act imputable to a Contracting State, wherever in the world that act may have been committed or its consequences felt, is thereby brought within the jurisdiction of that State for the purpose of Article 1 of the Convention.
The Court is inclined to agree with the Governments' submission that the text of Article 1 does not accommodate such an approach to "jurisdiction". Admittedly, the applicants accept that jurisdiction, and any consequent State Convention responsibility, would be limited in the circumstances to the commission and consequences of that particular act. However, the Court is of the view that the wording of Article 1 does not provide any support for the applicants' suggestion that the positive obligation in Article 1 to secure "the rights and freedoms defined in Section I of this Convention" can be divided and tailored in accordance with the particular circumstances of the extra-territorial act in question and, it considers its view in this respect supported by the text of Article 19 of the Convention. Indeed the applicants' approach does not explain the application of the words "within their jurisdiction" in Article 1 and it even goes so far as to render those words superfluous and devoid of any purpose. Had the drafters of the Convention wished to ensure jurisdiction as extensive as that advocated by the applicants, they could have adopted a text the same as or similar to the contemporaneous Articles 1 of the four Geneva Conventions of 1949 (see § 25 above).
Furthermore, the applicants' notion of jurisdiction equates the determination of whether an individual falls within the jurisdiction of a Contracting State with the question of whether that person can be considered to be a victim of a violation of rights guaranteed by the Convention. These are separate and distinct admissibility conditions, each of which has to be satisfied in the afore-mentioned order, before an individual can invoke the Convention

provisions against a Contracting State.
76. Secondly, the applicants' alternative suggestion is that the limited scope of the airspace control only circumscribed the scope of the respondent States' positive obligation to protect the applicants and did not exclude it. The Court finds this to be essentially the same argument as their principal proposition and rejects it for the same reasons.
77. Thirdly, the applicants make a further alternative argument in favour of the respondent States' jurisdiction based on a comparison with the Soering case (cited above). The Court does not find this convincing given the fundamental differences between that case and the present as already noted at paragraph 68 above.
78. Fourthly, the Court does not find it necessary to pronounce on the specific meaning to be attributed in various contexts to the allegedly similar jurisdiction provisions in the international instruments to which the applicants refer because it is not convinced by the applicants' specific submissions in these respects (see § 48 above). It notes that Article 2 of the American Declaration on the Rights and Duties of Man 1948 referred to in the above-cited *Coard* Report of the Inter-American Commission of Human Rights (§ 23 above), contains no explicit limitation of jurisdiction. In addition, and as to Article 2 § 1 the CCPR 1966 (§ 26 above), as early as 1950 the drafters had definitively and specifically confined its territorial scope and it is difficult to suggest that exceptional recognition by the Human Rights Committee of certain instances of extra-territorial jurisdiction (and the applicants give one example only) displaces in any way the territorial jurisdiction expressly conferred by that Article of the CCPR 1966 or explains the precise meaning of "jurisdiction" in Article 1 of its Optional Protocol 1966 (§ 27 above). While the text of Article 1 of the American Convention on Human Rights 1978 (§ 24 above) contains a jurisdiction condition similar to Article 1 of the European Convention, no relevant case-law on the former provision was cited before this Court by the applicants.
79. Fifthly and more generally, the applicants maintain that any failure to accept that they fell within the jurisdiction of the respondent States would defeat the *ordre public* mission of the Convention and leave a regrettable vacuum in the Convention system of human rights' protection.
80. The Court's obligation, in this respect, is to have regard to the special character of the Convention as a constitutional instrument of *European* public order for the protection of individual human beings and its role, as set out in Article 19 of the Convention, is to ensure the observance of *the engagements undertaken* by the Contracting Parties (the above-cited Loizidou judgment (*preliminary objections*), at § 93). It is therefore difficult to contend that a failure to accept the extra-territorial jurisdiction of the respondent States would fall foul of the Convention's *ordre public* objective, which itself underlines the essentially regional vocation of the Convention system, or of Article 19 of the Convention which does not shed any particular light on the territorial ambit of that system.
It is true that, in its above-cited *Cyprus v. Turkey* judgment (at § 78), the Court was conscious of the need to avoid "a regrettable vacuum in the system of human-rights protection" in northern Cyprus. However, and as noted by the Governments, that comment related to an entirely different situation to the present: the inhabitants of northern Cyprus would have found themselves excluded from the benefits of the Convention safeguards and system which they had previously enjoyed, by Turkey's "effective control" of the territory and by the accompanying inability of the Cypriot Government, as a Contracting State, to fulfil the obligations it had undertaken under the Convention.

In short, the Convention is a multi-lateral treaty operating, subject to Article 56 of the Convention[16], in an essentially regional context and notably in the legal space (*espace juridique*) of the Contracting States. The FRY clearly does not fall within this legal space. The Convention was not designed to be applied throughout the world, even in respect of the conduct of Contracting States. Accordingly, the desirability of avoiding a gap or vacuum in human rights' protection has so far been relied on by the Court in favour of establishing jurisdiction only when the territory in question was one that, but for the specific circumstances, would normally be covered by the Convention.

81. Finally, the applicants relied, in particular, on the admissibility decisions of the Court in the above-cited *Issa* and *Öcalan* cases. It is true that the Court has declared both of these cases admissible and that they include certain complaints about alleged actions by Turkish agents outside Turkish territory. However, in neither of those cases was the issue of jurisdiction raised by the respondent Government or addressed in the admissibility decisions and in any event the merits of those cases remain to be decided. Similarly, no jurisdiction objection is recorded in the decision leading to the inadmissibility of the *Xhavara* case to which the applicants also referred (cited above); at any rate, the applicants do not dispute the Governments' evidence about the sharing by prior written agreement of jurisdiction between Albania and Italy. The *Ilascu* case, also referred to by the applicants and cited above, concerns allegations that Russian forces control part of the territory of Moldova, an issue to be decided definitively on the merits of that case. Accordingly, these cases do not provide any support for the applicants' interpretation of the jurisdiction of Contracting States within the meaning of Article 1 of the Convention.

4. The Court's conclusion

82. The Court is not therefore persuaded that there was any jurisdictional link between the persons who were victims of the act complained of and the respondent States. Accordingly, it is not satisfied that the applicants and their deceased relatives were capable of coming within the jurisdiction of the respondent States on account of the extra-territorial act in question.

B. Remaining admissibility issues

83. In light of the above conclusion, the Court considers that it is not necessary to examine the remaining submissions of the parties on the admissibility of the application.

These questions included the alleged several liability of the respondent States for an act carried out by an international organisation of which they are members, whether the applicants had exhausted effective remedies available to them within the meaning of Article 35 § 1 of the Convention and whether the Court was competent to consider the case given the principles established by the above-cited *Monetary Gold* judgment of the ICJ.

C. Summary and conclusion

16. Article 56 § 1 enables a Contracting State to declare that the Convention shall extend to all or any of the territories for whose international relations that State is responsible.

84. Accordingly, the Court concludes that the impugned action of the respondent States does not engage their Convention responsibility and that it is not therefore necessary to consider the other admissibility issues raised by the parties.
85. The application must therefore be declared incompatible with the provisions of the Convention and, as such, inadmissible pursuant to Article 35 §§ 3 and 4 of the Convention.

For these reasons, the Court unanimously

Declares the application inadmissible.

Paul Mahoney — Registrar

Luzius Wildhaber — President

11.1 CONVENTIONAL WEAPONS

☛ Article 1 of the CCW (as amended on 21 December 2001)

1. This Convention and its annexed Protocols shall apply in the situations referred to in Article 2 common to the Geneva Conventions of 12 August 1949 for the Protection of War Victims, including any situation described in paragraph 4 of Article I of Additional Protocol I to these Conventions.

2. This Convention and its annexed Protocols shall also apply, in addition to situations referred to in paragraph 1 of this Article, to situations referred to in Article 3 common to the Geneva Conventions of 12 August 1949. This Convention and its annexed Protocols shall not apply to situations of internal disturbances and tensions, such as riots, isolated and sporadic acts of violence, and other acts of a similar nature, as not being armed conflicts.

3. In case of armed conflicts not of an international character occurring in the territory of one of the High Contracting Parties, each party to the conflict shall be bound to apply the prohibitions and restrictions of this Convention and its annexed Protocols.

4. Nothing in this Convention or its annexed Protocols shall be invoked for the purpose of affecting the sovereignty of a State or the responsibility of the Government, by all legitimate means, to maintain or re-establish law and order in the State or to defend the national unity and territorial integrity of the State.

5. Nothing in this Convention or its annexed Protocols shall be invoked as a justification for intervening, directly or indirectly, for any reason whatever, in the armed conflict or in the internal or external affairs of the High Contracting Party in the territory of which that conflict occurs.

6. The application of the provisions of this Convention and its annexed Protocols to parties to a conflict which are not High Contracting Parties that have accepted this Convention or its

annexed Protocols, shall not change their legal status or the legal status of a disputed territory, either explicitly or implicitly.

7. The provisions of paragraphs 2-6 of this Article shall not prejudice additional Protocols adopted after 1 January 2002, which may apply, exclude or modify the scope of their application in relation to this Article.

11.12 SMALL WEAPONS AND OTHERS

☛ Programme of Action to Prevent, Combat and Eradicate the Illicit Trade in Small Arms and Light Weapons in All Its Aspects (UN Document A/CONF.192/15)

I. Preamble

1. We, the States participating in the United Nations Conference on the Illicit Trade in Small Arms and Light Weapons in All Its Aspects, having met in New York from 9 to 20 July 2001,
2. *Gravely concerned* about the illicit manufacture, transfer and circulation of small arms and light weapons and their excessive accumulation and uncontrolled spread in many regions of the world, which have a wide range of humanitarian and socio-economic consequences and pose a serious threat to peace, reconciliation, safety, security, stability and sustainable development at the individual, local, national, regional and international levels,
3. *Concerned also* by the implications that poverty and underdevelopment may have for the illicit trade in small arms and light weapons in all its aspects,
4. *Determined* to reduce the human suffering caused by the illicit trade in small arms and light weapons in all its aspects and to enhance the respect for life and the dignity of the human person through the promotion of a culture of peace,
5. *Recognizing* that the illicit trade in small arms and light weapons in all its aspects sustains conflicts, exacerbates violence, contributes to the displacement of civilians, undermines respect for international humanitarian law, impedes the provision of humanitarian assistance to victims of armed conflict and fuels crime and terrorism,
6. *Gravely concerned* about its devastating consequences on children, many of whom are victims of armed conflict or are forced to become child soldiers, as well as the negative impact on women and the elderly, and in this context, taking into account the special session of the United Nations General Assembly on children,
7. *Concerned also* about the close link between terrorism, organized crime, trafficking in drugs and precious minerals and the illicit trade in small arms and light weapons, and stressing the urgency of international efforts and cooperation aimed at combating this trade simultaneously from both a supply and demand perspective,
8. *Reaffirming* our respect for and commitment to international law and the purposes and principles enshrined in the Charter of the United Nations, including the sovereign equality of States, territorial integrity, the peaceful resolution of international disputes, non-intervention and non-interference in the internal affairs of States,
9. *Reaffirming* the inherent right to individual or collective self-defence in accordance with Article 51 of the Charter of the United Nations,
10. *Reaffirming also* the right of each State to manufacture, import and retain small arms and

light weapons for its self-defence and security needs, as well as for its capacity to participate in peacekeeping operations in accordance with the Charter of the United Nations,

11. *Reaffirming* the right of self-determination of all peoples, taking into account the particular situation of peoples under colonial or other forms of alien domination or foreign occupation, and recognizing the right of peoples to take legitimate action in accordance with the Charter of the United Nations to realize their inalienable right of self-determination. This shall not be construed as authorizing or encouraging any action that would dismember or impair, totally or in part, the territorial integrity or political unity of sovereign and independent States conducting themselves in compliance with the principle of equal rights and self-determination of peoples,

12. *Recalling* the obligations of States to fully comply with arms embargoes decided by the United Nations Security Council in accordance with the Charter of the United Nations,

13. *Believing* that Governments bear the primary responsibility for preventing, combating and eradicating the illicit trade in small arms and light weapons in all its aspects and, accordingly, should intensify their efforts to define the problems associated with such trade and find ways of resolving them,

14. *Stressing* the urgent necessity for international cooperation and assistance, including financial and technical assistance, as appropriate, to support and facilitate efforts at the local, national, regional and global levels to prevent, combat and eradicate the illicit trade in small arms and light weapons in all its aspects,

15. *Recognizing* that the international community has a duty to deal with this issue, and acknowledging that the challenge posed by the illicit trade in small arms and light weapons in all its aspects is multi-faceted and involves, inter alia, security, conflict prevention and resolution, crime prevention, humanitarian, health and development dimensions,

16. *Recognizing also* the important contribution of civil society, including non-governmental organizations and industry in, inter alia, assisting Governments to prevent, combat and eradicate the illicit trade in small arms and light weapons in all its aspects,

17. *Recognizing further* that these efforts are without prejudice to the priorities accorded to nuclear disarmament, weapons of mass destruction and conventional disarmament,

18. *Welcoming* the efforts being undertaken at the global, regional, subregional, national and local levels to address the illicit trade in small arms and light weapons in all its aspects, and desiring to build upon them, taking into account the characteristics, scope and magnitude of the problem in each State or region,

19. *Recalling* the Millennium Declaration and also welcoming ongoing initiatives in the context of the United Nations to address the problem of the illicit trade in small arms and light weapons in all its aspects,

20. *Recognizing* that the Protocol against the Illicit Manufacturing of and Trafficking in Firearms, Their Parts and Components and Ammunition, supplementing the United Nations Convention against Transnational Organized Crime, establishes standards and procedures that complement and reinforce efforts to prevent, combat and eradicate the illicit trade in small arms and light weapons in all its aspects,

21. *Convinced* of the need for a global commitment to a comprehensive approach to promote, at the global, regional, subregional, national and local levels, the prevention, reduction and eradication of the illicit trade in small arms and light weapons in all its aspects as a contribution to international peace and security,

22. *Resolve* therefore to prevent, combat and eradicate the illicit trade in small arms and light weapons in all its aspects by:

(a) Strengthening or developing agreed norms and measures at the global, regional and national levels that would reinforce and further coordinate efforts to prevent, combat and eradicate the illicit trade in small arms and light weapons in all its aspects;
(b) Developing and implementing agreed international measures to prevent, combat and eradicate illicit manufacturing of and trafficking in small arms and light weapons;
(c) Placing particular emphasis on the regions of the world where conflicts come to an end and where serious problems with the excessive and destabilizing accumulation of small arms and light weapons have to be dealt with urgently;
(d) Mobilizing the political will throughout the international community to prevent and combat illicit transfers and manufacturing of small arms and light weapons in all their aspects, to cooperate towards these ends and to raise awareness of the character and seriousness of the interrelated problems associated with the illicit manufacturing of and trafficking in these weapons;
(e) Promoting responsible action by States with a view to preventing the illicit export, import, transit and retransfer of small arms and light weapons.

II. Preventing, combating and eradicating the illicit trade in small arms and light weapons in all its aspects

1. We, the States participating in this Conference, bearing in mind the different situations, capacities and priorities of States and regions, undertake the following measures to prevent, combat and eradicate the illicit trade in small arms and light weapons in all its aspects:

At the national level
2. To put in place, where they do not exist, adequate laws, regulations and administrative procedures to exercise effective control over the production of small arms and light weapons within their areas of jurisdiction and over the export, import, transit or retransfer of such weapons, in order to prevent illegal manufacture of and illicit trafficking in small arms and light weapons, or their diversion to unauthorized recipients.
3. To adopt and implement, in the States that have not already done so, the necessary legislative or other measures to establish as criminal offences under their domestic law the illegal manufacture, possession, stockpiling and trade of small arms and light weapons within their areas of jurisdiction, in order to ensure that those engaged in such activities can be prosecuted under appropriate national penal codes.
4. To establish, or designate as appropriate, national coordination agencies or bodies and institutional infrastructure responsible for policy guidance, research and monitoring of efforts to prevent, combat and eradicate the illicit trade in small arms and light weapons in all its aspects. This should include aspects of the illicit manufacture, control, trafficking, circulation, brokering and trade, as well as tracing, finance, collection and destruction of small arms and light weapons.
5. To establish or designate, as appropriate, a national point of contact to act as liaison between States on matters relating to the implementation of the Programme of Action.
6. To identify, where applicable, groups and individuals engaged in the illegal manufacture, trade, stockpiling, transfer, possession, as well as financing for acquisition, of illicit small arms and light weapons, and take action under appropriate national law against such groups and individuals.
7. To ensure that henceforth licensed manufacturers apply an appropriate and reliable

marking on each small arm and light weapon as an integral part of the production process. This marking should be unique and should identify the country of manufacture and also provide information that enables the national authorities of that country to identify the manufacturer and serial number so that the authorities concerned can identify and trace each weapon.

8. To adopt where they do not exist and enforce, all the necessary measures to prevent the manufacture, stockpiling, transfer and possession of any unmarked or inadequately marked small arms and light weapons.

9. To ensure that comprehensive and accurate records are kept for as long as possible on the manufacture, holding and transfer of small arms and light weapons under their jurisdiction. These records should be organized and maintained in such a way as to ensure that accurate information can be promptly retrieved and collated by competent national authorities.

10. To ensure responsibility for all small arms and light weapons held and issued by the State and effective measures for tracing such weapons.

11. To assess applications for export authorizations according to strict national regulations and procedures that cover all small arms and light weapons and are consistent with the existing responsibilities of States under relevant international law, taking into account in particular the risk of diversion of these weapons into the illegal trade. Likewise, to establish or maintain an effective national system of export and import licensing or authorization, as well as measures on international transit, for the transfer of all small arms and light weapons, with a view to combating the illicit trade in small arms and light weapons.

12. To put in place and implement adequate laws, regulations and administrative procedures to ensure the effective control over the export and transit of small arms and light weapons, including the use of authenticated end-user certificates and effective legal and enforcement measures.

13. To make every effort, in accordance with national laws and practices, without prejudice to the right of States to re-export small arms and light weapons that they have previously imported, to notify the original exporting State in accordance with their bilateral agreements before the retransfer of those weapons.

14. To develop adequate national legislation or administrative procedures regulating the activities of those who engage in small arms and light weapons brokering. This legislation or procedures should include measures such as registration of brokers, licensing or authorization of brokering transactions as well as the appropriate penalties for all illicit brokering activities performed within the State's jurisdiction and control.

15. To take appropriate measures, including all legal or administrative means, against any activity that violates a United Nations Security Council arms embargo in accordance with the Charter of the United Nations.

16. To ensure that all confiscated, seized or collected small arms and light weapons are destroyed, subject to any legal constraints associated with the preparation of criminal prosecutions, unless another form of disposition or use has been officially authorized and provided that such weapons have been duly marked and registered.

17. To ensure, subject to the respective constitutional and legal systems of States, that the armed forces, police or any other body authorized to hold small arms and light weapons establish adequate and detailed standards and procedures relating to the management and security of their stocks of these weapons. These standards and procedures should, inter alia, relate to: appropriate locations for stockpiles; physical security measures; control of access to stocks; inventory management and accounting control; staff training; security,

accounting and control of small arms and light weapons held or transported by operational units or authorized personnel; and procedures and sanctions in the event of thefts or loss.

18. To regularly review, as appropriate, subject to the respective constitutional and legal systems of States, the stocks of small arms and light weapons held by armed forces, police and other authorized bodies and to ensure that such stocks declared by competent national authorities to be surplus to requirements are clearly identified, that programmes for the responsible disposal, preferably through destruction, of such stocks are established and implemented and that such stocks are adequately safeguarded until disposal.

19. To destroy surplus small arms and light weapons designated for destruction, taking into account, inter alia, the report of the Secretary-General of the United Nations on methods of destruction of small arms, light weapons, ammunition and explosives (S/2000/1092) of 15 November 2000.

20. To develop and implement, including in conflict and post-conflict situations, public awareness and confidence-building programmes on the problems and consequences of the illicit trade in small arms and light weapons in all its aspects, including, where appropriate, the public destruction of surplus weapons and the voluntary surrender of small arms and light weapons, if possible, in cooperation with civil society and non-governmental organizations, with a view to eradicating the illicit trade in small arms and light weapons.

21. To develop and implement, where possible, effective disarmament, demobilization and reintegration programmes, including the effective collection, control, storage and destruction of small arms and light weapons, particularly in post-conflict situations, unless another form of disposition or use has been duly authorized and such weapons have been marked and the alternate form of disposition or use has been recorded, and to include, where applicable, specific provisions for these programmes in peace agreements.

22. To address the special needs of children affected by armed conflict, in particular the reunification with their family, their reintegration into civil society, and their appropriate rehabilitation.

23. To make public national laws, regulations and procedures that impact on the prevention, combating and eradicating of the illicit trade in small arms and light weapons in all its aspects and to submit, on a voluntary basis, to relevant regional and international organizations and in accordance with their national practices, information on, inter alia, (a) small arms and light weapons confiscated or destroyed within their jurisdiction; and (b) other relevant information such as illicit trade routes and techniques of acquisition that can contribute to the eradication of the illicit trade in small arms and light weapons in all its aspects.

At the regional level

24. To establish or designate, as appropriate, a point of contact within subregional and regional organizations to act as liaison on matters relating to the implementation of the Programme of Action.

25. To encourage negotiations, where appropriate, with the aim of concluding relevant legally binding instruments aimed at preventing, combating and eradicating the illicit trade in small arms and light weapons in all its aspects, and where they do exist to ratify and fully implement them.

26. To encourage the strengthening and establishing, where appropriate and as agreed by the States concerned, of moratoria or similar initiatives in affected regions or subregions on the transfer and manufacture of small arms and light weapons, and/or regional action

programmes to prevent, combat and eradicate the illicit trade in small arms and light weapons in all its aspects, and to respect such moratoria, similar initiatives, and/or action programmes and cooperate with the States concerned in the implementation thereof, including through technical assistance and other measures.

27. To establish, where appropriate, subregional or regional mechanisms, in particular trans-border customs cooperation and networks for information-sharing among law enforcement, border and customs control agencies, with a view to preventing, combating and eradicating the illicit trade in small arms and light weapons across borders.

28. To encourage, where needed, regional and subregional action on illicit trade in small arms and light weapons in all its aspects in order to, as appropriate, introduce, adhere, implement or strengthen relevant laws, regulations and administrative procedures.

29. To encourage States to promote safe, effective stockpile management and security, in particular physical security measures, for small arms and light weapons, and to implement, where appropriate, regional and subregional mechanisms in this regard.

30. To support, where appropriate, national disarmament, demobilization and reintegration programmes, particularly in post-conflict situations, with special reference to the measures agreed upon in paragraphs 28 to 31 of this section.

31. To encourage regions to develop, where appropriate and on a voluntary basis, measures to enhance transparency with a view to combating the illicit trade in small arms and light weapons in all its aspects.

At the global level

32. To cooperate with the United Nations system to ensure the effective implementation of arms embargoes decided by the United Nations Security Council in accordance with the Charter of the United Nations.

33. To request the Secretary-General of the United Nations, within existing resources, through the Department for Disarmament Affairs, to collate and circulate data and information provided by States on a voluntary basis and including national reports, on implementation by those States of the Programme of Action.

34. To encourage, particularly in post-conflict situations, the disarmament and demobilization of ex-combatants and their subsequent reintegration into civilian life, including providing support for the effective disposition, as stipulated in paragraph 17 of this section, of collected small arms and light weapons.

35. To encourage the United Nations Security Council to consider, on a case-by-case basis, the inclusion, where applicable, of relevant provisions for disarmament, demobilization and reintegration in the mandates and budgets of peacekeeping operations.

36. To strengthen the ability of States to cooperate in identifying and tracing in a timely and reliable manner illicit small arms and light weapons.

37. To encourage States and the World Customs Organization, as well as other relevant organizations, to enhance cooperation with the International Criminal Police Organization (Interpol) to identify those groups and individuals engaged in the illicit trade in small arms and light weapons in all its aspects in order to allow national authorities to proceed against them in accordance with their national laws.

38. To encourage States to consider ratifying or acceding to international legal instruments against terrorism and transnational organized crime.

39. To develop common understandings of the basic issues and the scope of the problems related to illicit brokering in small arms and light weapons with a view to preventing, combating and eradicating the activities of those engaged in such brokering.
40. To encourage the relevant international and regional organizations and States to facilitate the appropriate cooperation of civil society, including non-governmental organizations, in activities related to the prevention, combat and eradication of the illicit trade in small arms and light weapons in all its aspects, in view of the important role that civil society plays in this area.
41. To promote dialogue and a culture of peace by encouraging, as appropriate, education and public awareness programmes on the problems of the illicit trade in small arms and light weapons in all its aspects, involving all sectors of society.

III. Implementation, international cooperation and assistance

1. We, the States participating in the Conference, recognize that the primary responsibility for solving the problems associated with the illicit trade in small arms and light weapons in all its aspects falls on all States. We also recognize that States need close international cooperation to prevent, combat and eradicate this illicit trade.
2. States undertake to cooperate and to ensure coordination, complementarity and synergy in efforts to deal with the illicit trade in small arms and light weapons in all its aspects at the global, regional, subregional and national levels and to encourage the establishment and strengthening of cooperation and partnerships at all levels among international and intergovernmental organizations and civil society, including non-governmental organizations and international financial institutions.
3. States and appropriate international and regional organizations in a position to do so should, upon request of the relevant authorities, seriously consider rendering assistance, including technical and financial assistance where needed, such as small arms funds, to support the implementation of the measures to prevent, combat and eradicate the illicit trade in small arms and light weapons in all its aspects as contained in the Programme of Action.
4. States and international and regional organizations should, upon request by the affected States, consider assisting and promoting conflict prevention. Where requested by the parties concerned, in accordance with the principles of the Charter of the United Nations, States and international and regional organizations should consider promotion and assistance of the pursuit of negotiated solutions to conflicts, including by addressing their root causes.
5. States and international and regional organizations should, where appropriate, cooperate, develop and strengthen partnerships to share resources and information on the illicit trade in small arms and light weapons in all its aspects.
6. With a view to facilitating implementation of the Programme of Action, States and international and regional organizations should seriously consider assisting interested States, upon request, in building capacities in areas including the development of appropriate legislation and regulations, law enforcement, tracing and marking, stockpile management and security, destruction of small arms and light weapons and the collection and exchange of information.
7. States should, as appropriate, enhance cooperation, the exchange of experience and training among competent officials, including customs, police, intelligence and arms control officials, at the national, regional and global levels in order to combat the illicit trade in small arms and light weapons in all its aspects.

8. Regional and international programmes for specialist training on small arms stockpile management and security should be developed. Upon request, States and appropriate international or regional organizations in a position to do so should support these programmes. The United Nations, within existing resources, and other appropriate international or regional organizations should consider developing capacity for training in this area.
9. States are encouraged to use and support, as appropriate, including by providing relevant information on the illicit trade in small arms and light weapons, Interpol's International Weapons and Explosives Tracking System database or any other relevant database that may be developed for this purpose.
10. States are encouraged to consider international cooperation and assistance to examine technologies that would improve the tracing and detection of illicit trade in small arms and light weapons, as well as measures to facilitate the transfer of such technologies.
11. States undertake to cooperate with each other, including on the basis of the relevant existing global and regional legally binding instruments as well as other agreements and arrangements, and, where appropriate, with relevant international, regional and intergovernmental organizations, in tracing illicit small arms and light weapons, in particular by strengthening mechanisms based on the exchange of relevant information.
12. States are encouraged to exchange information on a voluntary basis on their national marking systems on small arms and light weapons.
13. States are encouraged, subject to their national practices, to enhance, according to their respective constitutional and legal systems, mutual legal assistance and other forms of cooperation in order to assist investigations and prosecutions in relation to the illicit trade in small arms and light weapons in all its aspects.
14. Upon request, States and appropriate international or regional organizations in a position to do so should provide assistance in the destruction or other responsible disposal of surplus stocks or unmarked or inadequately marked small arms and light weapons.
15. Upon request, States and appropriate international or regional organizations in a position to do so should provide assistance to combat the illicit trade in small arms and light weapons linked to drug trafficking, transnational organized crime and terrorism.
16. Particularly in post-conflict situations, and where appropriate, the relevant regional and international organizations should support, within existing resources, appropriate programmes related to the disarmament, demobilization and reintegration of ex-combatants.
17. With regard to those situations, States should make, as appropriate, greater efforts to address problems related to human and sustainable development, taking into account existing and future social and developmental activities, and should fully respect the rights of the States concerned to establish priorities in their development programmes.
18. States, regional and subregional and international organizations, research centres, health and medical institutions, the United Nations system, international financial institutions and civil society are urged, as appropriate, to develop and support action-oriented research aimed at facilitating greater awareness and better understanding of the nature and scope of the problems associated with the illicit trade in small arms and light weapons in all its aspects.

IV. Follow-up to the United Nations Conference on the Illicit Trade in Small Arms and Light Weapons in All Its Aspects

1. We, the States participating in the United Nations Conference on the Illicit Trade in Small Arms and Light Weapons in All Its Aspects, recommend to the General Assembly the following agreed steps to be undertaken for the effective follow-up of the Conference:
(a) To convene a conference no later than 2006 to review progress made in the implementation of the Programme of Action, the date and venue to be decided at the fifty-eighth session of the General Assembly;
(b) To convene a meeting of States on a biennial basis to consider the national, regional and global implementation of the Programme of Action;
(c) To undertake a United Nations study, within existing resources, for examining the feasibility of developing an international instrument to enable States to identify and trace in a timely and reliable manner illicit small arms and light weapons;
(d) To consider further steps to enhance international cooperation in preventing, combating and eradicating illicit brokering in small arms and light weapons.
2. Finally, we, the States participating in the United Nations Conference on the Illicit Trade in Small Arms and Light Weapons in All Its Aspects:
(a) Encourage the United Nations and other appropriate international and regional organizations to undertake initiatives to promote the implementation of the Programme of Action;
(b) Also encourage all initiatives to mobilize resources and expertise to promote the implementation of the Programme of Action and to provide assistance to States in their implementation of the Programme of Action;
(c) Further encourage non-governmental organizations and civil society to engage, as appropriate, in all aspects of international, regional, subregional and national efforts to implement the present Programme of Action.

BIBLIOGRAPHY

BIBLIOGRAPHY 2000-2001[1]

0. INTERNATIONAL HUMANITARIAN LAW IN GENERAL

Books

- Blank, L.R., *The Role of International Financial Institutions in International Humanitarian Law: Report from the International Humanitarian Law Working Group* (Washington, D.C., United States Institute of Peace 2002)
- Bosly, H., ed., *Actualité du Droit International Humanitaire* (Bruxelles, Charte 2001) 225 pp.
- Bouchet-Saulnier, F., *The Practical Guide to Humanitarian Law* [Dictionnaire pratique de droit humanitaire] (English) (Lanham, Rowman & Littlefield 2001) 488 pp.
- Centre de Recherches sur les Droits de l'Homme et le Droit Humanitaire, Universités de Paris-Sud et Rouen, *Collection du CREDHO* (Bruxelles, Bruylant 2001)
- Hasse, J., *Humanitäres Völkerrecht: Politische, Rechtliche und Strafgerichtliche Dimensionen* (Baden-Baden, Nomos 2001) 597 pp.
- Gardam, J. and M. Jarvis, *Women, Armed Conflict and International Law* (Dordrecht, Kluwer Law International 2001) 308 pp.
- Greppi, E., *I Crimini di Guerra e contro l'Umanita nel Diritto Internazionale* (Milan, UTET 2001) 264 pp.
- Green, L.C., *The Contemporary Law of Armed Conflict*, 2nd edn. (Melland Schill Studies in International Law, Juris Publishing 2000) 400 pp.
- Fleck, D., ed., *The Handbook of the Law of Visiting Forces* (Oxford, Oxford University Press 2001) 600 pp.
- Kalshoven, F. and L. Zegveld, *Constraints on the Waging of War: an Introduction to International Humanitarian Law*, 2nd edn. (Geneva, International Committee of the Red Cross 2001) 223 pp.
- Künzli, J., *Zwischen Rigidität und Flexibilität: der Verpflichtungsgrad Internationaler Menschenrechte: ein Beitrag zum Zusammenspiel von Menschenrechten, Humanitärem Völkerrecht und dem Recht der Staatenverantwortlichkeit* (Berlin, Duncker & Humblot 2001) 493 pp.
- Meron, T., *Bloody Constraint* (New York, Oxford University Press USA 2001) 256 pp.
- Ponte Iglesias, M.T., *Conflictos Armados, Refugiados y Desplazados Internos en el Derecho International Actual* (Santiago, Tórculo Edicions 2000) 285 pp.
- Provost, R., *International Human Rights and Humanitarian Law* (Cambridge, Cambridge University Press 2002) 418 pp.
- Tall, S.N., *Théories et Réalités du Droit International Humanitaire: Contribution à l'Étude de l'Application du Droit des Conflits Armés en Afrique Noire Contemporaine* (Dakar, Université Cheikh Anta Diop 2001) 41 pp.

1. The bibliography was compiled by Avril McDonald, Josephine Paulsson and Anna Danieli.

– Tavernier p. and L. Burgorgue-Larsen, eds., *Un Siecle de Droit International Humanitaire* (Brussels, Bruylant 2001) 272 pp.
– 3 *Yearbook of International Humanitarian Law* (The Hague, TMC Asser Press 2000) 873 pp.

Articles

– Abi-Saab, R., 'Le droit humanitaire et les troubles internes', *The International Legal System in Quest of Equity and Universality* (The Hague, Martinus Nijhoff Publisher 2001) p. 477
– Boll, A.M., 'The Asian values debate and its relevance to international humanitarian law', 83 *IRRC* (2001) p. 45
– Brett, R. and E. Lester, 'Refugee law and international humanitarian law: parallels, lessons and looking ahead: a non-governmental organization's view', 83 *IRRC* (2001) p. 713
– Bugnion, F., 'Réfugiés, personnes déplacées et droit international humanitaire', 11 *Schweizerische Zeitschrift für internationales und europäisches Recht* (2001) p. 277
– Condorelli, L., 'Les progrès du droit international humanitaire et la circulaire du secrétaire général des Nations Unies du 6 août 1999', *The International Legal System in Quest of Equity and Universality* (The Hague, Martinus Nijhoff Publisher 2001) p. 495
– Cowling, M.G., 'International humanitarian law and the armed struggle in South Africa', 26 *SAYIL* (2001) p. 221
– Day, L.E., M. Vandiver and W.R. Janikowski, 'The structure of obligations in international humanitarian law and its implications for conceptions of citizenship', *Anatomy of Genocide* (Lewiston, NY, Edwin Mellen Press 2001) p. 67
– Delooz, F. and S. Kolanowski, 'Introduction au droit international humanitaire', H. Bosly, ed., *Actualité du Droit International Humanitaire* (Bruxelles, Charte 2001) p. 5
– Desgagné, R., 'European Union practice in the field of international humanitarian law: an overview', V. Kronenberg, ed., *The European Union and the International Legal Order: Disord or Harmony* (The Hague, T.M.C. Asser Press 2001) p. 455
– Jaquemet, S., 'The cross-fertilization of international humanitarian law and international refugee law', 83 *IRRC* (2001) p. 651
– Kleffner, J.K., and L. Zegveld, 'Establishing an individual complaints procedure for violations of international humanitarian law', 3 *YIHL* (2001) p. 384
– Kritsiotis D., 'International humanitarian law and the disintegration of states', 30 *Israel YB HR* (2001) p. 17
– McDonald, A., 'The Year in Review', 3 *YIHL* (2001) p. 169
– Levrat, B., 'Le droit international humanitaire au Timor orientale : entre théorie et pratique', 83 *RICR* (2001) p. 77
– MacCoubrey, H., 'International humanitarian law and the Kosovo crisis', *The Kosovo tragedy* (London, Frank Cass 2001) p. 184
– Momtaz, D. and L., Condorelli, 'La compatibilité des sanctions du Conseil de Sécurité avec le droit internationale humanitaire', V. Gowlland-Debbas, ed., *United Nations Sanctions and International Law* (The Hague, Kluwer Law International 2001) p. 223
– Pivacet, S., 'De Interdepartementale Commissie voor humanitair recht', 10 *Zoeklicht* (2001) p. 21
– Rutinwa, B., 'Refugee claims based on violation of international humanitarian law: the "victim's" perspective', 15 *Georgetown Immigration Law Journal* (2001) p. 497

- Thakur, R., 'Global norms and international humanitarian law: an Asian perspective', 83 *IRRC* (2001) p. 19
- Thierry, H., 'Réflexions sur le "droit d'ingérence humanitaire"', *The International Legal System in Quest of Equity and Universality* (The Hague, Martinus Nijhoff Publisher 2001) p. 219
- Viljoen, F., 'Africa's contribution to the development of international human rights and humanitarian law', 1 *African HRJ* (2001) p. 18
- Wouters, J. and F. Naert, 'Internationaal humanitair recht na 11 september', 11 *Zoeklicht* (2002) p. 23
- Wouters, J. and F. Naert, 'Afghanistan en het internationaal humanitair recht', 11 *Zoek-licht* (2002) p. 25
- Xiaodong, H., 'The Chinese humanitarian heritage and the dissemination of and education in international humanitarian law in the Chinese People's Liberation Army', 83 *IRRC* (2001) p. 141

1.12 Hague Law

Books

- Tavernier, P., *Un Siècle de Droit International Humanitaire: Centenaire des Conventions de La Haye et Cinquantenaire des Conventions de Genève* (Bruxelles, Bruylant 2001) 262 pp.

1.13 Geneva Law

Books

- Tavernier, P., *Un siècle de droit international humanitaire: Centenaire des Conventions de La Haye et Cinquantenaire des Conventions de Genève* (Bruxelles, Bruylant 2001) 262 pp.

Articles

- Chlopak, E., 'Dealing with the detainees at Guantanamo Bay: humanitarian and human rights obligations under the Geneva Conventions', 9 *Amer. Univ. ILJ* (2002) http://www.wcl.american.edu/hrbrief/09/3guantanamo.cfm

1.15 Customary Law

Articles

- Henckaerts, J., 'The study on customary rules of international humanitarian law', *Protecting Civilians in 21st-Century Warfare: Target Selection, Proportionality and Precautionary Measures in Law and Practice, Speeches and Proceedings of the Red Cross Symposium* (The Hague, The Netherlands Red Cross 2001) p. 23

1.23 Principle of Distinction

Articles

- David. E., 'Respect for the principle of distinction in the Kosovo War', 3 *YIHL* (2001) p. 81

1.24 Principle of Proportionality

Articles

- Boyle, T., 'Proportionality in decision making and combat actions', *Protecting Civilians in 21st-Century Warfare: Target Selection, Proportionality and Precautionary Measures in Law and Practice, Speeches and Proceedings of the Red Cross Symposium* (The Hague, The Netherlands Red Cross 2001) p. 29
- Fenrick, W., 'The law applicable to targeting and proportionality after Operation Allied Force: a view from the outside', 3 *YIHL* (2001) p. 53
- Medenica, O., 'Protocol I and Operation Allied Force: did NATO abide by principles of proportionality?', 23 *Loyola of Los Angeles International and Comparative Law Review* (2001) p. 329

2.1 TYPES OF CONFLICT (general)

Articles

- Sassòli, M., 'The legal qualification of the conflicts in the former Yugoslavia: double standards or new horizons for international humanitarian law?', *International Law in the Post-Cold War World* (London, Routledge 2001) p. 307

2.11 International

Articles

- Condorelli, L., 'War crimes and international conflicts in the Statute of the International Criminal Court', in M. Politi, ed., *The Rome Statute of the International Criminal Court: a Challenge to Impunity* (Aldershot, Ashgate/Dartmouth 2001) p. 107

2.12 Non-international

Books

- Human Rights Watch, *Colombia: Beyond Negotiation: International Humanitarian Law and its Application to the Conduct of the FARC-EP* (New York, Human Rights Watch 2001) http://www.hrw.org/reports/2001/farc/
- Kessler, B., *Die Durchsetzung der Genfer Abkommen von 1949 in Nicht Internationalen Bewaffneten Konflikten auf Grundlage ihres Gemeinsamen Art. 1* (Berlin, Duncker & Humblot 2001) 281 pp.
- Moir, L., *The Law of internal Armed Conflict* (Cambridge, Cambridge University Press 2002) 306 pp.

Articles

- Aldykiewicz, J.E. and G.S., Corn, 'Authority to court-martial non-U.S. military personnel for serious violations of international humanitarian law committed during internal armed conflicts', 167 *Mil. LR* (2001) p. 74
- Fleck, D., 'Humanitarian protection in non-international armed conflicts: the new research project of the International Institute of Humanitarian Law', 30 *Israel YB HR* (2001) p. 1

– Hoffmann, M.H., 'The application of international humanitarian law in Sri Lanka: a compliance based case study on the rules of war', 30 *Israel YB HR* (2001) p. 209
– Kovacs, P., 'Authority and weakness of the 1977 Geneva Protocol II in the light of the conflict in Chechnya', 6 *International Peacekeeping* (2000) p. 137
– Walker, G.K., 'Responses to humanitarian law violations in non-international armed conflicts: historical perspectives and considerations on conflicts of jurisdiction', 30 *Israel YB HR* (2001) p. 79

2.13 Other

Books

– Molloy, I., *Rolling Back Revolution: The Emergence of Low Intensity Conflict* (London, Pluto Press 2001) 320 pp.

3.13 Civilian Population

Books

– Urbina, J.J., *Protección de las Victimas de los Conflictos Armados, Naciones Unadas y Derecho Internacional Humanitario* (Valencia, Cruz Roja Española/Tirant lo Blanch 2000) 439 pp.

3.132 Women and Children

Books

– Gardam, J. and M. Jarvis, *Women, Armed Conflict and International Law* (Dordrecht, Kluwer Law International 2001) 308 pp.
– Pradas, S.H., *El Niño en Los Conflictos Armados: Marco Jurid́ico para su Protección Internacional* (Valencia, Tirant lo Blanch 2001) 614 pp.

Articles

– Campanaro, J., 'Women, war and international law: the historical treatment of gender-based crimes', 89 *The Georgetown Law Journal* (2001) p. 2557
– Happold, M., 'The Optional Protocol to the Convention on the Rights of the Child on the Involvement of Children in Armed Conflict', 3 *YIHL* (2001) p. 226

3.22 Occupation

Articles

– Hassouna, H.A., 'The enforcement of the Fourth Geneva Convention in the occupied Palestinian territory, including Jerusalem', 7 *ILSA Journal of International and Comparative Law* (2001) p. 461

4.11 Basic Rules

Books

- *Protecting Civilians in 21st-Century Warfare: Target Selection, Proportionality and Precautionary Measures in Law and Practice, Speeches and Proceedings of the Red Cross Symposium* (The Hague, The Netherlands Red Cross 2001)

Articles

- Biegman, N., 'Political decision making and responsibility regarding the conduct of hostilities', *Protecting Civilians in 21st-Century Warfare: Target Selection, Proportionality and Precautionary Measures in Law and Practice, Speeches and Proceedings of the Red Cross Symposium* (The Hague, The Netherlands Red Cross 2001) p. 71
- Boyle, Tom, 'Proportionality in decision making and combat actions', *Protecting Civilians in 21st-Century Warfare: Target Selection, Proportionality and Precautionary Measures in Law and Practice, Speeches and Proceedings of the Red Cross Symposium* (The Hague, The Netherlands Red Cross 2001)p. 29
- Fenrick, W., 'The law applicable to targeting and proportionality after Operation Allied Force: a view from the outside', 3 *YIHL* (2001) p. 53
- Fenrick, W., 'Prosecuting violations of combat limitations', *Protecting Civilians in 21st-Century Warfare: Target Selection, Proportionality and Precautionary Measures in Law and Practice, Speeches and Proceedings of the Red Cross Symposium* (The Hague, The Netherlands Red Cross 2001) p. 77
- Henckaerts, J., 'The conduct of hostilities: target selection, proportionality and precautionary measures under international humanitarian law', *Protecting Civilians in 21st-Century Warfare: Target Selection, Proportionality and Precautionary Measures in Law and Practice, Speeches and Proceedings of the Red Cross Symposium* (The Hague, The Netherlands Red Cross 2001) p. 11
- Remacle, R., 'La conduite des opérations militaires au regard du droit des conflits armés', H. Bosly, ed., *Actualité du Droit International Humanitaire* (Bruxelles, Charte 2001) p. 27
- Tricarico, L., 'Identification of targets and precautions in attack in air warfare: Operation Allied Force as a case study', *Protecting civilians in 21st-century warfare: Target Selection, Proportionality and Precautionary Measures in Law and Practice, Speeches and Proceedings of the Red Cross Symposium* (The Hague, The Netherlands Red Cross 2001) p. 39

4.11111 Mines

Books

- Maslen, S., *Anti-personnel mines under humanitarian law: a view from the vanishing point*, (Antwerp, Intersentia 2001) 327 pp.

4.112 New Weapons

Articles
- Aldrich, G., 'The development of weapons and military strategy', *Protecting Civilians in 21st-Century Warfare: Target Selection, Proportionality and Precautionary Measures in Law and Practice, Speeches and Proceedings of the Red Cross Symposium* (The Hague, The Netherlands Red Cross 2001) p. 61

4.114 The Emblems and Safeguards of Persons *hors de combat*

Articles
- Meriboute, Z., 'The emblems of the 1949 Geneva Conventions: their content and meaning', 3 *YIHL* (2001) p. 258
- Pfirter, D., 'Attacking objects or persons using the distinctive emblems of the Geneva Conventions: article 8(2)(b)(xxiv)', The International Criminal Court (Ardsley, NY Transnational Publishers 2001) p. 201
- Hebel, H. von and C. Garaway, 'Improper use of a flag of truce or other flags, military insignia, uniforms or distinctive emblems: article 8(2)(b)(vii) 1-4', R. Lee and H. Friman, eds., *The International Criminal Court: Elements of Crimes and Rules of Procedure and Evidence* (Ardsley, NY, Transnational Publishers 2001) p. 154

4.144 The Natural Environment

Books
- Blom, E., W. Bergmans, I. Dankelman, p. Werweij, M. Voeten and p. Wit, eds., *Nature in War: Biodiversity Conservation during Conflicts* (Amsterdam, Nederlandse Commissie voor Internationale Natuurbescherming 2000) 174 pp.
- Boelaert-Suominen, S.A.J., *International Environmental Law and Naval War: The Effects of Marine Safety and Pollution Conventions During International Armed Conflicts* (Newport, RI, Naval War College 2000) 365 pp.
- P.F. Diehl and N.P. Gleditsch, eds., *Environmental Conflict* (Boulder, CO, Westview 2001) 343 pp.

Articles
- Desgagne, R., 'The prevention of environmental damage in time of armed conflict', 3 *YIHL* (2001) p. 109
- Kiss, A., 'International humanitarian law and the environment', 31 *Environmental Policy and Law* (2001) p. 223
- Lonergan, S.C., 'Water and conflict: rhetoric and reality', in P.F. Diehl and N.P. Gleditsch, eds., *Environmental Conflict* (Boulder, CO, Westview 2001) p. 109
- Payne, R.A., 'The limits and promise of environmental conflict prevention', in P.F. Diehl and N.P. Gleditsch, eds., *Environmental Conflict* (Boulder, CO, Westview 2001) p. 179
- Power, M.C., 'La protection de l'environnement en droit international humanitaire: le cas du Kosovo', 33 *Ottawa Law Review* (2001) p. 225
- Schwartz, D.M., T. Deligiannis and T. Homer-Dixon, 'The environment and violent conflict', in P.F. Diehl and N.P. Gleditsch, eds., *Environmental Conflict* (Boulder, CO, Westview 2001) p. 273

4.22 Air and Missile Warfare

Articles

- Boyle, Tom, 'Proportionality in decision making and combat actions', *Protecting Civilians in 21st-Century Warfare: Target Selection, Proportionality and Precautionary Measures in Law and Practice, Speeches and Proceedings of the Red Cross Symposium* (The Hague, The Netherlands Red Cross 2001) p. 29
- Tricarico, L., 'Identification of targets and precautions in attack in air warfare: Operation Allied Force as a case study', *Protecting Civilians in 21st-Century Warfare: Target Selection, Proportionality and Precautionary Measures in Law and Practice, Speeches and Proceedings of the Red Cross Symposium* (The Hague, The Netherlands Red Cross 2001) p. 39

4.23 Naval Warfare

Books

- Boelaert-Suominen, S.A.J., *International Environmental Law and Naval War: The Effects of Marine Safety and Pollution Conventions During International Armed Conflicts* (Newport, RI, Naval War College 2000) 365 pp.

5.1 CEASEFIRES, ARMISTICES AND PEACE AGREEMENTS

Books

- Bell, C., *Peace Agreements and Human Rights* (Oxford, Oxford University Press 2000) 434 pp.

Articles

- Wolff, S., 'The road to peace? The Good Friday Agreement and the conflict in Northern Ireland', 163 *World Affairs* (2001) p. 163

6.1 THE CRIMES (generally)

Articles

- Laucci, C., 'Juger et faire juger les auteurs de violations graves du droit international humanitaire', 83 *RICR* (2001) p. 407

6.11 War Crimes

Books

- Joki', A., ed., *War Crimes and Collective Wrongdoing: a Reader* (Malden, MA, Blackwell 2001) 313 pp.

Articles

- Condorelli, L.,'War crimes and international conflicts in the Statute of the International Criminal Court', in M. Politi, ed., *The Rome Statute of the International Criminal Court: a Challenge to Impunity* (Aldershot, Ashgate/Dartmouth 2001) p. 107

- Danieli, A.C., 'La repressione dei crimini sessuali nel diritto penale internazionale', *14 Rivista Internazionale del Diritti dell'Uomo* (2001) p. 844
- Ellis, A. 'What shall we do with war criminals?', in A. Jokić, ed., *War crimes and Collective Wrongdoing: a Reader* (Malden, MA, Blackwell 2001) p. 97
- Maravilla, Ch. S., 'Rape as a war crime: the implications of the International Criminal Tribunal for the Former Yugoslavia's decision in Prosecutor v. Kunarac, Kovac, & Vukovic on international humanitarian law', 13 *Florida JIL* (2001) p. 321
- Scharf, M.P., 'Defining terrorism as the peace time equivalent of war crimes: a case of too much convergence between international humanitarian law and international criminal law', 7 *ILSA JI &CL* (2001) p. 391

6.12 Genocide

Books

- Bloxham, D., *Genocide on Trial: War Crimes Trials and the Formation of Holocaust History and Memory* (Oxford, Oxford University Press 2001) 273 pp.
- Heidenrich, J.G., *How to Prevent Genocide: a Guide for Policymakers, Scholars and the Concerned Citizen* (Westport, CT, Praeger 2000) 275 pp.
- Ntezimana, V., *La justice Belge Face au Genocide Rwandis: L'Affaire Ntezimana* (Paris, L'Harmattan 2000) 214 pp.

Articles

- Fierens, J., 'La qualification de génocide devant le Tribunal pénal international pour le Rwanda et devant les juridictions rwandaises', *Actualité du droit international humanitaire* (2001) p. 181
- Labrin, J.B., 'Le crime contre l'humanité et le crime de génocide: généalogie et étude de deux cas emblématiques latino-américains', H. Bosly, ed., *Actualité du Droit International Humanitaire* (Brussels, Charte 2001) p. 41
- Mitchell, A., 'Is genocide a crime unknown to Australian law? *Nulyarimma* v. *Thompson*', 3 *YIHL* (2001) p. 362
- Morton, J.S., 'The international legal adjudication of the crime of genocide', 7 *ILSA Journal of International and Comparative Law* (2001) p. 329
- Schabas, W.A., 'The Jelisic case and the mens rea of the crime of genocide', 14 *Leiden JIL* (2001) p. 125

6.13 Crimes Against Humanity

Books

- Lattimer, M. and p. Sands, eds., *Justice for Crimes against Humanity: International Law after Pinochet* (Oxford, Oxford University Press 2001) 440 pp.

Articles

- Clark, R.S., 'Crimes against humanity and the Rome Statute of the international Criminal Court', M. Politi, ed., *The Rome Statute of the International Criminal Court: a Challenge to Impunity* (Ashgate/Dartmouth, Aldershot 2001) p. 75

- Labrin, J.B., 'Le crime contre l'humanité et le crime de génocide: généalogie et étude de deux cas emblématiques latino-américains', H. Bosly, ed., *Actualité du droit International Humanitaire* (Bruxelles, Charte 2001) p. 41

6.23 Superior/Command Responsibility

Articles

- Gavouneli, M. and I. Bantekas, 'Prefecture of Voiotia v. Federal Republic of Germany: Greek Supreme Court decision on sovereign immunity in action for injuries caused by humanitarian law violations during military occupation', 95 *AJIL* (2001) p. 198
- Jia., B.B., 'The doctrine of command responsibility: current problems', 3 *YIHL* (2001) p. 131
- Lippmann, M.R., 'Humanitarian law: the development and scope of the superior orders defense', 20 *Penn State ILR* (2001) p. 153

6.3 REPRESSION OF BREACHES

Books

- Bankekas, I., M. Mackarel and S. Nash, *International Criminal Law* (London, Cavendish Publishing 2001) 500 pp.
- Carnevali Rodríguez, R., *Derecho Penal y Derecho Sancionador de la Union Europea* (Granada, Editorial Comares 2001) 472 pp.
- Fischer, H., C. Kreß and S.R. Lüder, eds., *International and National Prosecution of Crimes under International Law: Current Developments* (Berlin, Spitz 2001) 873 pp.
- Gaboriau, S. and H. Pauliat, eds., *La Justice Pénale Internationale* (Limoges, Presse Universitaire de Limogesi 2001) 614 pp.
- Huet, A. and R. Koering-Joulin, *Droit Pénal International* (Paris, Press Universitaires de France 2001) 198 pp.
- Kittichaisaree, K., ed., *International Criminal Law* (Oxford, Oxford University Press 2001) 350 pp.
- Ratner, S. R., *Accountability for Human Rights Atrocities in International Law: Beyond the Nuremberg Legacy*, 2nd edn. (Oxford, Oxford University Press 2001) 435 pp.
- Report from the Freetown Conference on Accountability Mechanisms for Violations of International Humanitarian Law in Sierra Leone Freetown (2002) http://www.special-court.org/Outreach/SLConferenceReportFinal.htm
- Safferling, C., *Towards an International Criminal Procedure* (Oxford, Oxford University Press 2001) 450 pp.

Articles

- Buergenthal, T., 'Proliferation of international courts and tribunals: is it good or is it bad?' 14 *Leiden JIL* (2001) p. 267
- Cereste, S., 'The International Court of Justice, the International Criminal Court, and the *Ad Hoc* Tribunals', 17 *New York Law School Journal on Human Rights* (2001) p. 911
- Fenrick, W., 'Prosecuting violations of combat limitations', *Protecting Civilians in 21st-Century Warfare: Target Selection, Proportionality and Precautionary Measures in Law and Practice, Speeches and Proceedings of the Red Cross Symposium* (The Hague, The Netherlands Red Cross 2001) p. 77

- Schabas, W.A., 'Enforcing international humanitarian law: catching the accomplices', 83 *IRRC* (2001) p. 43
- Sharma, V.D., 'International crimes and universal jurisdiction', *42 Indian J. Int. Law* (2002) p. 139
- Wilde, R., 'Accountability and international actors in Bosnia and Herzegovina, Kosovo and East Timor', 7 *ILSA Journal of International and Comparative Law* (2001) pp. 583-606

6.31 International Courts (generally)

Articles

- Falk, R., 'Accountability for war crimes and the legacy of Nuremberg', A. Joki', ed., *War Crimes and Collective Wrongdoing: a Reader* (Malden, MA, Blackwell 2001) p. 113
- Gardam, J., 'The contribution of the International Court of Justice to international humanitarian law', 14 *Leiden JIL* (2001) p. 349
- Jansen, C., 'Het process van Neurenberg', 14 *VN Forum* (2001) p. 3
- Jansen, C., Het process van Tokio', 14 *VN Forum* (2001) p. 1
- Martin, F., 'Application du droit international humanitaire par la Cour interaméricaine des droits de l'homme', 83 *RICR* (2001) p. 1037
- Mundis, D.A., 'The creation of new ad hoc international criminal tribunals and other international efforts to prosecute violations of international humanitarian law', 35 *The International Lawyer* (2001) p. 631

6.312 International Criminal Tribunal for the Former Yugoslavia

Books

- *Due Process Protections Afforded Defendants: a Comparison between the Proposed U.S. Military Commissions and the International Criminal Tribunal for the Former Yugoslavia* (New York, Human Rights Watch 2001) http://www.hrw.org/press/2001/12/miltrib1204.htm
- May, R. et al, *Essays on ICTY Procedure and Evidence in Honour of Gabrielle Kirk McDonald* (The Hague, Kluwer Law International 2001) 579 pp.

Articles

- Ascensio, H. and R. Maison, 'L'activité des tribunaux pénaux internationaux *(2000)*', 46 *Annuaire Français de Droit International* (2000) p. 285
- Bothe, M., 'The protection of the civilian population and NATO bombing on Yugoslavia: comments on a report to the prosecutor of the ICTY', 6 *International Peacekeeping* (2000) p. 158
- Cassese, A., 'The impact of the European Convention on Human Rights on the International Criminal Tribunal for the Former Yugoslavia', p. Mahoney, et al, eds., *Protection des Droits de l'Homme: a Perspective Européenne*: Mélanges à la Mémoire de Rolv Ryssdal (Köln, Heymanns 2000) p. 213
- Kolb, R., 'The jurisprudence of the Yugoslav and Rwandan Criminal Tribunals on their jurisdiction and international crimes', 71 *BYIL* (2000) p. 259

- Maravilla, Ch.S., 'Rape as a war crime: the implications of the International Criminal Tribunal for the Former Yugoslavia's decision in Prosecutor v. Kunarac, Kovac & Vukovic on international humanitarian law', 13 *Florida JIL* (2001) p. 321
- McDonald, G.K., 'Reflections on the contributions of the International Criminal Tribunal for the Former Yugoslavia', 24 *Hastings International and Comparative Law Review* (2001) p. 155
- Nice, G., 'Trials of imperfection', 14 *Leiden JIL* (2001) p. 383
- Ponte, C. Del, 'Die UN-Tribunale für Ex-Jugoslawien und Ruanda: Herausforderungen fur die Anklagebehörde', 119 *Schweizerische Zeitschrift für Strafrecht* (2001) p. 317
- Sanna S., 'La testimonianza dei delegati del Comitato internazionale della Croce Rosssa davanti ai tribunali penali internazionali', 84 *Rivista di diritto internazionale* (2001) p. 393
- Shenk, M.D., B.J. Newquist, L. Stone and D.A. Mundis, 'International Tribunals for the Former Yugoslavia and for Rwanda', 35 *The International Lawyer* (2001) p. 622

6.313 International Criminal Tribunal for Rwanda

Articles

- Fierens, J., 'La qualification de génocide devant le Tribunal pénal international pour le Rwanda et devant les juridictions rwandaises', *Actualité du droit international humanitaire* (2001) p. 181
- Herik, L. van den, 'Het Rwanda Tribunaal', 14 *VN Forum* (2001) p. 23
- Ivokovi', S.K., 'Justice by the International Criminal Tribunal for the Former Yugoslavia', 37 *Stanford Journal of International Law* (2001) p. 255
- Kindiki, K., 'Contributions of the International Criminal Tribunal for Rwanda to the development of international humanitarian law', 33 *Zambia LR* (2001) p. 34
- Kolb, R., 'The jurisprudence of the Yugoslav and Rwandan Criminal Tribunals on their jurisdiction and international crimes', 71 *BYIL* (2000) p. 259
- Momeni, M., 'Why Barayagwiza is boycotting his trial at the ICTR: lesson in balancing due process rights and politics', 7 *ILSA Journal of International and Comparative Law* (2001) p. 329
- Nizich, I., 'International tribunals and their ability to provide adequate justice: lessons from the Yugoslav Tribunal', 7 *ILSA Journal of International and Comparative Law* (2001) p. 353
- Ponte, C. Del, 'Die UN-Tribunale für Ex-Jugoslawien und Ruanda: Herausforderungen fur die Anklagebehörde', 119 *Schweizerische Zeitschrift für Strafrecht* (2001) p. 317
- Swaak-Goldman, O., '*Kambanda* v. *Prosecutor*, No. ICTR 97-23-A: International Criminal Tribunal for Rwanda, Appeals Chambers, October 19, 2000', 95 *AJIL* (2001) p. 656

6.314 International Criminal Court

Books

- Bevers, H., ed., 'An independent Defence before the International Criminal Court: Proceedings of the Conference held in The Hague, 1-2 November 1999 (Amsterdam, Thela Thesis 2000) 106 pp.
- Bourdon, W., La Cour Pénale Internationale: le Statut de Rome (Paris, Editions du Seuil 2000) 369 pp.

- Cassese, A., *The Rome Statute for an International Criminal Court*, 2 vols. (Oxford, Oxford University Press 2001) 800 pp.
- Knoops, G-J., *Defenses in Contemporary International Criminal Law* (Irvington, NY., Transnational Publishers 2001) 326 pp.
- Lee, R. and H. Friman, eds., *The International Criminal Court: Elements of Crimes and Rules of Procedure and Evidence* (Ardsley, NY, Transnational Publishers 2001) 394 pp.
- Politi, M., ed., *The Rome Statute of the International Criminal Court: a Challenge to Impunity* (Aldershot, Ashgate/Dartmouth 2001) 319 pp.
- Schabas, W.A., *An Introduction to the International Criminal Court* (Cambridge, Cambridge University Press 2001) 336 pp.

Articles

- Britto, W., 'Tribunal Penal Internactional: uma Garantia jurisdictional para a protecção dos direitos da pessoa humana', 76 *Boletim da Faculdade de Direito* (2000) p. 81
- Cereste, S., 'The International Court of Justice, the International Criminal Court, and the *Ad Hoc* Tribunals', 17 *New York Law School Journal on Human Rights* (2001) p. 911
- Cottier, M., 'Verfaungsrechtliche aspekte der schweizerischen ratifizierung des Römer Statuts', 119 *Schweizerische Zeitschrift für Strafrecht* (2001) p. 328
- David, E., 'Les conséquences du statut de la Cour pénale internationale pour la répression en droit belge', H. Bosly, ed., *Actualité du Droit International Humanitaire* (Bruxelles, Charte 2001) p. 73
- Deen-Racsmàny, Z., 'The nationality of the offender and the jurisdiction of the International Criminal Court', 95 *AJIL* (2001) p. 606
- Delmont, A.T., 'The International Criminal Court: The United States should ratify the Rome Statute despite its objections', 27 *Journal of Legislation* (2001) p. 335
- Dugard, R., 'Independent defence before the ICC: the role of lawyers before international courts', in H. Bevers, ed., *An Independent Defence Before the International Criminal Court* (Amsterdam, Thela Thesis 2000) p. 19
- Fernández de Gurmendi, S. and H. Friman, 'The Rules of Procedure and Evidence of the International Criminal Court', 3 YIHL (2001) p. 289
- Galand, R. and F. Delooz, 'L'article par. 1c) du Statut de la Cour pénale internationale: une remise en cause des acquis du droit international humanitaire?', 83 *RICR* (2001) p. 533
- Halbertsma, T., 'De positie van het Internationale Gerechtshof', 14 *VU Forum* (2001) p. 45
- Hebel, H. von, 'Some comments on the Elements of crimes for the crimes of the ICC Statute', 3 YIHL (2001) p. 273
- Henzelin, M., 'La Cour pénale internationale: organe supranational ou otage des Etats?' 119 *Schweizerische Zeitschrift für Strafrecht* (2001) p. 221
- Kirsch, p. and D. Robinson, 'Sécurite humaine et puissance de la persuasion: la Conférence de Rome sur la Cour pénale internationale', 12 *Revue Québécoise de Droit International* (1999) p. 118
- Köpcke-Duttler, A., 'Nuklearwaffen-gutachten des internationalen gerichtshofes: seine bedeutung fur eine friedensethik', W.R. Vogt, ed., *Friedenskultur statt Kulturkampf: Strategien kultureller Zivilisierung und nachhaltiger Friedensstiftung* (Baden-Baden, Nomos 1999) p. 118

- Luder, S.R., 'Zur rechtsnatur des Internationalen Strafgerichtshofes', 14 *Humanitäres Völkerrecht* (2001) p. 136
- Ponte, C. Del and W. Blomeyer, 'Der Internationale Strafgerichtshof: vortrag, gehalten vor der juristischen gesellschaft mittelfranken zu Nürnberg e. V. am 9. November 2000 im *Historischen Gerichtssaal Nr. 600 des Jusitzgebäudes in Nürnberg* (Regensburg, Roderer 2001) p. 19
- Scharf, M.P., 'The United States and the International Criminal Court: a recommendation for the Bush Administration', 7 *ILSA Journal of International and Comparative Law* (2001) p. 385
- Schense, J. and J.L. Washburn, 'The United States and the International Criminal Court', 35 *The International Lawyer* (2001) p. 614
- Strijards, G.A.M., 'Nederland en "zijn" Internationaal Strafhof', 14 *VN Forum* (2001) p. 28
- Verhaegen, J., 'L'article 31.1.C. du statut de la Cour pénale internationale: un autre négationnisme?', H. Bosly, ed., *Actualité du Droit International Humanitaire* (Bruxelles, Charte 2001) p. 93
- Young, S.N.M., 'Surrendering the accused to the International Criminal Court', 71 *BYIL* (2000) p. 317

6.317 Special Court for Sierra Leone

Articles

- Scharf, M.P., 'The Special Court for Sierra Leone', 6 *International Peacekeeping* (2000) p. 156

6.32 National Courts

Books

- Ntezimana, V., *La Justice Belge Face au Genocide Rwandis: L'Affaire Ntezimana* (Paris, L'Harmattan 2000) 214 pp.

Articles

- Gavouneli, M., and I. Bantekas, 'Prefecture of Voiotia v. Federal Republic of Germany: Greek Supreme Court decision on sovereign immunity in action for injuries caused by humanitarian law violations during military occupation', 95 *American JIL* (2001) p. 198
- Kamminga, M.T., 'Lessons learned from the excise of universal jurisdiction in respect of gross rights offences', 23 *Human Rights Quarterly* (2001) p. 940
- Ntampaka, Ch., 'Le gacaca rwandais, une justice repressive participative', H. Bosly, ed., *Actualité du Droit International Humanitaire* (Bruxelles, Charte 2001) p. 211

7.21 Legislation to Implement IHL Treaties

Articles

- Mitchell, A., 'Is genocide a crime unknown to Australian law? *Nulyarimma* v. *Thompson*', 3 *YIHL* (2001) p. 362
- Scheirs, T.L.W., 'Het Rwanda-proces de Belgische wet ter bestraffing van inbreuken op het internationaal humanitair Recht in actie", 10 *Zoeklicht* (2001) p. 22

– Scheirs, T.L.W., 'Civiele Bescherming: een vergelijking tussen het Internationaal Humanitair Recht en de Belgische wetgeving terzake', 10 *Zoeklicht* (2001) p. 26

7.22 Legislation to Implement Obligations *vis-a-vis* the International Criminal Court and International Criminal Tribunals

Articles

– Cottier, M., 'Verfaungsrechtliche aspekte der schweizerischen Ratifizierung des Römer Statuts', 119 *Schweizerische Zeitschrift für Strafrecht* (2001) p. 328
– David, E., 'Les conséquences du statut de la Cour pénale internationale pour la répression en droit belge', *Actualité du droit international humanitaire* (2001) p. 73
– Lattanzi, F., 'The International Criminal Court and national jurisdictions', M. Politi, ed., *The Rome Statute of the International Criminal Court: a challenge to impunity* (Aldershot, Ashgate/Dartmouth 2001) p. 177
– Schabas, W.A., 'Canadian implementing legislation for the ICC Statute', 3 *YIHL (2000) p. 337*
– Vandermeersch, D., 'Les poursuites et le jugement des infractions de droit humanitaire en droit belge', *Actualité du droit international humanitaire* (Bruxelles, Charte 2001) p. 121

7.23 Military Manuals/National Instructions/Codes of Conduct

Articles

– Aldykiewicz, J.E. and G.S., Corn, 'Authority to court-martial non-U.S. military personnel for serious violations of international humanitarian law committed during internal armed conflicts', 167 *Mil LR* (2001) p. 74

7.4 ICRC

Books

– Caverzasio, S.G., *Strengthening Protection in War: a Search for Professional Standards: Summary of Discussions among Human Rights and Humanitarian Organizations: Workshops at the ICRC, 1996-2000* (Geneva, ICRC 2001) 127 pp.
– Harouel, V., *Histoire de la Crois Rouge* (Paris, Presses Universitaires de France 2001) 128 pp.

Articles

– Sandoz, Y., 'Role of the ICRC in the evolution and development of international humanitarian law', *Humanitäres Völkerrecht: Politische, Rechtliche und Strafgerichtliche Dimensionen* (Baden-Baden, Nomos 2001) p. 110
– Sanna S., 'La testimonianza dei delegati del Comitato internazionale della Croce Rosssa davanti ai tribunali penali internazionali', 84 *Rivista di Diritto Internazionale* (2001) p. 393

7.5 FACT-FINDING, INCLUDING THE INTERNATIONAL FACT-FINDING COMMISSION

Books

- Condorelli, L., 'La Commission internationale humanitaire d'établissement des faits: un outil obsolète ou un moyen utile de mise en oevre du droit international humanitaire?', 83 *RICR* (2001) p. 393

7.6 DISSEMINATION

Books

- Tall, S.N., *Théories et Réalités du Droit International Humanitaire: Contribution à l'Étude de l'Application du Droit des Conflits Armés en Afrique Noire Contemporaine* (Dakar, Université Cheikh Anta Diop 2001) p. 415

Articles

- Vierucci, L., 'Promoting the teaching of international humanitarian law in universities: the ICRC's experience in Central Asia', 83 *IRRC* (2001) p. 155
- Kadan, U., 'Teaching international humanitarian law in academic institutions in South Asia: an overview of an ICRC dissemination programme', 83 *IRRC* (2001) p. 167

9.11 United Nations Organization

Books

- *Humanitarian Law and the United Nations Organisation* (International Red Cross 2001) http://www.icrc.org/icrceng.nsf/c1256212004ce24e4125621200524882/
- Richmond, O. and J. Ker-Lindsay, eds., The Work of the UN in Cyprus (London, Palgrave 2001) 280 pp.

Articles

- Benvenuti, P., 'Le respect du droit international humanitaire par les forces des Nations Unies: la circulaire du Secrétaire Général', 105 *RGDIP* (2001) p. 355
- Condorelli, L., 'Les progrès du droit international humanitaire et la circulaire du secrétaire général des Nations Unies du 6 août 1999', L. Boisson de Chazournes and V Gowlland-Debbas, eds, *The International Legal System in Quest of Equity and Universality: Liber Amicorum Georges Abi-Saab* (The Hague, Martinus Nijhoff Publisher 2001) p. 495
- Momtaz, D. and L. Condorelli, 'La compatibilité des sanctions du Conseil de Sécurité avec le droit internationale humanitaire', V. Gowlland-Debbas, *United Nations Sanctions and International Law* (The Hague, Kluwer Law International 2001) p. 223
- Zacklin, R., 'Beyond Kosovo: The United Nations and humanitarian intervention', 41 *Virginia JIL* (2001) p. 923

9.12 Other

Books

- Wijk, R. de, B. Boxhoorn and N. Hoekstra, eds., *Nato after Kosovo* (Breda, Royal Netherlands Military Academy 2000) 154 pp.

Articles
- Mangala, J.M., 'L'OTAN et les personnes deplacées du Kosovo: une lecture humanitaire et stratégique', 80 *Revue de Droit International, de Sciences Diplomatiques et Politiques* (2002) p. 65
- Gray, Ch., 'The legality of Nato's military action in Kosovo: is there a right of humanitarian intervention?', S. Lee and W. Tieya, eds. *International Law in the Post-Cold War World,* (London, Routledge 2001) p. 240
- Leurdijk, D.A., 'Nato as a sub-contractor to the United Nations: the cases of Bosnia and Kosovo', in R. de Wijk, B. Boxhoorn and N. Hoekstra, eds., *Nato after Kosovo* (Breda, Royal Netherlands Military Academy 2000) p. 121
- Zaagman, R., 'A limited partnership: the relationship between Nato and the OSCE', R. de Wijk, B. Boxhoorn and N. Hoekstra, eds., *Nato after Kosovo* (Breda, Royal Netherlands Military Academy 2000) p. 109

9.21 Peacekeeping

Books
- Connaughton, R., *Military Intervention and Peacekeeping: The Reality,* (Aldershot, Ashgate 2001) 296 pp.
- Cousens, E.M. and C.K. Cater, *Towards Peace in Bosnia: Implementing the Dayton Accords* (Boulder, CO 2001) 189 pp.
- Richmond, O.P., *Maintaining Order, Making Peace* (New York, Palgrave 2001) 264 pp.

Articles
- Bothe, M. and T. Marauhn, 'The United Nations in Kosovo and East Timor: problems of a trusteeship administration', 6 *International Peacekeeping* (2000) p. 158
- Bullion, A., 'India in Sierra Leone: a case of muscular peacekeeping?' 8 *International Peaeckeeping* (2001) p. 77
- Carey, H.F., 'Women and peace and security: the politics of implementing gender sensitivity norms in peacekeeping', 8 *International Peacekeeping* (2001) p. 49
- Condorelli, L., 'Les progrès du droit international humanitaire et la circulaire du secrétaire général des Nations Unies du 6 août 1999', L. Boisson de Chazournes and V Gowlland-Debbas, eds, *The International Legal System in Quest of Equity and Universality: Liber Amicorum Georges Abi-Saab* (The Hague, Martinus Nijhoff Publisher 2001) p. 495
- Cooper, N., 'Conflict goods: the challenges for peacekeeping and conflict prevention', 8 *International Peacekeeping* (2001) p. 21
- Hills, A., 'The inherent limits of military forces in policing police operations', 8 *International Peacekeeping* (2001) p. 79
- Karamé, K.H., 'Military women and peace operations: experiences of the Norwegian battalion in UNIFIL 1978-98', 8 *International Peacekeeping* (2001) p. 85
- Kiehl, W.P., 'Peacekeeper or occupier? US experience with information operations in the Balkans', 8 *International Peacekeeping* (2001) p. 56
- Krishnasamy, K., '"Recognition" for third world peacekeepers: India and Pakistan', 8 *International Peacekeeping* (2001) p. 56
- Leeds, C.A., 'Culture, conflict resolution, peacekeeper training and the D mediator', 8 *International Peacekeeping* (2001) p. 92

- Mikula, S.R., 'Blue helmets in the next frontier: the future is now', 29 *Georgia Journal of International and Comparative Law* (2001) p. 531
- Rolfe, J., 'Peacekeeping the pacific way in Bougainville', 8 *International Peacekeeping* (2001) p. 38
- Skjelsb'k, I., 'Sexual violence in time of war: a new challenge for peace operations?', 8 *International Peacekeeping* (2001) p. 69
- Speiker, H., 'Challenging "peacekeeping in the new millennium": the recommendations of the panel on United Nations peace operations of August 2000', 6 *International Peacekeeping* (2000) p. 144
- Szurek, S., 'Sierra Leone: un état en attente de "paix durable": la communauté internationale dans l'engrenage de la paix en Afrique de l'Ouest', 46 *Annuaire Français de Droit International* (2000) p. 176
- Thakur, R., 'Cambodia, East Timor and the Brahimi Report', 8 *International Peacekeeping* (2001) p. 115

9.22 Peace Enforcement and Peace Building

Books

- Counsens, E.M., C. Kumar, and K. Wermester, *Peacebuilding as Politics: Cultivating Peace in Fragile Societies* (Boulder, CO., Lynne Riener 2001) 248 pp.
- Ikenberry, G.J., *After Victory: Institutions, Strategic Restraint and the Rebuilding of Order after Major Wars* (Princeton, NJ, Princeton University Press 2001) 293 pp.
- Jones, B.D., *Peacemaking in Rwanda: The Dynamics of Failure* (Boulder, CO., Lynne Riener 2001) 209 pp.
- Richmond. O.P., *Maintaining order, Making Peace* (New York, Palgrave 2001) 264 pp.

Articles

- Kirgis, F.L., 'Security Council goverance of postconflict societies: a plea for good faith and informed decision making', 95 *AJIL* (2001) p. 579
- Oswald, B., 'The Interfet Detainee Management Unit in East Timor', 3 *YIHL* (2001) p. 347
- Strohmeyer, H., 'Policing the peace: post-conflict judicial system reconstruction in East Timor', 24 *University of New South Wales Law Journal* (2001) p. 171
- Suhrke, A., 'Peacebuilders as nation-builders: UN dilemmas in East Timor', 8 *International Peacekeeping* (2001) p. 1

9.24 Humanitarian and Other Interventions

Books

- Chesterman, S., *Just War or Just Peace? Humanitarian Intervention and International Law* (Oxford, Oxford University Press 2001) 295 pp.
- Kreiger, H., ed., *The Kosovo Conflict and International Law: An Analytical Documentation 1974-1999* (Cambridge, Cambridge University Press 2001) 600 pp.
- Leiß, E., *Interventionen des Sicherheitsrates bei Innerstaatlich Begangenen Menschenrechtsverletzungen nach Kapitel VII der Charta der Vereinten Nationen: Versuch einer Standardisierung* (Frankfurt am Main, Peter Lang 2000) 321 pp.

Articles

- Berger, L.F., 'State practice evidence of the humanitarian intervention doctrine: the ECOWAS intervention in Sierra Leone', 11 *Indiana ICLR* (2001) p. 605
- Dee, M., '"Coalitions of the willing" and humanitarian intervention: Australia's involvement with *INTERFET*', 8 *International Peacekeeping* (2001) p. 1
- Egan, P.T., 'The Kosovo Intervention and collective self-defence', 8 *International Peacekeeping* (2001) p. 39
- Elshtain, J.B., 'The third annual Grotius lecture: just war and humanitarian intervention', 17 *The American University ILR* (2001) p. 1
- Elshtain, J.B., 'The third annual Grotius lecture: just war and humanitarian intervention', 95 Proceedings of the Annual Meeting of the American Society of International Law (2001) p. 1
- Gray, Ch., 'The legality of Nato's military action in Kosovo: is there a right of humanitarian intervention?', S. Lee and W. Tieya, eds. *International Law in the Post-Cold War World*, (London, Routledge 2001) p. 240
- Greenwood, Ch., 'Humanitarian intervention: the case of Kosovo', *Finland YIL* (1999) p. 141
- Harhoff, F., 'Unauthorised humanitarian interventions: armed violence in the name of humanity?' 70 *Nordic JIL* (2001) p. 65
- Hilpold, P., 'Humanitarian intervention: is there a need for a legal reappraisal?', 12 *EJIL* (2001) p. 437
- 'The Kosovo report: conflict, international response, lessons learned: international law and humanitarian intervention, The Independent International Commission on Kosovo', 14 *Humanitäres Völkerrecht* (2001) p. 44
- Matheson, M.J., 'Just war and humanitarian intervention: comment on the Grotius lecture by Professor Jean Bethke Elshtain', 17 *The American University ILR* (2001) p. 27
- McCullough, H.B., 'Intervention in Kosovo: Legal? Effective?' 7 *ILSA Journal of International and Comparative Law* (2001) p. 299
- Merriam, J.J., 'Kosovo and the law of humanitarian intervention', 33 *Case Western Rerserve JIL* (2001) p. 111
- Ocran, M. T., 'The doctrine of humanitarian intervention in light of robust peacekeeping', 25 *Boston College ICLR* (2002) p. 1
- Roberts, A., 'The so-called 'right' of humanitarian intervention', 3 *YIHL* (2001) p. 3
- Rytter, J.E., 'Humanitarian intervention without the Security Council: from San Francisco to Kosovo – and beyond', 70 *Nordic JIL* (2001) p. 121
- Tittemore, B.D., 'Evolving dynamics of intervention to end atrocities and secure accountability: security accountability for gross violations of human rights and the implications of non-intervention: the lessons of Cambodia', 7 *ILSA Journal of International and Comparative Law* (2001) p. 447
- Wheeler, N.J., 'Legitimating humanitarian intervention: Principles and procedures', 2 *Melbourne JIL* (2001) p. 550
- Zacklin, R., 'Beyond Kosovo: The United Nations and humanitarian intervention', 41 *Virginia JIL* (2001) p. 923

9.25 Sanctions

Books

- Gowlland-Debbas, V., *United Nations Sanctions and International Law* (The Hague, Kluwer Law International 2001) 408 pp.

Articles

- Sassòli, M., 'Sanctions and international humanitarian law – commentary', V. Gowlland-Debbas, *United Nations Sanctions and International Law* (The Hague, Kluwer Law International 2001) 408 p. 241

11. ARMS CONTROL AND DISARMAMENT

Books

- Myjer, E.P.J., *Issues of Arms Control Law and the Chemical Weapons Conventions Obligations Inter Se and Supervisory Mechanisms* (Dordrecht, Martinus Nijhoff Publishers 2001) 216 pp.

Articles

- Mubiala, M., 'The ECOWAS Moratorium on Small Arms in West Africa', 3 *YIHL* (2001) p. 245
- Vetschera, H., 'The negotiations on regional arms control under Annex 1-B, Art. V of the Dayton Agreement: a preliminary post-mortem', 12 *Helsinki Monitor* (2001) p. 177
- Yaffe, M.D., 'Promoting arms control and regional security in the Middle East', 2 *Disarmament forum* (2001) p. 9

12.1 CONFLICT PREVENTION

Books

- Hampson, F.O. and D. Malone, eds., *From Reaction to Conflict Prevention: Opportunities for the UN System* (Boulder, CO, Rienner 2002) 431 pp.
- Stevenson, J., *Preventing Conflict: the Role of the Bretton Woods Institutions* (Oxford, Oxford University Press for the International Institute for Strategic Studies 2000) 94 pp.

12.2 CONFLICT RESOLUTION

Books

- Deutsch, M and P.T. Coleman, *The Handbook of Conflict Resolution: Theory and Practice* (San Francisco, CA, Jossey-Bass 2000) 649 pp.

Articles

- Tinker, C., 'Dispute resolution and international law: the United Nations Dialogue among civilizations', 17 *New York Law School Journal of Human Rights* (2001) p. 985

12.3 THE PEACE MOVEMENT

Books
- Blight, J. and R.S. McNamara, eds., *Wilson's Ghost: Reducing the Risk of Conflict, Killing and Catastrophe in the 21st Century* (New York Perseus Books 2001) 288 pp.
- Crocker, C. A., F.O. Hampson, and p. Aall, eds., *Turbulent Peace: the Challenges of Managing International Conflict* (Washington, DC, United States Institute of Peace Press 2001) 894 pp.
- Williams, K.P., *Despite Nationalist Conflicts: Theory and Practice of Maintaining World Peace* (Westport, CT, Praeger 2001) 214 pp.

Articles
- Kennedy, S.S., 'A just world at peace', 11 *Indiana International and Comparative Law Review* (2001) p. 377
- Tomuschat, C., '"Uniting for Peace": ein ruckblick nach 50 Jahren', 76 *Die Friedenswarte* (2001) p. 289

13.1 JUS AD BELLUM

Books
- Cimbala, S.J., *Clausewitz and Chaos: Friction in War and Military Policy* (Westport, CT, Praeger Publishers 2001) 228 pp.
- Dinstein, Y., *War, Aggression, and Self-Defense,* 3rd edn., (Cambridge, Cambridge University Press 2001) 325 pp.
- Gray, C., *International Law and the Use of Force* (Oxford, Oxford University Press 2001) 256 pp.
- Hirst, P., *War and Power in the 21st Century* (Cambridge, Polity Press 2001) 169 pp.
- Tuck, R., *The Rights of War and Peace: Political Thought and the International Order From Grotius to Kant* (Oxford, Clarendon Press 2001) 272 pp.

12.5 THE PEACE MOVEMENT

Books

Blight, J. and R. S. McNamara, eds., *Wilson's Ghost: Reducing the Risk of Conflict, Killing,* [illegible]

[illegible]

[illegible]

TABLE OF CASES*

INTERNATIONAL

* The Table of Cases was compiled by Mrs. B.M. Hall, Elie, UK.

NATIONAL

INDEX

The index contains references to all matters of substance dealt with in the text of the articles. Detailed references to cases dealt with will be found in the accompanying Table of Cases. Multilateral agreements are indexed under *Agreements, multilateral*, classified by subject. The section on Correspondents' Reports is also indexed, but for information on the practice of individual states regarding detailed aspects of international humanitarian law the reader should consult the index under the states concerned. The index does contain, however, references to material from this section and the Documentation section which relate to the major topics of discussion in the present volume. Footnotes containing substantive material are also indexed, as are references to the work of scholars the first time such work is listed.

The index was compiled by Mrs. B.M. Hall, Elie, UK

Abbreviations frequently used

g.r.	general references
ICC	International Criminal Court
ICJ	International Court of Justice
ICTR	International Criminal Tribunal for Rwanda
ICTY	International Criminal Tribunal for the Former Yugoslavia
IHL	International humanitarian law
p.a.r.	parties, accessions, ratifications
UN	United Nations Organisation
US	United States of America

The manufacturer's authorised representative in the EU is Springer Nature Customer Service Centre GmbH, Europaplatz 3, 69115 Heidelberg, Germany. If you have any concerns regarding our products, please contact ProductSafety@springernature.com

Printed and bound by CPI Group (UK) Ltd, Croydon, CR0 4YY
30/09/2026
02225444-0020